Table of Contents

	PAGE
Preface to Revised Edition	v
Preface to First Edition	vii

Part 1. Nature and Classification of Property

CHAPTER
1. General Provisions, §§ 1-10 3
2. Fixtures, §§ 11-22.5 13

Part 2. Estates and Interests in Real Property

3. Estates Generally, § 23 33
4. Inheritable Estates, §§ 24-45 35
5. Freehold Estates Not Inheritable, §§ 46-63 57
6. Estates of Less Than Freehold, §§ 64-107 75
7. Concurrent Ownership, §§ 108-128 105

Part 3. Modes of Acquisition and Transfer of Title or Interests in Real Property

8. Real Estate Brokerage, §§ 129-134 141
9. Contracts for the Sale of Land, §§ 135-151 147
10. The Deed, §§ 152-209 171
11. Covenants for Title in Deeds, §§ 210-229 219
12. Leases, §§ 230-254 239
13. Mortgages and Deeds of Trust, §§ 255-285 265
14. Adverse Possession, §§ 286-302 309
15. Rights in the Lands of Others; Easements and Profits, §§ 303-345 ... 331
16. Rights of Enjoyment and Duties Incident to Ownership of Real Property, §§ 346-368 365
17. Priorities; Recordation, §§ 369-382 401
18. Private and Public Restrictions on the Use of Lands, §§ 383-399 417
19. Eminent Domain, §§ 400-408 457
20. Liens on Real Property, §§ 409-455 475

Part 4. Examination of Titles to Real Property in North Carolina

21. Title Examination Generally, §§ 456-459 541
22. The Chain of Title, §§ 460-463 545
23. Examination of the Sources of Title, §§ 464-487 563
24. Objections to Title, §§ 488-507 605
25. Marketable Title Act, § 508 635
26. Report of Title, § 509 643
27. Title Insurance, §§ 510-513 647

INDEX 651

Preface to Revised Edition

I never had the privilege of meeting Professor Webster, but I have grown to admire him very much in the course of revising his book. He had that rare ability of bringing clarity to a vast and sometimes confusing area of law. He could study a series of complicated and seemingly inconsistent court decisions and somehow manage to present their essence in an appropriate sentence or paragraph. He also made a special effort to write as a neutral observer and present an objective summary of property law. It is easily understandable why his straightforward, readable and accurate text became the recognized authority on North Carolina real property law.

This revision has been approached with the many strengths of the original edition in mind. Whenever possible, Professor Webster's analysis of North Carolina property law has been preserved. A special effort has been made by this revisor to present additions and revisions to the text in a manner and style consistent with the existing format.

Besides a general updating of footnotes and the incorporation of much of the former pocketpart into this revision, the original text has been augmented by an expansion of coverage in certain areas and by the addition of new issues and topics. Real estate contracts and options, real estate lbrokerage law, residential landlord and tenant law, lien law, implied warranties in new home sales, and deceptive practices legislation are some of the areas of additional and expanded coverage.

A comprehensive treatment of the North Carolina law of condominiums eludes this volume as it did the original, but for an entirely different reason. For the past year, a special committee appointed by the General Statutes Commission has been preparing a series of proposed new condominium laws that will hopefully meet the needs of both consumer and developer in a world where condominiums have become far more complicated than they used to be, and it is likely that the General Assembly will adopt some form of substantive revision. A decision was made, therefore, not to write a comprehensive treatment of condominium laws in North Carolina based upon statutes that may soon be obsolete.

I would like to express by gratitude to all who encouraged and assisted me in this revision project. Dean F. Leary Davis provided me with the facilities and support at Campbell University School of Law to do justice to this time-consuming task. Student research assistants put in long hours to aid the revision. Cheryl Poyner typed and re-typed page after page of manuscript.

One final but important note. I dedicate this revision to my lovely and understanding wife, Bernadette, who cheerfully supports me in all of my professional endeavors.

Patrick K. Hetrick

Preface to First Edition

This volume has been designed primarily for practicing lawyers and law students in North Carolina. Developed from the author's lectures and classroom materials, this one volume work does not have as its purpose the presentation of the whole law of real property in an encyclopedic manner. This work rather attempts to review in textual form the fundamental principles of the law of real property as developed and enunciated in the North Carolina courts and in the statutes. It is hoped that law students, members of the practicing bar, those engaged in real estate transactions and property owners generally may utilize this book and find it valuable as a handbook on the principles of real estate law in this State.

This work deals primarily with the creation, characteristics and incidents of possessory estates in land and with the modes of transferring and acquiring ownership of real property by formal conveyances, adverse possession and prescription. It also considers the acquisition of easements and rights in the lands of others by private arrangement and through the various public regulations of land use, such as zoning ordinances. Attention is given, in addition, to the devices utilized by the bar and landowners to assure title security with respect to real property. Covenants for title, the recordation system, and priorities are considered. Part 4 of the book outlines the procedures that must be followed in checking land titles in North Carolina, which should be of particular value to young attorneys just beginning to practice.

Certain areas of real property law have not been discussed in this work because of the author's belief that they are not of a sufficiently general interest to warrant their inclusion in a work of limited size. For instance, while North Carolina has adopted the Torrens System of land registration, it is only an auxiliary method of recordation in almost all instances and is not used to any large extent in the State. Hence, it was felt that few lawyers engaged in real estate practice are really interested in the Torrens System, and it was therefore excluded. Likewise, while subjects like "Condominiums" are capturing the fancy of law review writers over the country, it was thought that on a percentage basis the development and exposition of "condominium law" is not of a sufficiently universal interest in this State at this time to warrant its discussion in this type work.

It should be noted additionally that the subject of "Future Interests" has not been considered in any detail in this work. This omission is not from any lack of pertinency or interest with respect to real property law, but it arises from the author's desire to separate material primarily on "Possessory" or "Present" interests in real property from materials on "Future Interests." It is the author's present intent to write another book that gives particular emphasis to the subject of "Future Interests in North

Carolina," which in many cases will represent the "other side of the coin" with respect to the interests and principles set out in this work.

James A. Webster, Jr.

Part 1
Nature and Classification of Property

CHAPTER 1
GENERAL PROVISIONS

§ 1. Property Generally.
§ 2. Right of Disposition.
§ 3. Right of Exclusion.
§ 4. Right of User.
§ 5. Classes of Property.
§ 6. Significance of Distinctions Between Real and Personal Property.
§ 7. Lands Generally.
§ 8. Minerals.
§ 9. Fructus Naturales.
§ 10. Fructus Industriales.

§ 1. Property Generally.

Property is the term which describes the rights and interests which a person has in a thing as distinguished from the thing itself. It is sometimes referred to as a "bundle of rights," composed of all the various interests which are created and protectible by law.[1] Thus if a piece of land or a chattel is located in a place of anarchy, although a man be standing over it growling like a dog, there would be no property as thus defined.[2] Property can exist only where there is law which gives and protects persons' exclusive rights to own, possess, use and enjoy and to dispose of determinate things.

§ 2. Right of Disposition.

The term "ownership" involves the conception that a particular person or group of persons have all of the various interests in a thing and that the thing can be used according to their pleasure without accountability to any other person, so long as such use is not inconsistent with any law. One of the chief powers or privileges incident to the ownership of property is the power that an owner has to dispose of his interests as he sees fit. He may decide that he wants to look at the land in its natural state and may elect to keep the property for that purpose for as long as he lives.[3] If he elects to keep the property until his death, it will pass by operation of law to his heirs as provided by the laws of intestate succession [4] if he dies without a will. If he so elects, the owner may instead sell or give his

---

1. Jeremy Bentham, the great English legal reformer, once wrote: "Property and law are born together and die together. Before laws were made there was no property; take away laws and property ceases." BENTHAM, THEORY OF LEGISLATION, PRINCIPLES OF THE CIVIL CODE pt. I, 112 (Dumont ed. Hildreth transl. 1864).
2. CRIBBET, PRINCIPLES OF THE LAW OF PROPERTY 4 (1962).
3. Subject, however, to the government's power to take property under the power of eminent domain for governmental or public purposes.
4. N.C. GEN. STAT. § 29-1 et seq.

property away during his lifetime provided he complies with the laws establishing the form and manner for making conveyances or for disposing of the type and class of property involved.[5] Or he may make a will which will transfer his property interests to a particular person or group of persons upon his death, in which case the ownership of the property will shift to the beneficiary upon the owner's death.[6]

§ 3. Right of Exclusion.

Property rights are "in rem" rights. That is, they are rights which may be exercised and which are protectible "against all the world." Thus, if a person has a property right, he has a right to exclude others from the use of the determinate thing that is owned. If he chooses, however, he may give to others permission to use the thing owned under such terms and conditions as he elects, perhaps pursuant to a contract providing for the payment of a rent or compensation for the permission given. He will remain the owner and will retain important proprietary rights, but he will give up some of his "bundle of rights" to the permittee.

§ 4. Right of User.

An owner of land has the exclusive right to use and enjoy his land in any manner that he chooses so long as he acts in accordance with law. An owner may leave his lands unimproved or he may improve them as he sees fit. He may choose to allow his land to grow to weeds and brush, and this he may do unless there is some law or regulation that requires him to control such growth. He can, without obligation to anyone, cut and destroy his trees, dig gravel or minerals from his land and dispose of them as he sees fit, or he may build houses, factories, office buildings or stores on his land so long as he does not violate a zoning ordinance or other building regulation.

It should be noted, however, that the owner's rights to use his land as he sees fit is not unlimited. If he chooses to improve his land, he must comply with the provisions of zoning ordinances and building and safety codes which may apply in a particular locality. He must not use his land in such a way as to injure his neighbor. In addition, his right to use his land as he sees fit is subject to the paramount rights of the state to control the use of land for the interest of the public health, safety, morals and general welfare.

---

5. This is called an *inter vivos* transfer.
6. This is called a testamentary transfer.

§ 5. Classes of Property.

Property is divided into two great classifications: Real Property and Personal Property.[7]

Real property consists of lands, tenements and hereditaments. "Land" means the ground and air above it and all that is below the surface of the earth and all that is erected on it. Earth that is located underneath water is nevertheless "land" in contemplation of law. "Tenements" is a term that includes land but which embraces something more. For instance, while an easement or profit à prendre are not "lands," but are incorporeal interests in lands, and are not encompassed within the term "lands," they come within the definition of the term "tenements," which means anything of a permanent nature which was the subject of tenure at the common law. The term "hereditaments" is an even broader term and includes both "lands" and "tenements," embracing in its definition everything that could be inherited at the common law, whether corporeal or incorporeal. Even some items which were personal in nature, such as heirlooms, were deemed to be hereditaments at the common law and passed to the owner's heirs upon his death.[8]

Personal property may be defined negatively as all other property which is not real property, including moneys, goods, chattels, choses in action and evidences of debt, including all things capable of ownership which were not descendible to one's heirs at his death under the common law.[9] It should be noted, however, that a leasehold interest in real property is deemed personal property and is not real property.[10]

§ 6. Significance of Distinctions Between Real and Personal Property.

It is imperative that the distinctions between real and personal property be kept in mind because the classification of property as being either "real" or "personal" will often determine whether one set of laws is to be

---

7. The term "real" was derived from the name given to actions in connection with property whereby restitution of the very property itself could be effected. The term "personal" came from the name of actions whereby a plaintiff could not insist upon recovery of specific property but in which he could recover only its pecuniary value. The terms "real" and "personal" came to apply to things that were the subjects of the actions, those things which were specifically recoverable being called "real property" and those things for which only damages could be recovered being called "personal property." TIFFANY, REAL PROPERTY 3 (abr. ed. 1940); Williams, *The Terms Real and Personal in English Law*, 4 LAW Q. REV. 394.

8. 1 MORDECAI, LAW LECTURES 461 (1916).

9. Worth v. Trust Co., 151 N.C. 191, 65 S.E. 918 (1909).

10. A lease is called a "chattel real" and as such is a species of intangible personal property. Investment Co. v. Cumberland County, 245 N.C. 492, 96 S.E.2d 341 (1956). Since it is not real property a lease interest can be conveyed without a seal, although a writing *is* necessary if the lease has a duration of more than three years from the time of the making thereof. Moche v. Leno, 227 N.C. 159, 41 S.E.2d 369 (1947).

applied in a factual situation or whether another set of laws is to be applicable.

For instance, in some states, and in North Carolina prior to 1961 when North Carolina's new intestate succession law became effective, real property may pass to a decedent's "heirs" while his personal property may pass to his "distributees." In most states, however, and in North Carolina since 1961, the persons to whom real property and personal property passes upon intestacy have been assimilated and there is no longer any such distinction for purposes of inheritance.[11]

In the administration of estates prior to October 1, 1975, a decedent's personal property had to be subjected to payments of his debts or claims against the estate before resort could be made to his real property. Subsequent to October 1, 1975, pursuant to North Carolina General Statutes, §§ 28A-15-1 and 28A-17-1, all types of property of a decedent, both real and personal, equitable as well as legal, are deemed assets available for the discharge of debts and other claims against the estate of the decedent, without restriction. It is no longer essential for the personal property of the decedent to be exhausted prior to resort to his real property to pay decedent's debts or other claims against his estate. Since October 1, 1975, when North Carolina General Statutes, § 28-81 was repealed and Chapter 28A became effective with respect to the administration of decedent's estates, the personal representative of a decedent may make a determination concerning what property of decedent shall be sold, leased, pledged, mortgaged or exchanged for the purpose of paying the debts of the decedent and other claims against the estate. The personal representative shall select the assets which in his judgment are calculated to promote the best interests of the estate. In the absence of contrary provisions in a will, specifying that personal property shall be first resorted to, the personal representative of a decedent may bring a special proceeding before the clerk of the superior court to have a decedent's real property sold to pay the decedent's debts or claims against his estate.[12] The petition to sell real estate shall include a statement that the personal representative has determined that it is in the best interest of the administration of the estate to sell the real estate.[13]

During his life an owner of real property has a homestead exemption in real property in the amount of $1,000 valuation [14] and a personal property exemption in the amount of $500 valuation [15] which are free

---

11. N.C. Gen. Stat. § 29-3.
12. N.C. Gen. Stat. §§ 28A-15-1, 28A-17-1, 28A-17-2.
13. N.C. Gen. Stat. § 28A-17-2.
14. N.C. Gen. Stat. § 1-372; N.C. Const. art. X, § 2.
15. N.C. Gen. Stat. § 1-378; N.C. Const. art. X, § 1.

from execution, attachment or garnishment to satisfy any judgment procured against him.[16]

The modes of transferring real property and personal property are different. Title to personal property generally passes simply by delivery of possession of the item with the intention to transfer title. While written instruments frequently accompany the transfer of titles to personal property, in the form perhaps of bills of sale, instruments of gift and assignments, such writings are not usually necessary to pass title in the absence of particular requirements of special statutes. On the other hand title to real property cannot be transferred unless there is a writing to satisfy the Statute of Frauds which meets all of the formalities for the conveyance of real property. There must be a writing which describes the real property and which sets out words indicating the grantor's intention to grant the property. Such writing must be duly delivered with the intention to pass title, and must be signed and sealed by each grantor.

The determination that property is either "real" or "personal" may, in addition, determine what jurisdiction's law will apply to a transaction involving the property. If the property is deemed "real," the law of the place where it is located will govern the transaction. If the property is "personal," it is deemed "transitory" and the law of the domicile of the owner or the law of the place where the transaction takes place will control.[17] Actions involving real property are generally regarded as "local" actions in which the law of the jurisdiction in which the real property is located is applied. If the property involved is "personal," actions involving the property are deemed "transitory" and can be brought anywhere proper service can be had.[18]

---

16. It should be noted that a debtor is automatically entitled to have his homestead exemption in real property allotted before an execution sale is held. If he wishes to assert his personal property exemption he must request it and such is not automatic.

17. *See, e.g.*, In re Will of Marks, 259 N.C. 326, 130 S.E.2d 673 (1963), which holds that personalty has its situs at the domicile of the owner and a will valid in the state of his domicile will transfer title to the personalty irrespective of the physical location of the personal property. On the other hand, a will cannot dispose of real property effectively unless executed and probated in accordance with the laws of the state in which the real property is located. PAGE, WILLS § 60.11 (Bowe-Parker rev. 1962).

18. *See* Bunting v. Henderson, 220 N.C. 194, 16 S.E.2d 836 (1941), in which a change of venue was sought on the ground that the action, to recover the value of timber wrongfully cut from real property, was a local action. The court stated: "It is necessary to distinguish in each case what the particular cause of action is, as alleged. If the timber is cut and removed from the land, it becomes personalty, and the owner has the choice of several remedies. He may sue for the injury to the land by cutting the timber, in the nature of the old action of *quare clausum fregit,* and this is local; he may sue to recover possession of the specific articles of personalty and the venue is determined by where this particular article is located; he may sue for the value of the timber, as in trover or conversion, or for the wrongful taking, as in trespass *de bonis asportatis,* and these are transitory; or, if the article has been sold, he may sue, as in *assumpsit,* for the money received, and this is transitory." *See also* McLean v. Hardin, 56 N.C. 294 (1857); McGehee v. McGehee, 189 N.C. 558, 127 S.E. 684 (1925); Ellison v. Hunsinger, 237 N.C. 619, 75 S.E.2d 884 (1953).

With respect to venue within the state, actions to recover an estate or interest in real property, or actions brought for the purpose of determining one's right or interest in real property or to recover for injuries to real property, must be tried in the county in which the subject of the action, or some part thereof, is located.[19] The venue for actions to effect the foreclosure of mortgages or deeds of trust as well as partition proceedings is the county in which the real property is located.[20] An

---

19. N.C. GEN. STAT. § 1-76(1). While a lease is deemed "personal property" for some purposes, a lease creates an "interest in the real property." Since an action to terminate a lease requires the court to determine the respective rights of the parties with respect to the leasehold interest, such action must be tried in the county where the subject matter of the lease is located. Sample v. Towe Motor Co., Inc., 23 N.C. App. 742, 209 S.E.2d 524 (1974). But if the principal object involved in an action is monetary damages, and plaintiffs do not seek a judgment that would affect an interest in land but seek a judgment only in personam, it is not a local action within subdivision (1). Wise v. Isenhour, 9 N.C. App. 237, 175 S.E.2d 772 (1970). An action is not necessarily local because it incidentally involves the title to land or a right or interest therein. Hence, an action with respect to a note secured by a deed of trust is not an action involving an estate in land and does not have to be brought where the land is located. White v. Rankins, 206 N.C. 104, 173 S.E. 282 (1934); River Dev. Corp. v. Parker Tree Farms, Inc., 12 N.C. App. 1, 182 S.E.2d 211 (1971) (usury). But a suit to set aside a deed or deed of trust on lands or to establish a lien thereon involves an estate or interest in the lands and the venue is the place where the lands are located under N.C. GEN. STAT. § 1-76(1). Henrico Lumber Co. v. Dare Lumber Co., 180 N.C. 12, 103 S.E. 915 (1920); Wofford-Fain & Co. v. Hampton, 173 N.C. 686, 92 S.E. 612 (1917); Vaughan v. Fallin, 183 N.C. 318, 111 S.E. 513 (1922). An action to impress a parol trust upon lands involves a determination of an interest in such lands and establishes the venue as the county in which the lands are located. Williams v. McRackan, 186 N.C. 381, 119 S.E. 746 (1923). Likewise, actions for specific performance of contracts for the sale and purchase of real property have their proper venue in the county where the real property is located. Falls of Neuse Mfg. Co. v. Brower, 105 N.C. 440, 11 S.E. 313 (1890). But actions for damages for breach of contract need not be tried in the county in which the realty is located. Lamb v. Staples, 234 N.C. 166, 66 S.E.2d 660 (1951). An action to recover for the breach of covenants of seizin and the right to convey is not required to be tried in the county where the land is located. Eames v. Armstrong, 136 N.C. 392, 48 S.E. 769 (1904). Notwithstanding N.C. GEN. STAT. § 1-76(1), it has been held that actions brought to recover damages for injuries to land are transitory and need not be brought only in the county where the land lies. Cox v. Oakdale Cotton Mills, Inc., 211 N.C. 473, 190 S.E. 750 (1937) (action to recover damages for injuries to land caused by backing water); Perry v. Seaboard Air Line Ry., 153 N.C. 117, 66 S.E. 1060 (1910) (action to recover damages for burning timber); Harris Clay Co. v. Carolina China Clay Co., 203 N.C. 12, 164 S.E. 341 (1932) (action to recover damages for pollution of stream); Blevins v. Kitchen Lumber Co., 207 N.C. 144, 176 S.E. 262 (1934); Bunting v. Henderson, 220 N.C. 194, 16 S.E.2d 836 (1941) (actions to recover damages for cutting and removing of timber). *See* Wheatley v. Phillips, 228 F. Supp. 439 (W.D.N.C. 1964).

Under N.C. GEN. STAT. § 1-76(1), title to realty must be directly affected by the judgment in order to render the action local.

When the action puts in issue the title to land or the judgment which may be rendered thereon would affect an interest in the land, the action is removable as a matter of right upon motion aptly made to the county in which the land is situated. Rose's Stores v. Tarrytown Center, 270 N.C. 201, 154 S.E.2d 313 (1967).

20. N.C. GEN. STAT. § 1-76(2), (3).

action to enforce a laborer's or materialman's lien is not required to be brought in the county in which the realty subject to the lien is located.[21] It should be noted, however, that actions for the recovery of personal property must likewise be brought in the county where the property is located if recovery of the property is the sole or primary relief that is demanded.[22]

Recent due process protections in the personal property area render the ownership of personal property a more significant "bundle of rights" than it once was. This tends to erode part of the distinction between real and personal property.[23]

§ 7. Lands Generally.

The word "lands" is often used as a synonym for real property generally and as such includes the soil of the earth and whatever grows naturally thereon and those things attached, imbedded or annexed to or in the soil by natural causes. Since "land" is said to extend upward indefinitely and downward to the center of the earth,[24] the term includes growths and structures placed upon the soil by the hand of man with the intention that they should become a permanent addition and a part of the land. "Land" thus extends to include (1) the soil; (2) things growing naturally on the soil; (3) the minerals and waters beneath the surface of the soil; (4) the airspace that is above the soil so far as it may be reasonably reduced to possession and so far as it is reasonably necessary for the use or enjoyment of the surface; [25] and (5) those things that have been affixed by man to the

---

21. Investors, Inc. v. Berry, 293 N.C. 688, 239 S.E.2d 566 (1977).
22. N.C. GEN. STAT. § 1-76 (4).
23. *See* due process requirements enunciated in Sniadach v. Family Fin. Corp., 395 U.S. 337, 89 S. Ct. 1820, 23 L. Ed. 2d 349 (1969); Fuentes v. Shevin, 407 U.S. 67, 92 S. Ct. 1983, 32 L. Ed. 2d 556 (1972); Mitchell v. W.T. Grant Co., 416 U.S. 600, 94 S. Ct. 1895, 40 L. Ed. 2d 406 (1974).
24. This is often expressed in the phrase *"cujus est solum, ejus est usque ad coelum et ad inferos"* which is translated "to whomsoever the soil belongs, he owns also to the sky and to the depths." *See* Gilliam v. Bird, 30 N.C. 280 (1848); Ingold v. Phoenix Assur. Co., 230 N.C. 142, 52 S.E.2d 366 (1949). This rule of course does not apply where the ownership of land is divided by horizontal divisions, as where one person owns the surface and another has the right to minerals in the subsurface. It would also not apply in condominium ownership in cases where the ownership of buildings is divided horizontally.
25. *See* United States v. Causby, 328 U.S. 256, 66 S. Ct. 1062 (1946), a case involving a North Carolina chicken farm, which holds that a landowner owns at least as much of the space above the ground as he can use or occupy in connection with the land, and that airplane flights by the U.S. government that are so low and so frequent as to be a direct and immediate interference with the enjoyment and use of the land constituted a "taking" of the landowner's property. *Compare* Griggs v. County of Alleghany, Pennsylvania, 369 U.S. 84, 82 S. Ct. 531 (1962).

See also Lacey v. United States, 595 F.2d 614 (Ct. Cl. 1979); Palisades Citizens Ass'n. v. C.A.B., 420 F.2d 188 (D.C. Cir. 1969), holding that although Congress has declared exclusive national sovereignty in the airspace of the United States, a landowner, as an incident to

soil, such as houses, buildings, barns or fences, with the requisite legal intention that they shall become a permanent addition or improvement on the land.

§ 8. Minerals.

The word "land" includes unmined minerals and fossils imbedded in the earth.[26] While the minerals remain "in place" they are deemed real property, but when they are severed from the earth they become personal property.[27] This may have particular significance where the Statute of Frauds is involved.[28]

The minerals in place under the surface of the earth are susceptible of an ownership distinct from that of the surface.[29] Minerals and mining rights can, therefore, be conveyed or reserved separate from the surface of the land.[30] In such case, ownership of the land is divided horizontally.

After such separate conveyances of the minerals and the surface, two distinct estates are created which are governed by the laws of real property. Since two separate estates are created when minerals are conveyed or reserved separate from the surface of the land, possession of the surface thereafter will raise no presumption of possession of the subsurface containing the minerals for purposes of acquiring title by adverse possession.[31]

---

ownership, has a claim to the superadjacent airspace to the extent that a reasonable use of his land involves such space. If an invasion of the superadjacent airspace is destructive of the landowner's right to use and possess land, the invasion is compensable as a taking or through private tort actions. *But compare* Batten v. United States, 306 F.2d 580 (10th Cir. 1962), *cert. denied,* 372 U.S. 925, 83 S. Ct. 718, 9 L. Ed. 2d 731 (1963), which holds that no recovery can be had for aircraft noise, vibration and smoke when there is no physical invasion of the affected property. Unlike United States v. Causby, *supra,* no direct invasion of the landowner's domain took place.

26. Hoilman v. Johnson, 164 N.C. 268, 80 S.E. 249 (1913).
27. MINOR & WURTS, REAL PROPERTY § 49 (1910); State v. Burt, 64 N.C. 619 (1870).
28. Brown v. Morris, 83 N.C. 251 (1880).
29. *Compare* Sanders v. Wilkerson, 20 N.C. App. 331, 201 S.E.2d 571 (1974); Sanders v. Wilkerson, 285 N.C. 215, 204 S.E.2d 17 (1974). One cannot acquire a right, title or interest in the gravel, sand or dirt in the land of another without a valid writing. He may, however, acquire a license by oral grant.
30. Hoilman v. Johnson, 164 N.C. 268, 80 S.E. 249 (1913); Vance v. Guy, 223 N.C. 409, 27 S.E.2d 117 (1943); Davis v. Land Bank, 219 N.C. 248, 13 S.E.2d 417 (1941); Vance v. Pritchard, 213 N.C. 552, 197 S.E. 182 (1938); Banks v. Tennessee Mineral Products Corp., 202 N.C. 408, 163 S.E. 108 (1932).
31. Vance v. Pritchard, 213 N.C. 552, 197 S.E. 182 (1938); Vance v. Guy, 223 N.C. 409, 27 S.E.2d 117 (1943); Hoilman v. Johnson, 164 N.C. 268, 80 S.E. 249 (1913).

See Baltzley v. Wiseman, 28 N.C. App. 678, 222 S.E.2d 733 (1976), to the effect that when mineral rights in land are by deed or reservation severed from surface rights two distinct estates are created, and that an estate in mineral interests, being a part of the realty, is subject to the ordinary rules of law governing title to real property.

Where one has been granted mineral rights in land, the surface owner may use and deal

§ 9. Fructus Naturales.

Those things which are the natural and spontaneous growth of nature, which require little or no annual planting or cultivation, such as trees, grasses and shrubs, are generally recognized as part of the land to which they are attached; they are called "fructus naturales," and are deemed real property so long as they are unsevered.[32] Since "fructus naturales" are deemed real property, contracts and conveyances (including reservations) relating to trees, grasses and shrubs as they stand growing in the earth must be in writing under the real property section of the Statute of Frauds.[33] Even grants or reservations of fruit on trees must be in writing under the Statute of Frauds.[34] Since fructus naturales are real property they will pass to grantees of the land on which they are located and to mortgagees of the lands unless expressly reserved in writing and the other rules of law relating to real property apply to them.

It should be noted, however, that trees, grasses, shrubs and other fructus naturales become personal property upon their severance from the soil by the landowner.[35] For instance, if timber is cut down and a sale is made of the timber after it is cut, it is a sale of personal property and the formal requisites for a transfer of real property are not required.[36] In addition, although at the time the contract is made the timber is standing, if the landowner contracts to sell the timber and the contract contemplates that title to the timber is not to pass until after the timber is cut, whether it is to be cut by the vendor or by the vendee, the contract is simply a contract for the sale of personal property and the formalities required for the transfer of realty are not necessary.[37]

---

with his property in any legitimate manner not inconsistent with the rights acquired by the owner of the minerals. Conversely, the owner of the minerals has a limited right to use the surface in reaching and removing the minerals. The North Carolina Court of Appeals held in the *Baltzley* case, however, that the owner of mineral rights conveyed by severance deed which granted mineral rights for mining purposes and which contemplated the conducting of a conventional mining operation did not have a right, over the objections of the owner of the surface rights, to conduct on the land, or to grant to another the right to conduct thereon, a "rockhound" business of selling permits allowing persons to come upon the land to search for and remove mineral specimens.

32. Minor & Wurts, Real Property § 38 (1910); Flynt v. Conrad, 61 N.C. 190 (1867).

33. Flynt v. Conrad, 61 N.C. 190 (1867); Johnson v. Wallin, 227 N.C. 669, 44 S.E.2d 83 (1937); Winston v. Lumber Co., 227 N.C. 339, 42 S.E.2d 218 (1947); Westmoreland v. Lowe, 225 N.C. 553, 35 S.E.2d 613 (1945); Ives v. Railroad, 142 N.C. 131, 55 S.E. 74 (1906); 2 Mordecai, Law Lectures 834 (1916).

34. Flynt v. Conrad, 61 N.C. 190 (1867).

35. Lumber Co. v. Brown, 160 N.C. 281 (1912).

36. *Id.*

37. Walston v. Lowery, 212 N.C. 23, 192 S.E. 877 (1937); Johnson v. Wallin, 227 N.C. 339, 42 S.E.2d 218 (1937); Bishop v. Dubose, 252 N.C. 158, 113 S.E.2d 309 (1960).

§ 10. Fructus Industriales.

If vegetable products are the result of annual labor and cultivation, and especially if annually renewed and gathered, like cereals, garden products and other farm crops, they are called "fructus industriales." Fructus industriales are generally regarded as personalty while growing in the soil, although under some circumstances they may be regarded as real property. For instance, a growing crop will pass with a conveyance of land on which the crop is growing, from a vendor to a vendee, unless expressly excepted or reserved to the vendor.[38] For purposes of inheritance, testate succession and creditors' rights, however, they are deemed to be personal chattels.[39] Growing annual crops are likewise deemed to be personal property under the Statute of Frauds and may be transferred or reserved without compliance with the formalities required for the transfer or reservation of titles to real property.[40]

---

38. Flynt v. Conrad, 61 N.C. 190 (1867).
39. *Id.*
40. *Id.; see* Walton v. Jordan, 65 N.C. 170 (1871), and State v. Green, 100 N.C. 419, 5 S.E. 422 (1888). It should be noted, however, that under the Uniform Commercial Code enacted into law in North Carolina in 1965, there is a Statute of Frauds provision which requires contracts for the sale of goods in the amount of $500 or more to be in writing. N.C. GEN. STAT. § 25-2-201. *See also* N.C. GEN. STAT. § 25-2-107. Lowe's Companies, Inc. v. Lipe, 20 N.C. App. 106, 201 S.E.2d 81 (1973); Currituck Grain, Inc. v. Powell, 38 N.C. App. 7, 246 S.E.2d 853 (1978).

The Statute of Frauds provisions of the Uniform Commercial Code are entirely distinct from the Statute of Frauds relating to transfers of real property. N.C. GEN. STAT. § 22-2.

CHAPTER 2

FIXTURES

Article I. Definition and Nature

§ 11. Generally.

Article II. Real Fixtures

§ 12. Defined.
§ 13. Circumstances From Which Permanent Annexation May Be Deduced.
§ 14. Ways of Deducing Intention as to Permanent Annexation — Express Agreement.
§ 15. Same — Character of the Annexation.
§ 16. Same — Relationship of the Parties — Generally.
§ 17. Same — Same — Vendor and Vendee of Realty.
§ 18. Same — Same — Mortgagor and Mortgagee.
§ 19. Same — Same — When Dispute Arises Between Persons Claiming a Decedent's Personal Property and Persons Claiming a Decedent's Real Property.
§ 20. Same — Same — When Annexor Has Given Chattel Mortgage or Executed Conditional Sales Contract or Other Security Interest in Chattel Before Its Annexation.
§ 21. Same — Same — When Fixtures Annexed by Tenant.

Article III. Effect of Uniform Commercial Code

§ 22. Effect Generally; Regulation of Priority of Security Interests.
§ 22.1. Fixture Filing and Its Effect.
§ 22.2. Ten-Day Filing Period: Prior Real Estate Interests.
§ 22.3. Rule as to Subsequent Interests; Inapplicability of Ten-Day Filing Period.
§ 22.4. Priorities When Construction Mortgage Involved.
§ 22.5. Removability of Fixtures.

Article I. Definition and Nature

§ 11. Generally.

"Fixtures" are things located on land which owe their origin or annexation to the soil to the direct agency or hand of man. A fixture is a thing which was originally personal property but which has been attached to land in a more or less permanent manner and under such circumstances that it is considered in law to have become a part of the real property and thus belongs to the owner of the land to which it is attached.

For example, soil may be taken from one tract of land to make brick, stone may be taken from a quarry, or growing trees may be severed from the land to make lumber. So long as any of these items is a part of, imbedded in or attached to the land in its natural state, it is a part of the realty. But as soon as these items are severed or detached from the land they become personal property. Yet, all of these items may be reconverted into realty if the bricks, stone or lumber are used in the erection of a building upon that land from which they are taken or any other land.

Though personalty may be thus converted into realty by becoming fixed to land or to buildings thereon, it does not follow that such will always be the case. Many personal things when attached to realty do not become a part of the realty but remain personalty, depending on the circumstances of the case, or depending upon the relationship of the parties between whom the question arises and their relationship to the annexed items at the time of the annexation. The question that generally arises with respect to fixtures relates to the right of the original owner of the chattel in its chattel form (or his successor in interest) to sever the item from the land and restore it to its character as personalty when it becomes advantageous for him to do so.

It should be observed that the term "fixtures" is often used ambiguously because it is uncertain whether in using the term one is referring to chattels annexed to land which may be separated from the land (and are thus personalty), or whether the term refers to items annexed to land which may not be so separated from the land (and are thus realty). Both judges and text writers frequently use the term "fixtures" in these two opposite senses. The lawyer or student of the law should be careful to determine what precise meaning is attached to the term by judges or writers who use the term. As defined above, the term "fixture" in this work means an item that has become realty by its annexation. Perhaps it would be well, so as to avoid confusion, for the lawyer or student of the law to distinguish the two senses in which the word "fixtures" may be used by denominating or thinking of them as either "personal fixtures" or "real fixtures." "Personal fixtures" retain their character as personalty; "real fixtures" are those items which have become in law so inseparably a part of the land as to be deemed a part of the real property.

Article II. Real Fixtures

§ 12. Defined.

"Real fixtures" consist of things, originally chattels personal, which have been annexed to land, or to things permanently attached to land, by the owner of the chattels or with his assent, and with the intention to make the annexation permanent. All other annexations are "personal fixtures." [1]

It should be noted carefully that in the above definition of "real fixtures," for fixtures to be deemed real property by reason of their annex-

---

1. MINOR & WURTS, REAL PROPERTY § 23 (1910).

ation to the land or to something on the land, it is essential that the chattel should have been annexed permanently. There must have been an intention by the annexor that the annexed item should not thereafter be removed or severed from the land to which it is attached. This intention, however, need not be express or subjective, but may be drawn from the surrounding circumstances attending the annexation.

§ 13. Circumstances From Which Permanent Annexation May Be Deduced.

The following criteria may be utilized in deducing and determining whether a chattel annexed to land has become a part of the real property: (1) Is there an express agreement that the annexed chattel is to be either permanent or temporary? (2) What is the character of the annexation of the chattel to the land—will its severance tear or cause injury to the annexed item or to the realty to which it is attached? (3) What relationship exists between the annexor of the chattel to the land and what relationship exists between the annexor and other claimants—is the annexor's interest in the land a permanent estate since the probability of an intention to annex a chattel permanently to land is in proportion to the permanency of the interest that he claims in the land? (4) What is the nature and purpose of the annexation of the chattel to the land—is it for a "trade," "agricultural," "domestic," or "ornamental" purpose?

§ 14. Ways of Deducing Intention as to Permanent Annexation—Express Agreement.

Articles annexed to land, which might otherwise be considered real fixtures and a part of the land, may by express or implied agreement be made to retain their personal character.

An understanding between the owner of a chattel who affixes it to the land of another and the owner of the land to which it is affixed is binding on subsequent purchasers of the land who take with actual or constructive notice of the understanding.[2] To take another example, an agreement made between a lessor and a lessee that the lessee shall construct a

---

[2] Lee-Moore Oil Co. v. Cleary, 295 N.C. 417, 245 S.E.2d 720 (1978), in which gasoline dispensing equipment and storage tanks were claimed to have been installed under an oral agreement that the equipment would remain the property of the plaintiff-affixer but would be left on the premises "so long as the operator of Marley's Store purchased gasoline solely from plaintiff." When a subsequent purchaser of Marley's Store elected to purchase gasoline from another source, plaintiff insisted on either the return or purchase of its gasoline dispensing equipment. The court found evidence sufficient enough to survive the defendant's motion for a directed verdict holding that while, as a general rule, whatever is attached to the land is understood to be a part of the realty, this depends, to some extent, upon circumstances, and the rights involved must always be subject to explanation by evidence.

building on the leased lands owned by the lessor, and that the lessee shall have the right at the termination of the lease to remove the building and equipment installed by the lessee, will prevent the building and euqipment from becoming a real fixture and part of the realty.[3]

Contractual agreements may also be entered into between the owner of land and one who sells a chattel to the landowner or one who retains title to the chattel, perhaps by a conditional sales contract or by chattel mortgage. By retention of the title or security in the chattel in the conditional seller or chattel mortgagee, the parties evince their intention that the item is to remain personalty and that it shall not become realty upon its annexation to land.[4]

§ 15. Same—Character of the Annexation.

The mode or character of the annexation of a chattel will often be of weight in determining whether the intention of the annexor was to make an item a permanent part of the realty or whether it was to be only temporary and thus to retain its status as personalty.

If a chattel is actually attached to the land or building in such a way that it cannot be detached therefrom without seriously tearing or injuring the soil, land or building to which it is attached, there is strong evidence that the annexation was intended to be permanent and such fixtures will generally be considered real fixtures and nonremovable.[5] If an item affixed to realty cannot be removed without materially injuring the real property from which it is sought to be taken, it is usually a part of that real property.[6]

---

3. *See* Causey v. Orton, 171 N.C. 375, 88 S.E. 513 (1916), in which a lessee was held to have a right to remove houses and fences constructed on lands of the lessor because the lease provided for their removal at the expiration of the lease. *See also* Springs v. Atlantic Ref. Co., 205 N.C. 444, 171 S.E. 635 (1933); Ingold v. Phoenix Assur. Co., 230 N.C. 142, 52 S.E.2d 366 (1949); State v. Hicks, 233 N.C. 511, 64 S.E.2d 871 (1951); Feimster v. Johnson, 64 N.C. 259 (1870); Railroad v. Deal, 90 N.C. 110 (1884), which hold that whether a thing attached to land is a real fixture or chattel personal depends upon the agreement of the parties. The burden of proof is upon the party claiming that a building or structure is personalty to show that under the contract it retained that character. Ingold v. Phoenix Assur. Co., 230 N.C. 142, 52 S.E.2d 366 (1949); Woodworking Co. v. Southwick, 119 N.C. 611, 26 S.E. 253 (1896).

4. Finance Co. v. Weaver, 199 N.C. 178, 153 S.E. 861 (1930); Lancaster v. Ins. Co., 153 N.C. 285, 69 S.E. 214 (1910). The effectiveness of this agreement may vary, depending on who the contestant is against, the chattel mortgagee or conditional vendor, and depending upon the recordation statutes. *See* discussion relating to N.C. Gen. Stat. § 25-9-313, which is the Uniform Commercial Code provision concerned with fixtures, in note 18 *infra*.

5. Minor & Wurts, Real Property § 26 (1910). *E.g., see* Bryan v. Lawrence, 50 N.C. 337 (1858), in which the court held that stills, encased in brick and mortar work, which could not be removed without taking down the brickwork, were real fixtures. *See also* Horne v. Smith, 105 N.C. 322, 11 S.E. 373 (1890).

6. 1 Reeves, Real Property 23 (1909). *But see* Brunswick-Balke-Collender Co. v. Bowling Alleys, 204 N.C. 609, 169 S.E. 186 (1933), in which the court allowed the removal and sale of bowling alleys affixed to a building although their removal left holes that would have to be filled up. The court made provision, however, for the payment of damages to the owners of the building for the injuries caused by removal of the alleys.

§ 15 FIXTURES § 15

In addition, if the material or appliances built into a house or wall cannot be removed without dismembering or virtually destroying such material or appliances *themselves*, they will be deemed to have become real fixtures and they cannot be removed.[7]

On the other hand, the mode of physical attachment of an item to the land may not be a significant criterion in determining the intention of the party making the attachment, if the intention that the item is to be a part of the realty is provided by other means. For instance, chattels of a heavy and permanent character, even though not imbedded and not physically fastened to the land, but merely placed on the land and held in place by their own weight, such as buildings, fences, statuaries, monuments and machinery, may be real fixtures.[8]

---

7. Presumably on the theory that if their removal can be effected only by destroying the items and rendering them virtually worthless, an intention of the annexor that they shall be permanently affixed is indicated. *See* MORDECAI, LAW LECTURES 472 (1916). *Cf.* Ingold v. Phoenix Assur. Co., 230 N.C. 142, 52 S.E.2d 366 (1949), in which the court said: "To attempt to remove the additions thereto [brick walls] would require him substantially to destroy the very thing he claims. The court below was not required to assume the parties so intended." *But see* BROWN, PERSONAL PROPERTY § 144 (1955), in which the author states that modern authorities permit tenants to remove trade fixtures even if they are reduced to raw materials by removal.

8. REEVES, REAL PROPERTY 25 (1909); 1 MORDECAI, LAW LECTURES 474 (1916); Deal v. Palmer, 72 N.C. 582 (1875) (heavy machinery); Bryan v. Lawrence, 50 N.C. 337 (1858) (planks laid down unfastened in gin house); Latham v. Blakely, 70 N.C. 368 (1874) (cotton gin in building without being fastened thereto). As to statuary and monuments, *see* the leading case of Snedeker v. Waring, 12 N.Y. 170 (1854), in which a sculptor placed a statue of Washington, which with its pedestal weighed over three tons, in front of his house. The statue was simply set on a foundation of stone and was not otherwise fastened to the land. It, along with a two hundred pound sun dial also constructed on another stone block, was held to be a real fixture and a part of the realty.

It should be noted that the courts "pay more regard to the purposes which are to be served by the thing attached than to the manner of making the actual attachment." Latham v. Blakely, 70 N.C. 368 (1874). In other words, the chief value in considering the manner and mode of annexation of a chattel to realty is only for the purpose of showing the intention of the annexor. If the chattel item is fastened to the realty, this raises a presumption or inference of fact that the item was added to the realty for the purpose of becoming a part thereof. If the chattel item is not fastened to the realty, this raises a presumption or inference of fact that the item was *not* intended to be a part of the realty. Under the modern view that the intention of the annexor is the determining factor as to whether a chattel has become a part of the real property or remains personal property, either of the presumptions can be rebutted by the showing of a contrary intention. Such contrary intention can be shown either expressly or implied from attending circumstances. Following this analysis, the mode and manner of annexation, whether firm or flimsy, or by weight and gravity only, are important simply as they provide convincing evidence, one way or the other, that the annexor intended that the chattel item that he used in connection with real property was meant to become real property, or that he intended for it to be only a temporary addition and for it to remain personalty. *See generally* Brown v. Land Bank, 213 N.C. 594, 197 S.E. 140 (1938).

§ 16. Same—Relationship of the Parties—Generally.

The legal relation between the parties who are adversely claiming an item affixed to land is very often an important criterion for determining whether it is realty or personalty. The relationship which exists between the parties and between the annexing party and the land to which an item of personalty is annexed is often indicative of the reasonably presumable intention of the annexor at the time he made the annexation. The more permanent the interest of the annexor in the realty, the more likely is his intention that the item annexed is to become a part of the real property. Conversely, if one has only a temporary interest in the real property, it is reasonably presumable that he does not intend for an attachment to the realty to be more than temporary, to parallel his limited interest in the realty, and thus to remain personalty.

That the status of the parties, both as between themselves and as to the land to which items are annexed, often determines whether the items become realty or remain personalty can be demonstrated by analysis of a number of legal relationships. Analysis will show that the same article that may be regarded as a real fixture in one situation may be considered as personalty where a different relationship exists. The effect of the relationships of the parties as between themselves and as to the realty to which annexations are made will be separately considered in the following situations: (1) When a dispute arises between a vendor and a vendee of the realty to which an annexation has been made; (2) when a dispute arises between a mortgagor and a mortgagee of realty to which an annexation has been made; (3) when a dispute arises between persons entitled to a decedent's real property and persons entitled to the decedent's personal property; (4) when a dispute arises between one who holds or acquires title to real property and another who holds title to personal property which is affixed to the real property, title to the personalty being retained by a chattel mortgage or conditional sales contract; (5) when a dispute arises between a landlord and his tenant as to items annexed by the tenant; and (6) when a dispute arises between the representatives of a life tenant who has made an annexation of personalty to realty, and a reversioner, remainderman or other subsequent owner of the land.

§ 17. Same—Same—Vendor and Vendee of Realty.

It can be said generally that when an item of personalty is attached to realty by one who is both the owner of the realty and the owner of the chattel, the attached item becomes a part of the realty in the absence of positive evidence of his intention to the contrary. There is a natural

While the general rule is that a tenant may remove items which he annexes to real property in which he has a lease, there are dictum statements in certain cases decided by the North Carolina Supreme Court which suggest that there may be a difference in the degree of liberality to tenants making annexations depending on the purposes for which the annexations are made. For that reason, annexations for (1) trade purposes, (2) agricultural purposes, (3) mixed purposes of trade and agriculture, and (4) domestic and ornamental purposes, will be touched upon separately.

(b) *For trade purposes.* With respect to trade purposes, it is the purpose of the law to encourage trade, manufacture, industry and transportation and the law allows a tenant who places chattels on leased realty to remove whatever he has affixed to the premises for trade purposes.[23] They are called "trade fixtures" and remain personal property of the tenant. Thus machinery,[24] a brick depot,[25] a bar counter and bar fixtures,[26] poultry

---

23. *See* Railroad v. Deal, 90 N.C. 110 (1884), in which the court said: "It is the policy of the law to encourage trade, manufacture, and transportation, by affording them all reasonable facilities. Buildings, fixtures, machinery, and such things, certainly intended and calculated to promote them, are treated, not as part of the land, but distinct from it, belonging to the tenant, to be disposed of or removed at his will and pleasure. Hence if a house, or other structure, is erected upon land only for the exercise of trade or the mixed purpose of trade and agriculture, no matter how it may be attached to it, it belongs to the tenant, and may be removed by him during his term, and in some classes of cases, after it is ended." *See also* Horne v. Smith, 105 N.C. 322, 11 S.E. 373 (1890).

Ilderton Oil Co. v. Riggs, 13 N.C. App. 547, 186 S.E.2d 691 (1972), holds that a trade fixture may be removed by a tenant who has attached it for trade purposes *even after* termination of his lease. That case holds further that an oil company which placed an underground storage tank, pump and accessory equipment on leased premises under an agreement with the tenant had the same right to remove such trade fixtures as the tenant would have had if the tenant had owned them. It was held that an article may generally be regarded as a trade fixture if it is annexed for the purpose of aiding in the conduct by the tenant of a calling exercised on the leased premises for the purpose of pecuniary profit. A storage tank, pump and accessory equipment were held to be "trade fixtures."

The *Ilderton* case indicated that the liberality extended a tenant, in favor of trade and to encourage industry, may not apply as between vendor and vendee or mortgagor and mortgagee. When fixtures are annexed to the land by the *owner*, actual or potential, the purpose is to enhance the value of the freehold, and to be permanent. But with the tenant a different purpose is to be served; hence, for the encouragement of trade or manufacturing, the tenant is allowed to remove what has apparently become affixed to the land, if affixed for the purposes of trade and not merely for the better enjoyment of the premises. Stephens v. Carter, 246 N.C. 318, 98 S.E.2d 311 (1957), cited and distinguished.

24. Causey v. Plaid Mills, 119 N.C. 180, 25 S.E. 863 (1896); Railroad v. Deal, 90 N.C. 110 (1884); Horne v. Smith, 105 N.C. 322, 11 S.E. 373 (1890).

25. Railroad v. Deal, 90 N.C. 110 (1884).

26. Woodworking Co. v. Southwick, 119 N.C. 611, 26 S.E. 253 (1896).

§ 21 REAL ESTATE LAW IN NORTH CAROLINA § 21

houses and fences,[27] a gasoline service station building,[28] a warehouse,[29] and engines, gins or condensers [30] attached to land under proper circumstances have been held to be personal trade fixtures and thus removable by tenants who install them for trade purposes.

(c) *For agricultural purposes.* With respect to chattels placed on land for agricultural purposes, the common-law English doctrine was that they were not so easily removable as trade fixtures and that they were deemed real fixtures and not to be severed.[31]

The common-law English view has been carried forward in a North Carolina *dictum* statement [32] although no square holding on the point has been located.

There is no good reason for not granting to agricultural tenants the same rights of removal of agricultural fixtures as are accorded to tenants with respect to trade fixtures.[33] The tendency generally in the United States is to regard items annexed by a tenant for agricultural purposes as entitled to no less favor than those annexed for purposes of trade. Just as trade and manufacturing is to be promoted, there should also be a policy to promote the cultivation and improvement of the country through agriculture. A tenant who places a structure on land for his temporary use for

---

27. Causey v. Orton, 171 N.C. 375, 88 S.E. 513 (1916).
28. Springs v. Atlantic Ref. Co., 205 N.C. 444, 171 S.E. 635 (1933).
29. Haywood v. Briggs, 227 N.C. 108, 41 S.E.2d 289 (1946). In this case, while the court held that a tenant should be entitled to remove a warehouse placed on land for trade purposes as against his lessor (a life tenant), he should not be entitled to remove the building as against a remainderman after the death of the tenant's lessor. *Quaere* the correctness of the decision in light of the rule that the administrator or executor of a life tenant is entitled to remove trade fixtures placed on land by the life tenant. Should not the lessee of a life tenant have the same right?
30. *See generally* Overman v. Sasser, 107 N.C. 432, 12 S.E. 64 (1890).
31. Elwes v. Maw, 3 East (K.B.) (1802).
32. *See, e.g.,* Overman v. Sasser, 107 N.C. 432, 12 S.E. 64 (1890).
33. *See* 1 MORDECAI, LAW LECTURES 477 (1916): "it is palpably unjust and devoid of sound reason, and has been questioned by such able lawyers as Justice Story of the Supreme Court of the United States and Judge Putnam of the Supreme Court of Massachusetts and Judge Rogers of the Supreme Court of Pennsylvania. Our own court, while announcing the rule above stated, did so only in giving a correct summary of the English leading case of *Elwes v. Maw,* and did not have the question before it, nor did it specially discuss this branch of the law of fixtures. I do not regard the law to be settled on this point in this state, and trust that, when it shall be squarely presented, the views expressed by the learned gentlemen here referred to may be given careful consideration." *See* Van Ness v. Packard, 27 U.S. (2 Pet.) 137, 7 L. Ed. 374 (1829), for Justice Story's repudiation of *Elwes v. Maw.* He states the universal policy in this country has always been to procure its cultivation and improvement; "what tenant could afford to erect fixtures of such expense or value, if he was to lose his whole interest therein by the very act of erection?" *See also* BROWN, PERSONAL PROPERTY 747 (1955).

§ 21 FIXTURES § 21

agricultural purposes should be allowed to remove such item, provided he does not injure the premises by the removal.[34]

Particular notice should be taken of the law as it relates to manure.[35] In North Carolina, a tenant has a right to remove all manure made by his stock during his term,[36] apparently without regard to whether he feeds the stock making the manure from crops raised on the land or from crops raised elsewhere.[37]

(d) *For mixed purposes, both trade and agricultural.* Items annexed to land for the mixed purposes of trade and agriculture are governed by the law of trade fixtures and may be removed by the tenant making the annexation if the removal can be effected without injuring the premises.[38]

(e) *For domestic and ornamental purposes.* Items annexed to land by a tenant for the purpose of rendering it more comfortable and attractive during his term are generally deemed to be removable by the tenant provided the items can be removed without injury to the premises. For instance, windows and a window sash held in place by strips tacked to the window frame with shingle nails could be removed by a tenant.[39] Hence, mirrors, wardrobes, stoves, radiators, chandeliers, marble mantels and even wainscoting, fixed by screws, have been held frequently to be

---

34. Perhaps "agriculture" can itself be deemed a "trade" today. It is certainly true that agriculture affects "interstate commerce." See Wickard v. Filburn, 317 U.S. 111, 63 S. Ct. 82, 87 L. Ed. 122 (1942). Suggestive to lawyers seeking to have an item declared to be a trade fixture instead of an agricultural fixture is the 1916 case of Causey v. Orton, 171 N.C. 375, 88 S.E. 513 (1916), in which the court held poultry houses to be trade fixtures.

35. This subject is treated here, in the day of tractor use on the farm instead of horses, to exhibit, if nothing more, the propensity of persons to sue concerning almost anything!

36. Smithwick v. Ellison, 24 N.C. 326 (1842). The manure must be removed by the tenant during his term and care must be taken not to remove a part of the virgin soil in its removal. If virgin soil is removed with the "scraping" of manure, the landlord may maintain an action of trespass *de bonis asportatis,* or *trover,* for the removal of the virgin soil. If the tenant leaves the premises without removing the manure, it becomes the property of the reversioner. 1 MORDECAI, LAW LECTURES 547 (1916).

37. *See* TIFFANY, REAL PROPERTY § 432 (abr. ed. 1940), for the contrary view that manure derived from crops raised on the land becomes realty while manure produced from crops raised elsewhere remains personalty.

38. Overman v. Sasser, 107 N.C. 432, 12 S.E. 64 (1890). *See also* Ilderton Oil Co. v. Riggs, 13 N.C. App. 547, 186 S.E.2d 691 (1972). An article may generally be regarded as a trade fixture if it is annexed for the purpose of aiding in the conduct by the tenant of a calling exercised on the leased premises for the purpose of pecuniary profit. It was held that an oil company which placed an underground storage tank, pump and accessory equipment on leased premises under an agreement with the tenant had the same right to remove them as the tenant would have had if the tenant owned them. It was held that the storage tank, pump and accessory equipment were "trade fixtures."

The *Ilderton* case holds additionally that a trade fixture may be removed by a tenant *even after* termination of his lease. The oil company which placed the storage tank, pump and accessory equipment on the leased premises under an agreement with the tenant had the same rights of removal as the tenant would have had if the tenant had owned them.

39. State v. Whitener, 93 N.C. 590 (1885).

removable by tenants for years who made such annexations.[40] Note, however, that removal should be allowed only where circumstances indicate that the annexation was to be merely temporary, as where the chattel is easily detachable without tearing or injuring the premises to which attached.[41]

Article III. Effect of Uniform Commercial Code

§ 22. Effect Generally; Regulation of Priority of Security Interests.

The Uniform Commercial Code became effective in North Carolina on July 1, 1967.[42] The purpose of the Code's provisions relating to fixtures is to regulate the priority of security interests in such fixtures. These security interests in fixtures require legislative protection against certain conflicting interests of an encumbrancer or owner of realty. In 1975, the Code's treatment of fixtures was altered in a number of important respects by the amendment of Article 9.[43] The almost total revision of the priorities statute reads as follows:

> § 25-9-313. Priority of security interests in fixtures. — (1) In this section and in the provisions of part 4 of this article referring to fixture filing, unless the context otherwise requires
> (a) goods are "fixtures" when they become so related to particular real estate that an interest in them arises under real estate law;
> (b) a "fixture filing" is the filing of a financial statement covering goods which are or are to become fixtures and conforming to the requirements of subsection (5) of G.S. 25-9-402 or of a mortgage or deed of trust conforming to the requirements of subsection (6) of G.S. 25-9-402;
> (c) a mortgage is a "construction mortgage" to the extent that it secures an obligation incurred for the construction of an improvement on land including the acquisition cost of the land, if the recorded writing so indicates.
> (2) A security interest under this article may be created in goods which are fixtures or may continue in goods which become fixtures,

---

40. *See* 1 MORDECAI, LAW LECTURES 478 (1916); MINOR & WURTS, REAL PROPERTY § 32 (1910).

41. *See* 1 MORDECAI, LAW LECTURES 478 (1916), where the author states: "window glass and other things the removal of which would tend to expose the property to decay, etc., cannot be removed even by a tenant."

42. N.C. GEN. STAT. §§ 25-9-101 through 25-10-107.

43. *See* N.C. GEN. STAT. § 25-9-313 (Cum. Supp. 1977). To avoid confusion, all statutory references in the footnotes and body of Article III are to revised N.C. GEN. STAT. § 25-9-313 (Cum. Supp. 1977).

See generally Urban & Miles, *Mechanics' Liens for the Improvement of Real Property: Recent Developments in Perfection, Enforcement, and Priority,* 12 WAKE FOREST L. REV. 283, 290 et seq. (1976); Urban, *Future Advances Lending in North Carolina,* 13 WAKE FOREST L. REV. 297 (1977).

but no security interest exists under this article in ordinary building materials incorporated into an improvement on land.

(3) This article does not prevent creation of an encumbrance upon fixtures pursuant to real estate law.

(4) A perfected security interest in fixtures has priority over the conflicting interest of an encumbrancer or owner of the real estate where

(a) the security interest is a purchase money security interest, the interest of the encumbrancer or owner arises before the goods become fixtures, the security interest is perfected by a fixture filing before the goods become fixtures or within 10 days thereafter, and the debtor has an interest of record in the real estate or is in possession of the real estate; or

(b) the security interest is perfected by a fixture filing before the interest of the encumbrancer or owner is of record, the security interest has priority over any conflicting interest of a predecessor in title of the encumbrancer or owner, and the debtor has an interest of record in the real estate or is in possession of the real estate; or

(c) the fixtures are readily removable factory or office machines or readily removable replacements of domestic appliances which are consumer goods, and before the goods become fixtures the security interest is perfected by any method permitted by this article; or

(d) the conflicting interest is a lien on the real estate obtained by legal or equitable proceedings after the security interest was perfected by any method permitted by this article.

(5) A security interest in fixtures, whether or not perfected, has priority over the conflicting interest of an encumbrancer or owner of the real estate where

(a) the encumbrancer or owner has consented in writing to the security interest or has disclaimed an interest in the goods as fixtures; or

(b) the debtor has a right to remove the goods as against the encumbrancer or owner. If the debtor's right terminates, the priority of the security interest continues for a reasonable time.

(6) Notwithstanding paragraph (a) of subsection (4) but otherwise subject to subsections (4) and (5), a security interest in fixtures is subordinate to a construction mortgage recorded before the goods become fixtures if the goods become fixtures before the completion of the construction. To the extent that it is given to refinance a construction mortgage, a mortgage has this priority to the same extent as the construction mortgage.

(7) In cases not within the preceding subsections, a security interest in fixtures is subordinate to the conflicting interest of an encumbrancer or owner of the related real estate who is not the debtor.

(8) When the secured party has priority over all owners and encumbrancers of the real estate, he may, on default, subject to the provisions of part 5, remove his collateral from the real estate but he must reimburse any encumbrancer or owner of the real estate who is not the debtor and who has not otherwise agreed for the cost of repair of any physical injury, but not for any diminution in value of the real estate caused by the absence of the goods removed or by any necessity of replacing them. A person entitled to reimbursement may refuse

permission to remove until the secured party gives adequate security for the performance of this obligation. (1965, c. 700, s. 1; 1967, c. 562, s. 1; 1975, c. 862, s. 7.)

As evidenced by subsection (1) (a) of the above quoted priorities statute, the Code does not define when goods or chattels become fixtures, except to make it clear in subsection (2) that "ordinary building materials incorporated into an improvement on land" are not fixtures. It is the intent of the drafters of the revised Code that no inference may be drawn from a fixture filing that the secured party concedes that the goods are or will become fixtures; *i.e.*, the filing may be purely precautionary.

Although more complex than the former statute and laden with special rules and cross references, the statute can be generally summarized as having the following effect: (1) to make a "fixture filing" rather than "attachment" the crucial factor in most priorities problems; (2) to create a ten-day grace period for "fixture filing" as against *prior* real estate interests; and, (3) to give special priority status to a prior recorded construction mortgage. A more detailed discussion of these and other revisions is set forth in the following sections.

§ 22.1. Fixture Filing and Its Effect.

Under the former priorities statute, a security interest which *attached* in a chattel before it was annexed to the land of another prevailed over the landowner and prior mortgagees of the land. This could sometimes result in unsatisfactory consequences. A prior mortgagee of the land, for example, might grant extensions to a mortgagor in the belief that the real estate mortgage was the only encumbrance on the property. Later, the mortgagee might make the unhappy discovery that a number of fixtures had been installed which no filing or recording disclosed. With a few exceptions, the revised statute requires that a proper "fixture filing" be made for the protection of the secured party against both existing and future real estate interests, even where the security interest attaches to goods before installation. [44]

The term "fixture filing" is defined at (1) (b) of the revised statute and must be indexed and recorded in the real estate records so that a proper search of those records will reveal the filing. [45]

§ 22.2. Ten-Day Filing Period: Prior Real Estate Interests.

As against *prior* encumbrancers or owners, section (4) (a) of the revised statute provides for a ten-day filing period for the fixture filing of a purchase money security interest in a fixture. The fixture filing must take

---

[44]. Funk, *The Proposed Revision of Article 9 of The Uniform Commercial Code*, 26 THE BUS. LAWYER 1465, 1471, 1472 (1971).

[45]. *Id.* p. 1472; N.C. GEN. STAT. § 25-9-313 (4) (a), (b).

place either before the goods become fixtures or within ten days thereafter under this section. Note carefully the specific requirements of section (4) (a): The security interest must be a purchase money security interest and the debtor must have an interest of record in the real estate or be in possession of the real estate (*e.g.*, a lessee). [46]

§ 22.3. Rule as to Subsequent Interests; Inapplicability of Ten-Day Filing Period.

The ten-day filing period does not apply to *subsequent* purchasers or encumbrancers of the real estate. [47] As to them, the fixture security interest cannot defeat their interest unless it is properly filed and would prevail under the general principle of priority set forth in section (4) (b). [48] Thus the general standard or working rule as to priority is a familiar one: a prior, proper fixture filing prevails over subsequently filed real estate interests. [49]

§ 22.4. Priorities When Construction Mortgage Involved.

Special rules exist under the new statute where a recorded construction mortgage is involved. As the wording of section (6) of the statute indicates, "a security interest in fixtures is subordinate to a construction

---

46. Subject to the special construction mortgage rules of N.C. GEN. STAT. § 25-9-313 (6).
47. For this reason, a person with a purchase money security interest should file promptly for protection against subsequent interests in spite of the ten-day filing period allowed as against prior interests in N.C. GEN. STAT. § 25-9-13 (4) (a).
48. Under the priorities statute as it existed prior to the 1975 revision, if a subsequent purchaser of the realty for value, lienor or encumbrancer of the real property who made a subsequent advance had "knowledge" of the existence of the security interest in the item annexed to realty, interests in the real property in such case remained subordinate to the security interest even though such security interest had not been perfected by filing and recordation. This "knowledge" provision ran counter to the maxim long held in North Carolina that "no notice, however full and formal, will supply the place of registration." Under the revised statute, it appears that a combination of N.C. GEN. STAT. § 25-9-313 (4) (b) and (7) returns this specific area of priorities to a pure race concept. Knowledge of the existence of another unfiled or unrecorded interest does not affect the priority and the first to file prevails.
49. *See* the limiting language of several portions of this statute: N.C. GEN. STAT. § 25-9-313 (4) (b), requiring that the secured party have priority over any conflicting interest of a predecessor in title of the encumbrancer or owner. To cite one example, an assignee of a prior mortgage has an interest superior to a fixture security interest even though the assignment is recorded after the fixture filing. This is in accord with normal real estate practice and common sense. N.C. GEN. STAT. § 25-9-313 (4) (d) sets forth a special limitation allowing a fixture security interest to prevail as against a judgment lienor of the real estate even if the security interest has not been filed in the real estate records. The security interest may, in this situation, have been perfected by any method permitted by Article 9. Therefore, a proper chattel filing would enable the security interest to prevail over a later judgment lien. *See also* N.C. GEN. STAT. § 25-9-313 (4) (c) dealing with specific items of property and also allowing perfection "by any method permitted by this article."

mortgage recorded before the goods become fixtures if the goods become fixtures before the completion of the construction." Thus, a recorded construction mortgage is accorded a special priority during the construction period up to completion of the project. [50]

The statute defines the term "construction mortgage" as one that "secures an obligation incurred for the construction of an improvement on land including the acquisition cost of the land, if the recorded writing so indicates." The revised statute is intended to cover both optional advances and advances pursuant to commitment. Refinancing of a construction mortgage is to have the same priority as the mortgage itself. But additions to a building made long after completion of the improvement should not trigger the priority of section (6) simply because they are financed by an open end clause of the original construction mortgage.

§ 22.5. Removability of Fixtures.

The revised statute makes no substantive alteration of the removability provision in the former statute. [51] Therefore in all cases where a party has a security interest in an item affixed to realty and has priority over all other persons as to items affixed to the realty, the party with such superior security interest may, upon default, remove the item annexed from the real property, provided that the remover must reimburse any encumbrancer or owner of the real estate who is not the debtor and who has not otherwise agreed for the cost of repair of any physical injury resulting to the real estate caused by the removal. [52] As with the previous statute, the revised one allows a person entitled to reimbursement to refuse permission to remove until the secured party gives adequate security for the performance of the reimbursement obligation.

---

50. 1972 OFFICIAL TEXT WITH COMMENTS § 9-313, Comment 4 (e).

See generally Adams, *Security Interests in Fixtures Under Mississippi's Uniform Commercial Code*, 47 MISS. L.J. 831 (1976). *See also* Part III of this article, at 897 to 927 for an excellent summary of The 1972 Official Text of U.C.C. § 9-313.

51. N.C. GEN. STAT. § 25-9-313 (8).

52. The former rule was that one could not remove a fixture from real property if it caused "material injury to the freehold." *See* Cox v. New Bern Lighting & Fuel Co., 151 N.C. 62, 65 S.E. 648 (1909). The former rule is expressly abandoned, and substituted for it is the Code rule that a secured party entitled to priority in an item affixed to realty may in all cases sever and remove collateral, subject, however, to a duty to reimburse any real estate claimant (other than the debtor) for any physical injury caused by the removal.

Part 2
Estates and Interests in Real Property

CHAPTER 3

ESTATES GENERALLY

§ 23. History; Classification of Estates Under Common Law of England.

§ 23. History; Classification of Estates Under Common Law of England.

North Carolina retains the hierarchy of estates which were existent under the common law of England, although modified in some respects. The term "estate," originally derived from the Latin term "status,"[1] was and is descriptive of the quantum or potential duration of one's enjoyment of an interest in land that is or may become possessory.[2] As was the case under the common law, the degree, quantity, nature, duration, extent and incidents of one's possessory interest in land can be determined depending upon the classification of his interest under the scheme of estates.

Under the English common law, there were two great divisions of estates, the freehold estates and estates of less than freehold.[3] In tabulated form, the classification of estates is as follows:

I. Estates of Freehold.
   A. Estates of Inheritance.
      1. Fee Simple.
      2. Determinable, Base or Qualified Fee.
      3. Fee Conditional.
      4. Fee Tail.
   B. Estates Not of Inheritance (Life Estates).
      1. By Act of the Parties (Conventional).
         a. Estate for Tenant's Own Life.
         b. Estate for Life of Another (*Pur Autre Vie*).
         c. Estates Which May Last for Life but Terminate by an Uncertain Event.

---

1. MOYNIHAN, INTRODUCTION TO THE LAW OF REAL PROPERTY 28 (1962). "It speaks to us of a time when land holding was inseparably connected with personal status and a man's position in the community was determined by the estate he held." MOYNIHAN, PRELIMINARY SURVEY OF THE LAW OF REAL PROPERTY 16 (1940).

2. RESTATEMENT OF THE LAW OF PROPERTY § 9 (1936) defines "estate" as an interest in land which (a) is or may become possessory; and (b) is ownership measured in terms of duration.

3. Under the feudal law a "freehold" was a tenure in land requiring the rendition of services of such a nature that they were not beneath the dignity of a free man, such as the obligation to perform military services for the lord, or to pay a certain amount of money or to perform some honorary personal service. An "unfree tenure," on the other hand, was a tenure requiring the rendition of services of a menial or servile nature. The services required of the "unfree tenants" were not fixed, but subject to the lord's arbitrary will, such as plowing the lord's fields or building his hedges as serfs or peasants. Under the feudal law, only "freehold" estates were recognized as "real property" and only tenants of freehold tenures could sue and be sued in the king's courts in real actions with respect to title to land. The tenants of the unfree tenures had to seek their remedies in their lords' courts.

2. By Operation of Law.
    a. Estates Tail After Possibility of Issue Extinct.
    b. Curtesy.
    c. Dower.
II. Estates of Less Than Freehold.
  A. Estates for Years.
  B. Estates at Will.
  C. Estates From Year to Year.
  D. Estates by Sufferance.

These estates, to the extent that they or their counterparts are found in North Carolina law, will be discussed in the order of the above listing.

CHAPTER 4

INHERITABLE ESTATES

Article I. Fee Simple Estates

Division 1. General Provisions

§ 24. The Estate of Fee Simple Generally.
§ 25. Necessity for Word "Heirs" to Create at Common Law.
§ 26. Words of Inheritance Not Necessary Under Modern Statutes.
§ 27. Word "Heirs" Not Always Word of Limitation in North Carolina; Statutory and Constructional Exception.

Division 2. Incidents of the Fee Simple Estate

§ 28. Unlimited Power of Alienation.
§ 29. Descent to Heirs.
§ 30. Subject to Owner's Debts.
§ 31. Spouses' Rights.
§ 32. Escheats to State in Absence of Inheritable Blood.
§ 33. Forfeiture for Conviction of Treason or Felony Not Applicable in North Carolina.
§ 34. Subject to Power of Eminent Domain.

Division 3. Determinable, Base or Qualified Fee Simple Estates

§ 35. The Fee Simple Determinable.
§ 36. Same — Incidents.
§ 37. The Fee Simple Subject to a Condition Subsequent.
§ 38. Same — Incidents.
§ 39. The Fee Simple Subject to an Executory Interest.
§ 40. Same — Incidents.
§ 41. Effects of Illegal, Impossible or Repugnant Limitations and Conditions on Determinable, Base or Qualified Estates; Rule Against Perpetuities Applicable to Estates Subject to Executory Interests.

Article II. Fee Tail and Fee Conditional Estates

§ 42. Neither Fee Tail nor Fee Conditional Estates in Effect in North Carolina.
§ 43. Fee Tail Estates — Forms for Creating at Common Law — Generally.
§ 44. Same — Same — Rule in Wild's Case.
§ 45. Same — Statutory Change in North Carolina.

Article I. Fee Simple Estates

Division 1. General Provisions

§ 24. The Estate of Fee Simple Generally.

The estate of fee simple is the entire and absolute property in land. It is the most extensive estate or interest that can be owned in land and has a potentially infinite duration. A fee simple estate gives to the owner unconditional powers to dispose of the entire property during his life, and will pass by descent to his heirs or legal representatives upon his death.

§ 25. Necessity for Word "Heirs" to Create at Common Law.

At the early common law a fee simple estate could not be created unless the grantor made the conveyance "to the grantee *and his heirs.*"[1] If the words of inheritance "and his heirs" were omitted in the grant of land, the tenant's estate was not an inheritable estate but was limited to a life estate.[2] The words "and his heirs" thus became "magic" words indispensably necessary to evince the grantor's intention to create an inheritable estate in an individual by inter vivos conveyance; they were the only words which could serve this purpose. When the word "heirs" was thus used in a grant "to the grantee and his heirs," it was not considered a word of "purchase" vesting any estate or interest in the heirs themselves under the grant. The word "heirs," when used in a conveyance "to grantee and his heirs," was a word of "limitation," or a word marking out, limiting and describing the estate conveyed to the grantee, designating only that the grantee took an inheritable estate in fee.[3]

The rule requiring use of words of inheritance to create a fee was not applicable in conveyances to corporations,[4] conveyances by will,[5] conveyances to trustees,[6] conveyances referring to another deed "as fully as the land is conveyed to me by the within deed,"[7] equitable conveyances,[8] or conveyances to a government.[9]

§ 26. Words of Inheritance Not Necessary Under Modern Statutes.

While North Carolina followed the common law and held generally that a deed of conveyance which omitted the word "heirs" did not create a fee simple estate but created only a life estate in the grantee in conveyances prior to 1879,[10] and only conveyed a life estate, the North Carolina Supreme Court even before 1879 began to break away from the common-law rule and held that if the word "heirs" appeared anywhere in a deed that it could be transposed from the warranty clause of the deed

---

1. RESTATEMENT OF PROPERTY § 27 (1936).
2. *E.g.*, a conveyance "To *B*," "To *B* forever," or "To *B* in fee simple" created only life estates at the common law. RESTATEMENT OF PROPERTY § 27 (1936).
3. "Words of limitation are those marking or defining the quantum of interest given to the grantee; words of purchase indicate the grantee. Put another way, words of purchase indicate him who takes; words of limitation indicate what is taken. A purchaser is any person acquiring an estate in any way other than by descent. The term is not restricted to a grantee who pays value for the conveyance." MOYNIHAN, INTRODUCTION TO THE LAW OF REAL PROPERTY 31 (1962).
4. RESTATEMENT OF PROPERTY § 34 (1936); 2 MORDECAI, LAW LECTURES 1021 (1916).
5. RESTATEMENT OF PROPERTY § 37 (1936); 2 MORDECAI, LAW LECTURES 1021 (1916).
6. RESTATEMENT OF PROPERTY § 32 (1936); 2 MORDECAI, LAW LECTURES 1021 (1916).
7. RESTATEMENT OF PROPERTY § 28 (1936); 2 MORDECAI, LAW LECTURES 1021 (1916).
8. RESTATEMENT OF PROPERTY § 36 (1936); 2 MORDECAI, LAW LECTURES 1021 (1916).
9. RESTATEMENT OF PROPERTY § 35 (1936); 2 MORDECAI, LAW LECTURES 1021 (1916).
10. Anderson v. Logan, 105 N.C. 266, 11 S.E. 361 (1890).

to the habendum or premises clause in order that the deed would convey a fee simple title.[11] It was later held, relative to deeds executed before 1879, that a court in the exercise of its equitable jurisdiction could supply the omitted word "heirs" to make a deed convey a fee simple title if it appeared otherwise from the deed that the grantor intended to convey a fee simple title.[12]

In 1879 a statute was passed which provides that any deed with or without the word "heirs" will be construed as conveying a fee simple title "unless such conveyance shall in plain and express words show that the grantor meant to convey an estate of less dignity."[13] If, however, upon examination of a deed it clearly appears that the grantor intended to convey a life estate or some lesser estate, the deed will not be held to convey a fee simple.[14]

While it is no longer necessary to use the word "heirs" to create a fee simple in North Carolina or in most states, most deeds are still written "to grantee and his heirs." The effect is the same as at common law and conveys a fee simple title. Use of the word "heirs" in deeds precludes ambiguities and misinterpretations that a different estate was intended by the grantor. The word "heirs" used in such manner is still only a word of limitation designating the nature of the grantee's estate and creates no purchase interest in any heirs of the grantee.

§ 27. Word "Heirs" Not Always Word of Limitation in North Carolina; Statutory and Constructional Exception.

While it is stated in the preceding section that the word "heirs" when used in connection with the name of a grantee in a deed is a word of "limitation," there are certain instances in which the word "heirs" is a word of purchase, the granting instrument in which it appears creating

---

11. The ancient common-law rule was that the word "heirs" should appear, as indicating the grantee's estate, either in the premises or habendum. That the word could be transposed, see Carolina Real Estate Co. v. Bland, 152 N.C. 225, 67 S.E. 483 (1910); Tucker v. Williams, 117 N.C. 119, 23 S.E. 90 (1895).

12. Whichard v. Whitehurst, 181 N.C. 79, 106 S.E. 463 (1921); Vickers v. Leigh, 104 N.C. 248, 10 S.E. 308 (1889).

13. N.C. GEN. STAT. § 39-1. N.C. GEN. STAT. § 31-38 applies the same rule to wills. While the law does not favor a construction of the language contained in a deed which would constitute a condition subsequent and under N.C. GEN. STAT. § 39-1 when real estate is conveyed a conveyance in fee is presumed, where the words of the conveyance show in plain and express words that the grantor meant to convey an estate of less dignity his intent will be given effect. See Mattox v. State, 280 N.C. 471, 186 S.E.2d 378 (1972), wherein the court held that the language created a fee upon a condition subsequent.

In Pearson v. Chambers, 18 N.C. App. 403, 197 S.E.2d 42 (1973), it was held that a conveyance of a "right of way" in a particular tract described by metes and bounds "forty feet wide and thirteen hundred and fifty-eight feet long" indicated grantor's intention to convey merely an easement and not a fee simple estate in the described strip of land.

14. Boomer v. Grantham, 203 N.C. 230, 165 S.E. 698 (1932); Griffin v. Springer, 244 N.C. 95, 92 S.E.2d 682 (1956).

interests in the descendants of a named person *in their own right*. This may result from one of two reasons: (1) because North Carolina has a statute that has this effect, or (2) by reason of construction in certain instances.

North Carolina General Statutes, § 41-6,[15] states: "A limitation by deed, will, or other writing, to the heirs of a living person, shall be construed to be to the children of such person, unless a contrary intention appear by the deed or will." Under this statute if a conveyance is directly "to A's heirs," and if A is a living person at the time the conveyance is executed, A's living children will take a fee simple title by purchase.[16] At the common law, a deed "to the heirs of a named living person" was void because technically a living person has no heirs and there would be no identifiable grantee.[17] The statute, North Carolina General Statutes § 41-6, makes a deed "to the heirs of A" mean "to the children of A," thus making the conveyance to described persons *or descriptio personarium*. The living children of A will take titles by purchase.[18] If the conveyance is "to A and his heirs," however, the statute has been held not to apply.[19] It has likewise been held not to apply to a conveyance "To A for life and then to A's heirs," [20] while a conveyance "To A for life and then to B's heirs" [21] will create a remainder in the children of B if B is living at the time of the conveyance. It can be said generally that if the living ancestor of the "heirs" takes a concurrent or precedent freehold estate with his heirs the statute has no application and the word "heirs" is a word of limitation and the "heirs" take nothing by the conveyance.[22] If, however, the living ancestor of the "heirs" does not take a concurrent or precedent estate with the "heirs", the word "heirs" means "children" because the statute applies and in such case the "children-heirs" take estates by purchase in their own right.[23]

---

15. N.C. Gen. Stat. § 41-6.
16. Campbell v. Everhart, 139 N.C. 503, 52 S.E. 201 (1905).
17. *Id.*
18. *Id.*
19. Whitley v. Arenson, 219 N.C. 121, 12 S.E.2d 906 (1940); Marsh v. Griffin, 136 N.C. 333, 48 S.E. 735 (1904); Jones v. Ragsdale, 141 N.C. 200, 53 S.E. 842 (1906).
20. Whitley v. Arenson, 219 N.C. 121, 12 S.E.2d 906 (1940).
21. *Compare* Starnes v. Hill, 112 N.C. 1, 16 S.E. 1011 (1893).
22. Whitley v. Arenson, 219 N.C. 121, 12 S.E.2d 906 (1940); Starnes v. Hill, 112 N.C. 1, 16 S.E. 1011 (1893).
23. *Id.*

Division 2. Incidents of the Fee Simple Estate

§ 28. Unlimited Power of Alienation.

Perhaps the most important quality of a fee simple estate is that the owner may voluntarily dispose of his land as he sees fit either by deed or will free from the control of third persons so long as he complies with the legislative and constitutional requirements of the state and federal governments as they relate to land.[24] This absolute right to alien property is such an essential characteristic of the estate that any attempted restriction of the right is contrary to public policy and void.[25] Even a restriction on the power of alienation of a legal estate for a limited period of time is void.[26] Where such invalid restrictions appear in a conveyance, the grant

---

24. Williams v. Sealy, 201 N.C. 372, 160 S.E. 452 (1931). A condition or covenant in a deed that land shall not be conveyed to or occupied by a member of a certain race is not enforceable by a court of equity or a court of law. Shelley v. Kraemer, 334 U.S. 1, 68 S. Ct. 836 (1948); Barrows v. Jackson, 346 U.S. 249, 73 S. Ct. 1031 (1953).

25. Williams v. McPherson, 216 N.C. 565, 5 S.E.2d 830 (1939); Pilley v. Sullivan, 182 N.C. 493, 109 S.E. 359 (1921); Stokes v. Dixon, 182 N.C. 323, 108 S.E. 913 (1921); Brooks v. Griffin, 177 N.C. 7, 97 S.E. 730 (1918); Lee v. Oates, 171 N.C. 717, 88 S.E. 889 (1916); Trust Co. v. Nicholson, 162 N.C. 257, 78 S.E. 152 (1913); Christmas v. Winston, 152 N.C. 48, 67 S.E. 58 (1910); Wool v. Fleetwood, 136 N.C. 460, 48 S.E. 785 (1904); Dick v. Pitchford, 21 N.C. 480 (1837).

But see Wachovia Bank & Trust Co. v. John Thomasson Constr. Co., 275 N.C. 399, 168 S.E.2d 358 (1969), which holds that an absolute restraint against alienation in a deed of gift to a charitable trust is not invalid or void. A restraint on alienation is against public policy and void with respect to private trusts. *Compare* Cummings v. United States, 409 F. Supp. 1064 (M.D.N.C. 1976), a case involving a refund suit by a taxpayer in a dispute over the fair market value of a charitable contribution of land to a school unit, wherein the court held that language of a deed to the effect that taxpayers were precluded from disposing of property to any party other than the school unit constituted an unlawful restraint on alienation. Wachovia Bank & Trust Co. v. John Thomasson Constr. Co. is distinguished by the court at fn. 4, p. 1069. *See* Crockett v. Savings & Loan Ass'n, 289 N.C. 620, 224 S.E.2d 580 (1976) wherein the court states at p. 624: "We have also held that a condition against alienation annexed to the creation of a charitable trust is an exception to the restraints doctrine. [Citing *Wachovia Bank & Trust Co.* case] Of course, this restraint may be modified by the courts under their equitable powers in order to preserve the trust estate or protect the *cestuis que trustent* upon the happening of some exigency, contingency, or emergency not anticipated by the trustor." The *Crockett* court went on to hold that a "due-on-sale" clause in a deed of trust does not constitute an unlawful restraint on alienation.

26. That an attempted restriction or suspension of the power of alienation for a single day is void, *see* Christmas v. Winston, 152 N.C. 48, 67 S.E. 58 (1910). *See also* Wool v. Fleetwood, 136 N.C. 460, 48 S.E. 785 (1904) (restraint on alienation for life held void). In Brooks v. Griffin, 177 N.C. 7, 97 S.E. 730 (1918), Clark, C.J., sets out various restraints on alienation for limited periods which have been held void and cites numerous cases. *See* Twitty v. Camp, 62 N.C. 61 (1866), restraint on alienation until grantee attained age of thirty-five years held void; Wachovia Bank & Trust Co. v. John Thomasson Constr. Co., 3 N.C. App. 157, 164 S.E.2d 519 (1968), *modified*, 275 N.C. 399, 168 S.E.2d 358 (1969) citing and distinguishing Latimer v. Waddell, 119 N.C. 370, 26 S.E. 122 (1896), which states, "There cannot be a coexistence of a fee-simple estate and a total restriction upon its alienation during any period of time, however short it may be."

stands and the invalid condition or provision is rejected as nugatory.[27]

§ 29. Descent to Heirs.

Upon the death of the owner of a fee simple estate who dies without a will, the fee simple estate descends to the decedent's lineal or collateral heirs as provided by the statutes relating to intestate succession.[28] In North Carolina, the devolution of property by descent and distribution is entirely within the province of the General Assembly.[29]

§ 30. Subject to Owner's Debts.

The interests of a landowner who has a fee simple estate are liable to sale upon execution to satisfy judgments rendered against him for his debts.[30] A provision in a deed that the interest of the grantee shall not be subject to his debts is incompatible with and repugnant to the grant of a fee simple estate and such provision will be void.[31] Upon the death of the owner, the fee simple estate is liable to be sold to pay his debts.[32] Real property held in fee simple is also subject to sale for payment of the owner's taxes.[33]

---

27. "Prohibitions against alienation imposed by the transferor of legal and equitable fees and legal life estates upon the transferee are held by the common law to be invalid as against public policy." Wachovia Bank & Trust Co. v. John Thomasson Constr. Co., 3 N.C. App. 157, 164 S.E.2d 519 (1968), *modified,* 275 N.C. 399, 168 S.E.2d 358 (1969), citing BOGART, TRUSTS AND TRUSTEES § 349 (2d ed.). *See also* Lee v. Oates, 171 N.C. 717, 88 S.E. 889 (1916).
28. Chapter 29, N.C. GEN. STATS.
29. Newlin v. Gill, State Treasurer, 293 N.C. 348, 237 S.E.2d 819 (1977); Edwards v. Yearby, 168 N.C. 663, 85 S.E. 19 (1915); Hodges v. Lipscomb, 128 N.C. 57, 38 S.E. 281 (1901).
30. N.C. GEN. STAT. § 1-315.
31. Ricks v. Pope, 129 N.C. 52, 39 S.E. 638 (1901).
32. N.C. GEN. STAT. § 28-81 was repealed effective October 1, 1975, and new Chapter 28A became effective with respect to the Administration of Decedents' Estates. Under N.C. GEN. STAT. §§ 28A-15-1, 28A-17-1, and 28A-17-2 the personal representative of a decedent may make a determination concerning what property of his decedent shall be sold, leased, pledged, mortgaged or exchanged for the purpose of paying the debts of the decedent and other claims against his estate. The personal representative shall select the assets which in his judgment are calculated to promote the best interests of the estate. In the absence of contrary provisions in a will that specify that personal property shall be first resorted to, the personal representative of a decedent may bring a special proceeding before the clerk of court, to have decedent's real property sold to pay the decedent's debts or claims against his estate. The petition to sell real estate of the decedent shall include a statement that the personal representative has determined that it is in the best interest of the administration of the estate to sell the real estate. It is no longer mandatory that personal property be exhausted before resort to decedent's real property to pay a decedent's debts or other claims against his estate. *See* Aycock, *Article 17 — Sales, Leases or Mortgages of Real Property,* 11 WAKE FOREST L. REV. 35 (1975).
33. N.C. GEN. STAT. § 105-391, cited in this note in original, was renumbered by the North Carolina General Assembly in 1971. *See generally* N.C. GEN. STAT. §§ 105-369 to 105-378 for statutes authorizing the sale of real property for nonpayment of taxes. *See* Boone v. Sparrow, 235 N.C. 396, 70 S.E.2d 204 (1952), for an analysis of the two distinct methods provided by statute for the foreclosure of tax sale certificates.

§ 31. Spouses' Rights.

At the common law, and in North Carolina until 1959, the spouse of a deceased owner of a fee simple estate, was entitled to dower or curtesy, or legal life estates created by operation of law by reason of the existence of the marriage. In 1959 a new intestate succession law was enacted by the North Carolina General Assembly, abolishing both curtesy and dower.[34] The new intestate succession law also abolished the distinction between the devolution of personal property and the devolution of real property and provides that a surviving spouse is considered an heir for purposes of intestate succession [35] with respect to both types of property. If a surviving spouse does not desire to take an intestate share of the deceased spouse's property as provided under the intestate succession law, or in the event that a surviving spouse dissents from his or her deceased spouse's will, the surviving spouse has the option of taking, in lieu of such intestate share, a life estate in one third in value of all the real estate of which the deceased spouse was seized of an estate of inheritance at any time during the existence of the marriage.[36] The purpose of the statute is to allow the surviving spouse to accept either the intestate share in fee, as provided by the statute, or under the will of the dead spouse, or in lieu thereof to elect to take a life estate in one third in value of the real estate of which the deceased spouse was seized during coverture.[37]

---

34. N.C. GEN. STAT. § 29-4.

35. N.C. GEN. STAT. § 29-14. Prior to 1959, a surviving spouse was deemed a *distributee* and eligible to take personal property from a spouse, but a surviving spouse was *not an heir* for purposes of inheriting real property. As to real property, a surviving widow was entitled to a life estate in one third in value of any inheritable estate in real property that her husband was seized of during coverture. For the requisites of dower in North Carolina prior to 1959, *see* Gatewood v. Tomlinson, 113 N.C. 312, 18 S.E. 318 (1893). A husband was entitled to a life estate known as curtesy in all the real property of which his wife was seized of an inheritable estate during coverture, provided they had issue born alive during the marriage and provided his wife had not devised the real property before she died. For the law on curtesy prior to 1959, *see* the case of Fleming v. Sexton, 172 N.C. 250, 90 S.E. 247 (1916).

36. A present right of possession is not conferred on the owner's spouse by N.C. GEN. STAT. § 29-30. Thus a wife is not a real party in interest who can interpose a defense or counterclaim in an ejectment action instituted by her husband's grantee against her husband during the life of the husband. The statute only provides for a life estate at the election of the *surviving* spouse; it does not give a present right of possession. *See* People's Oil Co. v. Richardson, 271 N.C. 696, 157 S.E.2d 369 (1967).

37. A prospective purchaser of an estate from a married person, whether a husband or wife, should be careful to see that the grantor's spouse signs the deed. If the other spouse has not signed the deed, thus waiving or releasing his or her elective right to assert a life estate in one third of the deceased spouse's land upon his death, the grantee will take subject to a surviving spouse's right to assert such interest. While N.C. GEN. STAT. § 29-34 abolishes dower and curtesy N.C. GEN. STAT. § 29-30 preserves the benefits of dower and curtesy to surviving spouses. Smith v. Smith, 265 N.C. 18, 143 S.E.2d 300 (1965). If a married person signs a valid contract for the sale of land without the joinder of his or her spouse, specific performance of the contract can be decreed with respect to the property involved. The

Any or all of the marital rights under North Carolina General Statutes, § 29-30 may be surrendered by a properly drawn separation agreement complying with the requirements of Chapter 52 of the statutes.[38] Such agreements are ordinarily interpreted by the same rules which govern the interpretation of contracts generally.[39]

§ 32. Escheats to State in Absence of Inheritable Blood.

Since it is a maxim of general policy that no property in a state should be without an owner, if an owner of a fee simple title dies and leaves no heir capable of inheriting the land, it will escheat to the State. In North Carolina, if an owner of real or personal property dies without heirs or spouse capable of inheriting, it is provided by statute that the State Treasurer shall have the right to institute an action against any administrator, executor, unknown heirs or unknown claimants, by publication, to have the court declare unclaimed real or personal property as being escheated. When no answer is filed or no claim is made on behalf of the administrator, executor, unknown heirs or unknown claimants, or any answer admits or does not deny that no claim is made with respect to the property left by the deceased person, the clerk of the superior court may enter a default final judgment declaring the property escheated.[40] The State Treasurer may petition the court to have escheated property sold at a public sale and that a valid title be conveyed. Funds derived from the sale of escheated property shall be paid into the "Escheat Fund" maintained by the State Treasurer.[41] The income from the investment or deposit of the "Escheat Fund" shall be distributed annually to the State Education Assistance Authority for loans to aid worthy and needy resident students of the State who are enrolled in public institutions of higher

---

contract of the signing spouse is binding, but the rights of his nonsigning spouse under N.C. GEN. STAT. § 29-30 are not cut off or affected in any way. Hutchins v. Honeycutt, 286 N.C. 314, 210 S.E.2d 254 (1974). It has been held that where a wife joins in her husband's deed solely for the purpose of relinquishing her inchoate dower, she is not bound by any covenants contained therein, nor may she enforce as personal covenants restrictions contained therein, since she conveys nothing by deed. Maples v. Horton, 239 N.C. 394, 80 S.E.2d 38 (1954).

38. Lane v. Scarborough, 284 N.C. 407, 200 S.E.2d 622 (1973).
39. *Id.*
40. N.C. GEN. STAT. § 116A-2. *See generally* N.C. GEN. STAT. §§ 116A-1 through 116A-11. *See* Newlin v. Gill, State Treasurer, 293 N.C. 348, 237 S.E.2d 819 (1977), a case holding that the estate of an intestate escheated where the intestate was survived only by collateral kinsmen who did not descend from the intestate's parents or grandparents. In response to an argument that the manifest intent of the legislature was to prevent any property from escheating, the court notes, in part: "Had the Legislature desired to provide that no property would escheat, as appellants contend, it would seem that the reasonable method would have been to repeal G.S. 29-12 and G.S. 116A-2. This they did not do."

For an excellent history of escheats as deriving from the feudal system of England, *see* University v. High Point, 203 N.C. 558, 166 S.E. 511 (1932).

41. N.C. GEN. STAT. § 116A-1.

education.[42] Property, real or personal, which has escheated and of which the State Treasurer is custodian, shall be subject to refund for a period of seven years from the date that it first became due and payable to the Escheat Fund. After the expiration of seven years no property or funds may be returned to anyone claiming to be the rightful owner and no action may be brought for the return of the escheated property.[43]

§ 33. Forfeiture for Conviction of Treason or Felony Not Applicable in North Carolina.

While at the common law an attainder or conviction of treason or felony resulted in a forfeiture of the lands of the traitor or felon, on the theory that his blood was corrupted and deprived of its heritable quality by the commission of the treason or felony, this is not the law in North Carolina. One accused or convicted of commission of a felony or treason does not forfeit his property.[44]

Statutes exist in North Carolina which bar spouses, parents, devisees, legatees, heirs, and insurance beneficiaries from the receipt of interests in property by reason of the death of decedents as a result of acts of misconduct as specified in the statutes.[45] In addition to intentional homicide as a principal or accessory,[46] other specified acts of misconduct are enumerated including the wilful abandonment of care and maintenance of a child by a parent,[47] and a spouse who knowingly contracts a bigamous marriage.[48] The basic principle of common law, that a person should not be allowed to profit by his own wrong or acquire property as the result of his own crime, is not wholly supplanted by the statutes.[49]

---

42. N.C. GEN. STAT. § 116A-9.
43. N.C. GEN. STAT. § 116A-11.
44. *See* N.C. CONST. art. IV, § 5: "No conviction of treason or attainder shall work corruption of blood or forfeiture." As to forfeiture for crime, *see* White v. Fort, 10 N.C. 251, 264 (1824), in which it is stated that forfeiture for criminal offenses has not had any force in North Carolina since 1778. *See also* N.C. CONST. art. XI, § 1: "The following punishments *only* shall be known to the laws of this State, viz.: death, imprisonment with or without hard labor, fines, removal from office, and disqualification to hold and enjoy any office of honor, trust, or profit under this State." (Italics supplied.) This effectually excludes forfeiture of one's property as a punishment for the commission or conviction of any crime.
45. *See generally* N.C. GEN. STAT. §§ 31A-1 through 31A-15.
46. N.C. GEN. STAT. § 31A-3 (3); Quick v. United Benefit Life Ins. Co., 287 N.C. 47, 213 S.E.2d 563 (1975), a case barring a wife convicted of the involuntary manslaughter of her husband from taking life insurance proceeds as her husband's beneficiary.
47. N.C. GEN. STAT. § 31A-2.
48. N.C. GEN. STAT. § 31A-1 (a) (5).
49. Lofton v. Lofton, 26 N.C. App. 203, 215 S.E.2d 861 (1975); Garner v. Phillips, 229 N.C. 160, 47 S.E.2d 845 (1948). In Lofton v. Lofton, *supra*, although a minor child was not convicted in a criminal court of the willful killing of his parents, he was held to be barred from sharing in any of the property or benefits resulting from the death of his parents where the minor was adjudged a "delinquent child" in a juvenile proceeding upon the finding of the district court that the "child did willfully and with malice-aforethought murder his mother and father."

Rather, the common law still exists collateral to the provisions of North Carolina General Statutes, Chapter 31A and may apply to bar receipt of property in situations where the statutes are inapplicable.[50]

§ 34. Subject to Power of Eminent Domain.

Fee simple estates in land, like all other estates, are subject to the power of eminent domain.[51] Land may be taken for public or quasi-public purposes by the United States government, by the state, by cities, towns and other municipalities, and by quasi-public corporations such as railroads and public utilities authorized by statute.[52] There is no private right of eminent domain enabling one private citizen to require another to sell a portion of his property.[53]

When land is condemned under power of eminent domain, there are two conditions that must be met: (1) The "taking" must be for an authorized public purpose,[54] and (2) the condemnor must pay just compensation [55] to the owner whose interest is taken.[56]

---

50. *Id. See generally* Bolich, *Acts Barring Property Rights,* 40 N.C.L. REV. 175 (1962); Note, *Decedents' Estates — Forfeitures of Property Rights by Slayers,* 12 WAKE FOREST L. REV. 448 (1976); WIGGINS, WILLS AND ADMINISTRATION OF ESTATES, §§ 200-214 (1964).

51. The power of eminent domain is one of the inherent attributes of a sovereign state. Redevelopment Comm'n v. Hagins, 258 N.C. 220, 128 S.E.2d 391 (1962); Railroad v. Davis, 19 N.C. 451 (1837).

52. *See* N.C. GEN. STAT. § 40-2 for bodies politic in North Carolina which may under general law in North Carolina exercise the power of eminent domain and the purposes for which condemnation may be had. Other bodies may be given the power by the General Assembly by special act and for other purposes. For a recent example, *see* Colonial Pipeline Co. v. Neill, 296 N.C. 581, 251 S.E.2d 457 (1979), a case holding that interstate pipeline companies incorporated or domesticated under the laws of North Carolina have the power of eminent domain, regardless of whether their pipelines originate in North Carolina.

53. McCoy v. Peach, 40 N.C. App. 6, 251 S.E.2d 881 (1979).

54. The Supreme Court of North Carolina will determine as a matter of law whether a proposed use or purpose is a "public purpose" for which eminent domain can be exercised. Once the public purpose is established, the necessity or expediency of the taking is a legislative, and not a judicial question. Airport Authority v. Irvin, 36 N.C. App. 662, 245 S.E.2d 390 (1978).

55. Stamey v. Burnsville, 189 N.C. 39, 126 S.E. 103 (1925); Mount Olive v. Cowan, 235 N.C. 259, 69 S.E.2d 525 (1952); Virginia Elec. & Power Co. v. King, 259 N.C. 219, 130 S.E.2d 318 (1963).

56. The condemnor may either acquire an easement in property or may take the entire interest of the owner if the public exigency requires it, subject of course to the payment of an adequate and fair compensation.

Division 3. Determinable, Base or Qualified Fee Simple Estates

§ 35. The Fee Simple Determinable.

A fee simple determinable, though an estate of inheritance, is distinguished from the fee simple estate absolute by the characteristic that it may terminate upon the happening of some stated event. It is a fee simple and may therefore continue forever, but since it is subject to a limitation by which it may terminate at any moment upon the occurrence of some designated contingency, it is a fee simple defeasible rather than a fee simple absolute.[57]

The estate known as the fee simple determinable is created when apt and appropriate language is used by a grantor or devisor indicative of an intent on the part of the grantor or devisor that a fee simple estate conveyed or devised will expire *automatically* upon the happening of a certain event or upon the discontinuance of certain existing facts.[58] Typical language creating such estates may specify that a grantee or devisee shall have land "until" some event occurs, or "while," "during," or "for so long as" some state of facts continues to exist.[59] Upon the happening of the specified event, the fee simple determinable automatically terminates and reverts to the grantor or to his heirs.[60] The language in the creating instrument must clearly indicate that this automatic termination and reversion is intended.[61] Since there is a strong inclination in modern property law to disfavor the construction of a deed which would result in a fee simple determinable,[62] relying on past traditional language alone might not be sufficient. The grantor, in addition to using typical language such as "so long as" should include lan-

---

[57]. Elmore v. Austin, 232 N.C. 13, 59 S.E.2d 205 (1950); RESTATEMENT OF PROPERTY § 44 (1936).

[58]. *Id. See* Price v. Bunn, 13 N.C. App. 652, 187 S.E.2d 423 (1972), and Cummings v. United States, 409 F. Supp. 1064 (M.D.N.C.1976), both of which cite this section in the 1971 edition.

[59]. *See* RESTATEMENT OF PROPERTY § 44 (1936); McCall, *Estates on Condition and Special Limitation in North Carolina,* 19 N.C.L. REV. 334 (1941); Webster, *The Quest for Clear Land Titles — Whither Possibilities of Reverter and Rights of Entry?* 42 N.C.L. REV. 807 (1964). For a particularly good case setting out the distinctions between estates of fee simple determinable and estates in fee simple subject to a condition subsequent, *see* Board of Chosen Freeholders v. Buck, 79 N.J. Eq. 472, 82 A. 418 (1912).

[60]. RESTATEMENT OF PROPERTY § 44 (1936); Price v. Bunn, 13 N.C. App. 652, 187 S.E.2d 423 (1972). *Accord,* Cummings v. United States, 409 F. Supp. 1064 (M.D.N.C. 1976); Etheridge v. United States, 218 F. Supp. 809 (E.D.N.C. 1963).

[61]. Cummings v. United States, 409 F. Supp. 1064 (M.D.N.C. 1976).

[62]. "Conditions which restrict fee simple estates are not favored by the law and are strictly construed." Cummings v. United States, 409 F. Supp. 1064 (M.D.N.C. 1976); First Presbyterian Church v. Sinclair Refining Co., 200 N.C. 469, 157 S.E. 438 (1931).

guage unequivocally specifying that a fee simple determinable with an automatic reversion is intended.[63]

Until the occurrence of the limiting event the grantor (or devisor), or his heirs, have a future interest known as a "possibility of reverter." When the specified event occurrs, the possessory estate of the grantee or devisee ends by operation of law automatically and without the necessity of any act of re-entry, without the institution of any lawsuit or the intervention of any court.[64] The possibility of reverter of the grantor (or devisor) becomes a possessory estate upon the occurrence of the specified event.[65]

§ 36. Same — Incidents.

A fee simple determinable constitutes the entire estate throughout its continuance. It retains its defeasible quality, however, until the happening of the stated event by which it is to be determined, or until it is converted into a fee simple absolute.[66] A fee simple determinable is therefore alienable, but if an owner of a fee simple determinable conveys it, a grantee thereof will take it subject to the same limitations as existed prior to the grant.[67] The owner of a fee simple determinable holds his estate, and except for the limiting event the occurrence of which will result in its termination, has the same rights in the land as an owner of a fee simple estate.[68] An owner of an estate of fee simple determinable

---

63. Considering the difficulties often resulting from a choice of this type of estate, the grantor might as a matter of preventive law evaluate alternative methods of effectuating his intent.

64. RESTATEMENT OF PROPERTY § 56 (1936); SIMES & SMITH, FUTURE INTERESTS § 283 (2d ed. 1956). *See, e.g.,* Charlotte Park & Recreation Comm'n v. Barringer, 242 N.C. 311, 88 S.E.2d 114 (1955), *cert. denied,* 350 U.S. 983 (1956); Elmore v. Austin, 232 N.C. 13, 59 S.E.2d 205 (1950); Price v. Bunn, 13 N.C. App. 652, 187 S.E.2d 423 (1972); Cummings v. United States, 409 F. Supp. 1064 (M.D.N.C. 1976). *See also* Etheridge v. United States, 218 F. Supp. 809 (E.D.N.C. 1963). When grantee, the U. S. Government, conveyed land by deed that manifested grantor's intention that the U. S. Government was to have possession of certain land for the term of its use as a life saving station, it was held that the U. S. Government took a determinable fee. When it ceased to use the land for a life saving station, it automatically reverted to the grantor by operation of law. When, thereafter, the U. S. Government used the land for other purposes it became liable to the grantor for the rental value of the land under the Fifth Amendment of the United States Constitution prohibiting the taking of private property without the payment of a just compensation.

65. *Id.*

66. Elmore v. Austin, 232 N.C. 13, 59 S.E.2d 205 (1950).

67. *See* Jernigan v. Lee, 279 N.C. 341, 182 S.E.2d 351 (1971), which states: "The determinable quality of the fee of the first taker follows any transfer he may make, and the grantee can take no greater estate than that possessed by his grantor." Harrell v. Hagan, 147 N.C. 111, 60 S.E. 909 (1908); Williams v. Blizzard, 176 N.C. 146, 96 S.E. 957 (1918).

68. Hence all the incidents of the fee simple estate attach. MINOR & WURTS, REAL PROPERTY § 161 (1909).

may commit unlimited waste.[69] Upon the death of an owner of an estate of fee simple determinable his estate will pass to his heirs subject to the same limiting conditions of his estate.[70]

There are no cases since enactment of the 1959 Act giving a surviving spouse an option to elect to take a life estate in one third in value of the deceased spouse's property of which that spouse was seized of a defeasible estate of inheritance during coverture. Since North Carolina General Statutes, § 29-30 expressly provides that this right may be exercised in "inheritable" estates, it can be argued that, notwithstanding the happening of the specified limiting event terminating a spouse's estate, the surviving spouse should have the elective right in property held under a determinable fee simple.[71] On the other hand, the theory that "a stream can flow no higher than its source" and the position taken in the *Restatement of Property* on dower as a derivative estate can be mustered in favor of the conclusion that statutory substitutes for dower should logically be considered as subordinate to the limiting conditions of a defeasible fee.[72] The specific nature of the limitation involved, policy factors underlying the new concept, and legislative intent in enacting the new statute will play an important role in determining the outcome of a case involving this specific problem.[73]

§ 37. The Fee Simple Subject to a Condition Subsequent.

Another kind of defeasible or qualified fee simple estate is the fee simple estate subject to a condition subsequent. This estate very closely resembles the previously discussed fee simple determinable, but they are not the same and on occasion give rise to different legal consequences.

---

69. Poe v. Hardie, 65 N.C. 447 (1871).

70. But if the defeasible event is the grantee or devisee dying without issue at the time of his death, the heirs of the grantee or devisee can take nothing, as the event terminating the estate shall have happened upon the death of such grantee or devisee. Whitfield v. Garris, 131 N.C. 148, 45 S.E. 904 (1902).

71. *See* the analogous cases of Pollard v. Slaughter, 92 N.C. 72 (1885) and Alexander v. Fleming, 190 N.C. 815, 130 S.E. 867 (1925), which state that a wife had dower in a determinable estate of her husband because the husband was seized of an inheritable estate, both cases following the English case of Buckworth v. Thirkell, 3 Bos. & Pull. 652 (1804).

72. RESTATEMENT OF PROPERTY § 54. *See* AMERICAN LAW OF PROPERTY §§ 5.27, 5.29, 5.63 (Casner ed. 1952). As to dower, case law does not support the *Restatement* position on this point.

73. The cardinal principle of statutory construction is that the intent of the legislature is controlling. Quick v. Insurance Co., 287 N.C. 47, 213 S.E.2d 563 (1975).

See generally Webster, *The Quest for Clear Land Titles — Whither Possibilities of Reverter and Rights of Entry?* 42 N.C.L. REV. 807, 811, 812 (1964), in which various legal consequences are discussed wherein they may be different depending on whether a determinable fee is present or whether the estate involved is a fee simple subject to a condition subsequent. These relate to tax liability, liability for negligent maintenance of the premises pending any re-entry, entitlement to mesne profits, waiver, constitutional law, applicability of statutes of limitations and perhaps other procedural matters.

The primary distinguishing characteristic between the fee simple determinable and the fee simple subject to a condition subsequent is that the latter does not end *automatically*.[74] While a fee simple determinable is terminated *ipso facto* upon the occurrence of the limiting event, if the estate is a fee simple subject to a condition subsequent, the estate continues in the owner thereof until the grantor, his heir (or perhaps a devisor's heir) elects to exercise his power of termination by re-entering for breach of the condition, or elects to bring an action to terminate the estate by reason of the happening of the specified event.[75] Until the creator of the interest or his heirs elect to take action to terminate the estate, it will continue notwithstanding the fact that the terminating event has occurred. When in doubt as to a choice between a determinable fee and a fee simple subject to a condition subsequent, courts favor the later, apparently abhoring the automatic termination aspect of the former.

The reason for this distinction is that in the case of a fee simple determinable the words that provide for termination of the estate are regarded as a part of the original limitation of the estate; *i.e.*, the estate is to last "so long as," "while," "during," or to terminate "when" something exists or occurs.[76] Words of "condition," however, as distinguished from "limitation" words, are considered as words providing for the termination of an estate before its natural termination. Estates in fee simple determinable thus "expire"; estates of fee simple subject to a condition subsequent are "divested" at the option of the person having a "right of entry" or "power of termination."[77] Typical words introducing the estate of fee simple subject to a condition subsequent are: "on condition that," "provided that," "to be null and void if," or "to be forfeited if"

---

74. Charlotte Park & Recreation Comm'n v. Barringer, 242 N.C. 311, 88 S.E.2d 114 (1955), *cert. denied*, 350 U.S. 983 (1956).

75. RESTATEMENT OF PROPERTY § 45 (1936) provides:

An estate in fee simple subject to a condition subsequent is created by any limitation which in an otherwise effective conveyance of land,
  (a) creates an estate in fee simple, and
  (b) provides that upon the occurrence of a stated event the conveyor or his successor in interest shall have the power to terminate the estate so created.

See Brittain v. Taylor, 168 N.C. 271, 84 S.E. 280 (1915), where it is stated: "If the conditions subsequent were broken, it did not *ipso facto* produce a reversion of the title. The estate continued in full force until the proper step was taken to consummate the forfeiture." *Accord*, Mattox v. State, 280 N.C. 471, 186 S.E.2d 378 (1972).

76. RESTATEMENT OF PROPERTY § 44 (1936). *See* Price v. Bunn, 13 N.C. App. 652, 187 S.E.2d 423 (1972); Etheridge v. United States, 218 F. Supp. 809 (E.D.N.C. 1963).

77. RESTATEMENT OF PROPERTY, Introductory note, Chapter 4 (1936). *Compare* the outstanding case of Board of Chosen Freeholders v. Buck, 79 N.J. Eq. 472, 82 A. 418 (1912), setting out the distinctions between estates of fee simple determinable and estates in fee subject to a condition subsequent.

a certain event occurs or fails to occur.[78] A fee simple on a condition subsequent is not created unless the grantor expressly reserves the right to re-enter or provides for a forfeiture or for a reversion or that the instrument shall be null and void; *i.e.*, a deed must contain both the apt words to create a condition and an express clause of re-entry, reverter, or forfeiture in order for the estate to be properly created.[79]

§ 38. Same — Incidents.

The incidents of a fee simple estate subject to a condition subsequent as a possessory estate are substantially the same as the incidents of the fee simple determinable set out in § 36 *supra*.

As a consequence, however, of the characteristic of the fee simple subject to a condition subsequent that it does not terminate automatically but requires the holder of the power of termination or right of entry for condition broken to either re-enter or to bring an action to terminate the existing fee simple upon the happening of the specified event, the condition can thus be waived by the holder.[80]

When the action to terminate the estate is brought, a frequent question that arises is whether the acts of the holder of the fee simple upon a condition subsequent constitute such breach of the condition as to entitle the holder of the power of re-entry to recover the premises.[81] In a recent case, for example, land had been transferred to the State of North Carolina on the condition that the State "perpetually and continuously

---

78. RESTATEMENT OF PROPERTY § 45 (1936); Board of Chosen Freeholders v. Buck, 79 N.J. Eq. 472, 82 A. 418 (1912). *See* McCall, *Estates on Condition and Special Limitation in North Carolina,* 19 N.C.L. REV. 334 (1941); Webster, *The Quest for Clear Land Titles — Whither Possibilities of Reverter and Rights of Entry?* 42 N.C.L. REV. 807 (1964).
79. Mattox v. State, 280 N.C. 471, 186 S.E.2d 378 (1972).

See Brittain v. Taylor, 168 N.C. 271, 84 S.E. 280 (1915), to the effect that "the words which constitute a condition may be various, for in particular words there is no weight, as their operation and effect depend on the sense which they carry." *But see* Hall v. Quinn, 190 N.C. 326, 130 S.E. 18 (1925), where it is stated: "A clause in a deed will not be construed as a condition subsequent unless it expresses in *apt and appropriate language* the intention of the parties to this effect . . . and *a mere statement of the purpose for which the property is to be used* is not sufficient to create such condition." *Accord* Ange v. Ange, 235 N.C. 506, 71 S.E.2d 19 (1952). With reference to the question of whether a conveyance upon a condition subsequent *must* have a re-entry or forfeiture clause, *quaere? See also* Church v. Refining Co., 200 N.C. 469, 157 S.E. 438 (1931), in which the grant was "to a grantee *provided* always and *upon the condition that*" a certain status of facts continued, and the court held there was no condition, although repeating the statement that a condition subsequent will be found only if there is apt and appropriate language showing the intention of the parties to that effect.

If one intends to create a condition subsequent, it should be noted that forfeitures of estates are not favored by the law and will be construed strictly. Church v. Refining Co., 200 N.C. 469, 157 S.E. 438 (1931), and the other cases cited in this note.
80. Brittain v. Taylor, 168 N.C. 271, 84 S.E. 280 (1915).
81. Mattox v. State, 280 N.C. 471, 186 S.E.2d 378 (1972).

keep, maintain and operate" the premises as a highway patrol radio station and highway patrol headquarters. The State constructed a station and headquarters on the property. Subsequently, a slow-down in activities occurred at the property: the radio in the building was no longer regularly operated, the staff had diminished to two patrolmen on a regular basis who operated a license examination facility, and the main activities of the patrol in that vicinity had been transferred to another facility. The court, relying in part upon a *Webster's Dictionary* definition of the word "headquarters," held that the condition subsequent had clearly been breached and that the grantor was entitled to recover the premises.[82]

If the holder of the power of termination does not assert his right to terminate the estate for breach of the condition, it will continue, whereas the fee simple determinable terminates automatically and the title revests in the grantor or in the grantor's or devisor's heirs instantly upon the occurrence of the limiting event.[83]

§ 39. The Fee Simple Subject to an Executory Interest.

The third type of defeasible fee simple estate is the fee simple estate subject to an executory interest.[84] This type of estate is very similar to the fee simple subject to a condition subsequent. In a fee simple subject to an executory interest, however, upon the happening of the specified event the conveyance or devise provides that title will pass from the owner of the estate to some third person not the grantor or grantee or their heirs. For instance, a conveyance from *A* "to *B* and his heirs, but if *B* dies without issue living at his death, then to *C* and his heirs" conveys to *B* a fee simple subject to an executory interest.[85] Upon *B's* death without issue living at his death, *C* will be entitled to ownership of the real property involved. Whether or not *C's* interest will vest in him automatically or will require an entry or an action to effect entry will be dependent upon whether the creator of the interest has indicated that the succeeding estate is to take effect immediately and automatically or not.[86]

---

82. *Id.*
83. Brittain v. Taylor, 168 N.C. 271, 84 S.E. 280 (1915).
84. *See* Jernigan v. Lee, 279 N.C. 341, 182 S.E.2d 351 (1971); Elmore v. Austin, 232 N.C. 13, 59 S.E.2d 205 (1950).
85. The interest which *C* has in such conveyance is not a remainder because a remainder cannot be limited after a fee simple.
86. RESTATEMENT OF PROPERTY §§ 46, 47 (1936); A devise to testatrix' son and his heirs, but if he does "without issue or heirs by him begotten," then to testatrix' daughter in fee, and if she dies without "any heir of her body living at her death," then to another, was held to give the son a fee simple defeasible upon his death without surviving issue, and to give the daughter an executory interest contingent upon the son's death without surviving issue; and when the son died without issue, the daughter took a fee simple, defeasible upon her death without surviving issue, thus also subject to an executory interest. Jernigan v. Lee, 279 N.C. 341, 182 S.E.2d 351 (1971).

§ 40. Same — Incidents.

The incidents of the fee simple subject to an executory interest are substantially the same as those of the fee simple determinable and fee simple subject to a condition subsequent. The possessory incidents are the same, the only difference being that the succeeding estate is in a third person not the grantor, devisor or creator of the interest or their heirs.

§ 41. Effects of Illegal, Impossible or Repugnant Limitations and Conditions on Determinable, Base or Qualified Estates; Rule Against Perpetuities Applicable to Estates Subject to Executory Interests.

If an estate is created subject to being terminated upon the happening of an illegal event or an event that is contrary to public policy, the condition or limitation is deemed void and the estate becomes indefeasible.[87] For instance, conditions against alienation are opposed to public policy.[88] Therefore, conditions or provisions in a deed or will against alienation will not defeat the estate to which they are annexed.[89] It is likewise against public policy to set up conditions in restraint of marriage. If a deed provides for a grant to a person but a condition subsequent is provided that if said person marries the property will revert to the grantor, the condition subsequent is held invalid.[90]

If an estate is subject to being terminated because of a racial restriction, that restriction will be invalidated on public policy or constitutional grounds. This would appear to be the rule in North Carolina although a 1955 decision upheld a special limitation to a grantee city of land for use as a golf course with a racially restrictive condition.[91]

---

87. Brittain v. Taylor, 168 N.C. 271, 274, 84 S.E. 280 (1915).
88. Lee v. Oates, 171 N.C. 717, 88 S.E. 889 (1916).
89. Id.
90. Gard v. Mason, 169 N.C. 507, 86 S.E. 302 (1915). *But see In re* Miller, 159 N.C. 123 (1912), holding that a devise to one but in case she should "marry again, this becomes void" was valid, if for the purpose of taking care of the beneficiary while she was unmarried and not intended as a restraint against her remarrying.
91. *See* the case of Recreation Comm'n v. Barringer, 242 N.C. 311, 88 S.E.2d 114 (1955), *cert. denied,* 350 U.S. 983 (1956), which holds that a special limitation to a grantee city of land for use as a golf course upon the condition that the land "shall revert in fee simple to the undersigned donors" in the event the park is not maintained for members of the white race only was valid and that if Negroes played on the golf course title would revert automatically to the grantors. *But see* Robinson v. Mansfield, 2 RACE REL. REP. 445 (Ariz. Super. Ct. 1956); Capital Fed. Sav. & Loan Ass'n v. Smith, 136 Colo. 265, 316 P.2d 252 (1957); SIMES & SMITH, FUTURE INTERESTS § 285 at nn. 42.5, 42.10 (2d ed. 1956); 8 HASTINGS L.J. 96 (1956); and 9 VAND. L. REV. 561 (1956), in which the authors conclude that possibilities of reverter predicated to take effect upon the use of land by members of a particular race will not withstand challenges of constitutionality, their theories apparently being that whenever a determinable fee is based on an invalid limitation, one that is illegal or against public policy, such limitation is inoperative and that therefore any fee limited to

It should be noted, additionally, that unless the condition or limitation in a fee simple estate subject to an executory estate must necessarily occur or fail to occur at all events within the period of the Rule Against Perpetuities such condition or limitation is void and the grantee of the fee shall take free of the condition or limitation. It is the possibility, not the actuality, of an occurrence which postpones the vesting of the executory interest that the Rule Against Perpetuities is concerned with.[92]

Article II. Fee Tail and Fee Conditional Estates

§ 42. Neither Fee Tail nor Fee Conditional Estates in Effect in North Carolina.

The fee tail estate has not existed in North Carolina since 1784. In that year the legislature passed an act which provides that "Every person seized of an estate in tail shall be deemed to be seized of the same in fee simple." [93] Since the statute converts fee tail estates into fee simple

---

terminate if land is sold to Negroes should become a fee simple absolute in the grantee free of such limitation.

Compare Evans v. Abney, 396 U.S. 435 (1970), in which the United States Supreme Court upheld the decision of Georgia courts that a gift of a park to a city in trust for white women and white children reverted to the donor's heirs when Negroes were permitted to use the park facilities. The Georgia Supreme Court rejected the contention that this amounted to a judicial enforcement of racial discrimination amounting to a denial of equal protection in violation of the fourteenth amendment. 224 Ga. 826, 165 S.E.2d 160 (1968). The United States Supreme Court did not find sufficient "state action" in the Georgia court's decision that the land should revert to attribute racial discrimination to the state. *See* Note, 49 N.C.L. Rev. 148 (1970).

92. The Rule Against Perpetuities applies to executory interests and other contingent future interests but does not apply to possibilities of reverter following fees determinable nor to rights of entry for condition broken following estates of fee simple subject to conditions subsequent. Simes & Smith, Future Interests §§ 1238-39 (2d ed 1956); Charlotte Park & Recreation Comm'n v. Barringer, 242 N.C. 311, 88 S.E.2d 114 (1955), *cert. denied,* 350 U.S. 983 (1956).

Therefore if a fee is granted on condition that or so long as the land is used for residential purposes, and then to the grantor or his heirs, it is not necessary that the limiting event or breach of the condition occur within any specific time. But if land is granted in fee on condition that or so long as the land is used for residential purposes and upon cessation of such use to a *third person not the grantor,* the ultimate limitation to the third person will be void since the contingent event may not necessarily occur within the life or lives of persons in being and twenty-one years as is required by the Rule Against Perpetuities. Therefore, the condition is read out of the instrument and the previously vested estate will be deemed indefeasible.

93. N.C. Gen. Stat. § 41-1. *See* White v. Lackey, 40 N. C. App. 353, 253 S.E.2d 13 (1979), involving a clause in a will devising property to the testator's granddaughter "during her natural life and at her death to the lawful heir or heirs of her body." The court noted that if the Rule in Shelley's Case were applicable to this devise, then the granddaughter would be vested with a fee tail estate converted into a fee simple by operation of N.C. Gen. Stat. § 41-1. The court went on to decide that the Rule in Shelley's Case was not applicable because the testator did not use the term "lawful heir or heirs of her body" in the technical

estates, it is necessary to determine exactly what a fee tail estate was at the common law in order to make the statute meaningful.

Prior to 1285, a conveyance "to A and the heirs of his body" was deemed to convey to A a fee simple conditional.[94] The conveyance to A in such case was held to be upon a condition precedent, "to A and the heirs of his body, on condition that he have heirs of his body." If he never had heirs of his body the land reverted to the grantor. If he had issue born and he died survived by such issue, the land would go to such issue under the same conditions if he had not conveyed the land away before he died. The land would descend lineally forever to the heirs of the body (not to the heirs general) of the grantee if not conveyed away. If, however, issue was born to the grantee, the grantee (while he would not have a fee simple title) could convey the land in fee simple. It was deemed that the condition had been met. Consequently, the grantee of a fee simple conditional would generally hasten to convey the land in fee simple to some friend, taking back from him immediately a fee simple in lieu of the fee simple conditional which he had previously owned, thus frustrating the objects of the grantor who intended for the land to remain in the lineage of the grantee and not to be alienable to persons outside of such lineage.[95] Subsequent to such conveyance and reconveyance the grantee would have a fee simple estate which was not only alienable but also descendible to his heirs general; not limited to his lineal heirs.

To avoid this circumvention of the grantor's intention, the statute known as *De Donis Conditionalibus* was enacted.[96] The statute stated that henceforth the will of the donor (grantor) should be observed according to the form of the deed so that a person to whom land was given in the form "to A and the heirs of his body" should have no power to alien the land, but that it should revert to the donor (grantor) or the donor's heirs if the grantee's issue failed, either by absolute default of issue, or even after the birth of issue, by its subsequent extinction.[97] In other words, under a conveyance "to A and the heirs of his body" after the Statute *De Donis Conditionalibus* the grantee could no longer alien his estate simple upon the birth of issue. The "fee simple conditional" was not thereafter created by a conveyance in such form; a new kind of estate, the

---

sense but rather intended the term to mean issue of his granddaughter. In holding the Rule inapplicable, the court distinguished a number of North Carolina decisions: Morrisett v. Stevens, 136 N.C. 160, 48 S.E. 661 (1904); Benton v. Baucom, 192 N.C. 630, 135 S.E. 629 (1926); Tyson v. Sinclair, 138 N.C. 23, 50 S.E. 450 (1905); Ray v. Ray, 270 N.C. 715, 155 S.E.2d 185 (1967).

94. Not to be confused with the fee simple subject to a condition subsequent.

95. In a fee simple conditional, if the grantee died without heirs of his body surviving and if his lineage ever ran out, the land would revert to the original grantor or his heirs, if not previously aliened by the grantee after the *birth* of issue.

96. Westminster II, 13 Edw. I, c. 1 (1285).

97. DIGBY, HISTORY OF REAL PROPERTY 228 (4th ed. 1892).

"fee tail" had been developed as a result of enactment of the statute.[98] If the grantee had issue or heirs of his body, the land would descend to them. He could not convey a fee simple title either before or after the birth of issue. If he never had issue or if all of his lineal heirs ever became depleted or extinguished, the land reverted to the grantor or his heirs.

§ 43. Fee Tail Estates — Forms for Creating at Common Law — Generally.

The fee tail estate could be created in various forms. It could be created by a conveyance "to *A* and the heirs of his body generally" which was called a "fee tail general."[99] It could be created by a conveyance "to *A* and the heirs of his body by a particular spouse" which was a "fee tail special,"[100] meaning that only the lineal heirs of a particular husband or wife of the grantee would take. The fee tail could be created by a conveyance "to *A* and the heirs male of his body,"[101] called a "fee tail male," or "to *A* and the heirs female of his body," called a "fee tail female."[102] Or it could be "to *A* and the heirs male by a particular spouse," called a "fee tail male special";[103] or "to *A* and the heirs female of his body by a particular spouse," called a "fee tail female special."[104]

§ 44. Same — Same — Rule in Wild's Case.

A limitation of an estate "to *A* and his children" was construed to create a fee simple estate in *A* and his children living at the time of the conveyance, the word "children" in such conveyance being construed as a word of "purchase" designating that the children were to share in the estate.[105] If, however, the grantee had no children at the time of the conveyance, it was presumed that the word "children" was a word of limitation only, in the sense of "heirs of the body," and thus created a fee tail estate by implication.[106]

---

98. MINOR & WURTS, REAL PROPERTY § 165 (1910).
99. MINOR & WURTS, REAL PROPERTY § 168 (1910).
100. MINOR & WURTS, REAL PROPERTY § 168 (1910); Pittman v. Stanley, 231 N.C. 327, 56 S.E.2d 657 (1949).
101. MINOR & WURTS, REAL PROPERTY § 168 (1910).
102. *Id.*
103. *Id.*
104. *Id.*
105. Silliman v. Whitaker, 119 N.C. 89, 25 S.E. 742 (1896); Lewis v. Stancil, 154 N.C. 326, 10 S.E. 621 (1911); Tremblay v. Aycock, 263 N.C. 627, 139 S.E.2d 898 (1964); Davis v. Brown, 241 N.C. 116, 84 S.E.2d 334 (1954).
106. *Id.*
See generally for a comprehensive treatment of all aspects of the Rule in Wild's Case, see Link, *The Rule in Wild's Case in North Carolina,* 55 N.C. L. REV. 751 (1977). Professor Link's article deals, *inter alia,* with both resolutions of Wild's Case, rules of construction, time of determining existence of children, application to deeds or personalty, drafting suggestions and the status of reform of the Rule. At fn. 13, at 753 is a list compiled by Professor Link of North Carolina decisions relevant to the Rule in Wild's Case.

§ 45. Same — Statutory Change in North Carolina.

In most states of the United States the fee tail estate has either been abolished or modified by statute. In North Carolina in every instance in which a fee tail estate was created at the common law, a fee simple estate is created today by operation of statute.[107] There are no more fee tail estates in North Carolina.

---

107. N.C. GEN. STAT. § 41-1.

CHAPTER 5

FREEHOLD ESTATES NOT INHERITABLE

Article I. General Provisions

§ 46. Life Estates Generally.
§ 47. Conventional Life Estates Created by Acts of Parties.
§ 48. Estates Which May Last for Life but Which May Terminate upon the Happening of a Contingent Event.
§ 49. Estates for Life Which Arise by Operation of Law; Dower, Curtesy and Their Statutory Substitutes.
§ 50. The Marital Life Estates; Seisin Required.

Article II. Incidents of Life Estates

§ 51. Generally.
§ 52. Right to Alien.
§ 53. Right to Emblements.
§ 54. Right to Estovers.
§ 54.1. General Standard of Duty Owed by Life Tenant to Remainderman or Reversioner.
§ 55. Life Tenant's Duty to Pay Taxes.
§ 56. Life Tenant's Duty to Pay Local Assessments.
§ 57. Life Tenant's Duties with Respect to Encumbrances on Land; Duties with Respect to Interest.
§ 58. Life Tenant's Duty to Make Repairs; Improvements.
§ 59. Subject to Merger.
§ 59.1. Insurance on Land Subject to Life Estate.
§ 60. Life Tenant's Right to Possession; Profits.
§ 61. Subject to Life Tenant's Debts.
§ 62. Life Tenant's Disability to Acquire Outstanding Title Against Reversioner or Remainderman.
§ 63. Land Subject to Life Estate May Be Sold if Unproductive.

Article I. General Provisions

§ 46. Life Estates Generally.

A life estate is an estate the duration of which is limited by the length of the human life of some person or persons.[1] A life estate is a freehold estate but since it terminates upon the death of the tenant or of some other designated person it is not deemed an inheritable estate.[2]

---

1. 1 Restatement of Property § 18 (1936).

2. At the common law an estate in a tenant for the life of another could be retained by the first person who gained possession of the land upon the death of the tenant if he died before the death of the person whose life was the measuring life, if the life estate was measured by the life of another. This rule was changed in England by statute, 29 Chas. II, c. 3, § 12 (1677). See N.C. Gen. Stat. § 29-2, subsection (2)(a), which makes an estate for the life of another part of a decedent's "estate" for purposes of inheritance. Therefore today an estate for the life of another passes by descent to the heirs of the owner, at least for the life of the person whose life has been designated as the measuring life. 1 Restatement of Property § 151 (1936); Brown v. Brown, 168 N.C. 4, 84 S.E. 25 (1914). Such estates can be disposed of by will. Dew v. Shockley, 36 N.C. App. 87, 243 S.E.2d 177 (1978), noting that life estates *pur autre vie* are estates of inheritance.

Life estates may be classified in the following manner:

1. Estates for Life Created by Acts of the Parties (Conventional Life Estates.)
   a. Estates for Tenant's Own Life.
   b. Estates for the Life of Another (*Pur Autre Vie.*)
   c. Estates Which May Last for Life but Which Are Terminable upon Happening of Contingent Event.
2. Estates for Life Which Arise by Operation of Law (Legal Life Estates) or Life Estates Arising from Marital Relation.
   a. Dower.
   b. Curtesy.
   c. Statutory Substitutes for Dower and Curtesy.

§ 47. Conventional Life Estates Created by Acts of Parties.

A conventional life estate arises by act of the parties when it is the result of some agreement or express transfer. Thus a life estate may be created by transfers by deed or will or by reservations in such instruments.

The most typical life estate is for the tenant's own life; a conveyance "to *A* for life" creates an estate in *A* for the duration of his own life. A life estate may be created, however, which is to exist for the life of another person or persons.[3] A conveyance or devise which grants land "To *A* for the life of *B*" creates an estate for life *pur autre vie* (for the life of another).[4]

As discussed in § 25 *supra,* a life estate was created at early common law if the words of inheritance "and his heirs" were omitted in the grant of land. North Carolina statutes now presume that a full fee simple title passes absent a clear indication that an estate of less dignity was intended.[5] A grantor intending to create a life estate should take care to unequivocally indicate that intention. Care should be taken to avoid

---

3. A number of lives can be designated as limiting the duration of an estate. 1 RESTATEMENT OF PROPERTY § 107 (1936).

4. Brown v. Brown, 168 N.C. 4, 84 S.E. 25 (1914). The life estate *pur autre vie* is also created as the result of a conveyance of an ordinary life estate when the life tenant conveys his interest to a third party. When *A,* who owns a life estate for his own life, conveys it to *B,* the latter thereafter has a life estate for the duration of *A*'s life. Dew v. Shockley, 36 N.C. App. 87, 243 S.E.2d 177 (1978), at 36 N.C. App. 89: "Professor Link, in his illuminating article on the Rule in Wild's Case in North Carolina, suggests that a concurrent joint tenancy for life *might* be seen as a series of life estates *pur autre vie,* measured by the life of the last co-tenant to die. Life estates *pur autre vie* are estates of inheritance, and G.S. 41-2 abolishes survivorship. 55 N.C.L. REV. 751, 787-791. But such construction is clearly contrary to the case law as it now stands. 55 N.C.L. REV. 751, 790. Concurrent life estates still stand untouched by G.S. 41-2, and the old feudal presumption in favor of joint tenancies with survivorship remains."

5. N.C. GEN. STAT. § 39-1. *See* N.C. GEN. STAT. § 31-38 (as to wills).

conversion of the life estate to a fee by application of the Rule in Shelley's Case.[6] Certain descriptive words, such as giving a grantee "the use of" property, should be avoided and the nature of the estate should be specified.[7] A devise of a life estate with a power to sell or dispose of the property devised gives the grantee a life estate with a power of disposition, not a fee simple estate.[8]

§ 48. Estates Which May Last for Life but Which May Terminate upon the Happening of a Contingent Event.

A life estate may be created although it may be made terminable prematurely upon the happening of some specified contingency. For example, a conveyance may be made to a person for his life or the life of another but to be cut off upon the happening of a contingency. A conveyance "to a woman during her widowhood" or "to a man until he be promoted to a benefice" creates a defeasible life estate.[9] The life estate may be a determinable life estate, a life estate subject to a condition subsequent, or a life estate subject to an executory interest.

§ 49. Estates for Life Which Arise by Operation of Law; Dower, Curtesy and Their Statutory Substitutes.

(a) *Estates for life which arise by operation of law.* Estates for life

---

6. In re Grady, 33 N.C. App. 477, 235 S.E.2d 425 (1977), in which the Rule in Shelley's Case was applied to convert a devisee's life estate and remainder in her heirs into a fee simple estate. *Compare* White v. Lackey, 40 N.C. App. 353, 253 S.E.2d 13 (1979), a case holding the Rule in Shelley's Case inapplicable to a will devising property to testator's granddaughter "during her natural life and at her death to the lawful heir or heirs of her body."

7. Thompson v. Ward, 36 N.C. App. 593, 244 S.E.2d 485 (1978), holding that where the testatrix devised the "use of" the property so long as the beneficiaries "wish to live there," she showed an intent to devise less than the fee. The court rejected an argument that N.C. GEN. STAT. § 31-38 dictated the finding of a fee and distinguished earlier decisions holding that the devise of the "use of" property is the equivalent of a devise in fee. Poindexter v. Trust Co., 258 N.C. 371, 128 S.E.2d 867 (1963); Schwren v. Falls, 170 N.C. 251, 87 S.E. 49 (1915).

8. Atkins v. Burden, 31 N.C. App. 660, 230 S.E.2d 594 (1976): "A devise of a life estate with a power to sell or dispose of the property devised does not give the devisee a fee simple determinable but gives him a life estate coupled with a power of disposition." Citing Chewning v. Mason, 158 N.C. 578, 74 S.E. 357 (1912).

9. Jones v. Gooch, 36 N.C. App. 243, 243 S.E.2d 410 (1978).

See Blackwood v. Blackwood, 237 N.C. 726, 76 S.E.2d 122 (1953), which quotes from 2 BLACKSTONE'S COMMENTARIES § 121: "If an estate be granted to a woman during her widowhood, or to a man until he be promoted to a benefice; in these and similar cases, whenever the contingency happens, when the widow marries, or when the grantee obtains a benefice; the respective estates are absolutely determined and gone. Yet while they subsist, they are reckoned estates for life; may by possibility last for life, if the contingencies upon which they are to determine, do not sooner happen." *See* numerous cases cited in the *Blackwood* case *supra.*

arising by operation of law may be called "marital life estates." These life estates resulted from the marital relation at the common law for the purpose of giving surviving spouses a certain degree of security in the lands of a deceased spouse. They were a common-law attempt to provide "social security" for surviving spouses in the lands of deceased spouses.[10]

(b) *Dower.* One of these life estates which arose from the marital relation was the estate of dower. Dower was the right of a surviving widow to a life estate in one third in value of all of the real property of which her husband was seized of a freehold estate of inheritance during coverture.[11] The requisites for dower were: (1) a valid marriage; (2) the husband had to be seized of an estate of freehold of inheritance; and (3) death of the husband.[12] A husband's sole act of conveyance, mortgage, contract or will of his land could not defeat his wife's right of dower and if she survived her husband's death, she could have her dower allotted as against her husband's grantee, mortgagee, vendee or devisee.[13] The wife's right to dower was also superior to the claims of the creditors of the husband [14] and his heirs.

(c) *Curtesy.* The other marital life estate created by operation of law was the estate of curtesy. Like dower, the estate of curtesy existed in North Carolina until the enactment in 1959 of the currently existing Intestate Succession Act, which act became effective in 1960.[15] The estate of curtesy as it previously existed entitled a surviving husband to a life estate in all of the real property of which his wife was seized of an inheritable freehold estate during coverture. There were four requisites for a husband to be entitled to curtesy: (1) There had to be a valid marriage between the husband and wife; (2) the wife had to be seized of an inheritable freehold estate; (3) issue (children) must have been born alive to the marriage who were capable of inheriting the land; and (4) the wife must have died intestate.[16] The estate of curtesy, as such, has not been created by operation of law in North Carolina since 1960.[17]

---

10. CRIBBET, PRINCIPLES OF THE LAW OF PROPERTY 82 (1962).
11. *See former* statute, N.C. GEN. STAT. § 30-5, now repealed. This statute was repealed in 1959 when the present intestate succession statute was enacted. The present intestate succession statute had prospective effect only and consequently there are estates of dower still in force which resulted from decedents' deaths prior to 1959. *E.g., see* Coats v. Williams, 261 N.C. 692, 136 S.E.2d 113 (1964). The estate of dower has not been created, as such, by operation of law since 1960.
12. Pollard v. Slaughter, 92 N.C. 72 (1885); Houston v. Smith, 88 N.C. 312 (1883).
13. MINOR & WURTS, REAL PROPERTY § 283 (1910).
14. MINOR & WURTS, REAL PROPERTY §§ 301, 302 (1910).
15. *See* former statute, N.C. GEN. STAT. § 52-16, *repealed* by N.C. GEN. STAT. § 29-4 in 1959. Since the Intestate Succession Act had only prospective effect, estates of curtesy which arose as a result of the death of decedents prior to 1960 continue to exist.
16. Fleming v. Sexton, 172 N.C. 250, 90 S.E. 247 (1916). *See* former statute, N.C. GEN. STAT. § 52-16, *now repealed* by N.C. GEN. STAT. § 29-4.
17. *But see* the statutory substitutes for dower and curtesy in the following sections which preserve many of the characteristics and elements of common-law curtesy and dower.

(d) *Statutory substitutes for dower and curtesy.* The life estates of dower and curtesy have come to be regarded as anachronistic estates in modern times and legislatures almost everywhere have made modifications of the marital interests or, in some cases, have abolished them altogether, relying on other "social security" measures to protect surviving spouses.

In North Carolina the Intestate Succession Act enacted in 1959 purports to abolish curtesy and dower.[18] By another statute, however, in North Carolina General Statutes, § 29-30, the legislature of North Carolina has reinserted statutory provisions which indicate its desire that surviving spouses shall continue to have the same benefits as were formerly provided by dower and curtesy.[19] That statute provides a statutory substitute for curtesy and dower whereby a surviving spouse may elect to take a life estate in lieu of the share that he or she would take by intestate succession or by the will of the deceased spouse. That statute is set out in full at the end of this section.[20] By its terms the surviving spouse

---

18. N.C. GEN. STAT. § 29-4.
19. Smith v. Smith, 265 N.C. 18, 143 S.E.2d 300 (1965); Heller v. Heller, 7 N.C. App. 120, 171 S.E.2d 335 (1969).
20. N.C. GEN. STAT. § 29-30 provides:

§ **29-30. Election of surviving spouse to take life interest in lieu of intestate share provided.** — (a) In lieu of the share provided in G.S. 29-14 or 29-21, the surviving spouse of an intestate or the surviving spouse who dissents from the will of a testator shall be entitled to take as his or her intestate share a life estate in one third in value of all the real estate of which the deceased spouse was seised and possessed of an estate of inheritance at any time during coverture, except that real estate as to which the surviving spouse:
  (1) Has waived his or her rights by joining with the other spouse in a conveyance thereof, or
  (2) Has released or quitclaimed his or her interest therein in accordance with G.S. 52-10, or
  (3) Was not required by law to join in conveyance thereof in order to bar the elective life estate, or
  (4) Is otherwise not legally entitled to the election provided in this section.

(b) Regardless of the value thereof and despite the fact that a life estate therein might exceed the fractional limitation provided for in subsection (a), the life estate provided for in subsection (a) shall at the election of the surviving spouse include a life estate in the usual dwelling house occupied by the surviving spouse at the time of the death of the deceased spouse if such dwelling house were owned by the deceased spouse at the time of his or her death, together with the outbuildings, improvements and easements thereunto belonging or appertaining, and lands upon which situated and reasonably necessary to the use and enjoyment thereof, as well as a fee simple ownership in the household furnishings therein.

(c) The election provided for in subsection (a) shall be made by the filing of a notice thereof with the clerk of the superior court of the county in which the administration of the estate is pending, or, if no administration is pending, then with the clerk of the superior court of any county in which the administration of the estate could be commenced. Such election shall be made:
  (1) At any time within one month after the expiration of the time fixed for the filing of a dissent, or
  (2) In case of intestacy, then within twelve months after the death of the deceased spouse if letters of administration are not issued within that period, or
  (3) If letters of administration are issued within twelve months after the date of the death of the deceased spouse, then within one month after the expiration of the time limited for filing claims against the estate, or

§ 49　　　　　REAL ESTATE LAW IN NORTH CAROLINA　　　　　§ 49

of an intestate or a surviving spouse who dissents from the will of a testator shall be entitled to take as his or her intestate share a life estate in one third in value of all the real estate of which the deceased spouse was seized and possessed of an estate of inheritance at any time during coverture.[21]

---

(4) If litigation that affects the share of the surviving spouse in the estate is pending, then within such reasonable time as may be allowed by written order of the clerk of the superior court.

The notice of election shall:
  a. Be directed to the clerk with whom filed;
  b. State that the surviving spouse making the same elects to take under this section rather than under the provisions of G.S. 29-14 or 29-21, as applicable;
  c. Set forth the names of all heirs, devisees, legatees, personal representatives and all other persons in possession of or claiming an estate or an interest in the property described in subsection (a); and
  d. Request the allotment of the life estate provided for in subsection (a).

The notice of election may be in person, or by attorney authorized in a writing executed and duly acknowledged by the surviving spouse and attested by at least one witness. If the surviving spouse is a minor or an incompetent, the notice of election may be executed and filed by a general guardian or by the guardian of the person or estate of the minor or incompetent spouse. If the minor or incompetent spouse has no guardian, the notice of election may be executed and filed by a next friend appointed by the clerk. The notice of election, whether in person or by attorney, shall be filed as a record of the court, and a summons together with a copy of the notice of election shall be served upon each of the interested persons named in the notice of election.

(d) In case of election to take a life estate in lieu of an intestate share, as provided in either G.S. 29-14, G.S. 29-21, or G.S. 30-3 (a), the clerk of superior court, with whom the notice of election has been filed, shall summon and appoint a jury of three disinterested persons who being first duly sworn shall promptly allot and set apart to the surviving spouse the life estate provided for in subsection (a) and make a final report of such action to the clerk.

(e) The final report shall be filed by the jury not more than sixty days after the summoning and appointment thereof, shall be signed by all jurors, and shall describe by metes and bounds the real estate in which the surviving spouse shall have been allotted and set aside a life estate. It shall be filed as a record of court and a certified copy thereof shall be filed and recorded in the office of the register of deeds of each county in which any part of the real property of the deceased spouse, affected by the allotment, is located.

(f) In the election and procedure to have the life estate allotted and set apart provided for in this section, the rules of procedure relating to partition proceedings shall apply except insofar as the same would be inconsistent with the provisions of this section.

(g) Neither the household furnishings in the dwelling house nor the life estates taken by election under this section shall be subject to the payment of debts due from the estate of the deceased spouse, except those debts secured by such property as follows:
  (1) By a mortgage or deed of trust in which the surviving spouse has waived his or her rights by joining with the other spouse in the making thereof; or
  (2) By a purchase money mortgage or deed of trust, or by a conditional sales contract of personal property in which title is retained by the vendor, made prior to or during the marriage; or
  (3) By a mortgage or deed of trust made prior to the marriage; or
  (4) By a mortgage or deed of trust constituting a lien on the property at the time of its acquisition by the deceased spouse either before or during the marriage.

(h) If no election is made in the manner and within the time provided for in subsection (c) the surviving spouse shall be conclusively deemed to have waived his or her right to elect to take under the provisions of this section, and any interest which the surviving spouse may have had in the real estate of the deceased spouse by virtue of this statute shall terminate.

21. N.C. Gen. Stat. § 29-30 (a). A present right of possession is not conferred on the owner's spouse by N.C. Gen. Stat. § 29-30. Thus a wife is not a real party in interest who can interpose a defense or counterclaim in an ejectment action instituted by her husband's grantee against her husband. The statute only provides for a life estate at the election of the

The requirements for asserting this elective life estate created by statute are the same as those required at the common law and in North Carolina's former statute for the assertion of dower: (1) There must be a valid marriage between the spouses; (2) the decedent spouse must have been seized of an inheritable estate of freehold during the marriage; and (3) the spouse owning the inheritable estate during coverture must have died.[22]

Notwithstanding the value thereof and despite the fact that the surviving spouse ordinarily is entitled to a life estate in only one third in value of the land of which the deceased spouse was seized during coverture, a surviving spouse may, at his or her election, take his or her life estate in the usual dwelling house occupied by the deceased spouse at the time of his death, if the deceased spouse owned such dwelling house at the time of his death.[23] The surviving spouse gets a life estate in the whole dwelling, the outbuildings, improvements, and easements appurtenant thereto regardless of the value of such property.[24]

It can be stated generally that the life estates provided by these statutory provisions are not subject to the debts of the deceased spouse.[25] In addition, these life estates cannot be defeated by either spouse's sole conveyance. A spouse may, however, waive the marital rights conferred by this statute by joining the conveyance of the owning spouse by co-signing his deed, mortgage, or deed of trust.[26] Hence, any person buying real property from a married person will be well advised to determine the marital status of his grantor and to procure the signature of his grantor's spouse as well as that of the grantor himself on deeds, mortgages, and deeds of trust. It should be noted, however, that purchase money mortgages and purchase money deeds of trust executed by a spouse on real estate that he acquires during his marriage will take priority over

---

surviving spouse; it does not give a present right of possession in a living spouse's real property. *See* People's Oil Co. v. Richardson, 271 N.C. 696, 157 S.E.2d 369 (1967).

But see N.C. GEN. STAT. § 45-45 which permits a spouse to redeem real property conveyed by his or her spouse's mortgages, deeds of trust, and like security instruments and to have an assignment of the security instrument and the uncancelled obligation secured thereby. *Id.*

22. *Id.*
23. N.C. GEN. STAT. § 29-30 (b).
24. *Id.*
25. N.C. GEN. STAT. § 29-30 (g).
26. N.C. GEN. STAT. § 29-30 (a) (1), (2), (3), (4). Any or all of the marital rights under this section may be surrendered by a properly drawn separation agreement. If a married person signs a valid contract for the sale of land without the joinder of his or her spouse, specific performance of the contract can be decreed with respect to the property involved. The contract of the signing spouse is binding, but the rights of his nonsigning spouse under N.C. GEN. STAT. § 29-30 are not cut off or affected in any way. Hutchens v. Honeycutt, 286 N.C. 314, 210 S.E.2d 254 (1974).

a surviving spouse's right to assert a life estate pursuant to North Carolina General Statutes, § 29-30.[27]

Suffice it to say that dower and curtesy have not been abolished in North Carolina in any real sense; they have only been modified. The optional marital life estates that are permissible under the new statute are very much like the old estates of dower and curtesy.

§ 50. The Marital Life Estates; Seisin Required.

A surviving spouse could have neither curtesy nor dower under the common law or under statutory law previously in effect in North Carolina unless his or her spouse was seised of an estate of freehold of inheritance during coverture.[28] The result of this was that there was no curtesy or dower except when the decedent spouse had a present, possessory inheritable estate during the marriage.[29] Hence there could be no dower or curtesy in the lands of a deceased spouse if the spouse had only a life estate [30] or a term for years not of freehold. There could likewise be no dower or curtesy in a decedent spouse's future interest, such as a reversion or a remainder after a freehold estate in some other person.[31]

Since a determinable fee simple estate or a fee simple estate subject to a condition subsequent or subject to an executory interest *could* last forever, and *could* descend by inheritance to the heirs of the owner of any such estate, it has been held in North Carolina that a husband had curtesy and a widow had dower in his or her spouse's real property held upon such defeasible condition.[32] That the event happened that would terminate the deceased spouse's estate would not defeat the curtesy or dower of the surviving spouse.[33] Whether North Carolina General Stat-

---

27. N.C. GEN. STAT. § 29-30 (g) (1), (2), (3), (4).
28. *See former* statutes, N.C. GEN. STAT. §§ 30-5, 52-16 (both statutes now repealed). *See also* Houston v. Smith, 88 N.C. 312 (1883); Nixon v. Williams, 95 N.C. 103 (1886).
29. *Id.*
30. Alexander v. Cunningham, 27 N.C. 430 (1845); Gilmore v. Sellars, 145 N.C. 283, 59 S.E. 73 (1907).
31. *In re* Smith's Will, 249 N.C. 563, 107 S.E.2d 89 (1959); Royster v. Royster, 61 N.C. 226 (1867); *In re* Dixon, 156 N.C. 26, 72 S.E. 71 (1911); Thomas v. Bunch, 158 N.C. 175, 73 N.C. 899 (1912); Redding v. Vogt, 140 N.C. 562, 53 S.E. 337 (1906); 1 MORDECAI, LAW LECTURES 518 (1916). *But see* Weir v. Humphries, 39 N.C. 264 (1846), which held that an estate held by a husband subject to a mere estate for years in another gave to the husband sufficient seisin in the real property to make the land dowable for his wife. This conclusion was reached on the theory that the tenant for years was not seised; that since there is but one seisin in land, the husband who had a remainder after the term for years was seised.
32. North Carolina has followed the English case of Buckworth v. Thirkell, 3 Bos. & P. 652 (1804). *See* Pollard v. Slaughter, 92 N.C. 72 (1885); Allen v. Saunders, 186 N.C. 349, 119 S.E. 486 (1923); Alexander v. Fleming, 190 N.C. 815, 130 S.E. 867 (1925); American Yarn & Processing Co. v. Dewstoe, 192 N.C. 121, 133 S.E. 407 (1926).
33. *Id.*

utes, § 29-30 will receive a similar interpretation by the courts remains to be seen.[34]

There could be no dower or curtesy in real estate held by a partnership of which the deceased spouse was a member.[35] A spouse could, however, assert his marital life estate against the interest of the deceased spouse in a tenancy in common.[36]

These cases and authorities on the seisin requirements for curtesy and dower are significant because the seisin and estate requirements for the marital life estates created by the North Carolina Intestate Succession Act are essentially the same as formerly required for curtesy and dower. The reasoning applied in these dower and curtesy cases with reference to the seisin required by the deceased spouse should be carried over into the new statute.

Article II. Incidents of Life Estates

§ 51. Generally.

Life estates, whether created by operation of law or by the acts of the parties, have certain incidents which are annexed to them by operation of law, unless the parties, in case of the latter class of life estates, by stipulation deprive them of some of these incidents in the creating deed or will. The parties *may* annex to such estates by express covenants, conditions or stipulations such incidents as they may see fit, not contrary to law.[37]

§ 52. Right to Alien.

A life tenant may transfer his estate for life [38] or for any period not exceeding his life tenancy.[39] A life tenant may, however, be given, in addition to his life estate, a power to convey the fee, in which case he can convey a fee simple estate.[40] While at common law if a life tenant

---

34. *See* discussion of this point at § 36 *infra*, where the possibility of interpreting the statutory life estate as a derivative one is discussed.
35. N.C. GEN. STAT. § 59-55 (b) (5).
36. Jenkins v. Strickland, 214 N.C. 441, 199 S.E. 612 (1938); Dudley v. Tyson, 167 N.C. 67, 82 S.E. 1025 (1914).
37. MINOR & WURTS, REAL PROPERTY § 191 (1910).
38. Roe v. Journigan, 181 N.C. 180, 106 S.E. 680 (1921).
39. Haywood v. Briggs, 227 N.C. 108, 41 S.E.2d 289 (1946). A mortgage by a life tenant purporting to cover the fee is effective as to the life estate only. Thompson v. Watkins, 285 N.C. 616, 207 S.E.2d 740 (1974).
40. A life estate expressly created by the language of an instrument will not be converted into a fee or into any other form of estate greater than a life estate merely by reason of there being coupled with it a power of disposition, however general or extensive. Howell v. Alexander, 3 N.C. App. 371, 165 S.E.2d 256 (1969); Tillet v. Nixon, 180 N.C. 195, 104 S.E. 352 (1920). It should be noted, however, that the fact that the life tenant has a power to dispose of a fee simple does not give to the tenant a fee simple.

purported to convey a fee simple estate when he had only a life estate the life tenant's conveyance was deemed tortious and resulted in a forfeiture of the tenant's life estate, a conveyance by the life tenant at modern law operates only to convey his life tenancy; no forfeiture results.[41]

If a deed or will purports to restrain the alienation of a life estate created therein, such restraining condition is void.[42]

§ 53. Right to Emblements.

At the common law the personal representative of a life tenant was entitled,[43] upon the death of the life tenant, to reap crops previously sown and growing at the termination of the life tenancy. This right, called "emblements," gave to the personal representative of the life tenant the right of ingress and egress, not the right of possession, for the purpose of harvesting annual crops planted by the life tenant before the termination of his estate.[44] Since all parts of the common law are declared by statute to be in full force and effect if not abrogated or repealed,[45] this is apparently still the law in North Carolina.[46]

§ 54. Right to Estovers.

A life tenant, as well as a tenant for years or at will, is entitled to cut and use a reasonable amount of timber on the land for the purpose of repairing buildings, fences, equipment, machinery and the like or for use as fuel.[47] But a life tenant is not allowed to cut and sell timber from the land in which he has a tenancy merely for his own profit.[48]

---

41. A mortgage by a life tenant purporting to cover the fee is effective as to the life estate only. Thompson v. Watkins, 285 N.C. 616, 207 S.E.2d 740 (1974); 1 Mordecai, Law Lectures, 505, 701-702 (1916); Lovett v. Stone, 239 N.C. 206, 79 S.E.2d 479 (1953).
42. Wool v. Fleetwood, 136 N.C. 460, 48 S.E. 785 (1904).
43. The life tenant himself was entitled to emblements if the *cestui que vie* died and the life tenancy was *pur autre vie*.
44. Hayes v. Wrenn, 167 N.C. 229, 83 S.E. 356 (1914); Perry v. Terral, 21 N.C. 441 (1836); Poindexter v. Blackburn, 36 N.C. 286 (1840); King v. Foscue, 91 N.C. 116 (1884).
45. N.C. Gen. Stat. § 4-1.
46. N.C. Gen. Stat. § 42-7 is a statute providing for benefits in lieu of emblements for lessees from life tenants whose terms are terminated by the death of life tenants, and provides benefits for lessees from mortgagors whose terms are terminated by the foreclosure of a mortgage. The statute does not by its terms apply to the life tenants themselves.
47. Thomas v. Thomas, 166 N.C. 627, 82 S.E. 1032 (1914). Accord, Temple v. Carter, 3 N.C. App. 515, 165 S.E.2d 541 (1969).
48. *Id.* If the life tenant has cut wood in violation of the rights of a reversioner or remainderman, he may not recoup or set off against an action for waste the costs of repairs or improvements made by him at another time. The cutting of timber must be for the present purpose of making the necessary repairs or improvements. *But see* Temple v. Carter, 3 N.C. App. 515, 165 S.E.2d 541 (1969), which holds that the rule that a life tenant impeachable for waste may not cut timber for commercial purposes is subject to an exception in favor of the life tenant of a timber estate which, prior to the creation of the life estate, was cultivated merely for the production of salable timber. In other words, if the lands subject to the life

It should be noted, however, that every cutting of timber is not waste. If the tenant has acted with the same care as a prudent owner of the fee would have exercised if he had been in possession, his acts will not be deemed waste.[49]

§ 54.1. General Standard of Duty Owed by Life Tenant to Remainderman or Reversioner.

Disputes in this area often center around the following general issues: (1) What duties and obligations does a life tenant owe to the remainderman or reversioner? (2) To what extent can a life tenant use and reap the benefit of the life estate without such use constituting an unwarranted exploitation or surcharge?

The general relationship between a life tenant and remainderman is a quasi-fiduciary one.[50] A life tenant is not a pure trustee so as to invoke the rules of equity which govern trustees and cestuis que trustent, but acts as a limited trustee in the sense that the life tenant has a duty to act with due regard for the rights of the remainderman or reversioner, to refrain from injuring the property to the detriment of remainderman or reversioner, and to exercise reasonable precautions to preserve the property intact for transmission at the termination of the life estate.[51] Put another way, the quasi-fiduciary concept imposes upon the life tenant an enforceable legal duty of good husbandry; *i.e.*, the obligation to preserve the estate for the remainderman or reversioner in the condition in which the life tenant received it by paying taxes, making ordinary repairs, and paying interest on encumbrances.[52] A failure to perform these obligations falls under an extension of the rule which prohibits waste.[53]

§ 55. Life Tenant's Duty to Pay Taxes.

A life tenant has both a common law and statutory duty to pay taxes

---

tenancy have previously been used for tree farming and salable timber has been periodically cut and sold, the life tenant may continue the cultivation and sale of the trees from the land for his own profit. In such case the trees cut are deemed not a part of the inheritance but a part of the so-called annual fruits of the land when reforestation is pursued.

49. Thomas v. Thomas, 166 N.C. 627, 82 S.E. 1032 (1914). *Accord,* Temple v. Carter, 3 N.C. App. 515, 165 S.E.2d 541 (1969).

50. Thompson v. Watkins, 285 N.C. 616, 207 S.E.2d 740 (1974), a case which cites an excellent Supreme Court of Missouri decision on this subject; Muzzy v. Muzzy, 364 Mo. 373, 261 S.W.2d 927 (1953).

51. *Id.*

52. *Id. See* additional cases cited in the following sections.

53. Muzzy v. Muzzy, 364 Mo. 373, 261 S.W.2d 927 (1953). With regard to equitable life estates, *see* the North Carolina Principal and Income Act of 1973, N.C. Gen. Stat. §§ 37-16 to 37-40.

on real property in which the tenant has a life tenancy.[54] If compelled to pay the taxes on real property due to the omission of the life tenant to make such payment, a reversioner or remainderman is entitled to recover from the life tenant or his estate for the amount paid to discharge the taxes.[55] If a life tenant allows the property to be foreclosed and sold or sold under levy for failure to pay the taxes thereon, the life tenant is liable to the remainderman or reversioner for any damages incurred.[56]

§ 56. Life Tenant's Duty to Pay Local Assessments.

Whenever any real estate is in the possession or enjoyment of a tenant for life, or a tenant for a term of years, and an assessment is laid or levied by any city, town, county, township, municipal district, or the State, to cover the cost of permanent improvements ordered put thereon by the law or the ordinances of such city or town, township, or municipal district, such as paving streets and sidewalks, laying sewer and water lines, draining lowlands, and permanent improvements of a like character, which constitute a lien upon such property, the amount so assessed for such

---

54. See N.C. GEN. STAT. § 105-384:

§ **105-384. Duties and liabilities of life tenant.** — (a) If real or personal property is held by a tenant for life or by a tenant for the life of another, it shall be the duty of the life tenant to pay the taxes imposed on the property.
(b) Any remainderman or reversioner of real or personal property who pays the taxes thereon may recover the money so paid in an action against the life tenant of the property; in the case of real property, the action may be brought only in the appropriate division of the General Court of Justice of the county in which the real property is located.
(c) Any tenant for life of real or personal property who suffers the property to be foreclosed and sold or sold under levy for failure to pay the taxes thereon shall be liable to the remainderman or to the reversioner for any damages incurred.

Former N.C. GEN. STAT. § 105-410, relating to the forfeiture of life estates to remaindermen or reversioners was repealed by the Machinery Act of 1971. See N.C. GEN. STAT. § 105-271 et seq. The entire subchapter on "Listing, Appraisal, and Assessment of Property and Collection of Taxes on Property" was rewritten. The substance of N.C. GEN. STAT. § 105-387, referred to in this note in original, is now revised and renumbered as N.C. GEN. STAT. § 105-369. See generally CAMPBELL, PROPERTY TAX COLLECTION IN NORTH CAROLINA 112-114 (1974).

That the life tenant has the duty to list and pay taxes on the property in which he holds a life tenancy, in accord with the text, see Thompson v. Watkins, 285 N.C. 616, 207 S.E.2d 740 (1974). The life tenant cannot defeat the estate of the remainderman by allowing the land to be sold for taxes and taking title in himself by purchase at the tax sale. The life tenant's purchase at a tax sale is regarded as a payment of the tax, and the owner of the future interest is regarded as still holding under his original title. Being bound to pay the taxes, a life tenant cannot acquire a tax title or good title based on his failing to pay taxes. He becomes a quasi-trustee.

55. N.C. GEN. STAT. § 105-384 (b). It has been held by court decision that the interest of a life tenant will no longer be automatically forfeited because of nonpayment of taxes on the real estate during the life tenancy. Crandall v. Clemmons, 222 N.C. 225, 22 S.E.2d 448 (1942); Eason v. Spence, 232, N.C. 579, 61 S.E.2d 717 (1950).

56. N.C. GEN. STAT. § 105-384 (c).

See generally CAMPBELL, PROPERTY TAX COLLECTION IN NORTH CAROLINA 112-114 (1974).

purposes shall be paid by the tenant for life or for years, and the remaindermen after the life estate, or the owner in fee after the expiration of tenancy for a term of years, pro rata their respective interests in said real estate.[57]

§ 57. Life Tenant's Duties with Respect to Encumbrances on Land; Duties with Respect to Interest.

If property comes to a life tenant subject to a mortgage, deed of trust or other encumbrance, it is the duty of the life tenant to pay the annual interest on the debt secured by such mortgage, deed of trust or other encumbrance.[58] The life tenant is under no obligation, however, to pay off the principal of any lien indebtedness against the land; [59] he is only liable for the payment of interest which accrues during the existence of his life estate.

---

57. N.C. GEN. STAT. §§ 160A-234 and 160A-235. § 160A-234 provides:

§ 160A-234. **Assessments on property held by tenancy for life or years.** — (a) Assessments upon real property in the possession or enjoyment of a tenant for life, or a tenant for a term of years, shall be paid pro rata by the tenant and the remaindermen after the life estate, or the owner in fee after the expiration of the tenancy for years according to their respective interests in the land calculated as provided in G.S. 37-13.

(b) If any person having an interest in land held by tenancy for life or years shall pay more than his pro rata share of any assessment against the property, he shall have the right to maintain an action in the nature of a suit for contribution against the delinquent party to recover from him his pro rata share of the assessment, with interest thereon from the date of payment, and shall be subrogated to the right of the city to a lien on the property for the same.

(The reference in the above statute to N.C. GEN. STAT. § 37-13 as the mode for computation of the respective amounts to be paid by the tenant and the remainderman is no longer correct. See N.C. GEN. STAT. §§ 37-16 through 37-40.)

58. With respect to a mortgage encumbrance given prior to the creation of the life estate and remainder or reversion, in the absence of a different stipulation in the instrument creating the life estate, a life tenant owes a duty to the remainderman or reversioner to pay the interest accruing during the period of his life estate on the pre-existing mortgage encumbrance, at least to the extent of the income or rental value of the property. But the life tenant's only duty with respect to a prior lien on the whole estate is to pay the interest. He is under no obligation to pay any part of the principal. Thompson v. Watkins, 285 N.C. 616, 207 S.E.2d 740 (1974); Miller v. Marriner, 187 N.C. 449, 121 S.E. 770 (1924); Blount v. Hawkins, 57 N.C. 161 (1858); Jones v. Sherrard, 22 N.C. 179 (1838); 1 MORDECAI, LAW LECTURES 507 (1916).

59. In respect to a prior mortgage lien on the whole estate, unless obligated by the instrument creating his estate, the life tenant's only duty to the remainderman is to pay the interest. He is under no obligation to pay any part of the principal. When a life tenant, in order to preserve his estate, pays off an encumbrance upon the fee or estate property, whether the encumbrance is a mortgage, lien, charge or other type of encumbrance, he is entitled to reimbursement from the owners of future interests, such as reversioners or remaindermen, to the extent of their interest in the property which was subject to the encumbrance. He has a lien on the future interests for the amount which its owner is under a duty to pay. Thompson v. Watkins, 285 N.C. 616, 207 S.E.2d 740 (1974); Miller v. Marriner, 187 N.C. 449, 121 S.E. 770 (1924). That a life tenant is obligated to pay taxes and interest on encumbrances only to the extent of the income or annual value of the property, see Jones v. Sherrard and Miller v. Marriner, *supra* note 58, where it is stated that "one who is liable in respect of the occupation of land cannot be called on for more than the rents or actual annual value of the premises during his time."

§ 58. Life Tenant's Duty to Make Repairs; Improvements.

A life tenant has the duty to make all the ordinary repairs incident to the present enjoyment of the real property and such repairs as are necessary to prevent the property from passing into decay or waste.[60] If the life tenant neglects or omits to do what will prevent injury to the estate of freehold, by suffering a house thereon to become decayed for want of proper repair, he renders himself liable for permissive waste.[61]

A life tenant is under no obligation to make permanent or extraordinary improvements on the premises in which he has his life tenancy. If the life tenant makes improvements on the premises he cannot claim compensation therefor from the reversioner or remainderman.[62] It should be noted, however, that if the life tenant (or any other person) makes substantial and permanent improvements on lands, under circumstances affording him a well grounded or bona fide reasonable belief that he owned a fee simple at the time he made improvements to realty, he can recover from the remainderman or reversioner under the betterments statute [63] for the value of improvements placed on the land to the extent of the enhancement of the value of the land.[64]

---

60. Middleton v. Rigsbee, 179 N.C. 437, 102 S.E. 780 (1920).

61. Norris v. Laws, 150 N.C. 599, 64 S.E. 499 (1909).

62. Merritt v. Scott, 81 N.C. 385 (1879); Pendleton v. Williams, 175 N.C. 248, 95 S.E. 500 (1918); Middleton v. Rigsbee, 179 N.C. 437, 102 S.E. 780 (1920); Harriett v. Harriett, 181 N.C. 75, 106 S.E. 221 (1921); Smith v. Suitt, 199 N.C. 5, 153 S.E. 602 (1930); Hall v. Hall, 219 N.C. 805, 15 S.E.2d 273 (1941); Lovett v. Stone, 239 N.C. 206, 79 S.E.2d 479 (1953).

63. The presence or absence of color of title has significance with respect to claims for "betterments" under N.C. GEN. STAT. § 1-340. To be entitled to compensation for betterments under the statute the defendant must show that he made permanent improvements on the property under a bona fide belief of good title. *See* Hackett v. Hackett, 31 N.C. App. 217, 228 S.E.2d 758 (1976), citing Pamlico County v. Davis, 249 N.C. 648, 107 S.E.2d 306 (1959). Where all evidence showed that improvements made were made by defendant while he was a tenant, and not under color of title, defendant was not entitled to betterments.

The "Betterments" statute, N.C. GEN. STAT. § 1-340, is set out in full below:

§ 1-340. **Petition by claimant; execution suspended; issues found.** — A defendant against whom a judgment is rendered for land, may, at any time before execution, present a petition to the court rendering the judgment, stating that he, or those under whom he claims, while holding the premises under a color of title believed to be good, have made permanent improvements thereon, and praying that he may be allowed for the improvements, over and above the value of the use and occupation of the land. The court may, if satisfied of the probable truth of the allegation, suspend the execution of the judgment and impanel a jury to assess the damages of the plaintiff and the allowance to the defendant for the improvements. In any such action this inquiry and assessment may be made upon the trial of the cause.

See also Sweeten v. King, 29 N.C. App. 672, 225 S.E.2d 598 (1976), for a recent case involving betterments and applying N.C. GEN. STAT. § 1-340 where a life tenant thinking herself to be a fee simple owner of land under color of title in good faith made permanent improvements on the land. The North Carolina Court of Appeals held that her devisee as successor to her interest would be entitled to compensation for betterments upon a sale of the land for partition.

64. *Id.*

§ 59. Subject to Merger.

A life estate is subject to extinguishment by merger. That is, if the life estate (the lesser estate) and the remainder or reversion interest in expectancy (the greater estate) meet and coincide in one and the same person, without any intermediate estate, the general rule is that the greater freehold estate merges or extinguishes the lesser.[65]

§ 59.1. Insurance on Land Subject to Life Estate.

While it might be maintained that the concept of "good husbandry" discussed at § 54.1 *supra,* should include a duty on the part of the life tenant to keep the premises insured, this is not required of a legal life tenant by the caselaw. Both the life tenant and the remainderman or reversioner have insurable interests in the property which can be protected by insurance, but neither the holder of the present estate or future estate is required to protect the interest of the other by insurance.[66]

A life tenant who insures the property in the tenant's own name paying the premiums from his own funds and insuring for the full value of the fee is not precluded from recovering the full amount of the insurance policy proceeds.[67] The life tenant may retain as his own and the remainderman or reversioner will have no interest in the proceeds of a fire insurance policy covering the interests of the life tenant under the above mentioned circumstances, even though the insurance is for full value and the building is totally destroyed.[68]

§ 60. Life Tenant's Right to Possession; Profits.

A life tenant is entitled to possession and control of real property during the continuance of his life tenancy.[69] He is entitled to make the ordinary use and to take the ordinary profits delivered from the land provided his use and enjoyment of the premises does not constitute waste which will diminish the value of the reversion or remainder.[70]

---

65. 1 MORDECAI, LAW LECTURES 598 (1916); Trust Co. v. Watkins, 215 N.C. 292, 1 S.E.2d 853 (1939).
66. AMERICAN LAW OF PROPERTY § 2.23 (Casner ed. 1952).
67. Absent a special fiduciary responsibility or agreement between the life tenant and remainderman or reversioner as the procurement and maintenance of insurance coverage.
68. Stockton v. Maney, 212 N.C. 231, 193 S.E. 137 (1937); *In re* Will of Wilson, 224 N.C. 505, 31 S.E.2d 543 (1944); Forsyth County v. Plemmons, 2 N.C. App. 373, 163 S.E.2d 97 (1968).
69. Burwell v. Bank, 186 N.C. 117, 118 S.E. 881 (1923).
70. RESTATEMENT OF PROPERTY §§ 119, 120, 138 (1936).

§ 61. Subject to Life Tenant's Debts.

A life tenant's interest is subject to being reached for the satisfaction of the life tenant's debts in the same manner as other interests.[71]

§ 62. Life Tenant's Disability to Acquire Outstanding Title Against Reversioner or Remainderman.

If the property subject to a life tenancy is encumbered and is sold for satisfaction of the encumbrance or to satisfy taxes against the property, the life tenant cannot purchase the property for his own account but will be deemed to have purchased for the benefit of himself and the remainderman or reversioner.[72]

The Supreme Court of North Carolina has held, however, that if a life tenant purchases an outstanding title or encumbrance at a sale to satisfy the encumbrance he will be deemed to have made the purchase for the benefit of himself and the remainderman or reversioner only in case the latter will contribute his share of the sum paid by the life tenant *within a reasonable time.* If the life tenant purchases the property at a foreclosure sale and future interest holders do not contribute their proportionate parts of the purchase price within a reasonable time, the future interest holders will lose their rights to redeem their interests and the life tenant will acquire an exclusive unassailable title.[73] Likewise, while a

---

71. Burwell v. Bank, 186 N.C. 117, 118 S.E. 881 (1923).
72. Creech v. Wilder, 212 N.C. 162, 193 S.E. 281 (1937); Morehead v. Harris, 262 N.C. 330, 137 S.E.2d 174 (1964). *But see* Miller v. Marriner, 187 N.C. 449, 121 S.E. 770 (1924), to the effect that since a life tenant is obligated only to pay interest on encumbrances if land is sold by reason of default in payment of principal, the life tenant may purchase the land in his own right and not as a trustee, from a purchaser at a sale to foreclose the mortgage encumbrance.

Thompson v. Watkins, 285 N.C. 616, 207 S.E.2d 740 (1974), holds that a life tenant is not prohibited in all events from purchasing the property that is the subject of the life estate for his own exclusive benefit at a foreclosure sale. Even if a mortgage encumbrance existed prior to the creation of the life estate and a future interest, if the mortgage is foreclosed and the life tenant purchases the property at a foreclosure sale and the future interest owners do not contribute proportionate parts of the purchase price within a reasonable time, future interest owners will lose their rights to redeem their interests and the life tenant will own an exclusive unassailable title.

Thompson v. Watkins, *supra,* also states that when a remainderman for his own use places an encumbrance against his own vested interest (the remainder) and defaults, the life tenant may purchase the remainderman's interest for the life tenant's sole benefit at a foreclosure sale provided the transaction is free from fraud and the life tenant had no part in bringing about the foreclosure.

In Thompson v. Watkins, *supra,* the North Carolina Supreme Court also indicates that if encumbered property is devised to a life tenant with future interests to others, if it is necessary for the executor to sell the property to make assets for the decedent's estate, pursuant to a special proceeding to which all interested persons are made parties, the life tenant can purchase at the sale and obtain a fee simple title exclusively in himself upon the payment of full value.

73. Thompson v. Watkins, 285 N.C. 616, 207 S.E.2d 740 (1974).

life tenant's relation to the remainderman is a quasi-fiduciary one in the sense that he must exercise reasonable care to preserve the property intact for transmission to the remainderman and in that he can legally do nothing to prejudice or defeat the estate of the remainderman, the life tenant is not precluded from acquiring by gift or purchase from the remainderman his estate in remainder.[74]

§ 63. Land Subject to Life Estate May Be Sold If Unproductive.

In North Carolina, by statute,[75] a person who owns a life estate in lands which are unproductive and from which the income is insufficient to pay the taxes on and the reasonable upkeep of such lands is entitled to maintain an action, without the joinder of any of the remaindermen or reversioners,[76] to procure the sale of the lands under order of court for the purpose of obtaining funds to improve other nonproductive or unimproved real estate so as to make it profit bearing or in order to obtain a reinvestment of the funds for the benefit of the life tenant and remaindermen and reversioners.[77]

---

74. *Id.*

75. N.C. GEN. STAT. § 41-11; Stepp v. Stepp, 200 N.C. 237, 156 S.E. 804 (1930).

76. N.C. GEN. STAT. § 41-11 provides however that if the rights of minors or other persons not sui juris are involved, a competent and disinterested attorney shall be appointed by the court to file answer and represent their interests.

77. The purpose of this statute is not to destroy the interest of future interest holders but is to enable the present owners to sell the property and make a good title, subject to the claims of persons who may ultimately be entitled thereto and to safeguard their rights in all respects. Poole v. Thompson, 183 N.C. 588, 112 S.E. 323 (1922). *See* Lancaster v. Lancaster, 209 N.C. 673, 184 S.E. 527 (1936).

CHAPTER 6

ESTATES OF LESS THAN FREEHOLD

Article 1. General Provisions

§ 64. Estates of Less Than Freehold Generally.

Article II. Rights of Residential Tenants

§ 65. The Residential Rental Agreements Act — Introduction.
§ 66. Same — Mutuality of Obligations.
§ 67. Same — Landlord's Obligations.
§ 68. Same — Tenant's Obligations.
§ 69. Same — Tenant May Not Unilaterally Withhold Rent.
§ 70. Same — Remedies.
§ 71. Same — Statutory Prohibition Against Retaliatory Eviction.
§ 72. Tenant Security Deposit Act.
§ 73. Eviction of Tenants in Federally Assisted Low-Rent Housing Projects.

Article III. Estates for Years

Division 1. General Provisions

§ 74. The Estate for Years; Definition.
§ 75. Creation of the Tenancy for Years.
§ 76. Requirement That Lease for Years Be in Writing.
§ 77. Requirement That Lease for Years Be Recorded.

Division 2. Incidents of Estates for Years

§ 78. Generally.
§ 79. Tenant's Power of Alienation.
§ 80. Tenant's Right to Estovers.
§ 81. Tenant's Rights in Lieu of Emblements When Estate Terminated by Uncertain Event.
§ 82. Tenant's Exclusive Right of Possession and Enjoyment.
§ 83. Tenant's Liability for Waste.
§ 84. Tenant's Liability to Make Repairs.
§ 85. Merger.
§ 86. Termination Without Necessity of Notice.
§ 87. Effect of Tenant for Years Holding Over Beyond Stated Term.

Article IV. Tenancies from Period to Period

Division 1. General Provisions

§ 88. Estates from Year to Year, Quarter to Quarter, Month to Month, Week to Week; Definition.
§ 89. Ways Created.

Division 2. Incidents of Estates from Period to Period

§ 90. Generally.
§ 91. Right to Estovers.
§ 92. Right to Emblements.
§ 93. Right to Exclusive Possession.
§ 94. Right to Transfer Tenant's Interest.
§ 95. Tenant's Duty to Repair.
§ 96. Tenant's Liability for Waste.
§ 97. Termination; Necessity of Notice to Terminate.

Article V. Tenancies at Will

Division 1. General Provisions

§ 98. Tenancies at Will Generally.
§ 99. Creation by Express Agreement.
§ 100. Creation by Implication or Operation of Law.

Division 2. Incidents of Tenancies at Will

§ 101. Interest of Tenant at Will Is Personal.
§ 102. Tenant's Right to Estovers.
§ 103. Tenant's Right to Emblements.
§ 104. Tenant's Liability for Waste.
§ 105. Termination; No Prior Notice Required.

Article V. Tenancy at Sufferance

§ 106. General Provisions.
§ 107. Incidents of Tenancy at Sufferance.

Article I. General Provisions

§ 64. Estates of Less Than Freehold Generally.

Under the original feudal law, no estate of less than freehold was recognized as an interest in land.[1] The consequence of the tenant's not being recognized as the holder of a freehold interest in the land was that he did not have, at the early common law, any *in rem* rights in land held under a non-freehold possession.[2] For instance, if a lessor evicted his tenant, the tenant had no recourse against his lessor except an action for damages for breach of contract. Likewise, if a stranger put a lessee off his land held under lease, the lessee had no recourse or remedy whatever. The tenant of an estate of less than freehold was not recognized as holding any

---

1. MINOR & WURTS, REAL PROPERTY § 315 (1910); TIFFANY, REAL PROPERTY § 68 (abr. ed. 1940).

2. TIFFANY, REAL PROPERTY § 68 (abr. ed. 1940).

interest in real property and was not given the benefit of *real* actions by which he could recover possession of the land itself; his rights were strictly *in personam* and not *in rem*.[3]

With the passage of time, however, lessees of non-freehold estates were gradually given the right to recover the land itself, in actions against grantees of the lessor, against the lessor himself, and later against all the world, by the writ of *ejectione firmae,* which became the action of ejectment. The lessee came to be recognized as having a direct interest in the land itself.[4]

In modern law the estates of less than freehold — estates for years, estates at will, estates from period to period (year to year) and estates by sufferance — are recognized as interests in land but in some respects they retain some of the peculiarities which arose from their origin and early history.[5]

Because the relationship between landlord and tenant has been significantly changed in the area of residential non-freehold estates by the North Carolina Residential Rental Agreements Act that became effective on October 1, 1977,[6] a description and summary of this Act and related issues of tenants' rights will be discussed in the following sections. The remainder of this chapter will then be devoted to the traditional characteristics and incidents of non-freehold estates.

Article II. Rights of Residential Tenants

§ 65. The Residential Rental Agreements Act — Introduction.

By its passage of the Residential Rental Agreements Act,[7] the General Assembly materially altered what had been a seemingly unchangeable *status quo* in the area of residential landlord-tenant law. Effective on October 1, 1977, and applicable to rental agreements entered into,

---

3. MINOR & WURTS, REAL PROPERTY § 315 (1910).

4. *Id.*

5. *E.g.,* at the common law, non-freehold estates were treated as choses in action rather than as land. Hence, for various purposes non-freehold leasehold estates were, and are, regarded as personal property, and they are still called "chattels real."

A transfer of a lease, while it must be in writing, need not be under seal as is required for transfers of freehold estates. Moche v. Leno, 227 N.C. 159, 41 S.E.2d 369 (1947). A leasehold interest is taxable as personal property. Investment Co. v. Cumberland County, 245 N.C. 492, 96 S.E.2d 341 (1956). *But see* Cordell v. Stone Co., 247 N.C. 688, 102 S.E.2d 138 (1958).

For inheritance purposes, since 1960, in North Carolina, it is no longer significant that a leasehold interest is personal property, as both personal and real property descend in the same manner since the enactment of North Carolina's new Intestate Succession Act, in force since 1960.

6. N.C. GEN. STAT. § 42-38 et seq. (Supp. 1977).

7. N.C. GEN. STAT. § 42-38 et seq. (Supp. 1977). The Residential Rental Agreements Act will be referred to as "the Act" throughout Article II of this chapter.

extended, or renewed automatically or by the parties after that date, the Act revised the relationship between landlord and tenant in a number of important respects by imposing obligations on landlords and by according rights and remedies to tenants that were, for the most part, nonexistent under prior statutory or caselaw in North Carolina. In terms of application, the Act is stated as determining rights, obligations, and remedies under a rental agreement for a dwelling unit.[8] It is an Act aimed at residential landlord-tenant transactions only. In addition, "transient occupancy in a hotel, motel, or similar lodging subject to regulation by the Commission for Health Services" and any dwelling furnished rent-free are excluded from coverage under the Act.[9]

§ 66. Same — Mutuality of Obligations.

Under traditional landlord-tenant law, a lease of property was considered a transfer of an estate in land subject to the doctrine of *caveat emptor*. Covenants in the lease were considered mutually independent making the lessee's covenant to pay rent independent of the lessor's various obligations. The focus of the lease transaction was on the land itself, with structures on the property considered of little legal significance in the agrarian setting in which these rules developed.[10]

The Act makes a fundamental change in the above outdated notions by specifying that certain primary obligations are to be mutually dependent.[11] The tenant's obligation to pay rent and to comply with certain duties with respect to maintenance of the dwelling and the landlord's obligation to provide fit premises are made mutually dependent. The most consequential effect of this change, from a tenant's viewpoint, is that an "implied warranty of habitability" now applies to transactions covered by the Act.[12]

---

8. N.C. GEN. STAT. § 42-38 (Supp. 1977).

9. N.C. GEN. STAT. § 42-39 (Supp. 1977). *See also* N.C. GEN. STAT. § 42-40 (2) (Supp. 1977), defining "premises" as meaning "a dwelling unit and the structure of which it is a part and facilities and appurtenances therein and grounds, areas, and facilities normally held out for the use of residential tenants who are using the dwelling unit as their primary residence."

See generally Fillette, *North Carolina's Residential Rental Agreements Act: New Developments for Contract and Tort Liability in Landlord-Tenant Relations*, 56 N.C.L. REV. 785 (1978). This article discusses all aspects of the new Residential Rental Agreements Act and should be referred to for a comprehensive treatment of that subject.

10. Robbins v. Jones, 15 C.B.N.S. 221, 143 Eng. Rep. 768 (1863): "[F]raud apart, there is no law against letting a tumble-down house."

11. N.C. GEN. STAT. § 42-41 (Supp. 1977).

12. The standard of "habitability" is set forth, in part, in N.C. GEN. STAT. § 42-42 (a) (Supp. 1977).

§ 67. Same — Landlord's Obligations.

The Act sets forth the following obligations of a landlord: (1) to comply with current applicable building and housing codes;[13] (2) to make all repairs and do whatever is necessary to put and keep the premises in a fit and habitable condition; [14] (3) to keep the common areas of the premises in safe condition;[15] and (4) to "maintain in good and safe working order and promptly repair all electrical, plumbing, sanitary, heating, ventilating, air conditioning, and other facilities and appliances supplied or required to be supplied by him provided that notification of needed repairs is made to the landlord in writing by the tenant except in emergency situations." [16]

Although no reported Court of Appeals or Supreme Court cases exist interpreting the Act, it seems clear that the general obligation to keep the premises in a fit and habitable condition will plug any gaps that might exist in the enumeration of specific obligations in other parts of the same statute. The admonition to "do whatever is necessary" to render the premises habitable speaks for itself.[17] To the extent that the Act requires compliance with building and housing codes and then makes this obligation mutually dependent with the tenant's obligation to pay rent and maintain the dwelling unit, it makes the tenant an enforcer of the codes. Concerning the fourth obligation of the landlord set forth above, a special requirement of a written notice (except in emergency situations) is added. Presumably, the sweeping general obligation to keep the premises habitable will require that the landlord repair those defects or substandard conditions within the landlord's personal knowledge regardless of whether or not written notice of the matter in question has been received. The notice requirement will have utility, however, in a number of situations such as where only the tenant knows of the problem or where the landlord has been ignoring the problem.

§ 68. Same — Tenant's Obligations.

The Act sets forth the nature of a tenant's duty — both affirmative and negative — with respect to the dwelling.[18] Tenant's duties under the Act include, *inter alia,* keeping the premises as clean and safe as conditions

---

13. N.C. Gen. Stat. § 42-42 (a) (1) (Supp. 1977).
14. N.C. Gen. Stat. § 42-42 (a) (2) (Supp. 1977).
15. N.C. Gen. Stat. § 42-42 (a) (3) (Supp. 1977).
16. N.C. Gen. Stat. § 42-42 (a) (4) (Supp. 1977).

17. Although the precise legal meaning of "habitable" is certainly one that will require judicial interpretation to the extent that the specific requirements of N.C. Gen. Stat. § 42-42 (a) (Supp. 1977) do not cover the problem that arises.

18. N.C. Gen. Stat. § 42-43 (a) (Supp. 1977). As with all other sections of the new Act, no North Carolina Supreme Court or Court of Appeals decisions interpreting this section exist.

permit,[19] keeping plumbing fixtures clean,[20] disposing of all ashes, rubbish, garbage, and other waste in a clean and safe manner,[21] and complying with any obligations imposed upon the tenant by applicable building and housing codes.[22] The applicable statute also prohibits a tenant from causing unsafe or unsanitary conditions [23] and from deliberately or negligently damaging property.[24] Subject to a number of exceptions including "ordinary wear and tear," a tenant is made responsible for certain damage, defacement or removal of property.[25]

§ 69. Same — Tenant May Not Unilaterally Withhold Rent.

In a provision that could cause confusion in light of the "mutuality of obligations" language discussed at § 66 *supra,* the Act prohibits a tenant from unilaterally withholding rent prior to a judicial determination of the tenant's right to do so.[26] Since the unilateral withholding of rent prohibition appears to be referring solely to the entitlement of a tenant to remain in possession, there is arguably no inconsistency in the Act caused by this language. Upon material breach of the landlord's obligations, a tenant should be entitled to vacate the premises and cease paying rent without

---

19. N.C. GEN. STAT. § 42-43 (a) (1) (Supp. 1977), which provides that the tenant shall
[k]eep that part of the premises which he occupies and uses as clean and safe as the conditions of the premises permit and cause no unsafe or unsanitary conditions in the common areas and remainder of the premises which he uses; . . . .
20. N.C. GEN. STAT. § 42-43 (a) (3) (Supp. 1977), which reads:
Keep all plumbing fixtures in the dwelling unit or used by the tenant as clean as their condition permits; . . . .
21. N.C. GEN. STAT. § 42-43 (a) (2) (Supp. 1977).
22. N.C. GEN. STAT. § 42-43 (a) (5) (Supp. 1977).
23. N.C. GEN. STAT. § 42-43 (a) (1) (Supp. 1977). *See* the language of this subsection at note 19 *supra.*
24. N.C. GEN. STAT. § 42-43 (a) (4) (Supp. 1977), which reads: "[The tenant shall not] deliberately or negligently destroy, deface, damage, or remove any part of the premises or knowingly permit any person to do so."
25. N.C. GEN. STAT. § 42-43 (a) (6) (Supp. 1977), which notes that a tenant shall

[b]e responsible for all damage, defacement, or removal of any property inside a dwelling unit in his exclusive control unless said damage, defacement or removal was due to ordinary wear and tear, acts of the landlord or his agent, defective products supplied or repairs authorized by the landlord, acts of third parties not invitees of the tenant, or natural forces.

The Act requires written notice from the landlord to the tenant of any breaches of the tenant's obligations under this section except in emergency situations. N.C. GEN. STAT. § 42-43 (b) (Supp. 1977).

26. N.C. GEN. STAT. § 42-44 (c) (Supp. 1977) which reads:

The tenant may not unilaterally withhold rent prior to a judicial determination of a right to do so. The tenant shall be entitled to remain in possession of the premises pending appeal by continuing to pay the contract rent as it becomes due; provided that, in such case, the provisions of G.S. 42-34(b) shall not apply.

No official legislative history or commentary is available to explain the intended relationship between this "unilateral withholding" provision and other portions of the Act.

running afoul of this section.[27] Likewise, nothing stands in the way of a tenant obtaining a refund of all or a portion of past rents paid for breach by the landlord. The prohibition against unilateral withholding seems to be one aimed at precluding tenants from adopting self-help techniques such as outright withholding of rent, the payment of rent into escrow, or the repair of the premises with rent money in lieu of paying the same to the landlord.[28]

§ 70. Same — Remedies.

The Act provides: "Any right or obligation declared by this Chapter is enforceable by civil action, in addition to other remedies of law and equity."[29] The term "action" is defined as including "recoupment, counterclaim, defense, setoff, and any other proceeding including an action for possession." [30]

§ 71. Same — Statutory Prohibition Against Retaliatory Eviction.

A "retaliatory eviction" is an eviction or an eviction attempt by a landlord accompanied by a retaliatory motive on the part of the landlord because of a tenant's assertion of some legal right or engagement in some protected activity. Originally, the Act did not treat the subject of retaliatory eviction and thus continued the effect of reported caselaw in North Carolina that had not prohibited the practice.[31] By legislative additions to the Act in 1979, the General Assembly expressly recognized the retaliatory eviction doctrine.[32]

The North Carolina General Statutes, § 42-47 (a) begins by making clear the purpose behind the new statute: "It is the public policy of the State of North Carolina to protect tenants. . . who seek to exercise their rights to decent, safe, and sanitary housing." In a nutshell, this retaliatory

---

27. Although the tenant risks a later unfavorable judicial determination regarding whether or not the landlord in fact was derelict in complying with the landlord's statutory duties.

28. N.C. GEN. STAT. § 42-44 (c) (Supp. 1977) appears to leave the door open for a judicially mandated rent withholding. See N.C. GEN. STAT. § 42-40 (1) (Supp. 1977).

29. N.C. GEN. STAT. § 42-44 (a) (Supp. 1977). Certain limitations are set forth in this section including a prohibition of double damages and a statement that violation of the Act shall not constitute negligence *per se.*

30. N.C. GEN. STAT. § 42-40 (1) (Supp. 1977).

31. *See* Dockery v. Table Co., 36 N.C. App. 293, 244 S.E.2d 272 (1978), a case involving a claim of retaliatory discharge from employment where in the court states, at 36 N.C. App. 296: "However our courts have expressly rejected the use of 'retaliatory eviction' by a tenant as an affirmative defense in an action by a landlord for possession." (Citing Evans v. Rose, 12 N.C. App. 165, 182 S.E.2d 591, *cert. denied,* 279 N.C. 511, 183 S.E.2d 686 and 8 STRONG, N.C. INDEX 3d, *Landlord and Tenant,* § 17.1, p. 262.)

32. 1979 Sess. L. c. 807, creating N.C. GEN. STAT. §§ 42-37, 42-37.1 and 42-37.2.

eviction statute is designed to protect a tenant who in "good faith" does any of a number of protected activities including: requesting repairs that the landlord is obligated to make by statute; complaining to a government agency about a landlord's alleged violation of certain laws or regulations relating to the rented premises; attempting to exercise or enforce rights under the lease or rental agreement or under federal or state law; or, attempting to organize, join, or become involved with a tenants' rights organization. Also, a tenant is protected under this statute where a governmental agency issues a formal complaint to a landlord concerning the rented premises.

If a landlord brings an action for summary ejectment within twelve months of the occurrence of a protected tenant activity, the tenant is given the right to raise the retaliatory eviction defense. [33] The statute does not expressly trigger a presumption of retaliatory motive based on mere proximity of time between the protected tenant activity and the eviction attempt. The statute allows the tenant to raise the *affirmative defense* of retaliatory eviction and to present evidence that the eviction action is substantially in response to the protected tenant activity. [34] If the normal concept of an affirmative defense is adhered to, the tenant must plead the matter and meet at least an initial burden of proof.

As with many new statutes on the subject of tenants' rights, numerous questions of interpretation will have to be addressed by the judiciary. What of a mixed motive for eviction on the part of the landlord? When is the landlord's eviction action substantially in response to the tenant's protected activity? And what of other retaliatory actions such as the raising of rent or the cutting of services? The statute speaks in terms of an affirmative defense to an eviction action only.

Significant qualifications on the retaliatory eviction defense are set forth in the new statute. The North Carolina General Statutes, § 42-37 (c) (1) provides, in essence, that the landlord may prevail in a summary ejectment action in spite of a retaliatory motive where the tenant has breached the covenant to pay rent or any other substantial covenant in the lease for which the tenant may be evicted. [35] In addition, even if the tenant succeeds in raising the defense and the landlord's attempt at eviction is accordingly denied, the North Carolina General Statutes, § 42-37.1, a remedies section, provides in part that the dismissal "shall not prevent the landlord from receiving payments for rent due." These

---

33. N.C. GEN. STAT. § 42-47 (b).

34. Id.

35. Five additional exceptions are set forth in N.C. GEN. STAT. § 42-37 (c) (2) through (6).

provisions indicate that the General Assembly does not regard extra-judicial rent withholding as a permissible tenant remedy.[36]

§ 72. Tenant Security Deposit Act.

Security deposits of tenants in residential dwelling units are protected and regulated by the Tenant Security Deposit Act, effective on October 1, 1977.[37] Security deposits must be placed in a trust account with a licensed and insured North Carolina bank or savings institution or a bond may be furnished at the landlord's option.[38] Within 30 days after the lease term begins, the tenant must be notified of the name and address of the institution where the deposit is located or from which the bond was issued.[39]

The Tenant Security Deposit Act affects residential dwelling security deposits in a number of important ways including the following: permitted uses of and the amount of the deposit are restricted;[40] the landlord has a number of obligations upon termination of the tenancy with respect to refund and accounting for the security deposit;[41] require-

---

36. Thus, the language of N.C. GEN. STAT. § 42-44 (c) providing that a tenant may not unilaterally withhold rent appears reinforced.

See generally Comment, *Retaliatory Evictions and Housing Code Enforcement*, 49 N.C.L. REV. 568 (1971).

37. N.C. GEN. STAT. § 42-50 et seq. (Supp. 1977); N.C. GEN. STAT. § 42-56 (Supp. 1977) provides that the Tenant Security Deposit Acts applies "to all persons, firms, or corporations engaged in the business of renting or managing residential dwelling units, excluding single rooms, on a weekly, monthly or annual basis."

38. N.C. GEN. STAT. § 42-50 (Supp. 1977). The bond must be from an insurance company licensed to do business in North Carolina.

39. *Id.*

40. N.C. GEN. STAT. § 42-51 (Supp. 1977), which provides:

> § 42-51. **Permitted uses of the deposit.** — Security deposits for residential dwelling units shall be permitted only for the tenant's possible nonpayment of rent, damage to the premises, nonfulfillment of rental period, any unpaid bills which become a lien against the demised property due to the tenant's occupancy, costs of re-renting the premises after breach by the tenant, or court costs in connection with terminating a tenancy. Such security deposit shall not exceed an amount equal to two weeks' rent if a tenancy is week to week, one and one-half months' rent if a tenancy is month to month, and two months' rent for terms greater than month to month. These deposits must be fully accounted for by the landlord as set forth in G.S. 42-52.

41. N.C. GEN. STAT. § 42-52 (Supp. 1977), which provides:

> § 42-52. **Landlord's obligations.** — Upon termination of the tenancy, money held by the landlord as security may be applied as permitted in G.S. 42-51 or, if not so applied, shall be refunded to the tenant. In either case the landlord in writing shall itemize any damage and mail or deliver same to the tenant, together with the balance of the security deposit, no later than 30 days after termination of the tenancy and delivery of possession by the tenant. If the tenant's address is unknown the landlord shall apply the deposit as permitted in G.S. 42-51 after a period of 30 days and the landlord shall hold the balance of the deposit for collection by the tenant for at least six months. The landlord may not withhold as damages part of the security deposit for conditions that are due to normal wear and tear nor may the landlord retain an amount from the security deposit which exceeds his actual damages.

ments upon termination of the landlord's interest in the dwelling unit are set forth; [42] and remedies for tenants are provided, including a reasonable attorney's fee for willful noncompliance by the landlord. [43]

§ 73. Eviction of Tenants in Federally Assisted Low-Rent Housing Projects.

Tenants in federally assited low-rent housing projects may be entitled to additional legal rights and protections by virtue of federal law. [44] The United States Supreme Court, in a case involving the Housing Authority of the City of Durham, [45] has held that such tenants cannot be evicted prior to notification of the reasons for the eviction and without an opportunity to reply to the reasons given. The procedure required by the Supreme Court had been set forth in a Department of Housing and Urban Development circular issued after eviction proceedings had been initiated, but while the tenant was still residing in the project. [46]

Article III. Estates for Years

Division 1. General Provisions

§ 74. The Estate for Years; Definition

Every estate which by the terms of its creation must expire at a period certain and prefixed, by whatever words created, is an estate for years. [47] An estate for years arises from a contract whereby a tenant is to have the right to possession of lands or tenements for some determinate period. Whether the term be for a hundred years, or for only one year, or for a month or week or day even, still the estate of the lessee is termed in law an "estate for years." [48]

---

42. N.C. GEN. STAT. § 42-54 (Supp. 1977), which provides:

> § 42-54. **Transfer of dwelling units.** — Upon termination of the landlord's interest in the dwelling unit in question, whether by sale, assignment, death, appointment of receiver or otherwise, the landlord or his agent shall, within 30 days, do one of the following acts, either of which shall relieve him of further liability with respect to such payment or deposit:
>
> (1) Transfer the portion of such payment or deposit remaining after any lawful deductions made under this section to the landlord's successor in interest and thereafter notify the tenant by mail of such transfer and of the transferee's name and address; or
> (2) Return the portion of such payment or deposit remaining after any lawful deductions made under this section to the tenant.

43. N.C. GEN. STAT. § 42-55 (Supp. 1977).
44. Thorpe v. Housing Authority of the City of Durham, 393 U.S. 268, 89 S. Ct. 518 (1969).
45. Id.
46. Id.
47. 1 MORDECAI, LAW LECTURES 528 (1916).
48. See also 2 BLACKSTONE, COMMENTARIES *140; King v. Foscue, 91 N.C. 116 (1884). Accord, Gurtis v. City of Sanford, 18 N.C. App. 543, 197 S.E.2d 584 (1973), citing this section.

§ 75. Creation of the Tenancy for Years.

An estate for years is usually created by a conveyance or contract known as a lease. A lease for a term of years is a contract, by which one agrees, for a valuable consideration, to let another have the occupation and profits of land for a definite time.[49] The essentials of a lease creating a tenancy for years are (1) the names of the lessor and lessee; (2) a description of the real estate demised; (3) a statement of the term of the lease; and (4) the consideration or rent.[50] A devise of land to a devisee to hold for a certain number of years would likewise be sufficient to create an estate for years.

§ 76. Requirement That Lease for Years Be in Writing.

Under the Statute of Frauds in effect in North Carolina,[51] any lease which may extend for more than three years from the time of the making

---

49. Helicopter Corp. v. Cutter Realty Co., 263 N.C. 139, 139 S.E.2d 362 (1964); Gurtis v. City of Sanford, 18 N.C. App. 543, 197 S.E.2d 584 (1973); *See* Love v. Pressley, 34 N.C. App. 503, 239 S.E.2d 574 (1977), wherein the court holds that the rental of residential housing is "trade or commerce" for purposes of unfair or deceptive acts or practices legislation and cites Commonwealth v. Monumental Properties, Inc., 459 Pa. 450, 329 A.2d 812 (1974) for the following: "Functionally viewed, the modern apartment dweller is a consumer of housing services. The contemporary leasing of residences envisions one person (landlord) exchanging for periodic payments of money (rent) a bundle of goods and services, rights and obligations."

329 A.2d at 820.

Dixon v. Rivers, 37 N.C. App. 168, 245 S.E.2d 572 (1978), holding that a lease providing as follows involved a term for years with a valid and enforceable covenant for perpetual renewal:

    1. This lease shall begin as of the date hereof and shall exist and continue for a period of 10 years.

    2. Upon the expiration of the abovementioned period of 10 years, if said property has been kept in a good state of repair, and if said parties of the second part so desire, this lease shall be renewed for an additional period of 10 years and thereafter shall be renewable every 10 years for so long as parties of the second part so desire.

See also Board of Transportation v. Turner, 37 N.C. App. 14, 245 S.E.2d 233 (1978), holding that a reservation to the grantors in a deed of "the ownership of and right to bargain and sell" a right-of-way to the State for a period of 10 years gave the grantors a leasehold for a term for years and not a fee simple estate in the right-of-way.

50. Helicopter Corp. v. Cutter Realty Co., 263 N.C. 139, 139 S.E.2d 362 (1964). *See* Smith v. House of Kenton Corp., 23 N.C. App. 439, 209 S.E.2d 397, *cert. denied*, 286 N.C. 337, 211 S.E.2d 213 (1974), which sets out the requisites of a binding agreement to *execute a lease:* (1) The minds of the parties must have met as to the property to be included in the lease; (2) the terms of the lease should be agreed upon; (3) the parties should agree upon the rental; and (4) the time and manner of payment of rent should be stated. The *Smith* case held that an agreement to execute a lease was not binding since the agreement failed to provide for the time and manner of payment of rent notwithstanding a provision in the agreement that the "rental rate was to be $400.00 per month."

51. N.C. GEN. STAT. § 22-2.

thereof must be in writing in order to be valid.[52] Parol leases for exactly three years or for less than three years are valid if operative from the time the contract of lease is made.[53] If leases for exactly three years or for less than three years are to begin in the future so that they may "exceed in duration three years from the time of the making thereof," they will be void if not in writing.[54] Leases for life [55] or for other indefinite period [56] are void if not in writing since they may last beyond three years from the date of the making thereof.[57]

The invalidity of a lease because it violates the Statute of Frauds requirement of a writing leaves the lessee in the position of a tenant at will whose occupancy may be terminated *instanter* by demand for possession.[58]

Agreements to assign or to release leasehold estates which have more than three years to run, to be enforceable, must also be in writing.[59]

§ 77. Requirement That Lease for Years Be Recorded.

A lease for more than three years must be recorded in order to protect the lessee against lien creditors or purchasers for value of the lessor.[60] Assignments of leases for more than three years duration must likewise be recorded to protect the assignee of a lease against the lien creditors or purchasers for value of the assignor of the lease.[61] Leasehold estates of three years or less need not be recorded.[62] If a lessee is not in possession under a leasehold estate of three years or less and the lessor transfers the reversion to an innocent purchaser for value who has no notice of the tenancy, and nothing sufficient to put the purchaser on inquiry exists at

---

52. Investment Co. v. Zindell, 198 N.C. 109, 150 S.E. 704 (1929); Mauney v. Norvell, 179 N.C. 628, 103 S.E. 372 (1920).
53. Investment Co. v. Zindell, 198 N.C. 109, 150 S.E. 704 (1929).
54. *Id.*
55. Davis v. Lovick, 226 N.C. 252, 37 S.E.2d 680 (1946).
56. *See* Wright v. Allred, 226 N.C. 113, 37 S.E.2d 107 (1946), which holds that a parol agreement to lease realty for one year, with privilege of renewal thereafter for four successive years, was within the Statute of Frauds, and therefore void. *See also* Dixon v. Rivers, 37 N.C. App. 168, 245 S.E.2d 572 (1978), a case upholding a perpetual renewal clause.
57. *But see* Helicopter Corp. v. Cutter Realty Co., 263 N.C. 139, 139 S.E.2d 362 (1964), which held that a lease of a building roof for use as a heliport for one year, with an indefinite commencement date, to be effective "when the U.S. Government approved the roof for helicopter taxi service," was valid.
58. Davis v. Lovick, 226 N.C. 252, 37 S.E.2d 680 (1946).
59. Herring v. Merchandise, Inc., 249 N.C. 221, 106 S.E.2d 197 (1958). The latter case held, however, that if the lessee consummated his agreement to relinquish his lease interest and surrendered possession, accompanied by other conduct, that he may be estopped to deny the termination of the lease.
60. Mauney v. Norvell, 179 N.C. 628, 103 S.E. 372 (1920); Bourne v. Lay & Co., 264 N.C. 33, 140 S.E.2d 769 (1965).
61. Herring v. Merchandise, Inc., 249 N.C. 221, 106 S.E.2d 197 (1958).
62. Perkins v. Langdon, 237 N.C. 159, 74 S.E.2d 634 (1953).

the time of the sale, the transfer will destroy the leasehold estate of the tenant.[63] If the tenant is in possession under such a lease, a purchaser from the lessor will take subject to the lease.[64]

Division 2. Incidents of Estates for Years

§ 78. Generally.

The obligation and rights of the tenant of land held under a lease and of the landlord, respectively, are in part dependent upon rules of law and in part upon stipulations which are found in the lease. The incidents of estates for years which arise by operation of law will be first considered.

§ 79. Tenant's Power of Alienation.

A tenant of an estate for years may transfer the leasehold either by (1) assignment or (2) sublease, unless the tenant is restrained from doing so by an express covenant in the lease.[65] While the tenant may be restricted from alienating the leasehold term by express covenant or condition in the lease providing for termination of the leasehold estate upon any attempt by the tenant to assign or sublease the premises,[66] such restraints on alienation must be reasonable.[67] Where a lease permits assignment with the written consent of the lessor, the arbitrary withholding of consent by the lessor is invalid.[68] Refusal to give consent to an assignment should be based on reasons related to the purposes for which the tenancy was created.[69]

It should be noted that a covenant or provision against a lessee's "assignment" of his term does not prevent the lessee's "sublease" of his

---

63. Id. The lessee is relegated to an action for damages against the lessor.

64. Id. In such case, the purchaser will be charged with constructive notice of all that reasonable inquiry would disclose.

65. Rogers v. Hall, 227 N.C. 363, 42 S.E.2d 347 (1947).

66. J.D. Cornell Millinery Co. v. Little-Long Co., 197 N.C. 168, 148 S.E. 26 (1929); Hargrave v. King, 40 N.C. 430 (1848). In Carson v. Imperial '400' National, Inc., 267 N.C. 229, 147 S.E.2d 898 (1966), it was held that a provision of a lease that authorized the lessor to repossess the leased property if the lessee went bankrupt (or upon the appointment of a receiver for the lessee) was enforceable, notwithstanding that the lessee had subleased the property to a solvent sublessee before a receiver had been appointed for the original lessee.

67. Sanders v. Tropicana, 31 N.C. App. 276, 229 S.E.2d 304 (1976); L & H Investments, Ltd. v. Belvey Corporation, 444 F. Supp. 1321 (W.D.N.C. 1978), a case holding that a complaint alleging that the lessor of shopping center space refused to approve of an assignment of lease because it did not want the prospective assignee to compete with the lessor's own clothing business was sufficient to entitle the lessee-assignor to standing to sue under the Sherman Anti-Trust Act.

68. Id.

69. Id.

term, and vice versa.[70] It thus becomes important to distinguish "assignments" from "subleases." An "assignment" transfers the whole interest of the lessee, leaving no reversion or remaining part of the term in the lessee.[71] A "sublease" exists when the tenant aliens the land or subject of the lease for only a part of his time, leaving a reversion of the remainder of his term in himself.[72] A transfer of a part of the leased premises for the whole term is called an assignment *pro tanto*.[73]

§ 80. Tenant's Right to Estovers.

A tenant for years, unless it be otherwise stipulated in his lease, has the same rights as a tenant for life [74] to estovers — that is, the right to cut down, take and use a reasonable amount of timber as may be needed for repairs and fuel for use on the premises.[75]

§ 81. Tenant's Rights in Lieu of Emblements When Estate Terminated by Uncertain Event.

At the common law if a tenancy for years of an agricultural tenancy was terminated by the happening of some uncertain event not his own fault he was entitled to "emblements." [76] The term "emblements" denoted the right of the tenant to take and carry away, after his tenancy had ended, such annual products of the land as resulted from his care and labor. For example, if a person having a life tenancy in land leased land for years and his term was terminated by the death of the life tenant-lessor, the lessee had a continued right of ingress and egress for the purpose of

---

70. J.D. Cornell Millinery Co. v. Little-Long Co., 197 N.C. 168, 148 S.E. 26 (1929), involved a provision against sale or assignment of a lease. The court held that sublease of the property did not breach such restriction. In Rogers v. Hall, 227 N.C. 363, 42 S.E.2d 347 (1947), it was held that an assignment of a lease contract did not breach a covenant in a lease that the lessee should not sublease the premises. *See* Hargrave v. King, 40 N.C. 430 (1848), holding that a covenant against assignment would not prevent a lessee from taking in "associates" or "partners" to share his lease interest.

71. J.D. Cornell Millinery Co. v. Little-Long Co., 197 N.C. 168, 148 S.E. 26 (1929); Carson v. Imperial '400' National, Inc., 267 N.C. 229, 147 S.E.2d 898 (1966). A transfer of a part of the leased premises for the whole term is called an assignment *pro tanto*. J.D. Cornell Millinery Co. v. Little-Long Co., *supra*.

72. J.D. Cornell Millinery Co. v. Little-Long Co., 197 N.C. 168, 148 S.E. 26 (1929). If the tenant upon transferring his interest in leased property retains a reversionary interest, although only for one day, the transaction constitutes a "sublease" as distinguished from an assignment. 2 POWELL, REAL PROPERTY 306-07 (1950); 51 C.J.S. *Landlord & Tenant* § 37(1)b.

73. J.D. Cornell Millinery Co. v. Little-Long Co., 197 N.C. 168, 148 S.E. 26 (1929).

74. *See* § 54 *supra*.

75. 1 MORDECAI, LAW LECTURES 532 (1916). *Compare* Thomas v. Thomas, 166 N.C. 627, 82 S.E. 1032 (1914).

76. Hayes v. Wrenn, 167 N.C. 229, 83 S.E. 356 (1914); 1 MORDECAI, LAWS LECTURES 505-07 (1916).

cultivating and harvesting crops planted during his tenancy to compensate him for his labor and expenses for tilling, manuring, and sowing the lands and also for the encouragement of husbandry.[77] The tenant who had the right to emblements did not have a right to possession of the land but had only a right to ingress and egress to attend the crop; he did not have to pay for this right at common law.[78]

North Carolina now has a statute giving to tenants of agricultural tenancies rights in lieu of emblements.[79] North Carolina General Statutes, § 42-7 provides that any lessee for years [80] whose term is terminated by the happening of any uncertain event determining the estate of the lessor, including the sale of the premises under a mortgage foreclosure, may continue his occupation of the premises to the end of his current lease year.[81] The statute provides that the lessee shall pay to the succeeding owner of the property [82] the proportionate part of any rent accrued since the last payment became due and shall at the end of his current lease year give up possession to the succeeding owner. The statute also makes provision for reasonable compensation by the succeeding owner to the lessee for tillage and seed of any crop not gathered at the end of the tenant's current lease year.

§ 82. Tenant's Exclusive Right of Possession and Enjoyment.

The tenant in a lease for years is entitled to exclusive possession of the leased premises, not only as against third persons but also as against the lessor.[83] The tenant in a lease for years may recover against his landlord

---

77. *Id.*
78. 1 MORDECAI, LAW LECTURES 506 (1916).
79. N.C. GEN. STAT. § 42-7 provides:

> § 42-7. **In lieu of emblements, farm lessee holds out year, with rents apportioned.** — When any lease for years of any land let for farming on which a rent is reserved determines during a current year of the tenancy, by the happening of any uncertain event determining the estate of the lessor, or by a sale of said land under any mortgage or deed of trust, the tenant in lieu of emblements shall continue his occupation to the end of such current year, and shall then give up such possession to the succeeding owner of the land, and shall pay to such succeeding owner a part of the rent accrued since the last payment became due, proportionate to the part of the period of payment elapsing after the termination of the estate of the lessor to the giving up such possession; and the tenant in such case shall be entitled to a reasonable compensation for the tillage and seed of any crop not gathered at the expiration of such current year from the person succeeding to the possession.

80. This includes a lease for a single year since any lease for a certain and prefixed duration is technically an estate for years. King v. Foscue, 91 N.C. 116 (1884).
81. *Id.*
82. *E.g.*, remainderman, reversioner, or purchaser at mortgage foreclosure sale.
83. Produce Co. v. Currin, 243 N.C. 131, 90 S.E.2d 228 (1955); Rickman Mfg. Co. v. Gable, 246 N.C. 1, 97 S.E.2d 672 (1957); Love v. Pressley, 34 N.C. App. 503, 239 S.E.2d 574 (1977).

for entering and breaking the close during his term.[84] The tenant's right to possession and enjoyment of leased property includes everything properly appurtenant to, essential or reasonably necessary to the full beneficial use and enjoyment of the property conveyed in the absence of a lease provision indicating a contrary intention.[85]

§ 83. Tenant's Liability for Waste.

A tenant for years is liable for waste, the spoiling or destroying of the estate with respect to buildings, wood, or soil to the lasting injury of the property.[86]

§ 84. Tenant's Liability to Make Repairs.

A tenant for years is under an obligation, in the absence of a contrary agreement, to make ordinary repairs at his own expense, and failure to make such repairs may render the tenant liable to the lessor for permissive waste.[87] In the absence of an agreement on the part of the landlord to make repairs, the landlord is under no obligation to the tenant to keep the premises in repair.[88]

---

84. Produce Co. v. Currin, 243 N.C. 131, 90 S.E.2d 228 (1955); Rickman Mfg. Co. v. Gable, 246 N.C. 1, 97 S.E.2d 672 (1957); Barneycastle v. Walker, 92 N.C. 198 (1885); Love v. Pressley, 34 N.C. App. 503, 239 S.E.2d 574 (1977). The tenant may likewise bring an action against third parties for ejectment. Ingram v. Corbit, 177 N.C. 318, 99 S.E. 18 (1919).

85. Rickman Mfg. Co. v. Gable, 246 N.C. 1, 97 S.E.2d 672 (1957).

86. N.C. GEN. STAT. § 1-534. *See* 1 MORDECAI, LAW LECTURES 702-711 (1916) on waste generally. A residential tenant shall "[n]ot deliberately or negligently destroy, deface, damage, or remove any part of the premises or knowingly permit any person to do so; . . . ." N.C. GEN. STAT. § 42-43 (a) (4) (Supp. 1977).

87. Improvement Co. v. Coley-Bardin, 156 N.C. 255, 72 S.E. 312 (1911).

88. Duffy v. Hartsfield, 180 N.C. 151, 104 S.E. 139 (1920); Salter v. Gordon, 200 N.C. 381, 157 S.E. 11 (1931); Carolina Mtg. Co. v. Massie, 209 N.C. 146, 183 S.E. 425 (1936); Mercer v. Williams, 210 N.C. 456, 187 S.E. 556 (1936); Livingston v. Essex Inv. Co., 219 N.C. 416, 14 S.E.2d 489 (1941). *Accord,* Clark v. Kerchner, 11 N.C. App. 454, 181 S.E.2d 787 (1971), citing Thompson v. Shoemaker, 7 N.C. App. 687, 173 S.E.2d 627 (1970). Even if a landlord contracts to repair the leased premises, he is not liable for personal injuries to his tenant, the tenant's sublessee, family, servants, or guests resulting from disrepair or patent defects. The landlord will only be liable if he undertakes to make the repairs and does them negligently, which results in personal injury, or in the event the injury arises by reason of latent defect known to the landlord, or of which he should have known, and where the lessee was not aware of the latent defect and in the exercise of ordinary diligence could not discover it. *See* Phillips v. Stowe Mills, Inc., 5 N.C. App. 150, 167 S.E.2d 817 (1969); Robinson v. Thomas, 244 N.C. 732, 94 S.E.2d 911 (1956); Carson v. Cloninger, 23 N.C. App. 699, 209 S.E.2d 522 (1974).

As to tenancies covered by the Residential Rental Agreements Act, a violation of the Act does not constitute negligence *per se.* N.C. GEN. STAT. § 42-44 (d) (Supp. 1977). The Residential Rental Agreements Act would appear to change the holding of Knuckles v. Spaugh, 26 N.C. App. 340, 215 S.E.2d 825 (1975) insofar as residential tenancies are involved. That case holds that a tenant is not entitled to recover rents already paid on the theory that the rented dwelling was maintained by the landlord in violation of the city housing code and was unfit for human habitation. N.C. GEN. STAT. §§ 42-41 and 42-42 (a) (1) (Supp. 1977).

Concerning tenancies covered by the Residential Rental Agreements Act, the landlord must provide fit premises and make all repairs and do whatever is necessary to put and keep the premises in a fit and habitable condition.[89] The tenant has certain duties and obligations with respect to the leased premises,[90] but is not obligated to make ordinary repairs at the tenant's own expense.

A tenant for years is not liable, however, for damages to leased premises which occur accidentally and notwithstanding reasonable diligence on the lessee's part unless he specifically contracts to make himself liable in such event.[91] In addition, if either party expressly contracts to make repairs, such agreement shall not be construed to bind the contracting party to rebuild or repair a house or building destroyed or damaged by fire to the extent of more than one half of its value, if the fire is accidental and does not arise from want of ordinary diligence on the part of the contracting party. This rule is set out by North Carolina General Statutes, § 42-9.[92]

§ 85. Merger.

A term for years is destroyed by merger if the term and reversion or other expectant estate of freehold become vested in one person.[93] Merger never takes place, however, when it would have the effect of destroying vested estates in third persons.[94]

---

89. N.C. GEN. STAT. § 42-42 (a) (2) (Supp. 1977). See § 67 supra.
90. N.C. GEN. STAT. § 42-43 (Supp. 1977). See § 68 supra.
91. N.C. GEN. STAT. § 42-10 provides:

§ 42-10. Tenant not liable for accidental damage. — A tenant for life, or years, or for a less term, shall not be liable for damage occurring on the demised premises accidentially, and notwithstanding reasonable diligence on his part, unless he so contract.

While a lessee is not liable for accidental damages caused by fire under this statute, he is liable if the buildings are damaged by his negligence. Dixie Fire & Cas. Co. v. Esso Standard Co., 265 N.C. 121, 143 S.E.2d 279 (1965).

92. N.C. GEN. STAT. § 42-9 provides:

§ 42-9. Agreement to rebuild, how construed in case of fire. — An agreement in a lease to repair a demised house shall not be construed to bind the contracting party to rebuild or repair in case the house shall be destroyed or damaged to more than one half of its value, by accidental fire not occurring from the want of ordinary diligence on his part.

It should be noted that this statute, which limits the obligation of tenants to make repairs, applies only to situations where houses are destroyed by fire; it does not apply to cases in which the destruction is by ice and flood. Chambers v. North River Line, 179 N.C. 199, 102 S.E. 198 (1920). A residential tenant's agreement to make repairs to the leased premises is now subject to the restrictions of N.C. GEN. STAT. § 42-42 (b) (Supp. 1977).

93. Trust Co. v. Watkins, 215 N.C. 292, 1 S.E.2d 853 (1939); Lofton v. Berber, 226 N.C. 481, 39 S.E.2d 263 (1946); Logan v. Green, 39 N.C. 370 (1846); Mixon v. Coffield, 24 N.C. 301 (1842).

94. Logan v. Green, 39 N.C. 370 (1846).

§ 86. Termination Without Necessity of Notice.

An estate for years, since it is for a determinate period, terminates at the time fixed in the instrument creating it without the necessity of any notice by either party. A 1925 North Carolina Supreme Court decision elaborates on this rule as follows:

> It is a universal rule, both at the common law and by statute, that where the demise is for a fixed term and is to end on a day certain, no notice to quit is necessary. The reason for this rule is obvious. The object of notice is to terminate the tenancy, and when the lease itself fixes the time at which it is to expire, the necessity for any other notice by either party to terminate is done away with. Each party is apprised from the contract when the lease ends; further action by either to end it would be unnecessary and superfluous. If a tenant holds over after the expiration of a fixed demise without the lessor's consent, he becomes a mere tenant by sufferance, liable to be ejected without notice.[95]

The continuance of a term for years may be made to depend upon a condition whereby the lessor may terminate the lease and repossess the realty involved upon breach of covenants in the lease.[96] In addition, in North Carolina, there is a statute [97] which provides that the term of a tenant may be forfeited by the landlord if the tenant fails to pay past due rent within ten days after a demand is made therefor by the lessor.[98]

---

95. Midimis v. Murrell, 189 N.C. 740, 128 S.E. 150 (1925).

96. *E.g.*, an express provision in a lease that the lessor may terminate the lease if a receiver is appointed for the lessee or if the lessee is adjudicated a bankrupt is valid. Carson v. Imperial '400' National, Inc., 267 N.C. 229, 147 S.E.2d 898 (1966). The lease itself can provide that the lease will terminate upon the happening of any event or default and when the lease is terminated on the happening of the contingency, the happening of the contingent event determines the tenancy and ejectment will lie without further notice to quit. Midimis v. Murrell, 189 N.C. 740, 128 S.E. 150 (1925). In residential tenancies, the mutuality of obligations concept of N.C. GEN. STAT. § 42-41 (Supp. 1977) could alter traditional results. *See* § 66 *supra*.

97. N.C. GEN. STAT. § 42-3 provides:

> **§ 42-3. Term forfeited for nonpayment of rent.** — In all verbal or written leases of real property of any kind in which is fixed a definite time for the payment of the rent reserved therein, there shall be implied a forfeiture of the term upon failure to pay the rent within ten days after a demand is made by the lessor or his agent on said lessee for all past-due rent, and the lessor may forthwith enter and dispossess the tenant without having declared such forfeiture or reserved the right of reentry in the lease.

See Ryan v. Reynolds, 190 N.C. 563, 130 S.E. 156 (1925). That there can be no forfeiture until the expiration of ten days after the demand, *see* Reynolds v. Earley, 241 N.C. 521, 85 S.E.2d 904 (1955). *See also* Green v. Lybrand, 39 N.C. App. 56, 249 S.E.2d 443 (1978).

98. It should be noted that N.C. GEN. STAT. §§ 42-3 and 42-33 are in pari materia and should be construed together. The latter section provides that if tenant pays or tenders the rent due before judgment all further proceedings in such action shall cease. *See* Ryan v. Reynolds, 190 N.C. 563, 130 S.E. 156 (1925). N.C. GEN. STAT. § 42-33 provides:

> **§ 42-33. Rent and costs tendered by tenant.** — If, in any action, brought to recover the possession of demised premises upon a forfeiture for the nonpayment of rent,

§ 87 ESTATES OF LESS THAN FREEHOLD § 87

Where the lease contains no provision for termination before the end of the designated term, neither party may alone terminate the lease, but both parties may mutually consent to its termination and to a relinquishment of all relationships under the lease.[99] A surrender of the premises in order to be effective to relinquish future relationships under the lease must be accepted by both parties.[100] In addition, an executory parol offer by the lessee to surrender his leasehold estate which has more than three years to run must be put into writing to be valid under the Statute of Frauds.[101]

§ 87. Effect of Tenant for Years Holding Over Beyond Stated Term.

If a lessee for years wrongfully holds over and remains in possession after the expiration of the definite term set out in his lease, the lessor may

---

the tenant, before judgment given in such action, pays or tenders the rent due and the costs of the action, all further proceedings in such action shall cease. If the plaintiff further prosecutes his action, and the defendant pays into court for the use of the plaintiff a sum equal to that which shall be found to be due, and the costs, to the time of such payment, or to the time of a tender and refusal, if one has occurred, the defendant shall recover from the plaintiff all subsequent costs; the plaintiff shall be allowed to receive the sum paid into court for his use, and the proceedings shall be stayed.

In Green v. Lybrand, 39 N.C. App. 56, 249 S.E.2d 443 (1978), the court explains the relationship between the statutes at 39 N.C. App. 59 as follows:

Having determined that this is an action to repossess for nonpayment of rent, we conclude that the matter was properly dismissed. The lease is silent as to forfeiture for nonpayment of rent, and generally '[i]n the absence of a stipulation for a forfeiture, a lessee does not forfeit his term by the nonpayment of rent....' 49 Am. Jur. 2d, Landlord and Tenant § 1020. This rule is changed by G.S. 42-3, which provides that where the parties have failed to write the forfeiture into their lease, 'there shall be an implied forfeiture of the term upon failure to pay the rent within 10 days after a demand is made....' However, in the situation before us G.S. 42-3 must be read in conjunction with G.S. 42-33. *Ryan v. Reynolds*, 190 N.C. 563, 130 S.E. 156 (1925). G.S. 42-33 provides that if 'in any action brought to recover the possession of demised premises upon a forfeiture for the nonpayment of rent, the tenant, before judgment ..., pays or tenders the rent due and the costs of the action, all further proceedings in such action shall cease.' Here, the court found that the defendant tendered all rent due and all costs incurred by depositing the money with the Clerk of Court, and, according to G.S. 42-33, the action was properly dismissed. See *Hoover v. Crotts*, 232 N.C. 617, 61 S.E. 2d 705 (1950); *Coleman v. Carolina Theatres, Inc.*, 195 N.C. 607, 143 S.E. 7 (1928).

99. Monger v. Lutterloh, 195 N.C. 274, 142 S.E. 12 (1928).

100. *Id.* "When a tenant abandons premises, and returns the keys to the landlord, the latter may accept the keys as a surrender of possession, thereby determining the tenant's estate, and relet the premises on his own account, or he may accept the keys and resume possession conditionally by notifying the tenant or other person returning the keys that he will accept the keys but not the premises, and relet them on the tenant's account, in which case the tenant may be held for any loss in rent caused by his abandonment and the subsequent reletting." *Id.* at 277-78, 142 S.E. at 15.

101. Herring v. Merchandise, Inc., 249 N.C. 221, 106 S.E.2d 197 (1958), holds that while an executory offer to surrender a leasehold estate which has more than three years to run must be in writing under the Statute of Frauds in order to be enforceable, the lessee may be estopped by matters *in pais* or where the offer to surrender has been consummated by an actual surrender. *Accord,* Advertising, Inc. v. Harper, 7 N.C. App. 501, 172 S.E.2d 793 (1970).

consider him to be a tenant at sufferance and may bring ejectment against him to recover the premises.[102] If, however, in addition to the tenant's remaining in possession at the expiration of his lease for years, he continues to pay the same rent as paid under the lease and the landlord accepts the rent, it will be presumed that a tenancy from year to year has been created by operation of law.[103]

When a tenant holds over, the landlord has the initial option to treat the tenant who holds over as a trespasser and may eject him. If the landlord recognizes the tenant, however, by accepting rent, a presumption arises that a tenancy from year to year is intended and the law creates a tenancy from year to year between the parties under the same terms and conditions of the previously existing lease for years so far as the same may be applicable.[104]

This presumption of a tenancy from year to year is rebuttable, however, and will yield to an actual intention of the parties not to create such a tenancy. For instance, the fact that a tenant has been compelled to continue in possession of necessity due solely to his sickness or by reason of the sickness of some member of his family, making removal dangerous or impracticable, or pending negotiation of a new lease wherein the landlord acquiesces in the tenant's remaining in possession until the matter is determined, will rebut the presumption that a tenancy from year to year was intended.[105] If the lease itself provides that the tenant may hold over at the end of the lease, no tenancy from year to year will be presumed.[106] In addition, where the lease for years provides for the lessee to have an option to extend the lease for a certain number of years upon giving proper notice to the lessor prior to the expiration of the lease, if the lessee holds over and pays the rent called for in the extension provision, and the lessor accepts such rent, the parties are bound according to the terms of

---

102. Coulter v. Capitol Finance Co., 266 N.C. 214, 146 S.E.2d 97 (1966); Williams v. King, 247 N.C. 581, 101 S.E.2d 308 (1957).

103. Murrill v. Palmer, 164 N.C. 50, 80 S.E. 55 (1913); Cherry v. Whitehurst, 216 N.C. 340, 4 S.E.2d 900 (1939); Duke v. Davenport, 240 N.C. 652, 83 S.E.2d 668 (1954); Williams v. King, 247 N.C. 581, 101 S.E.2d 308 (1957); Kearney v. Hare, 265 N.C. 570, 144 S.E.2d 636 (1965); Coulter v. Capitol Finance Co., 266 N.C. 214, 146 S.E.2d 97 (1966). *Accord,* Treadwell v. Goodwin, 14 N.C. App. 685, 189 S.E.2d 643 (1972). *See also* Gurtis v. City of Sanford, 18 N.C. App. 543, 197 S.E.2d 584 (1973), which quotes from this section.

104. Murrill v. Palmer, 164 N.C. 50, 80 S.E. 55 (1913); Kearney v. Hare, 265 N.C. 570, 144 S.E.2d 636 (1965); Hannah v. Hannah, 21 N.C. App. 265, 204 S.E.2d 212 (1974).

105. Murrill v. Palmer, 164 N.C. 50, 80 S.E. 55 (1913).

106. In Harty v. Harris, 120 N.C. 408, 27 S.E. 90 (1897), the tenant's lease was for one year and "as much longer thereafter as the tenant should remain in business." When tenant's one year had expired he continued in possession. The court held that the presumption that holding over would create a tenancy from year to year could be rebutted by evidence that it was understood and agreed between the parties that the holding over was not to be under the original contract but only so long as the tenant remained in business; tenant was allowed to terminate at any time.

the extension agreement for a certain period and a tenancy from year to year is not created.[107]

Article IV. Tenancies from Period to Period
Division 1. General Provisions

§ 88. Estates from Year to Year, Quarter to Quarter, Month to Month, Week to Week; Definition.

An estate from year to year, month to month, or other fractional period of a year, referred to generally as "tenancies from period to period" are estates which continue to renew themselves from year to year, or for successive fractions of a year indefinitely until they are terminated at the end of one of the periods by a proper notice by either the lessor or the lessee in accordance with the law. The essential qualities of tenancies from period to period, whether from year to year, month to month, or other fractional part of a year, are the same.

§ 89. Ways Created.

Tenancies from year to year, or tenancies from period to period,[108] may be created either by an express contract or by implication of law.

The parties may contract that the lessee shall have an estate "From year to year, beginning at a specified date." Or the lease may provide that the lessee shall have possession "for one year and then at the expiration of one year, to hold from year to year." Such leases will create estates from year to year by express agreement.[109]

Perhaps more often, however, estates from year to year arise by implication of law. For instance, a tenancy from year to year is created by implication of law under a "general letting" in which the lease does not specify a definite term but provides for an annual rental amount to be paid by the lessee.[110]

---

107. Coulter v. Capitol Finance Co., 266 N.C. 214, 146 S.E.2d 97 (1966). Although the lease provided that 30 days' notice should be given to extend the lease, and payment should be increased from $175 per month to $225 per month, when the tenant held over and paid $225 per month and landlord accepted such amount without comment, the court held that the original lease was extended for two years and that the lessor had waived the notice requirement in the extension provision of the lease. The presumption that a tenancy from year to year was created was rebutted by the apparent intention of the parties.

108. What is here said of tenancies from year to year applies equally to tenancies from month to month, week to week, etc., the only difference between such estates being the length of notice required to terminate such tenancies.

109. Jones v. Willis, 53 N.C. 430 (1862).

110. *E.g.,* a lease to lessee for $1200 per year to commence on January 1, 1968, would be a "general letting" in which the parties agreed on everything except the term of the lease. The law in such case implies a tenancy from year to year. *Compare* Simmons v. Jarmon, 122 N.C. 195, 29 S.E. 332 (1898), where the lessee had rented from the lessor certain premises for $3 per month to commence on January 1, 1896, and it has held that the tenant had tenancy from month to month although he held until June, 1897.

In addition, the law implies a tenancy from year to year where a tenant for a fixed period (tenant for years) holds over after the termination of his original lease and continues to pay rent under the terms of the original lease, which rent is accepted by the lessor.[111] For example, if A holds under a lease for five years and at the end of his lease continues to hold over, and the lessor accepts the rental payment from A according to the terms of the expired lease, a tenancy from year to year may be created.[112]

Another instance where tenancies from period to period may be created by implication occurs when a tenancy for more than three years is entered without a writing in violation of the Statute of Frauds.[113] In such case the express lease is void but if the lessee goes into possession under such unenforceable lease and pays the rent pursuant to the agreement, a tenancy from period to period is created.[114]

Division 2. Incidents of Estates from Period to Period

§ 90. Generally.

The incidents of estates from year to year and other tenancies from period to period are for the most part the same as those of estates for years.

§ 91. Right to Estovers.

A tenant from year to year or other tenant from period to period may cut and appropriate as "estovers" a reasonable quantity of timber for the purpose of repairing buildings, fences, gates, implements of husbandry, and the like, and he may take sufficient wood for fuel for his house.[115]

---

111. See § 87 supra. See Gurtis v. City of Sanford, 18 N.C. App. 543, 197 S.E.2d 584 (1973), in accord with text.

112. The tenancy created is usually a tenancy from year to year if the original lease was for a year or more; if for less than a year, the periodic tenancy created is based on the way the rent was reserved, monthly, weekly, etc. See note in 108 A.L.R. 1464 (1937).

It should also be noted that the text above states "a tenancy from year to year *may* be created." This is because a periodic tenancy *may not* arise by implication in such case depending on the circumstances. Where the tenant holds over after expiration of his lease and pays rent to his landlord, a rebuttable presumption arises that the parties intend to create a tenancy from year to year. If the lessee has been compelled to remain in possession, however, and continued to pay rent to the lessor as a result of sickness or unavoidable necessity which prevented him from leaving, or the parties indicate an intention not to create such periodic tenancy by the holding over, payment and acceptance of rent, the presumption will be rebutted. See text supra following note 104. See, especially, Murrill v. Palmer, 164 N.C. 50, 80 S.E. 55 (1913). Accord, Gurtis v. City of Sanford, 18 N.C. App. 543, 197 S.E.2d 584 (1973).

113. N.C. Gen. Stat. § 22-2.

114. The tenancy from period to period that results will vary, that is, will be a tenancy from year to year or month to month, etc., depending on whether the lease reserved rent on an annual or monthly (or other) basis. Lesar, Landlord and Tenant § 3.27 (1957). See Ingram v. Corbit, 177 N.C. 318, 99 S.E. 18 (1919).

115. Tiffany, Real Property § 440 (abr. ed. 1940).

§ 92. Right to Emblements.

A tenant from year to year or other tenant from period to period, whose tenancy is terminated through an act of God, death of the tenant, or act of the landlord who expels him or terminates his tenancy, is entitled to the right of "emblements."[116] The tenant (or his administrator in case of the tenant's death) has the right to continue to enter upon the land and to cultivate crops planted and to harvest them when ripe.[117] The tenant does not have such right if he himself abandons the premises or voluntarily puts an end to his tenancy.[118]

While North Carolina has a statute[119] providing for the tenant's continued right of possession, with accompanying obligation to pay rent to a succeeding owner when a tenant's lease or estate terminates without fault of the tenant, this statute by its terms applies only to "estates for years." Therefore the common-law rule as to "emblements" may still be applicable to estates from year to year and other periodic tenancies.

§ 93. Right to Exclusive Possession.

Since a tenancy from year to year and other periodic tenancies are species of estates for years, the tenant therein has an exclusive right to possess the premises.[120]

§ 94. Right to Transfer of Tenant's Interest.

Although no North Carolina cases exist on point, a tenant from period to period may transfer all or part of the tenancy.[121] This is the general rule because, except for mode of termination, tenancies from period to period have the same incidents as estates for years.[122]

§ 95. Tenant's Duty to Repair.

A tenant from year to year or other periodic tenancy has the obligation to make repairs to the premises.[123] But in tenancies covered by the Residential Rental Agreements Act, the landlord must provide fit premises and make all repairs and do whatever is necessary to put and keep the

---

116. 1 WASHBURN, REAL PROPERTY § 254 (6th ed. 1902).
117. 1 WASHBURN, REAL PROPERTY § 259 (6th ed. 1902).
118. 1 WASHBURN, REAL PROPERTY § 260 (6th ed. 1902).
119. N.C. GEN. STAT. § 42-7. *See* § 81, note 79 *supra.*
120. MINOR & WURTS, REAL PROPERTY § 347 (1910). *See* § 82, notes 83, 84 and 85 *supra.*
121. 1 WASHBURN, REAL PROPERTY § 92 (6th ed. 1902). *See generally* AMERICAN LAW OF PROPERTY § 3.23 (Casner ed. 1952), where the editor cites Oxley v. James, 13 M. & W. 209, 153 Eng. Rep. 87 (Ex. 1844). In that case a tenant from year-to-year was allowed to sublease for a term for years.
122. AMERICAN LAW OF PROPERTY § 3.23 (Casner ed. 1952).
123. 1 WASHBURN, REAL PROPERTY § 92 (6th ed. 1902).

premises in a fit and habitable condition.[124] The tenant has certain duties an obligations with respect to the leased premises, but is not obligated to make ordinary repairs at the tenant's own expense.[125]

§ 96. Tenant's Liability for Waste.

A tenant from year to year or of other periodic tenancy, like any other tenant, is liable for waste, both voluntary and permissive.[126] As to tenancies covered by the Residential Rental Agreements Act, a tenant is prohibited from destroying, defacing, damaging, or removing any part of the premises or from knowingly permitting any person to do so.[127]

§ 97. Termination; Necessity of Notice to Terminate.

An estate from year to year or other tenancy from period to period does not terminate automatically at the end of any particular term. Such periodic tenancies are terminable only by the giving of an appropriate prior notice that the tenancy is to be ended. Such notice of termination must be given a specified time, depending upon the type of periodic tenancy involved, prior to the end of the current period.[128]

For instance, in North Carolina by statute, in order to terminate a lease from year to year, it is necessary for the party desiring to effect such termination to give to the other party notice to terminate at least one month before the end of the current year of the tenancy. A lease month to month is terminable only if the party desiring to terminate the tenancy gives the other party a notice of termination seven days prior to the end of the current month. A tenancy from week to week requires a notice of termination to be given two days prior to the end of the current week.[129] It should be noted that the notice must not only be for a certain number of days but that the notice must be given the specified length of time

---

124. *See* § 84 *supra*.
125. *Id.*
126. TIFFANY, REAL PROPERTY § 125 (abr. ed. 1940).
127. N.C. GEN. STAT. § 42-43 (a) (4) (Supp. 1977).
128. N.C. GEN. STAT. § 42-14 provides:

> § 42-14. **Notice to quit in certain tenancies.** — A tenancy from year to year may be terminated by a notice to quit given one month or more before the end of the current year of the tenancy; a tenancy from month to month by a like notice of seven days; a tenancy from week to week, of two days.

129. N.C. GEN. STAT. § 42-14 does not specify when notice to terminate must be given to terminate a tenancy from quarter to quarter. At the common law, except for the tenancy from year to year in which a six months' notice was required, the prior notice required to terminate a tenancy from period to period had to be equal to the length of the particular term. Since the statute is silent as to tenancies from quarter to quarter, presumably the common law would be applicable. *See* 1 MORDECAI, LAW LECTURES 540 (1916).

before the end of the current term of the tenancy.[130] If the proper notice is not given a sufficient length of time prior to the end of the current term, the parties will be bound for at least one additional term.[131]

While the notice of termination provided by North Carolina General Statutes, § 42-14 must be given the prescribed time prior to the end of the current tenancy, it need not be in any particular form and an oral notice that the tenancy is to be terminated will be sufficient.[132] In addition, the statute does not prevent the parties to a lease from period to period from making a different agreement prescribing the time for the giving of a notice to terminate the lease.[133]

Article V. Tenancies at Will

Division 1. General Provisions

§ 98. Tenancies at Will Generally.

A tenancy at will is a non-freehold tenancy which arises where lands or tenements are expressly or impliedly demised by one person to another to be held during the joint wills of both parties.[134] The tenancy at will is a tenancy held at the will or pleasure of both the landlord and tenant and either party can terminate the estate at any time, subject to certain wholesome restrictions such as the rights of emblements, ingress and egress to gather and remove crops, which the law bestows on the tenant when his estate is terminated by the lessor.[135] The distinguishing characteristics of the tenancy at will are (1) the indefiniteness or uncertainty of the term, (2) the right of either landlord or tenant to terminate the tenancy, and (3) that the tenant is in lawful possession with permission of the landlord.

§ 99. Creation by Express Agreement.

A tenancy at will may be created by express agreement of the parties. If an owner of land lets a tenant into possession "until you want to leave

---

130. 1 MORDECAI, LAW LECTURES 540 (1916). *E.g.*, assuming the tenancy is from month to month, and the tenancy started on January 1, a notice that he must leave must be given at least seven days prior to the last day of any month in order to terminate the tenancy on the last day of the month. If the notice is given only six days prior to the end of any current month, both parties are bound for at least another month. Nor can either party notify the other to vacate at any time other than the end of any current period. *See* Simmons v. Jarman, 122 N.C. 195, 29 S.E. 332 (1898).

131. Simmons v. Jarman, 122 N.C. 195, 29 S.E. 332 (1898).
132. Poindexter v. Call, 182 N.C. 366, 109 S.E. 26 (1921).
133. Cherry v. Whitehurst, 216 N.C. 340, 4 S.E.2d 900 (1939).
134. 1 MORDECAI, LAW LECTURES 533 (1916); Sappenfield v. Goodman, 215 N.C. 417, 2 S.E.2d 13 (1939).
135. 1 MORDECAI, LAW LECTURES 533 (1916).

for any reason"[136] or "until I rent or sell the premises,"[137] the tenancy created is a tenancy at will.

Although the traditional rule is that, if the estate is terminable at the will and option of either one of the parties, it is also terminable at the will and option of the other party,[138] a recent Court of Appeals decision has held that a properly executed lease for a definite term of fifteen years which expressly provided that the lessee should have the right to terminate the lease upon thirty-days' notice after the expiration of the first year did not create a tenancy at will giving the landlord a like right to terminate the lease.[139]

§ 100. Creation by Implication or Operation of Law.

A tenancy at will very often is created not by express intention or agreement but by operation of law or implication.

A tenancy at will arises when a lessee enters into possession of premises under a lease that is void because it is not in writing as required by the Statute of Frauds.[140] A tenancy at will is likewise created when a person takes possession of land preparatory to the execution of a lease which in fact is never completed or executed.[141] Possession taken under an unenforceable parol contract to purchase land also creates a tenancy at will.[142] In addition, a rental agreement providing that it would end if the tenant bought the house, but which gave no indication as to when the agreement would end if the tenant did not make the purchase, has been held to make the tenant a tenant at will.[143]

---

136. Sappenfield v. Goodman, 215 N.C. 417, 2 S.E.2d 13 (1939).
137. Choate Rental Co. v. Justice, 212 N.C. 523, 193 S.E. 817 (1937). *See* Stout v. Crutchfield, 21 N.C. App. 387, 204 S.E.2d 541 (1974), which holds that a rental agreement which would end if tenant bought house, but which gave no indication when agreement would end if tenant did not purchase house, would make the tenant a tenant at will and that the tenancy at will could be terminated at any time by either party. Since the tenant's estate was held to be a tenancy at will, the landlord could evict the tenant without giving the ten days' statutory notice required before a lease can be forfeited for nonpayment of rent under N.C. GEN. STAT. § 42-3.
138. Sappenfield v. Goodman, 215 N.C. 417, 2 S.E.2d 13 (1939); Mhoon v. Drizzle, 14 N.C. 414 (1832).
139. Jaynes v. Lawing, 12 N.C. App. 682, 184 S.E.2d 373 (1971).
140. Barbee v. Lamb, 225 N.C. 211, 34 S.E.2d 65 (1945); Davis v. Lovick, 226 N.C. 252, 37 S.E.2d 680 (1946).
141. Love v. Edmonston, 23 N.C. 152 (1840).
142. Love v. Edmonston, 23 N.C. 152 (1840). *See* Dowd v. Gilchrist, 46 N.C. 353 (1832), which holds that possession under a *written* contract for the sale of land creates a tenancy at will so as to estop the tenant from denying the title of the landlord until he surrenders possession. *See also* Walton v. File, 18 N.C. 567 (1836). *But see* Dail v. Freeman, 92 N.C. 351 (1885), which states that a vendee under a parol contract is a tenant at sufferance.
143. Stout v. Crutchfield, 21 N.C. App. 387, 204 S.E.2d 541 (1974).

Division 2. Incidents of Tenancies at Will

§ 101. Interest of Tenant at Will Is Personal.

The tenancy at will is a very precarious interest and since it is terminable at any moment at the mere caprice of either party, the tenant at will cannot assign his interest in the premises to a third person.[144] It is likewise terminated by the death of the tenant.[145]

§ 102. Tenant's Right to Estovers.

In the absence of a contrary stipulation, some authorities hold that a tenant at will is entitled to estovers; that is, he may cut and use such amount of timber from the premises as may be reasonably necessary for fuel or repairs, like any other tenant.[146] Other authoritative opinion holds that a tenant at will is not entitled to estovers.[147] There are no cases in North Carolina.

§ 103. Tenant's Right to Emblements.

Since the estate of a tenant at will is of uncertain duration, and since the law's general purpose is to encourage productivity of land, if a tenant at will who holds an agricultrual tenancy plants crops and his estate is terminated through no fault or act of the tenant, he will be entitled to harvest the crops in the ground, and to free ingress and egress for the purpose of cultivating, harvesting and carrying them away.[148]

§ 104. Tenant's Liability for Waste.

A tenant at will is liable to the owner for the commission of voluntary waste.[149] A tenant at will is not liable for permissive waste.[150]

---

144. 1 Mordecai, Law Lectures 534 (1916); Tiffany, Real Property § 121 (abr. ed. 1940).
145. 1 Washburn, Real Property § 771 (1902).
146. Minor & Wurts, Real Property § 338 (1910); 1 Washburn, Real Property § 768 (1902).
147. *See* Tiffany, Real Property § 440 (abr. ed. 1940), which states that a tenant at will is *not* entitled to estovers.
148. Minor & Wurts, Real Property § 339 (1910); 1 Washburn, Real Property § 769 (1902). N.C. Gen. Stat. § 42-7 (*see* note 79 *supra*) does not apply to tenancies at will and the rule of the common law giving a tenant at will a right to emblements presumably applies.
149. Tiffany, Real Property § 121 (abr. ed. 1940); Minor & Wurts, Real Property § 340 (1910). As to tenancies covered by the Residential Rental Agreements Act, *See* § 84 *supra*.
150. The Statute of Marlbridge, 52 Hen. III, c. 23, which created the action of waste declared all tenants for life or for years liable for waste but omitted tenants at will. Since at the common law an act of destruction as would be waste committed by the tenant at will terminated his tenancy, the tenant was then liable for his destructive act as for a trespass. This did not apply to permissive waste. North Carolina's waste statute, N.C. Gen. Stat. § 1-534, was derived from the Statute of Marlbridge. *See* 1 Mordecai, Law Lectures 709 (1916).

§ 105. Termination; No Prior Notice Required.

A tenancy at will may be terminated at any time at the will of either party.[151] Any act or declaration of either party indicating an intention to terminate the tenancy at will, will end it. For instance, the owner may expressly declare to the tenant that he shall no longer hold the premises and such declaration or demand for possession will terminate the tenancy.[152] Or the owner may terminate the tenancy by exercising acts of ownership that are inconsistent with the continuation of the tenancy, such as conveying or leasing the premises to another to commence immediately.[153]

The tenant at will may himself terminate the tenancy by express notice, by surrender, abandonment or desertion of the premises.[154] Tenancies at will are also terminated by the death of either the owner or the tenant.[155]

A tenancy at will may be terminated *instanter* upon demand for possession by the owner [156] without the necessity for a prior notice to terminate of any specified length of time.[157] A recent case, for example, has held that a landlord can evict a tenant at will without giving the ten days' statutory notice required before a lease can be forfeited for nonpayment of rent under North Carolina General Statutes, § 42-3.[158]

While it is sometimes stated that a tenant at will is entitled to a reasonable notice to quit, his estate is in fact immediately terminated by a demand for possession by the owner.[159] The tenant does, however, have a reasonable time to pack up and leave.[160] Any unreasonable delay by the tenant at will to remove himself or his effects after he has been given notice that his estate has been terminated will subject him to treatment as a trespasser.[161]

---

151. Choate Rental Co. v. Justice, 212 N.C. 523, 193 S.E. 817 (1937); Simons v. Lebrun, 219 N.C. 42, 12 S.E.2d 644 (1940); Barbee v. Lamb, 225 N.C. 211, 34 S.E.2d 65 (1945). *See* Stout v. Crutchfield, 21 N.C. App. 387, 204 S.E.2d 541 (1974).

152. Love v. Edmonston, 23 N.C. 152 (1846); Howell v. Howell, 29 N.C. 496 (1847).

153. Howell v. Howell, 29 N.C. 496 (1847); Barbee v. Lamb, 225 N.C. 211, 34 S.E.2d 65 (1945); Jones v. Potter, 89 N.C. 220 (1883).

154. MINOR & WURTS, REAL PROPERTY § 342 (1910).

155. *Id.* In addition, at the common law the assignment of the premises to another by the tenant or the commission of voluntary waste destroyed tenancies at will.

156. This would likewise be true if the tenant elects to terminate the tenancy at will.

157. Barbee v. Lamb, 225 N.C. 211, 34 S.E.2d 65 (1945); Sappenfield v. Goodman, 215 N.C. 417, 2 S.E.2d 13 (1939); Choate Rental Co. v. Justice, 212 N.C. 523, 193 S.E. 817 (1937); Humphries v. Humphries, 25 N.C. 362 (1843); Howell v. Howell, 29 N.C. 496 (1847); Love v. Edmonston, 23 N.C. 152 (1846).

158. Stout v. Crutchfield, 21 N.C. App. 387, 204 S.E.2d 541 (1974).

159. Howell v. Howell, 29 N.C. 496 (1847).

160. Jones v. Potter, 89 N.C. 220 (1883).

161. *Id.*

Article VI. Tenancy at Sufferance.

§ 106. General Provisions.

A tenancy or estate at sufferance is one which arises where one goes into possession of land lawfully but holds over without any consent of the owner, either express or implied, or under any title at all. The simplest illustration of this is where one has a lease for a specified period and holds over at the end of his lease without any consent or recognition by the owner.[162] The tenant at sufferance is not a trespasser as he must have come into possession lawfully,[163] nor is he a tenant at will since he does not continue in possession under permission or consent of the owner. His possession is in fact tortious since it is nonconsensual;[164] he is only "suffered" to remain in possession due to the laches or neglect of the owner.

§ 107. Incidents of Tenancy at Sufferance.

Since a tenant at sufferance is a wrongdoer, and in possession as a result of the landowner's laches or neglect, he has no term, and no estate or title, but only naked possession without right. He acquires no permanent rights because the landowner neglects to disturb his possession, and the landowner is entitled to resume possession, and the tenant is entitled to quit, at any time without notice.[165]

Since there is no privity of contract nor of estate between the owner and the tenant, the tenant at sufferance is not obligated to pay rent because a liability for rent supposes that the tenant is in possession by agreement. It has been held, however, that while a tenant at sufferance is not liable for rent as such, he may be liable for mesne profits accruing during his occupation in an action of trespass or of ejectment.[166]

A tenant at sufferance is not entitled to emblements upon termination of his tenancy.[167] He has no estate which he can transfer or transmit.[168]

---

162. A tenant at sufferance may at any time become a tenant at will upon the owner's recognition and consent to his being in possession. If the owner accepts rent and agrees to his remaining in possession, his tenancy will become one from period to period.

163. If the tenant comes in without any right, he is a mere trespasser.

164. It has been said that in only one respect does the position of a tenant by sufferance differ from that of a trespasser who has disseised the owner. He cannot be held in an action of trespass unless the owner first enters. *See* MINOR & WURTS, REAL PROPERTY § 344 (1910); TIFFANY, REAL PROPERTY § 127 (abr. ed. 1940).

165. Sappenfield v. Goodman, 215 N.C. 417, 2 S.E.2d 13 (1939).

166. *See* MINOR & WURTS, REAL PROPERTY § 346 (1910). A tenant at sufferance may also be liable for damages for use and occupation under N.C. GEN. STAT. § 42-4. *See also* 1 MORDECAI, LAW LECTURES 536 (1916).

167. MINOR & WURTS, REAL PROPERTY § 42 (1910); 2 BLACKSTONE, COMMENTARIES *146.

168. 1 MORDECAI, LAW LECTURES 534 (1916).

A tenant at sufferance likewise cannot acquire title as against his landlord or the owner by adverse possession, as his possession is deemed that of the owner and his assigns; he is estopped to dispute the title of his landlord until after he shall have surrendered the possession.[169] A tenant at sufferance is not entitled to estovers.

---

169. 1 MORDECAI, LAW LECTURES 535 (1916).

CHAPTER 7

CONCURRENT OWNERSHIP

Article I. General Provisions

§ 108. Concurrent Ownership Generally.
§ 109. Joint Tenancy.
§ 110. Tenancy in Common.
§ 111. Tenancy by the Entirety.

Article II. Incidents of Tenancy in Common

§ 112. Doctrine of Survivorship Does Not Apply.
§ 113. Alienability.
§ 114. Creditors' Rights.
§ 115. Rights to Possession Between Tenants in Common; Duty to Account.
§ 116. Fiduciary Aspects Between Tenants in Common.
§ 117. Taxes; Interest.
§ 118. Repairs and Improvements.
§ 119. Actions of Waste Between Co-Tenants.
§ 120. Actions of Ejectment Between Co-Tenants.
§ 121. Partition — Generally.
§ 122. Same — Voluntary.
§ 123. Same — Restrictions on Right.
§ 124. Same — Practice in Partition Proceedings.

Article III. Incidents of Tenancy by the Entirety

§ 125. Disability of Either Spouse to Convey His or Her Share During Coverture.
§ 126. Creditors' Rights.
§ 127. Termination.
§ 128. Survivorship.

Article I. General Provisions

§ 108. Concurrent Ownership Generally.

While the most usual way of holding an estate is in severalty, by a person in his own right only without any other person being connected with him in point of interest during his estate therein, estates of any quantity or duration, absolute or qualified, *in praesenti* or *in futuro*, may be held by a plurality of tenants who possess a common interest in the estate, whatever it is.

The kinds of concurrent ownership are joint tenancies, tenancies in common, and tenancies by the entireties. The rights of persons who own interests in concurrent estates depend upon the kind of concurrent ownership involved.

§ 109. Joint Tenancy.

(a) *In general.* At the common law any conveyance to two or more persons created a joint tenancy and not a tenancy in common unless there was an expression of a contrary intent.[1] The estate is always "conventional," meaning that it is always created by act of the parties and never arises by operation of law.[2] Each joint tenant is considered an owner of the undivided whole of the property as a part and parcel of the unit group which owns the whole; no joint tenant owns any fractional interest. To create the joint tenancy at the common law it was necessary for all of the "four unities" of *time, title, interest* and *possession* to be present. This meant that all tenants must receive their interest in the property at the same time; that all tenants must take their interest from the same source, by the same deed or same will; that all tenants must have the same identical kind of estate or interest in the property; and that the tenants each hold one collective undivided possession, meaning that the possession of one joint tenant is the possession of all the joint tenants and the possession of all the joint tenants is the possession of each respective joint tenant.

(b) *Survivorship.* The most important characteristic of the joint tenancy is the right of survivorship, which means that upon the death of one joint tenant, his interest in property jointly owned enures to the benefit of the surviving joint tenant or joint tenants. Upon the death of a joint tenant the surviving joint tenant or joint tenants take nothing from the decedent but instead take the whole by virtue of the original conveyance which created the joint tenancy; the surviving joint tenant or joint tenants take the whole which has been owned all the time. If all joint tenants die except one, the survivor owns the whole property in severalty. The heirs or spouse of a deceased joint tenant take nothing upon his death. A joint tenant cannot devise his interest upon his death.

(c) *Termination of joint tenancy.* A joint tenancy may be terminated or severed by the destruction of any of its unities. Each unity is essential to its continued existence. Since a joint tenant may convey his interest in real property, if he disposes of his interest to a stranger, he destroys the unity of title and thus terminates the joint tenancy. By his conveyance his grantee becomes a tenant in common with the other joint tenant.[3] An interest in a tenancy in common, of course, is descendible and is not subject to the doctrine of survivorship.

Since the destruction of any unity will terminate a joint estate, a volun-

---

1. 2 BLACKSTONE, COMMENTARIES *180.
2. 1 MORDECAI, LAW LECTURES 601 (1916).
3. If there are more than two joint tenants and one conveys his interest to a third person, the latter becomes a tenant in common with the others, who, however, remain joint tenants as between themselves. 2 BLACKSTONE, COMMENTARIES *186.

tary partition terminating the unity of possession between the two joint tenants will destroy the joint tenancy. Likewise a compulsory partition by judicial proceeding, to which each joint tenant is entitled as a matter of right, will result in destruction of the unity of possession and the joint tenancy.

Joint tenancies are not currently favored in the law. While they have not been abolished in North Carolina, the doctrine of survivorship has been abolished by statute since 1784 by North Carolina General Statutes, § 41-2, which states:

> **Survivorship in joint tenancy abolished; proviso as to partnership.** — In all estates, real or personal, held in joint tenancy, the part or share of any tenant dying shall not descend or go to the surviving tenant, but shall descend or be vested in the heirs, executors, or administrators, respectively, of the tenant so dying, in the same manner as estates held by tenancy in common: Provided, that estates held in joint tenancy for the purpose of carrying on and promoting trade and commerce, or any useful work or manufacture, established and pursued with a view of profit to the parties therein concerned, are vested in the surviving partner, in order to enable him to settle and adjust the partnership business, or pay off the debts which may have been contracted in pursuit of the joint business; but as soon as the same is effected, the survivor shall account with, and pay, and deliver to the heirs, executors and administrators respectively of such deceased partner all such part, share, and sums of money as he may be entitled to by virtue of the original agreement, if any, or according to his share or part in the joint concern, in the same manner as partnership stock is usually settled between joint merchants and the representatives of their deceased partners.

The effect of the statute is to make every fee simple interest held in joint tenancy descendible upon the death of a joint tenant in the same manner as interests in tenancies in common.

It should be noted, however, that it has been held that the statute abolishing the doctrine of survivorship in joint tenancies does not prevent or prohibit written contracts or provisions in deeds providing that a survivor shall take.[4] Nor does the statute abolish the right of survivorship in joint estates for life or estates held by the entirety.[5] Since life estates pur autre vie are estates of inheritance, they fall within the coverage of the statute.[6] The statute itself provides that the doctrine of survivorship still applies with respect to partnership property for the purpose of

---

4. Vettori v. Fay, 262 N.C. 481, 137 S.E.2d 810 (1964); Taylor v. Smith, 116 N.C. 531, 21 S.E. 202 (1895); Pope v. Burgess, 230 N.C. 323, 53 S.E.2d 159 (1949); Jones v. Waldroup, 217 N.C. 178, 7 S.E.2d 366 (1940).
5. Dew v. Shockley, 36 N.C. App. 87, 243 S.E.2d 177 (1978); Burton v. Cahill, 192 N.C. 505, 135 S.E. 332 (1926).
6. Dew v. Shockley, 36 N.C. App. 87, 243 S.E.2d 177 (1978).

winding up partnership business when one co-partner dies.[7] Other statutes retain the doctrine of survivorship upon the death of a joint trustee,[8] a joint mortgagee or joint trustee with a power of sale,[9] joint executor or joint representative.[10]

§ 110. Tenancy in Common.

(a) *In general.* The most common type of concurrent ownership existing in North Carolina between persons other than husband and wife is the tenancy in common. In a tenancy in common the tenants "hold by several and distinct titles but by unity of possession."[11] That is to say, each tenant in common owns a separate undivided interest in the land in his own right and each has an equal right to possession. Unity of possession is the only requisite unity — the tenants own distinct moieties in the land. Co-tenants need not have the same interest; they need not take from the same instrument, nor at the same time. One tenant may own an undivided one-half interest, another a one-fourth interest, and two others a one-eighth interest. One co-tenant may have acquired his interest by a will ten years ago, another by conveyance five years ago, and another may have acquired his interest by descent or operation of law yesterday.

(b) *Creation of tenancy in common.* A tenancy in common arises whenever the instrument creating the tenancy shows that the owner intended for the tenants to hold their interests as separate, undivided shares, or moieties, in the property. Thus, where an instrument provides that land shall be held by the tenants "equally" or that they are to "share and share alike," a tenancy in common is created.[12]

Tenancies in common may arise by deed, will or by operation of law. A deed or will may expressly limit an estate to two or more persons as tenants in common.[13] Or the devise or grant may be to two or more

---

7. N.C. GEN. STAT. § 41-2.
8. N.C. GEN. STAT. § 41-3.
9. N.C. GEN. STAT. § 45-8.
10. N.C. GEN. STAT. § 28-A-13-5.
Joint accounts with right of survivorship opened with banking institutions are governed by N.C. GEN. STAT. § 41-2.1. A recent Court of Appeals decision suggests that this statute must be strictly complied with in order to effectuate a valid survivorship feature. O'Brien v. Reece, 45 N.C. App. 610, 263 S.E.2d 817 (1980). For additional cases interpreting this statute as it applies to accounts open by two or more persons other than husband and wife see Moore v. Galloway, 35 N.C. App. 394, 241 S.E.2d 386 (1978); Harven v. First Union National Bank, 28 N.C. App. 75, 220 S.E.2d 136 (1975).
11. 1 MORDECAI, LAW LECTURES 612 (1916); 2 BLACKSTONE, COMMENTARIES *191.
12. Midgett v. Midgett, 117 N.C. 8, 23 S.E. 37 (1895). *Accord,* Dearman v. Bruns, 11 N.C. App. 564, 181 S.E.2d 809 (1971). A devise of land to testator's daughter and her husband "to share equally" creates a tenancy in common between the daughter and her husband, not an estate by the entireties.
13. 1 MORDECAI, LAW LECTURES 613 (1916).

persons to be shared "equally" or "share and share alike."[14] Or one grants a fractional part of one's land to a stranger without specifically describing it.[15] Or a tenancy by the entirety is severed by an absolute divorce.[16] Or a tenancy by the entirety is not created because the purported spouses are in fact not husband and wife at the time of the conveyance.[17] Or an ancestor's lands descend to his heirs in undivided fractional parts.[18]

It should be noted that a tenancy in common can exist only when two or more persons own "undivided" shares in the real property. If the creating instrument locates the lands by name or by metes and bounds so that each person knows his land, or if the shares are described with such certainty that a surveyor can take the instrument and locate them without other aid, then the parties hold in severalty and not as tenants in common.[19]

§ 111. Tenancy by the Entirety.[20]

(a) *In general.* North Carolina recognizes the common-law tenancy known as the tenancy by the entirety.[21] An estate by the entirety is a form of co-ownership held by husband and wife with the right of survivorship. It arises by virtue of title acquired by husband and wife jointly after their marriage. Any conveyance to a husband and wife by deed or will creates a tenancy by the entirety unless it is clear in the instrument that some other kind of tenancy is intended.[22] It can exist only between husband and wife.

---

14. Midgett v. Midgett, 117 N.C. 8, 23 S.E. 37 (1895). *See* Dearman v. Bruns, 11 N.C. App. 564, 181 S.E.2d 809 (1971).

15. Morehead v. Hall, 126 N.C. 213, 35 S.E. 428 (1900), where grantor conveyed "one half of well described tract." *See* Foreman v. Hough, 98 N.C. 386, 3 S.E. 912 (1887).

16. *See* notes 174, 175 *infra.*

17. *See* note 26 *infra.*

18. 1 MORDECAI, LAW LECTURES 613 (1916). The most usual method by which tenancies in common arise in this state is by descent because a person's land descends, when he dies intestate, to his nearest heirs in equal degree. It frequently happens that an estate descends to several co-heirs who become tenants in common.

19. Midgett v. Midgett, 117 N.C. 8, 23 S.E. 37 (1895); Locklear v. Martin, 245 N.C. 378, 96 S.E.2d 24 (1956); Mitchell v. Hoggard, 108 N.C. 353, 12 S.E. 844 (1891).

20. This estate is often expressed in the plural as an estate by the entireties.

21. Harris v. Parker, 17 N.C. App. 606, 195 S.E.2d 121 (1973); Combs v. Combs, 273 N.C. 462, 160 S.E.2d 308 (1968); Gas Co. v. Leggett, 273 N.C. 547, 161 S.E.2d 23 (1968). For a very excellent and complete exposition of the law relating to the tenancy by the entirety in North Carolina, see an article by Dr. Robert E. Lee in 41 N.C.L. REV. 67 (1962), which is excerpted from LEE, NORTH CAROLINA FAMILY LAW (1963).

22. A conveyance of land to a husband and his wife, nothing else appearing, creates an estate by the entireties. Dearman v. Bruns, 11 N.C. App. 564, 181 S.E.2d 809 (1971); Freeze v. Congleton, 276 N.C. 178, 171 S.E.2d 424 (1970); Jernigan v. Stokely, 34 N.C. App. 358, 238 S.E.2d 318 (1977), citing this section in original edition. *See* Davis v. Bass, 188 N.C. 200, 124 S.E. 566 (1924), for a comprehensive analysis of this estate in North Carolina. *See also* Moore v. Greenville Banking & Trust Co., 178 N.C. 118, 100 S.E. 269 (1919).

(b) *Creation of tenancy by the entirety.* When land is conveyed or devised to a husband and his wife, nothing else appearing, they take by the entirety, and upon the death of either one of them the other takes the whole by right of survivorship.[23] To create a tenancy by the entirety, it is customary to word the deed "To John Doe and Mary Doe, husband and wife, as tenants by the entirety," or "To John Doe and Mary Doe, husband and wife." It is not essential, however, to name the parties as husband and wife if they are actually man and wife at the time. Thus a conveyance "To John Doe and wife" will create a tenancy by the entirety in the grantee and his wife, if he has a wife.[24] A tenancy by the entirety will not, however, result if the grantees are not legally husband and wife at the time the conveyance takes effect even though they are so described in the conveyance.[25] A conveyance to a man and a woman who are not married but who afterwards intermarry will not create a tenancy by the entirety; even after they marry they will hold as tenants in common.[26]

To create the tenancy by the entirety, it is said that five unities must be present.[27] The *unity of time* requires that the husband and wife must take their interest in the premises at the same instant of time. The *unity of title* requires that the husband and wife take their interest from the same source, under the same deed or will. The *unity of interest* means that the husband and wife have the same identical interest in the land involved, whatever that is.[28] The *unity of possession* means that the

---

23. Dearman v. Bruns, 11 N.C. App. 564, 181 S.E.2d 809 (1971); Freeze v. Congleton, 276 N.C. 178, 171 S.E.2d 424 (1970); Moore v. Greenville Banking & Trust Co., 178 N.C. 118, 124, 100 S.E. 269, 272 (1919); Bowling v. Bowling, 252 N.C. 527, 114 S.E.2d 228 (1960); Edwards v. Batts, 245 N.C. 693, 97 S.E.2d 101 (1957); Byrd v. Patterson, 229 N.C. 156, 48 S.E.2d 45 (1948); see Smith v. Smith, 249 N.C. 669, 677, 107 S.E.2d 530, 535-36 (1959); Davis v. Bass, 188 N.C. 200, 124 S.E. 566 (1924).

24. Byrd v. Patterson, 229 N.C. 156, 48 S.E.2d 45 (1948); Bowden v. Bowden, 264 N.C. 296, 141 S.E.2d 621 (1965).

25. *See, e.g.,* Lawrence v. Heavener, 232 N.C. 557, 61 S.E.2d 697 (1950), where conveyance was to "Luther Heavener and wife, Reba Heavener," who supposed themselves to be husband and wife. The purported wife had another living and undivorced husband, however, and the purported marriage was declared void *ab initio.* The case held that since there was no legal marriage no tenancy by the entirety was created, that the conveyance made them tenants in common instead. *See also* Grant v. Toatley, 244 N.C. 463, 94 S.E.2d 305 (1956).

26. *See* Davis v. Bass, 188 N.C. 200, 124 S.E. 566 (1924). *Accord,* Combs v. Combs, 273 N.C. 462, 160 S.E.2d 308 (1968).

27. *Id.*

28. A tenancy by the entirety may exist in lands whether the estate be in fee, for life, or for years and whether the same be in possession, reversion or remainder. A tenancy by the entirety may likewise be held in equitable estates as well as legal estates. *See* Sprinkle v. Spainhour, 149 N.C. 223, 62 S.E. 910 (1908); *In re* Gardner, 20 N.C. App. 610, 202 S.E.2d 318 (1974) (involving life estates); Simonton v. Cornelius, 98 N.C. 433, 4 S.E. 38 (1887) (conveyance to husband and wife during their natural lives); Lanier v. Dawes, 255 N.C. 458, 461, 121 S.E.2d 857 (1961); Davis v. Bass, 188 N.C. 200, 209, 124 S.E. 566, 571 (1924). *See also* Stamper v. Stamper, 121 N.C. 251, 28 S.E. 20 (1897), where the court recognized a tenancy by the entirety in an equitable interest, under a contract to convey to a husband and wife.

possession of either the husband or the wife is the possession of the husband-wife entity, and the possession of the husband-wife entity is the possession of the individuals who make up the husband-wife entity. The *unity of person* involves the common-law concept that after marriage a husband and his wife are but one person, one legal entity. The tenancy by the entirety must be created either by deed or by will and never arises by descent or operation of law.

A conveyance to a husband and wife who are legally married and to another person, who is also named as grantee along with the husband and wife, will create a tenancy by the entirety in the husband and wife in a one-half undivided interest; the other person will take the other one-half undivided interest as a tenant in common with husband-wife entity.[29]

It is important to know when a tenancy by the entirety is *not* created. Nothing prevents a husband and wife from holding land as tenants in common, where there is no right of survivorship, if the conveyance by which they take title indicates this intention of the grantor or devisor.[30] Thus it would be sufficient to create a tenancy in common by stating that the conveyance is "To John Doe and his wife Mary Doe as tenants in common and not as tenants by the entirety." A conveyance "To John Doe and his wife Mary Doe, each one half interest" creates a tenancy in common and not a tenancy by the entirety.[31]

There is one peculiar situation in which a conveyance to a husband and wife, without further indication, will not create a tenancy by the entirety. That is where one of them, either the husband or the wife, is a tenant in common with another or others, and there is a partition deed, either pursuant to a judicial proceeding or by a voluntary exchange of deeds, naming the husband and wife as grantees. It has been held that such partition deed does not create a tenancy by the entirety in the spouses because one of the spouses was already entitled to the land; that the partition deed merely severed the possession and established the bound-

---

29. *See In re* Gardner, 20 N.C. App. 610, 202 S.E.2d 318 (1974), which states: "[A]nother peculiar incident of an estate by the entirety is, that if an estate be given to A, B, and C, and A and B are husband and wife, nothing else appearing, they will take a half interest in the property and C will take the other half." Darden v. Timberlake, 139 N.C. 181, 51 S.E. 895 (1905); Luther v. Luther, 157 N.C. 499, 73 S.E. 102 (1911); Hampton v. Wheeler, 99 N.C. 222, 6 S.E. 236 (1888); Davis v. Bass, 188 N.C. 200, 124 S.E. 566 (1924); Moore v. Greenville Banking & Trust Co., 178 N.C. 118, 100 S.E. 269 (1919). *See generally* 1 MORDECAI, LAW LECTURES 608 (1916).
30. Holloway v. Green, 167 N.C. 91, 83 S.E. 243 (1914); Eason v. Eason, 159 N.C. 539, 75 S.E. 797 (1912). *See* Davis v. Bass, 188 N.C. 200, 207, 124 S.E. 566, 570 (1924); 1 MORDECAI, LAW LECTURES 609 (1916).
31. Eason v. Eason, 159 N.C. 539, 75 S.E. 797 (1912). A devise of land to daughter and her husband "to share equally" creates a tenancy in common between the daughter and her husband and not an estate by the entireties. Dearman v. Bruns, 11 N.C. App. 564, 181 S.E.2d 809 (1971).

aries and did not create a new title. In such case it is held that there is no unity of time or title and therefore no tenancy by the entirety is created.[32] Where a clear intent that a tenancy by the entirety is to be created is indicated in the granting clause of the cross deed or deeds or in the judgment of partition, North Carolina General Statutes, § 39-13.5[33] changes the former law of North Carolina and allows the creation of the tenancy by the entirety. That statute reads as follows:

> § 39-13.5. **Creation of tenancy by entirety in partition of real property.** — When either a husband or a wife owns an undivided interest in real property as a tenant in common with some person or persons other than his or her spouse and there occurs an actual partition of the property, a tenancy by the entirety may be created in the husband or wife who owned the undivided interest and his or her spouse in the manner hereinafter provided:
> (1) In a division by cross-deed or deeds, between or among the tenants in common provided that the intent of the tenant in common to create a tenancy by the entirety with his or her spouse in this exchange of deeds must be clearly stated in the granting clause of the deed or deeds to such tenant and his or her spouse, and further provided that the deed or deeds to such tenant in common and his or her spouse is signed by such tenant in common and is acknowledged before a certifying officer in accordance with G.S. 52-10;
> (2) In a judicial proceeding for partition. In such proceeding, both spouses have the right to become parties to the proceeding and to have their pleadings state that the intent of the tenant in common is to create a tenancy by the entirety with his or her spouse. The order of partition shall provide that the real property assigned to such tenant and his or her spouse shall be owned by them as tenants by the entirety.

Another peculiarity arises relating to the creation of tenancies by the entirety depending on which spouse pays the purchase price for the property. If the husband pays the purchase price, and a deed of conveyance is made to himself and his wife, the law presumes the creation of a tenancy by the entirety, presuming that the husband intended to make a gift to the

---

32. In Smith v. Smith, 249 N.C. 669, 107 S.E.2d 530 (1959), the court said:

> This Court has consistently held that where tenants in common divide the common land and by exchange of deeds allot to each his or her share of the land, the deeds employed create no new title and serve only to sever the possession. And if any of such deeds names the tenant and his wife or the tenant and her husband as grantees, no estate by the entireties is thereby created, even if they are so named with the consent of the tenant.

Accord, Combs v. Combs, 273 N.C. 462, 160 S.E.2d 308 (1968); McLamb v. Weaver, 244 N.C. 432, 94 S.E.2d 331 (1956); Miller v. Miller, 34 N.C. App. 209, 237 S.E.2d 552 (1977). But distinguish the foregoing situation from the situation where one co-tenant conveys his own share of a co-tenancy to another co-tenant and his or her spouse. Morton v. Blades Lumber Co., 154 N.C. 278, 70 S.E. 467 (1911); *see* Smith v. Smith, 249 N.C. 669, 107 S.E.2d 530 (1959).

33. The original version of this statute was enacted in 1969 and became effective in that year. The statute quoted in the text reflects the 1977 amendments which, subject to a proviso that no pending litigation be affected, became effective on January 1, 1978.

benefit of the wife to the extent of her interest in the tenancy by the entirety.[34] On the other hand, if the wife furnishes the purchase price, the law makes no presumption that a tenancy by the entirety was created, but instead presumes that the wife intended to place title in the husband and herself on a resulting trust for the wife.[35]

At the common law, if a spouse owned real property individually, he or she could not directly convey the property to himself and his spouse by the entirety. This was because of the requirement that both spouses had to take their interest at the same time and by the same conveyance. Hence, if a spouse who owned land desired to have his wife share in the land as a tenant by the entirety, he had to convey it to a "straw man" or nominal party who would reconvey the land to the husband and wife. This is still possible and is perhaps still frequently done by some older lawyers.[36] But since the enactment of a statute in 1957,[37] direct conveyances between an individual husband or wife and the husband and wife entity have been specifically authorized by statute without the necessity of any "straw man" or nominal grantee.[38]

Article II. Incidents of Tenancy in Common

§ 112. Doctrine of Survivorship Does Not Apply.

The doctrine of survivorship does not apply as between tenants in common. Upon the death of one of the tenants in common, his share descends to his heirs or goes as he has provided in his will.[39]

---

34. Bowling v. Bowling, 252 N.C. 527, 114 S.E.2d 228 (1960); Morton v. Blades Lumber Co., 154 N.C. 278, 70 S.E. 467 (1911); *see* Honeycutt v. Citizens Nat'l Bank, 242 N.C. 734, 741, 89 S.E.2d 598, 604 (1955); *cf.* Akin v. First Nat'l Bank, 227 N.C. 453, 42 S.E.2d 518 (1947).

35. Sprinkle v. Spainhour, 149 N.C. 223, 226, 62 S.E. 910, 911 (1908); *see* Smith v. Smith, 249 N.C. 677, 107 S.E.2d 530, 536 (1959); Davis v. Vaughn, 243 N.C. 486, 492, 91 S.E.2d 165, 169 (1956); Ingram v. Easley, 227 N.C. 442, 444, 42 S.E.2d 624, 626 (1947); Carter v. Oxendine, 193 N.C. 478, 481, 137 S.E. 424, 425 (1927); Deese v. Deese, 176 N.C. 527, 528, 97 S.E. 475 (1918); Kilpatrick v. Kilpatrick, 176 N.C. 182, 185-86, 96 S.E. 988, 989 (1918); Speas v. Woodhouse, 162 N.C. 66, 68-69, 77 S.E. 1,000, 1,001 (1913).

If the wife furnishes only a part of the purchase price, there arises a resulting trust *pro tanto* in her favor. Cunningham v. Bell, 83 N.C. 328 (1880).

36. Certainly up until 1959. *See* Smith v. Smith, 249 N.C. 677, 678, 107 S.E.2d 530, 536 (1959), in which it is stated: "Indeed, this is the device customarily used in creating such an estate in land owned by one spouse, when it is desired that it be held by the entireties."

37. N.C. GEN. STAT. § 39-13.3.

38. This same result was foreshadowed by the decision of Woolard v. Smith, 244 N.C. 489, 94 S.E.2d 466 (1956), which held that a husband owning land could create a tenancy by the entirety by a direct conveyance to himself and his wife without the necessity of a "straw man."

39. 1 MORDECAI, LAW LECTURES 613 (1916); *see* N.C. GEN. STAT. § 41-2.

§ 113. Alienability.

Each tenant in common may convey, lease, or mortgage his interest in the common property,[40] either to another co-tenant or to a third person. But in making a conveyance a tenant in common acts only for himself and his share because he cannot bind his other co-tenants unless he has been empowered to act as their agent; the mere relationship of tenancy in common does not create an agency relationship.[41] When one of two co-tenants conveys his interest to a third party, the third party becomes a tenant in common with the other co-tenant.

§ 114. Creditors' Rights.

The interest of a tenant in common is subject to execution under judgment liens which may be obtained against him.[42]

§ 115. Rights to Possession Between Tenants in Common; Duty to Account.

In a tenancy in common, the co-tenants share equally in the land.[43] Each has a right to enter upon the land and to enjoy it jointly with the other.[44] Subject to the rights of his other co-tenants, one who is a tenant in common in real property may use and enjoy the common estate in the same manner as though he were the sole proprietor. He has a right to occupy and utilize every portion of the property at all times and in all circumstances provided he does not exclude his co-owners and does not appropriate to his sole use any particular portion of the land.[45] As each tenant in common is entitled to occupy the whole, the possession of the whole land by one co-tenant is looked upon as the possession in the interest of all co-tenants, unless the possession of the others is expressly negatived.[46]

A co-tenant is under no duty to compensate his fellow co-tenants if he

---

40. WASHBURN, REAL PROPERTY § 880 (6th ed. 1902).
41. Hinson v. Shugart, 224 N.C. 207, 29 S.E.2d 694 (1944); Bailey v. Howell, 209 N.C. 712, 184 S.E. 476 (1936); Herring v. Merchandise, Inc., 249 N.C. 221, 106 S.E.2d 197 (1958); Benbury v. Butts, 184 N.C. 23, 113 S.E. 499 (1922). However, acts by one tenant with relation to the common property may be presumed to have been done with authority and for the benefit of all co-tenants if there are circumstances under which to base the presumption. *See* Hinson v. Shugart, *supra*.
42. Jackson v. Baird, 148 N.C. 29, 61 S.E. 632 (1908); Southerland v. Cox, 14 N.C. 394 (1832); Holley v. White, 172 N.C. 77, 89 S.E. 1061 (1916).
43. Dearman v. Bruns, 11 N.C. App. 564, 181 S.E.2d 809 (1971).
44. *Id.*
45. 4 POWELL, REAL PROPERTY § 603 (1968). *See* Jones v. McBee, 222 N.C. 153, 22 S.E.2d 226 (1942); Dearman v. Bruns, 11 N.C. App. 564, 181 S.E.2d 809 (1971).
46. As *e.g.*, by an ouster or presumed ouster as discussed in text at § 120, note 81 *infra*. Collier v. Welker, 19 N.C. App. 617, 199 S.E.2d 691 (1973).

occupies the whole common property.[47] One is not chargeable for the enjoyment of his legal right. But if one co-tenant is dispossessed or excluded from possession by another, he may not only be restored to possession, but he is also entitled to recover damages from the tenant in common who occupies and uses the land.[48]

In addition, a tenant in common who rents common property to another and receives more than his just fractional share of the rents and profits of the land may be compelled to account to his co-owners.[49] In this regard, proof of ouster of a tenant in common is not a prerequisite to recovery.[50] But the co-tenant is not liable for the use and occupation of the lands; rather, the action is for rents and profits actually received that exceed a just fractional share.[51]

§ 116. Fiduciary Aspects Between Tenants in Common.

Although the mere relationship of tenants in common does not itself create a full complement of fiduciary and confidential relationships between the co-tenants, there frequently arises situations wherein the law imposes quasi-fiduciary obligations upon such co-tenants.[52] As a general principle, these quasi-fiduciary obligations require that co-tenants be true to each other and protect the rights of each other in the property.[53] The relationship between co-tenants has been described as a community of interest which gives rise to a community of duty.[54] For instance, if one

---

47. Whitehurst v. Hinton, 209 N.C. 392, 184 S.E. 66 (1936); Roberts v. Roberts, 55 N.C. 128 (1855); Pico v. Columbet, 12 Cal. 414 (1859); Mastbaum v. Mastbaum, 126 N.J. 366, 9 A.2d 51 (1939); Petrone v. Petrone, 248 App. Div. 908, 290 N.Y.S. 707 (1936); Kahnovsky v. Kahnovsky, 67 R.I. 208, 21 A.2d 569 (1941); see Etheridge v. Etheridge, 41 N.C. App. 44, 255 S.E.2d 729 (1979) and cases discussed therein.
48. Mastbaum v. Mastbaum, 126 N.J. 366, 9 A.2d 51 (1939); Sons v. Sons, 151 Minn. 360, 186 N.W. 811 (1922).
49. 4 POWELL, REAL PROPERTY § 604 (1968); Etheridge v. Etheridge, 41 N.C. App. 44, 255 S.E.2d 729 (1979); Dearman v. Bruns, 11 N.C. App. 564, 181 S.E.2d 809 (1971); Whitehurst v. Hinton, 209 N.C. 392, 184 S.E. 66 (1936); Hunt v. Hunt, 261 N.C. 437, 135 S.E.2d 195 (1964); Watson v. Carr, 9 N.C. App. 217, 175 S.E.2d 733 (1970).
50. For a full development of this issue and its historical development in North Carolina, see Etheridge v. Etheridge, 41 N.C. App. 44, 255 S.E.2d 729 (1979).
51. Lovett v. Stone, 239 N.C. 206, 79 S.E.2d 479 (1953); Hunt v. Hunt, 261 N.C. 437, 135 S.E.2d 195 (1964); Whitehurst v. Hinton, 209 N.C. 392, 184 S.E. 66 (1936); Watson v. Carr, 9 N.C. App. 217, 175 S.E.2d 733 (1970); Etheridge v. Etheridge, 41 N.C. App. 44, 255 S.E.2d 729 (1979).
52. 4 POWELL, REAL PROPERTY § 605 (1968). See Collier v. Welker, 19 N.C. App. 617, 199 S.E.2d 691 (1973); Moore v. Bryson, 11 N.C. App. 260, 181 S.E.2d 113 (1971).
53. Collier v. Welker, 19 N.C. App. 617, 199 S.E.2d 691 (1973); Cox v. Wright, 218 N.C. 342, 11 S.E.2d 158 (1940).
54. Moore v. Bryson, 11 N.C. App. 260, 181 S.E.2d 113 (1971); Gentry v. Gentry, 187 N.C. 29, 121 S.E.2d 188 (1924).

co-tenant buys in land under an outstanding title,[55] or under a mortgage,[56] tax claim,[57] or other encumbrance for which he is partially liable as a co-tenant, without giving his fellow co-tenants an opportunity to participate, such title will enure to the benefit of all the co-tenants, and they are entitled to pay their proportionate share and to receive the benefits of such title.[58]

The same may be true in the event of an indirect purchase. In one recent case,[59] for example, a husband and wife, who had been tenants by the entirety of their residence, became tenants in common upon divorce after they had entered into a deed of separation which gave the wife possession of the residence and obligated her to make the mortgage payments. The wife, after failing to make the mortgage payments, assigned her highest bid at the foreclosure sale to her mother who then purchased the property, obtained another loan, and reconveyed the property to the wife. The court ruled that the wife's indirect purchase of the residence inured to the benefit of the husband and that he was entitled to a one-half undivided interest in the property.[60] Thus, where the purchase by the third person is only nominal, a deed to the third person will be considered a mere matter of form and the co-tenant who acquires the title from such third person will be deemed to hold in trust for the other co-tenants.[61]

---

55. Gentry v. Gentry, 187 N.C. 29, 121 S.E. 188 (1924). *Accord,* Moore v. Bryson, 11 N.C. App. 260, 181 S.E.2d 113 (1971), which states that if one of several tenants in common should buy in an outstanding title affecting the common property, equity will declare him to have purchased for the benefit of the others. The foundation of the doctrine which disables a co-tenant from asserting an adverse title against the other co-tenants is that, while the relation continues, there is a community of interest which gives rise to a community of duty, and creates a relation of trust and confidence, which disables each co-tenant from doing anything which would prejudice the others in reference to the common property.

56. Gentry v. Gentry, 187 N.C. 29, 121 S.E. 188 (1924); McLawhorn v. Harris, 156 N.C. 107, 72 S.E. 211 (1911); Kelly v. Davis, 211 N.C. 1, 188 S.E. 853 (1936); Hatcher v. Allen, 220 N.C. 407, 17 S.E.2d 454 (1941); Sutton v. Sutton, 211 N.C. 472, 190 S.E. 718 (1937). *Accord,* Tilley v. Tilley, 24 N.C. App. 424, 210 S.E.2d 872 (1975).

57. Smith v. Smith, 150 N.C. 81, 63 S.E. 177 (1908), sets out the fiduciary relationship between tenants in common very clearly. That case states: "Tenants in common by descent are placed in confidential relations to each other by operation of law, as to the joint property, and the same duties are imposed as if a joint trust were created by contract between them or the act of a third party. Being associated in interest as tenants in common, an implied obligation exists to sustain the common interest. The reciprocal obligation will be enforced in equity as a trust. These relations of trust and confidence bind all to put forth their best exertions and to embrace every opportunity to protect and secure their common interest and forbid the assumption of a hostile attitude by either."

58. Tilley v. Tilley, 24 N.C. App. 424, 210 S.E.2d 872 (1975).

59. *Id.*

60. *Id.*

61. If a co-tenant purchases, either directly or indirectly, at a foreclosure sale under a mortgage or deed of trust binding on all the co-tenants, his purchase enures to the benefit of his co-tenants, and he will be regarded as a trustee for his other co-tenants. Hatcher v. Allen, 220 N.C. 407, 17 S.E.2d 454 (1941). If a third person, a stranger, buys in at the foreclosure sale and subsequently conveys to one of the co-tenants, a question arises as to

It should be noted, however, that the foregoing rule does not prevent an heir who is a tenant in common from purchasing the entire property at a foreclosure sale to pay an encumbrance executed by the ancestor of all the tenants in common. He acquires the whole title discharged of any trust for his co-heirs.[62] Nor does the rule prevent one co-tenant from acquiring the interest of another tenant in common under an execution sale to pay a debt of such other co-tenant.[63]

It should be further noted that frequently persons who are tenants in common are also members of the same family, or otherwise closely associated, which may give rise to particular confidential or fiduciary relationships that prevent one co-tenant from taking advantage of another co-tenant with respect to property held in common.[64]

§ 117. Taxes; Interest.

Since the payment of taxes is necessary to protect the common property, and each tenant is under an obligation to preserve the common property, if one tenant in common pays more than his proportionate share of the taxes to preserve the land from tax foreclosure, he is entitled to contribution from his co-owners. The tenant who pays the taxes will have a lien upon the common property to secure his reimbursement.[65] This has

---

the good faith of the purchasing co-tenant. If it appears that the purchase by the third person was only nominal, that in making the purchase he was merely acting as the agent of one of the co-tenants, a deed to the third person will be considered a mere matter of form and the co-tenant who acquires the title from such third person will be deemed to hold in trust for his fellow co-tenants. If, however, a third person, without collusion, purchases the common property at a sale for the debt of all the co-tenants, and afterwards conveys the title to one of the co-tenants, such co-tenant will take good title to the property in his own right, good as against his other co-tenants. Hatcher v. Allen, *supra;* Jackson v. Baird, 148 N.C. 29, 61 S.E. 632 (1908); McLawhorn v. Harris, 156 N.C. 107, 72 S.E. 211 (1911); Everhart v. Adderton, 175 N.C. 403, 95 S.E. 614 (1918). If upon the foreclosure the property is sold to a third party in good faith, and it has not been brought about by wilful and intentional default by one of the co-tenants, each of the former co-tenants is free to purchase from the third person who acquired title at the foreclosure sale. Hatcher v. Allen, *supra.*

62. Jackson v. Baird, 148 N.C. 29, 61 S.E. 632 (1908).
63. *Id.*
64. For instance, under some circumstances the relationship may be so close that one co-tenant is under an obligation to reveal facts with respect to the common property which he would be under no obligation to reveal to a stranger. *See* 4 POWELL, REAL PROPERTY § 605 (1968).
65. Holt v. Couch, 125 N.C. 456, 460, 34 S.E. 703 (1899); 1 MORDECAI, LAW LECTURES 627 (1916). *See* N.C. GEN. STAT. § 105-363 setting forth a procedure by which a tenant in common or joint tenant can obtain a release of a tax lien from his share by payment of a proportionate share of the taxes. The statute also allows a tenant in common or joint tenant to pay the entire amount of the taxes under specified conditions and thereby obtain a lien upon the shares of the other joint owners. This statute is apparently meant to refer to situations where all of the tenants are on the same footing; *i.e.,* with all or none being in possession. Smith v. Smith, 150 N.C. 81, 63 S.E. 177 (1908), a case dealing with former revisal, § 2860, a predecessor to N.C. GEN. STAT. § 105-363. *See also* CAMPBELL, PROPERTY

also been held to be true with respect to interest paid by one tenant in common on an existing encumbrance.[66] There are no cases in North Carolina on the point but it is generally held that if the co-tenant who pays the taxes is in exclusive possession of the common property, he is not entitled to contribution for expenditures made for ordinary taxes assessed against the property during his occupancy.[67] The same rule is applicable to payments of ordinary interest.

§ 118. Repairs and Improvements.

If repairs become necessary to the common property and one co-tenant pays for such necessary repairs which are made to preserve the property,[68] he is entitled to contribution from his fellow co-tenants in a court of equity. In most jurisdictions a co-tenant who is in possession of the common property is not entitled to compensation for expenditures made for repairs to the common property while he is in possession.[69] One recent North Carolina decision addresses this issue for the first time in this

---

TAX COLLECTION IN NORTH CAROLINA 116-18 (1974), which discusses rights of a tenant in common who pays taxes.

Wall v. Wall, 24 N.C. App. 725, 212 S.E.2d 238 (1975), holds that a former wife, upon partition of property which had been held by husband and wife as an estate by the entirety during their marriage, was not entitled to any reimbursement for sums paid by her on an indebtedness encumbering the property during the marriage. But with respect to sums paid by the wife in such case *after a judgment of absolute divorce,* the wife was entitled to credit for sums paid by her on the indebtedness. *See* Henson v. Henson, 236 N.C. 429, 72 S.E.2d 873 (1952), which holds that upon partition a tenant in common who has paid or assumed liens or encumbrances on the common property ordinarily is entitled to a proportionate reimbursement therefor from his other co-tenants.

66. *See* 2 AMERICAN LAW OF PROPERTY § 6.17 (Casner ed. 1952).

67. 2 AMERICAN LAW OF PROPERTY § 6.17 (Casner ed. 1952). *See* CAMPBELL, PROPERTY TAX COLLECTION IN NORTH CAROLINA 116-18 (1974), in which the author notes Smith v. Smith, 150 N.C. 81, 63 S.E. 177 (1908). The Supreme Court of North Carolina held that a tenant in common *in actual possession of the land* cannot allow the common property to be sold for taxes and purchase the title to the land for his exclusive benefit. His co-tenants are entitled to be let into possession with him and there should be an accounting with respect to waste, betterments, disbursements for taxes and receipts of rents and profits. This conclusion is based on the ground of the tenant's occupation of the entire property and his breach of duty in allowing the sale to take place, and in taking advantage of his own wrong by purchasing the property. *See* Ruark v. Harper, 178 N.C. 240, 252, 100 S.E. 584, 585 (1914); Bailey v. Howell, 209 N.C. 712, 184 S.E. 476 (1936). *See also* Craver v. Craver, 41 N.C. App. 606, 255 S.E.2d 253 (1979), holding that a co-tenant in exclusive possession of the property by virtue of a divorce decree was not entitled to compensation from the other co-tenant for expenditures made for repairs to the common property.

68. 1 MORDECAI, LAW LECTURES 626 (1916). *See* Holt v. Couch, 125 N.C. 456, 34 S.E. 703 (1899); MINOR & WURTS, REAL PROPERTY § 759 (1910).

69. Calvert v. Aldrich, 99 Mass. 74 (1868); Mastbaum v. Mastbaum, 126 N.J. Eq. 366, 9 A.2d 51 (1939).

jurisdiction and adopts this view.[70] In such cases the value of the possession and enjoyment of the common property is deemed to compensate the repairing co-tenant.[71] If the common property is income-producing property, however, compensation can be had. As a practical matter, the question of contribution usually arises upon a partition or when an action is brought against the repairing co-tenant to compel him to account for the rents and profits from the land involved; he is allowed credit for expenditures made for necessary repairs.[72] Statements are sometimes made indicating that no *affirmative* relief will be afforded to the co-tenant who makes repairs and that his right to equitable contribution will be limited to cases in which an accounting is required.[73]

With respect to *improvements,* as distinguished from repairs, however, the general rule is that a co-tenant who pays for such improvements is not entitled to affirmative contribution toward their cost. Nor is he credited with such payment in an accounting action for rents and profits.[74] But if there is a partition of the common lands, and one co-tenant has made expenditures for improvements to the lands, justice and fairness demand that the co-tenant who made the improvements entirely at his own expense should get the benefit of them if that result can be accomplished without injury to the others.[75] Thus, if the enhanced common property is actually divided, that part on which such improvements stand can be set off to the tenant who made the improvements if this can be done without unfairness to the others, each receiving his full share of the land as he would if the improvements had not been made. If an actual division cannot be made without injustice to any co-tenant, a sale can be ordered, and in the division of the proceeds the tenant who has made the improve-

---

70. *See* Craver v. Craver, 41 N.C. App. 606, 255 S.E.2d 253 (1979), citing this section in the original edition, and holding that a co-tenant in exclusive possession of the property by virtue of a divorce decree was not entitled to compensation from the other co-tenant for expenditures made for repairs to the common property.

71. *See* 4 AMERICAN LAW OF PROPERTY § 6.18 (Casner ed. 1952).

72. 4 AMERICAN LAW OF PROPERTY § 6.18 (Casner ed. 1952). Craver v. Craver, 41 N.C. App. 606, 255 S.E.2d 253 (1979), involved an affirmative action for contribution by the occupying co-tenant against the nonoccupying one. The final sentence of the decision reads: "The question of what the plaintiff's position would be upon a partition of the property is not before us."

73. *E.g.,* where there is a partition and the co-tenants seek an accounting of rents and profits from income-producing common property. *See* 4 AMERICAN LAW OF PROPERTY § 6.18 (Casner ed. 1952); Holt v. Couch, 125 N.C. 456, 34 S.E. 703 (1899).

74. 4 AMERICAN LAW OF PROPERTY § 6.18 (Casner ed. 1952).

75. Pope v. Whitehead, 68 N.C. 181 (1873); Holt v. Couch, 125 N.C. 456, 34 S.E. 703 (1899); Daniel v. Dixon, 163 N.C. 137, 79 S.E. 425 (1913); Cox v. Ward, 107 N.C. 507, 12 S.E. 379 (1890); Pipkin v. Pipkin, 120 N.C. 161 (1897).

ments can be awarded the additional amount which the property brings by reason of the improvements thereon.[76]

§ 119. Actions of Waste Between Co-Tenants.

While at the common law a tenant in common was not liable to his co-tenants for the commission of waste, under statute [77] in North Carolina an action may be maintained by one tenant in common against his co-tenant for the destruction of the common property.[78] In addition, a co-tenant may bring an action to restrain his fellow tenant in common from the commission of waste.[79]

§ 120. Actions of Ejectment Between Co-Tenants.

If one tenant in common ousts another or denies to him the right of possession of the common property, an action in the nature of ejectment can be brought by the co-tenant who is ousted to compel the tenant in possession to let the other into possession.[80] In order to maintain the action, it must be shown that there was an ouster by the possessing tenant.[81] In such cases the judgment, if in favor of the plaintiff, shall be that the plaintiff be let into possession as tenant in common with the defendant and not for the recovery of the whole tract.[82]

§ 121. Partition — Generally.

Each tenant in common is entitled, as a matter of right, to a partition of the common lands to the end that each may have and enjoy his share

---

76. *See generally* 4 AMERICAN LAW OF PROPERTY § 6.18 (Casner ed. 1952); 1 MORDECAI, LAW LECTURES 627 (1916). These results rest upon equitable principles and were recognized prior to the passage of N.C. GEN. STAT. § 1-340 relating to "betterments" which statute does not apply to improvements made by tenants in common. *But see* Harris v. Ashley, 38 N.C. App. 494, 248 S.E.2d 393 (1978), holding that where a tenant in common has a reasonable bona fide belief that he enjoys full ownership of property, he will be entitled to recover for betterments in a partition action.

77. N.C. GEN. STAT. § 1-536.

78. Hinson v. Hinson, 120 N.C. 400, 27 S.E. 80 (1897); Daniel v. Tallassee Power Co., 204 N.C. 274, 168 S.E. 217 (1933); Dearman v. Bruns, 11 N.C. App. 564, 181 S.E.2d 809 (1971), citing Jones v. McBee, 222 N.C. 152, 22 S.E.2d 226 (1942).

79. Morrison v. Morrison, 122 N.C. 598, 29 S.E. 901 (1898); 1 MORDECAI, LAW LECTURES 627, 628 (1916).

80. Jones v. Cohen, 82 N.C. 75 (1880); Witherow v. Biggerstaff, 82 N.C. 82 (1880); Harris v. Wright, 118 N.C. 422, 24 S.E. 751 (1896).

81. This can be shown by the tenant in possession denying the title of his co-tenant. *See* Jones v. Cohen, 82 N.C. 75 (1880); Witherow v. Biggerstaff, 82 N.C. 82 (1880); Harris v. Wright, 118 N.C. 422, 24 S.E. 751 (1896). Or by showning demand for possession and refusal to allow the plaintiff co-tenant to share possession. *See also* Huneycutt v. Brooks, 116 N.C. 788, 21 S.E. 558 (1895); Alexander v. Gibbon, 118 N.C. 796, 24 S.E. 748 (1896). A plea of sole seisin by the defendant will have the same effect. Alexander v. Gibbon, *supra*.

82. Vick v. Baker, 122 N.C. 98, 29 S.E. 64 (1898).

therein in severalty unless it is made to appear that an actual partition cannot be had without injury to some or all of the interested parties.[83] A "partition" is a division of the land between two or more tenants in common.[84] Every tenant in common is entitled, as a matter of right without the assignment of any reason for demanding such right, to obtain partition by instituting a special proceeding before the Clerk of the Superior Court.[85]

There are two distinct types of partition: partition in kind and partition by sale. A partition in kind is favored over a partition by sale, and a tenant in common is entitled, as a matter of right, to a partition in kind if it can be accomplished equitably.[86]

In the event it is made to appear by satisfactory proof that actual partition cannot be made of the land in kind by metes and bounds without injury to one or more of the co-tenants, the court may order a sale of the common lands in lieu of actual partition.[87] A sale will not, however, be ordered unless it is necessary to avoid injury to some of the parties.[88] The court has no jurisdiction to order a sale in the absence of allegation and proof that an actual partition cannot be had without injury to some or all of the parties.[89] The burden is on the party seeking sale for partition to

---

83. N.C. GEN. STAT. § 46-22; Seawell v. Seawell, 233 N.C. 735, 65 S.E.2d 369 (1951); Hyman v. Edwards, 217 N.C. 342, 7 S.E.2d 700 (1940); Talley v. Murchison, 212 N.C. 205, 193 S.E. 148 (1937); Foster v. Williams, 182 N.C. 632, 109 S.E. 834 (1931).

84. Edwards v. Batts, 245 N.C. 693, 97 S.E.2d 101 (1957); Smith v. Smith, 248 N.C. 194, 102 S.E.2d 868 (1958); Locklear v. Martin, 245 N.C. 378, 96 S.E.2d 24 (1956); Richardson v. Barnes, 238 N.C. 398, 77 S.E.2d 925 (1953); Murphy v. Smith, 235 N.C. 455, 70 S.E.2d 697 (1952).

85. N.C. GEN. STAT. §§ 46-1 through 46-34. *See generally* MCINTOSH, NORTH CAROLINA PRACTICE AND PROCEDURE §§ 2391-2407 (Wilson & Wilson ed. 1956). *See* Moore v. Baker, 22 N.C. 736, 24 S.E.2d 749 (1943); Chadwick v. Blades, 210 N.C. 609, 188 S.E. 198 (1936); Richardson v. Barnes, 238 N.C. 398, 77 S.E.2d 925 (1953); Coats v. Williams, 261 N.C. 692, 136 S.E.2d 113 (1964); Batts v. Gaylord, 253 N.C. 181, 116 S.E.2d 424(1960). An Assistant Clerk of Superior Court has the same powers as the Superior Court Clerk in partition proceedings under N.C. GEN. STAT. § 7A-102(b). Butler v. Weisler, 23 N.C. App. 233, 208 S.E.2d 905 (1974).

86. Phillips v. Phillips, 37 N.C. App. 388, 246 S.E.2d 41 (1978); Brown v. Boger, 263 N.C. 248, 139 S.E.2d 577 (1965).

87. N.C. GEN. STAT. § 46-22; Batts v. Gaylord, 253 N.C. 181, 116 S.E.2d 424 (1960); Coats v. Williams, 261 N.C. 692, 136 S.E.2d 113 (1964); Hyman v. Edwards, 217 N.C. 342, 7 S.E.2d 700 (1940); Butler v. Weisler, 23 N.C. App. 233, 208 S.E.2d 905 (1974).

88. 1 MORDECAI, LAW LECTURES 632 (1916); Seawell v. Seawell, 233 N.C. 735, 65 S.E.2d 369 (1951); Priddy & Co. v. Sanderford, 221 N.C. 422, 20 S.E.2d 341 (1942); Mineral Co. v. Young, 220 N.C. 287, 17 S.E.2d 119 (1941); Wolfe v. Galloway, 211 N.C. 361, 190 S.E. 213 (1937). A sale will not be ordered merely for the convenience of one of the co-tenants. Brown v. Boger, 263 N.C. 248, 139 S.E.2d 577 (1965); Butler v. Weisler, 23 N.C. App. 233, 208 S.E.2d 905 (1974).

89. Seawell v. Seawell, 233 N.C. 735, 65 S.E.2d 369 (1951); Butler v. Weisler, 23 N.C. App. 233, 208 S.E.2d 905 (1974).

show the necessity therefor.[90] He must show substantial injustice or material impairment of his rights or position by reason of a contemplated actual petition,[91] as where the value of his share would be materially less on actual partition than if the land was sold and the tenants were paid money equivalents for their shares.[92] If the court orders a sale in lieu of partition without first hearing evidence and finding facts to show the necessity of a sale to prevent injustices to some of the co-tenants, the cause will be remanded.[93] It should be noted, however, that the action of the court with respect to its determination that a sale for partition shall be held in lieu of actual partition, involves a finding of fact by the *court* to be determined by the trial judge alone, and does not raise an issue of fact for the jury.[94] The trial judge's finding of fact and order for a sale for partition is not subject to review except with respect to an error of law.[95]

§ 122. Same — Voluntary.

Co-tenants may voluntarily partition lands among themselves, and no particular form is required although a parol partition may not be enforced if the Statute of Frauds is invoked.[96] The power to convey, which is one of the self-evident incidents of land ownership, provides the basis for this right.[97] The most common method used to effect a voluntary partition is by exchange of deeds among the co-tenants. The process is repeated until

---

90. Brown v. Boger, 263 N.C. 248, 139 S.E.2d 577 (1965); Butler v. Weisler, 23 N.C. App. 233, 208 S.E.2d 905 (1974).

91. *Id.*

92. *See* Phillips v. Phillips, 37 N.C. App. 388, 246 S.E.2d 41 (1978), where the commissioners valued the property as a whole at $280,000, and as divided at $277,900. Concerning the question of whether actual division in kind would result in injury to the co-tenants, the court held that a $2,100 diminution in value, or $1,050 per co-tenant, was not a substantial or material impairment of the rights of the co-tenants. Therefore, an actual partition in kind would not be unconscionable under these circumstances. The court noted that court costs and commissioner's fees incurred in the conducting a sale would likely amount to more than the difference in values as found by the commissioners.

93. Wolfe v. Galloway, 211 N.C. 361, 190 S.E. 213 (1937); Seawell v. Seawell, 233 N.C. 735, 65 S.E. 2d 369 (1951); Butler v. Weisler, 23 N.C. App. 233, 208 S.E.2d 905 (1974). An attorney for a tenant in common has no inherent or imputed power or authority to consent to a sale in lieu of actual partition of his client's interest in property. There must be a finding that the attorney was given actual authority from his client to consent to a sale of his interest in the property.

94. Vanderbilt v. Roberts, 162 N.C. 273, 78 S.E. 156 (1913); Ledbetter v. Pinner, 120 N.C. 455, 27 S.E. 123 (1897); Brown v. Boger, 263 N.C. 248, 139 S.E.2d 577 (1965). This determination is made initially by the Clerk of Superior Court, without the necessity of a jury, subject to review by the judge on appeal, also without the necessity for a jury. Brown v. Boger, *supra*.

95. Albemarle Steam Nav. Co. v. Wovell, 133 N.C. 93, 45 S.E. 466 (1903); Tayloe v. Carrow, 156 N.C. 6, 72 S.E. 76 (1911); Brown v. Boger, 263 N.C. 248, 139 S.E.2d 577 (1965).

96. Miller v. Miller, 34 N.C. App. 209, 237 S.E.2d 552 (1977); Duckett v. Harrison, 235 N.C. 145, 69 S.E.2d 176 (1952).

97. 2 AMERICAN LAW OF PROPERTY § 6.19 (Casner ed. 1952).

each co-owner has a portion of the property set off to him by the deed of the other tenants. Traditionally, such partition deeds operate simply to sever the unity of possession and to separate the interests of the tenants in the common property.[98] Since 1969 the traditional rule has been altered by statute insofar as the creation of a tenancy by the entirety is concerned.[99]

§ 123. Same — Restrictions on Right.

Although the general rule is that each tenant in common is entitled, as a matter of right, to a partition of the common lands, it is equally well established in North Carolina that a co-tenant may expressly or impliedly waive the right to partition.[100] An agreement between tenants in common that common lands shall not be partitioned is enforceable, provided it is not for an unreasonable length of time.[101] Equity will not award partition at the suit of one in violation of his own agreement, or in violation of a condition or restriction imposed upon the estate by one from whom he claims, or where partition would be contrary to equitable principles.[102]

§ 124. Same — Practice in Partition Proceedings.

(a) *In general.* While compulsory partition by judicial action was historically a matter to be determined by a court of equity in North Carolina, since 1868 it has been governed by statute which provides for the parti-

---

98. Moore v. Baker, 224 N.C. 498, 31 S.E.2d 526 (1944); Valentine v. North Carolina Granite Corp., 193 N.C. 578, 137 S.E. 668 (1927); Virginia-Carolina Power Co. v. Taylor, 191 N.C. 329, 131 S.E. 646 (1926); Smith v. Smith, 249 N.C. 669, 107 S.E. 530 (1959); Combs v. Combs, 273 N.C. 462, 160 S.E.2d 308 (1968); *see* Scott v. Moser, 31 N.C. App. 268, 229 S.E.2d 222 (1976), in which three children of an intestate were tenants in common in intestate's lands and executed cross deeds of partition. The deed of one of the children was made to her and her daughter; the deeds of a second child's share was made to her and her husband; and all three deeds purported to convey remainder interests after a life estate or estates in the named grantee or grantees. The North Carolina Court of Appeals held that the cross deeds of partition operated only to sever the unity of possession and conveyed no title, and thus neither the first child's daughter, the second child's husband, nor any of the remaindermen obtained any title or interest by virtue of the partition deeds. The effect of the cross deeds was that the respective tenants in common thereafter held their shares in severalty.
99. N.C. GEN. STAT. § 39-13.5; *see* § 111, note 33 *supra*.
100. Mineral Co. v. Young, 220 N.C. 287, 17 S.E.2d 119 (1941); Chadwick v. Blades, 210 N.C. 609, 188 S.E. 198 (1936); Kayann Properties, Inc. v. Cox, 268 N.C. 14, 149 S.E.2d 553 (1966); *see* Hepler v. Burnham, 24 N.C. App. 362, 210 S.E.2d 509 (1975), which holds that a husband in a deed of separation can validly contract away his right to partition a home that was owned by him and his wife as tenants in common after a divorce decree terminated their tenancy by the entirety.
101. An agreement never to partition is void as an unreasonable restraint on alienation and therefore contrary to public policy. 2 AMERICAN LAW OF PROPERTY § 6.26 (Casner ed. 1952).
102. *See* a thorough discussion of these points in Kayann Properties, Inc. v. Cox, 268 N.C. 14, 149 S.E.2d 553 (1966).

§ 124 REAL ESTATE LAW IN NORTH CAROLINA § 124

tion of lands by a special proceeding instituted before the Clerk of the Superior Court.[103]

(b) *Venue.* The proper venue for a special proceeding to partition land is the county in which the land lies; if the land lies in different counties, the proceeding may be commenced in either county.[104]

(c) *Parties.* Anyone claiming a share in commonly held property may and should be made a party to a proceeding to partition the land. If a tenant in common is not made a party, he is not bound by the proceeding.[105] And if a tenant in common is named as a party, he is not bound by the partition proceeding unless he has been served with process.[106] Thus an unborn child is not bound by a decree of partition unless he has been represented by a class in which the interests are the same.[107]

While at the common law it was required that the action for partition could only be maintained by those having a possessory interest in the realty involved, in North Carolina remaindermen or holders of other future interests may maintain partition proceedings as between each other.[108] In no case, however, shall the partition interfere with the pos-

---

103. N.C. GEN. STAT. §§ 46-1 through 46-34; Brown v. Boger, 263 N.C. 248, 139 S.E.2d 577 (1965); MCINTOSH, NORTH CAROLINA PRACTICE AND PROCEDURE § 2391 (Wilson & Wilson ed. 1956). Even today, partition proceedings are consistently held to be equitable in nature, and as an incident to the exercise of general equitable jurisdiction the court will normally settle all the appropriate issues between the parties that are properly before the court. *See* Kayann Properties, Inc. v. Cox, 268 N.C. 14, 149 S.E.2d 553 (1966); Henson v. Henson, 236 N.C. 429, 72 S.E.2d 873 (1952); Raymer v. McLelland, 216 N.C. 443, 5 S.E.2d 321 (1939); Trust Co. v. Watkins, 215 N.C. 292, 1 S.E.2d 853 (1939); Roberts v. Barlow, 260 N.C. 239, 132 S.E.2d 483 (1963); Harris v. Ashley, 38 N.C. App. 494, 248 S.E.2d 393 (1978); Hepler v. Burnham, 24 N.C. App. 362, 210 S.E.2d 509 (1975). The rule that partition proceedings are equitable in nature does not require a divorced spouse to reimburse his former spouse for sums paid by the other spouse *during* their marriage to discharge an encumbrance on property that was owned by the entirety prior to their absolute divorce. Wall v. Wall, 24 N.C. App. 725, 212 S.E.2d 238 (1975). *But see* Henson v. Henson, 236 N.C. 429, 72 S.E.2d 873 (1952), which holds that a tenant in common who has paid or assumed liens or encumbrances on the property ordinarily is entitled on partition to a proportionate reimbursement therefor from the other tenants.

An Assistant Clerk of Superior Court has the same powers as the Superior Court Clerk in partition proceedings under N.C. GEN. STAT. § 7A-102 (b). Butler v. Weisler, 23 N.C. App. 233, 208 S.E.2d 905 (1974).

104. N.C. GEN. STAT. § 46-2; DuBose v. Harpe, 239 N.C. 672, 80 S.E.2d 454 (1954).

105. Henderson v. Wallace, 72 N.C. 451 (1875). *See* Carter v. White, 134 N.C. 466, 480, 46 S.E. 983 (1904); 1 MORDECAI, LAW LECTURES 631 (1916); Patillo v. Lytle, 158 N.C. 92, 23 S.E. 200 (1911).

106. *Id.*

107. Deal v. Sexton, 144 N.C. 157, 56 S.E. 691 (1907).

108. N.C. GEN. STAT. § 46-23; Moore v. Baker, 222 N.C. 736, 24 S.E.2d 749 (1943); Burton v. Cahill, 192 N.C. 505, 135 S.E. 332 (1926); Davis v. Griffin, 249 N.C. 26, 105 S.E.2d 119 (1959); Smith v. Smith, 248 N.C. 194, 102 S.E.2d 868 (1958); Richardson v. Barnes, 238 N.C. 398, 77 S.E.2d 925 (1953); Bunting v. Cobb, 234 N.C. 132, 66 S.E.2d 661 (1951); Priddy & Co. v. Sanderford, 221 N.C. 422, 20 S.E.2d 341 (1942).

session of the life tenant or lessee;[109] their rights shall remain unaffected.[110]

(d) *Pleadings in partition proceedings.*

(1) *The petition.* The petition for partition, in the form of an ordinary complaint in a civil action, must contain an allegation that the parties are tenants in common in the lands involved.[111] The petition should describe the lands involved and the interest of each tenant and state that the petitioner desires to hold his interest in severalty.[112]

(2) *The answer.* If the defendant co-tenant has been served and he does not file an answer to the petition for partition, the petitioner shall be entitled to an order for partition. Likewise, if the defendant co-tenant admits the tenancy in common, no question arises except with respect to the shares of the parties. If the defendant pleads *sole seisin* and denies the tenancy in common, this raises an issue of title and the proceeding for partition becomes in effect an action in the nature of ejectment, a civil action to try title.[113] When *sole seisin* is pleaded by the answer, an issue of fact as to the title arises which necessitates the transfer of the proceedings to the civil issue docket for trial before a jury.[114] When *sole seisin* is pleaded, the plaintiff petitioner has the burden of proving the existence of a tenancy in common.[115] The defendant co-tenant might also deny the existence of a tenancy in common by alleging that the co-tenancy involved is a tenancy by the entirety.[116]

---

109. Mineral Co. v. Young, 220 N.C. 287, 17 S.E.2d 119 (1941). *Accord,* Kayann Properties, Inc. v. Cox, 268 N.C. 14, 149 S.E.2d 553 (1966).

110. Bunting v. Cobb, 234 N.C. 132, 66 S.E.2d 661 (1951); Priddy & Co. v. Sanderford, 221 N.C. 422, 20 S.E.2d 341 (1942); Kayann Properties, Inc. v. Cox, 268 N.C. 14, 149 S.E.2d 553 (1966).

111. This is essential in order to confer jurisdiction. Gregory v. Pinnix, 158 N.C. 147, 73 S.E. 814 (1912); Pearson v. McKenney, 5 N.C. App. 544, 169 S.E.2d 46 (1969); 1 MORDECAI, LAW LECTURES 631 (1916).

112. Pearson v. McKenney, 5 N.C. App. 544, 169 S.E.2d 46 (1969). *See* 2 MORDECAI, LAW LECTURES 1413 (1916) for model forms of petitions and orders in partition proceedings. *See also* MCINTOSH, NORTH CAROLINA PRACTICE AND PROCEDURE § 2394 (Wilson & Wilson ed. 1956).

113. Ditmore v. Rexford, 165 N.C. 620, 81 S.E. 994 (1914); Sipe v. Herman, 161 N.C. 107, 76 S.E. 556 (1912); Gregory v. Pinnix, 158 N.C. 147, 73 S.E. 814 (1912); Graves v. Barrett, 126 N.C. 267, 35 S.E. 539 (1900); 1 MORDECAI, LAW LECTURES 631 (1916).

114. Gregory v. Pinnix, 158 N.C. 147, 73 S.E. 814 (1912).

115. Johnson v. Johnson, 229 N.C. 541, 50 S.E.2d 569 (1948); Lester v. Harward, 173 N.C. 83, 91 S.E. 698 (1917); Huneycutt v. Brooks, 116 N.C. 788, 21 S.E. 558 (1895).

116. Burke v. Harrington, 35 N.C. App. 558, 241 S.E.2d 715 (1978), where the defendant co-tenant answered the petition for partition alleging that the purported Florida divorce obtained by the plaintiff co-tenant was invalid because the plaintiff was not legally domiciled in the state of Florida at the time the divorce action was instituted and the decree rendered. The Court of Appeals held that the trial court erred in denying defendant co-tenant a trial by jury and in hearing the matter without a jury, since the defendant properly raised an issue as to the quality of plaintiff's title and was entitled to have a jury decide that issue.

(e) *Order for partition; functions and duties of commissioners.* If the pleadings raise no issues of fact requiring transfer of the partition proceedings to the civil issue docket, the Clerk will render a decree declaring the parties to be tenants in common in the land involved and will determine the respective interests of the parties. Pursuant to statute [117] the Clerk will appoint three disinterested persons as commissioners to make the partition of the land in kind if practicable.[118] If the land lies in more than one county the court may appoint additional commissioners from another county to join in making the partition.[119]

When the commissioners have been appointed and accept the commission under oath to do justice among the tenants in common according to their best skill and ability,[120] they meet on the premises and partition the land among the tenants in common by dividing the land into equal shares in point of value as nearly as is possible.[121] The commissioners then allot the shares to the tenants in common, either by specifically designating the person to receive each particular share, or where the shares are considered of equal value, the parties may be allowed to draw lots.[122]

If one tenant in common has made improvements on the property that tenant will be entitled, upon actual partition, to have that part of the property which he has improved allotted and assigned to him, and its value assessed as if no improvements had been made.[123] This procedure must not prejudice the interests of the other co-tenants.[124]

The commissioners shall, within a reasonable time, not to exceed sixty days after their appointment, make a full and ample report of their proceedings, specifying the manner of executing their trust and describing particularly the land or parcels of land divided and the share allotted to

---

117. N.C. GEN. STAT. § 46-7.
118. Sharpe v. Sharpe, 210 N.C. 92, 185 S.E. 634 (1936). *See* Dunn v. Dunn, 37 N.C. App. 159, 245 S.E.2d 580 (1978), holding that two commissioners could act for all in the purely ministerial duty of conducting a drawing for the allotment of shares.
119. N.C. GEN. STAT. § 46-7.
120. N.C. GEN. STAT. § 46-8. As to the form of the oath, *see* N.C. GEN. STAT. § 11-11.
121. N.C. GEN. STAT. § 46-10. The commissioners shall make their allotment by metes and bounds description. For the purpose of making a proper and accurate division, the commissioners are authorized to employ the county surveyor or other competent surveyor to survey and map the land shares involved. N.C. GEN. STAT. § 46-18.
122. Where there are tenants in common whose names are unknown or whose title is in dispute, such share or shares shall be set off together as one parcel so as to leave the other shares to be enjoyed by the owners without controversy. *See* N.C. GEN. STAT. § 46-13. Likewise, if two or more tenants in common petition to have their shares of partitioned lands allotted to them in common as one parcel, the commissioners may allot their several shares in common provided such division shall not be injurious or detrimental to any of the tenants. N.C. GEN. STAT. § 46-13. *See also* Dunn v. Dunn, 37 N.C. App. 159, 245 S.E.2d 580 (1978), holding that two commissioners could act for all in the purely ministerial duty of conducting a drawing for the allotment of shares.
123. Etheridge v. Etheridge, 41 N.C. App. 44, 255 S.E.2d 729 (1979).
124. *Id.*

each tenant in severalty, which report shall be filed with the Clerk of the Superior Court.[125] If, after the report is filed by the commissioners, there is no exception to the report within ten days of its filing, the same shall be confirmed by the court.[126] If exceptions are filed within the ten-day period, the Clerk shall hear and pass upon such exceptions, hearing such evidence as may be presented by affidavits or otherwise. If the Clerk sustains the exceptions, he shall make an order recommitting the report to the same commissioners for correction, or, where necessary, the Clerk may set aside the report in its entirety and appoint a new set of commissioners.[127] If the exceptions are not sustained by the Clerk, the report of the commissioners will be affirmed and from such ruling by the Clerk there may be an appeal to the judge, who may review the findings of the Clerk; but it should be noted that the judge on such appeal can consider only questions of law.[128]

When the commissioners' report is finally confirmed, such report and the decree of confirmation shall be enrolled in the Clerk's office and then certified to the Register of Deeds of the county in which the land is situated, and there registered as any other evidence of title. The registered report is binding upon all parties as a conveyance.[129] The unity of

---

125. N.C. GEN. STAT. § 46-17. The report may be made and signed by two of the three commissioners.

126. N.C. GEN. STAT. § 46-19; Floyd v. Rock, 128 N.C. 10, 38 S.E. 33 (1901). See Hewett v. Hewett, 38 N.C. App. 37, 247 S.E.2d 23 (1978), where the court refused to disturb the report of the commissioners because the exceptions were not filed within the ten day period. The decision notes that a report can be set aside after the ten day period only on grounds of fraud, collusion or mistake. A mere conclusory allegation that mistake existed will not suffice.

127. In a hearing on exceptions to the report of the commissioners the Clerk may (1) recommit the report for correction or further consideration, or (2) vacate the report and direct a reappraisal by the same commissioners, or (3) vacate the report, discharge the commissioners, and appoint new commissioners to view the premises and make partition thereof. Allen v. Allen, 258 N.C. 305, 128 S.E.2d 385 (1962).

128. When an order of the Clerk is appealed to a judge, the judge may not adjudge a partition of land different from that made by the commissioners. The judge may confirm the report in toto or he may vacate it and enter appropriate interlocutory orders in order that the same or other commissioners may make a new division. But the judge cannot, based on his findings, as to what would constitute an equitable division, adjudge a partition of the land different from that made by the commissioners. With reference to actual partition, it must be made by commissioners and not otherwise. Allen v. Allen, 258 N.C. 305, 128 S.E.2d 385 (1962). At any time prior to the confirmation decree, the court may also set aside the report of the commissioners and order a sale in lieu of actual partition. Hyman v. Edwards, 217 N.C. 342, 7 S.E.2d 700 (1940).

129. N.C. GEN. STAT. § 46-20; Weeks v. McPhail, 129 N.C. 73, 39 S.E. 732 (1901). Under the common law, a partition decree did not transfer or change legal title to any of the property, but the partition could be effected only by an exchange of deeds between the parties pursuant to the court's decree. Taylor v. Johnston, 289 N.C. 690, 224 S.E.2d 567 (1976).

possession of the tenants in common is severed and the title which the parties had before vests in them in severalty.[130]

(f) *Owelty of partition; applicable to actual partition.* Pursuant to statute [131] the commissioners are charged with the duty to equalize the shares of each tenant in common to the end that each shall receive an equitable partition. For this purpose the commissioners are empowered to place a charge on the more valuable tracts in an actual division with sums of money to be paid to those who receive less valuable tracts, in order to make the partition equitable. This charge, called "owelty of partition," is a lien on the land for which the land is responsible to prevent any injustice.[132] The recipient of a share charged with the owelty does not receive it completely until the charge is paid.[133] The owelty, which is not a personal debt, but an *in rem* charge, follows the land, bears interest, and may be enforced by execution.[134]

(g) *Petition and order for sale in lieu of actual partition; confirmation and decree.* If actual partition in kind cannot be accomplished equitably and fairly, a petition can be filed before the Clerk, describing the lands, the interests of the parties, and the fact that the land cannot be divided without injury and prejudice to the parties.[135] The burden of showing the necessity for the sale to prevent injury to one or more of the parties is on the party seeking the sale and the Clerk must decide whether or not the land is reasonably capable of actual division.[136] If the Clerk determines that the land cannot be divided in kind equitably and fairly without injury to one or more of the parties, he should make an order of sale.[137] The determination of whether or not the land is capable of actual division is a question of fact and not an issue of fact which requires a finding by a jury.[138] If it is deemed necessary, the court, either the Clerk or judge, may order that a part of the land may be divided in kind and the other sold for division.[139] As in the case of actual partition, the existence of a life estate in the land involved will not prevent the owners of a remainder

---

130. Carter v. White, 131 N.C. 14, 42 S.E. 442 (1902).
131. N.C. Gen. Stat. § 46-10.
132. Outlaw v. Outlaw, 184 N.C. 255, 114 S.E. 4 (1922).
133. *In re* Walker, 107 N.C. 340, 12 S.E. 136 (1890). A mere note given for the amount of the owelty will not discharge the lien until paid. Dobbin v. Rex, 106 N.C. 444, 11 S.E. 260 (1890).
134. N.C. Gen. Stat. § 46-11; Powell v. Weatherspoon, 124 N.C. 40, 32 S.E. 380 (1889); Newsome v. Harrell, 168 N.C. 295, 84 S.E. 337 (1915).
135. N.C. Gen. Stat. § 46-22; Seawell v. Seawell, 233 N.C. 735, 65 S.E.2d 369 (1951). For model form of petition, *see* 2 Mordecai, Law Lectures 1410 (1916).
136. Brown v. Boger, 263 N.C. 248, 139 S.E.2d 577 (1965); Kayann Properties, Inc. v. Cox, 268 N.C. 14, 149 S.E.2d 553 (1966).
137. *Id.*
138. Vanderbilt v. Roberts, 162 N.C. 273, 78 S.E. 156 (1913); Ledbetter v. Pinner, 120 N.C. 455, 27 S.E. 123 (1897).
139. N.C. Gen. Stat. § 46-16; Tayloe v. Carrow, 156 N.C. 6, 72 S.E. 76 (1911).

or reversion therein from procuring a sale for partition; such sale will not, however, affect the right of the life tenant to possession during his life tenancy.[140]

The court may direct either a public sale to the highest bidder,[141] or under certain circumstances may direct a private sale, where advisable.[142] No public or private sale of real property for partition will be consummated until confirmed (1) by the resident judge of the district or the judge regularly holding the courts of the district in those cases in which the sale was originally ordered by the judge, or (2) by the Clerk of the Superior Court in those cases in which the sale was originally ordered by the Clerk.[143] No confirmation can be had until the time for submitting any upset bid has expired.[144]

When the report of sale is confirmed, the decree shall apportion the funds among all of the co-tenants according to their respective interests, after making allowance to the commissioner who conducts the sale and for other costs of the proceeding.[145]

Article III. Incidents of Tenancy by the Entirety

§ 125. Disability of Either Spouse to Convey His or Her Share During Coverture.

While it was one of the incidents of the common-law joint tenancy that each joint tenant could convey to his co-tenant or to a stranger a distinct share in the property, the tenancy by the entirety differs radically from the common-law joint tenancy in this respect. In a tenancy by the entirety, neither spouse can individually transfer or encumber the real property in such a manner as will affect or defeat the other spouse's right of survivorship in the whole property.[145.1] Thus the assent and signatures

---

140. N.C. GEN. STAT. § 46-23; Kayann Properties, Inc. v. Cox, 268 N.C. 14, 149 S.E.2d 553 (1966).

141. N.C. GEN. STAT. § 1-339.33.

142. N.C. GEN. STAT. §§ 1-339.33, 1-339.35 through 1-339.38. *See* Ryder v. Oates, 173 N.C. 569, 92 S.E. 508 (1917).

143. N.C. GEN. STAT. §§ 1-339.28, 1-339.37.

144. N.C. GEN. STAT. §§ 1-339.28 (2) (b), 1-339.36 (b). If the sale involves the interest of a minor or incompetent, it must be confirmed by both the Clerk and judge.

145. The purchaser of lands at a sale for partition conducted by a commissioner appointed by the court is not under any obligation to see that the purchase price paid is properly disbursed. Perry v. Bassenger, 218 N.C. 838, 15 S.E.2d 365 (1948).

145.1. Stubbs v. Hardee, 461 F.2d 480 (4th Cir. 1972); Harris v. Parker, 17 N.C. App. 606, 195 S.E.2d 121 (1973); L. & M. Gas Co. v. Leggett, 273 N.C. 547, 161 S.E.2d 23 (1968); Moore v. Shore, 208 N.C. 446, 181 S.E. 275 (1935); Bank of Greenville v. Gornto, 161 N.C. 341, 77 S.E. 222 (1913); Gray v. Bailey, 117 N.C. 439, 23 S.E. 318 (1895); Meachem v. Boyce, 35 N.C. App. 506, 241 S.E.2d 880 (1978), citing this section in the original edition.

§ 125 REAL ESTATE LAW IN NORTH CAROLINA § 125

of both the husband and the wife are required to alien or encumber an absolute interest in entirety property.[146]

It should be noted, however, that in North Carolina where real property is owned by the entirety the husband has the absolute and exclusive right to the control, use, possession, rents, income and profits of the land during the joint lives of the husband and wife.[147] The result that flows from this

---

146. *See* First Nat'l Bank v. Hall, 201 N.C. 787, 161 S.E. 484 (1931), where husband alone had executed mortgage on entirety property. Husband predeceased the wife and when husband's mortgagee sought to foreclose his mortgage, the court restrained such foreclosure upon suit by the wife's mortgagee, who had taken mortgage from wife after the husband's death. *See also* Moore v. Shore, 208 N.C. 446, 181 S.E. 275 (1935), where the court held that a contract of the husband alone releasing land from a negative restriction was not binding on the wife since the husband and wife held a "negative easement" by the entirety. The court said: "[N]either can convey during their joint lives so as to bind the other, or defeat the right of the survivor to the whole estate," and that "Neither could encumber it or convey it so as to destroy the right of the other, if survivor, to receive the land itself unimpaired." *See generally* Bank of Greenville v. Gornto, 161 N.C. 341, 77 S.E. 222 (1913); Gray v. Bailey, 117 N.C. 439, 23 S.E. 318 (1895); Harrell v. Powell, 251 N.C. 636, 112 S.E.2d 81 (1954); Nesbitt v. Fairview Farms, 239 N.C. 481, 80 S.E.2d 472 (1954); Willis v. Willis, 203 N.C. 517, 166 S.E. 398 (1932); Capps v. Massey, 199 N.C. 196, 154 S.E. 52 (1930); Bryant v. Bryant, 193 N.C. 372, 137 S.E. 188 (1927); Davis v. Bass, 188 N.C. 200, 124 S.E. 566 (1924); Turlington v. Lucas, 186 N.C. 283, 119 S.E. 366 (1923).

See also Bryson v. Hutton, 41 N.C. App. 575, 255 S.E.2d 258 (1979), where a husband and wife owned land as tenants by the entirety. The husband established an account with his employer to provide materials and labor for the construction of a home on the entirety property, but the wife did not enter into any agreement with the employer. In a later suit brought by the employer against the wife on an unjust enrichment theory, the court held that where the employer knew of the legal status of ownership of the property, made advances based solely on the personal credit of the husband, and took no security interest in the land, it could not call upon a court of equity "to rescue it" from its predicament. The court distinguished Homes, Inc. v. Holt, 266 N.C. 467, 146 S.E.2d 434 (1966), where it was held that where a builder constructs a house through a reasonable mistake, and the landowner elects to keep the house rather than have it removed, the landowner must pay the value by which his property has been increased.

147. Hinton v. Hinton, 17 N.C. App. 715, 195 S.E.2d 319 (1973); Harris v. Parker, 17 N.C. App. 606, 195 S.E.2d 121 (1973); Dearman v. Bruns, 11 N.C. App. 564, 181 S.E.2d 809 (1971); Stubbs v. Hardee, 461 F.2d 480 (4th Cir. 1972); Koob v. Koob, 283 N.C. 129, 195 S.E.2d 552 (1973); Freeze v. Congleton, 276 N.C. 178, 171 S.E.2d 424 (1970); Lewis v. Pate, 212 N.C. 253, 193 S.E. 20 (1937); Moore v. Shore, 208 N.C. 446, 181 S.E. 275 (1935); First Nat'l Bank v. Hall, 201 N.C. 787, 161 S.E. 484 (1931); Johnson v. Leavitt, 188 N.C. 682, 125 S.E. 490 (1924); Dorsey v. Kirkland, 177 N.C. 520, 99 S.E. 407 (1919); Bank of Greenville v. Gornto, 161 N.C. 341, 77 S.E. 222 (1913); Bynum v. Wicker, 141 N.C. 95, 53 S.E. 478 (1906); West v. Aberdeen & R.R.R., 140 N.C. 620, 53 S.E. 477 (1906); *see In re* Perry's Estate, 256 N.C. 65, 70, 123 S.E.2d 99, 102 (1961); Smith v. Smith, 255 N.C. 152, 156, 120 S.E.2d 575, 579-80 (1961); Porter v. Citizens Bank, 251 N.C. 573, 577, 111 S.E.2d 904, 907-08 (1960); Nesbitt v. Fairview Farms, Inc., 239 N.C. 481, 486, 80 S.E.2d 472, 476-77 (1954); Williams v. Williams, 231 N.C. 33, 38, 56 S.E.2d 20, 24 (1949); Atkinson v. Atkinson, 225 N.C. 120, 129, 33 S.E.2d 666, 674 (1945); Wright v. Wright, 216 N.C. 693, 696, 6 S.E.2d 555, 557 (1940); Bryant v. Bryant, 193 N.C. 372, 378, 137 S.E. 188, 191 (1927); Davis v. Bass, 188 N.C. 200, 205-06, 124 S.E. 566, 569 (1924); Holton v. Holton, 186 N.C. 355, 361, 119 S.E. 751, 753 (1923); Moore v. Greenville Banking & Trust Co., 178 N.C. 118, 123-25, 100 S.E. 269, 272-73 (1919).

Control by the husband has come under increasing criticism in recent years and the

§ 125 CONCURRENT OWNERSHIP § 125

rule is that during their joint lives the husband may lease entirety lands without the joinder of his wife and his lease will be good against the wife during coverture and will fail only in the event the husband dies leaving the wife surviving.[148] The husband may likewise execute a mortgage or deed of trust on property held by the entirety without the joinder of the wife and mortgage or deed of trust will be effective during coverture, but it will not be effective to defeat or impair in any way the interest of the wife if she survives the husband.[149] Upon the death of the husband, if the wife survives, the mortgage executed by the husband will be automatically terminated and the entire estate, free of the security interest, will pass to the wife by survivorship unimpaired.[150] While the husband may also create an easement which will be valid during the joint lives of the husband and wife,[151] in no case can a conveyance by the husband affect or destroy the wife's right of survivorship without her written joinder and consent. Thus where a husband alone executed a mortgage on real property, the court enjoined the purchaser at the foreclosure sale under the husband's mortgage from cutting timber from the real property which would injure the wife's right of potential survivorship.[152] It should be noted, however, that a husband may validly execute a binding compromise settlement in a processioning proceeding with a contiguous landowner without the joinder of his wife.[153]

---

attorney dealing with a problem in this area should be aware of possible legislative developments. *Proposed* legislation, for example, would give the husband and wife equal right to use, possession, rents, income and profits of real property owned in tenancy by the entirety. It would also make judgment creditors of either spouse entitled to reach one half of rents, income and profits of tenancy by entirety property. *See* DAILY BULLETIN No. 56, Institute of Government, March 28, 1973.

148. The husband is entitled to the possession, use, income or usufruct of the property during their joint lives. He is not required to account to his wife for the rent received. Stubbs v. Hardee, 461 F.2d 480 (4th Cir. 1972); L. & M. Gas Co. v. Leggett, 273 N.C. 547, 161 S.E.2d 23 (1968); Bank of Greenville v. Gornto, 161 N.C. 341, 77 S.E. 222 (1913); Johnson v. Leavitt, 188 N.C. 682, 125 S.E. 490 (1924); Davis v. Bass, 188 N.C. 200, 124 S.E. 566 (1924); Moore v. Greenville Banking & Trust Co., 178 N.C. 118, 100 S.E. 269 (1919); Dorsey v. Kirkland, 177 N.C. 520, 99 S.E. 407 (1919); Bynum v. Wicker, 141 N.C. 95, 53 S.E. 478 (1906).

149. Subject to wife's right to take whole estate by entirety unaffected by husband's acts if she survives him, husband, during coverture, may, without joinder of wife, lease property, mortgage property, grant rights-of-way, and convey by way of estoppel. *See* L. & M. Gas Co. v. Leggett, 273 N.C. 547, 161 S.E.2d 23 (1968); Harris v. Parker, 17 N.C. App. 606, 195 S.E.2d 121 (1973); First Nat'l Bank v. Hall, 201 N.C. 787, 161 S.E. 484 (1931); Bynum v. Wicker, 141 N.C. 95, 53 S.E. 478 (1906); Willis v. Willis, 203 N.C. 517, 166 S.E. 398 (1932); Davis v. Bass, 188 N.C. 200, 124 S.E. 566 (1924); Moore v. Greenville Banking & Trust Co., 178 N.C. 118, 100 S.E. 269 (1919); Dorsey v. Kirkland, 177 N.C. 520, 99 S.E. 407 (1919).

150. Bynum v. Wicker, 141 N.C. 95, 53 S.E. 478 (1906); L. & M. Gas Co. v. Leggett, 273 N.C. 547, 161 S.E.2d 23 (1968).

151. Dorsey v. Kirkland, 177 N.C. 520, 99 S.E. 407 (1919); L. & M. Gas Co. v. Leggett, 273 N.C. 547, 161 S.E.2d 23 (1968).

152. Bynum v. Wicker, 141 N.C. 95, 53 S.E. 478 (1906).

153. Nesbitt v. Fairview Farms, Inc., 239 N.C. 481, 80 S.E.2d 472 (1954).

Another exception must be appended to the rule that neither spouse can individually convey his interest, in addition to the leases, mortgages, and easements executed by the husband that are effective during the joint lives of the husband and wife.[154] A spouse's conveyance of property held by the entirety may be effective to convey such a land in fee. Although a purported conveyance by a single tenant is ineffective to convey any fee simple interest in the estate if both spouses are living at the time of the conveyance, such an attempted transfer may become valid by the application of the concept of after-acquired title by estoppel.[155] Thus, if the husband, who holds land by the entirety with the wife, purports to convey the land in fee simple to a grantee while the wife is still living, the grantee will not take a fee simple title so long as the wife lives. If, however, the wife thereafter predeceases the husband, then the entire estate will vest in the husband as a result of survivorship, and his after-acquired title will enure to his grantee on the basis of title by estoppel.[156] Of course, if the wife survives the husband-grantor, the grantee will take nothing in fee by virtue of the husband's grant. The same principles apply if the wife makes a grant without the joinder of the husband.[157]

§ 126. Creditors' Rights.

In North Carolina, neither the individual creditors of the husband nor the individual creditors of the wife can reach entirety property by execution upon a judgment procured against either the husband or wife alone.[158] Joint creditors of both, however, can procure a joint judgment

---

154. By reason of the husband's right during coverture to the control, use, possession, rents, income, usufruct and profits, as set out in the text above.

155. On the general principles of title by estoppel, that when a grantor makes a conveyance when he does not have title and that a title subsequently acquired by the grantor enures to his grantee by estoppel, see Hallyburton v. Slagle, 132 N.C. 947, 44 S.E. 655 (1903); Willis v. Willis, 203 N.C. 517, 166 S.E. 398 (1932); Harris v. Parker, 17 N.C. App. 606, 195 S.E.2d 121 (1973).

156. Keel v. Bailey, 224 N.C. 447, 31 S.E.2d 362 (1944); Capps v. Massey, 199 N.C. 196, 154 S.E. 52 (1930); Harrell v. Powell, 251 N.C. 636, 112 S.E.2d 81 (1960).

157. Harrell v. Powell, 251 N.C. 636, 112 S.E.2d 81 (1960).

158. Stubbs v. Hardee, 461 F.2d 480 (4th Cir. 1972); L. & M. Gas Co. v. Leggett, 273 N.C. 547, 161 S.E.2d 23 (1968); Hodge v. Hodge, 12 N.C. App. 574, 183 S.E.2d 800 (1971); Grabenhofer v. Garrett, 260 N.C. 118, 131 S.E.2d 675 (1963); Edwards v. Arnold, 250 N.C. 500, 109 S.E.2d 205 (1959); Keel v. Bailey, 214 N.C. 159, 198 S.E. 654 (1938); Winchester-Simmons Co. v. Cutler, 199 N.C. 709, 155 S.E. 611 (1930); Southern Distrib. Co. v. Carraway, 189 N.C. 420, 127 S.E. 427 (1925); Johnson v. Leavitt, 188 N.C. 682, 125 S.E. 490 (1924); Martin v. Lewis, 187 N.C. 473, 122 S.E. 180 (1924); Harris v. Carolina Distrib. Co., 172 N.C. 14, 89 S.E. 789 (1916); Hood v. Mercer, 150 N.C. 699, 64 S.E. 879 (1909); Ray v. Long, 132 N.C. 891, 44 S.E. 652 (1903); Bruce v. Nicholson, 109 N.C. 202, 13 S.E. 790 (1891); see Davis v. Bass, 188 N.C. 200, 205, 124 S.E. 566, 569 (1924); Holton v. Holton, 186 N.C. 355, 361, 119 S.E. 751, 753 (1923); Bank of Glade Spring v. McEwen, 160 N.C. 414, 418-19, 76 S.E. 222, 224 (1912); cf. Lewis v. Pate, 212 N.C. 253, 193 S.E. 20 (1937).

See Produce v. Massengill, 23 N.C. App. 368, 208 S.E.2d 709 (1974), holding that, while

against the husband and wife on a joint obligation, and the judgment will become a lien on land held by the entirety and may be sold under execution to satisfy the judgment.[159]

The title to entirety property is not in the husband and wife individually or in shares. Title is in the husband and wife only as an entity. Thus, if a creditor of the husband procures a judgment against the husband on his individual debt, and another creditor procures a judgment against the wife on her individual debt, the two spouses could nevertheless convey a good title to a third person which is not subject to either of the judgments.[160] This is the reason that lenders and creditors compel husbands and wives to sign notes and obligations as co-makers, to make them jointly liable.

Since the husband has the exclusive right to possession and management of property held as tenants by the entirety, and is under no obligation to account to his wife for any rents or profits received from his use of the property,[161] it would seem logical for the husband's *possessory* rights in a tenancy by the entirety to be subject to execution to satisfy the claims of his individual creditors. While this is true in some states,[162] and the execution purchaser can acquire the husband's rights of possession and management during the joint lives of the husband and wife, subject

---

entirety property is not subject to execution to satisfy judgments against one spouse, proceeds of such property are the property of the husband and may be applied against the debts of the husband alone. The judgment creditor is not entitled to the appointment of a receiver, however. Note also the possibility of legislative reform in this area. *See also* § 125, note 147 *supra.*

159. L. & M. Gas Co. v. Leggett, 273 N.C. 547, 161 S.E.2d 23 (1968); North Carolina Nat'l Bank v. Corbett, 271 N.C. 444, 156 S.E.2d 835 (1967); Martin v. Lewis, 187 N.C. 473, 122 S.E. 180 (1924); *see* Edwards v. Arnold, 250 N.C. 500, 506, 109 S.E.2d 205, 209-10 (1959); Winchester-Simmons Co. v. Cutler, 199 N.C. 709, 712, 155 S.E. 611, 612-13 (1930); Johnson v. Leavitt, 188 N.C. 682, 685, 125 S.E. 490, 492 (1924); Davis v. Bass, 188 N.C. 200, 205, 124 S.E. 566, 569 (1924).

160. *See* L. & M. Gas Co. v. Leggett, 273 N.C. 547, 161 S.E.2d 23 (1968). *But see* Stubbs v. Hardee, 461 F.2d 480 (4th Cir. 1972), which indicates that a bankrupt husband and his wife, who owned a farm as tenants by the entirety, could not convey the farm away without substantial consideration so as to defeat the husband's creditors. This seems to conflict with North Carolina's law with respect to tenancies by the entirety as a basic proposition. It should be noted, however, that in Stubbs v. Hardee, *supra,* the husband had sought to retain possession of the property after his conveyance and had an understanding with his grantee that the husband could continue operation of the farm and that the farm would be reconveyed to the bankrupt husband and his wife after the claims of the creditors of the husband had been settled or barred. *See generally* Johnson v. Leavitt, 188 N.C. 682, 125 S.E. 490 (1924); Hood v. Mercer, 150 N.C. 699, 64 S.E. 897 (1909); *see* Edwards v. Arnold, 250 N.C. 500, 506, 109 S.E.2d 205, 209-10 (1959); Keel v. Bailey, 214 N.C. 159, 165, 198 S.E. 654, 658 (1938).

161. *See* § 125, note 147 *supra.*

162. *E.g., see* Raptes v. Cheros, 259 Mass. 37, 155 N.E. 787 (1927).

§ 126

to termination if the wife survives, in North Carolina a judgment creditor cannot reach the husband's possessory interest during coverture.[163]

It should be noted, however, that the husband's possessory interest *may* be reached and charged by court order for the support of the *wife* and his *minor children.*[164] The court may order the property to be rented to pro-

---

163. In Grabenhofer v. Garrett, 260 N.C. 118, 131 S.E.2d 675 (1963), the court held that a judgment creditor of the husband was not entitled to have a receiver appointed to rent entirety property to pay the husband's individual debt.

See Air Conditioning Co. v. Douglass, 241 N.C. 170, 84 S.E.2d 828 (1954), in which the court said that the husband alone could not make a contract with a laborer or materialman for which a laborer's or materialman's lien could attach to entirety property, in the absence of a showing of agency, ratification or estoppel which would bind the wife as well as the husband. H. & B. Co. of Statesville v. Hammond, 17 N.C. App. 534, 195 S.E.2d 58 (1973), accords with Air Conditioning Co. v. Douglass, 241 N.C. 170, 84 S.E.2d 828 (1954), to the effect that a materialman whose materials are furnished and annexed to entirety property is not entitled to have a lien enforced against the entirety property if the wife was not a party to the contract pursuant to which the materials were furnished. See also Leffew v. Orrell, 7 N.C. App. 333, 172 S.E.2d 243 (1970).

While property held by the entirety is not subject to execution to satisfy judgments against only one of the spouses, the *proceeds* of entirety property rented out by the husband are deemed to be the property of the husband in his own right against the wife and the rents paid to the husband may be reached by his creditors and applied in payment of the husband's individual debts. See Hodge v. Hodge, 12 N.C. App. 574, 183 S.E.2d 800 (1971), where entirety property had been rented out by the husband. When a judgment was procured by the creditor against the husband the court allowed the appointment of a receiver to receive all rental income due to be paid to the husband in excess of his personal property exemption. N.C. Gen. Stat. §§ 1-352 through 1-368. See also Stubbs v. Hardee, 461 F.2d 480 (4th Cir. 1972); Produce v. Massengill, 23 N.C. App. 368, 208 S.E.2d 709 (1974).

That the *proceeds* of a sale or insurance from real property held by the entireties are held by the husband and wife as tenants in common and thus one-half thereof is subject to the claims of the creditors of either spouse, *see* Stubbs v. Hardee, 461 F.2d 480 (4th Cir. 1972). *See also* Koob v. Koob, 283 N.C. 129, 195 S.E.2d 552 (1973); Forsyth County v. Plemmons, 2 N.C. App. 373, 163 S.E.2d 97 (1968).

But see Highway Comm'n v. Myers, 270 N.C. 258, 154 S.E.2d 87 (1967), in which the Supreme Court of North Carolina states with reference to compensation paid into the clerk's office in a condemnation proceeding that an involuntary transfer of title pursuant to a condemnation proceeding does not destroy or dissolve the estate by the entirety and that the compensation paid by the State Highway Commission to a husband and wife whose entirety property has been taken by condemnation continues to have the status of real property owned by the husband and wife as tenants by the entirety.

It should be noted that a judgment creditor is *not entitled* to have a receiver appointed to take possession of property held by the entireties in order to rent the property and to apply the rentals to the payment of his judgment. See Produce v. Massengill, 23 N.C. App. 368, 208 S.E.2d 709 (1974). *See also* the concurring opinion of Sharpe, J., in L. & M. Gas Co. v. Leggett, 273 N.C. 547, 161 S.E.2d 23 (1968).

164. Holton v. Holton, 186 N.C. 355, 119 S.E. 751 (1923); Wright v. Wright, 216 N.C. 693, 6 S.E.2d 555 (1939); Sellars v. Sellars, 240 N.C. 475, 82 S.E.2d 330 (1954); *see* Porter v. Citizens Bank of Warrenton, 251 N.C. 573, 577, 111 S.E.2d 904 (1960); *In re* Perry's Estate, 256 N.C. 65, 70, 123 S.E.2d 99 (1961). *Accord,* Hinton v. Hinton, 17 N.C. App. 715, 195 S.E.2d 321 (1973), which states that the rents and profits from entirety property which belong to the husband may be charged with the support of his wife since such rents and profits have the same status as other income and assets owned exclusively by the husband. *See also* Hodge v. Hodge, 12 N.C. App. 574, 183 S.E.2d 800 (1971).

duce an income to support the wife and children.[165] The court may also issue a writ of possession, pursuant to North Carolina General Statutes, § 50-17, giving the wife possession of the estate by the entirety in order that she may apply the rents and profits, as they shall accrue and become personalty, to the payment of alimony and counsel fees as fixed by the court.[166] The court has no power, however, to order a sale of the entirety property to procure funds to pay alimony to the wife or to pay her counsel fees.[167]

A tenancy by the entirety is not subject to sale under a tax foreclosure where the tax foreclosure is instituted against the husband alone, even though the tenancy by the entirety is listed for taxation by the husband in his own name alone as the owner.[168] The husband is not the owner of a divisible interest that is subject to execution. If an attempt is made to sell entirety property pursuant to a claim against only one of the spouses, an action may be maintained to restrain the sale because the purported execution sale would constitute a cloud on the title of the husband and the wife as an entity.[169]

§ 127. Termination.

The tenancy by the entirety may be terminated by a *voluntary partition* between the husband and the wife whereby they execute a joint instrument conveying the land to themselves as tenants in common or in severalty.[170] But neither party is entitled to a *compulsory partition* to sever the tenancy.[171] While an estate by the entirety can be destroyed and terminated by the voluntary joint acts of the husband and wife, as where the husband and wife voluntarily sell and convey real property owned by them as tenants by the entirety [172] (in which case the proceeds of the sale

---

165. Holton v. Holton, 186 N.C. 355, 119 S.E. 751 (1923).
166. Wright v. Wright, 216 N.C. 693, 6 S.E.2d 555 (1939); Sellars v. Sellars, 240 N.C. 475, 82 S.E.2d 330 (1954). *But note* that unless the wife claiming support is entitled to alimony or alimony pendente lite, she is not entitled to exclusive possession and use of her husband's entirety property. Hinton v. Hinton, 17 N.C. App. 715, 195 S.E.2d 321 (1973).
167. *See* Holton v. Holton, 186 N.C. 355, 362, 119 S.E. 751 (1923); Porter v. Citizens Bank of Warrenton, 251 N.C. 573, 577, 111 S.E.2d 904 (1960). The court has no authority to order the sale of land owned by the entirety in order to procure funds to pay alimony. Hinton v. Hinton, 17 N.C. App. 715, 195 S.E.2d 321 (1973); Koob v. Koob, 283 N.C. 129, 195 S.E.2d 552 (1973).
168. Duplin County v. Jones, 267 N.C. 68, 147 S.E.2d 603 (1966).
169. Harris v. Carolina Distrib. Co., 172 N.C. 14, 89 S.E. 789 (1916).
170. Moore v. Greenville Banking & Trust Co., 178 N.C. 118, 100 S.E. 269 (1919); Koob v. Koob, 283 N.C. 129, 195 S.E.2d 552 (1973).
171. Branstetter v. Branstetter, 36 N.C. App. 532, 245 S.E.2d 87 (1978); Miller v. Miller, 34 N.C. App. 209, 237 S.E.2d 552 (1977); Jones v. Smith, 149 N.C. 317, 62 S.E. 1092 (1908); Davis v. Bass, 188 N.C. 200, 124 S.E. 566 (1924).
172. *See* Koob v. Koob, 283 N.C. 129, 195 S.E.2d 552 (1973), citing Shores v. Rabon, 251 N.C. 790, 112 S.E.2d 556 (1960), and Wilson v. Ervin, 227 N.C. 396, 42 S.E.2d 468 (1947).

§ 127   REAL ESTATE LAW IN NORTH CAROLINA   § 127

become personal property and the husband and wife become tenants in common therein), an involuntary transfer of title pursuant to a condemnation proceeding does not terminate the tenancy by the entirety. The proceeds derived from a condemnation proceeding in which entirety property is taken retain the status of real property owned by the husband and wife by the entirety.[173]

A divorce *a vinculo,* an absolute divorce which destroys the unity of husband and wife that is essential to the existence of the tenancy, will convert an estate by the entirety into a tenancy in common.[174] The divorced spouses become equal co-tenants.[175]

A divorce *a mensa et thoro,* on the other hand, a divorce from bed and board which does not dissolve the marriage relation, does not sever the "unity of persons," and does not terminate or change the tenancy by the entirety in any way.[176] In this connection, it should be observed that an estate by the entirety is not terminated or dissolved by the acts of the parties which constitute mere grounds for an absolute divorce; there must be a final decree of absolute divorce for this effect to occur.[177]

A tenancy by the entirety is automatically terminated by the death of

---

173. *See* Highway Comm'n v. Myers, 270 N.C. 258, 154 S.E.2d 87 (1967); Koob v. Koob, 283 N.C. 129, 195 S.E.2d 552 (1973).

174. Waters v. Pittman, 254 N.C. 191, 118 S.E.2d 395 (1916); Smith v. Smith, 249 N.C. 669, 107 S.E.2d 530 (1959); Potts v. Payne, 200 N.C. 246, 156 S.E. 499 (1931); McKinnon v. Caulk, 167 N.C. 411, 83 S.E. 559 (1914); *see* Lanier v. Dawes, 255 N.C. 458, 462, 121 S.E.2d 857, 860 (1961); Smith v. Smith, 249 N.C. 669, 674-75, 107 S.E.2d 530, 535 (1959); Carter v. Continental Ins. Co., 242 N.C. 578, 580, 89 S.E.2d 122, 123 (1955); Wilson v. Ervin, 227 N.C. 396, 399, 42 S.E.2d 468, 469 (1947); Hatcher v. Allen, 220 N.C. 407, 409, 17 S.E.2d 454, 455 (1941); Fisher v. Fisher, 217 N.C. 70, 76, 6 S.E.2d 812, 816-17 (1940); Willis v. Willis, 203 N.C. 517, 520, 166 S.E. 398, 399-400 (1932); Davis v. Bass, 188 N.C. 200, 207, 124 S.E. 566, 570 (1924); Holton v. Holton, 186 N.C. 355, 362, 19 S.E. 751, 754 (1923); Turlington v. Lucas, 186 N.C. 283, 286, 119 S.E. 366, 367-68 (1923); Moore v. Greenville Banking & Trust Co., 178 N.C. 118, 126, 100 S.E. 269, 274 (1919); Finch v. Cecil, 170 N.C. 72, 75, 86 S.E. 992, 993-94 (1915); Jernigan v. Stokley, 34 N.C. App. 358, 238 S.E.2d 318 (1977), citing this section in the original edition. *Accord,* Koob v. Koob, 283 N.C. 129, 195 S.E.2d 552 (1973); Wall v. Wall, 24 N.C. App. 725, 212 S.E.2d 238 (1975). Where a husband and a wife own an estate for life by the entirety and are divorced, their estate is converted into a tenancy in common for life, and the survivor acquires only a life estate in an undivided one-half interest in the real property. Lanier v. Dawes, *supra.*

175. Wall v. Wall, 24 N.C. App. 725, 212 S.E.2d 238 (1975), holds that upon an absolute divorce, two former spouses become equal co-tenants in property that has been held as an estate by the entirety even though one of the former spouses paid the entire purchase price. Each spouse is entitled to an undivided one-half interest in the property and is entitled to partition the property. Lanier v. Dawes, 255 N.C. 458, 121 S.E.2d 857 (1961).

176. Freeman v. Belfer, 173 N.C. 581, 92 S.E. 486 (1917); Potts v. Payne, 200 N.C. 246, 156 S.E. 499 (1931); Davis v. Bass, 188 N.C. 200, 124 S.E. 566 (1924); Turlington v. Lucas, 186 N.C. 283, 119 S.E. 366 (1923).

177. *See* Hatcher v. Allen, 220 N.C. 407, 17 S.E.2d 454 (1941), in which it is stated: "The existence of an estate by entirety is not dependent upon the good conduct of the respective tenants and it is not destroyed by the bad conduct of either."

either spouse. Upon the death of one of the spouses, the title to land held by the entirety vests absolutely in the surviving spouse in severalty.[178]

§ 128. Survivorship.

(a) *In general.* Since the unity of person is required for there to be a tenancy by the entirety, each spouse is considered to be the owner of the entire estate with the other spouse. Consequently, when one of the spouses dies, the ownership continues in the surviving spouse, who becomes the sole owner. No title or interest passes to the estate of the deceased spouse.[179] Real property held by the entirety cannot be devised or reached by the creditors or heirs of the deceased spouse. As stated in the outstanding case, *Davis v. Bass*:[180]

> Upon the death of one, either the husband or the wife, the whole estate belongs to the other by right of purchase under the original grant or devise and by virtue of survivorship — and not otherwise — because he or she was seized of the whole from the beginning, and the one who died had no estate which was descendible or devisable. It does not descend upon the death of either, but the longest liver, being already seized of the whole, is the owner of the entire estate.

The significance of the doctrine of survivorship is that the surviving spouse does not take by reason of the Intestate Succession Act in North Carolina or by reason of the deceased spouse's will, but takes by virtue of the original conveyance that created the tenancy by the entirety.[181] That which the surviving spouse takes by survivorship will not in any way affect what the surviving spouse takes under the Intestate Succession Act or under the deceased spouse's will.[182]

---

178. Davis v. Bass, 188 N.C. 200, 124 S.E. 566 (1924). Land owned by husband and wife as tenants by the entirety passes to surviving spouse by purchase when one spouse dies. The dying spouse has no estate in the property that is descendible or devisable. Mansour v. Rabil, 277 N.C. 364, 177 S.E.2d 849 (1970); Olive v. Biggs, 276 N.C. 445, 173 S.E.2d 301 (1970).

179. Underwood v. Ward, 239 N.C. 513, 80 S.E.2d 267 (1954).

180. 188 N.C. 200, 204-205, 124 S.E. 566 (1924). *Accord,* Mansour v. Rabil, 277 N.C. 364, 177 S.E.2d 849 (1970); Olive v. Biggs, 276 N.C. 445, 173 S.E.2d 301 (1970).

181. Wollard v. Smith, 244 N.C. 489, 94 S.E.2d 466 (1966). It should be noted, however, that for purposes of the North Carolina Inheritance Tax real property held by the entirety shall nevertheless be taxable to the surviving tenant to the extent of one half of its value. N.C. GEN. STAT. § 105-2 (7). Detailed federal tax provisions should also be checked. *See* Cox, *Estate Planning for Farmers After the Reform Act of 1976,* 14 WAKE FOREST L. REV. 577 (1978) at 586-91.

182. A question of "election" may, however, arise if the testator purports to devise the entirety property to a third person and also devises other property to his spouse. "Election" is a concept in equity in which a party is compelled to make a choice between the acceptance of a benefit under a written instrument, and the retention of some property already his own, which is attempted to be disposed of in favor of a third party by virtue of the same paper. The doctrine of election rests upon the principle that a person claiming under any document shall not interfere by title paramount to prevent another part of the same instrument from

(b) *Rights of surviving spouse who willfully and unlawfully slays spouse.* When property is held by spouses by the entirety and one spouse willfully and unlawfully slays the other, the former law [183] has been rewritten in order to treat slaying spouses equally. Effective January 1, 1980, North Carolina General Statutes, § 31A-5 provides:

> Where the slayer and decedent held property as tenants by the entirety, one half of the property shall pass upon the death of the decedent to the decedent's estate, and the other one half shall be held by the slayer during his or her life, subject to pass upon the slayer's death to the slain decedent's heirs or devisees as defined in G.S. 28A-1-1.

The term "slayer" is defined by statute.[184]

(c) *Simultaneous death.* Since 1947, North Carolina has had the Uniform Simultaneous Death Act, which provides: "Where there is no sufficient evidence that two joint tenants or tenants by the entirety have died otherwise than simultaneously the property so held shall be distributed one half as if one had survived and one half as if the other had survived." [185]

---

having effect according to its construction; he cannot accept and reject the same writing. Elmore v. Byrd, 180 N.C. 120, 104 S.E. 162 (1920); Lamb v. Lamb, 226 N.C. 662, 40 S.E.2d 29 (1946); Honeycutt v. Citizens Nat'l Bank in Gastonia, 242 N.C. 734, 89 S.E.2d 598 (1955).

An election by a surviving spouse, either to take the property that the will gives to him or her or to take the entirety property by survivorship (and not under the will), is required only if the will of the decedent spouse discloses that it was the testator's manifest purpose to put the beneficiary to an election. The testator's intention to put the beneficiary to an election must appear clearly within the terms of the instrument. Taylor v. Taylor, 243 N.C. 726, 92 S.E.2d 136 (1956); Honeycutt v. Citizens Nat'l Bank in Gastonia, 242 N.C. 734, 89 S.E.2d 598 (1955); Lamb v. Lamb, 226 N.C. 662, 40 S.E.2d 29 (1946); Wright v. Wright, 198 N.C. 753, 153 S.E. 321 (1930); Olive v. Biggs, 276 N.C. 445, 173 S.E.2d 301 (1970); Mansour v. Rabil, 277 N.C. 364, 177 S.E.2d 849 (1970); Lambeth v. Fowler, 33 N.C. App. 596, 235 S.E.2d 914 (1977).

If it appears that the testator *erroneously* thought that the entirety property was his own to dispose of by will and devised it to a third person, and devised other property to his surviving spouse, the surviving spouse is not put to an election and can take both the entirety property by survivorship and the other property devised by the will. Burch v. Sutton, 266 N.C. 333, 145 S.E.2d 849 (1966); Bank v. Barbee, 260 N.C. 106, 131 S.E.2d 666 (1963).

For a complete discussion of the applicability and requisites of the doctrine of election, see the discussion of Sharpe, J., in Bank v. Barbee, *supra*. *See generally* WIGGINS, WILLS AND ADMINISTRATION OF ESTATES IN NORTH CAROLINA § 147 (1964) and LEE, NORTH CAROLINA FAMILY LAW § 118 (1963).

183. Under the former language of the statute, if the wife was the slayer, one half of the property passed to the husband's estate upon his death and the other half was held by the wife during her life and passed to the estate of the husband upon her death; if the husband was the slayer, he held all of the entirety property for the duration of his life and upon his death the property passed to the estate of the wife. The former version of N.C. GEN. STAT. § 31A-5 is discussed in Porth v. Porth, 3 N.C. App. 485, 165 S.E.2d 508 (1969), and is held to be constitutional in Homanich v. Miller, 28 N.C. App. 451, 221 S.E.2d 739 (1976).

184. N.C. GEN. STAT. § 31A-3.
185. N.C. GEN. STAT. § 28A-24-3.

Part 3

Modes of Acquisition and Transfer of Title or Interests in Real Property

CHAPTER 8
REAL ESTATE BROKERAGE

§ 129. Real Estate Brokers' Contracts Not Within the Statute of Frauds.
§ 130. Broker's Right to a Commission.
§ 131. Broker's Obligations as Agent of Seller.
§ 132. Liability of Broker to Purchaser for Misrepresentation.
§ 133. Liability of Seller to Purchaser Because of Misrepresentations of Agent.
§ 134. Regulation of Real Estate Brokerage.

§ 129. Real Estate Brokers' Contracts Not Within the Statute of Frauds.

A contract between an owner and a broker whereby the broker is to negotiate a sale of the former's real property is not required to be in writing and is not subject to the Statute of Frauds.[1] But use of an oral listing contract often leaves the precise terms of the sale open to future dispute, and where the parties have not agreed to all of the necessary sale terms, the owner-principal can terminate negotiations with a prospective purchaser without liability to the broker for a commission.[2] Courts will imply certain terms in the listing contract itself when the parties have failed to mention or adequately describe them. A broker who is the procuring cause of a sale has been allowed to recover the reasonable value of his services, for example, where no mention of the amount of the commission was made in the listing contract.[3] In addition, a listing contract is not invalid where it is for an indefinite time period although it is revocable by the principal prior to the finding of a purchaser by the broker.[4]

§ 130. Broker's Right to a Commission.

Under the most common listing contract situation, a broker with whom

---

1. Thompson-McLean, Inc. v. Campbell, 261 N.C. 310, 134 S.E.2d 671 (1964); Carver v. Britt, 241 N.C. 538, 85 S.E.2d 888 (1955); White v. Pleasants, 225 N.C. 760, 36 S.E.2d 227 (1945); Palmer v. Lowder, 167 N.C. 331, 83 S.E. 464 (1914).
2. Thompson-McLean, Inc. v. Campbell, 261 N.C. 310, 134 S.E.2d 671 (1964), citing the following from 12 AM. JUR. 2d, *Brokers* § 187:

> "Where the listing agreement fails to fix the terms for the sale or exchange of property, or specifies only part of the terms with the understanding that further details are subject to negotiation between the principal and the customer, the principal has been held free to terminate the negotiations without liability to the broker. Moreover, in such a case the broker may be denied compensation unless he produced a customer ready, able, and willing to buy on such terms as the principal may require, or as he accepts, or unless the principal and the customer reach a definitive oral or written agreement."

3. White v. Pleasants, 225 N.C. 760, 36 S.E.2d 227 (1945); Lindsey v. Speight, 224 N.C. 454, 31 S.E.2d 371 (1944).
4. The principal must, of course, act in good faith. White v. Pleasants, 225 N.C. 760, 36 S.E.2d 227 (1945). N.C. Real Estate Licensing Board Regulation .0104 now sets forth a requirement for a definite termination date for listing contracts.

§ 130 REAL ESTATE LAW IN NORTH CAROLINA § 130

an owner's property is listed for sale becomes entitled to a commission whenever that broker procures a purchaser who is ready, willing and able to purchase the property on the terms specified by the owner.[5] If any act of the broker in pursuance of the broker's authority to find a purchaser is the initiating act which is the procuring cause of a sale ultimately made by the owner, the owner must pay the commission.[6] Where the ultimate sale is the direct and proximate result of the broker's efforts or services, the broker is considered the procuring cause of the sale.[7]

The listing contract is the basis of the legal relationship between the seller and the broker. The North Carolina Supreme Court, in a 1949 decision,[8] has stated:

> Agency is the product of a mutual agreement. It is a situation which cannot be forced on a person *in invitum,* and no presumption or inference of agency arises from the fact that a realtor, with a buying client, has contacted a person willing to sell, and has consummated the sale. The defendant had not listed his property with plaintiff or initiated any relation of that sort.[9]

The broker's right to a commission therefore rests wholly upon performance in compliance with the terms and conditions imposed in the listing contract unless waived by the seller.[10]

---

5. Thompson-McLean, Inc. v. Campbell, 261 N.C. 310, 134 S.E.2d 671 (1964); Sparks v. Purser, 258 N.C. 55, 127 S.E.2d 765 (1962); Bonn v. Summers, 249 N.C. 357, 106 S.E.2d 470 (1959); Eller v. Fletcher, 227 N.C. 345, 42 S.E.2d 217 (1945); Bolich-Hall Realty & Ins. Co. v. Disher, 225 N.C. 345, 34 S.E.2d 200 (1945); Reams v. Wilson, 147 N.C. 304, 60 S.E. 1124 (1908). Since the relationship between seller and broker is established by contract, there is absolutely no legal impediment to the conditioning of the payment of commission in a listing contract to some standard other than the "ready, willing and able" rule. By way of example, a commission might be tied to the requirement of a consummated transaction. Where there is no dispute in respect to plain and unambiguous terms of a contract there is no room for construction and the contract is to be interpreted as written. Ross v. Perry, 281 N.C. 570, 189 S.E.2d 226 (1972); Jones v. Realty Co., 226 N.C. 303, 37 S.E.2d 906 (1946); Barham v. Davenport, 247 N.C. 575, 101 S.E.2d 367 (1957).

6. Realty Agency, Inc. v. Duckworth & Shelton, Inc., 274 N.C. 243, 162 S.E.2d 486 (1968); American Trust Co. v. Goode, 164 N.C. 19, 80 S.E. 62 (1913); Hecht Realty, Inc. v. Whisnaut, 41 N.C. App. 702, 255 S.E.2d 647 (1979).

7. Hecht Realty, Inc. v. Whisnaut, 41 N.C. App. 702, 255 S.E.2d 647 (1979); Realty Agency, Inc. v. Duckworth & Shelton, Inc., 274 N.C. 243, 162 S.E.2d 486 (1968), further defining the term procuring cause at 274 N.C. 243, 251 as follows:

> The term *procuring cause* refers to 'a cause originating or setting in motion a series of events which, without break in their continuity, result in the accomplishment of the prime object of the employment of the broker, which may variously be a sale or exchange of the principal's property, an ultimate agreement between the principal and a prospective contracting party, or the procurement of a purchaser who is ready, willing, and able to buy on the principals' terms.' 12 C.J.S. *Brokers* § 91, p. 209 (1938). Accord, 12 Am. Jur. 2d *Broker* § 190 (1964).

8. Johnson v. Orrell, 231 N.C. 197, 56 S.E.2d 414 (1949).

9. *Id.* at 231 N.C. 197, 201, 202.

10. Sparks v. Purser, 258 N.C. 55, 127 S.E.2d 765 (1962); Insurance Co. v. Disher, 225 N.C. 345, 34 S.E.2d 200 (1945).

§ 131. Broker's Obligations as Agent of Seller.

Under a real estate listing contract, the broker becomes an agent of the seller-principal and acts in a fiduciary capacity.[11] This agency relationship places upon the broker an obligation of utmost fidelity and good faith toward the principal.[12] There is a legal, ethical, and moral responsibility on the part of the broker to exercise reasonable care, skill, and judgment in securing for the principal the best bargain and terms possible;[13] to scrupulously avoid representing any interest antagonistic to that of the principal in transactions involving the listed property without the explicit and fully informed consent of the principal;[14] and to make a full, fair, and timely disclosure to the principal of all facts within the knowledge of the broker which are, or may be, material in connection with the transaction involved and which might affect the principal's actions with respect thereto.[15]

§ 132. Liability of Broker to Purchaser for Misrepresentation.

A broker who makes fraudulent misrepresentations or who conceals a

---

11. Carver v. Lykes, 262 N.C. 345, 137 S.E.2d 139 (1964).

12. Mersky v. Multiple Listing Bureau of Olympia, Inc., 73 Wash. 2d 225, 437 P.2d 897 (1968). While not a North Carolina decision, this case provides an excellent discussion of the meaning of the agency relationship in the real estate brokerage area.

13. Mersky v. Multiple Listing Bureau of Olympia, Inc., 73 Wash. 2d 225, 437 P.2d 897 (1968); Carver v. Lykes, 262 N.C. 345, 137 S.E.2d 139 (1964), holding that, as part of the broker's duty to exercise reasonable care and diligence to effect a sale to the best advantage of the owner, the broker must first determine the reasonable market value of the land. The seller-principal has a right to rely on the broker's expertise in this area without independently investigating the matter. In order to recover against the broker on a negligence theory, the seller-principal must show a substantial discrepancy between actual market value of the property and the price obtained by the broker. The seller-principal may not blindly rely on the broker in all matters, however. *See* Harris v. Bingham, 246 N.C. 77, 97 S.E.2d 453 (1957), holding that the sellers could not recover damages from a real estate broker for a mistake made when the broker failed to reveal a right-of-way easement in the contract of sale where the sellers signed the contract of sale without reading it.

14. Real Estate Exch. & Investors v. Tongue, 17 N.C. App. 575, 194 S.E.2d 873 (1973), holding that an agent employed to sell his principal's property may not himself become the purchaser absent both a good faith full disclosure to the principal of all material facts surrounding the transaction and consent by the principal after such full disclosure. *See* Cotton Mills v. Manufacturing Co., 221 N.C. 500, 20 S.E.2d 818 (1942).

15. Mersky v. Multiple Listing Bureau of Olympia, Inc., 73 Wash. 2d 225, 437 P.2d 897 (1968). In *Mersky,* the broker failed to disclose to the seller-principal that the prospective purchasers were the sister and brother-in-law of a salesperson who was handling the transaction involved in the broker's office. At 437 P.2d at 899, the Supreme Court of Washington declares:

> Against the backdrop of these general principles, we are satisfied that, as a matter of almost universal application, the duties of undivided loyalty, good faith and full disclosure, running from the broker and his subagents to the principal, embraces the obligation to timely reveal to the principal any close ties of kinship which may exist between the broker, or a participating subagent, and a prospective and proffered buyer or seller as the case might be.

material fact when there is a duty to speak to a prospective purchaser in connection with the sale of the principal's property is personally liable to the purchaser notwithstanding that the broker was acting in the capacity of agent for the seller.[16] However, a purchaser may not blindly and absolutely rely on the representations of the broker where the purchaser has the means and ability to independently ascertain the facts of the matter in question.[17]

§ 133. Liability of Seller to Purchaser Because of Misrepresentations of Agent.

A seller of property, as principal, is responsible to a purchaser for injuries caused by the fraud of the seller's broker committed during the existence of the agency and within the scope of the agent's actual or

---

16. Norburn v. Mackie, 262 N.C. 16, 136 S.E.2d 279 (1964), where the broker grossly misrepresented the number of acres of pasture in a tract to a purchaser who was unable to make a personal inspection of the tract. Folger v. Clark, 198 N.C. 44, 150 S.E. 618 (1929), involving a stock broker. Childress v. Nordman, 238 N.C. 708, 78 S.E.2d 757 (1953), holding that a purchaser who relied on a broker's representation that a house was free of termites must prove that the representation was untrue at the time it was made. See Griffin v. Wheeler-Leonard & Co., 290 N.C. 185, 225 S.E.2d 557 (1976), holding that a real estate broker's statement that water accumulated in the crawl space of a residence "was probably left over from construction and it should dry up in a short time now" did not present an issue of fraudulent nondisclosure where there was no evidence that the broker knew that the manner of construction of the residence was likely to create a continuing water problem. In addition to the real estate broker, other persons involved in the transfer of property may also be liable to the buyer on fraud or negligence theories. See, for example, Johnson v. Wall, 38 N.C. App. 406, 248 S.E.2d 571 (1978), involving the liability of a termite inspection company for the issuance of a false report.

See also 2 RESTATEMENT OF AGENCY 2d, § 348, where it is said that:

> An agent who fraudulently makes representations, uses duress, or knowingly assists in the commission of tortious fraud or duress by his principal or by others is subject to liability in tort to the injured person although the fraud or duress occurs in a transaction on behalf of the principal.

Although not directly discussed in a real estate broker case in North Carolina, liability of the broker for misrepresentation of fact can be imposed on a negligence principle. In PROSSER, TORTS (4th ed.) 704 it is stated that:

> A representation made with an honest belief in its truth may still be negligent, because of lack of reasonable care in ascertaining the facts, or in the manner of expression, or absence of the skill and competence required by a particular business or profession.

(Citations include Houston v. Thornton, 122 N.C. 365, 29 S.E. 827 (1898), a case involving directors of a bank.)

17. Griffin v. Wheeler-Leonard & Co., 290 N.C. 185, 225 S.E.2d 557 (1976); Marshall v. Keaveny, 38 N.C. App. 644, 248 S.E.2d 750 (1978), where the outcome might very well have been affected by the fact that the plaintiff is an attorney. Goff v. Realty & Ins. Co., 21 N.C. App. 25, 203 S.E.2d 65 (1974).

See generally, Annot., Liability of Vendor's Broker or Agent to Purchaser for Misrepresentation as to, or Nondisclosure of, Physical Defects of Property Sold, 8 A.L.R.3d 550 (1966).

apparent authority from the seller.[18] This is true even though the seller did not have knowledge of or authorize the actions of the broker.[19] A seller will be precluded from enforcing a contract to convey against a purchaser who has entered into the contract in justifiable reliance on the fraudulent, negligent or innocent material misrepresentations of the seller's agent.[20] In one recent decision,[21] for example, the real estate agent unintentionally but falsely represented to a purchaser that the property was zoned for business purposes. Although the seller-principal knew nothing of the misrepresentation, it was held that it would be unconscionable to allow the seller to enforce the contract to convey and thereby profit from the purchaser's reasonable reliance on the false representation of the seller's agent.[22]

§ 134. Regulation of Real Estate Brokerage.

Real estate brokerage is regulated by statute in North Carolina [23] and a license issued by the North Carolina Real Estate Licensing Board is necessary before any person, partnership, association or corporation may lawfully act as a real estate broker or real estate salesman.[24] The purpose

---

18. Norburn v. Mackie, 262 N.C. 16, 136 S.E.2d 279 (1964), citing Thrower v. Dairy Products, 249 N.C. 109, 105 S.E.2d 428 (1958); King v. Motley, 233 N.C. 42, 62 S.E.2d 540 (1950); and Dickerson v. Refining Co., 201 N.C. 90, 159 S.E. 446 (1931). 1 RESTATEMENT OF AGENCY 2d, §§ 257, 258. Illustration 1 to § 258 reads as follows:

> A, agent of P, sells P's land to T, representing that a nearby river does not overflow it, although knowing that this is untrue and having no authority to make the statement. Relying upon the statement, T purchases the land. P is subject to liability to T in an action of deceit.

19. Norburn v. Mackie, 262 N.C. 16, 136 S.E.2d 279 (1964).
20. MacKay v. McIntosh, 270 N.C. 69, 153 S.E.2d 800 (1967). Whether or not the seller was personally liable to the buyer for the representations of the broker was not at issue in this decision. See 1 RESTATEMENT OF AGENCY 2d, § 259 (1) which reads: "A transaction into which one is induced to enter by reliance upon untrue and material representations as to the subject matter, made by a servant or other agent entrusted with its preliminary or final negotiations, is subject to recission at the election of the person deceived."
21. MacKay v. McIntosh, 270 N.C. 69, 153 S.E.2d 800 (1967).
22. MacKay v. McIntosh, 270 N.C. 69, 153 S.E.2d 800 (1967). See 270 N.C. 69, 72, 73: "A principal cannot repudiate statements made by his agent in the course of employment, and fairly within the line of his real or apparent authority, and he is bound by the agent's material representations of fact to the same extent as if he had made them himself." (Citing 3 AM. JUR. 2d, *Agency* § 264).
23. Chapter 93A, N.C. GEN. STATS. This chapter was declared constitutional in State v. Warren, 252 N.C. 690, 114 S.E.2d 660 (1960). N.C. GEN. STAT. § 93A-3 creates the North Carolina Real Estate Licensing Board to, *inter alia,* issue licenses to real estate brokers and salesmen and to issue bylaws, rules and regulations not inconsistent with the chapter and the laws of North Carolina generally.
24. N.C. GEN. STAT. § 93A-3. A "real estate broker" is defined in N.C. GEN. STAT. § 93A-2. *See* Real Estate Licensing Board v. Aikens, 31 N.C. App. 8, 228 S.E.2d 493 (1976); McArver v. Gerukos, 265 N.C. 413, 144 S.E.2d 277 (1965); *In re* Dillingham, 257 N.C. 684, 127 S.E.2d 584 (1962); Western Carolina Realty Co. v. Rumbough, 90 S.E. 931, 172 N.C. 741 (1916).

of the statutory regulation is to protect sellers, purchasers, lessors and lessees of real property from fraudulent or incompetent brokers and salesmen and the statutes are to be construed accordingly.[25] The Real Estate Licensing Board is empowered to revoke or suspend the license of a licensee when that broker or salesman is found guilty of various acts enumerated by statute.[26]

---

25. McArver v. Gerukos, 265 N.C. 413, 144 S.E.2d 277 (1965); Real Estate Licensing Bd. v. Aikens, 31 N.C. App. 8, 228 S.E.2d 493 (1976).

26. N.C. GEN. STAT. § 93A-6. The Board is authorized by this statute to initiate a hearing and investigation on its own motion; or, the Board must do so upon the verified complaint in writing of any person, provided such complaint with the evidence presented in connection therewith makes out a prima facie case. *See* Carver v. Lykes, 262 N.C. 345, 137 S.E.2d 139 (1964), holding that a real estate broker could maintain an action for malicious prosecution against the complainant where the complaint to the Board is made with malice and without probable cause.

CHAPTER 9

CONTRACTS FOR THE SALE OF LAND

Article I. Options

§ 135. Options Distinguished.
§ 136. Options: Tender of Purchase Price as a Prerequisite to Exercise.
§ 137. Options: Necessity of Consideration.

Article II. Contracts for Sale

§ 138. Subcategories of Contracts for the Sale of Land: The "Interim" and "Long-Term" Contract.
§ 139. Statute of Frauds Generally.
§ 140. Sufficiency of the Memorandum; Writings Which May Constitute the Memorandum.
§ 141. The Signature Requirement.
§ 142. Description of the Land.
§ 143. Statement of Names of Parties, Terms and Conditions.
§ 144. Doctrine of Part Performance Not Applicable in North Carolina to Take Contracts Out of the Statute of Frauds.

Article III. Breach

§ 145. Remedies for Breach by Vendor: Generally.
§ 146. Vendor's Misrepresentations as to Acreage, Area or Square Footage.
§ 147. Vendor's Misrepresentations as to Quality or Character of Property.
§ 148. The Parol Evidence Rule: Contract Versus Tort Cause of Action.
§ 149. Implied Warranty Where Builder-Vendor Involved.
§ 150. Remedies for Breach by Vendee.
§ 151. Risk of Loss: Uniform Vendor and Purchaser Risk Act and Doctrine of Equitable Conversion.

Article I. Options

§ 135. Options Distinguished.

An option is a continuing offer to sell given by the optionor to the optionee.[1] The chief distinguishing feature of an option is that the optionee is not obligated to purchase the property and may freely accept or not accept the continuing offer according to the terms of the option. As a contractually binding offer to sell is involved, subsequent negotiations and counter proposals regarding the proposed purchase which do not result in an agreement to vary the terms of the option itself will not constitute a rejection of the option by the optionee.[2] Absent special circumstances, time is of the essence with respect to an option to purchase

---

1. Lawing v. Jaynes, 285 N.C. 418, 206 S.E.2d 162 (1974); Ward v. Albertson, 165 N.C. 218, 81 S.E. 168 (1914).
2. Kidd v. Early, 289 N.C. 343, 222 S.E.2d 392 (1976); Trust Co. v. Frazelle, 226 N.C. 725, 40 S.E.2d 367 (1946).

and acceptance and tender must be made within the time required by the option.[3]

Once properly exercised in accordance with its terms,[4] an option is transformed into a contract to convey.[5] It then becomes specifically enforceable if it is otherwise a proper subject for equitable relief[6] and assuming it meets the requirements of the Statute of Frauds.[7]

The unexercised option does not create the relationship of vendor and purchaser,[8] and the optionee has no interest in the land, legal or equitable, but only in *in rem* right to exercise the option.[9] A 1975 amendment to North Carolina's Conner Act requires that an option to purchase be

---

3. Harris v. Latta, 40 N.C. App. 421, 253 S.E.2d 28 (1979), where an option to purchase contained in a lease provided that notice of exercise of the option was to be given "at least sixty (60) days prior to March 15, 1976," and the optionees gave notice of their intent to exercise on January 15, 1976. The Court of Appeals' decision was that, since 1976 was a leap year and since use of the words "at least" denoted sixty full days of notice prior to March 15, 1976, the optionees failed to give adequate notice as January 14, 1976 was the last day available for them to make timely exercise of the option. The North Carolina Supreme Court reversed holding that, unless there is something to show an intention to count only "clear" and "entire" days, the use of the phrase "at least" did not alter the normal rule for computation of time. Harris v. Latta, 298 N.C. 555, 259 S.E.2d 239 (1979). *See* Trust Co. v. Medford, 258 N.C. 146, 128 S.E.2d 141 (1962); Douglass v. Brooks, 242 N.C. 178, 87 S.E.2d 258 (1955). Absent a special circumstance or provision to the contrary, time is *not* of the essence in a contract of sale and purchase of land. Brannock v. Fletcher, 271 N.C. 65, 155 S.E.2d 532 (1967); Douglass v. Brooks, 242 N.C. 178, 87 S.E.2d 258 (1955).

4. Winders v. Kenan, 161 N.C. 628, 77 S.E. 687 (1913); Harris v. Latta, 40 N.C. App. 421, 253 S.E.2d 28 (1979); Edward v. Kalnen, 14 N.C. App. 619, 188 S.E.2d 742 (1972); Builders, Inc. v. Bridgers, 2 N.C. App. 662, 163 S.E.2d 642 (1968).

5. Kidd v. Early, 289 N.C. 343, 222 S.E.2d 392 (1976); Lawing v. Jaynes and Lawing v. McLean, 285 N.C. 418, 206 S.E.2d 162 (1974); Passmore v. Woodard, 37 N.C. App. 535, 246 S.E.2d 795 (1978).

6. Kidd v. Early, 289 N.C. 343, 222 S.E.2d 392 (1976); Byrd v. Freeman, 252 N.C. 724, 114 S.E.2d 715 (1960); Samonds v. Cloninger, 189 N.C. 610, 127 S.E. 706 (1952); Craig v. Kessing, 36 N.C. App. 389, 253 S.E.2d 264 (1978). *See* Passmore v. Woodard, *supra.*

7. N.C. GEN. STAT. § 22-2. Kidd v. Early, 289 N.C. 343, 222 S.E.2d 392 (1976); Carr v. Good Shepard Home, 269 N.C. 241, 152 S.E.2d 85 (1967); Craig v. Kessing, 36 N.C. App. 389, 253 S.E.2d 264 (1978); Hurdle v. White, 34 N.C. App. 644, 239 S.E.2d 589 (1977); Watts v. Ridenhour, 27 N.C. App. 8, 217 S.E.2d 211 (1975). *See* § 139 *infra,* for a further discussion of the Statute of Frauds.

8. 3 AMERICAN LAW OF PROPERTY § 11.17 (Casner ed. 1952).

9. Lawing v. Jaynes, 285 N.C. 418, 206 S.E.2d 162 (1974), quoting from Christopher, *Options to Purchase Real Estate in North Carolina,* 44 N.C.L. REV. 63, 64 (1965). *See* Gentry Bros., Inc. v. Development Corp., 16 N.C. App. 386, 192 S.E.2d 100 (1972), where the following question of law is presented and answered by the court at 16 N.C. App. 386, 388:

> May a contractor enforce a lien on real property for labor performed pursuant to a contract with a party who has an option to purchase the land but never exercises the option or otherwise acquires any ownership in the land? We hold that the trial court correctly decided this question in the negative.

recorded in order to give it validity and priority as against lien creditors or purchasers of the land for value of the optionor.[10]

One recent North Carolina Supreme Court decision, *Davis v. McRee*,[11] deals with the contemporary problem of the status of an option to purchase in a lease where the lease term has been extended in a general fashion without express reference to the option. In *Davis,* the original lease contained an option to purchase the premises for a price of $12,000 with all payments made as rental to be applied as part of the purchase price in the event of exercise. The original lease term had expired, the lessee remained in possession, and the parties met months later to add the following language to the end of the original lease: "The term of this lease shall be from Jan. 31, 1974 through Jan. 31, 1976." No mention was made of the status of the option contained in the original lease. Rejecting a mechanical formula in use in some jurisdictions, the court instead adopted the following test to determine whether or not the option was incorporated into the extension agreement:

> The better view, and the one to which we adhere, is that the ultimate test in construing any written agreement is to ascertain the parties' intentions in light of *all* the relevant circumstances and not merely in terms of the actual language used . . . The parties are presumed to know the intent and meaning of their contract better than strangers, and where the parties have placed a particular interpretation on their contract after executing it, the courts ordinarily will not ignore that construction which the parties themselves have given it prior to the differences between them.[12]

Applying this test to the facts in *Davis,* the court found that, while the language of the extension agreement did not tend to shed any light on whether the parties intended to extend the option to purchase, the subsequent acts by both parties did clearly indicate an intent to extend the option in that the lessees had in fact exercised the option and the lessor had proceeded to have the deed of purchase drawn up.[13]

§ 136. Options: Tender of Purchase Price as a Prerequisite to Exercise.

Does the optionee have to tender to the optionor the purchase price as a prerequisite to exercise of the option? A recent North Carolina Supreme

---

10. N.C. GEN. STAT. § 47-18(a) was amended effective October 1, 1975, to change the result in Lawing v. Jaynes, 285 N.C. 418, 206 S.E.2d 162 (1974).
11. 299 N.C. 498, 263 S.E.2d 604 (1980).
12. 299 N.C. 498 at 502.
13. The court also found that the latter extension agreement created a new estate for years separate and distinct from the previous one. Only rental sums paid during the new period, therefore, would be applied toward the option price. 299 N.C. 498 at 503, 504.

See generally Christopher, *Options to Purchase Real Property in North Carolina,* 44 N.C.L. REV. 63 (1965).

Court decision [14] contains a comprehensive treatment of options and answers this question as follows:

> Whether tender of the purchase price is necessary to exercise an option depends upon the agreement of the parties as expressed in the particular instrument. The acceptance must be in accordance with the terms of the contract. Where the option requires the payment of the purchase money or a part thereof to accompany the optionee's election to exercise the option, tender of the payment specified is a condition precedent to the formation of a contract to sell unless it is waived by the optionor. On the other hand, the option may merely require that notice be given of the exercise thereof during the term of the option.[15]

§ 137. Options: Necessity of Consideration.

Where consideration has been given for the option, the continuing offer to sell may not be withdrawn by the optionor prior to expiration of the option period.[16] If based upon sufficient and valuable consideration, an option contract will normally be specifically enforceable [17] subject to the usual equitable principles intertwined with that remedy. The effect of options under seal is a more troublesome matter. While a series of North Carolina decisions follow the traditional rule that options under seal will be specifically enforced in equity in spite of no consideration or nominal consideration,[18] one recent decision suggests that courts will look beyond the seal and inquire as to consideration where the remedy of specific performance is sought.[19]

---

14. Kidd v. Early, 289 N.C. 343, 222 S.E.2d 392 (1976).
15. Kidd v. Early, 289 N.C. 343 at 361, citing Parks v. Jacobs, 259 N.C. 129, 129 S.E.2d 884 (1963) (*per curiam*); International Speedway Inc. v. Aman, 1 N.C. App. 227, 161 S.E.2d 50 (1968); Kottler v. Martin, 241 N.C. 369, 85 S.E.2d 314 (1955); First-Citizens Bank & Trust Co. v. Frazelle, 226 N.C. 724, 40 S.E.2d 367 (1946); Christopher, *Options to Purchase Real Property in North Carolina*, 44 N.C.L. REV. 63 (1966).

See generally Christopher, *Options to Purchase Real Property in North Carolina*, 44 N.C.L. REV. 63 (1966); Annot., Option — Necessity of Payment or Tender, 71 A.L.R.3d 1201 (1976).

16. First-Citizens Bank & Trust Co. v. Frazelle, 226 N.C. 724, 40 S.E.2d 367 (1946), in which the court notes that, where the option is contained in a lease, the lease is sufficient consideration to support specific performance of the option. The option supported by consideration may not be withdrawn, and the right of a lessee-optionee to enforce an option contained in a lease is not affected by the death of the lessor-optionor. 226 N.C. 724, 728. See Byrd v. Freeman, 252 N.C. 724, 114 S.E.2d 715 (1960).

17. Pearson v. Millard, 150 N.C. 303, 63 S.E. 1053 (1909).
18. See cases cited by Christopher, *Options to Purchase Real Property in North Carolina*, 44 N.C.L. REV. 63 (1966) at 73, 74.
19. In Craig v. Kessing, 36 N.C. App. 389, 244 S.E.2d 721 (1978), aff'd, 297 N.C. 32, 253 S.E.2d 264 (1979), the sole matter before the Supreme Court being a parol evidence issue) the obligation of the optionee to seek a buyer for the land was held to be valuable consideration although no money was paid for the option itself. The court at 36 N.C. App. at 394 notes:

> It is true ... that, under common law, a seal, which was present on the option

Article II. Contracts for Sale

§ 138. Subcategories of Contracts for the Sale of Land: The "Interim" and "Long-Term" Contract.

Two distinct subcategories of contracts for the sale of land are involved in North Carolina real estate transactions although the court decisions often do not clearly discuss the distinction. For lack of any consistently used and officially sanctioned terminology, these categories will be referred to herein as the "interim" and the "long-term" contracts of sale.

The interim contract for the sale of land is normally a printed form agreement intended to evidence the offer, acceptance, and basic agreement whereby vendor agrees to sell and vendee agrees to purchase real property. It is an interim contract because its reign soon ends with the closing of the transaction when the deed is delivered. It is not a financing device, but contemplates that the vendee will pay the balance due on the property at the closing date, either by securing permanent mortgage financing or by simply using the vendee's own funds. Under an interim contract for the sale of land, possession of the premises normally remains in the vendor until the closing date.[20] Because of its relatively short tenure and because possession has not transferred, special equities in favor of the vendee occur less frequently when disputes arise under the interim contract. This can affect the relief that a court accords to a vendee when the vendor has breached the contract, and vice versa.[21]

The long-term contract for the sale of land, on the other hand, is a financing device in addition to being a contract dealing with the necessary details of the sale and purchase. It is, in fact, an agreement under which the vendee is buying property on the installment method with delivery of the deed reserved for a later date. Although possession of the property remains in the vendor if the long-term contract is silent on the subject,[22] the vast majority of long-term contracts transfer possession to the vendee at the beginning of the payment period. Legal title remains in the vendor as security for payment of the purchase price. It is this

---

agreement, imports consideration, *Cruthis v. Steele*, 259 N.C. 701, 131 S.E.2d 344 (1963). However, where equitable relief is sought, the court will go back of the seal and will refuse to act unless the seal is supported by consideration. *Id.*

Since *Cruthis v. Steele* involved a deed, the reliance upon it by the *Craig v. Kessing* decision is open to question.

See generally Christopher, *Options to Purchase Real Property in North Carolina*, 44 N.C.L. Rev. 63 (1965).

20. Unless the contract provides otherwise, possession of the property remains in the seller until closing.
21. Remedies for breach of the contract of sale are discussed at § 145, *infra.*
22. Brannock v. Fletcher, 271 N.C. 65, 155 S.E.2d 532 (1967).

long-term contract that is properly described by North Carolina decisions as analogous to a mortgage. Because of its long-term nature and because possession has often passed by contractual agreement, equities in favor of a vendee may come into play in default situations. In plain terms, the vendee will more often receive the proverbial "benefit of the doubt" in a long-term contract fact situation.

In all other respects — such as the question of whether a contract was formed in the first place, the adequacy of legal descriptions and other statute of frauds issues, and matters of contract law generally — the distinction between interim and long-term contracts is unimportant.

§ 139. Statute of Frauds Generally.

It has been said that "There is no stake for which men will play so desperately. In men and nations there is an insatiable appetite for lands, for the defence or acquisition of which money, and even blood, sometimes are poured out like water. The evidence of land title ought to be as sure as human ingenuity can make it. But if left in parol, nothing is more uncertain, whilst the temptations to perjury are proportioned to the magnitude of the interest. The infirmity of memory, the honest mistakes of witnesses, and the misunderstanding of parties, these are all elements of confusion and discord which ought to be excluded." [23]

For these reasons, North Carolina, along with all other states in the United States, has enacted a statute for the prevention of fraud and perjury, known to all lawyers as the Statute of Frauds, which requires all contracts for the sale of real property to be in writing if they are to be enforceable. The North Carolina statute, a derivation from the English statute enacted in 1677,[24] states:

> All contracts to sell or convey any lands, tenements or hereditaments, or any interest in or concerning them, and all leases and contracts for leasing land for the purpose of digging for gold or other minerals, or for mining generally, of whatever duration; and all other leases and contracts for leasing lands exceeding in duration three years from the making thereof, shall be void unless said contract, or some memorandum or note thereof, be put in writing and signed by the party to be charged therewith, or by some other person by him thereto lawfully authorized.[25]

Pursuant to this statute all agreements to sell and purchase any inter-

---

23. Woodward, J., in Moore v. Small, 19 Pa. St. 461 (1852).
24. 29 Charles II (1677).
25. N.C. Gen. Stat. § 22-2.

est in real property [26] are voidable unless in writing. For the contract to be enforceable it must be evidenced by a written memorandum. Examples from recent decisions include the following: In order to be specifically enforceable, an option-contract must meet the requirements of the Statute of Frauds.[27] Likewise, an oral contract to devise real estate falls within that statute's purveiw.[28] In the absence of fraud, mistake, or undue influence, an oral agreement to reconvey land is unenforceable under the statute.[29] Not all agreements relating to real estate are subject to the

---

26. Some agreements relating to "interests in real property" other than contracts for the sale of land itself, and to which the Statute of Frauds is applicable, include: (1) Contracts relating to easements. Winston Brick Mfg. Co. v. Hodgin, 190 N.C. 582, 130 S.E. 330 (1925). (2) Contracts relating to *profits à prendre,* by which one is given the right to take timber or coal from the land of another, to fish in water belonging to another, or to shoot over land, or to take game or wild fowl from the land of another. Council v. Sanderlin, 183 N.C. 253, 111 S.E. 355 (1922). (3) Contracts relating to water rights whereby land is to be overflowed as a result of the construction of a milldam. Ebert v. Disher, 216 N.C. 36, 3 S.E.2d 301 (1939). (4) Contracts purporting to create equitable restrictions whereby the purposes for which land can be used is restricted. Pepper v. West End Dev. Co., 211 N.C. 166, 189 S.E. 628 (1936); Davis v. Robinson, 189 N.C. 589, 127 S.E. 697 (1925). (5) Contracts looking toward the conveyance or reservation of standing timber. Westmoreland v. Lowe, 225 N.C. 553, 35 S.E.2d 613 (1945). *But cf.* Bishop v. DuBose, 252 N.C. 158, 113 S.E.2d 309 (1960), and Walston v. Lowery, 212 N.C. 23, 192 S.E. 877 (1937), in which it is held that a contract for the passage of title to timber *after severance* need not be in writing. (6) Contracts releasing dower or curtesy interests, now dower or curtesy substitutes under N.C. GEN. STAT. § 29-30. Luther v. Luther, 234 N.C. 429, 67 S.E.2d 345 (1951). (7) Contracts between co-tenants wherein they attempt to partition realty among themselves. Williams v. Robertson, 235 N.C. 478, 70 S.E.2d 692 (1952), Duckett v. Harrison, 235 N.C. 145, 69 S.E.2d 176 (1952). (8) Agreements to establish disputed boundaries if unaccompanied with a change in possession. Andrews v. Andrews, 252 N.C. 97, 113 S.E.2d 47 (1960). (9) Agreements to arbitrate controversies relating to title to land. Cutler v. Cutler, 169 N.C. 482, 86 S.E. 301 (1915). (10) Contracts purporting to create, assign or release rights under leases the terms of which have more than three years to run. Investment Co. v. Zindell, 198 N.C. 109, 150 S.E. 704 (1929); Herring v. Merchandise, Inc., 252 N.C. 450, 113 S.E.2d 814 (1960). (11) A contract *to give* security in land, a mortgage. Harper v. Spainhour, 64 N.C. 629 (1870).

27. Kidd v. Early, 289 N.C. 343, 222 S.E.2d 392 (1976); N.C. GEN. STAT. § 22-2. *See also* Pierce v. Gaddy, 42 N.C. App. 622, 257 S.E.2d 459 (1979).

28. An agreement to devise realty is likewise within the Statute of Frauds and unenforceable if not in writing. Rape v. Lyerly, 287 N.C. 601, 215 S.E.2d 737 (1975); Hicks v. Hicks, 13 N.C. App. 347, 185 S.E.2d 430 (1971); Pickelsimer v. Pickelsimer, 257 N.C. 696, 127 S.E.2d 557 (1962); Gales v. Smith, 249 N.C. 263, 106 S.E.2d 164 (1958); Grady v. Faison, 224 N.C. 567, 31 S.E.2d 760 (1944). But failure to prove a special contract will not preclude recovery upon a theory of implied contract or *quantum meruit* when one has rendered services in reliance upon a promise made by another to devise real property to him, which promise is unenforceable because oral. *See* Hicks v. Hicks, *supra;* Wells v. Foreman, 236 N.C. 351, 72 S.E.2d 765 (1952); Stewart v. Wyrick, 228 N.C. 429, 45 S.E.2d 764 (1947); Nesbitt v. Donoho, 198 N.C. 147, 150 S.E. 875 (1929). Instead of the unenforceable promise the law will allow the recovery of the reasonable worth of services performed in reliance on the promise.

29. But if the vendee of land fraudulently induced vendor to sign a deed conveying the land by representing that an option had been executed and would promptly be delivered to the vendor, the vendee may be estopped from pleading the Statute of Frauds to defeat the vendor's action for specific performance. Dunn v. Dunn, 24 N.C. App. 713, 212 S.E.2d 407 (1975).

§ 140   REAL ESTATE LAW IN NORTH CAROLINA   § 140

statute. An oral promise to release real estate from the lien of a mortgage or deed of trust does not come within the Statute of Frauds and is enforceable although not in writing.[30] A lease required to be in writing by the statute may be rescinded orally by the mutual assent of both parties.[31] A guarantee of acreage by the grantor need not be in writing.[32]

§ 140. Sufficiency of the Memorandum; Writings Which May Constitute the Memorandum.

No special form or instrument is required in order to be a sufficient memorandum to satisfy the requirements of the Statute of Frauds.[33] Letters,[34] notes,[35] telegrams,[36] receipts,[37] sales records,[38] drafts,[39] deeds,[40] pleadings [41] or other documents [42] may be sufficient. The memorandum need not be contained in a single document but may consist of

---

30. Nye Dev. Co., 10 N.C. App. 676, 179 S.E.2d 795 (1971); Stevens v. Turlington, 186 N.C. 191, 119 S.E.2d 210 (1923).
31. Investment Properties of Asheville v. Allen, 281 N.C. 173, 188 S.E.2d 441 (1972).
32. Hoots v. Callaway, 282 N.C. 477, 193 S.E.2d 709 (1973).
33. Smith v. Joyce, 214 N.C. 602, 200 S.E. 431 (1939).
34. Hines v. Tripp, 263 N.C. 470, 139 S.E.2d 545 (1965); Heiland v. Lee, 207 F.2d 939 (4th Cir. 1953). That it is not necessary for the letter to be addressed to a party to the contract, see Nicholson v. Dover, 145 N.C. 18, 58 S.E. 444 (1907).
35. Gordon v. Collett, 102 N.C. 532, 9 S.E. 486 (1889).
36. Simpson v. Burnett County Lumber Co., 193 N.C. 454, 137 S.E. 311 (1927).
37. Lewis v. Allred, 249 N.C. 486, 106 S.E.2d 689 (1959).
38. A sales record and settlement sheet signed by a seller and accompanied by a plat, showing that a certain lot was sold and the terms of the sale, was deemed a sufficient compliance with the Statute of Frauds in Greenberg v. Bailey, 14 N.C. App. 34, 187 S.E.2d 505 (1972).
39. Neaves v. North State Mining Co., 90 N.C. 412 (1884); Hurdle v. White, 34 N.C. App. 644, 206 S.E.2d 162 (1977).
40. A deed, delivered in escrow, is a sufficient memorandum to meet the requirements of the Statute of Frauds. Oxendine v. Stephenson, 195 N.C. 238, 141 S.E. 572 (1928); Pope v. McPhail, 173 N.C. 238, 91 S.E. 947 (1917); Austin v. McCollum, 210 N.C. 817, 188 S.E. 646 (1936) (where the deed was found among the grantor's valuable papers it was held sufficient to evidence contract); Magee v. Blankenship, 95 N.C. 563 (1886). An instrument which is in form a deed but which is not operative as a deed because not under seal or other defect, may nevertheless operate as a contract *to convey*. Willis v. Anderson, 188 N.C. 479, 124 S.E. 834 (1924); Robinson v. Daughtry, 171 N.C. 200, 88 S.E. 252 (1916).
41. The admissions of parties in their pleadings may supply the writing requirement. Sandlin v. Kearney, 154 N.C. 596, 70 S.E. 942 (1911). A mere recital, however, of a parol agreement in a pleading, which is not an admission by the party to be charged, does not bar the plea of the Statute of Frauds. Davis v. Lovick, 226 N.C. 252, 37 S.E.2d 680 (1946).
42. *E.g.*, the writing, by an auctioneer, on the side of an advertisement for the sale of land at public auction, of the name of the person who made the last and highest bid, with the amount bid, satisfies the statute and will bind the purchaser. Proctor v. Finley, 119 N.C. 536, 26 S.E. 128 (1896); Smith v. Joyce, 214 N.C. 602, 200 S.E. 431 (1939). An auctioneer at a sale is, at the time and for that purpose, the agent of both seller and buyer. Greenberg v. Bailey, 14 N.C. App. 34, 187 S.E.2d 505 (1972).

several interconnected papers [43] if the contract provisions can be determined from the separate but related writings and are signed as required.[44]

A revoked will may be a sufficient memorandum of a contract to satisfy the requirements of the Statute of Frauds, provided it adequately expresses the intention of the parties to make a contract and sets out the contracted obligations.[45] If, however, the revoked will does not set out contractual language, it will not be a sufficient memorandum. In order for a revoked will to constitute a sufficient memorandum to satisfy the Statute of Frauds, it must state or make clear reference to the agreement so that the duties and obligations of the contracting parties are known.[46]

§ 141. The Signature Requirement.

The writing must be "signed by the party to be charged therewith, or

---

43. To comply with the Statute of Frauds it is not necessary that all of the provisions of a contract be set out in a single instrument. The memorandum required by the statute is sufficient if the contract provisions can be determined from separate but related writings. Greenberg v. Bailey, 14 N.C. App. 34, 187 S.E.2d 505 (1972).

There need not be a single document; the memorandum may consist of several papers. The papers need not be physically attached if they are connected by internal reference. Mezzanotte v. Freeland, 20 N.C. App. 11, 200 S.E.2d 410 (1973); Smith v. Joyce, 214 N.C. 602, 200 S.E. 431 (1939); Mayer v. Adrian, 77 N.C. 83 (1877).

44. "The note or memorandum required by the Statute of Frauds need not be contained in a single document, nor, when contained in two or more papers, need each paper be sufficient in contents and signature to satisfy the statute. Two or more writings properly connected may be considered together, matters missing or uncertain in one may be supplied or rendered certain by the other, and their sufficiency will depend upon whether, taken together, they meet the requirements of the statute as to contents and signature. The rule is frequently applied to two or more, or a series of letters or telegrams, or letters and telegrams sufficiently connected to allow their consideration together. But the rule is not confined in its application to letters and telegrams; any other documents can be read together when one refers to the other. The rule has been applied so as to allow the consideration together, when properly connected, of a letter and an order of court, a letter and an order for goods, letters and undelivered deeds, correspondence and accompanying papers, a check and a letter, a receipt and a check, a memorandum of agreement and a deed, and a contract, deed, and instructions to a depositary in escrow. Matters not contained in one paper, or not stated therein with sufficient definiteness and certainty, such as the name of a party, a description of the subject matter, a statement of the consideration, or the terms of payment, are frequently found to be adequately stated in another paper to justify their consideration together." Simpson v. Lumber Co., 193 N.C. 454, 137 S.E. 311 (1927). *See* Greenberg v. Bailey, 14 N.C. App. 34, 187 S.E.2d 505 (1972); Mezzanotte v. Freeland, 20 N.C. App. 11, 200 S.E.2d 410 (1973).

45. Rape v. Lyerly, 23 N.C. App. 241, 208 S.E.2d 712 (1974), *aff'd,* 287 N.C. 601, 215 S.E.2d 737 (1975); McGraw v. Llewellyn, 256 N.C. 213, 123 S.E.2d 575, 94 A.L.R.2d 914 (1962); Mansour v. Rabil, 277 N.C. 364, 177 S.E.2d 849 (1970); Olive v. Biggs, 276 N.C. 445, 173 S.E.2d 301 (1970); Hicks v. Hicks, 13 N.C. App. 347, 185 S.E.2d 430 (1971).

46. *See* Hicks v. Hicks, 13 N.C. App. 347, 185 S.E.2d 430 (1971); McGraw v. Llewellyn, 256 N.C. 213, 123 S.E.2d 575, 94 A.L.R.2d 914 (1962); Rape v. Lyerly, 23 N.C. App. 241, 208 S.E.2d 712 (1974), *aff'd,* 287 N.C. 601, 215 S.E.2d 737 (1975).

§ 141 REAL ESTATE LAW IN NORTH CAROLINA § 141

by some other person by him thereto lawfully authorized." The contract or memorandum may therefore be signed either by the party to be charged or by his agent. It is only "the party to be charged," the party against whom relief is sought, the defendant, who must have signed the contract or memorandum in order for it to be enforceable.[47] While the party who has not signed a writing may not be bound, the party who does sign is obligated on the contract.[48]

While a contract for the sale of land must be in writing and signed by the party to be charged or his authorized agent, an anomaly exists that the agent's authority to sign the contract may be shown by parol evidence.[49] For purposes of signing a contract for the sale and purchase of real property, an auctioneer at an auction sale is deemed the agent of both seller and purchaser.[50] If land is bid off at an auction sale, the auctioneer is the agent of the purchaser and is authorized to make the memorandum so as to bind the purchaser as to the terms of sale.[51]

It is not necessary that the signature be "subscribed" to the contract or memorandum, it being sufficient if the signature appears anywhere on

---

47. Hall v. Misenheimer, 137 N.C. 183, 49 S.E. 104 (1904); Love v. Atkinson, 131 N.C. 544, 42 S.E. 966 (1902); Durham Consol. Land & Improvement Co. v. Guthrie, 116 N.C. 381, 21 S.E. 952 (1895); Love's Ex'rs v. Welch, 97 N.C. 200, 2 S.E. 242 (1887); Davis v. Martin, 146 N.C. 281, 59 S.E. 700 (1907); Miller v. Carolina Monazite Co., 152 N.C. 608, 68 S.E. 1 (1910); Lewis v. Murray, 177 N.C. 17, 97 S.E. 750 (1919).

48. Lewis v. Murray, 177 N.C. 17, 97 S.E. 750 (1919); Mizell v. Burnett, 49 N.C. 249 (1857), wherein the court said, "if one agrees in writing to convey land in consideration of a verbal promise of the other party to pay the price, the contract is binding on the vendor, although the vendee may avoid the obligation on his part if he chooses to protect himself under the provisions of the statute."

49. Blacknall v. Parish, 59 N.C. 70 (1860); Wellman v. Horn, 157 N.C. 170, 72 S.E. 1010 (1911); Lewis v. Allred, 249 N.C. 486, 106 S.E.2d 689 (1959); Smith v. Browne, 132 N.C. 365, 43 S.E. 915 (1903); Flowe v. Hartwick, 167 N.C. 448, 83 S.E. 841 (1914); Lee v. Charitable Brotherhood, 191 N.C. 359, 131 S.E. 729 (1926); Yaggy v. B.V.D. Co., 7 N.C. App. 590, 173 S.E.2d 496 (1970); Reichler v. Tillman, 21 N.C. App. 38, 203 S.E.2d 68 (1974).

In Reichler v. Tillman, *supra,* where husband and wife owned land as tenants by the entirety, and husband entered a contract to sell the property "belonging to Ted Tillman," referring to the "seller" in the singular, the court nevertheless held that parol evidence was admissible to show that the wife had made the husband her agent to contract to sell the land belonging to the husband and wife as tenants by the entirety.

50. Smith v. Joyce, 214 N.C. 602, 200 S.E. 431 (1939); Woodruff v. Piedmont Trust Co., 173 N.C. 546, 92 S.E. 496 (1917); Love v. Harris, 156 N.C. 88, 72 S.E. 150 (1911); Cherry v. Long, 61 N.C. 466 (1868); Proctor v. Finley, 119 N.C. 536, 26 S.E. 128 (1896). *See* Greenberg v. Bailey, 14 N.C. App. 34, 187 S.E.2d 505 (1972).

51. *Id. See,* however, Smith v. Joyce, 214 N.C. 602, 200 S.E. 431 (1939), in which the auctioneer did not sign the name of the last and highest bidder until two or three days after the sale, *after* the bidder had repudiated the purchase. The Supreme Court of North Carolina held that the implied authority of the auctioneer had terminated and been revoked before the purchaser's name had been written on the memorandum and there was, therefore, no authorized signature.

§ 141 CONTRACTS FOR THE SALE OF LAND § 141

the instrument or in the body of the writing.[52] *What is a "signature"?* The actual signature of "the party to be charged" may take a variety of forms. Perhaps the making of any distinctive character upon an instrument with the intention that it shall serve as the signature of the maker will constitute a sufficient signing to satisfy the Statute of Frauds. There is no necessity for a formal signature. It has been stated that a cross mark, a straight or crooked line, a dot, or any other symbol will do.[53] Putting initials to a document will suffice.[54] One may authorize his agent in his presence and under his direction to sign his name and the act of the agent will be deemed the act of the principal who will be bound by the signature.[55] If one is illiterate or physically incapacitated another may sign for him and such signature becomes the signature of the illiterate or infirm person if he adopts it by attaching a cross or other mark.[56] Indeed it appears that one could elect to use a mark even though he is not illiterate

---

52. Farmers' Tobacco Warehouse Co. v. Eastern Carolina Warehouse Corp., 185 N.C. 518, 117 S.E. 625 (1923); Flowe v. Hartwick, 167 N.C. 448, 83 S.E. 841 (1914); Burris v. Starr, 165 N.C. 657, 81 S.E. 929 (1914); Wellman v. Horn, 157 N.C. 170, 72 S.E. 1010 (1911); Love v. Harris, 156 N.C. 88, 72 S.E. 150 (1911). *See* Proctor v. Finley, 119 N.C. 536, 26 S.E. 128 (1896), in which the signature was by an auctioneer who placed the name of the highest bidder in an inverted position on the side of a printed advertisement with an entry of the price bid. The Supreme Court of North Carolina held this to be a sufficient signing. *Accord,* Yaggy v. B.V.D. Co., 7 N.C. App. 590, 173 S.E.2d 496 (1970).

53. Devereux v. McMahon, 108 N.C. 134, 12 S.E. 902 (1891).

Affixing one's handwritten signature to a document is not the only method by which it may be considered "signed." A memorandum may be "signed" for purposes of the Statute of Frauds if his name is impressed on the paper by any of the known modes of writing, printing, lithographing, or other mode, provided the same is done with the intention of signing. A typewritten name can be a signature. *See* Yaggy v. B.V.D. Co., 7 N.C. App. 590, 173 S.E.2d 496 (1970), in which it is held that a teletyped or printed name of a vendor on a telegram constituted a "signing" of the telegram as a memorandum sufficient to satisfy the Statute of Frauds. *Compare* State v. Watts, 289 N.C. 445, 222 S.E.2d 389 (1976), wherein the question arose as to whether a mechanical reproduction could be a "signature" of a public officer. The Supreme Court of North Carolina states:

> In regard to a signature, it is the intent rather than the form of the act that is important. While one's signature is usually made by writing his name, the same purpose can be accomplished by placing any writing, indicia or symbol which the signer chooses to adopt and use as his signature and by which it may be proved; *e.g.*, by finger or thumb prints, by a cross or other mark, or by any type of mechanically reproduced or stamped facsimile of his signature, as effectively as by his own handwriting.
>
> ... A signature has also been defined as the act of putting down a person's name at the end of an instrument to attest its validity, any mark or sign made on an instrument or document in token of knowledge, approval, or device one may choose to employ as representative of himself. Stated in greater detail, in legal contemplation "to sign" means to attach a name or cause it to be attached by any of the known methods of impressing the name on paper with the intention of signing it.
>
> A signature consists of both the act of writing the person's name and the intention of thereby finally authenticating the instrument.

54. In Devereux v. McMahon, 108 N.C. 134, 12 S.E. 902 (1891), the initials "D.S.C." were held to mean "Solomon Davis." The "signer" testified: "... that is my name D.S. for Davis, C. for Solomon; that is the way I sign it; the rest was put there merely to fill in ...."

55. Devereux v. McMahon, 108 N.C. 134, 12 S.E. 902 (1891).

56. *Id.*

and is able to write.[57] It is not essential for the words "his mark" to be attached to the mark made and adopted; it is sufficient if it is made to appear that he made or adopted the mark as his signature.[58]

§ 142. Description of the Land.

The memorandum or instrument required to satisfy the Statute of Frauds in a contract for the sale of land must contain a description of the land that is the subject of the contract, either certain in itself, or capable of being reduced to a certainty by reference to something extrinsic to which the contract refers.[59] While the best manner of describing the land in the contract or memorandum is a complete legal description of the land in question by metes and bounds, by lot number, by plat or map, by monuments, by street number, or by reference to government survey if any, the ideal is not always achieved, particularly in contracts made without the aid of legal counsel. The inquiry therefore becomes: How much less than a complete legal description of the land will satisfy the Statute of Frauds in a contract for the sale of land?

The general rule is that if the description on its face identifies a particular tract of land as distinguished from other lands, it is adequate and parol evidence can be admitted and utilized to fit the description to the particular land.[60] In this situation, the description is said to be latently ambiguous; *i.e.*, it is insufficient in itself to identify the property but refers to something extrinsic by which identification might possibly be made.[61] On the other hand, it also may be said generally that if a description in a contract shows a patent ambiguity as written, parol evidence is inadmissible to fit the description to the land and the description will be held inadequate.[62] A patent ambiguity involves a

---

57. *Id.*

58. Sellars v. Sellars, 98 N.C. 13, 3 S.E. 917 (1887). A mark may be proven as adopted for a signature in the same manner that a signature is proved, by one who saw it made, or by one who heard the maker acknowledge it to be his. The maker himself, along with other witnesses, is a competent witness to prove that he made or adopted a mark as his signature. In addition, a mark may be so distinctive, peculiar and habitually used by the maker that it is as recognizable as a formal signature in handwriting would be. Devereux v. McMahon, 108 N.C. 134, 12 S.E. 902 (1891).

See Yaggy v. B.V.D. Co., 7 N.C. App. 590, 173 S.E.2d 496 (1970), where it is held that defendant's name affixed in print on a telegram constituted a "signing" of the telegram within the Statute of Frauds.

59. Lane v. Coe, 262 N.C. 8, 136 S.E.2d 269 (1964). *See* Yaggy v. B.V.D. Co., 7 N.C. App. 590, 173 S.E.2d 496 (1970).

60. Lewis v. Murray, 177 N.C. 17, 97 S.E. 750 (1918); Bateman v. Hopkins, 157 N.C. 470, 73 S.E. 133 (1911); Hurdle v. White, 34 N.C. App. 644, 239 S.E.2d 286 (1977).

61. Kidd v. Early, 289 N.C. 343, 222 S.E.2d 392 (1976); Lane v. Coe, 262 N.C. 8, 136 S.E.2d 269 (1964); Prentice v. Roberts, 32 N.C. App. 376, 232 S.E.2d 286 (1977).

62. Lane v. Coe, 262 N.C. 8, 136 S.E.2d 269 (1964); Taylor v. Bailey, 34 N.C. App. 290, 237 S.E.2d 918 (1977).

§ 142 CONTRACTS FOR THE SALE OF LAND § 142

description which leaves the land in question in a state of absolute uncertainty, and refers to nothing extrinsic by which the land might be identified with certainty.[63] Whether a description is patently ambiguous is a question of law.[64] It must be observed, however, that the cases in North Carolina relating to adequacy of descriptions, of which there are many, are not entirely consistent.

The following descriptions have been held sufficient as complying with the Statute of Frauds and parol testimony was admitted to specifically identify the real property involved: "You can have my timber on the tract of land known as the Walling tract, on Roanoke River . . .";[65] "My house and lot in the town of Jefferson";[66] "Mrs. Hooker to make a deed for her house and lot north of Kinston to the said J. R. Phillips";[67] an auctioneer's clerk's memorandum written simply as "Rayner Tract to James S. Long, at $40 per acre";[68] "Received of G.T. five hundred dollars on account of the sale of my interest in the 'Lenoir lands,' owned by myself and J.W.T.";[69] "Beginning at a stake on Grant's corner running north with the Rocky Ford road to Tate's line . . . and then with said line to the beginning; containing 1¼ acres, more or less";[70] "land on which the vendee now lives";[71] a note made by an auctioneer on the back of a notice of sale of lands reading, "sold to C.J. for $1,500.22 January, 1910";[72] "Received of W. E. Bateman $5, to confirm the bargain on the purchase of the farm on which I now live";[73] "Received on account of trade on homeplace one hundred dollars. From D. B. Lewis";[74] all that tract of land in two certain counties, lying on "both sides of old road between" designated points and bounded by lands of named owners "and others";[75] ". . . J. A. Smith has sold to W. H. Norton his entire tract or boundary of land consisting of 146 acres . . .";[76] a check stating that it was "payment on Watts Street House";[77] agreement by mother with her children that if they would convey her what their father had left them, she would

---

63. Kidd v. Early, 289 N.C. 343, 222 S.E.2d 392 (1976); Lane v. Coe, 262 N.C. 8, 136 S.E.2d 269 (1964).
64. Kidd v. Early, 289 N.C. 343, 222 S.E.2d 392 (1976); Carlton v. Anderson, 276 N.C. 564, 173 S.E.2d 783 (1970).
65. Mizell v. Burnett, 49 N.C. 249 (1857).
66. Carson v. Ray, 52 N.C. 609 (1860).
67. Phillips v. Hooker, 62 N.C. 193 (1867).
68. Cherry v. Long, 61 N.C. 466 (1868).
69. Thornburg v. Masten, 88 N.C. 293 (1883).
70. Gordon v. Collett, 102 N.C. 532, 9 S.E. 486 (1889).
71. Falls of Neuse Mfg. Co. v. Hendricks, 106 N.C. 485, 11 S.E. 568 (1890).
72. Love v. Harris, 156 N.C. 88, 72 S.E. 150 (1911).
73. Bateman v. Hopkins, 157 N.C. 470, 73 S.E. 133 (1911).
74. Lewis v. Murray, 177 N.C. 17, 97 S.E. 750 (1918).
75. Buckhorne Land & Timber Co. v. Yarbrough, 179 N.C. 335, 102 S.E. 630 (1920).
76. Norton v. Smith, 179 N.C. 553, 103 S.E. 14 (1920).
77. Harper v. Battle, 180 N.C. 375, 104 S.E. 658 (1920).

combine the whole of their father's estate with the greater part of her own estate and make an equal division to the children; [78] "agreement made . . . of sale of her home property on Pennsylvania Avenue and Cypress Street . . . Dr. Wright agrees to buy the vacant lot from Mrs. O. F. Gilbert, during the month of January, 1925, for the sum of fifteen hundred dollars"; [79] "Received of C.L. $50.00 for homeplace where he now lives which he has no deed for" dated and signed by the owner; [80] "3-23-63. Received of Jimmie Lane One Hundred Dollars as a binder on house and lots on 601 highway where his residence is . . . ." [81] For additional cases holding descriptions to be sufficient under the Statute of Frauds and admitting parol testimony to identify the specific property involved, see the note below.[82]

The following descriptions have been held *not* to be adequate compliance with the description requirements of the Statute of Frauds. Parol testimony was held inadmissible to specifically identify the property involved: "Received of Mr. Drury Allen two hundred and forty dollars, in part for a certain tract of land lying on Flat River, including Taylor Hicks' springhouse and lot, etc., and adjoining the land of Lewis Daniel; Womach, and others"; [83] "1841, W.P. to H.C.O. Dr. to 4 loads of Rock, one lot, at one year's credit, $125"; [84] "Received of A. C. Murdock . . . in part

---

78. McCall v. Lee, 182 N.C. 114, 108 S.E. 380 (1921).
79. Gilbert v. Wright, 195 N.C. 165, 141 S.E. 577 (1928).
80. Searcy v. Logan, 226 N.C. 562, 39 S.E.2d 593 (1946).
81. Lane v. Coe, 262 N.C. 8, 136 S.E.2d 269 (1964).
82. In Kidd v. Early, 23 N.C. App. 129, 208 S.E.2d 511 (1974), *aff'd in part, rev'd in part*, 289 N.C. 343, 222 S.E.2d 392 (1976), it was held that a description of land in an option referring to "200 acres or more or less of the C. F. Early farm. To be determined by a new survey furnished by sellers" was only latently ambiguous. Therefore parol and other evidence was held admissible to fit the description to the land. The Supreme Court of North Carolina held that the description was not invalid because the survey called for in the option contract was prepared subsequently to the execution of the option. Mezzanotte v. Freeland, 20 N.C. App. 11, 200 S.E.2d 410 (1973), holds that a description in a contract which refers to "a certain tract or parcel of land of approximately 85 acres in the County of Orange . . . said parcel of real estate being more particularly described in Attachment hereof" did not create a patent ambiguity even though five deeds that were to constitute the "attachment" were not physically attached to the contract of sale but were delivered contemporaneously with the execution of the contract.
Yaggy v. B.V.D. Co., 7 N.C. App. 590, 173 S.E.2d 496 (1970), holds that a description in a telegram referring to property to be conveyed as "BVD property in Carrboro, N.C. subject to reacquisition from Montvale Realty Corporation" is not patently ambiguous notwithstanding the vendor holds interests in two distinct tracts in Carrboro, N.C. separated by streets of the town, since the reference to property "subject to reacquisition from Montvale" makes it possible to show by extrinsic evidence the exact property intended to be sold.
83. Allen v. Chambers, 39 N.C. 125 (1845).
84. Plummer v. Owens, 45 N.C. 254 (1853).

§ 142   CONTRACTS FOR THE SALE OF LAND   § 142

payment of one house and lot in the town of Hillsboro"; [85] "Received of Henry Capps $100, in part payment . . . on a bargain made by us for a tract of land on the North side of the Watery Branch in the County of Johnston, and state of North Carolina, containing 150 acres . . ."; [86] "In settlement with A. E. Breaid, Kipp and Munger owed him $316.30 to be applied to his 100 acres of land and the lot where he now lives is paid in full"; [87] "Charles Crawford, Land . . . . $125.00, Paid . . . . $61.58, Balance due . . . . $63.48, 1 Jan. 1875, Gilbert Hale"; [88] bond for title to convey thirty acres of land of the "Deaver Tract," which tract contained more than thirty acres; [89] "19 April 1880 — James Harris has paid me $20 on his land, owes me six more on it." [90] For additional cases holding descriptions *not* to be adequate compliance with the description requirements of the Statute of Frauds and holding parol testimony to be inadmissible to specifically identify the property involved, see the note below.[91]

---

85. Murdock v. Anderson, 57 N.C. 77 (1858).
86. Capps v. Holt, 58 N.C. 153 (1859).
87. Breaid v. Munger, 88 N.C. 297 (1883).
88. Fortescue v. Crawford, 105 N.C. 29, 10 S.E. 910 (1890).
89. Falls of Neuse Mfg. Co. v. Hendricks, 106 N.C. 485, 11 S.E. 568 (1890). *See* Sheppard v. Andrews, 7 N.C. App. 517, 173 S.E.2d 67 (1970), which holds that a description of "4 acres of land fronting on Clover Leaf of Mt. Hope Church and NC-85 and Kivett Road" is an inadequate description in an option to sell land where the optionor owns over 40 acres. *See also* Carlton v. Anderson, 276 N.C. 564, 173 S.E.2d 783 (1970). *See generally* Overton v. Boyce, 26 N.C. App. 680, 217 S.E.2d 704 (1975), *rev'd on other grounds,* 289 N.C. 291, 221 S.E.2d 347 (1976), to the effect that a *deed* is void for uncertainty where it purports to convey part of a larger tract but there is an absence of any indication of intent to convey a specific part of the tract, citing State v. Brooks, 279 N.C. 45, 181 S.E.2d 553 (1971); Carlton v. Anderson, 276 N.C. 564, 173 S.E.2d 783 (1970); Cathey v. Lumber Co., 151 N.C. 592, 66 S.E. 530 (1909); Smith v. Proctor, 139 N.C. 314, 51 S.E. 889 (1905); Robeson v. Lewis, 64 N.C. 734 (1870). The same rule will be applicable to *contracts to sell* real property.

See also Kidd v. Early, 23 N.C. App. 129, 208 S.E.2d 511 (1974), *aff'd in part, rev'd in part,* 289 N.C. 343, 222 S.E.2d 392 (1976), which holds that a description of land in an option as *"200 acres or more or less of the C. F. Early farm. To be determined by a new survey furnished by sellers"* was only latently ambiguous. Parol and other evidence was held to be admissible to fit the description to the land. It was held that the description was not invalid because the survey called for in the option contract was prepared subsequently to the execution of the option. *Compare* Builders Supplies Co. v. Gainey, 282 N.C. 261, 192 S.E.2d 449 (1972), which states that a deed to a specified number of acres out of a larger tract with the right in the grantee to select the location of his acreage will be valid *provided the grantee makes a selection.* While no title passes until the grantee makes his selection, since a right given to a vendee to select a definite number of acres out of a larger tract affords the means of rendering the description certain, the vendee has a contractual right to acquire title.

90. Lowe v. Harris, 112 N.C. 473, 17 S.E. 539 (1893).
91. Barringer v. Weathington, 11 N.C. App. 618, 182 S.E.2d 239 (1971), holds that a description in a deed which referred to the tract in question as "containing 40 acres entered by Hugh Simpson" was patently ambiguous and could not be aided by parol evidence.

Bercegeay v. Realty Co., 16 N.C. App. 718, 193 S.E.2d 356 (1972), holds that a description in a purported contract to convey land describing the land as "Block 36, Lot 12 Sound Front" is insufficient to be aided by parol evidence to satisfy the Statute of Frauds when no map

If the court determines that the ambiguity is patent, parol evidence will not be admitted to aid in the identification of the property involved. If the ambiguity is identified as latent, on the other hand, evidence *dehors* the memorandum is competent to identify the property with certainty.[92]

§ 143. Statement of Names of Parties, Terms and Conditions.

It is generally stated that in order for a contract for the sale of real property to be enforceable under the Statute of Frauds the written contract or memorandum must contain all of the essential elements of a valid contract. This would require the writing to embody the terms of the contract, the names of the vendor and vendee,[93] a description of the

---

or plat is introduced into evidence showing a "Block 36." The memorandum sufficient to satisfy the Statute of Frauds must "contain a description of the land that is the subject of the contract, either certain in itself or capable of being reduced to a certainty by reference to something extrinsic to which the contract refers."

Watts v. Ridenhour, 27 N.C. App. 8, 217 S.E.2d 211 (1975), holds that a description in an option is inadequate under the Statute of Frauds where it purports to grant "the option to purchase additional acreage lying to the rear of Plot No. 8 for the price of $300 per acre, this acreage to lie primarily on the southeast side of a line running along the southeastern side of Plots Nos. 4, 5, 6 and 10 and extending on to the rear property line."

Overton v. Boyce, 289 N.C. 291, 221 S.E.2d 347 (1976), holds that a description in a deed which refers to "A certain tract of Pocosin Land adjoining the lands of the late Henry Luton and others, containing, by estimation, Three Hundred Acres" is patently ambiguous.

When it is apparent upon the face of the deed itself that there is uncertainty as to land intended to be conveyed and the deed itself refers to nothing extrinsic by which such uncertainty can be resolved the description is said to be patently ambiguous, and parol evidence may not be introduced to remove the ambiguity.

92. Lane v. Coe, 262 N.C. 8, 136 S.E.2d 269 (1964), wherein the Court said, "In such case plaintiff may offer evidence, parol and other, with reference to such extrinsic matter tending to identify the property, and defendant may offer evidence with reference thereto tending to show impossibility of identification, *i.e.,* ambiguity." *Accord,* Kidd v. Early, 23 N.C. App. 129, 208 S.E.2d 511 (1974), *aff'd in part, rev'd in part,* 289 N.C. 343, 222 S.E.2d 392 (1976); Overton v. Boyce, 289 N.C. 291, 221 S.E.2d 347 (1976); Barringer v. Weathington, 11 N.C. App. 618, 182 S.E.2d 239 (1971). In Prentice v. Roberts, 32 N.C. App. 379, 232 S.E.2d 286 (1977), it was held that a property sketch referred to in a sales agreement could be introduced to locate property and an easement thereon referred to in the sales agreement.

93. Yaggy v. B.V.D. Co., 7 N.C. App. 590, 173 S.E.2d 496 (1970); Carr v. Good Shepherd Home, Inc., 269 N.C. 241, 152 S.E.2d 85 (1967); Elliot v. Owen, 244 N.C. 684, 94 S.E.2d 833 (1956); Mayer v. Adrian, 77 N.C. 83 (1877). Where the memorandum of a contract to convey realty fails to identify the buyer in any manner, the memorandum is insufficient under the Statute of Frauds and the identity of the buyer cannot be shown by parol.

The Supreme Court of North Carolina has recently held in Kidd v. Early, 23 N.C. App. 129, 208 S.E.2d 511 (1974), *aff'd in part, rev'd in part,* 289 N.C. 343, 222 S.E.2d 392 (1976), that while the price to be paid for property is an essential term of an option agreement and must be agreed on by the parties, the option contract need not contain any expressions as to the manner and form of payment. Where an option does not specifically fix the time for payment of the purchase price, the law construes the offer to be for cash on delivery and before title passes. A sale on credit is never *implied.* Thus, absent a provision respecting the time of payment, a contract for the sale of realty will be construed as requiring payment in cash simultaneously with the tender or delivery of the deed. The court indicates, however, that if the memorandum relating to the sale of realty shows that the sale was to be upon

property, as well as the proper signature of the party to be charged. In North Carolina these general statements, while often repeated by the North Carolina Supreme Court, do not have unqualified application.

For instance, where the vendor is the party who institutes suit *against the vendee* as the party to be charged on a contract for the sale of real property, it *is* correct to say in North Carolina that the memorandum, to be sufficient, must contain all of the essential elements of the agreement, including a statement of the consideration or price.[94] On the other hand, if the vendee institutes the suit and the *vendor* is the party defendant to be charged, it is not necessary that the consideration or price appear in the instrument; it is sufficient if it discloses an agreement signed by the vendor that he will convey identified land.[95] If the vendor is the "party to be charged," the consideration to be paid by the vendee can be shown by parol evidence.[96] If the vendee is the "party to be charged," the consideration or price to be paid must appear in the written instrument before the Statute of Frauds is satisfied; it cannot be supplied by parol.[97]

The consequence of these foregoing rules is that a written contract that does not disclose the price or consideration may not be enforced against the vendee, even though he has signed it; in a suit by the vendee against the vendor, the same contract would be enforceable against the vendor who has signed a memorandum agreeing to convey the real property, even though the memorandum is silent as to the consideration or price.[98]

---

a credit, but fails to state the terms of such credit, or the statement relative to credit is indefinite or uncertain, specific performance of the contract will be refused. If the memorandum is entirely silent on the manner and form of payment, a sale for cash will be presumed to have been intended.

See Hurdle v. White, 34 N.C. App. 644, 239 S.E.2d 589 (1977), where the court found that a check was a sufficient memorandum of the contract under N.C. GEN. STAT. § 22-2. The check adequately described the vendor and vendee, the price was stated, and the designation of the property to be conveyed was sufficient enough to permit the introduction of extrinsic evidence. The fact that it was unclear as to whether the $500 paid by the check was intended as a down payment to be applied against purchase price or was intended only as consideration for the option involved did not deter the court from upholding the check as a valid memorandum of agreement.

94. *E.g., see* Keith v. Bailey, 185 N.C. 262, 116 S.E. 929 (1923); Hall v. Misenheimer, 137 N.C. 183, 49 S.E. 104 (1904).

95. *See* Bateman v. Hopkins, 157 N.C. 470, 73 S.E. 133 (1911), which held, in an action by a vendee against a vendor for specific performance of a contract to convey lands, that it is not necessary for the memorandum to set forth the obligation of the vendee to pay the purchase price. It is only necessary, if the action is against the vendor, that the memorandum show the vendor's duty to convey. It is not necessary that the price be set out; this can be shown by parol if the vendee is the plaintiff. *Accord,* Lewis v. Murray, 177 N.C. 17, 97 S.E.2d 750 (1918); Hall v. Misenheimer, 137 N.C. 183, 49 S.E. 104 (1904); Mizell v. Burnett, 49 N.C. 249 (1857); Thornburg v. Masten, 88 N.C. 293 (1883); Miller v. Irvine, 18 N.C. 104 (1834).

96. Hall v. Misenheimer, 137 N.C. 183, 49 S.E. 104 (1904).

97. *Id.*

98. *Id.;* Mizell v. Burnett, 49 N.C. 249 (1857).

§ 144. Doctrine of Part Performance Not Applicable in North Carolina to Take Contracts Out of the Statute of Frauds.

While most states hold that acts of partial performance of the plaintiff in reliance upon an oral contract for the sale of land take the contract out of the Statute of Frauds and make it enforceable, North Carolina disapproves of this doctrine in connection with real estate transactions.[99] Neither part payment,[100] nor rendition of services,[101] nor taking of possession by the vendee,[102] nor the vendee's making of improvements on real property [103] in reliance on a contract will suffice to make a contract for the sale of real property enforceable if it does not otherwise comply with the Statute of Frauds.

Article III. Breach

§ 145. Remedies for Breach by Vendor: Generally.

Although the uniqueness of real property no doubt adds a certain distinction to the contract to convey, it is nonetheless a contract governed by the basic doctrines and remedies of contract law.[104] Upon breach of a contract for the sale of land by the vendor, the most common remedies utilized in North Carolina by the vendee include: (1) standing on the contract and suing at law for damages for breach; [105] (2) affirming the contract by going into equity and seeking specific performance or specific performance with abatement; [106] or (3) rescinding the contract and recovering what the vendee has paid.[107]

---

99. Duckett v. Harrison, 235 N.C. 145, 69 S.E.2d 176 (1952); Ebert v. Disher, 216 N.C. 36, 3 S.E.2d 301 (1939); Grantham v. Grantham, 205 N.C. 363, 171 S.E. 331 (1933).

100. Barnes v. Saleeby, 177 N.C. 256, 98 S.E. 708 (1919). Indeed, payment of the *whole* price will not take a contract out of the Statute of Frauds. *See* Mauney v. Norvell, 179 N.C. 628, 103 S.E. 372 (1920).

101. Grantham v. Grantham, 205 N.C. 363, 171 S.E. 331 (1933).

102. Barnes v. Teague, 54 N.C. 277 (1854); Rhea v. Craig, 141 N.C. 602, 54 S.E. 408 (1906).

103. Dunn v. Moore, 38 N.C. 364 (1844).

104. *See* Brannock v. Fletcher, 271 N.C. 65, 155 S.E.2d 532 (1967) for a general summary of remedies for breach of a contract to convey. In addition to the most commonly utilized remedies, that case refers to 92 C.J.S., *Vendor & Purchaser* § 543 (1955), for other available remedies.

105. *Id.;* Emerson v. Carras, 33 N.C. App. 91, 234 S.E.2d 642 (1977); Pope v. McPhail, 173 N.C. 238, 91 S.E. 947 (1917).

106. Craig v. Kessing, 36 N.C. App. 389, 244 S.E.2d 721 (1978); Lawing v. Jaynes, 285 N.C. 418, 206 S.E.2d 162 (1974); Yaggy v. B.V.D. Co., 7 N.C. App. 590, 173 S.E.2d 496 (1970); *Compare* Nugent v. Beckham, 37 N.C. App. 557, 246 S.E.2d 541 (1978), dealing with and granting the remedy of specific performance with abatement, with Passmore v. Woodard, 37 N.C. App. 535, 246 S.E.2d 795 (1978), dealing with and denying the remedy of partial specific performance.

107. Hinson v. Jefferson, 287 N.C. 422, 215 S.E.2d 102 (1974). This case makes an important distinction between the granting of a rescission remedy based on mutual mistake

Once the vendor has breached, the vendee's actions are governed by the election of remedies doctrine. That is to say, the vendee must elect between affirming the contract through the damages or specific performance route, and disaffirming the contract through the remedy of rescission.[108]

§ 146. Vendor's Misrepresentations as to Acreage, Area or Square Footage.

As a general rule, a vendor's misrepresentation as to acreage or quantity of real property being sold is actionable by the vendee.[109] This rule assumes that the vendee has justifiably and reasonably relied on the misrepresentation.[110] Because the acreage of property is not considered something readily ascertainable by a purchaser, the North Carolina decisions have been tolerant in attitude toward vendees.[111] Where acreage has been misrepresented, the vendee has been given the election to either rescind or to keep the property and recover the difference between its actual value and its value as represented.[112] In sales made on an acreage basis, the vendee's action to recover the excess payment will most likely be treated as one for assumpsit for money had and received by the vendor

---

in completed, fully executed contracts to convey versus utilization of that remedy in the interim period prior to the closing of the transaction as was done in McKay v. McIntosh, 270 N.C. 69, 153 S.E.2d 800 (1967). In Hinson, at 287 N.C. 422, 432, 433, the Court explains the reason for the distinction:

> In any event, because of the uncertainty surrounding the law of mistake we are extremely hesitant to apply this theory to a case involving the completed sale and transfer of real property. Its application to this type of factual situation might well create an unwarranted instability with respect to North Carolina real estate transactions and lead to the filing of many non-meritorious actions. Hence, we expressly reject this theory as a basis for plaintiff's rescission.

Accord, Financial Servs. v. Capital Funds, 288 N.C. 122, 217 S.E.2d 551 (1975), where the vendee was denied rescission.

108. Stewart v. Salisbury Realty, 159 N.C. 230, 74 S.E. 736 (1912) where a purchaser sent written notice of "rescission and cancellation" to the vendor. The purchaser was held to have made a binding election to rescind that precluded him from recovering damages for breach of the contract. Rescission would not, however, preclude a recovery of special damages.

See generally Rabin, *A Proposed Black-Letter Rule Concerning Mistaken Assumptions in Bargain Transactions,* 45 TEX. L. REV. 1273 (1967), an article referred to in Hinson v. Jefferson, 287 N.C. 422, 215 S.E.2d 102 (1974).

109. Norburn v. Mackie, 262 N.C. 16, 136 S.E.2d 279 (1964); Swinton v. Realty Co., 236 N.C. 723, 73 S.E.2d 785 (1953); Shell v. Roseman, 155 N.C. 90, 71 S.E. 86 (1911); Hill v. Brower, 76 N.C. 124 (1877); Walsh v. Hall, 66 N.C. 233 (1872). A seller is also responsible to a purchaser for the misrepresentations as to acreage made by the seller's real estate broker. Norburn v. Mackie, 262 N.C. 16, 136 S.E.2d 279 (1964).

110. *Id.*

111. Marshall v. Keaveny, 38 N.C. App. 644, 248 S.E.2d 750 (1978).
112. Horne v. Cloninger, 256 N.C. 102, 123 S.E.2d 112 (1961).

to the vendee's use.[113] Thus, the vendee is not required to allege or prove fraud.[114]

In the one North Carolina case involving a vendor's misrepresentation as to the total square footage of a house,[115] the purchaser did not fare as well as his counterparts did in the acreage cases.[116] Conceding for purposes of the appeal that misrepresentations as to square footage took place, the Court of Appeals nonetheless concluded as a matter of law that the purchaser could not reasonably rely on them.[117] The court distinguished the acreage decisions noting that the purchaser had full opportunity to and did inspect the house, and that he could have easily determined the square footage for himself.[118]

§ 147. Vendor's Misrepresentations as to Quality or Character of Property.

North Carolina decisions have traditionally held the purchaser of real property to rather strict standards of personal inspection and evaluation of the property in cases involving alleged misrepresentations by the vendor as to the quality or character of the property purchased.[119] The right of a vendee to rely on representations of the vendor is inseparably connected in North Carolina to the vendee's correlative duty to use diligence in the matter. One of the assumptions made by the courts in these types of cases is that the parties to the contract to convey stand on equal footing and have the equal means of knowing the truth.[120] It is also

---

113. Hoots v. Calaway, 282 N.C. 477, 193 S.E.2d 709 (1973); Queen v. Sisk, 238 N.C. 389, 78 S.E.2d 152 (1953); Duffy v. Phipps, 180 N.C. 313, 104 S.E. 655 (1920).
114. Id.
115. Marshall v. Keaveny, 38 N.C. App. 644, 248 S.E.2d 750 (1978).
116. Id. This might in part be explainable by the fact that the purchaser was an attorney and therefore presumably sophisticated enough to ascertain on his own the total square footage of the dwelling.
117. Id.
118. Id. After an unsuccessful attempt during the interim period to be released from the contract, the purchaser elected to purchase the house (reserving his rights) and then brought suit for damages caused by the misrepresentations. Query: Would the court have been more sympathetic with the purchaser if he had brought a rescission action during the interim period prior to closing upon discovering the deficiency in square footage?
119. Marshall v. Keaveny, 38 N.C. App. 644, 248 S.E.2d 750 (1978); Goff v. Realty and Insurance Co., 21 N.C. App. 25, 203 S.E.2d 65 (1974); Calloway v. Wyatt, 246 N.C. 129, 97 S.E.2d 881 (1957). See Harding v. Insurance Co., 218 N.C. 129, 10 S.E.2d 599 (1940), where the court notes:

> Representations concerning the value of real property or its condition and the adaptation to particular uses will not support an action in deceit unless the purchaser has been fraudulently induced to forbear inquiries which he would otherwise have made, and if fraud of this latter description is relied on as an additional ground of action, it must be specifically set forth in the declaration.

120. Calloway v. Wyatt, 246 N.C. 129, 97 S.E.2d 881 (1957); Harding v. Ins. Co., 218 N.C. 129, 10 S.E.2d 599 (1940).

assumed that no fraud or artifice by the vendor has occurred that has induced the vendee to forego investigation.[121]

§ 148. The Parol Evidence Rule: Contract Versus Tort Cause of Action.

A common pattern in suits by a vendee against a vendor involves the attempt by the plaintiff-vendee to present evidence or oral statements and representations made by the vendor or the vendor's real estate agent prior to or at the time of the execution of the contract. The vendor usually resists the introduction of this parol testimony of prior or contemporaneous negotiations or conversations inconsistent with the written contract to convey under the parol evidence rule.[122] The vendor's objection is frequently bolstered by the commonplace boilerplate in most printed form contracts for the sale of realty to the effect that "no representations other than those expressed herein, either oral or written, are a part of this agreement." A careful distinction must be drawn, however, between an action for breach of contract and an action based on a tort theory. Where the vendee is proceeding against the vendor on a theory of fraudulent misrepresentation — a tort action — the rule that prior conversations and negotiations are merged into the written contract does not apply.[123] This is the case because evidence of the oral fraudulent misrepresentation is not offered to contradict the terms of the written contract; rather, the evidence is introduced to show that the contract was induced by fraud and is therefore invalid.

§ 149. Implied Warranty Where Builder-Vendor Involved.

In the 1974 decision of *Hartley v. Ballou*,[124] the North Carolina Supreme Court recognized the existence of an implied warranty of

---

121. *Id.* Rosenthal v. Perkins, 42 N.C. App. 449, 257 S.E.2d 63 (1979).
122. "A written agreement may not be varied, added to, taken from, or contradicted by parol evidence." Fox v. Southern Appliances, Inc., 264 N.C. 267, 141 S.E.2d 522 (1965); Parker v. Bennett, 32 N.C. App. 46, 231 S.E.2d 10 (1977).
123. Marshall v. Keaveny, 38 N.C. App. 644, 248 S.E.2d 750 (1978); Fox v. Southern Appliances, Inc., 264 N.C. 267, 141 S.E.2d 522 (1965); Parker v. Bennett, 32 N.C. App. 46, 231 S.E.2d 10 (1977).

See generally STANSBURY, NORTH CAROLINA EVIDENCE § 257 (2d ed. 1963).

124. Hartley v. Ballou, 286 N.C. 51, 209 S.E.2d 776 (1974) at 286 N.C. 51, 63, the court described the vendee's measure of damages for breach as either (1) the difference between the reasonable market value of the property as impliedly warranted and its reasonable value in its actual condition, or (2) the amount required to bring the property into compliance with the implied warranty. The Court cited the following sources and cases: 13 AM. JUR. 2d, *Building and Construction Contracts* § 79 (1964); D. DOBBS, REMEDIES, BUILDING CONTRACTS § 12.21 (1973). *Accord,* Leggette v. Pittman, 268 N.C. 292, 150 S.E.2d 420 (1966); Robbins v. Trading Post, Inc., 251 N.C. 663, 111 S.E.2d 884 (1960); Lumber Co. v. Constr. Co., 249 N.C. 680, 107 S.E.2d 538 (1959). *See* Salem Towne Apartments, Inc. v. McDaniel & Sons Roofing Co., 330 F. Supp. 906 (E.D.N.C. 1970). *See also* Stone v. Homes, Inc., 37 N.C. App. 97, 245 S.E.2d 801 (1978).

workmanlike construction and no major structural defects subject to the following guidelines and requirements: (1) the contract must be for the sale of a recently completed dwelling or a dwelling then under construction; (2) the vendor must be in the business of building such dwellings; [125] (3) the implied warranty is for the benefit of the initial vendee of the dwelling; (4) the implied warranty refers to the condition of the dwelling at the time of the passing of the deed or the taking of possession by the initial vendee (whichever first occurs); (5) under it, the builder-vendor warrants that the dwelling, together with all its fixtures, is sufficiently free from major structural defects, and is constructed in a workmanlike manner so as to meet the standard of workmanlike quality then prevailing at the time and place of construction;[126] and (6) the implied warranty is not extinguished under the doctrine of merger and survives the passing of the deed or the taking of possession by the vendee.[127]

125. *See, e.g.,* Griffin v. Wheeler-Leonard & Co., 290 N.C. 185, 225 S.E.2d 557 (1976), where the Court held that the wife of a builder-vendor was not liable under the implied warranty where the record contained no evidence that she was in the construction business even though she had signed the deed of conveyance as one of the vendors of the property. *See also* Jones v. Clark, 36 N.C. App. 327, 244 S.E.2d 183 (1978) where the court refused to impute the doctrine of implied warranty of workmanlike construction to a third party who had placed its seal of inspection on a modular home manufactured by someone else.

126. In Earls v. Link, 38 N.C. App. 204, 247 S.E.2d 617 (1978), for example, a builder-vendor was held to have impliedly warranted that a fireplace and attached chimney would adequately remove to the exterior smoke from a fireplace fire, when such fire was within the normal contemplated use of the fireplace. Furthermore, the court held that a county building inspector who also had been in the construction business for 20 years was properly permitted to testify by the trial court concerning the proper construction of chimneys and flues. *See* Stone v. Homes, Inc., 37 N.C. App. 97, 245 S.E.2d 801 (1978), where the Court of Appeals found no error in the trial court's permitting the vendee's witness, who held a Ph.D. in materials engineering, was a licensed building contractor, and had constructed homes within 25 miles of the vendee's home, to testify as an expert that the vendee's home was not built according to acceptable construction and engineering standards prevailing at the time and place of construction. In Lyon v. Ward, 28 N.C. App. 446, 221 S.E.2d 727 (1976), the Court of Appeals, at 28 N.C. App. 446, 450, held as follows regarding adequate water:

> Because an adequate supply of usable water is an absolute essential utility to a dwelling house, we believe that the initial purchaser of a house from the builder-vendor can reasonably expect that a well constructed on the premises by the builder-vendor will provide an adequate supply of usable water. We hold that at the time of the passing of the deed or the taking of possession the builder-vendor of a house impliedly warrants to the initial purchaser that a well constructed on the premises by him will provide water for the dwelling house which is adequate and usable.

127. *Id.* at 290 N.C. 185, 202, where the contract of purchase contained the following paragraph:

> Buyer hereby acknowledges that he has inspected the above described property, that no representations or inducements have been made other than those expressed herein, and that this contract contains the entire agreement between all parties hereto.

The court held that the above quoted language did not constitute an agreement that no warranty was to be implied. The implied warranty exists by operation of law, not by reason of a representation or inducement made by the builder-vendor. Although existing by operation of law and presumably based on public policy, the court nonetheless did note that a builder-vendor and a purchaser could enter into a binding agreement that excluded the applicability of an implied warranty.

The implied warranty falls short of an absolute guarantee as to the quality of construction and condition of the premises.[128] Thus, while a warranty might be implied that a dwelling has been sufficiently waterproofed to withstand water leakage under normal weather conditions, the implied warranty will not be expanded to include a guarantee that the waterproofing was sufficient to protect the dwelling from water damage caused by extreme weather conditions.[129]

At least as to defects not readily apparent to the vendee at the time of transfer of title or possession, the cause of action for breach of implied warranty has been held to accrue at the time the defect is discovered by the vendee.[130]

§ 150. Remedies for Breach by Vendee.

The North Carolina Supreme Court, in Brannock v. Fletcher,[131] enumerates the various possible remedies of a vendor upon breach by a vendee of a contract for the sale and purchase of real estate as follows:

> [He] may bring an action for damages for the breach, or may sue in equity for specific performance, or bring an action for the purchase price remaining unpaid, or proceed to enforce his vendor's lien for unpaid purchase money, or, if he has parted with possession of the land, he may sue to recover its possession or retake possession if the premises are vacant; he may retake possession and recover damages for the breach, or he may bring a suit for foreclosure of the vendee's interest or to quiet title, or he may rescind the contract *in toto* with the usual rights and duties attendant on such action, or he may accept the noncompliance as a forfeiture of the contract, or he may bring an action to rescind the contract or declare it at an end. Further, he may remain inactive and retain for his own use the moneys paid by the purchaser, and he may retain or recover a deposit made by the purchaser on the purchase price.[132]

§ 151. Risk of Loss: Uniform Vendor and Purchaser Risk Act and Doctrine of Equitable Conversion.

Concerning the problem of risk of loss during the interim period between the signing of the contract to convey and the closing date, North Carolina has adopted the Uniform Vendor and Purchaser Risk Act.[133] The provisions of this Act, which apply only where the contract has failed to expressly provide otherwise, may be summarized as follows: If *neither* legal title *nor* possession of the property has been transferred and all or

---

128. Hartley v. Ballou, 286 N.C. 51, 209 S.E.2d 776 (1974).
129. Id.
130. Earls v. Link, 38 N.C. App. 204, 247 S.E.2d 617 (1978), where the vendees acquired a new dwelling in June of 1971, but did not use a fireplace until early in 1974 at which time a defect in the chimney was discovered. The court found that the cause of action accrued in 1974, not 1971.
131. Brannock v. Fletcher, 271 N.C. 65, 155 S.E.2d 532 (1967).
132. *Id.*, quoting from 92 C.J.S., *Vendor & Purchaser* § 375 (1955).
133. N.C. GEN STAT. §§ 39-37 through 39-39.

a material part of the property is destroyed without fault of the *vendee*, then the vendor is not entitled to enforce the contract and the vendee is entitled to recover any portion of the price that has been paid.[134] If *either* legal title *or* possession of the property has been transferred and all or *any* part of the property is destroyed without fault of the *vendor*, then the purchaser is not relieved from a duty to pay the price, nor is the purchaser entitled to recover any portion of the price already paid.[135]

In the event that the contract is silent and the event or loss complained of is one that is not covered by the North Carolina Act (*e.g.*, rezoning or a taking by eminent domain), the question of which party will bear the risk of loss will be determined by the doctrine of equitable conversion or by contract law theory. The doctrine of equitable conversion, as applied to executory contracts for the sale of land, places the risk of loss on the vendee who is treated in equity as the owner of the property involved. This assumes, of course, an otherwise valid and binding contract to convey.[136] Several North Carolina decisions dealing with fires during the interim period adhere to this majority view,[137] but the Uniform Vendor and Purchaser Risk Act reverses the results of those cases.[138] Other North Carolina decisions have dealt with certain adverse changes in circumstances or losses during the interim period in terms of contract law doctrines and remedies.[139] By this approach, the risk of loss may fall upon the vendor, assuming that a material mistake of fact has been made and that a central and material part of the subject matter of the contract has been destroyed or no longer exists.[140]

One answer to any apparent uncertainties remaining in this area of law under either the uniform act or applicable equitable and contract law theories is careful draftsmanship of the "risk of loss" provision in the contract to convey.

---

134. N.C. GEN. STAT. § 39-39 (1).

135. N.C. GEN. STAT. § 39-39 (2).

136. Farmers Tobacco Warehouse Co. v. Eastern Carolina Warehouse Corp., 185 N.C. 518, 117 S.E. 625 (1923).

137. *Id.;* Poole v. Scott, 228 N.C. 464, 46 S.E.2d 145 (1948); Sutton v. Davis, 143 N.C. 474, 55 S.E. 844 (1906).

138. N.C. GEN. STAT. § 39-39.

139. *See* McKay v. McIntosh, 270 N.C., 69, 153 S.E.2d 800 (1967), a case involving misrepresentations as to zoning discovered during the interim period (rather than rezoning). The decision speaks of the right of a vendee to rescind based on mutual mistake of fact.

140. *Id.*

See generally Annot. 39 A.L.R.3d 362 (1971), dealing with, *inter alia,* rezoning during the interim period; Annot. 27 A.L.R.3d 572 (1969), regarding eminent domain matters.

CHAPTER 10

THE DEED

Article I. Definition and Nature

§ 152. The Deed Defined.
§ 153. Types of Deeds Generally.
§ 154. The Warranty Deed.
§ 155. The Quitclaim Deed.
§ 156. The Requisites of a Valid Deed.
§ 157. Essential Factors in Deeds.
§ 158. Nonessential Factors in Deeds.
§ 159. Legal and Orderly Execution of Deeds.

Article II. Parties to a Deed

Division 1. Grantors

§ 160. Requisites to Be a Grantor Generally.
§ 161. Persons Non Compos Mentis.
§ 162. Infants' Deeds.
§ 163. Married Infants' Deeds.
§ 164. Married Women's Deeds to Persons Other Than Husbands.
§ 165. Married Women's Deeds to Their Husbands.
§ 166. Corporations' Deeds.
§ 167. Partnerships' Deeds Generally.
§ 168. Partnership Real Property in Partnership Name.
§ 169. Partnership Real Property in Partnership Name Conveyed in Name of Individual Partner.
§ 170. Partnership Real Property Held in Name of One or More Partners Where Real Property Records Do Not Disclose Partnership.
§ 171. Partnership Real Property Held in Name of One or All Partners or by Third Person in Trust for Partnership.
§ 172. Partnership Real Property Held in Names of All Partners.
§ 173. Unincorporated Associations' Deeds.
§ 174. Trustees' Deeds.
§ 175. Aliens' Deeds.

Division 2. Grantees

§ 176. Requisites to Be a Grantee Generally.
§ 177. Grants to Persons *en Ventre sa Mere*.
§ 178. Grants to Dead Persons.
§ 179. Grants to "Heirs" of Living Persons.
§ 180. Grantees' Deed from Himself.
§ 181. Grants to Aliens.
§ 182. Sufficiency of Identification of Grantee.

Article III. Subject Matter of Deeds; Rules of Construction

§ 183. Sufficiency of Description of Subject Matter.
§ 184. Description by Monuments, Courses and Distances, or by Metes and Bounds.
§ 185. Rules of Construction in Cases of Conflicts and Ambiguities in Metes and Bounds Descriptions.

§ 186. The "Intention of the Parties."
§ 187. Rules That Monuments Control Distances and Courses; Courses Control Distances; Quantity Statement Least Reliable Guide.
§ 188. Rule That Boundaries Extend to Center of Monuments; Streets, Public Roads, Alleys, Ditches and Streams.
§ 189. Description by Reference to Plat or Map.
§ 190. Description by Reference to Streets and Numbers.
§ 191. Description by Reference to Prior Conveyance.
§ 192. Description by Reference to Quantity or Number of Acres.
§ 193. Miscellaneous Informal Descriptions.
§ 194. Necessity for Words of Conveyance.

Article IV. Execution of Deed

Division 1. Signing: Seal; No Witnesses Required

§ 195. Proper Execution of Deed by Grantor Generally.
§ 196. Signing.
§ 197. Seal.
§ 198. Witnesses Not Required; When Acknowledgment Required.

Division 2. Delivery

§ 199. Delivery Generally.
§ 200. Delivery Presumed from Possession of Deed by Grantee.
§ 201. Delivery Presumed from Recordation.
§ 202. Delivery to Third Person Not Grantee.
§ 203. Delivery in Escrow or Conditional Delivery.
§ 204. Delivery in Escrow; Necessity for Written Contract to Make Escrow Enforceable.
§ 205. Escrow's Wrongful Delivery to Grantee.
§ 206. Conditional Delivery Directly to Grantee.

Division 3. Acceptance

§ 207. Acceptance by Grantee Generally.

Division 4. Revenue Stamps

§ 208. Revenue Stamps Required on Deeds.

Division 5. Reading of Deed by Grantor Not Necessary

§ 209. No Necessity That Grantor Read Deed; Deed Effective in Absence of Fraud.

Article I. Definition and Nature

§ 152. The Deed Defined.

The most familiar method for the transfer of title to real property is by deed. A deed transfers real property "between the living" or by *inter vivos* conveyance as distinguished from a "will," which is a legal instrument that passes property from a dead person to a living person.

A deed may be defined as an instrument of *writing, signed, sealed* and *delivered* under which an interest in real property is transferred from a grantor to a grantee.[1]

---

1. Strain v. Fitzgerald, 128 N.C. 396, 38 S.E. 929 (1901); Ballard v. Ballard, 230 N.C. 629, 55 S.E.2d 316 (1949).

§ 153. Types of Deeds Generally.

There are two types of deeds of common commercial use in North Carolina — the warranty deed and the quitclaim deed. Other designations given to deeds, usually officials' deeds or deeds made in connection with court proceedings are sheriffs' deeds, commissioners' deeds, executors' deeds, guardians' deeds, trustees' deeds, or tax deeds. By reason of modern statutes and the Statute of Uses,[2] deeds which are properly executed and delivered will pass title from the grantor to the grantee.

§ 154. The Warranty Deed.

A warranty deed is a conveyance in which the grantor warrants or "guarantees" the title that he conveys to the grantee. There are two kinds of warranty deeds, (1) the deed with a *general warranty* in which the grantor warrants and guarantees to his grantee that the title that he conveys is good and unencumbered *as against all persons whomsoever,*[3] and (2) the deed with a *special warranty,* in which the grantor warrants and guarantees to his grantee that the title that he conveys is free from defects or encumbrances that have arisen since he acquired the title; the warranty is limited to those defects which may have occurred *"by, through or under the grantor"*[4] and is not a warranty against all potential defects. No warranty or guarantee is implied in a deed but must be express.[5]

§ 155. The Quitclaim Deed.

A quitclaim deed is one that purports to convey only the grantor's present interest in the land described, if the grantor *has* any interest. There is no warranty or guarantee from the grantor to the grantee but the deed merely transfers whatever right, title or interest the grantor happens to have in the land described.[6] Quitclaim deeds are frequently used to quiet title by serving to correct possible defects in title[7]; there may be doubt as to whether one has any interest in certain land and he "quitclaims" any interest that he may have, thus clearing the title of the grantee of his interest or potential claim, if any. Or sometimes a grantor has a doubtful title which he is reluctant to warrant and guarantee in any way. The title to realty may be as effectually transferred by quitclaim

---

2. N.C. Gen. Stat. § 41-7 (1950).
3. Spencer v. Jones, 168 N.C. 291, 84 S.E. 261 (1915).
4. *Id.*
5. Barden v. Stickney, 130 N.C. 62, 40 S.E. 842 (1902); Guy v. First Carolina Joint Stock Land Bank of Columbia, 205 N.C. 357, 171 S.E. 341 (1933).
6. Hayes v. Ricard, 245 N.C. 687, 97 S.E.2d 105 (1957).
7. Lake, North Carolina Practice Methods § 92 (1952).

deed as by any other form of conveyance and such a deed will convey whatever interest the grantor may have at the time it is given.[8]

§ 156. The Requisites of a Valid Deed.

In order for a conveyance to be valid in North Carolina it must be evidenced by an instrument in writing, signed by the grantor or by his authorized agent,[9] sealed,[10] and delivered.[11] It is not necessary, however, for a deed to be in any particular form in order to be valid so long as certain essential factors are present.[12]

§ 157. Essential Factors in Deeds.

Every deed must have the following: (1) a competent grantor; (2) a grantee capable of holding title to land; (3) a sufficient description of the property; (4) operative words of conveyance; (5) proper execution by the grantor; (6) proper delivery; and (7) an acceptance by the grantee that is adequate in law.

§ 158. Nonessential Factors in Deeds.

While desirable, it is not essential for a deed to be dated or acknowledged in order for the deed to be valid as between the grantor and grantee. It is also not a prerequisite to the deed's validity that it be witnessed.

Nor is it required that a recital of the consideration be included in a deed.[13] A deed in proper form is good and will pass title to land described therein without a recital of the amount of the consideration or that it has been paid.[14] The presence or lack of a recital of the consideration paid may become significant, however, if the deed is ever attacked as a fraudulent conveyance executed in fraud of the creditors of the grantor,[15] if it

---

8. Hayes v. Ricard, 245 N.C. 687, 97 S.E.2d 105 (1957). In this case it was held that a subsequently executed quitclaim deed which was recorded prior to a previously executed warranty deed would take precedence over the previously executed but subsequently recorded warranty deed.
9. N.C. GEN. STAT. § 22-2.
10. Strain v. Fitzgerald, 128 N.C. 396, 38 S.E. 929 (1901).
11. Ballard v. Ballard, 230 N.C. 629, 55 S.E.2d 316 (1949).
12. New Home Bldg. Supply Co. v. Nations, 259 N.C. 681, 131 S.E.2d 425 (1963). The Supreme Court of North Carolina states, however, that it would be "a very pernicious thing for a lawyer to experiment with legal writings by endeavoring to see how informal he can make them and how far he can with safety depart from known and customary forms." *See also* 2 MORDECAI, LAW LECTURES 797 (1916).
13. Howard v. Turner, 125 N.C. 107, 34 S.E. 229 (1899); New Home Bldg. Supply Co. v. Nations, 259 N.C. 681, 131 S.E.2d 425 (1963).
14. Howard v. Turner, 125 N.C. 107, 34 S.E. 229 (1899); Smith v. Smith, 249 N.C. 669, 107 S.E.2d 530 (1963); Little v. Little, 205 N.C. 1, 169 S.E. 799 (1933).
15. Howard v. Turner, 125 N.C. 107, 34 S.E. 229 (1899). For recent decisions dealing with the doctrine of fraudulent conveyances *see* Distributing Corp. v. Schofield, 44 N.C. App. 520, 261 S.E.2d 688 (1980), citing North Carolina National Bank v. Evans, 296 N.C. 374, 250 S.E.2d 231 (1979); Everett v. Gainer, 269 N.C. 528, 153 S.E.2d 90 (1967); Nytco Leasing, Inc. v. Southeastern Motels, Inc., 40 N.C. App. 120, 252 S.E.2d 826 (1979); Edwards v. Northwestern Bank, 39 N.C. App. 261, 250 S.E.2d 651 (1979); Tuttle v. Tuttle, 38 N.C. App. 651, 248 S.E.2d 896 (1978), *cert. denied*, 296 N.C. 589, 254 S.E.2d 32 (1979).

becomes necessary to determine whether the grantee is a purchaser for value in order to establish his priority under the recordation statutes,[16] or as evidence of fraud perpetrated on the grantor in the procuring of the deed.[17] While a statement in a deed of the amount and payment of the consideration is presumed to be correct, in the event that it becomes material parol evidence may be admitted to show the facts to be otherwise than as recited in a deed with respect to the consideration paid.[18]

§ 159. Legal and Orderly Execution of Deeds.

While many writings may suffice as deeds of conveyance of lands without containing the formal parts of deeds and without formalities of execution, since those formal parts of deeds and formalities of execution developed through the ages are calculated to convey meaning in the clearest, most distinct, and most effectual manner, and have been well considered and settled by the wisdom of successive ages, it is prudent not to depart from them without good reason or urgent necessity.[19] The various formal parts and formalities for a well-executed deed have been enumerated as follows: (1) sufficient parties, a grantor and a grantee; (2) proper subject matter; (3) apt words of conveyance; (4) a sufficient consideration; (5) a writing on paper or parchment duly stamped; (6) the conditions, if any; the warranties, if any; the covenants, if any; and the conclusion, which should include the date; (7) reading, if desired; (8) the signature and seal; (9) delivery; (10) attestation, if any.[20]

These formalities in the legal and orderly execution of deeds are discussed in the following sections.

---

16. Howard v. Turner, 125 N.C. 107, 34 S.E. 229 (1899).

17. McLeod v. Bullard, 84 N.C. 516 (1881). "As a general rule, a deed which is otherwise valid will not be invalidated by reason of a total or partial failure of consideration, and will nevertheless operate to convey title. The failure of consideration may, however, be accompanied by other circumstances which will justify setting aside the deed. . . ." Gadsden v. Johnson, 261 N.C. 743, 136 S.E.2d 74 (1964). *See* Jones v. Saunders, 254 N.C. 644, 119 S.E.2d 789 (1961), in which the court said: "The controlling principle established by our decisions is that inadequacy of consideration is a circumstance to be considered by the jury in connection with other relevant circumstances on an issue of fraud, but inadequacy of consideration standing alone will not justify setting aside a deed on the ground of fraud. However, if the inadequacy of consideration is so gross that it shows practically nothing was paid, it is sufficient to be submitted to the jury without other evidence." *See also* Garris v. Scott, 246 N.C. 568, 575, 99 S.E.2d 750 (1957).

18. Gadsden v. Johnson, 261 N.C. 743, 136 S.E.2d 74 (1964); Hinson v. Morgan, 225 N.C. 740, 36 S.E.2d 266 (1945); Willis v. Willis, 242 N.C. 597, 89 S.E.2d 152 (1955); *Ex parte* Barefoot, 201 N.C. 393, 160 S.E. 365 (1931); STANSBURY, N.C. EVIDENCE § 259 (2d ed. 1963).

19. MINOR & WURTS, REAL PROPERTY § 892 (1910).

20. 2 MORDECAI, LAW LECTURES 766 (1916).

Article II. Parties to a Deed

Division 1. Grantors

§ 160. Requisites to Be a Grantor Generally.

Every deed must have a competent grantor who is capable of entering into a valid contract.

§ 161. Persons Non Compos Mentis.

If a grantor makes a deed subsequent to a judicial determination that he is not mentally competent, his deed is absolutely *void* in the absence of proof that the grantor had been restored to sanity prior to his execution of the deed.[21] If the contract or conveyance was executed by a person who was *non compos mentis,* but who had not been adjudged insane or placed under guardianship, prior to the deed's execution, the deed is merely *voidable* and not *void.*[22] The measure of the capacity of a grantor is to be determined by his ability to understand the nature of the act in which he is engaged and its scope and effect, or its nature and consequences, not whether he is capable of acting wisely and discreetly so as to drive a good bargain, but that he should be in such possession of his faculties as to enable him to know at least what he is doing and to contract understandingly.[23] There may be an unnatural state of mental incapacity produced by intoxication and in North Carolina equity will in proper cases afford relief from contracts executed by a drunken man.[24] The mere fact, however, that a person is of weak understanding, if there is no fraud or surprise, is not cause for setting a deed aside.[25] If one is incompetent to make a deed his land may be conveyed only by his guardian as provided

---

21. Sprinkle v. Wellborn, 140 N.C. 163, 52 S.E. 666 (1905); Wadford v. Gillette, 193 N.C. 413, 137 S.E. 314 (1927); Tomlins v. Cranford, 227 N.C. 323, 42 S.E.2d 100 (1947). After a person has once been found to be mentally incompetent there is a presumption that the mental incapacity continues. Davis v. Davis, 223 N.C. 36, 25 S.E.2d 181 (1943).

22. Riggan v. Green, 80 N.C. 237 (1879); Allred v. Smith, 135 N.C. 443, 47 S.E. 597 (1904); Beeson v. Smith, 149 N.C. 142, 62 S.E. 888 (1908).

23. Sprinkle v. Wellborn, 140 N.C. 163, 52 S.E. 666 (1905); Carland v. Allison, 221 N.C. 120, 19 S.E.2d 245 (1942); Ludwig v. Hart, 40 N.C. App. 188, 252 S.E.2d 270 (1979).

24. *See* Morrison v. McLeod, 22 N.C. 221 (1839); Whitesides v. Greenlea, 17 N.C. 152 (1831); Calloway v. Witherspoon, 40 N.C. 128 (1847); Freeman v. Dwiggins, 55 N.C. 162 (1855); McCraw v. Davis, 37 N.C. 618 (1843).

25. Goins v. McLoud, 231 N.C. 655, 58 S.E.2d 634 (1950); Davis v. Davis, 223 N.C. 36, 56 S.E.2d 30 (1943); Bond v. Manufacturing Co., 140 N.C. 381 (1906). In Moffit v. Witherspoon, 32 N.C. 185, 192 (1849), the Supreme Court of North Carolina states: "If all persons are to be considered incapable of making contracts who do not manage their business with judgment and discernment, we apprehend there are many more disqualified by law than are now considered so."

by statute.[26] The law presumes that every person is sane in the absence of evidence to the contrary.[27]

§ 162. Infants' Deeds.

A person under eighteen years of age is an infant in North Carolina.[28] An infant's contracts and deeds are voidable and not void.[29] It is optional with an infant as to whether his deeds, leases or mortgages will be avoided or whether they will be ratified upon his reaching his majority. If he recognizes a deed executed during his minority as binding after he reaches his majority or takes any benefit under the conveyance, such will constitute a ratification of the deed, making it valid in every respect, provided the grantor is not then under some other disability.[30] An infant who has executed a deed cannot make the deed either void or valid by any act done by him while he remains a minor. An infant may make a deed valid, after coming of age, if he does some deliberate act by which he takes a benefit under the deed or expressly recognizes its validity. While under age, he cannot affirm or disaffirm, confirm or repudiate any act or deed for the obvious reason that he is supposed to have the same want of discretion, on account of which his first act or deed is voidable.[31] If the infant grantor does not disaffirm his deed within three years after he becomes of age he will be bound by the deed as an executed conveyance;[32] his inaction will become a ratification. During the three years after

---

26. N.C. GEN. STAT. § 33-31.
27. *See* Stewart v. Stewart, 25 N.C. App. 628, 214 S.E.2d 295 (1975), citing Davis v. Davis, 223 N.C. 36, 25 S.E.2d 181 (1943).
28. As a consequence of the enactment of N.C. GEN. STAT. § 48A-1, effective on July 5, 1971, the common-law definition of a "minor" was abrogated. N.C. GEN. STAT. § 48A-2 now defines a "minor" as any person who has not reached the age of eighteen years. Thus, since July 5, 1971, a person eighteen years or older is deemed capable of managing his own legal affairs and is therefore legally competent to execute a deed.
29. Weeks v. Wilkins, 139 N.C. 215, 51 S.E. 909 (1905); Baggett v. Jackson, 160 N.C. 26, 76 S.E. 86 (1912); Hogan v. Utter, 175 N.C. 332, 95 S.E. 565 (1918). *See* Personnel Corp. v. Rogers, 276 N.C. 279, 172 S.E.2d 19 (1970), which holds that an infant may not disaffirm a contract which he makes for "necessaries." Quoting from COKE ON LITTLETON 172 (13th ed. 1788), that "An infant may bind himselfe to pay for his necessary meat, drinke, apparell, necessary physicke, and such other necessaries, and likewise for his good teaching or instruction, whereby he may profit himselfe afterwards," the North Carolina Supreme Court held that the concept of "necessaries" should be enlarged to include such articles of property and such services as are reasonably necessary to enable the infant to earn the money required to provide the necessities of life for himself and those who are legally dependent upon him, including his wife and children. It is therefore conceivable that the execution of a deed by a minor might be part of a contractual obligation for "necessaries" and not voidable if made to provide the minor, his spouse or his child, with food, clothing, shelter, and medical attention, or to make it possible for the minor himself to earn money required to provide the necessities of life for himself or those legally dependent upon him.
30. Ward v. Anderson, 111 N.C. 115, 15 S.E. 933 (1892); *cf.* Gaskins v. Allen, 137 N.C. 426, 49 S.E. 919 (1905).
31. McCormick v. Leggett, 53 N.C. 425 (1862).
32. Baggett v. Jackson, 160 N.C. 26, 76 S.E. 86 (1912).

reaching his majority, however, the infant grantor may elect to disaffirm his deed notwithstanding the fact that upon the execution of the deed he fraudulently represented himself to be of legal age.[33] That the land has been transferred by the infant's grantee to a purchaser for value without notice does not preclude the infant grantor from disaffirming his deed when he reaches the age of eighteen.[34] Any act manifesting the infant's intention to disaffirm his deed will suffice as a disaffirmance. The execution of a deed aliening the land to one other than the prior grantee after the infant reaches his majority will operate as a disaffirmance.[35] The infant's denial of the execution of a deed in his answer when a suit against him is filed is a repudiation of his deed,[36] as is an action brought by the infant in ejectment against his grantee.[37] Returning the purchase money or bringing an action to remove cloud from his title would likewise be unequivocal acts of disaffirmance.[38] When the infant grantor, upon reaching his majority, seeks to avoid his conveyance because of his disability, he must restore any consideration he received for the deed, provided the money is then in hand or the property into which it has been converted can be reached.[39] If the infant has received money under a contract made during his minority, he must, if he has it or any part thereof, return it upon his disaffirmance, but if he does not have it, or the benefits therefrom, he need not return it or offer to put the parties in *statu quo.*[40]

In order for minors' conveyances of real property to be valid and enforceable it is necessary to follow the statutory procedures designed to protect incompetents.[41]

§ 163. Married Infants' Deeds.

While an infant's own deed's validity is governed by the rules of the foregoing section, in those instances where a married infant spouse's signature is required to validate the deed of the other spouse who has reached his majority, special rules apply in North Carolina. By statute, where a minor person under eighteen years of age is married to a spouse

---

33. Carolina Interstate Bldg. & Loan Ass'n v. Black, 119 N.C. 323, 25 S.E. 975 (1895).

34. Jackson v. Beard, 162 N.C. 105, 78 S.E. 6 (1913); Foster v. Williams, 182 N.C. 632, 109 S.E. 834 (1921).

35. Ward v. Anderson, 111 N.C. 115, 15 S.E. 933 (1892); Hoyle v. Stowe, 19 N.C. 320 (1837); Richmond Cedar Works v. Kramer Bros. & Co., 267 F. 723 (1920).

36. Ricks v. Wilson, 154 N.C. 282, 70 S.E. 476 (1911).

37. Jones v. Cohen, 82 N.C. 75 (1880).

38. Baggett v. Jackson, 160 N.C. 26, 76 S.E. 86 (1912).

39. Millsaps v. Estes, 137 N.C. 535, 50 S.E. 227 (1905).

40. Chandler v. Jones, 172 N.C. 569, 90 S.E. 580 (1916); Faircloth v. Johnson, 189 N.C. 429, 127 S.E. 346 (1925).

41. *See* N.C. Gen. Stat. § 33-31, which provides for special proceedings upon petition by guardian to sell interest of ward, requiring the approval of the superior court judge; Tate v. Mott, 96 N.C. 19, 2 S.E. 176 (1887).

over eighteen years of age, the married infant under eighteen is held to be competent to sign deeds and other instruments to which his signature is required in connection with the marital relationship. A minor spouse may waive, release or renounce any right or interest which he or she may have in the real or personal property of the other spouse. In addition, any married person under eighteen years of age may jointly execute with his or her spouse any note, contract of insurance, deed, deed of trust, mortgage, lien or other instrument held with the other spouse by the entirety, as joint tenants, tenants in common, or in any other manner, provided the spouse of the minor spouse is eighteen years of age or older.[42]

§ 164. Married Women's Deeds to Persons Other Than Husbands.

Prior to 1965, because of a constitutional provision and statutes, no conveyance of a married woman's real estate to a person other than her husband was valid unless made with the written assent of her husband. The deed of a married woman while married without her husband's written assent was inoperative and conveyed nothing.[43] The wife was not, during coverture, estopped to deny the validity of her deed even if she misrepresented herself as unmarried and capable of making a valid conveyance.[44] But where a married woman conveyed her real property without the written assent of her husband and thereafter survived her husband, she was estopped after his death to recover the land or defeat the title of her grantee on the ground that it was void because of the lack of written assent by her husband at the time of its execution.[45]

Under the law prior to 1965 a husband's signature under his wife's signature on the deed and his acknowledgment of the deed was deemed sufficient as showing his written assent to her conveyance.[46] It was not necessary that the husband's name appear in the body of the deed.[47] It was indicated in a dictum statement by the North Carolina Supreme Court that the husband's written assent might not be in the deed at all; that his signature on the deed as a witness or in a letter evincing his assent would be sufficient as the written assent required.[48] In deeds executed prior to 1965 it is essential to see that the husbands of married women grantors properly gave their written assent in order for the deed to be valid.

---

42. N.C. Gen. Stat. § 39-13.2.
43. Burford v. Mochy, 224 N.C. 234, 29 S.E.2d 729 (1944).
44. *Id.*
45. Harrell v. Powell, 251 N.C. 636, 112 S.E.2d 81 (1960).
46. Joiner v. Firemen's Ins. Co., 6 F. Supp. 103 (D.C.N.C. 1934).
47. *But see* Gray v. Matthis, 52 N.C. 503 (1860), in which the contrary was held in a case antedating the Constitution of 1868.
48. Stallings v. Walker, 176 N.C. 321, 324, 97 S.E. 25 (1918); *cf.* Hensley v. Blankenship, 174 N.C. 760, 94 S.E. 519 (1917).

Since 1965, by reason of an amendment of the North Carolina Constitution [49] and by reason of the repeal of a number of statutes,[50] it is no longer essential for deeds from married women to be signed or assented to by their husbands, in order to make them valid.[51]

§ 165. Married Women's Deeds to Their Husbands.

Prior to January 1, 1978, in order for a married woman's deed to her husband to be valid, either conveying to him a legal title [52] or creating a trust [53] for his benefit in real property, there was a statutory requirement in North Carolina that the deed be certified as not being unreasonable or injurious to the wife.[54] The purpose of this requirement was to protect the wife who was still presumed to be under the coercive influence of her husband.[55] Without such certificate any deed of a married woman to her husband was, in theory, void *ab initio*.[56]

North Carolina General Statutes, § 52-6 was repealed in 1977 effective January 1, 1978.[57] In its place, a new sex-neutral statute, North Carolina General Statutes, § 52-10, has been enacted. Various curative statutes also limit the effect of the former statute. North Carolina General Statutes, § 52-8, for example, reads as follows:

> Any contract between husband and wife coming within the provisions of G.S. 52-6 executed between January 1, 1930, and January 1, 1978, which does not comply with the requirement of a private examination of the wife and which is in all other respects regular is hereby validated and confirmed to the same extent as if the examination of the wife had been separate and apart from the husband. This section shall not affect pending litigation.[58]

---

49. N.C. CONST. art. X, § 6, amended on January 14, 1964 by a vote of the people, renumbered in 1971, art. X § 4.

50. Formerly N.C. GEN. STAT. §§ 52-1, 52-2, 52-4.

51. Since the newly enacted statutes have no retroactive effect it is still important to know that any deed executed prior to the effective date of the new statutes from a married woman to a third person without the written assent of her husband is absolutely void as a deed during coverture. Buford v. Mochy, 224 N.C. 234, 29 S.E.2d 729 (1944).

52. *In re* Estate of Loftin, 285 N.C. 717, 208 S.E.2d 670 (1974); Best v. Utley, 189 N.C. 356, 127 S.E. 337 (1925).

53. Garner v. Horner, 191 N.C. 539, 132 S.E. 290 (1926).

54. N.C. GEN. STAT. § 52-6, repealed by 1977 Sess. L., c. 375, s. 1, effective January 1, 1978.

55. Butler v. Butler, 169 N.C. 584, 86 S.E. 507 (1915). *Accord,* Kanoy v. Kanoy, 17 N.C. App. 344, 194 S.E.2d 201 (1973).

56. Caldwell v. Blount, 193 N.C. 560, 137 S.E. 578 (1927); Bolin v. Bolin, 246 N.C. 666, 99 S.E.2d 920 (1957). *Accord,* Kanoy v. Kanoy, 17 N.C. App. 344, 194 S.E.2d 201 (1973).

57. 1977 Sess. L., c. 375, s. 1, effective January 1, 1978.

58. *See* Spencer v. Spencer, 37 N.C. App. 481, 246 S.E.2d 805 (1978), n. 2, at 37 N.C. App. 488, where the court states:

> We note that G.S. 52-6 has been repealed effective 1 January 1978. The statute has been replaced by a new sex-neutral statute, G.S. 52-10. Also, over the years, the legislature has tried to limit the damage of G.S. 52-6 by passing curative statutes such as G.S. 52-8

§ 166. Corporations' Deeds.

A corporation is an artificial being which exists as a legal person or entity in contemplation of law. It has a legal existence separate and distinct from its shareholders and has its own rights and liabilities. A corporation may therefore own and convey real property in its own name upon compliance with the statutes provided.

If the transaction is one *in the ordinary course of the business* of the corporation its land may be deeded without any authorization of its board of directors, if signed on behalf of the corporation by its president, a vice-president or an assistant vice president and attested or countersigned by its secretary or an assistant secretary.[59] Such deed will pass the corporation's title notwithstanding anything to the contrary in the bylaws or charter of the corporation provided the instrument does not on its face disclose a potential breach of fiduciary obligation by the executing officer and provided the grantee has no notice of any lack of authority or breach of fiduciary obligation of the executing officer.[60]

As to conveyances of real property *not in the ordinary course of the business* of the corporation, it may be said generally that a corporation may not, in North Carolina, sell, exchange or lease all or substantially all of its property unless authorized by resolution of its board of directors and approved by its shareholders, either at an annual or special meeting as provided by statute.[61] If, however, the sale, exchange or lease is made pursuant to the judgment of the board of directors that the corporation is in a failing condition and a sale for cash or its equivalent is deemed by the directors to be advisable for the purpose of meeting the corporation's liabilities,[62] or if the corporation was formed for the purpose of liquidating its property and assets,[63] or if the sale, exchange or lease is not made to dispose of the corporate business but is merely a transaction, or one of a

---

as it stood at the time this suit was initiated. However, like Br'er Rabbit and the Tar Baby, the legislature found itself unable to turn the wretched creature loose.

See also N.C. GEN. STAT. § 39-13.1(b):

(b) Any deed, contract, conveyance, lease or other instrument executed prior to February 7, 1945, which is in all other respects regular except for the failure to take the private examination of a married woman who is a party to such deed, contract, conveyance, lease or other instrument is hereby validated and confirmed to the same extent as if such private examination had been taken, provided that this section shall not apply to any instruments now involved in any pending litigation.

In addition, *see* Johnson v. Burrow, 42 N.C. App. 273, 256 S.E.2d 811 (1979); Faucette v. Griffin, 35 N.C. App. 7, 239 S.E.2d 712 (1978).

59. N.C. GEN. STAT. § 55-36 (a). A 1979 amendment adds the assistant vice president to the earlier statute. A corporation deed will fail to pass title when it is not attested by its corporate secretary. *See* J. Perry Jones Realty, Inc. v. McLamb, 21 N.C. App. 482, 204 S.E.2d 880 (1974), citing this section in the original volume.

60. N.C. GEN. STAT. § 55-36 (a).
61. N.C. GEN. STAT. § 55-112 (c).
62. N.C. GEN. STAT. § 55-112 (b) (1).
63. N.C. GEN. STAT. § 55-112 (b) (2).

series of transactions, to further such business, whether usual or unusual, such sale, exchange or lease may be made on the authority of the board of directors without authorization from the shareholders.[64] A mortgage of or other security interest in all or any part of the property of a corporation may be made by authority of the board of directors without authorization of the shareholders, unless otherwise provided in the charter or in bylaws adopted by the shareholders.[65]

In addition to the officers specified above as capable of executing a deed for a corporation, any agent or corporate representative may bind the corporation pursuant to express, implied or apparent authority, ratification, or estoppel.[66]

If the corporation has been dissolved, its real property may still be conveyed by a majority of its last board of directors, then living, however reduced in numbers, acting directly themselves or through the last officers of the corporation.[67]

Foreign corporations shall have the same rights and privileges as domestic corporations with reference to conveyances of real estate.[68]

If any instrument purporting to be executed by a corporation bears a seal purporting to be the corporate seal, setting forth the name of the corporation, engraved, lithographed, printed, stamped, impressed upon, or otherwise affixed to the instrument, there is a prima facie presumption that the seal is the duly adopted corporate seal of the corporation, that the seal has been affixed by a person authorized to affix the seal and that such instrument was duly executed and signed by persons who were officers or agents of the corporation acting by authority duly given by the board of directors and that such instrument is the act of the corporation.[69] Such instrument is admissible into evidence without further proof of execution and will be binding and valid until evidence to the contrary is adduced.[70]

---

64. N.C. GEN. STAT. § 55-112 (b) (3). *See* Yaggy v. B.V.D. Co., 7 N.C. App. 590, 173 S.E.2d 496 (1970).
65. N.C. GEN. STAT. § 55-112 (a).
66. N.C. GEN. STAT. § 55-36 (e). *Compare* Barcello v. Hapgood, 118 N.C. 712, 24 S.E. 124 (1896), *and* Yaggy v. B.V.D. Co., 7 N.C. App. 590, 173 S.E.2d 496 (1970).
67. N.C. GEN. STAT. § 55-114 (f).
68. N.C. GEN. STAT. §§ 55-36 (d), 55-132.
69. N.C. GEN. STAT. § 55-36 (c). A corporate seal is a necessary prerequisite to a valid conveyance of real estate by a corporation. Investors Corp. v. Field Financial Corp., 5 N.C. App. 156, 167 S.E.2d 852 (1969); Caldwell v. Manufacturing Co., 121 N.C. 339, 28 S.E. 475 (1897). Note that a curative statute, N.C. GEN. STAT. § 47-71.1, is periodically updated; this statute validates corporate conveyances where the corporate seal has been omitted prior to the legislature's enactment of such curative statute. N.C. GEN. STAT. § 47-71.1 was updated by amendment in 1973; such amendments do not apply to pending litigation.
70. *Compare* the following cases, decided under prior statutes governing corporate conveyances: Lockville Power Corp. v. Power Co., 168 N.C. 219, 84 S.E. 398 (1915); Clark v. Hodge, 116 N.C. 761, 21 S.E. 562 (1895); Barcello v. Hapgood, 118 N.C. 712, 24 S.E. 124 (1896); Benbow v. Cook, 115 N.C. 324, 20 S.E. 453 (1894); Edwards v. Supply Co., 150 N.C. 173, 63 S.E. 740 (1909).

§ 167. Partnerships' Deeds Generally.

At the common law, prior to the adoption of the Uniform Partnership Act, legal title could not be vested in a partnership as such. In North Carolina, since 1941 when the Uniform Partnership Act was adopted, a partnership may acquire, hold and convey title to real property in the partnership name.[71] Partnership real property may now be held in the name of the partnership, in the name of an individual partner, in the name of all of the partners, or in the name of a trustee in trust for the partnership.

§ 168. Partnership Real Property in Partnership Name.

Every partner is an agent of the partnership for the purpose of carrying on the partnership's business. Therefore, if partnership real property is held in the partnership name, any one of the partners may make a valid conveyance of the partnership's title by a conveyance made in the partnership's name, if the partner who executes the deed has authority from his copartner or if the deed is excuted by him apparently for the purpose of carrying on the partnership's business in the usual way.[72] If the granting partner in fact has no authority to execute a deed and his immediate grantee has knowledge of his lack of authority, the deed is not binding as between the partnership and the immediate grantee who has such knowledge.[73] If, however, the grantee who has such knowledge himself transfers the property to another grantee who is a purchaser for value who has no knowledge that the partner's deed to the immediate grantee exceeded the granting partner's authority, the partnership may not recover the property conveyed.[74]

Individual partners have no authority, unless expressly authorized by the partners of a partnership, to assign partnership property in trust for creditors, to dispose of the good will of the partnership, to do any act that would make it impossible to carry on the partnership's ordinary business, to confess a judgment, or to submit a partnership claim or liability to arbitration or reference.[75]

§ 169. Partnership Real Property in Partnership Name Conveyed in Name of Individual Partner.

If title to partnership real property is in the name of the partnership, a conveyance by one of the partners in his own name, will pass the equitable interest of the partnership in such real property, provided the

---

71. N.C. GEN. STAT. § 59-38 (c).
72. N.C. GEN. STAT. § 59-39 (a).
73. Id.
74. N.C. GEN. STAT. § 59-40 (a).
75. N.C. GEN. STAT. § 59-39 (c).

deed is executed within the express or implied authority of the granting partner.[76]

§ 170. Partnership Real Property Held in Name of One or More Partners Where Real Property Records Do Not Disclose Partnership.

If title to partnership real property is held in the name of an individual partner or partners and the real estate records do not disclose the partnership, the partner or partners in whose name the title is held may convey title to the partnership property.[77] If, however, a grantee from the granting partner has knowledge that the property is partnership property and that the granting partner has no authority to make the conveyance, the partnership is not bound and may recover the property.[78]

§ 171. Partnership Real Property Held in Name of One or All Partners or by Third Person in Trust for Partnership.

If title to partnership real property is held in the name of one or all of the partners, or in the name of a third person in trust for the partnership, a conveyance by a partner in the partnership name or in the name of the granting partner will pass the partnership's equitable interest in the partnership real property if the deed's execution is within the express or implied authority of the granting partner.[79]

§ 172. Partnership Real Property Held in Names of All Partners.

Where title to real property is in the names of all the partners, a conveyance executed by all the partners passes all their rights in such real property.[80]

Under the Uniform Partnership Act a partner's right in specific partnership real property is not subject to dower, curtesy, or allowances to widows, heirs or next of kin.[81] Therefore it is not essential in a partner's deed conveying partnership real property that the partner's spouse sign the deed to cut off marital rights in the partnership real property. If title to partnership property has been placed in the name of an individual partner and conveyed by him, failure to require such partner's spouse to join in his deed may well result in a marketability problem or even future

---

76. N.C. GEN. STAT. §§ 59-40 (b), 59-39 (a).
77. N.C. GEN. STAT. § 59-40 (c).
78. N.C. GEN. STAT. §§ 59-40 (c), 59-39 (a).
79. N.C. GEN. STAT. §§ 59-40 (d), 59-39 (a).
80. N.C. GEN. STAT. § 59-40.
81. N.C. GEN. STAT. § 59-55 (b). *See* Ewing v. Caldwell, 243 N.C. 18, 89 S.E.2d 774 (1955).

§ 173   THE DEED   § 174

litigation respecting the rights of a partner's surviving spouse in the real property.[82]

§ 173. Unincorporated Associations' Deeds.

By statute in North Carolina,[83] voluntary organizations and associations of individuals organized for charitable, fraternal, religious, social or patriotic purposes may acquire and hold real estate in their common or corporate names. If real property has been acquired in the name of such organization or association in its common or corporate name, the organization or association may execute a deed of conveyance in its common or corporate name if the conveyance is authorized by resolution of the body of members duly constituted and if it is signed by its chairman or president, and its secretary or treasurer, or such officer as is the custodian of its common seal.[84]

It should be noted that under the foregoing statute voluntary organizations and associations not organized for charitable, fraternal, religious, social or patriotic purposes, such as associations, partnerships or copartnerships organized to engage in a business, trade or profession, may not acquire, hold and convey real estate in their common or corporate names.[85]

§ 174. Trustees' Deeds.

Where the validity of a deed of a trustee comes into question, the powers of the trustee to deal with the property which is the subject of the trust are of vital concern because the effects of trustees' deeds vary according

---

82. While North Carolina abolished curtesy and dower in 1959, there is retained a right in a surviving spouse to elect (in lieu of an intestate share) a life estate in one third in value of all real estate of which a deceased spouse was seised and possessed during his or her life unless the surviving spouse has waived his or her rights by joining with the other spouse in a conveyance. N.C. GEN. STAT. § 29-30.

83. N.C. GEN. STAT. § 39-24. *See* Goard v. Branscom, 15 N.C. App. 34, 189 S.E.2d 667 (1972). *See also* N.C. GEN. STAT. § 1-69.1, which provides that all unincorporated associations, organizations or societies, foreign or domestic, whether organized for profit or not, may sue or be sued under the name by which they are commonly known and called or under which they are doing business, to the same extent as any other legal entity established by law, and without naming any of the individual members composing it. Any judgments and executions against any such association, organization or society shall bind its real and personal property in like manner as if it were incorporated. N.C. GEN. STAT. § 1-69.1 does not apply to partnerships or corporations which are organized to engage in any business, trade or profession.

84. N.C. GEN. STAT. § 39-25.

85. N.C. GEN. STAT. § 39-24. *But see* Venus Lodge v. Acme Benevolent Ass'n, 231 N.C. 522, 58 S.E.2d 109 (1950), holding that a deed to an unincorporated association is not void at common law in North Carolina. Since it looks at substance rather than form the common law construes such a conveyance to be a grant to the members of the association, and adjudges that it vests the title to the property embraced by the conveyance in such members as individuals.

to the terms and objects of the trust. A trustee has no authority to convey land held by him in trust unless such authority is conferred under the instrument creating the trust.[86]

It should be noted, however, that pursuant to North Carolina General Statutes, §§ 43-63 and 43-64, enacted in 1975, when any instrument describes or designates a record owner of real property simply as "trustee" or "agent," without identifying the owner of any beneficial interest, or not setting forth the powers of such "trustee" or "agent" with respect to real property, the mere designation of the record owner as "trustee" or "agent" shall not be notice to any person thereafter dealing with the real property that there is any limitation on the powers of the party described in the instrument as "trustee" or "agent" nor put him upon inquiry. Unless the instrument by which the "trustee" or "agent" takes title or some other instrument in the recorded chain of title sets forth the name of the owner of a beneficial interest or specifies the powers of such "trustee" or "agent," the "trustee" or "agent" shall be deemed to have full power to convey or otherwise dispose of the real estate.[87]

While the terms of trusts are strictly construed to determine the extent of trustees' powers, the power of a particular trustee to make a conveyance of trust property need not be expressly conferred.[88] The trustee's power to make a conveyance may arise by implication from language in the trust instrument necessarily requiring the exercise of the power of sale, stating the purposes of the trust, or conferring other powers and duties to which a power of sale or to convey is essential.[89] A power of sale of real estate is implied in a trustee who is charged with the duty of "investing and keeping invested" the trust estate.[90] If the trustee's

---

86. *See* Immanuel Baptist Tabernacle Church v. Southern Emmanuel Tabernacle Church, 27 N.C. App. 127, 218 S.E.2d 223 (1975). Where the congregation was the church's governing body and the church was a congregational church in respect to its property, a meeting of the congregation would be necessary to authorize a conveyance of the church's property. The trustees of any religious body may mortgage or sell or convey in fee simple any land owned by such body, when directed to do so by such church, congregation, society or denomination, or its committee, board or body having charge of its finances. N.C. GEN. STAT. § 61-4. Hall v. Wardwell, 228 N.C. 562, 46 S.E.2d 556 (1948).

87. N.C. GEN. STAT. §§ 43-63 and 43-64 became effective on May 15, 1975, and apply to instruments recorded both prior and subsequent to that date. The statutes provide, however, that no claim shall be barred within one year of May 15, 1975, if a written notice of the claim is recorded and indexed which (a) identifies the place in the public records where the reference to a fiduciary may be found, and (b) names the person who is the record owner of the real estate affected. *See* Webster, *The Quest for Clear Land Titles — "Blind" and "Curtained" Trusts,* 46 N.C.L. REV. 305 (1968), for a description of the problems which prompted enactment of these statutes.

88. Shannonhouse v. Wolfe, 191 N.C. 769, 133 S.E. 93 (1926).

89. *Id.*

90. Foil v. Newsome, 138 N.C. 115, 50 S.E. 597 (1905); Powell v. Woodcock, 149 N.C. 235, 62 S.E. 1071 (1908); Dillon v. Cotton Mills, 187 N.C. 812, 123 S.E. 89 (1924); Bank v. Edwards, 193 N.C. 118, 136 S.E. 342 (1926).

§ 175 THE DEED § 175

authorization to make a conveyance is not clearly expressed or supported by necessary implication from the terms of the instrument creating the trust, appropriate proceedings may be instituted in the courts to determine whether the trustee has the power to make a valid conveyance of the trust property.[91] A court of equity may even direct a trustee to deviate from the terms of the trust in proper circumstances to save the beneficiaries from want or to prevent the loss or destruction of the estate arising from exigencies not contemplated by the party creating the trust.[92]

Authority given in a trust instrument for the trustee to sell or convey trust property does not ordinarily include the power to execute a mortgage on the trust property.[93]

When a trustee executes a deed, otherwise valid, conveying trust property, but the deed fails to recite that he is "trustee," the trustee's deed will nevertheless operate as a conveyance, both as between the parties and as to those holding by mesne conveyances.[94] When a trustee executes a deed conveying trust property, it is not necessary for the trustee's wife to join in the execution of the deed to waive her rights as a spouse.[95]

One trustee does not have the power to bind his cotrustee or the trust where property is held in trust by two trustees.[96] Unless otherwise provided by the trust instrument, however, any power vested in three or more trustees may be exercised by a majority of the trustees under the Uniform Trust Act unless otherwise provided in the trust instrument.[97]

Cotrustees hold title to trust property as joint tenants and not as tenants in common and when one of several original trustees dies, becomes disabled, or refuses to act, the whole trust estate and the trust powers devolve upon the survivors, down to the last survivor, and the survivors shall have the same powers to carry out the provisions of the trust as the original trustees had.[98]

§ 175. Aliens' Deeds.

By statute in North Carolina it is lawful for aliens to take, hold and convey real property according to the same rules as are applicable to

---

91. Trust Co. v. Rasberry, 226 N.C. 586, 39 S.E.2d 601 (1946).
92. Id.
93. Shannonhouse v. Wolfe, 191 N.C. 769, 133 S.E. 93 (1926).
94. Tocci v. Nowfall, 220 N.C. 550, 18 S.E.2d 225 (1941).
95. Blades v. Railroad, 224 N.C. 32, 29 S.E.2d 148 (1944).
96. BOGERT, TRUSTS AND TRUSTEES § 554 (1960).
97. N.C. GEN. STAT. § 36-34.
98. *See In re* Estate of Smith, 200 N.C. 272, 156 S.E. 494 (1931); N.C. GEN. STAT. § 41-3. *Compare* N.C. GEN. STAT. § 45-8, which gives to surviving trustees and mortgagees the same powers of sale as held by original trustees and mortgagees in deeds of trust and mortgages upon the death of one or more of the joint trustees or joint mortgagees.

citizens of the State.[99] A recent statute directs the Secretary of State "to collect all information obtainable from reports by aliens made to agencies of the federal government on ownership of real property interests in North Carolina."[100] This information on alien ownership is to be updated every three months and made available to the General Assembly and the public.[101]

Division 2. Grantees

§ 176. Requisites to Be a Grantee Generally.

In order for a deed to be valid it must designate an existing person or legal entity as the grantee who is capable of taking title to the real property at the time of the execution of the deed.[102] In general, however, the requirements for being a grantee are less stringent than for being a grantor as contractual capacity is not a prerequisite to one's being a competent grantee. Thus an infant or non-sane person can be a grantee.

Corporations are legal entities and have capacity to take and hold real property.[103] Partnerships may likewise be grantees in the partnership name.[104] Trustees may also take title to real property.[105] Deeds may also be executed to unincorporated organizations and associations organized for charitable, fraternal, social or patriotic purposes.[106]

---

99. N.C. GEN. STAT. § 64-1. *See* N.C. GEN. STAT. § 64-3, which provides that the right of nonresident aliens *to inherit* property or to take by testamentary disposition is dependent upon reciprocity accorded to United States citizens with respect to succession rights to property in the alien's nation of residence. *In re* Johnston, 16 N.C. App. 38, 190 S.E.2d 879 (1972). Under N.C. GEN. STAT. § 64-4, the burden of proving the existence of reciprocal rights required by N.C. GEN. STAT. § 64-3 is upon the nonresident alien who seeks to inherit real property in North Carolina or to take it by testamentary disposition.

While the United States Supreme Court has held, in Zshernig v. Miller, 389 U.S. 429, 88 S. Ct. 664, 19 L. Ed. 2d 683 (1968), that an Oregon "reciprocity" statute similar to North Carolina's was unconstitutional as applied because it constituted an impermissible intrusion into foreign affairs and international relations, matters which the Constitution entrusts solely to the Federal Government, the North Carolina Court of Appeals in the case of *In re* Johnston, *supra,* holds that N.C. GEN. STAT. § 64-3 is constitutional.

100. N.C. GEN. STAT. § 64-1.1. 1979 Sess. L., c. 610, s. 1, effective May 21, 1979.

101. *Id.* See generally with respect to the constitutionality of state laws restricting the rights of nonresident aliens to inherit property from American decedents, *see generally* Comment, *Alien Inheritance Statutes: An Examination of the Constitutionality of State Laws Restricting the Rights of Nonresident Aliens from American Decedents,* 25 SYR. L. REV. 597 (1974); Comment, *The Demise of the "Iron Curtain" Statute,* 18 VILL. L. REV. 49 (1972); Comment, *Iron Curtain Statutes — What is the Standard of Constitutionality?,* 9 DUQ. L. REV. 242 (1970).

102. Heath v. Heath, 114 N.C. 547, 19 S.E. 155 (1894); Byrd v. Patterson, 229 N.C. 156, 48 S.E.2d 45 (1948); Woodcock v. Merrimon, 122 N.C. 731, 30 S.E. 321 (1898).

103. N.C. GEN. STAT. § 55-17 (b) (1).
104. N.C. GEN. STAT. § 59-38 (c).
105. Ryan v. McGehee, 83 N.C. 500 (1880).
106. N.C. GEN. STAT. § 39-24.

§ 177. Grants to Persons en Ventre sa Mere.

An unborn infant, *in esse* or *en ventre sa mere* at the time of the execution of a deed, is capable of being a grantee just as if he had been born at the time of the execution of the deed.[107] A child is deemed *in esse* and capable of being a grantee in a deed if born within 280 days (ten lunar months) of the time that the deed is executed.[108] A deed made directly "to a designated person and her children" will create a tenancy in common in the designated person and a child born two months after execution of the deed but will not create any interest in a child born more than one year after execution of the deed.[109] On the other hand, *if the grant is not direct* to the children, but reserves a life estate in a parent or other person with a limitation of a remainder to the children of a designated person, *all* the children of such person who are alive at the termination of the first estate, whether born before or after execution of the deed, or whether *en ventre sa mere* or not at the time of the execution of the deed, will take as grantees under the deed.[110]

§ 178. Grants to Dead Persons.

If the named grantee is dead at the time the deed is executed, the deed is void.[111] The fact that the deed says "to A and his heirs" will not make the deed valid if A is dead at the time of its execution since the words "and his heirs" are words of limitation and not of purchase.[112] If, however, the deed is "to A *or* his heirs" and A is dead at the time of the execution of the deed, the deed is not void since A's heirs are identifiable living persons subsequent to A's death and are capable of owning real property.[113]

§ 179. Grants to "Heirs" of Living Persons.

At the common law there could be no grant to the heirs of a living person because it was reasoned that living persons have no heirs under the legal maxim *nemo est haeres viventis.*[114] By statute in North Carolina, however, this common-law rule has been changed.[115] It is provided by statute that "A limitation by deed, will, or other writing, to the heirs of a living person, shall be construed to be to the children of such person, unless a contrary intention appear by the deed or will." Therefore, today a conveyance directly "to A's heirs," A being alive at the time, will

---

107. N.C. GEN. STAT. § 41-5.
108. Mackie v. Mackie, 230 N.C. 152, 52 S.E.2d 352 (1949).
109. Heath v. Heath, 114 N.C. 547, 19 S.E. 155 (1894).
110. Powell v. Powell, 168 N.C. 461, 84 S.E. 860 (1915); Johnson Bros. v. Lee, 187 N.C. 753, 122 S.E. 839 (1924).
111. Neal v. Nelson, 117 N.C. 393, 23 S.E. 428 (1895); Thompson v. John L. Roper Lumber Co., 168 N.C. 226, 84 S.E. 289 (1915).
112. *Id.*
113. Neal v. Nelson, 117 N.C. 393, 23 S.E. 428 (1895).
114. Campbell v. Everhart, 139 N.C. 503, 52 S.E. 201 (1905).
115. N.C. GEN. STAT. § 41-6.

create an estate in *A's* children if *A* has children alive and born at the time the deed is executed or if *A* has a child *en ventre sa mere* at the time the deed is executed.[116] In a deed "to *A's* heirs" or "to *A's* children, adopted children as well as natural children should take.[117]

It should be noted, however, that the above statute does not change the word "heirs" in all cases to mean "children." For instance, a conveyance "to *A and* his heirs," the traditional manner of conveying an estate in fee simple to *A*, is not affected by the statute.[118] The words "and his heirs" in such deed of conveyance continue to be simply "words of limitation" indicating that *A* takes a fee simple estate and the children of *A* take nothing by the grant.[119]

A limitation in a deed "to *A* for life and then to his [*A's*] heirs" is likewise unaffected by the statute which converts the word "heirs" into children when there is a limitation to the heirs of a living person. Such limitation to the heirs of the life tenant *A* creates no estate in the heirs of *A* but, by application of the Rule in Shelley's Case in North Carolina, creates instead a fee simple estate in *A*.[120] The Rule in Shelley's Case was not in any way abrogated by this statute.[121]

If, on the other hand, a conveyance is made "to *B* for life, remainder to *A's* heirs," the statute will apply and cause the words "*A's* heirs" to mean "*A's* children" if *A* is alive at the time of the conveyance.[122]

Perhaps a handy method for determining when the word "heirs" is changed so as to mean "children" when found in a conveyance can be summed up in the following manner: The statute, providing that a limitation to the heirs of a living person shall be construed to be the children of such person, applies only when there is no precedent or concurrent freehold estate conveyed to such living person. Since *A* takes neither precedent nor concurrent estate with his heirs in a conveyance "to *A's* heirs," the statute makes "heirs" mean "children" in such case. For the

---

116. Campbell v. Everhart, 139 N.C. 503, 52 S.E. 201 (1905); Graves v. Barrett, 126 N.C. 267, 35 S.E. 539 (1900).

117. *See* Simpson v. Simpson, 29 N.C. App. 14, 222 S.E.2d 747 (1976), which holds that a devise to testator's daughter for life and "then to her children, if any" included her adopted children as well as her natural children under N.C. GEN. STAT. § 48-23 in the absence of an indication that adopted children were to be excluded. The same result should follow where there is a deed to one's children; adopted children as well as natural children should take under such deed. *See also* Stoney v. MacDougall, 28 N.C. App. 178, 220 S.E.2d 368, *aff'd*, 31 N.C. App. 678, 230 S.E.2d 592 (1976), which holds that a will provision for distribution of property to "my issue" includes adopted children of testator's son. Conversely, however, while an adopted child becomes legally a child of its new parents, the adoption makes him legally a stranger to the bloodline of his natural parents. *See* Crumpton v. Crumpton, 28 N.C. App. 358, 221 S.E.2d 390 (1976).

118. Marsh v. Griffin, 136 N.C. 333, 48 S.E. 735 (1904).

119. Whitley v. Arenson, 219 N.C. 121, 12 S.E.2d 906 (1941).

120. *Id. See* Marsh v. Griffin, 136 N.C. 333, 48 S.E. 735 (1904).

121. Starnes v. Hill, 112 N.C. 1, 16 S.E. 1011 (1893).

122. Condor v. Secrest, 149 N.C. 201, 62 S.E. 921 (1908). *See also* Starnes v. Hill, 112 N.C. 1, 16 S.E. 1011 (1893).

same reason the statute makes "heirs" mean "children" if the conveyance is "to *B* for life, remainder to *A's* heirs"; *A,* the living person, takes no estate either prior to or with his heirs and therefore the statute applies. On the other hand, a conveyance "to *A and* his heirs" seems to indicate that *A* is to take *with* his heirs and the statute does not apply to change the word "heirs" to "children" in such case; *A* takes a fee simple estate and the heirs take nothing, as the word "heirs" is not changed from a word of limitation to a word of purchase. Likewise, a conveyance "to *A* for life and then to his [*A's*] heirs does not call for application of the statute since the living person *A* takes a life estate precedent to the purported remainder estate to his heirs; since the word "heirs" is not changed from a word of limitation to a word of purchase in such case, the Rule in Shelley's Case applies to give *A* a fee simple estate.

§ 180. Grantee's Deed from Himself.

Since the law requires a grantor and a grantee, a person cannot be a grantee from himself.[123] This does not, however, prevent a husband from conveying his individual property to himself and his wife as tenants by the entirety or a grant of entirety property by both of the spouses to one spouse to hold individually. The husband-wife entity which takes or conveys real property by the entirety is considered a legal person separate and distinct from the spouses as individuals.[124] It is not necessary in such conveyances to use a "straw man" as is required in some jurisdictions and which was formerly widely practiced in North Carolina.[125]

§ 181. Grants to Aliens.

While at common law an alien could not take and hold real property, by statute in North Carolina aliens have the capacity to be grantees and to take and hold real property.[126] Information regarding real property ownership in North Carolina by aliens is to be obtained and made available to the General Assembly and the public according to North Carolina General Statutes, § 64-1.1. Presumably, an additional response would take place in the event that alien ownership increased to any alarming degree. Often citing economic reasons, legislatures in some states have restricted alien land ownership.[127]

---

123. Dupree v. Dupree, 45 N.C. 164 (1853).
124. Woolard v. Smith, 244 N.C. 489, 94 S.E.2d 466 (1956); N.C. GEN. SAT. § 39-13.3.
125. *Id.*
126. N.C. GEN. STAT. § 64-1.
127. *See* Weisman, *Restrictions on the Acquisition of Land by Aliens,* 28 AM. J. COMP. L. 39 (1980) where the author, at p. 43, quotes a portion of the introduction to a California bill on this subject, California Assembly Bill No. 3627, April 4, 1978. That introduction states, in part:

> The wise use of land is best encouraged through local ownership, such as through a farm system composed mainly of family farmers ... foreign absentee ownership is detrimental to such purposes ... foreign investment in California agricultural land tends to

§ 182. Sufficiency of Identification of Grantee.

The intended grantee must be designated in a deed with sufficient certainty so as to distinguish him from other persons, though it is not necessary for the specific name of the grantee to be set out. If the instrument shows who the grantee is or if it designates and so describes him that there is no uncertainty respecting the party who is intended to take under the deed, it is not of vital consequence that the matter which establishes his identity is not in the common or best form or expressed with technical nicety or accuracy in the usual or most appropriate position in the instrument.[128] While the correct name of the grantee is the best means of identifying the person intended, use of the Christian or surname of the grantee is not a prerequisite to the validity of the instrument.[129] If a living or legal person is intended as the grantee and is identifiable from the description used, the deed is valid, however he may be named in the deed.[130] A deed (like a legacy) to a person by his nickname will be sufficient if it can be shown by evidence *dehors* that he is the individual intended.[131] The grantee, individual or corporation, may take even if misnamed in the deed.[132] It should be noted, however, that

---

increase speculation of farm prices, to cause greater instability of market conditions, and to speed the further decline of family farming and rural development.

See generally Weisman, *Restrictions on the Acquisition of Land by Aliens,* 28 AM. J. COMP. L. 39 (1980); Morrison, *Limitations on Alien Investment in American Real Estate,* 60 MINN. L. REV. 621 (1976); Lowe, *Arizona Alien Land Law: Its Meaning and Constitutional Validity,* 1976 ARIZ. ST. L. J. 253 (1976). Notes at § 203 *infra.*

128. Campbell v. Everhart, 139 N.C. 503, 52 S.E. 201 (1905).

129. *See* 2 MORDECAI, LAW LECTURES 802 (1916), which quotes from 4 KENT, COMMENTARIES *462: "Conveyances are good, in many cases, when made to a grantee by a certain designation, without the mention of either the Christian or surname — as to 'the wife of A,' or to 'the eldest son of A,' for *id certum quod certum reddi potest*." (That is certain which can be made certain.)

130. *See* Byrd v. Patterson, 229 N.C. 156, 48 S.E.2d 45 (1948), and numerous cases there cited. *Accord,* Morton v. Thornton, 259 N.C. 697, 131 S.E.2d 378 (1963), which points out that if a grant be made to AB or CD, the grant would be void as to both, citing WASHBURN, REAL PROPERTY, 281. *See also* Neal v. Nelson, 117 N.C. 393, 23 S.E. 428 (1895), which indicates that while a conveyance to a person A (who is at the time dead) or his heirs is good if his heirs can be identified, a conveyance to A or B (both living) would create an uncertainty making the grant void.

131. *See* Institute v. Norwood, 45 N.C. 65 (1852), in which the court in considering a legacy stated that a legacy to "Le Petit Caporal" by a veteran of the army of Italy could have been recovered by Napoleon Bonaparte and a legacy to "Old Hickory" could have been recovered by Andrew Jackson.

132. *See* Institute v. Norwood, 45 N.C. 65 (1852), involving a legacy which was to the "Deaf and Dumb Institution." There was no institution by that name although there was a corporation known as "The President and Directors of the North Carolina Institute, for the Education of the Deaf and Dumb." The Supreme Court of North Carolina held that it is settled law that if an individual or corporation, in a will, deed or bond, is described by a nickname, that is, a short name, one *nicked* or cut off for the sake of brevity, it is competent to show that the individual whose true name was not used, was nevertheless meant to be

the grantee must be an identifiable living person, not a nonexistent fictional person. Thus, while a conveyance to "The Manassa Mauler" would operate to convey to the well known prizefighter Jack Dempsey, a conveyance to "Little Orphan Annie" or "Dick Tracy" would not be a valid conveyance because there are no such living persons. If a person or thing be named, and if after resorting to proof *dehors,* no such person or thing can be found, the instrument must fail for the want of a person or thing to fit the description of the grantee.[133] Even if there are two persons who can answer a description as grantee, however, the deed is not necessarily bad; while the question of the identity of the grantee becomes more complicated, it is still only a question of identity and must be decided by evidence outside the instrument.[134]

Article III. Subject Matter of Deeds; Rules of Construction

§ 183. Sufficiency of Description of Subject Matter.

In order for a deed or other instrument conveying or encumbering real property to be valid, it must describe the property conveyed or encumbered in such a way that it identifies the particular real property involved or furnishes the means for identifying it.[135]

It can be generally stated that every deed of conveyance must set forth

---

indicated by the nickname or soubriquet. *See also* Gold Mining Co. v. Lumber Co., 170 N.C. 273, 87 S.E. 40 (1915); Byrd v. Patterson, 229 N.C. 156, 48 S.E.2d 45 (1948), and numerous cases cited in those cases.

133. Institute v. Norwood, 45 N.C. 65 (1852).

134. *See* Institute v. Norwood, 45 N.C. 65 (1852), in which the court refers to this situation as the situation where there are two "Cousin Johns." Admissions and other parol testimony may be used to show that a particular individual was intended. The rules for the identification of a grantee in a deed are comparable to those for the identification of a devisee in a will. Where a testatrix devised and bequeathed property simply to "World Missions," and both the "Division of World Missions of the Board of Missions of the Methodist Church, Inc." and the "Board of World Missions of the Presbyterian Church in the United States, Inc." claimed to be the designated beneficiary, the North Carolina Supreme Court held that the latent ambiguity created in the description of the beneficiary of the will could be removed by parol testimony with respect to the testatrix's intention. Parol evidence was admitted to show that the testatrix was a lifelong Presbyterian, that the Presbyterians' Board of World Missions was commonly referred to as "World Missions" and sometimes designated in that manner in the church bulletin and on envelopes provided for donations. The parol evidence admitted *dehors* the instrument was held to indicate the testatrix's intention to benefit the "Board of World Missions of the Presbyterian Church in the United States, Inc." The court also held that the capitalization of the words "World Missions" negated any idea that testatrix was merely stating a purpose to aid world missions or foreign missions in general. *See* Redd v. Taylor, 270 N.C. 14, 153 S.E.2d 761 (1967).

135. Overton v. Boyce, 289 N.C. 291, 221 S.E.2d 347 (1975); State v. Brooks, 279 N.C. 45, 181 S.E.2d 553 (1971); Carrow v. Davis, 248 N.C. 740, 105 S.E.2d 60 (1958); Cathey v. Lumber Co., 151 N.C. 592, 66 S.E. 580 (1909); Edmundson v. Hooks, 33 N.C. 373 (1850). The material previously set out with reference to the descriptions required in contracts for the sale of real property is also pertinent to deeds.

a subject matter, either certain in itself or capable of being reduced to a certainty by recurrence to something extrinsic to which the deed refers.[136] The function of the description of land in conveyances and contracts is to describe the locus and boundaries of the real property to which the instrument relates in order that it can be located on the ground by a competent surveyor, with or without the introduction of competent extrinsic evidence.

Draftsmen of deeds of conveyance should take particular caution to see that every description is complete and accurate and, when made by metes and bounds, that the boundary lines of the description close. While it will be pointed out later that every deficiency or inaccuracy will not necessarily invalidate a deed, the many cases in the reports on descriptions are ample exhibits that descriptions that are less than perfect are prolific producers of clouded titles and disputes that end up in the courts.

The methods of description most usually employed in North Carolina to afford safe, accurate and permanent identification of real property in conveyances are the following: (1) descriptions by monuments, courses and distances, or by metes and bounds; (2) descriptions by reference to a plat or map; (3) descriptions of city lots by reference to streets and numbers; (4) descriptions by reference to prior conveyance; and (5) descriptions by reference to quantity of land or number of acres conveyed.

§ 184. Description by Monuments, Courses and Distances, or by Metes and Bounds.

In North Carolina the most usual method of describing land, particularly nonurban and irregularly shaped tracts, is by metes and bounds descriptions; that is, by the selection of certain ascertained landmarks or "monuments" that are as permanent in nature as possible which are situated at the angles of the boundary lines of the tract, and by stating the measurements between such "monuments." The accurate description of these permanent markers and the accurate statement of the courses and distances between them, as determined by a land survey, constitute perhaps the safest and best description practicable for country lands.

The purpose of metes and bounds descriptions is to mark out boundaries by mathematical lines. Usually a combination of forms of description are employed, references being made to ascertainable monuments, boundaries of adjoining lands, and statements of quantity or size of the tract of land involved in the conveyance.

A "monument" consists of any object or mark on the land that may serve to locate the boundary line at a given point. It may be a river, rock, tree, or other natural object, more or less permanent, or it may be artificial, as a wall, post, ditch, or road.[137]

---

136. Harris v. Woodard, 130 N.C. 580, 41 S.E. 790 (1902); Self Help Corp. v. Brinkley, 215 N.C. 615, 2 S.E.2d 889 (1939), and numerous other cases.
137. MINOR & WURTS, REAL PROPERTY § 933 (1909).

§ 185 THE DEED § 185

A "course" is the direction in which a line runs, stated with reference, not to its terminus, but to its correspondence with a certain point on the compass. The expressions "distance," "quantity," and "size" are self-explanatory.

In order for a draftsman of a deed to draw a reliable and valid metes and bounds description, he must first locate a stable and certain starting point or point of beginning, perhaps a monument such as an iron pipe, the intersection of two streets, or the corner of a lot shown on a recorded plat. When the point of beginning is established and located, the draftsman must trace the outline of the tract conveyed by reciting the courses and distances, the direction and length of each boundary line running continuously from one monument or point to another, until the point of beginning is again reached, enclosing the land to be conveyed.

Every description in a deed by metes and bounds should be made as certain as the means at hand will enable the draftsman to make it. He should take care to select a starting point that is as permanent as possible so that it can be readily located in the future.[138] The angles and distances of boundaries should be accurately surveyed to determine the bearings of lines and they should be carefully stated in the description to avoid confusion and future controversies.[139]

§ 185. Rules of Construction in Cases of Conflicts and Ambiguities in Metes and Bounds Descriptions.

As may be imagined, many descriptions by metes and bounds in deeds of conveyance are ambiguous, inconsistent and conflicting. The courts very frequently are called on to determine whether such descriptions are adequate to convey any land at all, or how much land is conveyed, or whether the deed completely fails because it does not describe the particular land to be conveyed. To resolve these cases involving ambiguous, inconsistent and conflicting descriptions, the courts have formulated var-

---

138. While such descriptions as "Beginning at a pine on the east side of Gum Swamp..." have been sustained (Broadwell v. Morgan, 142 N.C. 475, 55 S.E. 340 (1906)), even though the tree can no longer be located, the impermanency of such a monument will certainly lead to uncertainty in relocating the corners of tracts at some later date and should not be used. If the monument or marker is destroyed, however, its location may be determined by reversing the calls of the deed from another established monument or marker or by parol evidence. Andrews v. Andrews, 252 N.C. 97, 113 S.E.2d 47 (1960); Nelson v. Lineker, 172 N.C. 279, 90 S.E. 251 (1916).

139. In construing a deed, it is the duty of the court to ascertain the intent of the grantor as embodied in the entire instrument, and every part of the deed must be given effect if this can be done by any reasonable interpretation. Hardy v. Edwards, 22 N.C. App. 276, 206 S.E.2d 316 (1974). The intention of the grantor must be gathered from the whole instrument, and every part thereof must be given effect, unless the deed contains conflicting provisions that are irreconcilable, or a provision that is contrary to public policy or which runs counter to some rule of law. Pearson v. Chambers, 18 N.C. App. 403, 197 S.E.2d 42 (1973).

ious rules of construction and techniques to locate the boundaries of deeds whose descriptions are less than ideal.

§ 186. The "Intention of the Parties."

The first and foremost rule of construction employed by the courts, in cases where there is an ambiguity, inconsistency or conflict in a description, is to gather the intention of the parties from the four corners of the instrument.[140] This overriding constructional rule accounts for the upholding of certain weird descriptions and the seeming inconsistency in many cases involving descriptions. The courts seek to sustain a deed if possible on the assumption that the parties intended to convey and receive land or they would never have been involved in the first place.[141]

§ 187. Rules That Monuments Control Distances and Courses; Courses Control Distances; Quantity Statement Least Reliable Guide.

The "intention of the parties" criterion for establishing the meaning of a description when there is an ambiguity, inconsistency or conflict has resulted in the development of rules of construction by the courts, establishing a hierarchy or system of constructional preferences. These preferences, based upon presumed reliability, normally determine the relative supremacy of calls in deeds where there is ambiguity or discrepancy.

For instance, one constructional rule that has developed is the rule that where there is a conflict or ambiguity in the calls of a deed identifying land, the calls for natural or permanent monuments are given preference over calls for artificial or less permanent monuments.

The reason for this constructional preference is that a priority of reliability is established by the courts on the assumption that makers of deeds are less likely to be mistaken as to the location of a substantial physical monument referred to in a call than they would be as to mere imaginary lines indicated by references to courses and distances or recitals of quantity. In cases of ambiguity, therefore, references to physical objects are given more weight and control references to courses, distances, and quantity of land as being indicative of the grantor's intention in a description. The hierarchy of reliability established by the

---

140. Board of Transportation v. Pelletier, 38 N.C. App. 533, 248 S.E.2d 413 (1978) where the court, at 38 N.C. App. 536-537 notes: "In construing a deed description it is the function of the court to determine the true intent of the parties as embodied in the entire instrument." Citing Franklin v. Faulkner, 248 N.C. 656, 104 S.E.2d 841 (1958); Hardy v. Edwards, 22 N.C. App. 276, 206 S.E.2d 316 (1974).

141. "It is a general rule that the deed must be upheld, if possible, and the terms and phraseology of description will be interpreted with that view and to that end, if this can reasonably be done." Self Help Corp. v. Brinkley, 215 N.C. 615, 2 S.E.2d 889 (1939); Edwards v. Bowden, 99 N.C. 80, 5 S.E. 283 (1888).

§ 188 THE DEED § 188

courts ranks descriptions in cases of ambiguity in the following manner: references to natural monuments control references to artificial monuments; artificial monuments control courses; courses control distances; and recitals of quantity are the least reliable forms of description.[142] Calls to others' lines,[143] to a road or highway,[144] to a ditch,[145] or to marked trees[146] are calls to "monuments" within the meaning of these rules of construction. A call in a deed to a mere surveyor's stake is not a call to such a monument as will control course or distance or a call to a natural boundary.[147]

In determining the location of the true boundaries of a parcel, the location of the boundaries on the ground is a factual question for the jury. The determination of what the boundaries are is a question of law for the court.[148]

§ 188. Rule That Boundaries Extend to Center of Monuments; Streets, Public Roads, Alleys, Ditches and Streams.

It can be stated as a general rule that a call for a monument as a boundary line in a deed will convey the title of the land to the center of the monument if it has width. Thus if a street, public highway,[149] alley,[150] ditch,[151] stream,[152] or nonnavigable watercourse[153] is made the boundary in a description, the conveyance carries to the center of the street, public highway, alley, ditch, stream or nonnavigable watercourse unless there are words in the deed showing a contrary intent and provided the grantor at the time of the conveyance owns thereto. It should be noted,

---

142. 6 POWELL, REAL PROPERTY 202 (1958); Tice v. Winchester, 225 N.C. 673, 36 S.E.2d 257 (1945); Nelson v. Lineker, 172 N.C. 279, 90 S.E. 251 (1916); Queen v. Sink, 238 N.C. 389, 78 S.E.2d 152 (1953); Sherrod v. Battle, 154 N.C. 345, 70 S.E. 834 (1911).

143. Batson v. Bell, 249 N.C. 718, 107 S.E.2d 562 (1959); Franklin v. Faulkner, 248 N.C. 656, 104 S.E.2d 841 (1958); Carney v. Edwards, 256 N.C. 20, 122 S.E.2d 786 (1961); Hill v. Dalton, 140 N.C. 9, 52 S.E. 273 (1905); Board of Transportation v. Pelletier, 38 N.C. App. 533, 248 S.E.2d 413 (1978).

144. Franklin v. Faulkner, 248 N.C. 656, 104 S.E.2d 841 (1958); Brown v. Hodges, 232 N.C. 537, 61 S.E.2d 603 (1950); Board of Transportation v. Pelletier, 38 N.C. App. 533, 248 S.E.2d 413 (1978).

145. Franklin v. Faulkner, 248 N.C. 656, 104 S.E.2d 841 (1958).

146. Green v. Barker, 254 N.C. 603, 119 S.E.2d 456 (1961).

147. Tice v. Winchester, 225 N.C. 673, 36 S.E.2d 257 (1954); Clark v. Moore, 126 N.C. 1, 35 S.E. 125 (1900).

148. Cutts v. Casey, 271 N.C. 165, 155 S.E.2d 519 (1967); Mathias v. Brumsey, 27 N.C. App. 558, 219 S.E.2d 646 (1975).

149. Harris v. Carter, 189 N.C. 295, 127 S.E. 1 (1925); Brown v. Hodges, 232 N.C. 537, 61 S.E.2d 603 (1950).

150. Patrick v. Jefferson Standard Life Ins. Co., 176 N.C. 660, 97 S.E. 657 (1918).

151. White v. Woodard, 227 N.C. 332, 42 S.E.2d 94 (1947).

152. Rose v. Franklin, 216 N.C. 289, 4 S.E.2d 876 (1939), and numerous cases cited therein.

153. Id.

however, that if the description restricts the grant to the edge or shore of a public road or stream it does not carry to the center.[154]

§ 189. Description by Reference to Plat or Map.

A reference in a conveyance to a plat or map for the purpose of describing land conveyed makes the plat or map a part of the conveyance, and it may be used to identify the land.[155] Thereafter a lot may be described in all instruments by referring to the plat and lot number. It is customary to convey land in urban areas by reference to plats.[156] Care should be taken to see that plats referred to in deeds are recorded or else the means for identification of the property intended may be lost or destroyed.

§ 190. Description by Reference to Streets and Numbers.

While not advisable, buildings are sometimes described by reference to street and number in conveyances of city land.

§ 191. Description by Reference to Prior Conveyance.

A rather common method of describing real property is to refer to a prior deed conveying the same land, whereby the description in the prior deed is incorporated by reference into the latter.[157] If the first description in the prior deed referred to is accurate, the subsequent description satisfies the rules of law requiring certainty in deed descriptions. It has been held that where a deed or instrument conveying land refers to another for description, the principal deed should be considered and construed as if the description was written out therein in full.[158]

§ 192. Description by Reference to Quantity or Number of Acres.

Generally a description of land by quantity is not a description of

---

154. Kelly v. King, 225 N.C. 709, 36 S.E.2d 220 (1945).
155. Kelly v. King, 225 N.C. 709, 36 S.E.2d 220 (1945). *But see* Bercegeay v. Realty Co., 16 N.C. App. 718, 193 S.E.2d 356 (1972), which holds that a description of property as "Block 36" and "Lot 12 Sound Front" in a purported contract to convey real property was not sufficient to satisfy the Statute of Frauds when no record of any map or plat was introduced to show to what those descriptions referred. In Prentice v. Roberts, 32 N.C. App. 379, 232 S.E.2d 286 (1977), it was held that a property sketch referred to in a sales agreement could be introduced to locate property and an easement thereon referred to in the sales agreement.
156. Where a deed contains two descriptions, one by metes and bounds and the other by lot and block according to a certain plat or map, the controlling description is the lot according to the plan, rather than the one by metes and bounds. Kelly v. King, 225 N.C. 709, 36 S.E.2d 220 (1945); Hayden v. Hayden, 178 N.C. 259, 100 S.E. 515 (1919); Davidson v. Arledge, 97 N.C. 172, 2 S.E. 378 (1887).
157. Lumber Co. v. Swain, 161 N.C. 566, 77 S.E. 700 (1913).
158. Williams v. Bailey, 178 N.C. 630, 101 S.E. 105 (1919); Gudger v. White, 141 N.C. 507, 54 S.E. 386 (1906).

boundaries at all but is used merely as a subordinate or inferior mode of supplying cumulative information to aid other forms of description that may by themselves be inadequate.[159] If the statement of quantity in a description is inconsistent with the other more important and valuable elements of description, the statement of quantity must yield. If, however, the other elements of the description are uncertain and doubtful, the statement of quantity may become an important element in aid of the other descriptions. For instance, if a description sets out only three boundaries and the fourth boundary cannot be ascertained, if there is a statement of the quantity of land to be conveyed, the fourth line can be run so as to embrace the given quantity.[160]

A deed is void for uncertainty where it purports to convey part of a larger tract but there is an absence of any indication of intent to convey a specific part of the tract.[161] A grant of "200 acres of the marsh and islands," for example, was held to be patently and fatally defective.[162] Likewise, a devise of "25 acres of the home tract" was held void for vagueness and uncertainty where no means for determining the identity of the specific 25 acres was provided.[163]

On the other hand, a deed for a certain number of acres out of a large body of land is valid if it gives data by which the dividing line may be located.[164] A deed conveying "29 acres to be cut off the north end of a 129 acre tract" has been held to be adequate.[165] A devise of a "tract of 25 acres to be selected by her [the testatrix's daughter]" out of a specified larger tract was held not void for vagueness.[166] In another selection fact situation the grantee was given a specified number of acres out of a larger tract. The transfer was held to be valid if the grantee makes a selection.[167] Until the selection is made no title passes.[168] But a right given

---

159. *But see* Proctor v. Pool, 15 N.C. 370 (1833), in which the court says that if a grantor conveys his "acre-lot" in a town, when he owns two lots, one of an acre and the other larger or smaller, the "acre" lot will pass. In this instance the recital of quantity is crucial.

160. Clark v. Moore, 126 N.C. 1, 35 S.E. 125 (1900).

161. Overton v. Boyce, 26 N.C. App. 680, 217 S.E.2d 704 (1975), *rev'd on other grounds*, 289 N.C. 291, 221 S.E.2d 347 (1976), citing State v. Brooks, 279 N.C. 45, 181 S.E.2d 553 (1971); Carlton v. Anderson, 276 N.C. 564, 173 S.E.2d 783 (1970); Cathey Lumber Co., 151 N.C. 592, 66 S.E. 580 (1909); Smith v. Proctor, 139 N.C. 314, 51 S.E. 889 (1905); Robeson v. Lewis, 64 N.C. 734 (1870).

162. State v. Brooks, 279 N.C. 45, 181 S.E.2d 553 (1971).

163. Hodges v. Stewart, 218 N.C. 290, 10 S.E.2d 723 (1940).

164. Johnson v. Manufacturing Co., 165 N.C. 105, 80 S.E. 980 (1914); Builders Supplies Co. v. Gainey, 282 N.C. 261, 192 S.E.2d 449 (1972); Kidd v. Early, 289 N.C. 343, 222 S.E.2d 392 (1976).

165. Stewart v. Salmonds, 74 N.C. 518 (1876).

166. Cable v. Hardin Oil Co., 10 N.C. App. 569, 179 S.E.2d 829 (1971), *cert. denied*, 278 N.C. 521, 180 S.E.2d 863 (1971).

167. Builders Supplies Co. v. Gainey, 282 N.C. 261, 192 S.E.2d 449 (1972).

168. *Id.*

a vendee to select a definite number of acres out of a larger tract affords the means of rendering the description certain.[169] Prior to the vendee's selection, the vendee has at most only a contractual right to acquire the title pursuant to the description in the deed.[170]

§ 193. Miscellaneous Informal Descriptions.

Descriptions that are informal and general have been held sufficient by the courts. For instance, a parcel of land may be conveyed by its popular name.[171] The name of a place, like that of a man, may, and does serve to identify it to the apprehension of more persons than a description of coterminous lands and watercourses, and does it with equal certainty. For example, "Mount Vernon, the late residence of General Washington," is better known by that name than by a description of it, as situated on the Potomac River and adjoining the lands of A, B and C. Frequently, indeed, the name of a place, by which it is well known to those who know it at all, overrules a further and mistaken description.[172] Descriptions of tracts of land as "the Home Place," "the Lynn Place" and "The Leonard Greeson Place" have been held to be adequate descriptions.[173]

General descriptions such as "my house and lot in the town of A"[174] or "all of our lands in North Carolina"[175] have been held to be adequate descriptions. The possessive pronouns, coupled with a recital of the geographical location of the land — as the state, county or city in which it lies — serve to identify particular land. While it has been said that "A house and lot" or "one house and lot" in a particular town[176] would be inadequate as descriptions because too indefinite on the face of the instrument itself, the Supreme Court of North Carolina has at times indicated that it will supply the possessive pronoun even if "a" or "one" are used in lieu of the possessive pronoun.[177] While a description that indicates *"My"* house and lot imports a particular house and lot, which can be rendered certain under the maxim *id certum est quod certum reddi*

---

169. *Id.*

170. *Id.*

171. Smith v. Low, 24 N.C. 457 (1842); Hurdle v. White, 34 N.C. App. 644, 239 S.E.2d 589 (1977); 2 MORDECAI, LAW LECTURES 817 (1916).

172. Smith v. Low, 24 N.C. 457 (1842); 2 MORDECAI, LAW LECTURES 817 (1916).

173. *Id. See* Kidd v. Early, 289 N.C. 343, 222 S.E.2d 392 (1976); Carolina Power & Light Co. v. Waters, 260 N.C. 667, 133 S.E.2d 450 (1963); Scull v. Pruden, 92 N.C. 168 (1885); Maurice v. Motel Corp., 38 N.C. App. 588, 248 S.E.2d 430 (1978).

174. Carson v. Ray, 52 N.C. 609 (1860); Garrison v. Blakeney, 37 N.C. App. 73, 246 S.E.2d 144 (1978).

175. Janney v. Robbins, 141 N.C. 400, 53 S.E. 863 (1906); Garrison v. Blakeney, 37 N.C. App. 73, 246 S.E.2d 144 (1978).

176. Carson v. Ray, 52 N.C. 609 (1860); Murdock v. Anderson, 57 N.C. 77 (1858).

177. Farmer v. Batts, 83 N.C. 387 (1880); Perry v. Scott, 109 N.C. 374, 14 S.E. 294 (1891).

potest, "that is certain which can be made certain," the court has said: "the presence of the word 'my' or 'my lands' in such descriptions by the owner ... seems ... to be no longer recognized. [T]he assertion of title in the vendor is not less unequivocally involved in the very act of disposing of it as his property. It would indeed seem but charitable to assume that he who undertakes to convey property, intends to dispose of what he claims to be his own." [178] It should be noted, however, that subsequent cases have since been quoted with apparent approval in dictum statements from the previous cases which required the possessive pronoun without mentioning the cases which dispensed with the pronoun.[179]

Lands may also be conveyed by reference to an identifiable source of title. A description of land as "the land I purchased from *A.B.*" is a good description as is a conveyance of "all the lands described in the last will and testament of *O.*" [180] When, however, a general description could apply to one tract as well as another, or the land involved is not a distinct tract, or is a part of a larger tract, the description is void and cannot be aided by parol or other evidence *aliunde.*[181]

§ 194. Necessity for Words of Conveyance.

An effective deed must contain operative words of conveyance which indicate the grantor's intention to convey his property.[182] Such words are absolutely essential and the want of them is fatal and they cannot be supplied by parol proof.[183] The courts, however, have gone very far to sustain informal and nontechnical instruments purporting to convey interests in real estate and have held that words in common and ordinary parlance may be used if the intention of the grantor to convey his interest is manifest.[184]

---

178. Perry v. Scott, 109 N.C. 374, 14 S.E. 294 (1891).

179. Speed v. Perry, 167 N.C. 122, 83 S.E. 176 (1914); 2 Mordecai, Law Lectures 826 (1916).

180. *See* Peel v. Calais, 224 N.C. 421, 31 S.E.2d 440 (1944), and numerous cases cited therein.

181. *Id.*

182. New Home Bldg. Supply Co. v. Nations, 259 N.C. 681, 131 S.E.2d 425 (1963); Griffin v. Springer, 244 N.C. 95, 92 S.E.2d 682 (1956).

183. Tremaine v. Williams, 144 N.C. 114, 56 S.E. 694 (1907); Pope v. Burgess, 230 N.C. 323, 53 S.E.2d 159 (1949); 2 Mordecai, Law Lectures 804 (1916).

184. In New Home Bldg. Supply Co. v. Nations, 259 N.C. 681, 131 S.E.2d 425 (1963), the North Carolina Supreme Court held that the words "I transfer this deed to New Home Bldg. Supply Co.," written on the back of the deed and signed and sealed by the grantee named in the deed contained sufficient operative words of conveyance. In Waller v. Brown, 197 N.C. 508, 149 S.E. 687 (1929), the court held that the word "lend" was synonymous with the word

Article IV. Execution of Deed

Division 1. Signing; Seal; No Witnesses Required

§ 195. Proper Execution of Deed by Grantor Generally.

Technically speaking, "execution" in its legal signification includes signing, sealing and delivery when used in connection with a deed.[185]

§ 196. Signing.

The Statute of Frauds in North Carolina requires that instruments conveying lands shall be void unless in writing and signed by the party to be charged therewith or by some other person by him thereto lawfully authorized.[186] The signature may be that of the grantor himself or it may be written by his agent in his presence or under his direction, the act of an authorized agent being deemed the act of the principal.[187] If an agent, however, signs or executes a deed for his principal who is not present, such agent's deed or signature on behalf of his principal is not valid to pass title to real property purportedly conveyed unless the agent has been given authority under seal to act for his absent principal.[188] North Carolina's Statute of Frauds does not require that a deed be subscribed as is the requirement in some states. Therefore it is not essential that the signature be placed at the bottom or at the end of a deed as is required for the proper execution of some other instruments.[189] When a signature is

---

"convey" and was sufficient as a word of conveyance. In Armfield v. Walker, 27 N.C. 580 (1845), where the grantor stated in the deed that he would "warrant and defend" the grantee and that the grantee should "have and hold (the land) with all its profits and advantages," the court held the words to be adequate as words of conveyance.

See Cobb v. Hines, 44 N.C. 343 (1853), in which the court gave effect to an informal document stating: "The deed under which the defendant claims, and by virtue of which he seeks to defeat the recovery of the plaintiff's lessor, is, as must be admitted, very informal. It is untechnical, ungrammatical, and totally at variance with all recognized rules of orthography, and yet it may be valid, if 'there be sufficient words to declare clearly and legally the party's meaning.'"

185. Williams v. North Carolina State Bd. of Educ., 284 N.C. 588, 201 S.E.2d 889 (1974); Lee v. Parker, 171 N.C. 144, 88 S.E. 217 (1916); Turlington v. Neighbors, 222 N.C. 694, 24 S.E.2d 648 (1943); Muse v. Muse, 236 N.C. 182, 72 S.E.2d 431 (1952).

186. N.C. GEN. STAT. § 22-2.

187. Devereaux v. McMahon, 108 N.C. 134, 12 S.E. 902 (1891).

188. Kime v. Brooks, 31 N.C. 218 (1848); Cadell v. Allen, 99 N.C. 542 (1888). Authority to make a deed (a sealed instrument) cannot be conferred orally, but must be created by an instrument of equal dignity. He who executes a deed for another, whether for money or other property, must be armed with an authority under seal. *See also* Bank v. Wimbish, 192 N.C. 552, 135 S.E. 452 (1926).

189. Devereaux v. McMahon, 108 N.C. 134, 12 S.E. 902 (1891); Yaggy v. B.V.D. Co., 7 N.C. App. 590, 173 S.E.2d 496 (1974).

§ 196   THE DEED   § 196

essential to the validity of an instrument, it is not necessary that the signature appear at the end of the instrument unless the statute involved uses the word "subscribed."[190] Where another person has written the signature of one who is illiterate, such illiterate person may subsequently adopt the signing by attaching a cross or other mark used by him as a substitute.[191] The affixation of a mark by the grantor against his name written by another is a signing, even though it does not appear that he could not write his own name, and indeed, his mark is sufficient though he be able to write.[192] It is not essential that the words "his mark" be attached to the mark made. It is sufficient if it appears that the grantor in fact made the mark or adopted it.[193] Any cross mark, straight mark, crooked line, dot, or other symbol will do for a signature. Putting initials to a document, the name appearing elsewhere, may be a sufficient signing.[194] Whether a particular mark is intended as a signature is a question for the jury. The form of the mark or the number of the strokes of the pen is not material. It can make no difference whether it be an illegible attempt at writing, or simply designed as a mark.[195]

---

190. *In re* Will of Williams, 234 N.C. 228, 66 S.E.2d 902 (1951). *See* Burris v. Starr, 165 N.C. 657, 81 S.E. 929 (1914), which states that so far as the Statute of Frauds is concerned the signature may be at the top, or in the body, as well as at the foot, of the memorandum provided always that it is inserted in such a manner as to authenticate the instrument as his act so as to show the intention of the party to be bound.
191. Sellers v. Sellers, 98 N.C. 13, 3 S.E. 917 (1887).
192. Devereaux v. McMahon, 108 N.C. 134, 12 S.E. 902 (1891).
193. Sellers v. Sellers, 98 N.C. 13, 3 S.E. 917 (1887); Lee v. Parker, 171 N.C. 144, 88 S.E. 217 (1916). A mark is just as binding without a subscribing witness as with one, and it may be proved, as a signature may be, by one who saw it made, or who heard the maker acknowledge it to be his, and the maker himself is generally a competent witness to prove that he made it. State v. Byrd, 93 N.C. 625 (1885). *Compare* State v. Watts, 289 N.C. 445, 222 S.E.2d 389 (1976), wherein the question arose as to whether a mechanical reproduction could be a "signature" of a public officer. The North Carolina Supreme Court states:

> In regard to a signature, it is the intent rather than the form of the act that is important. While one's signature is usually made by writing his name, the same purpose can be accomplished by placing any writing, indicia or symbol which the signer chooses to adopt and use as his signature and by which it may be proved; *e.g.,* by finger or thumb prints, by a cross or other mark, or by any type of mechanically reproduced or stamped facsimile of his signature, as effectively as by his own handwriting.
> ... A signature has also been defined as the act of putting down a person's name at the end of an instrument to attest its validity, any mark or sign made on an instrument or document in token of knowledge, approval, or device one may choose to employ as representative of himself. Stated in greater detail, in legal contemplation "to sign" means to attach a name or cause it to be attached by any of the known methods of impressing the name on paper with the intention of signing it.

A signature consists of both the act of writing the person's name and the intention of thereby finally authenticating the instrument.
194. Devereaux v. McMahon, 108 N.C. 134, 12 S.E. 902 (1891). A form of mark may be so peculiar and so uniformly used by a person as to become well known as *his* mark and may be proved just as the signature of one who writes.
195. Hinsaman v. Hinsaman, 52 N.C. 510 (1860).

§ 197. Seal.

A seal is absolutely essential to the validity of an instrument to convey legal title to real property in North Carolina.[196] Originating in remote antiquity among the Persians and Jews, and introduced into England by the Normans as a substitute for signing their names because of their inability to write, the seal was usually employed on instruments to authenticate the due execution of the documents. Persons had their own seals with distinctive markings and the impression of a seal device on wax, wafers or other tenacious substance identified the grantor or maker of an instrument and marked his document as authentic.[197] Today, however, a seal need not be distinctive. A square piece of paper, affixed with a wafer, or a scrawl, or simply the word "Seal" in brackets is a seal.[198] It

---

196. 2 MORDECAI, LAW LECTURES 916 (1916). See Strain v. Fitzgerald, 128 N.C. 396, 38 S.E. 929 (1901), wherein the court said:

> A deed is an instrument of writing, signed, sealed and delivered. 2 Blk. Com., star page 395. The *seal* is what distinguishes it from a parol or simple contract. Land can only be delivered by a *deed*, that is, an instrument of writing signed, sealed and delivered. A paper, in form a deed, is *not a deed* without a seal . . . .

Willis v. Anderson, 188 N.C. 479, 124 S.E. 834 (1924); Morton v. Lumber Co., 154 N.C. 336, 70 S.E. 623 (1911); Pickens v. Rymer, 90 N.C. 282 (1884); Hinsdale v. Thornton, 74 N.C. 167 (1876). *Accord,* Williams v. North Carolina State Bd. of Educ., 284 N.C. 588, 201 S.E.2d 889 (1974). The *Williams* case holds, however, that the recital of the seal in the instrument raises a presumption that a seal was affixed to the original deed even though such does not appear on the face of the registered deed. *See* Hopkins v. Lumber Co., 162 N.C. 533, 78 S.E. 286 (1913), and Jones v. Coleman, 188 N.C. 631, 125 S.E. 406 (1924), in accord. *See also* N.C. GEN. STAT. § 47-108.11; Garrison v. Blakeney, 37 N.C. App. 73, 246 S.E.2d 144 (1978).

A corporate seal is a necessary prerequisite to a valid conveyance of real estate by a corporation. *See* Investors Corp. v. Field Financial Corp., 5 N.C. App. 156, 167 S.E.2d 852 (1969); Caldwell v. Morganton Mfg. Co., 121 N.C. 339, 28 S.E. 475 (1897).

197. *See* 2 MORDECAI, LAW LECTURES 913 (1916), in which the author describes the introduction of identifying coats of arms into seals by knights returning from the Crusades.

198. Hughes v. Debnam, 53 N.C. (8 Jones) 127 (1960); Williams v. Turner, 208 N.C. 202, 179 S.E. 806 (1935). *See* Ingram v. Hall, 2 N.C. 193 (1795), for an excellent history of the seal and the liberalization of its use, wherein it is stated:

> The people began at length, to forget the original use of this institution, and to seal with any impression they could get; and the law, rather than invalidate the whole transaction left it to the jury to decide whether that was the seal of the party or not. In this country the people have departed still further from the true use of seals, by not making any impression at all, scratching something like a seal upon the margin of paper, and making that pass for a seal. To the first of these abuses the law has conformed, and will now deem the sealing to be sufficient, if found by the jury to be the seal of the party. For fear of destroying some contracts improperly made at first, it has relaxed from strict propriety, and the practice of sealing with any impression has become general and is now, from necessity, allowed to be good in every instance . . . but still the contemplation of law is in conformity to the ancient use of seals. They are deemed signs of authenticity, are supposed to have an intrinsic evidence in themselves, and for that reason are carried out by the jury.

In other words, any mark *may* be a seal *if proved to be a seal.* But if additional proof is necessary to show that a mark is a seal, *i.e.,* that it is authentic, of what use is a seal? A large majority of the states in the United States have abolished private seals. *See also* Garrison v. Blakeney, 37 N.C. App. 73, 246 S.E.2d 144 (1978).

is a question for the jury to determine if a grantor or maker of any instrument has adopted a seal.[199]

It should be noted, however, that while an instrument cannot be a "deed" and pass legal title if it does not have a seal, it may be good as a *contract* for the sale of land and may be specifically enforced if supported by a consideration.[200]

Where there is no ambiguity on the face of an instrument which contains a printed seal, the parol evidence rule bars a signatory to that instrument from introducing parol testimony that he did not intend to adopt the printed seal as his own.[201]

§ 198. Witnesses Not Required; When Acknowledgment Required.

No witnesses are required in North Carolina in order to validate deeds.[202] While witnesses sometimes subscribe their signatures to deeds, such attestations are employed only as a convenient method of establishing their genuineness and authenticity and their testimony has no more weight than that of any other witness under oath.[203]

If the deed is to be recorded, however, in the land title records, in order to protect the grantee against lien creditors or purchasers for value of the grantor, the deed must be acknowledged by the grantor in the presence of a public officer authorized to take acknowledgments.[204] The word

---

199. *See, e.g.,* Harrell v. Butler, 92 N.C. 20 (1885), where the word "seal" was written by a subscribing witness' name instead of by the grantor's signature. It was held sufficient as the grantor's seal. In Pickens v. Rymer, 90 N.C. 282 (1884), there were two makers of an instrument and only one word "seal" by the two signatures. If both adopted the same seal, the instrument was a sealed instrument as to both. If both did not adopt the seal, it was a sealed instrument as to one party and a simple contract as to the other. The court held that it was a question for the jury to determine whether both parties adopted the same seal. *See also* Garrison v. Blakeney, 37 N.C. App. 73, 246 S.E.2d 144 (1978).

200. Williams v. Board of Educ., 284 N.C. 588, 201 S.E.2d 889 (1974); Dunn v. Dunn, 242 N.C. 234, 87 S.E.2d 308 (1955). This will require a lawsuit, however, and a "deed" without a seal at best creates a marketability problem.

201. Mobil Oil Corp. v. Wolfe, 297 N.C. 36, 252 S.E.2d 809 (1979); Bank of N.C. v. Cranfill, 297 N.C. 43, 253 S.E.2d 1 (1979). *Cf.* First Citizens Bank & Trust Co. v. Martin, 44 N.C. App. 261, 261 S.E.2d 145 (1979) where it was held that a material issue of fact existed as to the intent of the parties to enter into a sealed instrument where a corporate seal appeared on a promissory note but where there was no seal after the names of the individual defendants. *See generally* Webster, *Doubt Reduction Through Conveyancing Reform — More Suggestions in the Quest for Clear Land Titles,* 46 N.C.L. REV. 284 (1968).

202. Linker v. Linker, 167 N.C. 651, 83 S.E. 736 (1914). *See* Ingram v. Hall, 2 N.C. 193 (1795).

203. Linker v. Linker, 167 N.C. 651, 83 S.E. 736 (1914).

204. N.C. GEN. STAT. § 47-1. "Until a deed is proved in the manner prescribed by the statute, the public register has no authority to put it in his book . . . ." Withrell v. Murphy, 154 N.C. 82, 69 S.E. 748 (1910); *see* Duke v. Markham, 105 N.C. 131, 10 S.E. 1017 (1890); Todd v. Outlaw, 79 N.C. 235, 237 (1878). Instruments whose acknowledgment or proofs of probate are defective on their face will fail to impart constructive notice even if they are

"acknowledgment," as used with respect to the execution of instruments, describes the act of personal appearance before a proper officer and there stating to him the fact of the execution of the instrument as a voluntary act.[205] Before an instrument is entitled to be recorded, the Register of Deeds must approve the certificate of acknowledgment and order registration of the instrument.[206]

If there is an attesting witness to an instrument, it may be proved for the purpose of recordation without the maker's acknowledgment if the subscribing witness appears before an officer authorized to take acknowledgments and states under oath that the maker signed the instrument in his presence or acknowledged to him the execution

---

otherwise effectively recorded. If the acknowledgment or probate defect is *patent*, the recorded instrument will be treated as if unrecorded. McClure v. Crow, 196 N.C. 657, 146 S.E. 713 (1929); County Savings Bank v. Tolbert, 192 N.C. 126, 133 S.E. 558 (1926); Blanton v. Bostic, 126 N.C. 418, 35 S.E. 1035 (1900). When the incapacity of the acknowledging or probating officer is latent, *i.e.*, does not appear upon the record, a recordation of the instrument pursuant to such defective acknowledgment or probate is valid and suffices to impart record constructive notice. County Savings Bank v. Tolbert, 192 N.C. 126, 133 S.E. 558 (1926).

205. Freeman v. Morrison, 214 N.C. 240, 199 S.E. 12 (1938), sets out the requisites for a valid acknowledgment. N.C. GEN. STAT. § 47-38 provides the following form of acknowledgment:

§ 47-38. **Acknowledgment by grantor.** — Where the instrument is acknowledged by the grantor or maker, or where a married woman is a grantor or maker, the form of acknowledgment shall be in substance as follows:

North Carolina, ... County.
I (here give the name of the official and his official title), do hereby certify that (here give the name of the grantor or maker) personally appeared before me this day and acknowledged the due execution of the foregoing instrument. Witness my hand and (where an official seal is required by law) official seal this the . . . . day of . . . . (year).
(Official seal.)

. . . .
(Signature of officer.)

Certificates of acknowledgment will be liberally construed and will be upheld if in substantial compliance with the statute.

206. N.C. GEN. STAT. § 47-14. Prior to 1967 when the statute was changed, the Clerk of the Superior Court adjudged whether the certificate of acknowledgment was in due form and whether the instrument was entitled to recordation. This was called "probating" the instrument, *i.e.*, the Clerk passed upon the certificate of acknowledgment as furnishing proof of the execution of the instrument, adjudged the genuineness of the certificate, the authority of the officer making it, and whether the officer making the certificate was the officer he purported to be. *See* White v. Connelly, 105 N.C. 65, 11 S.E. 177 (1890). The omission of such adjudication by the Register of Deeds (formerly the Clerk of the Superior Court) will prevent the proper recordation of a deed of conveyance and it will thus be invalidated with respect to purchasers for value and lien creditors of the grantor. Champion Fibre Co. v. Cozard, 183 N.C. 600, 112 S.E. 810 (1922).

If the Register of Deeds does not approve a certificate of acknowledgment and denies recordation of an instrument the statute provides a means whereby a judge may be asked to pass on its validity.

thereof.[207] Even an unattested instrument may be proved and recorded by proof of the handwriting of the maker given under oath.[208]

Registration of an improperly acknowledged or defectively probated deed imports no constructive notice and the deed will be treated as if unregistered.[209]

Division 2. Delivery

§ 199. Delivery Generally.

No title to real property can pass by an instrument, though signed and sealed, until it is validly delivered.[210]

Whether there is a valid delivery of a deed is a mixed question of law and fact.[211] In North Carolina, there are two essentials to a valid delivery: (1) There must be an intention of the grantor to pass the deed from his possession and beyond his legal control, and (2) the grantor must actually pass the deed from his possession with the intent that it shall be taken by the grantee or someone for him.[212] Whether these facts have occurred in a real estate transaction are to be determined by the jury.[213]

Therefore, a mere intention of the grantor that the instrument shall be good as a deed will not suffice as a delivery if the intent is not accompanied by a "transmutation of possession," a physical transfer of the deed to the grantee or to someone on behalf of the grantee.[214] Even a manual passing of a deed from the grantor to the grantee is not conclusive of a delivery.[215] The intent to pass title and the act transferring pos-

---

207. N.C. GEN. STAT. § 47-12.

208. N.C. GEN. STAT. § 47-13.

209. New Home Bldg. Supply Co. v. Nations, 259 N.C. 681, 131 S.E.2d 425 (1963). See note 204 supra. See generally Webster, Toward Greater Marketability of Land Titles — Remedying the Defective Acknowledgment Syndrome, 46 N.C.L. REV. 56 (1967).

210. Williams v. North Carolina State Bd. of Educ., 284 N.C. 588, 201 S.E.2d 889 (1974); Tarlton v. Griggs, 131 N.C. 216, 42 S.E. 591 (1902); Gulley v. Smith, 203 N.C. 274, 165 S.E. 710 (1932); Newell v. Edwards, 7 N.C. App. 650, 173 S.E.2d 504 (1970).

211. Johnston v. Kramer Bros. & Co., 203 F. 733 (1913).

212. Tarlton v. Griggs, 131 N.C. 216, 42 S.E. 591 (1902); Newell v. Edwards, 7 N.C. App. 650, 173 S.E.2d 504 (1970).

213. Id.

214. See Penninger v. Barrier, 29 N.C. App. 312, 224 S.E.2d 245 (1976) where the Court of Appeals lists three requirements for the valid delivery of a deed: (1) an intention by the grantor to give the instrument legal effect according to its purport and tenor; (2) evidence of that intention by some word or act which discloses that the grantor put the instrument beyond his legal control; and (3) acquiescence by the grantees in such intention. Citing Jones v. Saunders, 254 N.C. 644, 119 S.E.2d 789 (1961). See also Elliot v. Goss, 250 N.C. 185, 108 S.E.2d 475 (1959); Barnes v. Aycock, 219 N.C. 360, 13 S.E.2d 611 (1941); Burton v. Peace, 206 N.C. 99, 173 S.E. 4 (1934); Fortune v. Hunt, 149 N.C. 358, 63 S.E. 82 (1908).

215. Foy v. Stephens, 168 N.C. 438, 84 S.E. 758 (1915); Gaylord v. Gaylord, 150 N.C. 222, 63 S.E. 1028 (1909); Blades v. Wilmington Trust Co., 207 N.C. 771, 178 S.E. 565 (1935).

session of the instrument must concur to make a valid delivery.[216] A deed passes no title unless the legal delivery of the deed, in its completed state, is perfected in the grantor's lifetime.[217] The grantor must intend to pass title presently and part with possession of the instrument and relinquish legal control of the instrument to the grantee or to someone on the grantee's behalf.[218] Thus, where the grantor gives the deed to a third person with direction to take it and keep it, and if the grantor never calls for it, to deliver it to the grantee, and the grantor dies without more being done, there is no delivery as there would have been had the grantor parted with control of the deed and given an unqualified direction that it be delivered, though after his death.[219] The deed must pass out of the legal control of the grantor and if the grantor retains the power to recall possession, there is no delivery.[220]

§ 200. Delivery Presumed from Possession of Deed by Grantee.

A presumption that there has been a valid delivery arises from the fact that the deed is in the possession of the grantee. When the deed, properly executed, is found out of the possession of the maker and in the possession of some other person, then the law presumes the fact to be that it was intentionally delivered to or for the grantee.[221] Conversely, no presumption of delivery arises so long as the deed remains in the possession of the maker; the presumption is that it had not been made. If the deed passed out of the maker's possession by accident, fraud or mistake, or was not intended to be delivered to the grantee or anyone for him, the presumption of delivery may be rebutted.

§ 201. Delivery Presumed from Recordation.

Where a deed is duly probated and recorded, the public record thereof is admissible in evidence and raises a presumption that the deed was duly executed and delivered on the date that it bears, and the burden of showing the contrary rests on one who asserts the contrary.[222] It has even

---

216. Foy v. Stephens, 168 N.C. 438, 84 S.E. 758 (1915).
217. Butler v. Butler, 169 N.C. 584, 86 S.E. 507 (1915).
218. Fortune v. Hunt, 149 N.C. 358, 63 S.E. 82 (1908); Huddleston v. Hardy, 164, N.C. 210, 80 S.E. 158 (1913).
219. Fortune v. Hunt, 149 N.C. 358, 63 S.E. 82 (1908); Smith v. Moore, 149 N.C. 185, 62 S.E. 892 (1908); Gaylord v. Gaylord, 150 N.C. 222, 63 S.E. 1028 (1909); Penninger v. Barrier, 29 N.C. App. 312, 224 S.E.2d 245 (1976).
220. Id.
221. Tarlton v. Griggs, 131 N.C. 216, 42 S.E. 591 (1902), and numerous cases cited.
222. Williams v. North Carolina State Bd. of Educ., 284 N.C. 588, 201 S.E.2d 889 (1974); Watson v. United States, 34 F. Supp. 777 (1940); Lance v. Coggins, 236 N.C. 134, 71 S.E.2d 918 (1952); Jones v. Saunders, 257 N.C. 118, 125 S.E.2d 350 (1962) (even if recorded after the death of the purported grantor); Wetherington v. Williams, 134 N.C. 276, 46 S.E. 728 (1904); Perry v. Suggs, 9 N.C. App. 128, 175 S.E.2d 696 (1970).

been held that delivery of a deed to a public officer *to be recorded, though never recorded,* was a valid delivery and that the grantor could not recall the deed even though the grantee knew nothing about the deed; the delivery was deemed complete upon delivery to the registry to be recorded.[223] While retention of possession of a deed by its grantor creates a presumption of no delivery, it should be noted that retention of possession of the deed by a grantor will not overcome the presumption of delivery arising from registration of the deed.[224] The presumption of delivery arising from the registration of a deed will, however, yield to and be rebutted by evidence which shows that the registration was inadvertent or fraudulent or not intended as a delivery.[225]

No presumption of delivery arises, apparently, from the fact that the deed was acknowledged by the grantor.[226]

§ 202. Delivery to Third Person Not Grantee.

A delivery of a deed may be absolute or it may be conditional. If the grantor delivers it to some third party for the grantee, parting with possession of it, without any condition, or any direction to hold it for the grantor, and without in some way reserving the right to repossess it, the delivery is complete and the title passes at once, though the grantee may be ignorant of the facts, and no subsequent act of the grantor or anyone else can defeat the effect of the delivery.[227] But it will be otherwise and title will not pass if the grantor or donor retains any control over the deed, as if he requests the third person to keep the deed and deliver it to the person for whom it is intended "unless the grantor shall call for it again." [228] The grantor must have relinquished all control over the deed in the hands of the third-party depositary in order for there to be a valid delivery.

---

223. Robbins v. Rascoe, 120 N.C. 79, 26 S.E. 807 (1897); Ballard v. Ballard, 230 N.C. 629, 55 S.E.2d 316 (1949); Philips v. Houston, 50 N.C. 302 (1858).

224. Federal Land Bank of Columbia v. Griffin, 207 N.C. 265, 176 S.E. 555 (1934); Faircloth v. Johnson, 189 N.C. 429, 127 S.E. 346 (1925); Helms v. Austin, 116 N.C. 751, 21 S.E. 556 (1895); Watson v. United States, 34 F. Supp. 777 (1940).

225. Gulley v. Smith, 203 N.C. 274, 165 S.E. 710 (1932). It can be shown that the grantor did not intend to make a delivery although he had the deed recorded. McMahon v. Hensley, 178 N.C. 587, 101 S.E. 210 (1919); Watson v. United States, 34 F. Supp. 777 (1940).

226. *See* Perkins v. Thompson, 123 N.C. 175, 31 S.E. 387 (1898). *See also* Williams v. North Carolina State Bd. of Educ., 284 N.C. 588, 201 S.E.2d 889 (1974) (citing this section in original text), holds that no presumption of delivery arises from the acknowledgment of a deed by the grantor.

227. Robbins v. Rascoe, 120 N.C. 79, 26 S.E. 807 (1897); McMahon v. Hensley, 178 N.C. 587, 101 S.E. 210 (1919); Buchanan v. Clark, 164 N.C. 56, 80 S.E. 424 (1913); Watson v. United States, 34 F. Supp. 777 (1940).

228. Buchanan v. Clark, 164 N.C. 56, 80 S.E. 424 (1913); Fortune v. Hunt, 149 N.C. 358, 63 S.E. 82 (1908); Huddleston v. Hardy, 164 N.C. 210, 80 S.E. 158 (1913).

It should be noted, however, that a delivery of a deed by the grantor to a third person to be delivered unconditionally by the third person to the grantee upon the grantor's death would be valid.[229] If the grantor unconditionally hands over the deed to the depositary, placing it beyond the control and dominion of the grantor, with instructions to transmit it to the grantee at grantor's death, there is then a valid, effective and irrevocable delivery of the instrument as a deed, and a present interest in the realty passes at that time to the grantee, although the enjoyment thereof is deferred until the death of the grantor. If, however, when the instrument is handed over to the depositary, the grantor retains control and dominion over it, and the instruction is to deliver the deed to the grantee at grantor's death, unless otherwise directed in the meantime, there is no delivery of a deed, but merely an effort to make a will in a manner not authorized by law; in such case the depositary remains the agent of the grantor only, and his authority to delivery is terminated by the death of the grantor, and the instrument will not be given effect unless it was executed with the formalities and intent required for the execution of a will.

In a 1976 Court of Appeals case,[230] for example, an attorney prepared certain deeds of gift for a grantor who later died. The attorney testified that the grantor told him to keep the deeds until the grantor's death and then deliver them to the grantees. The attorney also testified that if the grantor had ever requested him to change the deeds, "I imagine I would have but I don't know." He also testified that "I did whatever he instructed me to do" and that "I would have done what he wanted with these deeds to comply with his wishes." It was held that this testimony justified a reasonable inference that the grantor retained ultimate control over the deeds until his death and that the evidence supported a jury finding that there was no valid delivery.

§ 203. Delivery in Escrow or Conditional Delivery.

Another type of delivery to a third person is called a "delivery in escrow." In this type transaction the grantor deposits the deed with a third-person depositary, called an "escrow," with instructions to the third person to deliver it to the grantee only upon the performance or fulfillment of some stated condition.[231] Instead of the delivery by the depositary to the grantee depending only upon the lapse of time or the happening of an event certain to happen (the death of the grantor as previously discussed), the typical escrow situation depends upon the performance of some condition by the grantee — usually the payment of the

---

229. *Id.*
230. Penninger v. Barrier, 29 N.C. App. 312, 224 S.E.2d 245 (1976).
231. 2 MORDECAI, LAW LECTURES 951 (1916).

§ 203 THE DEED § 203

purchase price — and title does not pass until the condition has been performed.[232] Title does pass to the grantee, however, when the condition of the escrow is fully performed without the necessity of a second delivery by the depositary.[233] Prior to the happening of the specified event or the performance of the condition, the grantor remains the owner of the land.[234]

When the condition is finally performed, the question may arise as to when the delivery becomes effective — at the time of the delivery to the depositary or at the time of the delivery from the escrow to the grantee? When the condition is performed the rule is that the deed takes effect from the time of the first delivery if necessary to effectuate the intention of the parties.[235] For instance, if, after delivery of a deed to the escrow, but before the escrow delivers it to the grantee, the grantor comes under some disability such as mental incompetency, or gets married, or dies, the delivery date "relates back" to the date of delivery to the escrow and the deed is deemed delivered from that time.[236] A majority of the jurisdictions of the United States apparently follow this view. It should be noted, however, that the "relation back" doctrine relating to escrow deliveries will not become operative so as to defeat the rights of lien creditors or

---

232. Craddock v. Barnes, 142 N.C. 89, 54 S.E. 1003 (1906).

233. *Id.* "If a writing having the form of a deed is delivered as an escrow and the condition be afterwards performed, it takes effect by force of the first delivery and without any new delivery."

234. This may be significant to determine who has the right to maintain an action to protect or preserve the title. As continued owner, the grantor may bring such action prior to performance of the condition by the grantee. Board of Educ. v. Development Co., 159 N.C. 162, 74 S.E. 1015 (1912). In addition, while no cases have arisen in North Carolina, the status of the title in the grantor pending completion of the escrow condition entitles him to rents and profits during the pendency of the escrow. Stone v. Duvall, 77 Ill. 475 (1875); Blumenthal v. Liebman, 109 Cal. App. 374, 240 P.2d 699 (1952). The grantor would be liable for taxes during this period. Mohr v. Joslin, 162 Iowa 34, 142 N.C. 981 (1913); McMurtrey v. Bridges, 41 Okla. 264, 137 P. 721 (1913). The grantor is a proper party to sign a petition as "owner" during the pendency of the escrow for purposes of voting limited to landowners. Hull v. Sangamon River Drainage Dist., 219 Ill. 454, 76 N.E. 701 (1906). Similarly the escrow grantor is deemed "owner" for the purpose of insuring the property held in escrow and collecting thereof if destroyed. St. Paul Fire & Marine Ins. Co. v. Crump, 231 Ala. 127, 163 So. 651 (1935). A well thought out escrow arrangement can regulate the respective rights of the escrow grantor and the escrow grantee in the interim between delivery by the grantor to the escrow and a second delivery to the grantee. Questions concerning rents, profits, taxes, insurance, fortuitous losses, improvement liens and many others can be avoided by provisions in the escrow agreement.

235. Hall v. Harris, 40 N.C. 303 (1848).

236. *Id.* This has particular significance when the grantor has died after turning the deed over to the escrow. If he has died, unless the delivery "relates back" to the initial delivery to the escrow, he would be incapable of then making a delivery. The same reasoning applies to a supervening disability to the grantor in the interim. It is likewise applicable to cut off the marital rights of a spouse who marries the escrow grantor pending performance of the escrow condition which would otherwise render the deed defective.

purchasers for value of the grantor unless the deed delivered in escrow has been properly registered under the recording statute.[237]

§ 204. Delivery in Escrow; Necessity for Written Contract to Make Escrow Enforceable.

The leading case of *Campbell v. Thomas*,[238] a Wisconsin case, holds that the placing of a deed in escrow by the grantor does not take it out of the power of the grantor to revoke it unless an executory contract in writing, complying with the Statute of Frauds, exists between the grantor and grantee. A majority of the states apparently follow this view.[239] No cases have been found in North Carolina directly in point.[240]

§ 205. Escrow's Wrongful Delivery to Grantee.

In the case of a wrongfully delivered deed from the escrow agent, no title passes.[241] No delivery is intended until the condition is performed. Logically, therefore, if the third-party escrow wrongfully yields possession to the grantee, no title should be deemed transferred even where the rights of subsequent purchasers for value from such grantee are involved.[242] The wrongfully procured deed is analogous to a forged or other nondelivered deed procured by fraud.[243] There are, however, contrary holdings in favor of innocent purchasers from grantees who have wrongfully obtained deeds from escrows without performing the requisite conditions.[244] This question is one upon which there is much conflict of

---

237. N.C. GEN. STAT. § 47-18. An escrow deed, like any other deed, is not valid against lien creditors or purchasers for value of the grantor except from recordation.

238. 42 Wis. 437, 24 Am. Rep. 427 (1877).

239. *Compare* Main v. Pratt, 276 Ill. 218, 114 N.E. 576 (1916). *See* CRIBBET, PRINCIPLES OF THE LAW OF PROPERTY 170 (1962).

240. *But see* Pope v. McPhail, 173 N.C. 238, 91 S.E. 947 (1917), and Vinson v. Pugh, 173 N.C. 189, 91 S.E. 838 (1917), in which it is held that when parties enter into an oral contract to sell land, prepare and *sign a written deed substantially expressing the bargain,* and deliver the same in escrow, such a deed is a sufficient "memorandum" within the meaning and requirement of our Statute of Frauds, and the contract may be considered and dealt with as a valid and binding agreement.

241. State v. Pool, 27 N.C. 105 (1844), wherein the court said, "... when a deed is delivered as an escrow it is of no more force until the condition be performed, than if he, who made it, had kept it."

242. *See* the leading case of Everts v. Agnes, 4 Wis. 343, 65 Am. Dec. 314 (1885).

243. *Id.*

244. *See, e.g.,* Schurtz v. Colvin, 55 Ohio St. 274, 45 N.E. 527 (1896), in which the court said: "Where the grantee wrongfully procures the holder of a deed as an escrow to deliver it to him, he acquires no title, or at least a voidable one; but this is a very different case from where a third person without notice, afterward and while the grantee is in possession, deals with him in good faith as owner."

authority.[245] North Carolina has no cases directly in point but has merely said in other contexts that "no title passes" upon a wrongful delivery by the escrow.[246]

It should be noted, in any case, that if the grantor is negligent and knows of the wrongful delivery by the depositary and fails to take measures to cancel or to nullify the instrument after it has passed into the grantee's possession, he may be precluded by reason of such neglect from thereafter asserting title as against an innocent purchaser for value on the ground that the delivery was invalid for noncompliance with a condition.[247] If, after a wrongful delivery by the escrow to the grantee, the grantor does not promptly take action to protect himself or to set aside the instrument, he may be found to have ratified or waived the condition and may be estopped to set the conveyance aside against an innocent purchaser.[248]

§ 206. Conditional Delivery Directly to Grantee.

The great majority of the cases of other jurisdictions hold that if the grantor hands a completed deed directly to the grantee with the intention that it should be only a conditional delivery, it is nevertheless a valid absolute delivery. The delivery is deemed good but the condition is deemed a nullity. If the deed is absolute in form but is turned over to the grantee himself subject to the performance of a condition precedent before it is to become legally effective, it is nevertheless a complete and absolute

---

245. CRIBBET, PRINCIPLES OF THE LAW OF PROPERTY 178 (1962); 4 THOMPSON, COMMENTARIES ON THE MODERN LAW OF REAL PROPERTY §§ 3953-3955 (1924). Some authorities feel that the *bona fide* purchaser should be protected under the theory that "when a loss has occurred which must fall on one of two innocent persons, it should be borne by him who is the occasion of the loss." It is reasoned that a deed deposited with an escrow, regular on its face, is capable of clothing the grantee with apparent title; that since the grantor has made the instrument, parted with its possession voluntarily to a person of his choice, that the grantor should be responsible for any misdelivery by the escrow in any controversy between the grantor and a *bona fide* purchaser from the grantee. It is further theorized that the purposes of recordation would likewise be better effected and the merchantability of land aided by protecting the purchaser for value in such instances. On the other hand, other authorities take the position that a deed procured from an escrow without performance of the conditions for delivery is absolutely void and that the grantee has no title which he can pass to an innocent purchaser for value. *See* Clevenger v. Moore, 126 Okla. 246, 259 P. 219 (1927). The conflicting authorities are set out and analyzed in 4 TIFFANY, REAL PROPERTY § 1051 (1939) and in 8 THOMPSON, REAL PROPERTY § 4249 (1963). Excellent annotations appear in 48 A.L.R. 405 (1927) and in 54 A.L.R. 1246 (1928) collecting the authorities.

246. *See* note 241 *supra*.

247. Mays v. Shields, 117 Ga. 814, 45 S.E. 68 (1903).

248. *E.g.*, in Mays v. Shields, 117 Ga. 814, 45 S.E. 68 (1903), the grantee was let into possession wrongfully and the deed was wrongfully delivered to the grantee who had it recorded. The grantor did not act promptly upon learning of the recordation of the deed and was held to be estopped to set aside the conveyance. 8 THOMPSON ON REAL PROPERTY § 4249 (1963).

delivery in most states.[249] In other words, the grantee in a deed in most jurisdictions cannot be the escrow depositary for himself.[250]

In North Carolina, however, even though a deed is absolute in form and is placed directly into the hands of the grantee, if there is no intention that the deed is to become operative until the performance or occurrence of some condition, there is no effective delivery and no title to the realty described therein passes until the condition is performed.[251] The condition to be performed as a condition precedent to the validity of the delivery may be a parol condition and may be shown by parol evidence.[252]

There are apparently no cases in North Carolina concerning the rights of purchasers for value from grantees who have received deeds directly from the grantor upon conditions not performed. It would seem, however, that a purchaser for value who takes from a grantee named in an absolute deed should take free from any condition not referred to in the deed as in such case the grantor has clothed the grantee with apparent title which is capable of deceiving an innocent purchaser.[253]

Division 3. Acceptance

§ 207. Acceptance by Grantee Generally.

A conveyance by deed must be accepted by the grantee or by someone on his behalf in order to be valid to pass title to real property. In the normal arm's length land transaction between seller and buyer, acceptance is apparent and creates no legal problem. Where the deed is executed, however, to complete a gift, disputes may arise involving whether there has been an acceptance of the deed. Unconditional acceptance of the deed by the grantee is just as important to its validity as an unconditional

---

249. This rule was first declared in England in Whyddon's Case, Cro. Eliz. 520, 78 Eng. Rep. 769 (1596), and has been generally followed in the United States.

250. This holding is generally upon the ground that the written instrument is not subject to parol contradiction.

251. Lerner Shops v. Rosenthal, 225 N.C. 316, 34 S.E.2d 206 (1945), holds "... our Court has extended the doctrine of conditional delivery to cover instances where deeds or instruments affecting lands were so delivered directly by the grantor to the grantee *thus perhaps creating or adopting a minority rule*," citing Garrison v. Machine Co., 159 N.C. 285, 74 S.E. 821 (1912), and other cases.

252. *Id.* It is held that such parol condition respecting delivery does not violate the parol evidence rule by modifying, altering or contradicting a written instrument but goes to show that the deed or instrument never became legally operative or effective.

253. The grantor of such instrument should foresee that an absolute deed placed in the hands of the grantee on a condition not appearing in the deed might be conveyed by the grantee to a purchaser before the condition is performed. In this case the equities would not appear to be equal and the innocent purchaser from the grantee should be protected.

delivery. Actually, there is no complete "delivery" until the deed is "accepted." [254]

North Carolina follows the general rule that actual acceptance is not required but that acceptance will be presumed if the conveyance is beneficial to the grantee even though he may have no knowledge of the transaction.[255] Even if he dies without ever having knowledge that he was grantee in a deed, the conveyance will be valid and title thereunder can be asserted by his heirs.[256] The presumption is not that the grantee *will* accept but that he *does*.[257] Since it is not necessary that the grantee actually give a contractual assent to accept a deed for his benefit, it is further held generally that it is not necessary that the grantee be *sui juris* or capable of entering into a contract. Therefore an infant,[258] person *non compos mentis*, or grantee under other disability is presumed to accept as grantee although none of these would be competent to make a binding contract or conveyance.[259] It should be noted, however, that the presumption of delivery does not apply if the deed is subject to a condition or otherwise imposes an obligation on the grantee.[260] Furthermore, the presumption of acceptance will yield to and not be applicable to a case where there is a dissent or renunciation by the grantee or his heirs.[261] An actual

---

254. 2 Mordecai, Law Lectures 942 (1916); Perkins v. Isley, 224 N.C. 793, 32 S.E.2d 588 (1945); Ballard v. Ballard, 230 N.C. 629, 55 S.E.2d 316 (1949).

255. Ballard v. Ballard, 230 N.C. 629, 55 S.E.2d 316 (1949); Williams v. Herring, 15 N.C. App. 642, 190 S.E.2d 696 (1972).

256. Buchanan v. Clark, 164 N.C. 56, 80 S.E. 424 (1913).

257. *Id. See* Kirk v. Turner, 16 N.C. 14 (1826), in which the court says: "A delivery of a deed is in fact its tradition from the maker to the person to whom it is made, or to some person for his use; for his acceptance is presumed until the contrary is shown. It being for his interest, the presumption is, not that he *will accept* but that he *does.*" *See also* Corbett v. Corbett, 249 N.C. 585, 107 S.E.2d 85 (1959), and cases cited therein, and Williams v. Herring, 15 N.C. App. 642, 190 S.E.2d 696 (1972).

258. Buchanan v. Clark, 164 N.C. 56, 80 S.E. 424 (1913).

259. 2 Mordecai, Law Lectures 948 (1916), wherein it is said:

> A good conveyance may be made by deed poll to an infant, lunatic, or feme covert, although such grantee would be under legal disability to make a conveyance. It is true that in theory of law, the grantee in a deed poll is held to be a party by accepting the deed. But the deed does not derive its efficacy as a grant and conveyance from the act of the grantee in accepting it, but from the grantor in executing it. In case of a plain absolute conveyance, without conditions, either no special acceptance is necessary to give it effect, or, what is nearly the same thing, the acceptance of the grantee will be presumed.

260. *See, e.g.,* Beaver v. Ledbetter, 269 N.C. 142, 152 S.E.2d 165 (1967), in which it is held that a wife named as co-grantee in a deed with her husband is not liable for an agreement to assume an indebtedness against the land set forth in the deed when she did not assent thereto.

261. *See* Buchanan v. Clark, 164 N.C. 56, 80 S.E. 424 (1913), and cases there cited. When the grantee refuses to accept a first delivery, then a new delivery must be made. The first deed cannot thereafter be accepted by the grantee. Respass v. Latham, 44 N.C. 138 (1852). If the grantee does not agree to an acceptance of the deed it will become inoperative. Baxter v. Baxter, 44 N.C. 341 (1853). When the refusal to accept is made by the grantee, the deed becomes void *ab initio.* State v. Pool, 27 N.C. 112 (1844); Respass v. Latham, 44 N.C. 138 (1852). If the grantee is an infant his presumed acceptance cannot be repudiated or refused until his minority disability has been removed. Gaylord v. Respass, 92 N.C. 554 (1885).

assent to accept, of course, will supply the acceptance requirement to validate a deed and will also render the grantee liable to perform any conditions or covenants attached to the deed.[262] Probate and registration of a deed raise a rebuttable presumption of acceptance of a deed.[263] If deed is found in possession of the grantee, both delivery and acceptance are presumed.[264] It would seem also that an actual acceptance could be made out by showing that the grantee paid the consideration, asserted title, conveyed the title to another or mortgaged the title, assuming the elements of delivery are otherwise met.

If a deed is delivered to a trustee for the benefit of a third-person grantee, the delivery is complete notwithstanding the trustee's declination to serve as trustee or his refusal to accept the deed.[265] This rule is derived from a combination of two rules: (1) that there is a presumption that the *cestui que trust* will accept that which is to his advantage or to his beneficial interest,[266] and (2) that a trust shall not fail from want of a trustee and the court will appoint a trustee if necessary.[267]

Division 4. Revenue Stamps

§ 208. Revenue Stamps Required on Deeds.

Persons, firms, corporations, associations, societies and organizations that convey interests in real estate for a consideration must purchase and affix an excise tax stamp to each deed, instrument or writing by which land, tenements and other realty are transferred.[268] The tax rate for stamps required to be placed on conveyances is fifty cents for each five hundred dollars ($500.00), or fractional part thereof, of the consideration received.[269] The excise stamp is not required, however, on leases for a

---

262. The assumption of the mortgage debt on land by accepting a deed for the equity of redemption, such deed containing an express provision that the grantee assumes the debt, enures to the benefit of the mortgagee and all subsequent holders of the mortgage debt. Having actually accepted the deed, the grantee must assume its burdens, and a personal judgment may be rendered against him upon the debt thus assumed. Baber v. Hanie, 163 N.C. 588, 80 S.E. 57 (1913); Drake v. Howell, 133 N.C. 163, 45 S.E. 539 (1903); 2 Mordecai, Law Lectures 950 (1916). *But see* Beaver v. Ledbetter, 269 N.C. 142, 152 S.E.2d 165 (1967), which is *contra* when one of the grantees of the deed does not *actually* accept the deed made to her as a co-grantee with her husband who did actually accept.

263. Frank v. Heiner, 117 N.C. 79, 23 S.E. 42 (1895).
264. Whitman v. Shingleton, 108 N.C. 193, 12 S.E. 1027 (1891).
265. Frank v. Heiner, 117 N.C. 79, 23 S.E. 42 (1895).
266. Buchanan v. Clark, 164 N.C. 56, 80 S.E. 424 (1913).
267. Frank v. Heiner, 117 N.C. 79, 23 S.E. 42 (1895); McLean v. Nelson, 46 N.C. 396 (1854).
268. N.C. Gen. Stat. §§ 105-228.28 through 105-228.36. Prior to 1967 the Federal Government required the purchase of Federal Revenue Stamps for affixation to deeds of conveyance. *See* 26 U.S.C.A. § 4361, repealed in 1967. When the federal stamp requirements were removed, the State imposed a state excise stamp requirement.
269. N.C. Gen. Stat. § 105-228.30.

term of years, transfers by will, intestacy, gift, merger or consolidation, or for instruments which secure an indebtedness or any other transfer where no consideration is due or paid.[270] While failure to attach the necessary stamps to a conveyance will not invalidate the deed of conveyance, if they are omitted wilfully and knowingly, one failing to pay the correct amount of tax or one directing, aiding or abetting another to fail to pay the correct amount of tax shall be guilty of a misdemeanor.[271]

Division 5. Reading of Deed by Grantor Not Necessary

§ 209. No Necessity That Grantor Read Deed; Deed Effective in Absence of Fraud.

The law will not relieve one who can read and write from liability on a written instrument, upon the ground that he did not understand the purport of the writing, or that he has made an improvident contract when he could inform himself and understand the transaction and has not done so.[272] "The law aids those who are vigilant, not those who sleep on their rights" is the general rule.[273] It would thus appear that a grantor will be liable and his deed will be effective even though he fails to read his deed before executing it and delivering it. It has even been held that an illiterate or blind man who executes a deed or contract without having it read to him will not be relieved from his obligation on the instrument.[274]

---

270. N.C. GEN. STAT. § 105-228.29.
271. *See* N.C. GEN. STAT. § 105-228.34.
272. Leonard v. Power Co., 155 N.C. 10, 70 S.E. 1061 (1911); Isley v. Brown, 253 N.C. 791, 117 S.E.2d 821 (1960).
  See Creasman v. Savings & Loan Ass'n, 279 N.C. 361, 183 S.E.2d 115 (1971), in which plaintiff's son secured plaintiff's signature upon a blank note and deed of trust by falsely telling her that he wanted to mortgage a trailer located on her property for $600. The son of plaintiff then filled in the blanks so that the note was for $6,000 and the deed of trust encumbered plaintiff's home. The Supreme Court of North Carolina held that when one signs an instrument *in blank,* the plea of *non est factum* or fraud in the *factum* is not available to him against an innocent third party, notwithstanding he may have been induced to sign by false representations that the blank instrument would be filled in a certain way, since he cannot say that the instrument he signed was different from what he intended to sign.
  See also Brown v. Gurkin, 22 N.C. App. 456, 206 S.E.2d 504 (1974), which states: "The duty to read an instrument or to have it read before signing it, is a positive one, and the failure to do so, in absence of any mistake, fraud, or oppression, is a circumstance against which no relief may be had, either at law or in equity."
273. Leonard v. Power Co., 155 N.C. 10, 70 S.E. 1061 (1911); Creasman v. Savings & Loan Ass'n, 279 N.C. 361, 183 S.E.2d 115 (1971); Brown v. Gurkin, 22 N.C. App. 456, 206 S.E.2d 504 (1974).
274. School Committee v. Kesler, 67 N.C. 443 (1872). *Compare* Creasman v. Savings & Loan Ass'n, 279 N.C. 361, 183 S.E.2d 115 (1971), where plaintiff's son secured plaintiff's signature upon a blank note and deed of trust by falsely telling her that he wanted to mortgage a trailer located on her property for $600. The son of plaintiff then filled in the

§ 209 REAL ESTATE LAW IN NORTH CAROLINA § 209

This rule, however, does not apply if the grantor or maker of an instrument has been actively induced or lulled "to sleep" or into a false sense of security by false or fraudulent representations or prevented from making proper inquiry by trick, artifice or contrivance.[275]

---

blanks so that the note was for $6,000 and the deed of trust encumbered plaintiff's home. In holding for the lender the Supreme Court of North Carolina held that when one signs an instrument *in blank,* the plea of *non est factum* or fraud in the *factum* is not available to him against an innocent third party, notwithstanding he may have been induced to sign by false representations that the blank instrument would be filled in a certain way, since he cannot say that the instrument he signed was different from what he intended to sign. When an innocent third party becomes involved in the transaction, the loss must fall on those whose carelessness and neglect have occasioned the loss.

275. Isley v. Brown, 253 N.C. 791, 117 S.E.2d 821 (1960); Roberson v. Williams, 240 N.C. 696, 83 S.E.2d 811 (1954); Newbern v. Newbern, 178 N.C. 3, 100 S.E. 77 (1919); Taylor v. Edmunds, 176 N.C. 325, 97 S.E. 42 (1918). *Accord,* Turner v. Weber, 16 N.C. App. 574, 192 S.E.2d 601 (1972). The mere fact that a grantor who can read and write signs a deed does not preclude him from showing, as between the grantee and himself, that he was induced to sign by fraud on the part of the grantee, or that he was deceived and thrown off guard by the grantee's false statements and assurances designedly made at the time and reasonably relied on by him.

CHAPTER 11

COVENANTS FOR TITLE IN DEEDS

Article I. General Provisions

§ 210. Covenants in Deeds Respecting Title Generally.
§ 211. Types of Covenants Listed.

Article II. Covenants of Seisin and Right to Convey

§ 212. The Covenants of Seisin and Right to Convey in General.
§ 213. When the Covenants of Seisin and Right to Convey Are Breached.
§ 214. Same — When the Statute of Limitations Begins to Run.
§ 215. The Covenants of Seisin and Right to Convey Are Personal Covenants; Proper Party Plaintiff in Action to Recover for Breach.
§ 216. Damages Recoverable by Grantee Upon Breach of the Covenants of Seisin and Right to Convey.

Article III. The Covenant Against Encumbrances

§ 217. The Covenant Against Encumbrances Generally.
§ 218. Damages Recoverable by Grantee Upon Breach of the Covenant Against Encumbrances.
§ 219. When Breach of the Covenant Against Encumbrances Occurs; the Statute of Limitations.
§ 220. Proper Party Plaintiff in Action to Recover for Breach of the Covenant Against Encumbrances.

Article IV. The Covenants of Warranty and Quiet Enjoyment

§ 221. The Covenants of Warranty and Quiet Enjoyment Generally.
§ 222. When Breach of the Covenants of Warranty and Quiet Enjoyment Occur — Actual and Constructive Evictions.
§ 223. Same — The Statute of Limitations.
§ 224. Damages Recoverable Upon Breach of the Covenants of Warranty and Quiet Enjoyment.
§ 225. Covenants of Warranty and Quiet Enjoyment "Run With the Land"; Proper Parties Plaintiff to Bring Suit for Breach.

Article V. Title by Estoppel

§ 226. Estoppel by Deed — By Deed With Covenant of Warranty.
§ 227. Same — By Deed Without Covenant of Warranty.
§ 228. Persons Estopped by Deeds; "Estoppel" and "Rebutter."
§ 229. Title by Estoppel as Affected by Recordation Statutes.

Article I. General Provisions

§ 210. Covenants in Deeds Respecting Title Generally.

Most deeds of conveyance contain one or more covenants by the grantor whereby the grantor agrees that the grantee will be entitled to indemnity if the title which he purports to convey fails for some reason.[1] Purchasers of real property generally prefer to have the land rather than a return of the purchase price or a sum of money and utilize the recording system and the examination of vendors' titles to accomplish the objective of making certain that they get to keep the land itself if at all possible. The recording system is not entirely perfect, however, and in spite of due diligence it is still possible for title defects not to appear in land title records.[2] Therefore, in order to protect vendees from those risks not necessarily disclosed by the land title records, additional protection is desirable for a purchaser of lands as against his vendor in the event the title he purchases is defective. Covenants for title complement the recordation statutes in that they enable vendees to have a cause of action for damages if the covenants of the vendor are breached by the vendor's title turning out to be defective.

The covenant of "warranty" antedated the recording statutes and was the chief technique for protecting grantees prior to the development of the recording system. Under the common law, dating back to the feudal system, the grantor-lord was under an obligation to his grantee-vassal to give to the grantee-vassal land of equal value if the grantee-vassal was ousted under a title superior to that granted by the grantor-lord.[3] If the grantor-lord did not have sufficient land to reimburse the ousted grantee in kind, he was assessed damages to make up the difference. Modern

---

1. TIFFANY, REAL PROPERTY § 677 (abr. ed. 1940).

2. *E.g.,* the following hidden risks affecting land titles are not discoverable from an examination of the land title records: (1) The marital status of an owner in the chain of title. A grantor in the chain may have signed an instrument as a single person, though he was secretly married, which will give a claim to marital rights by a person whose existence was not suspected. (2) There may be undisclosed heirs of an owner whose rights have not been extinguished who can come in and claim their share of the property. (3) There is always the risk of a mistaken interpretation of title instruments which appear in the record. (4) Mental incompetence may not appear in the record. The person who executed the deed may have been a minor or under mental disability which does not appear of record; if so, the document is subject to cancellation and may be set aside. (5) A perfectly recorded instrument in the chain of title may be the result of impersonation or forgery and its perfect recordation does not validate it. (6) The deed may have been delivered without the consent of the owner or after his death. (7) The deed may not have been complete at the time of its delivery; the name of the grantee may have been inserted in the deed after its delivery. There are countless other possible risks of loss that will not necessarily be discoverable from the land title records.

3. *See* Phillips v. Smith, 4 N.C. 87 (1814).

covenants find their genesis in the feudal "warranty." But today covenants of title in real property transactions are contractual [4] and upon a branch of any covenant of title the grantee may recover a sum of money from his grantor measured by the damages suffered. The nature and scope of these covenants and the rights accruing upon their breach will be discussed in the following sections.

§ 211. Types of Covenants Listed.

The "usual covenants for title" included in deeds are:
1. The covenants of seisin and the right to convey.
2. The covenant against encumbrances.
3. The covenants of warranty and quiet enjoyment.

Article II. Covenants of Seisin and Right to Convey

§ 212. The Covenants of Seisin and Right to Convey in General.

The covenant of seisin at modern law is a covenant that the grantor has the estate, or the right to convey the estate, in quality and quantity,

---

4. There is no implied covenant of title with respect to real property; it must be express. TIFFANY, REAL PROPERTY § 681 (abr. ed. 1940). "The doctrine of *caveat emptor* finds its natural home in the law of real property. In the absence of express covenants for title the full risk of title falls on the purchaser." CRIBBET, PRINCIPLES OF THE LAW OF PROPERTY 204 (1962); Pridgen v. Long, 177 N.C. 189, 98 S.E. 451 (1919); Zimmerman v. Lynch, 130 N.C. 61, 40 S.E. 841 (1902); Huntley v. Waddell, 34 N.C. 32 (1851); 2 MORDECAI, LAW LECTURES 888 (1916). While "covenants for title" must be express and the doctrine of *caveat emptor* is still generally applicable with respect to the grantor's "title," recent cases indicate that "covenants of *quality*" in sales of real property may be *implied* in favor of purchasers in certain situations. *See, e.g.,* Hartley v. Ballou, 286 N.C. 51, 209 S.E.2d 776 (1974), in which the North Carolina Supreme Court holds that in every contract for the sale of a recently completed dwelling, and in every contract for the sale of a dwelling then under construction, the vendor, if he be in the business of building such dwellings, shall be held *impliedly* to warrant to the initial vendee that, at the time of the passing of the deed or the taking of possession by the initial vendee (whichever first occurs), the dwelling, together with all its fixtures, is sufficiently free from structural defects, and is constructed in a workmanlike manner, so as to meet the standard of workmanlike quality then prevailing at the time and place of construction.

See also Hinson v. Jefferson, 287 N.C. 422, 215 S.E.2d 102 (1975), which holds that a grantor breached an *implied* warranty where he conveyed land to a grantee subject to a restrictive covenant limiting its use to a single-family dwelling when the land could not be used for that purpose because it would not support a septic tank or on-site sewage disposal system, which fact was unknown to both the grantor and grantee at the time of the conveyance. The court discusses the inroads made into the doctrine of *caveat emptor* with respect to sales of real property. It should be noted, however, that Hartley v. Ballou, and Hinson v. Jefferson, *supra,* relate to implied warranties with respect to the "quality" of the real estate conveyed and not to "title." For a further discussion of implied warranties of quality, *see* § 149 *supra*.

which he purports to convey.[5] The covenant of the right to convey is substantially equivalent to the covenant of seisin.[6]

§ 213. When the Covenants of Seisin and Right to Convey Are Breached.

The covenants of seisin and the right to convey are deemed to be *in praesenti* undertakings that the grantor has the estate in quantity and quality which he purports to convey. Therefore, if he does not have an indefeasible title to the property with respect to which he covenants, his covenant is deemed broken as soon as made.[7] It is thus stated that the covenants are broken when made, if ever at all. If the grantor purports to convey a fee simple title when the fee or a part of the fee is outstanding in a third person, or if he has only a remainder or other future interest in the real property subject to a preceding estate,[8] the covenant is breached at the time the deed is delivered. It is a covenant or assurance that certain facts exist at the very time the deed is delivered; if the facts do not exist at that time there is an immediate breach upon delivery of the deed.[9] To maintain an action for breach of a covenant of seisin, it is not necessary to show that the grantee was evicted, as the mere existence of an outstanding paramount title to that conveyed by the grantor is a breach of the covenant.[10]

§ 214. Same — When the Statute of Limitations Begins to Run.

Since the covenant of seisin or right to convey is broken when made, if ever at all, the statute of limitations begins to run from the time the deed is executed and delivered.[11] Since the covenants appear in a deed, which is a sealed instrument, the ten-year statute of limitations applies to causes of action based on such covenants.[12]

---

5. Minor & Wurts, Real Property § 906 (1910); Tiffany, Real Property § 678 (abr. ed. 1940); Pridgen v. Long, 177 N.C. 189, 98 S.E. 451 (1919).
6. 2 Mordecai, Law Lectures 901 (1916); Pridgen v. Long, 177 N.C. 189, 98 S.E. 451 (1919).
7. Smith v. People's Bank, 254 N.C. 588, 119 S.E.2d 623 (1961); Cover v. McAden, 183 N.C. 641, 112 S.E. 817 (1922); Crowell v. Jones, 167 N.C. 386, 83 S.E. 551 (1914).
8. Tiffany, Real Property § 678 (abr. ed. 1940); Crowell v. Jones, 167 N.C. 386, 83 S.E. 551 (1914).
9. Pridgen v. Long, 177 N.C. 189, 98 S.E. 451 (1919); Newbern v. Hinton, 190 N.C. 108, 129 S.E. 181 (1925); Wilson v. Vreeland, 176 N.C. 504, 97 S.E. 427 (1918).
10. Cribbet, Principles of the Law of Property 207 (1962); Smith v. People's Bank, 254 N.C. 588, 119 S.E.2d 623 (1961); Eames v. Armstrong, 142 N.C. 506, 55 S.E. 405 (1906).
11. Shankle v. Ingram, 133 N.C. 255, 45 S.E. 578 (1903); Price v. Deal, 90 N.C. 290 (1884).
12. Shankle v. Ingram, 133 N.C. 255, 45 S.E. 578 (1903); 2 Mordecai, Law Lectures 901 (1916).

§ 215. The Covenants of Seisin and Right to Convey Are Personal Covenants; Proper Party Plaintiff in Action to Recover for Breach.

Since the covenants of seisin and right to convey relate to a presently existing fact, being assurances that the grantor has the title that he purports to convey, these covenants are always broken at the very instant they are made.[13] They therefore do not have the qualities of continuousness or prospectiveness. It is therefore said that the covenants of seisin and right to convey do not "run with the land." This means that the only person who can receive redress for breach of one of these covenants is the immediate grantee of the covenanting grantor or his personal representative. Remote grantees of land originally covenanted cannot recover for breach of a prior grantor's covenant of seisin or right to convey. A grantee can only recover for breach of the covenant if his own grantor made the covenant.[14] Nor can the grantee assign his right of action where there has been a breach of the covenant of seisin or right to convey.[15]

§ 216. Damages Recoverable by Grantee Upon Breach of the Covenants of Seisin and Right to Convey.

The usual recovery for breach of a covenant of seisin, or for breach of the covenant of the right to convey, is the purchase money paid to the covenantor, plus interest thereon.[16] But where the covenantee buys in the outstanding paramount title, the measure of damages recoverable against the covenantor for the breach is the reasonable price which he has fairly and reasonably paid for such paramount title, not exceeding the original consideration paid by him to the covenantor.[17]

Since the covenantee is only entitled to recover for the actual injury sustained to the extent of the amount of the consideration paid, if he goes into possession of the land involved and his defective title is rendered

---

13. Smith v. People's Bank, 254 N.C. 588, 119 S.E.2d 623 (1961).

14. Newbern v. Hinton, 190 N.C. 108, 129 S.E. 181 (1925); Eames v. Armstrong, 142 N.C. 506, 55 S.E. 405 (1906); Markland v. Crump, 18 N.C. 94 (1834); Wilder v. Ireland, 53 N.C. 85 (1860); Britton v. Ruffin, 123 N.C. 67, 26 S.E. 642 (1897); Pridgen v. Long, 177 N.C. 189, 98 S.E. 451 (1919); Wilson v. Vreeland, 176 N.C. 504, 97 S.E. 427 (1918); Cover v. McAden, 183 N.C. 641, 112 S.E. 817 (1922); Lockhart v. Parker, 189 N.C. 138, 126 S.E. 313 (1925).

15. 2 MORDECAI, LAW LECTURES 859, 860 (1916); Newbern v. Hinton, 190 N.C. 108, 129 S.E. 181 (1925); Lockhart v. Parker, 189 N.C. 138, 126 S.E. 313 (1925).

16. Pridgen v. Long, 177 N.C. 189, 98 S.E. 451 (1919); Eames v. Armstrong, 146 N.C. 1, 59 S.E. 165 (1907); Newbern v. Hinton, 190 N.C. 108, 129 S.E. 181 (1925); Price v. Deal, 90 N.C. 290 (1884); Wilson v. Forbes, 13 N.C. 30 (1828).

17. Atlantic Joint Stock Land Bank of Raleigh v. Williams, 209 N.C. 104, 182 S.E. 727 (1935); Campbell v. Shaw, 170 N.C. 186, 86 S.E. 1035 (1915); Pridgen v. Long, 177 N.C. 189, 98 S.E. 451 (1919); Bank v. Glenn, 68 N.C. 35 (1873).

perfect by the statute of limitations, he is entitled to recover only nominal damages.[18] In addition, where the grantor's covenant of seisin is broken because of his lack of title at the time of the conveyance, if his title is subsequently perfected in such a way that the grantor's title will enure to the benefit of his grantee by estoppel, damages for breach of the covenant of seisin will be nominal.[19] Where there is a failure of title to only part of the land purportedly conveyed, constituting a partial breach of the covenant of seisin, the grantee's measure of damages is the proportion that the value of such portion bears to the whole purchase price paid.[20] Neither increased value of the land nor the value of improvements placed on the land by the grantee can be considered in a suit for breach of the covenant of seisin.[21]

Article III. The Covenant Against Encumbrances

§ 217. The Covenant Against Encumbrances Generally.

The covenant against encumbrances is a covenant that there are no encumbrances outstanding against the premises at the time of the conveyance. This definition requires a consideration of what is an "encumbrance" in order to determine if there has been a breach of the covenant. The following have been held to be encumbrances, the existence of which will constitute a breach of the covenant against encumbrances: judgment liens against the real property;[22] mortgages; attachments; mechanics' and materialmen's liens; taxes; assessments;[23] rights of dower, whether inchoate or consummate;[24] covenants which run with the land and impose a burden on the owner or diminish the free use of the property, such as the covenant that no liquor should be sold on the land, or a covenant that fences shall be built or maintained, or restricting the character of buildings that may be erected on the land; easements and servitudes to which the land is subject, such as rights-of-way, water privileges, rights to back water by a dam, to run drains and sewers through

---

18. Wilson v. Forbes, 13 N.C. 30 (1828); Bank v. Glenn, 68 N.C. 35 (1873).
19. Meyer v. Thompson, 183 N.C. 543, 112 S.E. 328 (1922); Bank v. Glenn, 68 N.C. 35 (1873).
20. Campbell v. Shaw, 170 N.C. 186, 86 S.E. 1035 (1915).
21. Phillips v. Smith, 4 N.C. 87 (1814).
22. Thompson v. Avery County, 216 N.C. 405, 5 S.E.2d 146 (1939).
23. City of Winston-Salem v. Powell Paving Co., 7 F. Supp. 424 (1934). But where drainage assessments were levied, and both seller and buyer were fixed with legal notice of statutory proceedings for the formation of the drainage district, such subsequent assessments are public charges "which are not encumbrances" as contemplated by the seller's covenant against encumbrances. See Pate v. Banks, 178 N.C. 139, 100 S.E. 251 (1919). It is otherwise if payment of any assessment is past due. See Oliver v. Hecht, 207 N.C. 481, 177 S.E. 399 (1934).
24. Fishel v. Browning, 145 N.C. 71, 58 S.E. 759 (1907).

§ 217 COVENANTS FOR TITLE IN DEEDS § 217

the land, or to cut wood.[25] "Encumbrances" as used in the covenant against encumbrances has been said to mean "such as have some foundation in right, or at least color of right, such as would require in some proper way an expenditure of money to remove them, and not such as may be set up arbitrarily and groundlessly by a pretender." [26]

A restriction upon the use which may be made of land, or upon its transfer, which is imposed by a statute or ordinance enacted pursuant to the police power, such as a zoning ordinance or an ordinance regulating the size of lots, fixing building lines or otherwise regulating the subdivision of an area into lots, is not an encumbrance upon the land within the meaning of a covenant against encumbrances, being distinguishable in this respect from restrictions on the use of the land imposed by deed.[27] While the existence of this type of public ordinance or law is not an encumbrance on the property, a violation of a public restriction, existing at the time of the conveyance to the covenantee, does constitute an encumbrance within the meaning of the covenant.[28]

A grantor who makes a covenant against encumbrances will be liable on his covenant notwithstanding the fact that the grantee-covenantee has actual or record notice of an existing encumbrance at the time the grant is made.[29]

It should be noted, however, that a public road and a right-of-way of a railroad in operation are not considered encumbrances, it being presumed that a purchase of land through which a road or railway right-of-way runs

---

25. 2 MORDECAI, LAW LECTURES 903 (1916); TIFFANY, REAL PROPERTY § 680 (abr. ed. 1940); MINOR & WURTS, REAL PROPERTY § 909 (1910); Gerdes v. Shew, 4 N.C. App. 144, 166 S.E.2d 519 (1969).

26. Abernathy v. Stowe, 92 N.C. 213 (1885).

27. Fritts v. Gerukos, 273 N.C. 116, 159 S.E.2d 536 (1968); Marriott Financial Services, Inc. v. Capitol Funds, Inc., 23 N.C. App. 377, 209 S.E.2d 423 (1974), aff'd, 288 N.C. 122, 217 S.E.2d 551 (1975); Wilcox v. Pioneer Homes, 41 N.C. App. 140, 254 S.E.2d 214 (1979). Annot., 39 A.L.R.3d 362 (1971).

28. Wilcox v. Pioneer Homes, 41 N.C. App. 140, 254 S.E.2d 214 (1979). See 41 N.C. App. 142, 143, where the Court of Appeals decision reads:

There are no North Carolina cases which consider whether an existing violation of public restrictions on the use of real property constitutes an encumbrance. There is a split of authority among the jurisdictions which have considered this question. Annot., 39 A.L.R.3d 362 § 2 (1971). The majority of the jurisdictions have held that, although the existence of a public restriction on the use of real property is not an encumbrance rendering the title to the real property unmarketable, an existing violation of such an ordinance is an encumbrance within the meaning of a warranty against encumbrances. Lohmeyer v. Bower, 170 Kan. 442, 227 P. 2d 102 (1951), (minimum side lot violation); Oatis v. Delcuze, 226 La. 751, 77 So. 2d 28 (1954), (non-conforming building); Moyer v. De Vincentis Construction Co., 107 Pa. Super. 588, 164 A. 111 (1933), (violation of set-back requirement). See Hartman v. Rizzuto, 123 Cal. App. 2d 186, 266 P. 2d 539 (1954), (violation of rear-yard requirement); Miller v. Milwaukee, Odd Fellows Temple, Inc., 206 Wis. 547, 240 N.W. 193 (1932); Genske v. Jensen, 188 Wis. 17, 205 N.W. 548 (1925). Annot., 39 A.L.R.3d 362 §§ 5-6 (1971).

29. Philbin Invs. Inc. v. Orb Enterprises Ltd., 35 N.C. App. 622, 242 S.E.2d 176 (1978); Gerdes v. Shew, 4 N.C. App. 144, 166 S.E.2d 519 (1969).

was made with reference to the road or right-of-way and that the consideration was adjusted accordingly.[30]

§ 218. Damages Recoverable by Grantee Upon Breach of the Covenant Against Encumbrances.

The measure of damages for breach of the covenant against encumbrances is the reasonable amount required to remove the encumbrance from the land, not to exceed the purchase price paid to the covenantor.[31] While there are no North Carolina cases establishing the point, if the encumbrance consists of a servitude on the land that cannot be extinguished, as in the case of an easement where the holder refuses to release it, the general view is that the diminution in value of the estate by reason of the encumbrance can be recovered; in other words, the measure of damages would be the difference between the value of the land without the encumbrance and its value as it is conveyed subject to the encumbrance.[32] While a grantee has an action for breach of the covenant against encumbrances immediately upon delivery of the deed, if the encumbrance has inflicted no actual injury on the grantee, and he has paid nothing towards removing it, or extinguishing it, he can recover only nominal damages.[33]

Where a vendor represents in a contract or deed that property is free from encumbrances in order to make a sale when in fact the vendor knows that there is an outstanding indebtedness secured by a recorded deed of trust, there is a "false pretense" within the criminal statute making it unlawful to obtain money by false pretenses.[34]

§ 219. When Breach of the Covenant Against Encumbrances Occurs; the Statute of Limitations.

The covenant against encumbrances, like the covenant of seisin, is broken when made, if ever at all. The covenant against encumbrances is

---

30. Goodman v. Heilig, 157 N.C. 6, 72 S.E. 866 (1911). This latter rule may also be applicable, as in some states, to "visible easements." In the *Goodman* case the court said: "But there is a principle recognized by adjudged cases, and resting upon sound reason and policy, which holds that purchasers of property obviously and notoriously subjected at the time to some right of an easement or servitude affecting its physical condition, take it subject to such right without any express exceptions in the conveyance, and that the vendors are not liable on their covenants by reason of its existence."

31. Thompson v. Avery County, 216 N.C. 405, 5 S.E.2d 146 (1939).

32. Burby, Real Property § 127 (1965); Cribbet, Principles of the Law of Property 212 (1962).

33. Lane v. Richardson, 104 N.C. 642, 10 S.E. 189 (1889). In Fishel v. Browning, 145 N.C. 71, 58 S.E. 759 (1907), the court said: "If the encumbrance is contingent in its character, and if nothing has been paid by the plaintiff towards removing it or extinguishing it, and if it has inflicted no actual injury upon him, he can obtain but nominal damages, as he is not allowed to recover a certain compensation for running the risk of an uncertain injury."

34. State v. Wallace, 25 N.C. App. 360, 213 S.E.2d 420 (1975); State v. Banks, 24 N.C. App. 604, 211 S.E.2d 860 (1975).

a present assurance that there are no outstanding encumbrances against the land at the time it is conveyed and it is a "personal covenant" that does not "run with the land." Hence, if an encumbrance exists at the time the deed is delivered, the covenant is instantly broken at that time and the right of action for damages arises at that time in favor of the covenantee.[35] Therefore, for purposes of the statute of limitations, the cause of action for breach of the covenant against encumbrances, like the cause of action for breach of the covenants of seisin and right to convey, begins to run from the time of the delivery of the deed.[36]

§ 220. Proper Party Plaintiff in Action to Recover for Breach of the Covenant Against Encumbrances.

Since a covenant against encumbrances is a personal covenant and not a covenant that "runs with the land," it is not assignable at law and can be taken advantage of only by the immediate covenantee or his personal representative. It cannot pass to or be sued upon by his heir, his devisee, or by a subsequent purchaser.[37]

Article IV. The Covenants of Warranty and Quiet Enjoyment

§ 221. The Covenants of Warranty and Quiet Enjoyment Generally.

These two covenants are for all practical purposes the same and they should be considered together. They are assurances or guarantees of the grantor that he has title and that there are no outstanding paramount interests existing at the time of the conveyance and that he will protect and defend the estate of the covenantee against the lawful claims of all persons whomsoever in the future.[38] The covenants of warranty and quiet enjoyment therefore have the qualities of continuousness or prospectiveness, meaning that they are not simply *in praesenti,* present tense, guaranties, but that they operate *in futuro.* They promise that the grantee or grantees *will not be evicted by the holder of a paramount title*: that the grantor *will forever defend* the title which he has conveyed to his grantee against the lawful claims of all persons whomsoever. For that reason, they are sometimes called "future covenants" [39] to differentiate

---

35. Thompson v. Avery County, 216 N.C. 405, 5 S.E.2d 146 (1939); Lockhart v. Parker, 189 N.C. 138, 126 S.E. 313 (1925).
36. Since the covenant appears in a deed, which is a sealed instrument, the ten-year statute of limitations would apply from the date of delivery of the deed.
37. Lockhart v. Parker, 189 N.C. 138, 126 S.E. 313 (1925).
38. Cover v. McAden, 183 N.C. 641, 112 S.E. 817 (1922); Smith v. People's Bank, 254 N.C. 588, 119 S.E.2d 623 (1961); Fritts v. Gerukos, 273 N.C. 116, 159 S.E.2d 536 (1968); Shuford v. Phillips, 235 N.C. 387, 70 S.E.2d 193 (1952).
39. *See, e.g.,* CRIBBET, PRINCIPLES OF THE LAW OF PROPERTY 209 (1962). *See also* Cover v. McAden, 183 N.C. 641, 112 S.E. 817 (1922).

their effect from the covenants of seisin and right to convey and the covenant against encumbrances, which are all "present covenants." Covenants of general warranty and quiet enjoyment do not, however, extend to protect a grantee from the wrongful acts of strangers or tortious wrongdoers since the grantee has a legal remedy against a trespasser or disseisor.[40]

A distinction should be drawn between a general warranty and a special warranty. The general warranty guarantees the grantee and his successors in interest against the claims of all persons whomsoever who may successfully assert an adverse or paramount title. A special warranty, on the other hand, limits the protection afforded a grantee to claims arising "by, through, or under" the grantor, and goes no further.[41] A warranty executed by two covenantors may be general as to one covenantor and special as to the other,[42] depending upon the expressed intention of the parties. A special warranty has the same characteristics as a general warranty with respect to damages, its running with the land, the requirement of an eviction, and that any subsequent grantee can maintain an action for its breach.

§ 222. When Breach of the Covenants of Warranty and Quiet Enjoyment Occur — Actual and Constructive Evictions.

The covenants of warranty and quiet enjoyment, since they operate *in futuro,* and since they impose a continuing responsibility on the covenantor, are not breached until there has been an eviction of the grantee or grantees under a superior title.[43] This distinguishes the covenants of warranty and quiet enjoyment from the covenants of seisin and the right to convey and the covenant against encumbrances which are broken when made, if ever at all, without the necessity of an eviction. This distinction is significant in determining when a breach occurs.

In order to recover for a breach of a covenant of warranty or quiet enjoyment, the plaintiff must show an ouster or a disturbance of the peaceful possession by one who has an adverse superior title.[44] The ouster or distrubance may be total or partial. It may be actual or constructive. An actual eviction occurs when the grantee or his assigns withdraws from

---

40. Shimer v. Traub, 244 N.C. 466, 94 S.E.2d 363 (1956).

41. 2 MORDECAI, LAW LECTURES 858 (1916).

42. Spencer v. Jones, 168 N.C. 291, 84 S.E. 261 (1915).

43. Shimer v. Traub, 244 N.C. 466, 94 S.E.2d 363 (1956); Cover v. McAden, 183 N.C. 641, 112 S.E. 817 (1922); Shuford v. Phillips, 235 N.C. 387, 70 S.E.2d 193 (1952); Pridgen v. Long, 177 N.C. 189, 98 S.E. 451 (1919); Smith v. People's Bank, 254 N.C. 588, 119 S.E.2d 623 (1961).

44. Shuford v. Phillips, 235 N.C. 387, 70 S.E.2d 193 (1952).

or surrenders the land upon the demand of the true owner.[45] While there must be an ouster or disturbance of the possession of the covenantee or his assignee,[46] it is not essential that the yielding of possession be pursuant to legal process.[47] It is sufficient that the claim is asserted, that it is valid, and that the covenantee yields to it. If the covenantee yields possession to one who does not have superior title, it is his folly and no recovery can be had for breach of warranty.[48] If possession is yielded pursuant to a judicial decision, the covenantor is not necessarily bound unless he has been given proper notice of such proceedings in order that he could appear and defend the title.[49]

A constructive eviction occurs when a covenantee buys in a superior title instead of yielding possession.[50] A constructive eviction also occurs when the covenantee is unable to obtain possession of purchased premises because another person having a superior title is in possession.[51] The covenantee is not required to take forcible possession of the premises in order to maintain his action against the warrantor.[52]

The mere existence of a better title without a disturbance of the grantee's possession or an ouster,[53] even if there is a judgment that the

---

45. Mizzell v. Ruffin, 118 N.C. 69, 23 S.E. 927 (1896). The title or right to which the covenantee yields must be not only paramount to his own but must be paramount to that of anyone else. Wilson v. Vreeland, 176 N.C. 504, 97 S.E. 427 (1918). Where covenantee left the premises for a short time and returned to find them in possession of one who held paramount title, this constituted a sufficient eviction to entitle him to bring an action for breach of warranty against the warrantor. See Hodges v. Latham, 98 N.C. 239, 3 S.E. 495 (1887).

46. Fishel v. Browning, 145 N.C. 71, 58 S.E. 759 (1907); Lockhart v. Parker, 189 N.C. 138, 126 S.E. 313 (1925); Shuford v. Phillips, 235 N.C. 387, 70 S.E.2d 193 (1952).

47. TIFFANY, REAL PROPERTY § 681 (abr. ed. 1940).

48. See 2 MORDECAI, LAW LECTURES 891 (1916).

49. It is not always essential to the covenantee's right of action for breach of the covenant of warranty that he should give his covenantor notice to come in to defend the title. If no notice is given to the covenantor that an action has been brought to oust the covenantee by a claimant of a superior title, however, the judgment against the covenantee does not make out a prima facie case against the covenantor that the eviction of the covenantee was under a superior title. The covenantee, in order to prevail over the covenantor, has the burden of showing that he was in fact ousted under a paramount title. See Culbreth v. Britt Corp., 231 N.C. 76, 56 S.E.2d 15 (1949); Jones v. Balsley, 154 N.C. 61, 69 S.E. 827 (1910). If notice *is* given to the covenantor that a suit has been instituted by one claiming under paramount title, and the covenantor does not defend the suit and judgment is rendered against the covenantee, who is in fact ousted, the covenantor is bound by the judgment as if he were a party to the suit. Culbreth v. Britt Corp., *supra*.

50. Herrin v. McEntyre, 8 N.C. 410 (1821).

51. Cover v. McAden, 183 N.C. 641, 112 S.E. 817 (1922); Grist v. Hodges, 14 N.C. 200 (1831).

52. Id.

53. Shuford v. Phillips, 235 N.C. 387, 70 S.E.2d 193 (1952).

grantee has a defective title,[54] does not by itself ordinarily constitute a breach of the covenants of warranty and quiet enjoyment. There must be an ouster, or a disturbance of the possession equivalent to an ouster, for there to be a breach. There is an exception to the foregoing rule, however, where the true owner of the premises is the State or the United States. Where the paramount title holder is the State or the United States there is a constructive eviction at once without the necessity for a formal assertion of title.[55]

§ 223. Same — The Statute of Limitations.

Since a breach of the covenants of warranty and quiet enjoyment does not occur until there has been an eviction, either actual or constructive, the statute of limitations does not begin to run until the covenantee has been ousted or until his possession has been disturbed.[56] Since assignees of the original covenantee can bring an action for breach of the covenants of warranty and quiet enjoyment, it is clearly apparent that a grantor may be called upon to honor these covenants many years after the date of the conveyance in which they appear.

§ 224. Damages Recoverable Upon Breach of the Covenants of Warranty and Quiet Enjoyment.

(a) *Consideration paid, plus interest.* The usual and ordinary measure of damages where there is a breach of the covenants of warranty and quiet enjoyment is the amount of the consideration paid to the covenantor for the land,[57] plus interest.[58]

Where there is only a partial breach of the covenants of warranty and quiet enjoyment, and the grantee is ousted or evicted only as to part of the land, the measure of damages is limited to a proportionate part of the

---

54. Ravenal v. Ingram, 131 N.C. 549, 42 S.E. 967 (1902); Lockhart v. Parker, 189 N.C. 138, 126 S.E. 313 (1924).

55. Cover v. McAden, 183 N.C. 641, 112 S.E. 817 (1922).

56. Shankle v. Ingram, 133 N.C. 254, 45 S.E. 578 (1903); Mizzell v. Ruffin, 118 N.C. 69, 23 S.E. 927 (1896); Wiggins v. Pender, 132 N.C. 628, 44 S.E. 362 (1903). *See* dissenting opinion in Cover v. McAden, 183 N.C. 641, 112 S.E. 817 (1922). In the *Cover v. McAden* case, title to land conveyed with a covenant of warranty was in the United States. In that case, the court held that since title was in the United States there was a constructive eviction immediately upon delivery of the deed and that the statute of limitations on the action for breach of such warranty commenced to run immediately without further ouster of the grantee.

57. *See, e.g.,* Grist v. Hodges, 14 N.C. 198 (1831); Pridgen v. Long, 177 N.C. 189, 98 S.E. 451 (1919).

58. Interest is usually allowed only in cases in which the grantee has not had the benefit of the possession, rents, or profits of the land, or has had to surrender the rents and profits to the paramount title holder. CRIBBET, PRINCIPLES OF THE LAW OF PROPERTY 212 (1962). *See* Williams v. Beeman, 13 N.C. 483 (1830).

consideration paid to the covenantor, that part of the consideration paid for the part of the land lost.[59]

The maximum recovery against the covenantor, then, is the value of the land at the time of the conveyance, or in other words, the consideration paid to the covenantor by the covenantee. The enhanced value of the real property, either by reason of improvements placed thereon or by reason of the development of the neighborhood or increasing land values generally, are not factors to be considered in fixing damages.[60]

The rule establishing the amount of consideration paid to the covenantor as the measure of damages recoverable for breach of the covenants of warranty and quiet enjoyment is subject to a further rule that only actual loss or injury can be recovered from the covenantor.[61] For instance, where grantor *A* sells land to *B* for $1,000 with a covenant of warranty, and then *B* sells the same land to *C* for $500 with a covenant of warranty, the remote grantee *C* can recover from the original grantor *A* upon *A's* covenant of warranty, but *C's* recovery will be limited to the $500 that he has lost, which was the consideration he paid to *B*. *C* cannot recover the $1,000 amount which was the consideration received by *A* from *B*.[62]

A further incident of the rule that only actual loss or injury to the evicted grantee can be recovered, up to the amount of the consideration received by the warrantor, is the rule that an intermediate vendor cannot recover of an original vendor on his breach of the covenants of warranty and quiet enjoyment until he has first been damnified by making good the damages of the remote grantee of the land who has been evicted. For example, if *A* sells land to *B* for $1,000 with a covenant of warranty, and *B* later sells the same land to *C* with a covenant of warranty for $500, and *C* is subsequently evicted under a paramount title to that conveyed by *A*, the intermediate vendor *B* cannot sue *A* for breach of the covenant of warranty until *B* has first made good the damages of *C*, in which case the

---

59. Dickens v. Shepherd, 7 N.C. 526 (1819); Lemly v. Ellis, 146 N.C. 221, 59 S.E. 683 (1907).

60. Phillips v. Smith, 4 N.C. 87 (1814). The latter case ably discusses the reason for the rule. If one sold land at a small price with a covenant of warranty or quiet enjoyment and its value subsequently increased unexpectedly, a rule that would make the measure of damages payable by the covenantor the amount of the value of the land at the time of the eviction would cause great and unforeseeable liability. The court says the "purchase price paid to the covenantor" rule as a measure of damages for breach of the covenants of warranty and quiet enjoyment will prevent unforeseeable hardships. It says that any other rule would cause "glaring injustice and the widespread ruin and impoverishment of families." The measure of damages that the *Phillips* case adopts is that adopted by an overwhelming majority of the jurisdictions of the United States.

61. 2 MORDECAI, LAW LECTURES 894 (1916).

62. Williams v. Beeman, 13 N.C. 483 (1830); Markland v. Crump, 18 N.C. 94 (1834).

damages would be only $500.[63] Since a remote grantee may sue not only his immediate grantor for breach of the covenants of warranty and quiet enjoyment but can sue all previous grantors in his chain of title who have executed covenants of warranty and quiet enjoyment, and since each covenantor is individually liable only in the amount of the consideration he has respectively received from his immediate grantee, the amount of recoveries will be as variable as the various amounts received by each covenantor. In no case, however, will a warrantor be liable for more than the consideration which he has received from his immediate grantee, and in no case is the warrantor subject to suit until his covenantee has been evicted or compelled to pay damages to a person evicted.[64] In addition, in no case will the covenantor have to pay more than once upon a breach of the covenants of warranty and quiet enjoyment.

(b) *Counsel fees and costs.* The covenantee who recovers for breach of the covenants of warranty and quiet enjoyment can usually recover the costs, including reasonable attorney's fees, for his unsuccessful defense of his title against the paramount owner who brings an action to eject him, provided he has given the covenantor notice to come in and defend the action in order that the covenantor might have the opportunity to decide whether or not he will go to the expense of resisting the claim for title set up by the person who sues the covenantee for the land.[65] The covenantee is not entitled to attorney's fees in defending an action of ejectment brought by the paramount titleholder where he has not notified the warrantor to come in and defend the title.[66]

(c) *Damages where covenantee buys in outstanding paramount title.* If the covenantee buys up the outstanding paramount title instead of surrendering the land pursuant to an ejectment, his damages are that amount which he reasonably paid for that purpose, provided such amount does not exceed the purchase price for the land.[67]

(d) *No damages recoverable where covenantee subsequently acquires title by adverse possession.* Where a grantor warrants title in a deed and the grantee goes into possession of the land under the deed and stays there

---

63. Markland v. Crump, 18 N.C. 94 (1834).

64. Markland v. Crump, 18 N.C. 94 (1834). *See* Taylor v. Wallace, 20 Colo. 211, 37 P. 963 (1894). *E.g.,* if A warrants and conveys to B for $1,000; and B warrants and conveys to C for $500; and C warrants and conveys to D for $800; and D is evicted, D could recover of either A or C for $800. D could recover of B for $500. C could recover of A in the amount of $800 if C had paid D $800. C could recover of B in the amount of $500 if he had paid D that amount or more. B could recover of A in the amount of $500 if he had paid that amount to either C or D. The judgments against all the prior grantors will vary in amount since the land sold for different prices in successive transfers.

65. Jones v. Balsley, 154 N.C. 61, 69 S.E. 827 (1910); Culver v. Jennings, 157 N.C. 565, 72 S.E. 1005 (1911); Culbreth v. Britt Corp., 231 N.C. 76, 56 S.E.2d 15 (1949).

66. Wiggins v. Pender, 132 N.C. 628, 44 S.E. 362 (1903).

67. Lemly v. Ellis, 146 N.C. 221, 59 S.E. 683 (1907); Price v. Deal, 90 N.C. 290 (1884).

for the period required for acquiring title by adverse possession, his title becomes absolute. If he thereafter surrenders the land to the prior paramount titleholder, he has no action for breach of the covenants of warranty and quiet enjoyment, as he himself has acquired the superior title and it was folly for him to surrender the land to the record paramount titleholder.[68] In such case he has not been damaged by breach of the covenants of warranty and quiet enjoyment.

§ 225. Covenants of Warranty and Quiet Enjoyment "Run With the Land"; Proper Parties Plaintiff to Bring Suit for Breach.

The covenants of warranty and quiet enjoyment are said to "run with the land" before they are breached and therefore their benefits enure to remote grantees. Unlike the covenant of seisin and the covenant against encumbrances, the covenants of warranty and quiet enjoyment have prospective effect and continue in effect until there is an eviction. Thus, if there is a chain of deeds from A to D through intermediate grants via B and C, if the remote grantee D is evicted by one having a paramount title he can sue any of the prior grantors whose deed of conveyance contained a covenant of warranty or quiet enjoyment. It is not necessary for every deed in the chain of deeds to contain a covenant of warranty or quiet enjoyment; the remote grantee can sue any grantor above him who has warranted title even though there are intermediate quitclaim deeds or deeds without warranties.[69] Of course any grantee who is evicted is entitled to only one satisfaction.

"Running with the land" is not to be taken literally. If it were, the land itself would not "run" upon a total failure of the grantor's title even though he warranted that he had title; the covenants therefore could not "run" with a nonexistent estate. One court has stated clearly what the "run with the land" concept actually means. It has stated:[70]

> We should be inclined rather to say that although the covenant of warranty is attached to the land, and for that reason is said in the books, to pass to the assignee, yet this certainly does not mean that it is attached to the paramount title, or to possession, and only passes with that, but it means simply, that it passes by virtue of the privity of estate, created by successive deeds, each grantor being estopped by his own deed from denying that he has conveyed an estate to which the covenant would attach.

---

68. Britton v. Ruffin, 122 N.C. 113, 26 S.E. 642 (1897). *See* Wilson v. Forbes, 13 N.C. 30 (1828); Bank v. Glenn, 68 N.C. 35 (1873).

69. Ravenal v. Ingram, 131 N.C. 549, 42 S.E. 967 (1902); Markland v. Crump, 18 N.C. 94 (1834). *See* Lewis v. Cook, 35 N.C. 193 (1851), in which the purchaser at a sheriff's sale under execution, who took his title from the sheriff without a warranty, was allowed to sue the remote grantor through whom a judgment debtor's title was developed for breach of warranty in such remote grantor's deed of conveyance. *See also* Winders v. Sutherland, 174 N.C. 235, 93 S.E. 726 (1917), in which it is held that two or more grantors can be joined in a breach of warranty suit.

70. Wead v. Larkin, 54 Ill. 489, 499 (1870).

Article V. Title by Estoppel

§ 226. Estoppel by Deed — By Deed with Covenant of Warranty.

Where a grantor purports to convey certain land that he does not in fact own by a deed with a covenant of warranty, it does not pass title at that time due to his total lack of title. If the grantor subsequently acquires the title to that specific property, however, as an outgrowth of common-law rules relating to warranty of title, the after-acquired title of the grantor enures to the benefit of the grantee. A grantor who has executed a warranty deed is estopped from asserting in himself a subsequently acquired title to the same property as against his grantee. [71] The doctrine may work in a number of ways. In one recent Court of Appeals decision, for example, it was held that, where a grantor had warranted to the defendant's predecessor in title that the land was free and clear of all encumbrances and that the grantor would defend title to the property against the claim of all persons whomsoever, the grantor was held to be estopped to assert a right-of-way easement which he subsequently acquired over the land from an independent source. [72]

Thus the covenant of warranty is said to have not only the indemnity aspect, whereby the warrantor must pay damages to the grantee or his successors, but there is also an "estoppel" aspect. For instance, if *A* has conveyed certain described land to *B* with a covenant of warranty, and *A* did not own the land in fact at the time of the conveyance, if *A* subsequently acquires title to the land from an ancestor or vendor, or otherwise, *A's* title enures immediately to his prior grantee *B*, and *A* is estopped to set up his after-acquired title as against *B*. [73]

§ 227. Same — By Deed Without Covenant of Warranty.

While the common law would not estop the grantor in a deed from asserting his after-acquired title against his prior grantee unless such deed contained a covenant of warranty, the law in North Carolina today seems clearly to be that a grantor is estopped from asserting an after-acquired title as against his prior grantee under a prior deed even

---

71. Farmers' Bank v. Glenn, 68 N.C. 35 (1873); Bell v. Adams, 81 N.C. 118 (1879); Foster v. Hackett, 112 N.C. 546, 17 S.E. 426 (1893); Cooley v. Lee, 170 N.C. 18, 86 S.E. 720 (1915); Ford v. McBrayer, 171 N.C. 420, 88 S.E. 736 (1916); James v. Griffin, 192 N.C. 285, 134 S.E. 849 (1926); Crawley v. Stearns, 194 N.C. 15, 138 S.E. 403 (1927); Baker v. Austin, 174 N.C. 433, 93 S.E. 949 (1917); Kelly v. Davis, 211 N.C. 1, 188 S.E. 853 (1936); Woody v. Cates, 213 N.C. 792, 197 S.E. 561 (1938).

72. Sparks v. Choate, 22 N.C. App. 62, 205 S.E.2d 624 (1974).

73. *See, e.g.,* Baker v. Austin, 174 N.C. 433, 93 S.E. 949 (1917).

though the deed did not contain a covenant of warranty.[74] In the case of *Weeks v. Wilkins*,[75] the North Carolina Supreme Court has stated:

> Where the conveyance purports, as in this case, to pass a title in fee to the entire body of land, the grantor is estopped thereafter to say it does not. The consensus of all the authorities is to the effect that where the deed bears upon its face evidence that the entire estate and title in the land was intended to be conveyed, and that the grantee expected to become vested with such estate as the deed purports to convey, then, although the deed may not contain technical covenants of title, still the legal operation and effect of the deed is binding on the grantors and those claiming under them, and they will be estopped from denying that the grantee became seized of the estate the deed purports to vest in him.

Under the foregoing statement even a quitclaim deed could operate to estop the grantor if "the deed bears upon its face evidence that the entire estate and title in the land was intended to be conveyed and that the grantee expected to become vested with such estate as the deed purports to convey ...."[76] The general rule, however, is that a grantor in a quitclaim deed is not estopped.[77]

§ 228. Persons Estopped by Deeds; "Estoppel" and "Rebutter."

The grantor who executes a deed to his grantee when he has no title or only a defective title at the time of the conveyance, but who thereafter acquires the title, is estopped to assert his after-acquired title as against his grantee; his after-acquired title is said to "feed the estoppel" and by operation of law the title vests *eo instante* in the grantee by operation of law.[78] Thus the *grantor himself* is *estopped*.

In addition, where a grantor purports to convey property which he does

---

74. Crawley v. Stearns, 194 N.C. 15, 138 S.E. 403 (1927); Woody v. Cates, 213 N.C. 792, 197 S.E. 561 (1938).

75. 139 N.C. 215, 51 S.E. 909 (1905).

76. *See* Harrell v. Powell, 251 N.C. 636, 112 S.E.2d 81 (1959). *See also* Dixieland Realty Co. v. Wyson, 272 N.C. 172, 158 S.E.2d 7 (1967), where the Supreme Court, at 272 N.C. 178, 179, summarizes the status of the law on this point as follows:

> In North Carolina, whether a quitclaim deed or a deed of bargain and sale without technical covenants creates an estoppel depends upon its language, *Harrell v. Powell*, 251 N.C. 636, 112 S.E.2d 81; and there is substantial authority in this jurisdiction for the position that the principle of estoppel will apply when the deed shows that the grantor intended to convey and the grantee expected to acquire a particular estate, although the deed contains no technical covenants. *Keel v. Bailey*, 224 N.C. 447, 31 S.E.2d 362; *Capps v. Massey*, 199 N.C. 196, 154 S.E. 52; *Willis v. Willis*, 203 N.C. 517, 166 S.E. 398; *Weeks v. Wilkins*, 139 N.C. 215, 51 S.E. 909; *Crawley v. Stearns*, 194 N.C. 15, 138 S.E. 403; *Williams v. R. R.*, 200 N.C. 771, 158 S.E. 473; *Woody v. Cates*, 213 N.C. 792, 197 S.E. 561.

grantor from subsequently acquiring title against his grantee by adverse possession. Chatham v. Lansford, 149 N.C. 363, 63 S.E. 81 (1908).

78. Morrell v. Building Management, 241 N.C. 264, 84 S.E.2d 910 (1954).

not own or to which he has a defective title and thereafter acquires a good title to that property, the *grantor's heirs* are precluded from denying that their ancestor's deed conveyed the land, if their claim to the land comes by, through or under the grantor-ancestor. Thus if *A* purports to convey land to *B* to which he does not have title, and thereafter acquires title and then dies leaving heirs or devisees, the heirs of *A* are precluded (just as *A* would be) from denying that title passed by *A's* prior deed. The heirs are said to be precluded by "*rebutter.*" "Estoppel" operates *inter partes* to estop the grantor himself. "Rebutter" has the same effect as "estoppel" except that it operates to bind the third person heirs, as well as their parties and privies, from asserting any claim to the land which has come to them by, through or under their ancestor who acquired title to the land after purporting to convey it away when he did not have a good title in fact.[79]

Now it should be noted that the doctrine of "rebutter" does not have the effect of "barring" or "estopping" the heirs of the grantor where they do not derive their claim to the land in question "by, through, or under" the grantor-ancestor. If they take their claim to the land from some other source than the grantor, they are not barred, rebutted or estopped, or precluded in any way, from denying the validity of their ancestor's deed, nor are they personally bound in any way on his warranty.[80]

At the common law, if an ancestor granted land to a grantee with a warranty, his heirs were rebutted from asserting title to the land after his death, even though they derived their title through a source other than the granting ancestor.[81] Today, however, pursuant to the statute which abolishes collateral warranties,[82] where a tenant for life of lands, tenements or hereditaments, conveys lands which come to those persons who would be his heirs by reversion or remainder, the warranties do not estop those heirs whose claim to the land is by way of remainder or reversion and who do not claim by, through or under the granting life tenant.[83]

---

79. Olds v. Cedar Works, 173 N.C. 161, 91 S.E. 846 (1917). *See generally* McGehee, *Estoppel and Rebutter in North Carolina,* 1 N.C.L. Rev. 152 (1923).

80. Of course the estate of the grantor-ancestor may be liable for breach of warranty and the heirs may be liable for breach of the warranty to the extent that they have shared in the estate of the grantor-ancestor.

81. Southerland v. Stout, 68 N.C. 446 (1873); 2 Mordecai, Law Lectures 877 (1916).

82. N.C. Gen. Stat. § 41-8.

83. Hauser v. Craft, 134 N.C. 319, 46 S.E. 756 (1904); Sprinkle v. Reidsville, 235 N.C. 140, 69 S.E.2d 179 (1952); Johnson v. Bradley, 37 N.C. 36 (1849); Starnes v. Hill, 112 N.C. 1, 16 S.E.1011 (1893); 2 Mordecai, Law Lectures 879 (1916). Nor is the heir liable to respond in money in payment for his ancestor's warranty except to the extent that he has shared in the assets of the ancestor upon his ancestor's death. 2 Mordecai, Law Lectures 878 (1916).

§ 229. Title by Estoppel as Affected by Recordation Statutes.

A further limitation on the doctrines of estoppel and rebutter by deed should also be noted as a consequence of the recordation statutes. While an after-acquired title of a grantor will enure to the grantee, the grantor's after-acquired title will not enure to his prior grantee so as to defeat the title of a purchaser for value who purchases the title subsequent to the grantor's acquisition, and who first records his title subsequent to the grantor's acquisition. For instance, assume the following situation: Grantor *A* purports to convey land by a warranty deed to *B* when *A* does not in fact have good title. *B* immediately records his deed from *A*. Thereafter *A* acquires good title after his deed to *B* has been delivered and recorded. *A* then subsequently executes and delivers a deed conveying the land to *C*, who subsequently records his deed. Notwithstanding the doctrine of enurement by estoppel and notwithstanding *B's* prior recordation, *C*, as a purchaser for value who purchased subsequent to *A's* acquisition of title and because he recorded first after *A's* acquisition of title, will prevail.[84]

A caveat should be noted, however, with respect to mortgages on property *to be acquired* subsequent to the date of the mortgage. As between the mortgagor and mortgagee such "after-acquired property clause" in a mortgage is valid, and when the mortgagor acquires real property it immediately enures to the benefit of the mortgagee for security purposes. In addition, prior to the enactment of recent legislation, if an "after-acquired property mortgage" was recorded *before* the mortgagor's acquisition of title, the recordation established the mortgagee's priority over purchasers for value, lien creditors and other encumbrancers who acquired their rights and who relied on the records *subsequent* to the mortgagor's acquisition of title.[85] This necessitated a search of every "out" conveyance of every grantor in a particular chain of title, both before and after each acquired title, to make sure that no grantor had made a valid

---

84. A purchaser for value, therefore, with respect to *deeds,* must check the real estate records only back to the time that the records show that a particular vendor or grantor acquired the title. The purchaser for value need not have the records checked prior to the date that a particular grantor actually acquired record title. *See* Door Co. v. Joyner, 182 N.C. 518, 109 S.E. 259 (1909). In the latter case the Supreme Court of North Carolina said: ". . . a purchaser having the prior registry is not affected with constructive notice by reason of deeds or claims arising against his immediate or other grantor prior to the time when such grantor acquired the title, but the deed or instrument first registered after such acquisition shall confer the better right." The court also stated: ". . . the doctrine of title by estoppel no longer prevails as against the provision and policy of our registration acts."

85. Hickson v. Lumber Co., 150 N.C. 282, 63 S.E. 1045 (1909). In the latter case the Supreme Court said: "In North Carolina a mortgage upon after-acquired property, being enforcible *inter partes,* becomes, upon registration, valid and enforcible against subsequent purchasers, because the registration is an effectual notice as against the world."

"after-acquired property mortgage" which was still viable because recorded prior to his acquisition of title.

With respect to "after-acquired property mortgages" subsequent to 1969, however, and because of legislation enacted in the 1969 General Assembly,[86] an after-acquired property clause is not effective to pass title to after-acquired real property as against lien creditors or purchasers for value from the grantor unless and until such instrument has been registered or reregistered at or subsequent to the time such after-acquired property is acquired by such grantor. Thus, since September 30, 1969, a purchaser for value or a lien creditor of a particular grantor does not take subject to an after-acquired property mortgage recorded before a particular grantor acquired the property unless it is rerecorded subsequent to his acquisition of title and prior to the date the purchaser for value records or the lien creditor's right attaches.

---

86. N.C. GEN. STAT. § 47-20.5. *See generally* McDermott, *Title by Estoppel as Affected by Recordation*, 27 N.C.L. REV. 380 (1949).

CHAPTER 12

LEASES

Article I. General Provisions

§ 230. The Landlord-Tenant Relationship Generally.
§ 231. Definition of Lease.

Article II. Essential Elements for Creating Lease; Formalities of Execution

§ 232. Generally.
§ 233. Names of the Parties.
§ 234. Description of the Leased Premises.
§ 235. Designation of the Term of the Lease.
§ 236. Statement of Rent.

Article III. Covenants in Leases

§ 237. The Usual Covenants Contained in Leases; Provisions Placed in Leases Generally.
§ 238. The Covenant of Title and Quiet Enjoyment.
§ 239. The Covenant to Deliver Possession.
§ 240. The Covenant to Repair.
§ 241. Covenant with Respect to Assignment and Subletting.
§ 242. The Covenant of Fitness of Purpose.
§ 243. Covenant That Lease May Be Terminated for Default in Payment of Rent or for Breach of Any Other Covenant in the Lease; Statutory Forfeiture for Nonpayment of Rent; Destruction of Premises.
§ 244. Covenant Limiting Use of Premises by Lessee.
§ 245. Covenant to Pay Taxes.
§ 246. Covenant to Insure Premises.
§ 247. Covenant to Renew Lease.
§ 248. Provision in Lease Giving Tenant Option to Purchase Leased Premises.
§ 249. Provision in Lease Relating to Alterations by Tenant.
§ 250. Provision in Lease Giving Landlord Right of Entry to Inspect, to Repair, or for Other Purposes.
§ 251. Covenants That "Run with the Land" in Leases; Effect.

Article IV. Contractual Aspects of Leases; the Rule in Dumpor's Case

§ 252. Doctrine of Mitigation of Damages Applicable.
§ 253. Doctrine of Anticipatory Breach of Contract Applicable.
§ 254. The Rule in Dumpor's Case.

Article I. General Provisions

§ 230. The Landlord-Tenant Relationship Generally.

The law of landlord and tenant is often described as a synthesis of property concepts with contractual doctrines. But this traditional formula can no longer be applied in a vacuum. During the decade of the 1970s, firm notions of consumer-oriented public policy also began to play a substantial role in the resolution of certain types of landlord-tenant disputes.[1] A triumvirate of property law, contract law, and public policy provides the more accurate framework within which to view this area today. In this regard, a distinction must be drawn today between residential and commercial tenancies.[2] For it is in the former category that public policy will most frequently intervene to protect the consumer-tenant from a body of law that historically granted him few rights. In the commercial area, on the other hand, the courts and legislature of North Carolina appear quite willing to allow the parties to a lease to determine their legal rights and obligations pursuant to the rules of property and contract law alone.[3]

Until about the middle of the thirteenth century when the writ of *quare eject infra terminum* was developed, a lessee-tenant was not deemed to have an interest in the land held under a lease. The only remedy in the event of a wrongful ejectment was for the ejected tenant to bring an action against his lessor on the contract.[4] If a leasehold tenant was put off the land by one other than his landlord, the leasehold tenant did not have the standing to sue the tort-feasor as lessees did not have protectible interests in real property which was the subject of a lease. Today, however, a lessee is clearly recognized as having an interest in the land itself and not merely a right by way of contract.[5] Thus today a lease, as it pertains to

---

1. *See* Chapter 6 *supra* where the North Carolina Residential Rental Agreements Act is discussed beginning at § 65. It is the intention of this revisor to devote Chapter 11 to the traditional property and contract issues associated with leases. Except by occasional cross-reference, no emphasis will be placed on reforms relating chiefly to the residential tenant in this chapter.

2. By the term "commercial," the entire realm of the non-residential tenancy is meant to be referred to.

3. This approach is most often rationalized on the basis that more sophisticated parties are dealing at arm's length with legal representation, and, under these circumstances, they are rightfully compelled to abide by the legal consequences of the lease agreement they have entered into. A recent Supreme Court of Mississippi decision illustrates this point well. In Smith v. Smith, 375 So. 2d 1041 (Miss. 1979), the court upheld the validity of an exculpatory clause in a lease (holding the lessor harmless for damage to the lessee). At 375 So. 2d 1043, the court notes: "This contract is unaffected by any public interest. There is no evidence of unequal bargaining power or of any overreaching by the lessors-appellees. There exists no problem as to the validity of the clause. (Citations omitted.)"

4. 2 Powell, Real Property § 221 (1967).

5. At the common law a bare lease did not vest any *estate* in the lessee; he received only a right of entry in the tenement involved, called *interesse termini*. Only after entering into possession was he vested of an estate even after development of the action for wrongful ejectment. While the tenant is deemed to have an estate in the real property and can maintain ejectment after he enters into possession, even today there is some question in North Carolina as to whether he can maintain an action in the nature of ejectment if he is kept out by the landlord or a third person before he actually occupies the premises. *See* Bunch v. Elizabeth City Lumber Co., 134 N.C. 116, 46 S.E. 24 (1903); 1 Mordecai, Law Lectures 530 (1916); and Barneycastle v. Walker, 92 N.C. 198 (1885), all of which indicate that before the lessee enters and takes possession, his right lies only in contract; after entry his estate is vested absolutely in him and he can bring an action in ejectment for interference with his possession.

real property, is a *grant* or conveyance by the owner of an estate to another person of a portion of his interest for a term less than his own. At the same time a lease is also a *contract* between the lessor and lessee giving rise to rights and obligations to the respective parties for which actions may be maintained for their enforcement as in the case of other contracts. A lease has two sets of rights and obligations, those growing out of the relation of landlord and tenant which are based on *privity of estate,* and those growing out of the express stipulations of the lease provisions based on *privity of contract.*

§ 231. Definition of Lease.

A lease is a contract whereby one person, called the lessor, grants to another person, called the lessee, the right to use a definite parcel of land for a term specified in the contract, in consideration of payments called rent.[6]

A leasehold interest in real property is categorized as a "chattel real" and is subject to rules of law applying to personal property.[7] Thus it is considered a species of personal property that is outside the scope of the anti-deficiency statute;[8] it need not be under seal to be valid,[9] and it receives a tax treatment consistent with its "chattel real" status.[10]

Article II. Essential Elements for Creating Lease; Formalities of Execution

§ 232. Generally.

In order to create a valid lease of real property in North Carolina that exceeds three years in duration from the time of the making thereof, it must be in writing and signed by the party to be charged therewith under North Carolina's Statute of Frauds.[11] This would include a lease for exactly three years but to commence *in futuro,*[12] and would even include

---

6. Helicopter Corp. v. Realty Co., 263 N.C. 139, 139 S.E.2d 362 (1964); Moche v. Leno, 227 N.C. 159, 41 S.E.2d 369 (1947); Moring v. Ward, 50 N.C. 272 (1858); Stallings v. Purvis, 42 N.C. App. 690, 257 S.E.2d 664 (1979).

7. Moche v. Leno, 227 N.C. 159, 41 S.E.2d 369 (1947); Waddell v. Cigar Stores, 195 N.C. 434, 142 S.E. 585 (1928); Real Estate Trust v. Debnam, 41 N.C. App. 256, 254 S.E.2d 638 (1979), *aff'd* and cited with approval on the "chattel real" issue at 299 N.C. 510, 263 S.E.2d 595 (1980).

8. Real Estate Trust v. Debnam, 299 N.C. 510, 263 S.E.2d 595 (1980).
9. Moche v. Leno, 227 N.C. 159, 41 S.E.2d 369 (1947).
10. Investment Co. v. Cumberland County, 254 N.C. 492, 96 S.E.2d 341 (1957).
11. N.C. Gen. Stat. § 22-2. Barbee v. Lamb, 225 N.C. 211, 34 S.E.2d 65 (1945).
12. Mauney v. Norvell, 179 N.C. 628, 103 S.E. 372 (1920).

a lease for a period of less than three years if it can endure for more than three years from the time of the making thereof.[13]

In addition, all leases of whatever duration for the purpose of digging gold or other minerals, or for mining generally, must be in writing.[14] If the lease is not for the purpose of mining, however, and is to run for a period not exceeding three years from the time of the making thereof, it is valid although oral.[15]

While no particular form of words is necessary to create a valid lease, the contract's words should show the intention of the parties that the lessor is to give up his possession and that the lessee will assume such possession for the agreed period under specified terms and conditions. The purpose of the lease contract, besides conveying the use of the real property, is to set forth the agreement between the parties as to the letting and rental of the premises and to outline the reciprocal rights, duties and obligations of the respective parties. For this reason, a draftsman of the lease should take careful precautions to include all the terms of the parties' agreement in order to avoid subsequent disagreements. In the case of long term leases, considerable foresight is required of the parties and by the draftsmen of such leases as the contingencies not considered are the ones that frequently occur.

A binding agreement *to execute a lease* must be certain as to terms of lease, minds of parties must have met as to property to be included in lease, terms of lease should be agreed upon, parties should agree upon rental, and time and manner of payment of rent should be stated.[16]

While many additional provisions may be added to leases that are both practical and desirable, the provisions discussed in the following sections are essential to every valid lease.

§ 233. Names of the Parties.

The lease instrument must identify the lessor and the lessee. Since an original lessee-tenant has, in the absence of a restriction in the lease to the contrary, a right to sublease his interest in real property, the lessor

---

13. Investment Co. v. Zindel, 198 N.C. 109, 150 S.E. 704 (1929). A lease of land for a life tenant's life, since indefinite and since it could last for more than three years from the time of the making is void if not in writing. Davis v. Lovick, 226 N.C. 252, 37 S.E.2d 680 (1946). Likewise, an oral assignment or surrender of a lease that has more than three years to run is void. Alexander v. Morris, 145 N.C. 22, 58 S.E. 600 (1907); Herring v. Volume Merchandise, Inc., 249 N.C. 221, 106 S.E.2d 197 (1958). *But see* Investment Properties of Asheville, Inc. v. Allen, 281 N.C. 174, 188 S.E.2d 441 (1972), which holds that a lease which is required by the Statute of Frauds to be in writing may be rescinded orally by the mutual assent of the parties.

14. N.C. Gen. Stat. § 22-2.

15. Rhodes v. Smith-Douglass Fertilizer Co., 220 N.C. 21, 16 S.E.2d 408 (1941).

16. Smith v. House of Kenton Corp., 23 N.C. App. 439, 209 S.E.2d 397 (1974).

does not necessarily have to be the owner of the fee in the property.[17] In order for the lease to be valid the same requisites of contractual capacity apply to the parties to a lease as apply to ordinary contracts.

§ 234. Description of the Leased Premises.

As in the case of other conveyances, the description of the premises being leased is one of the most important elements of a lease because it specifies the boundaries and extent of possession to which the lessee is entitled. Therefore every lease should state clearly and definitely the exact property and appurtenances that are the subject of the letting since the lessee has an exclusive right to possession of that specific property described in the agreement and no other. The tenant has an exclusive right to enter and to have possession of the described premises, and he has this right against the landlord as well as against third persons; any unauthorized entry by the landlord is as much a trespass as if he were a stranger.[18]

The method of description of the property leased may be the same as used in other conveyances and any description by which the identity of the leased land can be established will be sufficient.[19] A street address or a description by lot or block number in accordance with tax maps may meet the minimum requirements, but a careful draftsman will often want to make a more complete legal description to reduce the possibility of controversy. For instance, a description of the leased interest as "A lot about 37 feet wide, fronting on Hillsboro Street, with a depth of about 200 feet on which a building approximately 27 feet 8 inches by 65 feet will be erected at 747 Hillsboro St., Raleigh, North Carolina, comprising an area of 1772 square feet, for use as offices . . ." was held to be an ambiguous description requiring the jury's determination of whether the lessee was entitled to use the basement of the building.[20]

It should be noted, however, that it is well settled that the lease of a building or a part thereof ordinarily passes with it, as an incident thereto, everything necessarily used with or reasonably necessary to the enjoyment of what is granted, although not mentioned in the lease, unless the same has been reserved to the lessor.[21]

§ 235. Designation of the Term of the Lease.

A lease must specify the term of the lease, the period of time for which

---

17. Stallings v. Purvis, 42 N.C. App. 690, 257 S.E.2d 664 (1979) citing this section (§ 206 in the original edition).
18. Barneycastle v. Walker, 92 N.C. 198 (1885); State v. Piper, 89 N.C. 551 (1883); Krider v. Ramsay, 79 N.C. 354 (1878); Rickman Mfg. Co. v. Gable, 246 N.C. 1, 97 S.E.2d 672 (1957).
19. Root v. Insurance Co., 272 N.C. 580, 158 S.E.2d 829 (1968).
20. Id.
21. Manufacturing Co. v. Gable, 246 N.C. 1, 97 S.E.2d 672 (1957); State v. Foster, 196 N.C. 431, 146 S.E. 69 (1929).

the lessee shall have the right of possession. It must designate when the term is to begin, either by specifying some particular date or by referring to some definite future event which will establish the time that the term commences [22] and how long it shall endure. When no term is designated, only a tenancy at will is created.[23]

In *Helicopter Corp. v. Realty Co.*,[24] for example, the plaintiff was promised a one year rent-free lease of a roof for a heliport if plaintiff would secure the necessary equipment and governmental approval. Although plaintiff performed the necessary acts, defendant denied the existence of a valid lease pointing, *inter alia,* to the cardinal principle that the term must be certain as to commencement and duration. Citing the general rule that a thing is certain which is capable of being made certain, the Supreme Court held that a lease term may commence on the happening of a stated event. After the occurrence of the event all uncertainty is removed and a valid lease results. The commencement of term decisions involve different considerations than the duration of term ones. This is true because a definite commencement date will result if the event occurs whereas a terminating event may never occur leaving the lease term in the prohibited status of open-endedness. Therefore an agreement to rent a house until such time as the tenant decides to buy it results in a tenancy at will because of the indefinite duration.[25]

The problem of perpetual leases has recently surfaced in North Carolina.[26] Both Court of Appeals decisions addressing this issue have adopted the majority view that perpetual leases are not to be favored and that the intention to create one must appear in clear and unequivocal language.[27]

§ 236. Statement of Rent.

A lease must specify the amount which the parties agree upon as the rent.[28] The lease agreement should also specify when the rent is due,

---

22. Helicopter Corp. v. Realty Co., 263 N.C. 139, 139 S.E.2d 362 (1964); Stallings v. Purvis, 42 N.C. App. 690, 257 S.E.2d 664 (1979); Stout v. Crutchfield, 21 N.C. App. 387, 204 S.E.2d 541 (1974).

23. Choate Rental Co. v. Justice, 212 N.C. 523, 193 S.E. 817 (1937); Sappenfield v. Goodman, 215 N.C. 417, 2 S.E.2d 13 (1939); Simuns v. Labrun, 219 N.C. 42, 12 S.E.2d 644 (1940); Barbee v. Lamb, 225 N.C. 211, 34 S.E.2d 65 (1945); Stout v. Crutchfield, 21 N.C. App. 387, 204 S.E.2d 541 (1974).

24. 263 N.C. 139, 139 S.E.2d 362 (1964).

25. Stout v. Crutchfield, 21 N.C. App. 387, 204 S.E.2d 541 (1974).

26. Oglesby v. McCoy, 41 N.C. App. 735, 255 S.E.2d 773 (1979); Dixon v. Rivers, 37 N.C. App. 168, 245 S.E.2d 572 (1978).

27. *Id.*

28. Lawrence v. Stroupe, 263 N.C. 618, 139 S.E.2d 885 (1964); Helicopter Corp. v. Realty Co., 263 N.C. 139, 139 S.E.2d 362 (1964); Stallings v. Purvis, 42 N.C. App. 690, 257 S.E.2d 664 (1979).

because in the absence of an agreement providing otherwise rent is not due until the end of the rental period.[29] The rent consists of all forms of return to the lessor, usually a fixed and specified sum of money payable at regular stated intervals by the lessee to the lessor. It may, however, take the form of payments of taxes and assessments on the land, insurance premiums, or a fraction of the crops grown on the land in the case of agricultural leases. The rent may be a fixed amount to be paid periodically or it may be a percentage of the business done by the lessee, or, in some cases, a combination of a fixed minimum amount coupled with a percentage clause based on the quantity of business done by the lessee on the premises above a certain amount.

The lease should designate the place where the rent shall be paid; if it fails to do so the place of payment is at the leased premises.[30]

Article III. Covenants in Leases

§ 237. The Usual Covenants Contained in Leases; Provisions Placed in Leases Generally.

In addition to the foregoing four essential elements that must be in all valid leases, many other provisions are often put into lease agreements which frequently shift a duty from one party to the other. These provisions appear under the so-called "covenants and conditions" sections of the lease. If the parties to a lease wish to bind themselves or each other to duties not required of them by the general law of landlord and tenant, they may do so by inserting stipulations in the lease (1) in the form of a condition, upon the breach of which the lease may be made to terminate; or (2) in the form of a personal covenant, upon the breach of which the injured party is entitled to sue the other for damages.[31]

Covenants arising from leases may be either implied or express, and they may relate to any lawful subject in the contemplation of the parties. No attempt will be made here to enumerate all of the various covenants which may, or should be, in leases, as this will depend upon the condition and situation of the leased premises and the circumstances and desires of the parties. Only a few of the more important and frequently occurring will be mentioned.

---

29. BURBY, REAL PROPERTY § 73 (1965); MINOR & WURTS, REAL PROPERTY § 362 (1910). Thus, if a landlord wishes his lessee to pay the rent before it is due under this rule, he must be sure to specify the words "in advance" after providing when the payment shall be made. For instance, a statement "payable on the first day of each month, *in advance"* is necessary to make the payment become due in advance.

30. MINOR & WURTS, REAL PROPERTY § 362 (1910).

31. As with all sections of this chapter, an assumption is being made that the lease involved is *not* covered by the Residential Rental Agreements Act (Chapter 6 *supra*). This distinction is extremely important because of the numerous obligations under the Residential Rental Agreements Act that cannot be altered by lease provisions. For an exhaustive treatment of all aspects of the topic of leases, *see generally* FRIEDMAN ON LEASES (Practising Law Institute, New York City 1974).

§ 238. The Covenant of Title and Quiet Enjoyment.

A covenant of title is a stipulation on the part of the lessor, in one form or another, that he is transferring to his lessee a good title to the land leased, and that the lessee shall enjoy quiet and undisturbed possession of the same throughout his tenancy. While such covenants may be express, in North Carolina in the absence of a provision to the contrary there is an implied covenant that the lessee shall have quiet and peaceable possession of the leased premises during his term, including those easements and appurtenances necessary and essential to the enjoyment of the leased premises.[32] The covenant of quiet enjoyment affords protection to the lessee only against the wrongful acts of the lessor, someone claiming under the lessor, or one who has a title paramount to the title of the lessor. If the tenant is disturbed in his possession by the landlord,[33] or by one claiming under the landlord, or by one who has a superior title to the landlord's title, the landlord is liable for breach of the covenant of quiet enjoyment. It should be noted, however, that the covenant of quiet enjoyment does not protect the lessee against acts of a stranger wrongdoer who ousts him or interferes with his possession after the lessee has taken possession.[34] If a stranger wrongdoer disturbs the lessee's possession after he has taken possession, the lessee has his remedies against the wrongdoer and not against his lessor.[35]

§ 239. The Covenant to Deliver Possession.

In a majority of jurisdictions of the United States when a lessor makes a lease, he only impliedly covenants to confer upon the lessee the *right to possession* of the leased premises, that neither he nor one holding title paramount will withhold possession from the lessee. In a majority of jurisdictions the lessor is not deemed to impliedly warrant against the acts of wrongdoers who keep the tenant out of possession.[36]

In North Carolina, however, the lessor is held to impliedly warrant that

---

32. Andrews & Knowles Produce Co. v. Currin, 243 N.C. 131, 90 S.E.2d 228 (1955); Helicopter Corp. v. Realty Co., 263 N.C. 139, 139 S.E.2d 362 (1964); Improvement Co. v. Coley-Bardin, 156 N.C. 255, 72 S.E. 312 (1911); Huggins v. City of Goldsboro, 154 N.C. 443, 70 S.E. 842 (1911). *See* Oestreicher v. Stores, 290 N.C. 118, 225 S.E.2d 797 (1976), holding that a lease provision guaranteeing the lessee peaceful and uninterrupted possession of the premises "so long as it occupies, complies with, and performs the covenants and conditions of the lease" reflected the lessor's obligation to the lessee with regard to quiet enjoyment only and did not expressly or impliedly require the lessee to occupy the premises.

33. Hendrix v. Guin, 42 N.C. App. 36, 255 S.E.2d 604 (1979).

34. Huggins v. City of Goldsboro, 154 N.C. 443, 70 S.E. 842 (1911); Sloan v. Hart, 150 N.C. 269, 63 S.E. 1037 (1909).

35. MINOR & WURTS, REAL PROPERTY § 368 (1910).

36. *See* Hannan v. Dusch, 154 Va. 356, 153 S.E. 824, 70 A.L.R. 141 (1930), and Sloan v. Hart, 150 N.C. 269, 63 S.E. 1037 (1909), for cases in which both the majority (American) and the minority (English) rules are set forth.

the tenant shall have *possession* at the commencement of his leasehold estate and not a mere "right to possession," that is, the lessee is entitled to enjoy the property and "not a mere chance of a lawsuit." North Carolina follows the minority or English rule and if the tenant is precluded from taking possession at the commencement date of his lease by reason of a wrongdoer's remaining in possession, the landlord is liable for breach of his implied covenant to the lessee that the premises shall be open to entry by the lessee at the time fixed for the beginning of the term.[37]

§ 240. The Covenant to Repair.

In the absence of a provision in the lease expressly imposing the duty to make repairs, the lessor, in a tenancy *not* subject to the Residential Rental Agreements Act,[38] has no duty to keep the leased premises in good repair.[39] The occupant and not the lessor is under an obligation to keep the leased premises in repair. If the landlord retains control over parts of the leased property, he is, however, under a duty to use reasonable care to keep in a safe condition the premises over which he retains control. Therefore, where the landlord leases separate portions of a building to different tenants and reserves control of parts of the building leased, such as hallways and elevator shafts, which are used in common by all of the tenants, the landlord is bound to use reasonable care to keep those parts in a safe condition.[40]

To avoid the common-law rules relating to the obligation to make repairs, the parties to a non-residential lease may make a covenant specifying who is to make the repairs, either (1) placing the duty of all repairs on the landlord, (2) placing the duty of all repairs on the tenant or tenants, or (3) distributing the duty of repairs between the landlord and the tenant or tenants.

It should be noted, however, that even if the landlord contracts to make repairs to premises leased to a single tenant, he will not be held liable in

---

37. Sloan v. Hart, 150 N.C. 269, 63 S.E. 1037 (1909); Shelton v. Clinard, 187 N.C. 664, 122 S.E. 477 (1924).

38. Chapter 6 *supra. See* Haga v. Childress, 43 N.C. App. 302, 258 S.E.2d 836 (1979), where the Court of Appeals expressed no opinion as to whether the Residential Rental Agreements Act would give rise to liability for personal injuries caused by a lessor's breach of statutorily imposed duties (the Act was not applicable in *Haga*).

39. Improvement Co. v. Coley-Bardin, 156 N.C. 255, 72 S.E. 312 (1911); Jordan v. Miller, 179 N.C. 73, 101 S.E. 550 (1919); Duffy v. Hartsfield, 180 N.C. 151, 104 S.E. 139 (1920); Salter v. Gordon, 200 N.C. 381, 157 S.E. 11 (1931); Carolina Mtg. Co. v. Massie, 209 N.C. 146, 183 S.E. 676 (1936); Mercer v. Williams, 210 N.C. 456, 187 S.E. 556 (1936); Livingston v. Essex Inv. Co., 219 N.C. 416, 14 S.E.2d 489 (1941). *Accord,* Haga v. Childress, 43 N.C. App. 302, 258 S.E.2d 836 (1979); Thompson v. Shoemaker, 7 N.C. App. 687, 173 S.E.2d 627 (1970); Knuckles v. Spaugh, 26 N.C. App. 340, 215 S.E.2d 825 (1975); Clarke v. Kirchner, 11 N.C. App. 454, 181 S.E.2d 787 (1971).

40. PROSSER, TORTS 648-65 (1941); Drug Stores v. Gur-Sil Corp., 269 N.C. 170, 152 S.E.2d 77 (1966); Thompson v. Shoemaker, 7 N.C. App. 687, 173 S.E.2d 627 (1970).

North Carolina to the tenant, the tenant's sublessee, family, servants or guests for personal injuries resulting from disrepair or patent defects.[41] This is true even if the dangerous condition has been brought to the lessor's attention and he has agreed to repair it.[42] The contract of the lessor to make repairs to the leased premises simply creates a *contractual* liability to make the repairs; if he fails to abide by his agreement the tenant may himself make the repairs and recover the costs of the repairs in an action for that purpose or upon a counterclaim in an action for rent.[43] It has been held that a contract to repair made by the landlord does not contemplate, as damages for the failure to perform it, that any liability for personal injuries shall grow out of the defective condition of the premises or the landlord's failure to perform his promise.[44] But if the landlord leases the premises with a latent, as distinguished from patent, defect known to the landlord, or of which the landlord should have known, involving a menace or danger, and of which defect the tenant was unaware or could not by ordinary diligence discover, the landlord will be liable for personal injuries resulting from such defect.[45] In addition, if the landlord undertakes to make the repairs pursuant to his contract and does

---

41. Manufacturing Co. v. Gable, 246 N.C. 1, 97 S.E.2d 672 (1957); Mercer v. Williams, 210 N.C. 456, 187 S.E. 556 (1936); Williams v. Strauss, 210 N.C. 200, 185 S.E. 676 (1936); Salter v. Gordon, 200 N.C. 381, 157 S.E. 11 (1931); Harrell v. Refining Co., 225 N.C. 421, 35 S.E.2d 240 (1945). *Accord,* Haga v. Childress, 43 N.C. App. 302, 258 S.E.2d 836 (1979); Thompson v. Shoemaker, 7 N.C. App. 687, 173 S.E.2d 627 (1970); Floyd v. Jarrell, 18 N.C. App. 418, 197 S.E.2d 229 (1973); Phillips v. Stowe Mills, Inc., 5 N.C. App. 150, 167 S.E.2d 817 (1969); Clarke v. Kirchner, 11 N.C. App. 454, 181 S.E.2d 787 (1971).

42. Leavitt v. Rental Co., 222 N.C. 81, 21 S.E.2d 890 (1942); Moss v. Hicks, 240 N.C. 788, 83 S.E.2d 890 (1954); Harrill v. Refining Co., 225 N.C. 421, 35 S.E.2d 240 (1945). *Accord,* Thompson v. Shoemaker, 7 N.C. App. 687, 173 S.E.2d 627 (1970); Floyd v. Jarrell, 18 N.C. App. 418, 197 S.E.2d 229 (1973); Clarke v. Kirchner, 11 N.C. App. 454, 181 S.E.2d 787 (1971).

43. Jordan v. Miller, 179 N.C. 73, 101 S.E. 550 (1919). *Accord,* Cato Ladies Modes of North Carolina, Inc., 21 N.C. App. 133, 203 S.E.2d 405 (1974), citing this section; Thompson v. Shoemaker, 7 N.C. App. 687, 173 S.E.2d 627 (1970).

44. *Id.*

45. Harrill v. Refining Co., 225 N.C. 421, 35 S.E.2d 240 (1945). *Accord,* Floyd v. Jarrell, 18 N.C. App. 418, 197 S.E.2d 229 (1973); Clarke v. Kirchner, 11 N.C. App. 454, 181 S.E.2d 787 (1971), holding that where the tenant has knowledge of a patent defect in the premises and continues to occupy the premises, he may be considered to have assumed the risk, and, in case of injury resulting from such defects, he will be held guilty of contributory negligence. Thompson v. Shoemaker, 7 N.C. App. 687, 173 S.E.2d 627 (1970). *Cf.* the recent case of Boyer v. Agapion, 46 N.C. App. 45, 264 S.E.2d 364 (1980), holding that a landlord is subject to liability for injuries to third persons on the leased premises in accordance with the general rule set forth in § 17.1 of THE RESTATEMENT (SECOND) OF PROPERTY. That section states that the landlord is liable only if:

> the tenant does not know or have reason to know of the condition of the risk involved; and (b) the landlord knows or has reason to know of the condition, realizes or should realize the risk involved, and has reason to expect that the tenant will not discover the condition or realize the risk.

the repairs negligently, resulting in injury to the tenant, he will be held liable for his misfeasance.[46]

With respect to covenants to repair, whether by the lessor or lessee, North Carolina General Statutes, § 42-9 should be observed. That statute provides:

> An agreement in a lease to repair a demised house shall not be construed to bind the contracting party to rebuild or repair in case the house shall be destroyed or damaged to more than one half of its value, by accidental fire not occurring from the want of ordinary diligence on his part.

Therefore an agreement to repair a demised house shall not be construed to bind the contracting party to repair or rebuild it when it is destroyed or damaged to the extent of more than one half of its value by accidental fire not occurring from want of ordinary diligence on his part. However, it should be further observed that the statute is limited in its effect to damage or destruction by fire. The case of *Chambers v. North River Line,* 170 N.C. 199, 102 S.E. 198 (1920), where a wharf was destroyed by ice and flood, held that if there is a covenant to repair by one of the parties to a lease, and the destruction or damage occurs from causes other than fire, the covenanting party will remain under a duty to repair the structure even though it may necessitate a complete restoration of an unprofitable structure; North Carolina General Statutes, § 42-9 has no application in non-fire destruction or damage to the leased premises. With respect to the covenant for repairs, therefore, the lease should provide clearly the intention of the parties with regard to imposing rights and duties on the parties to the lease in the event the building is destroyed or damaged.[47]

§ 241. Covenant with Respect to Assignment and Subletting.

The interests of all lessees, except the tenancy at will, may be assigned or subleased without the consent of the lessor, provided there is no restric-

---

46. Livingston v. Investment Co., 219 N.C. 416, 14 S.E.2d 489 (1941); Mercer v. Williams, 210 N.C. 456, 187 S.E. 556 (1936); Haga v. Childress, 43 N.C. App. 302, 258 S.E.2d 836 (1979). *See* Carson v. Cloninger, 23 N.C. App. 699, 209 S.E.2d 522 (1974). The prevailing rule places a duty upon the landlord to exercise reasonable care in the actual repair of leased premises regardless of any covenant to repair.

47. *See* Discount Corp. v. Mangel's, 2 N.C. App. 472, 163 S.E.2d 295 (1968). In that case the lessor made a covenant to repair. The court held that generally the landlord's covenant to repair would require the replacement and restoration of the structures on the leased premises should they be totally destroyed by fire. But the court held that the landlord was *not* under a duty to repair or replace a whole building by reason of his covenant to repair where the lessee had leased only a one-fourth portion of the building destroyed. *See generally* Fillette, *North Carolina's Residential Rental Agreements Act: New Developments for Contract and Tort Liability in Landlord-Tenant Relations,* 50 N.C.L. REV. 785 (1978).

tion in the lease to the contrary.[48] Therefore, it is a frequent practice for the lease to contain a provision to the effect that the lessee shall not assign or sublet the premises without the consent of the lessor in order to protect the latter from having undesirable and financially irresponsible occupants forced upon him and placed in possession of the premises.[49]

While a covenant in a lease not to assign or sublet the premises is valid and enforceable, since it is a restraint upon alienation it is subject to strict construction. The recent case of *Jones v. Andy Griffith Products, Inc.*[50] provides guidance for determining whether or not a lessor has been reasonable in withholding consent to a proposed sublease. The lease involved contained the commonly used provision that subletting was subject to the lessor's approval and that such approval would not be *unreasonably withheld.* Finding no specific guidance in North Carolina caselaw on the issue of reasonableness, the Court of Appeals turned to decisions of other

---

48. BURBY, REAL PROPERTY § 60 (1965).

49. While an assignment of the lease does not relieve the original lessee from his contractual obligations under the lease, his assignment may result in the premises being turned over to one who is irresponsible and whose financial condition will make collection of damages difficult. Therefore it is to the advantage of the landlord to place a covenant against assignment into the lease. That the lessee continues to be liable for his contractual obligations notwithstanding his assignment, see Alexander v. Harkins, 120 N.C. 454, 27 S.E. 120 (1897); 1 MORDECAI, LAW LECTURES 542 (1916). The lessee continues to be liable even if the landlord assents to the assignment unless the lessor expressly releases him or unless there is such conduct on the part of the landlord from which a novation may be inferred. Bank v. Bloomfield, 246 N.C. 492, 98 S.E.2d 865 (1957); Williams v. King, 247 N.C. 581, 101 S.E.2d 308 (1957); Coulter v. Capitol Fin. Co., 266 N.C. 214, 146 S.E.2d 97 (1966).

See Sanders v. Tropicana, 31 N.C. App. 276, 229 S.E.2d 304 (1976), which holds that a cooperative apartment may impose reasonable restraints prohibiting alienation of the cooperative's stock and prohibiting assignment of a tenant-shareholder's lease without the written consent of a majority of the cooperative's board of directors under N.C. GEN. STAT. § 54-120. The *Sanders* case cites and quotes with approval the case of Weisner v. 791 Park Avenue Corp., 6 N.Y.2d 426, 190 N.Y.S.2d 70, 160 N.E.2d 720 (1959), to the effect that absent a violation of statutory standards prohibiting discrimination because of race, color, religion, national origin or ancestry, under the cooperative plan of organization in effect "there is no reason why the owners of the cooperative apartment house could not decide for themselves, with whom they wished to share their elevators, their common halls and facilities, their stockholders' meetings, their management problems and responsibilities, and their homes." In the *Sanders* case the North Carolina Court of Appeals, in a case of first impression, held that the refusal of the board of directors of a cooperative apartment to approve the sale of stock and an assignment of a tenant-shareholder's proprietary lease to a party who indicated that he would sublease before taking occupancy was not arbitrary or capricious, but was in line with the social purposes of the cooperative apartment to limit apartment occupancy to owners.

50. 35 N.C. App. 170, 241 S.E.2d 140, *cert. denied,* 295 N.C. 90, 244 S.E.2d 258 (1978). The Court of Appeals affirmed the lower court's holding that the lessor's refusal to consent to a sublease of premises designed for and operated as a restaurant to a sublessee who proposed to operate an electronics business on the premises was reasonable.

jurisdictions.[51] The general standard of a reasonable man in the landlord's position was cited with apparent approval by the court.[52] Specific objective criteria which might form a basis upon which to predicate a reasonable refusal of a subtenant were listed as: (1) financial responsibility of the proposed subtenant; (2) identity or business character of the subtenant — his suitability for the particular building; (3) legality of the proposed use of the premises; and (4) nature of the occupancy, such as office, factory, clinic, etc.[53] The reasonable man standard and the objective criteria should be equally appropriate in a withholding of consent to an assignment of lease case.

Because of the strict construction rule mentioned above, a prohibition against assignment is not breached by a sublease [54] and a prohibition against a sublease is not breached by an assignment.[55] Therefore it is necessary to distinguish an "assignment" from a "sublease." An "assignment" is a conveyance of the lessee's entire interest in the demised premises, without retaining any reversionary interest in the term in himself.[56] A "sublease," on the other hand, is a conveyance of only a part of the term of the lessee, the lessee retaining a reversion of some portion of the term.[57] A transfer by the lessee of a part of the leased premises only, but for the full term, is called an "assignment pro tanto."[58]

In the absence of a provision in the lease, an assignment creates "privity of estate" at once between the lessee's assignee and the original lessor, and the original lessor has a right of action directly against the

---

51. Broad & Branford Place Corp. v. J. J. Hockenjos Co., 132 N.J.L. 229, 39 A. 2d 80 (1944); American Book Co. v. Yeshiva University Development Foundation, Inc., 59 Misc. 2d 31, 297 N.Y.S. 2d 156 (Sup. Ct. 1969).

52. The full text of the quotation from Broad & Branford Place Corp. v. J. J. Hockenjos Co., 39 A.2d at 82, with emphasis added by the Court of Appeals is as follows:

> Arbitrary considerations of personal taste, sensibility, or convenience do not constitute the criteria of the landlord's duty under an agreement such as this [not to unreasonably withhold consent to a sublease]. Personal satisfaction is not the sole determining factor. Mere whim or caprice, however honest the judgment, will not suffice. (citations omitted) *The standard is the action of a reasonable man in the landlord's position* . . . . The term "reasonable" is relative and not readily definable. As here used, it connotes action according to the dictates of reason — such as is just, fair and suitable in the circumstances.

53. American Book Co. v. Yeshiva Univ. Dev. Foundation, Inc., 297 N.Y.S.2d at 160.

54. Millinery Co. v. Little-Long Co., 197 N.C. 168, 148 S.E. 26 (1929).

55. Rogers v. Hall, 227 N.C. 363, 42 S.E.2d 347 (1947).

56. *E.g.*, if A has a lease for 10 years, has been in possession for 2 years, and transfers the remainder of his lease term, the transfer is an "assignment," regardless of what the parties call such transfer.

57. *E.g.*, if A has a lease for 10 years, has been in possession for 2 years, and transfers his term for 6 years to a transferee, leaving 2 years of the term undisposed of to be enjoyed after the expiration of the 6-year term of the transferee, there is a reversion of a part of the term and the transfer is a "sublease," regardless of what the parties call such transfer. Millinery Co. v. Little-Long Co., 197 N.C. 168, 148 S.E. 26 (1929).

58. MORDECAI, LAW LECTURES 541 (1916).

assignee on all covenants running with the land.[59] If, instead of assigning, however, the lessee sublets the premises, reserving or retaining a reversion in the term, however short, "privity of estate" is not established between the original landlord and the sublessee and the landlord has no direct action with respect to the covenants in the original lease as against the sublessee; there is neither privity of estate nor privity of contract as between the original landlord and a sublessee, and the sublessee can sue only his immediate lessor and the original landlord can sue only his immediate lessee with respect to the lease.[60]

§ 242. The Covenant of Fitness of Purpose.

In tenancies *not* governed by the Residential Rental Agreements Act, there is no implied covenant on the part of the landlord that the premises at the time of the letting are fit for any particular purpose.[61] Therefore the lessee cannot complain that the premises were not in a habitable condition or that they were not adapted to the tenant's purposes.[62] The doctrine of *caveat emptor* still applies to non-residential leases;[63] if a lessee wishes to hold the landlord responsible for the premises being fit for a specific purpose he must make provision therefor in his lease by express provision.

§ 243. Covenant That Lease May Be Terminated for Default in Payment of Rent or for Breach of Any Other Covenant in the Lease; Statutory Forfeiture for Nonpayment of Rent; Destruction of Premises.

Under the case law relating to landlord and tenant a breach of covenants by either party does not work a forfeiture of the lease or authorize a surrender of the leased premises by the lessee.[64] It is thus quite usual to place in the lease provisions which in effect convert "covenants" into "conditions," the breach of which permit the termination of the lessee's estate instead of leaving the injured party to an action for damages for breach of contract.[65]

---

59. MINOR & WURTS, REAL PROPERTY § 374 (1910).
60. *Id.*
61. Gaither v. Hascall-Richards Steam Generator Co., 121 N.C. 384, 28 S.E. 546 (1897); Improvement Co. v. Coley-Bardin, 156 N.C. 255, 72 S.E. 312, 36 L.R.A. (n.s.) 907 (1911); Williams v. Strauss, 210 N.C. 200, 185 S.E. 676 (1936).
62. Improvement Co. v. Coley-Bardin, 156 N.C. 255, 72 S.E. 312, 36 L.R.A. (n.s.) 907 (1911).
63. The Residential Rental Agreements Act, Chapter 6 *supra,* does not alter the *caveat emptor* doctrine expressed in cases such as Harrill v. Sinclair Refining Co., 225 N.C. 421, 35 S.E.2d 240 (1945) except in residential tenancies covered by that Act.
64. Brewington v. Loughran, 183 N.C. 558, 112 S.E. 257 (1922); Carson v. Imperial 400' Nat'l, Inc., 267 N.C. 229, 147 S.E.2d 898 (1966).
65. *Cf.* Friendly Center, Inc. v. Robinson, 233 F. Supp. 274 (1964).

§ 243

It should be noted that with respect to rent, where there is a definite time specified for the payment of rent, even though the lease is silent as to a forfeiture for nonpayment, upon the tenant's failure to pay all past due rent within ten days from demand therefor the lessor may reenter and dispossess the tenant [66] even though no right of reentry or forfeiture provision has been reserved in the lease. In this connection, however, if, during the hearing and before judgment on a petition made for forfeiture of a lease under North Carolina General Statutes, § 42-3, all rents and costs lawfully incurred are tendered to the petitioner, the petition will be denied.[67]

There is also a statute[68] which provides that if the use of a building was the main inducement for the execution of a lease and the building is destroyed without the fault of the lessee, or is so damaged that it cannot be made reasonably fit for the intended use as contemplated by the lease without the expenditure of more than one year's rent, the lessee may surrender the remainder of the term, provided the lease does not contain contrary stipulations.[69] In order to terminate the lease by surrender

---

66. N.C. Gen. Stat. § 42-3; Ryan v. Reynolds, 190 N.C. 563, 130 S.E. 156 (1925). Concepts of commercial impracticability of performance and frustration of purpose did not apply to excuse payment of rent by the lessee of a bus ticket agency where a labor dispute affected the lessee's commissions. Therefore, the lease could be terminated for defaults in rent payments. Knowles v. Carolina Coach Co., 41 N.C. App. 709, 255 S.E.2d 576 (1979).

67. N.C. Gen. Stat. § 42-33; Coleman v. Carolina Theaters, 195 N.C. 607, 143 S.E. 7 (1928); Hoover v. Crotts, 232 N.C. 617, 61 S.E.2d 705 (1950). If the lease contains a clear provision for forfeiture which negatives the right to retain the possession to a later date, the lessor may have a forfeiture notwithstanding N.C. Gen. Stat. § 42-33 and payments made thereunder if in fact late. Tucker v. Arrowood, 211 N.C. 118, 189 S.E. 180 (1937). In Green v. Lybrand, 39 N.C. App. 56, 249 S.E.2d 443 (1978), the Court of Appeals does an excellent job of summarizing this area. It notes that N.C. Gen. Stat. § 42-3 alters the common-law rule by providing for an implied forfeiture of the term upon failure to pay the rent within 10 days after a demand is made. Where the lease is silent, N.C. Gen. Stat. § 42-3 must be read in conjunction with N.C. Gen. Stat. § 42-33. Thus by tendering all rent due and all costs incurred by depositing the money with the Clerk of Court, the defendant-tenant will be able to avoid forfeiture of the leasehold. Cf. Menache v. Management Corp., 43 N.C. App. 733, 260 S.E.2d 100 (1979), where the lease agreement provided that, should the lessee remain in default of the lease for 30 days following notice of default, the lessor could thereupon "enter upon the premises and expel the lessee therefrom, without prejudice to any other remedy which the lessor ... may have on account of such default." The lessee contended that as a result of tendering the amounts of rent due in accordance with N.C. Gen. Stat. § 42-33, a complete defense to the lessor's summary ejectment action existed. The lessor responded that the tender of rent should not abate an action where the lease provides that the landlord shall have the option to declare the lease void upon the failure of the lessee to pay the rent when due. The Court of Appeals concluded at 43 N.C. App. 738: "Whether G.S. 42-33 applies in our opinion is a defense to be determined at the hearing on this matter on the merits."

68. N.C. Gen. Stat. § 42-12.

69. Grant v. Borden, 204 N.C. 415, 168 S.E. 492 (1933), holds that the parties to a lease may stipulate different provisions that will control N.C. Gen. Stat. § 42-12. Compare, Industrial Metal Treating v. T. & D. Realty, 30 N.C. App. 620, 228 S.E.2d 63 (1976).

§ 244   REAL ESTATE LAW IN NORTH CAROLINA   § 244

under this statute, the lessee may exercise his option to terminate by giving written notice of his election to terminate the lease and by paying all rent due to the date of the damage; the notice of surrender and termination must be tendered or delivered to the lessor within ten days from the date of the destruction or damage. A lease provision as to the rights of the parties upon damage or destruction of the premises can prevent the statute from having application; the parties can establish in detail specific rights with respect to the leased premises.[70]

§ 244. Covenant Limiting Use of Premises by Lessee.

If a lease does not place a limitation or restriction on the use of the leased premises, the lessee has a right to use it for any lawful purposes as he pleases.[71] However, the lessor may restrict the use of the premises as he sees fit as an incident to his right to control his property and may provide that the property is to be used *only* for a designated purpose in a specified way, which is a common practice, particularly in commercial leases.[72] Since the law does not favor restrictions upon the use of land, restrictive clauses are construed most strongly against the grantor or lessor and thus a mere statement of the purpose for which leased premises shall be used will not generally prevent the lessee from using the premises for other purposes; the mere statement of the purpose is deemed permissive and not restrictive unless followed by unambiguous words indicating an intention to limit the uses to which the property may be put.[73]

While it has been often argued that a lease which provides that rent is to be computed on a percentage basis implies a covenant on the part of the lessee to make use of the leased property for the purpose for which it is leased, North Carolina has held that there is no obligation on the lessee to use a commercial building for operation of a store during the life of the lease in the absence of a specific provision that the lessee should operate his store in that building,[74] especially where the lease requires the lessee

---

70. Grant v. Borden, 204 N.C. 415, 168 S.E. 492 (1933). *Compare* Industrial Metal Treating v. T. & D. Realty, 30 N.C. App. 620, 228 S.E.2d 63 (1976).

71. BURBY, REAL PROPERTY § 66 (1965).

72. Equity will enforce a clear restriction on the use of the property if the clause is unambiguous. CRIBBET, PRINCIPLES OF THE LAW OF PROPERTY 193 (1962). Capital City Oil Co., Inc. v. Humble Oil & Ref. Co., 25 N.C. App. 82, 212 S.E.2d 49 (1975) (citing this section), holds that the owner of a leasehold estate has the right to require that premises leased to a sublessee be used exclusively for the sale of the owner's products. A lessor has the right to impose a restriction on a lessee's use of the leased premises.

73. CRIBBET, PRINCIPLES OF THE LAW OF PROPERTY 193 (1962). *Compare* Samia v. Oil Co., 25 N.C. App. 601, 214 S.E.2d 222 (1975).

74. *See* Jenkins v. Rose's 5, 10 and 25¢ Stores, 213 N.C. 606, 197 S.E. 174 (1938), where the lease of a store building guaranteed a minimum rental of $2,400 for a one-year term, payable in monthly installments of $200, and providing that if sales should exceed $48,000 at the expiration of the term the lessee should account to the lessors and pay five percent

to pay an unconditional minimum rental that is substantial in nature in light of all the surrounding circumstances.[75] Thus a covenant against a noncomplying use must be carefully distinguished from a covenant to use. A continuous operation clause in the lease should be utilized by a lessor who desires to impose an obligation on the tenant to continue to use the premises for a specified purpose. Even with this clause problems relating to the lessor's remedy in the event of breach by the lessee can develop.[76]

§ 245. Covenant to Pay Taxes.

In the absence of a covenant to pay taxes, the lessee is under no obligation to pay any tax levied on leased lands. It is ordinarily the duty of the lessor to pay the taxes on leased premises in the absence of a contrary express provision.[77] Even if there is a contract provision that requires the tenant to pay the taxes, this does not relieve the landlord from liability with respect to the taxing authority.[78]

§ 246. Covenant to Insure Premises.

In the absence of a covenant or agreement in a lease, neither the lessee

---

on any sales in excess of $48,000. The lessee did not operate its store or business at the demised premises, but conducted its business in another location for one year. The lessor sued, contending that the lessee was obligated not only to pay the minimum rent agreed to but was obligated to do business at the store building and to pay a percentage of the gross sales after $48,000; the lessor showed that for several years the amount paid in rent had exceeded $2,400 under the percentage clause of the lease. The court held that there was no implied covenant to operate the store in the leased building in the absence of a specific provision that the lessee should occupy the building and operate a store therein; that the payment of the minimum of $2,400 rental was a full settlement of rent due for that year. *Accord,* Oestreicher v. American Nat'l Stores, Inc., 290 N.C. 118, 225 S.E.2d 797 (1976); Lowe's of Shelby, Inc. v. Hunt, 30 N.C. App. 84, 226 S.E.2d 232 (1976).

75. Burby, Real Property § 66 (1965). *Compare* Samia v. Oil Co., 25 N.C. App. 601, 214 S.E.2d 222 (1975).

76. *See, e.g.,* the recent Court of Appeals of Indiana case of Madison Plaza, Inc. v. Shapira Corp., 387 N.E.2d 483 (1979), where the court held that inability to earn a profit did not excuse a tenant from complying with a continuous operation clause but that the trial court did not abuse its discretion in refusing to grant the lessor an injunction. At 387 N.E.2d 486, part of the reasoning of the trial court in denying the injunctive relief is set forth as follows:

> The lease provides for the operation by the defendant of a junior department store on the leased premises for a period of ten years commencing October 21, 1974, and ending October 31, 1984. In order to operate a junior department store, the defendant must exercise special knowledge, taste, skill and judgment in selecting and investing in inventory, selecting and training and compensating adequate personnel needed to operate the store, and in making innumerable other day-to-day business decisions. A decree of specific performance would require the Court to maintain constant supervision over a long period of time and acts involving taste, skill, judgment and technical knowledge in order to enforce the decree.

77. Cordell v. Stone & Sand Co., 247 N.C. 688, 102 S.E.2d 138 (1958). *But see* Willard v. Blount, 33 N.C. 624 (1850), where it is held that a tenant who occupies land without any obligation to pay rent *is* under an obligation to pay taxes.

78. Hunt v. Cooper, 194 N.C. 265, 139 S.E. 446 (1927); Outlaw v. Cooper, 194 N.C. 268, 139 S.E. 447 (1927).

nor the lessor is under any obligation to insure the leased property against damage or loss by fire or other hazard.[79] But if there is a covenant by either the landlord or tenant to obtain insurance for the benefit of the other party with respect to the leased premises and there is a breach of this covenant, the defaulting party may be held accountable for actual damage caused to the leased interest that is not compensated for by insurance. In addition, the liability of the defaulting party who fails to procure proper insurance [80] pursuant to his covenant is not limited to the amount of premiums involved. Furthermore, if the covenantee becomes aware that the covenantor has failed to procure the proper insurance, he may secure the insurance himself and hold the covenantor liable to the extent of the premiums involved.[81]

Both the landlord and the tenant have insurable interests in leased property and either or both may insure to the extent of their respective individual interests. If either the lessor or lessee insures his own interest in the leased premises and thereafter collects from the insurance company upon the destruction or damage to the property, the other party has no claim to the proceeds from such insurance policy.[82] Of course, if the insurance policy has been procured for the mutual or joint benefit of the landlord and tenant a different accounting will be indicated.[83]

§ 247. Covenant to Renew Lease.

Covenants to renew the terms of leases upon the expiration of the initial term are often put into leases for a definite term.[84] But in the absence of a provision giving to the lessee the option to renew his lease for additional time, there is no implied right to renew.[85] When the term of the lease for a definite time expires it is the duty of the lessee to vacate the premises; the landlord is not required to give to the lessee any notice

---

79. Helicopter Corp. v. Cutter Realty Co., 263 N.C. 139, 139 S.E.2d 362 (1964); BURBY, REAL PROPERTY § 65 (1965).

80. *See* Industrial Metal Treating Corp. v. Realty Co., 30 N.C. App. 620, 228 S.E.2d 63 (1976), holding, *inter alia,* that a lease provision, which required the lessor to pay fire, windstorm, and hail insurance but which did not specify the amount of insurance to be carried, created by reasonable implication a requirement that the insurance should be in a reasonable amount relative to the value of the property, the cost of the premiums, and the risk involved. *See also* Indiana Lumbermens Mut. Ins. Co. v. Gallos Plastics Corp., 46 N.C. App. 335, 264 S.E.2d 736 (1980) holding that coverage on the leased premises was clearly excluded by a clause of the insurance policy excluding coverage for property damage to property owned or occupied or rented to the insured. (A separate policy providing coverage to lessees for leased premises had not been purchased.)

81. BURBY, REAL PROPERTY § 65 (1965).

82. Batts v. Sullivan, 182 N.C. 129, 108 S.E. 511 (1921).

83. *Id.;* Ingold v. Phoenix Assur. Co., 230 N.C. 142, 52 S.E.2d 366 (1949).

84. A renewal clause is not necessary where the tenancy is one from period to period. *See* section 235, notes 26, 27 *supra* concerning the perpetual renewal issue.

85. Barnes v. Saleeby, 177 N.C. 256, 98 S.E. 708 (1919).

§ 247　　　　　　　　　　　LEASES　　　　　　　　　　　§ 247

of the expiration of the term or to take any action against the lessee.[86] At the expiration of the lease, in the absence of a valid extension or renewal, the lessor has the right to treat the lessee as a trespasser and may bring an action to have him evicted without notice.[87] The omission of a renewal provision could work a serious hardship on a tenant who has made an expensive improvement of the leased property in reliance on an expectation of continuing in possession for a longer period.

In order for a renewal clause to be valid, it must be supported by a consideration. Thus where the lease provides that the lessee may renew the lease at its expiration for a stipulated period at a specified rental amount upon giving notice of intention to so renew it on or before a stipulated time before the expiration of the term, the provision will be given effect.[88] Additional guidelines with respect to lease renewal include the following:

1. Where the lease provides that the tenant may extend its terms by giving notice to the landlord of such intent in a specified manner by a specified time, the giving of such notice is a condition precedent to the extension of the term and if such notice provision is not complied with within the time specified he has no right to the renewal or extension.[89]

2. If the lease contains a provision which requires the lessee to give a notice to the landlord at a specified time of his election to renew, his right of renewal will be lost irrespective of whether the failure to give such notice caused the lessor to suffer any loss.[90]

3. If there is a renewal provision which does not require the lessee to give any notice to the landlord at a specified time of his election to renew, if he remains in possession after expiration of the term and pays the specified rent to the landlord as provided in the renewal agreement, such is by itself deemed to indicate the tenant's intention to extend the term of the lease and to suffice to notify the landlord of that intention. The acceptance of the specified rent may, under the circumstances, constitute a waiver on the part of the landlord of any further notice.[91]

4. If the lease contains a renewal provision specifying that the lessee shall give notice to the landlord within a specified period if he intends to

---

86. Duke v. Davenport, 240 N.C. 652, 83 S.E.2d 660 (1954); Realty Co. v. Demetreles, 213 N.C. 52, 194 S.E. 897 (1937).

87. *Id.*

88. Bank of Greenville v. Gornto, 161 N.C. 341, 77 S.E. 222 (1913). *See* Merchants Oil Co. v. Mecklenburg County, 212 N.C. 642, 194 S.E. 114 (1937); Kearney v. Hare, 265 N.C. 570, 144 S.E.2d 636 (1965); and Coulter v. Capitol Fin. Co., 266 N.C. 214, 146 S.E.2d 97 (1966).

89. Coulter v. Capitol Fin. Co., 266 N.C. 214, 146 S.E.2d 97 (1966).

90. Merchants Oil Co. v. Mecklenburg County, 212 N.C. 642, 194 S.E. 114 (1937).

91. Kearney v. Hare, 265 N.C. 570, 144 S.E.2d 636 (1965). *See* Treadwill v. Goodwin, 14 N.C. App. 685, 189 S.E.2d 643 (1972), which states that whether or not there has been a waiver of written notice of lessee's intention to renew is a question of fact to be determined by the circumstances indicating the intention of the parties.

extend the period of his lease, if he fails to give such notice within the time specified but holds over and pays rent to the landlord in the same amount as specified in the original lease, he is deemed to be only a tenant from year to year and is not deemed in possession under the renewal clause. On the other hand, if there is a renewal clause and the tenant remains in possession without giving the notice of renewal within the specified time but pays the landlord an increased rent in the amount that the lease specifies would be paid in the event of a renewal, it has been held that this is affirmative evidence that the tenant has exercised his option to take the lease for an additional term.[92]

While an option in the original lease to renew would not be without consideration and thus would be valid, a promise made by the lessor to the lessee after the inception of the lease, or during the lease period, to give to the tenant such option to renew is without consideration and will not be enforceable.[93] Likewise a provision purporting to grant the lessee a right of renewal at a rent "satisfactory to the lessor"[94] or at a rent "subject to adjustment at the beginning of the option period"[95] is void because of the uncertainty of the consideration.

It should be noted that in construing the terms of a renewal clause in a lease, the general rule is that ambiguities will be resolved in favor of the tenant and against the landlord, upon the principle that every man's grant is to be taken most strongly against himself since he has the power of stipulating in his own favor.[96]

§ 248. Provision in Lease Giving Tenant Option to Purchase Leased Premises.

Many leases, particularly those involving commercial or industrial property, give to the tenant the option to buy the leased property. The general consideration of the lease, such as the covenant to pay rent or do other acts, supports the option to purchase.[97] The draftsman of a lease with a provision therein giving to the tenant an option to purchase the real property should see that the option provision states clearly the time

---

92. Coulter v. Capitol Fin. Co., 266 N.C. 214, 146 S.E.2d 97 (1966).
93. Barnes v. Saleeby, 177 N.C. 256, 98 S.E. 708 (1919).
94. R.J. Reynolds Realty Co. v. Logan, 216 N.C. 26, 3 S.E.2d 280 (1939).
95. Young v. Sweet, 266 N.C. 623, 146 S.E.2d 669 (1966).
96. Winston-Salem Masonic Temple Co. v. Union Guano Co., 162 N.C. 87, 77 S.E. 1106 (1913); Trust Co. v. Frazelle, 226 N.C. 724, 40 S.E.2d 367 (1946); Kearney v. Hare, 265 N.C. 570, 144 S.E.2d 636 (1965). *But see* Coulter v. Capitol Fin. Co., 266 N.C. 214, 146 S.E.2d 97 (1966), to the effect that if the lessee's attorney has drawn the lease, ambiguous language is considered in favor of the lessor on the principle that "an ambiguity in a written contract is to be inclined against the party who prepared the writing."
97. Pearson v. Millard, 150 N.C. 303, 63 S.E. 1053 (1909); Crotts v. Thomas, 226 N.C. 385, 38 S.E.2d 158 (1946); Reynolds v. Earley, 241 N.C. 521, 85 S.E.2d 904 (1955).

§ 249   LEASES   § 249

within which the option may be exercised,[98] how and where the notice of the lessee's election to exercise it is to be given, the purchase price to be paid, the terms of payment or security,[99] whether or not an extension of the lease term automatically revives the option,[100] any items to be prorated, the type of deed to be executed, and all other material terms and conditions.[101] In order to effect priority over purchasers for value and lien creditors of the landlord, options to purchase in leases should be recorded as other grants of real property.

§ 249. Provision in Lease Relating to Alterations by Tenant.

In the absence of a provision therefor in the lease, a tenant is not authorized to make any substantial alteration in leased property without the consent of the lessor.[102] Since certain alterations may be desirable to accomplish the purposes of the lease, express provisions can be put into

---

98. Time is of the essence with respect to a lease contract provision which gives to the tenant an option to purchase leased premises, and any conditions imposed therein must be fully complied with by the tenant within the time specified. Atlantic Greyhound Corp. v. Smithfield, 98 F. Supp. 385, *rev'd,* 192 F.2d 453, *cert. denied,* 72 S. Ct. 761, 343 U.S. 929, 96 L. Ed. 1338 (1951); Barham v. Davenport, 247 N.C. 575, 101 S.E.2d 367 (1957).

99. Tender of the purchase price by the tenant optionee is not necessary until the lessor tenders a good and sufficient deed in the absence of a contractual provision requiring tender of the purchase price as a part of the "exercise" of the option. Kottler v. Martin, 241 N.C. 369, 85 S.E.2d 314 (1954); Trust Co. v. Frazelle, 226 N.C. 724, 40 S.E.2d 367 (1946). The lease contract may require that the payment of the purchase money, or a part thereof, accompany the optionee's election to exercise the option. Trogden v. Williams, 144 N.C. 192, 56 S.E. 865 (1907); Land Co. v. Smith, 191 N.C. 619, 132 S.E. 593 (1926); Hudson v. Cozart, 179 N.C. 247, 102 S.E. 278 (1920).

100. *See* the recent Supreme Court case of Davis v. McRee, 299 N.C. 498, 263 S.E.2d 604 (1980), where the original lease involved a term from January 31, 1972 through January 31, 1974 and also contained an option to purchase. The original lease term expired and the lessee remained in possession continuing to make rental payments until August 13, 1974 when the parties added the following handwritten language to the end of the original typewritten lease: "The term of this lease shall be from Jan. 31, 1974 through Jan. 31, 1976." When the lessees thereafter gave notice that they were exercising the option to purchase, the lessors eventually argued that the handwritten endorsement did not revive the option to purchase contained in the original lease. The Supreme Court ascertained that the intention of the parties in light of all of the relevant circumstances including the subsequent acts of the parties clearly indicated their intent to extend the option. It was also held that the later handwritten endorsement created a new estate for years which was separate and distinct from the previous one. Therefore, only those rental sums paid subsequent to the original term could be applied toward the purchase price.

101. Since an option given a tenant the right to purchase leased realty is unilateral and is binding only on the landlord until exercised by the tenant, it is construed strictly in favor of the landlord. Atlantic Greyhound Corp. v. Smithfield, 98 F. Supp. 385, *rev'd,* 192 F.2d 453, *cert. denied,* 72 S. Ct. 761, 343 U.S. 929, 96 L. Ed. 1338 (1951).

102. A material alteration of a building, such as removing interior partitions or cutting openings therein by a tenant, constitutes waste in most jurisdictions without reference to the question of actual injury or damages to the inheritance. This is called meliorating waste and the change of the character of the inheritance is the offense. *See* TIFFANY, REAL PROPERTY § 443 (abr. ed. 1940).

leases which authorize the lessee to make specified alterations within the contemplation of the parties in order to keep the premises modern and attractive for the tenant's purposes. In the absence of an agreement between the landlord and the tenant there is no obligation of the landlord to pay the tenant for improvements erected by the tenant upon leased premises although the improvements are such that by reason of annexation to the freehold they become a part of the realty and cannot be removed by the tenant.[103]

§ 250. Provision in Lease Giving Landlord Right of Entry to Inspect, to Repair, or for Other Purposes.

If the lease does not provide to the contrary, the lessor has no right of entry upon leased premises during the term of the lease. The landlord may be sued by the tenant in trespass for any unauthorized entry.[104] A complaint stating a claim for trespass will also present a claim for the recovery of at least nominal damages.[105] One recent Court of Appeals decision notes that punitive damages may be recovered for a willful, wanton, malicious or reckless and forcible trespass to rightful possession of the leased premises.[106]

If the landlord desires a right of entry for inspection, to make repairs, or for other purposes, he must insert a provision in the lease to that effect. While it would seem that if the landlord has made an agreement to make repairs on the leased premises, he should have a right of entry by implication for the purpose of making the repairs, it is advisable for a landlord to place in leases specific provisions authorizing his entry during the term.

§ 251. Covenants That "Run with the Land" in Leases; Effect.

Covenants contained in a lease or conveyance of land are said to "run with the land" when they are of such character that the benefits and burdens thereof pass with the land to an assignee, into whosoever hands the land may come.[107] It is thus important to determine whether a partic-

---

103. Haywood v. Briggs, 227 N.C. 108, 41 S.E.2d 289, 171 A.L.R. 480 (1947); Brown v. Ward, 221 N.C. 344, 20 S.E.2d 324 (1942). The creditors of the tenant have no greater right to charge land with the value of improvements made by the tenant than the tenant himself would have. Pitt v. Speight, 222 N.C. 585, 24 S.E.2d 350 (1943).

104. Barneycastle v. Walker, 92 N.C. 198 (1885); Manufacturing Co. v. Gable, 246 N.C. 1, 97 S.E.2d 672 (1957); Andrews & Knowles Produce Co. v. Currin, 243 N.C. 131, 90 S.E.2d 228 (1955).

105. Hendrix v. Guin, 42 N.C. App. 36, 255 S.E.2d 604 (1979); Hutton v. Cook, 173 N.C. 496, 92 S.E. 355 (1917).

106. Hendrix v. Guin, 42 N.C. App. 36, 255 S.E.2d 604 (1979), citing Matthews v. Forrest, 235 N.C. 281, 69 S.E.2d 553 (1952); and Binder v. Acceptance Corp., 222 N.C. 512, 23 S.E.2d 894 (1943).

107. Minor & Wurts, Real Property § 375 (1910).

ular covenant "runs with the land" in the landlord-tenant relationship because on this conclusion rests the determination of whether an assignee or successor in interest of either the landlord or the tenant can recover on or be liable for a breach of a particular covenant in the lease.

In order that a covenant may run with the land, and for the benefits and burdens of such covenant to pass with the assignment of the respective interests of the landlord and the tenant, two circumstances must concur: (1) The covenant must refer to something which affects the nature, quality, or value of the particular land leased or conveyed;[108] and (2) there must be privity of estate between the parties involved.[109]

Hence, if a lessor leases land to a tenant, stipulating in the lease that the tenant will make repairs,[110] or that the tenant shall pay taxes on the leased land, or that he shall keep the premises insured, or that he shall pay a designated rent, or that the lessee shall have a right to renew or to extend the lease,[111] or that he shall have an option to purchase the leased premises,[112] or that the lessor shall repair, these stipulations are all covenants that "touch or concern" the nature, quality, or value of the leased premises itself, and if either the lessor or lessee should subsequently assign all of his respective interests in the leased premises his assignee must bear the burdens and may enjoy the benefits of each of these covenants.[113] It is not necessary for the lease to expressly mention that the assignee is to benefit or to be an obligor of the covenants; the benefits and burdens of covenants that affect the nature, quality or value of the leased premises "run with the land" and are enforceable between assignees and successors in the respective interests of lessors and lessees.

---

108. *See* Bigelow, *The Content of Covenants in Leases,* 12 MICH. L. REV. 639 (1914), which states: "If the covenant tends to increase or diminish the rights, privileges, or powers of the tenant in connection with the enjoyment of the leased land, then the covenant is one that touches and concerns the leasehold estate, and may be enforced by and against any subsequent assignee of the estate."

> Opposed to the covenant which meets this test is the collateral or personal promise which does not run with the land. If the promises are those you would normally expect to find in a lease and if they relate to the subject matter of the lease — a covenant to build on the land, to repair, to pay rent, to renew or extend, etc. — they undoubtedly "touch and concern" the land. If they are abnormal and seem to relate to the personal relationship of the parties rather than the lease relationship — a promise to marry the lessor's daughter or buy ale at his pub — they are collateral. Thus a covenant by the tenant to pay taxes on the leased property "touches and concerns" the land, while a covenant to pay taxes on other than leased land does not "touch and concern" the estate and cannot be enforced by or against remote parties.

CRIBBET, PRINCIPLES OF THE LAW OF PROPERTY 183 (1962).

109. MINOR & WURTS, REAL PROPERTY § 375 (1910). See text at note 59 *supra*.

110. Which will be implied in the absence of a provision to the contrary in a tenancy not subject to the Residential Rental Agreements Act, Chapter 6 *supra.*

111. Bank of Greenville v. Gornto, 161 N.C. 341, 77 S.E. 222 (1913); Trust Co. v. Frazelle, 226 N.C. 724, 40 S.E.2d 367 (1913).

112. Smithfield Oil Co. v. Furlonge, 257 N.C. 388, 126 S.E.2d 167 (1962).

113. MINOR & WURTS, REAL PROPERTY § 375 (1910).

It should be noted that while covenants which run with the land can be enforced between the original parties to the lease and as between the original lessor, his successors, and assignees of the lessee, covenants are not enforceable either in favor of or against sublessees since there is no privity of estate between a sublessee and the original lessor.[114]

Article IV. Contractual Aspects of Leases; the Rule in Dumpor's Case

§ 252. Doctrine of Mitigation of Damages Applicable.

Since it is a basic principle of contract law that damages are compensatory and not punitive, North Carolina holds that the nonbreaching party to a lease cannot recover damages which he could have averted by reasonable activity on his part; he must mitigate or lessen the damages of the breaching party by using reasonable diligence to find a new tenant where the tenant has wrongfully abandoned the premises and also by doing whatever reasonable prudence requires in order to lessen his damages.[115] The party charged with responsibility for breach of the contract has the burden of showing matters in mitigation of damages; for in the absence of such proof, nothing else appearing save the wrongful breach of the agreement, prima facie the plaintiff would be entitled to recover the amount fixed by the terms of the lease.[116]

The mitigation of damages rule does not seem to preclude the use of a liquidated damages clause or lease termination fee subject to the well established rule of damages that such clauses not be intended as a penalty.[117]

§ 253. Doctrine of Anticipatory Breach of Contract Applicable.

While some jurisdictions do not follow the doctrine of anticipatory

---

114. WASHBURN, REAL PROPERTY § 674 (1902).
115. Monger v. Lutterloh, 195 N.C. 274, 142 S.E. 12 (1928). U.S.I.F. Wynewood Corp. v. Soderquist, 27 N.C. App. 611, 219 S.E.2d 787 (1975).
116. Id.
117. See, e.g., Milner Hotels, Inc. v. Mecklenburg Hotel, Inc., 42 N.C. App. 179, 256 S.E.2d 310 (1979) where the lease contained a $7,500 liquidated damages provision triggered in the event of premature termination by the lessee. For an example of a provision determined to be a penalty, see Jones v. Clark, 147 Ga. App. 657, 249 S.E.2d 619 (1978), where a lease provision allowed the landlord to accelerate remaining rental payments for the entire term of a five-year lease in the event of breach and also to repossess the leased premises with the option of reletting them for the lessee's benefit. The Georgia Court of Appeals held that this provision was a penalty and not a liquidated damages provision where the lease did not refer to the provision as one for liquidated damages or otherwise manifest an intent to treat it as such and where it would be unreasonable and oppressive to allow the landlord to collect in advance the remaining four-and-a-half years' worth of rental payments while also allowing him to retake the leased premises with no obligation to relet them for the lessee's benefit. See generally Note, Landlord's Duty to Re-rent Premises, 6 N.C.L. REV. 68 (1927).

breach where a lease is repudiated by the tenant after he has taken possession, North Carolina does apply the doctrine. If the lessee wrongfully repudiates the lease contract, and the landlord rightfully reenters for the purpose of diminishing the damage thus caused, he is entitled to recover the rental value from the lessee for the unexpired term as fixed by the contract, diminished by the fair rental value of the leased premises in the open market for the remainder of the term.[118]

§ 254. The Rule in Dumpor's Case.

The ancient rule, known as the Rule in Dumpor's Case, dating from 1603,[119] may still be in effect in North Carolina. While repudiated in a number of states,[120] North Carolina has not expressly repudiated the rule and has one decision which is susceptible of the interpretation that the rule still exists and will apply under proper circumstances.[121]

The Rule in Dumpor's Case is to the effect that where there is a covenant or condition in a lease, a license once given for breach of the covenant or condition discharges it forever. In *Dumpor's Case*[122] a lease contained a provision that the lessee "*or* his assigns" should not "alien the premises" without the license of the lessors. The lessee Bolde, after securing consent of the lessors, assigned the lease to Tubbe, who devised the lease to his son. The son died testate and the administrator of his estate assigned the lease to defendant. The lessor claimed a right to enter for breach of the condition. The claim was denied upon the ground that a condition is entire and indivisible and having once been waived cannot be enforced again. In other words, if a lessor once gives his assent to breach of a covenant or condition against assignment of the lease, such assent is deemed to be a waiver of the provision prohibiting assignment and the control of the lessor over his property is forever gone with respect to that covenant or condition.

In the case of *Childs v. Theatres, Inc.*,[123] a case similar in facts to

---

118. Womble v. Leigh, 195 N.C. 282, 142 S.E. 17 (1928). *See* Comment, 6 N.C.L. Rev. 495 (1927). *See* Kearns v. Gay Apparel Corp., 232 F. Supp. 475 (1964), in which the court states in a broken lease case:

> The total breach of a contract partly performed creates a cause of action in favor of the aggrieved party, entitling him to recover all damages sustained by the breach which include past, present and prospective damages, reasonably flowing from such breach fairly within contemplation of the parties and capable of being ascertained with a reasonable degree of certainty.

The latter case involved a lease with eleven years to run. It was affirmed in 341 F.2d 297 (1965). *See also* Eutaw Shopping Center, Inc. v. Glenn, 39 N.C. App. 67, 249 S.E.2d 459 (1978); U.S.I.F. Wynewood Corp. v. Soderquist, 27 N.C. App. 611, 219 S.E.2d 787 (1975), citing Weinstein v. Griffin, 241 N.C. 161, 84 S.E.2d 549 (1954).

119. 4 Coke 119b, 76 Eng. Rep. 1110 (1603).
120. Burby, Real Property § 54 (1965).
121. Childs v. Theatres, Inc., 200 N.C. 333, 156 S.E. 923 (1931).
122. 4 Coke 119b, 76 Eng. Rep. 1110 (1603).
123. 200 N.C. 333, 156 S.E. 923 (1931).

Dumpor's Case, the lease provided: "said R. D. Craver (lessee), his executors, administrators and assigns ... covenant ... that said R. D. Craver shall not convey this lease or underlet the premises without the written consent of the lessors...." The original lessee Craver transferred the premises to Warner Brothers Theatres, with the assent of the lessors. Thereafter, Warner Brothers Theatres reassigned the same lease to Carolina Theatres. The lessors sought to reenter under a provision in the lease giving the right of reentry upon the breach of any covenants in the lease. The North Carolina Supreme Court held, without repudiating the Rule in Dumpor's Case, that since the covenant against assignment ran to the lessee "*and assigns*" it was not a "single" covenant but was a "multiple" covenant to which the Rule in Dumpor's Case does not apply. The Rule in Dumpor's Case applies only when the covenant is "single." Thus, this archaic rule, if followed, could be a trap for the unwary or uninitiated. A covenant imposed on the "lessee" alone, or on the "lessee *or* his assigns," as was the case in the original *Dumpor's Case,* once waived for the original lessee could never be reasserted against successive assignees of the lease. But a covenant imposed on the "lessee *and* his assigns" is a multiple covenant, and assent to one breach does not waive the right of the lessor to insist that there be no subsequent breach of the covenant.[124]

It should be noted that the Rule in Dumpor's Case does not have application to covenants in any case where the covenants are continuous or recurrent in nature, such as the covenant to pay a stipulated rent each month. In such case, there are repeated or periodical possibilities of breach and the fact that the landlord excuses the lessee from one such payment would not discharge the entire condition, or rather series of conditions.[125]

Moreover, the Rule in Dumpor's Case can easily be circumvented in every case by the landlord giving only a qualified consent, that is, consent conditioned on there being no further breach.[126] This ancient and arbitrary rule seems to have nothing to commend it.

---

124. Childs v. Theatres, Inc., 200 N.C. 333, 156 S.E. 923 (1931). The whole question is discussed and the authorities assembled in the leading case of Investors' Guaranty Corp. v. Thompson, 225 P. 590, 32 A.L.R. 1071 (1924). *See also* Spitz v. Nunn, 171 N.E. 117 (1930); Klein v. Niezer, 169 N.E. 688 (1930); Gusman v. Mathews, 163 N.E. 636 (1928); Burby, Real Property § 54 (1965).

125. Minor & Wurts, Real Property § 497 (1910); Childs v. Theatres, Inc., 200 N.C. 333, 156 S.E. 923 (1931).

126. Cribbet, Principles of the Law of Property 183 (1962).

CHAPTER 13

MORTGAGES AND DEEDS OF TRUST

Article I. General Provisions

§ 255. The Nature and Effect of Mortgages and Deeds of Trust Generally.
§ 256. "Title Theory" of Mortgages in Effect in North Carolina; Mortgagee Obtains Legal Title by Mortgage.
§ 257. Form of Mortgages and Deeds of Trust.

Article II. The Nature and Effects of the "Equity of Redemption"

§ 258. The Equity of Redemption as Essential Feature of Every Mortgage Generally.
§ 259. Persons Who Have the Right to Redeem.
§ 260. Amount Necessary to Be Paid for Redemption of Property From Mortgage.
§ 261. Termination of Right to Redeem by Foreclosure; Statutory Termination.

Article III. Rights and Duties as Between Mortgagor and Mortgagee

§ 262. Rights of Mortgagor and Mortgagee to the Possession and Use of Mortgaged Property Generally.
§ 263. Mortgagor in Possession.
§ 264. Mortgagee in Possession.
§ 265. Duty to Pay Taxes as Between Mortgagor and Mortgagee.
§ 266. Either Mortgagor or Mortgagee May Insure Mortgaged Property.

Article IV. Transfer of Mortgagor's Interest

§ 267. Mortgagor's Right to Transfer Interest in Mortgaged Property Generally.
§ 268. Where Transfer of Mortgagor's Interest Recites That the Property Is "Subject to" the Mortgage.
§ 269. Where Transfer of Mortgagor's Interest Recites That the Mortgagor's Grantee "Assumes" the Mortgage.
§ 270. Conveyance of Mortgagor's Interest in Mortgaged Property to the Mortgagee.
§ 271. Acquisition of Mortgage Security by Owner of the Mortgaged Property; When Doctrine of Merger Applies.

Article V. Transfer of Mortgagee's Interest

§ 272. Transfer of Mortgagee's Interest in Mortgaged Property Generally.
§ 273. Where the Mortgagee Transfers the Mortgage Debt Only.
§ 274. Where the Mortgagee Transfers the Mortgage Only Without Transferring the Mortgage Debt.
§ 275. Where the Mortgagee Transfers the Mortgage and Note or Indebtedness at the Same Time by Written Instruments.

Article VI. Right of Mortgagee to Foreclose

§ 276. Nature of Mortgagee's Right to Foreclose Generally.
§ 277. When Right to Foreclosure Accrues; Acceleration Clause.
§ 278. Due-On-Sale Clause.
§ 279. Types of Foreclosure Available in North Carolina Generally.
§ 280. Foreclosure by Action.
§ 281. Foreclosure of Mortgages and Deeds of Trust Under Power of Sale.
§ 282. Deficiency Judgment.
§ 283. Statutes of Limitations Relating to Foreclosures.

Article VII. Payment and Discharge of Mortgages

§ 284. Discharge of Mortgage by Payment or Tender of Payment; Discharge of Record.
§ 285. Effect of Tender of Payment.

Article I. General Provisions

§ 255. The Nature and Effect of Mortgages and Deeds of Trust Generally.

A mortgage on real property is a written conveyance of land which represents the security for the payment of a debt or the performance of some duty. A mortgage is most usually given by a debtor, called the *mortgagor,* to a creditor, called the mortgagee, as security for the payment of a debt, with a provision that the conveyance shall become void on the payment of the debt by a specified date.[1]

The *mortgagor* is the person who owns the title or interest in the land that is being mortgaged; he is the debtor who owes the debt that is being secured by the mortgage. The *mortgagee* is the person to whom the indebtedness is owed and to whom the land is conveyed as security for the debt; he is the creditor who receives title to the land to secure the debt.[2] A mortgage which purports to secure payment of a debt has no validity if the debt has no existence.[3]

The debt for which a mortgage is given may be an antecedent debt, an existing debt, or one that is to arise in the future. The debt may be evidenced either by (1) a promise to pay included in the mortgage, or (2) by an instrument or agreement separate and apart from the mortgage, usually in the form of a promissory note or a bond.

The mortgage is a means of acquiring a loan on land, and represents to the borrower-mortgagor a mode of financing. To the lender-mortgagee, a mortgage represents security for his investment.

---

1. *See* 4 DENT, COMMENTARIES *133, which provides: "A mortgage is the conveyance of an estate by way of pledge for the security of a debt; and to become void on payment of it."

2. In North Carolina a mortgagee does not receive a mere "lien" on mortgaged real property, but he receives legal "title" to the land for security purposes. North Carolina is therefore considered a "common law" or "title" theory state with respect to mortgages. In a majority of jurisdictions in the United States a real estate mortgage creates only a "lien" in the mortgagee. That legal title passes in North Carolina, see Hemphill v. Ross, 66 N.C. 477 (1872); Fraser v. Bean, 96 N.C. 327, 2 S.E. 159 (1887); Kiser v. Combs, 114 N.C. 640, 19 S.E. 664 (1894); Cauley v. Sutton, 150 N.C. 327, 64 S.E. 3 (1909); Modlin v. Atlantic Fire Ins. Co., 151 N.C. 35, 65, S.E. 605 (1909); Hogan v. Udder, 175 N.C. 332, 95 S.E. 565 (1918); Lewis v. Nunn, 180 N.C. 159, 104 S.E. 470 (1920); Alexander v. Virginia-Carolina Joint Stock Land Bank, 201 N.C. 449, 160 S.E. 460 (1931); Stevens v. Turlington, 186 N.C. 191, 119 S.E. 210, 32 A.L.R. 870 (1923); Crews v. Crews, 192 N.C. 679, 135 S.E. 784 (1926); Riddick v. Davis, 220 N.C. 120, 16 S.E.2d 662 (1941); Simms v. Hawkins, 1 N.C. App. 168, 160 S.E.2d 514 (1968).

3. Walston v. Twiford, 248 N.C. 691, 105 S.E.2d 62 (1958); Bradham v. Robinson, 236 N.C. 589, 73 S.E.2d 555 (1953).

§ 256. "Title Theory" of Mortgages in Effect in North Carolina; Mortgagee Obtains Legal Title by Mortgage.

The mortgage in a "title theory state," such as North Carolina, is a conveyance of legal title to the land involved for security purpses on the condition that the conveyance is to be void if a specified sum of money is paid or collateral act done, by a designated time.[4] The legal title of the mortgagee is in the nature of a determinable fee.[5] The performance of the condition of payment divests the mortgagee of his estate and restores the right of possession to the mortgagor without the necessity of a reconveyance.[6] At the common law a mortgagee, in his character as the legal owner, was entitled to the immediate possession of the mortgaged premises even before breach of condition in the mortgage, unless this right had been waived or it had been otherwise stipulated in the mortgage.[7] See, however, the recent case of *Brannock v. Fletcher*,[8] in which the following statement appears: "Under the modern equitable doctrines, however, the mortgagor is entitled to remain in the possession of the property at least until breach of condition." *After default* in performance of conditions, after default of the mortgagor in paying the debt secured by the mortgage, the mortgagee is entitled to the possession.[9] The present law in North Carolina appears to be that so long as the mortgagor complies with the contract for which the mortgage is given, so long as he makes the payments as they become due, he is entitled to possession of the mortgaged land even in the absence of a stipulation to the contrary.[10]

---

4. Gregg v. Williamson, 246 N.C. 356, 98 S.E.2d 481 (1957); Barbee v. Edwards, 238 N.C. 215, 77 S.E.2d 646 (1953); Manufacturing Co. v. Malloy, 217 N.C. 666, 9 S.E.2d 403 (1940); Blake v. Broughton, 107 N.C. 220, 12 S.E. 127 (1890); Complex Inc. v. Furst, 43 N.C. App. 95, 258 S.E.2d 379 (1979). See 43 N.C. App. 101, where the court states:
   > A mortgage or deed of trust to secure a debt passes legal title to the mortgagee or trustee, as the case may be, but the mortgagor or trustor is looked on as the equitable owner of the land with the right to redeem at any time prior to foreclosure. This right, after the maturity of the debt, is designated as his equity of redemption.

(Citing Riddick v. Davis, 220 N.C. 210, 16 S.E.2d 662 (1941).)

5. *Id.*

6. Payment of the debt secured by the mortgage or deed of trust prior to foreclosure extinguishes the power of sale and terminates the title of the mortgagee or trustee, and a foreclosure sale made thereafter is invalid and ineffectual to convey title to the purchaser. Dobias v. White, 240 N.C. 680, 83 S.E.2d 785 (1954); Barbee v. Edwards, 238 N.C. 215, 77 S.E.2d 646 (1953); Crook v. Warren, 212 N.C. 93, 192 S.E. 684 (1937). The mortgage or deed of trust is extinguished upon payment notwithstanding that it is not canceled of record. *See, e.g.,* Blake v. Broughton, 107 N.C. 220, 12 S.E. 127 (1890).

7. *See* 1 MORDECAI, LAW LECTURES 575 (1916), citing Hinson v. Smith, 118 N.C. 503, 24 S.E. 541 (1896), to the effect that this was the law of North Carolina at that time. *See also* Crews v. Crews, 192 N.C. 679, 135 S.E. 284 (1926).

8. 271. N.C. 65, 155 S.E.2d 532 (1967).

9. *Id.*

10. *Id.*

§ 257. Form of Mortgages and Deeds of Trust.

(a) *Form of mortgages.* There is no particular form required to constitute a mortgage,[11] but the conventional form is an instrument of conveyance similar to a deed except that it recites the indebtedness and that the purpose of the instrument is to secure the payment of the indebtedness. In addition, the conventional mortgage contains a defeasance clause which states that the instrument is intended to secure the payment of a debt and is to be void upon such payment.

(b) *Form of deeds of trust.* In North Carolina most mortgage transactions take the form of deeds of trust. Instead of executing a mortgage in the ordinary form to the mortgagee directly, the borrower conveys the land to a third-party trustee to hold for the mortgagee-lender, subject to the condition that the conveyance shall be void on payment of the debt at maturity. Most deeds of trust contain a power of sale giving the trustee the power to sell the land in case of default and to apply the proceeds from the sale to payment of the debt. The deed of trust, while in the form of a trust, is essentially only a mortgage since the land is conveyed to the trustee to secure a debt, and the courts will construe it as a mortgage. The deed of trust differs from the ordinary mortgage in that instead of the conveyance being directly to the creditor, the conveyance is to a third person for the benefit of the creditor. By the utilization of the third-person trustee, in the event of a foreclosure by power of sale, the mortgagee-creditor can purchase at the foreclosure sale which would render the purchase voidable if he purchased at his *own* sale.

Since both mortgages and deeds of trust are conveyances of land, they must meet all of the requirements previously discussed for transferring land.[12] All of the requisites for conveying land titles must be met. The first requirement is that a mortgage or deed of trust must be in writing to satisfy the Statute of Frauds. Since a mortgage or deed of trust is essentially a deed, it must name the grantor-mortgagor and also the grantee-mortgagee (or grantee-trustee). It should recite that the consideration is the debt or obligation which the instrument is to secure, stating the amount of the indebtedness if practicable; if given for future advances, it may not be practicable to state the amount of the indebtedness. The mortgage or deed of trust must contain a granting clause which is necessary to convey legal title. The same rules applicable to descriptions in deeds are equally applicable to mortgages and deeds of

---

11. Excellent forms developed by the North Carolina Bar Association and forms developed by various lending institutions are utilized by many members of the real estate bar.
12. Complex, Inc. v. Furst, 43 N.C. App. 95, 258 S.E.2d 379 (1979), citing this section (§ 230 in the original edition).

trust.[13] In each, the instrument must describe the property conveyed with sufficient certainty to identify it or to furnish the means by which it can be identified. The mortgage or deed of trust may likewise contain covenants and conditions in the same manner as warranty deeds. There may be a provision in the mortgage or deed of trust, and in the accompanying promissory note or bond, whereby the maturity of the obligation of the mortgage is accelerated in case of some default by the mortgagor. This clause, called an "acceleration clause," simply provides that the entire indebtedness shall become due and payable upon the occurrence of any of certain enumerated defaults. The whole debt may be made to mature immediately upon a failure to pay a single installment of principal or interest when due; or upon a failure to pay taxes or assessments, or to procure insurance or for failure to pay an insurance premium when due, for failure to repair the premises, or because of an unauthorized alteration of the premises, or for any other act or omission of the mortgagor specified in the instrument which may be thought to impair the value of the security. The acceleration clause gives to the mortgagee the right to call for immediate payment of the entire indebtedness and if not paid to immediately start foreclosure proceedings.

If it is desired that the mortgagee or trustee shall have the power to sell the mortgaged premises upon a default in performance of the conditions of the mortgage or deed of trust, in order that foreclosure will not have to be perfected by judicial action in the courts, it is necessary to provide in the mortgage or deed of trust that the mortgagee or trustee is empowered to sell the mortgaged property to effect foreclosure. In the absence of such clause conferring the power of sale on the mortgagee or trustee, foreclosure cannot be effected except by a judicial foreclosure.

To constitute a legal mortgage or deed of trust, it must be signed and sealed by the mortgagor or his authorized agent, just as in the case of a deed.[14]

In addition, there must be an adequate delivery of the instrument and an acceptance thereof in the same manner as for deeds.

---

13. Matter of Norton, 41 N.C. App. 529, 255 S.E.2d 287 (1979), holding that a deed of trust was not rendered invalid where it erroneously referred to a plat and deed of the property conveyed as security as being recorded in the Clerk's Office rather than in the Office of the Register of Deeds.

14. *See* Ludwig v. Hart, 40 N.C. App. 188, 252 S.E.2d 270 (1979), where the Court of Appeals found defendants' evidence sufficient to survive a motion for directed verdict granted to the plaintiff by the trial court where it was alleged that the note and deed of trust were unenforceable because of the mental incapacity of one of the defendants.

Article II. The Nature and Effects of the "Equity of Redemption"

§ 258. The Equity of Redemption as Essential Feature of Every Mortgage Generally.

(a) *"Equity of redemption" generally.* An "equity of redemption" is the equitable right which the mortgagor, or one claiming through him, has after the execution of the mortgage to recover back his title to the mortgaged property as it existed prior to the execution of the mortgage. The "right" or "equity" of redemption is the right of the mortgagor, or those claiming through him, to regain complete title by paying the mortgage debt, plus any interest and any costs accrued. At any time before foreclosure is perfected, the mortgagor may "redeem" his title by paying to the holder of the mortgage or deed of trust the total indebtedness owed.[15] The payment discharges the mortgage and satisfies it, putting the title back as it was at the time the mortgage was executed. Even after the mortgage indebtedness is overdue and in default, the mortgagor, or those claiming through him, may pay off the indebtedness and get the mortgaged land back, free of the encumbrance.[16] The reason for the allowance of the equity of redemption is to be found in the general maxim of courts of equity that penalties and forfeitures are always to be relieved against when the substantial object in view can be attained and the other party put substantially in *status quo* without enforcing them.[17] Since a mortgage is intended only for security for an indebtedness, if the total indebtedness is paid at any time before foreclosure is complete,[18] plus interest and costs,[19] although not within the time limited, the object of the transaction will be attained and the creditor-mortgagee will have no complaint. No redemption can be had, however, after a valid foreclosure either by judicial foreclosure or under power of sale.

The right of redemption is an inseparable incident of every mortgage and is jealously guarded by the courts in the exercise of their equitable jurisdiction. No agreement is permitted between a mortgagor and mortgagee at the inception of an instrument in the form of a mortgage security whereby the mortgagor waives his equity of redemption in any way.[20]

---

15. Riddick v. Davis, 220 N.C. 120, 16 S.E.2d 662 (1941); Crews v. Crews, 192 N.C. 679, 135 S.E. 784 (1926); Complex, Inc. v. Furst, 43 N.C. App. 95, 258 S.E.2d 379 (1979).
16. *Id.*
17. Minor & Wurts, Real Property § 535 (1910).
18. Anderson v. Moore, 233 N.C. 299, 63 S.E.2d 641 (1951).
19. Osborne, Mortgages § 305 (1951).
20. *See* Wilson v. Fisher, 148 N.C. 535, 62 S.E. 622 (1908), to the effect that no one can deprive the mortgagor of his equitable right of redemption and, as a result, he cannot — when he executes the mortgage — agree with the mortgagee that he will waive or release his right. The court states:

> If the transaction be a mortgage in substance, the most solemn engagement to the contrary, made at the time, cannot deprive the debtor of his right to redeem. Nor can a mortgagor, by any agreement at the time of the execution of the mortgage that the

This concept is expressed in the statement "once a mortgage, always a mortgage" which means that the mortgagee cannot in any way bar or clog the right of redemption of the mortgagor.[21] The only way that the equity of redemption can be effectively cut off is by a proper foreclosure.

(b) *Absolute deed accompanied by oral agreement of grantee to reconvey upon performance of specified condition or payment of specified sum of money within specified time.* An exception to the foregoing rule should be noted, however. This exception which in effect makes it possible to cut off the mortgagor's equity of redemption arises from North Carolina's anomalous rule [22] that if a lender, A, insists upon and takes a deed in absolute form from borrower B, to secure the obligation owed to A, upon an oral promise or representation that A will reconvey the land to B upon payment of the indebtedness at the appropriate time, parol evidence will not be admissible to show that the absolute deed and the oral agreement to reconvey upon payment of the indebtedness were intended to constitute a mortgage for security purposes only. In the absence of fraud, mistake, ignorance, or undue influence, parol evidence is inadmissible to show that such deed in absolute form was intended as a mere mortgage.[23] But if the grantor in the deed in question alleges and

---

right to redeem shall be lost if the money be not paid by a certain day, debar himself of such right.

It should be noted, however, *that after creation of the mortgage,* the mortgagor *can* sell and convey his equity of redemption, if he wishes, either to third parties or to the mortgagee. Any such subsequent transaction with the mortgagee whereby the mortgagor sells his equity of redemption to the mortgagee will be closely scrutinized by the courts because of the peculiar relationship of the parties and the possibility of oppression by the mortgagee. There is a presumption of fraud and the mortgagee who buys the mortgagor's equity of redemption has the burden of showing that the transaction was fair and honest and free of undue influence. *See* Alford v. Moore, 161 N.C. 382, 77 S.E. 343 (1913).

21. *See* MORDECAI, LAW LECTURES 574 (1916), where the author states:

If the people and their attorneys would just learn and heed this maxim, and cease to draw mortgages with stipulations that the mortgagor shall not redeem after a certain time — or stipulations having a similar intent, though not so candidly expressed — they would be saved much trouble, cost, and in some instances, mortification. The courts are not so blind that they can be deceived by these schemes; nor are they so vacillating that they will permit a principle so thoroughly established to be swept away or evaded by a juggling with technical rules or terms . . . .

See also Ray v. Patterson, 170 N.C. 226, 87 S.E. 212 (1915).

22. North Carolina is in a distinct minority with respect to this rule. *See* OSBORNE, MORTGAGES § 72 (1951), where it is indicated that the majority and better rule admits parol testimony to show that an absolute deed between the parties was intended as a security instrument.

23. In Williamson v. Rabon, 177 N.C. 302, 98 S.E. 830 (1919), the court said: "Since the case of Streator v. Jones, 10 N.C. 433, there has been a uniform current of decisions by which these two principles are established in reference to bills which seek to correct a deed, absolute on its face, into a mortgage or security for a debt: (1) It must be alleged, and of course proven, that the clause of redemption was omitted by reason of ignorance, mistake, fraud, or undue advantage; (2) the intention must be established, not merely by proof of

proves that the redemption clause was omitted by mistake, fraud, ignorance or undue advantage and such proof is *clear, strong and convincing*,[24] the deed in absolute form can be corrected and reformed into a mortgage, in which case the grantor-mortgagor will have his right to redemption as in the case of other mortgages.[25]

At least one recent Court of Appeals case raises the possibility of invoking the doctrine of equitable estoppel because of fraud to compel reconveyance of lands.[26]

---

declarations, but by proof of facts and circumstances *dehors* the deed, inconsistent with the idea of an absolute purchase. Otherwise titles evidenced by solemn deeds would be at all times exposed to the slippery memory of witnesses . . . ." *See also* Isley v. Brown, 253 N.C. 791, 117 S.E.2d 821 (1960); Perkins v. Perkins, 249 N.C. 152, 105 S.E.2d 663 (1958); Davenport v. Phelps, 215 N.C. 326, 1 S.E.2d 824 (1939); Briley v. Roberson, 214 N.C. 295, 199 S.E. 73 (1938); Newbern v. Newbern, 178 N.C. 3, 100 S.E. 77 (1919); Newton v. Clark, 174 N.C. 393, 93 S.E. 951 (1917). *See* Brown v. Gurkin, 22 N.C. App. 456, 206 S.E.2d 504 (1974), which holds that a directed verdict in favor of defendants was proper in an action to have a deed reformed and declared to be a deed of trust where there was no evidence tending to show that a clause of redemption was omitted from the grantor's deed, which she signed as the result of ignorance, mistake, fraud or undue advantage, and where there was no evidence that the grantor was prevented from ascertaining that the paper writing she signed was a deed.

24. Perkins v. Perkins, 249 N.C. 152, 105 S.E.2d 663 (1958); Davenport v. Phelps, 215 N.C. 326, 1 S:E.2d 824 (1939).

25. Ray v. Patterson, 170 N.C. 226, 87 S.E. 212 (1915); Davenport v. Phelps, 215 N.C. 326, 1 S.E.2d 824 (1939).

26. *See* Dunn v. Dunn, 24 N.C. App. 713, 212 S.E.2d 407 (1975), where the Court of Appeals states at 24 N.C. App. 716:

It is clear that an oral agreement to acquire legal title to land and thereafter reconvey to the grantor upon specified terms and conditions is within the statute of frauds, (G.S. 22-2), and is unenforceable in the absence of fraud, mistake or undue influence. A parol trust in favor of a grantor cannot be engrafted upon such a deed. *Conner v. Ridley,* 248 N.C. 714, 104 S.E. 2d 845 (1958).

But in proper cases an equitable estoppel based upon grounds of fraud may override the statute of frauds. *McKinley v. Hinnant, supra.* In *McNinch v. Trust Co.,* 183 N.C. 33, 38, 110 S.E. 663, 666 (1922), an action based on breach of a constructive trust to hold land and obtain the best price therefor, the Court said, "[i]t is not necessary that actual fraud be shown, but the establishment of such conduct and bad faith . . . as would shock the conscience of a chancellor will suffice to invoke the aid of a court of equity." See also 73 Am. Jur. 2d, Statute of Frauds, § 567 (1974).

We do not find a case in this State where the relief sought is the specific performance of a contract to reconvey lands based on equitable estoppel because of fraud. There are numerous cases where the grantor sought to have a transaction of this nature declared a mortgage. *Ferguson v. Blanchard,* 220 N.C. 1, 16 S.E. 2d 414 (1941); *Ricks v. Batchelor,* 225 N.C. 8, 33 S.E. 2d 68 (1945); *McKinley v. Hinnant, supra; Hardy v. Neville,* 261 N.C. 454, 135 S.E. 2d 48 (1964). Our Supreme Court has recognized the doctrine of equitable estoppel and there is some indication in *McNinch v. Trust Co., supra,* that in an appropriate case of estoppel based on fraud, it would uphold the specific performance of such a contract to reconvey.

In other jurisdictions it has been held that the conveyance of land by the plaintiff to the defendant, under an oral agreement by the latter to reconvey to the plaintiff, has been held to constitute a sufficient part performance to entitle the plaintiff to a specific performance of the contract to reconvey. See Annot. 101 A.L.R. 923 at 1108 (1936). In *Cloniger v. Cloniger,* 261 S.C. 603, 193 S.E. 2d 647 (1973), the court upheld the right of the plaintiff to the specific performance of defendant's oral promise to reconvey land to the plaintiff when he was able to repay costs incurred by defendant, together with interest.

(c) *Absolute deed accompanied by collateral written agreement of grantee to reconvey upon performance of specified condition or payment of specified sum of money within specified time.* If a grantee receives an absolute deed and contemporaneously executes another written instrument by which he agrees to reconvey the land to the grantor of the deed upon the payment of a specified amount of money by a specified time, or agrees to perform some other act or condition, the transaction is susceptible of being construed in more ways than one. Such deed and contract to reconvey upon the performance of some act or the payment of money within a specified time may be what at first blush it appears to be; it may be a grant coupled with an option to repurchase if payment or performance of the condition is complied with within the specified time. In such case if the conditions are not met within the specified time, the grantor in the deed is not entitled to make the specified payment later and to recover his land. Time is of the essence with respect to an option to purchase and if the conditions are not fulfilled according to its terms the right to exercise and enforce the option is terminated.[27] On the other hand, if the grantee receives an absolute deed and he executes another written instrument by which he agrees to reconvey to the grantor upon the payment of a specified amount of money at a specified time, extrinsic parol testimony may be introduced by the grantor to show that the two instruments, the deed and the agreement to reconvey, were executed for the purpose of security and therefore constitute a mortgage.[28]

The intention of the parties at the time an agreement to execute a deed is consummated is determinative of whether the title is irrevocably transferred, or is merely a security for the payment of a debt or the performance of an obligation. Factors considered in order to ascertain the intention of the parties where there is a deed to the grantee and an agreement by the grantee to reconvey to the grantor upon payment within a specified time are:

1. Was there a debtor-creditor relationship between the parties at the time the deed was executed, either created then or pre-existing and continued thereafter?[29]

---

27. Winders v. Kenan, 161 N.C. 628, 77 S.E. 687 (1913); Gaylord v. McCoy, 161 N.C. 685, 77 S.E. 959 (1913); McKinley v. Hinnant, 242 N.C. 245, 87 S.E.2d 568 (1955).
28. O'Briant v. Lee, 214 N.C. 723, 200 S.E. 865 (1938).
29. O'Briant v. Lee, 214 N.C. 723, 200 S.E. 865 (1938). Where there is no debtor-creditor relationship between the parties to a deed absolute in form, and the grantee contemporaneously agrees in writing to reconvey to the grantor upon the payment of a certain amount at a certain time, the transaction will not be held a mortgage in law or equity. If the agreement to reconvey leaves it entirely optional with the grantor as to whether he will make such payment and take the reconveyance, and does not bind him to do so, there is no mortgage. *See* McKinley v. Hinnant, 242 N.C. 245, 87 S.E.2d 568 (1955); Ricks v. Batchelor, 225 N.C. 8, 33 S.E.2d 68 (1945); Ferguson v. Blanchard, 220 N.C. 1, 16 S.E.2d 414 (1941); Watkins v. Williams, 123 N.C. 170, 31 S.E. 388 (1898); King v. Kincey, 36 N.C. 187 (1840); Trust Co. v. Morgan-Schultheiss, 33 N.C. App. 406, 235 S.E.2d 693 (1977).

2. Did the parties between themselves intend for the absolute deed and the instrument of the grantee agreeing to reconvey to be only security for the debt? The character of the conveyance is to be determined by the intention of the parties, and if the intention, however ascertained, was that it should operate as a security, the court so regards it, and the debtor will be entitled to redeem.[30]

3. How does the sum paid by the grantee compare with the value of the land conveyed? If the amount is disproportionate, it will generally show that the parties intended the conveyance to be a mortgage.[31] If the money advanced is grossly inadequate under ordinary circumstances for an absolute conveyance of land of the value in question, this indicates that the transaction is a mortgage and not an absolute conveyance with an option to repurchase. If the price to be paid upon reconveyance is not the value of the land but is exactly the amount the grantee has advanced plus an amount equal to interest, insurance and taxes, this indicates a mortgage and not a sale with an option to repurchase.[32]

4. Does the grantor remain in possession of the land after the conveyance to the grantee who executes the agreement to reconvey? If the grantor in such absolute deed remains in possession,[33] particularly if he pays rent that is equivalent to what interest on a loan would be,[34] the factual presumption is raised that a mortgage and not an absolute deed was intended.

5. Was the grantor of the absolute deed under the pressure of need and distressed, hard pressed for money, at the time of its execution? If he was, this gives support to the idea that the deed, accompanied by a contemporaneous agreement by the grantee to reconvey, together constitute a mortgage transaction. Since lenders are less under the pressure of circumstances which control the perfect and free exercise of judgment than are borrowers, it is recognized by the courts that the lender may have taken advantage of his superiority of bargaining power and omitted the usual redemptive clause to his own advantage.[35]

6. Did the instruments originate out of an application for a loan? If so, this tends to support the conclusion that the deed given was intended as a mortgage, regardless of how the parties label their transaction.[36]

7. In addition, other conduct of the parties before, at, and after the time of the execution of the instruments are circumstances to be considered in determining whether a mortgage was intended.

---

30. O'Briant v. Lee, 214 N.C. 723, 200 S.E. 865 (1938); Gillis v. Martin, 17 N.C. 470 (1833).

31. O'Briant v. Lee, 214 N.C.723, 200 S.E. 865 (1938); Hodges v. Hodges, 37 N.C. App. 459, 246 S.E.2d 812 (1978).

32. Hardy v. Neville, 261 N.C. 454, 135 S.E.2d 48 (1964).

33. *Id. See also* Hodges v. Hodges, 37 N.C. App. 459, 246 S.E.2d 812 (1978).

34. *See, e.g.,* Beeler v. American Trust Co., 24 Cal. 2d 1, 147 P.2d 583 (1944). *Compare* Henderson v. Finance Co., 273 N.C. 253, 160 S.E.2d 39 (1968).

35. O'Briant v. Lee, 214 N.C. 723, 200 S.E. 865 (1938).

36. *Id.*

It should be noted that only a preponderance of the evidence is required to show that an absolute deed accompanied by a written agreement of the grantee to reconvey to the grantor upon the payment of a certain amount within a specified time is a mortgage in fact. Unlike the situation where the absolute deed is accompanied only by an oral promise to reconvey,[37] no fraud, mistake, undue advantage or ignorance must be shown where the deed is accompanied by a *written* agreement to reconvey. In addition the quantum of proof is less, only a preponderance of the proof being required and not evidence that is "clear, strong and convincing." [38] But the intention to create a mortgage must be established by more than the simple declaration of the parties; *i.e.,* by proof of facts and circumstances *dehors* the deed inconsistent with the idea of an absolute purchase.[39]

It should be further noted that where the execution of a deed in absolute form and a written agreement to reconvey raise doubt and ambiguity, the transaction is construed to be a mortgage.[40] The courts lean toward the mortgage construction since to construe the instruments as an absolute deed and an independent option to repurchase may result in a forfeiture of the grantor's option rights if not performed within the specified time. If, however, the instruments are construed in doubtful cases as a mortgage, redemption can be had by the grantor by paying the specified amount even after the due date, at any time before foreclosure. Oppression can be prevented and substantial justice more often accomplished.[41]

If a "mortgage" is construed from the absolute deed accompanied by a written agreement of the grantee to reconvey, all the consequences that follow a mortgage follow this transaction. The mortgagor has a right to an accounting, a right to redemption, and the like, notwithstanding any stipulation in the instruments to the contrary, "for the power of redemption is not lost by any hard conditions, nor shall it be fettered to any point of time not according to the course of the Court." [42] If the instruments together are found to constitute a mortgage, all the incidents of mortgages apply. The real character of the transaction and the true intention of the parties may be inquired into and govern notwithstanding the parties may have adopted the form of an absolute conveyance and a bond for resale.[43]

---

37. O'Briant v. Lee, 212 N.C. 793, 195 S.E. 15 (1937).
38. O'Briant v. Lee, 214 N.C. 723, 200 S.E. 865 (1938).
39. *Id. See also* Hodges v. Hodges, 37 N.C. App. 459, 246 S.E.2d 812 (1978).
40. O'Briant v. Lee, 214 N.C. 723, 200 S.E. 865 (1938).
41. OSBORNE, MORTGAGES § 89 (1951).
42. O'Briant v. Lee, 214 N.C. 723, 200 S.E. 865 (1938).
43. In O'Briant v. Lee, 214 N.C. 723, 200 S.E. 865 (1938), the court said:

> Courts of equity, therefore, will carefully examine any transaction between debtor and creditor, where there is a possibility of oppression to the end that justice may be done to him whose circumstances of need place him in a position to be imposed upon by an unscrupulous creditor. A Shylock can no longer demand his pound of flesh.

§ 259. Persons Who Have the Right to Redeem.

Generally the equitable right of redemption belongs to one who has an interest in the mortgaged premises and whose interest would be extinguished or prejudiced by a foreclosure of the mortgage.[44] This would include the mortgagor or anyone who may have acquired any interest in the premises through the mortgagor, legal or equitable, by operation of law or otherwise. In addition to the mortgagor[45] who is entitled to redeem, the mortgagor's heirs,[46] his judgment creditors,[47] transferee or purchaser of the equity of redemption,[48] including one who becomes owner of a fractional part of the mortgagor's interest,[49] junior mortgagees of the mortgaged premises,[50] the wife or widow of the mortgagor,[51] are each entitled to redeem the premises from a mortgage. Others generally accorded the right to redeem are tenants for life or for years, remaindermen, reversioners, and easement holders; anyone whose interest in the mortgaged premises will be prejudiced by foreclosure can redeem.[52]

Even after a foreclosure of a mortgage, persons who are entitled to redeem may still redeem the premises from the mortgage if the foreclosure was not valid for some reason. For instance, if the foreclosure is by judicial action, if a junior encumbrancer, lienor or other person entitled to redeem is not made a party to the foreclosure proceedings, his equitable right of redemption is not extinguished by the purported foreclosure; he can still get the premises back, freed from the mortgage, by tendering the amount of the mortgage debt, accrued interest and costs; his right to redeem is not cut off as it would have been had he been made a party.[53] Likewise, if the foreclosure is under a *power of sale,* and the sale is irregular in that there has been some failure to comply with statutory or contractual requirements for the holding of the sale, the equity of redemption will not be extinguished.[54] The person who had the equity of redemption before the purported foreclosure can redeem the premises from the person who purchased the land at the invalid foreclosure sale.

---

44. OSBORNE, MORTGAGES § 304 (1951).
45. Crews v. Crews, 192 N.C. 679, 135 S.E. 784 (1926).
46. Jessup v. Nixon, 199 N.C. 122, 154 S.E. 18 (1930).
47. Stainback v. Geddy, 21 N.C 479 (1837); Tucker v. White, 22 N.C. 289 (1839).
48. Pearce v. Watkins, 219 N.C. 636, 14 S.E.2d 653 (1941).
49. Dickerson v. Simmons, 141 N.C. 325, 53 S.E. 850 (1906).
50. Wilson v. Union Trust Co., 200 N.C. 788, 158 S.E. 479 (1931).
51. Oil Co. v. Richardson, 271 N.C. 696, 157 S.E.2d 369 (1967). *See also* N.C. GEN. STAT. § 45-45.
52. OSBORNE, MORTGAGES § 304 (1951).
53. Wilmington v. Merrick, 231 N.C. 297, 56 S.E.2d 643 (1949); Riddick v. Davis, 220 N.C. 120, 16 S.E.2d 662 (1941).
54. Jessup v. Nixon, 199 N.C. 122, 154 S.E. 18 (1930).

§ 260. Amount Necessary to Be Paid for Redemption of Property From Mortgage.

Where a mortgagor or other person who has an equity of redemption wishes to redeem the premises from the mortgage, he must tender the entire amount of the mortgage plus legal interest.[55]

Since a mortgagee who takes possession of the mortgaged property is chargeable to account for rents and profits he receives for the premises after he takes possession, the mortgagor has a right, as an incident of his right to redeem, to compel the mortgagee to deduct from the mortgage indebtedness owed the amount of rents and profits received by the mortgagee.[56] Since the rents and profits received by the mortgagee who takes possession of the mortgaged premises are chargeable to the mortgagee in diminutation of the mortgage indebtedness, the mortgagor or other person having a right of redemption has a right to insist that the mortgagee in possession give an accounting to determine whether or not there is anything remaining due on the mortgage. If the mortgagee in possession has received sufficient rents and profits to liquidate the indebtedness secured by the mortgage, the mortgagor or person entitled to redeem is entitled, without more, to have an entry of satisfaction entered on a judgment in a foreclosure suit, the mortgage or deed of trust cancelled, and the premises surrendered to the mortgagor free and clear of the mortgage indebtedness.[57]

§ 261. Termination of Right to Redeem by Foreclosure; Statutory Termination.

The right to redeem is terminated by a valid foreclosure sale.[58] The right to redeem may also be terminated in the mortgagor if he conveys his interest in the mortgaged premises to a third party; the transferee of the mortgagor's interest thereafter has the right to redeem.[59] Likewise, if the mortgagor, subsequent to the execution of the mortgage, transfers his equity of redemption to the mortgagee for a valuable consideration, the equity of redemption will be terminated.[60] In addition, if the mortgagee buys in at his own foreclosure sale, which sale is voidable and does not extinguish the mortgagor's equity of redemption, the mortgagor's equity of redemption may be terminated if the mortgagor (1) releases his right of redemption under seal, (2) engages in such conduct as would make assertion of his right of redemption fraudulent as against the mortgagee

---

55. MINOR & WURTS, REAL PROPERTY § 551 (1910).
56. Anderson v. Moore, 233 N.C. 299, 63 S.E.2d 641 (1951).
57. Id.
58. OSBORNE, MORTGAGES § 306 (1951).
59. Pullen v. Mining Co., 71 N.C. 567 (1874).
60. Alford v. Moore, 161 N.C. 382, 77 S.E. 343 (1913).

or one claiming under the mortgagee, thus estopping him, or (3) if he acquiesces or ratifies a foreclosure sale by failing to act thereon for a long time after having knowledge of its irregularity or invalidity.[61]

A North Carolina statute [62] also provides that if the mortgagee takes and remains in actual possession of the mortgaged premises for more than ten years after the right to redeem accrues, the mortgagor's equity of redemption will be barred.[63]

Article III. Rights and Duties as Between Mortgagor and Mortgagee

§ 262. Rights of Mortgagor and Mortgagee to the Possession and Use of Mortgaged Property Generally.

Since legal title passes to a mortgagee upon delivery of the mortgage, the common-law rule was that the mortgagee as legal owner was entitled to immediate possession of the mortgaged premises even before breach of condition in the mortgage, unless the right was waived or it was otherwise stipulated in the mortgage.[64] In a recent decision, however, the North Carolina Court stated: "Under the modern equitable doctrine, however, the mortgagor is entitled to remain in the possession of the property at least until breach of condition." [65] Thus, in North Carolina today, since legal title is vested in the mortgagee only for security purposes, the mortgagee is entitled to enter and hold the land until redemption or foreclosure only *after default* by the mortgagor, unless there is an agreement to the contrary.[66]

§ 263. Mortgagor in Possession.

The mortgagor who remains in possession of the mortgaged premises may be liable for waste.[67] The mortgagor in possession is entitled to the

---

61. Denson v. Davis, 256 N.C. 658, 124 S.E.2d 827 (1962).
62. N.C. GEN. STAT. § 1-47 (4).
63. Gay v. J. Exum & Co., 234 N.C. 378, 67 S.E.2d 290 (1951); Anderson v. Moore, 233 N.C. 299, 63 S.E.2d 641 (1951).
64. *See* 1 MORDECAI, LAW LECTURES 575 (1916), in which the author indicated this to be the law of North Carolina.
65. Brannock v. Fletcher, 271 N.C. 65, 155 S.E.2d 532 (1967).
66. Federal Land Bank v. Jones, 211 N.C. 317, 190 S.E. 479 (1937); Gregg v. Williamson, 246 N.C. 356, 98 S.E.2d 481 (1957).
67. 1 MORDECAI, LAW LECTURES 574 (1916); OSBORNE, MORTGAGES § 128 (1951). *In re* Castillian Apartments, 281 N.C. 709, 190 S.E.2d 161 (1972), which holds that a default on a first deed of trust which results in foreclosure of the first deed of trust is not "waste" within the meaning of a provision in a second deed of trust which stated that the indebtedness of the latter deed of trust would become due and payable if the mortgagor permits "any waste or injury to such extent as to impair the value of the premises as security." The Supreme Court of North Carolina held that the word "waste" referred only to waste in the traditional sense of destruction, impairment or injury to the property itself, citing Thomas v. Thomas, 166 N.C. 627, 82 S.E. 1032 (1914).

rents and profits which the mortgaged premises produce in the absence of a stipulation to the contrary.[68] Even after default, the mortgagor is entitled to the rents and profits of mortgaged premises prior to the time the mortgagee takes possession of the mortgaged premises.[69]

While entitled to possession prior to default in the absence of contrary stipulation, the mortgagor may so use the land that he will be liable for waste if his use substantially impairs the security.[70] The mortgagor also has such an interest in the mortgaged premises as will entitle him to maintain an action against the mortgagee or a third party for waste or injury to the mortgaged premises.[71]

§ 264. Mortgagee in Possession.

If the mortgagee takes possession of the mortgaged premises, which he is entitled to do upon default in payment of the mortgage indebtedness upon the date that it is due, in the absence of contrary stipulations, he is chargeable on an accounting for the rents and profits which the land produces,[72] or in the exercise of reasonable diligence could produce.[73] The mortgagee who takes possession has the duty of applying rentals received to the mortgage debt and is chargeable for a reasonable rental to be so applied.[74] This accounting will be made only in an action to redeem or in a foreclosure action.[75]

The mortgagee who takes possession of mortgaged premises is under an obligation to keep them in ordinary repair.[76] In his accounting for rents

---

68. Kistler v. Wilmington Dev. Co., 205 N.C. 755, 172 S.E. 413 (1934).
69. Gregg v. Williamson, 246 N.C. 356, 98 S.E.2d 481 (1957).
70. Tiffany, Real Property § 886 (abr. ed. 1940); Federal Land Bank v. Jones, 211 N.C. 317, 190 S.E. 479 (1937).
71. Id.
72. Green v. Rodman, 150 N.C. 176, 63 S.E. 732 (1909); Weathersbee v. Goodwin, 175 N.C. 234, 95 S.E. 491 (1918); Brannock v. Fletcher, 271 N.C. 65, 155 S.E.2d 532 (1967); Anderson v. Moore, 233 N.C. 299, 63 S.E.2d 641 (1951); Gregg v. Williamson, 246 N.C. 356, 98 S.E.2d 481 (1957). "Under North Carolina law, absent a special provision giving the mortgagee a right to receive the rents, a mortgagee must take possession of the mortgaged property in order to be entitled to the rents which issue therefrom." Golden Enterprises, Inc. v. United States, 566 F.2d 1207 at 1210 (4th Cir. 1977), citing Gregg v. Williamson, 246 N.C. 356, 98 S.E.2d 491 (1957); Kistler v. Development Co., 205 N.C. 755, 172 S.E. 413 (1934); Killibrew v. Hines, 104 N.C. 182, 10 S.E. 159 (1889).
73. Tiffany, Real Property § 878 (abr. ed. 1940); 1 Mordecai, Law Lectures 579 (1916).
74. Fleming v. Land Bank, 215 N.C. 414, 2 S.E.2d 3 (1939); Mills v. Bldg. & Loan Ass'n, 216 N.C. 664, 6 S.E.2d 549 (1939); Gregg v. Williamson, 246 N.C. 356, 98 S.E.2d 481 (1957). See Green v. Rodman, 150 N.C. 176, 63 S.E. 732 (1909), which states that a mortgagee who takes possession of mortgaged land "must account to the mortgagor for the 'highest fair rental and he becomes responsible for all such acts or omissions as would under the usual leases constitute claims on an ordinary tenant.'"
75. Brannock v. Fletcher, 271 N.C. 65, 155 S.E.2d 532 (1967).
76. Gregg v. Williamson, 246 N.C. 356, 98 S.E.2d 481 (1957).

and profits, he is credited with expenditures for necessary repairs.[77] The general rule is that a mortgagee in possession of real property is not entitled to be compensated or credited for improvements placed on the premises while he is in possession, without the consent of the mortgagor. The reason for this rule is that otherwise the mortgagee might "improve the mortgagor out of his estate" by rendering it more difficult for the mortgagor to redeem the premises.[78] Since an accounting is an equitable proceeding, however, in some circumstances where the mortgagee in possession in good faith places improvements on the land after being in possession for a long period of time, thinking himself to have an absolute estate in the land, the court may allow an accounting for the benefit of the mortgagee to prevent an unjust result where the land has been appreciably enhanced in value.[79] In any case, the improving mortgagee should not be charged on an accounting with an increased rental because of the enhanced value of the premises as a result of improvements made by the mortgagee in possession.[80]

§ 265. Duty to Pay Taxes as Between Mortgagor and Mortgagee.

The mortgagor in possession of mortgaged premises is the substantial owner of the property and the duty of paying taxes falls on him in all states.[81] If the mortgagor defaults in payment of the taxes, the mortgagee can make the payment and the money paid by the mortgagee to discharge such taxes shall become a lien prior to all other liens, and this lien may be enforced by action in the Superior Court.[82]

When the mortgagee is in possession, however, he is under a duty to pay the taxes, at least to the extent of the rents and profits received.[83] But since his payment of the taxes enures to the benefit of the mortgagor, upon an accounting in a suit for redemption or a suit for foreclosure, the mortgagee in possession who has paid the taxes is entitled to credit for the amount of taxes paid on the mortgaged property.

---

77. WALSH, MORTGAGES § 21 (1934). It has even been held that a mortgagee in possession is entitled to the costs of improvements made if the improvement made is of a permanent and beneficial nature and has been made by the mortgagee under the belief that his estate was absolute, if such improvement was made for the purpose of making the premises productive. *See* Gillis v. Martin, 17 N.C. 470 (1833).

78. OSBORNE, MORTGAGES § 169 (1951); Gillis v. Martin, 17 N.C. 470 (1833).

79. Wilson v. Fisher, 148 N.C. 535, 62 S.E. 622 (1908); Gillis v. Martin, 17 N.C. 470 (1833).

80. Gillis v. Martin, 17 N.C. 470 (1833).

81. WALSH, MORTGAGES § 24 (1934); Wooten v. Sugg, 114 N.C. 295, 19 S.E. 148 (1894).

82. N.C. GEN. STAT. § 105-386 (having the same effect as the former statute N.C. GEN. STAT. § 105-409). While this statute gives the mortgagee the right to protect himself by paying the taxes in the event of default of the mortgagor, he is under no duty to make the payment. He may instead stand by and permit the land to be sold at a tax foreclosure and may even buy in at the tax foreclosure sale. Redic v. Bank, 241 N.C. 152, 84 S.E.2d 542 (1954).

83. OSBORNE, MORTGAGES § 173 (1951).

In most modern mortgage transactions today an express provision is placed in the mortgage instrument that in case of a default in payment of the taxes for a certain period of time after they are due, the mortgagee may by notice to the mortgagor declare the entire debt due and he may then proceed to foreclose the mortgage as to the entire amount, including the taxes.

§ 266. Either Mortgagor or Mortgagee May Insure Mortgaged Property.

Both the mortgagor and the mortgagee of mortgaged real property have distinct insurable interests in the real property and each may therefore protect his undivided interest in the property by insurance against loss or other casualty.[84]

In the absence of an agreement in the mortgage requiring the insurance of the property by one of the parties for the benefit of the other, there is no duty on either to insure for the benefit of the other.[85] Each can protect his own interest.

It is a common practice today, however, for the usual mortgage to expressly include a provision for the mortgagor to keep the premises insured for the benefit of the mortgagee, insurance being taken by the mortgagor for the benefit of both the mortgagor and the mortgagee as their interests may appear. It is usually provided that if the mortgagor fails to maintain the insurance for the specified amount or fails to pay the premiums in accordance with the agreement, that the mortgagee shall have the right to take out such insurance and to charge the premiums paid against the mortgagor by adding them to the mortgage debt, enforceable by foreclosure along with the mortgage debt.[86]

Article IV. Transfer of Mortgagor's Interest

§ 267. Mortgagor's Right to Transfer Interest in Mortgaged Property Generally.

Since the mortgagor remains the substantial owner of real property after it is mortgaged, he has an interest in the property that can be transferred by sale, mortgage, lease, or otherwise.[87] While the mortgagee has legal title to mortgaged premises in North Carolina, the mortgagor has a beneficial title in his equity of redemption which he can freely alien.

---

84. WALSH, MORTGAGES § 25 (1934).
85. Id.
86. Id.
87. McKinney v. Sutphin, 196 N.C. 318, 145 S.E. 621 (1928); Gregg v. Williamson, 246 N.C. 356, 98 S.E.2d 481 (1957). The interest of the mortgagor is also subject to sale under execution by creditors. Schoffner v. Fogleman, 60 N.C. 564 (1864). See also N.C. GEN. STAT. § 1-315(3).

It should be noted, however, that if the mortgage has been properly executed and recorded it will attach to the property in the hands of whomsoever it comes; thus every transfer of the mortgaged premises is made subject to the mortgagee's rights.[88] What is actually transferred, then, is the mortgagor's equity of redemption or his right to pay the mortgage debt and to regain the title which he had at the time the mortgage was executed. If the transferee does not redeem by paying the debt, he may have his rights extinguished by foreclosure.[89]

§ 268. Where Transfer of Mortgagor's Interest Recites That the Property Is "Subject to" the Mortgage.

The mortgagor may transfer his interest in the mortgaged land to a purchaser who takes "subject to" the mortgage, which means that the transferee agrees, as between him and his transferor, that the transferee is not to be personally liable for payment of the mortgage debt;[90] if there is a mortgage on land and the mortgagor grants the land without noting the existence of the mortgage and no reference is made to it, the purchaser takes "subject to" the mortgage in the absence of any agreement to that effect. Where a transferee takes "subject to," or without mentioning, an existing mortgage on the land, the mortgage debt can be satisfied only out of the land or by suit against the transferor; the transferee does not become personally liable either to the mortgagor or the mortgagee to pay the mortgage debt. While the land remains subject to the mortgage and may be reached by the mortgagee in foreclosure to satisfy the mortgage debt, the grantee of the mortgagor does not become personally liable to pay a mortgage debt unless he expressly assumes to pay the debt.[91] Of course, the original mortgagor remains personally liable on the mortgage debt after transferring the mortgaged property.[92]

§ 269. Where Transfer of Mortgagor's Interest Recites That the Mortgagor's Grantee "Assumes" the Mortgage.

The mortgagor's grantee may become personally liable for the mortgage debt by expressly assuming and promising to pay the debt.[93] If he

---

88. McKinney v. Sutphin, 196 N.C. 318, 145 S.E. 621 (1928).
89. Pearce v. Watkins, 219 N.C. 636, 14 S.E.2d 653 (1941).
90. OSBORNE, MORTGAGES § 252 (1951).
91. Harvey v. Knitting Co., 197 N.C. 177, 148 S.E. 45 (1929). *Accord,* Arnold v. Howard, 29 N.C. App. 570, 225 S.E.2d 149 (1976), citing Henry v. Heggie, 163 N.C. 523, 79 S.E. 982 (1913).
92. Keller v. Parrish, 196 N.C. 733, 147 S.E. 9 (1929).
93. Parlier v. Miller, 186 N.C. 501, 119 S.E. 898 (1923); Baber v. Hanie, 163 N.C. 588, 80 S.E. 57 (1913); Sanders v. Griffin, 191 N.C. 447, 132 S.E. 157 (1926); Keller v. Parrish, 196 N.C. 733, 147 S.E. 9 (1929); Brown v. Turner, 202 N.C. 227, 162 S.E. 608 (1932); Beaver v. Ledbetter, 269 N.C. 142, 152 S.E.2d 165 (1967).

takes the mortgagor's deed and "assumes" the mortgage, not only is the land subject to foreclosure to satisfy the mortgage debt, but the mortgagor's transferee who makes such assumption becomes personally obligated to pay the debt. The mortgagee may proceed against the transferee to recover the indebtedness either by obtaining a deficiency judgment after foreclosure or by proceeding directly to obtain an *in personam* judgment for payment of the debt.[94] Even if there is an "assumption" by the mortgagor's transferee, however, the mortgagor remains liable for the mortgage debt to the mortgagee.[95]

The "assumption" of the mortgage debt may be either by agreement in writing or by parol[96] and can be enforced by the mortgagee against the one who assumes either upon third-party beneficiary contract principles or upon equitable principles.[97] Ordinarily the mere acceptance of a deed by a grantee will bind the grantee to pay the mortgage indebtedness if the deed has a provision therein whereby it is stated that the grantee assumes to pay the debt.[98]

Upon the assumption of the mortgage debt, the grantee becomes the principal obligor on the indebtedness and the grantor-mortgagor becomes, as between himself and the assuming grantee, a surety.[99] If the transferring mortgagor has to pay the mortgage because of a default by the assuming transferee, he is entitled to indemnification from the assuming transferee.[100]

---

94. Beaver v. Ledbetter, 269 N.C. 142, 152 S.E.2d 165 (1967).

95. Keller v. Parrish, 196 N.C. 733, 147 S.E. 9 (1929); Brown v. Turner, 202 N.C. 227, 162 S.E. 608 (1932).

96. Rector v. Lyda, 180 N.C. 577, 105 S.E. 170 (1966).

97. Baber v. Hanie, 163 N.C. 588, 80 S.E. 57 (1913); Keller v. Parrish, 196 N.C. 733, 147 S.E. 9 (1929).

98. Beaver v. Ledbetter, 269 N.C. 142, 152 S.E.2d 165 (1967). The latter case held, however, that where a mortgagor conveyed to a husband and wife as tenants by the entirety, and the husband alone assumed to pay the mortgage indebtedness without the knowledge of the wife, that the husband alone and not the wife was liable on the assumption. The case held that while the acceptance by the husband on behalf of the wife was sufficient to constitute a delivery, it did not bind the wife on the mortgage assumption.

99. Meredith College v. Lee, 212 N.C. 327, 193 S.E. 269 (1937); Brown v. Turner, 202 N.C. 227, 162 S.E. 608 (1932); Green v. Elias, 198 N.C. 256, 151 S.E. 247 (1930); Land Bank v. Page, 206 N.C. 18, 173 S.E. 312 (1934); Bank v. Whitehurst, 203 N.C. 302, 165 S.E. 795 (1932); State Planters Bank & Trust Co. v. Randolph, 207 N.C. 241, 176 S.E. 561 (1934).

100. The suretyship analogy can also be significant if the mortgagee releases a part of the security from a part of the obligations. To the extent of the value of the security that is released the mortgagor-transferor is released as a surety would be. In addition, if the mortgagee gives to the assuming transferee a binding extension of time for the payment of the mortgage debt, under suretyship law the mortgagor-transferor will be relieved of liability. *See* OSBORNE, MORTGAGES § 270 (1951); Bank v. Whitehurst, 203 N.C. 302, 165 S.E. 795 (1932).

With respect to a mortgage indebtedness which is a negotiable instrument, the Uniform Commercial Code provision N.C. GEN. STAT. § 25-3-606 would apply. If the obligee grants a binding extension of time to a grantee of the mortgaged premises who has assumed the mortgage such will discharge the mortgagor-maker of the negotiable instrument, unless the

If there is a novation, that is, if the mortgagee for a consideration agrees to a substitution of the mortgagor's transferee who assumes in lieu of the mortgagor, then the mortgagor who has assigned his interest in mortgaged property can be relieved of all liability.

§ 270. Conveyance of Mortgagor's Interest in Mortgaged Property to the Mortgagee.

While the preceding sections relate to the conveyance of the mortgagor's interest to third persons, can the mortgagor convey his equity of redemption to the mortgagee himself? As previously stated, courts of equity jealously guard a mortgagor's equity of redemption and will not allow the mortgagor, *at the inception of a mortgage* to contract it away or to clog or fetter it in any way.[101] If the purported mortgage in any way attempts to forfeit the mortgagor's interest upon default in payment upon a certain date, or attempts to tie it up in any way, requiring additional payment or providing that the mortgagee can purchase the absolute title by paying an additional amount, such provisions are invalid and unenforceable.[102] Wherever there is a mortgage the mortgagor must be entitled to receive back his land as free and unencumbered as it was before he executed the mortgage simply by paying the amount of the mortgage debt, plus interest and any costs accrued by reason of default. This, therefore, prevents any anticipatory conveyance of the mortgagor's equity of redemption at the time the mortgage is executed. But *subsequent* conveyances of the mortgagor's equity of redemption to the mortgagee are permissible under proper circumstances. For instance, if the mortgagor finds it difficult or impossible to pay the mortgage debt, he may desire to convey his interest in the property directly to the mortgagee to obviate the necessity of a foreclosure and to eliminate the possibility of a deficiency judgment if the foreclosure sale does not bring an amount equal to the amount of the indebtedness. This procedure may appeal to the mortgagee because of the expense and time consumption connected with foreclosure. Thus the parties may reach an understanding whereby the mortgagor, after the mortgage has been in force, conveys to the mortgagee his equity of redemption. If the mortgagee pays to the mortgagor a consideration for this conveyance and cancels the mortgage, the conveyance of the equity of redemption by the mortgagor to the mortgagee will be upheld.[103] It should be noted, however, that courts will regard the equity

---

obligee in making the extension expressly reserves his rights against the maker of the instrument (the transferring mortgagor). *But see* to the contrary Commercial Nat'l Bank v. Carson, 207 N.C. 495, 177 S.E. 335 (1934), which was decided before the Uniform Commercial Code was written and adopted.

101. Wilson v. Fisher, 148 N.C. 535, 62 S.E. 622 (1908).
102. *Id.*
103. Alford v. Moore, 161 N.C. 382, 77 S.E. 343 (1913).

of redemption as a precious right and even *subsequent* conveyances of the mortgagor to the mortgagee of the equity of redemption will be presumed fraudulent. Feeling that "Necessitous men are not, truly speaking, free men, but to answer any present emergency will submit to any terms the crafty may impose upon them,"[104] the courts presume that when the mortgagor conveys his equity of redemption to the mortgagee the transaction is fraudulent, even if it is subsequent to the execution of the mortgage as outlined. The mortgagee who buys the mortgagor's equity of redemption has the burden of proving that the transaction was fair and free of undue influence.[105]

§ 271. Acquisition of Mortgage Security by Owner of the Mortgaged Property; When Doctrine of Merger Applies.

When the owner of mortgaged land, who is primarily liable for payment of a debt secured by the mortgage, becomes also the owner of the indebtedness secured by the mortgage, and the security interest incident thereto, the debt is deemed paid and the land is discharged from the lien of the mortgage.[106] But the rule is not the same *where the owner of the mortgaged property who acquires the mortgage security is not personally liable for the payment of the mortgage debt.* In such case when the ownership of the mortgagor's interest in the real property and the ownership of the mortgagee's security interest therein become united in one person there is not deemed to be a merger as will extinguish the mortgage unless there is proof of an intention by the parties to merge the two interests. The intention of the holder of the two interests is the decisive consideration and no merger will take place if there is proof of an intention on his part to the contrary. In the absence of any intention as to whether the two interests will merge, the presumption is against the existence of an intention to merge on the part of the owner of the two interests in such case.[107]

---

104. Vernon v. Bethell, 2 Eden 113 (1762).

105. Alford v. Moore, 161 N.C. 382, 77 S.E. 343 (1913). This proof can be sustained by a showing that the transfer of the mortgagor's equity of redemption was at his initiative, that there was a consideration paid, and that the mortgagee did not use his power and position to drive an unfair bargain. *See also* Barnes v. Brown, 71 N.C. 507 (1874); McLeod v. Bullard, 84 N.C. 515 (1881); Cole v. Boyd, 175 N.C. 555, 95 S.E. 778 (1918); Jones v. Williams, 176 N.C. 245, 96 S.E. 1036 (1918).

106. Waff Bros., Inc. v. Bank of N.C., N.A., 289 N.C. 198, 221 S.E.2d 273 (1976), citing Hussey v. Hill, 120 N.C. 312, 26 S.E. 919 (1897).

107. *See* Waff Bros., Inc. v. Bank of N.C., N.A., *supra,* citing and quoting Furniture Co. v. Potter, 188 N.C. 145, 124 S.E. 122 (1924).

Article V. Transfer of Mortgagee's Interest

§ 272. Transfer of Mortgagee's Interest in Mortgaged Property Generally.

The mortgagee's interest in mortgaged land is transferable. The mortgagee's interest is composed of two things: (1) the debt or obligation, usually evidenced by a negotiable promissory note, and (2) his interest in the land which secures the obligation. It is often said that the debt or obligation is the principal thing and the security for the debt is the "incident" or "accessory" of the obligation.[108] This idea is of fundamental significance in considering the law relating to the transferability of the mortgagee's interest in the mortgage. This concept means that the security is inseparable from the obligation and that the person who holds the note or obligation is also entitled to the mortgage. Since the mortgagee owns a duality of interests, difficulties may arise when the mortgagee purports to transfer those interests to different persons. The various modes of transferring the mortgagee's interest and their effects will be considered in the following sections.

§ 273. Where the Mortgagee Transfers the Mortgage Debt Only.

Since a mortgage is a mere security for the debt, an assignment of the debt, which is the principal, carries with it the mortgage security, which is only the accessory.[109] As long as the debt exists, the security will follow it. Thus where the mortgagee assigns or negotiates a note secured by a mortgage to another, the mortgage is also automatically assigned, even though the assignee does not know that there is a mortgage when he takes the note.[110] The assignment of the mortgage, therefore, can be without a writing, and while the legal title to the real property does not pass, the assignee can nevertheless bring a suit to have the mortgage foreclosed to satisfy the debt.[111]

---

108. OSBORNE, MORTGAGES § 224 (1951).

109. *Id.;* MINOR & WURTS, REAL PROPERTY § 565 (1910). *See* Weil v. Davis, 168 N.C. 298, 84 S.E. 395 (1915); Stevens v. Turlington, 186 N.C. 191, 119 S.E. 210 (1923); Jenkins v. Wilkinson, 113 N.C. 532, 18 S.E. 696 (1893).

It should be noted that the transfer of the mortgagee's interest in the form of a release of the lien of a mortgage or deed of trust is valid and enforceable although not in writing. An oral agreement, made by a mortgagee, for a valuable consideration, to release a real estate mortgage does not come within the Statute of Frauds. *See* Nye v. Dev. Co., 10 N.C. App. 676, 179 S.E.2d 795 (1971), citing Stevens v. Turlington, 186 N.C. 191, 119 S.E. 210 (1923).

110. OSBORNE, MORTGAGES § 224 (1951).

111. If the assignment of the mortgage results from an assignment of the debt only, without a writing also assigning the mortgage instrument, signed, sealed and delivered, the mortgagee's assignee can only foreclose by judicial action. In order for the assignee of a mortgage to foreclose by exercising a power of sale in the mortgage, it must appear that there has been a valid written assignment of the mortgage by the mortgagor to the assignee. *Compare* Weil v. Davis, 168 N.C. 298, 84 S.E. 395 (1915).

Of course, if the mortgage transaction is evidenced by a deed of trust instead of a two-party

§ 274. Where the Mortgagee Transfers the Mortgage Only Without Transferring the Mortgage Debt.

Since the mortgage is only the incident of the mortgage debt, and since the person who holds the note or obligation is also entitled to the mortgage security, it has been held that a transfer of the mortgage without transfer of the indebtedness is a nullity, and that the transferee who takes an assignment of the mortgage without the note or obligation takes nothing.[112] Some authorities hold, however, that if the intent to assign the debt appears affirmatively although not expressed in the instruments, the debt will also pass with the assignment of a mortgage and there is a complete assignment of both.[113] Of course, even under the latter view, if the evidence of the indebtedness is a negotiable instrument, the prior assignee of the mortgage and indebtedness should not prevail against a holder in due course of the negotiable instrument if the mortgagor has been allowed to keep and negotiate the note subsequent to his prior transfer; the holder in due course, since he has the right on the debt, should also have the prior right in the mortgage security.[114]

---

mortgage, since the trustee of the deed of trust has legal title, the assignee of the debt could call on the trustee to foreclose the deed of trust under its power of sale without the necessity of a judicial action to foreclose.

It should be noted that the transfer of the mortgagee's interest in the form of a release of the lien of a mortgage or deed of trust is valid and enforceable although not in writing. An oral agreement, made by a mortgagee, for a valuable consideration, to release a real estate mortgage does not come within the Statute of Frauds. *See* Nye v. Dev. Co., 10 N.C. App. 676, 179 S.E.2d 795 (1971), citing Stevens v. Turlington, 186 N.C. 191, 119 S.E. 210 (1923).

112. If the transferee of the mortgagee takes only the mortgage, without taking the note or other obligation, and the mortgagee subsequently negotiates the note to another transferee, the transferee of the mortgage only would have nothing while the transferee of the note only would have the benefit of the note *and* the security.

113. WALSH, MORTGAGES § 58 (1934) states: "Though the debt is the principal thing and the mortgage its incident, nevertheless the security which the mortgage gives to the creditor is the element of greatest importance and value in the secured debt as property, and an assignment of the mortgage, therefore, is universally regarded, by laymen and lawyers alike, as an assignment of both debt and mortgage. Certainly very definite proof that an assignment of the debt was not intended should be required to rebut the inference to the contrary which arises from the formal assignment of the mortgage."

114. The majority view in the United States is that a mortgage securing a negotiable instrument has imparted to it the qualities of negotiability of the obligation it secures. Thus, a negotiation of a negotiable instrument secured by a mortgage, to a holder who takes it in good faith, for value and without notice before maturity will take the mortgage as he takes the note free from personal defenses that would have been available to the mortgagor against the mortgagee. Carpenter v. Longan, 83 U.S. 271, 21 L. Ed. 313 (1872); OSBORNE, MORTGAGES § 231 (1951); WALSH, MORTGAGES § 61 (1934). *See* Parker v. Thomas, 192 N.C. 798, 136 S.E. 118 (1926); Coor v. Spicer, 65 N.C. 401 (1871). If the note secured by the mortgage is nonnegotiable in character, all defenses available to the mortgagor against the original mortgagee are available as against the mortgagee's assignee. WALSH, MORTGAGES § 59 (1934).

§ 275. Where the Mortgagee Transfers the Mortgage and Note or Indebtedness at the Same Time by Written Instruments.

The usual and better way of assigning a mortgage is to assign the note or other mortgage indebtedness at the same time the mortgage is assigned by formal writing, signed and sealed by the mortgagee. Formal written assignment of both the indebtedness and the mortgage is advisable in order to permit the assignee to record the assignment in the public registry, to enable him to foreclose under power of sale where provided in the instrument, and to avoid possible problems which may arise from transfer of the mortgage to one person and transfer of the indebtedness to another.

Article VI. Right of Mortgagee to Foreclose

§ 276. Nature of Mortgagee's Right to Foreclose Generally.

Foreclosure is a proceeding whereby the mortgagee, upon default of the mortgagor in payment of the obligation, can terminate the mortgagor's equity of redemption and have the mortgaged property subjected to the payment of the mortgage debt. It is the procedure developed in equity and in law whereby the mortgagee may realize on his security by having the mortgaged property sold and the proceeds applied to the mortgage indebtedness, thus permitting the mortgagee to protect his investment when the mortgagor fails to pay the debt or otherwise fails to adhere to the mortgage agreement. Like the right to redeem given the mortgagor, the right to foreclose given to the mortgagee upon the default of the mortgagor is an inherent right flowing from the mortgage relationship.

§ 277. When Right to Foreclose Accrues; Acceleration Clause.

The right of the mortgagee to foreclose accrues only when the mortgagor defaults or breaches a stipulation with respect to the mortgage obligation. Most frequently, the default consists of the mortgagor's failure to pay the mortgage debt when it becomes due, on "law day," but under some mortgages the default authorizing a foreclosure may amount to something else. For instance, modern mortgages usually include "acceleration clauses" whereby the mortgagor is obligated to perform specified acts and if the mortgagor fails to perform such acts the whole mortgage is made to become due and payable immediately.[115] A type of acceleration clause — the due-on-sale provision — is discussed in the next section.

---

115. *E.g.*, an express stipulation may confer the right to foreclose upon the mortgagor's failure to pay one installment on the obligation, his failure to pay the taxes, or to procure or pay the premiums on insurance. Nonperformance of the stipulated condition will advance the maturity of the debt at the option of the mortgagee. *See* Sanders v. Hamilton, 229 N.C. 43, 47 S.E.2d 472 (1942).

See Furst v. Loftin, 29 N.C. App. 248, 224 S.E.2d 641 (1976), which holds that a clause

§ 278. Due-On-Sale Clause.

In 1976, the North Carolina Supreme Court upheld the validity of a "due-on-sale" clause in a deed of trust.[116] It was held that the clause involved did not result in the type of substantial or direct restraint on alienation that would render it invalid under traditional property law concepts.[117] It was also held that the clause was validly exercised even though the security was not impaired and its transfer did not affect repayment of the original loan.[118] Absent fraud, duress, inequitable or unconscionable conduct on the part of the lender, the clause was found to be *reasonable per se*. Thus, it could be validly exercised for the sole purpose of obtaining higher interest rates or for accelerating repayment of the loan.[119] In addition, the Court rejected a contention that North Carolina General Statutes, § 25-1-208 precluded acceleration of the debt. The good faith standard of that Uniform Commercial Code statute (assuming *arguendo* its applicability to contracts involving land), according to the Court, applied only to insecurity-type clauses. "These clauses are clearly distinguished from default-type clauses (such as the due-on-sale clause involved in our case) where the right to accelerate is *conditioned* upon the occurrence of a condition which is within the control of the debtor." [120]

The decision also noted that policy and equitable factors were not unfavorably affected by the use of the clause.[121] Indeed, the majority opinion seemed to favor use of it as a fair arrangement for both lender and borrower, assuming no prepayment penalty was involved.[122]

---

in a deed of trust is valid where it specified that the lender shall have the option of declaring the entire mortgage indebtedness due and payable immediately in the event certain conditions and covenants required of the borrower (procurement and payment for insurance on the mortgaged property) are not complied with. *See also In re* Foreclosure of Deed of Trust, 41 N.C. App. 563, 255 S.E.2d 260 (1979) (failure to pay ad valorem taxes as required by deed of trust).

116. Crockett v. Savings & Loan Assoc., 289 N.C. 620, 224 S.E.2d 580 (1976). The pertinent clause reads, in part, as follows:

> or if the property herein conveyed is transferred without the written assent of Association, then in all or any of said events the full principal sum with all unpaid interest thereon shall at the option of Association, its successors or assigns, become at once due and payable without further notice and irrespective of the date of maturity expressed in said note.

117. *Id.*
118. *Id.*
119. *Id.*
120. *Id.* at 289 N.C. 631.
121. *Id.*
122. *Id. Cf.* a strongly worded dissent by Justice Lake beginning at 289 N.C. 632. *See also* N.C. GEN. STAT. §§ 24-1.1A(b) & 24-10(d). For a law review article highly critical of the *Crockett v. Savings & Loan Assoc.* decision *see generally* Real Property Security — North Carolina Deals Mortgagors a Bad Hand, 13 WAKE FOREST L. REV. 490 (1977).

The *Crockett* decision cites the following law review articles as dealing with the economic

§ 279. Types of Foreclosure Available in North Carolina Generally.

There are two types of foreclosure available in North Carolina: (1) foreclosure by action, and (2) foreclosure under power of sale.[123]

---

and legal problems involved with due-on-sale clauses: Bonanno, *Due on Sale and Prepayment Clauses in Real Estate Financing in California in Times of Fluctuating Interest Rates — Legal Issues and Alternatives,* 6 U. OF SAN. FRAN. L. REV. 267 (1971-72); Volkmer, *The Application of the Restraints on Alienation Doctrine to Real Property Security Interests,* 58 IOWA L. REV. 750 (1973); Warren, *Is the Practice of Raising the Interest Rate in Return for Not Exercising an Acceleration Clause on Assumption of a Mortgage Illegal in Texas as a Restraint on Alienation?* 13 S. TEX. L.J. 296 (1971-72); Comment, *Mortgages — A Catalogue and Critique on the Role of Equity in the Enforcement of Modern-Day "Due-on-Sale" Clauses,* 26 ARK. L. REV. 485 (1972-73); Comment, *Mortgages: Restrictions on Transfer of the Fee — Effect of Due-on-Sale Clauses,* 28 OKLA. L. REV. 418 (1975); Comment, *Acceleration Clauses as a Protection for Mortgagees in a Tight Money Market,* 20 S.D.L. REV. 329 (1975); Comment, *Judicial Treatment of the Due-on-Sale Clause: The Case for Adopting Standards of Reasonableness and Unconscionability,* 27 STAN. L. REV. 1109 (1974-75); Comment, *Debt Acceleration on Transfer of Mortgaged Property,* 29 U. OF MIAMI L. REV. 584 (1975); Note, *The Case for Relief from Due-on-Sale Provisions: A Note to Hellbaum v. Lytton Savings and Loan Association,* 22 HASTINGS L.J. 431 (1970-71).

123. North Carolina does not recognize the common-law "strict foreclosure" whereby the mortgagee procures a decree that if payment is not made by a certain date that the mortgagee will get title free of the mortgagor's equity of redemption. In North Carolina, the mortgagee procures a decree that the land be sold and that the proceeds be applied to the payment of the encumbrance and costs. *See* Bradburn v. Roberts, 148 N.C. 214, 61 S.E. 617 (1908); 1 MORDECAI, LAW LECTURES 584 (1916).

As a consequence of the decision in Turner v. Blackburn, 389 F. Supp. 1250 (W.D.N.C. 1975), the North Carolina General Assembly in 1975 enacted N.C. GEN. STAT. §§ 45-21.16, 45-21.16A, 45-21.17, 45-21.21, 45-21.29, and 45-21.33, setting out new procedures to effect valid foreclosures under powers of sale. The case of Turner v. Blackburn, *supra,* held that a foreclosure of a deed of trust under a power of sale was an unconstitutional deprivation of the mortgagor's property where the mortgagor had not been given prior notice of the foreclosure and had not been given an opportunity for a timely hearing prior to the foreclosure. The three-judge court of the United States District Court for the Western District of North Carolina found that the requirements of former N.C. GEN. STAT. § 45-21.17 that a public notice of foreclosure need only be posted at the courthouse door for thirty days and that an advertisement should be run in a newspaper published or generally circulated in the county as specified by the statute were not sufficient to meet due process requirements under the fourteenth amendment of the United States Constitution.

Notwithstanding the decision of Turner v. Blackburn, *supra,* the North Carolina Court of Appeals held in the case of Britt v. Britt, 26 N.C. App. 132, 215 S.E.2d 172 (1975), decided subsequent to the *Turner* case, that notice of a foreclosure sale posted at the courthouse door and advertised in a newspaper as provided in the former statute (N.C. GEN. STAT. § 45-21.17) was sufficient to meet due process requirements. The North Carolina Court of Appeals cited Armeta v. Nussbaum, 519 S.W.2d 673 (Texas Civ. Ct. App. 1975), to the effect that a personal notice and a hearing is not necessary to make a foreclosure under a power of sale valid under the Constitution provided notice of the foreclosure is published as provided by the statute.

With respect to foreclosures under powers of sale subsequent to the 1975 legislation, however, statutory provisions relating to giving notice that a foreclosure sale is to be held and providing an opportunity for a hearing in connection with the foreclosure should be followed strictly.

Foreclosure by action is available in every mortgage upon default, whereas foreclosure under power of sale is not available except where the mortgage or deed of trust expressly confers the power.

§ 280. Foreclosure by Action.

(a) *In general.* The mortgagee may bring an action to foreclose the mortgagor's equity of redemption by bringing an action to have the mortgaged property sold at a judicial sale. The mortgagee brings his action, praying that the land be sold under judicial process and that the proceeds be applied to the mortgage debt. Upon the sale of the property on foreclosure sale pursuant to a judicial decree, assuming there are no valid defenses, the purchaser at the foreclosure sale obtains the legal title to the property free of any claims of the mortgagor or holder of the equity of redemption.

(b) *Jurisdiction and venue in actions to foreclose.* The action must be brought in the county in which some part of the land lies.[124] Depending on the amount of the indebtedness or the amount in controversy, it would seem that the action may be brought in either the District Court or in the Superior Court in the county in which the land lies.[125]

(c) *Parties to foreclosure action.* The mortgagee, or trustee in a deed of trust, is an indispensable party plaintiff in an action to foreclose the mortgage.[126] As previously indicated, every person who has any interest in the equity of redemption that may be cut off by a valid foreclosure must be made a party defendant in an action to foreclose,[127] including the mortgagor's widow,[128] his heirs or devisees,[129] subsequent transferees, judgment creditors and other lien holders.[130] If they are not made parties

---

[124] N.C. GEN. STAT. § 1-76. A foreclosure proceeding under an order of court is a civil action, an equitable proceeding. Since a Clerk of Superior Court has no general equity jurisdiction, an attempted foreclosure by a special proceeding before a Clerk of the Superior Court was held to be a nullity in Shaw v. Wolf, 23 N.C. App. 73, 208 S.E.2d 214 (1974).

[125] *See* N.C. GEN. STAT. § 7A-243. A "special proceeding" in the Superior Court is not the proper proceeding for foreclosure of a mortgage or deed of trust. Shaw v. Wolf, 23 N.C. App. 73, 208 S.E.2d 214 (1974).

[126] Grady v. Parker, 228 N.C. 54, 44 S.E.2d 449 (1947); East Carolina Lumber Co. v. Pamlico County, 250 N.C. 681, 110 S.E.2d 278 (1959). If the trustee in a deed of trust refuses to act as plaintiff, he must nevertheless be joined as a party defendant. Underwood v. Otwell, 269 N.C. 571, 153 S.E.2d 40 (1967).

[127] Riddick v. Davis, 220 N.C. 120, 16 S.E.2d 662 (1947).

[128] Oil Co. v. Richardson, 271 N.C. 696, 157 S.E.2d 369 (1967). *See also* N.C. GEN. STAT. § 45-45.

[129] Jessup v. Nixon, 199 N.C. 122, 154 S.E. 18 (1930); Hinkle v. Walker, 213 N.C. 657, 197 S.E. 129 (1938).

[130] Stainback v. Gaddy, 21 N.C. 479 (1837); Tucker v. White, 22 N.C. 289 (1839); Pearce v. Watkins, 219 N.C. 636, 14 S.E.2d 653 (1941); Dickerson v. Simmons, 141 N.C. 325, 53 S.E. 850 (1906); Wilson v. Union Trust Co., 200 N.C. 788, 158 S.E. 479 (1931). *See* LAKE, NORTH CAROLINA PRACTICE METHODS § 144 (1952).

defendant in the foreclosure proceeding, there will be no valid foreclosure as to their interests and their respective rights of redemption will not be terminated.[131]

(d) *Proceedings in foreclosure by action; pleadings; sales.* The complaint in a foreclosure action must set forth the mortgage contract, alleging facts entitling the plaintiff to a money judgment by reason of a breach or default, identifying the mortgaged property, and asking for a foreclosure of the mortgage security. Process is served on the defendant mortgagor and any other person entitled to redeem who may answer the complaint as in the case of any other civil action or who may submit to a default judgment. If the mortgagor or other person entitled to redeem has any defenses to the action, such as payment, release, satisfaction, binding extension of time given by the mortgagee, or other defense, he may raise them by his answer. If a defense is raised by the answer, a hearing is had upon the issues and if the court finds for the plaintiff mortgagee a decree or judgment of foreclosure is rendered establishing the existence of the debt and its nonpayment when due and that the plaintiff should have the relief that he seeks. The court finds the exact amount of the mortgage indebtedness due the complainant and that it was secured by a mortgage which identifies specific real property. In addition, since the primary object of a foreclosure proceeding is to satisfy the indebtedness out of the mortgaged property, the court will order that the property subject to the mortgage be sold to pay the amount of the mortgage debt. The decree contains not only an order for a sale of real property to satisfy the debt, but it sets out the court's directions for conduct of the sale.

The decree may name the trustee of a deed of trust as commissioner to hold the sale or it may name some other person to act as commissioner.[132] It may require the commissioner to give a bond.[133] The judge shall fix the compensation to the commissioner for conducting the foreclosure sale and shall provide that his payment shall come from the proceeds of the sale.[134]

---

131. If any person who owns any part of the equity of redemption is not made a party to the foreclosure proceeding, there is no valid foreclosure and his respective share of the right of redemption is not cut off. He will still have the right to redeem the land from the purchaser at the foreclosure sale by paying the mortgage debt, plus interest and costs accrued. It is therefore necessary for the mortgagee's attorney to check the status of the title of the mortgagor to determine if his equity of redemption or any part thereof has been transferred, either as a result of the transfer of the mortgagor's interest or by reason of his death or transfer of his title or any interest therein by operation of law. This impairs the utility and convenience of the *action* to foreclose and is the principal reason that most mortgages today include a provision authorizing foreclosure by power of sale without the necessity of a judicial action.

132. N.C. GEN. STAT. § 1-339.4. *See generally* LAKE, NORTH CAROLINA PRACTICE METHODS §§ 141-152 (1952).

133. N.C. GEN. STAT. § 1-339.10.

134. N.C. GEN. STAT. § 1-339.11.

§ 280   MORTGAGES AND DEEDS OF TRUST   § 280

Directions concerning the sale include the manner and extent of notice that must be given of the time, place and manner of the sale and any terms or conditions of the sale. The court may direct that the purchaser must pay cash, make a cash deposit, or order the land to be sold in separate parcels or in gross.[135]

Public sales to foreclose must be held in accordance with the chapter on "Judicial Sales" in the General Statutes of North Carolina.[136] After a public sale has been held, the commissioner who holds it must report the sale within five days to the Clerk of the Superior Court in the county where the action was brought.[137] At any time within ten days after the filing of the report of the sale, anyone may come in and file an "upset bid" with the Clerk of the Superior Court with respect to the sale, which has the effect of requiring a resale of the property after readvertisement as required by statute.[138] The upset bid requires an advanced bid of at least 10 percent of the first $1,000 of the last highest bid plus 5 percent of any excess over the original $1,000 bid, with a minimum advanced bid of $25 being required.[139] Upon a resale as a result of the upset bid, the amount of the upset bid is the initial bid at the resale and, in the absence of any other bidding at the resale, the commissioner holding such resale shall report the upset bid amount as the last highest bid within five days of such resale, where it is again subject to upset bid requiring possible resales. Finally, when there are no more upset bids and the time for upset bids has expired and there are no further resales, the sale can be confirmed by the court.

No foreclosure sale under judicial foreclosure is final and no title passes to the purchaser until the court confirms the sale,[140] which cannot be done until the time for upset bids has elapsed under the statute.[141] When the sale is confirmed, however, the court's decree will order that a deed be prepared and delivered to the purchaser at the foreclosure sale by the commissioner holding the foreclosure sale, and such deed will pass title to the purchaser.[142]

---

135. N.C. GEN. STAT. §§ 1-339.9, 1-339.13.
136. N.C. GEN. STAT. §§ 1-339.1 through 1-339.40. *See generally* LAKE, NORTH CAROLINA PRACTICE METHODS §§ 141-152 (1952), for detailed procedures for foreclosing by judicial action.
137. N.C. GEN. STAT. § 1-339.24 provides what must be shown in such report.
138. N.C. GEN. STAT. § 1-339.27.
139. N.C. GEN. STAT. § 1-339.25.
140. N.C. GEN. STAT. § 1-339.28. *See* Baker v. Murphry, 250 N.C. 346, 108 S.E.2d 644 (1959); Anderson v. Moore, 233 N.C. 299, 63 S.E.2d 641 (1951); Bank v. Stone, 213 N.C. 598, 197 S.E. 132 (1938).
141. N.C. GEN. STAT. § 1-339.28.
142. N.C. GEN. STAT. § 1-329.29. The deed shall include the authority of the person making the deed, the title of the action in which it is made, the name of the person making the deed, the fact that the sale was duly advertised, the date of the sale, the name of the highest bidder and the price bid, that the sale has been confirmed, that the terms of the sale

The person holding the foreclosure sale as commissioner must file with the Clerk of the Superior Court an account of his receipts and disbursements in connection with the foreclosure sale.[143] The foreclosure sale may produce more or less than the amount of the mortgage debt. If there is a surplus beyond what is due on the mortgage debt, the mortgagor-debtor is entitled to the surplus.[144] If the sale does not bring the total amount of the indebtedness, the typical judgment in the foreclosure action provides for a personal judgment as well as an *in rem* judgment authorizing sale of the mortgaged property; when the sale does not bring the entire amount of the mortgage debt, the deficiency may be recovered pursuant to the personal judgment in the same manner as other judgments. This statement assumes the inapplicability of anti-deficiency legislation.[145]

§ 281. Foreclosure of Mortgages and Deeds of Trust Under Power of Sale.

(a) *In general.* To obviate the necessity of bringing an action in the courts to foreclose, most deeds of trust and mortgages executed in North Carolina today contain a "power of sale" whereby the instruments confer upon the trustee or mortgagee the "power" to sell the real property mortgaged without any order of court in the event of a default. This power to foreclose without judicial proceedings is available, however, only when provided in the deed of trust or mortgage and the provisions in the instrument creating the power must be followed strictly.[146] In addition,

---

have been complied with, and that the person executing the deed has been duly authorized to execute it.

The doctrine *caveat emptor* applies to judicial sales to foreclose mortgages or deeds of trust and a bidder at a foreclosure sale will not be relieved of his bid and liability therefor due to shortage in acreage or lack of access to the property when he had an opportunity to discover the facts. Walton v. Cagle, 269 N.C. 177, 152 S.E.2d 312 (1967). *See* N.C. Gen. Stat. § 1-339.30, which makes provisions for liabilities of bidders who fail to comply with their bids.

143. N.C. Gen. Stat. § 1-339.31.

144. Gahagan v. Whitehurst, 211 N.C. 280, 189 S.E. 765 (1937). Since it may be difficult to determine exactly who is entitled to any such surplus, it is wise for any person holding the sale to pay the amount of the surplus to the Clerk of the Superior Court to hold for such persons as may appear and establish their claims thereto. *See* Lake, North Carolina Practice Methods §§ 152, 180 (1952) and N.C. Gen. Stat. § 45-21.31. *Compare* Koob v. Koob, 283 N.C. 129, 195 S.E.2d 552 (1973).

145. N.C. Gen. Stat. § 45-21.38. *See* § 282 *infra*.

146. *See* Eubanks v. Becton, 158 N.C. 230, 73 S.E. 1009 (1912); Worley v. Worley, 214 N.C. 311, 199 S.E. 82 (1938); Spain v. Hines, 214 N.C. 432, 200 S.E. 25 (1938). It is particularly important to a purchaser at the foreclosure sale to see that all conditions specified by the instrument and the requirements of the statute are complied with. If they have not been complied with the purchaser will not receive a good title and the equity of redemption of the mortgagor or his assignees will not be extinguished. *See* General Realty Co. v. Lewis, 212 N.C. 45, 192 S.E. 902 (1937).

notwithstanding what the provisions in the deed of trust or mortgage state, there are certain minimum requirements specified by statute that must be complied with in the conduct of a sale under a power of sale which have been designed to protect the holder of the mortgagor's interest.

Although foreclosure by sale remains advantageous to the lender from the standpoint of relative simplicity of procedure, a new statutory scheme has been in effect in North Carolina since 1975 providing for notices and hearings where foreclosure sales are held under powers of sale in deeds of trust and mortgages.[147] These statutes were enacted as a consequence of the decision of Turner v. Blackburn,[148] which held that the previously existing power of sale foreclosure statutes violated procedural due process and were unconstitutional in that they did not require personal notice to be given to the mortgagor and an opportunity for a hearing prior to having his property sold on a foreclosure sale. This new statutory scheme is discussed in the next subsection.

(b) *Procedure for exercising power of sale to foreclose.*[149] The mortgage or deed of trust may itself provide for the notice that must be given by the mortgagee or trustee by advertisement or otherwise before a valid foreclosure can be had under a power of sale. *In addition,* there are statutes that set out the procedures that a mortgagee or trustee must take in order to foreclose a mortgage or deed of trust under a power of sale.

Prior to the decision of *Turner v. Blackburn, supra,* the North Carolina Supreme Court held, in the absence of a contrary stipulation in the instrument, that it was not necessary to give personal notice to the mortgagor-debtor of an intention to foreclose a mortgage or deed of trust. If the mortgage or deed of trust contained a power of sale and the obligor defaulted, the mortgagee or trustee could simply post a notice on the courthouse door for thirty days and publish a notice in a newspaper circulated in the county where the land was located once per week for four weeks that a sale for foreclosure was to be held.

Since June 6, 1975, however, as a consequence of *Turner v. Blackburn, supra,* the statutes of North Carolina now require that a hearing shall be held before the Clerk of the Superior Court in the county where the land is situated prior to any foreclosure sale under a power of sale in a mortgage or deed of trust.[150] A mortgagee or trustee who seeks to exercise a

---

147. N.C. Sess. Laws 1975, c. 492, codified as N.C. Gen. Stat. §§ 45-21.9, 45-21.16, 45-21.16A, 45-21.17, 45-21.21, 45-21.29, 45-21.33, and 45-21.45. The new statutes became effective on June 6, 1975.

148. 389 F. Supp. 1250 (W.D.N.C. 1975).

149. *See* Turner v. Blackburn, 389 F. Supp. 1250 (W.D.N.C. 1975); N.C. Gen. Stat. §§ 45-21.16, 45-21.16A, 45-21.17, 45-21.21, 45-21.29, 45-21.29A, 45-21.30, 45-21.33 and 45-21.45. For an article setting out an analysis of the 1975 legislation and a suggested procedure for effecting a foreclosure under the new statutes, *see* Glover, *Real Property — Changes in North Carolina's Foreclosure Law,* 54 N.C.L. Rev. 903 (1976).

150. N.C. Gen. Stat. § 45-21.16(d).

power of sale to foreclose a mortgage or deed of trust must serve a notice of the hearing upon each party entitled to notice as set out in the statute.[151] Service of the notice of the hearing may be in any manner provided by the Rules of Civil Procedure for the service of summons, by registered or certified mail, or in some instances through the posting of notice upon the property involved.[152] The notice of hearing must apprise a party entitled to notice of the following: (1) the particular real estate security interest being foreclosed, with a description sufficient to identify the real property, including its date; (2) the name and address of the holder of the security interest, and if different from the original holder, his name and address; (3) the nature of the default claimed; (4) the fact, if such be the case, that the secured creditor has accelerated the maturity of the debt; (5) any right of the debtor to pay the indebtedness if such is permitted; (6) the right of the debtor (or other party served) to appear before the Clerk of the Superior Court at a time and on a date specified, at which appearance he shall be afforded the opportunity to show cause as to why the foreclosure should not be allowed to be held; the notice shall contain a statement that if the debtor does not intend to contest the creditor's allegations of default, the debtor does not have to appear at the hearing and that his failure to attend the hearing will not affect his right to pay the indebtedness and thereby prevent the proposed sale, or to attend the actual sale, should he elect to do so; (7) that if the foreclosure sale is consummated the purchaser will be entitled to possession of the real estate as of the date of delivery of his deed, and that the debtor, if still in possession, can then be evicted; (8) that the debtor should keep the trustee or mortgagee notified in writing of his address so that he can be mailed copies of the notice of foreclosure setting forth the terms under which the sale will be held, and notice of any postponements or resales; (9) if the notice of hearing is intended to serve also as a notice of sale it should include such additional information as is set forth in North Carolina General Statutes, § 45-21.16A.[153]

Upon the hearing, the Clerk of the Superior Court shall consider the evidence of the parties and if he finds the existence of (i) a valid debt of which the party seeking to foreclose is the holder, (ii) default; (iii) a right to foreclose under the instrument, and (iv) notice to those entitled to notice as provided by North Carolina General Statutes, § 45-21.16 (b), the

---

151. N.C. GEN. STAT. § 45-21.16(a), (b). This notice shall be served upon (1) any person to whom the security instrument directs notice to be sent in case of default; (2) any person obligated to pay the indebtedness against whom the holder of the indebtedness intends to assert liability; and (3) the record owner or owners of the real estate as defined by the statute. *See* Ludwig v. Hart, 40 N.C. App. 188, 252 S.E.2d 270 (1979) voiding a portion of a judgment directing foreclosure where the trustee was not made a party to the action. *See also In re* Foreclosure of Norton, 41 N.C. App. 529, 255 S.E.2d 287 (1979).

152. N.C. GEN. STAT. § 45-21.16(a).
153. N.C. GEN. STAT. § 45-21.16(c).

Clerk shall find that the trustee or mortgagee can proceed under the instrument, and can give notice of and conduct a sale under the power of sale.[154]

A hearing cannot be waived simply as a result of the lapse of time or failure of a person entitled to notice to respond. In order to waive a hearing one entitled to notice of the hearing must *affirmatively* sign a waiver on a form mailed to him *by the Clerk* upon the request of the trustee or mortgagee subsequent to the notice of hearing. If one entitled to a notice of the hearing signs such waiver, the Clerk in his discretion may dispense with the hearing and proceed to issue the order authorizing the foreclosure sale.[155] Of course, if the party entitled to notice does not appear, the hearing can proceed in his absence on evidence adduced by the mortgagee or trustee and the Clerk can make his findings and the appropriate order. The statute denominates the Clerk's finding with respect to foreclosure as a "judicial act" and provides that the Clerk's finding or refusal to find may be appealed to the judge of the appropriate district or superior court within ten days after said act.[156]

In addition to the "notice of hearing" provisions as set out above, North Carolina General Statutes, § 45-21.17 provides for the "notice of sale" prerequisites which must be adhered to pursuant to the Clerk's findings as set out in North Carolina General Statutes, § 45-21.16 (b). In addition to complying with such provisions with respect to the posting or publishing the notice of sale as are contained in the security instrument, the statute requires the posting of the notice of sale at the courthouse door in the county where the land is situated for twenty days immediately preceding the sale. In addition, the notice of sale must be published in a newspaper qualified for legal advertising in the county once per week for at least two successive weeks. Furthermore, the Clerk may in his discretion upon application of any interested party authorize such additional advertisement as in the opinion of the Clerk will serve the interests of the parties. The period from the date of the first publication in the newspaper to the date of the last publication shall not be less than seven days, including Sundays, and the date of the last publication in the newspaper

---

154. N.C. GEN. STAT. § 45-21.16(d). *See* the recent Court of Appeals decisions of Golf Vistas v. Mortgage Investors, 39 N.C. App. 230, 249 S.E.2d 815 (1978) and *In re* Watts, 38 N.C. App. 90, 247 S.E.2d 427 (1978) discussing the proper method for invoking equitable jurisdiction to enjoin a foreclosure sale. The Golf Vistas decision, at 39 N.C. App. 232, summarizes as follows:

> We hold, simply, as we did in *In re Watts* ... that the hearing provided for in G.S. 45-21.16 was not intended to settle all matters in controversy between the parties and that the appropriate means for invoking equity jurisdiction is an action pursuant to G.S. 45-21.34.

155. N.C. GEN. STAT. § 45-21-16(f).

156. N.C. GEN. STAT. § 45-21.16(d). *See* Hassell v. Wilson, 44 N.C. App. 434, 261 S.E.2d 227 (1980) discussing briefly the impropriety of an independent action seeking to attack a judgment ordering foreclosure entered by the Clerk of Superior Court.

shall not be more than ten days preceding the date of the sale. The notice of sale shall be mailed at least twenty days prior to the date of the sale to each party entitled to notice of the hearing as provided in North Carolina General Statutes, § 45-21.16 whose address is known to the mortgagee or trustee or any other person who desires a copy of the notice of sale who has complied with North Carolina General Statutes, § 45-21.17 (5) (a).

As a result of the enactment of the foregoing amendments to the statutes relating to foreclosures of mortgages and deeds of trust under powers of sale, the former laws and practices prevalent in North Carolina have been drastically changed. There is no longer simply a "contractually permitted" foreclosure without the intervention of the judicial process. Pursuant to the decision of *Turner v. Blackburn* [157] and North Carolina General Statutes, Chapter 45, Article 2A, which was amended in 1975, *every foreclosure, even under power of sale, is in effect a "judicial foreclosure."* While a foreclosure under a power of sale can be more promptly and expeditiously effected than can a foreclosure by ordinary civil action, perhaps, the current statutes require that a "notice of hearing" be served in a defined way on designated parties whose interests are to be foreclosed or affected. Such parties are entitled to a hearing before the Clerk of the Superior Court, who must make specific findings establishing grounds for the foreclosure before he can authorize the foreclosure sale. The Clerk's findings, or refusal to find, as to the facts that entitle a mortgagee or trustee to hold a foreclosure sale are expressly declared to be "judicial acts" that can be appealed to the courts.

The mortgagee or trustee who seeks to foreclose a mortgage or deed of trust under a power of sale contained in the security instrument should follow strictly the provisions of North Carolina General Statutes, Chapter 45, Article 2A, as amended, to make certain (1) that all requisite parties have adequate and timely notice of the foreclosure hearing as set out in the statutes; (2) that all requirements for the hearing before the Clerk and the requisite findings are made by the Clerk; and (3) that the notices of sale are published, posted and mailed at the appropriate times to the persons and in the manner specified by the statutes, in order to meet all due process and substantive requirements to which the statutes are aimed.[158]

There must, of course, be a default entitling the creditor to foreclose.[159] Acceleration clauses are generally placed in mortgages and deeds of trust which make the whole indebtedness become due upon default in the

---

[157]. 389 F. Supp. 1250 (W.D.N.C. 1975).

[158]. An article by Glover, *Real Property — Changes in North Carolina's Foreclosure Law*, 54 N.C.L. REV. 903, at 921, sets out a "suggested procedure" for foreclosing under a power of sale pursuant to the amended statutes.

[159]. Oliver v. Piner, 224 N.C. 215, 29 S.E.2d 690 (1944).

performance of some part of the obligation. If there has been no default, or in the absence of an acceleration clause if a missed installment is paid before the foreclosure sale is completed, a sale under the power of sale can be restrained.[160]

After the default and after serving notice of a hearing on any person entitled to notice of hearing under North Carolina General Statutes, § 45-21.16 (b), and after a hearing has been held by the Clerk of the Superior Court who finds the mortgagee or trustee is authorized to conduct a foreclosure sale pursuant to North Carolina General Statutes, § 45-21.16 (d), and after the proper posting and publishing of the notice of sale to foreclose under North Carolina General Statutes, §§ 45-21.16A and 45-21.17, the person designated as having the power of sale conducts the sale.[161] The sale is commonly held at the courthouse door and the seller, often through an auctioneer, invites offers from those attending and then accepts the bid of the highest bidder who meets the legal requirements — that he is an eligible purchaser, able to pay any cash deposit as may be required, and able to pay the remainder of the purchase price in the medium required. The bidder on the property is bound from the moment his bid is accepted.[162]

A lender *cestui que trust* may purchase at a trustee's sale under a power of sale in a deed of trust [163] but a purchase by a mortgagee lender at his own sale under a two-party mortgage containing a power of sale, either

---

160. Frink v. Tyre, 170 N.C. 41, 86 S.E. 773 (1915); Oliver v. Piner, 224 N.C. 215, 29 S.E.2d 690 (1944).

161. Turner v. Blackburn, 389 F. Supp. 1250 (W.D.N.C. 1975). *See* Sloop v. London, 27 N.C. App. 516, 219 S.E.2d 502 (1975), to the effect that the power to sell under a deed of trust cannot be exercised by the holder of the obligation secured if he is not the trustee. Under a deed of trust, the secured party can only demand that the *trustee* sell the property and cannot conduct the sale himself or through agents. Where the secured party *himself* exercises the power of sale under a deed of trust, even though the trustee subsequently ratifies the sale, there is a wrongful foreclosure. Only the person named as having the power of sale, or his legal successor, may exercise the power of sale. If the deed of trust grants the trustee the power of sale, holders of notes secured by the deed of trust do not have the power. Likewise, if the power is given to the holders of the notes, the trustee cannot exercise the power of sale. General Realty Co. v. Lewis, 212 N.C. 45, 192 S.E. 902 (1937). If a mortgagee or trustee has a power of sale pursuant to a mortgage or deed of trust and dies, his executor or administrator may exercise the power. N.C. GEN. STAT. § 45-4. When there are two or more mortgagees or trustees with the power of sale and one dies, the survivor has the power of sale. N.C. GEN. STAT. § 45-8. If the trustee in a deed of trust has the power and renounces his trust, or is removed from any reason, the Clerk of Superior Court can substituted a trustee to exercise the power of sale. N.C. GEN. STAT. § 45-6. *See also* KAKE, NORTH CAROLINA PRACTICE METHODS §§ 171, 172 (1952); Pearce v. Watkins, 219 N.C. 636, 14 S.E.2d 653 (1941).

162. N.C. GEN. STAT. § 45-21.30.

163. DeBruhl v. Harvey & Son, 250 N.C. 161, 108 S.E.2d 469 (1959); *In re* Sale of Land of Sharpe, 230 N.C. 412, 53 S.E.2d 302 (1949); Graham v. Graham, 229 N.C. 565, 50 S.E.2d 294 (1948); Hare v. Weil, 213 N.C. 484, 196 S.E. 869 (1938); Hill v. Fertilizer Co., 210 N.C. 417, 187 S.E. 577 (1936); Bunn v. Holliday, 209 N.C. 351, 183 S.E. 278 (1935).

personally or through an agent, is voidable at the option of the mortgagor or holder of the mortgagor's interest or any part thereof.[164]

The trustee or mortgagee who exercises a power of sale to foreclose must make a report of the sale to the Clerk of the Superior Court of the county where the sale was held [165] within five days after the date of the sale. Any person may make an upset bid on the property within ten days after the filing of the report of the sale.[166] The effect of the upset bid is that the property must be resold and the bidding at the resale starts with the amount of the upset bid. The resale must be advertised again in accordance with statute.[167] After the highest bid is submitted, it too must be reported within five days of the resale and is also subject to upset bid for ten days from the time of the refiled report. This resale procedure may be repeated any number of times until no further upset bids are forthcoming or until the time for filing upset bids expires.[168] At any time before the time for upset bids has expired, foreclosure is incomplete and the mortgagor or any successor to the mortgagor's interest has the right to pay off the mortgage indebtedness plus all costs of sale and resale and to redeem the land.[169]

The proceeds of a sale under a power of sale contained in a mortgage or deed of trust are applied in the following order: First, they are applied to pay the costs and expenses of holding the sale, including the cost of advertising, the auctioneer's fees, any trustee's commissions provided in the instrument, and the fees of the Clerk of the Superior Court for auditing the final account. Next, taxes due and unpaid on the property are paid from the proceeds as are special assessments due on the property. Then the proceeds are applied to payment in full of the obligation secured by the mortgage or deed of trust, including interest and any other expenditures the obligee has paid as a result of the mortgagor's default pursuant to the mortgage or deed of trust, such as insurance or taxes. Lastly, if there is any surplus after paying the foregoing, the trustee or mortgagee pays it to the person or persons entitled thereto. If he does not know who is entitled to the remaining proceeds, he shall pay it to the Clerk for

---

164. Thompson v. Insurance Co., 234 N.C. 434, 67 S.E.2d 444 (1951); Peedin v. Oliver, 222 N.C. 665, 24 S.E.2d 519 (1943); Mills v. Building & Loan Ass'n, 216 N.C. 664, 6 S.E.2d 549 (1939); Smith v. Land Bank, 213 N.C. 343, 196 S.E. 481 (1938); Council v. Land Bank, 213 N.C. 329, 196 S.E. 483 (1938); Shuford v. Bank, 207 N.C. 428, 177 S.E. 408 (1934). Likewise a trustee's purchase at his own sale is voidable. These sales may be avoided regardless of good faith or the absence of fraud, the rule being founded upon the opportunity for oppression arising out of the relationship.

165. N.C. GEN. STAT. § 45-21.26.
166. N.C. GEN. STAT. § 45-21.27.
167. N.C. GEN. STAT. § 45-21.29.
168. *In re* Sale of Land of Sharpe, 230 N.C. 412, 53 S.E.2d 302 (1949). The purpose of the resales is to encourage the maximum price for the land to the advantage of both the mortgagor and the mortgagee.
169. N.C. GEN. STAT. § 45-21.20.

the benefit of such persons as may establish their right to such funds in order to discharge himself from all liability to the extent of the payment.[170] The safest course for a trustee or mortgagee to follow when there is a surplus is to pay any surplus in every case to the Clerk of the Superior Court. The trustee or mortgagee must file a final account of his receipts and disbursements within thirty days after receipt of the proceeds of the sale, which shall be accompanied by a copy of the notice of sale or resale, if any, which were posted, and also a copy of the notice of sale or resale published in a newspaper, together with the affidavit of publication by the authorized officer of the newspaper. This final report is audited by the Clerk of the Superior Court.[171]

§ 282. Deficiency Judgment.

Unless the mortgage or deed of trust was executed to secure the purchase price of land, the mortgagee creditor may recover a judgment against the mortgagor or grantor in the deed of trust for the unpaid balance due on the mortgage indebtedness after applying the amount realized at the sale. He may bring an action on the notes, or other obligation, for the difference between the amount of the indebtedness and the amount credited as a result of the foreclosure sale, subject, of course, to applicable statutes of limitations and issues relating thereto.[172]

---

170. N.C. GEN. STAT. § 45-21.31 (b). Koob v. Koob, 283 N.C. 129, 195 S.E.2d 552 (1973); In re Foreclosure of Deed of Trust, 20 N.C. App. 610, 202 S.E.2d 318 (1974).

171. LAKE, NORTH CAROLINA PRACTICE METHODS § 181 (1952). See N.C. GEN. STAT. § 45-21.33. See generally Glover, Real Property — Changes in North Carolina's Foreclosure Law, 54 N.C. L. REV. 903 (1976).

172. See, i.e., Trust Co. v. Martin, 44 N.C. App. 261, 261 S.E.2d 145 (1979) where the plaintiff bank sued defendants for a deficiency. Defendants, who were makers of the promissory note but who did not pledge any collateral as security, raised the one-year statute of limitations under N.C. GEN. STAT. § 1-54(6) as a bar to plaintiff's action for a deficiency. The Court of Appeals ruled that the defendants should not be allowed to assert the one-year statute because they were not parties with an interest in the mortgaged property. At 44 N.C. App. 263-64, the decision provides an excellent summary of this area:

> We have found no case in this jurisdiction which defines the term deficiency judgment in a manner relevant to the situation at hand. Other jurisdictions are divided on the issue and some have held the term "deficiency judgment" applicable to all debtors while others have limited the term to mortgagors only . . .
>
> First adopted by the General Assembly in 1933, G.S. 1-54(6) was obviously intended to restrict the personal liability of debtors upon the foreclosure of property during the depression. 1933 N.C. Sess. Laws, ch. 529. See, 2 Glenn, Mortgages § 150, pp. 840-841 (1943); Osborne, Nelson and Whitman, Real Estate Finance Law § 8.3, pp. 528-529 (1979); Perlman, Mortgage Deficiency Judgments During an Economic Depression, 20 Va. L. Rev. 771 (1934). In that same year the General Assembly adopted other legislation affecting deficiency judgments. A statute was adopted prohibiting actions for a deficiency in purchase money mortgages. G.S. 45-21.38.
>
> The General Assembly also adopted an Act which allowed the mortgagee or other person with an interest in the mortgaged property to enjoin the sale of the collateral where the price offered was inadequate or inequitable. Where the property was purchased by the mortgagee, the mortgagor was permitted to show, as a defense to an action by the mortgagee for a deficiency, that the purchase price was less than the land's

By statutory provision, however, if the debt secured by the mortgage or deed of trust is the balance of the purchase price owed to the vendor for the land involved, no deficiency judgment can be recovered against the mortgagor, provided the evidence of the indebtedness shows on its face that it is for the balance of the purchase money for the real estate.[173] The manifest intention of the legislature in enacting this anti-deficiency statute, according to recent judicial interpretation, was to leave foreclosure as the only remedy in purchase money situations.[174] Thus the statute has been construed broadly by the courts to preclude creditors from utilizing the option of suing upon the note in a purchase money transaction without foreclosure.[175] Since the protection of the statute was designed for the benefit of the general public, it is not intended as a right which can be waived or which is generally subject to the doctrine of estoppel.[176]

Certain limitations concerning the scope of the anti-deficiency statute should be noted. It bars a suit for a deficiency judgment after foreclosure and bars suit on the note in lieu of foreclosure only in sales of *real property* to secure to the seller payment of the balance of the purchase price of said *real property*.[177] The statute therefore does not bar an *in personam* suit and judgment on a purchase money note securing the assignment of a leasehold interest since a lease which is a chattel real is considered as personal property for purposes of the statute.[178] In addition, the statute is applicable only to mortgages given by the vendee to the vendor and does not apply to prevent a deficiency judgment in the case of a note and deed of trust or mortgage securing a third-party lender.[179]

In addition, there is another statute which should be noted with respect

---

fair market value. 1933 N.C. Sess. Laws, ch. 275, presently codified as G.S. 45-21.36. This defense was explicitly granted only when the mortgagee sued "to recover a deficiency judgment against the mortgagor, trustor, or other maker of any such obligation *whose property has been so purchased.* [Emphasis added.]" *Id.* From this Act it seems clear that the General Assembly intended to limit protection to those persons who held a property interest in the mortgaged property, and that such protection was not applicable to other parties liable on the underlying debt.

173. N.C. GEN. STAT. § 45-21.38. The parties may expressly contract that there shall be no deficiency judgment and that payment will be made exclusively out of funds derived from foreclosure in the event of default. Jones v. Casstevens, 222 N.C. 411, 23 S.E.2d 303 (1942). *See* Gambill v. Bare, 32 N.C. App. 597, 232 S.E.2d 870 (1977) holding that N.C. GEN. STAT. § 45-21.38 does not apply, even by implication, where it was nowhere indicated on the note or deed of trust that the indebtedness was for the balance of purchase money for real estate.

174. Ross Realty v. First Citizens Bank & Trust Co., 296 N.C. 366, 250 S.E.2d 271 (1979); Real Estate Trust v. Debnam, 299 N.C. 510, 263 S.E.2d 595 (1980).

175. Ross Realty v. First Citizens Bank & Trust Co., 296 N.C. 366, 250 S.E.2d 271 (1979). *See* 296 N.C. 370-71 for a discussion of the legislative intent behind N.C. GEN. STAT. § 45-21.38.

176. Chemical Bank v. Belk, 41 N.C. App. 356, 255 S.E.2d 421 (1979).

177. Real Estate Trust v. Debnam, 299 N.C. 510, 263 S.E.2d 595 (1980).

178. *Id.*

179. Childers v. Parker's, Inc., 274 N.C. 256, 162 S.E.2d 481 (1968); Dobias v. White, 239 N.C. 409, 80 S.E.2d 23 (1954); Armel Management Corp. v. Stanhagen, 35 N.C. App. 571, 241 S.E.2d 713 (1979).

to deficiency judgments where foreclosure has been effected by power of sale without judicial action. That statute,[180] which relates only to foreclosures under powers of sale and not to judicial foreclosures, provides that if the mortgagee, payee, or other holder of the indebtedness becomes the purchaser at the foreclosure sale, the defendant debtor may show as a defense, but not as a counterclaim, that the property was, at the time and place of the sale, fairly worth more than the amount bid for it at the sale. Therefore, under the statute the creditor's deficiency judgment, when the mortgagee creditor buys at his own sale or at a trustee's sale under a deed of trust, cannot exceed the difference between the fair market value of the property at the time of the foreclosure sale and the amount of the indebtedness, regardless of what was actually bid by him at the foreclosure sale. The statute does not entitle the debtor to have credited upon the note whatever profit the purchaser at the sale realizes upon the subsequent sale of the property, although such subsequent sale is a circumstance indicating the fair market value of the property at the time of the foreclosure.[181] As stated, the statute does not apply when an independent third person buys the land in at the foreclosure sale under a power of sale, and it does not apply in any case to purchases made pursuant to an order or decree of court in a foreclosure action.[182]

§ 283. Statutes of Limitations Relating to Foreclosures.

Both foreclosure by action and under power of sale may be barred by statute in North Carolina where the mortgagor or grantor in a deed of trust has been in actual possession of the mortgaged land for more than ten years after default or after the power of sale became absolute or after the last payment was made on the mortgage indebtedness.[183]

In addition to the statutory bar of the action to foreclose or to foreclose by power of sale, there is another statute which may bar the right to foreclose by either of these methods, irrespective of possession of the land

---

180. N.C. GEN. STAT. § 45-21.36.
181. Wachovia Realty Investments v. Housing, Inc., 292 N.C. 93, 232 S.E.2d 667 (1977). The weight to be given to a subsequent sale will depend on other circumstances such as the lapse of time between foreclosure and subsequent sale and known probability, at the time of the foreclosure sale, that such subsequent sale could be made.
182. Richmond Mortgage & Loan Corp. v. Wachovia Bank, 210 N.C. 29, 185 S.E. 482 (1936); Briggs v. Lassiter, 220 N.C. 761, 18 S.E.2d 419 (1942).
183. N.C. GEN. STAT. §§ 1-47 (3), 45-21.12. *See* Woodlief v. Wester, 136 N.C. 162, 48 S.E. 578 (1904); Ownbey v. Parkway Properties, 222 N.C. 54, 21 S.E.2d 900 (1942); Lowe v. Jackson, 263 N.C. 634, 140 S.E.2d 1 (1964). Moreover, even though the statute does not expressly so provide, it has been held that a written acknowledgement of the debt after default will renew the indebtedness and extend the period of time required for barring foreclosure under the statute. In other words, a mortgagee has ten years from a written acknowledgment of the deed within which to bring his action to foreclose or within which to exercise a power of sale, even though the mortgagor is in possession. *See* Royster v. Farrell, 115 N.C. 306, 20 S.E. 475 (1894).

or payments on the indebtedness. This is North Carolina General Statutes, § 45-37 (b), which provides that a mortgage or deed of trust is presumed paid in full in favor of creditors and purchasers for value from the mortgagor or grantor in a deed of trust after the expiration of fifteen years from the date when the last installment of the obligation became due, unless the holder has filed an affidavit with the Register of Deeds stating the amount of the debt still unpaid which is entered on the margin of the record of the deed of trust or mortgage; or unless the creditor-mortgagee has entered on the margin of the record of the mortgage or deed of trust a statement of payments made on the mortgage indebtedness and the balance remaining unpaid, signed and witnessed by the Register of Deeds. With respect to purchasers for value and creditors of the mortgagor, trustor or grantor in a deed of trust, the statute [184] establishes a conclusive presumption that the mortgage indebtedness has been paid irrespective of whether the credit was extended or the purchase was made before or after the expiration of the said fifteen years from the date that the obligation was due to be fully performed. It should be noted, however, that the statute does not apply to bar the mortgagee's right to foreclose as against the mortgagor, trustor or grantor in a deed of trust himself, or as against his heirs, devisees, or donees.

In further considering statutes of limitation, it should be observed that a statute of limitations which may bar the bringing of an action directly upon an obligation will not bar a foreclosure of the mortgage or deed of trust securing the obligation to effect payment unless foreclosure of the mortgage or deed of trust is also barred under one of the statutes discussed in the preceding two paragraphs. For instance, if a simple note is secured by a mortgage or deed of trust, the fact that an action is barred on the note because the three-year statute of limitations has run against the note will not preclude foreclosure on the mortgage or deed of trust securing the note, provided one of the statutes of limitations has not run which specifically bars foreclosure.[185]

Article VII. Payment and Discharge of Mortgages

§ 284. Discharge of Mortgage by Payment or Tender of Payment; Discharge of Record.

A mortgagor is entitled to pay off his mortgage debt and to have his land released from the security at any time and returned to him free,

---

[184]. N.C. Gen. Stat. § 45-37 (b).
[185]. Jenkins v. Griffin, 175 N.C. 184, 95 S.E. 166 (1918); Jenkins v. Wilkinson, 113 N.C. 532, 18 S.E. 696 (1893); Demai v. Tart, 221 N.C. 106, 19 S.E.2d 130 (1942).

clear, and unencumbered.[186] Where a mortgage or deed of trust has been given to secure a specific debt, payment of the debt extinguishes the power of sale and terminates the title of the mortgagee or trustee, and all outstanding interests in the realty revert immediately to the mortgagor by operation of law without the necessity of any reconveyance to the mortgagor.[187] After satisfaction of the mortgage indebtedness by payment, the mortgage or deed of trust securing it has no further validity and the debtor is entitled to have the mortgage or deed of trust cancelled.[188] Once satisfaction of the provisions of any deed of trust or mortgage has occurred, a recently enacted statute [189] requires within 60 days that the holder of the evidence of indebtedness (if it is a single instrument) or a duly authorized agent or attorney of such holder shall:

(1) Discharge and release of record such documents and forward the cancelled documents to the grantor or mortgagor; or,

(2) Alternatively, at the request of the mortgagor or grantor, acknowledge the satisfaction of said instrument's terms in writing on the face of it and forward it and the deed of trust or mortgage instrument, marked "paid and satisfied," to the grantor or mortgagor.[190]

Payment must be made to the holder of the indebtedness or his authorized agent, and payment to a trustee of a deed of trust does not discharge the debt unless the trustee is in addition the agent of the *cestui que trust*

---

186. It should be noted that the creditor may legally charge a premium in North Carolina, in addition to the legal rate of interest, for permitting the debtor to exercise the privilege of prepaying the notes secured by the mortgage before their maturity. *See* Bakeries v. Ins. Co., 245 N.C. 408, 96 S.E.2d 408 (1956). *But see* N.C. GEN. STAT. § 24-1.1A(b) which reads:

> No prepayment fees shall be contracted by the borrower or lender with respect to any home loan where the principal amount borrowed is one hundred thousand dollars ($100,000) or less; otherwise a lender and a borrower may agree on any terms as to prepayment of a home loan.

See also N.C. GEN. STAT. § 24-10(b), which limits prepayment fees on other loans.

187. Barbee v. Edwards, 238 N.C. 215, 77 S.E.2d 646 (1953); Kyler v. Holding Corp., 5 N.C. App. 465, 168 S.E.2d 502 (1969).

188. Walston v. Twiford, 248 N.C. 691, 105 S.E.2d 62 (1958); Dobias v. White, 240 N.C. 680, 83 S.E.2d 785 (1954); Barbee v. Edwards, 238 N.C. 215, 77 S.E.2d 646 (1953); Bradham v. Robinson, 236 N.C. 589, 72 S.E.2d 555 (1952); Manufacturing Co. v. Malloy, 217 N.C. 666, 9 S.E.2d 403 (1940); Crook v. Warren, 212 N.C. 93, 192 S.E. 684 (1939); Kyler v. Holding Corp., 5 N.C. App. 465, 168 S.E.2d 502 (1969).

189. N.C. GEN. STAT. § 45-36.3, effective Jan. 1, 1980.

190. N.C. GEN. STAT. § 45-36.3(b) provides for a civil penalty of $100 in addition to attorneys' fees "and any other damages awarded by the court to the grantor or mortgagor" with the proviso that prior to the institution of an action under this section notice shall be given to the mortgagee, obligee or other responsible party who shall have an additional 30 days to fulfill the requirements of this statute.

creditor for the purpose of receiving payment.[191] The burden of proving payment is on the mortgagor.[192] If the mortgagee, as either mortgagee in possession or pursuant to an agreement, has collected rents sufficient to pay the mortgage debt, the mortgage will be discharged.[193] If the mortgage or deed of trust has been extinguished by payment, any purchase thereafter under a foreclosure sale is invalid and ineffectual to pass title to the foreclosure purchaser.[194]

The methods for cancelling mortgages and deeds of trust of record are set out by statute. The two principal methods are by "personal" cancellation and "exhibition" cancellation. "Personal" cancellation is accomplished when the mortgagee or trustee appears before the Register of Deeds and personally acknowledges the satisfaction of the provisions of the deed of trust or mortgage, whereupon the Register of Deeds makes a marginal entry on the record signed by the mortgagee or trustee showing that the deed of trust or mortgage indebtedness has been satisfied.[195] "Exhibition" cancellation is effected when the mortgagor or grantor of a deed of trust exhibits the note and mortgage or deed of trust which is marked "paid" or "satisfied," signed by payee of payee the note (or in the case of a bearer instrument, signed by the bearer). The Register of Deeds will mark the mortgage or deed of trust "satisfied" on the margin of the record thereof, and the mortgagor who pays the mortgage debt is entitled in North Carolina to retain possession of the bond, mortgage or other instrument so marked "satisfied." [196]

It should be noted that when the owner of mortgaged land, who is primarily liable for payment of a debt secured by the mortgage, becomes also the owner of the indebtedness secured by the mortgage, and the security interest incident thereto, the debt is deemed paid and the land is discharged from the lien of the mortgage.[197]

---

191. Monteith v. Welch, 244 N.C. 415, 94 S.E.2d 345 (1956). An unauthorized receipt of payment or cancellation can be set aside as between the parties. Monteith v. Welch, *supra;* McKinley v. Hinnant, 242 N.C. 245, 87 S.E.2d 568 (1955); Burney v. Holloway, 225 N.C. 633, 36 S.E.2d 5 (1945); Hill v. Street, 215 N.C. 312, 1 S.E.2d 850 (1939). If due cancellation is made on the record by the trustee, however, it may be relied upon by innocent purchasers of the realty for value. *See* Manufacturing Co. v. Malloy, 217 N.C. 666, 9 S.E.2d 403 (1940); Parham v. Hinnant, 206 N.C. 200, 178 S.E. 26 (1934).

192. Combs v. Porter, 231 N.C. 585, 58 S.E.2d 100 (1950).

193. Wilson v. Allsbrook, 203 N.C. 498, 166 S.E. 313 (1932); Fleming v. Land Bank, 215 N.C. 414, 2 S.E.2d 3 (1939).

194. Dobias v. White, 240 N.C. 680, 83 S.E.2d 785 (1954); Barbee v. Edwards, 238 N.C. 215, 77 S.E.2d 646 (1953); Crook v. Warren, 212 N.C. 93, 192 S.E. 684 (1937).

195. N.C. Gen. Stat. § 45-37 (a) (1).

196. N.C. Gen. Stat. § 45-37 (a) (2), (3), (4). It should again be noted that an unauthorized cancellation can be set aside as between the parties. If after an unauthorized cancellation, however, by a trustee in a deed of trust, the land is sold to an innocent purchaser for value, the unauthorized cancellation cannot thereafter be set aside. *See* note 191 *supra.*

197. Waff Bros., Inc. v. Bank of N.C., N.A., 289 N.C. 198, 221 S.E.2d 273 (1976), citing Hussey v. Hill, 120 N.C. 312, 26 S.E. 919 (1897).

But the rule is not the same, however, *where the owner of the mortgaged property who*

§ 285. Effect of Tender of Payment.

The question sometimes arises as to whether a mere tender of payment by the obligor that is not accepted by the lender will extinguish the mortgage indebtedness. In some states which follow the "lien theory" of mortgages, as distinguished from the "title theory" which is followed in North Carolina, mere tender of payment without more will discharge the mortgage. In North Carolina, however, the answer to this question apparently depends on *when the tender is made.* If an unconditional tender of payment is made exactly when due, on the date when the mortgage debt falls due, called the "law day," the lien of the mortgage is discharged although the debt itself survives as a personal liability.[198] But if a tender is made after "law day," after maturity of the debt, the lien of the mortgage is not discharged by mere tender, although a refused tender of payment will have the effect of arresting the accrual of any further interest on the obligation and will free the debtor-mortgagor from any future costs which may be necessitated by an action to redeem or an action of foreclosure as a result of the refusal to accept the proffered tender.[199] If the debtor-mortgagor desires by his tender to discharge the mortgage lien when it is not accepted, he must keep his tender good, bring his suit to redeem, and pay the money into court.[200] If he makes a tender which is refused and does not keep it good, and the mortgage is subsequently foreclosed, if a bona fide purchaser for value purchases at the foreclosure sale he can get good title.[201]

---

acquires the mortgage security is not personally liable for the payment of the mortgage debt. In such case when the ownership of the mortgagor's interest in the real property and the ownership of the mortgagee's security interest therein become united in one person there is not deemed to be a merger as will extinguish the mortgage unless there is proof of an intention by the parties to merge the two interests. The intention of the holder of the two interests is the decisive consideration and no merger will take place if there is proof of an intention on his part to the contrary. In the absence of any intention as to whether the two interests will merge, the presumption is against the existence of an intention to merge on the part of the owner of the two interests in such case. *See* Waff Bros., Inc. v. Bank of N.C., N.A., *supra,* citing and quoting Furniture Co. v. Potter, 188 N.C. 145, 124 S.E. 122 (1924).

198. Dickerson v. Simmons, 141 N.C. 325, 53 S.E. 850 (1906).

199. *Id.;* Debnam v. Watkins, 178 N.C. 238, 100 S.E. 336 (1919); Parker v. Beasley, 116 N.C. 1, 21 S.E. 955 (1895).

200. Dickerson v. Simmons, 141 N.C. 325, 53 S.E. 850 (1906).

201. *Id.;* Debnam v. Watkins, 178 N.C. 238, 100 S.E. 336 (1919). A mortgagor may preserve his right to redeem by giving any purchaser at the foreclosure sale notice of the tender made to the mortgagee before or at the sale.

CHAPTER 14

ADVERSE POSSESSION

Article I. General Provisions
§ 286. Adverse Possession as Means of Acquiring Title Generally.

Article II. Elements of Adverse Possession
§ 287. Generally.
§ 288. Actual Possession Required.
§ 289. Hostility; Exclusiveness Required.
§ 290. Open and Notorious Possession Required.
§ 291. Continuous and Uninterrupted Possession for Statutory Period Required; Periods Required Against Individuals, State.
§ 292. Tacking.
§ 293. Intent to Claim Title to Land Occupied; Occupation by Mistake.

Article III. Adverse Possession Under Color of Title
§ 294. Constructive Adverse Possession.
§ 295. Proof of Possession Under Known and Visible Lines and Boundaries.
§ 296. Lappage or Interlocker.

Article IV. Nature and Extent of Title Acquired by Adverse Possession
§ 297. Generally.
§ 298. Adverse Possession of Minerals.
§ 299. Property That Cannot Be Acquired by Adverse Possession.

Article V. Persons Who May Acquire Title by Adverse Possession; Disabilities
§ 300. Persons Who May Acquire Title by Adverse Possession.
§ 301. Adverse Possession as Between Tenants in Common.
§ 302. Disabilities That Will Delay or Prevent the Passage of Title by Adverse Possession.

Article I. General Provisions

§ 286. Adverse Possession as Means of Acquiring Title Generally.

Adverse possession is a means for acquiring title when a person occupies and possesses real property for a period of time specified by a statute of limitation applicable [1] to the recovery of real property. Adverse possession may be defined as the actual, open, notorious, exclusive, continuous and hostile occupation and possession of the land of another under claim of right or under color of title for the entire period required by the statute. At the expiration of the period specified by statute, such possession ripens into a fee simple title in the possessor. A new title is created in the adverse possessor and the title of the record owner is extinguished.

---

1. *See* N.C. GEN. STAT. §§ 1-35, 1-38, 1-39, 1-40.

The doctrine of the title by adverse possession serves two salutary purposes: (1) It encourages persons to make maximum use of land. If persons who own land do not attend it and leave it fallow, and make no attempt to watch after it and use it, it is deemed better for the community and society in general for the title to be shifted after a specified period of time to those who undertake to use it and make it productive. (2) Land title defects, often resulting from transactions which have occurred many years in the past, might be shown long after all witnesses or parties to such transactions are dead or have passed from the scene or forgotten the facts. The law deems it preferable to allow persons in long uninterrupted possession of land under claims of title to be protected from suits concerning their titles because of the difficulty which might be had even in the case of valid titles to prove claims as a result of the lapse of time, the loss of records, defective memories, death of witnesses and the like.

Article II. Elements of Adverse Possession

§ 287. Generally.[2]

Every possession of land will not ripen into title. Each one of the following elements must be proved by a claimant in order for him to obtain title by adverse possession.

There must be an *actual possession* of the real property claimed; the possession must be *hostile* to the true owner; the claimant's possession must be *exclusive;* the possession must be *open and notorious;* the possession must be *continuous* and *uninterrupted for the statutory period;* and the possession must be with *an intent to claim title to the land occupied.*

§ 288. Actual Possession Required.

A mere intention on the part of a claimant "to claim land adversely," unaccompanied by a physical entry or a taking of possession of the land, will never ripen into title.[3] The test of whether land is "actually pos-

---

2. The entire text of this section in the original edition (§ 258) is quoted in Mizzell v. Ewell, 27 N.C. App. 507, 219 S.E.2d 513 (1975). *See* Stone v. Conder, 46 N.C. App. 190, 264 S.E.2d 760 (1980).

3. For instance, mere listing and payment of taxes on land does not constitute an actual possession as will support a claim to title by adverse possession. Chisholm v. Hall, 255 N.C. 374, 121 S.E.2d 726 (1961); Ruffin v. Overby, 88 N.C. 369 (1883); *In re* King, 9 N.C. App. 369, 176 S.E.2d 394 (1970). *See* Price v. Tomrich Corp., 275 N.C. 385, 167 S.E.2d 766 (1969), to the effect that one's granting of permission to hunt to another is not possession. While the granting of a permission to hunt is evidence of an adverse claim, like the payment of taxes, it is not possession. Taylor v. Johnston, 289 N.C. 690, 224 S.E.2d 567 (1976), holds that mere posting of signs on property which read "Wildlife Game Management Area" was not sufficient to constitute adverse possession.

sessed" is whether the acts of the claimant were such as to subject the claimant continually during the whole statutory period to an action in the nature of trespass in ejectment instead of making him subject only to one or several actions of trespass *quare clausum fregit* for damages.[4] While occupying land for a residence, fencing it, farming, or making permanent improvements on land are ideal methods of showing actual possession, neither of these acts is essential. Any usage of land will be regarded as an actual possession of the land if the claimant makes such use of the land as its quantity, character, nature, location and circumstances will permit, and if the use of such land is the same as is customary in the community by the title owners of similar land. For instance, in *Locklear v. Savage*,[5] the North Carolina Court has said: "What is adverse possession within the meaning of the law has been well settled by our decisions. It consists in actual possession, with an intent to hold solely for the possessor to the exclusion of others, and is denoted by the exercise of acts of dominion over the land, in making the ordinary use and taking the ordinary profits of which it is susceptible in its present state, such acts to be so repeated as to show that they are done in the character of owner, in opposition to right or claim of any other person, and not merely as an occasional trespasser. It must be decided and notorious as the nature of the land will permit, affording unequivocal indication to all persons that he is exercising thereon the dominion of owner . . . ."

It has been held that making shingles in a swamp unfit for cultivation,[6] keeping fish traps in a stream during fishing season and erecting and repairing dams across a stream,[7] cutting timber from land with frequency and regularity,[8] entering upon, ditching, and making roads in a cypress swamp and working timber into shingles,[9] mining items from lands,[10] allowing one's cattle to use another's land for pasture,[11] using lands to make turpentine,[12] are acts sufficient to evidence the actual possession required for obtaining title by adverse possession. In short, actual pos-

---

4. Mallett v. Huske, 262 N.C. 177, 136 S.E.2d 553 (1964), citing Shaffer v. Gaynor, 117 N.C. 15, 23 S.E. 154 (1895); Mizzell v. Ewell, 27 N.C. App. 507, 219 S.E.2d 513 (1975).

5. Wilson County Bd. of Educ. v. Lamm, 276 N.C. 487, 173 S.E.2d 281 (1970); Price v. Tomrich Corp., 275 N.C. 385, 167 S.E.2d 766 (1969); Locklear v. Savage, 159 N.C. 236, 74 S.E. 347 (1912); Wiggins v. Taylor, 31 N.C. App. 79, 228 S.E.2d 476 (1976); State v. Brooks, 2 N.C. App. 115, 162 S.E.2d 579 (1968).

6. Loftin v. Cobb, 46 N.C. 406 (1854).

7. Williams v. Buchanan, 23 N.C. 535 (1841).

8. Berry v. Coppersmith, 212 N.C. 50, 193 S.E. 3 (1937); Brown v. Hurley, 243 N.C. 138, 90 S.E.2d 324 (1955); Poe v. Bryan, 12 N.C. App. 462, 183 S.E.2d 790 (1971).

9. Treadwell v. Reddick, 23 N.C. 56 (1841); Alexander v. Cedar Works, 177 N.C. 137, 98 S.E. 312 (1919); Poe v. Bryan, 12 N.C. App. 462, 183 S.E.2d 790 (1971).

10. Hoilman v. Johnson, 164 N.C. 268, 80 S.E. 249 (1913).

11. Moore v. Curtis, 169 N.C. 74, 85 S.E. 132 (1915); Everett v. Sanderson, 238 N.C. 564, 78 S.E.2d 408 (1953).

12. Bynum v. Carter, 26 N.C. 310 (1844).

session means subjecting the land to the will and dominion of the claimant, to the exclusion of others, and in making the ordinary use and taking the ordinary profits of which it is susceptible, such acts to be so repeated as to show that they are done in the character of owner, and not merely as an occasional trespasser.[13]

What is sufficient to constitute the necessary actual possession will not be the same in all cases. What is sufficient actual possession depends upon the character of the land and also upon the circumstances of its use. In *Alexander v. Cedar Works*,[14] the North Carolina Supreme Court has said:

> Actual possession of land consists in exercising acts of dominion over it and in making the ordinary use of it, and in taking the profits of which it is susceptible. This dominion may consist in and be shown by a great number and almost endless combination of acts, and where the statute of limitations has not designated certain things as requisites the law has prescribed no particular manner in which possession shall be maintained and made manifest. Nor, on the other hand, has the law attempted to lay down any precise rules by which the sufficiency of a given set of facts to constitute possession may be determined. It is ordinarily sufficient, if the acts of ownership are of such nature as the claimant would exercise over his own property and would not exercise over another's. Whether there has been sufficient adverse possession to ripen title is a mixed question of law and fact, and its solution must necessarily depend upon the situation of the parties, the nature of the claimant's title, the character of the land, and the purpose for which it is adapted and for which it has been used. All these circumstances must be taken into consideration by the jury, whose peculiar province it is to pass upon the question. The only rule of general applicability is that the acts relied upon to establish such possession must always be as distinct as the character of the land reasonably admits of and be exercised with sufficient continuity to acquaint the true owner with the fact that a claim of ownership, in denial of his title, is being asserted.

§ 289. Hostility; Exclusiveness Required.

In order for a title to be conferred by adverse possession the claimant's possession must be hostile to the true owner. His possession must be under circumstances that exclude any recognition of the true owner's rights or that the possessor holds in subordination to the owner. Mere

---

13. Lindsay v. Carswell, 240 N.C. 45, 81 S.E.2d 168 (1954). *See* Poe v. Bryan, 12 N.C. App. 462, 183 S.E.2d 790 (1971), which holds that maintaining a drainage ditch and cleaning the ditch once per year where tract is a wooded tract, the taking of logs by a predecessor in title to build his home, the taking of clay and sticks from the tract to build other people's chimmneys, selling timber from the tract, gathering firewood, setting out trees on the tract and advising others not to cut timber from the tract constituted sufficient evidence of adverse possession to ripen into good title. *Accord,* Price v. Tomrich Corp., 275 N.C. 385, 167 S.E.2d 766 (1969).

14. 177 N.C. 137, 98 S.E. 312 (1919); Wiggins v. Taylor, 31 N.C. App. 79, 228 S.E.2d 478 (1976).

possession does not amount to adverse possession;[15] every possession of land is presumed to be under the true title and permissive until it is proved that the occupant intended to claim against and exclusive of the true owner.[16] It is the occupation with the intent to claim against the true owner which renders an entry and possession hostile and adverse.[17] The "hostility" of possession required in order to ripen title by adverse possession does not import ill will or animosity; it simply means that the possessor claims the land exclusively in his own right and that he is not holding it in subordination to the owner.[18] Conscious intent to claim the land of another is a prerequisite to adverse possession in North Carolina. In this state if the possession is by mistake or is equivocal in character, and not with the intent to claim against the true owner, it is not adverse.[19]

In some relationships there is a presumption that a possession by one of the parties is with the permission of the true owner, and in subordination to the true owner's title. Hence, in such cases any possession is presumed not to be hostile and adverse and does not start the statute of limitations running. For example, the possession of a trustee with respect to his *cestui que trust*,[20] the possession of an agent with respect to his principal,[21] the possession of one in a fiduciary relationship

---

15. Barbee v. Edwards, 238 N.C. 215, 77 S.E.2d 646 (1953).

16. Brewer v. Brewer, 238 N.C. 607, 78 S.E.2d 719 (1954); Gibson v. Dudley, 233 N.C. 255, 63 S.E.2d 630 (1951).

17. Parker v. Banks, 79 N.C. 480 (1878); Gibson v. Dudley, 233 N.C. 255, 63 S.E.2d 630 (1951).

18. State v. Brooks, 275 N.C. 175, 166 S.E.2d 70 (1969); Brewer v. Brewer, 238 N.C. 607, 78 S.E.2d 719 (1954); Garris v. Butler, 15 N.C. App. 268, 189 S.E.2d 809 (1972). *See* Lea v. Dudley, 25 N.C. App. 251, 220 S.E.2d 828 (1976), which holds that declarations of defendants' predecessor, since deceased, to the effect that he had bought land and that it "belonged to him," which declarations were made when he was in possession of the land, were admissible to show that he claimed to possess as the real owner, in proceedings in which defendants claimed title to land by adverse possession.

19. Gibson v. Dudley, 233 N.C. 255, 63 S.E.2d 630 (1951). The weight of authority is to the contrary. As a matter of fact, in the case of adverse possession under color of title, this does not appear to be the law of North Carolina as in almost all color-of-title cases the claimant is a good faith claimant who claims pursuant to a mistake.

Where a grantee went into possession of a tract of land conveyed and also a contiguous tract under the mistaken belief that the contiguous tract was included within the description in his deed, it was held that no act of the grantee, however exclusive, open and notorious, constitutes adverse title of the contiguous tract so long as he thought his deed covered the contiguous tract, since there was no intent on his part to claim adverse to the true owner. Garris v. Butler, 15 N.C. App. 268, 189 S.E.2d 809 (1972). *See* Williamson v. Vann, 42 N.C. App. 569, 257 S.E.2d 102 (1979).

20. Miller v. Bingham, 36 N.C. 423 (1841).

21. Tiffany, Real Property § 1181 (1939).

with respect to a landowner,[22] the possession of one spouse with respect to another spouse,[23] if the spouses are living together, the possession of a tenant with respect to his landlord,[24] and the possession of one cotenant with respect to his fellow cotenants [25] are all deemed, by reason of the special relationships, to be permissive, nonhostile and nonadverse. In order for such possessions to become hostile and adverse so as to start the statute of limitations running, it is essential for the possessor to bring home to the owner some clear, definite and unequivocal notice of the adverse claimant's intention to assert an exclusive ownership in himself. In other words, where the possession of the occupant is in a relationship not inconsistent with the owner's title, it is not antagonistic to the owner's title and will not ripen into title by adverse possession.[26]

But in all such cases this consistency of possessions lasts only so long as the possessions are not distinctly antagonistic. Immediately upon a clear, positive, and open disclaimer or disavowal by the occupant that he is holding in privity with the true owner the possession becomes adverse.[27] Declarations and acts of disclaimer, in order to change a

---

22. Clendenin v. Clendenin, 181 N.C. 465, 107 S.E. 458 (1921). Watson v. Chilton, 14 N.C. App. 7, 187 S.E.2d 482 (1972), states that the general rule is that an adverse possession cannot be predicated on the possession of a child as against its parent. "In order that a possession by a parent against a child, or vice versa, may become adverse, the owner must have had some clear, definite, and unequivocal notice of the adverse claimant's intention to assert an exclusive ownership in himself."
23. Hancock v. Davis, 179 N.C. 282, 102 S.E. 269 (1920).
24. Taylor v. Kelly, 56 N.C. 240 (1857). *But see* Williams v. Robertson, 235 N.C. 478, 70 S.E.2d 692 (1952), which holds that the tenant's possession is deemed that of the landlord only twenty years after termination of the tenancy.
25. Morehead v. Harris, 262 N.C. 330, 137 S.E.2d 174 (1964); Williams v. Robertson, 235 N.C. 478, 70 S.E.2d 692 (1952). *See, however,* Watson v. Chilton, 14 N.C. App. 7, 187 S.E.2d 482 (1972), to the effect that if one cotenant does some act to show that a hostile relation exists and that he intends to hold alone, the adverse possession statute begins to run against the other cotenants. If the other cotenants attempt to assert their claim, as to enter, or to demand an account for rents, etc., which is resisted by the occupant, then his possession becomes adverse and if it continues for seven years his title will ripen against his cotenants, quoting Thorpe v. Holcombe, 126 N.C. 365, 35 S.E. 608 (1900).
26. The possession of a vendee of land under a contract of sale is presumed to be in subordination to the rights of his vendor. McNeill v. Fuller, 121 N.C. 209, 28 S.E. 299 (1897).
27. *E.g.,* a tenant in common may adversely possess land against his cotenants by an actual ouster of his cotenants which arises from some clear, positive and unequivocal act equivalent to an open denial of his cotenants' rights and putting them out of seisin. See Morehead v. Harris, 235 N.C. 478, 70 S.E.2d 692 (1952); Dobbins v. Dobbins, 141 N.C. 210, 53 S.E. 870 (1906). In addition, even in the absence of an actual ouster, the ouster of one tenant in common by a cotenant will be presumed from an exclusive use of the common property and the appropriation of its profits for his own use for twenty years. *See* Williams v. Robertson, 235 N.C. 478, 70 S.E.2d 692 (1952); Winstead v. Woolard, 223 N.C. 814, 28 S.E.2d 507 (1943); Morehead v. Harris, 262 N.C. 330, 137 S.E.2d 174 (1964); Collier v. Welker, 19 N.C. App. 617, 199 S.E.2d 691 (1973) citing this section (§ 260 in original edition).

relation originally permissive into an adverse holding, must be unequivocal and must be brought home to the true owner.[28]

§ 290. Open and Notorious Possession Required.

The possession required for the acquisition of title by adverse possession must not only be actual possession but must be open and notorious. This means that the record owner of the real property involved must be given actual notice of the hostile possession of the claimant or the possession must be so open, visible or notorious that he is presumed to have constructive notice of the adverse claim. If the acts of possession are of such a nature that everyone in the community, including the owner, knows or by observing *could* know that the claimant is claiming the land as his own and that the acts are not merely acts of temporary trespass, the requisite openness and notoriety are made out. The possession must be decided and as notorious as the nature of the land will permit, affording unequivocal indication to all persons that the claimant is exercising the dominion of owner over the land involved.[29]

The possession required for the acquisition of title by adverse possession must not be clandestine or equivocal but must be of such a continuous, open and notorious nature as would apprise the true owner and the world of the adverse claim and the extent of the possession claimed.[30]

What will amount to a clear and satisfactory possession for the acquisition of title from the point of view of notoriety and openness will depend on the nature and location of the land and the uses to which it is adapted. The possession required in an old and heavily populated section will differ from that required in remote or unimproved lands. But in any case, the possession must be definite; not doubtful, fugitive, desultory, or equivocal. The possession must always be of such a character as to warrant the inference that the owner ought to know that one is asserting dominion over his land.[31]

On the issue of adverse possession, general reputation that the land is

---

28. Clendenin v. Clendenin, 181 N.C. 465, 107 S.E. 458 (1921). *See* Wilson County Bd. of Educ. v. Lamm, 276 N.C. 487, 173 S.E.2d 281 (1970); Lea v. Dudley, 25 N.C. App. 251, 220 S.E.2d 828 (1975).

29. Shelly v. Granger, 204 N.C. 488, 168 S.E. 736 (1933); Owens v. Lumber Co., 210 N.C. 504, 187 S.E. 504 (1936); Locklear v. Savage, 159 N.C. 237, 74 S.E. 347 (1912); Berry v. Coppersmith, 212 N.C. 50, 193 S.E. 3 (1937); Cothran v. Akers Motor Lines, Inc., 257 N.C. 782, 127 S.E.2d 578 (1962).

30. Bowers v. Mitchell, 258 N.C. 80, 128 S.E.2d 6 (1962); McDaris v. Breit Bar "T" Corp., 265 N.C. 298, 144 S.E.2d 59 (1965); Cothran v. Akers Motor Lines, Inc., 257 N.C. 782, 127 S.E.2d 578 (1962); May v. Manufacturing Co., 164 N.C. 262, 80 S.E. 380 (1912); Alexander v. Cedar Works, 177 N.C. 137, 98 S.E. 312 (1919).

31. Locklear v. Savage, 159 N.C. 236, 74 S.E. 347 (1912).

owned by the person in possession is admissible as showing the notoriety of the possession.[32]

§ 291. Continuous and Uninterrupted Possession for Statutory Period Required; Periods Required Against Individuals, State.

(a) *In general.* Possession of the land claimed must be continuous and uninterrupted for the period required by statute.[33] In North Carolina the statutory period of possession required for acquisition of title against an individual is twenty years if the possession is without color of title [34] and seven years if the possession is under color of title.[35] To acquire title as against the State, possession without color of title must be maintained for thirty years; [36] if the possession is against the State and under color of title, it must be continued for twenty-one years.[37]

Intermittent, occasional, or periodic possessions do not constitute the continuity of possession required to gain title by adverse possession.[38] While the possession need not be *unceasing,* there must be evidence that warrants the inference that the actual use and occupation of the land have extended over the required period, and that during that time the claimant has from time to time, continuously subjected some part of the disputed land to the only use of which it was susceptible.[39] The following cases illustrate that the possession need not be unceasing: It was held in *Bynum v. Carter* [40] that the occupation of pine land by annually making turpentine thereon was a sufficiently continuous possession. In *Tredwell v. Reddick* [41] continuous possession was shown by the entering upon, ditching and making roads in a cypress swamp and working up timber into shingles. In *Williams v. Buchanan* [42] the keeping of fish traps in a

---

32. Hedden v. Hall, 23 N.C. App. 453, 209 S.E.2d 358 (1974); STANSBURY, N.C. EVIDENCE, § 149, p. 501 (Brandis Rev. 1973).

33. Newkirk v. Porter, 237 N.C. 115, 74 S.E.2d 235 (1953); Sessoms v. McDonald, 237 N.C. 720, 75 S.E.2d 904 (1953); Alexander v. Richmond Cedar Works, 177 N.C. 137, 98 S.E. 312 (1919); Cross v. Seaboard Ry., 172 N.C. 119, 90 S.E. 14 (1916).

34. N.C. GEN. STAT. §§ 1-39, 1-40. Schell v. Rice, 37 N.C. App. 377, 246 S.E.2d 61 (1978); Campbell v. Mayberry, 12 N.C. App. 469, 183 S.E.2d 867 (1971).

35. N.C. GEN. STAT. § 1-38.
36. N.C. GEN. STAT. § 1-35.
37. N.C. GEN. STAT. § 1-35.

38. Sessoms v. McDonald, 237 N.C. 720, 75 S.E.2d 904 (1953); Gudger v. Hensley, 82 N.C. 482 (1880).

39. Cross v. Seaboard Ry., 172 N.C. 119, 90 S.E. 14 (1916); Price v. Tomrich Corp., 275 N.C. 385, 167 S.E.2d 766 (1969); Cutts v. Casey, 278 N.C. 390, 180 S.E.2d 297 (1971); Mizzell v. Ewell, 27 N.C. App. 507, 219 S.E.2d 513 (1975); Wiggins v. Taylor, 31 N.C. App. 79, 228 S.E.2d 476 (1976); Helton v. Cook, 27 N.C. App. 565, 219 S.E.2d 505 (1975).

40. 26 N.C. 310 (1844).
41. 23 N.C. 56 (1840).
42. 23 N.C. 535 (1841).

nonnavigable stream, erecting and repairing dams over it and using the stream every year during the fishing season were held sufficient. On the contrary, continuous possession was not made out by simply cutting timber for a sawmill and feeding hogs upon land susceptible for other uses in the case of *Loftin v. Cobb*.[43] Nor was the making of pole bridges over a ditch on the side of a public road for driving cattle into a swamp and the occasional cutting and getting timber therein.[44] The cutting of timber for rails every year for a few weeks at a time on land valuable only for its growth of timber was not an adequate continuous possession.[45] Occasional entries upon land at long intervals for the purpose at one time of cutting timber, at another for firewood, making rails at another, making bricks at still another, all occasional and at long intervals, unaccompanied by a continuous possession of public notoriety, did not constitute the requisite continuity in the case of *Williams v. Wallace*.[46] Similarly, *Campbell v. Mayberry*[47] holds that intermittent acts of ownership over disputed property between the years 1935 through 1952 — the selling of timber in 1935 and the planting of tobacco beds and bean patches in 1938, 1939, 1950, 1951 and 1952 — were insufficient to establish a continuous possession of the property for a twenty-year period.

Thus the existence and establishment of the continuity of possession required for the acquisition of title by adverse possession depends upon the character of the property and the purposes for which it is suitable, the use to which the property is adapted, the actual manner of its use over the prescribed period, the circumstances of the occupant and, to some extent, the possessor's intention throughout the period. Put another way, whether the possession is sufficiently continuous depends in large measure upon the unique facts and circumstances of each case.[48]

If there is a break in the continuity of possession, the law carries the possession to the holder of the legal title[49] and destroys the effectiveness of the prior possession. Not every extended absence from the property by the adverse possessor breaks the continuity of possession for purposes of this rule. In a 1975 Court of Appeals decision,[50] for example, it was held that an adverse possessor's temporary absence from the property for two periods of four months and nine months to serve two criminal sentences in the penitentiary did not interrupt the continuity of possession where the adverse possessor locked the house on the disputed property during her absence, where the adverse possessor's daughter looked after the

---
43. 46 N.C. 406 (1854).
44. Morris v. Hayes, 47 N.C. 93 (1854).
45. Bartlett v. Simmons, 49 N.C. 295 (1857).
46. 78 N.C. 354 (1878).
47. 12 N.C. App. 469, 183 S.E.2d 867 (1971).
48. Locklear v. Savage, 159 N.C. 236, 74 S.E.2d 347 (1912).
49. Williams v. Wallace, 78 N.C. 354 (1878); Newkirk v. Porter, 237 N.C. 115, 74 S.E.2d 235 (1953).
50. *See* Helton v. Cook, 27 N.C. App. 565, 219 S.E.2d 505 (1975).

house while the adverse possessor was in prison, and where the true owner had clear and unequivocal notice of the adverse possessor's occupancy and of the temporary nature of the absences. Absent circumstances such as the unique facts of this case present, a gap or interruption in the continuity of the possession results in a rehabilitation of the owner's possession and necessitates a resumed possession by the adverse claimant for the period of the statute of limitations, the continuity of the adverse possession running only from the time of such renewed possession.[51]

Just as it is not every absence by the adverse possessor from the property that will break the continuity of possession, it is not every entrance by the true owner onto the property that will interrupt the continuity. A recent Court of Appeals case has held in this regard that the occasional going onto the property by one of the record owners to cut a Christmas tree or rake pinestraw for a dog house was not sufficient to interrupt the continued adverse possession.[52]

§ 292. Tacking.

The possession of an adverse claimant, before he has been in possession of land as against the true owner for the full statutory period, may be "tacked"[53] to the possession of a subsequent adverse possessor to make up the continuous and uninterrupted adverse possession required for the acquisition of title if there is "privity" between successive possessors of the land. It is not necessary for the possession to be continuous in the same person throughout the statutory period if privity of successive possessions can be proved.

The "privity" requirement for tacking simply means that there is a succession of relationship to the land possessed, that a successor possessor has derived or received his possession from a predecessor possessor, either by some act of the predecessor or by operation of law, giving rise to a continued possession under the same claim, in order that there will be no interval during which the true owner would be constructively possessed under his legal title.[54] This "privity" or relational connection of possessions serves to blend successive possessions and to make them one continuous holding under one continuous claim although by two or more persons.

The privity requirement is made out and tacking is thus permitted where an initial adverse possessor transfers his possession to a successor

---

51. MINOR & WURTS, REAL PROPERTY § 826 (1910).
52. Stone v. Conder, 46 N.C. App. 190, 264 S.E.2d 760 (1980).
53. "Tacking" is defined in Dickinson v. Pake, 284 N.C. 576, 201 S.E.2d 897 (1974), in which this work is cited. In a prescription case, the Supreme Court of North Carolina holds that tacking is the legal principle whereby successive adverse users in privity with prior adverse users can tack successive adverse possessions of land so as to aggregate the prescriptive period of twenty years.
54. Vanderbilt v. Chapman, 172 N.C. 809, 90 S.E. 993 (1916).

adverse possessor by some recognized connection. Thus the privity connection is made out if an adverse possessor transfers his possession to another by deed or will or even by a parol transfer.[55] There is also privity of possession between an initial adverse possessor who lived upon land with his family and the members of his family who continued to occupy the land after his death by descent.[56] The possession of a tenant may be tacked to that of his landlord to show title by adverse possession in the landlord.[57]

Successive adverse possessions cannot be tacked if there is no privity between the possessions. For instance, if one in adverse possession is disseised by another, the subsequent adverse possession cannot be tacked to the prior possession.[58] Likewise, where land has been held beyond the proper boundary by a grantor, a conveyance of land described by a description of the proper boundary only, will not entitle a grantee to tack the possession of his grantor with respect to the land beyond the proper boundary, since the grantee's possession of that land will be deemed independent of the deed and without privity.[59] In such case the deed does not itself create privity between the grantor and the grantee as to the land not described in the deed but which has been occupied by the grantor and this is true even though the grantee may enter into possession of the land not described and even though he uses the land in connection with that described in his deed.[60]

§ 293. Intent to Claim Title to Land Occupied; Occupation by Mistake.

Overlapping the elements of hostility and exclusiveness is the require-

---

55. Vanderbilt v. Chapman, 172 N.C. 809, 90 S.E. 993 (1916). *See* Sipe v. Blankenship, 37 N.C. App. 499, 246 S.E.2d 527 (1978) where the claimants failed to show the requisite privity.

A will beneficiary, being in privity with testator, is entitled to tack her adverse possession to the prior adverse possession by the testator. Price v. Tomrich Corp., 275 N.C. 385, 167 S.E.2d 766 (1969).

56. Vanderbilt v. Chapman, 172 N.C. 809, 90 S.E. 993 (1916); Barrett v. Brewer, 153 N.C. 547, 69 S.E. 614 (1910); Newkirk v. Porter, 237 N.C. 115, 74 S.E.2d 235 (1953). International Paper Co. v. Jacobs, 258 N.C. 439, 128 S.E.2d 818 (1963). The possession of land by a widower as a tenant by curtesy consummate inures to the benefit of children of himself and his wife for purposes of tacking the possession of an ancestor to the possession of his heirs to make out the statutory period.

57. Alexander v. Gibbon, 118 N.C. 796, 24 S.E. 748 (1896).

58. Jennings v. White, 139 N.C. 22, 51 S.E. 799 (1905).

59. Newkirk v. Porter, 237 N.C. 115, 74 S.E.2d 235 (1953); Ramsey v. Ramsey, 229 N.C. 270, 49 S.E.2d 476 (1948).

60. *But see* Vanderbilt v. Chapman, 172 N.C. 809, 90 S.E. 993 (1916), wherein the court said that if in addition to the deed there had been a parol agreement with respect to a transfer of the land beyond the deed's boundary description, privity would be made out between the grantor and the grantee which would permit the tacking of the grantee's adverse possession to that of the grantor previously existing.

ment that the possessor must occupy the land in question with the intent to claim title to the land occupied to the exclusion of any recognition of the true owner's rights.[61] This intention is of prime importance and must exist for the entire statutory period.

Contrary to the weight of American authority, a conscious intention to claim title to the land of the true owner is required to make out adverse possession in North Carolina if there is no color of title. In this state, if the possession is by mistake due to a mistaken boundary, or if the possession is equivocal in character, and without color of title, it is not adverse.[62] The existence of mistake negates the requisite intent to establish adverse possession.[63]

Article III. Adverse Possession Under Color of Title

§ 294. Constructive Adverse Possession.

Adverse possession under "color of title" is occupancy under a writing that purports to pass title to the occupant but which does not actually do so either because the person executing the writing fails to have title or capacity to transfer the title or because of the defective mode of conveyance that is used.[64] The "color of title" may be a deed, will, or judicial decree, which purports to convey and apparently passes title to land but

---

61. Bland v. Beasley, 145 N.C. 168, 58 S.E. 993 (1907); Richmond Cedar Works v. Stringfellow, 236 F. 264 (1916); Williamson v. Vann, 42 N.C. App. 569, 257 S.E.2d 102 (1979).

62. Gibson v. Dudley, 233 N.C. 255, 63 S.E.2d 630 (1951). If possession is under color of title, the actual conscious intent is apparently not required. An intention to claim title is implied where one possesses under color of title. Since virtually all claims under color of title are mistaken claims, the rule of *Gibson v. Dudley, supra,* if applicable, would practically extinguish the laws permitting the acquisition of title by adverse possession under color of title. *See* Garris v. Butler, 15 N.C. App. 268, 189 S.E.2d 809 (1972). Where a grantee went into possession of the tract of land conveyed and also a contiguous tract under the mistaken belief that the contiguous tract was included within the description in his deed, no act of the grantee, however exclusive, open and notorious, constituted adverse possession of the contiguous tract so long as he thought his deed covered the contiguous tract, since there was no intent on his part to claim adversely to the true owner.

63. Williamson v. Vann, 42 N.C. App. 569, 257 S.E.2d 102 (1979). Criminal intent to steal the land of another is not an essential element of establishing adverse possession. *See* Sipe v. Blankenship, 37 N.C. App. 377, 246 S.E.2d 527 (1978) where one of the claimants testified: "I am not claiming any of Mr. Sipe's land. Just ours. I'm claiming where the old line was set up. What's always been the old line. My mother pointed out to me where this old line was." (This mistaken possession was held not to be adverse.)

64. Price v. Tomrich Corp., 275 N.C. 385, 167 S.E.2d 766 (1969); Hensley v. Ramsey, 283 N.C. 714, 199 S.E.2d 1 (1973); Seals v. Seals, 165 N.C. 409, 81 S.E. 613 (1914); Trust Co. v. Parker, 235 N.C. 326, 69 S.E.2d 841 (1952); Norwood v. Totten, 166 N.C. 648, 82 S.E. 951 (1914); Smith v. Proctor, 139 N.C. 314, 51 S.E. 889 (1905); Stuart v. Bryant, 40 N.C. App. 206, 252 S.E.2d 286 (1979); Adams v. Severt, 40 N.C. App. 247, 252 S.E.2d 276 (1979).

which is in fact defective.[65] Even a fraudulent deed from one who has no title whatsoever may be color of title and a fraudulent grantee can acquire title by adverse possession for the statutory period against the true owner.[66]

The presence or absence of color of title has significance in adverse possession under North Carolina law because if possession is under color of title the statutory period of possession is a shorter period than if entry and possession is without color of title. As previously stated, adverse possession under color of title will ripen title in a claimant against an individual in seven years.[67] If the possession is without color of title, no title will be acquired against an individual landowner until the possession is maintained for twenty years.[68]

In addition to the shorter period of possession required to obtain title by adverse possession, if the possession is under color of title, perhaps even more significant is the applicability of the fiction of constructive adverse possession when color of title is present. When one enters into adverse possession *without* color of title, he must *actually* possess *all* that he claims in order to acquire title thereto.[69] If he possesses *with* color of title, so long as he has *some actual* possession of a *part* of the land, his color of title makes him the constructive possessor of the remainder of the land described in the instrument constituting color of title,[70] provided the land is a single tract owned by a single owner and is not actually occupied by another.[71] In order for constructive adverse possession to apply, how-

---

65. It should be noted, however, that the writing, in order to constitute "color of title" must include an adequate description of the land involved. Katz v. Daughtry, 198 N.C. 393, 151 S.E. 879 (1930); Carrow v. Davis, 248 N.C. 741, 105 S.E.2d 60 (1958); Barringer v. Weathington, 11 N.C. App. 618, 182 S.E.2d 239 (1971), citing McDaris v. Breit Bar "T" Corp., 265 N.C. 298, 144 S.E.2d 59 (1965); Stuart v. Bryant, 40 N.C. App. 206, 252 S.E.2d 286 (1979).

66. Trust Co. v. Parker, 235 N.C. 326, 69 S.E.2d 841 (1952); Seals v. Seals, 165 N.C. 409, 81 S.E. 613 (1914). A deed obtained from the purchase of land at a mortgage foreclosure sale constitutes color of title even though the foreclosure sale was defective or void. Scott Poultry Co. v. Bryan Oil Co., 272 N.C. 16, 157 S.E.2d 693 (1967).

67. Trust Co. v. Miller, 243 N.C. 1, 89 S.E.2d 765 (1955); Washington v. McLawhorn, 237 N.C. 449, 75 S.E.2d 402 (1953); Newkirk v. Porter, 237 N.C. 115, 74 S.E.2d 235 (1953).

68. Newkirk v. Porter, 237 N.C. 115, 74 S.E.2d 235 (1953); Ward v. Smith, 223 N.C. 141, 25 S.E.2d 463 (1943); Carrow v. Davis, 248 N.C. 740, 105 S.E.2d 60 (1958).

69. Carswell v. Morganton, 236 N.C. 375, 72 S.E.2d 748 (1952).

70. Lenoir v. South, 32 N.C. 237 (1849); Carswell v. Morganton, 236 N.C. 375, 72 S.E.2d 748 (1952).

71. Vance v. Guy, 223 N.C. 409, 27 S.E.2d 117 (1943); Wachovia v. Miller, 243 N.C. 1, 89 S.E.2d 765 (1955); Bowers v. Mitchell, 258 N.C. 80, 128 S.E.2d 6 (1962); Morehead v. Harris, 262 N.C. 330, 137 S.E.2d 174 (1964). But that land is across a creek will not prevent the doctrine of constructive adverse possession from applying if it is otherwise in the same tract. Pheeny v. Hughes, 158 N.C. 463, 74 S.E. 321 (1912). Nor will the subdivision of land into lots shown on a map prevent possession of part of the land from extending constructively to the whole land when it had been previously conveyed as one entire undivided tract. Alsworth v. Richmond Cedar Works, 172 N.C. 17, 89 S.E. 1008 (1916).

ever, the instrument purporting to be color of title must adequately describe the land involved [72] and constructive possession does not extend to lands not described in the instrument nor to lands in the actual possession of another.[73]

The presence or absence of color of title has significance with respect to claims for *betterments* under North Carolina General Statutes § 1-340.[74] To be entitled to *betterments* under this statute, the defendant must show that he made permanent improvements on the property under a bona fide belief of good title.[75]

§ 295. Proof of Possession Under Known and Visible Lines and Boundaries.

In 1973, the General Assembly added two new subsections to the color of title statute [76] designed to facilitate proof of possession under known and visible lines and boundaries, which is often difficult with respect to farmland and woodland not actually occupied. The statute provides that:

(1) The marking of boundaries on the property by distinctive markings on trees or by the implacement of visible metal or concrete boundary markers in the boundary lines surrounding the property, such markings to be visible to a height of 18 inches above the ground, *and*

---

72. Where a deed is insufficient to identify the land, it cannot operate as color. Carrow v. Davis, 248 N.C. 740, 105 S.E.2d 60 (1958). A deed is color of title only for the land designated and described in it. Harris v. Raleigh, 251 N.C. 313, 111 S.E.2d 329 (1959); Shingleton v. Wildlife Comm'n, 248 N.C. 89, 103 S.E.2d 402 (1958); Stuart v. Bryant, 40 N.C. App. 206, 252 S.E.2d 286 (1979); Adams v. Severt, 40 N.C. App. 247, 252 S.E.2d 276 (1979).

73. Locklear v. Oxendine, 233 N.C. 710, 65 S.E.2d 673 (1951); Wallin v. Rice, 232 N.C. 371, 61 S.E.2d 82 (1950); Vance v. Guy, 224 N.C. 607, 31 S.E.2d 766 (1944); Stuart v. Bryant, 40 N.C. App. 206, 252 S.E.2d 286 (1979).

74. **§ 1-340. Petition by claimant; execution suspended; issues found.** — A defendant against whom a judgment is rendered for land may, at any time before execution, present a petition to the court rendering the judgment, stating that he, or those under whom he claims, while holding the premises under a color of title believed to be good, have made permanent improvements thereon, and praying that he may be allowed for the improvements, over and above the value of the use and occupation of the land. The court may, if satisfied of the probable truth of the allegation, suspend the execution of the judgment and impanel a jury to assess the damages of the plaintiff and the allowance to the defendant for the improvements. In any such action this inquiry and assessment may be made upon the trial of the cause.

75. *See* Hackett v. Hackett, 31 N.C. App. 217, 228 S.E.2d 758 (1976), citing Pamlico County v. Davis, 249 N.C. 648, 107 S.E.2d 306 (1959). Where all of the evidence showed that improvements were made by defendant while he was a tenant, and not under color of title, defendant was not entitled to betterments.

76. N.C. GEN. STAT. § 1-38(b), (c). Further amendments were added in 1975. *See* Stone v. Conder, 46 N.C. App. 190, 264 S.E.2d 760 (1980) where the claimants utilize these new subsections.

(2) The recording of a map prepared from an actual survey by a surveyor under the laws of North Carolina, in the book of maps in the office of the register of deeds in the county where the real property is located, with a certificate attached to said map by which the surveyor certifies that the boundaries as shown by the map are those described in the deed or other title instrument or proceeding from which the survey was made, the surveyor's certificate reciting the book and page or file number of the deed, other title instrument or proceeding from which the survey is made, *and*

(3) The listing and paying of taxes on the real property marked, and for which a survey and map have been certified and recorded

shall constitute prima facie evidence of possession of real property under known and visible lines and boundaries.

§ 296. Lappage or Interlocker.

Occasionally the question of the extent of constructive adverse possession is raised where the title deeds of two rival claimants lap upon each other. To make out a superior title to the land by adverse possession, it is necessary to ascribe exclusive possession to one or the other of the claimants. Certain rules have been formulated by the court establishing possession of that part of the land within the lappage the possession of which is in dispute. If the deeds of the two rival claimants to land lap over the same land and neither claimant is in actual possession of any part of the land covered by both deeds, the law adjudges the possession of the whole lappage to be in the senior title holder or in the holder of the better title.[77] If the deeds of two rival claimants lap and one of the claimants actually possesses some part of the land covered by the lappage, and the other claimant is in possession of none of the land in dispute, the claimant in possession of a part of the lappage is deemed constructively possessed of the whole lappage, irrespective of whether the claimant in possession is the junior claimant or senior claimant.[78] Such constructive possession by a junior claimant for seven years under color of title will confer title upon him to the whole lappage. If both the senior claimant and the junior claimant are each seated on a part of the lappage but neither is seated on

---

77. McLean v. Smith, 106 N.C. 172, 19 S.E. 279 (1890); Currie v. Gilchrist, 147 N.C. 648, 61 S.E. 581 (1908); Lindsay v. Carswell, 240 N.C. 45, 81 S.E.2d 168 (1954); Vance v. Guy, 224 N.C. 607, 31 S.E.2d 766 (1944); Bostic v. Blanton, 232 N.C. 441, 61 S.E.2d 443 (1950); Shelly v. Grainger, 204 N.C. 488, 168 S.E. 736 (1933). *See* Price v. Tomrich Corp., 275 N.C. 385, 167 S.E.2d 766 (1969). *See also* King v. United States, 585 F.2d 1213 (4th Cir. 1978).

78. McLean v. Smith, 106 N.C. 172, 19 S.E. 279 (1890); Whitehurst v. Grubbs, 232 N.C. 236, 60 S.E.2d 101 (1950); Berry v. Coppersmith, 212 N.C. 50, 193 S.E. 3 (1937); Price v. Tomrich Corp., 275 N.C. 385, 167 S.E.2d 766 (1969); King v. United States, 585 F.2d 1213 (4th Cir. 1978).

the whole lappage, the junior claimant is deemed in possession of that on which he is actually seated and the senior claimant is deemed in possession of all the rest of the lappage, including that on which he is actually seated plus all of that part of the lappage not actually occupied by the junior claimant.[79]

Article IV. Nature and Extent of Title Acquired by Adverse Possession

§ 297. Generally.

An adverse possession of land for the period of time prescribed by the statutes of limitation not only bars the remedy but completely extinguishes the rights and title of the person having the true paper title to the land, and vests a perfect title in the adverse holder.[80] Once title is acquired by adverse possession, it continues in the claimant just as any other title until he conveys it to another or loses it through the adverse possession of another. His title cannot be divested by his abandonment of the land or by a conveyance by the record owner or even if the claimant orally declares or admits that he does not own the land.[81]

§ 298. Adverse Possession of Minerals.

Mines and mineral rights can be acquired by adverse possession. As in other cases of adverse possession, there must be shown acts of dominion done in the character of owner in opposition to the rights and claims of all other persons, under known and visible lines and boundaries, for the statutory period.[82]

When title to the mineral rights in land has been severed from the title of the surface of the land, the owner of the surface can acquire no title to the minerals thereafter simply by his exclusive and continuous possession of the surface.[83] After severance of the ownership of the surface of land from the subsurface mineral rights thereunder, subsequent possession of the surface land alone will not give title by adverse possession to the

---

79. McLean v. Smith, 106 N.C. 172, 19 S.E. 279 (1890); Currie v. Gilchrist, 147 N.C. 648, 61 S.E. 581 (1908); Price v. Tomrich Corp., 275 N.C. 385, 167 S.E.2d 766 (1969); King v. United States, 585 F.2d 1213 (4th Cir. 1978).
80. Covington v. Stewart, 77 N.C. 148 (1877); Clayton v. Cagle, 97 N.C. 300, 1 S.E. 523 (1887); Christenbury v. King, 85 N.C. 229 (1881); Morse v. Freeman, 157 N.C. 385, 72 S.E. 1056 (1911).
81. Bell v. Adams, 81 N.C. 118 (1879). *But see* Eaton v. Doub, 190 N.C. 14, 128 S.E. 494 (1925), to the effect that if the adverse possession is under an unrecorded deed it will not prevail as against a purchaser for value or lien creditor of the record owner of the land, where the instrument under which the claim is made has been executed by the record owner.
82. Davis v. Land Bank, 219 N.C. 248, 13 S.E.2d 417 (1941).
83. Vance v. Pritchard, 213 N.C. 552, 197 S.E. 182 (1938); Vance v. Guy, 223 N.C. 409, 27 S.E.2d 117 (1943).

minerals; there must be an actual adverse possession of the minerals themselves.[84]

§ 299. Property That Cannot Be Acquired by Adverse Possession.

No one can acquire title by adverse possession in any property belonging to the United States Government.[85] Title can be acquired, however, against the State of North Carolina pursuant to statute.[86] Land can likewise be acquired by adverse possession against municipalities, which are considered governmental agencies of the State.[87] It should be noted, however, with respect to the State and municipalities, that no person can acquire any part of a public road, street, land, alley, square or public way by adverse possession,[88] provided such road, street, lane, alley, square or public way has been accepted by the public authorities and has not been abandoned.[89] Nor can any title by adverse possession be acquired in a railroad, plank road, turnpike, or canal company's real estate which has been acquired by condemnation for use as a right-of-way, depot, station house, or place of landing.[90] Title to land that has been registered

---

84. Where one enters into possession of land under a deed, his deed constitutes color of title to the entire interest and estate in the land and he may acquire title to the minerals by adverse possession for seven years under color of title provided he actually uses and possesses the minerals or some part thereof in addition to his possession of the surface. Vance v. Guy, 223 N.C. 409, 27 S.E.2d 117 (1943); Vance v. Guy, 224 N.C. 607, 31 S.E.2d 766 (1944). *See generally* Stoebuck, *Adverse Possession of Severable Minerals*, 68 W. VA. L. REV. 274 (1966).

85. United States v. Burnette, 103 F. Supp. 645 (1952); United States v. 7,405.3 Acres of Land, 97 F.2d 417 (1938).

86. N.C. GEN. STAT. § 1-35.

87. N.C. GEN. STAT. § 1-35; Threadgill v. Wadesboro, 170 N.C. 641, 87 S.E. 521 (1916).

88. N.C. GEN. STAT. § 1-45. *See* the interpretation of this statute in Saddle Club, Inc. v. Gibson, 9 N.C. App. 565, 176 S.E.2d 846 (1970) where a restaurant recovered damages for the wrongful cutting of trees on a strip of land in the possession of the restaurant but also located within a right-of-way. At 9 N.C. App. 568, the court notes:

> While G.S. 1-45 prevents plaintiff or any other person from acquiring an *exclusive* right to the land, it does not prevent plaintiff from acquiring a right superior to that of all other persons save the State, and the stipulation that the land was within the right-of-way of the Highway Department indicates only that the State has a superior right, if it chooses to exercise it, to the land. The rights of the State do not preclude plaintiff from acquiring actual, lawful possession, and the evidence was sufficient to support a finding of fact to that effect.

89. Salisbury v. Barnhardt, 249 N.C. 549, 107 S.E.2d 297 (1959); Steadman v. Town of Pinetops, 251 N.C. 509, 112 S.E.2d 102 (1960). *See* Owens v. Elliott, 258 N.C. 314, 128 S.E.2d 583 (1962), that the acceptance for the public must be by the proper authorities, *e.g.*, the governing board of a municipality or the State Highway Commission. If not accepted by the proper authorities in a recognized legal manner it would follow that an adverse possession and use of land could extinguish a street, road, alley, etc., which might otherwise appear to be dedicated to the State or to a municipality.

90. N.C. GEN. STAT. § 1-44.

under the Torrens System cannot be thereafter acquired by adverse possession.[91]

Article V. Persons Who May Acquire Title by Adverse Possession; Disabilities

§ 300. Persons Who May Acquire Title by Adverse Possession.

Any person, artificial or natural, capable of owning real property, may acquire title to land by adverse possession. Thus private individuals, corporations,[92] municipal corporations,[93] the state government[94] and the federal government[95] may acquire title to land by adverse possession.

§ 301. Adverse Possession as Between Tenants in Common.

Since each tenant in common is entitled to occupy and possess the whole land in which his tenancy in common is shared, the possession of the land by one tenant in common is not deemed adverse to his cotenants until there has been an ouster and adverse holding for twenty years.[96] It should be noted that one cotenant may not be deprived of his rights in real property by another cotenant by adverse possession unless the alleged disseized cotenant has actual knowledge or constructive notice of a coowner's intent to dispossess. The adverse nature of a cotenant's possession must be "manifested by some clear, positive and unequivocal act equivalent to an open denial of the co-tenants' rights, and putting them out of seizin." Ordinarily, a particular action or activity falls outside the

---

91. N.C. GEN. STAT. § 43-21. *See* State v. Johnson, 278 N.C. 126, 179 S.E.2d 371 (1971). *Cf.* the Marketable Title Act, N.C. GEN. STAT. § 47B-3 which provides that it does not affect or extinguish the following rights: "(3) Rights, estates, interests, claims or charges of any person who is in present, actual and open possession of the real property so long as such person is in such possession. *See also* Taylor v. Johnston, 289 N.C. 690, 224 S.E.2d 567 (1976).

92. Cross v. Seaboard Air Line Ry., 172 N.C. 119, 90 S.E. 14 (1916).

93. City of Raleigh v. Durfey, 163 N.C. 154, 79 S.E. 434 (1913); *In re* Southern Ry. Co. Paving Assessment, 196 N.C. 756, 147 S.E. 301 (1929).

94. Williams v. North Carolina State Bd. of Educ., 266 N.C. 761, 147 S.E.2d 381 (1966).

95. United States v. Chatham, 208 F. Supp. 220 (1962), *aff'd*, 323 F.2d 95 (1962).

96. Morehead v. Harris, 262 N.C. 330, 137 S.E.2d 174 (1964); Williams v. Robertson, 235 N.C. 478, 70 S.E.2d 692 (1952); Whitehurst v. Hinton, 230 N.C. 16, 51 S.E.2d 899 (1949); Hardy v. Mayo, 224 N.C. 558, 31 S.E.2d 748 (1944); Parham v. Henley, 224 N.C. 405, 30 S.E.2d 372 (1944); Winstead v. Woolard, 223 N.C. 814, 28 S.E.2d 507 (1944); Carswell v. Creswell, 217 N.C. 40, 7 S.E.2d 58 (1940); Stephens v. Clark, 211 N.C. 84, 189 S.E. 191 (1937); Stallings v. Keeter, 211 N.C. 298, 190 S.E. 473 (1937); Bailey v. Howell, 209 N.C. 712, 184 S.E. 476 (1936); Collier v. Welker, 19 N.C. App. 617, 199 S.E.2d 691 (1973), citing this section (§ 260(b) in the original edition). Hi-Fort, Inc. v. Burnette, 42 N.C. App. 428, 257 S.E.2d 85 (1979).

§ 301 ADVERSE POSSESSION § 301

purview of this test unless it exposes the actor to an action by the cotenants for a breach of fealty.[97]

The above rule is true even though a parol partition has been attempted [98] or when a tenant in common has executed a deed to a grantee who takes possession; the grantee in such case becomes a tenant in common and his possession is presumed to be in the interest of his other cotenants and will not mature into title by adverse possession without an ouster and possession for twenty years.[99] In other words, the deed of one tenant in common to a grantee will not constitute color of title which will mature title by adverse possession in the grantee against the other tenants in common short of twenty years. It should be noted, however, that if the grantee receives his deed pursuant to a judicial sale for partition or tax foreclosure or from a commissioner or stranger, the grantee can acquire title as against all cotenants by seven years adverse possession, the deed in such cases being deemed color of title.[100]

It should be further noted that where one tenant in common has been in sole possession of land for more than twenty years without any acknowledgment on his part of title in his cotenants [101] and without any demand or claim on the part of such cotenants to rents, profits or possession, there being no disability during the time, the law in such cases raises a presumption that such sole possession is rightful, and will protect

---

97. Collier v. Welker, 19 N.C. App. 617, 199 S.E.2d 691 (1973), citing numerous cases and this work. See Harris v. Parker, 17 N.C. App. 606, 195 S.E.2d 121 (1973), which holds that the possession of entirety property by a grantee of the husband cannot be adverse to the wife nor cut off her survivorship rights so long as the marriage is not dissolved by death or absolute divorce. The reason for this result is that during the existence of the marriage and the tenancy by the entirety the husband, and not the wife, has the absolute and exclusive right to the control, use, possession, rents, income and profits of the lands.

98. Williams v. Robertson, 235 N.C. 478, 70 S.E.2d 692 (1952); Duckett v. Harrison, 235 N.C. 145, 69 S.E.2d 176 (1952).

99. Morehead v. Harris, 262 N.C. 330, 137 S.E.2d 174 (1964); Johnson v. McLamb, 247 N.C. 534, 101 S.E.2d 311 (1958).

100. *See* Johnson v. McLamb, 247 N.C. 534, 101 S.E.2d 311 (1958), and cases there cited. Such deeds are deemed color of title where there is a sale pursuant to a judicial proceeding or tax foreclosure even if all the cotenants are not made parties to the proceeding or foreclosure. *See also* Yow v. Armstrong, 260 N.C. 287, 132 S.E.2d 620 (1963).

101. On the issue of acknowledgment of title of cotenants see Hi-Fort, Inc. v. Burnette, 42 N.C. App. 428, 257 S.E.2d 85 (1979). In that case, a cotenant claiming the concurrently owned property by adverse possession contended that the trial court's findings that "she did openly, notoriously and exclusively possess the lands involved" and that "she took the rents and profits from 1929 to 1969 and that she made no accounting to any person for the same" were sufficient to raise a presumption of ouster. The Court of Appeals held that the presumption of ouster did not arise in spite of the above findings because the claimant testified: "I never intended to claim this land to the exclusion of my children," and that, "I never intended to claim this land to the exclusion of Babe Burnette's heirs." These statements amounted to a recognition of the cotenancy by the claimant and prevented the presumption of ouster from arising.

it.[102] In such case, where one tenant in common in possession of land takes exclusively to himself the rents and profits from the land openly and notoriously for twenty years, the law presumes an ouster of his cotenants and title may ripen in such possessing tenant by adverse possession.[103]

§ 302. Disabilities That Will Delay or Prevent the Passage of Title by Adverse Possession.

(a) *In general.* Statutes of limitations generally do not begin to run against persons who are under legal disabilities until such time as the disabilities are removed. Thus the statutes of limitations with respect to the acquisition of title by adverse possession are extended where the owner of land is under a legal disability at the time the adverse possession begins.

In North Carolina, if the owner of the land is under eighteen years of age or insane at the time the adverse possession commences, no title passes to the adverse possessor until after three years from the time of the removal of the disability even though the statutory period for the acquisition of title by adverse possession might otherwise be complete.[104] In other words, while it cannot be said that the statute of limitations does not run against a person under disability at the time the cause of action accrues, a period of three years must have expired after removal of the disability before title can mature by adverse possession.

In order to extend the time for the acquisition of title by adverse possession because of the owner's disability, the disability must exist at the time the adverse possession begins, at the time when the cause of action accrues.[105] If the statute of limitations begins to run in favor of a claimant by adverse possession against an owner not under disability, it will continue to run and will not be tolled or extended if the owner dies leaving minor heirs or heirs under other disability.[106] But if two or more

---

102. Brewer v. Brewer, 238 N.C. 607, 78 S.E.2d 719 (1953); Covington v. Stewart, 77 N.C. 148 (1877); Woodlief v. Woodlief, 136 N.C. 133, 48 S.E. 583 (1904); Hi-Fort, Inc. v. Burnette, 42 N.C. App. 428, 257 S.E.2d 85 (1979); Collier v. Welker, 19 N.C. App. 617, 199 S.E.2d 691 (1973).
103. Brewer v. Brewer, 238 N.C. 607, 78 S.E.2d 719 (1953); Hi-Fort, Inc. v. Burnette, 42 N.C. App. 428, 257 S.E.2d 85 (1979); Collier v. Welker, 19 N.C. App. 617, 199 S.E.2d 691 (1973). *See generally* Note, *Adverse Possession Between Tenants in Common and the Rule of Presumptive Ouster,* 10 WAKE FOREST L. REV. 300 (1974).
104. *See* N.C. GEN. STAT. § 1-17, as amended. Campbell v. Crater, 95 N.C. 156 (1886); Clendenin v. Clendenin, 181 N.C. 465, 107 S.E. 458 (1921); Clayton v. Rose, 87 N.C. 106 (1882); Warlick v. Plonk, 103 N.C. 81, 9 S.E. 190 (1889). *See* Cross v. Craven, 120 N.C. 331, 26 S.E. 940 (1897), which holds that a minor is under a disability with respect to adverse possession even though she has a guardian and she is entitled to the benefit of the statute. Stone v. Conder, 46 N.C. App. 190, 264 S.E.2d 760 (1980).
105. N.C. GEN. STAT. § 1-20.
106. Battle v. Battle, 235 N.C. 499, 70 S.E.2d 492 (1952); Frederick v. Williams, 103 N.C. 189, 9 S.E. 298 (1889); Caskey v. West, 210 N.C. 240, 186 S.E. 324 (1936).

disabilities coexist *at the time the right of action accrues* (at the time adverse possession begins) or if one disability exists at the time the right of action accrues and another disability supervenes an existing one, the statute of limitations does not bar the owner's rights until all the disabilities are removed.[107]

(b) *No disseisin of one whose right to possession is future.* A rule that is universally applicable is that the statute of limitations conferring title by adverse possession does not begin to run against one who has no right of possession to the land involved. Hence one who has only a future interest in land cannot have his title affected by an adverse possessor prior to the time that he has a right to possession. Thus the interest of a remainderman or reversioner whose interest is subject to a life estate will not be extinguished until the statutory period of adverse possession has run after termination of the life estate.[108]

---

107. N.C. Gen. Stat. § 1-19; Epps v. Flowers, 101 N.C. 158, 7 S.E. 68 (1888); Cross v. Craven, 120 N.C. 331, 26 S.E. 940 (1897).

108. Narron v. Musgrave, 236 N.C. 388, 73 S.E.2d 6 (1952); Lovett v. Stone, 239 N.C. 206, 79 S.E.2d 479 (1953); Sprinkle v. Reidsville, 235 N.C. 140, 69 S.E.2d 179 (1952); Walston v. Applewhite, 237 N.C. 419, 75 S.E.2d 138 (1953); Loftin v. Barber, 226 N.C. 481, 39 S.E.2d 263 (1946). *See* Thompson v. Watkins, 285 N.C. 616, 207 S.E.2d 740 (1974). *See also* Harris v. Parker, 17 N.C. App. 606, 195 S.E.2d 121 (1973), which holds that the possession of entirety real property by a grantee of the husband cannot be adverse to the wife nor cut off her survivorship rights so long as the marriage is not dissolved by death or absolute divorce. The reason for this result is that during the existence of the marriage and the tenancy by the entirety the husband, and not the wife, has the absolute and exclusive right to the control, use, possession, rents, income and profits of the lands. *And see* the recent Court of Appeals decision, Stone v. Conder, 46 N.C. App. 190, 264 S.E.2d 760 (1980) referring to the well established rule that possession of real property cannot be adverse to remaindermen until the death of the life tenant, even though during the lifetime of the life tenant he gave a deed purporting to convey a fee.

CHAPTER 15

RIGHTS IN THE LANDS OF OTHERS; EASEMENTS AND PROFITS

Article I. Definition and Nature

§ 303. Defined.
§ 304. Classification of Easements Generally.
§ 305. Easements in Gross.
§ 306. Easements Appurtenant.
§ 307. Construction as Easements Appurtenant in Case of Ambiguity.
§ 308. Affirmative Easements.
§ 309. Negative Easements.

Article II. Ways of Creating and Modes of Acquisition of Easements

§ 310. Generally.
§ 311. Express Grant.
§ 312. Express Reservation.
§ 313. Implied Grants Generally.
§ 314. Implied Grants Arising by Necessity.
§ 315. Easements Arising From Quasi-Easements; "Doctrine of Visible Easements."
§ 316. Easements by Estoppel.
§ 317. Easements by Dedication.
§ 318. Acquisition of Easements by Prescription — Generally.
§ 319. Same — Necessity That Use Be Adverse.
§ 320. Same — Necessity of Openness and Notoriety.
§ 321. Same — Requirement of Continuity for Prescriptive Period.
§ 322. Same — "Tacking" Applies.
§ 323. Same — Effect of Disabilities.
§ 324. Same — Extent of Use; Extent of Easement.
§ 325. Same — No Prescriptive Easement May be Acquired Against the State, Municipalities or Counties in Public Roads, Streets, etc.; No Easement by Prescription Against United States Government.
§ 326. Acquisition of Easements by Condemnation.
§ 327. Acquisition of Easements by Statutory Cartway Proceeding in North Carolina.

Article III. Extent of Easements; Scope of Rights of User; Actions

§ 328. Generally.
§ 329. Servient Owner's Right to Use Lands Subject to Easement.
§ 330. Actions to Enforce Rights of Dominant and Servient Owners; Injunctions and Damages.

Article IV. Transferability of Easements

§ 331. Appurtenant Easements.
§ 332. Easements in Gross.

Article V. Termination of Easements

§ 333. Generally.
§ 334. Cessation of Purposes of Easement.
§ 335. Express Release.
§ 336. Abandonment.
§ 337. Merger of Dominant and Servient Tracts into Single Ownership.
§ 338. Extinguishment of Easements by Servient Owner's Adverse User.
§ 339. Termination of Easements by Expiration of Period.
§ 340. Termination of Easements by Transfer of Servient Land to Purchaser for Value; Lien Creditors; Exceptions.
§ 341. Termination of Easements Under Power of Eminent Domain.

Article VI. Profits a Prendre

§ 342. Generally.

Article VII. Licenses

§ 343. Generally.
§ 344. Creation of Licenses.
§ 345. Revocability and Transferability of Licenses.

Article I. Definition and Nature

§ 303. Defined.

An easement is an incorporeal hereditament or nonrevocable right to use or enjoy land of another person for a special purpose not inconsistent with a general property in the owner.[1] An easement is a nonpossessory interest in the real property of another for a limited purpose; it is not an estate.[2]

§ 304. Classification of Easements Generally.

Easements are classified as either *affirmative* easements or *negative* easements. They are either *appurtenant* easements or easements *in gross*. They may be either *express* or *implied*. The significance of these classifications, depending on the purposes of the classifier, will be set out in the sections following.

---

1. Builders Supplies Co. v. Gainey, 282 N.C. 261, 192 S.E.2d 449 (1972), citing this section (in the original edition § 270), defines an easement as a right to make some use of land owned by another without taking a part thereof, distinguishing an easement from a profit a prendre. *See* Davis v. Robinson, 189 N.C. 589, 127 S.E. 697 (1925).

2. *See* RESTATEMENT OF PROPERTY § 450 (1944), which lists the following six factors as the essential characteristics of an easement: (1) It is an interest in land which is in the possession of another; (2) It is a limited use or enjoyment; (3) It is an interest which can be protected against interference by third persons; (4) The possessor of the land cannot terminate the interest at will; (5) It is not a natural right; and (6) It is capable of being created by conveyance. In a *Special Note* following this section, it is explained that the RESTATEMENT OF PROPERTY section includes the term "profit" within its definition of the term "easement." North Carolina continues to distinguish the two interests.

§ 305. Easements in Gross.

An easement in gross is an easement created in land for the benefit of an individual or entity irrespective of the ownership of any estate in other land. A servitude is imposed upon servient land and the benefit of the easement runs to the person and not to any particular or dominant tract of land.[3]

An easement in gross to pass over land is purely personal and ends with the death of the grantee; it is neither assignable nor inheritable, even though it may be limited to a person and his heirs and assigns forever.[4]

§ 306. Easements Appurtenant.

An appurtenant easement is an easement created for the purpose of benefitting particular land. An appurtenant easement is one that is attached to and passes with a dominant tenement as an appurtenance thereof; it is owned in connection with other real estate and as an incident of such ownership.[5] An appurtenant easement requires two tracts of land owned by two different persons. The *dominant* tract is the tract whose owner is benefitted by the easement.[6] The *servient* tract is the tract that is burdened by the easement created for the benefit of the dominant

---

[3]. *See* Gibbs v. Wright, 17 N.C. App. 495, 195 S.E.2d 40 (1973), where the North Carolina Court of Appeals held that easement created in a deed that stated that grantors "agree for the party of the second part herein to get water by conveying the same from a spring above the tract" was an easement appurtenant to the land conveyed and was not an easement in gross that would only amount to a personal license limited to the original grantee. The court stated: "Whether an easement in a given case is appurtenant or in gross depends mainly on the nature of the right and the intention of the parties creating it. If the easement is in its nature an appropriate and useful adjunct to the land conveyed, having in view the intention of the parties as to its use, and there is nothing to show that the parties intended it to be a mere personal right, it should be held to be an easement appurtenant and not an easement in gross. Easements in gross are not favored by the courts, however, and an easement will never be presumed as personal when it may fairly be construed as appurtenant to some other estate. If doubt exists as to its real nature, an easement is presumed to be appurtenant, and not in gross."

An example of an easement in gross would be where A, owner of land, gives to B, Power Company, a right to use his lands to maintain its transmission lines across his lines. *See* Davis v. Robinson, 189 N.C. 589, 127 S.E. 697 (1925), for a definition of "easement in gross." *See also* Shingleton v. State, 260 N.C. 451, 133 S.E.2d 183 (1963); 1 Mordecai, Law Lectures 469 (1916).

[4]. 1 Mordecai, Law Lectures 469 (1916); Shingleton v. State, 260 N.C. 451, 133 S.E.2d 183 (1963).

[5]. 1 Mordecai, Law Lectures 469 (1916); Shingleton v. State, 260 N.C. 451, 133 S.E.2d 183 (1963); Davis v. Robinson, 189 N.C. 589, 127 S.E. 697 (1925); Gibbs v. Wright, 17 N.C. App. 495, 195 S.E.2d 40 (1973).

[6]. *See* Lovin v. Crisp, 36 N.C. App. 185, 243 S.E.2d 406 (1978) holding that a deed conveying a parcel of land which also provided that water rights "shall run with the lands" of the grantees created an easement appurtenant only to the land conveyed in such deed and not appurtenant to other lands owned by the grantees.

tract.[7] After the creation of the easement for the benefit of a dominant tract, the easement appurtenant becomes an incident of the ownership of the dominant tract and inheres in the land and passes to subsequent owners of the land as an appurtenance thereof.[8]

An easement appurtenant cannot exist separate from the dominant land to which it is appurtenant. Nor can an easement appurtenant be converted into an easement in gross by the easement holder's attempt to transfer it to a separate and distinct parcel of land. An appurtenant easement cannot be conveyed separate from the land to which it is appurtenant, but only by a transfer of ownership of such land.[9]

§ 307. Construction as Easements Appurtenant in Case of Ambiguity.

The law favors appurtenant as opposed to easements in gross and if there is any doubt as to whether an easement is appurtenant or in gross, it is construed to be an appurtenant easement.[10] The general rule is, however, that the intention of the parties, as derived from the terms of the grant, the situation of the parties and the surrounding circumstances, will determine whether an easement is one in gross or appurtenant.[11] As a recent Court of Appeals decision [12] has stated:

> Whether an easement in a given case is appurtenant or in gross depends mainly on the nature of the right and the intention of the parties creating it. If the easement is in its nature an appropriate and

---

7. An example of an easement appurtenant occurs where the grantor conveys a lot to A and grants to A, and his heirs and assigns, a right of ingress and egress over an adjacent lot retained by the grantor. An easement appurtenant passes to A and will pass with the lot to whomever it may be conveyed or may come to by descent or devise. Wood v. Woodley, 160 N.C. 17, 75 S.E. 719 (1912).

8. Davis v. Robinson, 189 N.C. 589, 127 S.E. 697 (1925); Wood v. Woodley, 160 N.C. 17, 75 S.E. 719 (1912); Shingleton v. State, 260 N.C. 451, 133 S.E.2d 183 (1963); Yount v. Lowe, 288 N.C. 90, 215 S.E.2d 563 (1975). See also Hensley v. Ramsey, 283 N.C. 714, 199 S.E.2d 1 (1973), which states: "A deed which conveys a portion of the grantor's property and in addition grants the right of ingress and egress over other lands of the grantor to a highway creates an easement in favor of and appurtenant to the land conveyed and subjects the remaining land of the grantor to the burden of such easement. . . . An appurtenant easement is one which is attached to and passes with the dominant tenement as an appurtenance thereof."

9. Yount v. Lowe, 288 N.C. 90, 215 S.E.2d 563 (1975); Wood v. Woodley, 160 N.C. 17, 75 S.E. 719 (1912). A right-of-way appurtenant to specified lands cannot be used for the benefit of other lands, even though such other lands are within the same enclosure with the dominant estate. State v. Shingleton, 260 N.C. 451, 133 S.E.2d 183 (1963). See Hales v. Atlantic Coast Line R.R., 172 N.C. 104, 90 S.E. 11 (1916).

10. Shingleton v. State, 260 N.C. 451, 133 S.E.2d 183 (1963); Gibbs v. Wright, 17 N.C. App. 495, 195 S.E.2d 40 (1973).

11. Id.

12. Gibbs v. Wright, 17 N.C. App. 495 at 497-98 quoting from 25 AM. JUR. 2d, *Easements and Licenses* § 13, p. 427.

useful adjunct to the land conveyed, having in view the intention of the parties as to its use, and there is nothing to show that the parties intended it to be a mere personal right, it should be held to be an easement appurtenant and not an easement in gross. Easements in gross are not favored by the courts, however, and an easement will never be presumed as personal when it may fairly be construed as appurtenant to some other estate. If doubt exists as to its real nature, an easement is presumed to be appurtenant, and not in gross.

§ 308. Affirmative Easements.

An *affirmative* easement is an easement which entitles the holder thereof to do affirmative acts on the land of another whose land is servient land. For example, if an owner of a lot has been given the right to maintain a passageway, ditch, drain or other servitude across an adjacent owner's tract of land, an affirmative easement exists over the land of the adjacent owner.[13]

§ 309. Negative Easements.

A *negative* easement is one which prohibits or restricts a landowner from doing some things which, were it not for the existence of such easement, the landowner would have a right to do on his own land. For example, if one landowner by restrictive covenant binds himself in a contractual agreement or deed with another not to build a certain type of structure on his own land, his land becomes subject to a negative servitude which curtails his rights so as to prevent the use of his land in a manner that would otherwise be lawful. While the other party to such an easement has no right affirmatively to use the land of the servient owner, he can maintain an action to prevent the servient owner from using the land in violation of the restrictive provision — the negative easement.[14]

Article II. Ways of Creating and Modes of Acquisition of Easements

§ 310. Generally.

Easements may be created in at least nine ways. They may result from express grant, express reservation, by implication, by necessity, by estoppel, by dedication, by prescription, by condemnation, and by statutory cartway proceeding.[15]

---

13. *See* Davis v. Robinson, 189 N.C. 589, 127 S.E. 697 (1925).
14. *See* Davis v. Robinson, 189 N.C. 589, 127 S.E. 697 (1925), which holds that a building restriction is a negative easement. *Accord,* Callaham v. Arenson, 239 N.C. 619, 80 S.E.2d 619 (1954); Turner v. Glenn, 220 N.C. 620, 18 S.E.2d 197 (1941). Since a negative easement is an interest in land, it cannot be created by parol. *Accord,* Simmons v. Morton, 1 N.C. App. 308, 161 S.E.2d 222 (1968).
15. 1 Mordecai, Law Lectures 464 (1916); Davis v. Robinson, 189 N.C. 589, 127 S.E. 697 (1925).

§ 311. Express Grant.

An easement may be created by an express grant. Since an easement is an interest in land it is necessary for such easement created by express grant to be in writing under the Statute of Frauds.[16] While an easement is generally created by deed,[17] a writing signed, sealed and delivered, it has been held that a writing not under seal will create an easement right which can be enforced in equity if acted upon.[18] The written instrument creating an easement by grant must describe with reasonable certainty the easement created and must also describe the dominant and servient tracts involved.[19] An attempt to create an easement by oral grant is void under the Statute of Frauds.[20]

---

16. Shingleton v. State, 260 N.C. 451, 133 S.E.2d 183 (1963); Simmons v. Morton, 1 N.C. App. 308, 161 S.E.2d 222 (1968).

17. Borders v. Yarbrough, 237 N.C. 540, 75 S.E.2d 541 (1953); Prentice v. Roberts, 32 N.C. App. 379, 232 S.E.2d 286 (1977). *See* Lovin v. Crisp, 36 N.C. App. 185, 243 S.E.2d 406 (1978) stating that an easement deed is a contract, and, when such contracts are plain and unambiguous, their construction is a matter of law for the courts.

18. Hammond v. Schiff, 100 N.C. 161, 6 S.E. 753 (1888).

19. *See* Hensley v. Ramsey, 283 N.C. 714, 199 S.E.2d 1 (1973); Oliver v. Ernul, 277 N.C. 591, 178 S.E.2d 393 (1973), to the effect that an instrument creating an easement should describe with reasonable certainty the easement created and the dominant and servient tenements. *Accord,* Prentice v. Roberts, 32 N.C. App. 379, 232 S.E.2d 286 (1977).

But compare Builders Supplies Co. v. Gainey, 282 N.C. 261, 192 S.E.2d 449 (1972). Where a grant of an easement of way does not locate the way upon the grantor's land, which land is described sufficiently, a subsequent, actual location of the way upon the described tract by the grantee, acquiesced in by the owner of the servient estate, locates the way sufficiently to enable the courts to protect the right of the grantee therein. *See also* Prentice v. Roberts, 32 N.C. App. 379, 232 S.E.2d 286 (1977).

See also Borders v. Yarbrough, 237 N.C. 540, 75 S.E.2d 541 (1953). The creation of an easement by deed must not be so uncertain, vague and indefinite as to prevent identification with reasonable certainty. But if the location of a way granted is not located in the instrument, if there is practical location and user of a reasonable way by the grantee, acquiesced in by the grantor or owner of the servient estate, such user sufficiently locates the way. *But see* Thompson v. Umberger, 221 N.C. 178, 19 S.E.2d 484 (1942), wherein the court said that if there is a patent ambiguity in a deed purporting to grant an easement, so that a court reading the language is unable to derive therefrom the intention of the parties as to the location of the easement, it will be ineffective to create the easement. The description must either be certain in itself or capable of being reduced to a certainty by a recurrence to something extrinsic to which it refers.

Adams v. Severt, 40 N.C. App. 247, 252 S.E.2d 276 (1979) discusses many of the above-cited cases.

Besides the location cases, there is the issue of whether or not a given document creates an easement. In Mason v. Anderson, 33 N.C. App. 568, 235 S.E.2d 880 (1977), for example, it was held that a deed transferred subject to certain restrictive covenants did not create an easement for use of a lake referred to in such restrictions.

20. Davis v. Robinson, 189 N.C. 589, 127 S.E. 697 (1925); Simmons v. Morton, 1 N.C. App. 308, 161 S.E.2d 222 (1968).

§ 312. Express Reservation.

As in the case of an express grant of an easement, an owner who sells one tract of land and retains another may expressly "except" or "reserve" an easement over the tract conveyed to his grantee.[21] The reservation of the easement must be in writing and the description of such easement must not be too uncertain, vague or indefinite.[22]

§ 313. Implied Grants Generally.

In certain cases, the law will imply an easement when there is no express grant. This easement created by implication occurs where there is a conveyance of land and the land cannot be reasonably used or beneficially enjoyed for the purpose for which it is granted unless an easement is inferred. The law will imply an easement under a theory of inferred intention — that one is always understood to intend, as an incident of his grant, to convey everything reasonably necessary to the enjoyment of the thing granted which is in the grantor's power to bestow.[23]

Easements arising thusly by implied grant divide themselves into two classes: (1) Easements arising by necessity; and (2) easements arising from quasi-easements upon a grant of a quasi-dominant tract. These two types of implied easements are discussed in the following sections.

§ 314. Implied Grants Arising by Necessity.

In some instances property granted could not be used for the purpose for which granted or for any beneficial purpose unless an easement is implied. For example, where a grantor conveys land entirely surrounded by his own land, and there is no outlet for ingress and egress, the law will imply an "easement of necessity" for the grantee to pass over the grantor's land so as to reach the public road.[24] The same rule applies if the grantee's

---

21. State v. Suttle, 115 N.C. 784, 20 S.E. 725 (1894); U.S. v. Sea Gate, Inc., 397 F. Supp. 1351 (N.C.D.C. 1975).

22. Gruber v. Eubank, 197 N.C. 280, 148 S.E. 246 (1929); Adams v. Severt, 40 N.C. App. 247, 252 S.E.2d 576 (1979); United States v. Sea Gate, Inc., 397 F. Supp. 1351 (N.C.D.C. 1975) holding, *inter alia,* that a deed creating an easement by express reservation is a contract.

23. Carmon v. Dick, 170 N.C. 305, 87 S.E. 224 (1915); MINOR & WURTS, REAL PROPERTY § 95 (1910). *See generally* Glenn, *Implied Easements in the North Carolina Courts: An Essay on the Meaning of "Necessary,"* 58 N.C.L. REV. 223 (1980).

24. *Accord,* Oliver v. Ernul, 277 N.C. 591, 178 S.E.2d 393 (1970), which states: "A way of necessity arises when one grants a parcel of land surrounded by his other land, or when the grantee has no access to it except over grantor's other land or land of a stranger. In such cases, grantor impliedly grants a right-of-way over his land as an incident to purchaser's occupation and enjoyment of the grant." *See* Wilson v. Smith, 18 N.C. App. 414, 197 S.E.2d 23 (1973), to the same effect. In the *Wilson* case, the North Carolina Court of Appeals held that even though the grantees had a *permissive* right-of-way over the lands of strangers, they were entitled to a way of necessity over the lands of their grantor in order to get to a

land is surrounded by the lands of the grantor and the lands of others.[25] Implied easements of necessity arise only by implication in favor of grantees and their privies as against grantors and their privies.[26] No implied easement of necessity can be presumed or acquired over the land of a stranger; it can only arise where there is privity of title. Hence a devisee of land cannot establish a way of necessity over the lands of other devisees even though the land devised to him has no access to a public road.[27] If the grantor-grantee relationship is not present and an owner has no access to a public road, his remedy is to proceed under the statutory provisions for the establishment of a "cartway." [28]

An easement of necessity will not be implied for mere convenience; there must be a necessity.[29]

---

public highway. In the *Wilson* case it appeared that the grantees could not obtain a loan on their property to finance their home because they lacked a legally enforceable right of access to the public way even though they had a permissive right-of-way over the lands of strangers. *See also* Lumber Co. v. Cedar Works, 158 N.C. 161, 73 S.E. 902 (1912); White v. Coghill, 201 N.C. 421, 160 S.E. 472 (1931); Pritchard v. Scott, 254 N.C. 277, 118 S.E.2d 890 (1961).

25. White v. Coghill, 201 N.C. 421, 160 S.E. 472 (1931).
26. Lumber Co. v. Cedar Works, 158 N.C. 161, 73 S.E. 902 (1912); Wilson v. Smith, 18 N.C. App. 414, 197 S.E.2d 23 (1973).
27. White v. Coghill, 201 N.C. 421, 160 S.E. 472 (1931).
28. *See* N.C. GEN. STAT. §§ 136-68, 136-69.
29. Lumber Co. v. Cedar Works, 158 N.C. 161, 73 S.E. 902 (1912); Winston Brick Mfg. Co. v. Hodgin, 190 N.C. 582, 130 S.E. 330 (1925). The easement of necessity should be distinguished from implied easements created where a grantor's quasi-easement is converted into an easement when he sells a quasi-dominant tract of land and retains a quasi-servient tract which he has previously used for the benefit of the quasi-dominant tract. In such case the quasi-easement is converted into an easement for the benefit of the grantee of the quasi-dominant tract if necessary to reach the public road. *See* Pritchard v. Scott, 254 N.C. 277, 118 S.E.2d 890 (1961). In the latter case the implied easement arising from a quasi-easement is distinguished from an easement of necessity. An implied easement arising from conversion of a visible quasi-easement into an easement does not require an absolute necessity. It is sufficient to show such physical conditions and such use as would reasonably lead one to believe that the grantor intended that the grantee should have the right to continue to use the road in the same manner and to the same extent that his grantor had used it, because such use was reasonably necessary to the "fair," "full," "convenient and comfortable" enjoyment of his property. Smith v. Moore, 254 N.C. 186, 118 S.E.2d 436 (1961). In other words, it would appear that the "necessity" requirement for establishing an implied easement through the conversion of a quasi-easement into an easement is less strict than if the easement arises as an "easement of necessity" *per se. See also* Wilson v. Smith, 18 N.C. App. 414, 197 S.E.2d 23 (1973); Oliver v. Ernul, 277 N.C. 591, 178 S.E.2d 393 (1970); and Dorman v. Wayah Valley Ranch, Inc., 6 N.C. App. 497, 170 S.E.2d 509 (1969), which hold that to establish the right to use a way of necessity it is not necessary to show *absolute* necessity. It is sufficient to show such physical conditions and such use as would lead one to believe that the grantor intended that the grantee should have a right of access. It is sufficient to show only that the easement is reasonably necessary to just enjoyment of properties affected thereby.

The location of an easement of necessity, when the grantor conveys land entirely surrounded by the grantor's land or by the lands of the grantor and others, is initially for the grantor to select.[30] If the grantor or vendor fails to point out the route for the easement of necessity, the grantee may select the route, and if he once selects the route of the easement he must stick to that route.[31]

§ 315. Easements Arising From Quasi-Easements; "Doctrine of Visible Easements."

When one uses one part of his own land for the benefit of another part of his own land, there is no true easement, by definition, so long as he owns both tracts of land and is not using "the land of another." There is, however, a "quasi-easement" over a "quasi-servient" tract for the benefit of a "quasi-dominant" tract. If the owner of the land has used a part of his land for the benefit of other dominant land which he owns, when he grants the quasi-dominant tract, it is implied that he intends to grant an easement over the servient tract if the existence of such easement is reasonably necessary for the beneficial enjoyment of the land conveyed. The "quasi-easement" which existed when the land was in the ownership of the grantor is converted by implication into an easement in the grantee when the dominant tract is granted.

There are three essentials for the creation of this type of implied easement:[32] (1) It must be shown that the prior owner of two or more tracts of land previously used one part of his own land for the benefit of another part of his own land; that while there was a unity of title there was an obvious and manifest use of the servient land for the benefit of the dominant land and that the use had been so long continued as to indicate that it was to be permanently enjoyed for the benefit of a certain tract of land; (2) the owner of two or more tracts must have conveyed a part of his land; there must be a separation of the titles of the dominant and servient tracts; and (3) it must be shown that the existence of the easement is

---

30. White v. Coghill, 201 N.C. 421, 160 S.E. 472 (1931); Oliver v. Ernul, 277 N.C. 591, 178 S.E.2d 393 (1970).

31. Id. See generally Glenn, *Implied Easements in the North Carolina Courts: An Essay on the Meaning of "Necessary,"* 58 N.C.L. Rev. 223 (1980).

32. Carmon v. Dick, 170 N.C. 305, 87 S.E. 224 (1915); Ferrell v. Durham Bank & Trust Co., 221 N.C. 432, 20 S.E.2d 329 (1942); Packard v. Smart, 224 N.C. 480, 31 S.E.2d 517 (1944); Green v. Barbee, 238 N.C. 77, 76 S.E.2d 307 (1953); Spruill v. Nixon, 238 N.C. 523, 78 S.E.2d 323 (1953); Goldstein v. Wachovia Bank & Trust Co., 241 N.C. 583, 86 S.E.2d 84 (1955); Barwick v. Rouse, 245 N.C. 391, 95 S.E.2d 869 (1956); Bradley v. Bradley, 245 N.C. 483, 96 S.E.2d 417 (1956); Smith v. Moore, 254 N.C. 186, 118 S.E.2d 436 (1961); McGee v. McGee, 32 N.C. App. 726, 233 S.E.2d 675 (1977), citing this section in the original edition (§ 282); Dorman v. Wayah Valley Ranch, Inc., 6 N.C. App. 497, 170 S.E.2d 509 (1969).

"necessary"[33] for the beneficial enjoyment of the land granted; the grant of an easement "cannot be implied from convenience, but is only implied where it is necessary to the full enjoyment of the thing granted."

§ 316. Easements by Estoppel.

In some situations easements may be created by estoppel. An easement may arise where one cognizant of his own right keeps silent in the knowledge that another will be innocently and ignorantly induced to make a land purchase or otherwise expend money or labor in reliance on the existence of such an easement.[34]

An easement by estoppel also arises, perhaps more frequently, when a grantor sells lands with reference to a map which shows streets or alleys or squares.[35] This estoppel creates and vests in the purchasers of lots and their privies in estate, an easement in the streets, alleys or squares which is irrevocable and will be protected just as any other property is protected.[36]

§ 317. Easements by Dedication.

(a) *In general.* An easement may be created by dedication. Dedication is a form of transfer, either formal or informal, whereby an individual grants to the public rights of user in his lands. An easement may be created either by implied or express dedication in North Carolina.[37]

---

33. It is not necessary to show absolute necessity. It is sufficient to show such physical conditions and such use as would reasonably lead one to believe that the grantor intended the grantee should have the right to use the servient land in the same manner and to the same extent that his grantor had used it, because such use was reasonably necessary to the "fair," "full," "convenient and comfortable" enjoyment of his property. See Smith v. Moore, 254 N.C. 186, 118 S.E.2d 436 (1961), and cases there cited. *But see* Goldstein v. Wachovia Bank & Trust Co., 241 N.C. 583, 86 S.E.2d 84 (1955), in which it is stated that easements by implication will not be *reserved* to the *grantor* when he has conveyed a servient tract in the absence of a showing of "strict or imperious necessity." *See also* Dorman v. Wayah Valley Ranch, Inc., 6 N.C. App. 497, 170 S.E.2d 509 (1969); McGee v. McGee, 32 N.C. App. 726, 233 S.E.2d 675 (1977) holding, in part, that the presence of a second or alternative way onto the property is not conclusive proof that an implied easement is unnecessary. In McGee v. McGee, *supra,* the alternative route was described as being "totally unsuitable" by the court. *See generally* Glenn, *Implied Easements in the North Carolina Courts: An Essay on the Meaning of "Necessary,"* 58 N.C.L. Rev. 223 (1980).

34. 3 Powell, Real Property § 411 (1970).

35. *See* "Easements by Dedication," § 317 *infra. See also* Oliver v. Ernul, 277 N.C. 591, 178 S.E.2d 393 (1970), which states that the reason for the rule is that the grantor, by making such a conveyance of his property, induces the purchasers to believe that the streets and alleys, squares, courts and parks will be kept open for their use and benefit, and having acted upon the faith of his implied representations, based upon his conduct in platting the land and selling accordingly, he is equitably estopped from denying the existence of the easement. The basis of the rule is *estoppel in pais.*

36. Broocks v. Muirhead, 223 N.C. 227, 25 S.E.2d 889 (1943), and cases cited therein. *Accord,* Commercial Fin. Corp. v. Langston, 24 N.C. App. 706, 212 S.E.2d 176 (1975).

37. Spaugh v. Charlotte, 239 N.C. 149, 79 S.E.2d 748 (1953).

(b) *Implied dedication of easement.*

A sale of a lot or lots in accordance with, and in recognition of a map or plat in which streets are laid out, constitutes a dedication of the streets to the use of the purchasers,[38] and under some circumstances to the public.[39] The grantor who grants land described with reference to a plat showing a street is "equitably estopped" to deny the existence of an easement as to a purchaser.[40] The purchaser has an easement irrespective of whether streets are in fact opened or accepted by the governing board of

---

38. Home Real Estate Loan & Ins. Co. v. Town of Carolina Beach, 216 N.C. 778, 7 S.E. 2d 13 (1939), and numerous cases there cited.

> In a strict sense it is not a dedication for a dedication must be made to the public and not to part of the public. It is a right in the nature of an easement appurtenant. Whether it be called an easement or a dedication, the right of the lot owners to the use of the streets, parks and playgrounds may not be extinguished or diminished except by agreement or estoppel. This is true because the existence of the right was an inducement to and part of the consideration for the purchase of the lots.

Commercial Fin. Corp. v. Langston, 24 N.C. App. 706, 212 S.E.2d 176 (1975), quoting from Land Corp. v. Styron, 7 N.C. App. 25, 27-28, 171 S.E.2d 215, 217 (1969).

This principle applies to a situation where separate owners of separate but contiguous lots have placed on record a plat showing the subdivision of both tracts. Each owner who thereafter sells lots by reference to the recorded plat effectively represents to purchasers from either tract that the streets as shown on the entire plat would be available and remain open for reasonable use, each of the separate owners in effect thereby creating a joint and reciprocal easement which becomes both a burden and benefit for his separate tract, and a purchaser of a lot or lots from either owner by such purchase would acquire the benefit of the appurtenant easement over all of the streets shown on the plat and not merely over those portions of the streets which are located on the tract owned separately by his immediate grantor. *See* Commercial Fin. Corp. v. Langston, *supra.*

39. So far as the general public is concerned, there is no dedication of a street, either express or implied, until there has been an acceptance. If the land involved is within a municipality, there is no dedication to the *public* until the governing authorities accept on behalf of the municipality by official action or unless acceptance is effected by public user as a matter of right, by the making of improvements, or by some other means recognized by law. Town of Blowing Rock v. Gregorie, 243 N.C. 364, 90 S.E.2d 898 (1955). It is possible, therefore, for purchasers in a subdivision located in a municipality to have an easement in platted streets without the public having an easement in such streets. Oliver v. Ernul, 277 N.C. 591, 178 S.E.2d 393 (1970), states that a dedication to the public without acceptance is merely a revocable offer and is not complete until accepted, and neither burdens nor benefits with attendant duties may be imposed on the public unless in some proper way it has consented to assume them.

Once properly dedicated and accepted, it is possible for the property so dedicated to be used for additional public purposes assuming an enabling ordinance. *See, e.g.,* Sampson v. City of Greensboro, 35 N.C. App. 148, 240 S.E.2d 502 (1978) holding that, where an ordinance provided that all property shown on a plat as dedicated for a public use would be deemed to be dedicated for any other public use approved by the city council in the public interest, a contention that an easement shown on a recorded plat was dedicated for storm sewer purposes only and not for sanitary sewer purposes fell on deaf judicial ears.

40. *See* Home Real Estate Loan & Ins. Co. v. Town of Carolina Beach, 216 N.C. 778, 7 S.E.2d 13 (1939), and cases there cited. *Accord,* Oliver v. Ernul, 277 N.C. 591, 178 S.E.2d 393 (1970); Commercial Fin. Corp. v. Langston, 24 N.C. App. 706, 212 S.E.2d 176 (1975).

a town or city if the land involved is located within a municipality.[41] These rules do not apply, however, when the grantor expressly reserves to himself and to his heirs and assigns title to and control of streets referred to in the subdivision plat.[42]

(c) *Express dedication of easement.*

An easement may be created by an express dedication.[43] If the owner of land expressly indicates by his words or acts an intention to dedicate his land to a public use, and his offer is accepted by the public, the dedication becomes irrevocable. The requisites for an express dedication are: (1) Indication of an unequivocal intention on the part of the owner of land to make a dedication,[44] and (2) an acceptance of the offer of dedication by the public in some recognized legal manner.[45] If these two requisites are present there is no required period of user and the dedication becomes effective and irrevocable immediately.[46]

It should be observed that since a dedication may arise either from words or conduct, the Statute of Frauds should have no application in the creation of easements by dedication. But since dedication is an exceptional and peculiar mode of passing title to an interest in land, the courts will not lightly declare a dedication to public use.[47]

---

41. Steadman v. Town of Pinetops, 251 N.C. 509, 112 S.E.2d 102 (1960); Home Real Estate Loan & Ins., Co. v. Town of Carolina Beach, 216 N.C. 778, 7 S.E.2d 13 (1939); Hine v. Blumenthal, 239 N.C. 537, 80 S.E.2d 266 (1954); Broocks v. Muirhead, 223 N.C. 227, 25 S.E.2d 889 (1943); *Accord,* Commercial Fin. Corp. v. Langston, 24 N.C. App. 706, 212 S.E.2d 176 (1975).

Under N.C. GEN. STAT. § 136-96, if a developer has dedicated a street or alley to a municipality but the municipal authorities fail to improve and open to public use the street or alley for a period of 15 years, the dedicator or some one or more claiming under him may file and record a declaration withdrawing the street or alley from dedication. By failure to develop or use, the municipality's right to insist on the dedication is lost. Osborne v. Town of North Wilkesboro, 280 N.C. 696, 187 S.E.2d 102 (1972). But where the continued use of any strip of land dedicated for street or highway purposes shall be necessary to afford convenient ingress or egress to any lot or parcel of land sold and conveyed by the dedicator of such street or highway, the street or highway may not be withdrawn under N.C. GEN. STAT. § 136-96. *See* Andrews v. Country Club Hills, Inc., 18 N.C. App. 6, 195 S.E.2d 584 (1973).

42. *See* Todd v. White, 246 N.C. 59, 97 S.E.2d 439 (1957).

43. Spaugh v. Charlotte, 239 N.C. 149, 79 S.E.2d 748 (1953).

44. Owens v. Elliott, 257 N.C. 250, 125 S.E.2d 589 (1962); Nicholas v. Furniture Co., 248 N.C. 462, 103 S.E.2d 837 (1958); Milliken v. Denny, 141 N.C. 224, 53 S.E. 867 (1906).

45. Owens v. Elliott, 258 N.C. 314, 128 S.E.2d 583 (1962). *See* Oliver v. Ernul, 277 N.C. 591, 178 S.E.2d 393 (1970) reaffirming the principle that a dedication without acceptance is a mere revocable offer and is not complete until accepted by some competent public authority (mere permissive use being insufficient). Citing Gault v. Lake Waccamaw, 200 N.C. 593, 158 S.E. 104 (1931); Chesson v. Jordan, 224 N.C. 289, 29 S.E.2d 906 (1944); 2 THOMPSON ON REAL PROPERTY (Grimes ed. 1961) § 372.

46. "if there is a dedication by the owner, completed by acceptance on the part of the public, or by persons in a position to act for them, the right at once arises, and the time of user is no longer material." Nicholas v. Furniture Co., 248 N.C. 462, 103 S.E.2d 837 (1958).

47. *Id.*

§ 318. Acquisition of Easements by Prescription — Generally.

An easement may be acquired by prescription or adverse user for a specified length of time. Prescription means literally "before written" and the law of prescriptive rights had its genesis in courts' application of a legal fiction that immemorial usage of land by a claimant must have been based originally on a "lost grant."[48] Today, however, courts have discarded for the most part any reliance on the lost-grant theory and have adopted, by analogy, the statute of limitations applicable for acquiring title to land by adverse possession as the basis for presuming a grant of an easement.[49] An open, continuous adverse use of land for a period of twenty years will create an easement in the user in North Carolina.[50]

§ 319. Same — Necessity That Use Be Adverse.

In order for an easement to arise by prescription, the claimant must show an adverse or hostile use.[51] A use by permission or license for the period of the statute of limitations will be insufficient to establish an easement by prescription; the use must be with the intent to hold to the exclusion of others.[52] A mere permissive use of a way over another's land, no matter how long continued, cannot ripen into an easement by prescription.[53] A party asserting an easement by prescription has the burden of showing that his use was adverse, as every use will be presumed permissive until the contrary is shown.[54] To show that a use is "hostile" rather

---

48. Draper v. Conner & Walters Co., 187 N.C. 18, 121 S.E. 697 (1924).
49. N.C. GEN. STAT. § 1-40 is the basic adverse possession statute in North Carolina.
50. Draper v. Conner & Walters Co., 187 N.C. 18, 121 S.E. 697 (1924); Nash v. Shute, 184 N.C. 383, 114 S.E. 470 (1922); Weaver v. Pitts, 191 N.C. 747, 133 S.E. 2 (1926); Grant v. Tallassee Power Co., 196 N.C. 617, 146 S.E. 531 (1929). *See generally* Dickinson v. Pake, 19 N.C. App. 287, 198 S.E.2d 467, *rev'd,* 284 N.C. 576, 201 S.E.2d 897 (1973), citing §§ 285-291 of the original edition (§§ 318-324 in this edition). *See also* Adams v. Severt, 40 N.C. App. 247, 252 S.E.2d 276 (1979); Watkins v. Smith, 40 N.C. App. 506, 253 S.E.2d 354 (1979); Coggins v. Fox, 34 N.C. App. 138, 239 S.E.2d 594 (1977), the latter two cases listing all elements of the doctrine of easements by prescription.
51. Nicholas v. Furniture Co., 248 N.C. 462, 103 S.E.2d 837 (1958); Weaver v. Pitts, 191 N.C. 747, 133 S.E. 2 (1926). *Accord,* Dickinson v. Pake, 19 N.C. App. 287, 198 S.E.2d 467, *rev'd on other grounds,* 284 N.C. 576, 201 S.E.2d 897 (1973); Watkins v. Smith, 40 N.C. App. 506, 253 S.E.2d 354 (1979); Coggins v. Fox, 34 N.C. App. 138, 237 S.E.2d 332 (1977).
52. Colvin v. Tallassee Power Co., 199 N.C. 353, 154 S.E. 678 (1930); Gruber v. Eubank, 197 N.C. 280, 148 S.E. 246 (1929).
53. Nicholas v. Furniture Co., 248 N.C. 462, 103 S.E.2d 837 (1958); Henry v. Farlowe, 238 N.C. 542, 78 S.E.2d 244 (1953); Speight v. Anderson, 226 N.C. 492, 39 S.E.2d 371 (1946); Chesson v. Jordan, 224 N.C. 289, 29 S.E.2d 906 (1944); Darr v. Aluminum Co., 215 N.C. 768, 3 S.E.2d 434 (1939); Railroad v. Ahoskie, 202 N.C. 585, 163 S.E. 565 (1932). *Accord,* Dickinson v. Pake, 19 N.C. App. 287, 198 S.E.2d 467, *rev'd on other grounds,* 284 N.C. 576, 201 S.E.2d 897 (1973).
54. Nicholas v. Furniture Co., 248 N.C. 462, 103 S.E.2d 837 (1958); Weaver v. Pitts, 191 N.C. 747, 133 S.E. 2 (1926); Dickinson v. Pake, 19 N.C. App. 287, 198 S.E.2d 467, *rev'd on other grounds,* 284 N.C. 576, 201 S.E.2d 897 (1973); Adams v. Severt, 40 N.C. App. 247, 252 S.E.2d 276 (1979); Watkins v. Smith, 40 N.C. App. 506, 253 S.E.2d 354 (1979); Coggins v. Fox, 34 N.C. App. 138, 237 S.E.2d 332 (1977).

than permissive, however, it is not necessary to show that there was a heated controversy, or a manifestation of ill will, or that the claimant was in any sense the owner of the servient estate.[55] "Hostility" can be sufficiently shown by demonstrating a use exercised under such circumstances as to manifest and give notice that the use was made under a claim of right.[56]

§ 320. Same — Necessity of Openness and Notoriety.

In order for an adverse use of land to ripen into an easement by prescription, it is necessary for the use to be open and notorious.[57] The general principle is the same as in the case of adverse possession. It is not essential that the owner should actually know that his land is being adversely used, but it is necessary that the acts of user be open so that the owner may have notice that the land is being so used.[58] The use must not be concealed, clandestine, secretive or under cover of darkness so that the servient owner can have no opportunity to know of the use being made of his land. The requirement of openness and notoriety is for the purpose of assuring the owner whose land is being used that he should protect himself against the creation of an easement over his land by prescription. If the landowner actually knows of an adverse use being made of his land, or if the use is such that a reasonable inspection of his land would indicate such usage, the openness and notoriety requirement is met.[59]

§ 321. Same — Requirement of Continuity for Prescriptive Period.

In order for an easement to be created by prescription, the adverse use of the land must be continuous and uninterrupted throughout the prescriptive period, twenty years in North Carolina.[60]

The terms "continuous" and "uninterrupted" are not synonymous. "Continuous" refers to the claimant's behavior and activity, while "uninterrupted" refers to the behavior and activity of the potential servient landowner.[61] The "continuous" usage required of a claimant of

---

55. Dulin v. Faires, 266 N.C. 257, 145 S.E.2d 873 (1965); Snowden v. Bell, 159 N.C. 497, 75 S.E. 721 (1912). *Accord,* Dickinson v. Pake, 19 N.C. App. 287, 198 S.E.2d 467, *rev'd on other grounds,* 284 N.C. 576, 201 S.E.2d 897 (1973).

56. *Id.*

57. Dulin v. Faires, 266 N.C. 257, 145 S.E.2d 873 (1965). *Accord,* Dickinson v. Pake, 19 N.C. App. 287, 198 S.E.2d 467, *rev'd on other grounds,* 284 N.C. 576, 201 S.E.2d 897 (1973), citing this section in the original edition (§ 287).

58. 3 POWELL, REAL PROPERTY 486 (1966). *Accord,* Dickinson v. Pake, 19 N.C. App. 287, 198 S.E.2d 467, *rev'd on other grounds,* 284 N.C. 576, 201 S.E.2d 897 (1973).

59. *Id.*

60. Ingraham v. Hough, 46 N.C. 39 (1853); Speight v. Anderson, 226 N.C. 492, 39 S.E.2d 371 (1946); Adams v. Severt, 40 N.C. App. 247, 252 S.E.2d 276 (1979); Dickinson v. Pake, 19 N.C. App. 287, 198 S.E.2d 467, *rev'd on other grounds,* 284 N.C. 576, 201 S.E.2d 897 (1973), citing this section in the original edition (§ 288).

61. 3 POWELL, REAL PROPERTY 487 (1966).

an easement by prescription does not mean a perpetually unceasing use, but has been construed reasonably to depend on the nature of the easement asserted.[62] The continuity required is that the use be exercised more or less frequently, according to the purpose and nature of the easement.[63] It is necessary, however, that the use be often enough and with such regularity as to constitute notice to the potential servient owner that the user is asserting an easement.[64] It should also be noted that this continuity of usage requirement dictates that the acts of usage relate to the same area of land for the prescriptive period. For example, the claim of a prescriptive right-of-way will be denied unless the user is confined to definite and specific lines for the whole time.[65]

In addition to the continuous use requirement, it is essential that there be no break in the claimant's attitude of mind, such as would be evidenced by a recognition of subordination to the servient owner's consent, or an abandonment of the use in response to the servient owner's demand, or a payment to the servient owner for a privilege of continuing the use.[66]

The requirement that an adverse user's usage of land must be "uninterrupted" for the prescriptive period in order to create an easement by prescription means that the evidence must show that the potential servient owner has not succeeded, either by threats or the construction of physical barriers, in causing a discontinuance of the use of the land. If the owner of the land blocks the usage of the land, however briefly, this

---

62. *E.g., see* the old case of Williams v. Buchanan, 23 N.C. 535 (1841), for an analogous analysis. In that case, involving adverse possession which also requires "continuity," the court held that the placing of fish traps in a river every year only during the fishing season for the purpose of catching fish constituted sufficiently "continuous" possession to pass title by adverse possession. *See generally* Dickinson v. Pake, 19 N.C. App. 287, 198 S.E.2d 467, *rev'd on other grounds,* 284 N.C. 576, 201 S.E.2d 897 (1973).

63. *E.g.,* certain uses, such as for overhanging eaves, are unceasing, while others, such as easements of way, are used only intermittently according to the needs of the claimant. While perpetual and unceasing use is not required, there must be a frequency and regularity of usage. *See* Romans v. Nadler, 217 Minn. 174, 14 N.W.2d 482 (1944), in which it is held that the mere entering of alleged servient land twice per year and resting ladders thereon for the purpose of cleaning rain gutters was too infrequent to support a claim of an easement. The usage must be of such frequency as to apprise the alleged servient owner that he should take steps to prevent himself from being subject to an easement.

64. 3 POWELL, REAL PROPERTY 488 (1966).

65. While there may be slight deviations in the line of travel there must be substantial identity of the thing enjoyed. *See* Speight v. Anderson, 226 N.C. 492, 39 S.E.2d 371 (1946) in which the court said: "One who uses one path or track for a portion of the prescriptive period and thereafter abandons all or nearly all of such path or track and uses another cannot tack the period of the use of the new way onto that of the use of the old way in order to acquire a way by prescription." *See also* Watkins v. Smith, 40 N.C. App. 506, 253 S.E.2d 354 (1979) and Coggins v. Fox, 34 N.C. App. 138, 237 S.E.2d 332 (1977) listing this requirement.

66. 3 POWELL, REAL PROPERTY 488 (1966).

destroys the continuity of usage required.[67] While the erection of actual physical barriers preventing usage and the prosecuting of a lawsuit to judgment will constitute "interruptions," mere ineffective protests or disregarded remonstrances should serve only to strengthen the evidence of adverse use and should have no significance as interruptions of the easement claimant's use.[68]

§ 322. Same — "Tacking" Applies.

It should be observed that successive adverse users, like successive adverse possessions of land, may be tacked together so as to aggregate the prescriptive period if there is privity between prior and successive adverse users.[69] The requisite privity exists when a subsequent user succeeds to the interest of an earlier user by deed, descent, will, contract or other voluntary or involuntary conveyance and continues to use the land in the manner of his predecessor.[70] Successive uses under a common claim, as for example, by a tenant for his landlord, or by a life tenant for a remainderman, will also provide the necessary privity.[71] Of course, these tacked uses must all be adverse, continuous and uninterrupted, and there must be no hiatus. No period of use may be included that is permissive, and the extent of use by the successor user must correspond to the usage of the prior user.[72]

If an adverse use of land starts against an owner and continues for the prescriptive period, the fact that a receiver is appointed for the owner before the prescriptive period lapses will not prevent the acquisition of an easement by prescription.[73]

---

67. 3 POWELL, REAL PROPERTY 491 (1966). *But see* MINOR & WURTS, REAL PROPERTY § 848 (1910), which states that if passage is only rendered less convenient, without blocking it altogether, the continuity is not broken.

An "interruption" to an easement for a right-of-way would be any act, done by the owner of the servient tenement, which would prevent the full and free enjoyment of the easement by the owner of the dominant tenement. *See* Dickinson v. Pake, 284 N.C. 576, 201 S.E.2d 897 (1973), quoting from Ingraham v. Hough, 46 N.C. 39 (1853).

68. 3 POWELL, REAL PROPERTY 490 (1966).

69. RESTATEMENT OF PROPERTY § 464 (1944); MINOR & WURTS, REAL PROPERTY § 848 (1910).

"Tacking" is defined in Dickinson v. Pake, 284 N.C. 576, 201 S.E.2d 897 (1973) (citing this section) as the legal principle whereby successive adverse users in privity with prior adverse users can tack successive adverse possessions of land so as to aggregate the prescriptive period of twenty years.

It should be noted from the *Dickinson* case that if an easement has already ripened in a person by his adverse use of the land of another, his easement passes upon his death by succession to his heirs and the principle of 'tacking" is no longer involved.

70. 3 POWELL, REAL PROPERTY 496 (1966).

71. *Id.*

72. 3 POWELL, REAL PROPERTY 497 (1966).

73. Nicholas v. Furniture Co., 248 N.C. 462, 103 S.E.2d 837 (1958).

§ 323. Same — Effect of Disabilities.

Since the prescriptive period for acquiring easements by prescription is drawn by analogy to the period specified in the statute of limitations relating to the acquisition of title to land by adverse possession, it is customary for the analogy to carry over and to apply the same rules of disability to prescription as apply to adverse possession.[74] Thus, if the owner is under eighteen years of age or insane at the time the adverse user starts, the prescriptive period will not bar the owner until three years after such disability is removed. If, however, no such disability exists at the time the adverse user commences, any subsequent disability occurring will not prevent the running of the prescriptive period.

§ 324. Same — Extent of Use; Extent of Easement.

For the creation of an easement by prescription, it is necessary that the easement have boundaries sufficiently definite to be located and identified with reasonable certainty.[75]

Since an easement by prescription is based upon continuous user for the prescriptive period, the extent of the easement created thereby arises only to the extent of the customary user.[76] While in the case of easements arising by express grant the language of the grant is to be examined to define and limit the rights of the parties, as to easements created by prescription the only way to determine the extent is by reference to the accustomed user. Thus, whether one claiming a way over another's land by prescription is entitled to a footway, horseway, carriageway, or way for other vehicle or purpose, depends upon the mode in which he has been accustomed to using the land during the prescriptive period.[77]

§ 325. Same — No Prescriptive Easement May Be Acquired Against the State, Municipalities or Counties in Public Roads, Streets, etc.; No Easement by Prescription Against United States Government.

Pursuant to statute in North Carolina no exclusive easement or title can be acquired by any person by adverse use or possession against the State, any municipality or county in any public road, street, lane, alley,

---

74. *See* N.C. GEN. STAT. §§ 1-17, 1-19, 1-20 (1966). MINOR & WURTS, REAL PROPERTY § 846 (1910). *See generally* the discussion of disabilities with respect to adverse possession at § 302 *supra*.

75. Fremont v. Baker, 236 N.C. 253, 72 S.E.2d 666 (1952); Speight v. Anderson, 226 N.C. 492, 39 S.E.2d 371 (1946); Cahoon v. Houghton, 215 N.C. 116, 1 S.E.2d 362 (1939). *Accord,* Dickinson v. Pake, 284 N.C. 576, 201 S.E.2d 897 (1973).

76. 2 THOMPSON, REAL PROPERTY § 349 (1961).

77. MINOR & WURTS, REAL PROPERTY § 847 (1910).

square, or public way.[78] The foregoing rule does not apply, however, to prevent the acquisition of an easement or title by adverse user or possession of land dedicated to public ways, squares, commons, streets, alleys or parks if there has been no acceptance by a municipality.[79]

Another statute [80] prevents the creation of any right-of-way, easement, or title by adverse possession in any land condemned or acquired in any other way by a railroad, plank road, turnpike, or canal company for use as a right-of-way, depot, station house or place of landing.[81]

An easement by prescription cannot be obtained against the United States.[82]

§ 326. Acquisition of Easements by Condemnation.

Easements may be acquired by condemnation under the laws conferring the right of eminent domain.[83] The State and its agencies and public service corporations which are given the power of eminent domain may condemn and take easement rights in lands for public roads, streets, rights-of-way and for other necessary purposes upon following the statutory proceedings and paying just compensation to the owner therefor.[84] While a fee simple title may be condemned, very often condemnations for railway rights-of-way, and for telephone or power lines and for other purposes are of easements only.[85]

---

78. N.C. GEN. STAT. § 1-45 (1966); Lenoir County v. Crabtree, 158 N.C. 357, 74 S.E. 105 (1912); Steadman v. Town of Pinetops, 251 N.C. 509, 112 S.E.2d 102 (1960); Salisbury v. Barnhardt, 249 N.C. 549, 107 S.E.2d 297 (1959). *But see* Saddle Club, Inc. v. Gibson, 9 N.C. App. 565, 176 S.E.2d 846 (1970). While N.C. GEN. STAT. § 1-45 prevents a person from acquiring an exclusive right to land against the State in a highway right-of-way, it does not prevent a person from acquiring a right therein superior to all other persons save the State. Thus, where plaintiff had possessed a 20-foot strip within the right-of-way of a State highway for seven years under color of title, it was held that plaintiff's rights to the strip were superior to all other parties except the State. Defendant was compelled to pay damages for cutting trees within the State's right-of-way which had been possessed by plaintiff.

The statute likewise does not prevent an adverse possessor from acquiring title in property that has been conveyed to trustees for the benefit of members of the community for use as a community house or playground. *See* Carswell v. Creswell, 217 N.C. 40, 7 S.E.2d 58 (1940).

79. Lee v. Walker, 234 N.C. 687, 68 S.E.2d 664 (1952); Salisbury v. Barnhardt, 249 N.C. 549, 107 S.E.2d 297 (1959); Hall v. Fitzgerald, 248 N.C. 474, 103 S.E.2d 815 (1958).

80. N.C. GEN. STAT. § 1-44.

81. Withers v. Long Mfg. Co., 259 N.C. 139, 129 S.E.2d 886 (1963).

82. 2 THOMPSON, REAL PROPERTY § 339 (1961).

83. *See* N.C. GEN. STAT. §§ 40-11, 40-20, 40-32.

84. Virginia & Carolina Southern R.R. v. McLean, 158 N.C. 498, 74 S.E. 461 (1912); City of Statesville v. Bowles, 6 N.C. App. 124, 169 S.E.2d 467 (1969). *See* Power Co. v. Ham House, Inc., 43 N.C. App. 308, 258 S.E.2d 815 (1979) discussing the proper measure of damages in the condemnation of an easement.

85. *E.g.*, only an easement passes to a railroad upon its condemnation of a right-of-way. Virginia & Carolina Southern R.R. v. McLean, 158 N.C. 498, 74 S.E. 461 (1912).

§ 327. Acquisition of Easements by Statutory Cartway Proceeding in North Carolina.

In North Carolina there is a peculiar mode provided by statute [86] for the establishment of cartways of not less than eighteen feet in width for ingress and egress to a public highway over intervening lands when there is no reasonable access to lands which are used for the purposes of cultivation, cutting and removing timber, working of any quarries, mines or minerals, operating industrial or manufacturing plants, public or private cemeteries, or for purposes preparatory to such uses. The procedures provided by the statutes specify that the Clerk of the Superior Court shall appoint a jury of view made up of three disinterested freeholders [87] who shall lay off the cartway and assess damages which the petitioner for the cartway must pay to the owner for the establishment of such cartway.[88]

Being in derogation of the common law, North Carolina General Statutes § 136-69 is strictly construed by the courts.[89] Thus, no cartway will be established under it unless the petitioner's land is used or is being

---

86. N.C. GEN. STAT. §§ 136-68, 136-69.

87. The laying off of a cartway, its location, its termini, the land to be burdened, and the adjudication of damages are matters for the jury of view to determine. Candler v. Sluder, 259 N.C. 62, 130 S.E.2d 1 (1963); Garris v. Byrd, 229 N.C. 343, 49 S.E.2d 625 (1948). The Clerk of the Superior Court determines the right to a cartway and the mechanics of locating it and laying it off is for the jury of view. Candler v. Sluder, 259 N.C. 62, 130 S.E.2d 1 (1963); Dailey v. Bay, 215 N.C. 652, 3 S.E.2d 14 (1939). But see Taylor v. West Virginia Pulp & Paper Co., 262 N.C. 452, 137 S.E.2d 833 (1964), which states that while the location of the way is the task of the jury of view, its acts are reviewable by the court.

88. The establishment of a cartway is in the nature of a condemnation for which compensation must be paid. See N.C. GEN. STAT. § 136-68; Garris v. Byrd, 229 N.C. 343, 49 S.E.2d 625 (1948); Kanupp v. Land, 248 N.C. 203, 102 S.E.2d 779 (1958).

89. Brown v. Glass, 229 N.C. 657, 50 S.E.2d 912 (1948); Opinion of Atty. Gen. to Bessie J. Cherry, 46 N.C.A.G. 222 (1977). See also Pritchard v. Scott, 254 N.C. 277, 118 S.E.2d 890 (1961); Candler v. Sluder, 259 N.C. 62, 130 S.E.2d 1 (1963); Warlick v. Lowman, 103 N.C. 122, 9 S.E. 458 (1889). But see Candler v. Sluder, supra, which holds that once a legitimate purpose for the establishment of a cartway is determined, the cartway that is laid off may be used for purposes other than those set forth in the statute. In that case the cartway was established to "cultivate" fruit trees and for the removal of timber. It was held that the cartway could also be used for hunters who rented a cabin on the land after its location.

In accord with Brown v. Glass, 229 N.C. 657, 50 S.E.2d 912 (1948), that the cartway statute N.C. GEN. STAT. § 136-69 must be strictly construed, see Taylor v. Askew, 17 N.C. App. 620, 195 S.E.2d 316 (1973).

See Yount v. Lowe, 24 N.C. App. 48, 209 S.E.2d 867 (1974), which indicates that once a cartway has been acquired under N.C. GEN. STAT. § 136-69 the landowner who has acquired a cartway to a public highway is not limited in the uses he can make of the property. On appeal of the case of Yount v. Lowe, 288 N.C. 90, 215 S.E.2d 563 (1975), the Supreme Court of North Carolina held that since a *consent judgment* was entered by the parties pursuant to the cartway proceeding, whereby plaintiffs' predecessor in title agreed that defendants should have a perpetual right and easement of ingress and egress without limitation as to the purpose of its use, such consent judgment made inapplicable any limitations of N.C. GEN. STAT. § 136-69 with respect to the purposes for which a cartway may be laid out. The court

prepared for one of the uses specified in the statute.[90] Nor will a cartway be allowed if the petitioner has another reasonable or adequate means of ingress and egress to a public road.[91] This has been held to prevent the acquisition of a cartway if the petitioner's land is surrounded entirely by the lands of his grantor or by the lands of his grantor and others; in such case, the law gives him an easement by necessity and he must seek his way out over his vendor's lands and not by the cartway statute.[92] With respect to "permissive" rights-of-way, whether they are "in all respects reasonable and adequate as a proper means of ingress and egress" must be determined. If the permissive nature of the way renders it insufficient to meet the requirement of "other adequate means of transportation affording necessary and proper means of ingress thereto and egress therefrom" within the meaning of the statute, the relief should be granted.[93]

Article III. Extent of Easements; Scope of Rights of User; Actions

§ 328. Generally.

Assuming that an easement exists, by whatever means created, its extent and scope is a frequently litigated issue. The extent and scope of

---

emphasized that a consent judgment is a contract and since the consent judgment between the parties specified that defendants were to have an easement over plaintiffs' lands in general terms, without any limitations, there was an enforceable contractual agreement that defendants were to have an easement of unlimited reasonable use.

90. Id.

91. See Taylor v. Askew, 17 N.C. App. 620, 195 S.E.2d 316 (1973), which holds that a petitioner is not entitled to have a cartway laid out over the lands of another under N.C. GEN. STAT. § 136-69 simply because it would give him a shorter and better outlet to the public road. Warlick v. Lowman, 104 N.C. 403, 10 S.E. 474 (1889).

92. Pritchard v. Scott, 254 N.C. 277, 118 S.E.2d 890 (1961).

93. With respect to "permissive" rights-of-way, however, see Wilson v. Smith, 18 N.C. App. 414, 197 S.E.2d 23 (1973), which holds that the fact plaintiffs had a *permissive* right-of-way to a public highway across the lands of strangers would not prevent them from obtaining a *way of necessity* over the lands of the grantor in order to get to the highway where it was shown that grantees could not obtain a loan on their property to finance the construction of their home because they lacked a legally enforceable right of access to the public way where the requisites for obtaining an easement of necessity were present. The same reasoning is apparently applicable where a "cartway" is sought by one who has a "permissive" outlet to a highway. *Cf.* earlier decisions holding that access pursuant to permission and not as a matter of right will preclude operation of the cartway statute. Garris v. Byrd, 229 N.C. 343, 49 S.E.2d 625 (1948); Pritchard v. Scott, 254 N.C. 277, 118 S.E.2d 890 (1961); Taylor v. West Virginia Pulp & Paper Co., 262 N.C. 452, 137 S.E.2d 833 (1964). The latter case held that access to a navigable creek was sufficient access for the transportation of timber to market in that the timber could be rafted or floated to market. *But see* Mayo v. Thigpen, 107 N.C. 63, 11 S.E. 1052 (1890), which says that if a passageway is impassable to get to a public road, even if owned by the petitioner himself, he is entitled to a cartway over the lands of another.

use that may be made of land by an easement holder of an easement created by express grant is determined by the words of the deed or instrument creating such easement.[94] If the terms of an instrument creating an easement are ambiguous, the court will interpret the scope and extent of the easement so as to effect a rational purpose and to effectuate the intention of the parties.[95] In determining the extent of an easement created by contract, consideration must be given to the purpose for which it was granted, the subject matter of the contract, and the situation of the parties.[96] Easements of grant therefore have a built-in elasticity in that the courts can assume that certain permissible variations of use were within the contemplation of the parties if such uses would reasonably serve the purposes of the grant.[97]

In the case of easements arising by prescription, the character and pattern of the user during the whole prescriptive period during which the easement came into being determines its extent.[98]

If the easement is created by implication through the prior use of a quasi-easement,[99] its scope and extent is measured by the scope and extent of the use of the land involved which gave rise to the quasi-easement, since the courts in such cases are merely attempting to effectuate the unexpressed intention of the parties.[100]

If the easement is one of necessity,[101] its scope and extent depends on what use is reasonably essential for the beneficial use of the dominant tract to which it is appurtenant.[102]

---

94. Hine v. Blumenthal, 239 N.C. 537, 80 S.E.2d 266 (1954); Weyerhaeuser Co. v. Light Co., 257 N.C. 717, 127 S.E.2d 539 (1962). *See, e.g.,* Hanner v. Power Co., 34 N.C. App. 737, 239 S.E.2d 594 (1977) where a clear easement agreement was enforced as written and the argument of the servient owner that the right to grow "crops" on a power-line right-of-way included trees was flatly rejected.

95. *Id.*

96. Shingleton v. State, 260 N.C. 451, 133 S.E.2d 183 (1963). *Compare,* City of Statesville v. Bowles, 6 N.C. App. 124, 169 S.E.2d 467 (1969), which states with respect to an easement taken by eminent domain that an easement "extends to all uses directly or incidentally conducive to the advancement of the purpose for which the land was acquired, and to no others; and the owner retains the title to the land in fee and the right to make any use of it that does not interfere with the full and free exercise of the public easement." *See* Sampson v. City of Greensboro, 35 N.C. App. 148, 240 S.E.2d 502 (1978) holding that, where an ordinance provided that all property shown on a plat as dedicated for a public use would be deemed to be dedicated for any other public use approved by the city council in the public interest, a contention that an easement shown on a recorded plat was dedicated for storm sewer purposes only and not for sanitary sewer purposes fell on deaf judicial ears.

97. 3 POWELL, REAL PROPERTY 508 (1966); Shingleton v. State, 260 N.C. 451, 133 S.E.2d 183 (1963).

98. MINOR & WURTS, REAL PROPERTY § 847 (1910); Powell v. Lash, 64 N.C. 456 (1870).

99. *See* § 315 *supra.*

100. 3 POWELL, REAL PROPERTY 519 (1966).

101. *See* text at note 24, § 314 *supra.*

102. 3 POWELL, REAL PROPERTY 518 (1966).

In general, once an easement has been established, the easement holder must not change the use for which the easement was created so as to increase the burden of the servient tract.[103] For instance, where an easement is created for the purpose of running a power transmission line over land, the easement holder is not authorized to erect other types of utility lines across the servient premises.[104] The easement holder cannot "increase the servitude" by making greater use of the premises than is contemplated by the purpose for which the easement has been created.[105] It should be noted, however, that increased usage has been allowed in some cases, making allowances for normal evolutionary expectations in the development of land and certain technological advances. For example, no wrongful increase in land burden is necessarily present where a footpath for a single dwelling house is converted into a path for dwellers of a multi-family apartment house erected on the site.[106] The grantee of an easement is not limited to the methods of use current at the time of creation of the easement but may avail himself of modern improvements.[107] It has been held that ways created for carriages may be used for motor vehicles and that such usage does not constitute an increase of the servitude.[108] That the holder of an easement may make use of modern inventions in order to fully exercise and enjoy the purpose for which the easement was granted.[109] It is sometimes said that easement usage may be changed in degree, but that changes in kind of uses are not authorized.[110]

---

103. 1 MORDECAI, LAW LECTURES 469 (1916).

104. Grimes v. Power Co., 245 N.C. 583, 96 S.E.2d 713 (1956); Cooke v. Electric Membership Corp., 245 N.C. 453, 96 S.E.2d 351 (1956). See also McCullock v. North Carolina R.R., 146 N.C. 316, 59 S.E. 882 (1907), which states that a railroad which has an easement cannot lease another railroad company and expand the use of its right-of-way to handle increased business appertaining to the leased company. Railroad v. Railroad, 120 N.C. 520, 26 S.E. 913 (1896), holds that the running of streetcars over a railway bridge already constructed for railway purposes imposes an additional servitude on the easement involved and for which compensation had to be paid.

See Van Leuven v. Motor Lines, 261 N.C. 539, 135 S.E.2d 640 (1964), which holds that the fact that the State Highway Commission has acquired an easement over lands for highway purposes does not allow it to permit another agency to construct a sewer line within the easement without the payment of further compensation.

105. 1 MORDECAI, LAW LECTURES 469 (1916).

106. Baldwin v. Boston & M.R., 181 Mass. 166, 63 N.W. 428 (1901); 2 THOMPSON, REAL PROPERTY 693 (1961).

107. McDonnell v. Sheets, 234 Iowa 1148, 15 N.W.2d 252 (1944). See other cases collected in Note, 156 A.L.R. 1050, 1053 (1945).

108. See Diocese of Trenton v. Toman, 74 N.J. Eq. 702, 70 A. 606 (1908), and McDonnell v. Sheets, 234 Iowa 1148, 15 N.W.2d 252 (1944). But see Clarkin v. Duggan, 292 Mass. 263, 198 N.E. 170 (1935), which holds that an easement for "teams only" did not permit use by motor vehicles.

109. 2 THOMPSON, REAL PROPERTY 694 (1961).

110. Baldwin v. Boston & M.R., 181 Mass. 166, 63 N.W. 428 (1901).

The use of land for an easement is limited to a reasonable use and for the purpose only for which the easement is created.[111] If the easement is an appurtenant easement, appurtenant to specific land, it cannot be extended to any other land or converted into an easement in gross without the consent of the owner of the servient tract.[112] The right to make a reasonable use of land subject to an easement would logically carry with it by implication certain secondary rights essential to its enjoyment, such as the right to make repairs, renewals and replacements in connection with the easement so long as the easement holder uses reasonable care, does not increase the servitude and burden of the servient estate, and does not go beyond the authorized boundaries of his easement.[113]

§ 329. Servient Owner's Right to Use Lands Subject to Easement.

The owner of land that is subject to an easement has a right to continue to use his land in any manner and for any purpose which is not inconsistent with the reasonable use and enjoyment of the existing easement.[114] If, however, the owner of the servient estate makes a use of his

---

111. *E.g.,* an easement to transport sewage in a proper manner through underground pipes does not grant the right to cart sewage in an open watercourse across land. Veazey v. Durham, 231 N.C. 357, 57 S.E.2d 377 (1949). An easement for power lines and poles to one party, with the right to increase or decrease the number of wires, does not entitle the owner of the easement to grant to another utility a license to attach its crossarms and wires to the poles without payment of additional compensation to the landowner for the additional burden. Grimes v. Power Co., 245 N.C. 583, 96 S.E.2d 713 (1956). Nor can a railway company lease a part of its right-of-way to a private business for a nonrailroad use merely because such business is a customer and such use by the customer might incidentally enhance the expectation of additional freight business for the railroad. Sparrow v. Tobacco Co., 232 N.C. 589, 61 S.E.2d 700 (1950). *See also* Hildebrand v. Telegraph Co., 219 N.C. 402, 14 S.E.2d 252 (1941). *Compare,* City of Statesville v. Bowles, 6 N.C. App. 124, 169 S.E.2d 467 (1969), which states with respect to an easement taken by eminent domain that an easement "extends to all uses directly or incidentally conducive to the advancement of the purpose for which the land was acquired, and to no others; and the owner retains the title to the land in fee and the right to make any use of it that does not interfere with the full and free exercise of the public easement." *Compare also* Sampson v. City of Greensboro, 35 N.C. App. 148, 240 S.E.2d 502 (1978) involving the expansion of the scope of an easement by dedication by a public ordinance.

112. Wood v. Woodley, 160 N.C. 17, 75 S.E. 719 (1912). *See* Lovin v. Crisp, 36 N.C. App. 185, 243 S.E.2d 406 (1978) holding that a deed conveying a parcel of land which also provided that water rights "shall run with the lands" of the grantees created an easement appurtenant only to the land conveyed in such deed and not appurtenant to other lands owned by the grantees.

113. Lamb v. Lamb, 177 N.C. 150, 98 S.E. 307 (1919); RESTATEMENT OF PROPERTY § 485 (1944).

114. Railroad v. Sturgeon, 120 N.C. 225, 26 S.E. 779 (1897); Hildebrand v. Telegraph Co., 219 N.C. 402, 14 S.E.2d 252 (1941); Light Co. v. Bowman, 229 N.C. 682, 51 S.E.2d 191 (1948); Bivens v. Railroad, 247 N.C. 711, 102 S.E.2d 128 (1958); Chesson v. Jordan, 224 N.C. 289, 29 S.E.2d 906 (1944). *Accord,* City of Statesville v. Bowles, 6 N.C. App. 124, 169 S.E.2d 467 (1969), to the effect that an owner whose land is subject to an easement has the right to make any use of it that does not interfere with the full and free exercise of the easement.

land in such a way as to obstruct or interfere with the exercise of the easement, or inconsistent with its purposes, such usage may be enjoined.[115]

§ 330. Actions to Enforce Rights of Dominant and Servient Owners; Injunctions and Damages.

The usual remedies for wrongful interference with easement holders' use and enjoyment of easements are to bring an action at law for damages [116] or a suit in equity to procure a mandatory [117] or prohibitory [118] injunction either compelling the removal of the interference or forbidding the continuance of the objectionable conduct.[119]

If the easement holder makes an unwarranted use of the land of the servient owner in excess of the easement rights held, such use will consti-

---

Compare, Setzer v. Annas, 286 N.C. 534, 212 S.E.2d 154 (1975), which indicates that the owner of land subject to an easement is not precluded generally from maintaining gates across a way if they are not constructed so as to interfere unreasonably with the easement holder's right of passage. *See also,* Commercial Fin. Corp. v. Langston, 24 N.C. App. 706, 212 S.E.2d 176 (1975), to the effect that a grant of "an easement of way for the use of pedestrians and vehicles" on a 24-foot wide strip did not preclude servient owners from subsequently granting similar easements to others in the same way. *See* United States v. Sea Gate, Inc., 397 F. Supp. 1351 (N.C.D.C. 1975) where the court at 1358 states:

> The owner of an estate subject to an easement cannot use the fee in a fashion that obstructs or materially impairs the easement holder's use and enjoyment of his rights under the easement. Any activity by the fee owner which would result in increased cost or inconvenience to the easement holder in exercise of his rights or which would create a safety hazard should those rights be exercised amounts to a material impairment of the easement interest.

See also Hanner v. Power Co., 34 N.C. App. 737, 239 S.E.2d 594 (1977).

115. *E.g.,* where landowner erected and maintained theater and dwelling on right-of-way which an electric company had acquired, which were found to obstruct and interfere with the company's transmission lines, it was held that a mandatory or prohibitory injunction will lie to remove or prevent encroachment upon the easement. *See* Light Co. v. Bowman, 229 N.C. 682, 51 S.E.2d 191 (1948); United States v. Sea Gate, Inc., 397 F. Supp. 1351 (N.C.D.C. 1975).

116. Strickland v. Shew, 261 N.C. 82, 134 S.E.2d 137 (1963). The measure of damages for interference with an easement is (1) the difference between the value of the easement holder's right before and after the doing of the wrongful act, or (2) compensation for injuries suffered by the easement holder as the proximate result of the wrongful act or obstruction. *See* 3 POWELL, REAL PROPERTY § 420 (1966).

117. Carolina Power & Light Co. v. Bowman, 229 N.C. 682, 51 S.E.2d 191 (1948); Packard v. Smart, 224 N.C. 480, 31 S.E.2d 517 (1944). *Accord,* Pruitt v. Williams, 25 N.C. App. 376, 213 S.E.2d 369 (1975), which holds that a preliminary injunction may be issued to restrain the obstruction of a roadway easement where there is reasonable apprehension of irreparable loss unless interlocutory injunctive relief is granted. *See* U.S. v. Sea Gate, Inc., 397 F. Supp. 1351 (N.C.D.C. 1975).

118. *Id.*

119. 3 POWELL, REAL PROPERTY § 420 (1966).

tute an excessive user and likewise may be enjoined [120] or an action for damages may be brought.[121]

Article IV. Transferability of Easements

§ 331. Appurtenant Easements.

Where an easement is annexed as an appurtenance to land, it will pass as an appurtenance to the land when the land is transferred, by implication, whether the land is transferred by grant, devise or descent.[122] The appurtenant easement follows every part of the land into whatever hands the same may come, either by purchase or descent.[123] It should be noted, however, that use of the easement is limited in favor of the land to which it is appurtenant and cannot be extended to other land nor converted into a public way without the consent of the owner of the servient estate.[124] Nor can an appurtenant easement ever be transferred separate from the land to which it is appurtenant; it adheres in the particular land to which it is appurtenant and cannot exist separate from it.[125]

§ 332. Easements in Gross.

It has been stated that an easement in gross to pass over or to use land is purely personal and ends with the death of the easement holder and is neither inheritable nor assignable.[126]

---

120. Hales v. Atlantic Coast Line R.R., 172 N.C. 104, 90 S.E. 11 (1916).

121. *See, e.g.,* Bane v. Railroad Co., 259 N.C. 285, 130 S.E.2d 406 (1963); Waters v. Greenleaf-Johnson Lumber Co., 115 N.C. 648, 20 S.E. 718 (1894); Hanner v. Power Co., 34 N.C. App. 737, 239 S.E.2d 594 (1977).

122. Bowling v. Burton, 101 N.C. 176, 7 S.E. 701 (1888); Shingleton v. State, 260 N.C. 451, 133 S.E.2d 183 (1963); Hensley v. Ramsey, 283 N.C. 714, 199 S.E.2d 1 (1973); Yount v. Lowe, 288 N.C. 90, 215 S.E.2d 563 (1975); Gibbs v. Wright, 17 N.C. App. 495, 195 S.E.2d 40 (1973).

123. Wood v. Woodley, 160 N.C. 17, 75 S.E. 719 (1912).

124. *Id. See* Lovin v. Crisp, 36 N.C. App. 185, 243 S.E.2d 406 (1978) holding that a deed conveying a parcel of land which also provided that water rights "shall run with the lands" of the grantees created an easement appurtenant only to the land conveyed in such deed and not appurtenant to other lands owned by the grantees.

125. 1 MORDECAI, LAW LECTURES 470 (1916). *Accord,* Yount v. Lowe, 288 N.C. 90, 215 S.E.2d 563 (1975). *See* Gibbs v. Wright, 17 N.C. App. 495, 195 S.E.2d 40 (1973), which holds that when there is doubt as to whether an easement is an "easement in gross" or an "easement appurtenant," the easement will be presumed to be an easement appurtenant.

126. 1 MORDECAI, LAW LECTURES 469 (1916); Shingleton v. State, 260 N.C. 451, 133 S.E.2d 183 (1963); Davis v. Robinson, 189 N.C. 589, 127 S.E. 697 (1925).

See 3 POWELL, REAL PROPERTY § 419 (1966), for that author's views that easements in gross should be freely transferable except in those cases where the easements were demonstrably intended to benefit only the first recipient. Numerous cases decided in America are cited, particularly involving easements in gross created for commercial purposes (railroads, telephone, telegraph and electric power lines, pipelines, stream facilities, water ditches, and for business structures) in which such easements have been

Article V. Termination of Easements

§ 333. Generally.

Easements may be terminated or extinguished as the result of the acts of the easement owner alone, by action of the servient landowner alone, by mutual action, or in some cases even against the wishes of both parties. The following sections will set out the various ways in which easements may be terminated or extinguished.

§ 334. Cessation of Purposes of Easement.

If the particular purpose for which an easement is created is fulfilled, or otherwise ceases to exist, the easement also ceases. This is a corollary to the rule that an easement holder's right to use the property is a right to use it only for the purposes for which the easement is created; when the easement purpose ceases, the easement ceases. To determine if an easement is terminated by cessation of its purpose will, therefore, require a study of the terms of the grant or the circumstances under which the easement arose if the easement is one created by implication or operation of law.[127]

---

held transferable. In RESTATEMENT OF PROPERTY § 491 (1944), the position is taken that the transferability of easements in gross should be determined by reference to the terms of their creation.

See Gibbs v. Wright, 17 N.C. App. 495, 195 S.E.2d 40 (1973), in which it was held that an easement in a deed stating that grantors "agree for the party of the second part herein to get water by conveying the same from a spring above the tract" (retained by the grantors) was an easement appurtenant to the land conveyed, not an easement in gross amounting to no more than a personal license limited to the original grantee. The court stated:

> Whether an easement in a given case is appurtenant or in gross depends mainly on the nature of the right and the intention of the parties creating it. If the easement is in its nature an approriate and useful adjunct to the land conveyed, having in view the intention of the parties as to its use, and there is nothing to show that the parties intended it to be a mere personal right, it should be held to be an easement appurtenant and not an easement in gross. Easements in gross are not favored by the courts, however, and an easement will never be presumed as personal when it may fairly be construed as appurtenant to some other estate. If doubt exists as to its real nature, an easement is presumed to be appurtenant. 25 Am. Jur. 2d, Easements and Licenses, § 13, p. 427.

127. MINOR & WURTS, REAL PROPERTY § 103 (1910); TIFFANY, REAL PROPERTY § 567 (abr. ed. 1940); Railroad v. Way, 172 N.C. 774, 90 S.E. 937 (1916).

E.g., if an easement was created to maintain a staircase on adjoining land in order for the easement holder to get to his building, or in order that he might use a party wall for the benefit of a dominant building, if the dominant building is destroyed the purpose of the original grant creating the easement must be looked at to determine whether the easement was intended to be appurtenant only to that particular building or whether another building may be substituted to which the easement will attach. See Douglas v. Coonley, 156 N.Y. 521, 51 N.E. 283 (1898); Rudderham v. Emery Bros., 46 R.I. 171, 125 A. 291 (1924); Annot., 34 A.L.R. 606 (1925). As to destruction of buildings having a common party wall, in North Carolina it has been held that their destruction ordinarily puts an end to any easement. See George v. Smathers, 198 N.C. 212, 151 S.E. 194 (1929). See Price v. Bunn, 13 N.C. App.

Rights-of-way created by necessity terminate as soon as the necessity which has called them into existence ceases. For instance, when an easement holder who holds an easement of necessity acquires another mode of access, his easement is terminated.[128]

§ 335. Express Release.

The owner of an easement, usually the owner of the dominant tract, may expressly release to the servient owner his outstanding right to use the latter's land for the purposes of the easement.[129] This release is most satisfactorily effected by the execution of a deed of release or by quitclaim deed, as such instruments are recordable and can afford record notice of the easement's termination. Other methods of termination of easements, discussed *infra*, may not give indication in the land title records of the extinction of the easement and may make title unmarketable.

In North Carolina, while a mere unexecuted parol agreement will not extinguish an easement, if the parol agreement between the dominant and servient owners is accompanied by other facts, such as a reliance by the servient owner on the parol release, the easement may be extinguished.[130]

§ 336. Abandonment.

An easement may be extinguished through its abandonment by its owner.[131] In order to constitute an "abandonment" of an easement, there must be a concurrence of the easement holder's intention to abandon the easement and the external act by which such intention is carried into effect.[132] There must be a showing that the acts relied on as abandonment were voluntarily done by the owner of the dominant tenement, or by his express authority; that such party was the owner of the inheritance and had authority to bind the estate by his grant or release; and that the acts were of such a decisive character as to indicate and prove his intent to abandon the easement.[133]

652, 189 S.E.2d 523 (1972), citing this work. The North Carolina Court of Appeals held that a determinable easement was created where a deed granted to plaintiff an easement for so long as he and his heirs and assigns used the easement and specified that the easement would become null and void and revert to grantors in the event the plaintiff, his heirs or assigns failed to maintain a dam over a named creek for the period of five years.

128. Pritchard v. Scott, 254 N.C. 277, 118 S.E.2d 890 (1961).

129. 3 POWELL, REAL PROPERTY § 423 (1966); Hine v. Blumenthal, 239 N.C. 537, 80 S.E.2d 458 (1954).

130. Combs v. Brickhouse, 201 N.C. 366, 160 S.E. 355 (1931); Miller v. Teer, 220 N.C. 605, 18 S.E.2d 173 (1941); Moore v. Shore, 206 N.C. 699, 175 S.E. 117 (1934).

131. Moore v. Shore, 206 N.C. 699, 175 S.E. 117 (1934).

132. Miller v. Teer, 220 N.C. 605, 18 S.E.2d 173 (1941); Combs v. Brickhouse, 201 N.C. 366, 160 S.E. 355 (1931).

133. Miller v. Teer, 220 N.C. 605, 18 S.E.2d 173 (1941), and numerous cases there cited.

The question of abandonment is largely a matter of intention and is for the jury to decide.[134] A mere lapse of time or other delay in asserting rights under an easement, unaccompanied by acts clearly inconsistent with his rights, will not amount, by themselves, to a waiver or abandonment of an easement holder's rights.[135]

§ 337. Merger of Dominant and Servient Tracts into Single Ownership.

Since an easement is a privilege enjoyed in the land of *another,* when there is a coming together of the dominant and servient tracts into one ownership, the easement is permanently extinguished, because a person obviously cannot have an easement in his own land.[136]

§ 338. Extinguishment of Easements by Servient Owner's Adverse User.

An easement may be extinguished through adverse user by the servient owner for the prescriptive period.[137] Since easements may be created by prescription, by a reverse process they may also be lost if the servient owner refuses to recognize the rights of the easement holder and prevents the use of the easement for the statutory period.[138] In order to extinguish an easement, the interference or user by the servient owner must be adverse to the easement holder, continuous, uninterrupted, and for the prescriptive period.[139]

§ 339. Termination of Easements by Expiration of Period.

An easement may be created for a definite period. Upon expiration of such period the easement will expire naturally. For instance, if one is given an easement for fifty years, the easement will expire at the end of that period automatically.[140] An easement may likewise be a

---

134. Miller v. Teer, 220 N.C. 605, 18 S.E.2d 173 (1941).
135. *Id. See also* Railroad v. McGuire, 171 N.C. 277, 88 S.E. 337 (1916). Since, however, the intention to abandon may be proved by an infinite variety of acts and is a question for the jury to determine, the fact of long continued nonassertion of rights should be relevant evidence when accompanied with other facts going to show abandonment. RESTATEMENT OF PROPERTY § 504, comment d (1944).
136. Patrick v. Jefferson Standard Life Ins. Co., 176 N.C. 660, 97 S.E. 657 (1918); Barringer v. Virginia Trust Co., 132 N.C. 409, 43 S.E. 910 (1903); McAllister v. Devane, 76 N.C. 57 (1877).
137. 3 POWELL, REAL PROPERTY § 424 (1966).
138. Hunter v. West, 172 N.C. 160, 90 S.E. 130 (1916); Duke Power Co. v. Toms, 118 F.2d 443 (4th Cir. 1941).
139. 3 POWELL, REAL PROPERTY § 424 (1966); Duke Power Co. v. Toms, 118 F.2d 443 (4th Cir. 1941).
140. *See* 3 POWELL, REAL PROPERTY § 422 (1966); Leigh v. Garysburg Mfg. Co., 132 N.C. 167, 43 S.E. 632 (1903). *See* the recent Court of Appeals decision of Williams v. Southern Bell Tel. & Tel. Co., 47 N.C. App. 176, 266 S.E.2d 700 (1980) holding that a life tenant could not create an easement or estate to endure beyond her lifetime.

determinable easement or an easement subject to a condition subsequent, created under such conditions that the easement will be terminable upon the occurrence of some event, in which case the easement ends in accordance with the terms of its creation.[141]

§ 340. Termination of Easements by Transfer of Servient Land to Purchaser for Value; Lien Creditors; Exceptions.

Under some circumstances, when an easement has been created by express grant, the easement may be terminated if the servient land is conveyed to a purchaser for value without notice, provided the instrument has not been previously recorded under the land recordation statutes.[142]

Easements which arise by implication or operation of law, however, such as easements of necessity, easements arising out of the conversion of previously existing quasi-easements upon the severance of titles, and easements by prescription, are outside the terms and application of the recordation statutes and will not be extinguished by the conveyance of the servient tract to purchasers for value.[143] So, too, an easement created in equity by estoppel will not be extinguished by sale of the servient land to a purchaser for value even though such easement is not recorded.[144]

---

141. Dees v. Pipeline Co., 266 N.C. 323, 146 S.E.2d 50 (1966); Wallace v. Bellamy, 199 N.C. 759, 155 S.E. 856 (1930); McDowell v. Railroad Co., 144 N.C. 721, 57 S.E. 520 (1907); Hall v. Turner, 110 N.C. 292, 14 S.E. 791 (1892).

142. N.C. GEN. STAT. § 47-18. *See* Davis v. Robinson, 189 N.C. 589, 127 S.E. 697 (1925), and Clark v. Railroad, 192 N.C. 280, 135 S.E. 26 (1926). In Davis v. Robinson, *supra,* the court states: "... no notice, however full and formal, will supply the place of registration," thus making recordation the only notice that will protect an easement holder against a purchaser for value from the servient owner. *But see* Gas Co. v. Day, 249 N.C. 482, 106 S.E.2d 678 (1958), in which the court seems to indicate that actual notice of an unrecorded easement will prevent a purchaser for value from a servient owner from taking free of the easement. In the latter case, however, the deed conveying the servient tract referred to the existence of the easement. In Packard v. Smart, 224 N.C. 480, 31 S.E.2d 517 (1944), the statement is made that "one who purchases land with notice, actual or constructive, that it is burdened with an existing easement takes the estate subject to the easement." It would therefore seem that if an easement is in use and apparent from an observation of the property, a purchaser for value will take subject thereto, notwithstanding that it is not recorded. But it should be observed that in the *Packard* case the easement was one which arose by implication.

See Hensley v. Ramsey, 283 N.C. 714, 199 S.E.2d 1 (1973), to the effect that grantees take title to lands subject to duly recorded easements which have been granted to their predecessors in title. *Accord,* Yount v. Lowe, 288 N.C. 90, 215 S.E.2d 563 (1975), which states: "The purchaser of lands upon which the owner has imposed an easement of any kind takes the title subject to all easements, however created, of which he has notice."

143. 3 POWELL, REAL PROPERTY § 424 (1966).

144. *See* Reid v. King, 158 N.C. 85, 73 S.E. 168 (1911), in which the original owners of two tracts made a parol agreement for one to build a party wall, partly on the land of both, providing that when the other later attached to the wall he would share the original expense of construction. Thereafter the servient owner conveyed his land to a purchaser for value who had notice of the prior agreement. The court held that cross-easements were created

§ 341   REAL ESTATE LAW IN NORTH CAROLINA   § 342

For purposes of recordation and in the determination of whether interests in real property are extinguished as a result of nonrecordation, lien creditors who have affixed their liens by judicial proceedings are treated in the same manner as purchasers for value.

§ 341. Termination of Easements Under Power of Eminent Domain.

Easements, like other real property interests, are subject to being taken under condemnation for public purposes by the sovereign or by public service corporations upon the payment of just compensation to the easement holder.[145]

Article VI. Profits à Prendre

§ 342. Generally.

A right that is closely akin to the easement is the profit à prendre, which is a right created in its owner to take a part of the soil or the products of the soil from the land of another person. Examples of profits à prendre are the right to take timber from the land of another, or to mine coal, or to fish in waters belonging to another or to shoot over lands or

---

that bound the servient lands in the hands of all successive owners who took with notice even though the easement was not recorded. *See also* Packard v. Smith, 224 N.C. 480, 31 S.E.2d 517 (1944). *But see* Green v. Miller, 161 N.C. 24, 76 S.E. 505 (1912), which held that an easement created by estoppel will not continue as against a purchaser for value who has no notice of the easement's existence.

145. Duke Power Co. v. Toms, 118 F.2d 443 (4th Cir. 1941); Restatement of Property § 507, comment a (1944); 3 Powell, Real Property § 426 (1966); Hedrick v. Graham, 245 N.C. 249, 96 S.E.2d 129 (1956); Power Co. v. Ham House, Inc., 43 N.C. App. 308, 258 S.E.2d 815 (1979).

See Raleigh v. Edwards, 235 N.C. 671, 71 S.E.2d 396 (1952), which holds that restrictive covenants in deeds to purchasers within a development create negative easements constituting vested interests in land. When a particular parcel of land is appropriated for a public use that violates the restrictions created for the benefit of surrounding lands, such appropriation amounts in a constitutional sense to a taking or damaging of property of the other landowners for whose benefit the restrictions were imposed.

That a board of education which purchased land subject to restrictive covenants cannot be *enjoined* to comply with the restrictive covenants requiring the land to be used exclusively for residential purposes, see Carolina Mills v. Catawba County Bd. of Educ., 27 N.C. App. 524, 219 S.E.2d 509 (1975). It was held that since the board of education is a corporate entity that has the power of eminent domain its use of the property in such a manner as to violate the restrictive covenant would involve the inverse condemnation of negative easements and constitute a taking; that *damages* to such negative easements *could* be recovered as a result of the violation of the restrictive covenants, while an injunction of the government entity that had the power of eminent domain would not be granted.

§ 342 RIGHTS IN THE LANDS OF OTHERS § 342

take game or wild fowl from the lands of another.[146] Profits à prendre, sometimes called "rights of commons" were numerous at the common law and had their origin in the feudal law.[147] The "common of pasture" was the right to pasture one's cattle upon another man's land; the "common of turbary" was the right to take peat or turf from another's land; the "common of piscary" was the right to fish in another man's waters; the "common of digging" was the right to take for one's own use part of the soil or minerals (most often sand, gravel, stones and clay) from another's land; the "common of fowling" was the right to take wild animals from the land of another; the "common of estovers" or "botes" was the right to take wood from the land of another for use as fuel (called "fire bote"), for repairing houses (called "house bote"), for making and repairing agricultural tools (called "plough bote" or "cart bote"), or for making and repairing hedges or fences (called "hedge bote").[148]

The distinguishing feature between an easement and a profit à prendre is that the easement gives its owner only a right to use the land of another with no right to take anything from the land, while a profit à prendre gives its owner the right to remove some specified product of the soil from the land.[149] The profit à prendre may be granted to be enjoyed in common with the landowner or with others.[150] Profits à prendre may exist in gross and may be held independently of any ownership in other land, or they may be held as appurtenances of other "dominant" lands as is the case with easements.[151]

Profits in gross, unlike easements in gross, are assignable and inheritable.[152] Appurtenant profits à prendre pass upon a transfer of the dominant tract.[153]

Profits à prendre, like easements, may be acquired by grant,

---

146. Council v. Sanderlin, 183 N.C. 253, 111 S.E. 365, 32 A.L.R. 1527 (1922). *Accord,* Builders Supplies Co. v. Gainey, 14 N.C. App. 678, 189 S.E.2d 657, *aff'd,* 282 N.C. 261, 192 S.E.2d 449 (1972), citing this section in original edition (§ 309).

147. MINOR & WURTS, REAL PROPERTY §§ 68, 69 (1910). *See* Builders Supplies Co. v. Gainey, 282 N.C. 261, 192 S.E.2d 449 (1972).

148. *Id. See generally* BLACK'S LAW DICTIONARY 366 (3d ed. 1933). *See* N.C. GEN. STAT. § 74-49 (6), the Mining Act of 1971. "Sand" and "gravel" are now included in the definition of "minerals."

149. Council v. Sanderlin, 183 N.C. 253, 111 S.E. 365, 32 A.L.R. 1527 (1922). *Accord,* Builders Supplies Co. v. Gainey, 14 N.C. App. 678, 189 S.E.2d 657, *aff'd,* 282 N.C. 261, 192 S.E.2d 449 (1972).

150. TIFFANY, REAL PROPERTY § 839 (3d ed. 1939).

151. Council v. Sanderlin, 183 N.C. 253, 111 S.E. 365, 32 A.L.R. 1527 (1922); TIFFANY, REAL PROPERTY § 843 (3d ed. 1939). *Accord,* Builders Supplies Co. v. Gainey, 14 N.C. App. 678, 189 S.E.2d 657, *aff'd,* 282 N.C. 261, 192 S.E.2d 449 (1972).

152. Council v. Sanderlin, 183 N.C. 253, 111 S.E. 365, 32 A.L.R. 1527 (1922); TIFFANY, REAL PROPERTY § 843 (3d ed. 1939).

153. TIFFANY, REAL PROPERTY § 843 (3d ed. 1939). *Accord,* Builders Supplies Co. v. Gainey, 14 N.C. App. 678, 189 S.E.2d 657, *aff'd,* 282 N.C. 261, 192 S.E.2d 449 (1972).

reservation or prescription.[154] Since a profit à prendre is an interest in land, it cannot be created by parol, and if created by express grant or reservation there must be a writing to satisfy the Statute of Frauds.[155]

Profits à prendre are closely analogous to easements in most respects and the principles applicable to one are generally applicable for the other. It should be noted, however, that a profit à prendre cannot be assigned in portions to several persons so as to allow each to take the profits from the soil. A profit à prendre is indivisible and cannot be apportioned so as to permit numerous persons to exercise the profit to the injury of the land.[156]

Article VII. Licenses

§ 343. Generally.

Licenses should be carefully distinguished from easements and profits á prendre. A license is not an estate and creates no substantial interest in land but merely serves to authorize one to do certain specified acts upon the lands of the licensor. A license operates merely as a permission or waiver permitting the licensee to do acts upon the land which would otherwise be a trespass.[157] A license is generally revocable, while easements and profits à prendre are not.[158]

§ 344. Creation of Licenses.

A license arises upon a consent given by the owner of land or by one in possession of the land. While easements and profits à prendre are substantial interests in real property which require a writing to validate their creation under the Statute of Frauds, a license does not require a

---

154. Council v. Sanderlin, 183 N.C. 253, 111 S.E. 365, 32 A.L.R. 1527 (1922); TIFFANY, REAL PROPERTY § 843 (3d ed. 1939).

155. Council v. Sanderlin, 183 N.C. 253, 111 S.E. 365, 32 A.L.R. 1527 (1922). *Accord,* Sanders v. Wilkerson, 20 N.C. App. 331, 201 S.E.2d 571 (citing this work), *modified,* 285 N.C. 215, 204 S.E.2d 17 (1974).

156. TIFFANY, REAL PROPERTY § 847 (3d ed. 1939); MINOR & WURTS, REAL PROPERTY § 70 (1910); 1 MORDECAI, LAW LECTURES 470 (1916).

157. Lee-Moore Oil Co. v. Cleary, 295 N.C. 417, 245 S.E.2d 720 (1978); Sanders v. Wilkerson, 20 N.C. App. 331, 201 S.E.2d 571 (citing this work), *modified,* 285 N.C. 215, 204 S.E.2d 17 (1974). MINOR & WURTS, REAL PROPERTY § 122 (1910). That a licensee has no protectible interest against the owner or any third person, *see* TIFFANY, REAL PROPERTY § 829 (3d ed. 1939).

158. Railroad v. Battle, 66 N.C. 541 (1872); State v. Fisher, 117 N.C. 733, 23 S.E. 158 (1895); Hutchins v. Durham, 118 N.C. 457, 24 S.E. 723 (1896); Elizabeth City v. Banks, 150 N.C. 407, 64 S.E. 189 (1909). It should be noted, however, that if the license is "coupled with an interest," a license that is incidental to ownership of property located on the land or is created pursuant to some other legal relation, such license is irrevocable. RESTATEMENT OF PROPERTY § 513 (1944); Railroad v. Battle, 66 N.C. 541 (1872). *See* Sanders v. Wilkerson, 20 N.C. App. 331, 201 S.E.2d 571 (citing this work), *modified,* 285 N.C. 215, 204 S.E.2d 17 (1974).

writing.[159] For instance, while an oral grant of a right to fish in a stream on one's lands cannot be either an easement or profit à prendre, it can constitute a license. A license may also arise by implication or by tacit consent, as, for example, when a shopkeeper or business man impliedly invites the public to enter his store or office during business hours.[160] A license may also result from an ineffective attempt to create an easement or estate if the deed purporting to make such conveyance is defective.[161] In addition, a license may be created by a writing if the owner expresses as his intention that he is creating a revocable relationship.[162] Holders of theater tickets and tickets to other amusements or spectacles, hotel guests and renters of stalls in markets, are generally deemed to be mere licensees whose licenses are revocable at the option of the owners.[163]

§ 345. Revocability and Transferability of Licenses.

A license is the least important of the rights in the lands of another. As a matter of fact, a license does not create "rights" in land but gives one only a personal, revocable privilege to do an act or series of acts upon the land of another without conferring any estate or interest in the land. Hence, licenses are, in general, freely revocable by the licensor. They are revocable at the option of the lessor even though the revocation may violate the terms of a contract and render the lessor liable in damages for breach of contract.[164] While it is sometimes stated that a license may have become irrevocable because of acts done in reliance on the continued existence of the license, accurate analysis indicates that this means only that an irrevocable easement (not a license) has been created by estoppel.[165] Licenses coupled with an interest, however, are not revocable by the licensor. Where one has been given a license in connection with other

---

159. Lee-Moore Oil Co. v. Cleary, 295 N.C. 417, 245 S.E.2d 720 (1978). *See* dissent in Sanders v. Wilkerson, 20 N.C. App. 331, 201 S.E.2d 571 (citing this work), *modified,* 285 N.C. 215, 204 S.E.2d 17 (1974). MINOR & WURTS, REAL PROPERTY § 124 (1910); 3 POWELL, REAL PROPERTY § 429 (1966).

160. HOPKINS, REAL PROPERTY § 99 (1896); TIFFANY, REAL PROPERTY § 830 (3d ed. 1939).

161. 3 POWELL, REAL PROPERTY § 429 (1966); Whitaker v. Cawthorne, 14 N.C. 389 (1832). *See* dissent in Sanders v. Wilkerson, 20 N.C. App. 331, 201 S.E.2d 571 (citing this work), *modified,* 285 N.C. 215, 204 S.E.2d 17 (1974), stating that when an attempt to create an easement or profit à prendre is ineffective because of defects in the written document or because there is no written document, a license is created.

162. 3 POWELL, REAL PROPERTY § 428 (1966).

163. Hutchins v. Durham, 118 N.C. 457, 24 S.E. 723 (1896); 3 POWELL, REAL PROPERTY § 428 (1966); TIFFANY, REAL PROPERTY § 829 (1939); 1 MORDECAI, LAW LECTURES 464 (1916). While ticketholders, hotel guests and renters of stalls in markets and the like may recover damages for wrongful ouster, they cannot recover the premises in ejectment. *See* 1 MORDECAI, LAW LECTURES 464 (1916).

164. 1 MORDECAI, LAW LECTURES 464 (1916); Hutchins v. Durham, 118 N.C. 457, 24 S.E. 723 (1896).

165. CRIBBET, PRINCIPLES OF THE LAW OF PROPERTY 277 (1962).

property in which he has an interest, as where one has been given a license to remove his own chattels or fixtures from the lands of the licensor, the licensor cannot revoke the license.[166]

Licenses are not assignable [167] and normally terminate upon the death of either the licensor or the licensee.[168] It has been held that licensees do not have a right to sue third persons for interference the exercise of the privilege given under licenses.[169]

---

166. MINOR & WURTS, REAL PROPERTY § 127 (1910); Railroad v. Railroad, 104 N.C. 658, 669, 10 S.E. 659 (1889). If a licensee has been given, pursuant to an oral contract, a license to cut timber, and has actually cut the timber and transformed it into personalty before the license is revoked, the owner of the land will not be permitted to revoke the license as to such trees as have been cut. 1 MORDECAI, LAW LECTURES 835 (1916).

167. 3 POWELL, REAL PROPERTY 428 (1966).

168. Id.

169. Id. There have been some decisions to the contrary, however, and it would seem that licensees should be entitled to court protection against persons who interfere with licensees' possession under licenses, since even naked trespassers may maintain actions against subsequent trespassers. See, i.e., Lee-Moore Oil Co. v. Cleary, 295 N.C. 417, 245 S.E.2d 720 (1978) where a licensee oil company had placed certain chattels on the real property of another with the understanding that these chattels were to remain the personal property of the licensee. It was held that a subsequent purchaser of the real property could be sued by the licensee for conversion of the chattels where the subsequent purchaser had knowledge of the license agreement at the time of purchase.

CHAPTER 16

RIGHTS OF ENJOYMENT AND DUTIES INCIDENT TO OWNERSHIP OF REAL PROPERTY

Article I. General Provisions

§ 346. Rights of Enjoyment and Duties Incident to Ownership of Real Property Generally.

Article II. Lateral and Subjacent Support

§ 347. The Right to Lateral and Subjacent Support Generally.

Article III. Water Rights

§ 348. Water Rights Generally.
§ 349. Defining "Navigable."
§ 350. Ownership of Submerged Lands; Under Navigable Waters.
§ 351. Ownership of Submerged Lands; Under Nonnavigable Waters.
§ 352. The Right of Riparian Owners to Take Water From Known and Well Defined Channels of Water Above the Surface of the Earth.
§ 353. Accretion; Avulsion; Reliction; Erosion.
§ 354. Rights in Subterranean and Percolating Waters.
§ 355. Drainage of Surface Water.
§ 356. Public Water Rights; Public Trust Doctrine.
§ 357. Sovereign Prerogative Doctrine Recognized in North Carolina.
§ 358. Governmental Regulation: Federal.
§ 359. Governmental Regulation: State.

Article IV. Rights of Adjoining Landowners; Nuisances

§ 360. Generally.
§ 361. Classification of Nuisances.
§ 362. Public Nuisances.
§ 363. Private Nuisances.
§ 364. Nuisances Per Se.
§ 365. Nuisances Per Accidens.
§ 366. Persons Entitled to Relief Because of Nuisances; Persons Liable for Nuisances.
§ 367. Remedies for Nuisance.
§ 368. Spite Fences.

Article I. General Provisions

§ 346. Rights of Enjoyment and Duties Incident to Ownership of Real Property Generally.

Real property consists of lands, tenements and hereditaments.[1] "Lands" means the ground and the air above it and all that is below the surface of the earth and all that is erected *on* it. "Lands" means not only the face of the earth, but everything under it or over it,[2] whether put there by nature, as trees and grass, or by the hand of man, as houses and other

---
1. 1 Mordecai, Law Lectures 461 (1916).
2. 2 Blackstone, Commentaries* 19.

buildings.[3] "Tenements" and "hereditaments" are broader terms than "lands," and the term "tenements" embraces anything that could have been "holden" under feudal law, anything subject to feudal tenure, including incorporeal interests such as easements and profits à prendre. The term "hereditaments" is a still broader term, broader than either "lands" or "tenements," encompassing both of those terms and embracing anything which was capable of being inherited at the common law.[4]

Suffice it to say that the ownership of real property as above defined, particularly the ownership of lands, carries with it certain inherent rights. Among these "natural" or "inherent" rights that are incident to the ownership of real property are (1) the right to lateral and subjacent support; (2) water rights which attach to real property; and (3) the right of an owner not to have a nuisance maintained by his neighbor as will unreasonably interfere with the use or enjoyment of his land. Of course, these rights carry with them correlative duties to other owners of real property who have the same rights. The following sections will discuss these and other rights and duties incident to the ownership and possession of real property which exist in owners by the operation of law and without the necessity of having been created by any grant, stipulation or agreement.

Article II. Lateral and Subjacent Support

§ 347. The Right to Lateral and Subjacent Support Generally.

Every landowner has an absolute inherent right to have his land supported *in its natural state,* from the sides, by the lands of adjoining owners. This is called the right of "lateral" support. If the land is in its "natural state," that is, if there is no artificial structure or building located on the land, and one excavates neighboring lands so as to cause another's land to subside and be damaged, the injured owner can recover from the excavator without any proof of negligence. Neighboring landowners [5] owe an *absolute* duty not to excavate their own lands in such a way as to cause the subsidence of soil on another's land which is in its natural condition.

---

3. Gilliam v. Bird, 30 N.C. 284 (1848).

4. "Hereditaments" included even some items of personal property called "heirlooms" which passed by "inheritance" to "heirs" and not to the "distributees" of a decedent as was the general custom as to personal property items.

See generally for a comprehensive treatment of the law of trespass to land in North Carolina, Dobbs, *Trespass to Land in North Carolina — Part I. The Substantive Law,* 47 N.C.L. Rev. 31 (1968) and Dobbs, *Trespass to Land in North Carolina — Part II. Remedies for Trespass,* 47 N.C.L. Rev. 334 (1969).

5. The burden of this support extends to so much of the adjacent land, whether owned entirely by one person or not, as is naturally required to afford the proper support. *See* Minor & Wurts, Real Property § 113 (1910); Keating v. City of Cincinnati, 38 Ohio St. 141, 43 Am. R. 421 (1882).

If, on the other hand, land is not in its natural state and has structures erected thereon, there is no absolute right to have the land laterally supported so far as the additional structures are concerned.[6] If there are structures on the land, however, adjoining excavators may be liable for damages which naturally and proximately flow from *negligence* in making the excavation, and recovery can be had for damages to both land and any artificial structures where such negligence is made to appear.[7]

If it can be shown that a neighbor's excavation would have caused an owner's land to fall away — even if in its natural condition without the additional weight of a building — and the excavation was not accompanied by negligence on the part of the excavator, some jurisdictions allow recovery for damages both to the land and to the building on the theory that the proximate cause of the total injury was invasion of the right of lateral support of his soil and that the injury was not the result of the weight of the building.[8] Other jurisdictions limit recovery to land damages only as would have occurred had the land been in its natural state when there is a subsidence of land with artificial structures located thereon and the excavation is unaccompanied by negligence.[9] The better view appears to be the former view.

Landowners also have a right to subjacent support. This right-duty relationship arises when ownership of land is divided horizontally into surface and subsurface ownership, where one person owns the surface and another person owns the subsurface (for the purpose of mining or

---

6. Minor & Wurts, Real Property § 114 (1910). If a right to support is claimed for the added weight of buildings, there must be an express grant or reservation of an easement to that effect.

7. Davis v. Summerfield, 131 N.C. 352, 42 S.E. 818 (1902), *rehearing denied,* 133 N.C. 325, 45 S.E. 654 (1903); 4 Restatement of Torts § 819.

The negligence for which an action may be had may consist of a failure to make necessary preliminary tests and investigations; a defective plan for the work; excavating in too great lateral sections; leaving the excavation open for an unreasonable length of time; and any other conduct that shows a failure to use reasonable care, skill and prudence in carrying on the work. Dykstra & Dykstra, The Business Law of Real Estate 666 (1956). In addition, there may be negligence if the party intending to make the excavation fails to notify the adjoining owner of his intention to excavate. Although the excavator has no duty to the adjoining owner to provide lateral support to structures on the land, he does owe the duty to give such adjoining owner timely notice of his intention to excavate in order to enable the adjoining owner to shore up his buildings for their protection. Davis v. Summerfield, 131 N.C. 352, 42 S.E. 818 (1902).

8. This view is called the "English Rule." Prete v. Cray, 49 R.I. 209, 141 A. 609 (1928), gives a clear exposition of this view.

9. This view is called the "American Rule." *See, e.g.,* Gildersleeve v. Hammond, 109 Mich. 431, 67 N.W. 519, 33 L.R.A. 46 (1896); Gilmore v. Driscoll, 122 Mass. 199, 23 Am. R. 312 (1877).

otherwise). The same principles applicable to lateral support apply equally to subjacent support.[10]

Article III. Water Rights

§ 348. Water Rights Generally.

The law of waters and water courses is a vast expanse of legal beach that this brief survey cannot possibly hope to do justice to. General areas of water rights that will be discussed in the ensuing sections may be summarized as follows:

1. *Water rights incident to the ownership of land.* Among the so-called "natural" rights that are incident to the ownership of land are water rights. By virtue of ownership of a parcel bordering on a stream, lake, or the ocean, a landowner has something akin to a "property right" with respect to the water.[11] This area of riparian rights has become increasingly important by reason of the population explosion in the last half of the twentieth century and because of the vastly increased usage of water for developing industries and agricultural needs.

2. *Water rights of the public.* The public also enjoys certain water rights — not as an incident to riparian land ownership — but by virtue of custom and various legal theories.

3. *Governmental regulation.* All types of water rights have become increasingly subject to state and federal legislation and regulation. Superimposed upon the almost quaint common law of watercourses, these contemporary enactments have come into being as a response to society's concern for the environment.

§ 349. Defining "Navigable."

In the following sections, it will be seen that it is necessary to draw a

---

10. Novel questions have arisen as to when the statute of limitations begins to run in the case of excavation of subsurfaces which do not result in immediate subsidence of the surface but which subsidence occurs much later. Does the statute of limitations begin to run at the time of the excavation or at the time of the falling in? Some jurisdictions make the statute of limitations begin to run at the time of the excavation. *See* Noonan v. Pardee, 200 Pa. 474, 50 A. 255 (1901). Others take the view that the statute of limitations does not begin to run in favor of the defendant excavator until the subsidence. *See* 4 RESTATEMENT OF TORTS § 820, comment g; Western Coal & Mining Co. v. Randolph, 191 Ark. 1115, 89 S.W.2d 741 (1936).

See generally for a comprehensive treatment of the law of trespass to land in North Carolina, Dobbs, *Trespass to Land in North Carolina — Part I. The Substantive Law,* 47 N.C.L. REV. 31 (1968) and Dobbs, *Trespass to Land in North Carolina — Part II. Remedies for Trespass,* 47 N.C.L. REV. 334 (1969).

11. 5 POWELL ON REAL PROPERTY § 710 (1979). At § 710, Powell goes on to state that the temporary and usufructuary character of this water right has been properly stressed, citing, *inter alia,* the case of United States v. Fallbrook Pub. Util. Dist., 165 F. Supp. 806 (S.D. Cal. 1958). *See* the recent case of Conservation Council of North Carolina v. Froehlke, 435 F. Supp. 775 (M.D.N.C. 1977), holding that the flow of a stream is in no sense a private property right when that stream is subject to the United States navigational servitude.

distinction between "navigable" and "nonnavigable" waters to determine the ownership of submerged lands. While at the common law and in England a navigable body of water was one in which the tide ebbs and flows, in North Carolina, and in the United States generally, a navigable body of water is that is navigable in fact.[12] The rule is variously stated. In *Development Co. v. Parmele*,[13] it is stated that "all waters which are actually navigable for sea vessels are to be considered navigable waters." And in *Parmele v. Eaton*,[14] the test is said to be: "whether, in its ordinary state, a body of water has capacity and suitability for the usual purpose of navigation by vessels or boats such as are employed in the ordinary course of water commerce, trade, and travel."

§ 350. Ownership of Submerged Lands; Under Navigable Waters.

Where one's land borders upon a navigable body of water, upon the ocean or an arm thereof or upon a navigable stream, the ownership of the land under the water does not belong to the bordering owner, but belongs to the various states.[15] Private property bordering upon the ocean ends at the mean or average high water mark.[16] Title to the foreshore, *i.e.*, that "strip of land between the high- and low-tide lines,"[17] is in the State and not in the littoral owner, although the littoral owner may have certain rights to make use of the foreshore subject to noninterference with general rights of the public.[18]

Subject to specific reservations concerning navigation, flood control, or the production of power by the federal government,[19] and subject to the restrictions of the Commerce Clause of the United States Constitution, lands beneath the coastal waters to a line three geographical miles from its coast line belong to the State of North Carolina.[20]

In North Carolina, title to submerged lands under navigable waters

---

12. Development Co. v. Parmele, 235 N.C. 689, 71 S.E.2d 474 (1952).
13. *Id.*
14. 240 N.C. 539, 83 S.E.2d 93 (1954).

See generally note, *Defining Navigable Waters and the Application of the Public Trust Doctrine in North Carolina: A History and Analysis,* 49 N.C.L. REV. 888 (1971).

15. Miller v. Coppage, 261 N.C. 430, 135 S.E.2d 1 (1964); Land Co. v. Atlantic Hotel, 132 N.C. 517, 44 S.E. 39 (1903); Railroad v. Way, 172 N.C. 774, 90 S.E. 937 (1916); Home Real Estate Loan & Ins. Co. v. Parmele, 214 N.C. 63, 197 S.E. 714 (1938); Wilson v. Forbes, 13 N.C. 30 (1828).
16. Carolina Beach Fishing Pier, Inc. v. Town of Carolina Beach, 277 N.C. 297, 177 S.E.2d 513 (1970).
17. *Id.*, citing 1 POWELL ON REAL PROPERTY § 163.
18. *Id.*
19. *Id.*
20. *Id.* Citing the Submerged Lands Act of 1953, 43 U.S.C. § 1312; 67 Stat. 31.

cannot be granted to individuals by the State.[21] While title to such submerged lands under navigable waters cannot be conveyed by the State, it can grant easements in such lands to adjoining riparian owners [22] for various purposes, provided such easements do not interfere with navigation, which is subject to the rights and control of the federal government. In addition, riparian owners whose lands border on navigable waters have a right, along with other members of the public, to fish in the waters and to use them for travel purposes either for business or pleasure, subject, of course, to a like right in others. It should be noted, however, that the rights of members of the public to use navigable waters do not give any license to members of the public to go or come through riparian owners' lands, nor to use the banks of streams except at public landings, unless the bank owner consents, since the banks of navigable streams are private property.[23]

§ 351. Ownership of Submerged Lands; Under Nonnavigable Waters.

The bed of a private or nonnavigable stream or body of water belongs to the owner of the soil through which it flows. If the banks of such nonnavigable stream or body of water are owned by different persons, each owns prima facie to the middle of the stream.[24] This presumption that owners on different banks own to the middle of a nonnavigable stream or waterway may be rebutted by proof of a grant or exception of the whole bed by one of the owners to the other, or by or to their predecessors in the title.[25]

§ 352. The Right of Riparian Owners to Take Water From Known and Well Defined Channels of Water Above the Surface of the Earth.

Riparian proprietors of real property are proprietors who own land on

---

21. Swan Island Club, Inc. v. Yarbrough, 209 F.2d 698 (1954). See N.C. GEN. STAT. § 146-3. *But see* N.C. GEN. STAT. § 146-6, which makes land which is raised from navigable water subject to N.C. GEN. STAT. § 146-4, which section provides for the sale and transfer of vacant and unappropriated lands which belong to the State. In addition, it seems that lands lying between the high-water mark and the low-water mark of an arm of the ocean may be conveyed by the State. Home Real Estate Loan & Ins. Co. v. Parmele, 214 N.C. 63, 197 S.E. 714 (1938); Land Co. v. Atlantic Hotel, 132 N.C. 517, 44 S.E. 39 (1903); Carolina Beach Fishing Pier, Inc. v. Town of Carolina Beach, 277 N.C. 297, 177 S.E.2d 513 (1970).

22. N.C. GEN. STAT. § 146-12; Land Co. v. Atlantic Hotel, 132 N.C. 517, 44 S.E. 39 (1903); Home Real Estate Loan & Ins. Co. v. Parmele, 214 N.C. 63, 197 S.E. 714 (1938); Carolina Beach Fishing Pier, Inc. v. Town of Carolina Beach, 277 N.C. 297, 177 S.E.2d 513 (1970).

23. Gaither v. Albemarle Hosp., 235 N.C. 431, 70 S.E.2d 680 (1952); Carolina Beach Fishing Pier, Inc. v. Town of Carolina Beach, 277 N.C. 297, 177 S.E.2d 513 (1970).

24. Rose v. Franklin, 216 N.C. 289, 4 S.E.2d 876 (1939), and numerous cases cited therein.

25. MINOR & WURTS, REAL PROPERTY § 57 (1910); Kelly v. King, 225 N.C. 709, 36 S.E.2d 220 (1945).

the banks of streams.[26] Such proprietors of lands that border upon streams have certain valuable rights in the streams that are a part of their property and that are natural incidents of their estates.[27] These rights are called "riparian rights" and are in the nature of incorporeal hereditaments. A recent federal case has summarized these rights as follows:

> In North Carolina, a riparian landowner has a right to the agricultural, recreational, and scenic use and enjoyment of the stream bordering his land, subject, however, to the rights of upstream riparian owners to make reasonable use of the water without excessively diminishing its quality. Though he does not own the fish in the stream, the riparian owner's rights include the opportunity to catch them. Interference with riparian rights is an actionable tort, and a riparian owner may join several polluters as joint tort-feasors.[28]

Subject to certain customary uses of the water itself by the general public, the right to use waters discussed in this section is a form of property interest to be adjusted only among those whose lands front upon the waters. As later sections in this chapter will illustrate, the common law rights of riparian owners are subject to federal and state legislation and regulation.[29]

North Carolina follows the "reasonable use" doctrine of water usage which embodies the principle that all riparian owners on a watercourse have equal rights with respect to the removal and use of water from the

---

26. *See* Young v. Asheville, 241 N.C. 618, 86 S.E.2d 408 (1955), which states that a riparian owner's land must be in contact with the water; proximity without contact is insufficient. For lands to be riparian to a stream, there must be actual contact of land with the water. *See also* Pernell v. Henderson, 220 N.C. 79, 16 S.E.2d 449 (1941), and Durham v. Cotton Mills, 141 N.C. 615, 54 S.E. 453 (1906), to the effect that a municipality which pumps water to its inhabitants is not in the exercise of the traditional rights of riparian owners.

27. Durham v. Cotton Mills, 141 N.C. 615, 54 S.E. 453 (1906), wherein the court held: "A riparian owner is entitled to a reasonable use of the water flowing by his premises in a natural stream, as an incident to his ownership of the soil, and to have it transmitted to him without sensible alteration in quality or unreasonable diminution in quantity. While he does not own the running water, he has the right to a reasonable use of it as it passes his land." *See* Smith v. Morganton, 187 N.C. 801, 123 S.E. 88 (1924), in which it is stated: "the right to have a natural water course continue its physical existence upon one's property is as much property as is the right to have the hills and forests remain in place, and while there is no property right in any particular particle of water or in all of them put together, a riparian proprietor has the right of their flow past his lands for ordinary domestic, manufacturing, and other lawful purposes, without injurious or prejudicial interference by an upper proprietor." *See also* Braswell v. State Highway Comm'n, 250 N.C. 508, 108 S.E.2d 912 (1959); Jones v. Home Bldg. & Loan Ass'n, 252 N.C. 626, 114 S.E.2d 638 (1960); Midgett v. State Highway Comm'n, 260 N.C. 241, 132 S.E.2d 599 (1963).

28. Springer v. Joseph Schlitz Brewing Co., 510 F.2d 468 at 470 (4th Cir. 1975).

29. See §§ 358 & 359 *infra*.

watercourse.[30] Every riparian owner has a property right in the reasonable use of water flowing in a natural watercourse as it passes through or along his land, such right being qualified, however, by an accompanying requirement that it must be enjoyed with reference to the similar rights of other riparian proprietors who own land on the stream.[31] A riparian owner has a right to make all the use he can of a stream flowing through his lands so long as he does not pollute it or divert it from its natural channel and abstract so much of the water as to prevent other people from having equal enjoyment with himself, or does not use the same in such an unreasonable manner as to materially damage or destroy the rights of other riparian owners.[32] The rights of riparian owners in a running stream above and below are equal; each has a right to the reasonable use and enjoyment of the water, and each has a right to the natural flow of the stream, subject to such disturbance and consequent inconvenience and annoyance as may result to him from reasonable use of the waters by others. There may be a diminution in quantity or a retardation or acceleration of the natural flow indispensable for the general valuable use of the water perfectly consistent with the existence of the common right, and this may be done so long as the retardation and acceleration is reasonably necessary in the lawful and beneficial use of the stream.[33]

The extent to which an upper riparian owner may use waters from a stream, thus diminishing the stream, is determined by the "reasonableness" of the use to which the waters are put by the upper riparian owner. What constitutes a reasonable use is a question of fact, having regard to the subject matter and the use; the occasion and manner of its application; its object and extent of necessity; the nature and size of the stream; the kind of business to which it is subservient; the importance and necessity of the use claimed by one party and the extent of the injury caused by it to the other.[34]

Only riparian owners have a right to take waters from a stream. The use of the waters of a stream to supply the inhabitants of a municipality with water for domestic purposes is not in the exercise of the traditional right of a riparian owner to make a reasonable domestic use of the water without accountability to other riparian owners who may be injured by its diversion or diminution.[35]

Under the "reasonable use" doctrine relating to waters, every extraction of water by an upper riparian owner is not actionable. A right

---

30. Dunlap v. Light Co., 212 N.C. 814, 195 S.E. 43 (1937); Pugh v. Wheeler, 19 N.C. 50 (1836).
31. Id.
32. Id.
33. Id.
34. Id.
35. Pernell v. City of Henderson, 220 N.C. 79, 16 S.E.2d 449 (1941).

of action accrues to a lower riparian owner only when water is taken or diverted in such an unreasonable quantity as to materially and substantially injure the lower proprietor in some legitimate use he is making of the water; there is no cause of action unless the lower riparian owner has been actually injured by the usage of the upper riparian owner.[36] Since rights of extraction and diversion of waters can be acquired by prescription,[37] however, it would seem that *any* extraction or diversion by one who is not a riparian owner should be unlawful and actionable, even without the showing of material injury or unreasonableness. The burden is on lower riparian owners to prove alleged unlawful, wrongful or unreasonable usage of the waters of a stream by an upper proprietor.[38]

It should be noted that since riparian rights are property rights it is not necessary to show negligence in a diversion or unreasonable use of water of a stream for the plaintiff to win.[39]

Riparian owners also have a property right to have water flow through their lands "without sensible alteration in quality"[40] which means that the water should flow through their lands free from pollution. No individual, industry or municipal corporation can contaminate waters with sewage, industrial waste or refuse without liability to lower riparian owners who are injured by the pollution.[41] But it has been held that an industry that uses a municipal sewage system to dispose of its waste is not

---

36. Harris v. Railway Co., 153 N.C. 542, 69 S.E. 623 (1910).
37. Young v. Asheville, 241 N.C. 618, 86 S.E.2d 408 (1955).
38. Dunlap v. Light Co., 212 N.C. 814, 195 S.E. 43 (1937).
39. Braswell v. State Highway Comm'n, 250 N.C. 508, 108 S.E.2d 912 (1959); McKinney v. Deneen, 231 N.C. 540, 58 S.E.2d 107 (1950).
40. Durham v. Cotton Mills, 141 N.C. 615, 54 S.E. 453 (1906); Cook v. Mebane, 191 N.C. 1, 131 S.E. 407 (1926); Nance v. Fertilizer Co., 200 N.C. 702, 158 S.E. 486 (1931); Little v. Furniture Co., 200 N.C. 731, 158 S.E. 490 (1931). *Accord,* Springer v. Joseph Schlitz Brewing Co., 510 F.2d 468 (4th Cir. 1975).
41. *Id. But see* Hampton v. Spindale, 210 N.C. 546, 187 S.E. 775 (1936), which holds that where an industrial corporation empties industrial waste into a municipal sewage system, the industrial corporation is not liable to lower riparian owners for injuries from the waste since the industrial corporation has no control over the municipality's sewerage system. *See also* Clinard v. Kernersville, 215 N.C. 745, 3 S.E.2d 267 (1939). In such cases, the municipality alone is liable. *Accord,* Springer v. Joseph Schlitz Brewing Co., 510 F.2d 468 (4th Cir. 1975). In the *Springer* case the federal court of appeals held that it is not reasonable for an industry to expect a city to safely treat *prohibited* sewage. Thus where evidence disclosed that municipality's sewage ordinance was violated and the sewer overloaded, resulting in water pollution of stream that killed fish, the court held that the corporation could be held liable to downstream riparian owners damaged by the pollution. The court indicates that the immunity of an industrial corporation from liability where it empties its waste into a municipal sewage system, as applied in Hampton v. Spindale, 210 N.C. 546, 187 S.E. 775 (1936), relates only to "those persons who use the sewers in the way prescribed by law." If an industrial corporation violates a statute or ordinance designed to protect persons or property and expels waste into a municipal sewage system which causes pollution that proximately causes damages to lower riparian property, the violation becomes actionable notwithstanding the fact that the waste was discharged through the municipality's sewage treatment facility.

liable to a riparian landowner for the pollution caused by a city's failure to provide adequate treatment [42] unless in the exercise of reasonable care the industry should have ascertained that the municipal treatment plant could not adequately treat its sewage or unless an ordinance is violated in the process.[43]

Lower riparian owners who are injured by unlawful extractions, diversions and pollution of waters, may recover damages [44] or procure injunctive relief [45] to restrain the activities of upper riparian owners.[46]

It should be noted in closing that while the right of a riparian owner to use waters is in the nature of a property right that can be protected from private interference, a recent Federal District Court decision has confirmed the proposition that, as between a riparian owner and the federal government, there is no private property right in the flow of a stream which is subject to the navigational servitude of the United States.[47] The Court quoted the following with approval from a 1945 United States Supreme Court decision:

> Rights, property or otherwise, which are absolute against all the world are certainly rare, and water rights are not among them. Whatever rights may be as between equals such as riparian owners, they are not the measure of riparian rights on a navigable stream relative to the function of the Government in improving navigation. Where these interests conflict they are not to be reconciled as be-

---

42. Springer v. Joseph Schlitz Brewing Co., 510 F.2d 468 (4th Cir. 1975).
43. Id.
44. Spaugh v. Winston-Salem, 249 N.C. 194, 105 S.E.2d 610 (1958).
45. Durham v. Cotton Mills, 141 N.C. 615, 54 S.E. 453 (1906); Anderson v. Waynesville, 203 N.C. 37, 164 S.E. 583 (1932).
46. An action for temporary damages may be maintained under proper circumstances. Likewise, an action to obtain a permanent injunction may be maintained along with an action for temporary damages which occur prior to abatement. Anderson v. Waynesville, 203 N.C. 37, 164 S.E. 583 (1932). If the defendant is a municipality, an action for unlawful extraction, diversion or pollution of waters may be treated as a "taking" of property under condemnation for the maintenance of a continuing nuisance, and permanent damages may be recovered by the lower riparian owners injured. Spaugh v. Winston-Salem, 249 N.C. 194, 105 S.E.2d 610 (1958); Clinard v. Kernersville, 215 N.C. 745, 3 S.E.2d 267 (1939). A lower riparian owner injured by an unreasonable extraction, diversion or pollution of a stream is not limited to an action for permanent damages as against a municipality but may sue for temporary damages as well as an injunction. Municipal corporations who damage lower riparian owners by unreasonable extraction, diversion or pollution of waters are not exempt from liability, notwithstanding that they resulted from the exercise of a governmental function and irrespective of any negligence. Clinard v. Kernersville, *supra;* Rhodes v. Durham, 165 N.C. 679, 81 S.E. 938 (1914).

"A municipal corporation has no more right than an individual to maintain a nuisance, and is equally liable for damages resulting therefrom; and authorized acts of a governmental character which create a nuisance causing damage to a private owner are regarded and dealt with as an appropriation of property to the extent of the injury thereby inflicted." Sandlin v. Wilmington, 185 N.C. 257, 116 S.E. 733 (1923); Young v. Asheville, 241 N.C. 618, 86 S.E.2d 408 (1955).

47. Conservation Council of N. C. v. Froehlke, 435 F. Supp. 775 (M.D. 1977).

tween equals, but the private interest must give way to a superior right, or perhaps it would be more accurate to say that as against the Government such private interest is not a right at all.[48]

§ 353. Accretion; Avulsion; Reliction; Erosion.

"Accretion" denotes an increase in the amount of riparian land by the gradual depositing of solid material causing area formerly covered by water to become dry land.[49] "Avulsion" constitutes a "sudden and perceptible gain or loss of riparian land."[50] "Reliction" involves the gradual exposure of land by the permanent recession of a body of water.[51] "Erosion" is the loss of soil by the action of running water or tidal ebbs and flows.[52]

Blackstone described the legal effect of accretion and reliction as follows:

> And as to lands gained from the sea, either by *alluvion,* by the washing up of sand and earth, so as in time to make *terra firma;* or by *dereliction,* as when the sea shrinks back below the usual water mark; in these cases the law is held to be, that if this gain be by little and little, by small and imperceptible degrees, it shall go to the owner of the land adjoining. For *de minimis non curat lex;* and besides, these owners being often losers by the breaking in of the sea, or at charges to keep it out, this possible gain is therefore a reciprocal consideration for such possible charge or loss.[53]

Thus, it has been held in North Carolina that, where the waters of a navigable lake recede "gradually and insensibly," the riparian owner obtains title to such land.[54] And where the gradual and imperceptible forces of accretion add to the boundary of a tract of land, the riparian owner is entitled to the increased boundary.[55]

While enjoying the possible benefits of the doctrines of accretion and reliction, a riparian or littoral landowner may lose part or all of his property by erosion. In a recent North Carolina Supreme Court case, for example, the lots of the plaintiff were gradually worn away by the

---

48. United States v. Willow River Power Co., 324 U.S. 499, 510, 65 S. Ct. 761, 767, 89 L. Ed. 1101 (1945).

See generally Aycock, *Introduction to Water Use Law in North Carolina,* 46 N.C.L. REV. 1 (1967).

49. State v. Johnson, 278 N.C. 126, 179 S.E.2d 371 (1971), citing 5A THOMPSON ON REAL PROPERTY (Grimes ed., 1957), § 2560 and 6 POWELL ON REAL PROPERTY, § 983 *et seq.,* Jones v. Turlington, 243 N.C. 681, 92 S.E.2d 75 (1956).

50. State v. Johnson, 278 N.C. 126, 179 S.E.2d 371 (1971), citing 5A THOMPSON ON REAL PROPERTY (Grimes ed., 1957), § 2561.

51. State Engineer v. Cowles Bros., Inc., 86 Nev. 872, 478 P.2d 159 (1970).

52. CARTWRIGHT, GLOSSARY OF REAL ESTATE LAW, p. 318 (1972).

53. 2 BLACKSTONE'S COMMENTARIES, § 262 (Cooley ed. 1899).

54. *See* Murray v. Sermon, 8 N.C. (1 Hawks) 56 (1820).

55. State v. Johnson, 278 N.C. 126, 179 S.E.2d 371 (1971).

churning of the ocean.[56] In a brief sojourn into the literary world, the court noted that title was divested by "the sledgehammering seas ... the inscrutable tides of God."[57]

Finally, where sudden, powerful, natural forces, such as a flood or hurricane, cause a "sudden and perceptible gain or loss of riparian land,"[58] no change in legal title occurs.[59]

§ 354. Rights in Subterranean and Percolating Waters.

Underground waters or subterranean waters are generally classified as (1) streams or bodies of water flowing in fixed or definite channels, the existence and location of which are known or ascertainable from surface indications or other means without excavations for that purpose, and (2) percolating waters, which ooze, seep or filter through the soil beneath the surface, or which flow in a course which is unknown or undefined and are not discoverable from surface indications without excavations for that purpose.[60] In the absence of proof to the contrary, it is presumed that underground water is percolating water and that it does not flow in a defined and known channel.[61]

With respect to subterranean streams flowing in fixed channels, the rights and liabilities of adjacent landowners are governed so far as practicable by the rules applicable to surface streams.[62]

With respect to percolating waters, North Carolina follows the "reasonable use" doctrine.[63] It is to be remembered that "percolating waters" are

---

56. Fishing Pier v. Town of Carolina Beach, 277 N.C. 297, 177 S.E.2d 513 (1970).
57. State v. Johnson, 278 N.C. 126, 179 S.E.2d 371 (1971), citing 5A THOMPSON ON REAL PROPERTY (Grimes ed., 1957), § 2561.
58. Id.
59. See generally Maloney & Ausness, *The Use and Legal Significance of the Mean High Water Line in Coastal Boundary Mapping*, 53 N.C.L. REV. 185 (1974). (See the excellent discussion at 53 N.C.L. REV. at pp. 234-37 of state and federal common law of water boundaries.)
60. Jones v. Home Bldg. & Loan Ass'n, 252 N.C. 626, 114 S.E.2d 638 (1960).
61. Id. The burden of establishing the existence of an underground stream rests upon the party who alleges such fact.
62. In addition to the rules relating to extraction, diversion and pollution of streams, it has long been settled in North Carolina that a lower owner cannot obstruct a surface stream of water, so as to prevent the water from flowing as it naturally would, and thereby flood the lands and buildings above him, and if he does so, he incurs liability for the damage done by such flooding. Pugh v. Wheeler, 19 N.C. 50 (1836); Overton v. Sawyer, 46 N.C. 308 (1854); Railroad v. Wicker, 74 N.C. 220 (1876); Porter v. Durham, 74 N.C. 767 (1876); Cagle v. Parker, 97 N.C. 271, 2 S.E. 76 (1887); Ridley v. Railroad, 118 N.C. 996, 24 S.E. 730 (1896); Mullen v. Canal Co., 130 N.C. 496, 41 S.E. 1027 (1902); Chaffin v. Manufacturing Co., 135 N.C. 95, 47 S.E. 226 (1904); Clark v. Guano Co., 144 N.C. 64, 56 S.E. 858 (1907); Winchester v. Byers, 196 N.C. 383, 145 S.E. 774 (1928); Braswell v. State Highway Comm'n, 250 N.C. 508, 108 S.E.2d 912 (1959).
63. Rouse v. City of Kinston, 188 N.C. 1, 123 S.E. 482 (1924); Bayer v. Teer Co., 256 N.C. 509, 124 S.E.2d 552 (1962).

§ 354   RIGHTS AND DUTIES OF OWNERS   § 354

those that ooze or filtrate through the soil or flow in undefined and unknown channels. While at the common law an owner was deemed to own all that lies beneath the surface of the earth, whether solid rock, porous earth, veins or strata of stone or ore, or veins or percolations of water, this rule did not allow for the difference between substances which underlie the surface of the earth. While solid rock under the soil remains stable and stationary, water is mobile, and because of its oozing and filtrating mobility a landowner could pump all the water from under his neighbors' lands as well as from under his own, and through the same pump. For that reason, the "American rule" has been developed relating to the use of percolating waters, which is the "reasonable use" rule applicable in North Carolina.[64] The "reasonable use" rule means that a landowner may use percolating waters that are subjacent to his soil for manufacturing, agriculture, mining, irrigation or otherwise, provided such is done in connection with any beneficial ownership or enjoyment of the land from which the waters are taken.[65] Any [66] such use is deemed "reasonable," but any withdrawal of waters for distribution or sale, or for uses not connected with any beneficial ownership or enjoyment of the land from which they are taken, will be deemed "unreasonable" if adjoining landowners are injured thereby.[67] Any use may be made that is reason-

---

64. *Id.*
65. *Id.*
66. In Rouse v. City of Kinston, 188 N.C. 1, 123 S.E. 482 (1924), the court states: "This rule does not prevent the private use by any landowner of percolating waters subjacent to his soil, in manufacturing, agriculture, irrigation, or otherwise; nor does it prevent any reasonable development of his land by mining, or the like, although by such use the underground percolating waters of his neighbor may be thus interfered with or diverted; but it does prevent the withdrawal of underground waters for distribution or sale, for uses not connected with any beneficial ownership or enjoyment of the land from which they are taken, if it thereby follows that the owner of adjacent lands is interfered with in his right to the reasonable use of subsurface water upon his own land, or if his wells, springs or streams are thereby materially diminished in flow or his land rendered less valuable for agriculture, pasturage, or for legitimate uses. . . . I therefore charge you that, in the absence of contract or legislative enactment, whatever is reasonable for the owner to do with his subsurface water, he may do. He may make the most of it that he reasonably can. It is not unreasonable for him to dig wells and take therefrom all of the waters that he needs in order to get the fullest enjoyment and usefulness from his land, for the purposes of abode, productiveness of the soil, or manufacture, or whatever else the land is capable of. He may consume it at will; but, to fit it up with wells and pumps of such pervasive and potential reach that from their base he can tap the waters stored in the lands of others, and thus lead them to his own land, and by merchandising it, prevent its return, to the injury of adjoining landowners, is an unreasonable use of the soil, and in such event the injured neighbor may bring his action for damages."
67. In Rouse v. City of Kinston, 188 N.C. 1, 123 S.E. 482 (1924), the City of Kinston was held liable for damages where it dug artesian wells and piped water from the land to the city to furnish the water supply of its inhabitants. Since the piping of the water from the city's wells practically exhausted the supply of water in wells of an adjoining owner, injuring the productiveness of his land and the health of his tenants, recovery of damages from the city was allowed.

able and legitimate in the natural enjoyment or improvement of one's land, provided he does not waste the water, use it for purposes unconnected with the improvement or enjoyment of his land, or act maliciously or negligently.[68]

§ 355. Drainage of Surface Water.

The rules applicable to rights in water flowing in natural watercourses or channels have been considered in the preceding sections. For the most part, the law with respect to water flowing in defined streams has been designed to maximize the beneficial use of waters. "Surface water" is water that comes from rain, snow and the like, which is diffused and not flowing in defined channels. The law with respect to "surface water" has been designed to "get rid of it" and to establish the rights and duties of landowners, as between themselves, when water is expelled or discharged.

Under the common law, the rule for getting rid of surface waters was called the "common-enemy rule," which meant that surface water was considered a common enemy of all landowners and that each landowner should have an unqualified right to fend off surface waters without regard to the consequences of other landowners, who also had a right to protect themselves as best they could.[69] While this rule was applied in its original vigor in many states during the pioneer period of settlement when the country was largely undeveloped and sparsely settled, North Carolina has never applied the "common-enemy rule."[70] Instead, North Carolina traditionally adhered to a modified version of the so-called "civil-law rule" with respect to surface waters until the 1977 North Carolina Supreme

---

68. In Bayer v. Teer Co., 256 N.C. 509, 124 S.E.2d 552 (1962), defendant's quarry operations resulted in the diminution and contamination of neighboring landowners' wells. In denying recovery the court stated: "There is no evidence on defendant's part of malice, or of negligence, or of waste, or of an intentional contamination or interference with plaintiffs' supply of percolating waters to their well. Defendant was not required to let its rock quarry remain unworked because of percolating waters in order to protect the underground waters on plaintiffs' land."

See, however, Masten v. Texas Co., 194 N.C. 540, 140 S.E. 89 (1927), where recovery was allowed against an oil company which allowed gasoline to leak from its tanks and to pollute a neighbor's well. *See also* Clark v. Lawrence, 59 N. C. 83 (1960), in which the court enjoined the burying of dead persons at a point where it would corrupt the water of wells or springs.

See generally Aycock, *Introduction to Water Use Law in North Carolina,* 46 N.C.L. REV. 1 (1967).

69. Midgett v. State Highway Comm'n, 260 N.C. 241, 132 S.E.2d 599 (1963).

70. *Id.;* Davis v. Cahoon, 5 N.C. App. 46, 168 S.E.2d 70 (1969).

Court case of *Pendergrast v. Aiken*[71] in which the "reasonable use" rule was adopted with the following language:

> Accordingly, we now formally adopt the rule of reasonable use with respect to surface water drainage. That rule is expressed as follows: Each possessor is legally privileged to make a reasonable use of his land, even though the flow of surface water is altered thereby and causes some harm to others, but liability is incurred when his harmful interference with the flow of surface waters is unreasonable and causes substantial damage.[72]
>
> Analytically, a cause of action for unreasonable interference with the flow of surface water causing substantial damage is a private nuisance action, with liability arising where the conduct of the landowner making the alterations in the flow of surface water is either (1) intentional and unreasonable or (2) negligent, reckless or in the course of an abnormally dangerous activity.[73]

For purposes of this rule, the *Pendergrast* decision went on to define "reasonableness" as follows:

> Reasonableness is a question of fact to be determined in each case by weighing the gravity of the harm to the plaintiff against the utility of the conduct of the defendant.... Determination of the gravity of the harm involves consideration of the extent and character of the harm to the plaintiff, the social value which the law attaches to the type of use which is invaded, the suitability of the locality for that use, the burden on plaintiff to minimize the harm, and other relevant considerations arising upon the evidence. Determination of the utility of the conduct of the defendant involves consideration of the purpose of the defendant's conduct, the social value which the law attaches to that purpose, the suitability of the locality for the use defendant makes of the property, and other relevant considerations arising upon the evidence.[74]

---

71. Pendergrast v. Aiken, 293 N.C. 201, 236 S.E.2d 787 (1977). At 293 N.C. 218, the court explains:

    > We do not view the formal adoption of the rule of reasonable use as an innovation in the law of North Carolina. In the past, modifications in drainage water law have been piecemeal as required by time and circumstance. Our action today simply recognizes that fact and approves a rule by which adjustments in the rights and duties of landowners may be made fairly and justly without disrupting the consistency of the law. Thus we adopt the reasonable use rule as an act of clarification — not innovation.

72. *Id.* at 293 N.C. 216, citing Armstrong v. Francis Corp., 20 N.J. 320, 120 A.2d 4 (1956) and Weinberg v. Northern Alaska Development Corp., 384 P.2d 450 (Alaska 1963).

73. *Id.* at 293 N.C. 216, 217 citing RESTATEMENT OF TORTS § 833 (1939); RESTATEMENT (SECOND) OF TORTS § 822 (Tent. Draft No. 17, 1971); *accord,* Watts v. Manufacturing Co., 256 N.C. 611, 124 S.E.2d 809 (1962); Morgan v. Oil Co., 238 N.C. 185, 77 S.E.2d 682 (1953); City of Houston v. Renault, Inc., 431 S.W.2d 322 (Tex. 1968); Sanford v. University of Utah, 26 Utah 2d 285, 488 P.2d 741 (1971); and State v. Deetz, 66 Wis. 2d 1, 224 N.W.2d 407 (1974).

74. *Id.* at 293 N.C. 217, citing Armstrong v. Francis Corp., 20 N.J. 320, 120 A.2d 4 (1956); State v. Deetz, 66 Wis. 2d 1, 224 N.W.2d 407 (1974); and RESTATEMENT (SECOND) OF TORTS § 826 (Tent. Draft No. 18, 1972) for the general rule and citing the following with respect to determination of the gravity of the harm: Rodrigues v. State, 52 Haw. 156, 472 P.2d 509 (1970); Armstrong v. Francis Corp., 20 N.J. 320, 120 A.2d 4 (1956); Watts v. Manufacturing

§ 356. Public Water Rights; Public Trust Doctrine.

While the state owns the tidelands and beds under navigable waters, it does so subject to what is known as the public trust doctrine.[75] Under this doctrine, the state is required to preserve the property for use by and in trust for the general public, and the state cannot generally destroy this trust by devoting the tidelands and beds to non-public uses.[76] Members of the public, therefore, enjoy certain rights with respect to navigable waters separate and distinct from water rights incident to the ownership of riparian or littoral property. Using waters for navigational purposes and fishing purposes constitute traditional public rights.[77] Certain rights of salvage might be deemed another public interest in such waters.[78] With regard to the ocean, members of the public have a right to travel over and utilize the foreshore in connection with swimming, fishing and other recreational activities related to use of the water.[79] They do not, however,

---

Co., 256 N.C. 611, 124 S.E.2d 809 (1962); Jones v. Boeing Company, 153 N.W.2d 897 (N.D. 1967); RESTATEMENT OF TORTS §§ 829-831 (1939); RESTATEMENT (SECOND) OF TROTS §§ 827, 828 (Tent. Draft No. 17, 1971); RESTATEMENT (SECOND) OF TORTS § 829A (Tent. Draft No. 18, 1972); Note, 50 KY. L.J. 254 (1961-62).

The Court went on to emphasize that, "even should alteration of the water flow by the defendant be 'reasonable' in the sense that the social utility arising from the alteration outweighs the harm to the plaintiff, defendant may nevertheless be liable for damages for a private nuisance 'if the resulting interference with another's use and enjoyment of land is greater than it is reasonable to require the other to bear under the circumstances without compensation.'" Citing RESTATEMENT (SECOND) OF TORTS (Tent. Draft No. 17, 1971); RESTATEMENT (SECOND) OF TORTS §§ 826, 829A (Tent. Draft No. 18, 1972).

See also Board of Transportation v. Terminal Warehouse Corp., 44 N.C. App. 81, 260 S.E.2d 696 (1979) holding the reasonable use rule applicable to cases in which a condemnation authority is involved. Specifically, the court held that the reasonable use rule governed the rights and liabilities of the parties with respect to changes in drainage surface waters resulting from the construction of a highway.

See generally Note, *Real Property — Adoption of the Reasonable Use Rule in North Carolina for Surface Water Drainage Between Adjoining Landowners*, 14 WAKE FOREST L. REV. 866 (1978); Comment, The Application of Surface Water Rules in Urban Areas, 42 MO. L. REV. 76 (1977). [Referred to by the Court in Pendergrast v. Aiken.]

75. Maloney & Ausness, *The Use and Legal Significance of the Mean High Water Line in Coastal Boundary Mapping*, 53 N.C.L. REV. 185, 188 (1974).

76. Id.

77. 5 POWELL ON REAL PROPERTY § 723.2 (1979).

78. Subject to applicable laws. See, for example, § 357 infra discussing the sovereign prerogative doctrine.

79. While citizens of a state may collectively have certain rights in the tidewaters, their use of such waters may of course be regulated. Recently, a surfboard enthusiast's challenge to a county ordinance prohibiting surfboard riding in specified coastal waters was rejected in McDonald v. Newsome, 437 F. Supp. 796 (E.D.N.C. 1977). The court held, inter alia, that a member of the general public does not have a "property" or "liberty" interest in the waters off of Carteret County sufficient to warrant a due process hearing before enforcement of the ordinance prohibiting surfboarding. (But see the final paragraph of the decision where the court questioned whether the state delegated to the county the right to enact an ordinance regulating coastal property and whether the county could delegate to riparian owners the right to regulate and control the use of coastal waters which flow on their lands.)

enjoy any right in North Carolina to cross over private littoral property to get to the foreshore and ocean.

Banks of navigable streams are private property and the rights of members of the public to use navigable waters do not give any license to them to go or come through riparian owners' lands, nor to use the banks except at public landings unless the owner consents.[80]

§ 357. Sovereign Prerogative Doctrine Recognized in North Carolina.

"Sovereign prerogative" is an English common-law principle placing sole ownership of certain wrecked and abandoned vessels at sea in the sovereign.[81] Claiming successorship to this prerogative right of the crown, both the United States government [82] and the State of North Carolina [83] have recently laid claim to treasure, historical items and other goods found wrecked or derelict at sea. Following judicial recognition of the doctrine in 1968,[84] the North Carolina General Assembly codified a form of the doctrine at North Carolina General Statutes, § 121-22. Subject to certain other statutes and the possibility of federal preemption, the enactment declares that "the title to all bottoms of navigable waters within one marine league seaward from the Atlantic seashore measured from the extreme low watermark; and the title to all shipwrecks, vessels, cargoes, tackle, and underwater archeological artifacts which have remained unclaimed for more than 10 years lying on the said bottoms, or on the bottoms of any other navigable waters of the State, is hereby declared to be in the State of North Carolina, and such bottoms, shipwrecks, vessels, cargoes, tackle, and underwater archeological artifacts shall be subject to the exclusive dominion and control of the State."

This statute has been interpreted as covering all archeological artifacts found in navigable waters and not merely items associated with shipwrecks.[85]

---

80. Gaither v. Albemarle Hosp., 235 N.C. 431, 70 S.E.2d 680 (1952).

See generally Schoenbaum, *Public Rights and Coastal Zone Management*, 51 N.C.L. Rev. 1 (1972); Maloney & Ausness, *The Use and Legal Significance of the Mean High Water Line in Coastal Boundary Mapping*, 53 N.C.L. Rev. 185 (1974).

81. State ex rel. Wade v. Flying "W" Enterprises, 273 N.C. 399, 160 S.E.2d 482 (1968).
82. Treasure Salvors, Inc. v. Unidentified Wreck, 569 F.2d 330 (5th Cir. 1978).
83. State ex rel. Wade v. Flying "W" Enterprises, 273 N.C. 399, 160 S.E.2d 482 (1968).
84. Id.
85. State v. Armistead, 19 N.C. App. 704, 200 S.E.2d 226 (1973). Defendants in this case determined that the Confederate Army had in 1856 abandoned certain items of military hardware at Fort Branch, N.C., by rolling them into the Roanoke River. They discovered and brought to the surface 3 cannons, remnants of artillery carriages, and pieces of hardware. N.C. Gen. Stat. § 121-22 was held to cover the artifacts. See generally N.C. Gen. Stat. §§ 121-22 through 121-28.

§ 358. Governmental Regulation: Federal.

As mentioned earlier in this chapter, water rights have become increasingly subject to state and federal legislation and regulation.[86] At the federal level, legislation in areas of navigation, environmental law, land use planning, water power development and irrigation has had a significant impact on the rights of individuals with respect to all aspects of water use and use of riparian and littoral property.[87]

The paramount role of the federal government in this area is based upon a number of constitutional and legislative grounds.[88] A recent environmental law case [89] describes the federal-state relationship in the navigational area as follows:

> While states undeniably possess broad power to regulate their own navigable waters for the general welfare, the power clearly is, and should be subordinate to the federal navigational power unless Congress expressly defers to the state authority in the context of a specific statute.[90]

The Submerged Lands Act,[91] which vested in states the power to regulate tidelands property except for purposes relating to navigation, flood control and hydroelectric power, has been held to not constitute a relinquishment by Congress of its constitutional powers over commerce to regulate submerged riparian property for conservation purposes.[92]

A summary of some of the federal legislation in this area of water law is as follows:

(a) The *Rivers and Harbors Act of 1899 (Refuse Act)* [93] prohibits the creation of any obstruction to the navigable capacity of any of the waters of the United States. It applies to both the building of structures and the excavating and filling in of navigable waters.[94] All users of navigable waters — including private parties who suffer special injury because of unauthorized obstructions — are beneficiaries of this Act.[95]

---

86. Introductory remarks at § 348 *supra*.
87. *See* the discussion of various statutes including the Federal Water Power Act of 1920 and other examples of water power legislation at 5 POWELL ON PROPERTY § 723.
88. See the excellent summary at 5 POWELL ON PROPERTY § 723.
89. Sierra Club v. Andrus, 610 F.2d 581 (9th Cir. 1979).
90. *Id.* at 599.
91. 43 U.S.C.A. § 1301 *et seq.*
92. Zabel v. Tabb, 430 F.2d 199 (5th Cir. 1970).
93. 33 U.S.C.A. §§ 401-413 (§ 407 is also known as the *Refuse Act of 1899*.)
94. Zabel v. Tabb, 430 F.2d 199 (5th Cir. 1970). The Rivers and Harbors Act prohibits navigational capacity obstructions unless approval is issued by the Secretary of the Army upon recommendation of the Chief of Engineers, Corps of Engineers.
95. Sierra Club v. Andrus, 610 F.2d 581 (9th Cir. 1979) citing Neches Canal Co. v. Miller & Vidor Lumber Co., 24 F.2d 763 (5th Cir. 1928); Tatum v. Blackstock, 319 F.2d 397 (5th Cir. 1963); and Leslie Salt Co. v. Froehlke, 578 F.2d 742 (9th Cir. 1978). Specifically, the Sierra Club v. Andrus decision gave parties who suffered special injury a private right of action to enforce the permit requirements of Section 10 of the River and Harbors Act of 1899, 33 U.S.C.A. 403.

(b) The *Federal Water Pollution Control Act* (as amended by the *Clean Water Act of 1977*)[96] has as its general objective the restoration and maintenance of the chemical, physical and biological integrity of the nation's waters, and the Act contains extensive requirements and standards designed to achieve this goal. The Act requires, for example, the issuance of a permit by the Secretary of the Army for the discharge of material into bodies of water covered by it.[97]

(c) The *National Environmental Policy Act of 1969*[98] requires every federal agency to consider ecological factors when dealing with activities which may have an impact on the environment. Based on this Act, it has been held that a permit under the Rivers and Harbors Act can be denied on conservation grounds,[99] and an environmental impact statement may be required before the Corps of Engineers can lawfully issue a permit for certain water projects.[100] Likewise, in the recent case of *Sierra Club v. Alexander*,[101] where construction of a New York shopping center mall was to involve the filling in of approximately thirty-eight acres of wetlands, it was held that the Army Corps of Engineers has an affirmative obligation under the National Environmental Policy Act of 1969 to consider alternatives to the shopping mall's fill proposal when issuing a permit under the Federal Water Pollution Control Act.[102] Thus, in many instances the obstruction or filling of navigable water of the United States will involve both an application for the necessary permit from the Corps of Engineers and an analysis and taking into account of the environmental considerations set forth in the National Environmental Policy Act.

(d) The *Coastal Zone Management Act of 1972*[103] was enacted to establish a national policy and develop a national program for the management, beneficial use, protection, and development of the land and water resources of the nation's coastal zones. Coastal states become eligible for federal grants and assistance under this Act if they develop a management program for the land and water resources of their coastal

---

96. 33 U.S.C.A. § 1251 *et seq.*
97. 33 U.S.C.A. § 1344.
98. 42 U.S.C.A. §§ 4331-4347.
99. Zabel v. Tabb, 430 F.2d 199 (5th Cir. 1970).
100. *Id.*
101. 484 F. Supp. 455 (1980).
102. *Id. See also* Conservation Council of North Carolina v. Costanzo, 398 F. Supp. 653 (E.D.N.C. 1975) where it was held that the Corps of Engineers was required to comply with the requirements of the National Environmental Protection Act including preparation and filing of a detailed environmental impact statement where the issuance of a marina permit on Bald Head Island would have a significant effect on the environment in that it would accelerate development and cause a population increase of 15,000 part-time residents. The filling activities of the developer onto wetlands regularly or periodically inundated by tidal waters constituted a discharge into waters of the United States and violated the Federal Water Pollution Control Act. (Injunctive relief was held to be inappropriate.)
103. P.L. 92-583 as amended by P.L. 94-370 and P.L. 95-372.

zones in accordance with federal guidelines. In North Carolina, the state Coastal Area Management Act of 1974 [104] was tailored with a view to complying with this federal Act.[105]

§ 359. Governmental Regulation: State.

A summary of some of the more significant State Acts affecting water law is as follows:

(a) *The Water Use Act of 1967* [106] has as its declared purpose "that the water resources of the State be put to beneficial use to the fullest extent to which they are capable, subject to reasonable regulation in order to conserve these resources and to provide and maintain conditions which are conductive to the development and use of water resources." [107] The Act is administered by the Environmental Management Commission [108] which is authorized to declare and delineate "capacity use areas" in the State pursuant to specified administrative procedures.[109] A "capacity use area" is defined as one where the Commission "finds that the aggregate uses of groundwater or surface water, or both, in or affecting said area (i) have developed or threatened to develop to a degree which requires coordination and regulation, or (ii) exceed or threaten to exceed, or otherwise threaten or impair, the renewal or replenishment of such waters or any part of them." [110]

The significance of declaration of a "capacity use area" is that, subject to procedural and notice requirements, the Commission is given significant powers to regulate users of surface and ground waters in the area.[111]

---

104. N.C. GEN. STAT. §§ 113A-100 to 113A-129.

105. Schoenbaum, *The Management of Land and Water Use in the Coastal Zone: A New Law is Enacted in North Carolina*, 53 N.C.L. REV. 275, 282 (1974).

Note: This discussion in § 358 is not intended to be an exhaustive exposition of water-related federal legislation. Additional legislation includes: *Federal Water Power Act of 1920*, 16 U.S.C.A. § 790 *et seq.*; *Wild and Scenic Rivers Act*, 16 U.S.C.A. § 1274 *et seq.*; *Marine Mammal Protection Act*, 16 U.S.C.A. § 1361; and the *National Flood Insurance Act* of 1968, 42 U.S.C.A. § 4001 *et seq.* Various federal Executive Orders and a myriad of regulations have not been discussed herein.

106. N.C. GEN. STAT. § 143-215.11 *et seq. See generally*, Article 21, *Water And Air Resources*, of Chapter 143 of N.C. GEN. STATS.

107. N.C. GEN. STAT. § 143-215.12.

108. N.C. GEN. STAT. § 143-214.1.

109. N.C. GEN. STAT. § 143-215.13(c). *High Rock Lake Association v. Environmental Management Commission*, 39 N.C. App. 699, 252 S.E.2d 109 (1979) holding that a fact finding hearing of the Environmental Management Commission to consider whether to initiate proceedings to declare a certain river basin as a "capacity use area" constituted rule-making type procedure under N.C. GEN. STAT. § 143-215.13(c) and was not a contested case entitling a party to judicial review under the Administrative Procedure Act.

110. N.C. GEN. STAT. § 143-215.13(b).

111. N.C. GEN. STAT. § 143-215.14(a) which provides:

(a) Following the declaration of a capacity use area by the Environmental Management Commission, it shall prepare proposed regulations to be applied in said area,

Whether or not a "capacity use area" has been declared, the Commission has the power, again subject to notice and hearing, to regulate water withdrawal and water pollution if it believes that the withdrawal of water from or the discharge of water pollutants is having "an unreasonably adverse effect upon such waters." [112]

The Act is not intended to change or modify existing relative rights of riparian owners concerning the use of surface water under existing common or statutory law.[113]

(b) The *Dam Safety Law of 1967*[114] provides for the certification and inspection of dams by the Department of Natural Resources in the interest of public safety and the prevention of damage to property.[115] It also calls for the approval and regulation of certain projects by the Envi-

---

containing such of the following provisions as the Environmental Management Commission finds appropriate concerning the use of surface waters or groundwaters or both:

(1) Provisions requring water users within the area to submit reports not more frequently than at 30-day intervals concerning quantity of water used or withdrawn, sources of water and the nature of the use thereof.
(2) With respect to surface waters, groundwaters, or both: provisions concerning the timing of withdrawals; provisions to protect against or abate salt water encroachment; provisions to protect against or abate unreasonble adverse effects on other water users within the area, including but not limited to adverse effects on public use.
(3) With respect to groundwaters: provisions concerning well-spacing controls; and provisions establishing a range of prescribed pumping levels (elevations below which water may not be pumped) or maximum pumping rates, or both, in wells or for the aquifer or for any part thereof based on the capacities and characteristics of the aquifer.
(4) Such other provisions not inconsistent with this Part as the Environmental Management Commission finds necessary to implement the purposes of this Part.

See also N.C. GEN. STAT. §§ 143-215.15 and 143-215.16.

112. N.C. GEN. STAT. § 143-215.13(d). Powers of the Commission include:

(1) Prohibiting any person withdrawing waters in excess of 100,000 gallons per day from increasing the amount of the withdrawal above such limit as may be established in the order.
(2) Prohibiting any person from constructing, installing or operating any new well or withdrawal facilities having a capacity in excess of a rate established in the order; but such prohibition shall not extend to any new well or facility having a capacity of less than 10,000 gallons per day.
(3) Prohibiting any person discharging water pollutants to the waters from increasing the rate of discharge in excess of the rate established in the order.
(4) Prohibiting any person from constructing, installing or operating any facility that will or may result in the discharge or water pollutants to the waters in excess of the rate established in the order.
(5) Prohibiting any agency or political subdivision of the State from issuing any permit or similar document for the construction, installation, or operation of any new or existing facilities for withdrawing water from or discharging water pollutants to the waters in such area in excess of the rates established in the order.

113. N.C. GEN. STAT. § 143-215.22.
114. N.C. GEN. STAT. § 43-215.23 *et seq.*
115. N.C. GEN. STAT. § 143-215.23. Wells v. Benson, 40 N.C. App. 704, 253 S.E.2d 602 (1979).

ronmental Management Commission.[116] Construction of any dam covered by the *Dam Safety Law* [117] cannot begin until certain information and a certification as to safety are filed with the Department of Natural Resources.[118] Likewise, subject to enumerated exceptions, a repair, alteration or improvement of a dam must be preceded by application to the appropriate state agency.[119]

(c) The *Coastal Area Management Act of 1974 (CAMA)* establishes a cooperative state-local scheme of coastal area management [120] with the basic objective of establishing a comprehensive plan for the coastal area of North Carolina that will protect, preserve, and cause the orderly development of it.[121] Specifically, the goals of the coastal area management system are set forth as follows: [122]

> (b) Goals. — The goals of the coastal area management system to be created pursuant to this Article are as follows:
>
>> (1) To provide a management system capable of preserving and managing the natural ecological conditions of the estuarine system, the barrier dune system, and the beaches, so as to safeguard and perpetuate their natural productivity and their biological, economic and esthetic values;
>>
>> (2) To insure that the development or preservation of the land and water resources of the coastal area proceeds in a manner consistent with the capability of the land and water for development, use, or preservation based on ecological considerations;
>>
>> (3) To insure the orderly and balanced use and preservation of our coastal resources on behalf of the people of North Carolina and the nation;
>>
>> (4) To establish policies, guidelines and standards for:
>>
>>> a. Protection, preservation, and conservation of natural resources including but not limited to water use, scenic vistas, and fish and wildlife; and management of transitional or intensely developed areas and areas especially suited to intensive use or development, as well as areas of significant natural value;
>>>
>>> b. The economic development of the coastal area, including but not limited to construction, location and design of

---

116. N.C. GEN. STAT. §§ 143-215.26 through 143-215.31. *See* Wells v. Benson, 40 N.C. App. 704, 253 S.E.2d 602 (1979) holding that the Environmental Management Commission is not authorized to deny a removal of a private washed out dam by the owners where there was no threat of physical damage to surrounding property owners.

117. N.C. GEN. STAT. § 143-215.25(2) defines "dam."

118. N.C. GEN. STAT. § 143-215.26.

119. N.C. GEN. STAT. § 143-215.27.

120. N.C. GEN. STAT. § 113A-101. See the listing of helpful law review articles that follows at the end of citations.

121. N.C. GEN. STAT. § 113A-102(a).

122. N.C. GEN. STAT. § 113A-102(b). Adams v. Dept. of N.E.R., 295 N.C. 683, 249 S.E.2d 402 (1978).

industries, port facilities, commercial establishments and other developments;

 c. Recreation and tourist facilities and parklands;

 d. Transportation and circulation patterns for the coastal area including major thoroughfares, transportation routes, navigation channels and harbors, and other public utilities and facilities;

 e. Preservation and enhancement of the historic, cultural, and scientific aspects of the coastal area;

 f. Protection of present common-law and statutory public rights in the lands and waters of the coastal area;

 g. Any other purposes deemed necessary or appropriate to effectuate the policy of this Article.

Part 2 of CAMA,[123] titled "Planning Processes," involves the development of State guidelines for the coastal area which are to consist of statements of objectives, policies and standards to be followed in the public and private use of land and water areas within the coastal area.[124] These guidelines are to be developed by the Coastal Resources Commission. Local land-use plans are to be developed for each county within the coastal area consistent with the State guidelines,[125] and these plans are to serve as criteria for the issuance or denial of development permits under Part 4 of CAMA.[126]

Under Part 3 of CAMA,[127] the Coastal Resources Commission is directed to designate by rule geographic areas of the coastal area as "areas of environmental concern,"[128] a term which is defined by statute.[129] Notice and hearing requirements must be complied with prior to the adoption of a rule designating an area of environmental concern.[130] The significance of the "area of environmental concern" designation is that any person undertaking any development in such an area must obtain in advance a permit pursuant to the provisions of CAMA.[131] An expedited procedure is set forth for the obtaining of a permit for a "minor development" from the appropriate local governmental unit.[132] A quasi-judicial procedure is specified for any "major development," and

---

123. N.C. GEN. STAT. §§ 113A-106 to 113A-112.
124. N.C. GEN. STAT. §§ 113A-106 and 113A-107.
125. N.C. GEN. STAT. § 113A-108.
126. *Id.* Part 4, titled "Permit Letting and Enforcement," is located at §§ 113A-116 — 113A-128 of the N.C. GEN. STATS. If the city or county has not developed an approved implementation and enforcement program, permits are to be obtained from the Secretary of Natural Resources and Community Development. N.C. GEN. STAT. § 113A-118.
127. N.C. GEN. STAT. §§ 113A-113 to 113A-115, titled "Areas of Environmental Concern."
128. N.C. GEN. STAT. § 113A-113.
129. N.C. GEN. STAT. § 113A-113(b).
130. N.C. GEN. STAT. § 113A-115.
131. N.C. GEN. STAT. § 113A-118.
132. *Id. See also* N.C. GEN. STAT. §§ 113A-119, 113A-120, 113A-121, and 113A-122.

permits for "major developments" are obtained from the Coastal Resources Commission.[133]

Miscellaneous provisions of CAMA of general interest include the judicial review statute,[134] an injunctive relief and penalties section,[135] and a statute titled "Protection of Landowners' Rights"[136] which states: "Nothing in this Article authorizes any governmental agency to adopt a rule or regulation or issue any order that constitutes a taking of property in violation of the Constitution of this State or of the United States."

Finally, it should be noted that in a recent North Carolina Supreme Court decision[137] an attack on the constitutionality of CAMA was made on a number of grounds. The Court upheld the general constitutionality of CAMA, rejecting arguments that it was a prohibited local act, that the coastal counties constituted an invalid legislative class, that the General Assembly did not properly define the inland limits of the coastal sounds, and that legislative authority had been improperly delegated.[138] Additionally, the court found no justiciable controversy concerning contentions that CAMA effected an unconstitutional taking of land and that it authorized warrantless searches.[139]

Article IV. Rights of Adjoining Landowners; Nuisances

§ 360. Generally.

While it is a general rule that the owner of land, as an incident of his ownership, has the right to make such use of his own property as he sees fit, this rule applies only so long as he does not injure his neighbors who have the same right. While every landowner has a right to the free enjoyment and use of his own property, his neighbors have the same rights and privileges, and he must so use his property as not unreasonably to hurt or hinder his neighbors' rights to the use and enjoyment of their

---

133. Id.
134. N.C. GEN. STAT. § 113A-123.
135. N.C. GEN. STAT. § 113A-126.
136. N.C. GEN. STAT. § 113A-128.
137. Adams v. Dept. of N.E.R., 295 N.C. 683, 249 S.E.2d 402 (1978).
138. Id.
139. Id.

See generally Schoenbaum, *Public Rights and Coastal Zone Management*, 51 N.C.L. REV. 1 (1972); Maloney & Ausness, *The Use and Legal Significance of the Mean High Water Line in Coastal Boundary Mapping*, 53 N.C.L. REV. 185 (1974); Schoenbaum, *The Management of Land and Water Use in the Coastal Zone: A New Law Is Enacted in North Carolina*, 53 N.C.L. REV. 275 (1974); Glenn, *The Coastal Area Management Act in the Courts: A Preliminary Analysis*, 53 N.C.L. REV. 303 (1974); Heath, Jr., *A Legislative History of the Coastal Area Management Act*, 53 N.C.L. REV. 345 (1974).

property.[1] An improper use of one's real property in such a way as results in injury to the land or property of another, constitutes a nuisance under the maxim *sic utere tuo ut alienum non laedas* (use your own property in such a manner as not to injure that of another).[2]

A "nuisance" involves an act done on one's own land, unaccompanied by trespass, which causes hurt, inconvenience or damage, or which interferes with the enjoyment of life or property of another.[3] Every person is bound to make a reasonable use of his property so as to occasion no unnecessary damage or annoyance to his neighbor.[4] If he makes an unreasonable, unwarrantable or unlawful use of it, so as to produce a material annoyance, inconvenience, discomfort or hurt to his neighbor, he will be guilty of a nuisance to his neighbor. To constitute a nuisance, the use must be such as to produce a tangible, appreciable injury to neighboring property, or such as to render its enjoyment specially uncomfortable or inconvenient.[5]

---

1. Watts v. Manufacturing Co., 256 N.C. 611, 124 S.E.2d 809 (1962), wherein the court said: "The precise limits of one's rights to do as he pleases with his own property are difficult to define. The use must be a reasonable one, and the right implies and is subject to a like right in every other person. One cannot use his property so as to cause a physical invasion of another's property, or unreasonably to deprive him of the lawful use and enjoyment of the same, or so as to create a nuisance to adjoining property owners . . . and any unreasonable . . . use which produces material injury or great annoyance to others, or unreasonably interferes with their lawful use and enjoyment of their property, is a nuisance which . . . will render him liable for the consequent damages." Pendergrast v. Aiken, 293 N.C. 201, 236 S.E.2d 787 (1977), holding that the essential inquiry into any nuisance action is whether the conduct of the defendant is unreasonable.

2. Watts v. Manufacturing Co., 256 N.C. 611, 124 S.E.2d 809 (1962); Andrews v. Andrews, 242 N.C. 382, 88 S.E.2d 88 (1955); Morgan v. Oil Co., 238 N.C. 185, 77 S.E.2d 682 (1953).

3. Holton v. Northwestern Oil Co., 201 N.C. 744, 161 S.E. 391 (1931); King v. Ward, 207 N.C. 782, 178 S.E. 577 (1935); Barrier v. Troutman, 231 N.C. 47, 55 S.E.2d 973 (1949). See Jones v. Queen City Speedways, Inc., 276 N.C. 231, 172 S.E.2d 42 (1970), to the effect that mere noise may be so great at certain times and under certain circumstances as to amount to an actionable nuisance and entitle the party subjected to it to an injunction. (The court held that the operation of a motor vehicle race track could be enjoined as a nuisance because the noise was so loud as to cause plaintiffs discomfort and annoyance. It was alleged and the jury found that the noise of the racing vehicles on defendant's track caused plaintiffs to lose sleep at night, impaired the use and enjoyment of their homes, and that lights and dust from the race track, coupled with the noise, caused plaintiffs' property to depreciate in value and made their homes virtually uninhabitable while the races were in progress.)

4. Watts v. Manufacturing Co., 256 N.C. 611, 124 S.E.2d 809 (1962).

5. "Before plaintiffs may recover the injury to them must be substantial. By substantial invasion is meant an invasion that involves more than slight inconvenience or petty annoyance. The law does not concern itself with trifles. Practically all human activities, unless carried on in a wilderness, interfere to some extent with others or involve some risk of interference, and these interferences range from mere trifling annoyances to serious harms. Each individual in a community must put up with a certain amount of annoyance, inconvenience or interference, and must take a certain amount of risk in order that all may get on together. But if one makes an unreasonable use of his property and thereby causes another substantial harm in the use and enjoyment of his, the former is liable for the injury

A nuisance may arise either from intentional conduct or by reason of negligence.[6] It may flow from either a lawful or unlawful act.[7] Even though an act is lawful, it may be unreasonable or unwarranted under the circumstances and thus may constitute a nuisance.[8] A nuisance is "nontrespassory";[9] this means that the objectionable condition exists on the owner's property without any trespassing encroachment beyond his own boundaries onto his neighbor's land, although the activity or condition affects the neighbor's use and enjoyment of his land.[10]

§ 361. Classification of Nuisances.

Nuisances are classified according to their extent or the scope of their injurious effect and also according to the nature and character of the thing or condition causing the injury.

Nuisances are either (1) *public,* or (2) *private,* depending on the scope or extent of their injurious effect.

In addition, nuisances are either (1) *nuisances per se,* or (2) *nuisances per accidens,* according to the nature or character of the thing or condition causing the injury.

§ 362. Public Nuisances.

Acts or conditions which injure the public health, morals, safety or general welfare are *public* nuisances.[11] Public nuisances affect an

---

inflicted." Watts v. Manufacturing Co., 256 N.C. 611, 124 S.E.2d 809 (1962). *See* 4 RESTATEMENT OF TORTS § 822, comments g and j, pp. 229, 231. *Accord,* Jones v. Queen City Speedways, Inc., 276 N.C. 231, 172 S.E.2d 42 (1970).

6. Morgan v. Oil Co., 238 N.C. 185, 77 S.E.2d 682 (1953), in which the court said: "A person who creates or maintains a private nuisance is liable for the resulting injury to others regardless of the degree of care or skill exercised by him to avoid such injury.... One of America's greatest jurists, the late Benjamin N. Cardozo, made this illuminating observation on this aspect of the law: 'Nuisance as a concept of the law has more meanings than one. The primary meaning does not involve the element of negligence as one of its essential factors. One acts sometimes at one's peril. In such circumstances, the duty to desist is absolute whenever conduct, if persisted in, brings damage to another. Illustrations are abundant. One who emits noxious fumes or gases day by day in the running of his factory may be liable to his neighbor though he has taken all available precautions. He is not to do such things at all, whether he is negligent or careful.' McFarlane v. City of Niagara Falls, 247 N.Y. 340, 160 N.E. 391."

7. Morgan v. Oil Co., 238 N.C. 185, 77 S.E.2d 682 (1953).

8. *Id. Accord,* Jones v. Queen City Speedways, Inc., 276 N.C. 231, 172 S.E.2d 42 (1970).

9. It has been said in the famous case of Village of Euclid v. Ambler Realty Co., 272 U.S. 365, 47 S. Ct. 114, 71 L. Ed. 303 (1926), that "A nuisance may be merely a right thing in the wrong place, like a pig in the parlor instead of the barnyard."

10. Morgan v. Oil Co., 238 N.C. 185, 77 S.E.2d 682 (1953).

See generally Warren, *Nuisance Law as an Environmental Tool,* 7 WAKE FOREST L. REV. 211 (1971).

11. Wilcher v. Sharpe, 236 N.C. 308, 72 S.E.2d 662 (1952).

indefinite number of people; they offend the people and the state collectively and are subject to abatement upon suit being brought by the proper public officials.[12] Since public nuisances involve offenses to the public at large, as distinghished from offenses to individual property rights,[13] they will not be dealt with in any detail in this work. Suffice it to say that one may be enjoined from using even his own property in such a way as to cause a public nuisance.

§ 363. Private Nuisances.

A *private* nuisance is an act done unaccompanied by an act of trespass which causes a substantial prejudice to the hereditaments, corporeal or incorporeal, of another.[14] A private nuisance affects only a limited number of persons, usually one or a few, in their use or enjoyment of some private right or interest.[15] Where one uses his land unreasonably in such a manner as to annoy and disturb another in the possession of his property, so as to render its ordinary use or occupation physically uncomfortable, or so as injuriously to affect the peace or menace the health and safety of an adjoining landowner, there is a private nuisance

---

12. 6A AMERICAN LAW OF PROPERTY § 28.23 (Casner ed. 1954). Certain acts and conditions have been declared to be public nuisances by the North Carolina General Assembly. *See, e.g.,* N.C. GEN. STAT. §§ 19-1 through 19-8, which make certain acts or conditions public nuisances because injurious to public morals. *See also* Carpenter v. Boyles, 213 N.C. 432, 196 S.E. 850 (1937).

Suits to abate public nuisances must be brought by the State on the relation of the Attorney General and not on the relation of the Solicitor of the District, except where there is a statute (such as N.C. GEN. STAT. § 19-2) which permits another to bring the action to abate. McLean v. Townsend, 227 N.C. 642, 44 S.E.2d 36 (1947).

Under express statutory authority, a citizen and resident of a county may maintain an action in the name of the State to enjoin certain nuisances, without the necessity of showing that the relator would suffer any direct injury or invasion of his property rights. State *ex rel.* Summrell v. Carolina-Virginia Racing Ass'n, 239 N.C. 591, 80 S.E.2d 638 (1954).

13. It should be noted, however, that an individual may bring an action to abate a nuisance or to procure damages because of a public nuisance if he can show he has suffered unusual or special damages as an individual different from those suffered by the general public. *See* Barrier v. Troutman, 231 N.C. 47, 55 S.E.2d 923 (1949), and cases there cited. In other words, a public nuisance may be an individual or private nuisance, as well, for which an individual may maintain an action. *See also* N.C. GEN. STAT. § 1-539; and especially McManus v. Railroad, 150 N.C. 655, 64 S.E. 766 (1909), and Elliott v. Power Co., 190 N.C. 62, 128 S.E. 730 (1925). *See generally* Warren, *Nuisance Law as an Environmental Tool,* 7 WAKE FOREST L. REV. 211 (1971).

14. King v. Ward, 207 N.C. 782, 178 S.E. 577 (1935); Holton v. Oil Co., 201 N.C. 744, 161 S.E. 391 (1931); Morgan v. Oil Co., 238 N.C. 185, 77 S.E.2d 682 (1953).

15. The nature of the protectable interest would seem to be immaterial. For instance, a fee owner, a life tenant, tenant for years, tenant from period to period, or even an adverse possessor should be entitled to maintain an action to have a private nuisance enjoined which affected his interest. SMITH, REAL PROPERTY SURVEY 234 (1956).

for which the law provides the injured persons redress, either remedial or preventive.[16]

§ 364. Nuisances Per Se.

A nuisance *per se*, or a nuisance in law, is an act, occupation, or structure which is a nuisance at all times and under any circumstances, regardless of location or surroundings.[17] Nuisances *per se* must always be in violation of some law; nothing that is legal in its erection can be a nuisance *per se*.[18] There are very few nuisances *per se* today. The original concept of nuisance *per se* at the common law enbraced only those things which by their nature and inherent qualities made obvious their dangers and indicated that the probability of injury from their presence was almost a certainty. Today, the concept of nuisance *per se* is generally limited to behavior and activities made unreasonable *per se* by statutes or ordinances, particularly those relating to disorderly conduct, immorality and breaches of the peace.[19]

§ 365. Nuisances Per Accidens.

Nuisances *per accidens,* or nuisances in fact, are those acts, occupations or structures which are not always nuisances, but which may become nuisances by reason of their location or by reason of the manner in which they are constructed, maintained or operated.[20] Nuisances *per accidens* are the result of lawful enterprises which are objectionable because one's use of his own land has become unreasonable under the circumstances of a particular case, and interferes with another's use and enjoyment of his land.[21] Most nuisances which occur in the cases are nuisances *per accidens*, which arise as the result of someone carrying on operations in

---

16. Morgan v. Oil Co., 238 N.C. 185, 77 S.E.2d 682 (1953); Jones v. Queen City Speedways, Inc., 276 N.C. 231, 172 S.E.2d 42 (1970).
17. Morgan v. Oil Co., 238 N.C. 185, 77 S.E.2d 682 (1953).
18. Pharr v. Garibaldi, 252 N.C. 803, 115 S.E.2d 18 (1960). An airport is not a nuisance *per se.* 79 A.L.R.3d 264.
19. 6A AMERICAN LAW OF PROPERTY § 28.27 (Casner ed. 1954). For instance, use of property for houses of prostitution or gambling establishments would be nuisances *per se*. Other statutes or ordinances proscribing certain activities can also have the effect of making the proscribed activity be treated as a nuisance *per se,* the main advantage of which is that the petitioner need only show the activity without the necessity of showing the consequences of the activity in his particular situation.
20. Morgan v. Oil Co., 238 N.C. 185, 77 S.E.2d 18 (1960); Swinson v. Realty Co., 200 N.C. 276, 156 S.E. 545 (1930); Cherry v. Williams, 147 N.C. 452, 61 S.E. 267 (1908); Dargan v. Waddill, 31 N.C. 244 (1848).
21. Morgan v. Oil Co., 238 N.C. 185, 77 S.E.2d 18 (1960). *See* Jones v. Queen City Speedways, Inc., 276 N.C. 231, 172 S.E.2d 42 (1970), which holds that the operation of a motor vehicle speedway is a lawful enterprise and is not a nuisance *per se,* but under varying circumstances the operation may become a private nuisance *per accidens.* Moody v. Lundy Packing Co., 7 N.C. App. 463, 172 S.E.2d 905 (1970), held that the operation of a hog buying station in close proximity to a church was not a nuisance *per se,* but that it could become a nuisance *per accidens* when improperly maintained or conducted.

an area that is not congenial to such business, as a result of one not conducting his business properly, or because he contemplates starting a business in an area that another landowner thinks will cause him and his land injury.

What is a nuisance *per accidens* depends upon a qualitative evaluation related more to public policy than to legal theory. Is a particular use of land reasonable or unreasonable in a particular locality? Most harm-producing activities are lawful in themselves and most even produce social benefits to the community in varying degrees.[22] Yet they may be nuisances. In determining if a particular activity constitutes a nuisance it is necessary to look at each individual situation and determine what activities are reasonable or essential on land in a particular locality. What is a reasonable or essential use of land in a particular locality and under certain circumstances may be entirely unreasonable (and thus a nuisance) in another. Therefore the "reasonable-unreasonable," "nuisance-nonnuisance" concept is a relative concept depending on a balancing of the social needs of a community with the harm or hardships which may be caused to an individual landowner by the carrying on of a particular activity in a particular environment.[23]

In considering nuisances *per accidens*, it is always necessary to ask the following questions: (1) Is the particular activity in an improper location considering the surrounding circumstances? (2) Is the particular activity being conducted improperly, assuming it is in the proper location? (3) Is the activity causing the plaintiff-landowner substantial injury?[24] If ques-

22. 6A AMERICAN LAW OF PROPERTY § 28.26 (Casner ed. 1954).
23. *See* Watts v. Manufacturing Co., 256 N.C. 611, 124 S.E.2d 809 (1962), in which the court said: "What is reasonable in one locality and in one set of circumstances may be unreasonable in another. The circumstances which are to be considered by the jury in determining whether or not defendant's conduct is unreasonable include: the surroundings and conditions under which defendant's conduct is maintained, the character of the neighborhood, the nature, utility and social value of defendant's operation, the nature, utility and social value of plaintiff's use and enjoyment which have been invaded, the suitability of the locality for defendant's operation, the suitability of the locality for the use plaintiffs make of their property, the extent, nature and frequency of the harm to plaintiffs' interest, priority of occupation as between the parties and other considerations arising upon the evidence. No single factor is decisive; all the circumstances in the particular case must be considered."
24. *See* Watts v. Manufacturing Co., 256 N.C. 611, 124 S.E.2d 809 (1962), wherein the court said: "Before plaintiffs may recover the injury to them must be substantial. By substantial invasion is meant an invasion that involves more than slight inconvenience or petty annoyance. The law does not concern itself with trifles. Practically all human activities, unless carried on in a wilderness, interfere to some extent with others or involve some risk of interference, and these interferences range from mere trifling annoyances to serious harms. Each individual in a community must put up with a certain amount of annoyance, inconvenience or interference, and must take a certain amount of risk in order that all may get on together. But if one makes an unreasonable use of his property and thereby causes another substantial harm in the use and enjoyment of his, the former is liable for the injury inflicted." *See also* Holton v. Northwestern Oil Co., 201 N.C. 744, 161 S.E. 391 (1931); Taylor v. Railroad, 145 N.C. 400, 59 S.E. 129 (1907).

tions (1) or (2) are either answered in the affirmative, and question (3) is answered in the affirmative, an actionable nuisance exists.

1. *Improper location.* While every man has a right to use his own land as he sees fit in accordance with law, it is his duty to locate any business that he establishes in a place where it will not injure or offend others in their use of their own land.[25]

It is thus the duty of a landowner who proposes to carry on a business on his land to locate it where it is compatible with the surroundings so as to make it as innocuous as possible to other nearby landowners.[26] A thing that is lawful and proper in one locality may be a nuisance in another. In other words, a nuisance may consist merely of the right thing in the wrong place. If one engages in an activity, of itself lawful, which being done in a particular place necessarily tends to damage another's property, it is a nuisance; for it is incumbent on him to find some other place to do that activity where it will not be injurious or offensive.[27]

---

25. Wilcher v. Sharpe, 236 N.C. 308, 72 S.E.2d 662 (1952); Barrier v. Troutman, 231 N.C. 47, 55 S.E.2d 973 (1949). It should be noted that "The locality, the condition of property and the habits and tastes of those residing there, divested of any fanciful notions or such as are dictated by 'dainty modes and habits of living,' is the test to apply in a given case." Cherry v. Williams, 147 N.C. 452, 61 S.E. 267 (1908).

26. Duffy v. Meadows, 131 N.C. 32, 42 S.E. 460 (1902), wherein the court said: "A slaughterhouse located in a thickly populated town or city, or a manufactory of guano similarly situated, in which the chief material used was decayed fish, not having gone through a process of deodorization, would be a nuisance *per se* [sic] and there may be others. But if a slaughterhouse was situated in a place remote from residences and public highways it would not be a nuisance unless it was shown that the business was conducted in an improper manner, as by allowing or permitting the escape of gases, stenches or vapors, thereby producing serious and substantial discomfort and annoyance to those residing in the neighborhood, from a want of proper care in the removal or burning of the offal from the premises. Such a guano manufactory as we have mentioned, so remotely situated from residences as not to affect the health or comfort of the community by means of odors, would not be a nuisance." *See* Cherry v. Williams, 147 N.C. 452, 61 S.E. 267 (1908), in which the court affirmed an injunction restraining the conduct of a sanatorium for the treatment of tuberculosis and other infectious and contagious diseases in a residential area. *See* Moody v. Lundy Packing Co., 7 N.C. App. 463, 172 S.E.2d 905 (1970), which holds the operation of a hog buying station in close proximity to a church is not a nuisance *per se,* but that it could become a nuisance *per accidens* when improperly maintained or conducted.

27. *See* Hooks v. International Speedways, Inc., 263 N.C. 686, 140 S.E.2d 387 (1965), in which the court enjoined construction of an automobile race track near a church because races would be held on Sundays during times of worship and because the noise from the automobiles racing would render practically impossible the conduct of Sunday church services. *But see* Moody v. Lundy Packing Co., 7 N.C. App. 463, 172 S.E.2d 905 (1970), in which the North Carolina Court of Appeals refused to enjoin the construction and operation of a hog buying station in close proximity to a church. The court held that a hog buying station is not a nuisance *per se.* The court held that the operation of the hog buying station *could become* a nuisance *per accidens* by being operated in such a manner as to become a nuisance. The court held that introduction of evidence that the defendants had other hog buying stations that gave off offensive odors causing annoyance and discomfort to people in other neighborhoods was insufficient to show that the proposed hog buying station would be a

2. *Improper operation or maintenance.* If a given activity or business is lawful and its location is proper, it will not be a nuisance unless it is conducted or operated in such an unreasonable manner as to cause substantial interference with another's use and enjoyment of his land. A nuisance may arise from an unreasonable operation or maintenance of a lawful enterprise even if it is properly located.[28]

It should be noted, however, that if a plaintiff complains and brings an action to enjoin the *establishment* of a business or activity in a proper location, alleging that it will *become* a nuisance, the courts will not ordinarily enjoin its construction, as it is possible that the business will be operated without creating an interference or annoyance.[29]

But under certain circumstances a court of equity may enjoin a threatened or anticipated nuisance where the contemplated enterprise must necessarily result in an unreasonable interference with another's use of his property. Thus the Supreme Court of North Carolina has upheld an injunction restraining the construction of an automobile race track near a church on the ground that anticipated noise from the motors and squealing tires of racing cars would disturb and disrupt the church's services, weddings, funerals and other functions.[30] Where it is sought to enjoin an anticipated nuisance, it must be shown: (1) that the proposed construction or the use to be made of the property will be a nuisance *per se;* (2) or that, while it may not amount to a nuisance *per se,* under the circumstances of the case, a nuisance must necessarily result from the contemplated act or thing. The injury must be actually threatened, not merely anticipated, it must be practically certain, not merely probable. It

---

nuisance when constructed; there was no showing of substantial grounds for anticipating that the proposed hog buying station would create a nuisance and annoyance to plaintiffs or others similarly situated.

28. Watts v. Manufacturing Co., 256 N.C. 611, 124 S.E.2d 809 (1962); Morgan v. Oil Co., 238 N.C. 185, 77 S.E.2d 682 (1953); Hooks v. International Speedways, Inc., 263 N.C. 686, 140 S.E.2d 387 (1965); Mewborn v. Rudisill Mine, Inc., 211 N.C. 544, 191 S.E. 28 (1937); Jones v. Queen City Speedways, Inc., 276 N.C. 231, 172 S.E.2d 42 (1970); Moody v. Lundy Packing Co., 7 N.C. App. 463, 172 S.E.2d 905 (1970).

29. Hooks v. International Speedways, Inc., 263 N.C. 686, 140 S.E.2d 387 (1965), wherein the court said: "Where the thing complained of is not a nuisance *per se*, but may or may not become a nuisance, according to the circumstances, and the injury apprehended is merely eventual or contingent, equity will not interfere." *See also* Wilcher v. Sharpe, 236 N.C. 308, 72 S.E.2d 662 (1952); Cherry v. Williams, 147 N.C. 452, 61 S.E. 267 (1908). *See* Moody v. Lundy Packing Co., 7 N.C. App. 463, 172 S.E.2d 905 (1970).

30. Hooks v. International Speedways, Inc., 263 N.C. 686, 140 S.E.2d 387 (1965). *But see* Moody v. Lundy Packing Co., 7 N.C. App. 463, 172 S.E.2d 905 (1970), in which the North Carolina Court of Appeals refused to enjoin the construction and operation of a hog buying station in close proximity to a church.

must further be shown that the threatened injury will be an irreparable one which cannot be compensated by damages in an action at law.[31]

§ 366. Persons Entitled to Relief Because of Nuisances; Persons Liable for Nuisances.

Any person who suffers injury, either to his person or to his property, is entitled to relief against a party who injures him by the maintenance of a nuisance, and he may sue that person in law to recover damages or in equity to have the nuisance abated.[32]

Any person who creates a nuisance is liable for it regardless of whether he is the owner of the land on which it is maintained. But it should be noted that a lessor-owner is not liable to have his premises padlocked to abate a public nuisance maintained by his tenant unless it is established that the lessor knew, or by due diligence could have known, that the nuisance was being maintained.[33] Two or more persons may be liable for the maintenance of a nuisance; if their acts are separate and distinct as to place or time, but culminate in producing a public nuisance which injures the person or property of another, such persons are jointly and severally liable.[34]

§ 367. Remedies for Nuisance.

(a) *Categories of remedies.* The remedies for nuisances fall into three categories: (1) damages; (2) equitable relief by way of temporary injunction; and (3) equitable relief by way of permanent injunction.

(b) *Damages.* Anyone who suffers injury as the consequence of a nuisance may sue at law to recover damages.[35]

What can be recovered as damages will vary depending on the nature of the nuisance, whether it is permanent or temporary, and whether maintained by an ordinary individual or by a municipality, governmental entity or public service corporation. If the nuisance is maintained by a

---

31. Wilcher v. Sharpe, 236 N.C. 308, 72 S.E.2d 662 (1952). In Cherry v. Williams, 147 N.C. 452, 61 S.E. 267 (1908), *construction* of a building for use as a sanitorium for treatment of tuberculosis and other infectious and contagious diseases in a residential section was not restrained although its *use* for those purposes was restrained. *Accord,* Moody v. Lundy Packing Co., 7 N.C. App. 463, 172 S.E.2d 905 (1970).

32. Barrier v. Troutman, 231 N.C. 47, 55 S.E.2d 973 (1949); Pernell v. City of Henderson, 220 N.C. 79, 16 S.E.2d 449 (1941); Welsh v. Todd, 260 N.C. 527, 133 S.E.2d 171 (1963).

33. *See* Bowman v. Fipps, 266 N.C. 535, 146 S.E.2d 395 (1965); Bowman v. Malloy, 264 N.C. 396, 141 S.E.2d 796 (1965); Sinclair, Solicitor v. Croom, 217 N.C. 526, 8 S.E.2d 834 (1940).

34. Moses v. Morganton, 192 N.C. 102, 133 S.E. 421 (1926).

35. Rhodes v. City of Durham, 165 N.C. 679, 81 S.E. 938 (1914); Pernell v. City of Henderson, 220 N.C. 79, 16 S.E.2d 449 (1941); Barrier v. Troutman, 231 N.C. 47, 55 S.E.2d 973 (1949).

§ 367 RIGHTS AND DUTIES OF OWNERS § 367

private individual or corporation, only those damages which have been caused to the time of the trial of the action may be recovered, even if the nuisance is a continuing nuisance.[36] Separate actions must be brought for continuing or recurrent nuisances, and damages are recoverable to the time of the trial only. But the issue of permanent damages may be submitted in the case of an individual's nuisance if the parties consent.[37]

If the nuisance is maintained by a municipal corporation, governmental entity or public service corporation which has the power of eminent domain, either the injured party or the defendant may treat such nuisance as a "taking" of the injured person's land to the extent of its injury by the nuisance, and demand that permanent damages, both past and prospective, be allotted, in which case the action is converted into an action in the nature of condemnation.[38]

The amount of damages recoverable for the maintenance of a nuisance will also vary depending on the circumstances. For instance, if the action is against one who has the power of eminent domain and for permanent damages, the measure of damages is the diminished pecuniary value of the property incident to the wrong, the difference in the market value of the plaintiff's land before and after the injury.[39] But if the action is against a private individual or corporation, the measure of damages is not limited to the diminished pecuniary damage to the land's market value,

---

36. Langley v. Staley Hosiery Mills Co., 194 N.C. 644, 140 S.E. 440 (1927).

37. Id. See also Clinard v. Kernersville, 215 N.C. 745, 3 S.E.2d 267 (1939).

38. Clinard v. Kernersville, 215 N.C. 745, 3 S.E.2d 267 (1939), wherein it is said: "The decisions of this State are in approval of the principle that the owner can recover such (permanent) damage for a wrong of this character (damages resulting from the operation of a sewage plant which polluted a stream crossing plaintiff's land), and that the right is not affected by the fact that the acts complained of were done in the exercise of governmental functions or by express municipal or legislative authority, the position being that the damage arising from the impaired value of the property is to be considered and dealt with to that extent as a 'taking or appropriation,' and brings the claim within the constitutional principle that a man's property may not be taken from him even for the public benefit except upon compensation duly made. (Citing cases.)"

39. Clinard v. Kernersville, 215 N.C. 745, 3 S.E.2d 267 (1939), wherein the court held: "The damages are confined to the diminished pecuniary value of the property incident to the wrong or to the continued maintenance of the nuisance in the nature of an easement." See also Moser v. Burlington, 162 N.C. 141, 78 S.E. 74 (1913); Hines v. Rocky Mount, 162 N.C. 409, 78 S.E. 510 (1913); Metz v. Asheville, 150 N.C. 748, 64 S.E. 881 (1909); Williams v. Greenville, 130 N.C. 93, 40 S.E. 977 (1902); Rhodes v. City of Durham, 165 N.C. 679, 81 S.E. 938 (1914); Aydett v. Carolina By-Products Co., 215 N.C. 700, 2 S.E.2d 881 (1939). It should be noted that if the suit is for permanent damages for the maintenance of a permanent nuisance, since the suit is in the nature of a proceeding to condemn the plaintiff's property, any special benefits arising out of the establishment of the nuisance may be set off in diminution of the damages. See Brown v. Virginia-Carolina Chemical Co., 162 N.C. 83, 77 S.E. 1102 (1907).

but the plaintiff may recover other damages which come directly and immediately from the nuisance.[40]

(c) *Temporary injunction.* Courts have broad discretionary powers to restrain or give other appropriate relief against existing or threatened public and private nuisances upon application of one who can show that irreparable injuries threaten him and that damages would not adequately compensate him for his threatened losses, or that their recovery in any event would necessitate a multiplicity of suits.[41] The suit in equity for injunction is the traditional method of abating a nuisance. A temporary restraining order may be granted to a complainant when he introduces facts which give good reason to believe that another landowner is about to devote his land permanently to a use which imports a serious menace to the health of the complainant or other occupants of adjacent property; such user will be restrained until the facts on which the rights of the parties depend can be properly determined in a final hearing.[42] When the interposition by injunction is sought to restrain that which it is apprehended will create a nuisance, the proof must show that the apprehension of material and irreparable injury is well grounded upon a state of facts from which it appears that the danger is real and immediate.[43] Thus, when the proof tends to show with reasonable certainty that there is a well-grounded apprehension of danger to health or life by reason of the threatened use of adjacent property, such user will be temporarily restrained until the final hearing to determine if an activity is or is not a nuisance.[44]

(d) *Permanent injunction.* In proper cases, where irreparable injury is caused to one's health or property, the maintenance of nuisances may be

---

40. King v. Ward, 207 N.C. 782, 178 S.E. 577 (1935), approves a charge that specifies that "The damages ... that plaintiff is entitled to recover must be damages which come directly and immediately from the nuisance caused by the defendant, and from nothing else." For private nuisances created and maintained by private persons, beyond his property losses, the injured party is permitted to recover additional damages for such injuries to the health and comfort of his family as cause expense or inconvenience to himself. 6A AMERICAN LAW OF PROPERTY § 28.33 (Casner ed. 1954). *See* Oates v. Manufacturing Co., 217 N.C. 488, 8 S.E.2d 605 (1940), measuring damages from a nuisance by comparing the productiveness of land before and after the nuisance (flooding of the land). In Downs v. High Point, 115 N.C. 182, 20 S.E. 385 (1894), plaintiff recovered for both injuries to his property and the health of his family as a result of the maintenance of a filthy drain.
41. 6A AMERICAN LAW OF PROPERTY § 28.35 (Casner ed. 1954); Bradsher v. Lea's Heirs, 38 N.C. 301 (1844); Barrier v. Troutman, 231 N.C. 47, 55 S.E.2d 973 (1949); Cherry v. Williams, 147 N.C. 452, 61 S.E. 267 (1908); Brown v. Carolina Cent. Ry., 83 N.C. 128 (1880).
42. Cherry v. Williams, 147 N.C. 452, 61 S.E. 267 (1908).
43. Durham v. Cotton Mills, 141 N.C. 615, 54 S.E. 453 (1906).
44. Causby v. Oil Co., 244 N.C. 235, 93 S.E.2d 79 (1956); Cherry v. Williams, 147 N.C. 452, 61 S.E. 267 (1908); Evans v. Railroad, 96 N.C. 45, 1 S.E. 529 (1887); Elliott v. Swartz Industries, 231 N.C. 425, 57 S.E.2d 305 (1950). *See* Huskins v. Hospital, 238 N.C. 357, 78 S.E.2d 116 (1953), setting out the province and availability of the temporary injunction.

permanently restrained either by mandatory or prohibitive injunctive relief as might be required to prevent the continuance of such nuisances.[45] "Irreparable injury" simply means injury from a nuisance that is constantly recurring and one which is, from its nature, not susceptible of adequate compensation in damages in an action at law.[46] In addition, there is no reason why damages may not be awarded in the same action in which an injunction is allowed.[47]

§ 368. Spite Fences.

Occasionally acts of nuisance proceed from a malicious desire to do harm for its own sake. Into this category fall "spite fences." While a man ordinarily may erect any improvements on his own land as he sees fit, if he erects an unsightly "spite fence" on his own land for the *sole* malicious purpose of inflicting needless injury to his neighbor, without profit or benefit to himself, he can be enjoined or held liable in damages.[48] It should be noted, however, that even a fence erected for "spite," out of malicious motives, may not give rise to an action for damages or abatement if, in addition, it is erected to screen out objectionable noises, odors or unseemly conduct.[49]

---

45. Morgan v. Oil Co., 238 N.C. 185, 77 S.E. 682 (1953); Redd v. Edna Cotton Mills, 136 N.C. 342, 48 S.E. 761 (1904).

46. Brown v. Railroad, 83 N.C. 128 (1880); Reyburn v. Sawyer, 135 N.C. 328, 47 S.E. 761 (1904); Hooks v. International Speedways, Inc., 263 N.C. 686, 140 S.E.2d 387 (1965); Barrier v. Troutman, 231 N.C. 47, 55 S.E.2d 973 (1949).

47. Anderson v. Town of Waynesville, 203 N.C. 37, 164 S.E. 583 (1932); Burris v. Creech, 220 N.C. 302, 17 S.E.2d 123 (1941); Welsh v. Todd, 260 N.C. 527, 133 S.E.2d 171 (1963).

48. *See* 1 Mordecai, Law Lectures 468 (1916); Barger v. Barringer, 151 N.C. 433, 66 S.E. 439 (1909), wherein the court said: "No one ought to have the legal right to make a malicious use of his property for no benefit to himself, but merely to injure his fellowman. To hold otherwise makes the law an engine of oppression with which to destroy the peace and comfort of a neighbor, as well as to damage his property for no useful purpose but solely to gratify a wicked and debasing passion." *See also* Welsh v. Todd, 260 N.C. 527, 133 S.E.2d 171 (1963); Burris v. Creech, 220 N.C. 302, 17 S.E.2d 123 (1941).

49. *See* Welsh v. Todd, 260 N.C. 527, 133 S.E.2d 171 (1963). *Cf.* Bell v. Danzer, 187 N.C. 224, 121 S.E. 448 (1924). *See generally* Annot., *Fence as Nuisance*, 80 A.L.R.3d 962.

CHAPTER 17
PRIORITIES; RECORDATION

§ 369. Generally; History.
§ 370. Priorities — North Carolina's "Race" Type Recordation Statute.
§ 371. Same —- Effect of Failure to Record as Against Purchasers for Value and Lien Creditors.
§ 372. Same — Effect of Failure to Record as Between Grantors and Grantees Inter Se; Donees, Heirs and Devisees.
§ 373. Persons Protected by the Recording Acts — Purchasers for Value.
§ 374. Same — Lien Creditors.
§ 375. Constructive Notice From Recordation.
§ 376. Office Where Deeds, Deeds of Trust, and Mortgages are Recorded.
§ 377. Requirements for Recordation — Effect of Recording Defective or Unauthorized Instruments.
§ 378. Same — Indexing, Use of Indices.
§ 379. Instruments Required to Be Recorded to Effect Priority Under Recordation Statutes.
§ 380. Use of the Recording System; the Chain of Title.
§ 381. Deeds of Gift Must Be Recorded Within Two Years.
§ 382. Recordation of Easements.

§ 369. Generally; History.

North Carolina has, as does every state in the United States, a recording system for the recordation of real estate transactions. The common-law rule for determining priorities between successive claimants to the same land was that prior in time was prior in right; *e.g.*, at the common law, if an owner of land conveyed it to *A*, and later conveyed the same land to *B*, in the absence of unusual circumstances such as an estoppel, the latter acquired no title whatsoever. The prior grantee prevailed because the grantor, after he once conveyed, had nothing left that he could transfer to a second or third grantee. This common-law rule has been changed in every state by statute.

In North Carolina the recordation statutes in use today are known as the Conner Act and were enacted in 1885.[1] Prior to the Conner Act, North Carolina had two different "period of grace" recording statutes. The pre-Conner Act rules are described in a 1974 North Carolina Supreme Court case [2] and may be summarized as follows:

(a) *The Act of 1715, chapter 7, § 1.* [Laws of North Carolina, Potter (1821)] This was North Carolina's first registration law and provided a period of up to twelve months after the date of the deed for its registration. For purposes of priority, a deed properly registered within the twelve month period related back to the time of execution and delivery of it.

(b) *The Act of 1756, chapter 58, § 2.* [Laws of North Carolina, Potter

---
1. *See* N.C. GEN. STAT. §§ 47-18, 47-20.
2. Williams v. Board of Education, 284 N.C. 588, 201 S.E.2d 889 (1974).

(1821)] The period of grace in this statute was extended to two years with the relation doctrine for purposes of determining priority applicable. This act remained in effect until the passage of the Conner Act in 1855.

The distinctive feature of the recording system under the Conner Act in North Carolina, as applied to conveyances of land, may be summarized as follows: Conveyances of real property may be recorded in the office of the Register of Deeds in the county where the real property is situated, and from the time of recording impart constructive notice to purchasers for value and creditors and establish priority in such real property from the time of recordation. If a conveyance is not recorded by a grantee, it is considered absolutely void with respect to purchasers for value or lien creditors of the same grantor who record their conveyances or docket their liens.

§ 370. Priorities — North Carolina's "Race" Type Recordation Statute.

While most jurisdictions have a form of recordation statute which protects *subsequent* grantees from prior conveyances only if they have paid value and purchased without actual notice of a prior unrecorded conveyance, the recordation statute in effect in North Carolina protects *any* purchaser for value of specific land who records first, whether he has notice of a prior unrecorded conveyance or not, and irrespective of whether he is a prior or subsequent purchaser. A number of legal writers [3] call North Carolina's statute a "pure race" statute meaning that the one who wins the race to the Register of Deeds' office will have priority. This concept is frequently expressed in the following manner: "No notice, however full or formal, will supply the want of registration of a deed." [4] Thus in North Carolina, if a grantor conveys real property to A and later conveys the same interest to B for a valuable consideration, and B records first, he will have the superior right in the real property even though B had actual notice of the prior conveyance.[5] Although the grantor has conveyed good title to A and has no further title to convey, the grantor retains a *power* to defeat his earlier conveyance, if it is not recorded, by another conveyance to a second grantee.

The "pure race" aspect of North Carolina's recordation statute, that supreme importance is attached to being the first to record when the same

---

3. *See, e.g.,* CRIBBET, PRINCIPLES OF THE LAW OF PROPERTY 220 (1962). For a detailed history and analysis of the recording acts utilized in the United States, *see* 4 AMERICAN LAW OF PROPERTY §§ 17.4-17.36 (Casner ed. 1952).

4. Bourne v. Lay & Co., 264 N.C. 33, 140 S.E.2d 769 (1965); Dulin v. Williams, 239 N.C. 33, 79 S.E.2d 213 (1953); Beasley v. Wilson, 267 N.C. 95, 147 S.E.2d 577 (1966); Quinnerly v. Quinnerly, 114 N.C. 145 (1894); Patterson v. Bryant, 216 N.C. 550, 5 S.E.2d 849 (1939).

5. Bourne v. Lay & Co., 264 N.C. 33, 140 S.E.2d 769 (1965); Patterson v. Bryant, 216 N.C. 550, 5 S.E.2d 849 (1939).

real property is taken from the same grantor, can be demonstrated by another holding of the North Carolina Supreme Court. In the case of *Chandler v. Cameron*,[6] an owner *A* contracted to convey to *B*. *B* did not record his contract at the time it was made.[7] Subsequently *A* conveyed the land to *C*, who also did not record at the time of the conveyance. Subsequently *B* recorded his earlier contract. The North Carolina Supreme Court held that since *B* was the first to record, although he was not a *subsequent* purchaser, *B* should prevail over *C* with respect to the real property involved. In other words, if a prior conveyance from a grantor is not recorded, and the grantor makes another conveyance to a subsequent purchaser who delays in recording, if the prior grantee is also a purchaser for value and records before the subsequent purchaser, the prior purchaser who has won the "race" to the Register of Deeds' office will have priority.[8] Thus it is all important for a grantee to immediately record any deed which he receives in order to protect himself against prior or subsequent purchasers from the same grantor with respect to the land granted.

§ 371. Same — Effect of Failure to Record as Against Purchasers for Value and Lien Creditors.

If a conveyance is not recorded, it is considered void as against prior or subsequent purchasers of the same property for value who record first and as against lien creditors of the grantor.[9] Priority of registration determines priority of rights deriving from deeds, mortgages, deeds of trusts and judgments, regardless of the dates that they were executed or became effective.[10]

§ 372. Same — Effect of Failure to Record as Between Grantors and Grantees Inter Se; Donees, Heirs and Devisees.

Registration is not required as between original grantors and grantees;

---

6. 229 N.C. 62, 47 S.E.2d 528 (1948). *See* Note, 27 N.C.L. REV. 376 (1949).

7. Contracts to convey land are treated the same as conveyances for purposes of recordation. N.C. GEN. STAT. § 47-18; Combes v. Adams, 150 N.C. 64, 63 S.E. 186 (1908).

8. The majority view in the United States would reach a contrary result. *See, e.g.,* Swanstrom v. Washington Trust Co., 41 Wash. 561, 83 P. 1112 (1906), where it is stated: "It is not necessary that the subsequent conveyance should be recorded in order to gain priority." *See also* WEBB, RECORD OF TITLE § 13 (1891), where the author states: "[W]here through the neglect of the first grantee to record his deed, a subsequent party has been led to part with a valuable consideration, a race for registry between the two does not afford a proper criterion by which their rights should be determined." For a critical comment on the case of Chandler v. Cameron, *supra* note 6, *see* 27 N.C.L. REV. 376 (1949).

9. N.C. GEN. STAT. §§ 47-18, 47-20; Bourne v. Lay & Co., 264 N.C. 33, 140 S.E.2d 769 (1965).

10. Hayes v. Ricard, 245 N.C. 687, 97 S.E.2d 105 (1957); Clark v. Butts, 240 N.C. 709, 83 S.E.2d 885 (1954); Dulin v. Williams, 239 N.C. 33, 79 S.E.2d 213 (1953); Bank v. Mitchell, 203 N.C. 339, 166 S.E. 69 (1932).

an unrecorded conveyance is valid as between the parties thereto.[11] Thus a previously executed deed, though not registered, will prevail over all persons who are not purchasers for value or lien creditors.[12] The recordation statutes are not designed for the protection of the grantor and do not affect any equities which might exist between the grantor and those to whom he has sold his land. As between a grantor and grantee, a deed of conveyance is valid and it is of no consequence whether it is registered at all.[13] A grantee in a deed given without consideration, a donee, does not come under the protection of the statute.[14] Therefore a prior unrecorded conveyance by a grantor to A will be valid and effective as against a subsequent donee of the grantor who takes a deed of conveyance without paying a consideration.[15] The same rule applies with respect to an unrecorded deed as against a devisee or heirs of the grantor.[16] Such unrecorded deed of the grantor will be effective as against *all* persons who cannot show that they are purchasers for value or lien creditors of the grantor.[17]

§ 373. Persons Protected by the Recording Acts — Purchasers for Value.

The persons the recording statutes are designed to protect are prospective purchasers and encumbrancers of land.[18] Recording protects a grantee from the claims of other purchasers [19] and encumbrancers and, conversely, a grantee's failure to record an instrument which he receives may create rights in another purchaser or encumbrancer superior to those of the grantee. The potential effect of an omission to record an instrument of conveyance is derived from the wording of the recordation statute,[20] which states in part:

(a) No (i) conveyance of land, or (ii) contract to convey, or (iii)

---

11. Patterson v. Bryant, 216 N.C. 550, 5 S.E.2d 849 (1939); Glass v. Shoe Co., 212 N.C. 70, 192 S.E.2d 899 (1937); Hargrove v. Adcock, 111 N.C. 166, 16 S.E. 16 (1892).
12. Tyner v. Barnes, 142 N.C. 110, 54 S.E. 1008 (1906).
13. Patterson v. Bryant, 216 N.C. 550, 5 S.E.2d 849 (1939).
14. McRary v. McRary, 228 N.C. 714, 47 S.E.2d 27 (1948); Sansom v. Warren, 215 N.C. 432, 2 S.E.2d 459 (1939); Twitty v. Cochran, 214 N.C. 265, 199 S.E.29 (1938).
15. Twitty v. Cochran, 214 N.C. 265, 199 S.E.29 (1938).
16. Bowden v. Bowden, 264 N.C. 296, 141 S.E.2d 621 (1965).
17. Tyner v. Barnes, 142 N.C. 110, 54 S.E. 1008 (1906); Harris v. Lumber Co., 147 N.C. 631, 61 S.E. 604 (1908); Spence v. Pottery Co., 185 N.C. 218, 117 S.E. 32 (1923); Eaton v. Doub, 190 N.C. 14, 128 S.E. 494 (1925); Gosney v. McCullers, 202 N.C. 326, 162 S.E. 746 (1932).
18. *See* Hayes v. Richard, 245 N.C. 687, 97 S.E.2d 105 (1957), which states: "The purpose of the statute is to point out to prospective purchasers the one place where they must go to find the condition of land titles — the public registry." The *Hayes* case holds that a grantee under a quitclaim deed may qualify as a purchaser for value.
19. The statutes do not specify *subsequent* purchasers.
20. N.C. GEN. STAT. § 47-18. While N.C. GEN. STAT. § 47-20 is not quoted, its effect is identical.

option to convey,[21] or (iv) lease of land for more than three years shall be valid to pass any property interest as against lien creditors or purchasers for a valuable consideration from the donor, bargainor or lessor but from the time of registration thereof in the county where the land lies, or if the land is located in more than one county, then in each county where any portion of the land lies to be effective as to the land in that county.

That raises the question: Who is a "purchaser for value"? A person who is a purchaser for value under the statute must be in fact a purchaser; that is, he must have paid a valuable consideration for the execution of the instrument.[22] While no exact criterion exists as to what will be a sufficient consideration to make a grantee a "purchaser for value" in all instances, the consideration must be more than merely nominal. In the case of *King v. McRackan*,[23] the North Carolina Supreme Court has stated:

> We use the term "purchaser for a valuable consideration" in the sense in which it is defined by the Court in Fullenwider v. Roberts, 20 N.C. 278, "A fair and reasonable price according to the common mode of dealing between buyers and sellers," or, as said by *Pearson, C. J.,* in Worthy v. Caddell, 76 N.C. 82, "The party assuming to be a purchaser for a valuable consideration must prove a fair consideration, not up to the full price, but a price paid which would not cause surprise or make any one exclaim, 'He got the land for nothing! There must have been some fraud or contrivance about it.'"

The burden of proof is on the parties claiming under a prior recorded instrument to show that they are purchasers for value so as to bring themselves within the recordation laws.[24] That they are purchasers for value must be shown by a preponderance of the evidence.[25] Even if the deed recites that a substantial consideration has been paid, the recital does not establish that the amount of the consideration stated has actually been paid and is inadmissible as evidence of the fact recited as against one who was not a party nor a privy to the deed.[26]

---

21. The 1975 amendment to N.C. GEN. STAT. § 47-18, adding *options to convey* to those instruments which must be recorded to effect priority over lien creditors or purchasers for value under North Carolina's recording statute was prompted by the case of Lawing v. Jaynes, 285 N.C. 418, 206 S.E.2d 162 (1974). That case held, *before the amendment* of N.C. GEN. STAT. § 47-18, that the registration of an option to purchase land was not essential to its validity against lien creditors or purchasers for a valuable consideration from the optionor.
22. Sansom v. Warren, 215 N.C. 432, 2 S.E.2d 459 (1939).
23. 168 N.C. 621, 84 S.E. 1027 (1915).
24. Waters v. Pittman, 254 N.C. 191, 118 S.E.2d 395 (1961); Lawing v. Jaynes, 285 N.C. 418, 206 S.E.2d 162 (1974).
25. Waters v. Pittman, 254 N.C. 191, 118 S.E.2d 395 (1961); King v. McRackan, 171 N.C. 752, 88 S.E. 621 (1916); Lawing v. Jaynes, 285 N.C. 418, 206 S.E.2d 162 (1974).
26. Waters v. Pittman, 254 N.C. 191, 118 S.E.2d 395 (1961); Hughes v. Fields, 168 N.C. 520, 84 S.E. 804 (1915).

A person who takes a mortgage in lands to secure a pre-existing debt is treated as a purchaser for value and if he takes an absolute conveyance in consideration of the cancellation of such pre-existing debt the grantee in the conveyance will also be considered a purchaser for value.[27]

§ 374. Same — Lien Creditors.

The recordation statutes [28] do not protect every creditor against unrecorded deeds and mortgages. They protect only (1) purchasers for a valuable consideration from the grantor who records first and (2) creditors who have first fastened a lien upon the property in some manner sanctioned by law.[29] The creditors, in order to be protected must be "lien" creditors and not mere general creditors.[30] If a judgment is obtained against a grantor of land subsequent to the execution of the conveyance, but prior to the time of its registration, the lien of the judgment has priority over the title of the grantee and the lands conveyed are subject to execution under the judgment.[31]

§ 375. Constructive Notice From Recordation.

The recordation of deeds and mortgages impart to all purchasers and creditors constructive notice of the execution and recordation of such instruments.[32] The recordation statutes require persons intending to purchase real estate or to lend money on mortgages or deeds of trust on land to examine the public records relating to the tract of land in question. Whether or not such purchaser or mortgagee actually examines the records, the law presumes that he knows everything he would have learned by such examination and will not permit him to say that actually no such examination was made.[33]

---

27. Sansom v. Warren, 215 N.C. 432, 2 S.E.2d 459 (1939); Brem v. Lockhart, 93 N.C. 191 (1885).
28. Cf. Wachovia Bank & Trust Co. v. Wayne Finance Co., 262 N.C. 711, 138 S.E.2d 481 (1964); National Bank of Goldsboro v. Hill, 226 F. 102 (1915). While both of these cases relate to personal property, the same rule applies to real property recordation.
29. Id.
30. A judgment creditor acquires a lien on the judgment debtor's real estate by docketing the judgment. N.C. GEN. STAT. § 1-234. No lien is acquired on personalty until there has been a valid levy. N.C. GEN. STAT. § 1-312 (1); Credit Co. v. Norwood, 257 N.C. 87, 125 S.E.2d 369 (1962).
31. Maxton Realty Co. v. Carter, 170 N.C. 5, 86 S.E. 714 (1915); Dula v. Parsons, 243 N.C. 32, 89 S.E.2d 797 (1955).
32. Dorman v. Goodman, 213 N.C. 406, 196 S.E. 352 (1938). See Fleming v. Mann, 23 N.C. App. 418, 209 S.E.2d 366 (1974), to the effect that the recording of a document not required or authorized to be recorded gives no constructive notice of its contents, citing Chandler v. Cameron, 229 N.C. 62, 475 S.E.2d 528 (1948).
33. A purchaser is charged with notice of the contents of every recorded instrument constituting a link in his chain of title and is put on notice of any fact or circumstance affecting his title which any of such instruments would reasonably disclose. Randle v.

§ 376. Office Where Deeds, Deeds of Trust, and Mortgages Are Recorded.

To be validly recorded, deeds, deeds of trust, mortgages, and contracts relating to real property must be registered in the office of the Register of Deeds in the county where the land lies, and if the land is located in more than one county, then the instrument must be registered in each county.[34]

§ 377. Requirements for Recordation — Effect of Recording Defective or Unauthorized Instruments.

While a duly recorded instrument constitutes constructive notice, an instrument not entitled to record does not have that effect although the instrument has in fact been recorded.

For instance, before an instrument may be recorded in the public registry it is necessary for it to be acknowledged before an officer authorized to take acknowledgments.[35] If there is no acknowledgment or there is a defective acknowledgment which appears on its face, any recordation thereof does not constitute due recordation under the recording statutes so as to give constructive notice to purchasers for value or for establishing priority over lien creditors of the grantor.[36] Thus, where the certificate of

---

Grady, 224 N.C. 651, 32 S.E.2d 20 (1944); Insurance Co. v. Knox, 220 N.C. 725, 18 S.E.2d 436 (1942); Turner v. Glenn, 220 N.C. 620, 18 S.E. 197 (1942); Bank v. Mitchell, 203 N.C. 339, 166 S.E. 69 (1932).

34. N.C. GEN. STAT. §§ 47-18, 47-20.1.

35. An acknowledgment of an instrument is the act of the grantor or maker of the instrument going before an officer designated by statute and declaring that he executed the instrument as his voluntary act and deed. Its primary purpose is to give authenticity to the instrument by attesting to its due execution. The term "acknowledgment" is also a shorthand expression descriptive of the act of personal appearance before a proper officer and there stating to him the fact of the execution of the instrument as a voluntary act. It is often used to mean the official certificate that such declaration was made. Freeman v. Morrison, 214 N.C. 240, 199 S.E. 12 (1938). Under N.C. GEN. STAT. § 47-1, instruments may be proved or acknowledged before any one of the following state officials: the justices, judges, magistrates, clerks, assistant clerks, and deputy clerks of the General Court of Justice, and notaries public. In addition, N.C. GEN. STAT. § 47-2 provides that instruments may be proved and acknowledged outside of North Carolina in other states and in foreign countries by judges and clerks of courts of record, notaries public, commissioners of deeds, commissioners of oaths, mayors and magistrates of incorporated municipalities, ambassadors, ministers, consuls, vice-consuls, consuls general, vice-consuls general, commercial agents, justices of the peace, and by officers of the United States Army, Navy, Marines, Air Force, Coast Guard, or Merchant Marine, with the rank of warrant officer or higher.

36. New Home Bldg. Supply Co. v. Nations, 259 N.C. 681, 131 S.E.2d 425 (1963); Todd v. Outlaw, 79 N.C. 235 (1878); PATTON, LAND TITLES § 354; P. BAYSE, CLEARING LAND TITLES § 241 (1953); Webster, *Toward Greater Marketability of Land Titles — Remedying the Defective Acknowledgment Syndrome,* 46 N.C.L. REV. 56 (1967). The North Carolina view, and the view of most jurisdictions, is that instruments whose acknowledgments or proofs of probate are defective on their face will fail to impart constructive notice of their execution

a notary public who takes an acknowledgment shows that the notary's commission has expired, any recordation made on the basis of such acknowledgment is void.[37] Likewise, a complete lack of an acknowledgment,[38] an acknowledgment taken before an officer outside of his territorial jurisdiction,[39] the making of an acknowledgment before an officer who is disqualified because he has an interest in the property involved or because he is a party to the transaction,[40] or where the acknowledgment does not show the officer's authority to make such acknowledgment,[41] will each render a recordation based on such acknowledgment void. The defect may result from a particular kind of acknowledgment, such as the requirement of a separate acknowledgment of married women with respect to contracts and conveyances with their own husbands.[42]

It should be noted that the Supreme Court of North Carolina has stated that certificates of acknowledgment will be liberally construed and will

---

even if they are otherwise effectively recorded. If the acknowledgment or probate defect is patent, the recorded instrument will be treated as if unrecorded. McClure v. Crow, 196 N.C. 657, 146 S.E. 713 (1929); County Sav. Bank v. Tolbert, 192 N.C. 126, 133 S.E. 558 (1926); Blanton v. Bostic, 126 N.C. 410, 35 S.E. 1035 (1900); PATTON, LAND TITLES § 356, n. 21; Annot., 59 A.L.R.2d 1299 (1958). When the incapacity of the acknowledging or probating officer is *latent*, *i.e.*, does not appear upon the record, a recordation of the instrument pursuant to such defective acknowledgment or probate is valid and suffices to impart constructive notice. County Sav. Bank v. Tolbert, 192 N.C. 126, 133 S.E. 558 (1926); PATTON, LAND TITLES § 356, n. 25; Annot., 59 A.L.R.2d 1299 (1958). See Fleming v. Mann, 23 N.C. App. 418, 209 S.E.2d 366 (1974), to the effect that a document not authorized to be recorded gives no constructive notice of its contents. *See also* Lawing v. Jaynes, 285 N.C. 418, 208 S.E.2d 162 (1974), wherein it is stated: "The registration or record of an instrument operates as constructive notice only when the statute authorizes its registration; and then only to the extent of those provisions which are within the registration statutes. Therefore, the registration of a deed or other instrument not entitled or required to be recorded is not constructive notice to subsequent purchasers." And in the recent Court of Appeals case of Hi-Fort, Inc. v. Burnette, 42 N.C. App. 428, 257 S.E.2d 85 (1979), the court notes at 42 N.C. App. 432: "The same reasoning which prevents a party from introducing into evidence against a lien creditor or purchaser for value a deed invalidly registered does not apply to exclude an invalidly registered deed introduced against a party claiming interest to the land by descent. An heir is not a purchaser for value entitled to the protection of the recording act." (Citations omitted.)

37. Crissman v. Palmer, 225 N.C. 472, 35 S.E.2d 422 (1945).
38. New Home Bldg. Supply Co. v. Nations, 259 N.C. 681, 131 S.E.2d 425 (1963).
39. Wood v. Lewey, 153 N.C. 401, 69 S.E. 268 (1910); DeCourcy v. Burr, 45 N.C. 181 (1853); Dixson v. Robbins, 134 N.C. 102, 19 S.E. 239 (1894); Ferebee v. Hinton, 102 N.C. 93, 8 S.E. 922 (1889).
40. *See generally* Webster, *Toward Greater Marketability of Land Titles — Remedying the Defective Acknowledgment Syndrome,* 46 N.C.L. REV. 56, 62 (1967); Long v. Crews, 113 N.C. 256, 18 S.E. 499 (1893); Cowan v. Dale, 189 N.C. 684, 128 S.E. 155 (1925); White v. Connelly, 105 N.C. 65, 11 S.E. 177 (1890); Turner v. Connelly, 105 N.C. 72, 11 S.E. 179 (1890).
41. Withrell v. Murphy, 154 N.C. 82, 69 S.E. 748 (1910); Bernhardt v. Brown, 122 N.C. 587, 29 S.E. 884 (1898).
42. *See* N.C. GEN. STAT. § 52-6.

be upheld if in "substantial compliance" with the statute.[43] In the case of *Freeman v. Morrison*,[44] the court suggests the following minimum requirements for a valid acknowledgment of a deed: (1) Name and title of the official taking the acknowledgment; (2) name of the grantor; (3) personal appearance of the grantor before the officer; (4) acknowledgment of grantor to the officer of the execution of the instrument; (5) date; and (6) signature of the officer, and, if required by law otherwise, his seal.[45]

Certain curative statutes have been framed and passed by the North Carolina General Assembly to afford relief to landowners and to title lawyers by validating many defective acknowledgments on deeds in order to make their recordations likewise valid.[46]

§ 378. Same—Indexing, Use of Indices.

Proper indexing and cross-indexing of instruments required to be registered is an essential part of their registration.[47]

The Register of Deeds is required to index a recorded instrument in alphabetically arranged "grantor" and "grantee" indices, showing the names of the parties, the type of instrument recorded, the date of filing, and the book and page number where a copy of the recorded instrument may be found. Therefore, a deed or other instrument relating to real property is not effectively recorded unless indexed in such a manner as to disclose to a careful and prudent title examiner the existence and location of the recorded instrument.[48]

It should be noted, however, that a perfect indexing is not required in order to make out a complete and effective recordation. Since the function of the index is to point out the book and page where the recorded instrument may be found, it is sufficient if it discloses enough to put a careful and prudent examiner upon inquiry which, if made, would lead to

---

43. Freeman v. Morrison, 214 N.C. 240, 199 S.E. 12 (1938).
44. 214 N.C. 240, 199 S.E. 12 (1938).
45. While the stated case is helpful in setting out guidelines for one seeking to procure an acknowledgment of an instrument, what is a "substantial" defect may give a title-searching attorney more concern. In P. BAYSE, CLEARING LAND TITLES § 249 (1953), the author states: "Until some sure light can be furnished by the courts or legislatures as to the point of demarcation in certificates of acknowledgment between fatal defects and minor irregularities of no consequence title examiners will continue to hesitate in assuring purchasers and mortgagees as to which side of the line a given case will fall on."
46. *See* N.C. GEN. STAT. §§ 47-47 through 47-108.16. There are additional curative statutes in other places in the statutes relating to similar defects. For an analysis of the statutes and their inadequacy in general, *see* Webster, *Toward Greater Marketability of Land Titles — Remedying the Defective Acknowledgment Syndrome*, 46 N.C.L. REV. 56, 68 (1967).
47. Cuthrell v. Camden County, 254 N.C. 181, 118 S.E.2d 601 (1961); Cotton Co. v. Hobgood, 243 N.C. 227, 90 S.E.2d 541 (1955); Tocci v. Nowfall, 220 N.C. 550, 18 S.E.2d 225 (1941); Dorman v. Goodman, 213 N.C. 406, 196 S.E. 352 (1938).
48. *Id.*

the discovery of the recorded instrument. For instance, if a conveyance is by a corporation and the index shows the grant but does not indicate that the corporation is a trustee,[49] which fact appears in the recorded deed, the indexing has been held sufficient. Likewise, where a wife owned land and she and her husband executed a deed of trust which was indexed in the name of the husband "et ux,"[50] the index was held to be sufficient. Where a husband and his wife owned land by the entirety and executed a deed of trust which was indexed "Jesse Hinton and wife,"[51] the court has held that the indexing met the requirements and constituted an adequate record along with the recorded deed of trust. And where the index book had alphabetical subdivisions of each letter and a deed of trust executed by one Harrison was misplaced in the subdivision "Haa to Hap" instead of the subdivision "Har to Haz,"[52] the court stated that this would not prevent the deed of trust from being considered properly recorded. Even if the index erroneously refers to an incorrect page in the correct book where an instrument is recorded,[53] the court has held that the indexing is sufficient to make out proper recording to constitute constructive notice.[54]

The following, however, have been held not to be sufficient indexing to impart constructive notice under the recordation statutes: Where a deed was indexed under the name of "J. L. Crowell" as grantor instead of "J. Frank Crowell" the true grantor, and there was a J. L. Crowell and his name appeared in the grantor index more than a hundred times, the court said the indexing was too far from substantial compliance with statutory requirements to constitute constructive notice.[55] And where a wife owned land and she and her husband executed a mortgage, and the mortgage was indexed only in the name of the husband the indexing prevented the mortgage from being properly recorded and it did not constitute notice to purchasers for value or establish priority over lien creditors.[56] If an instrument creating a lien on real estate is indexed and cross-indexed only in the chattel mortgage index it is not properly recorded with respect to the real estate.[57] And where a public officer gave a mortgage in lieu of an official bond and the mortgage was indexed only in the bond book, the

---

49. Tocci v. Nowfall, 220 N.C. 550, 18 S.E.2d 225 (1941).
50. Prudential Ins. Co. v. Forbes, 203 N.C. 252, 165 S.E. 699 (1932).
51. West v. Jackson, 198 N.C. 693, 153 S.E. 257 (1930).
52. Clement v. Harrison, 193 N.C. 825, 138 S.E. 308 (1927).
53. Cuthrell v. Camden County, 254 N.C. 181, 118 S.E.2d 601 (1961).
54. Even though the index refers to an *incorrect page and book,* it has been held sufficient in a case where the cross-index shows the correct page and book. Cotton Co. v. Hobgood, 243 N.C. 227, 90 S.E.2d 541 (1955).
55. Dorman v. Goodman, 213 N.C. 406, 196 S.E. 352 (1938).
56. Heaton v. Heaton, 196 N.C. 475, 146 S.E. 146 (1928).
57. Bank v. Harrington, 193 N.C. 625, 137 S.E. 712 (1925) (court equally divided, no precedent).

mortgage was not sufficiently indexed to make out a due recordation.[58] To like effect is a holding that a judgment, which must be "docketed" or indexed to constitute a lien on land, indexed in favor of "J. A. Quick" when the judgment was in favor of "J. A. Curry," is not properly indexed so as to establish priority in the judgment creditor.[59]

The general rule to be applied in determining the sufficiency of an irregular indexing has been stated by the North Carolina Supreme Court to be as follows:

> ... [T]he primary purpose of the law requiring the registration and indexing of conveyances is to give notice, and it has been repeatedly stated by those writing on this subject that an index will hold a subsequent purchaser or encumbrancer to notice if enough is disclosed by the index to put a careful and prudent examiner upon inquiry, and if upon such inquiry the instrument would be found.... The cardinal purpose of the registration and indexing laws is to provide records that shall of themselves be sufficient, under careful and proper inquiry, to disclose the true state of the title to real estate.[60]

§ 379. Instruments Required to Be Recorded to Effect Priority Under Recordation Statutes.

The effect of the recordation statutes is that any written instrument by which an interest in real property is created, transferred, mortgaged or assigned, or by which the title to real property may be affected, except a will,[61] or a lease for a term not exceeding three years from the time of its making,[62] must be recorded in order to achieve priority over other purchasers for value and subsequent lien creditors. This includes deeds,[63] deeds of trust,[64] mortgages,[65] leases for periods exceeding three years in

---

58. Hooper v. Tallassee Power Co., 180 N.C. 651, 105 S.E. 327 (1920).
59. Trust Co. v. Currie, 190 N.C. 260, 129 S.E. 605 (1925).
60. *See* Dorman v. Goodman, 213 N.C. 406, 196 S.E. 352 (1938), in which the court made this statement in holding that an index of the name "J. Frank Crowell" erroneously as "J. L. Crowell," among a hundred other conveyances properly indexed under "J. L. Crowell's" name, was not properly indexed so as to give constructive notice. The court stated: "The most prudent and careful searcher of titles would not be expected to examine the more than one hundred deeds referred to in the index as having been executed by J. L. Crowell to ascertain if by chance one of them had been erroneously indexed.... That would be a task comparable to the proverbial search for a needle in a haystack." *See also* West v. Jackson, 198 N.C. 693, 153 S.E. 257 (1930); Cuthrell v. Camden County, 254 N.C. 181, 118 S.E.2d 601 (1961).
61. That a will is not a "conveyance" within the terms of the recordation statutes, *see* Cooley v. Lee, 170 N.C. 18, 86 S.E. 720 (1915); Barnhardt v. Morrison, 178 N.C. 563, 101 S.E. 218 (1919); Bell v. Couch, 132 N.C. 346, 43 S.E. 911 (1903); Harris v. Dudley Lumber Co., 147 N.C. 631, 61 S.E. 604 (1908).
62. N.C. GEN. STAT. § 47-18; Perkins v. Langdon, 237 N.C. 159, 74 S.E.2d 634 (1953).
63. N.C. GEN. STAT. § 47-18; Spence v. Foster Pottery Co., 185 N.C. 218, 117 S.E. 32 (1923).
64. N.C. GEN. STAT. § 47-20; First Nat'l Bank v. Sauls, 183 N.C. 165, 110 S.E. 865 (1922).
65. *Id.*

duration from the time of the making,[66] executory contracts for the sale of any estate or interest in the real property [67] or any part thereof.[68]

Parol trusts, and other trusts created by operation of law, called "constructive" trusts under the laws of North Carolina, do not come within the meaning and purview of the recording statutes since they are not written interests capable of registration.[69] Therefore beneficiaries under such trusts will lose their equitable interests in property subject to such trusts only when the trust property is conveyed by the record legal titleholder to a *bona fide* purchaser for a valuable consideration who takes without notice of the existence of the equitable interest.[70]

---

66. Bourne v. Lay & Co., 264 N.C. 33, 140 S.E.2d 769 (1965); Mauney v. Norvell, 179 N.C. 628, 103 S.E. 372 (1920).

67. Winston v. Williams & McKeithan Lumber Co., 227 N.C. 339, 42 S.E.2d 218 (1947); Chandler v. Cameron, 229 N.C. 62, 47 S.E.2d 528 (1948); Dulin v. Williams, 239 N.C. 33, 79 S.E.2d 213 (1953). This would also include a contract giving to a broker the exclusive right to sell real property. Eller v. Arnold, 230 N.C. 418, 53 S.E.2d 266 (1949). *See* Beasley v. Wilson, 267 N.C. 95, 147 S.E.2d 577 (1967), which holds that an unregistered contract to convey is not enforceable against a grantee of the owner, even though the grantee had knowledge of the existence of such contract at the time of his purchase.

N.C. GEN. STAT. § 47-18 was amended in 1975 and now provides that *options* to convey land must be recorded in order to be valid against lien creditors or purchasers for a valuable consideration of the optionor. In the case of Lawing v. Jaynes, 285 N.C. 418, 206 S.E.2d 162 (1974), the Supreme Court of North Carolina had held prior to the statute's amendment that registration of an option to purchase land was not essential to its validity against lien creditors or purchasers for a valuable consideration.

See also Cities Serv. Oil Co. v. Pochna, 30 N.C. App. 360, 226 S.E.2d 884 (1976), which holds that an unrecorded assignment of an interest in an oil or gas lease is invalid as against a subsequent third-party purchaser for a valuable consideration under N.C. GEN. STAT. § 47-18 (a).

68. An assignment of accruing rents from real property is an assignment of an incorporeal hereditament and therefore an assignment of real property which, if for more than three years, must be in writing and recorded in order to be effective as against a purchaser for value. First & Citizens Nat'l Bank v. Sawyer, 218 N.C. 142, 10 S.E.2d 656 (1940). Easements created by grant, including negative easements in the form of building restrictions, must likewise be recorded in order to be valid as against purchasers of the servient tract and lien creditors of the grantor. Davis v. Robinson, 189 N.C. 589, 127 S.E. 697 (1925). Cities Serv. Oil Co. v. Pochna, 30 N.C. App. 360, 226 S.E.2d 884 (1976), holds that under N.C. GEN. STAT. § 47-18 (a) an unrecorded assignment of an interest in an oil or gas lease is invalid as against a subsequent third-party purchaser for a valuable consideration who records.

69. Spence v. Foster Pottery Co., 185 N.C. 218, 117 S.E. 32 (1923); Wood v. Tinsley, 138 N.C. 507, 51 S.E. 59 (1905); Pritchard v. Williams, 175 N.C. 319, 95 S.E. 570 (1918); Roberts v. Massey, 185 N.C. 164, 116 S.E. 407 (1923); Eaton v. Doub, 190 N.C. 14, 128 S.E. 494 (1925); Sansom v. Warren, 215 N.C. 432, 2 S.E.2d 459 (1939).

70. It should be noted that if *A* holds legal title to real property on a parol or constructive trust for *B* and *A,* who is the record title-holder of the real property, conveys it to *C,* the *cestui que trust B* will not have his equitable rights cut off unless *C* is a *bona fide purchaser for value* without notice, *either actual or constructive.* This is one instance in which actual notice is still significant in North Carolina, contrary to the often stated rule that "no notice however full and formal will supply the place of registration." It should be further noted in the above factual illustration that *only bona fide purchasers for value* can cut off the trust beneficiary's interest, *not creditors.* Therefore, if *A,* the constructive trustee who has record

In addition, while they may be in writing and thus recordable, the North Carolina Supreme Court has held that express written declarations of trust are not conveyances or contracts to convey or leases requiring registration as against creditors.[71]

§ 380. Use of the Recording System; the Chain of Title.

As stated earlier, deeds and instruments of conveyance are indexed under an official index of names, called the "Grantor-Grantee Index." If one desires to purchase land from *A,* the supposed owner, he must check back on the grantee index until he finds the recording reference to the instrument by which *A* acquired the title. The title searcher will then look up the name of *A's* grantor in like manner in the grantee index and other predecessors in title in the grantee index back to time when the original title was acquired from the State or back to the point of time for which the title is to be searched.[72]

After this chain of acquisitions by grant has been determined the name of each owner in the chain of title must be checked in the grantor indices subsequent to the date of his acquisition of ownership in order to determine whether or not he has executed a deed or encumbrance on the real property that would prevent his being able to convey good title.

A deed, although recorded at the time of its execution, does not constitute constructive notice and is not within the chain of title of a particular grantor or grantee if it is recorded prior to such person's acquisition of title. Hence, if a deed purports to pass title to land, and such deed is executed prior to the grantor's acquisition of title, its recordation prior to the date of acquisition of the title gives no notice to purchasers for value and lien creditors of the grantor; only grants out of the grantor *subse-*

---

title, has a judgment docketed against him, such judgment lien does not cut off the interest of the *cestui que trust* under the parol or constructive trust. *See* Spence v. Foster Pottery Co., 185 N.C. 218, 117 S.E. 32 (1923), in which the court said: "And, it has been held with us consistently that these trusts, though resting in parol, or not evidenced by any writing, may be enforced against the holder of the legal title, unless it appear that such holder, or someone under whom he claims, has acquired his title for a fair and reasonable value without notice of the trust. Here it will be observed that a bona fide purchaser for value without notice (but not a creditor) is protected against the claim of one in whose favor the trust is sought to be established, not by virtue of the terms of the Connor Act, but on the broad principles of equity."

71. Crossett v. McQueen, 205 N.C. 48, 169 S.E. 829 (1933).
72. Information elicited by the author from various real estate attorneys in North Carolina indicates that the period of ordinary title searches varies depending on locality. In most areas a search of the records for forty years is the standard while in other localities searches for thirty and even twenty years are deemed sufficient. For title insurance companies to insure title to real estate, a search of fifty or sixty years is required by the principal companies doing business in North Carolina.

§ 380 REAL ESTATE LAW IN NORTH CAROLINA § 380

quent to his acquisition of title must be searched with respect to deeds.[73] This has particular significance in cases of title by estoppel. While the doctrine of title by estoppel is applicable in North Carolina, that when one purports to convey title to land which he does not own the title enures to his grantee when the grantor subsequently acquires title to that land,[74] the doctrine of estoppel does not prevail as against the provision and policy of the recording statutes.[75]

It should be noted, however, that prior to a statute enacted in 1969 a mortgage or deed of trust containing an after-acquired property clause created special problems for title searchers. If a mortgage or deed of trust, as distinguished from a deed, contained a clause mortgaging or encumbering *property to be acquired by the mortgagor* (as distinguished from property that he currently had), and such mortgage or deed of trust was recorded *even before the mortgagor acquired the property,* such recordation gave constructive notice to subsequent claimants of the property who acquired their claims subsequent to the mortgagor's acquisition of title.[76] Thus prior to 1969 in cases of mortgages or deeds of trust executed by a mortgagor on property to be after acquired, it was necessary for a title searcher thereafter not only to check the grantor-grantee indices for conveyances out of the owner-grantor subsequent to his acquisition of title, but the searcher also had to determine whether any predecessor in title had made a mortgage or deed of trust on his real property before he acquired it in the form of an after-acquired property clause in a mortgage.[77] Since the foregoing rule with respect to mortgages and deeds of trust had the serious effect of lengthening the period of time for which each grantor in a chain of title had to be checked in order that land titles could be certified, the North Carolina General Assembly passed a statute [78] in 1969 which provides that an after-acquired property clause in a real property security instrument shall not be effective against purchasers for value and lien creditors unless recorded or re-recorded subsequent to the owner-mortgagor's acquisition of title.[79]

---

73. Intending purchasers of land are only required to search against each grantor during the time that the record title remains in him. See 4 AMERICAN LAW OF PROPERTY §§ 17.19, 17.20 (Casner ed. 1952); Maddox v. Arp, 114 N.C. 585 (1894).
74. Olds v. Richmond Cedar Works, 173 N.C. 161, 91 S.E. 846 (1917).
75. Builders Sash & Door Co. v. Joyner, 182 N.C. 518, 109 S.E. 259 (1921); Maddox v. Arp, 114 N.C. 585 (1894). See Notes, 1 N.C.L. REV. 56 (1923); *see also* McGhehee, *Estoppel and Rebutter in North Carolina,* 1 N.C.L. REV. 152, 162 (1923); Notes, 27 N.C.L. REV. 376, 380 (1949).
76. Hickson Lumber Co. v. Gay Lumber Co., 150 N.C. 282, 63 S.E. 1045 (1909).
77. Hickson Lumber Co. v. Gay Lumber Co., 150 N.C. 282, 63 S.E. 1045 (1909). It should be observed that this necessitated the same search as against every owner who had held the land within the period for which the title search was made.
78. N.C. GEN. STAT. § 47-20.5.
79. N.C. GEN. STAT. § 47-20.5 (c), (d).

§ 381. Deeds of Gift Must Be Recorded Within Two Years.

Special notice should be taken of a statute in effect in North Carolina which requires all deeds of gift to be recorded within two years from the time of their making. The statute, North Carolina General Statutes, § 47-26, provides:

> All deeds of gift of any estate of any nature shall within two years after the making thereof be proved in due form and registered, or otherwise shall be void, and shall be good against creditors and purchasers for value only from the time of registration.

Unlike the other recordation statutes, the statute requiring the recordation of deeds of gift makes such deeds absolutely *void*[80] as against *everyone* unless they are recorded within two years from the time of the making.[81] If a deed of gift is not recorded within two years from the time of its execution it revests in the grantor.[82] A deed of gift deposited in escrow which is not recorded within two years from the time of its execution is void.[83] If a consideration has been paid for the deed, however, it is not a deed of gift and its recordation is necessary only as against purchasers for value and lien creditors under North Carolina General Statutes, §§ 47-18 and 47-20; it is valid as between the parties and their heirs though not recorded. This involves a determination of what is "consideration"? There must be some value given by the grantee to the grantor in return for the deed to prevent its being a deed of gift.[84] In

---

80. Booth v. Harrison, 195 N.C. 8, 141 S.E. 480 (1928), *aff'g* 193 N.C. 278, 136 S.E. 879, 57 A.L.R. 1186 (1927); Ferguson v. Ferguson, 225 N.C. 375, 35 S.E.2d 231 (1945). After the expiration of two years from the time of the making of such deed the legislature is without power to lengthen the period within which it may be registered. Booth v. Harrison, *supra;* Cutts v. McGhee, 221 N.C. 465, 20 S.E.2d 376 (1942).

81. "Making," as used in N.C. GEN. STAT. § 47-26, means date of execution by signing, sealing and delivering. Turlington v. Neighbors, 222 N.C. 694, 24 S.E.2d 648 (1943); Muse v. Muse, 236 N.C. 182, 72 S.E.2d 431 (1952). An acknowledgment by the donor three and a half years after its delivery to the donee was not a re-execution of a deed of gift and since it was not recorded within two years of its delivery it was held void in Cutts v. McGhee, 221 N.C. 465, 20 S.E.2d 376 (1942).

82. Winstead v. Woolard, 223 N.C. 814, 28 S.E.2d 507 (1944); Kirkpatrick v. Sanders, 261 F.2d 480 (4th Cir. 1958).

83. Allen v. Allen, 209 N.C. 744, 184 S.E. 485 (1936); Harris v. Briley, 244 N.C. 526, 94 S.E.2d 476 (1956).

84. *See* Cannon v. Blair, 229 N.C. 606, 50 S.E.2d 732 (1948), in which the court indicates the criterion to be whether the grantee gave to the grantor "some legal rights ... to which he would not otherwise have been entitled." In Sprinkle v. Ponder, 233 N.C. 312, 64 S.E.2d 171 (1951), the court held that an agreement by a wife to perform ordinary marital duties was not sufficient consideration to make a deed out of N.C. GEN. STAT. § 47-26. *But see* Kirkpatrick v. Sanders, 261 F.2d 480, *cert. denied,* 359 U.S. 1000, 79 S. Ct. 1138, 3 L. Ed. 2d 1029 (1959), where the court held that payment of $100 for a conveyance of land worth $27,000 was not a valuable consideration sufficient to negate a gift under N.C. GEN. STAT. § 47-26. Where a deed recites the payment and receipt of a consideration it is presumed to be correct and is prima facie evidence of that fact. Pelaez v. Pelaez, 16 N.C. App. 604, 192 S.E.2d 651 (1972), citing Speller v. Speller, 273 N.C. 340, 159 S.E.2d 894 (1968), and Randle v. Grady, 224 N.C. 651, 32 S.E.2d 20 (1944).

addition, a mere recital of a consideration, if not in fact paid, does not negate the existence of a gift deed.[85] A deed of gift, properly registered, within two years from its execution is valid as against the grantor and his heirs,[86] and is valid as against purchasers for value from the same grantor or his lien creditors from the time of recordation.[87]

§ 382. Recordation of Easements.

Easements created by deeds or right-of-way agreements must be recorded in order to be valid as against purchasers for value from the owner of the servient tract or as against his lien creditors.[88] Where the owner of land conveys a portion thereof together with an easement over his remaining lands by deed duly recorded, grantees of the servient tenement, directly or by mesne conveyances, take title subject to the duly recorded easement, notwithstanding that no deed in their chain of title refers to such easement.[89] If an easement is created by implication or operation of law, however, it is outside the purview and application of the recordation statutes and will not be extinguished due to lack of recordation.[90]

---

85. Harris v. Briley, 244 N.C. 526, 94 S.E.2d 476 (1956). Where a deed recites the payment and receipt of a consideration, it is presumed to be correct and is prima facie evidence of that fact. Pelaez v. Pelaez, 16 N.C. App. 604, 192 S.E.2d 651 (1972), citing Speller v. Speller, 273 N.C. 340, 159 S.E.2d 894 (1968), and Randle v. Grady, 224 N.C. 651, 32 S.E.2d 20 (1944).
86. Edwards v. Batts, 245 N.C. 693, 97 S.E.2d 101 (1957).
87. Provided, of course, it is not in fraud of creditors under N.C. GEN. STAT. § 39-15.
88. N.C. GEN. STAT. § 47-27; North Carolina State Highway Comm'n v. Nuckles, 271 N.C. 1, 155 S.E.2d 772 (1967).
89. Waldrop v. Brevard, 233 N.C. 26, 62 S.E.2d 512 (1950). Yount v. Lowe, 288 N.C. 90, 215 S.E.2d 563 (1975), holds that the purchaser of lands upon which the owner has imposed an easement takes the title subject to all easements, however created, of which he has notice. A consent judgment granting a cartway over specified land, duly recorded, constitutes notice.
90. *See* § 340 *supra;* POWELL, REAL PROPERTY § 424 (1966); Reid v. King, 158 N.C. 85, 73 S.E. 168 (1911); Packard v. Smith, 224 N.C. 480, 31 S.E.2d 517 (1944). Yount v. Lowe, 288 N.C. 90, 215 S.E.2d 563 (1975), holds that the purchaser of lands upon which the owner has imposed an easement takes the title subject to all easements, however created, of which he has notice. A consent judgment granting a cartway over specified land, duly recorded, constitutes notice.

CHAPTER 18

PRIVATE AND PUBLIC RESTRICTIONS ON THE USE OF LANDS

Article I. Private Restrictions on the Use of Lands
§ 383. Generally.
§ 384. Conditions and Limitations on the Estate Granted.
§ 385. Restrictive Covenants Generally.
§ 386. Creation of Restrictive Covenants.
§ 387. Persons Entitled to Enforce Restrictive Covenants.
§ 388. Construction of Restrictive Covenants.
§ 389. Modes of Termination of Restrictive Covenants.
§ 390. Validity of Particular Restrictions; Racial Restrictions; Restraints on Alienation.
§ 391. Conditions and Restrictions in Restraint of Marriage.

Article II. Public Restrictions on the Use of Lands

Division 1. Planning and Zoning

§ 392. Planning and Zoning Generally.
§ 393. Zoning Ordinances Generally.
§ 394. Types of Zones.
§ 395. The Validity of Zoning Ordinances; the Police Power Source.
§ 396. Historical Preservation Zoning; Constitutionality.
§ 397. Operation of Zoning Ordinances.
§ 398. Enforcement and Remedies Under Zoning Ordinances.

Division 2. Subdivision Regulations

§ 399. Subdivision Regulations Generally.

Article I. Private Restrictions on the Use of Lands

§ 383. Generally.

Landowners and developers frequently desire to make their lands more attractive and desirable to purchasers by establishing a protected residential community free from the inroads of commercial enterprises, substandard dwellings and obnoxious uses. This purpose is frequently accomplished by the utilization of restrictive conditions or restrictive covenants which limit the uses to which the land may be put. To that end lands are frequently conveyed by deeds which impose limitations on the potential uses of lands by specifying that the land conveyed will be used for residential,[1] noncommercial purposes only;[2] that buildings erected on

---

1. Edney v. Powers, 224 N.C. 441, 31 S.E.2d 372 (1944); Starmount Co. v. Greensboro Memorial Park, 233 N.C. 613, 65 S.E.2d 134 (1951).

2. Ingle v. Stubbins, 240 N.C. 382, 82 S.E.2d 388 (1954); Tull v. Doctor's Bldg., Inc., 255 N.C. 23, 120 S.E. 817 (1961). *Compare* Quadro Stations v. Gilley, 7 N.C. App. 227, 172 S.E.2d 237 (1970), which holds that a restrictive covenant between the grantor of a lot and a grantee, the predecessor in title of an oil company, providing that a four-acre tract adjoining the lot will not be used for the sale and advertising of any petroleum products for a period

the land will be single family dwellings only;[3] that the lot sizes will be of a certain size and will not be resubdivided to make lots of a smaller size;[4] that any dwelling erected on the land will cost not less than a certain sum [5] or be less than a certain size;[6] that any dwelling erected will be set back a certain distance from the street [7] and a certain distance from the sidelines of the lot;[8] that any dwelling erected on the land will be of a certain architectural design [9] or conform to a certain height; and the like.

The courts hold that any landowner, in disposing of his land, may impose restrictions on the uses to which the land conveyed may be put provided the beneficial enjoyment of the estate is not materially impaired and the public good and interest are not violated.[10] The right to acquire and possess property includes the right to dispose of all or any part of it, and to impose upon the grant whatever reservations or restrictions the grantor may see fit, provided they are not contrary to law or public policy.

Private restrictions with respect to the use of land fall into one of three main categories: (1) those imposing a limitation or condition on the estate granted; (2) those imposing a covenant or promise as to the use of the land conveyed; and (3) a combination of the first two types. The distinction between these categories of restrictions is primarily in the different modes of enforcement in the event of a breach.

As contradistinguished from zoning ordinances which also restrict the use of land, private restrictions need not be promotive of public health, safety, morals or public welfare; their purpose may be simply to create a particular type of neighborhood deemed desirable to the individual tract owner, and may be based solely on aesthetic considerations.

---

of twenty-five years, which covenant was executed simultaneously with the conveyance to the grantee of the lot as a site for a filling station, was legally enforceable by the oil company and not in violation of the statute prohibiting monopolies and trusts, N.C. GEN. STAT. § 75 (b) (6), where (1) the covenant was reasonably necessary to protect the oil company's investment in the filling station from future competition on the four-acre tract and (2) the restrictions as to area and duration were not unreasonable or injurious to the public.

3. Bailey v. Jackson-Campbell Co., 191 N.C. 61, 131 S.E. 567 (1926). But a covenant merely specifying "dwelling house" would not preclude erection of an apartment house. *See* DeLaney v. Van Ness, 193 N.C. 721, 138 S.E. 28 (1927).

4. Callaham v. Arensen, 239 N.C. 619, 80 S.E.2d 619 (1954); Ingle v. Stubbins, 240 N.C. 382, 82 S.E.2d 388 (1954).

5. *Id.*

6. *Id.*

7. *Id.*

8. *Id.*

9. Julian v. Lawton, 240 N.C. 436, 82 S.E.2d 210 (1954).

10. Hinton v. Vinson, 180 N.C. 393, 104 S.E. 897 (1920); Reed v. Elmore, 246 N.C. 221, 98 S.E. 360 (1957); Sheets v. Dillon, 221 N.C. 426, 20 S.E.2d 344 (1942); Davis v. Robinson, 189 N.C. 589, 127 S.E. 897 (1925); Boiling Spring Lakes v. Coastal Servs. Corp., 27 N.C. App. 191, 218 S.E.2d 476 (1975), citing this section (§ 344) in the original edition.

§ 384. Conditions and Limitations on the Estate Granted.

If a grantor transfers his land "To *A* and his heirs so long as it is used for noncommercial purposes and no longer," *A* receives a fee simple determinable and the grantor retains a possibility of reverter. If the premises are used for commercial purposes at any time in the future the title will revert automatically, "upon the happening of the event," to the grantor or his heirs or successors in interest [11] without the necessity of any court action.[12] Likewise, if the grantor transfers his land "To *A* and his heirs in fee but if the premises are ever used for commercial purposes, the grantor shall have the right to re-enter and terminate the estate granted," the grantor, his heirs or successors in interest [13] will have the right to re-enter and terminate the estate of the grantee or his sucessors if the prohibited event ever occurs.[14] In the latter case, the estate created in *A* is called an estate in fee simple subject to a condition subsequent.[15] The significant characteristic of restrictions created either by way of a fee simple determinable or a fee simple subject to a condition subsequent is that if the land is used for a prohibited purpose the grantor may get his land back; the grantor or his heirs or successors may divest the grantee's title, or that of the grantee's successors without paying any compensation upon the happening of the specified contingent event irrespective of any mortgages or interests created in the land subsequent to the creation of the restrictive limitation. Since restrictions created by such conditions operate so harshly and may terminate vested fee simple estates, the courts do not lightly construe a clause in a deed as a condition subsequent which qualifies or limits the duration of the estate conveyed thereby, unless the clause clearly expresses in "apt and appropriate language" the intention of the parties to that effect.[16] A mere statement of the purpose

---

11. While at the common law possibilities of reverter and rights of entry for condition broken were not assignable by the grantor but could be exercised only by the grantor or his heirs, under North Carolina law since the adoption of N.C. GEN. STAT. § 39-6.3 in 1961, rights of entry for condition broken and possibilities of reverter are assignable both before and after breach of the condition. Therefore assignees of the grantor who has a possibility of reverter or right of entry can take advantage of breach of the specified condition to effect a reverter or to revest title.

12. RESTATEMENT OF PROPERTY § 56 (1956); SIMES & SMITH, THE LAW OF FUTURE INTERESTS § 293 (1956). *See, e.g.,* Charlotte Park & Recreation Comm'n v. Barringer, 242 N.C. 311, 88 S.E.2d 114 (1955), *cert. denied,* 350 U.S. 983 (1956); Elmore v. Austin, 232 N.C. 13, 59 S.E.2d 205 (1950). *Accord,* Price v. Bunn, 13 N.C. App. 652, 187 S.E.2d 423 (1972), quoting Section 35 of this text; Cummings v. United States, 409 F. Supp. 1064 (M.D.N.C. 1976), citing Sections 35, 37, and 346 of the original edition of this work.

13. *See* note 1 *supra.*

14. Cummings v. United States, 409 F. Supp. 1064 (M.D.N.C. 1976) citing §§ 35, 37, and 346 of the original edition of this work.

15. RESTATEMENT OF PROPERTY § 45 (1956).

16. Church v. Refining Co., 200 N.C. 469, 157 S.E. 438 (1931); Hall v Quinn, 190 N.C. 326, 130 S.E. 18 (1925); Brittain v. Taylor, 168 N.C. 271, 84 S.E. 280 (1915); Washington v. Board of Educ. of Edgerton, 244 N.C. 576, 94 S.E.2d 661 (1956); Cummings v. United States, 409 F. Supp. 1064 (M.D.N.C. 1976).

for which the land is to be used, without more, is not sufficient to create a condition.[17] Very clear language of condition, indicating that title is subject to revert upon the occurrence of a specified event, must be used. While express language of reverter is not required, anything less may cause the court to construe the language to create simply a covenant, charge or trust, or to be mere surplusage.[18]

§ 385. Restrictive Covenants Generally.

The second principal device for the private regulation of land use is the restrictive *covenant*. A restrictive covenant is a servitude commonly referred to as a negative easement.[19] While both conditions and covenants are called "restrictions," the "covenant" differs from the "condition" with respect to the manner of relief afforded upon a breach. Upon the happening of an event which constitutes a breach of a "condition" set forth in the deed, the grantee may lose his title. Upon breach of a "covenant," on the other hand, the grantee simply subjects himself to liability for damages or to a decree in equity for enforcement of the covenant or promise.[20] Damages may be recoverable for its breach or compliance with the covenant may be enforced by injunction in appropriate cases.[21] It is

---

17. Church v. Refining Co., 200 N.C. 469, 157 S.E. 438 (1931); Shaw Univ. v. Life Ins. Co., 230 N.C. 526, 53 S.E.2d 656 (1949); Ange v. Ange, 235 N.C. 506, 71 S.E.2d 19 (1952); Roten v. State, 8 N.C. App. 643, 175 S.E.2d 384 (1970). *Cf.* Y.W.C.A. v. Morgan, 281 N.C. 485, 189 S.E.2d 169 (1972), which holds that the mere statement of the purpose for which a gift is made does not *per se* show an intent to make the donee a trustee to accomplish that purpose.

18. SIMES, FUTURE INTERESTS, Hornbook Series, § 13 (2d ed. 1966).

Mattox v. State, 280 N.C. 471, 186 S.E.2d 378 (1972), holds that a fee upon a condition subsequent is *not* created unless the grantor expressly reserves the right to reenter or provides for a forfeiture or for a reversion or that the instrument shall be null and void. The law does not favor a construction of the language contained in a deed which would constitute a condition subsequent unless the intention of the parties to create such a restriction upon the title is clearly manifested.

See Moore v. Tilley, 15 N.C. App. 378, 190 S.E.2d 243 (1972), where language was held to create an equitable lien on land. A provision in a will for support of a named person may be construed as constituting a personal covenant, as a charge upon only the rents and profits from lands devised, or as creating an equitable lien or charge upon the land itself which will follow the land into the hands of purchasers, depending upon the language used.

See generally for a distinction between the fee simple determinable and the fee simple subject to a condition subsequent, *see* Webster, *The Quest for Clear Land Titles — Whither Possibilities of Reverter and Rights of Entry?* 42 N.C.L. REV. 807 (1964). *See also* an excellent article by Professor Fred B. McCall, *Estates on Condition and on Special Limitation in North Carolina,* 19 N.C.L. REV. 334 (1941).

19. Hawthorne v. Realty Syndicate, Inc., 43 N.C. App. 436, 259 S.E.2d 591 (1979). This renders the servitude an incorporeal hereditament and a six-year statute of limitations is applicable for an action for injury to this type of interest. N.C. GEN. STAT. § 1-50(3).

20. The courts have shown considerable hostility to the termination of vested estates as a result of powers of termination and reverter provisions. SIMES, FUTURE INTERESTS, Hornbook Series, § 13 (2d ed. 1966). *See* note 4 *infra*.

21. Ingle v. Stubbins, 240 N.C. 382, 82 S.E.2d 388 (1954).

not always easy to determine whether a particular restriction is a "condition" or a mere "covenant" as the nomenclature used by the parties is not always decisive. The intention of the parties as derived from the imposing instrument is crucial. If the intention is expressed clearly that the continuation of the estate granted is to be dependent upon the happening or nonhappening of some specified event, the restriction will be construed a "condition"; if the restriction evinces the intention of the parties that it merely exacts a promise from the grantee that the land will not be used other than in a designated manner for a designated purpose, or that some other act will be performed, the restriction will be construed to be simply a "covenant."[22]

§ 386. Creation of Restrictive Covenants.

Where an owner of adjoining lots conveys one of the lots to a grantee upon the grantee's agreement contained in the deed that he will not use the land except in a specified manner, a covenant is created, the breach of which can be enjoined in equity[23] or for which damages can be recovered.[24]

In order for a restrictive covenant or condition to be valid and enforceable, it must be in writing since it constitutes an interest in land in the nature of a negative easement.[25] A grantee in a deed, however, who accepts a deed poll containing covenants or conditions restricting the use of the land or requiring him to perform some act becomes bound by such covenants or stipulations even though he does not execute or sign the instrument.[26] Since a restrictive covenant is deemed an interest in land it likewise cannot be released by parol.[27]

The grantor may set forth the use restrictions in each deed of convey-

---

22. A restriction will be construed to be a mere covenant rather than a condition if the words will reasonably admit such interpretation. See Minor v. Minor, 232 N.C. 669, 62 S.E.2d 60 (1950); Hinton v. Hinton, 180 N.C. 393, 104 S.E. 897 (1920). Accord, Cummings v. United States, 409 F. Supp. 1064 (M.D.N.C. 1976).

23. See Ingle v. Stubbins, 240 N.C. 382, 82 S.E.2d 388 (1954), in which a *mandatory* injunction compelled the removal of a building constructed in violation of a restrictive covenant. Accord, Franzle v. Waters, 18 N.C. App. 371, 197 S.E.2d 15 (1973), which states: "It is well settled in North Carolina that injunctive relief is available as a remedy to enforce restrictive covenants. Realty Company v. Barnes, 197 N.C. 6, 147 S.E. 617 (1929)." See Higgins v. Builders & Fin., Inc., 20 N.C. App. 1, 200 S.E.2d 397 (1973), in which defendant was ordered to remove buildings constructed in violation of restrictive covenants.

24. Minor v. Minor, 232 N.C. 669, 62 S.E.2d 60 (1950).

25. Cummings v. Dosam, Inc., 273 N.C. 28, 159 S.E.2d 513 (1968); Hege v. Sellers, 241 N.C. 240, 84 S.E.2d 892 (1954); Callaham v. Arenson, 239 N.C. 619, 80 S.E.2d 619 (1954); Pepper v. Development Co., 211 N.C. 166, 189 S.E. 628 (1937); Moore v. Shore, 206 N.C. 699, 175 S.E. 117 (1934); Turner v. Glenn, 220 N.C. 620, 18 S.E.2d 197 (1941); Cogburn v. Holness, 34 N.C. App. 253, 237 S.E.2d 905 (1977).

26. Barrier v. Randolph, 260 N.C. 741, 133 S.E.2d 655 (1963); Williams v. Joines, 228 N.C 141, 44 S.E.2d 738 (1947); Cummings v. Dosam, Inc., 273 N.C. 28, 159 S.E.2d 513 (1968).

27. See note 25 supra.

ance. Or, if he is a subdivider of land, he may record a plat of the tract of land being developed, along with an indenture or master set of the restrictive covenants or conditions, perhaps in an initial deed or pursuant to statute,[28] which restrictions carefully describe the limitations with respect to the uses to which the lots conveyed may be put. Thereafter, as subsequent deeds are given to grantees relating to separate parcels within the development, references can be made stating that each grant is subject to the recorded restrictions recorded in a specific book. In order for restrictions to be binding on subsequent purchasers they must be duly recorded and indexed.[29]

A commissioner appointed by a court to conduct a judicial sale has no authority to create a restriction on land sold. Such restriction is null and void and a purchaser at the judicial sale can transfer title free of restrictions.[30]

§ 387. Persons Entitled to Enforce Restrictive Covenants.

In ascertaining the enforceability of restrictive covenants by persons not originally a party to them, it must be determined whether the grantor intended to create a negative easement for their benefit.[31] This intent can be ascertained by certain circumstances surrounding the creation of the covenants. Where the owner of a tract of land subdivides it and sells distinct parcels thereof to separate grantees, imposing restrictions on its use pursuant to a general plan of development or improvement, such restrictions may be enforced by any grantee against any other grantee, either on the theory that there is a mutuality of covenant and consideration or on the ground that mutual negative equitable easements are created.[32] The right to enforce the restrictions in such case is not confined to immediate purchasers from the original grantor. It may be exercised by subsequent owners who acquire lots in the subdivision covered by the general plan through *mesne* conveyances from such immediate pur-

---

28. *See, e.g.,* N.C. GEN. STAT. § 47-21.
29. Davis v. Robinson, 189 N.C. 589, 127 S.E. 697 (1925); Goodnite v. Gurley, 40 N.C. App. 45, 251 S.E.2d 908 (1979); Cogburn v. Holness, 34 N.C. App. 253, 237 S.E.2d 905 (1977).
30. White v. Moore, 11 N.C. App. 534, 181 S.E.2d 734 (1971).
31. Lamica v. Gerdes, 270 N.C. 85, 153 S.E.2d 814 (1967); Beech Mountain Property Owners' Assoc. v. Current, 35 N.C. App. 135, 240 S.E.2d 503 (1978); Hawthorne v. Realty Syndicate, Inc., 43 N.C. App. 436, 259 S.E.2d 591 (1979).
32. Sedberry v. Parsons, 232 N.C. 707, 62 S.E.2d 88 (1950); Higdon v. Jaffa, 231 N.C. 242, 56 S.E.2d 661 (1949); Brenizer v. Stephens, 220 N.C. 395, 17 S.E.2d 471 (1941); Bailey v. Jackson, 191 N.C. 61, 131 S.E. 567 (1925); Homes Co. v. Falls, 184 N.C. 426, 115 S.E. 184 (1922). *Accord,* Shipton v. Barfield, 23 N.C. App. 58, 208 S.E.2d 210 (1974). *See* Sleepy Creek Club, Inc. v. Lawrence, 29 N.C. App. 547, 225 S.E.2d 167 (1976), to the effect that for a covenant to be enforceable by a stranger it must be shown to have been impressed on land for his benefit. Thus if a restrictive covenant inserted in a deed is not made pursuant to a general plan of development, persons other than the grantor cannot enforce such covenant unless it is shown that the provision was made for the benefit of such persons. *See also* Beech Mountain Property Owners' Assoc. v. Current, 35 N.C. App. 135, 240 S.E.2d 503 (1978).

chasers.[33] The restrictions limiting the use of land in the subdivision embraced by the general plan can be enforced against a subsequent purchaser who takes title to the land with notice of the restrictions.[34] A purchaser of land in a subdivision is chargeable in law with notice of restrictions limiting the use of the land adopted as a part of a general plan for the development or improvement of the subdivision if such restrictions are contained in any recorded deed or other instrument in his chain of title, even though they do not appear in his immediate deed.[35]

Whether there is a common plan or scheme of development depends upon the intention of the grantor in making the grants, which may be evidenced by the fact that substantially common restrictions apply to all lots of like character in the particular subdivision.[36]

---

33. Sedberry v. Parsons, 232 N.C. 707, 62 S.E.2d 88 (1950); Higdon v. Jaffa, 231 N.C. 242, 56 S.E.2d 661 (1949); Starmount Co. v. Greensboro Memorial Park, 233 N.C. 613, 65 S.E.2d 134 (1951).

Accord, Shipton v. Barfield, 23 N.C. App. 58, 208 S.E.2d 210 (1974), which states:

> The law of third-party beneficiary as it relates to that of restrictive covenants is designed to provide a remedy to the various grantees of a subdividing grantor *inter se.* "Where land within a given area is developed in accordance with a . . . uniform scheme of restriction, ordinarily anyone purchasing in reliance on such restriction may sue and enforce the restriction against another lot owner taking with record notice" . . . Craven County v. Trust Co., 237 N.C. 502, 513, 75 S.E.2d 620, 628 (1953). This is so because the law treats each landowner as a promisor, promising to abide by the restrictions for the benefit of the third-party beneficiary landowners. The concepts of mutuality of covenant and consideration as well as mutual negative equitable easements have been applied to give landowners the right to sue *inter se.* Maples v. Horton, 239 N.C. 394, 80 S.E.2d 38 (1953)."

In the absence of a general plan of subdivision, development and sales subject to uniform restrictions, restrictions limiting the use of a portion of the property sold are deemed to be personal to the grantor and for the benefit of land retained. Stegall v. Housing Authority, 278 N.C. 95, 178 S.E.2d 824 (1971).

34. Sedberry v. Parsons, 232 N.C. 707, 62 S.E.2d 88 (1950); Higdon v. Jaffa, 231 N.C. 242, 56 S.E.2d 661 (1949); Davis v. Robinson, 189 N.C. 589, 127 S.E. 697 (1925); Shipton v. Barfield, 23 N.C. App. 58, 208 S.E.2d 210 (1974).

35. Sedberry v. Parsons, 232 N.C. 707, 62 S.E.2d 88 (1950); Sheets v. Dillon, 221 N.C. 426, 20 S.E.2d 344 (1942); Long v. Branham, 271 N.C. 264, 156 S.E.2d 235 (1967); Cummings v. Dosam, Inc., 273 N.C. 28, 159 S.E.2d 513 (1968); Quadro Stations v. Gilley, 7 N.C. App. 227, 172 S.E.2d 237 (1970).

36. Lamica v. Gerdes, 270 N.C. 85, 153 S.E.2d 814 (1967); Sedberry v. Parsons, 232 N.C. 707, 62 S.E.2d 88 (1950); Higdon v. Jaffa, 231 N.C. 242, 56 S.E.2d 661 (1949). It is not necessary for the restrictions to be exactly the same with respect to lots in a particular subdivision. There must be "substantial" uniformity. *See* Stegall v. Housing Authority, 278 N.C. 95, 178 S.E.2d 824 (1971), which holds that a grantee of land cannot benefit from covenants contained in his deed to his vendor "except such as attach to, and run with, the land." A restriction which is merely a personal covenant with the grantor does not run with the land and can be enforced by him only. McCotter v. Barnes, 247 N.C. 480, 101 S.E.2d 330 (1958). Whether restrictions imposed upon land by a grantor create a personal obligation or impose a servitude upon the land enforceable by subsequent purchasers from his grantee is determined by the intention of the parties at the time the deed containing the restriction was delivered. Ordinarily this intention must be ascertained from the deed itself, but when the language used is ambiguous it is proper to consider the situation of the parties and the

If the owner of a large tract of land subdivides in into numerous tracts and files a separate map as to each tract, which map shows a general plan for each respective tract, it has been held that each tract is a separate subdivision for the purpose of construing the restrictive covenants.[37] A recent court of appeals case suggests that the inquiry into determining whether divisional or single unit development was intended involves the following four factors: (1) the way in which the land in question is platted; (2) the scope of any provision for altering the restrictions imposed; (3) the express limitations on the extent of the restrictions imposed by the conveyance; and (4) the similarity of restrictions between subdivisions.[38]

As between the original parties to the covenants and those owning title by *mesne* coveyances from them, restrictive covenants are enforceable irrespective of any general scheme of development.[39] For the purpose of enforcing restrictive covenants between purchasers of the land *inter se,* or between subsequent purchasers of the original parties, a purchaser is chargeable with notice of restrictive covenants if such covenants are contained in any recorded deed or other instrument in this line of title, even though they do not appear in his immediate deed, since he is charged with notice of every fact affecting his title which an examination of his record chain of title would disclose.[40] Further, it has been held that the purchaser of lands is chargeable with notice that his grantor had previously conveyed contiguous land by registered deed creating a negative easement running with the land and constituting a limitation of the use of land then retained.[41]

---

circumstances surrounding their transaction. However, this intention may not be established by parol. Neither the testimony nor the declarations of a party is competent to prove intent.

See also Sleepy Creek Club, Inc. v. Lawrence, 29 N.C. App. 547, 225 S.E.2d 167 (1976), to the effect that for a covenant to be enforceable by a stranger it must be shown to have been impressed on land for his benefit. Thus if a restrictive covenant inserted in a deed is not made pursuant to a uniform plan of development, persons other than the grantor cannot enforce such covenant unless it is shown that the provision was made for the benefit of such persons.

37. Tull v. Doctor's Bldg., Inc., 255 N.C. 23, 120 S.E.2d 817 (1961).

38. Hawthorne v. Realty Syndicate, Inc., 43 N.C. App. 436, 259 S.E.2d 591 (1979), citing 52 CORNELL LAW QUARTERLY 611, 613 (1967).

39. Starmount Co. v. Greensboro Memorial Park, Inc., 233 N.C. 613, 65 S.E.2d 134 (1951). See Sleepy Creek Club, Inc. v. Lawrence, 29 N.C. App. 547, 225 S.E.2d 167 (1976), to the effect that for a covenant to be enforceable by a stranger it must be shown to have been impressed on land for his benefit. Thus if a restrictive covenant inserted in a deed is not made pursuant to a uniform plan of development, persons other than the grantor cannot enforce such covenant unless it is shown that the provision was made for the benefit of such persons.

40. Sedberry v. Parsons, 232 N.C. 707, 62 S.E.2d 88 (1950); Higdon v. Jaffa, 231 N.C. 242, 56 S.E.2d 661 (1949); Sheets v. Dillon, 221 N.C. 426, 20 S.E.2d 344 (1942); Quadro Stations v. Gilley, 7 N.C. App. 227, 172 S.E.2d 237 (1970); Strickland v. Overman, 11 N.C. App. 427, 181 S.E.2d 136 (1971).

41. Reed v. Elmore, 246 N.C. 221, 98 S.E.2d 860 (1957); Waldrop v. Brevard, 233 N.C. 26, S.E.2d 512 (1950).

Some covenants are merely personal in nature and do not run with the land.[42] If this is the case, subsequent owners of the property burdened by the personal covenant are not bound by it.[43] Even a statement that a covenant is to run with the land will not effectively achieve that result unless the covenant possesses the essential characteristics of a real covenant,[44] which may be summarized by the following three-part test: (1) Is there an intention that the covenant run with the land as evidenced by the instruments of record? (2) Is there a close connection between the covenant and the real property so that it can be said that the covenant "touches and concerns" the land? (3) Is there privity of estate between the parties to the covenant?[45]

§ 388. Construction of Restrictive Covenants.

Many cases have been concerned with the interpretation and construction of language used in instruments which purport to limit the uses to which the land may be put. The North Carolina Supreme Court, in the case of *Long v. Branham*,[46] has stated:

> Covenants and agreements restricting the free use of property are strictly construed against limitations upon such use. Such restrictions will not be aided or extended by implication or enlarged by construction to affect lands not specifically described, or to grant rights to persons in whose favor it is not clearly shown such restrictions are to apply. Doubt will be resolved in favor of the unrestricted use of property, so that where the language of a restrictive covenant is capable of two constructions, the one that limits, rather than the

---

42. Raintree Corp. v. Rowe, 38 N.C. App. 664, 248 S.E.2d 904 (1978); Beech Mountain Property Owners' Assoc. v. Current, 35 N.C. App. 135, 240 S.E.2d 503 (1978).
43. Raintree Corp. v. Rowe, 38 N.C. App. 664, 248 S.E.2d 904 (1978); Nesbit v. Nesbit, 1 N.C. 490 (1801).
44. *Id.*
45. Raintree Corp. v. Rowe, 38 N.C. App. 664, 248 S.E.2d 904 (1978), citing 20 AM. JUR. 2d *Covenants, Conditions, etc.* § 30 (1965).
46. 271 N.C. 264,156 S.E.2d 235 (1967). *Accord,* Edney v. Powers, 224 N.C. 441, 31 S.E.2d 372 (1944); Starmount Co. v. Greensboro Memorial Park, 233 N.C. 613, 65 S.E.2d 134 (1951); Craven County v. First Citizens Bank & Trust Co., 237 N.C. 502, 75 S.E.2d 620 (1953); Julian v. Lawton, 240 N.C. 436, 82 S.E.2d 210 (1954); Hege v. Sellers, 241 N.C. 240, 84 S.E.2d 892 (1954); Shuford v. Asheville Oil Co., 243 N.C. 636, 91 S.E.2d 903 (1956); Hullett v. Grayson, 265 N.C. 453, 144 S.E.2d 206 (1965); Lamica v. Gerdes, 270 N.C. 85, 153 S.E.2d 814 (1967); Cummings v. Dosam, Inc., 273 N.C. 28, 159 S.E.2d 513 (1968); Boiling Spring Lakes v. Coastal Servs. Corp., 27 N.C. App. 191, 218 S.E.2d 476 (1975); Robinson v. Investment Co., 19 N.C. App. 590, 200 S.E.2d 59 (1973); Franzle v. Waters, 18 N.C. App. 371, 197 S.E.2d 15 (1973); Berryhill v. Morgan, 16 N.C. App. 584, 192 S.E.2d 599 (1972); Stegall v. Housing Authority, 278 N.C. 95, 178 S.E.2d 824 (1971); Bank v. Morris, 45 N.C. App. 281, 262 S.E.2d 674 (1980). *See* Sleepy Creek Club, Inc. v. Lawrence, 29 N.C. App. 547, 225 S.E.2d 167 (1976), which states that restrictive covenants are to be strictly construed against limitations on use, and the same principle should be observed when attempting to determine *who* may enforce a restrictive covenant.

§ 388 REAL ESTATE LAW IN NORTH CAROLINA § 388

one which extends it, should be adopted, and that construction should be embraced which least restricts the free use of the land.

Such construction in favor of the unrestricted use, however, must be reasonable. The strict rule of construction as to restrictions should not be applied in such a way as to defeat the plain and obvious purposes of a restriction.

Therefore, in North Carolina the fundamental rule in construing restrictive covenants is that the intention of the parties governs, and their intention must be gathered from study and consideration of *all* the covenants contained in the instrument or instruments creating the restrictions.[47] Where the meaning of restrictive covenants is doubtful, the "surrounding circumstances existing at the time of the creation of the restriction are taken into consideration in determining the intention."[48]

That restrictive covenants will be strictly construed against limitations upon the use of land is illustrated by North Carolina holding that the phrase "for dwelling purposes" does not necessarily mean that the land may be used only for single family dwellings; while the land may be used only for residential purposes, a person would be free to erect an apartment house on the land unless the restriction narrows the permissible use to "single family dwellings" or expressly negates multiple family residences.[49] A restriction in a deed prohibiting the erection of a "temporary

---

47. Callaham v. Arensen, 239 N.C. 619, 80 S.E.2d 619 (1954); Franzle v. Waters, 18 N.C. App. 371, 197 S.E.2d 15 (1973); Robinson v. Investment Co., 19 N.C. App. 590, 200 S.E.2d 59 (1973); Berryhill v. Morgan, 16 N.C. App. 584, 192 S.E.2d 599 (1972); Bank v. Morris, 45 N.C. App. 281, 262 S.E.2d 674 (1980).

48. Long v. Branham, 271 N.C. 264, 156 S.E.2d 235 (1967); Stegall v. Housing Authority, 278 N.C. 95, 178 S.E.2d 824 (1971); Boiling Spring Lakes v. Coastal Servs. Corp., 27 N.C. App. 191, 218 S.E.2d 476 (1975).

49. DeLaney v. Van Ness, 193 N.C. 721, 138 S.E. 28 (1927); Construction Co. v. Cobb, 195 N.C. 690, 143 S.E. 522 (1928). *But see* Bailey v. Jackson-Campbell Co., 191 N.C. 61, 131 S.E. 567 (1926), in which the court held that an apartment house is not "one residence." *See also* Muilenburg v. Blevins, 242 N.C. 271, 87 S.E.2d 493 (1955). A restriction against an "apartment house" is not violated by alterations and the renting of two rooms without kitchen facilities. Huffman v. Johnson, 236 N.C. 225, 72 S.E.2d 236 (1952).

A restrictive covenant prohibiting the construction of "more than one single unit family residence" on lots in a subdivision precludes the construction of duplexes in the subdivision. Rodgerson v. Davis, 27 N.C. App. 173, 218 S.E.2d 471 (1975). A subdivision restrictive covenant stating "No duplexes or apartment houses for rental property" was held to prohibit the construction of a two-family duplex dwelling for rental purposes on property within the subdivision. Berryhill v. Morgan, 16 N.C. App. 584, 192 S.E.2d 599 (1972). Higgins v. Builders & Fin., Inc., 20 N.C. App. 1, 200 S.E.2d 397 (1973), holds that a subdivision restrictive covenant providing that "no structure shall be erected, altered, placed or permitted to remain on any lot other than for use as a single family residential dwelling" is not merely a "use" restriction prohibiting the occupancy of each house by more than one family but would be violated by the *erection* of a duplex house on any lot, even though it remained vacant and unoccupied by even one family. It was held that the builder's mere cutting of a three-foot-wide opening between the two portions of two duplex houses and the finishing of but one complete kitchen in each house did not constitute a sufficient modifica-

§ 388 RESTRICTIONS ON USE OF LANDS § 388

building, garage, garage apartment, or trailer for temporary or permanent use" did not prohibit owners from constructing a detached garage of permanent rather than temporary nature.[50] Convenants purporting to impose restrictive servitudes in derogation of the free and unfettered use of land are to be strictly construed against limitation on use, and they may not be enlarged by implication or extended by construction, but they must be given effect as written.[51] Thus, a restriction which said only that "there shall not be constructed on said lot more than one (1) dwelling house" was held not to limit the use of the property to residential uses only or to prohibit the erection of a residence or other building on more than one lot.[52] Likewise, a restriction in a deed that "no building shall be

---

tion of the duplexes to prevent them from violating a restrictive covenant prohibiting use of land in a subdivision for other than single-family residential dwellings. The court rendered a mandatory injunction ordering the builder to remove the offending buildings from the subdivision.

See Van Poole v. Messer, 19 N.C. App. 70, 198 S.E.2d 106 (1972), which states that a "mobile home" is a "trailer" within the intendment of a restrictive covenant that prohibits the use of a "trailer" as a residence on a lot in a subdivision; City of Asheboro v. Auman, 26 N.C. App. 82, 214 S.E.2d 621 (1975), a *zoning case,* which holds that the removal of the wheels and tongue from a mobile home, and the erection of a foundation for it, did not change its nature where the *zoning ordinance* forbade mobile homes.

Franzle v. Waters, 18 N.C. App. 371, 197 S.E.2d 15 (1973), holds that a restrictive covenant limiting subdivision lots to residential use precludes a construction company from building a roadway across a lot in the subdivision that would connect a street in the subdivision with a street in an adjoining subdivision. The North Carolina Court of Appeals indicates, however, that each case involving the construction of roadways over property restricted solely to residential use must be determined on its own facts. If it appears that a restrictive covenant was placed on a subdivision to preserve a quiet residential area in which noise and hazards of traffic would be kept at a minimum, construction of a roadway to carry traffic to and from another subdivision may constitute a violation of the restrictive covenant. While restrictive covenants are strictly construed against limitations on use, such construction must be reasonable and should not be applied to defeat the plain and obvious purposes of the restriction.

See also Boiling Spring Lakes v. Coastal Servs. Corp., 27 N.C. App. 191, 218 S.E.2d 476 (1975), which holds that a restrictive covenant requiring building plans to be submitted to and approved by the grantor is valid and enforceable, even though the covenant does not in itself impose standards of approval. The North Carolina Court of Appeals holds, however, that the exercise of the authority to approve building plans cannot be arbitrary and where standards are not set out within the restrictive covenant itself, they must be in other stated or designated covenants or they must be otherwise clearly established in connection with some general plan or scheme of development. The court further states that a restrictive covenant requiring approval of house plans is enforceable only if the exercise of the power in a particular case is reasonable and in good faith.

See also J. T. Hobby & Son, Inc. v. Family Homes of Wake County, Inc., 46 N.C. App. 231, 266 S.E.2d 32 (1980) holding that a family care home for retarded adults was an "institution" and not a "single family dwelling" required on the property by restrictive covenants.

50. Hullett v. Grayson, 265 N.C. 453, 144 S.E.2d 206 (1965).
51. Callaham v. Arensen, 239 N.C. 619, 80 S.E.2d 619 (1954).
52. Scott v. Board of Missions, 252 N.C. 443, 114 S.E.2d 74 (1960).

constructed nearer than fifteen feet from the side line of a lot" does not prevent one from purchasing three lots and constructing a building on the three lots provided the building erected is not nearer than fifteen feet from the outside lines of the tract consisting of the three lots.[53] Where a grantor develops his land by its division into more than one tract, his imposition of restrictions on land within one tract does not preclude his development of other subdivisions for entirely different uses.[54]

The strict construction rule that is invoked in the area of restrictions on land must be kept in proper perspective. It is a rule of construction that must be applied in a reasonable manner so as not to defeat the plain and obvious purpose of a restriction.[55] Thus a family care home for two to five retarded adults supervised by a married couple has been held to be an "institution" in violation of a restrictive covenant requiring a "single family dwelling" on the property.[56] In addition, a restriction against commercial use of land extends to preclude use of the land as an entrance or driveway to commercial property on adjacent land.[57] And a restriction providing that land shall be used for a golf course will preclude the granting of an easement across the golf course for a street for ingress and egress for adjacent landowners, since such use is inconsistent with the use

---

53. *Id.* Robinson v. Investment Co., 19 N.C. App. 590, 200 S.E.2d 59 (1973), holds that restrictive covenants on subdivision lots which required that buildings be located no closer than given distances from the front and interior lot lines did not prohibit the resubdivision of the property or prevent the relocation of interior side lines of lots.

54. Starmount Co. v. Greensboro Memorial Park, Inc., 233 N.C. 613, 65 S.E.2d 134 (1951).

55. J. T. Hobby & Son, Inc. v. Family Homes of Wake County, Inc., 46 N.C. App. 231, 266 S.E.2d 32 (1980); Long v. Branham, 271 N.C. 264, 156 S.E.2d 235 (1967); 20 AM. JUR. 2d, *Covenants, Conditions and Restrictions* § 187 (1965).

56. J. T. Hobby & Son, Inc. v. Family Homes of Wake County, Inc., 46 N.C. App. 231, 266 S.E.2d 32 (1980). The court of appeals rejected a contention that the restriction was contrary to public policy and in violation of N.C. GEN. STAT. § 168-9 (a statute providing that handicapped citizens shall have the same right to live and reside in residential communities, homes and group homes as other citizens).

57. Cleveland Realty Co. v. Hobbs, 261 N.C. 414, 135 S.E.2d 30 (1964). *Compare* Franzle v. Waters, 18 N.C. App. 371, 197 S.E.2d 15 (1973), which holds that a restrictive covenant limiting subdivision lots to residential use precludes a construction company from building a roadway across a lot in the subdivision that would connect a street in the subdivision with a street in an adjoining subdivision. The court indicates, however, that each case involving the construction of roadways over property restricted solely to residential use must be determined on its own facts. If it appears that a restrictive covenant was placed on a subdivision to preserve a quiet residential area in which noise and hazards of traffic would be kept at a minimum, construction of a roadway to carry traffic to and from another subdivision may constitute a violation of the restrictive covenant. While restrictive covenants are strictly construed against limitations on use, such construction must be reasonable and should not be applied to defeat the plain and obvious purposes of the restriction. *See also* Bank v. Morris, 45 N.C. App. 281, 262 S.E.2d 674 (1980) holding that a fifteen-foot wide driveway did not violate a restrictive covenant.

contemplated by the restrictive covenants.[58] These cases do not mean, however, that the grant of a right-of-way over restricted property will always constitute a violation of the restrictive covenants. Rather, the language of the restriction must be analyzed in light of the objects sought to be obtained, and the conditions and circumstances surrounding the premises involved.[59] Thus, it has been held that the creation of a fifteen foot driveway along the boundary of a restricted lot did not result in a restrictive covenant violation where it was reasonable to expect that easements would be necessary for access to other lots and where the court determined that the purposes of the restrictions as originally established were not interfered with.[60]

§ 389. Modes of Termination of Restrictive Covenants.

The question of how long restrictive covenants on lands last is frequently of prime importance. Provisions are often drafted whereby they will expire by their own terms after twenty, thirty or forty years.[61] Since the extent of restrictive covenants should not exceed the judicially determined intent of the parties, any statement by the parties in a deed creating a restriction with respect to its natural expiration at the end of a definite period will be effective.

Under the Real Property Marketable Title Act,[62] some covenants will be extinguished by the 30-year marketable record title rule set forth in North Carolina General Statutes, § 47B-2(c). A broad exception to the Act insofar as restrictive covenants are concerned may be found at North Carolina General Statutes, § 47B-3(13) which excepts from coverage of the 30-year rule: "Covenants applicable to a general or uniform scheme of development which restrict the property to residential use only, provided said covenants are otherwise enforceable. The excepted covenant may restrict the property to multi-family or single-family residential use or simply to residential use." [63]

---

58. Craven County v. First Citizens Bank & Trust Co., 237 N.C. 502, 75 S.E.2d 620 (1953); Higdon v. Jaffa, 231 N.C. 242, 56 S.E.2d 661 (1949); East Side Builders v. Brown, 234 N.C. 517, 67 S.E.2d 489 (1951). *Compare* Franzle v. Waters, 18 N.C. App. 371, 197 S.E.2d 15 (1973).

59. Bank v. Morris, 45 N.C. App. 281, 262 S.E.2d 674 (1980).

60. *Id.* The court of appeals distinguished the leading case of Long v. Branham, 271 N.C. 264, 156 S.E.2d 235 (1967) which involved a proposed road which would have connected two subdivisions and thus converted a quiet access road into a thoroughfare. In Bank v. Morris, a driveway easement at the boundary of a restricted lot was to provide access to a street for only one house.

61. Edney v. Powers, 224 N.C. 441, 31 S.E.2d 372 (1944).

62. N.C. Gen. Stat. ch. 47B. *See* chapter 25 *infra*.

63. N.C. Gen. Stat. 47B-3(13) goes on to state: "Restrictive covenants other than those mentioned herein which limit the property to residential use only are not excepted from the provisions of chapter 47B."

Increasingly, creators of restrictive covenants are wisely drafting time limitations and provisions for renewal of the covenants in the creating instrument. There remain numerous instances, however, where no limitation on duration has been stated. Since it is highly likely that these restrictive covenants will be covered by the exception of North Carolina General Statutes, § 47B-3(13) discussed above, they have a potentially infinite duration. Where there is a restrictive covenant without any limitation as to how long it will endure, equity may refuse to enforce the covenant when there has been a change of circumstances in the restricted area or a change in the character of the neighborhood to such an extent that the objectives of the covenant have in fact been frustrated or made impossible or impracticable of accomplishment.[64] The burden of showing that changed conditions and changes in the character of the property have been so substantially changed as to make enforcement of the restrictions inequitable and unjust is on the party contending that the restriction should not be enforced.[65] All persons who may have a right to enforce the covenants *inter se* or otherwise should be made parties in any action to declare restrictive covenants unenforceable by reason of changed circumstances.[66]

While there is some authority to the contrary,[67] the general rule in North Carolina is that changes in the character or use of land adjacent to but outside the area of a subdivision restricted to residential purposes do not affect the validity and enforceability of the residential restrictions if there has been no change in use within the covenanted area.[68]

The fact that a municipality opens up a street on a part of a lot in a

---

64. Muilenburg v. Blevins, 242 N.C. 271, 87 S.E.2d 493 (1955); Shuford v. Asheville Oil Co., 243 N.C. 636, 91 S.E.2d 903 (1956); Bengel v. Barnes, 231 N.C. 667, 58 S.E.2d 371 (1950); McLeskey v. Heinlein, 200 N.C. 290, 156 S.E. 489 (1930); Caldwell v. Bradford, 248 N.C. 48, 102 S.E.2d 399 (1958); Sheets v. Dillon, 221 N.C. 426, 20 S.E.2d 344 (1942); Bass v. Hunter, 216 N.C. 505, 5 S.E.2d 558 (1939); Elrod v. Phillips, 214 N.C. 472, 199 S.E. 722 (1938); Synder v. Caldwell, 207 N.C. 626, 178 S.E. 83 (1934); Oldham v. McPheeters, 203 N.C. 141, 164 S.E. 731 (1932). *Accord,* Cotton Mills v. Vaughn, 24 N.C. App. 696, 212 S.E.2d 199 (1975); Lewis v. Wiggs, 5 N.C. App. 95, 167 S.E.2d 813 (1969). *See generally,* Starkey v. Gardner, 194 N.C. 74, 138 S.E. 408 (1927).
65. Sheets v. Dillon, 221 N.C. 426, 20 S.E.2d 344 (1942).
66. Muilenburg v. Blevins, 242 N.C. 271, 87 S.E.2d 493 (1955).
67. Elrod v. Phillips, 214 N.C. 472, 199 S.E. 722 (1938).
68. Tull v. Doctor's Bldg., Inc., 255 N.C. 23, 120 S.E.2d 817 (1961); Higdon v. Jaffa, 231 N.C. 242, 56 S.E.2d 661 (1949); Vernon v. R.J. Reynolds Realty Co., 226 N.C. 58, 36 S.E.2d 710 (1945); Turner v. Glenn, 220 N.C. 620, 18 S.E.2d 197 (1941); Brenizer v. Stephens, 220 N.C. 395, 17 S.E.2d 471 (1941); Cauble v. Bell, 249 N.C. 722, 107 S.E.2d 557 (1959); Lamica v. Gerdes, 270 N.C. 85, 153 S.E.2d 814 (1967); Mills v. Enterprises, Inc., 36 N.C. App. 410, 244 S.E.2d 469 (1978); Cotton Mills v. Vaughn, 24 N.C. App. 696, 212 S.E.2d 199 (1975), which states: "It is generally held that the encroachment of business and changes due thereto, in order to undo the force and vitality of the restrictions, must take place within the convenated area. [Quoting Tull v. Doctor's Bldg., Inc., 255 N.C. 23, 120 S.E.2d 817 (1961), and Brenizer v. Stephens, 220 N.C. 395, 17 S.E.2d 471 (1941).]"

subdivision in which all the lots are restricted to residential purposes does not violate or negate the residential restrictions.[69] Nor does a subsequently enacted zoning ordinance nullify or supersede them [70] although such ordinance may be considered with other competent evidence in determining whether or not there has been a fundamental change in the restricted subdivision.[71]

Equity will not relieve a grantee of his covenants merely because they have become burdensome, but will give them full effect unless changed conditions within the covenanted area are so radical as to destroy the essential objects of the scheme of development and such changes have been acquiesced in by the owners of other lots so as to constitute a waiver or abandonment of their rights to enforce the restrictions.[72]

The party who has the right to enforce a restrictive covenant may, of course, contract to release his right to enforce the covenant just as any other interest in land may be surrendered to the fee holder.[73] Or the party who has the right to enforce the covenant may estop himself from enforcing the terms of the covenant if he himself executes a deed to other land within the covenanted area which deed permits a use restricted as to other lots in the covenanted area.[74] But acquiescence in a violation by one owner of land entitled to enforce a covenant does not estop other owners of land subject to the same restrictions from enforcing those restrictions.[75] In addition, not every acquiescence to a use in technical violation of a covenant will constitute "waiver" or "estoppel" in the legal sense of those terms.[76]

---

69. Tull v. Doctor's Bldg., Inc., 255 N.C. 23, 120 S.E.2d 817 (1961).
70. *Id.* Hawthorne v. Realty Syndicate, Inc., 43 N.C. App. 436, 259 S.E.2d 591 (1979); Mills v. Enterprises, Inc., 36 N.C. App. 410, 244 S.E.2d 469 (1978).
71. Shuford v. Asheville Oil Co., 243 N.C. 636, 91 S.E.2d 903 (1956).
72. Tull v. Doctor's Bldg., Inc., 255 N.C. 23, 120 S.E.2d 817 (1961); Cotton Mills v. Vaughn, 24 N.C. App. 696, 212 S.E.2d 199 (1975); Van Poole v. Messer, 25 N.C. App. 203, 198 S.E.2d 106 (1975).
73. Shuford v. Asheville Oil Co., 243 N.C. 636, 91 S.E.2d 903 (1956); Hawthorne v. Realty Syndicate, Inc., 43 N.C. App. 436, 259 S.E.2d 591 (1979); Goodnite v. Gurley, 40 N.C. App. 45, 251 S.E.2d 908 (1979).
74. *See* Logan v. Sprinkle 256 N.C. 41, 123 S.E.2d 209 (1961), in which lots in subdivision were restricted for residential uses only. The developer then sold six lots within the subdivision for the construction of a motel. The court held that a motel is a commercial purpose and when the owner sold the land for motel purposes he abandoned his general scheme with respect to residences and therefore waived his right as against a purchaser of one of the lots to enforce the residential restriction. Rodgerson v. Davis, 27 N.C. App. 173, 218 S.E.2d 471 (1975), holds that where restrictions have been imposed according to a general plan and one of the grantees of lots subject thereto has himself violated such restrictions, he will not be allowed in equity to complain against similar violations by other grantees.
75. Tull v. Doctor's Bldg., Inc., 255 N.C. 23, 120 S.E.2d 817 (1961).
76. Mills v. Enterprises, Inc., 36 N.C. App. 410, 244 S.E.2d 469 (1978).

§ 390. **Validity of Particular Restrictions; Racial Restrictions; Restraints on Alienation.**

(a) *Racial restrictions.* Prior to 1948 when the United States Supreme Court decided the case of *Shelley v. Kraemer* [77] it was a general practice for grantors to include in their deeds covenants prohibiting the use and occupancy of the land by designated racial groups. Frequently owners in an area entered into separate contracts whereby they agreed not to convey their land to non-Caucasians and not to permit their lands to be used or occupied by members of such classes. Or developers sold land in subdivisions with restrictions providing that members of certain racial groups could not be owners of land within the subdivisions.[78] In 1948, however, the *Shelley v. Kraemer* case held that racial restrictive covenants could not be enforced *in equity* against Negro purchasers who purchased realty in violation of racial restrictions because enforcement would constitute "state action" denying equal protection of the laws to the Negroes in violation of the Fourteenth Amendment of the United States Constitution. It was subsequently held in the case of *Barrows v. Jackson* [79] that restrictive racial covenants were likewise unenforceable *in law actions for damages* since to permit recovery of damages would also constitute "state action" and deprive non-Caucasians of the equal protection of the laws under the Fourteenth Amendment of the United States Constitution.

Therefore racial restrictive covenants, prohibiting the sale or use of real property by a particular racial group, are unenforceable today either in equity or at law in a suit for damages. Where a conveyance is made which contains such void covenants, full effect is given to the conveyance but the invalid restriction or limitation is read out and eliminated from consideration.[80]

(b) *Restraints on alienation — Fee simple estates.* Dating back to the common law there has been a policy in favor of the free alienation of land. As a consequence any provision in a deed, whether a "disabling," [81]

---

77. 334 U.S. 1, 68 S. Ct. 836 (1948).

78. *See, e.g.,* Vernon v. R.J. Reynolds Realty Co., 226 N.C. 58, 36 S.E.2d 710 (1946).

79. 346 U.S. 249, 73 S. Ct. 1031 (1953). Discrimination on the basis of race, color, religion or national origin with respect to the sale or rental of real property has been made unlawful by various statutes enacted by the United States Congress and as a result of significant federal court decisions. *E.g., see* the Civil Rights Act of 1968, Title VIII, Fair Housing, 42 U.S.C.A. §§ 3601-3619, and Jones v. Alfred H. Mayer Co., 392 U.S. 409, 88 S. Ct. 2186 (1968). As a result of far-reaching federal legislation and decisions of the federal courts, racial covenants are now totally invalid.

80. Hawthorne v. Realty Syndicate, Inc., 43 N.C. App. 436, 259 S.E.2d 591 (1979).

81. A "disabling" restraint is a direction that the property which is conveyed or devised shall not thereafter be aliened. SIMES & SMITH, THE LAW OF FUTURE INTERESTS § 1131 (1956). *Accord,* Crockett v. First Fed. Sav. & Loan Ass'n, 289 N.C. 620, 224 S.E.2d 580 (1976).

"promissory," [82] or "forfeiture" [83] restraint, which undertakes to directly restrict the right of transfer of the fee simple title to real estate in any way is void.

The *jus disponendi* or right of alienation being an inseparable incident of every estate in fee, any restriction of this right is deemed to be repugnant to the estate granted and therefore void.[84] Any restriction against alienation of the fee is held invalid even if it is only for a limited time.[85] Likewise, a restriction which permits alienation of the fee only to a limited group of persons is void.[86] Contrary to the holdings of a number of jurisdictions,[87] the court of appeals has recently held that any restriction on a landowner's right to freely alienate his property, even though

---

82. A "promissory" restraint is a covenant or contract in an instrument of conveyance in which the promisor agrees not to alien the land. SIMES & SMITH, THE LAW OF FUTURE INTERESTS § 1131 (1956). *Accord,* Crockett v. First Fed. Sav. & Loan Ass'n, 289 N.C. 620, 224 S.E.2d 580 (1976).

83. A "forfeiture" restraint is a condition or limitation imposed on an estate by deed or will whereby the estate granted will be forfeited if there is an attempted alienation. A forfeiture restraint always purports to create a future interest. SIMES & SMITH, THE LAW OF FUTURE INTERESTS § 1131 (1956). *Accord,* Crockett v. First Fed. Sav. & Loan Ass'n, 289 N.C. 620, 224 S.E.2d 580 (1976).

84. Buckner v. Hawkins, 230 N.C. 99, 52 S.E.2d 16 (1949); Douglass v. Stevens, 214 N.C. 688, 200 S.E. 366 (1938); Monroe v. Hall, 97 N.C. 206, 1 S.E. 651 (1887). *See* Crockett v. First Fed. Sav. & Loan Ass'n, 289 N.C. 620, 224 S.E.2d 580 (1976), which states: "The policy against restraints on alienation is said to be based upon the belief that restraints remove property from commerce, concentrate wealth, prejudice creditors, and discourage property improvements."

85. *See* Twitty v. Camp, 62 N.C. 61 (1866) (until grantee attains 25); Pritchard v. Bailey, 113 N.C. 521, 18 S.E. 668 (1893) (life of grantee); Latimer v. Waddell, 219 N.C. 370, 26 S.E. 122 (1896) (five years); Holloway v. Green, 167 N.C. 91, 83 S.E. 243 (1914) (life of co-tenant); Welch v. Murdock, 192 N.C. 709, 135 S.E. 611 (until third generation); Buckner v. Hawkins, 230 N.C. 99, 52 S.E.2d 16 (1949); Elder v. Johnston, 227 N.C. 592, 42 S.E.2d 904 (1947); Johnson v. Gaines, 230 N.C. 653, 55 S.E.2d 19 (1949) (35 years). *See* Trust Co. v. Construction Co., 275 N.C. 399, 168 S.E.2d 358 (1969), which holds, however, that an absolute restraint against alienation in a gift to a charitable trust is not void. The case states that a restraint on alienation is void as to private trusts. *Accord,* Crockett v. First Fed. Sav. & Loan Ass'n, 289 N.C. 620, 224 S.E.2d 580 (1976).

86. Langston v. Wooten, 232 N.C. 124, 59 S.E.2d 605 (1950); Brooks v. Griffin, 177 N.C. 7, 97 S.E. 730 (1919); Williams v. McPherson, 216 N.C. 565, 5 S.E.2d 830 (1939). *See* Jenkins v. Coombs, 21 N.C. App. 683, 205 S.E.2d 728 (1974), which holds that a paper writing executed contemporaneously by a grantee, whereby the grantee stated, "If I, or my heirs or assigns, decide to sell the Jenkins Homeplace in Northampton County, I will give Andrew T. Jenkins (grantor), Robert D. Jenkins, and Clyde W. Jenkins, first chance to buy the above said property," was void as an unlawful restraint upon alienation. The *Jenkins* case quoted from Hardy v. Galloway, 111 N.C. 519, 15 S.E. 890 (1892), with approval. It should be noted that in neither case was there a statement of a fixed price for the repurchase of the land nor a time specified for performance of the provision.

That restraints are void where alienation is restricted to a single class, *see* Crockett v. First Fed. Sav. & Loan Ass'n, 289 N.C. 260, 224 S.E.2d 580 (1976).

87. *See* SIMES & SMITH, THE LAW OF FUTURE INTERESTS § 1154 (1956). *But see* Hardy v. Galloway, 111 N.C. 519, 15 S.E. 890 (1892). Annot., 40 A.L.R.3d 943 (1971).

limited as to time and certain as to duration, is void as an invalid restraint on alienation.[88] The restrictive covenant involved read:

> If any future owner of lands herein described shall desire to sell the lands owned by him, he shall offer the parties of the first part the option to repurchase said property at a price no higher than the lowest price he is willing to accept from any other purchaser. Parties of the first part agree to exercise said option or to reject same in writing within 14 days of said offer. This covenant shall be binding on the parties of the first part and their heirs, successors, administrators, and executors or assigns for as long as W. Osmond Smith, Jr. shall live and for 20 years from the date of his death unless sooner rescinded.[89]

The court reaffirmed what it called the longstanding principles of *Hardy v. Galloway*[90] and interpreted that case " ... to establish for this State the sound policy that a grant of the estate in fee vests the owner with the inseparable and unlimited right of free alienation. No restraint, however, slight, whether direct or indirect, express or implied, may be imposed to frustrate or diminish that right." [91]

Similarly, a restriction to the effect that the grantee or devisee is not to convey the land except with consent of some other person is void.[92] And a restriction in a deed conveying a fee which purports to prevent the land from being subject to the debts of the grantee is void as being incompatible with the grant of a fee simple estate therein.[93]

---

88. Smith v. Mitchell, 44 N.C. App. 474, 261 S.E.2d 231 (1980) citing this section (§ 346) in the original work.

89. *Id.*

90. 111 N.C. 519, 15 S.E. 890 (1892).

91. Smith v. Mitchell, 44 N.C. App. 474, 261 S.E.2d 231 (1980).

92. Schwren v. Fall, 170 N.C. 251, 87 S.E. 49 (1916). *But see* Crockett v. First Fed. Sav. & Loan Ass'n, 289 N.C. 620, 224 S.E.2d 580 (1976), which held valid a provision in a deed of trust which specified that the principal sum of the mortgage indebtedness plus interest should become due and payable at the option of the lender in the event the mortgaged property was conveyed without the written assent of the lender. It was contended that such provision was an unlawful restraint on alienation since the lender could refuse his assent to the borrower's conveyance unless the borrower's purchaser would agree to pay a higher interest than that provided for in the original mortgage loan. The Supreme Court of North Carolina held that a mortgage deed of trust containing a "due-on-sale clause" was valid. A lender secured by a mortgage deed of trust can specify that upon a sale of the mortgaged property without the written assent of the lender the entire mortgage debt and interest shall become due and payable at the option of the lender. That the mortgage-lender can require a purchaser of the mortgaged property to agree to pay an increased rate of interest as a condition precedent to the lender's granting its assent to a transfer of the security property is not deemed unreasonable or invalid as a restraint on alienation.

93. Ricks v. Pope, 129 N.C. 52, 39 S.E. 638 (1901); Mizell v. Bazemore, 194 N.C. 324, 139 S.E. 453 (1927); TIFFANY, REAL PROPERTY § 830 (abr. ed. 1940).

(c) *Same — Life estates.* Any restriction in a deed or will which attempts to restrict the alienation of a life estate, prohibiting either voluntary or involuntray conveyance of the life estate, or designed to prevent the life tenant's creditors from reaching the life tenant's interest to satisfy his debts, is void in North Carolina.[94] While most jurisdictions will give effect to a forfeiture restriction which provides that a life estate will be terminated if it is sold or executed upon by the life tenant's creditors,[95] it appears in North Carolina that a condition or limitation with respect to a life tenancy which purports to prohibit its transfer, or which attempts to prevent its being reached by judgment to satisfy the life tenant's debts, is invalid.[96]

(d) *Same — Leasehold estates.* Restrictive covenants which provide that lessees' interests under leasehold estates shall not be aliened are held to be valid everywhere.[97]

(e) *Same — Restrictions on the power to partition.* A provision in a deed or will which provides that the land shall not be partitioned is valid, if for a reasonable time.[98] Of course, if the restriction against partition purports to last for a period in excess of the period of the rule against perpetuities, beyond the period of a life or lives in being at the effective date of the instrument and twenty-one years, it would probably be void.[99]

---

94. Wool v. Fleetwood, 136 N.C. 460, 48 S.E. 785 (1904); Pilley v. Sullivan, 182 N.C. 493, 109 S.E. 359 (1921); Mizell v. Bazemore, 194 N.C. 324, 139 S.E. 453 (1927); Crockett v. First Fed. Sav. & Loan Ass'n, 289 N.C. 620, 224 S.E.2d 580 (1976).
95. SIMES & SMITH, THE LAW OF FUTURE INTERESTS § 1157 (1956).
96. Mizell v. Bazemore, 194 N.C. 324, 139 S.E. 453 (1927).
97. SIMES & SMITH, THE LAW OF FUTURE INTERESTS § 1157 (1956). *See* Sanders v. Tropicana, 31 N.C. App. 276, 229 S.E.2d 304 (1976), which holds that a cooperative apartment may impose reasonable restraints prohibiting alienation of the cooperative's stock and prohibiting assignment of a tenant-shareholder's lease without the written consent of a majority of the cooperative's board of directors under N.C. GEN. STAT. § 54-120. The *Sanders* case cites and quotes with approval the case of Weisner v. 791 Park Ave. Corp., 6 N.Y.2d 426, 190 N.Y.S.2d 70, 160 N.E.2d 720 (1959), to the effect that absent a violation of statutory standards prohibiting discrimination because of race, color, religion, national origin or ancestry, under the cooperative plan of organization in effect "there is no reason why the owners of the cooperative apartment house could not decide for themselves, with whom they wished to share their elevators, their common halls and facilities, their stockholders' meetings, their management problems and responsibilities, and their homes." In the *Sanders* case the North Carolina Court of Appeals, in a case of first impression, held that the refusal of the board of directors of a cooperative apartment to approve the sale of stock and an assignment of a tenant-shareholder's proprietary lease to a party who indicated that he would sublease before taking occupancy was not arbitrary or capricious, but was in line with the social purposes of the cooperative apartment to limit apartment occupancy to owners.
98. Green v. Stadiem, 198 N.C. 445, 152 S.E. 398 (1930); Anderson v. Edwards, 239 N.C. 510, 80 S.E.2d 260 (1954). *But see dictum* statement of Copeland, J. in Crockett v. First Fed. Sav. & Loan Ass'n, 289 N.C. 620, 224 S.E.2d 580 (1976), in which it is stated that restraints against partition or division are void without differentiating between restraints against partitions or division for a reasonable time and absolute restraints.
99. 2 RESTATEMENT OF PROPERTY § 173 (1936).

§ 391. Conditions and Restrictions in Restraint of Marriage.

Since conditions subsequent and restrictive covenants are void if they are contrary to law, conditions and restrictions in direct restraint of marriage are generally held void because the policy of the law encourages marriages.[100] Thus if a conveyance or devise to a person is on a condition that his estate will terminate if he marries, it is in general restraint of marriage and the condition is void.[101] Even if there is no positive prohibition against marriage, if the condition operates to occasion a probable prohibition, or is so rigid as to cause a virtual restraint, it is void.[102] Any restraint on marriage that is without limitation as to time or person will be disregarded as void.[103]

It has been held, however, that a condition which operates only as a partial restraint of marriage, as incidental to another lawful purpose, is not illegal or void.[104] For instance, suppose a grantor or devisor desires to make a conveyance to his widow only "so long as she remains my widow," meaning that if she remarries it is the grantor's desire that her second husband shall then support her, and provides that upon her remarriage the subject of the deed or gift is to go to someone else, perhaps the grantor's children. In such case, it has been held that the condition is not invalid. The rule has developed that a restraint on marriage which is merely incidental to another lawful purpose and which is no more extensive in time or more burdensome in its nature than is reasonably necessary for the proper fulfillment of such purpose, is not unlawful. There are numerous recognitions of estates "during widowhood" or "so long as she shall remain unmarried." [105] The cases make no distinction between the widow and the widower, and hold that the wife has the same right as the husband to make her gift conditional upon the husband remaining single.[106] As stated in the case of *In re Miller's Will*,[107] "If it is apparent from the will that he [testator] did not intend to prevent a marriage or to condemn the legatee to a life of celibacy, but that he intended solely to provide for her support while unmarried, and that as soon as she was in a position to be supported by her husband, he desired the provision to cease and the property to be devoted others, it is valid." The desire to take

---

100. 1 MORDECAI, LAW LECTURES 557 (1916).
101. Gard v. Mason, 169 N.C. 507, 86 S.E. 302 (1915). The invalid provision is disregarded, making the grant indefeasible.
102. Watts v. Griffin, 137 N.C. 572, 50 S.E. 218 (1905).
103. *In re* Miller's Will, 159 N.C. 123, 74 S.E. 888 (1912).
104. RESTATEMENT OF CONTRACTS § 581 (1932); LEE, NORTH CAROLINA FAMILY LAW § 7 (1963). *See, e.g., In re* Miller's Will, 159 N.C. 123, 74 S.E. 888 (1912).
105. Beddard v. Harrington, 124 N.C. 51, 32 S.E. 377 (1899); *In re* Miller's Will, 159 N.C. 123, 74 S.E. 888 (1912); Bryan v. Harper, 177 N.C. 308, 98 S.E. 822 (1919); Blackwood v. Blackwood, 237 N.C. 726, 76 S.E.2d 122 (1953).
106. Bryan v. Harper, 177 N.C. 308, 98 S.E. 822 (1919).
107. 159 N.C. 123, 74 S.E. 888 (1912).

care of the widow in her widowhood only, to protect her only during her need, and then to care for the children of the testator's marriage after his widow has remarried, is deemed the primary objective of the testator to which the partial restraint of marriage is only a reasonable incident.

A grant to one's child on a condition subsequent that he shall not marry before he reaches his majority should be held valid.[108] It is reasoned that a grantor parent has a legitimate objective in mind when he makes a grant to his child conditioned upon his not making a rash and improvident marriage because of his youth and inexperience. Likewise, the Supreme Court of North Carolina has held that a devise is valid which leaves property to the testator's widow, contingent upon her remaining unmarried until their youngest child reaches twenty-one years of age.[109] In determining whether a condition in partial restraint of marriage is valid, the court's questions are: What was the purpose of the gift? What did the grantor or devisor intend to accomplish? If his purpose was to accomplish a legitimate objective, such as to provide support for a certain length of time when such support was needed, or to protect minors from their own discretion and/or to insure their support, and not to restrain marriage, the courts will uphold reasonable partial restraints of marriage.[110]

Since no contract in restraint of marriage will be enforced,[111] it would seem that no "promissory" or "disabling" restrictive covenant, as distinguished from the foregoing examples of reasonable partial "forfeiture" conditions, in restraint of marriage, would be enforceable under any circumstance.[112]

Article II. Public Restrictions on the Use of Lands

Division 1. Planning and Zoning

§ 392. Planning and Zoning Generally.

As elsewhere in the United States the municipalities of North Carolina have developed and adopted master plans for the systematic and orderly development of the communities of the State. For the purpose of promoting the common interest, the State has adopted laws providing for the systematic growth and development of the communities of the future with particular respect to the location of future major street systems,

---

108. *See* Watts v. Griffin, 137 N.C. 572, 578, 50 S.E. 218 (1905).
109. Bryan v. Harper, 177 N.C. 308, 98 S.E. 822 (1919).
110. *Id.*
111. RESTATEMENT OF CONTRACTS § 581 (1932).
112. For discussion of provisions generally in restraint of marriage appearing in wills and deeds, in addition to the cases cited above, *see* LEE, NORTH CAROLINA FAMILY LAW § 7, n. 85, citing Munroe v. Hall, 97 N.C. 206, 1 S.E. 651 (1887); Griffin v. Doggett, 199 N.C. 706, 155 S.E. 605 (1930); Note, 37 N.C.L. REV. 494 (1959); Annot., 122 A.L.R. 7-132 (1939).

transportation systems, parks, recreational areas, industrial and commercial undertakings and residential developments, the creation and preservation of civic beauty, the preservation of historic districts, public convenience and the like. The zoning ordinance was invented to implement and preserve the purposes of this planning with regard not only to the present but with a view to the orderly maximum beneficial use of lands not yet developed.

§ 393. Zoning Ordinances Generally.

Zoning ordinances are ordinances designed to enable the governments of municipal corporations (and sometimes counties) to divide the municipality into districts or zones for the purpose of regulating the uses of each parcel of land in the municipality. By the passage of such an ordinance, municipal authorities may properly allocate and regulate business in one section of a town or city, restrict other lands to residential uses only, and provide that industrial development shall be limited to still other sections.

§ 394. Types of Zones.

The earliest zoning ordinances simply divided the municipality into three districts or zones; residential, commercial and industrial. Uses permitted in the respective zones were cumulative and many ordinances still operate in this manner. While only residences were allowed in residential districts, both stores and residences were allowed in commercial zones, and all types of uses, including residences, stores and manufacturing were allowed in industrial zones. Today modern comprehensive zoning ordinances are more sophisticated and usually create a greater number of use classifications. Residential districts are no longer simply residential but are often further classified into "single family districts," "multifamily zones," "apartment zones," or in some cases may be further restricted for "walk up" or "high rise" (elevator building) zones. Commercial districts may be divided into retail zones or wholesale zones. Industrial zones may be divided so as to permit light manufacturing in some districts and heavy manufacturing in others. Zoning ordinances are becoming more and more complex as they attempt to do more and more. For instance, while initial zoning ordinances only attempted to keep commercial and manufacturing uses out of residential zones, not bothering to keep residences out of commercial and industrial zones, modern ordinances in some states today are attempting to keep residences out of commercial and industrial zones.[113]

---

113. *E.g., see* People *ex rel.* Skokie Town House Builders, Inc. v. Village of Morton Grove, 16 Ill. 2d 183, 157 N.E.2d 33 (1959). Initial zoning ordinances were framed so as to incorporate the "progressively less restrictive" theory. Under this concept less intensive uses such

§ 395. The Validity of Zoning Ordinances; the Police Power Source.

The constitutional basis and validity of every zoning ordinance rests upon the police power.[114] This is "that power which inheres in the legislature to make, ordain and establish all manner of reasonable regulations and laws whereby to preserve the peace and order of society and the safety of its members, and to prescribe the mode and manner in which everyone may use and enjoy that which is his own as not to preclude the corresponding use and enjoyment of their own use by others."[115] The core of the police power concept is the promotion of public health, safety, welfare and morals of the community.[116] Legislation purporting to be pursuant to the police power must be to protect or to promote these broad general concepts and the means adopted by the legislation must be neither unreasonable, arbitrary, discriminatory nor confiscatory in order to be valid.[117] While

---

as residences and light commerical uses have been allowed to continue without restriction in industrial and other districts zoned for very intensive uses. While there are apparently no cases in North Carolina on the point, the trend in modern zoning today is to exclude residences from industrial districts. This modern tendency in legislation can be sustained as a valid exercise of the police power to prevent urban blight, to prevent the intermixing of building types which so often frustrates the process of self-renewal and results in deteriorating neighborhoods. In addition, the patterns of utilities and streets for residential areas are different from those required for industrial areas. The construction of residences on lands that would otherwise be available for industrial uses makes the packaging and acquisition of industrial lands more difficult and results in fragmentation of industrial areas. Furthermore, if industrial uses are objectionable near residential developments because of smoke, fumes, fire or health hazards, the reverse is equally true. See Mott & Wehrly, *The Prohibition of Residential Development in Industrial Districts*, URBAN LAND INST. TECH. BULL. NO. 10 (Nov. 1948). It should be stated, however, that the prohibition of residences from industrial districts has not been generally sustained. See Katobimar Realty Co. v. Webster, 118 A.2d 824, 20 N.J. 114 (1955).

114. Euclid v. Ambler Realty Co., 272 U.S. 365, 47 S. Ct. 114, 71 L. Ed. 303 (1926); Elizabeth City v. Aydlett, 201 N.C. 602, 161 S.E. 78 (1931); Schloss v. Jamison, 262 N.C. 108, 136 S.E.2d 691 (1964); State v. Joyner, 23 N.C. App. 27, 208 S.E.2d 233 (1974), *aff'd*, 286 N.C. 366, 211 S.E.2d 320 (1975).

115. COOLEY, PRINCIPLES OF CONSTITUTIONAL LAW 338 (1898).

116. The "police power" should be distinguished from the concept of "eminent domain." In the former, as related to land use controls, the governmental entity regulates the use of property or impairs the owner's rights in it because an unregulated usage would be detrimental to the public interest. "Eminent domain," however, takes the property from the owner for use of the public for public purposes. Under the latter concept, compensation must be given to the owner for property taken while under the police power no payment is made to the landowner whose usage of his land is restricted because compensation is assumed for such interference or restraint in that the restrained owner shares in the advantages derived from the regulation along with other members of society.

117. The burden of proof that there is no rational connection between an ordinance and a police power objective is on the individual attacking the ordinance rather than the municipality. Furthermore, the inclusion of a reasonable margin to insure enforcement will not invalidate the ordinance. See In re Appeal of Parker, 214 N.C. 51, 197 S.E. 706 (1938), *appeal dismissed sub nom.*, Parker v. City of Greensboro, 305 U.S. 568, 59 S. Ct. 150, 83 L. Ed. 358 (1938). Courts will resolve the issue in favor of the validity of a zoning ordinance and will not substitute their judgment for that of the legislative body where debatable

municipal zoning ordinances are presumed to be valid, they may be shown to be unreasonable, arbitrary, discriminatory or confiscatory by clear evidence.[118] When zoning regulations are adopted in the proper exercise of the police power, any resultant loss is misfortune which nearby property owners must suffer as members of society.[119] And although the mere fact that a zoning ordinance seriously depreciates the value of realty is not enough, standing alone, to establish invalidity of the ordinance; [120] a zoning ordinance will be held invalid if it has the effect of completely depriving an owner of the beneficial use of his property by precluding all practical uses or the only use to which it is reasonably adapted.[121] Although it has been held that a municipality has no inherent power to zone its territory and restrict to specified purposes the use of private property in each such zone, such power has been delegated to the cities and incorporated towns of North Carolina by its General Assembly.[122] The State enabling act is the key to zoning authority and any municipal ordinance which exceeds the municipality's grant of power in the enabling act is void. [123]

North Carolina General Statute, § 160A-381 provides:

> For the purpose of promoting health, safety, morals or the general welfare of the community, any city is hereby empowered to regulate and restrict the height, number of stories and size of buildings and other structures, the percentage of lots that may be occupied, the size of yards, courts and other open spaces, the density of population, and the location and use of buildings, structures and land for trade, indus-

---

divergent conclusions may be reasonably reached as to whether the ordinance is unreasonable, arbitrary or discriminatory. If, however, it is clearly so, or confiscatory in its application to particular land, it will be held to be unconstitutional. Helms v. Charlotte, 255 N.C. 647, 122 S.E.2d 817, 96 A.L.R.2d 439 (1962); Schloss v. Jamison, 262 N.C. 108, 136 S.E.2d 691 (1964).

See also A-S-P Associates v. City of Raleigh, 298 N.C. 207, 258 S.E.2d 444 (1979); Orange County v. Heath, 278 N.C. 688, 180 S.E.2d 810 (1971); Allgood v. Town of Tarboro, 281 N.C. 430, 189 S.E.2d 255 (1972).

118. Kinney v. Sutton, 230 N.C. 404, 53 S.E.2d 306 (1949); Helms v. City of Charlotte, 255 N.C. 647, 122 S.E.2d 817, 96 A.L.R.2d 439 (1962); Durham County v. Addison, 262 N.C. 280, 136 S.E.2d 600 (1964); Elizabeth City v. Aydlett, 201 N.C. 602, 161 S.E. 78 (1931).

119. Allgood v. Town of Tarboro, 281 N.C. 430, 189 S.E.2d 255 (1972) (case involving rezoning of residential district to commercial shopping district).

120. Zopfi v. City of Wilmington, 273 N.C. 430, 160 S.E.2d 325 (1968); Michael v. Guilford County, 269 N.C. 515, 153 S.E.2d 106 (1967); Roberson's Beverages, Inc. v. City of New Bern, 6 N.C. App. 632, 171 S.E.2d 4 (1969).

121. Helms v. Charlotte, 255 N.C. 647, 122 S.E.2d 817 (1961); Roberson's Beverages, Inc. v. City of New Bern, 6 N.C. App. 632, 171 S.E.2d 4 (1969).

122. The General Assembly of North Carolina adopted a new chapter 160A of N.C. Gen. Stat. in 1971. The zoning statutes relative to municipalities now appear in N.C. Gen. Stat. §§ 160A-381 through 160A-392. The General Assembly adopted a new chapter 153A of N.C. Gen. Stat. in 1973. The zoning statutes relative to counties now appear in N.C. Gen. Stat. §§ 153A-340 through 153A-347.

123. Schloss v. Jamison, 262 N.C. 108, 136 S.E.2d 691 (1964); Sellers v. City of Asheville, 33 N.C. App. 544, 236 S.E.2d 283 (1977).

try, residence or other purposes. These regulations may provide that a board of adjustment may determine and vary their application in harmony with their general purpose and intent and in accordance with general or specific rules therein contained. The regulations may also provide that the board of adjustment or the city council may issue special use permits or conditional use permits in the classes of cases or situations and in accordance with the principles, conditions, safeguards, and procedures specified therein and may impose reasonable and appropriate conditions and safeguards upon these permits. Where appropriate, such conditions may include requirements that street and utility rights-of-way be dedicated to the public and that provision be made of recreational space and facilities.

North Carolina General Statutes, § 160A-382 provides:

> For any or all these purposes, the city may divide its territorial jurisdiction into districts of any number, shape, and area that may be deemed best suited to carry out the purposes of this Article; and within those districts it may regulate and restrict the erection, construction, reconstruction, alteration, repair or use of buildings, structures, or land. All regulations shall be uniform for each class or kind of building throughout each district, but the regulations in one district may differ from those in other districts.[124]

North Carolina General Statutes, § 160A-383 provides:

> Zoning regulations shall be made in accordance with a comprehensive plan and designed to lessen congestion in the streets; to secure safety from fire, panic and other dangers; to promote health and the general welfare; to provide adequate light and air; to prevent the overcrowding of land; to avoid undue concentration of population; and to facilitate the adequate provision of transportation, water, sewerage, schools, parks, and other public requirements. The regulations shall be made with reasonable consideration, among other things, as to the character of the district and its peculiar suitability for particular uses, and with a view to conserving the value of buildings and encouraging the most appropriate use of land throughout such city.

§ 396. Historical Preservation Zoning; Constitutionality.

In conformity with a national concern for the preservation of historically significant districts, municipal governing bodies in North Carolina have been delegated the power to designate one or more historic districts

---

124. *See* Walker v. Town of Elkin, 254 N.C. 85, 118 S.E.2d 1 (1961), that restrictions on use must be uniform in all areas in defined class or district under zoning ordinance, even though various areas in the same class might not be contiguous. *See* Berger v. Smith, 156 N.C. 323, 72 S.E. 376 (1911). An ordinance which prohibits the erection of certain types of buildings without first obtaining the consent of members of the board of aldermen is void as arbitrary and unconstitutional as vesting arbitrary powers without prescribing a uniform rule of action. Bizzell v. Board of Aldermen, 192 N.C. 348, 135 S.E. 50, 49 A.L.R. 755 (1926).

§ 396 REAL ESTATE LAW IN NORTH CAROLINA § 396

as part of their general zoning ordinances.[125] In a case of first impression in North Carolina, the Supreme Court recently upheld the validity of historic district preservation zoning and sustained two ordinances passed by the City of Raleigh creating a 98 acre, overlay historic district in that city's Oakwood neighborhood against a battery of constitutional and legal challenges.[126] This zoning decision constitutes an important landmark in North Carolina property law because the decision contains a general constitutional stamp of approval on the concept of historic preservation zoning.

The Court ruled that a historic preservation ordinance passed in conformity with state enabling legislation constitutes a valid exercise of the police power. Distinguishing regulation for purely aesthetic purposes, the Court held that "the police power encompasses the right to control the exterior appearance of private property when the object of such control is the preservation of the State's legacy of historically significant structures."[127] It went on to uphold the means chosen to implement the legislative objective of historic preservation holding that the comprehensive regulation of the "construction, moving of buildings, structures, appurtenant fixtures, or outdoor advertising signs in the historic district which would be incongruous with the historic aspects of the district" was the only feasible method of maintaining the historical integrity of an entire district.[128]

Finally, the Court rejected the following contentions: that the ordinance resulted in an improper delegation of legislative power to a municipal governing authority,[129] that the setting of boundaries of the district denied the plaintiff property owner equal protection of the laws,[130] that the categorization of the plaintiff's property as part of a historic district constituted spot zoning,[131] and that certain statutory

---

125. N.C. GEN. STAT. § 160A-395.

126. A-S-P Associates v. City of Raleigh, 298 N.C. 207, 258 S.E.2d 444 (1979). The question of the constitutionality of historic district preservation was a matter of first impression for the Court.

127. *Id.* The court cited the following cases from other jurisdictions upholding the validity of use of the police power to regulate private property in the interest of historic preservation: Maher v. City of New Orleans, 516 F.2d 1051 (5th Cir. 1975); Bohannan v. City of San Diego, 31 Cal. App. 3d 416, 106 Cal. Rptr. 333 (1973); Figarsky v. Historic District Comm., 171 Conn. 198, 368 A.2d 163 (1976); Rebman v. City of Springfield, 111 Ill. App. 2d 430, 250 N.E.2d 282 (1969); City of New Orleans v. Levy, 223 La. 14, 64 So. 2d 798 (1953); Opinion of the Justices, 333 Mass. 773, 128 N.E.2d 557 (1955); Opinion of the Justices, 333 Mass. 783, 128 N.E.2d 563 (1955); and City of Santa Fe v. Gamble-Skogmo, Inc., 73 N.M. 410, 389 P.2d 13 (1964).

128. *Id.*
129. *Id.*
130. *Id.*
131. *Id.*

requirements of the historic preservation enabling legislation were not met by the City of Raleigh.[132]

§ 397. Operation of Zoning Ordinances.

(a) *Planning agency.* As noted, the power of a municipality to enact zoning ordinances has been expressly granted by statute. The enabling act and zoning ordinance provide for the creation or designation of a planning agency. The planning agency [133] shall prepare a zoning plan, including both the full text of a zoning ordinance and maps showing proposed district boundaries, and upon its completion shall certify the plan to the city council. The planning agency does not itself *enact* the zoning ordinance but merely prepares it and submits it to the city council, which may adopt the ordinance after the appropriate hearings as prescribed by the statutes.[134]

(b) *The board of adjustment.* To make the zoning ordinance more flexible and to prevent its causing practical difficulties and unnecessary hardships to certain individuals' property by a strict application of the ordinance to the letter, the enabling statutes which permit zoning in municipalities provide for the appointment of a "board of adjustment" by the legislative body of the municipality.[135] The provision for appointment of such a board, composed of five appointees who are empowered to exercise quasi-judicial functions, is a recognition that the zoning ordinance in question may be unreasonable in certain situations as related to particular land, requiring some adjustment in order to prevent injustice in certain circumstances. For the purpose of effecting a just result, the board

---

132. *Id. See generally* Comment, *Historic Preservation Cases: A Collection*, 12 WAKE FOREST L. REV. 227 (1976); Beckwith, *Developments in the Law of Historic Preservation and a Reflection on Liberty*, 12 WAKE FOREST L. REV. 93, 95 n.18 (1976); Wilson & Winkler, *The Response of State Legislation to Historic Preservation*, 36 LAW & CONTEMP. PROB. 329 (1971).

133. Frequently called "planning board," "planning commission," "zoning board" or "zoning commission." The planning agency (board) has no legislative, judicial or quasi-judicial power. Its recommendations do not restrict or otherwise affect the legislative power of the city council. Allred v. City of Raleigh, 277 N.C. 530, 178 S.E.2d 432 (1971).

134. N.C. GEN. STAT. § 160A-387 provides:

In order to exercise the powers conferred by this Part, a city council shall create or designate a planning agency under the provisions of this Part or of a special act of the General Assembly. The planning agency shall prepare a zoning plan, including both the full text of a zoning ordinance and maps showing proposed district boundaries. The planning agency may hold public hearings in the course of preparing the plan. Upon completion, the planning agency shall certify the plan to the city council. The city council shall not hold its required public hearing or take action until it has received a certified plan from the planning agency. Following its required public hearing, the city council may refer the plan back to the planning agency for any further recommendations that the agency may wish to make prior to final action by the city council in adopting, modifying and adopting, or rejecting the ordinance.

135. N.C. GEN. STAT. § 160A-388.

of adjustment shall have the power to correct errors or abuse in administration of the zoning enforcement officer. Such board shall have the power to consider certain cases where the municipal governing board has given it power to grant permits if specified conditions are fulfilled. In addition, the board of adjustment may grant relief to a landowner when hardship results from strict application of the ordinance's terms.[136] For instance, in the latter situation, an aggrieved property owner who feels that his land will suffer an unnecessary particular hardship if the zoning law is strictly enforced as against his land may apply to the board of adjustment for a "variance" whereby he will be entitled to "vary" the use of his land to some extent from the strict letter of the zoning ordinance. The concept of the board of adjustment is a recognition that in particular cases the rigors of generally drawn zoning regulations need to be ameliorated to prevent extreme and unreasonable hardship which may result from a slavish adherence to the precise letter of the regulations. In a given case where little or no public good will result, because of the situation of particular land, but severe and undue hardship will result to the landowner if the ordinance is literally enforced, if the board of adjustment finds these to be the facts, it may waive strict enforcement of the ordinance.[137]

The provision for "variances" by the board of adjustment provides an important "safety valve" for zoning ordinances whereby the comprehensive plan of a particular ordinance can be saved by making certain exceptions from the ordinance's application. Otherwise, in cases of severe hardships, unless there is some way to vary the strict terms of the ordinance, it might be held invalid *in toto* as being unreasonable when weighed against the public benefit derived. The power to make selective variances permits the board to preserve a substantial property right of the landowner and at the same time it will not subvert the purposes of the zoning ordinance or be detrimental to the public welfare. The variance concept gives to the law of zoning an elasticity in its administration. The lack of such elasticity for exceptional circumstances would result in practical difficulties or unnecessary hardship in many cases and might otherwise result in having a whole ordinance held to be unconstitutional.

---

136. In Lee v. Board of Adjustment, 226 N.C. 107, 37 S.E.2d 128 (1946), the Supreme Court of North Carolina states that the granting of variances is the main function of the board of adjustment. *See also* Zopfi v. City of Wilmington, 273 N.C. 430, 160 S.E.2d 282 (1968).

137. For instance, if sometimes a lot is so small or so peculiarly shaped that the owner would have great difficulty in complying with the yard requirements and yet constructing a suitable building. Or perhaps his lot is located in a cluster of nonconforming uses which will prevent the owner from securing any reasonable return from his land if he is compelled to comply strictly with the zoning ordinance (as where a lot in a residential zone is surrounded by nonconforming business structures). When the board grants exemption from harsh provisions, it is "granting a variance." *See* GREEN, ZONING IN NORTH CAROLINA (Inst. of Gov't Pub., Univ. of N.C.) 339 (1952).

In order for a variance to be supported, the petitioning landowner must show to the board of adjustment that strict application of the zoning ordinance will result in an unnecessary hardship peculiar to the owner; that granting the variance will not be contrary to the public interest or be contrary to the spirit and purposes of the ordinance, and that by granting the variance substantial justice will be done.[138] The board of adjustment is not unlimited in its power, however, to grant variances. It simply has the power to "determine and vary" the application of the terms of a zoning ordinance with the power to make only such variations and modifications as are in harmony with the general purposes and intent of the ordinance and which do no violence to its spirit.[139]

(c) *Amendments and rezoning; "spot zoning."* The zoning enabling act provides that zoning ordinances may be amended from time to time by the legislative body of the municipality.[140] Any amendment, just like the original ordinance, must be made in accordance with the enabling legisla-

---

138. Five general rules have been developed to show whether there are "practical difficulties or unnecessary hardships" within the meaning of N.C. GEN. STAT. § 160A-388. Courts have required the applicant for a variance to show (a) that if he complies with the provisions of the ordinance, he can secure no reasonable return from, or make no reasonable use of, his property; (b) that the hardship results from the application of the ordinance to his property; (c) that the hardship of which he complains is suffered by the property directly, and not merely by others; (d) that the hardship is not the result of his own actions; and (e) that the hardship is peculiar to the property of the applicant. The burden of proving that these exist is on the applicant. *See* GREEN, ZONING IN NORTH CAROLINA (Inst. of Gov't Pub., Univ. of N.C.) 343 (1952).

139. In the exercise of its discretion, the board of adjustment is not left free to make any determination whatever that appeals to its sense of justice. It must abide by and comply with the rules of conduct provided by its charter — the local ordinance enacted in accord with and by permission of the State zoning law. *See* Lee v. Board of Adjustment, 226 N.C. 107, 37 S.E.2d 128 (1946). The mere deprivation of better earnings by means of a nonconforming use is not an unnecessary hardship within the meaning of the law. The hardship that is required to be shown is that the landowner is prevented from making *any* reasonable use of his property by reason of the application of the ordinance strictly. GREEN, ZONING IN NORTH CAROLINA (Inst., of Gov't Pub., Univ. of N.C.) 339 (1952). *See In re* Markham, 259 N.C. 566, 131 S.E.2d 329, *cert. denied,* 84 S. Ct. 332 (1963), to effect that the board of adjustment's power is *"quasi-judicial."*

140. N.C. GEN. STAT. § 160A-385. The statute provides:

§ **160A-385. Changes.** — Zoning regulations and restrictions and zone boundaries may from time to time be amended, supplemented, changed, modified or repealed. In case, however, of a protest against such change, signed by the owners of twenty percent (20%) or more either of the area of the lots included in a proposed change, or of those immediately adjacent thereto either in the rear thereof or on either side thereof, extending 100 feet therefrom, or of those directly opposite thereto extending 100 feet from the street frontage of the opposite lots, an amendment shall not become effective except by favorable vote of three fourths of all the members of the city council.

See Davis v. Zoning Board of Adjustment, 41 N.C. App. 579, 255 S.E.2d 444 (1979) dismissing an appeal from a county board of adjustment where the questions presented were rendered moot by amendments to the zoning ordinance.

tion [141] and must not contravene constitutional limitations on the zoning power.[142] Amendments usually come about as a result of some significant error in the original zoning plan or because of some substantial change in a zoned community after adoption of the ordinance which warrants an alteration in the zoning ordinance. The police power is not static and the legislative body can make any change in the zoning ordinance that it could have written into it initially, provided that it does not act arbitrarily and capriciously but seeks only to promote in a rational way the public health, safety, morals and general welfare.[143] Where conditions existing at the time of a proposed change are such as would have originally justified the proposed alteration in the zoning plan, the legislative body has the power to act.[144]

One of the potential abuses of the amending power and one which is subject to being struck down by the courts is the "spot zoning" amendment whereby a small tract or plot of land is rezoned for some purpose

---

141. The statutory requirements relating to notice and hearings that must be given prior to the adoption or amendment of any zoning ordinance are set out in N.C. GEN. STAT. § 160A-364.

There must be compliance with the statutory requirements of notice and public hearing in order to adopt or amend a zoning ordinance. A rezoning ordinance adopted by a municipal governing body without compliance with the enabling statute's notice provisions is invalid and ineffective. Keiger v. Board of Adjustment, 281 N.C. 715, 190 S.E.2d 175 (1972). *See also* Orange County v. Heath, 278 N.C. 688, 180 S.E.2d 610 (1971). If the ordinance or amendment as finally adopted contains alterations substantially different (amounting to a new proposal) from those originally advertised and heard, there must be additional notice and opportunity for additional hearing before the ordinance may be enacted or amended. No further notice or hearing is required after a properly advertised and properly conducted public hearing when the alteration of the initial proposal is insubstantial. Moreover, additional notice and public hearing will not be required when the initial notice is broad enough to indicate that there is a possibility of substantial change and substantial changes are made fundamentally similar to those contained in the initial notice of hearing, provided such changes result from objections, debate and discussion at the properly noticed initial hearing. Heaton v. City of Charlotte, 277 N.C. 506, 178 S.E.2d 352 (1971). *See also* Walker v. Elkin, 254 N.C. 85, 118 S.E.2d 1 (1961); Freeland v. Orange County, 273 N.C. 452, 160 S.E.2d 282 (1968); Kass v. Hedgepeth, 226 N.C. 405, 38 S.E.2d 164 (1946).

142. Allgood v. Town of Tarboro, 281 N.C. 430, 189 S.E.2d 255 (1972); Walker v. Elkin, 254 N.C. 85, 118 S.E.2d 1 (1961).

143. *Id.* Zopfi v. City of Wilmington, 273 N.C. 430, 160 S.E.2d 325 (1968); Blades v. City of Raleigh, 280 N.C. 533, 187 S.E.2d 35 (1972).

144. Walker v. Elkin, 254 N.C. 85, 118 S.E.2d 1 (1961); Elizabeth City v. Aydlett, 201 N.C. 602, 161 S.E. 78 (1931); Eggebeen v. Sonnenburg, 239 Wis. 213, 1 N.W.2d 84, 138 A.L.R. 495 (1941). *Accord,* Allgood v. Town of Tarboro, 281 N.C. 430, 189 S.E.2d 255 (1972). In the *Allgood* case, the Supreme Court of North Carolina held that the annexation of an area to the city, construction of a new school, installation of water and sewer service in the area and the widening and construction of existing and new highways, and the construction of twenty-four multiple family apartment units on adjoining property since the adoption of an original zoning ordinance furnished the town council with reasonable grounds and plausible basis for adopting an amendment which rezoned a twenty-five acre tract from a residential to a community shopping district.

inconsistent with the uses for which the surrounding area is zoned under a comprehensive plan. If such an amendment were permitted it would result in small "flecks" or "islands" of business establishments in otherwise residential districts, violating the requirement of the State enabling act that zoning regulations "shall be made in accordance with a comprehensive plan" and also violating the due process clauses of the State and federal constitutions in that they are transparently discriminatory. With respect to amendments to zoning ordinances, property owners have the right to rely on the rule of law that a classification made by an ordinance will not be changed unless a change is required for the public good — that a change will not be made merely to accommodate by special treatment some one or more landowners at the expense of their less fortunate neighbors.[145] No amendment should be made to accommodate private interests so as to be detrimental to the welfare of other property owners in the same district nor should a postage stamp size district be set up simply to benefit some private interest. Every amendment, just as every original zoning ordinance, should have a demonstrable relationship to the police power objectives of public health, safety, morals or general welfare in order to be valid.[146] If it can be shown that an amendment does not bear such relationship and is arbitrary, preferential, or discriminatory, it can be attacked as invalid and will not remove the designated area from the effect of the comprehensive zoning ordinance previously in effect.[147] The adjoining owners have a right and standing to bring an action to enjoin the use permitted by the amendment and the "spot zoning" amendment will have no effect.

Only the legislative body of a municipality is authorized to amend a zoning ordinance. While in proper circumstances the zoning board of

---

145. Zopfi v. City of Wilmington, 273 N.C. 430, 160 S.E.2d 325 (1968). A zoning ordinance, or amendment, which singles out or reclassifies a relatively small tract owned by a single person and surrounded by a much larger area uniformly zoned so as to impose upon the small tract greater restrictions that those imposed upon the larger area, or so as to relieve the small tract from restrictions to which the rest of the area is subjected, is "spot zoning" and is beyond the authority of the municipality, in the absence of a clear showing of a reasonable basis for such distinction. Blades v. City of Raleigh, 280 N.C. 533, 187 S.E.2d 35 (1972). *Accord,* Stutts v. Swaim, 30 N.C. App. 611, 228 S.E.2d 750 (1976); Lathan v. Bd. of Commissioners, 47 N.C. App. 357, 267 S.E.2d 30 (1980).

146. Allgood v. Town of Tarboro, 281 N.C. 430, 189 S.E.2d 255 (1972); Walker v. Elkin, 254 N.C. 85, 118 S.E.2d 1 (1961). *See* GREEN, ZONING IN NORTH CAROLINA (Inst. of Gov't Pub., Univ. of N.C.) 391 (1952).

147. Zopfi v. City of Wilmington, 273 N.C. 430, 160 S.E.2d 325 (1968). *Accord,* Allgood v. Town of Tarboro, 281 N.C. 430, 189 S.E.2d 255 (1972).

A municipality may not engage in "contract zoning." If an ordinance rezones a five-acre tract surrounded by a very extensive area of land zoned and occupied for single-family residences so as to permit a less restrictive classification of the five-acre tract on the basis of a specific plan or proposal by the owner of the tract to construct "luxurious townhouses," it is not only "spot zoning" but is also unlawful as "contract zoning." *See* Blades v. City of Raleigh, 280 N.C. 533, 187 S.E.2d 35 (1972).

adjustment can vary the strict application of an ordinance and permit a "variance" from the terms of the ordinance when it finds an undue hardship or practical difficulty as previously set out, the board of adjustment is not a law making body and cannot change city maps or amend the zoning ordinance under which it functions.[148] Amendments must be effected by the legislative body of the municipality.

(d) *Nonconforming uses.* It is customary for most zoning ordinances to provide that upon adoption of the zoning ordinance a pre-existing use of land or a structure may be continued for the current purposes for which it is being employed when the ordinance becomes effective, although the remainder of the district in which it is located is zoned for other purposes. These uses which do not comply with the ordinance and which are permitted to continue are called "nonconforming uses." They are allowed to continue because of a feeling by the courts and legislators alike that it would often be inequitable and unjust, and perhaps unreasonable and illegal, to substantially destroy property values by prohibiting the continuation of existing uses made of land and structures already in operation.[149]

The ordinances recognize that the imposition of a zoning ordinance to municipal property is almost never effected in advance of the establishment of some business or other use with respect to some property within a particular district that does not conform with the regulations imposed on that district. To prevent a possible invalidation of the ordinance as being an unreasonable restriction on the use of such pre-existing establishments [150] and structures, and evincing the fairness

---

148. Lee v. Board of Adjustment, 226 N.C. 107, 37 S.E.2d 128 (1946); Bryan v. Wilson, 259 N.C. 107, 130 S.E.2d 68 (1963); *In re* Application of Rea Constr. Co., 272 N.C. 715, 158 S.E.2d 887 (1968).

149. "There has been persistent doubt of the lawfulness of a statute which requires the cessation of a use which is not a nuisance . . ." 6 POWELL, REAL PROPERTY 109 (1958); YOKLEY, ZONING LAW AND PRACTICE § 50 (2d ed. 1956). *See* dissenting opinion of Lake, J. in State v. Joyner, 286 N.C. 366, 211 S.E.2d 320 (1975). The *Joyner* case holds that a municipality may provide in the exercise of its police powers that nonconforming uses shall be terminated within a specified period of time ("amortized") provided such period of time is reasonable. It was held that a municipal zoning ordinance that required a nonconforming use to be removed within three years was not unconstitutionally arbitrary, unreasonable or confiscatory *per se* or as applied to a nonconforming building materials salvage yard. The court held that restrictions on the continuation of nonconforming uses will be enforced if reasonably designed to avoid loss to the owner and where his prospective loss is relatively slight. On the other hand, they might not be enforced if such enforcement would cause serious loss to property owners and destroy valuable businesses built up over many years. State v. Joyner, 23 N.C. App. 27, 208 S.E.2d 233 (1974), *aff'd,* 286 N.C. 366, 211 S.E.2d 320 (1975). When an ordinance deals with nonconforming uses, it is an attempt by the municipality to balance the right to the use of private property with the paramount public interest.

150. What is a "pre-existing use" may be the subject of some debate. For instance, the Supreme Court of North Carolina held in In re Appeal of Supply Co., 202 N.C. 496, 163 S.E. 462 (1932), that the "placing of a grease dispenser and goods to be sold out of a filling

§ 397 RESTRICTIONS ON USE OF LANDS § 397

of the authorities, zoning ordinances have provided rather generally that

station" on the premises in good faith with the intention to construct a filling station had "started" to construct the filling station sufficient to make out a pre-existing nonconforming use. On the other hand, where an optionee of real property after a zoning ordinance was enacted but before its effective date, hurried to cut down trees and employed an architect and procured a building permit before the effective date of the ordinance in order to be engaged in a nonconforming use at the time the ordinance became effective, the Supreme Court of North Carolina held that his acts, use and expenditures would not be sufficient to entitle him to continue a "pre-existing" use after the ordinance became effective. *See* Warner v. W. & O., Inc., 263 N.C. 37, 138 S.E.2d 782 (1964).

In the Appeal of Tadlock, 261 N.C. 120, 134 S.E.2d 177 (1964), the court held that although a nonconforming trailer park was only partially complete, due to financial considerations, where the owners had graded the land for additional trailers and dug wells for expansion of the park, there was a pre-existing nonconforming use for the whole trailer park, to the extent that such improvements had been made. The court held, however, that land with respect to which no improvements had been made, still in the planning stage, could not be added to the trailer park as a nonconforming use unless the board of adjustment found reason to grant a variance on the basis of hardship. *But see* Town of Hillsborough v. Smith, 276 N.C. 48, 170 S.E.2d 904 (1969), which holds that one who in good faith and in reliance upon a building permit lawfully issued to him makes expenditures or incurs contractual obligations, substantial in amount, incidental to or as part of acquisition of a building site or construction or equipment of proposed building for proposed use authorized by the permit, may not be deprived of his right to continue such construction and use by revocation of such permit, whether revocation be by enactment of an otherwise valid zoning ordinance or by other means.

It should be noted that only "legal" pre-existing nonconforming uses may be contined. In City of Raleigh v. Fisher, 232 N.C. 629, 61 S.E.2d 897 (1950), the owner of land procured a permit to build a residence in a residence zone. He thereafter carried on a bakery business in the residence zone and when the city reenacted its zoning ordinance permitting continuation of uses previously existing, the owner sought to continue the bakery in the residential zone as a pre-existing nonconforming use. The court held that he was entitled to continue only pre-existing "legal" uses and he was denied the right to carry on the bakery business in the residential zone. The court pointed out that he had been in violation of the zoning regulations at all times. *See* Properties, Inc. v. Board of Adjustment, 18 N.C. App. 712, 198 S.E.2d 1 (1973), in accord with Town of Hillsborough v. Smith, 276 N.C. 48, 170 S.E.2d 904 (1969), to the effect that one who has obtained a building permit acquires a vested right to carry on a nonconforming use of his land under the issued permit if he has made a substantial beginning of construction and has incurred substantial expense. It is not required that construction be completed prior to the passage or amendment of the zoning ordinance, or that there by any visible change in the condition of the land. *See also In re* Campsites Unlimited, 23 N.C. App. 250, 208 S.E.2d 717 (1974), *aff'd,* 287 N.C. 493, 215 S.E.2d 73 (1975), to the effect that the incurring of expenses under binding contractual obligations is the same as the actual expenditure of money for purposes of showing a change of position in bona fide reliance upon a lawfully issued building permit. Hence, actual expenditure of money or the incurring of binding obligations for the acquisition of land, for the acquisition of building materials or services, and for making of visible, physical changes in the condition of the land will suffice if done in good faith pursuant to a building permit lawful when issued. One incurring such expenses or incurring obligations acquires a vested right to carry on a nonconforming use. In Thomasville v. City of Thomasville, 17 N.C. App. 483, 195 S.E.2d 79 (1973), it was held that where plaintiff committed itself to a $60,000 earth moving contract and obligated itself by a promissory note and security agreement to the repayment of a $1,142,400 loan, such substantial contractual obligations, if incurred in good

§ 397 REAL ESTATE LAW IN NORTH CAROLINA § 397

such existing "nonconforming uses" may be continued in the same manner as before the passage of the zoning ordinance.

While nonconforming uses are generally provided for in zoning ordinances,[151] the ultimate objective of zoning is the eventual elimination of all such nonconforming uses since their existence is often subversive of the purposes of zoning. To the end of eventual elimination of the nonconforming uses, most zoning ordinances contain provisions that limit

---

faith, vested in plaintiff the right to proceed with its apartment building project irrespective of any subsequent changes in zoning classification made by defendant city.

In accord with Warner v. W. & O., Inc., 263 N.C. 37, 138 S.E.2d 782 (1964), and Hillsborough v. Smith, 276 N.C. 48, 170 S.E.2d 904 (1969), see In re Campsites Unlimited, 287 N.C. 493, 215 S.E.2d 73 (1975), to the effect that the "good faith" incurring of obligations or the expenditure of funds with respect to a building permit are not present for the purpose of giving the owner a vested right to carry on a nonconforming use if at the time he makes the expenditure or incurs the obligation, the owner has knowledge that the adoption of a zoning ordinance is imminent and that if it is adopted it will forbid his proposed construction and use of his land. He is not permitted to hasten, in a race with the town commissioners, to make expenditures or incur obligations before the town can take its contemplated action so as to avoid what would otherwise be the effect of the ordinance upon him. In the Campsites case, supra, however, the Supreme Court of North Carolina held that notwithstanding the fact that developer had admitted that he had been aware that zoning "had been in the planning stage for a year or so" and that he was "trying to beat it" there was no showing of bad faith in his proceeding with his proposed development. At the time the expenditures were made and the obligations incurred the owner of the land did not know that the zoning ordinance was imminent *nor did he know that if adopted it would forbid his proposed construction and use of his land.* To negate his good faith, the rule of Hillsborough v. Smith, supra, requires knowledge on the part of the landowner that a zoning ordinance will prohibit the contemplated use to which he was putting the land. *See In re* Campsites Unlimited, 23 N.C. App. 250, 253, 208 S.E.2d 717 (1974). It thus appears that a landowner is not deemed to be acting in bad faith if he incurs obligations or makes expenditures "to beat zoning" if he does so while a proposed ordinance, which may or may not be adopted, is being "studied" or while it is in the debating stage preliminary to its possible adoption, especially where the ordinance *if adopted may or may not* restrict the landowner's proposed use of his land. In other words, "the right of landowners to develop their properties in ways then lawful cannot be frozen by a county's or a municipality's announcement of its undertaking of a general study of zoning which, at some future date, may or may not lead to the adoption of an ordinance restricting the landowner's proposed use of his land." *In re* Campsites Unlimited, 287 N.C. 493, at 504, 215 S.E.2d 73 (1975).

151. *See, e.g., In re* O'Neal, 243 N.C. 714, 92 S.E.2d 189 (1956), which sets out the nonconforming use provisions of the zoning ordinance of the City of Charlotte as follows:

> The lawful use of any building or land existing at the time of the adoption of this ordinance may be continued, but not enlarged or extended although the use of such building or land does not conform to the regulations of the district in which such use is maintained. An existing non-conforming use of a building or premises may be changed to another non-conforming use of the same or higher classification, but may not at any time be changed to a use of a lower classification.
>
> No non-conforming use may be reestablished in any building or on any premises where such non-conforming use has been discontinued for a period of one year.
>
> Any non-conforming building or structure damaged by fire, explosion, flood, riot or act of God may be reconstructed and used as before any such calamity, provided such reconstruction takes place within one year of the calamity.

the enlargement and expansion of nonconforming uses,[152] that prohibit resumption of the use of a nonconforming structure or establishment after it has been discontinued for a specified period of time, that they may not be changed to other nonconforming uses of a lower order, and relating to whether or not they may be rebuilt if destroyed and under what conditions.[153]

If a landowner's property was used prior to the effective date of an ordinance so as to bring him within the permission of the ordinance to use his land although it does not conform to the uses for which other lands in the district may be put, he is entitled to make such use as a matter of right and it is neither dependent on a showing of hardship nor upon any discretion on the part of the zoning administrative officer or the board of appeals.[154]

---

152. Application & Appeal of Hasting, 252 N.C. 327, 113 S.E.2d 433 (1960). *See* City of Brevard v. Ritter, 14 N.C. App. 207, 188 S.E.2d 41 (1972), which holds that construction of a building to be used as a lounge or club for pilots and as space for storage of an airplane constituted an enlargement or expansion of a previously existing nonconforming airport in violation of the city's ordinance prohibiting extension of nonconforming uses. *See also* Clark v. Richardson, 24 N.C. App. 556, 211 S.E.2d 530 (1975), which holds that the enclosing of a roofed porch on a building used as a grocery store, which building was a nonconforming building under the town's zoning ordinance, did not constitute an enlargement or extension of the pre-existing nonconforming use within the meaning of the ordinance.

153. *See* numerous typical examples of the limitations that appear in zoning ordinances in North Carolina with respect to nonconforming uses in GREEN, ZONING IN NORTH CAROLINA (Inst. of Gov't Pub., Univ. of N.C.) 163-70 (1952).

Diggs v. City of Wilson, 25 N.C. App. 464, 213 S.E.2d 443 (1975), holds that where the city issued a building permit for remodeling a restaurant building which constituted a nonconforming use in an area zoned for residential use, and the building permit set no limitation with respect to when the remodeling had to be completed, the closing of the restaurant to the general public for over one hundred and eighty days while the remodeling process was being completed did not constitute, as a matter of law, a "discontinuance" of the nonconforming use within the meaning of the zoning ordinance.

154. *See In re* O'Neal, 243 N.C. 714, 92 S.E.2d 189 (1956), which is an excellent case on a number of aspects of zoning. That one is entitled to a nonconforming use in specified circumstances and need not ask for a variance is significant also in that it is not necessary to have four concurring votes of the board of appeals to procure a variance. The zoning administrator has no option with respect to a nonconforming use permitted under the ordinance. Town of Hillsborough v. Smith, 276 N.C. 48, 170 S.E.2d 904 (1969).

Compare Application of Ellis, 277 N.C. 419, 178 S.E.2d 77 (1970) *and* Keiger v. Board of Adjustment, 278 N.C. 17, 178 S.E.2d 616 (1971), with respect to "special use" or "special exception" permits. If an applicant for a "special use" or "special exception" permit shows facts and conditions specified in the ordinance as entitle him to a "special use" or "special exception" permit, there is no discretion in the board of adjustment and it must grant such permit, upon a finding that the specified conditions have been satisfied.

With respect to "special use" or "special exception" permits, *see* Jackson v. Board of Ajustment, 275 N.C. 155, 166 S.E.2d 78 (1969), which states:

> When a statute, or ordinance, provides that a type of s structure may not be erected in a specified area, except that such structure may be erected therein when certain conditions exist, one has a right, under the statute or ordinance, to erect such structure upon a showing that the specified conditions do exist. The legislative body may confer upon an

§ 398. Enforcement and Remedies Under Zoning Ordinances.

(a) *In general.* Landowners and their attorneys should be particularly interested in the legislative, administrative and judicial procedures connected with the application of zoning regulations with respect to real property. A large number of governmental authorities have had a hand in the application of a particular ordinance restricting the use of land to particular uses. The legislative body of the State has passed the statute initially enabling the municipal authorities to pass the ordinance pursuant to the enabling legislation. The municipal planning or zoning commission has developed the comprehensive master plan and recommended the passage of the zoning ordinance to implement it. The municipal legislative body, after giving affected citizens the opportunity to be heard with respect to the ordinance, has enacted the zoning ordinance specifying the types of and limitations on uses to which land may be put in the respective districts of the municipality. The legislative body of the municipality has the power to amend a zoning ordinance when to do so appears desirable to accomplish some object of zoning.

Another legal entity, the zoning board of adjustment, has been established under the enabling act to hear petitions for variances where strictly literal enforcement of the ordinance will result in undue hardship or practical difficulties on particular landowners. The board of adjustment also has the duty of making interpretive rulings to determine if the administrative official has made errors with respect to specific properties and to determine if he has correctly applied the ordinance. The chief administrative official, usually the building inspector of the municipality, has the duty of initially interpreting the ordinance and the duty to issue building and/or occupancy permits when the use contemplated by an owner complies with the ordinance; he likewise has the duty to refuse to issue such permits when his contemplated use will violate the ordinance. The courts are occasionally called upon to pass upon the validity of ordinances or to interpret them, to aid in the enforcement upon petition of municipal authorities and individuals, or to excuse individual landowners from their application where the situation warrants.

(b) *The enforcement officer's function.* When a landowner desires to

---

administrative officer, or board, the authority to determine whether the specified conditions do, in fact, exist and may require a permit from such officer, or board, to be issued when he or it so determines, as a further condition precedent to the right to erect such structure in such area. Such permit is not one for a variance or departure from the statute or ordinance, but is the recognition of a right established by the statute or ordinance itself. Consequently, the delegation to such officer, or board, of authority to make such determination as to the existence or nonexistence of the specified conditions is not a delegation of the legislative power to make law.

Accord, Kenan v. Board of Adjustment, 13 N.C. App. 688, 187 S.E.2d 49 (1972); Refining Co. v. Board of Adjustment, 284 N.C. 458, 202 S.E.2d 129 (1974); Neighborhood Assoc. v. Board of Adjustment, 35 N.C. App. 449, 241 S.E.2d 872 (1978); Robinhood Trails Neighbors v. Bd. of Adjustment, 44 N.C. App. 539, 261 S.E.2d 682 (1980).

make a particular use of land and applies for a permit, the chief administrative officer of the zoning ordinance, usually the building inspector, must determine from the ordinance whether he should issue or deny the permit.[155] He must follow the literal provisions of the zoning regulations as a purely administrative agent.[156] He has no authority to refuse a permit for a structure for a use which the ordinance allows.[157] The administrative officer may suggest to the landowner the manner in which he could comply with the ordinance by making modifications in his plans. The administrative officer has no authority, however, to permit any violation of the ordinance simply because he thinks that it is unduly harsh as applied in a particular case.

After the building permit has been issued, the enforcement officer by periodic inspections determines whether the actual construction is being carried out as represented by the application for the building permit. Items such as the size and dimensions of the lot, the percentage of the lot that the structure will occupy, the size of the yards and the like, are checked. The administrative officer may detect any noncompliance with the ordinance and recommend changes with respect to offending structures before they become too expensive. When the building is complete and ready for occupancy, the enforcement officer determines if the structure complies in all respects with the zoning ordinance. If it does, he will indicate his approval or give a certificate of occupancy for the owner to move in. If the structure fails in some way to conform to the requirements of the zoning ordinance, the administrator will refuse permission to occupy the building until brought into compliance.

(c) *Appeals from enforcement officer's decision; the board of adjust-*

---

155. *See* City of Winston-Salem v. Concrete Co., 37 N.C. App. 186, 245 S.E.2d 536 (1978) holding that, if a zoning officer acting in accordance with authority given to him under an ordinance determined that a concrete mixing operation was a permitted use within an I-2 (limited industrial) district, then the city could not enjoin the concrete mixing business from operating on the premises. The concrete mixing business was a use not specifically listed in any of the zoning categories of the city, and the ordinance gave the zoning officer authority to determine the category within which the proposed use was most similar. The court distinguished this fact situation from those where past decisions have held that a city cannot be estopped to enforce a zoning ordinance due to the conduct of a city official in encouraging or permitting the violation. Helms v. Charlotte, 255 N.C. 647, 122 S.E.2d 817, 96 A.L.R.2d 439 (1961); Raleigh v. Fisher, 232 N.C. 629, 61 S.E.2d 897 (1950).

156. Lee v. Board of Adjustment, 226 N.C. 107, 37 S.E.2d 128 (1946); *In re* Application of Rea Constr. Co., 272 N.C. 715, 158 S.E.2d 887 (1968).

157. There is even a possibility that he could be held liable for refusing to issue such permit. *See* Clinard v. Winston-Salem, 173 N.C. 356, 91 S.E. 1039 (1917). Where the applicant meets all the requirements of the zoning ordinance he is entitled to the issuance of a permit as a matter of right and it may not lawfully be withheld. *In re* Application of Rea Constr. Co., 272 N.C. 715, 158 S.E.2d 887 (1968). *Mandamus* lies to compel the issuance of a building permit when an applicant has a clear right to its issuance under the zoning ordinance. Mitchell v. Barfield, 232 N.C. 325, 59 S.E.2d 810 (1950); Quadrant Corp. v. City of Kinston, 22 N.C. App. 31, 205 S.E.2d 324 (1974).

ment. If the enforcement officer denies or revokes a building permit or permission to occupy a building, the owner may make such modifications in his structure as will bring it into conformity with the regulations or he may decide to take an appeal to the board of adjustment. If the landowner constructs his building or uses it after being denied a building or occupancy permit by the enforcement officer, he will be subject to prosecution under a criminal proceeding.[158] On appeal to the board of adjustment, the board has the authority to review any order, requirement, decision, or determination of such officer, provided the appeal is taken within the time specified by the rules of the ordinance or pursuant to the general rules of the board of adjustment.[159] Appeals must be made pursuant to applications for appeal as prescribed by the board and pursuant to procedures set forth in the ordinance. Appeals may be either from alleged erroneous interpretations of the ordinance or because of alleged hardships caused from strict interpretations of the ordinance from which the administrative officer could not veer. The board of adjustment is a *quasi-judicial* administrative body and has the power to hold hearings and to receive evidence with respect to appeals before it. The board of adjustment can either affirm the enforcement of the enforcement officer's decision or can reverse it in favor of the appealing landowner. For the board of adjustment to reverse any order, requirement, decision or determination of any such administrative officer, however, or to decide in favor of any applicant on any matter upon which the board is required to pass or to effect any variance from the terms of the ordinance, there must be a concurring vote of four of the five members of the board.[160]

The board of adjustment is clothed with judicial or "quasi-judicial" power but may not disregard zoning regulations adopted by the city council. It can vary them only when it finds that their strict letter application will cause injustice or unnecessary hardship.[161] Nonconforming use permits on the basis of hardship are discretionary with the board.[162] While hearings before the board of adjustment may be informal and technical rules of evidence and procedure may be dispensed with upon the

---

158. *See* State v. Roberson, 198 N.C. 70, 150 S.E. 674 (1929). Not only will he be subject to prosecution but he will be barred from showing that the ordinance was invalid as a defense to prosecution if he constructs or occupies without exhausting his remedies on appeal.

159. N.C. GEN. STAT. § 160A-388.

160. *Id.* The board of adjustment is not required to sound record its hearings under the North Carolina Administrative Procedures Act. Neighborhood Assoc. v. Board of Adjustment, 35 N.C. App. 449, 241 S.E.2d 872 (1978).

161. *In re* Markham, 259 N.C. 566, 131 S.E.2d 329 (1963). *Accord, In re* Application of Rea Constr. Co., 272 N.C. 715, 158 S.E.2d 887 (1968), which states: "The board is not a lawmaking body and has no power to amend the zoning ordinance either to permit the construction of a building prohibited by the ordinance or to prohibit the construction of one permitted by the ordinance."

162. Town of Garner v. Weston, 263 N.C. 487, 139 S.E.2d 642 (1965).

§ 398 RESTRICTIONS ON USE OF LANDS § 398

board's hearings, any party whose rights are being determined must be given the opportunity to offer evidence, cross-examine witnesses and inspect other evidence in explanation and rebuttal and no essential of a fair trial can be disregarded.[163]

(d) *Appeals from the board of adjustment to the courts; scope of appeal.* Any aggrieved property owner whose property owner whose property is affected by a ruling of the board of appeals may seek a review of the board's action by proceedings in the nature of *certiorari* in the courts.[164] The court to which such a case is appealed will hear it upon only the evidence presented in the record before the board of adjustment. Review is limited to errors of law and the courts will give relief only against the board's orders that are illegal, arbitrary, oppressive or which are attended by a manifest abuse of authority.[165] Questions of fact which are not a part of the record made before the board of adjustment are not subject to review in the courts.[166] The decision of the board is not subject to collateral attack.[167]

---

163. Humble Oil & Ref. Co. v. Board of Aldermen of Town of Chapel Hill, 284 N.C. 458, 202 S.E.2d 129 (1974). A zoning board of adjustment, or a board of aldermen conducting a quasi-judicial hearing, cannot dispense with an essential element of a fair trial. In a hearing before a zoning board of adjustment or board of aldermen, parties whose rights are being determined must be given the opportunity to offer evidence, cross-examine adverse witnesses and inspect documents; the board may not base findings upon the existence or nonexistence of crucial facts upon unsworn statements, and crucial findings of facts which are unsupported by competent evidence cannot stand. *See also* Humble Oil & Ref. Co. v. Board of Aldermen of Town of Chapel Hill, 286 N.C. 170, 209 S.E.2d 447 (1974); Jarrell v. Board of Adjustment, 258 N.C. 476, 128 S.E.2d 879 (1963).

164. *See* N.C. GEN. STAT. § 160A-388; Lee v. Board of Adjustment, 226 N.C. 107, 37 S.E.2d 128 (1946). *See* Quadrant Corp. v. City of Kinston, 22 N.C. App. 31, 205 S.E.2d 324 (1974), to the effect that N.C. GEN. STAT. § 160A-388(e) provides that all decisions of a board of adjustment are subject to review by the superior court by proceedings in the nature of certiorari.

See also Davis v. Zoning Board of Adjustment, 41 N.C. App. 579, 255 S.E.2d 444 (1979) dismissing an appeal from a county board of adjustment where the questions presented were rendered moot by amendments to the zoning ordinance.

165. *In re* Pine Hill Cemeteries, 219 N.C. 735, 15 S.E.2d 1 (1941); *In re* Campsites Unlimited, 23 N.C. App. 250, 208 S.E.2d 717 (1974), *aff'd,* 287 N.C. 493, 215 S.E.2d 73 (1975); Deffet Rentals, Inc. v. City of Burlington, 27 N.C. App. 361, 219 S.E.2d 223 (1975).

166. Jarrell v. Board of Adjustment, 258 N.C. 476, 128 S.E.2d 879 (1963). The decision of a board of adjustment is final as to facts found provided there is some evidence to support such facts. The courts are empowered to review errors in law, but not facts. The court can give relief against orders which are abitrary, oppressive or attended with manifest abuse of authority and ones which are unsupported by evidence. *In re* Campsites Unlimited, 23 N.C. App. 250, 208 S.E.2d 717 (1974), *aff'd,* 287 N.C. 493, 215 S.E.2d 73 (1975); Deffet Rentals, Inc. v. City of Burlington, 27 N.C. App. 361, 219 S.E.2d 223 (1975). It is error for the reviewing court to find facts.

167. City of Hickory v. Machinery Co., 39 N.C. App. 236, 249 S.E.2d 851 (1978) where a property owner failed to seek judicial review by way of petition for writ of certiorari of the actions of the board of adjustment in requiring him to remove a canopy from his property. When the city sought to enjoin the property owner's continuing violation of the zoning

Division 2. Subdivision Regulations

§ 399. Subdivision Regulations Generally.

In order to provide for more orderly development of subdivisions, many municipalities, in the exercise of their police powers, have been given the power to adopt subdivision regulations within the municipalities and often beyond their boundaries. The purposes of such regulations can be effected by requiring the dedication or reservation of rights-of-way or easements for street and utility purposes,[168] by providing for the distribution of population and traffic which shall avoid congestion and overcrowding. A subdivision control ordinance may require a developer of land to prepare and file a plat that shows sufficient data in order that a determination may be readily made as to the location, bearing, and length of every street and alley line, lot line, easement boundary line and other boundary lines. The subdivision control ordinance may provide that the developer shall construct community service facilities in connection with his subdivision development in accordance with municipal policies and standards and may require the posting of a bond to assure compliance with such conditions imposed.[169]

Where subdivision regulations are in effect, no subdivision plat shall be filed or recorded until it shall have been submitted to and approved by the legislative body of the municipality.[170] Furthermore, any sale of land in a subdivision by reference to a plat that has not been properly approved shall render the seller guilty of a misdemeanor. In addition, the municipality may enjoin the sale of land with respect to a plat of a subdivision that has not been properly approved.[171]

---

ordinance, the owner argued that the court should not grant relief to the city because the canopy should have been allowed as a permissible non-conforming use. The court of appeals held that this constituted an impermissible collateral attack.

168. *E.g.*, some regulations in some states require provision for utilities, curbs, gutters, sidewalks, storm and sanitary sewers, fire hydrants, street lighting, street signs. *See* Ayres v. Los Angeles, 34 Cal. 2d 31, 207 P.2d 1 (1949).

169. N.C. GEN. STAT. § 160A-372. Subdivision controls have been sustained in other states as a valid exercise of the police power of the states and municipalities. Some counties also have the power to regulate subdivisions. *See* N.C. GEN. STAT. §§ 153A-330 through 153A-331.

170. N.C. GEN. STAT. § 160A-373.

171. N.C. GEN. STAT. § 160A-375.

See Financial Servs. v. Capitol Funds, 23 N.C. App. 377, 209 S.E.2d 423 (1974), *aff'd*, 288 N.C. 122, 217 S.E.2d 551 (1975), which involved the subdivision control ordinance of the City of Raleigh. It held that an enabling statute and city ordinance making it a misdemeanor to describe land in any contract of sale, deed or other instrument of transfer by reference to a subdivision plat that has not been properly approved and recorded does not render void or voidable a contract for the sale of land on the ground that the seller did not comply with the ordinance.

See also the 1977 amendment to N.C. GEN. STAT. § 160A-375 rewriting the third sentence to read: "The city may bring an action for injunction of any illegal subdivision, transfer, conveyance, or sale of land, and the court shall, upon appropriate findings, issue an injunction and order requiring the offending party to comply with the subdivision ordinance."

CHAPTER 19

EMINENT DOMAIN

Article I. Eminent Domain Generally

§ 400. Nature of Power of Eminent Domain Generally.
§ 401. Inverse Condemnation.
§ 402. Statutory Provisions Authorizing Appropriation of Property Under Eminent Domain.
§ 403. Those Authorized to Exercise Power of Eminent Domain.

Article II. Procedure in Condemnation

§ 404. The Attempt to Purchase.
§ 405. Special Proceedings.
§ 406. Rules Relating to Compensation in Eminent Domain Proceedings.
§ 407. Evidence Admissible in Determining "Market Value."
§ 408. Right of Condemnor to Offset Benefits to Realty Condemned.

Article I. Eminent Domain Generally

§ 400. Nature of Power of Eminent Domain Generally.

Eminent domain is defined as the power vested in a sovereign to take, to authorize the taking of, or to damage, the private property of an individual without his consent for a public purpose upon the payment of a just compensation.[1] The right to take property for public use, the power of eminent domain, is one of the prerogatives of a sovereign state. The right is inherent in sovereignty; it is not conferred by constitutions.[2] Both state and federal governments have the power of eminent domain. It is a power that may be delegated to others who perform "public purposes" under appropriate legislation, subject only to the constitutional limitations that a just compensation must be paid to the owner and that due process be complied with.[3]

---

1. Virginia Elec. & Power Co. v. King, 259 N.C. 219, 130 S.E.2d 318 (1963); Redevelopment Comm'n v. Hagins, 258 N.C. 220, 128 S.E.2d 391 (1962).
2. State v. Club Properties, 275 N.C. 328, 167 S.E.2d 385 (1969); Redevelopment Comm'n v. Hagins, 258 N.C. 220, 128 S.E.2d 391 (1962). A public service corporation, however, has no power of eminent domain unless a valid statute gives it such power. Statutes which authorize the exercise of the power of eminent domain must be strictly construed. See, e.g., Carolina-Tennessee Power Co. v. Hiawassee River Power Co., 175 N.C. 668, 96 S.E. 99 (1918); Mount Olive v. Cowan, 235 N.C. 259, 69 S.E.2d 525 (1952).
3. State v. Club Properties, 275 N.C. 328, 167 S.E.2d 385 (1969). Pipeline Co. v. Neill, 296 N.C. 503, 251 S.E.2d 457 (1979); Development Co. v. County of Wilson, 44 N.C. App. 469, 261 S.E.2d 275 (1980).

Wholly at the discretion of the appropriate public official involved, a person displaced as the result of public works programs may be entitled to relocation assistance payments. N.C. GEN. STAT. § 133-8. Henry v. Dept. of Transportation, 44 N.C. App. 170, 260 S.E.2d 438 (1979).

While the North Carolina Constitution does not have an express provision requiring compensation upon a taking of property by eminent domain, such is implied. See N.C.

The power of eminent domain extends to every kind of property. The word "property" comprehends not only the thing possessed, but also the right of the owner to possess, use, enjoy, and dispose of the *res* and the corresponding right to exclude others from its use.[4] Whether the totality of ownership, the fee title, is appropriated, or whether a mere easement is condemned for a particular purpose, is usually a question of the construction of the particular enabling statute. This would be significant in case the public use is changed or abandoned. If the taking was of fee simple, upon a change or abandonment of the public use the land can be disposed of by the government agency or condemnor without limitation as to any rights of the former owner. If an easement only was condemned, however, the title to the underlying fee remains in the landowner or his successor in interest.[5]

The creation of a nuisance by a governmental agency and the emission of sewage into a stream injuring the value of contiguous lands and lower proprietors has been held to be a "taking" requiring compensation.[6] The erection of a structure by a municipality which violates restrictive covenants in a development constitutes a "taking" of property which is compensable.[7] A concussion caused by use of explosives in construction of

---

CONST. art. I, § 17. Requirement of compensation is also guaranteed under the Fourteenth Amendment of the United States Constitution.

It has been held that an agency may not condemn land unless it has the money on hand, or the present authority to obtain the money, for payment of just compensation. Horton v. Redevelopment Comm'n of High Point, 264 N.C. 1, 140 S.E.2d 728 (1965).

4. Hildebrande v. Telephone Co., 219 N.C. 402, 14 S.E.2d 252 (1941).

5. *See* Frink v. Board of Transp. 41 N.C. App. 751, 255 S.E.2d 746 (1979) where the Court of Appeals found that an earlier acquisition by the State of land for a canal right-of-way gave the State the inherent right to construct bridges and roadways across the property without payment of additional compensation to the landowners involved. The court elected not to couch the issue in terms of whether the State originally acquired title in fee or merely an easement.

6. That a permanent and continuing nuisance created and maintained by the sovereign may be a taking, *see* Cogdill v. Highway Comm'n, 279 N.C. 313, 182 S.E.2d 373 (1973). *See also* Eller v. Board of Educ., 242 N.C. 584, 89 S.E.2d 144 (1955); Ivester v. Winston-Salem, 215 N.C. 1, 1 S.E.2d 88 (1939); Clinard v. Kernersville, 215 N.C. 745, 3 S.E.2d 267 (1939); Wagner v. Conover, 200 N.C. 82, 156 S.E. 167 (1930).

7. *See* Carolina Mills v. Catawba County Bd. of Educ., 27 N.C. App. 524, 219 S.E.2d 509 (1975), which is in accord with Raleigh v. Edwards, 235 N.C. 671, 71 S.E.2d 396 (1952), to the effect that a governmental board's use of land in such a way as to violate and impair the value of restrictive covenants running with the property is a taking *whether the property is purchased or condemned* and the owner of the easements created by covenant are entitled to compensation for the "taking"; they are not entitled to injunctive relief to prevent the governmental board from using the property for an otherwise legitimate public purpose.

The owner of a right of re-entry from breach of condition has no compensable interest in a condemnation award where the fee owner had no intention to abandon the allowed use of the property. Board of Transp. v. Recreation Comm., 38 N.C. App. 708, 248 S.E.2d 909 (1978).

a sewer which damages one's dwelling is a "taking" of property.[8] Likewise, interference with an owner's access to a public roadway may be a taking for which compensation must be paid.[9]

§ 401. Inverse Condemnation.

The legal doctrine of "inverse condemnation" is well established in North Carolina. Where private property is taken for a public purpose by a municipality or other agency having the power of eminent domain under circumstances such that no procedure provided by statute affords an applicable or adequate remedy, an owner may maintain an action to obtain just compensation therefor.[10] "Inverse condemnation" is a device which forces a governmental body to exercise its power of condemnation even though it may have no desire to do so.[11]

§ 402. Statutory Provisions Authorizing Appropriation of Property Under Eminent Domain.

North Carolina has various statutes [12] authorizing the exercise of emi-

---

8. Guilford Realty & Ins. Co. v. Blythe Bros. Co., 260 N.C. 69, 131 S.E.2d 900 (1963).

9. State Highway Comm'n v. Raleigh Farmers Market, Inc., 263 N.C. 622, 139 S.E.2d 904, adhered to in 264 N.C. 139, 141 S.E.2d 10 (1965). See Smith Co. v. Highway Comm'n, 279 N.C. 328, 182 S.E.2d 383 (1971), to the effect that the owner of land abutting a highway has a right beyond that which is enjoyed by the general public for access purposes and that this right of access is an easement appurtenant which cannot be damaged or taken from him without compensation. *Accord,* Guyton v. North Carolina Bd. of Transp., 30 N.C. App. 87, 226 S.E.2d 175 (1976).

See also Board of Transp. v. Brown, 34 N.C. App. 266, 237 S.E.2d 854 (1977) where it was held that the trial court erred in excluding evidence of traffic noise and of a lack of direct access from the landowner's remaining land to the highway as factors to be considered in determining the fair market value of the remaining land. And see Highway Comm. v. Rose, 31 N.C. App. 28, 228 S.E.2d 664 (1976) holding, *inter alia,* that, if a landowner retains reasonable means of ingress and egress to and from his property after the construction of traffic islands by the highway commission, then there is no compensable interference with the property rights of the landowner. A case appearing to have been decided on similar reasoning is Board of Transp. v. Warehouse Corp., 44 N.C. App. 81, 260 S.E.2d 696 (1979).

10. Charlotte v. Spratt, 263 N.C. 656, 140 S.E.2d 341 (1965); Hoyle v. City of Charlotte, 276 N.C. 292, 172 S.E.2d 1 (1970).

11. *See* Bohannon, *Airport Easements,* 54 VA. L. REV. 355, 373 (1968).

12. It should be noted that the General Statutes Commission has been working with regularity on a proposed law revision project that would consolidate and make uniform the many existing eminent domain statutes. It is possible that this important change in the statutory framework of the eminent domain law could be approved and adopted by the General Assembly in 1982.

The present statutes dealing with eminent domain are numerous and varied. *See* N.C. GEN. STAT. § 40-2 setting out the general purposes for which eminent domain can be had. Many other general statutes authorize specific kinds of condemnation for various purposes. *See, e.g.,* N.C. GEN. STAT. § 62-220 (relating to railroads); N.C. GEN. STAT. §§ 160A-240 through 160A-263 (relating to municipal corporations); N.C. GEN. STAT. § 115-125 (relating to school buildings); N.C. GEN. STAT. § 131-15 (relating to hospitals); N.C. GEN. STAT.

nent domain through special proceedings in the Superior Court.[13] These statutes prescribe who may exercise the power,[14] the purposes for which property may be acquired,[15] the nature of the interest acquired,[16] and the requisite steps and procedures to be followed to effect a valid condemnation or "taking" of an individual's property under eminent domain.[17] Statutes granting the power of eminent domain must be strictly construed and followed.[18]

§ 403. Those Authorized to Exercise Power of Eminent Domain.

A state has an inherent right to subject the private proeprty of its citizens to public uses.[19] The power is deemed essential to the due exercise of the powers of government and to the promotion of the public welfare. The power of eminent domain may be exercised by the State itself or it may be delegated to a corporation or body politic engaged in the performance of some public function or purpose. The power of eminent domain rests in the legislature and it may exercise the power either directly or through the medium of a municipality or quasi-public corporation or other appropriate agency engaged in the performance of some public function.[20] The power of eminent domain, however, lies dormant

---

§§ 136-19, 136-52, 136-103 et seq. (relating to roads); N.C. GEN. STAT. § 73-5 (relating to mills built on stream where two sides of stream are owned by different persons); N.C. GEN. STAT. § 73-14 (relating to races and waterways); N.C. GEN. STAT. § 156-1 (relating to drainage districts).

13. N.C. GEN. STAT. § 7A-248.

14. Such as cities, counties, the State, other governmental agencies, as well as corporations engaged in public uses to whom the power has been delegated, such as public utility corporations.

15. For such purposes as streets, railroads, drainage, schools, public buildings, and the like.

16. Whether a fee simple title or a mere easement for specific purposes. See City of High Point v. Farlow, 28 N.C. App. 343, 220 S.E.2d 841 (1976), which holds that the city's resolution for condemnation of property for construction of overhead transmission line was fatally defective where it did not clearly provide whether condemnation was of easement or of a fee. A city's resolution of condemnation must state clearly the public purpose for a taking and the interest sought to be taken.

17. Basic procedures to be followed when the various statutes make no contrary provision for specific procedures to be followed are those provided in N.C. GEN. STAT. §§ 40-11 through 40-29. A major exception to the procedures found in Chapter 40 are the procedures for State Highway Department acquisitions under art. 9, ch. 136 of N.C. GEN. STAT.

18. State v. Club Properties, 275 N.C. 328, 167 S.E.2d 385 (1969); Mont Olive v. Cowan, 235 N.C. 259, 69 S.E.2d 525 (1952); Development Co. v. County of Wilson, 44 N.C. App. 469, 261 S.E.2d 275 (1980).

See generally Phay, *The Eminent Domain Procedure of North Carolina: The Need for Legislation,* 45 N.C.L. REV. 587 (1967), in which the author states that the law of eminent domain is scattered through twenty-six chapters of the General Statutes, in addition to the many instances authorizing eminent domain under local legislation.

19. Jeffress v. Greenville, 154 N.C. 490, 70 S.E. 919 (1911).

20. Yarborough v. Park Comm'n, 196 N.C. 284, 145 S.E. 563 (1928).

§ 403   EMINENT DOMAIN   § 403

until legislative action determines the occasion, conditions, and proper agencies for its exercise.[21] No state agency, municipal corporation or public service corporation has the power to condemn or take the property of an individual until there is some act of the legislature conferring such power.[22] Legislative action is required to confer any right to appropriate private property. Even if an agency or corporation is given the power to acquire property for its functions, if no power to condemn is expressed or necessarily implied from the power given, it is presumed that the necessary property should be acquired by contract and not by condemnation.[23] The power of eminent domain is one of the highest attributes of sovereignty and the extent of its exercise is limited to the express terms or to the necessary implication of the statute delegating the power.[24] Statutes granting the power of eminent domain, being in derogation of common rights, must be strictly construed, both as to the extent of the power and as to its exercise.[25]

The power of eminent domain may be created in or delegated to a state agency, municipal corporation, quasi-public corporation or body politic by either general or special act. North Carolina General Statutes, § 40-2 enumerates certain state agencies and quasi-public corporations which have been delegated the power of eminent domain by the general eminent domain statute. Various other organizations and bodies politic have been given the power of eminent domain elsewhere in the General Statutes.[26] The power of eminent domain may be exercised *only* for a public purpose, and only for a public purpose which has been authorized and in the manner and on the conditions specified by the General Assembly.[27] These "public purposes" and "public uses" for which property may be condemned have come to be numerous.

A partial list of the purposes for which condemnation may be had follows: Appropriate agencies may exercise condemnation for the purpose of constructing and maintaining public buildings for the direct adminis-

---

21. Lloyd v. Venable, 168 N.C. 531, 84 S.E. 855 (1915).
22. Mount Olive v. Cowan, 235 N.C. 259, 69 S.E.2d 525 (1952).
23. Lloyd v. Venable, 168 N.C. 531, 84 S.E. 855 (1915).
24. Griffith v. Southern Ry., 191 N.C. 84, 131 S.E. 413 (1925).
25. Proctor v. Highway Comm'n, 230 N.C. 687, 55 S.E.2d 479 (1949); Sechrist v. Thomasville, 202 N.C. 108, 162 S.E. 212 (1932); Griffith v. Southern Ry., 191 N.C. 84, 131 S.E. 413 (1925); Johnson City Southern Ry. v. South & W.R. Co., 148 N.C. 59, 61 S.E. 683 (1908); State v. Jones, 139 N.C. 613, 52 S.E. 240 (1905).
26. *See, e.g.,* N.C. Gen. Stat. §§ 160A-240 through 160A-263 which replaced the former statutes with respect to the powers and procedures applicable to municipalities with respect to eminent domain.
27. State v. Core Banks Club Properties, Inc., 275 N.C. 328, 167 S.E.2d 385 (1969). What is a public use is a judicial quesiton to be determined by the court as a matter of law, reviewable on appeal. Development Co. v. Wilson, 44 N.C. App. 469, 261 S.E.2d 275 (1980); Highway Commission v. Batts, 265 N.C. 346, 144 S.E.2d 126 (1965).

tration of governmental affairs;[28] for purposes relating to public travel (for the construction and maintenance of highways and turnpikes,[29] for offices, shops, garages, places for the storage of supplies and for the purpose of quartering workmen and prisoners employed in the construction and maintenance of public roads,[30] for railroads,[31] depots, yards, terminals,[32] and for airports);[33] for purposes connected with communications (for telephone and telegraph lines, towers, poles, conduits, and offices);[34] for purposes relating to navigation (for wharves,[35] canals,[36] improvements of streams, piers and docks); [37] for purposes relating to public health (for water supply,[38] public hospitals and asylums,[39] public parks and playgrounds,[40] public cemeteries,[41] drainage,[42] sewers and sewage disposal plants,[43] and for the eradication of substandard, outmoded, unsanitary, or dangerous dwellings for slum clearance);[44] for purposes relating to education (for the provision of schools, playgrounds, athletic fields, institutions of higher learning,[45] and for historic sites);[46] and for other purposes, the performance of which the legislature has found to be for the public interest (such as condemnation for the transportation of oil, gas and petroleum products through pipe lines,[47] the establishment of public parking lots and garages,[48] the production and distribution of electric power and light,[49] and the building and maintenance of public markets).[50]

---

28. N.C. GEN. STAT. § 40-2.
29. N.C. GEN. STAT. §§ 136-19, 136-52, 136-103 et seq.
30. N.C. GEN. STAT. § 40-2(9).
31. N.C. GEN. STAT. § 62-192.
32. N.C. GEN. STAT. § 40-4.
33. N.C. GEN. STAT. §§ 63-5, 63-6.
34. N.C. GEN. STAT. § 62-183.
35. N.C. GEN. STAT. § 40-7.
36. N.C. GEN. STAT. §§ 40-2(1), 40-29.
37. N.C. GEN. STAT. § 143-220.
38. N.C. GEN. STAT. §§ 162A-6(10), 162A-7.
39. N.C. GEN. STAT. § 131-15.
40. N.C. GEN. STAT. § 160A-353.
41. N.C. GEN. STAT. § 160A-345.
42. See N.C. GEN. STAT. § 156-1 et seq. (individual drainage statute); N.C. GEN. STAT. §§ 160A-240 through 160A-263 (powers and procedures applicable to municipal corporations).
43. N.C. GEN. STAT. § 130-162.
44. N.C. GEN. STAT. § 157-50.
45. N.C. GEN. STAT. § 115-125.
46. N.C. GEN. STAT. § 121-9 contains the authorization for the acquisition of property under eminent domain where such property has peculiar historical, architectural, archeological or other cultural importance to the State.
47. N.C. GEN. STAT. § 62-190.
48. N.C. GEN. STAT. §§ 160-481, 160-482.
49. N.C. GEN. STAT. § 62-183.
50. See N.C. GEN. STAT. §§ 160A-240 through 160A-263 with respect to eminent domain

An owner of property cannot be compelled to surrender his property to another against his will, even though he may be fully compensated, unless the taking of his property is for a public use, some use in which the public interest is involved.[51] To be a "public use" and one which will justify the taking of private property, the use must be one by or for the government, or for the benefit of the general public, or some portion of the general public *as such,* and not a use by or for particular individuals or for the benefit of particular estates.[52] The use must be one for furnishing the general public with some necessity or convenience which cannot be readily furnished without the aid of some govenmental power. What constitutes a public purpose or use is a question of law and a judicial question.[53] While deference will be paid to legislative judgment as to whether a particular use of property is a "public use," the question ultimately is a question for the courts,[54] but once the judiciary determines that a use is public, then condemnation under eminent domain will be allowed and the wisdom, necessity, expedience or extent of condemnation for such purpose is not reviewable.

Article II. Procedure in Condemnation [55]

§ 404. The Attempt to Purchase.

Under the general condemnation statute found in Chapter 40 of the North Carolina General Statutes, an authorized corporation or body

---

powers and procedures applicable to municipal corporations. *See also* N.C. GEN. STAT. § 160A-311 for list of "public enterprises" for which condemnation may be had.

51. Charlotte v. Heath, 226 N.C. 750 (1946), wherein the court said: "In the exercise of the right of eminent domain private property can be taken only for a public purpose and upon just compensation." *See also* Cozard v. Hardwood Co., 139 N.C. 283, 51 S.E. 932 (1905); N.C. State Highway Comm'n v. Asheville School, Inc., 276 N.C. 556, 173 S.E.2d 909 (1970).
52. *Id.*
53. Cozard v. Hardwood Co., 139 N.C. 283, 51 S.E. 932 (1905).
54. *Id.* Cobb v. Railroad, 172 N.C. 58, 89 S.E. 807 (1916).
55. This discussion is limited to procedures under Chapter 40 of the General Statutes, the section under which most condemnation is made in North Carolina. It should be remembered that the legislature may authorize entirely different modes of condemnation by special act or special charter so long as a hearing is provided for the property owner and "just compensation" is assured. The requirement that property shall not be taken except by "due process of law" or by the "law of the land" does not control the power of the State to determine the process by which the legal right may be asserted or legal obligations enforced if the method of procedure gives reasonable notice to the landowner and a fair opportunity to be heard before the issues are decided. *See* Yarborough v. Park Comm'n, 196 N.C. 284, 145 S.E. 563 (1928). It is the exclusive prerogative of the legislature, limited only by the organic law which requires that just compensation shall be paid for the land appropriated, to prescribe the method of taking land for public use. *See* Board of Educ. v. Allen, 243 N.C. 520, 91 S.E.2d 180 (1956). When there is a particular manner provided for condemning land, this method and not that prescribed by the general law must be followed. *See* Railroad v. Ely, 95 N.C. 77 (1886); Railroad v. Warren, 92 N.C. 620 (1885). *See also* N.C. GEN. STAT. § 136-103 et seq., which will govern condemnations by the State Highway Commission.

politic which possesses the power of eminent domain may acquire lands for its public purposes by purchase at such sum as may be agreed upon between the property owner and the condemnor.[56] If, however, no agreement can be reached and the lands required for the public purpose cannot be purchased, the condemnor shall have the right to acquire the property it needs by following the procedures set out in North Carolina General Statutes, §§ 40-11 through 40-29.

§ 405. Special Proceedings.

(a) *In general.* If the lands required by the authorized corporation or body politic cannot be acquired by negotiation with the owner by purchase, the corporation or body politic empowered to exercise eminent domain may institute *special proceedings* to obtain the property required by filing a petition with the Clerk of the Superior Court in the county where the property is located.[57] Likewise, an owner whose land has been taken by one claiming the power of eminent domain can file a petition with the Clerk in order to obtain compensation.[58]

(b) *What petition must include.* The petition filed with the Clerk must be signed and verified. If it is filed by the condemnor, it must describe the lands to be condemned,[59] it must state the due incorporation of the corporation (if it is a corporation), that its intention is to conduct and carry on its public business, stating the nature of the public business and the specific use to be made of the lands. The petition must state that the condemnor has been unable to acquire the property and the reason for its inability to do so. The petition, whether filed by the condemnor or the owner, must state the names and places of residence of all parties, so far as can be ascertained by reasonable diligence, who own or have estates or interests in the lands to be condemned. If any such parties in interest are infants, their ages must be stated and if any such persons are idiots or persons of unsound mind or are unknown, that fact must be stated, together with other statements of liens or encumbrances on said property as the condemnor or owner may see fit to make. The petition asks for the appointment of commissioners for appraisal to ascertain the value of the property condemned for public purposes.[60]

---

56. N.C. Gen. Stat. § 40-3.

57. N.C. Gen. Stat. § 40-11; Airport Authority v. Irvin, 36 N.C. App. 662, 245 S.E.2d 390 (1978).

58. N.C. Gen. Stat. § 40-12; Proctor v. Highway Comm'n, 230 N.C. 687, 55 S.E.2d 479 (1949).

59. Under Article 9, Chapter 136 of the North Carolina statutes, a single condemnation proceeding may include more than one tract of land, and the applicable statutes do not require that multiple tracts be contiguous. Board of Transp. v. Royster, 40 N.C. App. 1, 251 S.E.2d 921 (1979). If the condemnation is for railroad right-of-way purposes, a map and profile must be filed with petition. *See* N.C. Gen. Stat. § 62-192.

60. N.C. Gen. Stat. § 40-12.

§ 405 EMINENT DOMAIN § 405

(c) *Summons in condemnation proceedings.* A summons, as in other cases of special proceedings, together with a copy of the petition, must be served on all persons whose interests are to be affected by the proceedings at least ten days prior to the hearing of the same by the Clerk. If there are persons whose names are unknown or whose residence cannot be located by the exercise of reasonable diligence, the Clerk may direct that service be made by publication of a notice stating the time and place within which such person must appear and plead, the object of the action, with a description of the property to be affected by the proceedings. Such notice should be published in a paper published in the county where the land lies, once in each week for four weeks previous to the time fixed by the Clerk for the hearing, and if there is no paper printed in the county where the property is located, then such notice shall be printed in a newspaper printed in the City of Raleigh.[61]

(d) *Answer to petition in condemnation proceeding — hearing.* When a petition is presented to the Superior Court by a condemnor, with proof of service of a copy thereof and of the summons, all or any of the persons whose estates or interests will be affected by the proceedings may file answers to show cause why the property should not be appraised and why condemnation should not be allowed.[62] The court shall appoint an attorney to appear for and protect the rights of any party in interest who is unknown, and who has not appeared by an attorney or agent.[63] If an answer is filed to the petition, a hearing is ordered and the burden is on the petitioner to establish the facts alleged as warranting appraisal of the property and its condemnation. Upon denial of the allegations in the petition, the condemnor is put to his proof on the following issues: (1) Is the condemnor one authorized by general law, special act or charter to condemn property under the power of eminent domain? (2) Is the petition signed and verified? (3) Is the property which is the subject of the condemnation proceeding sufficiently described?[64] (4) Is the property being condemned in good faith to conduct public business?[65] (5) Has there been

---

61. N.C. GEN. STAT. §§ 40-13, 40-14.
62. N.C. GEN. STAT. § 40-16.
63. N.C. GEN. STAT. § 40-24.
64. The recipe for taking property by condemnation begins by saying: "First locate the property." *See* Gastonia v. Glenn, 218 N.C. 510, 11 S.E.2d 459 (1940).
65. *See* Power Co. v. Wissler, 160 N.C. 269, 76 S.E. 267 (1912), which indicates that bad faith on the part of the condemnor or an oppressive or manifest abuse of the condemnor's discretion may raise an issuable question for the court's determination. *Accord,* City of Charlotte v. McNeely, 281 N.C. 684, 190 S.E.2d 179 (1972). A city council's choice of a route, or the land to be condemned for a street will not be reviewed on the ground that another route may have been more appropriately chosen unless it appears that there has been an abuse of the discretion. Upon specific allegation tending to show bad faith, malice, wantoness, or oppressive and manifest abuse of discretion by the condemnor, the issue raised becomes the subject of judicial inquiry as a question of fact to be determined by the judge. *See also* Airport Auth. v. Irvin, 36 N.C. App. 662, 245 S.E.2d 390 (1978).

§ 405

the mandatory attempt by the condemnor to acquire the property by negotiation and purchase which has failed?[66] Until these averments of facts are made and found to be true by the court (the Clerk), the right to exercise the power of eminent domain is not established. The determination of the truth of these facts is a matter for the Clerk and not subject to jury determination.[67] Unlike other special proceedings, when factual issues are raised by the pleadings in a condemnation proceeding, the cause is not transferred to the civil issue docket. These are preliminary jurisdictional questions of fact which must be decided by the Clerk.[68]

If the Clerk finds against the condemnor upon any of these essential averments, he dismisses the proceeding. The petitioner may immediately except and appeal from the Clerk's dismissal to the judge of the Superior Court who will hear and decide petitioner condemnor's appeal upon these preliminary questions. If the judge affirms the Clerk, an appeal lies to the North Carolina Court of Appeals upon conclusions of law. There is no right to a trial by jury at any stage upon these preliminary issues even though they are issues of fact.[69]

If the Clerk finds the condemnor's averments to be true, he makes an order for the appointment of commissioners to view the premises involved and to assess the benefits and damages from the condemnation.[70] There can be no appeal by the condemnee from an order of the Clerk merely appointing commissioners to assess damages, this being only an interlocutory order. An appeal can be had by the condemnee only after a final judgment upon the report of the commissioners.[71]

---

66. In the absence of proof thereof the petition should be dismissed. Railroad v. Railroad, 148 N.C. 59, 61 S.E. 683 (1908). *But see* Power Co. v. Moses, 191 N.C. 744, 133 S.E. 5 (1926), where it is said that no attempt need be shown to purchase from one who is under disability.

Under N.C. GEN. STAT. § 160A-241, the power of a municipality to acquire property by condemnation shall not depend on any prior effort to acquire the same property by grant or purchase, nor shall the power to negotiate for the grant or purchase of property be impaired by initiation of condemnation proceedings for acquisition of the same property.

See Power & Light Co. v. Merritt, 41 N.C. App. 438, 438, 255 S.E.2d 225 (1979) holding that a property owner could not prevent condemnation by asserting the doctrine of *res judicata* based on a final judgment entered in an earlier condemnation proceeding since the so-called final judgment in the earlier matter was in reality a voluntary dismissal. Abandonment of the earlier proceeding in which no interest was taken could not extinguish the right of eminent domain.

67. Railroad v. Railroad, 148 N.C. 59, 61 S.E. 683 (1908).

68. *Id.* Selma v. Nobles, 183 N.C. 322, 111 S.E. 543 (1922); Abernathy v. Railroad, 150 N.C. 97, 63 S.E. 180 (1908).

69. Railroad v. Railroad, 148 N.C. 59, 61 S.E. 683 (1908).

70. N.C. GEN. STAT. § 40-17.

71. N.C. GEN. STAT. § 40-19; Selma v. Nobles, 183 N.C. 322, 111 S.E. 543 (1922); Abernathy v. Railroad, 150 N.C. 97, 63 S.E. 180 (1908); Railroad v. Railroad, 148 N.C. 59, 61 S.E. 683 (1908). For miscellaneous procedural issues see Power & Light Co. v. Merritt, discussed at note 66 *supra;* Development Co. v. County of Wilson, 44 N.C. App. 469, 261

(e) *Appraisal and report of commissioners.* The commissioners shall be three disinterested and competent freeholders who reside in the county. They are required to take an oath that they will fairly and impartially appraise the value of the lands mentioned in the petition. They are empowered to issue subpoenas, to administer oaths to witnesses and to adjourn the proceedings before them from time to time. They view the premises, hear the proofs and allegations and reduce testimony, if any is taken, to writing. They are empowered to ascertain and determine the compensation which ought justly to be paid by the condemnor of the property condemned. The commissioners are not required to be unanimous in their report but their report need be signed only by a majority of the commissioners, all of them being present and voting.[72]

(f) *Appeals from commissioners' appraisal.* As mentioned above, there can be no appeal by the landowner from an order of the Clerk merely appointing commissioners to appraise property. An appeal by the condemnee will lie only from a final judgment upon the report of the commissioners.[73] If the report is made by the commissioners, however, either condemnor or condemnee may file exceptions to the report within twenty days from the filing thereof. The Clerk shall make a determination as to the exceptions to the report and make such orders as may be necessary.[74] From this determination by the Clerk, either party may appeal to the judge of the Superior Court *during a session.*[75] The judge of the Superior Court has the power in his discretion to set aside the commissioners' report and to direct a new appraisement by the same or other commissioners if he thinks the damages assessed are excessive, or he may modify or confirm the report or make such order in the premises as to him shall seem right and proper. The judge does *not* have the power to modify the commissioners' report by substituting a smaller sum.[76] There is no right of appeal from an order by the judge remanding a condemnation proceeding to the Clerk for reappraisal by the commissioners, this being interlocutory and appeals lying only from final judgments.[77]

Once the commissioners' report is made and upon exception approved by the Clerk and not remanded by the Superior Court judge for

---

S.E.2d 275 (1980) holding that landowners could not seek to enjoin Wilson County from proceeding to condemn their land where the appeal procedures in the applicable condemnation statute gave them an adequate remedy at law.

72. N.C. Gen. Stat. §§ 40-16, 40-17.

73. Note, however, that the condemnor has an immediate right of appeal from the Clerk to the judge of the Superior Court if the Clerk *dismisses* the condemnor's action for failure of the petitioner to allege and prove preliminary questions essential to maintenance of condemnation proceeding. *See* Railroad v. Railroad, 148 N.C. 59, 61 S.E. 683 (1908).

74. McIntosh, North Carolina Practice and Procedure § 2371 (1956).

75. N.C. Gen. Stat. § 40-19; Railroad v. Stewart, 132 N.C. 248, 43 S.E. 638 (1903).

76. Hanes v. Railroad, 109 N.C. 490, 13 S.E. 896 (1891).

77. Cape Fear R.R. v. King, 125 N.C. 454, 34 S.E. 541 (1899).

§ 405   REAL ESTATE LAW IN NORTH CAROLINA   § 405

reappraisal, the parties upon appeal are entitled to have the issue of compensation to be awarded determined by a jury if demanded. This is a right to have the matter of compensation tried *de novo*.[78] This means that when either party appeals to the Superior Court in term and demands that the damages be determined by a jury, the trial must proceed in the Superior Court insofar as the question of damages is concerned as though no commissioners of appraisal had ever been appointed. This being true, it necessarily follows that the Superior Court at term is vested with authority to enter judgment for the landowner for the amount of damages fixed by the verdict of the jury, regardless of whether the same be greater or smaller than the sum originally awarded by the commissioners of appraisal and regardless of whether the landowner or the condemnor took the appeal.[79] From any errors in law, appeals may be had from the Superior Court's decision to the North Carolina Court of Appeals.

(g) *Rights of condemnor pending appeal.* Notwithstanding the pendency of an appeal from the commissioners' or jury's verdict as to damages to be awarded, if the condemnor at the time of the appraisal, shall pay into court the sum appraised by the commissioners, the said condemnor corporation may enter, take possession of and hold the lands. Therefore, appeal as a dilatory tactic is not available. By simply paying into court the amount of the appraisal, the condemnor corporation can proceed to take and use the property for its public purposes.[80] This rule is applicable to corporations and is designed to secure definite and certain compensation to the landowner and at the same time to prevent delays by appeals which might bring the work of the condemnor to a standstill and stand in the way of obviously necessary public works. In cases of condemnation by the State Highway Commission for highway purposes, the Commission may enter and take possession of lands after filing a complaint and declaration of a taking and by depositing in court a sum of money estimated to be just compensation for the property taken. The Commission may proceed and use the property to be condemned pending the final determination of the action.[81]

(h) *When no appeal is taken by owner.* If there is no appeal by the owner and the final judgment is in favor of the condemnor at a certain sum adjudged, and the condemnor pays into court this amount plus costs and counsel fees allowed, all parties who have been made parties to the proceedings shall be divested and barred of all rights, estates and interests in the property condemned to the extent specified by the petition for

---

78. Ayden v. Lancaster, 195 N.C. 297, 142 S.E. 18 (1925); Light Co. v. Reeves, 198 N.C. 404, 151 S.E. 871 (1930).
79. Proctor v. Highway Comm'n, 230 N.C. 687, 55 S.E.2d 479 (1949).
80. N.C. GEN. STAT. § 40-19.
81. N.C. GEN. STAT. § 136-103 et seq.

condemnation.[82] In the event that the appraised value of the land is not paid by the condemnor within one year from the final judgment fixing the petitioner's right to condemn, the petitioner's right to take the property shall end.[83]

§ 406. Rules Relating to Compensation in Eminent Domain Proceedings.

It has been said that in the exercise of the right of eminent domain, private property can be taken only for a public purpose and only upon "just compensation" being paid. [84] What is the owner entitled to when his property is taken from him under the foregoing procedures and for the purposes for which condemnation is allowed? The determination of this question becomes especially important when the attorney for the property owner considers and prepares evidence for use in a condemnation proceeding.

The market value of the property is the yardstick by which compensation for the taking of land or any interest therein is to be measured.[85] The landowner is entitled to receive a just equivalent of that which is taken from him.[86] The citizen landowner should suffer no financial loss which may be prevented by awarding him damages.[87] He is entitled to recover the present market value of the property taken from him as of the date that the condemnation proceeding is instituted or the property is taken. No subsequent change in value, upward or downward, can be considered.[88]

In determining the "market value" of property, it is said that it is the hypothetical sum which probably would be arrived at as a result of fair

---

82. Depending upon whether a fee or merely an easement in the property is condemned.

83. N.C. GEN. STAT. § 40-19. *See* Nantahala Power Co. v. Whiting Mfg. Co., 209 N.C. 560, 184 S.E. 48 (1936).

84. *See* § 403, note 84 *supra*. *See also* Department of Transp. v. Container Co., 45 N.C. App. 638, 263 S.E.2d 830 (1980), holding that litigation expenses and costs incurred by a landowner in a condemnation proceeding do not constitute part of "just compensation" required to be paid by the Fifth Admendment and holding that such expenses and costs may be taxed only if authorized by statute. (Citing United States v. Bodcaw Company, 440 U.S. 202, 59 L. Ed. 2d 257, 99 S. Ct. 1066 (1979)).

85. Light Co. v. Moss, 220 N.C. 200, 17 S.E.2d 10 (1941). *Accord,* City of Kings Mountain v. Cline, 19 N.C. App. 9, 198 S.E.2d 64 (1973). In North Carolina the taking of land by eminent domain does not contemplate compensation for loss of business maintained on that land, or for cost in moving a business and its attendant personal property to another location. *See* Williams v. Highway Comm'n, 252 N.C. 141, 113 S.E.2d 263 (1960); Power Co. v. Ham House, Inc., 43 N.C. App. 308, 258 S.E.2d 815 (1979).

86. State v. Suncrest Lumber Co., 199 N.C. 199, 154 S.E. 72 (1930).

87. A term apparently used interchangeably in condemnation proceedings with "compensation." *See* Railroad v. Manufacturing Co., 169 N.C. 156, 85 S.E. 390 (1915).

88. Power Co. v. Hayes, 193 N.C. 104, 136 S.E. 353 (1927); Ayden v. Lancaster, 197 N.C. 556, 142 S.E. 18 (1929). City of Greensboro v. Sparger, 23 N.C. App. 81, 208 S.E.2d 230 (1974), holds that occurrences or events which may affect the value of property after the date of taking are not cognizable in assessment of damages in eminent domain proceedings.

negotiations between an owner willing to sell and a purchaser willing to buy after due consideration of all elements reasonably affecting the value of the property.[89]

If a landowner's entire tract is taken, he should receive the market value of the whole tract. If, however, his whole tract is not taken, but only a small part thereof is taken, or the condemnor only acquires an easement over a portion of the owner's total tract, the landowner is entitled to the difference between the fair market value of the entire tract immediately before the taking and the fair market value of what is left after the taking.[90] It is obvious that the extent of the taking is important. If a fee or very onerous easement is taken, the compensation will be much greater than if an easement of very limited purposes is taken and the condemnee is allowed to continue to own and use the fee.

§ 407. Evidence Admissible in Determining "Market Value."

The condemnee owner is only entitled to be indemnified to the extent that he has *lost* by the taking. The just compensation rule merely requires that the owner of the property taken shall be paid for what is taken from him. The value of the property to the condemnor for his particular use may not be considered.[91]

In determining what the condemnee has lost, he is entitled to have considered all the capabilities of the property and all the uses to which it *may* be applied, or for which it is adapted, which affects its value in the market. He is not limited merely to compensation for the value of his property in its present application. The landowner should be allowed to state, and have his witnesses state, every fact concerning the property which he would naturally be disposed to adduce in order to place it in an advantageous light if he were attempting to negotiate a sale of it to a

---

89. Light Co. v. Moss, 220 N.C. 200, 17 S.E.2d 10 (1941). *Accord,* City of Kings Mountain v. Cline, 19 N.C. App. 9, 198 S.E.2d 64 (1973).

90. Gallimore v. Highway Comm'n, 241 N.C. 350, 85 S.E.2d 392 (1955); Statesville v. Anderson, 245 N.C. 208, 95 S.E.2d 591 (1956). *Accord,* City of Kings Mountain v. Cline, 19 N.C. App. 9, 198 S.E.2d 64 (1973); City of Greensboro v. Sparger, 23 N.C. App. 81, 208 S.E.2d 230 (1974); Duke Power Co. v. Ribet, 25 N.C. App. 87, 212 S.E.2d 182 (1975); Board of Transp. v. Harvey, 28 N.C. App. 327, 220 S.E.2d 815 (1976).

See Board of Transp. v. Brown, 34 N.C. App. 266, 237 S.E.2d 854 (1977) where it was held that the trial court erred in excluding evidence of traffic noise and of a lack of direct access from the landowner's remaining land to the highway as factors to be considered in determining the fair market value of the remaining land. *See also* Highway Comm. v. Rose, 31 N.C. App. 28, 228 S.E.2d 664 (1976) holding *inter alia,* that, if a landowner retains reasonable means of ingress and egress to and from his property after the construction of traffic islands by the highway commission, there is no compensable interference with the property rights of the landowner. Board of Transp. v. Warehouse Corp., 44 N.C. App. 81, 260 S.E.2d 696 (1979); Board of Transp. v. Jones, 297 N.C. 436, 255 S.E.2d 185 (1979).

91. State v. Johnson, 282 N.C. 1, 191 S.E.2d 641 (1972); Light Co. v. Moss, 220 N.C. 200, 17 S.E.2d 10 (1941).

private individual.[92] Likewise, the jury and the opposing counsel should be allowed to make every inquiry touching the property that one about to buy it would feel it to his interest to make.[93] The owner is entitled to compensation for the highest and most profitable use for which the property is adaptable in the reasonably near future but mere imaginary or speculative schemes are to be excluded. Any witness who has knowledge of value gained from experience, information and observation may give his opinion of the value of specific property.[94] He need not be an expert if he has sufficient knowledge and experience as to enable him intelligently to place a value on the property.[95]

In the recent decision of *Power Co. v. Winebarger*,[96] the North Carolina Supreme Court, in order to clarify the law concerning valuation of property in eminent domain proceedings, restated the controlling principles as follows:

> (1) Where the value of a particular parcel of realty is directly in issue, the price paid at voluntary sales of land similar in nature, location, and condition to the land involved in the suit is admissible as independent evidence of the value of the land in question, if the sales are not too remote in time. Whether two properties are sufficiently similar to admit the sales price of one as circumstantial evidence of the value of the other is a question to be determined by the trial judge, usually upon *voir dire*.[97]
>
> (2) Conversely, where a particular property is markedly dissimilar

---

92. Brown v. Power Co., 140 N.C. 333, 52 S.E. 954 (1905); Light Co. v. Rogers, 207 N.C. 751, 178 S.E. 575 (1935). *Accord,* Charlotte v. Recreation Comm'n, 278 N.C. 26, 178 S.E.2d 601 (1970); State v. Johnson, 282 N.C. 1, 191 S.E.2d 641 (1972). *See* Barnes v. Highway Comm'n, 250 N.C. 378, 109 S.E.2d 219 (1950), a particularly complete and comprehensive opinion with respect to the establishment of "market value." *See also* Power Co. v. Winebarger, 300 N.C. 57, 265 S.E.2d 227 (1980) discussed later in this section.

93. *Id.*

94. STANSBURY, NORTH CAROLINA EVIDENCE § 128 (1946); Railroad v. Manufacturing Co., 169 N.C. 156, 85 S.E. 390 (1915). Expert real estate appraisers should be given great latitude in determining the value of property. Board of Transp. v. Jones, 297 N.C. 436, 255 S.E.2d 185 (1979); Power Co. v. Ham House, Inc., 43 N.C. App. 308, 258 S.E.2d 815 (1979). *See also* Power Co. v. Winebarger, 300 N.C. 57, 265 S.E.2d 227 (1980); Department of Transp. v. Rogers, 44 N.C. App. 56, 259 S.E.2d 775 (1979).

95. Highway Comm'n v. Fry, 6 N.C. App. 370, 170 S.E.2d 91 (1969).

96. 300 N.C. 57, 265 S.E.2d 227 (1980).

97. Citing State v. Johnson, 282 N.C. 1, 191 S.E.2d 641 (1972). That case holds that it is the rule in North Carolina that the price paid at voluntary sales of land, similar in nature, location, and condition to the condemnee's land, is admissible as independent evidence of the value of the land taken if prior sale was not too remote in time. Whether two properties are sufficiently similar to admit evidence of the purchase price of one as a guide to the value of the other is a question to be determined by the trial judge in the exercise of a sound discretion guided by law. The approved practice is for the judge to conduct a *voir dire,* to hear testimony in the absence of the jury as a basis for determining the admissibility of such evidence. *Accord,* Highway Comm'n v. Helderman, 285 N.C. 645, 207 S.E.2d 720 (1974).

to the property at issue, the sales price of the former may not be introduced or alluded to in any manner which suggests to the jury that it has a bearing on the estimation of the value of the latter.

(3) Where a witness has been offered to testify to the value of the property directly in issue, the scope of that witness' *knowledge* of the values and sales prices of dissimilar properties in the area may be cross-examined for the limited purposes of impeachment to test his credibility and expertise.[98]

(4) Under these limited impeachment circumstances, however, it is improper for the cross-examiner to refer to specific values or prices of noncomparable properties in his questions to the witness.[99] Moreover, if the witness responds that he does not know or remember the value or price of the property asked about, the impeachment purpose of the cross-examination is satisfied and the inquiry as to that property is exhausted.[100] If, on the other hand, the witness asserts his knowledge on cross-examination of a particular value or sales price of noncomparable property, he may be asked to state that value or price only when the trial judge determines in his discretion that the impeachment value of a specific answer outweighs the possibility of confusing the jury with collateral issues. In such a rare case, however, the cross-examiner must be prepared to take the witness' answer as given.[101]

As one might guess, numerous cases exist dealing with this subject. A sampling of them is included in the following summary. Concerning value of property, unaccepted offers to buy or sell are deemed too uncertain, shadowy and speculative to shed any light on the true value of property.[102] The price paid in settlement of other condemnation proceedings of land similarly situated is not admissible to show the value of land to be condemned.[103] Tax assessment valuations prepared by tax assessors are not admissible as evidence of the value of land,[104] but if the property is personal property and the valuation has been made by the owner

---

98. Citing Templeton v. Highway Commission, 254 N.C. 337, 118 S.E.2d 918 (1961).

99. Citing Carver v. Lykes, 262 N.C. 345, 137 S.E.2d 139 (1964).

100. Citing Highway Commission v. Privett, 246 N.C. 501, 99 S.E.2d 61 (1957).

101. Citing Carver v. Lykes, 262 N.C. 345, 137 S.E.2d 139 (1964).

102. Canton v. Harris, 177 N.C. 10, 97 S.E. 748 (1918). *Accord,* Highway Comm'n v. Helderman, 285 N.C. 645, 207 S.E.2d 720 (1974).

103. Light Co. v. Sloan, 227 N.C. 151, 41 S.E.2d 361 (1947). *Accord,* State v. Johnson, 282 N.C. 1, 191 S.E.2d 641 (1972), which quotes from WIGMORE, EVIDENCE § 463 (3d ed., Supp. 1962) as follows: "Evidence of amounts paid by the condemnor for property similarly situated, in the absence of extraordinary circumstances, is inadmissible, because such sales are involuntary and therefore, under the substantive law, run counter to the essential ingredient of fair market value."

104. Ridley v. Railroad, 124 N.C. 37, 32 S.E. 379 (1899); Railroad v. Land Co., 137 N.C. 330, 49 S.E. 350 (1904); STANSBURY, NORTH CAROLINA EVIDENCE § 100 (1946).

himself, such valuation may be used as evidence of value, being an admission of the owner.[105]

If by reasons of its surroundings, its natural advantages or its artificial improvements, or its intrinsic character, property is peculiarly adapted to some particular use, all the circumstances which make up this adaptability may be shown for the jury's consideration in determining the compensation to be paid.[106] The rental value of property is competent upon the question of fair market value at the time of the taking.[107] That property may be joined with other properties to become adaptable for a certain use may be admissible on the issue of damages if such is of reasonable probability and not too remote.[108]

In condemnation proceedings, the determinative question is: In its condition on the day of the taking, what was the value of the land for the highest and best use to which it would be put by owners possessed of prudence, wisdom, and adequate means? The owner's actual plans or hopes for the future are considered irrelevant and regarded as too remote and speculative to merit consideration.[109] In other words, the value of the property may not be enhanced by reason of the frustration of the owner's particular plans with respect to the property. The burden of establishing value in eminent domain proceedings is on the landowner condemnee.[110]

§ 408. Right of Condemnor to Offset Benefits to Realty Condemned.

In the determination of the compensation to be paid a condemnee when his property is taken, the condemnor is often entitled to have evidence of benefits accruing to the condemnee considered in diminution of the sum to be paid by the condemnor. The condemnor may be entitled to offset an increase in the value of the condemnee's property by reason of the condemnation as against the compensation found to be due the condemnee,

---

105. Daniels v. Fowler, 123 N.C. 35, 31 S.E. 598 (1898). *Compare,* Highway Comm'n v. Helderman, 285 N.C. 645, 207 S.E.2d 720 (1974), to the effect that while a mere offer to sell is inadmissible as evidence to prove market value, an offer to sell by the owner, made at or about the time of a taking, is competent for the purpose of contradicting his contention that it is worth more than the amount for which he offered to sell the property.

106. Light Co. v. Rogers, 207 N.C. 751, 178 S.E. 575 (1935). *Accord,* State v. Johnson, 282 N.C. 1, 191 S.E.2d 641 (1972).

107. Palmer v. Highway Comm'n, 195 N.C. 1, 141 S.E. 338 (1927); Brown v. Power Co., 140 N.C. 333, 52 S.E. 954 (1905). *Accord,* Ross v. Perry, 281 N.C. 570, 189 S.E.2d 226 (1972), citing Kirkman v. Highway Comm'n, 257 N.C. 428, 432, 126 S.E.2d 107, 110 (1966).

108. *See* Light Co. v. Moss, 220 N.C. 200, 17 S.E.2d 10 (1941), Justice Clarkson's concurring opinion.

109. *See* State v. Johnson, 282 N.C. 1, 191 S.E.2d 641 (1972), citing 4 NICHOLS, THE LAW OF EMINENT DOMAIN § 12.314 (3d ed. 1971). Improbable, theoretical schemes may not be admitted. Light Co. v. Clark, 243 N.C. 577, 91 S.E. 569 (1956).

110. Statesville v. Anderson, 245 N.C. 208, 95 S.E.2d 591 (1956).

depending upon whether the benefit to the landowner is "general" or "special."[111]

"Special benefits" are those which directly increase the value of a particular piece of property by reason of the condemnation for a certain purpose.[112] "General benefits" are those which affect the value of the property of the whole community or neighborhood.[113]

If the condemnation is by a municipality[114] or the State Highway Commission,[115] both general and special benefits can be assessed and offset in diminution of the sum to be paid to the condemnee by reason of statutes where only a part of the landowner's land is taken. If, however, the condemnation is by a quasi-public corporation not a municipal corporation nor the State, the benefits which can be offset as against the compensation due the condemnee are limited to special benefits to his land not shared in by the community at large.[116]

The decision as to whether the condemnor shall be allowed to offset *all* the benefits to the land of a landowner accruing from a condemnation or only *special benefits* or *no benefits* at all rests with the sovereign.[117] The legislature has the power to determine what benefits can be offset and specific statutes authorizing condemnation must always be consulted to determine the admissibility of benefit evidence. In no event will the owner be compelled to pay for special or general benefits if they exceed the damages to the owner.

---

111. For a recent discussion of general and special benefits, see Board of Transp. v. Rand, 299 N.C. 476, 263 S.E.2d 800 (1980). *See also* Board of Transp. v. Jones, 297 N.C. 436, 255 S.E.2d 185 (1979).
112. *Id.*
113. *Id.*
114. N.C. Gen. Stat. § 160A-250 makes provision for the consideration of both "special" and "general" benefits to property affected by the condemnation. *See* City of Kings Mountain v. Cline, 19 N.C. App. 9, 198 S.E.2d 64 (1973), decided under previously existing N.C. Gen. Stat. § 160-204 *et seq.* which states: "If the statute under which the condemnor has taken land authorizes the deduction of benefits to the land remaining, the total compensation to the landowner must be diminished by any such benefit to his remaining land arising out of the use to which the condemned land is put."
115. N.C. Gen. Stat. § 136-112. *See* Templeton v. Highway Comm'n, 254 N.C. 337, 118 S.E.2d 918 (1961), to the effect that the condemnor under N.C. Gen. Stat. § 136-112 is entitled to have its witnesses to testify as to the increase in value of the condemnee's remaining land as a result of highway construction for which the condemnation is made. If the jury finds either "special" or "general" benefits to the condemnee's remaining land as a result of the condemnation, such benefits shall be offset against damages payable to the condemnee.
116. Town of Hillsborough v. Bartow, 38 N.C. App. 708, 248 S.E.2d 909 (1978) holds that, when condemnation is pursuant to Chapter 40 of the General Statutes, the benefits that can be offset are limited to the special benefits to the condemnee's land.
117. Wade v. Highway Comm'n, 188 N.C. 210, 124 S.E. 193 (1924).

CHAPTER 20

LIENS ON REAL PROPERTY

Article I. General Provisions

§ 409. Liens on Real Property Generally.

Article II. Judgment Liens

§ 410. Judgment Liens Generally.
§ 411. Inception of Judgment Liens.
§ 412. Extent of Judgment Liens.
§ 413. Judgments of Various Courts May Be Docketed.
§ 414. Priority of Judgment Liens Where Judgment Debtor Owns Real Property at Time Judgment Docketed.
§ 415. Priority of Judgment Liens Where Judgment Debtor Acquires Real Property After the Docketing of Judgment.
§ 416. Enforcement of Judgment Liens — Execution.
§ 417. Termination of Judgment Liens.

Article III. Mechanics' Liens

Division 1. General Provisions

§ 418. Mechanics' Liens Generally.

Division 2. Liens Arising in Favor of Those Dealing Directly with the Owner of Real Property

§ 419. Introduction.
§ 420. Architects, Engineers, Land Surveyors, and Landscape Architects.
§ 421. Materialmen; Relationship of Article 9 of the Uniform Commercial Code.
§ 422. The Requirement of a Contract with the Owner of Real Property.
§ 423. Perfection of the Lien; Amendments; Assignment.
§ 424. Enforcement of the Lien.
§ 425. Priority and Extent of Lien; Introduction.
§ 426. Extent of Lien; Blanket Lien.
§ 427. Priority of Contractors' Lien as Against Subcontractors' Lien.
§ 428. Priority of Contractors' Lien as Against Purchase Money Mortgage or Deed of Trust.
§ 429. Priority of Contractors' Lien as Against Security Instrument Securing Presently Owned and After Acquired Property.
§ 430. Priority of Mechanics' Liens as Against Instruments Securing "Future Advances."
§ 431. Priority of Contractors' Lien Against Federal Tax Liens.
§ 432. Priority of Contractors' Lien Against Interests Arising Under the Bankruptcy Act.
§ 433. Priority of Mechanics' Lien Against Owners' Homestead Exemption.
§ 434. Priority of Contractors' Lien Against Federal Mortgages or Deeds of Trust.
§ 435. Waiver of the Lien.
§ 436. Discharge of the Lien.

Division 3. Liens of Mechanics, Laborers, and Materialmen Dealing with One Other than the Owner of Real Property

§ 437. Introduction.
§ 438. Nature of Lien; Statutory Definitions.
§ 439. General Applicability of Part I of Article 2 of Chapter 44A.

§ 440. Grant of Lien upon Funds: The First Tier Subcontractor.
§ 441. Grant of Lien upon Funds: Second and Third Tier Subcontractors.
§ 442. Direct Lien Rights of Second and Third Tier Subcontractors upon Funds.
§ 443. Subrogation Rights Available to Second and Third Tier Subcontractors.
§ 444. Grant of Lien: Remote Tier Subcontractors.
§ 445. Lien upon Funds: Perfection.
§ 446. Lien upon Funds: Amount Secured.
§ 447. Lien upon Funds: Effect of One Person's Waiver upon Another Person's Rights.
§ 448. Lien upon Funds: Duties and Liabilities of the "Obligor."
§ 449. Lien upon Funds: Priorities.
§ 450. Lien upon Funds: Enforcement.
§ 451. Liens upon the Owner's Interest in Real Property.

Division 4. Other Matters Concerning Mechanics' Lienors

§ 452. Applicability of Federal Truth in Lending Act.
§ 453. Criminal Sanctions Applicable to Lien Claimants.

Article IV. Tax and Assessment Liens

§ 454. Tax Liens.
§ 455. Assessment Liens.

Article I. General Provisions

§ 409. Liens on Real Property Generally.

A lien is defined as a right conferred on certain classes of creditors to have their debts paid out of specific property belonging to the debtor. A lien is a right to impose a charge or claim against specific property as security for the performance of an act, usually the payment of an obligation. If the obligation is not paid, the property may be subjected to payment of the owner's debts, usually by means of a sale of the property. Liens may be created by voluntary act such as the execution of a mortgage or deed of trust or they may arise involuntarily by operation of law as a result of a judgment, by a tax assessment, or by the filing of a laborer's or materialman's lien.[1]

Article II. Judgment Liens

§ 410. Judgment Liens Generally.

A judgment procured against the owner of real property, which is docketed on the judgment docket of the superior court of the county where the land is located, constitutes a lien on the real property of the judgment debtor.[2] In addition, a judgment properly docketed becomes a lien on any

---

[1]. These liens will be discussed fully at Article III of this chapter. Liens will also be discussed in Part 4, chapters 21 to 27 *infra,* which relate to searching land titles.

[2]. N.C. GEN. STAT. §§ 1-233, 1-234. *See* N.C. GEN. STAT. § 7A-193, which provides for the same procedure in district courts.

real property acquired by the judgment debtor subsequent to the docketing of the judgment and during the life of the judgment.[3]

§ 411. Inception of Judgment Liens.

A judgment lien does not take effect from the mere rendition or pronouncement of the judgment. It must be "docketed"[4] on the judgment docket of the superior court of the county where the judgment roll was filed and where the real property is located in order to constitute a lien on the real property of the judgment debtor.[5] The judgment "docket" is a book of index to judgments which are alphabetically arranged according to the name of the judgment debtor which is maintained by the Clerk of the Superior Court. The judgment docket is a convenience to purchasers, mortgagees and title searchers and obviates the necessity of reading the judgment rolls at large and readily discloses whether or not there are any judgment liens affecting specific property. The requirements of docketing must be strictly complied with in order to perfect a judgment lien[6] but when the lien becomes fixed the debtor cannot escape it; if he sells his real property thereafter his purchaser takes subject to the statutory lien.[7]

A judgment in one county cannot be docketed in another county so as to constitute a lien in such other county in which the real property is located unless it has first been docketed in the county where it was rendered.[8]

§ 412. Extent of Judgment Liens.

A judgment lien extends only to the real property owned by the judgment debtor located in the county where the judgment is docketed.[9] But if the judgment debtor owns real property in some other county, the judgment can be made a lien thereon by docketing of the judgment in such

---

3. *Id.*

4. *See* McIntosh, North Carolina Practice and Procedure § 1752 (Wilson & Wilson ed. 1956) for the methods of docketing.

5. Southern Dairies v. Banks, 92 F.2d 282 (1937); Alsop v. Moseley, 104 N.C. 60, 10 S.E. 124 (1889).

6. Southern Dairies v. Banks, 92 F.2d 282 (1937).

7. Moore v. Jordan, 117 N.C. 86, 23 S.E. 259 (1895); Moore v. Jones, 226 N.C. 149, 36 S.E.2d 920 (1946); Moses v. Major, 201 N.C. 613, 160 S.E. 890 (1931); Cowan v. Witherow, 112 N.C. 736, 17 S.E. 575 (1893). A docketed judgment also gives a lien over subsequent judgments. Perry v. Morris, 65 N.C. 221 (1871), as well as against subsequent mortgages, Moore v. Jones, 226 N.C. 149, 36 S.E.2d 920 (1946).

8. Essex Inv. Co. v. Pickelsimer, 210 N.C. 541, 187 S.E. 813 (1936); McAden v. Banister, 63 N.C. 479 (1869).

9. N.C. Gen. Stat. § 1-234.

other county in addition to the county where the judgment is originally docketed.[10]

The statutory judgment lien creates a lien in the nature of a statutory mortgage.[11] It applies not only to legal interests in real property but contemplates a lien in any "present, subsisting estate, legal or equitable, in the real property of the judgment debtor that may be enforced in some proper manner."[12] The lien will embrace "lands, tenements and hereditaments"[13] owned by the judgment debtor and includes equitable estates in real property which are subject to sale under execution or which may be reached by supplemental proceedings or by civil action in the nature of equitable execution.[14]

The lien of judgment does not extend to real property held by a husband and wife by the entireties where the judgment is against only one of the spouses, but it will attach where the judgment is against both spouses on a joint debt.[15]

§ 413. Judgments of Various Courts May Be Docketed.

Judgments of the North Carolina Supreme Court, inferior courts and federal courts become liens on the real property of the judgment debtor if they are properly docketed in the county where the real property is located.[16]

§ 414. Priority of Judgment Liens Where Judgment Debtor Owns Real Property at Time Judgment Docketed.

The priority of lien is generally established by priority of docketing of the judgment and where there are several judgments the order of their

---

10. Essex Inv. Co. v. Pickelsimer, 210 N.C. 541, 187 S.E. 813 (1936); McAden v. Banister, 63 N.C. 479 (1869); Lee v. Bishop, 89 N.C. 256 (1883); Brown v. Harding, 171 N.C. 686, 89 S.E. 222 (1916); McIntosh, North Carolina Practice and Procedure § 1752 (3) (Wilson & Wilson ed. 1956).

11. James v. Markham, 128 N.C. 380, 38 S.E. 917 (1901); Gambrill Mfg. Co. v. Wilcox, 111 N.C. 42, 15 S.E. 885 (1892).

12. Bruce v. Nicholson, 109 N.C. 202, 13 S.E. 790 (1891).

13. Rogers v. Kimsey, 101 N.C. 559, 8 S.E. 159 (1888).

14. Mayo v. Staton, 137 N.C. 670, 50 S.E. 331 (1905); Trimble v. Hunter, 104 N.C. 129, 10 S.E. 291 (1889); Mannix v. Ihrie, 76 N.C. 299 (1877); McKeithan & Sons v. Walker & Brown, 66 N.C. 95 (1872).

15. Johnson v. Leavitt, 188 N.C. 682, 125 S.E. 490 (1924); Martin v. Lewis, 187 N.C. 473, 122 S.E. 180 (1924); Bruce v. Nicholson, 109 N.C. 202, 13 S.E. 790 (1891).

16. *See, e.g.,* N.C. Gen. Stat. § 1-235, which provides for the docketing of judgments from the North Carolina Supreme Court. *See* Alsop v. Moseley, 104 N.C. 60, 10 S.E. 124 (1889). N.C. Gen. Stat. § 7A-225 provides for the docketing of a magistrate's judgment. N.C. Gen. Stat. § 1-237 provides for the docketing of judgments of the federal courts in order to create liens. *See* Riley v. Carter, 165 N.C. 334, 81 S.E. 414 (1914). *But see* United States v. Norman Lumber Co., 127 F. Supp. 518 (1955), to the effect that condemnation judgments in favor of the United States Government do not have to be recorded in the county where the land condemned lies.

docketing will control.[17] For instance, where priority is to be established with respect to judgments from different courts or from different counties, the exact time of docketing may be important to determine priority.

If more than one judgment is rendered against the judgment debtor during the same term of Superior Court, the doctrine of relation back is applied as between the competing judgment creditors. If two or more judgments are rendered in the same term of court and they are docketed within ten days after the term of court terminates, all the judgments are deemed to have been rendered and docketed on the first day of the term of court, as between the competing judgment creditors who obtain their judgments at the same term of court.[18] In such case, each judgment creditor has an equal lien with the others and they share pro rata.

§ 415. Priority of Judgment Liens Where Judgment Debtor Acquires Real Property After the Docketing of Judgment.

(a) *In general.* Where two or more judgment creditors procure judgments against a judgment debtor and docket their judgments prior to his acquisition of real property, when he subsequently acquires real property the judgments attach to the real property when he acquires it.[19] Priority as between the judgment liens in this case, as distinguished from the situation where the judgment debtor already owns the real property, is not determined by priority of docketing but the previously docketed judg-

---

17. National Surety Corp. v. Sharpe, 236 N.C. 35, 72 S.E.2d 109 (1952); Perry v. Morris, 65 N.C. 221 (1871); Cannon v. Parker, 81 N.C. 320 (1879). If a judgment is docketed prior to the recording of a transfer of the title to realty by the judgment debtor, the judgment lien has priority. *See* Moses v. Major, 201 N.C. 613, 160 S.E. 890 (1931).

18. N.C. GEN. STAT. § 1-233. This rule was adopted as a rule of court and later as a statute to "prevent an indecent rush to get a judgment docketed first, and to cut off the favoritism on the part of the clerk" and "to prevent the rights of the parties from depending upon the chance as to which plaintiff should first get the ear of the court." *See* McKinney v. Street, 165 N.C. 515, 81 S.E. 757 (1914). This rule only applies where more than one judgment is acquired during some term of court and both judgments are docketed within ten days. If they are not docketed within ten days of the term of court's expiration, the regular rule of priority prevails. Furthermore, the relation back doctrine does not apply to give a judgment priority over any type of lien interest acquired during the court term other than another judgment rendered by the same court at such term. *E.g.*, where a mortgage is procured after the court term has begun, or a judgment from another court is rendered and docketed after a specific court term has begun, the judgment rendered and docketed does not relate back to take priority over such mortgage or judgment from another court, where the latter is recorded or docketed first. Fowle v. McLean, 168 N.C. 537, 84 S.E. 852 (1915); McKinney v. Street, 165 N.C. 515, 81 S.E. 757 (1914); Perry v. Morris, 65 N.C. 221 (1871).

19. N.C. GEN. STAT. § 1-234.

ments constitute equal liens on the real property acquired by the judgment debtor after the docketing.[20]

(b) *Docketed judgments not prior where judgment debtor acquires property subject to purchase money mortgage or purchase money deed of trust.* With respect to the priority of docketed judgments against other lien claimants, a special rule applies where the contest is between a prior judgment creditor and a vendor who has conveyed real property to the judgment debtor subsequent to the docketing of the judgment against the judgment debtor, and has taken a purchase money mortgage or deed of trust to secure the purchase money. In such case, notwithstanding the priority of docketing of the judgment, it has been held that the liens of judgment creditors do not attach to such after acquired real property under these circumstances.[21] The Supreme Court of North Carolina has said: "The title vests, but does not rest; but 'like the borealis race, that flits ere you can point the place.' "[22] The mortgage or deed of trust for the purchase money will prevail over previously docketed judgments whether made to the vendor of the real property or to a third person.[23]

§ 416. Enforcement of Judgment Liens — Execution.

A creditor who procures a judgment against his debtor has a right, subject to constitutional limitations, to have the debtor's property sold under execution to satisfy the judgment debt.[24] An execution is an order signed by the Clerk of the Superior Court directing the sheriff to sell the property of the judgment debtor to pay off or satisfy the judgment.[25]

All legal interests of the judgment debtor in real property, including freehold interests such as life estates and nonfreehold interests such as leasehold estates are subject to execution as are vested and contingent

---

20. Moore v. Jordan, 117 N.C. 86, 23 S.E. 259 (1895). This rule applies where a judgment is procured against a husband who owns realty with his wife as tenants by the entirety. There is no lien on entireties property during his wife's life. If another judgment is docketed against the husband before the wife's death, both liens will attach equally upon the wife's death, neither having priority. Johnson v. Leavitt, 188 N.C. 682, 125 S.E. 490 (1924).

21. Smith Builders Supply, Inc. v. Rivenbark, 231 N.C. 213, 56 S.E.2d 431 (1949); Virginia-Carolina Chem. Co. v. Walston, 187 N.C. 817, 123 S.E. 196 (1924); Humphrey Bros. v. Buell-Crocker Lumber Co., 174 N.C. 514, 93 S.E. 971 (1917).

22. Bunting v. Jones, 78 N.C. 242 (1878).

23. Smith Builders Supply, Inc. v. Rivenbark, 231 N.C. 213, 56 S.E.2d 431 (1949); Savings Bank & Trust Co. v. Brock, 196 N.C. 24, 144 S.E. 365 (1928); Weil v. Casey, 125 N.C. 356, 34 S.E. 506 (1899); Moring v. Dickerson, 85 N.C. 466 (1881); Pegram-West, Inc. v. Hiatt Homes, Inc., 12 N.C. App. 519, 184 S.E.2d 65 (1971).

24. N.C. GEN. STAT. § 1-315.

25. *See* McINTOSH, NORTH CAROLINA PRACTICE AND PROCEDURE §§ 1931-1941 (Wilson & Wilson ed. 1956) for procedures for levying and sales under execution. *See also* N.C. GEN. STAT. § 1-313.

interests in real property.[26] While there are older cases which indicate that contingent remainders are not subject to levy of execution to satisfy the debts of judgment debtors, under recent statutes making them freely alienable along with other contingent interests in real property, it would seem that they should now be subject to execution for the satisfaction of judgment debts.[27] The purchaser of such interest, however, would take subject to the specified contingency. In addition to *legal* interests in real property, equitable rights of redemption may be levied on as can the interests of *cestuis que trust* in passive trusts.[28]

While the interests of tenants in common are subject to execution, the interests of a husband and wife in a tenancy by the entirety are not subject to execution except upon a joint debt on which both the husband and wife are liable.[29]

It should be noted, however, that under the North Carolina Constitution,[30] a judgment debtor has the right to have certain property exempted from sale to satisfy his judgment creditors. By constitutional provision the judgment debtor is entitled to have real property not exceeding one thousand dollars in value laid off as his "homestead" and exempted from the reach of his judgment creditors.[31] The judgment debtor is not required to demand that his homestead be allotted but is entitled to the allotment automatically since it is a constitutional right.[32] A purported sale under

---

26. The North Carolina Supreme Court has held that a vested remainder in lands is subject to sale under execution for the debts of the remainderman during the term of the life tenant. Elwood v. Plummer, 78 N.C. 392 (1878); Bristol v. Hallyburton, 93 N.C. 384 (1885).

27. *See* N.C. GEN. STAT. § 39-6.3. *See also* Jernigan v. Lee, 279 N.C. 341, 182 S.E.2d 351 (1971), which states that contingent interests — executory interests, contingent remainders, springing uses, and executory devises — may be sold, assigned, transmitted, or devised provided the identity of the person who will take the estate upon the happening of the contingency be ascertained. The Supreme Court of North Carolina has said they may be assigned . . . both in real and personal estate, *and by any mode of conveyance by which they might be transferred had they been vested remainders.*

28. That property held for a debtor under a passive trust is subject to sale under execution pursuant to N.C. GEN. STAT. § 1-315 (a) (4), *see* Ferguson v. Morgan, 282 N.C. 83, 191 S.E.2d 817 (1972); Fishel and Taylor v. Church, 22 N.C. App. 647, 207 S.E.2d 330 (1974).

29. Johnson v. Leavitt, 188 N.C. 682, 125 S.E. 490 (1924); Martin v. Lewis, 187 N.C. 473, 122 S.E. 180 (1924); Harris v. Carolina Distrib. Co., 172 N.C. 14, 89 S.E. 789 (1916); Hood v. Mercer, 150 N.C. 699, 64 S.E. 897 (1909).

For a very complete analysis and collection of cases with respect to the kinds of property which may be subject to execution *see* MCINTOSH, NORTH CAROLINA PRACTICE AND PROCEDURE § 1922 (Wilson & Wilson ed. 1956).

30. N.C. CONST. art. X, § 2.

31. The procedure for allotting a homestead exemption is set out in MCINTOSH, NORTH CAROLINA PRACTICE AND PROCEDURE § 2026 (Wilson & Wilson ed. 1956). *See* Printery, Inc. v. Schinhan, 34 N.C. App. 637, 239 S.E.2d 744 (1977) which contains a thorough history and discussion of the homestead exemption.

32. *See* Gardner & Clark v. McConnaughey, 157 N.C. 481, 73 S.E. 125 (1911); Williams v. Johnson, 230 N.C. 338, 53 S.E.2d 277 (1949). The homestead exemption with respect to real property should be distinguished from the personal property exemption provided by

execution without laying off the debtor's homestead in his real property is void.[33]

It should be further noted that certain debts are not subject to the debtor's homestead exemption. For instance, a forced sale of property may be compelled to pay taxes,[34] to pay off a laborer's lien for work done on the premises,[35] or to pay obligations contracted for the purchase of the premises,[36] without any allotment of a homestead exemption.

Otherwise, however, even a specific provision in a contract that the debtor will not take advantage of the homestead exemption as against a particular debt is invalid.[37]

When property is sold pursuant to an execution, the judgment debtor's title is divested and it is vested in the purchaser at the execution sale subject to any liens that have priority over the judgment under which the sale is made.[38]

§ 417. Termination of Judgment Liens.

The lien which arises from a docketed judgment is lost by the lapse of ten years from the date of the rendition of the judgment.[39] A judgment

---

N.C. CONST. art. X, § 1. With respect to the personal property exemption the debtor must demand that personal property of no more than $500 valuation be allotted as his personal property exemption from judgment. If he does not make such demand, a levy and sale of his personal property in whatever amount is valid and his personal property exemption is waived and lost.

33. The sheriff must lay off a judgment debtor's homestead before levy and if it is not laid off in accordance with the mandatory provision of the statute the sale is absolutely void. Williams v. Johnson, 230 N.C. 338, 53 S.E. 277 (1949); Stokes v. Smith, 246 N.C. 694, 100 S.E.2d 85 (1957); Ferguson v. Wright, 113 N.C. 537, 18 S.E. 691 (1893); Long v. Walker, 105 N.C. 90, 10 S.E. 858 (1890); Mebane v. Layton, 89 N.C. 396 (1883); MCINTOSH, NORTH CAROLINA PRACTICE AND PROCEDURE § 2026 (Wilson & Wilson ed. 1956).

34. N.C. CONST. art. X, § 2.

35. N.C. CONST. art. X, § 3. *See* Stevens v. Hicks, 156 N.C. 239, 72 S.E. 313 (1911), for definition of a "laborer." *See also* Mebane v. Layton, 89 N.C. 396 (1883).

36. N.C. GEN. STAT. § 1-313 (5). *See* Toms v. Fite, 93 N.C. 274 (1885); Durham v. Bostick, 72 N.C. 353 (1875).

37. Beavan v. Speed, 74 N.C. 544 (1876).

38. Glass Co. v. Forbes, 258 N.C. 426, 128 S.E.2d 875 (1962).

39. N.C. GEN. STAT. § 1-234. Cheshire v. Drake, 223 N.C. 577, 27 S.E.2d 627 (1943); North Carolina Joint Bank v. Bland, 231 N.C. 26, 56 S.E.2d 30 (1949). Even if execution has been issued on a judgment, if the execution sale is not consummated before the expiration date of the judgment, within ten years of its recordation, the lien expires. McMullen v. Durham, 229 N.C. 418, 50 S.E.2d 511 (1948).

It should be noted, however, that the time during which the creditor is prevented from enforcing his lien due to a court order, because of the operation of an appeal, or because of a statutory prohibition, or because the property is in the *custodia legis* of a bankruptcy court, does not count as a part of the ten years so as to bar the judgment creditor with respect to the judgment defendant or any other person not a purchaser, creditor or mortgagee for value in good faith.

In addition, if the judgment debtor's homestead is laid off, the life of the judgment is extended as to the land included within the homestead until the homestead right is ended

§ 418 LIENS ON REAL PROPERTY § 418

may be kept in force beyond ten years by the judgment creditor if within the ten year period from the rendition of the original judgment he brings an independent action upon the initial judgment.[40] Neither part payment nor agreement will operate to extend a judgment lien[41] and if the judgment creditor procures a judgment upon a previously docketed judgment, the subsequent judgment does not relate back to the original judgment to take priority over intervening liens.[42]

Article III. Mechanics' Liens[43]

Division 1. General Provisions

§ 418. Mechanics' Liens Generally.

The term "mechanic's lien" generally refers to the lien rights of mechanics, laborers, materialmen, surveyors, architects, and professional engineers who have rendered services for improvement of real property pursuant to a contractual obligation.[44] The mechanic's lien statutes

---

with respect to the land laid off in the homestead but not with respect to other lands of the judgment debtor. See N.C. GEN. STAT. §§ 1-234, 1-306; Blow v. Harding, 161 N.C. 375, 77 S.E. 340 (1913); McCaskill v. Graham, 121 N.C. 190, 28 S.E.2d 264 (1897); Pipkin v. Adams, 114 N.C. 201, 19 S.E. 105 (1894); Adams v. Guy, 106 N.C. 275, 11 S.E. 535 (1890); Fox v. Kline, 85 N.C. 173 (1881); N.C. GEN. STAT. § 1-369; Kirkwood v. Peden, 173 N.C. 460, 92 S.E. 264 (1917); Brown v. Harding, 171 N.C. 686, 89 S.E. 222 (1916); Bevan v. Ellis, 121 N.C. 224, 28 S.E. 471 (1897).

40. See Reid v. Bristol, 241 N.C. 699, 86 S.E.2d 417 (1955); see N.C. GEN. STAT. § 1-47 (1) to effect that only one action upon a judgment may be brought.

41. McDonald v. Dickson, 87 N.C. 404 (1882).

42. Springs v. Pharr, 131 N.C. 191, 42 S.E. 590 (1902).

43. It was the revisor's opinion that a more comprehensive treatment of lien law would be desirable in this revised edition of WEBSTER. Normally, the task of adding substantial amounts of new material on a complex subject further complicated by statutory changes in 1969 and 1971 would be a formidable one to anyone but a seasoned expert on liens. Fortunately for this revisor and for practising lawyers in North Carolina, two experts on the subject of lien law decided to devote a significant amount of their time to produce a clearly organized, extensive law review treatment of the subject titled: *Mechanics' Liens for the Improvement of Real Property: Recent Developments in Perfection, Enforcement, and Priority.* The article may be found at 12 WAKE FOREST L. REV. 283 (1976). A brief note about its authors is in order: Edmund T. Urban, J.D., Wake Forest University was a legal counsel at Jefferson-Pilot Title Insurance Company at the time of his co-authorship of the article. He has recently become Vice-President and Southeast Regional Counsel for Safeco Title Insurance Company, Tampa, Florida. James W. Miles, Jr., J.D., University of North Carolina School of Law, was an Assistant City Attorney in Greensboro at the time of his co-authorship. He is presently a practicing attorney in Greensboro, North Carolina.

The entire Article III of this chapter is a reprint or paraphrase of portions of the Urban, Miles article. In addition, the revisor has adopted much of the organization of this subject developed by Urban and Miles.

The revisor wishes to both acknowledge the source of the following lien law discussion and to publicly convey his grateful appreciation to Messrs. Urban and Miles, to the Wake Forest Law Review and to the present holder of the copyright, Fred B. Rothman & Co., Littleton, Colorado, for their permission to utilize this article in this revision.

44. 12 WAKE FOREST L. REV. at 286.

remained relatively unchanged for almost a century after the initial laws were enacted in the mid-nineteenth century. Substantial changes then occurred with the enactment of parts 1 and 2 of Article 2 of Chapter 44A of the North Carolina General Statutes.[45]

Division 2. Liens Arising in Favor of Those Dealing Directly with the Owner of Real Property

§ 419. Introduction.

Liens of mechanics, laborers and materialmen dealing directly with the owner of real property are governed by Part 1, Article 2 of the North Carolina General Statutes.[46] North Carolina General Statutes, § 44A-8 grants the mechanic's, laborer's, and materialman's lien and reads as follows:

> Any person who performs or furnishes labor or professional design or surveying services or furnishes materials pursuant to a contract, either express or implied, with the owner of real property, for the making of an improvement thereon shall, upon complying with the provisions of this Article, have a lien on such real property to secure payment of all debts owing for labor done or professional design or surveying services or material furnished pursuant to such contract.[47]

Since the liens which are granted by this statutory provision vary, it is necessary to examine the potential lienors on the basis of the divisions of the statute. The following sections of this chapter, therefore, will examine the parties to whom the statutory lien is granted, the contract which is a prerequisite to the obtaining of the lien, and the type of materials or labor which need to be furnished. Mechanical aspects of the lien obtained and the problems of attachment, duration, enforcement, satisfaction, priorities, and discharge will also be discussed.

§ 420. Architects, Engineers, Land Surveyors, and Landscape Architects.

Because their services did not fall under the accepted definition of "labor" under the former lien statute,[48] statutory liens were denied to architects, supervisors, and bookkeepers.[49] A 1975 amendment to North Carolina General Statutes, §§ 44A-7(1) and 44A-8 grants the right to a

---

45. *Id.* at 286 and 287. Part 1 became effective Jan. 1, 1970 and Part 2 on October 1, 1971.
46. N.C. GEN. STAT. §§ 44A-7 through 44A-16.
47. As the authors of 12 WAKE FOREST L. REV. 283 note at 287, n.8, N.C. GEN. STAT. § 44A-8 has codified the case law rule that one who has not performed the labor himself but who has provided or furnished the labor of others is entitled to the protection of the mechanics' lien statute. Citing Lester v. Housten, 101 N.C. 605, 8 S.E. 366 (1888).
48. N.C. GEN. STAT. § 44-1, repealed by N.C. Sess. L. c. 1112, § 4 (1969). *See* 12 WAKE FOREST L. REV. at 288.
49. *See* citations of authority at 12 WAKE FOREST L. REV. at 288.

mechanic's lien to any person who performs or furnishes professional design or surveying services.[50] Amended North Carolina General Statutes, § 44-7(1) defines the term "improve" to include "any design or other professional or skilled services furnished by architects, engineers, land surveyors and landscape architects registered under Chapter 83, 89, or 89A of the General Statutes."[51]

§ 421. Materialmen; Relationship of Article 9 of the Uniform Commercial Code.[52]

North Carolina General Statutes, § 44A-8 grants a materialman's lien to any person who "furnishes materials pursuant to a contract . . . with the owner of real property, for the making of an improvement thereon."

Because the statute does not expressly define the term "materials furnished," one cannot definitively ascertain which materialmen are entitled to the protection of the lien. It is clear, however, that the materials must be capable of becoming incorporated into an "improvement" upon "real property," terms which are defined in North Carolina General Statutes, § 44A-7. Consequently, the furnishing of items that cannot by their nature lose their legal status as personalty are incapable of being secured by a mechanic's lien. The statute, then, focuses on the character of the article furnished, rather than on the person who furnished it.[53]

Is it possible that fixtures to which a materialman's lien may attach might also be within the purview of Article 9 of the Uniform Commercial Code dealing with secured transactions?[54] The 1975 amendment to Article 9 of the U.C.C. reads as follows:

"A security interest under this article may be created in goods which are fixtures or may continue in goods which become fixtures, but no security interest exists under this article in ordinary building materials incorporated into an improvement on land."[55]

From the exception spelled out in the amended statute quoted above, a mechanic's lien, but not a U.C.C. security interest, may be perfected with respect to the furnishing of "ordinary building materials incorporated into an improvement upon land."[56]

---

50. *Id.* at 289.
51. *Id.* at 289. *See* Smith and Associates v. Properties, Inc., 29 N.C. App. 447, 224 S.E.2d 692 (1976), holding that planning, design, and consulting services rendered incident to the development and construction of a resort community were not covered by the pre-1975 lien laws. *See also* Bryan v. Projects, Inc., 29 N.C. App. 453, 224 S.E.2d 689 (1976) holding that the services of a landscape architect were not lienable prior to the 1975 amendments.
52. This section is quoting 12 Wake Forest L. Rev. 289-94.
53. 12 Wake Forest L. Rev. 289.
54. *Id.* at 290.
55. N.C. Gen. Stat. § 25-9-313(2).
56. 12 Wake Forest L. Rev. at 290.

Is the supplier of articles which become "fixtures" other than "ordinary building materials" entitled to a mechanic's lien in addition to, or in lieu of, a U.C.C. Article 9 security interest?[57] While North Carolina General Statutes § 44A-8 does not seem to preclude this result, the status of the lien law in this regard is in need of clarification.[58]

The statute lacks clarity also in its failure to specify whether the materials furnished by the lien claimant must reach the site of the improvement. North Carolina General Statutes, § 44A-8 makes no express requirement that the materials be furnished at the site of the improvement by the lien claimant. Since the statute only mentions the furnishing of materials in general terms, questions arise as to whether the materials must reach the site and if so, by whom they must be brought.[59]

§ 422. The Requirement of a Contract with the Owner of Real Property.

(a) *The Statutory Requirements in General.* Pursuant to North Carolina General Statutes, § 44A-8, the contractor who renders an otherwise lienable performance will not qualify for the security of a mechanic's lien unless the contractor has performed pursuant to an express or implied contract with the owner of the real property.[60] An *owner of real property* is one who has an interest in *real property,* a term that is defined by the lien statutes as "the real estate that is improved, including lands, leaseholds, tenements and hereditaments, and improvements placed thereon."[61] The statutory definition of real property quoted immediately above encompasses both the lessee's interest and the lessor's interest as capable of being subjected to a mechanic's lien.[62]

---

57. *Id.* at 291. The authors of the law review article describe this as a much more difficult question that is important owing to the differences in priorities, and the prerequisites of perfection and enforcement of the U.C.C. Article 9 security interest and the mechanic's lien. (12 WAKE FOREST L. REV. 291, n.27.)

58. *Id.* at 292. The authors suggest that an amendment to Article 2 of Chapter 44A is necessary to set forth expressly whether or not a vendor of fixtures is entitled to a mechanic's lien. "Until such time as such an amendment is passed, however, the authors suggest that vendors of fixtures make certain that they perfect a security interest pursuant to Article 9 of the U.C.C. so as definitely to have the benefit of at least one type of security interest." 12 WAKE FOREST L. REV. at 292.

59. *See* full discussion of this point at 12 WAKE FOREST L. REV. 293 & 294.

60. This section is quoting 12 WAKE FOREST L. REV. 294. At p. 295, n.45 of that article, the authors note that the requirement that there be an express or implied contract was established by case law prior to the inclusion of the requirement in the statute, citing Wilkie v. Bray, 71 N.C. 205 (1874). The term "owner" is defined by N.C. GEN. STAT. § 44A-7(3).

61. 12 WAKE FOREST L. REV. at 295. N.C. GEN. STAT. § 44A-7(4).

62. *Id.* at 296. N.C. GEN. STAT. § 44A-7(4). As the authors note at p. 296: "The lien claimant who contracts with a lessee, therefore, can file and enforce a mechanic's lien against whatever interest the lessee had under the lease, even if the lien is prevented from attaching to the lessor's fee simple interest." Citing Hayward Lumber & Inv. Co. v. Graham, 104 Ariz. 103, 449 P.2d 31 (1968); Levine v. McCollum, 245 Ore. 418, 425 P.2d 755 (1967). *See generally* Annot., 87 A.L.R. 1290 (1933); 53 AM. JUR. 2d *Mechanics' Liens* §§ 44, 110, 240 (1970).

(b) *The Owner of Real Property.* The statutory definition of owner includes an owner's agent acting within his authority.[63] A lessor-lessee relationship may give rise to an agency sufficient enough so that one contracting with the lessee may be able to subject the lessor's fee simple interest to the lien.[64] Property held by a husband and wife as tenants by the entirety can also cause problems of agency. If, for example, the interest to be subjected to the lien is vested in husband and wife as tenants by the entirety, a contract with only one of the spouses will be insufficient to subject the property to the claimant's lien.[65] It appears, therefore, that a contract with both owner-spouses must be alleged and proved in order to subject entirety property to a mechanic's lien.[66]

One final problem concerning the requirement of an express or implied contract with the owner or the owner's agent involves a lien claimant who has contracted with someone else who has contracted with the owner.[67] In such case, the lien claimant will be unable to enforce a contractor's lien against the owner's interest in the real property improved.[68] In *Suffolk Lumber Co. v. White*,[69] it was held that where there exists a contract between a contractor and a subcontractor for the furnishing of goods or services to the owner's property, the owner is not liable on an implied contract merely because he has received such goods or services. The requisite owner-agent relationship is not thereby established unless a claimant can allege and prove a contract with the owner or his agent, and the claimant will be unable to enforce a contractor's lien against the owner's interest in the real property. There are circumstances, however, in which the claimant may still have some sort of a remedy where he has not contracted with the owner but has merely contracted with someone else who has contracted with the owner. Such a party may be able to exercise rights of subrogation and enforce the lien of the party who

---

63. 12 WAKE FOREST L. REV. at 296. N.C. GEN. STAT. § 44A-7(3).

64. For a complete discussion of this, *see* 12 WAKE FOREST L. REV. at 297-99.

65. For a complete discussion of husband-wife agency problems, see 12 WAKE FOREST L. REV. at 299-300.

66. 12 WAKE FOREST L. REV. at 299. The authors also point out that an intervening event may aid the lien claimant dealing with entirety property. At 12 WAKE FOREST L. REV. 299 and 300, the authors state:

> Even though a lien claimant has contracted with only one of the owner-spouses, there may still be the opportunity to establish the lien if there is an intervening event which destroys the tenancy by the entirety. For example, if a person has a contract for the making of an improvement with one of the spouses and the other spouse dies within the life of the judgment obtained for enforcement, the lien of the judgment will at that time attach to property formerly held by the entirety. The lien of the judgment, however, will not relate back to the date of the judgment's docketing or to an earlier date preceding the death of the noncontracting spouse. [Citations omitted.]

67. *See* discussion of this issue at 12 WAKE FOREST L. REV. 300.

68. *Id.* at 300.

69. 12 N.C. App. 27, 182 S.E.2d 215 (1971). *See also* Outer Banks Contractors, Inc. v. Forbes, 267 S.E.2d 63 (1980).

contracted directly with the owner [70] or may be able to enforce a lien to the extent of wrongful payments made by the owner.[71]

(c) *The Requirement of an Express or Implied Contract.* The statutory requirement of North Carolina General Statutes, § 44A-8 of a contract, express or implied, under which the materials, labor or services for which a lien is claimed must have been furnished, is worthy of brief mention.[72] When materials are furnished at the site by the lien claimant, it becomes imperative to analyze the nature of the claimant's contract with the owner; more specifically, the contractual intent of the parties *at the inception of the transaction* must be discerned.

One important question that arises in the context of the contract requirement is whether a sale of materials in the ordinary course of business or on a general open account vests in the vendor the right to a mechanic's lien when the vendor at the time of the sale does not know for what purpose the materials are to be used or what land is to be improved.[73] An 1879 North Carolina decision contains dictum to the effect that an "unqualified sale" of materials will not give the vendor a right to a mechanic's lien upon the property ultimately improved with such materials.[74] It has been contended that the specific wording of North Carolina General Statutes, § 44A-8 would justify the denial of a mechanic's lien to a materialman who at the time of the making of the contract is unaware both of the express purpose for which the materials were to be used and where they were to be used.[75]

It should be noted that the validity of the lien should not have to depend upon the contract with the owner of the real property being in writing.[76] North Carolina General Statutes, § 44A-8, the general statute of frauds (North Carolina General Statutes, § 22-2) and the Uniform Commercial Code do not require that contracts of persons furnishing labor or materials be in writing in order for a lien to be valid.[77]

§ 423. Perfection of the Lien; Amendments; Assignment.

(a) *Place of Filing.* Lien claims against real property must be filed in the office of the Clerk of Superior Court in each county wherein the real

---

70. N.C. GEN. STAT. § 44A-23.
71. *Id.* § 44A-20(d).
72. For a thorough discussion of this matter, *see* 12 WAKE FOREST L. REV. 300-03. *See also* Lowes v. Quigley, 46 N.C. App. 770, 266 S.E.2d 378 (1980).
73. 12 WAKE FOREST L. REV. at 301.
74. Lanier v. Bell, 81 N.C. 337 (1879).
75. 12 WAKE FOREST L. REV. at 302. The authors state:

> The fact that upon delivery to the site the materialman discovered the intended use of the materials would be irrelevant. Frequently at the time of the making of the contract, the materialman will necessarily discover what property is to be improved by a provision to deliver the materials at the correct site and consequently, he will be in a better position to obtain a mechanic's lien than if he did not contract to deliver the materials.

76. See 12 WAKE FOREST L. REV. at 305.
77. *Id.*

property subject to a claim of lien is located.[78] This means that, in a situation where the tract of land is located in two adjoining counties but labor or materials are furnished only to that portion of the property located in one of the counties, the claim of lien still must be filed within the prescribed period in *both counties* in order to subject the entire tract to the claim of lien.[79]

(b) *Time of Filing.*[80] Claims of lien may be filed "at any time after the maturity of the obligation secured thereby but not later than 120 days after the last furnishing of labor or materials at the site of the improvement by the person claiming the lien."[81] The time period for filing has therefore been shortened from the former six-month period.[82]

In order to determine when the 120-day period begins to run one must determine whether the contract is "entire and indivisible" or is in fact a series of separate and independent contracts. In one type of arrangement, a contract is entered into for the furnishing of all labor or materials in the making of an improvement or improvements for the consideration of a fixed price or a "cost plus" price.[83] On the other hand, some transactions, which have been loosely referred to as "continuing transactions," involve several separate furnishings of labor or material to a building site, without any meeting of the minds at the time of the first furnishing that any further furnishings will be required in the future. An example of such a "continuing transaction" arises when a buyer goes to a lumber yard on several different occasions and purchases individual quantities of lumber to incorporate into the same improvement. Obviously, the intent of the parties at the time of the first furnishing will determine the type of transaction or transactions involved. It has been held in some jurisdictions that a continuous transaction will be secured by a single claim of lien, notwithstanding the fact that separate distinct contracts are involved.[84] However, the more widely accepted view in jurisdictions where the statutes refer to "a contract" is that a claim of lien must be filed for that which was furnished under each separate contract within the statutory period after its completion.[85] It seems that North Carolina

---

78. N.C. Gen. Stat. § 44-38. The former statute allowed the lien claim to be filed in the office of the clerk of superior court in *any county* where the labor was performed or the materials furnished. 12 Wake Forest L. Rev. 305.

79. 12 Wake Forest L. Rev. 305-06.

80. This subsection is quoting 12 Wake Forest L. Rev. 306, 307 and 308.

81. N.C. Gen. Stat. § 44A-12(b).

82. Former N.C. Gen. Stat. § 44-39, N.C. Sess. L. c. 1112 § 4 (1969).

83. *See, e.g.,* Priddy v. Lumber Co., 258 N.C. 653, 129 S.E.2d 256 (1963). *See also* Mebane Lumber Co. v. Avery & Bullock Builders, Inc., 270 N.C. 337, 154 S.E.2d 665 (1970).

84. *See generally* 53 Am. Jur. 2d *Mechanics' Liens* § 199, n.17 (1970).

85. *Id.* n.19.

would be in accord with this view,[86] since its present statute expressly refers to a contract for the making of an improvement,[87] rather than to a "continuous transaction" between the parties.

Even when the contract is deemed to be entire, in order for the statutory filing period to commence running from the date of the furnishing of the last item at the site, such last item must be lienable. If it is not and the claim of lien is filed after the statutory period, as computed from the date on which the last lienable item was furnished, the *entire* claim of lien will be invalid.[88] However, if the last item furnished is lienable, it is immaterial that such item has been paid for, and the statutory period will still commence to run from the date of that furnishing, rather than from any earlier date.[89]

The time of filing is in issue also when there is controversy on the purpose for which the item or items were furnished. In *Priddy v. Lumber Co.*,[90] the claimant informed the owner that the claimant's time for filing a lien was about to expire and, therefore, unless the owner brought another item, the claimant would proceed to file his claim of lien. The claimant testified at trial that he had furnished the last item and several others for the sole purpose of extending the period within which to file a claim of lien. The court held that the claim of lien had been filed too late in this case, refusing to hold that the additional furnishing had extended the time within which a claim of lien could be filed.[91] Within the purview of the rule announced in *Priddy* additional labor or materials furnished will extend the period within which a claim of lien may be filed only when the following conditions have been met: (1) the additional labor or materials are embraced within the terms of the original contract; (2) the owner assents to or requires the additional items; (3) the items are not of a trivial nature furnished for the sole purpose of extending the time within which to file a claim of lien, rather than for the purpose of performing the original contractual obligation.[92]

Another potential timing problem has been resolved not by case law but by the North Carolina statute. Other jurisdictions have faced difficulties in determining how the period for filing is affected by an abandonment or

---

86. *See* N.C. GEN. STAT. § 44A-8 (Cum. Supp. 1975); Note, *Liens — Mechanics, Laborers, Materialmen — Acquisition and Priorities*, 29 N.C.L. REV. 480, 481-82 (1951), citing King v. Elliot, 197 N.C. 93, 147 S.E. 701 (1929).

87. N.C. GEN. STAT. § 44A-8.

88. *See* Downtowner of Atlanta, Inc. v. Dunham-Bush, Inc., 120 Ga. App. 342, 170 S.E.2d 590 (1969); Mawson-Peterson Lumber Co. v. Sprinkle, 59 Wyo. 334, 140 P.2d 588 (1943).

89. *See* 53 AM. JUR. 2d *Mechanics' Liens* § 196, n.11 (1970).

90. 258 N.C. 653, 129 S.E.2d 256 (1963).

91. *Id.*

92. *Id.;* Beamon v. Elizabeth City Hotel Corp., 202 N.C. 418, 163 S.E. 117 (1932). *See also* Note, *Liens — Mechanics, Laborers, Materialmen — Acquisition and Priorities*, 29 N.C.L. REV. 480, 481-82 (1951).

cessation of construction in terms of ascertaining when abandonment has occurred.[93] Assuming the abandonment was not the fault of the contractor so that his right to a lien is not prejudiced, North Carolina provides that the lien period commences to run from the time of the last lienable performance [94] and has therefore avoided the problem.

(c) *Contents of the Claim of Lien to Be Filed.*[95] North Carolina General Statutes, § 44A-12(c) requires substantial compliance with the suggested form of a claim of lien. The name and address of the "record owners" must be provided. A sufficient description of the real property is also required. The claimant may use the street address, tax lot and block number, a reference to a recorded instrument, or any other description of the real property, "whether or not it is specific, if it *reasonably* identifies what is described." [96]

The claim of lien must also include the name and address of the person with whom the claimant contracted.[97] This information will include agents of the owner, and in the case of subcontractors, the name of a general independent contractor or subcontractor with whom the claimant dealt.

In addition to the information pertaining to the persons and real property involved, the statute requires the claimant to set forth the date upon which labor or materials were first furnished at the site of the improvement by the claimant.[98] That date will determine the effective date [99] and concomitant priority [100] of the claimant's claim of lien.[101]

In light of the North Carolina Supreme Court decision of *Canady v. Creech,*[102] it appears that any error or omission in a claim of lien which could not have misled the party asserting the invalidity of the claim of lien will not render the claim invalid *per se* or invalid and unenforceable against the party asserting the invalidity of the claim.[103]

---

93. *See generally* Annot., 52 A.L.R.3d 797 (1973) (notes the difference between the states holding that physical abandonment commences by running of the filing period, and the states that require intent to abandon).
94. N.C. GEN. STAT. § 44A-12(b).
95. Substantial portions of this subsection are quoting 12 WAKE FOREST L. REV. 308, 309 and 310.
96. N.C. GEN. STAT. § 44A-12(c)(3) (emphasis added). *See also* Southern Sash, Inc. v. Jean, 285 Ala. 705, 235 So. 2d 842 (1970); James Weller, Inc. v. Hansen, 21 Ariz. App. 217, 517 P.2d 1110 (1973).
97. N.C. GEN. STAT. § 44A-12(c)(4).
98. *Id.* § 44A-12(c)(5).
99. *Id.* § 44A-10.
100. *Id.* § 44A-14(a).
101. There is no statutory requirement that the claim of lien include the date upon which the lien claimant last furnished labor or materials at the site. *See* a more complete discussion of this point at 12 WAKE FOREST L. REV. 311.
102. 288 N.C. 354, 218 S.E.2d 383 (1975).
103. 12 WAKE FOREST L. REV. 311.

A final requirement for the contents of the claim concerns the materials themselves. A general description of the labor or materials furnished is sufficient and it is not necessary for the lien claimant to file an itemized list of materials or a detailed statement of the labor performed.[104] Various North Carolina Supreme Court decisions interpreting the former statute have held that although the statute demanded more than a mere summary statement, it did not require overly detailed itemization.[105] The amount of specificity required in a claim of lien remained unclear,[106] prior to the express provisions of the current mechanic's lien statute.[107]

(d) *Amendment of Claim of Lien.* Before the enactment of the current statute, it had been stated that a defective claim of lien could not be cured by an amendment after the filing period had expired.[108] The current statute goes even further by stating that "[a] claim of lien may not be amended."[109] Instead, the claimant must cancel the original claim of lien and substitute a new one within the time allowed for the original filing.[110]

(e) *Assignment of Claim of Lien.* North Carolina General Statutes, § 44A-12(e) provides:

> When a claim of lien has been filed, it *may* be assigned of record by the lien claimant in a writing filed with the clerk of superior court who shall note said assignment in the margin of the judgment docket containing the claim of lien. Thereafter the assignee becomes the lien claimant of record. [Emphasis added.]

Although the word "may" in the statute could indicate an intent of the General Assembly to provide an optional guideline rather than to impose a mandatory duty with respect to the notation of assignments of claims of lien upon the record, other sections of the current statute seem to

---

104. N.C. Gen. Stat. § 44A-12(c)(6).
105. *See* Mangum, *Mechanics' Liens in North Carolina,* 41 N.C.L. Rev. 173, 181-82 and cases cited at nn. 43-47 (1963).
106. *See, e.g.,* Mebane Lumber Co. v. Avery & Bullock Builders, Inc., 270 N.C. 337, 154 S.E.2d 665 (1967). *See generally* Annot., 27 A.L.R.2d 1169 (1953); 53 Am. Jur. 2d *Mechanics' Liens* §§ 217, 219 (1970).
107. For a case dealing with the situation where non-lienable items are included with lienable items in an unsegregated manner, see Hays v. Pigg, 267 Ore. 143, 315 P.2d 924 (1973). *See also* Atlee Elec. Co. v. Johnson Constr. Co., 14 Ill. App. 716, 301 N.E.2d 192 (1973) (errors or overcharging by lien claimants will not invalidate their liens absent a clear intent to defraud).
108. 12 Wake Forest L. Rev. 311. Mebane Lumber Co. v. Avery & Bullock Builders, Inc., 270 N.C. 337, 154 S.E.2d 665 (1967); Jefferson v. Bryant, 161 N.C. 404, 77 S.E. 341 (1913).
109. N.C. Gen. Stat. § 44A-12(d).
110. *Id.* Some jurisdictions permit amendments even after the time for filing a claim has expired. 53 Am. Jur. 2d *Mechanics' Liens* § 225 (1970). *See also* Lowe's for Muscle Shoals, Inc. v. Dillard, 53 Ala. App. 669, 304 So. 2d 12 (1974).

indicate that the name of the person claiming the lien must appear of record.[111]

§ 424. Enforcement of the Lien.

(a) *Where Action Must Be Instituted.* An action to enforce a lien may be instituted in "any county in which the lien is filed."[112] Since under North Carolina General Statutes, § 44A-12(a) the claim of lien must be filed in each county in which the real property is located, the commencement of the action to enforce the lien must appear in one of those counties to be effective as against third persons entitled to constructive notice of record.[113]

(b) *When Action Must Be Filed.*[114] The statute stipulates that the action may not be commenced later than "180 days after the last furnishing of labor or materials at the site of the improvement by the person claiming the lien."[115] Under the former statute the period for the commencement of the action was within six months from the date of the filing of the notice of the lien.[116] Thus under the present statute, the action must be commenced within a particular period regardless of when the claim of lien is filed; a claimant proceeding under the former statute had six months from the date of the last furnishing of labor or materials to file a claim of lien and an additional six months from that date to commence the action of enforcement.[117]

Although a different rule applies in a few jurisdictions, it is normally held that when the statute defines the duration of the lien and the suit is not brought within that time, the lien expires regardless of alleged

---

111. 12 WAKE FOREST L. REV. 311, citing the requirement of N.C. GEN. STAT. § 44A-12(c)(1) that the name and address of the person claiming the lien appear of record. Also citing N.C. GEN. STAT. §§ 44A-16(1) and (2) — discharge of a record lien. The authors provide the following example at 12 WAKE FOREST L. REV. 311:

> Thus, if *A* files a claim of lien and subsequently assigns the indebtedness secured thereby to *B*, and *A*, the "lien claimant of record" acknowledges satisfaction of the indebtedness to the clerk of superior court (N.C. GEN. STAT. § 44A-16(1)), or the owner exhibits an instrument of satisfaction of the indebtedness signed and acknowledged by the lien claimant of record (N.C. GEN. STAT. § 44A-16(2)), persons entitled to rely upon the status of record title should take the same unencumbered by *B*'s interest.

(The authors note that this problem is somewhat analogous to problems surrounding assignments of mortgages or deeds of trust and the applicability of the recording acts thereto.) *See generally* OSBORNE, HANDBOOK OF THE LAW OF MORTGAGES §§ 235, 238 (2d ed. 1970). North Carolina's recording act does not specifically require the recordation of assignments of mortgages or deeds of trust. N.C. GEN. STAT. § 47-20.

112. N.C. GEN. STAT. § 44A-13(a).
113. *See* 12 WAKE FOREST L. REV. 312 for additional discussion of this subject. The authors also discuss the relationship of the lis pendens statute to the mechanic's lien statute.
114. Adapted from 12 WAKE FOREST L. REV. 314.
115. N.C. GEN. STAT. § 44A-13(a).
116. N.C. Sess. L. c. 117, § 7 (1868-69).
117. *See* 12 WAKE FOREST L. REV. 314-15 for a discussion of the effect of the real property involved being vested in a receiver or trustee in bankruptcy. N.C. GEN. STAT. § 44A-13(a).

agreements of waivers to the contrary. The rationale for this holding is that the statutes do not merely govern the remedy as statutes of limitation but rather limit the right to a mechanic's lien.[118]

(c) *Parties to the Action.*[119] The owner of the property is obviously a necessary party in an action to enforce a contractor's lien. The question often arises as to who else must be made a party to the action.

In some jurisdictions the statutes contain provisions which require the additional joinder of all parties claiming of record any right, title, or interest in the real property.[120] In North Carolina, however, the statute does not undertake to specify who shall be made a party to the action; instead, the answer to this question rests with the nature and object of the action to enforce the lien. Such an action is designed to enforce the lien by sale of the interest in the real property improved which the owner held at the time the lien attached.[121] For example, in *Childers v. Powell*[122] the plaintiff filed a complaint seeking to enforce a lien. When the sole defendant, the owner, failed to answer, a mortgagee then filed a petition seeking to intervene and answer the plaintiff's complaint. The court held that the petitioner-mortgagee was not a necessary party to a complete determination of the controversy between the plaintiff and the owner. The plaintiff could obtain complete relief sought, *i.e.,* the sale of the interest owned by the defendant, without having the rights of the petitioner determined. The petitioner was deemed a proper rather than a necessary party, and the court stated that it was within its discretion to allow the petitioner to intervene.[123] If such a mortgagee is not originally joined or permitted to intervene, he will not be bound by the judgment; and subsequent purchasers under the execution sale pursuant to the mechanic's lien judgment will take subject to the rights of the mortgagee. Thus, while not necessary parties, subsequent mortgagees are not only proper parties, but are also highly desirable parties.[124]

When a contractor institutes an action against the owner in order to enforce his lien, the owner will be permitted to file a motion to join all subcontractors dealing with the plaintiff. Such a motion results in the issuance of an order requiring the subcontractors to answer and assert

---

118. 12 WAKE FOREST L. REV. 315, *citing* 53 AM. JUR. 2d *Mechanics' Liens* §§ 358 & 359 (1970). Curtis Lumber Co. v. Sortor, 9 Wash. App. 762, 515 P.2d 554 (1973). *But see* Peterson v. W.T. Grant Co., 41 Cal. App. 3d 217, 115 Cal. Rptr. 874 (1974) (statutory period is a mere statute of limitations which may be waived if not affirmatively pleaded, rather than a limitation on the right to a mechanic's lien itself.)
119. This entire subsection has been taken directly from 12 WAKE FOREST L. REV. 315-16.
120. *See, e.g.,* WASH. REV. CODE § 60.04.120 (1974).
121. *See generally* 53 AM. JUR. 2d *Mechanics' Liens* § 359 (1970).
122. 243 N.C. 711, 92 S.E.2d 65 (1956).
123. *Id.* at 713, 92 S.E.2d at 67.
124. *Id.*; Equitable Life Assur. Soc'y v. Basnight, 234 N.C. 347, 67 S.E.2d 390 (1951). *See also* N.C. GEN. STAT. § 1A-1, Rule 19(b) (1969).

any claims that they might have against the plaintiff which they contend to be a lien against either the property or the funds.[125]

(d) *Attachment.*[126] The remedy of attachment is afforded lien claimants by North Carolina General Statutes, § 44A-15. After summarily including other grounds for attachment, the statute provides:

> [I]n all cases where the owner removes or attempts or threatens to remove an improvement from real property subject to a lien under this article, without the written permission of the lien claimant or with the intent to deprive the lien claimant of his lien, the remedy of attachment of the property subject to the lien shall be available to the lien claimant *or any other person.*[127]

It should be noted that not only may the lien claimant take advantage of this provision, but also "any other person." Additionally, one need not allege one of the traditional grounds for attachment.[128] In order to come within the protection of the above quoted section, mere removal or a threat of removal of the improvement without the written permission of the lien claimant will constitute a statutory ground for attachment.

Under the general attachment provision the lien of attachment will relate back to the time the notice of the issuance of the order of attachment is noted on the lis pendens docket.[129] In regard to mechanic's lien claimants, however, the liens would seem to relate back to the first furnishing of labor or materials at the site.[130]

(e) *Judgment; Amount; Content.*[131] The statute provides that a judgment rendered in an action to enforce a contractors' lien may be entered "for the principal amount shown to be due, not exceeding the principal amount stated in the claim of lien enforced thereby."[132] However, the statute does not treat the amount recoverable when the contract is not fully performed. In these situations, one must consult the law of contracts to ascertain the principal amount recoverable which may be secured by a mechanic's lien. In fact, in absence of substantial performance by the contractor, the right to collect anything from the owner and to have a lien for that amount may be denied.[133] But in an action against the owner for substantial, though not exact, performance of a building contract, a certain amount is recoverable. The amount recoverable depends upon the

---

125. T.A. Loving Co. v. Latham, 15 N.C. App. 441, 190 S.E.2d 248 (1972).
126. This subsection is quoting 12 WAKE FOREST L. REV. 316-17.
127. N.C. GEN. STAT. § 44A-15 (emphasis added).
128. *See id.* §§ 1-440.2, -440.3 (1969).
129. *Id.* § 1-440.33.
130. *See id.* §§ 44A-10, -11, -14(a).
131. This subsection is quoting 12 WAKE FOREST L. REV. 317-18. For additional discussion of the judgment, see those pages.
132. N.C. GEN. STAT. § 44A-13(b).
133. *See* Rozena v. Quinn, 51 Ill. App. 2d 479, 201 N.E.2d 649 (1964); Widenhouse v. Russ, 234 N.C. 382, 67 S.E.2d 287 (1951).

nature of the defect or omissions. In *T.C. Allen Construction Co. v. Stratford*,[134] a federal court construing North Carolina law held that:

> Where the defects or omissions are of such a character as to be capable of being remedied, the proper rule for measuring the amount recoverable by the contractor is the contract price less the reasonable cost of remedying the defects or omissions so as to make the building conform to the contract.[135]

In conjunction, if the reasonable cost of supplying the omissions or remedying the defects exceeds the unpaid portion of the contract price, the owner may by counterclaim recover the amount of such excess.[136]

The judgment rendered in the enforcement of a mechanic's lien "shall direct a sale of the real property subject to the lien thereby enforced."[137] The consequences of failing to comply with that statutory mandate may be illustrated by the North Carolina Court of Appeals decision of *H & B Co. v. Hammond*.[138] The court ruled against the plaintiff in his action to correct a default judgment which erroneously did not include a provision declaring a specific lien. The court felt it would be inequitable to penalize the appellants, innocent purchasers, for a clerical mistake made by the plaintiff's counsel which afforded them no notice of the plaintiff's lien. But if the plaintiff's action had been commenced in a proper county, with a proper filing of lis pendens describing the real property, the parties, and the nature and purpose of the action, the technical failure to refer to and direct the sale of the property may not have precluded recovery by the plaintiff. It is suggested that the omission of the required direction would then not have been prejudicial to the appellants; in that case, the result might well have been different.[139]

(f) *Sale of Property in Satisfaction of Judgment*.[140] North Carolina General Statutes, § 44A-14(b) allows one claiming a lien to sell the real property upon notice to all interested parties and after a hearing and upon a finding that a sale prior to judgment is necessary to prevent substantial waste, destruction, depreciation, or other damage to the real property prior to the final determination of the action of enforcement. Furthermore, the rights of all parties shall be transferred to the proceeds of the sale. This provision is somewhat similar to the North Carolina statutory provisions pertaining to the sale of attached property prior to rendition of judgment.[141]

---

134. 384 F.2d 653 (4th Cir. 1967).
135. *Id.* at 658. *See also* Durham Lumber Co. v. Wrenn-Wilson Constr. Co., 249 N.C. 680, 684, 107 S.E.2d 538, 540-41 (1959).
136. 384 F.2d at 658.
137. N.C. Gen. Stat. § 14A-13(b).
138. 17 N.C. App. 534, 195 S.E.2d 58 (1973).
139. *See* Canady v. Creech, 23 N.C. App. 673, 209 S.E.2d 511 (1974), *rev'd*, 288 N.C. 354, 218 S.E.2d 383 (1975).
140. This subsection is quoting 12 Wake Forest L. Rev. 319-20.
141. N.C. Gen. Stat. § 1-440.44 (1969).

With respect to sales made after the rendition of the judgment, North Carolina General Statutes, § 44A-14(a) states that sale and distribution of the proceeds are to be governed by North Carolina General Statutes, § 1-339.41 through .76. It is also provided that the sale to satisfy the lien shall operate so as to pass all title and interest of the owner to the purchaser, "good against all claims or interests recorded, filed or arising after the first furnishing of labor or materials at the site of the improvement."[142]

§ 425. Priority and Extent of Lien; Introduction.[143]

Assuming that a lien is validly perfected [144] and subsequently enforced within the statutory period,[145] Article 2 of Chapter 44A further provides that the liens "shall relate to and take effect from the time of the first furnishing of labor or materials at the site of the improvement by the person claiming the lien" [146] and will be deemed perfected as of that time.[147] This legislation represents a codification of the established North Carolina case law doctrine of "relation back" [148] as applied to priority contests between a contractors' lien and a lien of a different nature, such as the lien of a conventional mortgage or deed of trust.[149] Yet, the statute also represents a fundamental change in the former provisions [150] which ordained that competing contractors' liens were to be accorded priority as against each other by the order of filing.

Although the statute makes no express requirement that there must be a *visible* commencement [151] of the improvement, it should be noted that insofar as the lien rights of laborers and materialmen are concerned, the statutory definition of the term "improve" [152] includes undertakings, the

---

142. N.C. Gen. Stat. § 44A-14(a). At 12 Wake Forest L. Rev. 320, the authors note that it appears to have been the intent of the draftsmen of the new statute by repeal of the former statute to remove the requirement that the lien claimant execute first on the property subject to the mechanic's lien before levying upon other assets of the owner. (See authorities cited therein.)

143. This section is quoting 12 Wake Forest L. Rev. 320-21.

144. *See* N.C. Gen. Stat. §§ 44A-11, -12.

145. *See id.* § 44A-13(a).

146. *Id.* § 44A-10.

147. *Id.* § 44A-11.

148. For a good discussion of the history and application of the rule of "relation back" in North Carolina, *see* Note, *Liens — Mechanics, Laborers, Materialmen — Acquisition and Priorities,* 29 N.C.L. Rev. 480, 484-88 (1951).

149. *See* Equitable Life Assur. Soc'y v. Basnight, 234 N.C. 347, 67 S.E.2d 390 (1951) (deed of trust recorded subsequent to commencement of performance by the lien claimant held subordinate to the claimant's mechanics' lien); Chadborne v. Williams, 71 N.C. 444 (1874).

150. N.C. Sess. Laws ch. 117, § 11 (1868-69).

151. *Cf.* Minn. Stat. Ann. § 514.05 (1971).

152. *See* N.C. Gen. Stat. § 44A-7(1).

commencement of which will likely be apparent upon an examination of the construction site. It was the intent of the draftsmen that persons interested in the subject lot or tract should be able to examine the property and ascertain the extent to which it was possibly encumbered.[153] A recent North Carolina Supreme Court decision, *Conner Co. v. Spanish Inns*,[154] agrees with this "visible commencement of the improvement" interpretation. In that case, the Court held that the partial clearing of a building site and the staking of the outlines of the building constituted a visible commencement of an improvement sufficient to put a prudent person on notice that a possible improvement was underway and that the property might be subject to a lien under North Carolina General Statutes, § 44A-8. This clearing and staking was held to be the first furnishing of labor at the site so that the general contractor's lien related back to and took effect from the date this labor was first performed.[155]

§ 426. Extent of Lien; Blanket Lien.[156]

N.C. GEN. STAT. § 44A-9 provides:

> Liens authorized under the provisions of this article shall extend to *the improvement* and to *the lot or tract* on which the improvement is situated, to the extent of the interest of the owner. When *the lot or tract* on which a building is erected *is not surrounded* at the time of the making of the contract with the owner by an *enclosure* separating it from *adjoining land* of the same owner, *the lot or tract* to which any lien extends shall be such area as is reasonably necessary for the convenient use and occupation of such building, but in no case shall the area include a building, structure, or improvement not normally used or occupied or intended to be used or occupied with the building with respect to which the lien is claimed.[157]

It has been noted that the intended application of this statute to situations in which a single lot or tract is improved by the lien claimant pursuant to a single contract with the owner is not as clear as it should be.[158]

---

153. Humphrey, *Position, Priorities and Protection of Parties and Statutory Liens* in N.C. BAR ASS'N FOUNDATION INSTITUTE ON TROUBLED REAL ESTATE VENTURES AND NEW USE AND OWNERSHIP CONCEPTS, IV-1 through IV-23 (May 1975). *See* 12 WAKE FOREST L. REV. 321-22 discussing the problem of priority and effective dates of lien rights of architects, engineers, land surveyors, and landscape architects.

154. 294 N.C. 661, 242 S.E.2d 785 (1978).

155. *Id.* Citing with approval the suggested interpretation of the authors of 12 WAKE FOREST L. REV. 283, 321.

156. This section is quoting 12 WAKE FOREST L. REV. 323-28.

157. N.C. GEN. STAT. § 44A-9.

158. 12 WAKE FOREST L. REV. 323. The authors explain the problem as follows at 12 WAKE FOREST L. REV. 324:

> Less certain is N.C. GEN. STAT. § 44A-9's intended application to a situation in which a contractor improves a single lot or tract belonging to the owner and there exists no adjoining property of that owner. If a contract is made to erect a building on one corner of a large tract, the other corner of which already has a building which will not be

If on a single-building lot or tract it is undisputed that the entire lot or tract upon which an improvement is situated is reasonably necessary for the convenient use and occupation of the building, the only question left for determination is whether, in addition to the lot or tract improved, the claim of lien may be extended to adjoining lands of the same owner, if such extension is reasonably necessary. In such a situation North Carolina General Statutes, § 44A-9 is rather easy to apply. For example, North Carolina General Statutes, § 44A-9 allows a lien claimant to extend the lien to the adjoining lot if he can prove that a lot adjoining the one upon which he built a house is reasonably necessary for the convenient use and occupation of the house. In order for the operation of a lien to be extended to adjoining land of the owner-obligor, it must appear that at the time of the making of the contract, as distinguished from the first furnishing of labor or materials, the lot or tract improved is not surrounded by an enclosure separating it from the adjoining land and that title to the adjoining land is vested in the owner with whom the claimant contracted.

Problems of statutory interpretation can arise in the "blanket lien" area when a contractor, pursuant to a single contract with the owner of several lots, furnishes labor or materials to each lot for the making of separate improvements, and the improvement erected upon each lot is not used or occupied in conjunction with the improvement erected upon another lot.[159]

The difficulty arises primarily because Article 2 of Chapter 44A does not clearly address the following questions:

(1) Does Article 2 of Chapter 44A permit a contractor to file a single claim of lien against all lots improved under the same contract with the owner?

---

utilized or occupied in conjunction with the building to be erected, the statutes of certain jurisdictions preclude the extension of the claim of lien to include the entire area of the tract. [VA. CODE ANN. § 43-3 (1968)] A literal reading of the first and second sentences of N.C. GEN. STAT. § 44A-9 seems not to so limit the extent of the claim of lien. The rationale for this assumption can be summarized in this way: the first sentence of N.C. GEN. STAT. § 44A-9 sets forth the minimum area to which the lien extends, *i.e.,* "[t]he lot or tract upon which the improvement is situated." The second sentence of N.C. GEN. STAT. § 44A-9, commencing with the phrase, "[w]hen *the lot or tract* on which a building is erected *is not surrounded,"* seems to indicate that the utilization in the forth line of the phrase "the lot or tract to which any lien extends" refers only to the *entire* lot or tract on which the building is situated *and* adjoining land of the same owner. This reasoning is justified since if the phrase "the lot or tract to which any lien extends" had been intended to include in certain instances only *a portion* of the lot or tract, it would be irrelevant that the *entire* lot or tract improved was surrounded by an enclosure separating it from adjoining land. If, however, the intent of the draftsmen was to make N.C. GEN. STAT. § 44A-9 applicable to situations similar to the example set forth immediately above, so as to limit the extent of a particular lien in certain instances to only that portion of the lot or tract improved, the second sentence of N.C. GEN. STAT. § 44A-9 could have been drafted to make clear that in certain instances the phrase "the lot or tract" was meant to include *a portion* of "the lot or tract." Moreover, if the intent was to limit the application of the second sentence of N.C. GEN. STAT. § 44A-9 to situations in which the claimant seeks to extend the lien to lands adjoining the lot or tract improved, it should so state.

159. *See* discussion of this issue at 12 WAKE FOREST L. REV. 324-28. *See* Annot., 15 A.L.R.3d 73 (1967).

(2) If a single claim of lien may be filed, to what extent is each lot encumbered thereby?

(3) When do the periods for perfecting and enforcing the contractors' lien rights commence to run as against each lot?

(4) What is the effective date and priority of the contractors' lien rights as against each lot?

North Carolina General Statutes, § 44A-8 grants a lien for the furnishing of labor or materials "pursuant to a contract... with the owner of real property for the making of an improvement thereon ...." North Carolina General Statutes, § 44A-9, which sets forth the extent of a lien, repeatedly refers to "the improvement" and to "the lot or tract"; and the sections of the article setting forth the periods within which a lien must be perfected [160] and enforced [161] and the effective date [162] and priority of a lien [163] refer to "the site of the improvement." "Improvement" is defined [164] to include the singular of such terms as building, structure, erection, etc., but not expressly to include the plural of such terms.

Other jurisdictions have construed mechanics' lien statutes phrased in the singular as including by implication the plural as well as the singular of such terms, thereby providing justification for the filing of a blanket lien against all lots or tracts improved pursuant to a single contract with the owner.[165] Still other jurisdictions have refused to sanction the blanket lien procedure.[166] While there is some authority to the contrary,[167] most of the jurisdictions allowing the filing of blanket liens have further held that each lot may not be encumbered by a blanket lien to an extent greater than that portion of the entire contract indebtedness owing for the labor or materials furnished to the particular lot in question.[168] There is little probative case law regarding the application of a particular statute's lien perfection and enforcement periods and the ascertainment of the

---

160. N.C. Gen. Stat. § 44A-12(b) (Cum. Supp. 1975).
161. *Id.* § 44A-13(a).
162. *Id.* § 44A-10.
163. *Id.* § 44A-14(a).
164. *Id.* § 44A-7(2).
165. *See generally* Annot., 15 A.L.R.3d 73, 149-52 (1967).
166. *Id.*
167. Werner v. Fordham, 246 Ore. 200, 424 P.2d 673 (1967).
168. Weaver v. Harland, 176 Va. 224, 10 S.E.2d 547 (1940) (also illustrating that in some of the jurisdictions a failure of the lien claimant to so apportion his claim of lien will render it invalid against third parties). *See* Del. Code Ann. tit. 25, § 2713 (1953); Cal. Civ. Code Ann. § 3130 (Deering 1969) (if the claimant does not know the exact amount owed on each lot, he must estimate an equitable apportionment of the entire contractual indebtedness). However, other courts have held that the claimant's failure to make such an apportionment will not render the claim of lien invalid, and that, if necessary, the court will make the apportionment. *See* Annot., 15 A.L.R.3d 73 (1967). *See also* Chadbourne v. Williams, 71 N.C. 444, 448 (1874) (the court stated that if it was necessary to apportion the materials then it could be done and thus at least recognized apportionment of a single claim of lien).

priority of a blanket lien with respect to each lot improved though the following case offers some elucidation.

In *Chadbourne v. Williams*,[169] the North Carolina Supreme Court clearly upheld the filing of a blanket lien under the former statute; but while the court intimated that the amount of a blanket lien could be apportioned among the lots if necessary, the court failed to discuss the important issue of priority as against each lot. This upholding implies that the date upon which the materials were first furnished to any one of the lots improved establishes the effective date of the plaintiff's lien as against all lots. It is suggested that in order to avoid confusion and inequity, the consistent utilization in Article 2 of Chapter 44A of the singular of such terms as "the improvement," "the lot or tract," "the site of the improvement," and "building" be construed to mean that the Article requires each lot to be considered separately when determining all aspects of lien perfection, enforcement, and priority, notwithstanding the existence of only one contract with the owner and further notwithstanding the lien claimant's contract providing that he is to be paid for his performance upon each particular lot as each is completed,[170] or instead, that he is not to be paid anything until he completes the entire contract with the owner. Admittedly, in situations in which the contract provides that the owner's obligation to pay the entire contract price does not mature until the lien claimant completes his last lienable performance upon the last lot improved, the lien claimant might in certain instances be precluded from filing a claim of lien against one of the lots in question because the owner's obligation to pay matures subsequent to 120 days after the last furnishing of labor or materials to the lot in question. It is therefore suggested that, wherever possible, persons entitled to liens pursuant to Article 2 of Chapter 44A make it clear to the obligor that they are to be paid for each lot improved immediately after the rendition of their lienable performance. It is further suggested that Article 2 of Chapter 44A be amended so as to preclude uncertainty when

---

169. 71 N.C. 444 (1874).

170. *See* 4. A. Corbin, Contracts § 949 (1951) (regarding one contract covering several obligations to pay in installments), where it is stated:

> The failure to perform any one of the installments when it is due is now regarded as breach of contract for which an action will lie; and if there are several definite and independent performances which are to take place at different times, the contractor is regarded as under duties to render these performances that are separately enforceable.

The period fixed by the statute of limitations begins to run from the accrual of the cause of action. N.C. Gen. Stat. § 1-15(a) (1971); 4 A. Corbin, Contracts § 951 (1951) citing authority to the effect that:

> [W]here separate actions would lie for a series of such breaches, the statute operates against each one separately as of the time when each one could have been brought, and that this rule is not affected by the fact that after two or more such breaches have occurred the plaintiff must join them all in one action. Of course, if an action for a first installment is barred by the statute, it can not properly be included in an action for later installments that are not yet barred.

pursuant to a single contract with the owner of several lots, the lien claimant furnishes labor or materials or other lienable services to each lot for the making of separately utilized improvements.

§ 427. Priority of Contractors' Lien as Against Subcontractors' Lien.[171]

It appears that a subcontractor will be able to enforce the lien of the contractor to the extent of the subcontractor's claim.[172] Thus, as under the former statute,[173] it can be said that the lien of the subcontractor will be preferred to the lien of the contractor.

§ 428. Priority of Contractors' Lien as Against Purchase Money Mortgage or Deed of Trust.[174]

On occasion, a contractor will enter into an agreement for the making of an improvement with a person who does not yet have fee simple title to the real property in question. This situation usually involves a person who is in possession of the subject property under a contract to purchase the property or under a lease containing an option to purchase. When the purchase is concluded and a mortgage or deed of trust to secure the purchase price is given simultaneously with acceptance of the deed by the purchaser, does the security instrument in question have priority over claims of lien filed for work done or materials furnished by a contractor for the purchaser prior to the acceptance of the deed and the giving of the security instrument by the purchaser? Under certain circumstances the answer is "yes."

In *Supply Co. v. Riverbark*,[175] the claimant contracted with a lessee in possession with an option to purchase, furnishing the lessee materials shortly thereafter. The lessee exercised the option and executed a deed of trust to secure the balance of the purchase price simultaneously with the receipt of the deed. Both instruments were recorded simultaneously. The court held that the purchase money deed of trust recorded subsequently to the claimant's initial lienable performance had priority over the claimant's mechanics' lien since the deed and the deed of trust were executed, delivered, and recorded as part of the same transaction.[176]

Similarly, in *Pegram West, Inc. v. Homes, Inc.*[177] the deed and deed of trust were executed and delivered on the same date, but the different outcome is explained because the deed of trust was recorded eleven days

---

171. *See* 12 WAKE FOREST L. REV. 328-29; 354 *et seq.*
172. N.C. GEN. STAT. § 44A-23 (Cum. Supp. 1975).
173. N.C. Sess. L. c. 44, §§ 1, 3 (1880).
174. This section is quoting 12 WAKE FOREST L. REV. 329-30.
175. 231 N.C. 213, 56 S.E.2d 431 (1949).
176. *Id.* at 214, 56 S.E.2d at 432.
177. 12 N.C. App. 514, 184 S.E.2d 65 (1971).

after the date of the deed's recordation. For that reason, the court refused to apply the doctrine of "instantaneous seizin" and awarded priority to the mechanics' lien claimant. However, it would seem that as long as the deed and the deed of trust in the *Pegram West* decision were executed and delivered as part of the same transaction, the doctrine of "instantaneous seizin" should have been applied in favor of the purchase money mortgagee since the act of recordation is not a prerequisite to the vesting of title as between the mortgagor and mortgagee. The doctrine of "instantaneous seizin" prescribes only that the purchase money mortgagee prevail if the deed and the deed of trust be executed and delivered virtually simultaneously as part of one transaction so that it can be said that title vested in the borrower only for an instant.[178] This result follows notwithstanding someone's lien being prior to the purchase money security instrument insofar as what an examination of the record and the property might reveal. Recordation, as a prerequisite to priority, is only designed to protect those parties who could have taken, but did not, some affirmative action toward perfection of their own interest in the real property prior to the recordation of the purchase money security instrument.[179] The mechanics' lienors in the *Pegram West* case do not come within that class of persons since they had taken their affirmative action, namely, the commencement of furnishing labor or materials which would have otherwise established the effective date and priority of their liens prior to the deed of trust's recordation.

§ 429. Priority of Contractors' Lien as Against Security Instrument Securing Presently Owned and After Acquired Property.[180]

On occasion, a mortgagor will execute a security instrument which not only encumbers property described which is presently owned by the mortgagor, but also contains an "after acquired property clause" which seeks to create a security interest in real property to be acquired by the mortgagor subsequent to the instrument's recordation.[181] The priority of such security instruments as against mechanics' liens arising against the after acquired property is determined by applying North Carolina General Statutes, § 47-20.5 in conjunction with North Carolina General Statutes, § 44A-10 and North Carolina General Statutes, § 44A-14(a). If a contractor commences the furnishing of labor or materials to the "after acquired property"[182] prior to the re-registration of the security

---

178. *See* Bunting v. Jones, 78 N.C. 242 (1878).
179. N.C. GEN. STAT. § 47-20 (Cum. Supp. 1975) (mortgages and deeds of trust recorded to be effective against lien creditors and purchasers for value).
180. This section is quoting 12 WAKE FOREST L. REV. 330-31.
181. *See* N.C. GEN. STAT. § 47-20.5(a).
182. *Id.* § 47-20.5(b).

instrument containing the after acquired property clause after the acquisition of the property by the mortgagor,[183] or in lieu of re-registration, prior to registration of a "notice of extension,"[184] the contractors' lien should have priority as against the after acquired property.[185]

§ 430. Priority of Mechanics' Liens as Against Instruments Securing "Future Advances." [186]

(a) General Comments. Ordinarily as against purchasers for value and lien creditors, the priority of a security instrument is determined as of the time and date of recordation,[187] provided that all loan proceeds are disbursed at that time. However, when a construction loan or other future-advances security instrument is involved, the loan proceeds of which are disbursed at intervals subsequent to closing and recordation, questions arise as to whether the time and date of the security instrument's recordation should establish the effective date of lien priority with respect to loan proceeds subsequently disbursed as against mechanics' liens arising out of the project and as against other encumbrances intervening between the time of the recordation of the security instrument and the making of one or more subsequent future advances.[188]

In an effort to provide a guideline in this area of the law, the North Carolina General Assembly in 1969 enacted Article 7 of Chapter 45 of the General Statutes, entitled, "Instruments to Secure Future Advances and Future Obligations."[189]

(b) Definition of the Term "Security Instrument". Article 7 defines the term "security instrument" as follows:

> As used in this article, "security instrument" means a mortgage, deed of trust, or *other instrument* relating to real property securing an obligation or obligations to a person, firm, or corporation specifically named in such instrument, as distinguished from being included in a class of security holders referred to therein, for the payment of money.[190]

---

183. *Id.* § 47-20.5(c).
184. *Id.* § 47-20.5(d).
185. *Id.* §§ 47-20.5(c), (d), (g). *But see, id.* § 47-20.5(h) (for an exception to the rule of priority of instruments containing after acquired property clauses). *See generally* Note, 6 WAKE FOREST L. REV. 378 (1970).
186. This section is quoting 12 WAKE FOREST L. REV. 331-39.
187. *See* N.C. GEN. STAT. § 47-20.
188. *See generally* Annot., 80 A.L.R.2d 179 (1961); 53 AM. JUR. 2d *Mechanics' Liens* §§ 269-70 (1970); OSBORNE, *supra* note 153, § 113 *et seq.;* G. THOMPSON, COMMENTARIES ON THE MODERN LAW OF REAL PROPERTY § 4747 *et seq.* (1958).
189. N.C. Sess. Laws ch. 736, § 3 (1969) made the act effective October 1, 1969. The Article was amended in 1971 with the addition of G.S. 45-70(d).
190. N.C. GEN. STAT. § 45-67 (emphasis added).

This definition and the caption of the article seem to indicate an intent of the General Assembly to address itself basically to two types of instruments: the "open end" mortgage or deed of trust and the "future advances" construction security instrument.

The essence of the former is that the borrower has the distinct advantage of being able to obtain successive loans for various purposes secured by the same security instrument, thereby avoiding multiple closing costs while the lender usually has the advantage of not being obligated at the date of the security instrument's execution and recordation to advance the maximum amount set forth in the instrument.[191] The essence of the latter type of security instrument is that the advances are used for one originally contemplated purpose — namely the construction of a particular project. The lender at the time of the execution and recording of the security instrument usually obligates himself to make advances provided either that certain conditions precedent are met or certain conditions subsequent do not occur.

(c) Statutory Requirements. Article 7 in part provides that a security instrument, otherwise valid, shall secure future obligations [192] which may be incurred so as to give priority if the security instrument [193] shows that:

(A) it is given wholly or partly to secure future obligations which may be incurred thereunder; [194]

(B) [t]he amount of present obligations secured, and the maximum amount, including present and future obligations, which may be secured thereby at any one time; [195] and

---

191. *See* Wolfman, *Legal Problems Involved in Open End Mortgages,* appearing in *Real Estate in Mid-Century: Transition Taxation and Trends* 16 (1974). *See also* North v. J.W. McClintock, Inc., 208 Miss. 289, 44 So. 2d 412 (1950).

192. "Future obligations," as used throughout Article 7, refers to the borrower's obligation to repay future advances. *See* N.C. GEN. STAT. § 45-67. OSBORNE, HANDBOOK ON THE LAW OF MORTGAGES § 114 (2d ed. 1970). OSBORNE points out that the borrower's promise to repay future advances is really a present obligation.

193. The requirements set forth in N.C. GEN. STAT. § 45-68(1)(a), (b), and (c) apparently must appear in the security instrument itself, rather than in an allied instrument incorporated by reference therein. *Accord,* CONN. GEN. STAT. ANN. §§ 49-2, -3, -4(a) (Supp. 1973); FLA. STAT. ANN. § 697.04(1) (Supp. 1973). *But see* DEL. CODE ANN. tit. 25, § 2118(a) (1974).

194. N.C. GEN. STAT. § 45-68(1)(a) (Cum. Supp. 1975). *Accord,* CONN. GEN. STAT. ANN. §§ 49-2(c)(1), (2), -3(a)(1) *et seq.* (Supp. 1973); FLA. STAT. ANN. § 697.04(1) (Supp. 1973); MD. ANN. CODE art. 66, § 2 (1969). If an instrument does not contain this information, it might not secure future advances as against third parties relying upon the record. *See* Western Pa. Nat'l Bank v. Peoples Union Bank & Trust Co., 439 Pa. 304, 266 A.2d 773 (1970); OSBORNE, *supra* note 151, § 116.

195. N.C. GEN. STAT. § 45-68(1)(b). *See* statutes from other jurisdictions cited in notes 195 and 196 *supra. See also* OSBORNE, *supra* note 151, § 116. G.S. 45-69 sets forth the rule regarding "fluctuating balances." This rule is quite common. *Cf.* DEL. CODE ANN. tit. 25, § 2118(a) (Supp. 1973).

(C) [t]he period within which such future obligations may be incurred, which period shall not extend more than ten years beyond the date of the security instrument.[196]

In addition to the requirements for the security instrument itself, Article 7 prescribes: "At the time of incurring any such future obligations each obligation is evidenced by a written instrument or notation signed by the obligor and stipulating that such obligation is secured by such security instrument."[197] On this point, Article 7 seems a bit inconsistent, in that while the requirements section demands notations of receipt of advances as a prerequisite to the application of the Article's rules of priority, it makes no requirement that such notations appear upon the security agreement. Furthermore, the priority section makes reference to "any security instrument which conforms to the requirements of [the Article]" [198] when referring to instruments to which the Article's rule of priority pertain, but makes no reference to the receipt of advances which might not be noted upon the security instrument. Article 7 should be amended to clarify this inconsistency.

An additional requirement is that at the time of the assignment of a security instrument the amount, date, and due date of each bond or other undertaking for the payment of money representing a future obligation secured by the security instrument must be noted in writing thereon.[199]

(d) Priority of Security Instrument. Article 7 of Chapter 45 conditions the priority of security instruments by these stipulations:

> Any security instrument which conforms to the requirements of this Article and which *on its face* shows that the making of *future advances is obligatory,* shall, from the time and date of registration thereof, have the same priority *to the extent of all obligatory future advances secured by it,* as if all the advances had been made at the time of the execution of the instrument.[200]

Thus, several statutory prerequisites for according priority to the advances are evident:

1. The security instrument must conform to the requirements of Article 7; [201]

2. The *security instrument on its face* must show that the making of future advances is obligatory; [202] and

---

196. N.C. GEN. STAT. § 45-68(1)(c) (Cum. Supp. 1975). *Cf.* DEL. CODE ANN. tit. 25, § 2118(b) (Supp. 1973); FLA. STAT. ANN. § 697.04(1) (Supp. 1973).
197. N.C. GEN. STAT. § 45-68(2).
198. *Id.* §§ 45-70(a), (b),
199. *Id.* § 45-68(3).
200. *Id.* § 45-70(a) (emphasis added).
201. *Id.* § 45-68.
202. *Id.* § 45-70(a).

3. The future advances made must in fact be "obligatory," whatever that term is intended to mean.[203]

The Article also provides that:

> Any security instrument which conforms to the requirements of this Article, which *on its face does not show that the making of future advances is obligatory,* shall, from the time and date of registration thereof, have the same priority to the extent of all obligations secured by it, as if all the advances had been made at the time of the execution of the instrument, except that when an intervening lienor or encumbrancer gives *actual notice as hereinafter provided* that an intervening lien or encumbrance *has been perfected* on the property covered by the security instrument, *or is being incurred and when perfected will relate back to the time when incurred,* any future advances made subsequent to the receipt of such notice shall not take priority over such intervening perfected lien or encumbrance. Such notice shall be in writing and shall be given to the secured creditor named in the security instrument; but if the security instrument is registered and if any assignment of the security instrument has been noted on the margin of the record showing the name and address of the assignee, such notice shall be given to the last assignee so noted at the address so shown.[204]

The above quoted sections of the Article are mute with respect to the rule of priority to be applied when the security instrument complies with the "requirements" section of the Article and on its face purports to secure obligatory advances but in fact, for one reason or another, does not. It is suggested that North Carolina General Statutes, § 45-70(b) would apply to such a situation, although in the phrasing of that section of the Article does not do so expressly. It seems clear, however, that if the security instrument in question complies with the requirements section of the Article but does not on its face show that the making of future advances is obligatory, the advances secured may be subordinate to intervening mechanics' liens arising either from labor or materials furnished at the construction site or from certain professional services rendered for construction and to other liens or encumbrances, notwithstanding the actual obligatory nature of the advances.[205]

(e) *Obligatory vs. Optional Advances.* Most open end security instruments,[206] as well as certain construction loan security instruments,[207] allow clearly optional future advances to be made at the sole discretion

---

203. *Id.*
204. *Id.* § 45-70(b) (emphasis added).
205. *See* the additional discussion of related issues at 12 WAKE FOREST L. REV. 335, 336.
206. *See* Kimmell v. Bathy, 168 Colo. 431, 451 P.2d 751 (1969); North v. J.W. McClintock, Inc., 208 Miss. 280, 44 So. 2d 412 (1950); Western Pa. Nat'l Bank & Trust Co. v. Peoples Union Bank, 439 Pa. 304, 266, A.2d 773 (1970); Peoples Sav. Bank v. Champlin Lumber Co., 106 R.I. 225, 258 A.2d 82 (1969).
207. Imhoff v. Title Ins. Co., 113 Cal. App. 2d 139, 247 P.2d 851 (1952); W. Fuller & Co. v. McClure, 48 Cal. App. 162, 191 P. 1027 (1920).

of the lender. Most construction loan security instruments provide that the lender is obligated to make future advances up to a maximum amount specified in the security instrument if certain conditions precedent occur or if certain conditions subsequent do not occur. Although there appears to be authority to the contrary,[208] the prevailing view is that the mere inclusion of conditions precedent to the making of future advances in a security instrument will not render the advances optional.[209] If a condition precedent to the making of future advances does not occur or if a condition subsequent occurs, thereby relieving the lender of his obligation to make subsequent advances, the prevailing view is that future advances thereafter made are optional rather than obligatory.[210] However, a minority rule holds that in such instances the nature of the advances remains obligatory.[211] To date, there are no North Carolina cases defining the term "obligatory" or interpreting Article 7 of Chapter 45.[212]

(f) Statutory Exceptions. If the security instrument secures the obligations of an electric or telephone membership corporation incorporated or domesticated in North Carolina, all future advances will have priority as if made at the time of the execution of the security instrument even though the instrument neither complies with the requirements section of Article 7 nor shows that the making of future advances is obligatory.[213]

The statute covers all other exceptions pertaining to the priority of advances in this manner:

> Payments made by the secured creditor for fire and extended coverage insurance, taxes, assessments, *or other necessary expendi-*

---

208. *See* National Bank of Washington v. Equity Investors, 81 Wash. 2d 886, 506 P.2d 20 (1973).

209. Annot., 80 A.L.R.2d 179, 197-98 (1961).

210. *See* Yost-Linn Lumber Co. v. Williams, 121 Cal. App. 571, 9 P.2d 324 (1932); J.I. Kislack Mtg. Corp. v. William Matthews Builders, Inc., — Del. Super. —, 287 A.2d 686 (1972), *aff'd*, — Del. —, 303 A.2d 648 (1973) (DEL. CODE ANN. tit. 25, § 2118 (Supp. 1973) essentially overrules the case); Housing Mfg. Corp. v. Allied Constr. Co., 374 Pa. 321, 97 A.2d 802 (1953); Elmendorf-Anthony v. Dunn, 10 Wash. 2d 29, 116 P.2d 253 (1941).

211. Landers-Morrison-Christenson Co. v. Ambassador Holding Co., 171 Minn. 445, 214 N.W. 503 (1927); Hyman v. Hauff, 138 N.Y. 48, 33 N.E. 735 (1893). *See also* Tony Schloos Properties Corp. v. Union Fed. Sav. & Loan, 223 Md. 224, 196 A.2d 458 (1967), where the court treated full disbursement to a construction loan account under control of a trustee for the lender as a full disbursement at closing, notwithstanding that payments made from that account to the borrower were to be made upon fulfillment of certain conditions precedent and that advances from the account were made subsequent to the non-occurrence of a condition precedent. The court strongly refused to view the arrangement as a future advance loan.

212. The various jurisdictions have varying rules of priority. Florida and Delaware grant all optional and obligatory future advances priority as if they were all made at the time of the execution of the security instrument. *See* DEL. CODE ANN. tit. 25, §§ 2118(a), (c) (Supp. 1973); FLA. STAT. ANN. § 697.04(1) (Supp. 1973). Connecticut has a similar rule but apparently restricts its application to construction loans. CONN. GEN. STAT. ANN. §§ 49-3(a), -2(c)(8) (1958). Other jurisdictions discern between obligatory and optional advances as does North Carolina. *See e.g.,* OHIO REV. CODE ANN. § 5301.232(b) (1967).

213. N.C. GEN. STAT. § 45-70(d).

tures for the preservation of the security shall be secured by the security instrument and shall have the same priority as if such payments had been made at the time of the execution of the instrument, whether or not notice has been given as provided in subsection (b) of this section. The provisions of G.S. 45-68(2) and (3) shall not be applicable to such payments, nor shall such payments be considered in computing the maximum amount which may be secured by the instrument.[214]

(g) The Provisions of Article 7 Are Not Exclusive. Article 7 expressly provides that:

> The provisions of this article shall not be deemed exclusive, and no security instrument securing future advances or future obligations which is otherwise valid shall be invalidated by failure to comply with the provisions of this article.[215]

North Carolina case law does not indicate how priorities will be determined absent a security instrument's compliance with Article 7 of Chapter 45. For instance, in *McAdams v. Piedmont Trust Co.,*[216] the court held that the lien of a deed of trust securing funds to be disbursed as construction progressed was superior to the claims of laborers and materialmen attaching subsequent to the deed of trust's registration. The facts of the opinion do not clearly indicate whether or not the advances made were obligatory, nor do the facts relate when each advance was made. Since the provisions of Article 7 are not exclusive, one can only speculate as to what rules of priority the North Carolina courts will apply.

§ 431. Priority of Contractors' Lien Against Federal Tax Liens.[217]

The tax lien imposed by federal law[218] arises at the time the tax is assessed and continues until the amount assessed (or a judgment against the taxpayer arising out of such liability) is paid or becomes enforceable because of "lapse of time."[219]

---

214. *Id.* § 45-70(c) (emphasis added).

215. One writer interpreted a similar provision contained in an ill-fated 1953 Senate bill [S. 27, N.C. Assembly (1953)] to mean that the law regarding priorities existing prior to the statute would apply if a security instrument did not comply with the statute. Note, 31 N.C.L. REV. 504, 508 (1953).

216. 167 N.C. 494, 83 S.E. 623 (1924).

217. This section is quoting 12 WAKE FOREST L. REV. 339-42.

218. INT. REV. CODE OF 1954, § 6321 provides:

> If any person liable to pay any tax neglects or refuses to pay the same after demand, the amount (including any interest, additional amount, addition to tax, or assessable penalty, together with any costs that may accrue in addition thereto) shall be a lien in favor of the United States upon all property and rights to property, whether real or personal, belonging to such person.

219. By statute, a "lapse of time" is six years from the date of assessment (or a longer period if the taxpayer waives restrictions on collection) during which time the Commissioner has not attempted to collect the tax either by suit or distraint. INT. REV. CODE OF 1954, § 6502(a).

Prior to the enactment of the Federal Tax Lien Act of 1966,[220] a federal tax lien had priority over a statutory mechanics' lien which had not been reduced to judgment even though the mechanics' lien was perfected at the time the tax claim arose.[221] The Federal Tax Lien Act of 1966, however, expanded the class of interests to which priority over unfiled tax liens was granted to include mechanics' liens.[222]

The general rule seems to be that unless the notice of the federal tax lien has been filed in the office of the clerk of superior court of the county where the real property is situated [223] prior to the first furnishing of labor or materials at the site by the contractor, the contractor's lien will be superior in priority to the federal tax lien.[224] This result would hold true even though the tax lien had been filed before the contractor's lien. It should also be noted that if the contract price with the owner is $1000 or less and if the contract is for the repair or improvement of a personal residence (containing not more than four dwelling units) occupied by the owner of such residence, the mechanics' lien will be superior in priority to the federal tax lien even though notice of the federal tax lien has been filed prior to the commencement of the contractor's lienable performance.[225]

§ 432. Priority of Contractors' Lien Against Interests Arising Under the Bankruptcy Act.[226]

The Federal Bankruptcy Reform Act of 1978 establishes the following priorities:

> The trustee may avoid the fixing of a statutory lien on property of the debtor to the extent that such lien —
>
>> (2) is not perfected or enforceable on the date of the filing of the petition against a bona fide purchaser that purchases such property on the date of the filing of the petition, whether or not such a purchaser exists;[227]

---

220. Pub. L. No. 89-719, tit. I, § 113(b), 80 Stat. 1146 (1966).
221. United States v. White Bear Brewing Co., 350 U.S. 1010, *rehearing denied,* 351 U.S. 958 (1965).
222. INT. REV. CODE OF 1954, § 6323(a).
223. *Id.* § 6323(f)(1)(A); N.C. GEN. STAT. § 44-68.1 (Cum. Supp. 1975).
224. INT. REV. CODE OF 1954, § 6323(a). Section 6323(h)(2) states that under the tax lien act "a person has a lien on the earliest date such lien becomes valid under local law against subsequent purchasers without actual notice, but not before he begins to furnish the services, labor, or materials."
225. *Id.* § 6323(b)(7).
226. Parts of this section have been taken directly from portions of 12 WAKE FOREST L. REV. 342-43.
227. Bankruptcy Reform Act of 1978, 11 U.S.C. § 545(2) (1978).

The 1978 amendment retains the basic approach of the former section.[228]

It is generally accepted that state law governs the existence or validity of statutory liens in bankruptcy proceedings.[229] Thus, if a contractor begins furnishing labor or materials at the site of the improvement prior to the date of the filing of the petition and if the contractors' lien for materials would have priority over the interest of a subsequent purchaser for value, the contractors' lien filed subsequent to the date of the bankruptcy proceeding will not be invalidated by that proceeding.[230] Under the facts set forth above, a contractors' lien in North Carolina would not be invalidated since the effective date of the contractors' lien relates back to the date of the first lienable performance as against purchasers for value and lien creditors.[231]

§ 433. Priority of Mechanics' Lien Against Owners' Homestead Exemption.[232]

Article X section 3 of the North Carolina Constitution grants laborers' and mechanics' liens priority over the homestead exemption of the land owner in the following terms:

> The General Assembly shall provide by proper legislation for giving to *mechanics* and *laborers* an adequate lien on the subject matter of their *labor*. The provisions of Sections 1 and 2 of this Article shall not be so construed as to prevent a *laborer's lien for work done and performed* for the person claiming the exemption or a mechanic's lien for work done on the premises (emphasis added).

It has been held, however, that a lien for materials furnished does not have priority over the homestead exemption since the constitution provides such priority only for mechanics' liens for work done or labor performed.[233] Although the decisions were rendered under Article X section 4 of the Constitution of 1868, it would appear that they are still good law since the prior provision is practically identical to the current Article X section 3.

---

228. Bankruptcy Act §§ 67(c)(1)(B), 11 U.S.C. §§ 107(c)(1)(B) (1970). This former section declared liens that did not qualify "invalid" against the trustee. The new section states that the trustee "may avoid" the fixing of the lien.
229. Diamond Nat'l Corp. v. Lee, 333 F.2d 517 (9th Cir. 1964); *In re* Kobiela, 152 F. Supp. 489 (D. Neb. 1957); *In re* Venarsky, 287 F. Supp. 446 (N.D.N.Y. 1968).
230. Sandusky Foundry & Mach. Co. v. City of Wickliffe, 369 F. Supp. 439, 445-46 (W.D. Ky. 1972); *In re* Chesterfield Developers, Inc., 285 F. Supp. 689 (S.D.N.Y. 1968).
231. N.C. GEN. STAT. §§ 44A-10, -14(a) (Cum. Supp. 1975).
232. This section is quoting 12 WAKE FOREST L. REV. 343.
233. Broyhill v. Gaither, 119 N.C. 443, 26 S.E. 31 (1896); Cumings v. Bloodworth, 87 N.C. 83 (1882).

§ 434. Priority of Contractors' Lien Against Federal Mortgages or Deeds of Trust.[234]

Under the relation-back doctrine embodied in most state statutes, contractors have priority from the first date of furnishing labor and materials as against conventional mortgages. This rule does not apply, however, with regard to federal mortgages or deeds of trust. It has been held that the mortgage liens of the Farmers Home Administration had priority over subsequently filed contractors' liens even though material and labor had been furnished to the site prior to the recordation of such mortgages and notwithstanding state law provisions for the relation back of such liens.[235] The rationale for this result is that federal law governs the priority of federal liens on the basis of "first in time, first in right."[236] In order for a nonfederal lien to acquire priority over the federal lien, it must become "choate" prior to the federal lien. The "choateness" of such nonfederal lien is determined by federal law.[237] From the cases, it would appear that choateness is met only if the identity of the lienor, the property subject to the lien, and the amount of the lien are established with certainty so as to preclude a judicial contest over the validity and amount of the lien.[238] In view of the foregoing, it appears that unless a North Carolina contractors' lien has been reduced to final judgment, it will be subordinate to the lien of a federal mortgage.

§ 435. Waiver of the Lien.[239]

Lien rights can be lost even prior to lien perfection by the execution of a valid lien waiver [240] by the prospective lien claimant. The lien claimant must receive consideration for his waiver; therefore, if a lien waiver is obtained from a contractor after the execution of the original contract, additional consideration must pass to him for the waiver to be valid and binding unless estoppel is involved.[241] Under the better reasoned cases, lien waivers given by a contractor without having received adequate consideration from the owner have been upheld as to mortgagees

---

234. This section is quoting 12 WAKE FOREST L. REV. 343-44.
235. Rogers Lumber Co. v. Apel, 468 F.2d 14 (10th Cir. 1972); Bellegarde Custom Kitchens v. Select-A-Home, Inc., 385 F. Supp. 318 (S.D. Me. 1974).
236. Rogers Lumber Co. v. Apel, 468 F.2d 14 (10th Cir. 1972); Bellegarde Custom Kitchens v. Select-A-Home, Inc., 385 F. Supp. 318 (S.D. Me. 1974).
237. United States v. New Britain, 347 U.S. 81 (1954); United States v. Waddill, Holland & Flynn, Inc., 323 U.S. 353 (1945).
238. United States v. New Britain, 347 U.S. 81 (1954); United States v. Waddill, Holland & Flynn, Inc., 323 U.S. 353 (1945). *See also* United States v. Security Trust & Sav. Bank, 340 U.S. 47 (1950).
239. This section is quoting 12 WAKE FOREST L. REV. 350-51.
240. *See* Homebuilding, Inc. v. Nash, 200 N.C. 430, 157 S.E. 134 (1931) (recognizing validity of lien waivers). *See generally* 53 AM. JUR. 2d *Mechanics' Liens* §§ 290-314 (1970).
241. G.R. Sponagle & Sons, Inc. v. McKnight Constr. Co., —— Del. Super. ——, 304 A.2d 339 (1973).

advancing loan proceeds to an owner or otherwise changing their positions in good faith reliance upon lien waivers.[242]

It has been held that the taking of an unsecured note by a potential lien claimant does not constitute a waiver of the right to file a mechanics' lien if the maturity date of the note falls within the period within which a claim of lien may be filed.[243]

§ 436. Discharge of the Lien.[244]

Article 2 of Chapter 44A sets forth a number of methods by which a lien may be discharged. One obvious method involves a failure to enforce the lien within the period prescribed by Article 2.[245] A lien may also be discharged "[b]y filing in the office of the clerk of superior court the original or certified copy of a judgment or decree of a court of competent jurisdiction showing that the action by the claimant to enforce the lien has been dismissed or finally determined adversely to the claimant."[246] Both of these methods of discharge had counterparts in the statute previously applicable.[247]

Additionally, the lien claimant of record, his agent, or attorney may acknowledge the satisfaction of the lien indebtedness in the presence of the clerk of superior court. The clerk will then enter on the record of such lien an acknowledgment of satisfaction which must be signed by the lien claimant of record, his agent, or attorney and witnessed by the clerk.[248] The statute which was formerly applicable contained a similar provision.[249] However, the present version is a distinct improvement in that it specifies the claimant's function before the clerk: the acknowledgment of satisfaction, which is made by the clerk upon the record, must be signed by the claimant of record, his agent, or attorney.

The present law makes it clear as well that the owner may bring before the clerk of superior court an instrument of satisfaction which is signed

---

242. St. Louis Flexicone, Inc. v. Lintezenich, 414 S.W.2d 787 (Mo. App. 1967).
243. Raeford Lumber Co. v. Rockfish Trading Co., 163 N.C. 314, 79 S.E. 627 (1913); 53 AM. JUR. 2d *Mechanics' Liens* § 299 (1970); Annot., 91 A.L.R.2d 425, 442, § 9(b) (1963).
244. This section is quoting 12 WAKE FOREST L. REV. 351 & 352.
245. N.C. GEN. STAT. § 44A-16(3). *See also id.* § 44A-13(a), which indicates that no action to enforce a lien created by Article 2 "may be commenced later than 180 days after the last furnishing of labor or materials at the site of the improvement by the person claiming the lien."
246. *Id.* § 44A-16(a).
247. *See id.* § 44-48(4) (1966), *as amended, id.* § 44-48(4) (discharge occurs from failure to enforce the lien within six months from the time of the filing of the notice of the lien); *id.* § 44-48(3) (1966), *as amended, id.* § 44-48(3) (discharge occurs by an entry in the lien docket to the effect that the action by the claimant to enforce the lien has been dismissed or has resulted in a judgment against the claimant).
248. *Id.* § 44A-16(1).
249. *Id.* § 44-48(1) (1966), *as amended, id.* § 44-48(1).

and acknowledged by the claimant of record, whereupon the clerk will cancel the lien by making an entry of satisfaction on the record of lien.[250] Although there is no equivalent provision in old G.S. 44-48, the same result could probably have been achieved under the statute.

Discharge of a lien may also occur "[w]hevever a sum equal to the amount of the lien or liens claimed is deposited with the clerk of court, to be applied to the payment finally determined to be due . . . ." After such deposit is made, the clerk is required to cancel the lien or liens of record.[251] In such a situation it would seem that a deposit of the principal amount due would suffice so as to require the lien's discharge since a judgment enforcing the lien cannot be entered for a sum exceeding the principal amount shown to be due.[252] It should be noted that in lieu of cash, a corporate surety bond conditioned upon the payment of the amount finally determined to be due in satisfaction of the lien or liens, in a sum equal to one and one-fourth times the amount of the lien or liens claimed may be deposited with the clerk.[253]

Division 3. Liens of Mechanics, Laborers, and Materialmen Dealing with One Other than the Owner of Real Property

§ 437. Introduction.[254]

One who has furnished labor or materials at the site of the improvement is generally referred to as a "subcontractor" if he did not contract directly with the owner or indirectly with the owner through the owner's agent. Subcontractors at common law were not allowed liens on land or buildings as security for the debt owed them by the owner for their labor and materials.[255] Accordingly, the North Carolina Supreme Court held in *Wilkie v. Bray*[256] that unless the laborer or materialman could allege and prove a contract with the owner of the real property improved by the laborer's or materialman's performance, no lien could be perfected and enforced against the owner's real property. In 1880, the General Assembly altered the harshness of the common law by enacting a statute which expressly provided for subcontractors' liens.[257]

In 1971, in an effort to clarify the rights and priorities applicable to subcontractors' liens, the General Assembly enacted Part 2 of Article 2 of Chapter 44A of the General Statutes.[258]

---

250. *Id.* § 44A-16(2).
251. *Id.* § 44A-16(5); *id.* § 44-48(2) (contains an equivalent provision).
252. *Id.* § 44A-13(b).
253. *Id.* § 44A-16(6).
254. This section is quoting 12 Wake Forest L. Rev. 352 & 353.
255. 53 Am. Jur. 2d *Mechanics' Liens* § 2 (1970).
256. 71 N.C. 205 (1874).
257. N.C. Sess. Laws ch. 44 §§ 1, 3 (1880) (repealed 1971). That provision was eventually designated as G.S. § 44-6.
258. N.C. Gen. Stat. §§ 44A-17 through 44A-23.

§ 438. Nature of Lien; Statutory Definitions.[259]

In contrast to the prior law,[260] Part 2 of Article 2 of Chapter 44A grants three remedies which inure to the subcontractor at various times and which may be summarized as follows:

(a) statutory lien upon funds [261] — the subcontractor's initial remedy;
(b) lien upon owner's interest in real property by virtue of subcontractor's right of subrogation to contractor's lien rights [262] — this remedy is not available to a subcontractor until the owner's obligation to the contractor is matured; and
(c) lien upon owner's interest in real property by virtue of owner's personal liability to subcontractor [263] — this remedy is not available until the owner incurs personal liability to the subcontractor.

Unlike the former statute, the present law states when and to what extent the various remedies are available to the claimant. Before discussing those remedies, however, it is imperative to set forth the definition of terms utilized in the statute and to ascertain *who* is entitled to the benefit of those remedies.

§ 44A-17. *Definitions.* — Unless the context otherwise requires in this Article:
 (1) "Contractor" means a person who contracts with an owner to improve real property.
 (2) "First tier subcontractor" means a person who contracts with a contractor to improve real property.
 (3) "Obligor" means an owner, contractor or subcontractor in any tier who owes money to another as a result of the other's partial or total performance of a contract to improve real property.
 (4) "Second tier subcontractor" means a person who contracts with a first tier subcontractor to improve real property.
 (5) "Third tier subcontractor" means a person who contracts with a second tier subcontractor to improve real property.

§ 439. General Applicability of Part I of Article 2 of Chapter 44A.[264]

The basic requirements for lien perfection and enforcement by the contractor are set forth at Part B of Article III of this chapter. As a general rule, it can be stated that those requirements also pertain to the perfection of the subcontractors' various remedies.[265] For example, the subcontractor and his immediate obligor must have entered into a

---

259. This section is quoting 12 WAKE FOREST L. REV. 353-54.
260. *See* 12 WAKE FOREST L. REV. 353.
261. N.C. GEN. STAT. § 44A-18.
262. *Id.* § 44A-23.
263. *Id.* § 44A-20(d).
264. This section is taken directly from portions of 12 WAKE FOREST L. REV. 354-55. *See id.* 355-56 for a discussion of problems caused by the failure of the General Assembly to address expressly liens of subcontractors dealing with contractors who are among the class of new lienors (architects, surveyors, and engineers).
265. N.C. GEN. STAT. §§ 44A-20(d) to -23 would seem to support this assertion.

contract for the express purpose of improving the real property against which a lien is asserted, rather than for a general sale of materials for purposes unknown until delivery at the site.[266] The labor or materials must also have been furnished at the site by the claimant.[267] If the materials are furnished at the site in accordance with the requisite contractual intent, the better rule seems to be that the materials so furnished need not have become incorporated into the improvement in order for the mechanics' lien to arise. The rationale behind such a rule is that a contract for the furnishing of materials for the making of an improvement is the pertinent requirement and that the statute does not expressly require incorporation or use of the materials.[268] The rule would be applied when the subcontractor furnishes the materials at the site, but the contractor, or a subcontractor in a tier higher than the claimant, does not incorporate the materials into a building or other structure. In such a case the claimant-subcontractor should not have to bear the burden of loss, nonuse, or misuse of the materials furnished, nor should he be forced to refrain from enforcing his contract by taking back undamaged materials, unless he elects to do so. His *contractual performance* should be entitled to the security of a mechanics' lien.

§ 440. Grant of Lien upon Funds: The First Tier Subcontractor.[269]

Chapter 44A expressly provides that upon compliance with Article 2:

> A first tier subcontractor who furnished labor or materials as the site of the improvement shall be entitled to a lien upon funds which are owed to the contractor with whom the first tier subcontractor dealt and which arise out of the improvement on which the first tier subcontractor worked or furnished materials.[270]

The lien will attach to funds due at the time of the owner's receipt of notice and to those funds which thereafter become due, a result indicated by decisions rendered in interpretation of both the former and current

---

266. N.C. Gen. Stat. § 44A-17 defines the various tier subcontractors as persons who contract "to improve real property."

267. *Id.* § 44A-18 indicates that the labor or materials must be furnished "at the site of the improvement" by the subcontractor-claimant.

268. *See* Kobayashi v. Meehleis Steel Co., 28 Colo. App. 327, 472 P.2d 724 (1972); Gaster v. Wilmington Plumbing Supply Co., — Del. —, 321 A.2d 504 (1974); American Blower Corp. v. James Talcott, Inc., 18 Misc. 2d 1031, 194 N.Y.S.2d 630 (Sup. Ct. 1959), *aff'd mem.*, 11 App. Div., 2d 654, 203 N.Y.S.2d 1018 (1960), *aff'd*, 19 N.Y.2d 282, 176 N.E.2d 833, 219 N.Y.S.2d 263 (1961); Houston Fire & Cas. Co. v. Hales, 279 S.W.2d 389 (Tex. Civ. App. 1955). *See also* Hinkle v. Creek, 113 Ill. App. 2d 454, 251 N.E.2d 111 (1969) (construing Ill. Ann. Stat. ch. 82, § 7 (Smith-Hurd 1966), which expressly does not require use or incorporation). *See generally* Annot., 39 A.L.R.2d 394 (1955).

269. This section has been taken from portions of 12 Wake Forest L. Rev. 366.

270. N.C. Gen. Stat. § 44A-18(1).

statutes.[271] This result would also follow with regard to lien rights inuring to subcontractors more remote than those of the first tier.[272]

§ 441. Grant of Lien upon Funds: Second and Third Tier Subcontractors.[273]

In contrast to the ambiguities of the former statute,[274] the current statute makes it clear that only second and third tier subcontractors (in addition to first tier subcontractors) have rights of subrogation against funds held by the owner.[275] Unlike under the former statute, second and third tier subcontractors have also been granted lien rights against funds held by people lower in the construction hierarchy than the owner.

§ 442. Direct Lien Rights of Second and Third Tier Subcontractors upon Funds.[276]

North Carolina General Statutes, § 44A-18(2) provides in part:

> A second tier subcontractor who furnished labor or materials at the site of the improvement shall be entitled to a lien upon funds which are owed to the first tier subcontractor with whom the second tier subcontractor dealt and which arise out of the improvement on which the second tier subcontractor worked or furnished materials.

With respect to third tier subcontractors, North Carolina General Statutes, § 44A-18(3) similarly provides:

> A third tier subcontractor who furnished labor or materials at the site

---

271. Norfolk Bldg. Supplies Co. v. Elizabeth City Hosp. Co., 176 N.C. 87, 97 S.E. 1 (1918); Blue Pearl Granite Co. v. Merchants Bank, 172 N.C. 354, 90 S.E. 312 (1916); Borden Brick & Tile Co. v. Pulley, 168 N.C. 371, 84 S.E. 513 (1915). *See* Builders Supply v. Bedros, 32 N.C. App. 209, 231 S.E.2d 199 (1977) holding, *inter alia,* that no funds were owed by the owner to the contractor at the time of receipt of notice of lien claim from the first tier subcontractor. The subcontractor had argued that, since the owner's architect had approved a progress payment to the general contractor in the amount of $15,284.66, this approval constituted irrebuttable evidence that the owner owed the contractor this sum which had not been paid at the time the first tier subcontractor had filed his notice of claim of lien for $13,366.98 with the owner. The court rejected this theory noting that the amount owed by the owner to the contractor at any particular time was to be determined "in the light of existing circumstances and the contract between owner and contractor." And where the contractor subsequently breached the construction contract, the amount due from owner to contractor had to be determined in light of the damages suffered by the owner from the contractor's breach. The court went on to hold that, where the owner mitigated damages by completing the construction, the owner was entitled to set-off any amount he may have owed the contractor. *See also* Mace v. Construction Co., 48 N.C. App. 297, 269 S.E.2d 191 (1980) where the first tier subcontractor filed a claim of lien on August 26, 1974, but did not give notice to the original property owners until October 4, 1974.

272. *See* North Carolina Supreme Court cases cited in note 271 *supra.*

273. This section is quoting 12 WAKE FOREST L. REV. 356-57.

274. *See id.* for a summary of ambiguities existing under the former statute with respect to the lien rights of those persons classified as second, third, or more remote tier subcontractors.

275. N.C. GEN. STAT. § 44A-18(4).

276. This section is quoting 12 WAKE FOREST L. REV. 357-58.

of the improvement shall be entitled to a lien upon funds which are owed to the second tier subcontractor with whom the third tier subcontractor dealt and which arise out of the improvement on which the third tier subcontractor worked or furnished materials.

Accordingly, upon compliance with perfection requirements particular to subcontractors' liens, the second tier subcontractor can perfect a lien upon funds in the hands of the contractor, which the latter owes or may owe to the first tier subcontractor.

§ 443. Subrogation Rights Available to Second and Third Tier Subcontractors. [277]

Because of North Carolina General Statutes, § 44A-18(2), second tier subcontractors will have a right of subrogation with respect to certain funds:

> A second tier subcontractor, *to the extent of his lien* provided in this subdivision, shall be entitled to be subrogated to the lien of the first tier subcontractor with whom he dealt provided for in subdivision (1) and shall be entitled to perfect it by notice to the extent of his claim. (emphasis added)

In regard to similar rights available to third tier subcontractors, North Carolina General Statutes, §§ 44A-18(3) states:

> A third tier subcontractor, *to the extent of his lien* provided in this subdivision, shall also be entitled to be subrogated to the lien of the second tier subcontractor with whom he dealt and to the lien of the first tier subcontractor with whom the second tier subcontractor dealt to the extent that the second tier subcontractor is entitled to be subrogated thereto, and in either case shall be entitled to perfect the same by notice to the extent of his claim. (emphasis added)

The above principal of subrogation represents a substantial and worthwhile change in the law. For example, in more than one decision rendered in interpretation of the former statute, the North Carolina Supreme Court held that the state of accounts between the principal contractor and the first tier subcontractor was irrelevant when ascertaining the right of the second tier subcontractor to assert a lien upon funds in the hands of the owner.[278]

---

277. This section is quoting 12 WAKE FOREST L. REV. 358-61.
278. *See, e.g., Atlas Powder Co. v. Denton,* 176 N.C. 426, 97 S.E. 372 (1918); Norfolk Bldg. Supplies Co. v. Elizabeth City Hosp. Co., 176 N.C. 87, 97 S.E. 146 (1918); Borden Brick & Tile Co. v. Pulley, 168 N.C. 371, 84 S.E. 513 (1915); Parnell-Martin Supply Co. v. High Point Motor Lodge, Inc., 7 N.C. App. 701, 173 S.E.2d 623, aff'd, 277 N.C. 312, 77 S.E.2d 392 (1970).

At 12 WAKE FOREST L. REV. 359, the authors give the following illustration of how the new statute alters the former law:

> For example, in *Atlas Powder Co. v. Denton,* the first tier subcontractor owed the second tier subcontractor $1,526.67. The contractor owed the first tier subcontractor $1,028.69, and the owner owed the contractor an amount in excess of $1,526.67. The court held that the plaintiff-second tier subcontractor was entitled to a lien upon the owner's land and upon the funds not paid to the contractor to the extent of $1,526.67. This decision resulted in the contractor having to pay $497.98 (the difference between

§ 444. Grant of Lien: Remote Tier Subcontractors.[279]

The statute treats not only first, second, and third tier subcontractors, but also others whose position is more remote. For example, North Carolina General Statutes, § 44A-18(4) explains:

> Subcontractors more remote than the third tier who furnished labor or material at the site of the improvement shall be entitled to a lien upon funds which are owed to the person with whom they dealt and which arise out of the improvement on which they furnished labor or material, but such remote tier subcontractors shall not be entitled to subrogation to the rights of other persons.

The Drafting Committee on Lien Laws of the General Statutes Commission felt that the third tier of subcontractors provided a reasonable cutoff point for the right of subrogation, correctly reasoning that permitting subrogation without any cutoff would compound the practical difficulties existing in a multi-tier construction project.[280] It is obvious that one consequence of this provision is that construction lenders, owners, contractors, and first tier subcontractors have no statutory duty to hold back funds at the request of fourth tier subcontractors.

§ 445. Lien upon Funds: Perfection.[281]

The statute elucidates that "[t]he liens granted under this section are perfected upon the giving of notice in writing to the obligor as hereinafter provided and shall be effective upon the receipt thereof by such obligor."[282] Thus, the current statute does not require the filing of the notice of claim of lien in the land records in order to perfect a lien upon the funds

---

$1,526.67 and $1,028.69) twice for the same performance since that amount was paid first to the first tier subcontractor and as a result of the suit had to be paid to the second tier subcontractor. If *Atlas Powder Co.* were decided today, the amount of the second tier subcontractor's lien would be limited to $1,028.69 since he would be subrogated to the first tier subcontractor's right to a lien upon funds in the hands of the owner; and the first tier subcontractor's lien would be limited to $1,028.69 — the amount owed to the first tier subcontractor by the contractor. Thus, the inequities of which the *Atlas Powder Co.* court were apparently cognizant have been eliminated. [Citations omitted.]

At 12 WAKE FOREST L. REV. 359-61, the authors discuss in some detail the question of whether the claimant seeking a right of subrogation must perfect his own lien. The authors conclude their discussion of this problem by suggesting that both N.C. GEN. STAT. §§ 44A-18(2) and 44A-18(3) be amended to prevent possible misinterpretations.

279. This section is quoting 12 WAKE FOREST L. REV. 361.
280. Memorandum of the Drafting Committee on Lien Laws of the North Carolina General Statutes Commission, Subject — A Bill to Be Entitled an Act to Rewrite the Laws Governing Liens of Mechanics, Materialmen, and Laborers who Deal with One Other than the Owner, 9 (1971).
281. This section is quoting 12 WAKE FOREST L. REV. 362-64.
282. N.C. GEN. STAT. § 44A-18(6).

§ 445   REAL ESTATE LAW IN NORTH CAROLINA   § 445

in the hands of the owner. This interpretation is in accord with prior statutory and case law.[283]

The current statute also sets forth the form of the notice of claim of lien. Both the contractors' claim of lien and the subcontractors' notice of claim of lien must contain: (1) the name and address of the person claiming the lien; [284] (2) a general description of the real property improved; [285] (3) the name and address of the person with whom the lien claimant contracted to improve the real property; [286] (4) a general description of the contract and the person against whose interest a lien is claimed; [287] and (5) the amount claimed by the lien claimant under his contract.[288] For obvious reasons, the requirement of the inclusion of the name and address of each person against or through whom subrogation rights are claimed [289] has no counterpart in the contractors' lien statute. It should be observed that the subcontractor's notice of claim of lien need *not* contain the date upon which the claimant first furnished labor or materials at the site as must the claim of lien filed by the contractor. The reason for this omission is that it is entirely possible to perfect a lien against funds in the hands of the owner or someone else lower than the owner in the construction hierarchy without at the time perfecting a lien against the owner's interest in the real property or, as will be subsequently discussed, without being entitled to perfect a lien against the owner's interest in the real

---

283. As mentioned previously, N.C. Sess. L. c. 44, § 1 (1880) (repealed 1971), indicated that the lien of the subcontractor, perfected upon the giving of notice to the owner, was on the owner's real property. Additionally, in Atlas Powder Co. v. Denton, 176 N.C. 426, 97 S.E. 372 (1918), it was held that the lien was not only on the owner's interest in the real estate but also on the funds in the hands of the owner. In Porter v. Case, 187 N.C. 629, 122 S.E. 483 (1924) and Campbell v. Hall, 187 N.C. 464, 121 S.E. 761 (1924) it was held that the lien upon land (and in effect, the lien upon funds) need not be filed in the land records. In regard to the perfection of a subcontractors' lien against the owner's real property, *compare* Porter v. Case, 187 N.C. 629, 122 S.E. 483 (1924) *and* Campbell v. Hall, 187 N.C. 464, 121 S.E. 761 (1924), *with* N.C. Gen. Stat. §§ 44A-20(d), -23 (Cum. Supp. 1975). *See also* N.C. Gen. Stat. § 44A-19(b) (Cum. Supp. 1975) for the form notice of claim of lien by the first, second, and third tier subcontractors, and *id.* § 44A-19(c) for the form notice of claim of lien for subcontractors more remote than the third tier.

284. *Id.* § 44A-12(c)(1) (contractors' claim of lien); *id.* § 44A-19(a)(1) (subcontractors' notice of claim of lien).

285. *Id.* § 44A-12(c)(3) (contractors' claim of lien); *id.* § 44A-19(a)(2) (subcontractors' notice of claim of lien).

286. *Id.* § 44A-12(c)(4) (contractors' claim of lien); *id.* § 44A-19(a)(3) (subcontractors' notice of claim of lien).

287. *Id.* §§ 44A-12(c)(2) and (6) (contractors' claim of lien); *id.* § 44A-19(a)(5) (subcontractors' notice of claim of lien).

288. *Id.* § 44A-12(c)(6) (contractors' claim of lien); *id.* § 44A-19(a)(6) (subcontractors' notice of claim of lien).

289. *Id.* § 44A-19(a)(4).

property at the time the notice of claim of lien is first given to and received by the owner.[290]

Another question concerning perfection is whether the time limitation placed on the period within which a subcontractor may perfect a lien upon the owner's interest in real property is applicable, either expressly or by implication, to perfection of a lien upon funds in the hands of the owner or anyone else. For example, suppose that the entire project is completed on June 1, that the owner still owes the contractor $10,000, and that the contractor owes the first tier subcontractor $2000. On December 1, more than 120 days after the contractor last furnished labor or materials at the site on June 1, the situation has not changed, except that the first tier subcontractor is now reviewing his rights and remedies against the owner and contractor. The first tier subcontractor will not be able to file a claim of lien against the owner's interest in the improved real property either in his own right [291] or in subrogation to the contractor's right to do so,[292] since the 120-day period has expired. Can the first tier subcontractor still perfect a lien upon funds held by the owner which the latter owes to the contractor? It would seem that he could, notwithstanding the unavailability of a claim of lien against the owner's interest in the real property, since one can obviously perfect a lien upon funds without electing to perfect a lien upon real property, or in some instances, without being legally entitled to perfect the latter. If the contractor's obligation to pay the first tier subcontractor matured on May 1, the first tier subcontractor would have three years from May 1, the date of the contractor's breach of contract, to commence an action against the contractor.[293] If the first tier subcontractor's action were commenced within that three-year period, it would seem that he would have three years from the date on which the owner's obligation to pay the contractor arose (June 1) to give the owner notice of claim of lien upon funds and to join the owner as a party defendant.

Case law formulated prior to the enactment of the current statute held that if the owner was given cursory notice of a lien claim and wrote a letter to the subcontractor-claimant admitting the validity of the claim,

---

290. *Id.* § 44A-20(d). This section provides that the lien set forth therein cannot be perfected prior to the time that the owner incurs personal liability to the lien claimant pursuant to N.C. GEN. STAT. § 44A-20(b). N.C. GEN. STAT. 44A-23 makes it fairly clear that a subcontractor cannot perfect the lien of the contractor until the contractor is able to do so; *i.e.,* upon the maturity of the owner's obligation to pay the contractor.

291. *Id.* § 44A-20(d).

292. *Id.* § 44A-23.

293. *Id.* § 1-52(1). If the contract is for the furnishing of labor and materials, and is under seal, the statute of limitations would be ten years. *Id.* § 1-47(2) (1969). If only materials are sold, a seal would be inoperative and thus not extend the statute of limitations. *See id.* § 25-2-105(1) (1965) for a definition of what constitutes "goods." *See id.* § 25-2-203 (1965) for effect of a seal. *See id.* § 25-2-725(1) for the statute of limitations on the sale of goods.

the requirement of receipt of a proper notice of claim of lien was waived, and the lien was deemed perfected without the requisites of formal perfection.[294] With that precedent in mind, in *Interior Distributors, Inc. v. Promae, Inc.*[295] the court decided that if the owner acknowledges the validity of several subcontractors' claims and proposes a proration of funds held among all such subcontractors, a subcontractor who has perfected a notice of claim of lien pursuant to Part 2 of Article 2 of Chapter 44A will be unable to preclude the subcontractors who have not perfected notices of claim of lien from participating in such a proration.

It should be noted that the provision of the former statute [296] which required the *contractor* to submit to the owner notice of claim of various subcontractors has no counterpart in the present law.

§ 446. Lien upon Funds: Amount Secured. [297]

The amount secured by liens upon funds is treated in North Carolina General Statutes, § 44A-18(5):

> The liens granted under this section shall secure amounts *earned* by the lien claimant as a result of his having furnished labor or materials at the site of the improvement under the contract to improve real property, *whether or not such amounts are due and whether or not performance or delivery is complete* (emphasis added).

The Drafting Committee, in its memorandum in explanation of Part 2 of Article 2 of Chapter 44A, stated that under the above quoted section, "[a] subcontractor may give notice of claim of lien at any time during or before the performance of his work, but the lien secures only the amounts earned under the contract to improve real property."[298] The Committee emphasized that the lien secures amounts earned, whether or not payment is due. It should be observed initially that the statute states that subcontractors "who furnished labor or materials at the site of the improvement shall be entitled to a lien upon funds . . . ."[299] It seems as though that section precludes lien perfection prior to the time that the claimant commenced the furnishing of labor or materials pursuant to his immediate contract. If the Committee's memorandum reflects an accurate construction of the statute, the claimant may give statutory notice at any time subsequent to the making of his contract, and the lien will be deemed perfected as of that time, attaching to funds subsequently earned. The

---

294. Bain v. Lamb, 167 N.C. 304, 83 S.E. 466 (1914).
295. 27 N.C. App. 418, 219 S.E.2d 281 (1975).
296. N.C. Sess. L. c. 67, § 1 (1887) (repealed 1971).
297. This section is quoting 12 Wake Forest L. Rev. 364-66.
298. Memorandum of Drafting Comm., note 282 *supra*, at 9.
299. N.C. Gen. Stat. §§ 44A-18(1) through (4).

statute is in obvious need of amendment to clarify the original legislative intent.[300]

That portion of North Carolina General Statutes, § 44A-18(5) pertaining to amounts secured by the lien upon funds works well when the entire project (and as a consequence, all subcontracts) is completed prior to the time when the claimant perfects his notice of claim of lien. In that instance, the amounts of all contracts and subcontracts will not only be earned but also will be due unless there has been a deficiency in performance.[301]

---

300. At 12 WAKE FOREST L. REV. 365, n. 437, the authors suggest that it may very well be that a court would hold contrary to the intention of the draftsmen based upon the express language of the statute. Accordingly, they recommend the following addition to N.C. GEN. STAT. § 44A-18(6): "Said notice of claim of lien may be given to the obligor at any time after the making of the claimant's contract either prior or subsequent to the claimant's commencement of furnishing labor or materials at the site thereunder." They cite FLA. STAT. ANN. § 713.06(2)(a) (1969) as an example of a statute which states that the notice to be served upon the owner may be served prior to the commencement of furnishing of labor or materials.

301. But consider the following example.
On December 31, 1974, an owner contracts with a contractor to build a $100,000 structure. On January 1, 1975, the contractor hires a first tier subcontractor to do the grading and foundation work for $10,000. The first tier subcontractor interprets the statute in such a way that he gives notice of claim of lien on January 1 to the owner for $10,000. On January 1, prior to the first tier contractor's commencement of performance, his notice of claim of lien secures nothing since he has not *earned* any amount of his contract. Assume further that on February 1, the owner owed the contractor $30,000, payment not being due, and that the first tier subcontractor has *earned* $8,000, payment also not being due. On that date, the first tier subcontractor's lien secures $8,000. Apparently, he need only submit the initial claim of lien in order for all amounts then earned or subsequently earned to be secured. If his contract with the contractor was such that he was to be paid on a "cost plus" basis, the statute is silent with regard to the amount that he should put in his notice of claim of lien. It would seem that the first tier subcontractor could estimate the final amount of the contract, but would thereafter be bound by this estimate if the owner acted in reliance thereon. It could be argued that the first tier subcontractor could merely state in his notice of claim of lien that his contract was for cost plus a certain percent. Once again, the lien would only secure the amount *earned* by the first tier subcontractor under his contract with the contractor.

The Drafting Committee freely admitted that "[n]o attempt is made by [the] statute to provide any expedient method (other than litigation) to resolve the amount *earned* in case of a dispute." Thus, while it is obviously more difficult to maintain records of what amounts are earned on any given date by the various subcontractors submitting the early notice of claim of lien than it is to make a determination of the amounts earned and due at the end of the entire project upon receipt of the notices, the owner will be under a statutory duty to do the former in order to protect the interests secured by various notices of claim of lien. To restate the effect of this important provision, the statute apparently allows the first, second, and third tier subcontractors to put the owner on notice at the beginning of the project that he know what amount has been earned by each claimant at any given time as the project progresses. The same is true with regard to obligors other than the owner who receive

§ 447. Lien upon Funds: Effect of One Person's Waiver upon Another Person's Rights.[302]

Since the concept of a lien upon funds is based upon subrogation, it might well be that in certain situations, the waiver of one person's rights will totally preclude the assertion of another person's rights based upon subrogation. This result would not occur if the contractor waived his right to a lien upon the owner's *real property;* in that case the first tier subcontractor's right to a lien upon *funds* which the owner owes the contractor would not be extinguished since the contractor's security in the form of a mechanics' lien upon the improved property has only been waived.

However, if the contractor waived the owner's obligation to pay the balance due on their construction contract *prior* to the owner's receipt of notice of claim of lien from a first, second, or third tier subcontractor, the subcontractor giving such notice would, as in the case of the owner's payment to the contractor prior to the owner's receipt of notice of claim of lien, have nothing against which to assert a lien upon funds. But if the contractor takes the action described above *subsequent* to the owner's receipt of notice of claim of lien from the subcontractor, such action should have no more effect than payment to the contractor by the owner after the owner's receipt of notice of claim of lien.

If the first tier subcontractor waives his right to a lien upon the real property of the owner, this action should not affect the second and third tier subcontractors' lien rights against funds in the hands of the contractor or owner since, once again, only a lien upon land is waived.

If the first tier subcontractor waives his lien upon funds in the owner's hands prior to the receipt by the owner of notice of claim of lien from the second or third tier subcontractor, the second tier subcontractor will still be able to assert successfully a lien upon funds in the contractor's hands; but the second tier subcontractor's right of subrogation to the first tier subcontractor's lien upon funds in the owner's hand will be precluded; and the third tier subcontractor's right of subrogation to the first tier subcontractor's right to a lien upon funds in the hands of the owner — to the extent that the second tier subcontractor is entitled to be subrogated thereto — will also be effectively precluded.

---

statutory notice. Accordingly, the owner and other obligors receiving notice will have to do one of the following, or some combination thereof:

   (1) consult with the parties and pay the claimant directly when payment is due;
   (2) consult with the parties and adopt a "joint payee system";
   (3) consult with the parties and hold back funds sufficient to fulfill duties of retention imposed by statute; or
   (4) be able to trust the person to whom the obligor makes payment, without following procedures 1-3 above, to apply the funds paid in an honest manner.

302. This section is quoting 12 WAKE FOREST L. REV. 366-67. *See* Mace v. Construction Co., 48 N.C. App. 297, 269 S.E.2d 191 (1980).

If the first tier subcontractor waives his lien upon funds in the hands of the owner subsequent to the receipt by the owner of notice of claim of lien from the second or third tier subcontractor, the rights of subrogation so asserted by the second or third tier subcontractor will be unimpaired. However, if instead of waiving his lien upon funds the first tier subcontractor waives the contractor's obligation to pay, the second tier subcontractor's lien upon funds in the hands of the contractor will be voided; the waiver will preclude the second tier subcontractor's right of subrogation to the lien rights of the first tier subcontractor; and the waiver will preclude the third tier subcontractor's rights of subrogation to the lien rights of the second tier subcontractor.

§ 448. Lien upon Funds: Duties and Liabilities of the "Obligor." [303]

After receiving statutory notice of a claim of lien, "the obligor [is] under a duty to retain any funds subject to the lien or liens ... up to the total amount of such liens as to which notice has been received." [304] If the obligor breaches this duty to retain and makes a payment to his immediate obligee in violation of the lien, he becomes personally liable for the amount so paid.[305]

The duty to retain funds does not arise until the obligor receives statutory notice. North Carolina case law, interpreting the former statute, exempts the obligor from personal liability when he has paid his immediate obligee prior to receiving notice.[306] Unlike the statutes of other jurisdictions,[307] the current North Carolina statute has not overruled these decisions.

The common-law rules of "application of payments" also have a direct bearing both on the amount of the lien which a subcontractor may claim and on the amount which the obligor must retain in order to protect himself from incurring personal liability to the claimant. This doctrine applies when the debtor (general contractor) owes a number of debts to the creditor (subcontractor). Upon receiving a payment, the creditor may make an application of the funds to any of the debts he chooses unless the debtor has specified a particular debt to which the funds are to be applied.

---

303. This section is quoting 12 WAKE FOREST L. REV. 368-70.
304. N.C. GEN. STAT. § 44A-20(a).
305. *Id.* § 44A-20(b).
306. Roberts & Johnson Lumber Co. v. Horton, 232 N.C. 419, 61 S.E.2d 100 (1950); Dixon v. Ipock, 212 N.C. 363, 193 S.E. 392 (1937); Rose v. Davis, 188 N.C. 355, 124 S.E. 576 (1924); Orinoco Supply Co. v. Masonic Home, 163 N.C. 513, 79 S.E. 964 (1913). The North Carolina Supreme Court has also held that, for purposes of the mechanics' lien statutes, where the obligor makes payment by check prior to notice, he is under no duty to stop payment on the check, even if the notice is received before the check is paid by the drawee bank. Parnell-Martin Supply Co. v. High Point Motor Lodge, Inc., 277 N.C. 312, 177 S.E.2d 392 (1970).
307. *See, e.g.,* N.Y. LIEN LAW § 7 (McKinney 1966).

Application of payment was in issue in *Rural Plumbing & Heating Co. v. Hope Dale Realty Co.*[308] In that case the North Carolina Supreme Court recognized the applicability of the doctrine to the mechanics' and materialmen's lien situation.

> [W]here money is paid by a contractor or the seller of property to a mechanic or materialman out of funds received by the contractor or seller of property from an owner or purchaser whose property is subject to a mechanics' or materialmen's lien, or both, and the purpose of the payment to the contractor or seller was to discharge the indebtedness against a specific house, the mechanic or materialman must apply the payment to discharge the indebtedness *if he had knowledge* of the source and purpose of the payment.[309]

If the subcontractor accepts a payment from the general contractor knowing that it is for the purpose of discharging all or part of an indebtedness on a specific piece of real estate, the subcontractor's right to assert a lien relating to that property is cut off to the extent of the payment received. The obligor's duty to retain funds pertaining to that subcontractor would similarly be extinguished.

The obligor is apparently required to retain funds sufficient to pay only the amounts *earned* by the claimant since the liens perfected pursuant to the subcontractor's statute secure "amounts *earned* by the lien claimant."[310] Accordingly, if a subcontractor gives notice of a claim of lien for $5,000 to the owner but has "earned" only $1,000 on the date the owner pays the general contractor, the owner need retain only $1,000 to avoid personal liability to the subcontractor.

The force of the section on retention of funds is enhanced by the provisions for personal liability. Once an obligor has received notice of a claim of lien, the statute provides that if he makes

> further payments to a contractor or subcontractor against whose interest the lien or liens are claimed, the lien shall continue upon the funds in the hands of the contractor or subcontractor who received the payment, and *in addition the obligor shall be personally liable* to the person or persons entitled to liens *up to the amount of such wrongful payments,* not exceeding the total claims with respect to which the notice was received prior to payment.[311]

This section is a codification of prior case law which held an *owner* personally liable to a subcontractor when and to the extent that he failed to retain sufficient funds when paying the general contractor.[312] This

---

308. 263 N.C. 641, 140 S.E.2d 330 (1965).
309. *Id.* at 654-55, 140 S.E.2d at 340 (emphasis added).
310. N.C. GEN. STAT. § 44A-18(5) (emphasis added).
311. *Id.* § 44A-20(b) (emphasis added).
312. Grier-Lawrence Constr. Co. v. Winston-Salem Journal Co., 198 N.C. 273, 151 S.E. 631 (1930); Porter v. Case, 187 N.C. 629, 122 S.E. 483 (1924); Cambell v. Hall, 187 N.C. 464, 121 S.E. 761 (1924); Hilderbrand v. Vanderbuilt, 147 N.C. 639, 61 S.E. 626 (1908).

personal liability continues even if the lien on the property is lost by failure to enforce it within the statutory period.

Obligors lower in the construction hierarchy may also incur personal liability under the present statute.[313] This represents a significant change from the prior law. In *Borden Brick & Tile Co. v. Pulley*,[314] the North Carolina Supreme Court refused to uphold the lower court's rendering a personal judgment in favor of the plaintiff, a second tier materialman, against a general contractor. The plaintiff had served the statutory notice upon both the owner and the general contractor. The general contractor thereafter proceeded to pay the first tier subcontractor, the plaintiff's immediate obligor. The court held that the above described payment by the general contractor after receipt of notice did not constitute a "breach of duty, under the statute." [315]

There will, no doubt, be numerous instances where all of the obligors receiving notice of a claim of lien consider each other amply solvent and trustworthy or consider a notice of claim of lien exaggerated or frivolous. In such a case, the parties receiving notice may wish to continue making orderly progress payments and not retain funds to satisfy the lien claim. In that instance, the statute provides that:

> If an obligor shall make a payment after receipt of notice and incur personal liability therefor, the obligor shall be entitled to reimbursement and indemnification from the party receiving such payment.[316]

Thus, if the owner pays the contractor after he receives notice of claim of lien from the subcontractor, the contractor must indemnify the owner and save him harmless to the extent that the owner actually pays the subcontractor to discharge his personal liability.

§ 449. Lien upon Funds: Priorities.[317]

(a) *Among Subcontractors.* North Carolina General Statutes, § 44A-21 addresses the problem of inadequate funds for lien claims in this way:

> In the event that the funds in the hands of the obligor and the obligor's personal liability, if any ... are less than the amount of valid lien claims that have been filed with the obligor under this Article the parties entitled to liens shall share the funds on a pro rata basis.

The sharing of the funds by only those lien claimants who have filed a notice of claim of lien and the sharing on a prorata basis are continuations

---

313. N.C. GEN. STAT. § 44A-17(3) defines "obligor" as "an owner, contractor or subcontractor in any tier who owes money to another as a result of the other's partial or total performance of a contract to improve real property."
314. 168 N.C. 371, 84 S.E. 513 (1915).
315. *Id.* at 376, 84 S.E. at 515.
316. N.C. GEN. STAT. § 44A-20(c).
317. This section has been taken directly from portions of 12 WAKE FOREST L. REV. 370-73.

of former North Carolina General Statutes, § 44-11.[318] The new statute, however, applies to all *obligors* — not just *owners* — as did the former statute.[319]

(b) *Between Subcontractors and Other Persons.* Although the rule of prorata payments applies among subcontractors, with respect to other persons with a claim on funds against which a subcontractor's lien is asserted, the statute provides that:

> Liens perfected under this Article have priority over all other interests or claims theretofore or thereafter created or suffered in the funds by the person against whose interest the lien is asserted, including, but not limited to, liens arising from garnishment, attachment, levy, judgment, assignments, security interests, and any other type of transfer, whether voluntary or involuntary. Any person who receives payment from an obligor in bad faith with knowledge of a claim of lien shall take such payment subject to the claim of lien.[320]

The first sentence of the above quoted statute grants to the perfected subcontractors' lien upon funds absolute priority over *all other* interests or claims created or suffered in the funds.[321]

The intent of the second sentence of the statute is not altogether clear. According to the first sentence, persons having "other interests or claims theretofore or thereafter created or suffered in the funds by the person against whose interest a lien is asserted" apparently need not receive payment from the obligor "in bad faith with knowledge of a claim of lien" in order to take payment subject to the subcontractors' perfected lien upon funds. The first sentence contains no express reference to bad faith. Perhaps the vague rule set forth in the second sentence is intended as a "catch all" provision, whereby creditors and assignees of the obligor — the person with whom the lien is filed — as distinguished from creditors and assignees of the person against whose interest a lien is asserted, will be precluded from being paid prior to the subcontractor-claimant in a fraudulent or preferential manner.[322]

§ 450. Lien upon Funds: Enforcement.[323]

If for some reason the subcontractor is precluded from asserting a lien upon the owner's real property and the owner has incurred no personal

---

318. N.C. Sess. L. c. 67, § 3 (1887) (repealed 1971). *See also* Morganton Mfg. & Trading Co. v. Andrews, 165 N.C. 285, 81 S.E. 418 (1914).

319. *See* 12 WAKE FOREST L. REV. 371-72 for a chart and several examples illustrating the concept of prorata distribution among subcontractor-claimants.

320. N.C. GEN. STAT. § 44A-22.

321. This result, reached under N.C. GEN. STAT. § 44A-22, is substantially the same as that reached under prior case law. *See* Blue Pearl Granite Co. v. Merchants Bank, 172 N.C. 354, 90 S.E. 312 (1916). *See also* 12 WAKE FOREST L. REV. 373 for several examples of how the absolute priority rule of the first sentence of the statute works.

322. The authors conclude that, if this is the intent, the draftsmen of the statute should have been more precise. 12 WAKE FOREST L. REV. 373.

323. This section is quoting 12 WAKE FOREST L. REV. 373 & 374.

liability, the subcontractor's only recourse to enforce his lien upon funds is to sue the contractor in contract and join the owner as a party defendant. It would seem that the claimant could take this action as soon as the contractor's obligation to pay matures, notwithstanding the fact that the owner's obligation to pay the contractor has not matured. The only remedy that the subcontractor would be entitled to is an order directing the owner to pay him the funds upon maturity of the owner's obligation to pay the contractor.

Time limitations on enforcement of liens upon funds force the claimant to sue the contractor within the appropriate statute of limitations [324] after maturity of the contractor's obligation. He must enforce the lien upon funds within the statute of limitations after maturity of the *owner's* obligation to pay the contractor.

If the owner pays the contractor in full, breaching his duty to retain funds and incurring personal liability to the subcontractor, the subcontractor could sue the owner on the latter's personal liability within three years after the wrongful payment.[325] In addition, since the lien on the funds in the hands of the owner continues in the hands of the contractor,[326] the subcontractor would have an additional claim against the contractor.

§ 451. Liens upon the Owner's Interest in Real Property.[327]

There are two prevalent theories which grant the subcontractor a lien upon the improved real property of the owner: the "New York System" and the "Pennsylvania System." Under the "New York System," the subcontractor's lien is derived from and dependent upon the contractor.[328] The "Pennsylvania System" grants a lien to the subcontractor directly, independent of the lien granted to the contractor.[329] Both systems are incorporated in the North Carolina statutes.

A North Carolina subcontractor may obtain two types of liens against the owner's interest in real property: a lien by virtue of *subrogation* to the

---

324. *Id.* § 1-52(1) (three years); *id.* § 1-47(2) (1966) (ten years, if contractor signs and seals the contract). If a sale of "goods" only is involved, N.C. Gen. Stat. § 25-2-725(1) provides that the statute of limitations is four years, unless the parties agree to reduce it to not less than one year; they may not extend it. Seals are inapplicable to sales of goods. *Id.* § 25-2-203 (1965).

325. *Id.* § 1-52(2). The owner in this instance would be able to bring the contractor into the suit by virtue of the owner's right to indemnification. *Id.* § 44A-20(c).

326. *Id.* § 44A-20(b).

327. This section is quoting 12 Wake Forest L. Rev. 374-80. *See also* 12 Wake Forest L. Rev. 380-82 where the authors discuss additional aspects of this area of lien law.

328. *See* 53 Am. Jur. 2d *Mechanics' Liens* § 8 (1970); Fla. Stat. Ann. § 713.06(1) (1969); N.Y. Lien Law § 4(1) (McKinney 1966); Central Valley Concrete Corp. v. Montgomery Ward & Co., 34 App. Div. 2d 860, 310 N.Y.S.2d 925 (1970).

329. *See* 53 Am. Jur. 2d *Mechanics' Liens* § 8 (1970); Cal. Civ. Code Ann. §§ 3110, 3123 (Deering 1971).

lien rights inuring to the contractor [330] and a lien by virtue of the owner's *personal liability* to the subcontractor.[331]

(a) *Lien by Virtue of Subrogation.* North Carolina General Statutes, § 44A-23 states:

> A first, second or third tier subcontractor, who gives notice as provided in this Article, may, to the extent of his claim, enforce the lien of the contractor created by Part 1 of Article 2 of this Chapter. The manner of such enforcement shall be as provided by North Carolina General Statutes, § 44A-7 through North Carolina General Statutes, § 44A-16. Upon the filing of the notice and claim of lien and the commencement of the action, no action of the contractor shall be effective to prejudice the rights of the subcontractor without his written consent.

The statute has blurred the distinctions between the terms "perfection" and "enforcement" as those terms are defined in Part 1 of Article 2 of Chapter 44A pertaining to contractors' liens.[332] The statute appears to permit the subcontractor to *perfect* the lien of the contractor pursuant to the right of subrogation granted in North Carolina General Statutes, § 44A-23 and to *enforce* that lien once perfected.[333] The subcontractor must give the owner notice of claim of lien prior to filing a claim of lien in subrogation. There seems to be no prohibition against combining the form for the claim of lien with the subcontractor's notice, provided that the statutory requirements for the content and perfection of both are satisfied.

Since the subcontractor's lien on the owner's real property by virtue of North Carolina General Statutes, § 44A-23 is subrogated to the rights of the contractor, the requirements of Part 1 of Article 2 of Chapter 44A pertinent to the contractor must be fulfilled.[334] For example, the owner's obligation to pay the *contractor* must have matured at the time of filing.[335] The claim of lien filed by the subrogating subcontractor must be filed within 120 days after the *contractor* last furnished labor or materials at the site.[336] And, the enforcement of the lien must be commenced within 180 days after the *contractor* last furnished labor or materials at the site.[337]

---

330. N.C. Gen. Stat. § 44A-23.

331. *Id.* § 44A-20(d).

332. A lien is "perfected" by filing a claim of lien and is "enforced" by instituting an action. *Id.* §§ 44A-11, -13(a).

333. Humphrey, *Position, Priorities and Protection of Parties and Statutory Liens* in N.C. Bar Ass'n Foundation Institute on Troubled Real Estate Ventures and New Use and Ownership Concepts, IV-17, note 15.

334. N.C. Gen. Stat. § 44A-23 (Cum. Supp. 1975).

335. *Id.* § 44A-12(b).

336. *Id.*

337. *Id.* § 44A-13(a).

The effective date and priority of the subcontractor's lien obtained through subrogation relates back to and takes effect from the date upon which the *contractor* first furnished labor or materials, the date and priority to which the contractor is entitled. This provision possibly effectuates a change in the prior law. While the former statute provided that the lien of the subcontractor would be preferred to the lien of the contractor, and North Carolina Supreme Court decisions interpreted this provision as granting the subcontractor a right of subrogation to the lien of the contractor,[338] there apparently existed some uncertainty regarding whether, as against an encumbrance other than a contractors' lien, the effective date of a subcontractors' lien related back to the date upon which the contractor first furnished labor or materials.[339]

In order for the subcontractor to protect his lien upon the owner's real property pursuant to North Carolina General Statutes, § 44A-23 against the actions of the contractor, he must file notice and claim of lien and commence an enforcement action.[340] Actions of the contractor which might prejudice the subcontractor's rights in this regard include waiver of the right of lien and acceptance of payment. If the contractor accepts payment or waives his right to a lien upon the owner's real property, he no longer has a right to a lien and the subcontractor has no right to which he may be subrogated.[341]

(b) *Lien by Virtue of Owner's Personal Liability.* By North Carolina General Statutes, § 44A-20(d), the extent of the claimant's lien depends on the owner's personal liability:

> If the obligor is an owner of the property being improved, the lien claimant shall be entitled to a lien upon the interest of the obligor in the real property to the extent of the owner's personal liability under subsection (b), which lien shall be enforced only in the manner set

---

[338]. N.C. Sess. L. c. 44 § 1 (1880) (repealed 1971), *construed in,* Schnepp v. Richardson, 222 N.C. 220, 22 S.E.2d 555 (1942).

[339]. *See* Clark v. Edwards, 119 N.C. 115, 25 S.E. 794 (1896); Lookout Lumber Co. v. Mansion Hotel, 109 N.C. 650, 14 S.E. 35 (1891), discussed in Note, 30 N.C.L. REV. 83, 86 (1950). *See also* Blue Pearl Granite Co. v. Merchants Bank, 172 N.C. 354, 90 S.E. 312 (1916).

[340]. N.C. GEN. STAT. § 44A-23.

[341]. *See* Mace v. Construction Corp., 48 N.C. App. 297, 269 S.E.2d 191 (1980), discussing the subrogation rights of a first tier subcontractor and stating as follows at 48 N.C. App. 303:

> This statute [G.S. 44A-23] grants to a first tier subcontractor a lien upon improved real property based upon a right of subrogation to the direct lien of the general contractor on the improved real property as provided for in G.S. 44A-8. Because the subcontractor is entitled to a lien under G.S. 44A-23 only by way of subrogation, his lien rights are dependent upon the lien rights of the general contractor. Thus, if the general contractor has no right to a lien, the first tier subcontractor likewise has no such right. As the language of G.S. 44A-23 indicates, no action of the contractor will be effective to prejudice the rights of the subcontractor without his written consent "[u]pon the filing of the notice and claim of lien and the commencement of the action." Prior to that time, however, the general contractor is free to waive its lien rights and to bar effectively the subcontractor's rights by way of subrogation. (Citations Omitted)

The Court of Appeals went on to hold that, by virtue of a waiver by the general contractor, the claimant had no right to a lien on the realty pursuant to N.C. GEN. STAT. § 44A-23.

forth in G.S. 44A-7 through G.S. 44A-16 and which lien shall be entitled to the same priorities and subject to the same filing requirements and periods of limitation applicable to the contractor.

As quoted above, North Carolina General Statutes, § 44A-20(d) provides in part that the lien asserted thereunder "shall be *enforced* only in the manner set forth in North Carolina General Statutes, § 44A-7 through North Carolina General Statutes, § 44A-16." Once again, the term "enforce" is loosely utilized so as apparently to include "perfection" as well as "enforcement." The phrase obviously means that the technical requirements set forth in North Carolina General Statutes, § 44A-7 through North Carolina General Statutes, § 44A-16 must be met in order for the subcontractor, entitled to a lien upon real property pursuant to North Carolina General Statutes, § 44A-20(d), to perfect and enforce the same.

North Carolina General Statutes, § 44A-20(d) further provides that the lien asserted thereunder "shall be entitled to the same priorities and subject to the same filing requirements and periods of limitation *applicable to the contractor.*" This phrase is susceptible to different interpretations. The requirements of North Carolina General Statutes, § 44A-7 through North Carolina General Statutes, § 44A-16 are to be measured as they pertain either to the acts of the *subcontractor* or to the acts of the *contractor; e.g.,* the lien pursuant to North Carolina General Statutes, § 44A-20(d) must be filed either within 120 days after the *subcontractor* last furnishes labor or materials or within 120 days after the *contractor* does so. The requirements of the enforcement action, effective date of the lien, and priorities would similarly be affected by which interpretation is selected.[342]

Division 4. Other Matters Concerning Mechanics' Lienors

§ 452. Applicability of Federal Truth in Lending Act.[343]

Federal Reserve Board Regulation Z,[344] promulgated pursuant to Title I of the Federal Consumer Credit Protection Act,[345] better known as the Truth in Lending Act, requires mechanics' lienors extending credit to persons for whom a finance charge either is or may be imposed or which, pursuant to an agreement, is or may be payable in more than four installments,[346] to make certain disclosures concerning any finance charges imposed [347] and the consumer's right of rescission under the Act.[348] Inten-

---

342. *See* 12 WAKE FOREST L. REV. 377-80 for an extensive discussion of this problem and for suggested solutions by the authors.
343. This section is quoting 12 WAKE FOREST L. REV. 382-83.
344. FRB Reg. Z, 12 C.F.R. § 226 (1973).
345. Consumer Credit Protection Act (Truth in Lending Act), 15 U.S.C. §§ 1601-77 (1970).
346. 12 C.F.R. § 226.2(s) (1975).
347. *Id.* §§ 226.6 through 226.8.
348. The consumer is entitled to receive notice that he has three business days following

tional violation of the Act's disclosure requirements can result in civil liability to the consumer in an amount equal to the sum of twice the amount of the finance charge plus reasonable costs and attorneys' fees incurred by the consumer; [349] in addition, criminal liability may be imposed.[350] Upon rescission, all finance charges imposed and all security interests that are or may be retained are forfeited.[351]

Regulation Z expanded the scope of the Truth in Lending Act to include a security interest that "*is or will be retained or acquired* in any real property which is used or expected to be used as the personal residence of the customer." [352] Regulation Z also specifically includes mechanics' and materialmen's liens within its definition of the terms "security interest" and "security." [353] The initial United States district court decision pertaining to the applicability of the Truth in Lending Act to mechanics' liens held that section 125(a) of the Act applied only to consensual liens and did not include liens which arose by operation of law, such as mechanics' and materialmen's liens.[354] This decision was reversed by the Second Circuit,[355] and an intervening case from another circuit [356] has also upheld the application of the Truth in Lending Act to mechanics and materialmen who extend credit for home improvements.

§ 453. Criminal Sanctions Applicable to Lien Claimants.[357]

Part 3 of Article 2 of Chapter 44A has been amended to extend the criminal sanctions for the misdemeanor of the furnishing of a false statement by the contractor or person receiving payment from an obligor of sums due or claimed to be due, so that not only obligors, but also purchasers, lenders obtaining security interests in the real property improved, and title insurance companies insuring the same will be protected.[358] The amendment also raised the maximum amount of the fine and length of prison term from $500 and six months respectively to $1,000 and two years.[359]

---

the consummation of the transaction or the delivery of the required disclosures required by the Act to rescind the contract. 15 U.S.C. § 1635(a) (1970); 12 C.F.R. § 226.9(b) (1973).
349. 15 U.S.C. § 1640(a) (1970).
350. *Id.* § 1611.
351. *Id.* § 1635(b); 12 C.F.R. § 226.9(d) (1973).
352. *Compare* FRB Reg. Z, 12 C.F.R. § 226.9(a) (1973) *with* 15 U.S.C. § 1635(a) (1970).
353. 12 C.F.R. § 226.2(gg) (1975).
354. N.C. Freed Co., Inc. v. Board of Governors, [1969-1973 Transfer Binder] CCH Consumer Credit Guide ¶ 99,356 (W.D.N.Y. 1971).
355. N.C. Freed Co., Inc. v. Board of Governors, 473 F.2d 1210 (2d Cir.), *cert. denied*, 414 U.S. 827 (1973).
356. Gardner & North Roofing & Siding Corp. v. Board of Governors, 464 F.2d 838 (D.C. Cir. 1972). *See also* Hobbs Lumber Co. v. Shidell, 42 Ohio Misc. 21, 326 N.E.2d 706 (1974).
357. This section is quoting 12 Wake Forest L. Rev. 384.
358. N.C. Gen. Stat. § 44A-24.
359. *Id.*

Lastly, the second sentence of the first paragraph of the amendment providing that reimbursement of a party suffering loss may be made a condition precedent to the granting of a suspended sentence to the defendant is new.[360] It is important to note that the misleading of or injury to the obligor, purchaser, lender, or title insurance company to whom the false statement was furnished is not a necessary element of the criminal offense prohibited by Part 3 of Article 2 of Chapter 44A.[361]

Article IV. Tax and Assessment Liens

§ 454. Tax Liens.

Taxes levied by a county or municipality which are unpaid constitute a lien on all real property belonging to the taxpayer which is located within the taxing unit.[362] A change in ownership of the real property will not relieve the real property from the lien for unpaid taxes and consequently any person who desires to purchase specific real property must determine if there are any outstanding delinquent taxes because the governmental authorities may enforce collection of such taxes by foreclosing the tax lien.[363] In addition, since taxes are levied on property for the purpose of collecting revenue to support the government and since these revenues are necessary to the very existence of government, it is imperative that the lien for taxes shall take precedence over all private encumbrances such as mortgages, deeds of trust and similar claims. Consequently, the general rule is that the lien of the property tax on real estate is superior to all other liens and rights except liens for other taxes, whether such liens or rights are created prior or subsequent to the levy

---

360. *Id.*

361. *Id.*

362. Former N.C. GEN. STAT. § 105-340 was repealed by the Machinery Act of 1971. The substance of former § 105-340 was renumbered and currently appears as N.C. GEN. STAT. § 105-355. *See generally* CAMPBELL, PROPERTY TAX COLLECTION IN NORTH CAROLINA 193, 194 (1974). The tax lien on real property shall continue until the principal amount of the taxes plus penalties, interest, and costs allowed by law have been fully paid. N.C. GEN. STAT. § 105-362.

363. Former N.C. GEN. STAT. § 105-422 was repealed by the Machinery Act of 1971. N.C. GEN. STAT. § 105-378 currently states the statutory limitation that no county or municipality may maintain an action or procedure to enforce any remedy for the collection of taxes or the enforcement of any tax lien unless such action or procedure is instituted within ten years from the date the taxes become due. *See generally* CAMPBELL, PROPERTY TAX COLLECTION IN NORTH CAROLINA 303, 304.

The tax lien secures not only the tax amount due but includes interest and penalties for delay in payment as well as the original amount of the tax. The lien, which is for property, poll, dog and other taxes, extends to all the real property owned by the taxpayer in the taxing unit.

of the taxes.[364] While there is no state statute imposing a lien on real estate for state taxes,[365] such as inheritance taxes, license taxes, franchise taxes, state income taxes and other taxes, liens may become operative with respect to real property of the delinquent taxpayer if the State Commissioner of Revenue dockets a summary judgment or certificate for the delinquent taxes in the office of the Clerk of the Superior Court in the county where the land is located.[366]

Taxes due the United States Government under the Internal Revenue Laws may also be made liens upon the real property of the taxpayer by the proper filing in the office of the Register of Deeds in the county in which the land lies, a certificate of lien against the landowner.[367]

§ 455. Assessment Liens.

In addition to annual taxes levied on real estate for the general support of local government, real property may also be assessed for its share of special levies assessed by counties, municipalities and other authorized bodies politic.[368] While these are often thought of as taxes, they are not actually taxes although they spring from the construction of authorized public works. The costs of such improvements are allocated to abutting lands on the theory that those particular lands have special benefits

---

364. *See generally* CAMPBELL, PROPERTY TAX COLLECTION IN NORTH CAROLINA. N.C. GEN. STAT. § 105-408 was repealed by the Machinery Act of 1971. N.C. GEN. STAT. § 105-383 currently provides that it shall be the duty of every guardian, executor, administrator, agent, trustee, receiver, or other fiduciary having care or control of any real or personal property to pay the taxes thereon out of the trust funds in his hands. Any fiduciary who fails to pay the taxes on property in his care or control when trust funds are available to him for that purpose shall be personally liable for the taxes. This liability may be enforced by a civil action brought in the name of the tax collector of the taxing unit to which the taxes are owed against the fiduciary in an appropriate division of the General Court of Justice of the county in which the taxing unit is located.

365. There is currently no ad valorem taxation imposed on real property by the State of North Carolina.

366. N.C. GEN. STAT. §§ 105-241, 105-242. Priority dates from the docketing.

367. N.C. GEN. STAT. §§ 44-65 through 44-67 were repealed effective October 1, 1969. N.C. GEN. STAT. § 44-68.1 through 44-68.7 became effective October 1, 1969. N.C. GEN. STAT. § 44-68.1 provides for the filing of certificates and notices of such tax liens in the office of the Clerk of the Superior Court in the county in which the real property subject to a federal tax lien is situated. This is pursuant to the Uniform Federal Tax Lien Registration Act. N.C. GEN. STAT. § 44-68.3 provides for the filing of certificates of release, nonattachment, discharge or subordination of tax liens with the Clerk of the Superior Court.

368. *See* N.C. GEN. STAT. §§ 160A-216 through 160A-238 for general authority given to municipal corporations to make special improvements. In addition to these general statutes applicable to all cities and towns there may be numerous authorities granted to specific governmental entities by special or local laws. The power of a municipality to make assessments upon property for local improvements is dependent upon a grant from the legislature and is not to be implied as an incident of municipal existence nor to the general power to tax. City of Winston-Salem v. Smith, 216 N.C. 1, 3 S.E.2d 328 (1939); City of Charlotte v. Kavanaugh, 221 N.C. 259, 20 S.E.2d 97 (1942).

which arise from the local improvements.[369] These assessments may be for the construction or installation of streets, sidewalks, curbs, gutters, drains, sewers and similar purposes.[370]

Special assessments for local improvements are liens upon real property abutting upon or benefiting from the improvement.[371] This lien for special improvements is superior to all other liens and encumbrances, except city and county tax liens, on the theory that the property which is assessed is improved to the extent of the assessment.[372]

The lien for local improvements does not render the owner of the real property charged with the lien personally liable for the assessment. The land itself is subject to the lien and any action to collect the amount of the assessment is an action in rem; a personal judgment cannot be obtained against anyone.[373] Liens for local improvements may be enforced only by

---

369. Saluda v. Polk County, 207 N.C. 180, 176 S.E. 298 (1934). *Accord,* Southern Ry. v. City of Raleigh, 277 N.C. 709, 178 S.E.2d 422 (1971).

370. N.C. GEN. STAT. § 160-85 was repealed effective January 1, 1972. N.C. GEN. STAT. §§ 160A-216 and 160A-217 replaced the former statute in setting out various purposes for which special assessments may be made. Assessments for similar purposes may be authorized. *E.g.,* see N.C. GEN. STAT. § 160A-238 which authorizes special assessments for beach erosion control projects and for the construction of flood and hurricane protection. Special legislation can likewise be enacted permitting special assessments of benefited property for the purpose of making various improvements.

371. N.C. GEN. STAT. § 160-88 was repealed effective January 1, 1972. N.C. GEN. STAT. § 160A-218, now in effect, does not require abutment in order for real property benefited to be assessed. Assessments may be made on the basis of: (1) frontage abutting on the project at an equal rate per foot of frontage; *or* (2) the area of land served, or subject to being served, by the project, at an equal rate per unit of area, *or* (3) the value added to the land served by the project, or subject to being served by it, being the difference between the appraised value of the land without improvements as shown on the tax records of the county, and the appraised value of the land with the improvement according to the appraisal standards and rules adopted by the county at its last reevaluation, at an equal rate per dollar of value added, *or* (4) the number of lots served, or subject to being served, where the project involves extension of an existing system to a residential or commercial subdivision, at an equal rate per lot, *or* (5) a combination of two or more of these bases.

372. N.C. GEN. STAT. § 160-88 was repealed effective January 1, 1972. N.C. GEN. STAT. §§ 160A-228 and 160A-233 (c), now in effect, declare that special assessment liens are superior to all other liens except prior and subsequent liens for State, local and federal taxes. *See* N.C. GEN. STAT. § 105-356(a). *See also* Town of Saluda v. Polk County, 207 N.C. 180, 176 S.E. 208 (1934); City of Kinston v. Atlantic & N.C.R. Co., 183 N.C. 14, 110 S.E. 645 (1934). While the lien of an assessment does not take effect until the assessment roll is confirmed, when it is so confirmed it prevails over prior as well as subsequent liens other than tax liens.

373. City of Charlotte v. Kavanaugh, 221 N.C. 259, 20 S.E.2d 97 (1942); Town of Wadesboro v. Coxe, 215 N.C. 708, 2 S.E.2d 870 (1939); City of Statesville v. Jenkins, 199 N.C. 159, 154 S.E. 14 (1930); Carawan v. Barnett, 197 N.C. 511, 149 S.E. 740 (1929); Town of Morganton v. Avery, 179 N.C. 551, 103 S.E. 138 (1920); City of Raleigh v. Peace, 110 N.C. 32, 14 S.E. 521, 17 L.R.A. 330 (1892). N.C. GEN. STAT. § 160A-233 states that the city shall not be entitled to a deficiency judgment in an action to foreclose an assessment lien.

foreclosure against the land. An action is brought in the nature of an action to foreclose a mortgage [374] and where the lien is valid as against the owner at the time of his transfer of title, the land in the hands of his grantee is likewise subject to foreclosure.[375] No city may maintain an action or proceeding to enforce any remedy for the foreclosure of special assessment liens unless the action or proceeding is begun within ten years from the date that the assessment, or the earliest installment thereof included in the action or proceeding, becomes due.[376]

---

374. The assessing authority may maintain an action to foreclose its lien by alleging the making of the improvements, the levying of the assessment for such improvements, that some part of the assessments remain due and unpaid, and that all statutory procedures have been complied with. Town of Wadesboro v. Coxe, 215 N.C. 708, 2 S.E.2d 870 (1939). N.C. GEN. STAT. § 160A-233 (c) now provides that assessment liens may be foreclosed under any procedure prescribed by law for the foreclosure of tax liens, except that lien sales and lien sale certificates shall not be required, and foreclosure may be begun at any time after 30 days after the due date.

375. Insurance Co. v. Charlotte, 213 N.C. 497, 196 S.E. 809 (1938).

376. N.C. GEN. STAT. § 160A-233 (d) provides that no action or proceeding to enforce any remedy for the foreclosure of a special assessment may be maintained unless the action or proceeding is begun within 10 years from the date the assessment becomes due or from the date the *earliest* installment thereof becomes due.

Part 4

Examination of Titles to Real Property in North Carolina

CHAPTER 21

TITLE EXAMINATION GENERALLY

§ 456. Importance of Title Examination.
§ 457. Purpose and Scope of Part 4.
§ 458. Responsibilities and Duties of Title Attorneys.
§ 459. Information to Be Obtained Prior to Title Search.

§ 456. Importance of Title Examination.

A substantial portion of the practice of many lawyers in North Carolina consists of the examination and certification of titles to real property. "Property Law" has long been considered a main branch of the law of North Carolina and is a subject in which every lawyer should be thoroughly grounded. As the State progresses and becomes more and more commercial and industrialized, the volume of real estate work continues to increase. A large percentage of the legal work done in the State of North Carolina is related to real estate practice, conveyancing, mortgages and deeds of trust, and the examination of titles in connection with purchases and loans. Purchasers want to know that they are secure when they take title from vendors. The financial institutions, savings and loan associations, insurance companies, banks and mortgage companies, and individuals who lend money on real estate security desire to know that they are secure in the titles that they take as security. They desire to know that any deed of trust or mortgage they take is not defective due to the existence of some preceding encumbrance, judgment or other lien.

The work of title searching has always been an important phase of the practice of most practitioners of law in North Carolina. Title work, while not generally lucrative, is considered by many lawyers as the "rent payer" or as "bread and butter" work. Since searching a land title is *ex parte* work it can be engaged in without the pressures and nervous strain usually attendant to courtroom employment. Almost all lawyers and law firms find that they must do some title work at one time or another for their regular clients.

§ 457. Purpose and Scope of Part 4.

The purpose of Part 4 of this volume is to outline the steps, routines, and procedures which the title-searching practitioner should follow in making an examination of a land title. The reader is cautioned that in making a title search one must carry all of the substantive law of real property into every search. However, in this Part the inclusion of substantive law with respect to real property will not be more than incidental and fragmentary. The purpose of this Part is simply to set out the routines or system to be observed in searching a title.

§ 458. Responsibilities and Duties of Title Attorneys.

Another further word of caution is in order. Title practice carries with it a great deal of responsibility. Title-searching attorneys, even if they try, cannot be too careful! Purchasers and lenders look upon their title attorney as an insurer that they are taking a good title. Since it is very difficult at best to assure a client that a proffered title is good, and almost impossible to assure a client that a title is perfect, it is clear that a title attorney must do all of his work thoroughly and painstakingly in order that it may be as free from error as is humanly possible. The title attorney in certifying land titles must not only protect his client to the fullest extent but he must also protect himself from potential liability in a malpractice suit and he must protect his reputation for competence generally.

The highest level of caution is required of the attorney in every title search. Since most clients who have titles searched do consider the title attorney as the insurer of the title searched and certified, the title-searching attorney can not afford to take any chance on any questionable point with respect to the title. The title attorney has as his duty the ascertainment of the status of the title involved, its potential defects, and any questions which relate to the quality or quantity of the title being certified. The attorney then should report the status of the title completely as he discovers if from the records and let the client decide for himself whether he desires to run any risks that may exist.

Fees for attorneys searching titles are not usually large enough to warrant any gambling on the part of the title-searching attorney with respect to any doubtful question. Most title attorneys take the position that it is not sufficient simply to certify a record title that will stand up in later litigation; most title attorneys are careful not to certify titles which will raise questions in the minds of subsequent title searchers, requiring a lengthy citation of cases or perhaps a lawsuit to clarify the status of the title.

§ 459. Information to Be Obtained Prior to Title Search.

(a) *In general.* The attorney for the prospective purchaser or mortgage lender can greatly simplify his work and save a great deal of time and labor by collecting from his client as much information as he can with respect to a particular title before the title search begins. This information can usually be obtained by a carefully planned conference with the prospective buyer and the present owner of the land before enbarking on the title search at the courthouse. The title searcher will find that every bit of information that he can receive about the land will prove beneficial to him with respect to his search. Perhaps an actual visual visit on the land will help the attorney to fix in his mind how the property lies with reference to other lands and monuments.

§ 459   TITLE EXAMINATION GENERALLY   § 459

The information outlined in the following subsections can be important and useful to the title searcher and should be obtained prior to the title searcher's visit to the courthouse.

(b) *Proposed use of land.* What use is to be made of the land? This information is especially important if the land is within a municipality or if it is found to be subject to a restrictive covenant. The title attorney may determine whether any applicable zoning regulation or building or use restriction will interfere with or prevent some desired utilization of the land.

(c) *Location of land.* Where is the land? What is its exact location? Many false starts and much work can be averted by the attorney when he gets to the courthouse if he has a rather specific idea of where the land lies. It is important to determine what township the land lies in, what street, road or other monument it adjoins. When the title searcher goes to the books and discovers descriptions of land to and from grantors located in other townships or on other roads, highways and monuments far from those in which his particular land is supposed to be located, he can usually ignore such descriptions and know that these records do not involve the land in which he is interested.

Is the property "town" or "city" property? Or is it "country" or "rural" property? Whether it is one or the other is often important in determining if there are potential assessments for local improvements by a municipality and in determining if there are potential municipal land use restrictions which affect the land. The preliminary location of the property is also important in that it will probably establish the manner in which descriptions of the land are recorded. "Municipal" or "town" property will more than likely be described in the form of "lot" and "block" and "street number" references and not in the form of "metes and bounds" descriptions which are common if the property involved is "country" or "rural" property.

If possible, the title-searching attorney should obtain a copy of the deed of the present owner of the land, or at least a sufficiently accurate description of the land by street and number, township, lot number, by metes and bounds, or by its proximity to relatively permanent monuments such as a road, school, church, or stream. The title searcher should get such information as will enable him to locate the specific land in the records of the Register of Deeds even if the records disclose that the land has been variously and inconsistently described in the various deeds of conveyance which are recorded.

(d) *Known encumbrances or restrictions.* What existing encumbrances or restrictions are known to the prospective seller, buyer, or mortgage borrower?

(e) *Recent improvements on land.* Have any improvements been made on the land recently? Have there been any building improvements or repairs recently which might form the basis for unfiled laborers' or materialmen's liens? Have there been any street, sidewalk, sewer or other local improvements made in connection with the land which might form the basis for an unfiled assessment lien?

(f) *Age and marital status of prospective grantor or mortgagor.* What is the age and marital status of the prospective seller or mortgagor? Is the prospective grantor of a competent age, and is he married so as to require his spouse's signature to waive spousal rights? Is there any other circumstance which might affect his legal capacity to convey his real property, such as mental incompetency?

(g) *Known history of prospective grantor's or mortgagor's title.* What is the history of the prospective grantor's or mortgagor's title so far as it is known either by the buyer, prospective vendor, or prospective mortgagor? Where did the land come from, if the parties know? When did the present owner take title? Did some predecessor in title, either immediate or remote, take the land as one of the "links" in the "chain of title" by descent, by intestate succession? If someone has taken title to land by descent, it is advisable to procure the names of the heirs of the decedent from whom the land was descended if they are known or can be obtained conveniently.[1]

(h) *Present occupant of the land.* Who is now in possession of the land and upon what terms does he occupy it?

---

1. Where a decedent has died without a will his land passes to his lineal heirs as provided by the intestate succession statutes. *See* N.C. GEN. STAT. §§ 29-1 through 29-30. If a decendent has no lineal heirs, his land passes to his collateral heirs upon his death intestate pursuant to the statute. Where a decedent has died intestate the records of the courthouse frequently do not show who were the heirs of the decedent and thus do not show to whom the land devolved. It is therefore frequently necessary to procure affidavits from persons in the community who know that a particular person was the heir of a deceased owner when title has been derived at some point in the chain of title by intestate succession. It is helpful to the attorney in examining the records if he can obtain this information and leads before he starts his search.

CHAPTER 22
THE CHAIN OF TITLE

§ 460. Running the Chain of Title.
§ 461. Period of Time for Which Chain of Title Is Searched.
§ 462. Checking the "Out" or "Adverse" Conveyances of Each Owner in the Chain of Title.
§ 463. Compilation of the Abstract of Title.

§ 460. Running the Chain of Title.

The examination of real estate titles usually begins in the office of the Register of Deeds.[1] The attorney should have his client furnish him with the last deed executed to the present owner, if it is available. Deeds are frequently written with a back reference to the next preceding link in the chain of title, stating from whom the grantor acquired title and the book and page number where the conveyance is recorded.[2]

In every case, the title searcher needs to have an exact description of the land that he is searching and the name of the prospective grantor or mortgagor. The title searcher should be equipped before he goes to the courthouse with printed blank abstract forms in order that he may record vital and pertinent information concerning every link in the chain of title. These abstract forms should be filled in methodically for complete future reference so as to avoid the inconvenience of unnecessary return trips to the courthouse. These abstracts can be filed and preserved. Not only do they assure thoroughness on the part of the certifier of the record title but these filed abstracts may be quite valuable at later times when the attorney is employed to certify title to the same land in subsequent transactions. In no event should a title attorney ever rely on his memory with respect to a title which he has searched and placed on abstract sheets; he should rely only on the notes and information that he has put down at the time he has searched a particular recorded instrument.

The purpose of the title search is to determine if a proposed grantor or

---

1. If the present owner, the prospective vendor or prospective borrower, has taken by will or descent, however, the search will have to begin in the office of the Clerk of the Superior Court in the county where the land lies. When the name of the intestate or devisor is ascertained and the fact established that the land came to the present owner through the deceased person, then the normal search carries the title attorney to the office of the Register of Deeds unless the decedent also took title through a will or by descent.

In addition, it should be noted that some counties have excellent mapping departments and tax supervisors who keep an index system on real property and its owners by tracts or "tax blocks." By utilizing these tax indexes before starting in the office of the Register of Deeds, the title searcher can often save time.

2. The practice of including a back-link reference in every deed drafted and recorded, which requires little effort on the part of the title attorney drafting a deed, would greatly facilitate title searches. Local bar associations and individual practitioners should encourage the practice. A simple reference on the deed, perhaps after the descriptive clause, to the previous conveyance of the land is sufficient. The following back reference is frequently used: "The above land was conveyed to grantor . . . . by . . . ., see Book . . . ., Page . . . ."

mortgagor has taken a good record title to the land that he seeks to convey or mortgage. It is also to determine if the grantor or mortgagor or any of his predecessors in title have ever made any conveyance or created any encumbrance, lien or other charge on the land that will prevent his giving a good, indefeasible and marketable title of record.

The first procedure which a title searcher follows is to "run the chain of title." "Running the chain of title" is to find in reverse chronological order the names of all the persons who have owned the land for a given period of time, working backward from the current owner to his predecessor in title and backward successively to preceding owners to the date that the examiner deems sufficient.

In the office of the Register of Deeds there are two principal types of books. The first types of books are the "Index" books. The "Index" books are simply books which enable the title searcher to locate documents which are copied verbatim in other volumes. They point to the other type of volumes where the actual deeds, deeds of trust, mortgages, contracts and other agreements are copied. By checking the "chain of grantees" in the "Index" books, which point to the places where the actual instruments involving the land in question are recorded, the searcher can determine if a person has taken a title to real property regularly and without a defect that appears in the records. By then checking the "grantors" in the chain of title in the "Grantor Index" books and the recorded instruments to which they point, the searcher can determine if any owner of the land has done anything with respect to the land while he owned it that will impair the title in any way in the hands of subsequent grantees. This procedure is called "running" or "tracing" the "chain of title."

As instruments are received in the office of the Register of Deeds for the purpose of recordation, they are stamped with the date and hour and minute that they are received. They are immediately entered on a "Temporary Index Book," which lists each document, the name of the grantor, the name of the grantee, and the nature of the instrument, whether a deed, mortgage, deed of trust, contract or otherwise. The "Temporary Index Book" contains only those transactions which are so recent that they have not been permanently indexed and placed in permanent registration books. As soon as practicable, each document is indexed in the permanent index books, both under the "Grantor Index" and under the "Grantee Index."

The permanent "Grantor Index" books contain eight columns, headed so as to indicate the date of the receipt of the instrument for recordation, the surname of the grantor, the book (the volume where the instrument is copied), the kind of instrument, the name of the grantee, and a brief description of the land. The permanent "Grantee Index" books are just like the "Grantor Index," except that the names of the grantors and grantees are transposed and arranged alphabetically according to the grantee's surname. (See example on page 547)

GRANTEE General Index to Real Estate Conveyances — Forsyth County, N. C. 105 (A)

DATE OF INST.	SURNAMES	GRANTEES ABCDEFGH	GRANTEES IJKLMNO	GIVEN NAMES PQRSTUVWXYZ	GRANTORS	KIND OF INSTRUMENT	RECORDED Book	RECORDED Page	BRIEF DESCRIPTION, LOCATION, ETC.	CANCELLED
1951	Thorpe	E W	Mary L		William S & Martha Surratt	Deed	654	96	Lt 7 B E Chandler Prop	
1953	do	Baleka W		Philip L	Foss T Smithdeal etal	Deed	671	378	Lt 36 Strathmore	
1953	do	E G			Johnnie M L & Oscar W Swaim	Deed	677	240	Lts 60 to 63 Incl Sec #1 J Lindsay Walker Est	
1955	do			Roger F Pauline C	P G & Ethel L Barker	Deed	700	42	Lt 128 Reynolds Place	
1955	do			Roger F Pauline C	W H & Mable L Wilson	Deed	704	229	Pt Lt 9 Parkview	
1955	do			Roger F Pauline C	Harvey E & Mary M McGee Harrison	Deed	706	26	Lt 172 Fairview	
1955	do	A J	Margaret H		David T & Virginia W	Deed	709	260	Lt 4 Economy Homes Inc Prop	
1956	do	Grace B			E S Burke Sr Charles	Deed	723	12	Lt 21 E S Burke Prop	
1956	do			Roger F Pauline C	Russell C & Betty H	Deed	723	125	Lt 304 Montview	
1956	do			Roger F Pauline C	James C & Maggie L T Hall	Deed	730	427	Lts 34 to 38 Incl Blk A Tallywood	
1956	do			Roger F Pauline C	Sarah E Bovender	Deed	731	7	Lt 190 Montview	
1956	do			Roger F Pauline C	Win-Sal Corporation	Deed	735	343	Lt 7 Greenway Heights	
1956	Thorp	Ada		Wilton S	Homer B & Aileen M Idol	Deed	737	480	Lts 16 & Pt Lt 15 Linville Smith & Breece Prop &	
1956	do	Ada		Wilton S	do	Deed	737	480	Water Right Easement	

§ 460   REAL ESTATE LAW IN NORTH CAROLINA   § 460

In beginning a title search, as suggested before, it is easier if the searcher has the last deed of conveyance to the present owner, the prospective grantor or prospective mortgagor. If the deed is available, it of course will include the names of the grantor, the grantee, the date of the grant, the exact description of the land, and the book and page number where the instrument is recorded. With the current owner's deed, the searcher can go immediately to the "Grantee Index" book for the year in which the deed has been recorded.[3] If the searcher does not have the current owner's deed, it will be necessary to examine the "Grantee Index" book to locate his name as "grantee." Several attempts may be necessary to locate the name of the present owner as a "grantee" where the date of the conveyance to him is unknown at the time the title search begins.

When the name of the present owner is located, however, in the "Grantee Index," it will show the book and page number where the deed to the present owner is copied and recorded. The copy of the present owner's deed will not only show that the present owner was in fact a grantee of the property at a certain time but will also disclose the identity of his grantor. The searcher will then look up the name of the present owner's grantor, likewise in the "Grantee Index"; this in turn will show the book and page number where the owner's grantor was a "grantee" and who *his* grantor was. By working backward in this way, the complete chain of title can frequently be built up quickly.

For instance, assuming that the prospective grantor of property to be searched is Wilton S. Thorpe, the title searcher will look up the name of Wilton S. Thorpe in the "Grantee Index" in the time period which the searcher knows or has reason to believe that Wilton S. Thorpe took title to the property.[4] By checking the "Grantee Index" for the period within which the searcher knows or estimates that Wilton S. Thorpe took his title, the searcher finds the entry shown on page 550.

When the searcher looks at Deed Book 737, page 480, he discovers the deed from Homer B. Idol. To determine if Homer B. Idol had a title to convey, his name will in turn be looked up in the "Grantee Index" in the book that contains records of instruments prior to 1956 as Idol would have been a grantee prior to 1956, which was the date when he granted title out. In the same manner as before the searcher will find the entry shown on page 551.

The foregoing leads the searcher to Deed Book 650, page 205, which discloses that Hendrix conveyed to Idol as grantor and therefore Hendrix

---

3. The searcher should determine if the deed has been recorded and properly indexed by his immediate grantor, since if it has not been duly recorded and indexed the present owner's title may be defeated by another conveyance to a purchaser for value or by judgment creditors of the present owner's grantor.

4. It becomes apparent why it is very important for a title examiner to know the approximate date that the owner of the land took his title.

and each of his predecessors in title must be looked up in order pursuant to the same pattern, backward for the period of time for which the title is to be searched and certified.

If, in checking the "Grantee Index" books, the name of one who has been a "grantor" cannot be located, a search *dehors* the record books may be necessitated. A grantor in the chain of title whose name does not appear in the "Grantee Index" as a "grantee" may have taken his title by an unrecorded deed which was valid to pass title but which has not been placed on the records. In such cases the missing deed should be placed on the records so as not to be vulnerable under North Carolina's Connor Act if the land is conveyed to a purchaser for value by the prior owner or if the former owner's creditor affixes a lien to the property.[5]

---

5. An unregistered deed is ineffectual to pass title as against other purchasers for value and lien creditors of the same grantor who first record their deeds or docket their liens in the county where the land lies.

N.C. GEN. STAT. § 47-18(a) was amended effective October 1, 1975. The current statute provides:

> No (i) conveyance of land, or (ii) contract to convey, or (iii) option to convey, or (iv) lease of land for more than three years shall be valid to pass any property interest as against lien creditors or purchasers for a valuable consideration from the donor, bargainor or lessor but from the time of registration thereof in the county where the land lies, or if the land is located in more than one county, then in each county where any portion of the land lies to be effective as to the land in that county.

Thus, subsequent to the 1975 amendment, contrary to the holding of Lawing v. Jaynes, 285 N.C. 418, 206 S.E.2d 162 (1974), which held otherwise under the pre-existing statute, an option to purchase land must be recorded in order to give it validity and priority as against lien creditors or purchasers of the land for value of the optionor.

See also N.C. GEN. STAT. § 47-20.

DATE OF INST.	SURNAMES	GRANTEES GIVEN NAMES ABCDEFGH	GIVEN NAMES IJKLMNO	GIVEN NAMES PQRSTUVWXYZ	GRANTORS	KIND OF INSTRUMENT	RECORDED Book	Page	BRIEF DESCRIPTION, LOCATION, ETC.	CANCELLED
1956	THORP	ADA		WILTON S	HOMER B. & AILEEN M. IDOL	DEED	737	480	SMITH & BREECE PROP. &	
1956	"	ADA		WILTON S	" "	DEED	737	480	WATER RIGHT EASEMENT	

GRANTEE General Index to Real Estate Conveyances — Forsyth County, N. C.

§ 460 THE CHAIN OF TITLE § 460

GRANTEE General Index to Real Estate Conveyances — Forsyth County, N. C.

DATE OF INST.	SURNAMES	GRANTEES GIVEN NAMES ABCDEFGH	GIVEN NAMES IJKLMNO	GIVEN NAMES PQRSTUVWXYZ	GRANTORS	KIND OF INSTRUMENT	RECORDED Book	Page	BRIEF DESCRIPTION, LOCATION, ETC.	CANCELLED
1952	Do	Aileen Homer B			Roy L & Hazel Hendrix	Deed	650	205	Lt 16 Linville, Smith & Breece Prop	
1952	Do	ETAL		W B	C J Phipps	Affidavit	D B 650	296	Pt A Old Salem & Greensboro Rd	
1951	Do	G D Peggy			J A & Minnie Phipps	Deed	655	196	27,400 Sq Ft Arbotis Creek Tp	
1952	Do	Aileen M Homer B			Garland S & Gladys Idol	Cont & Agmnt	D B 656	19	Water Right & Easement Lts 16-1 Linville Smith & Breece Prop	

When the name of one who has been a "grantor" cannot be located in the "Grantee Index" it may mean that such person acquired his title not by grant but by devise or descent. The records of devises and descents are maintained in the office of the Clerk of the Superior Court of the county and not in the office of the Register of Deeds. Where a particular grantor does not appear to have taken by deed and his name is not discoverable by a search of the "Grantee Index," the searcher may have to look for his name as a "Devisee" or it may be necessary to determine if a particular person is an heir who inherited the property from a deceased owner. The Clerk of the Superior Court maintains a record of all persons who take property as "Devisees" and these are locatable in the "Devisee Index to Wills." [6]

If a grantor in the chain of title did not take by deed and cannot be located as having taken his title by devise, he may have taken by descent as an "heir." This determination that one took title by descent and not by deed or will is frequently not readily discoverable from the records except by trial and error. This is true because the Clerk of the Superior Court does not maintain an "Index of Heirs" of decedents, as such. While there *is* an "Index of Estates," setting out the names of decedents, which directs a searcher to records which usually disclose the names of the decedent's heirs, this does not systematically assist the title searcher in connecting a particular person to the estate of a deceased person as his heir unless the searcher already has other information disclosing that the property was inherited from a particular deceased person.[7]

The Clerk of the Superior Court also maintains an "Index of Administrators and Executors," and if the name of a grantor in the chain of title is the administrator or executor, and he is also one of the heirs of the decedent, his status as an "heir" will be discoverable in the "Index of Administrators and Executors," which will point to the book, page and file number where the decedent's estate was administered and will indicate whether a particular grantor in the chain of title was an heir and whether he took title by descent [8] and when. It becomes clear that if the searcher knows at the beginning of his title search that there is a descent in his

---

6. The Clerk of the Superior Court also maintains a cross-index of "Devisors" in the "Devisor Index to Wills." Both the "Devisee Index" and the "Devisor Index" are arranged according to the family-name indexing system and direct the title searcher to the recorded copy of the will involved according to the book, page, or file number where it is recorded.

7. This again points up the advisability of obtaining all the information that it is possible to acquire at the preliminary conference.

8. North Carolina's Intestate Succession Act is set out in Chapter 29 of the North Carolina General Statutes. This act was passed in 1959 and became effective on July 1, 1960. Since it was made applicable only to estates of persons dying after July 1, 1960, the title attorney must consult the statutes relating to "Descents" which existed prior to the effective date of this statute with reference to titles by descent derived from persons dying before 1960.

chain of title, he can and should make inquiry as to the name of any decedent, the name of the administrator of the estate, and the names of any known heirs, in order that he may discover the files concerning the administration of the estate either by searching the "Index of Estates" under the name of the decedent or by searching the "Index of Administrators and Executors," which indexes will point to the files of the estate from which the title was descended. The files of the estate will disclose an inventory of the real property of which the decedent was seized at the time of his death, whether a particular person (one who appears as a grantor in the searcher's chain of title) was an heir of the decedent, and what such person inherited from the decedent. The files of the estate will also disclose whether the estate was properly administered and closed in accordance with law.

If a particular grantor is found to have taken his title by descent from an ancestor or by will, and further time is required to complete the chain of title for the requisite number of years, the title searcher can again resume his search in the office of the Register of Deeds, looking up the decedent ancestor or devisor (from whom the heir or devisee derived his title) in the "Grantee Index" to determine if the land was transmitted to the ancestor or devisor by deed or grant. The same procedure can be continued backwards for the period of time which the search is to encompass.

§ 461. Period of Time for Which Chain of Title Is Searched.

The title searcher should run the chain of title back in point of time as far as he deems necessary to give him assurance that the record title he is certifying is sufficiently certain to be free of question. In fact, the length of the search may be determined by the client's wishes and his willingness to pay. Some purchasers or lenders require very lengthy title searches because of the nature, location and value of the property involved. Title searches going all the way back to the time when the State conveyed the land for the first time are very rare because they are necessarily expensive and in many cases impossible.

In the past, the practice prevailing in a locality often had a primary influence on the length of time for which land titles were searched. With the increased use of title insurance in North Carolina, the requirements of the particular title company involved in the transaction will most often dictate the requisite length of search. Most title insurance companies in North Carolina require either a forty-year or fifty-year chain of title. If title insurance coverage already exists on the property, however, a number of title companies are presently allowing an attorney to update title since the date of the existing policy. Thus a lengthy search will often not be necessary.

The title attorney should not certify a record title unless he has made a title search of at least thirty years and preferably only if he has checked it for a minimum of forty years. While some attorneys apparently rely on shorter searches on the theory that various statutes of limitations diminish any risk in certifying a title if the record title is searched for twenty years or more, they do not take into consideration that the statutes of limitations do not bar persons who are minors or insane persons until three years after the removal of the disability,[9] and do not even begin to run against remaindermen and holders of other future interests so long as a life tenant is living or so long as the future interest remains a nonpossessory interest.[10] Or there may be important restrictions or conditions that have been placed on the title which were recorded at some remote time more than twenty years before the title search which are still viable.[11] In addition, the mere existence of a record title for twenty years or more does not mean that all of the requisites for acquiring title by adverse possession can be proved. In short, the title searcher should not take the risk of relying on either the doctrines of adverse possession or color of title to support his certificate of record title. And while the adoption of the Marketable Title Act[12] will have a positive effect on the elimination of certain title problems, there are a number of reasons why a title searcher cannot completely rely on this legislation and examine recent records only.[13] There is still much wisdom, therefore, in the principle that the longer the period of the attorney's search, the more likely it is that the certificate will be free of question.

If the client desires a shorter search than the title attorney would ordinarily deem sufficient, the client should be apprised of the risks that are involved in not having a more extensive search made. The client should also be apprised of the amount of the lawyer's fee that would be required if an adequate title search were made. If the client then elects to have a shorter search made than the attorney deems safe, there is, of course, no reason why the attorney should not make the shorter search. If the shorter title search is made, however, the attorney should be extremely careful, and should make a complete record of the fact that the shorter search was at the election of his client, and should see that his certificate of record title is limited to the specific time for which the search was requested.

---

9. *See* N.C. GEN. STAT. §§ 1-17, 1-19, 1-20.

10. Eason v. Spence, 232 N.C. 579, 61 S.E.2d 717 (1950); Hauser v. Craft, 134 N.C. 319, 46 S.E. 756 (1904).

11. While the rule against perpetuities will not vitiate restrictive covenants, rights of entry for condition broken, or possibilities of reverter, these interests will no longer have the potentiality of continuing forever to the extent that they are now limited by the Marketable Title Act, N.C. GEN. STAT. §§ 47B-1 through 47B-9.

12. N.C. GEN. STAT. §§ 47B-1 through 47B-9.

13. *See* Chapter 25 *infra,* discussing the Marketable Title Act.

§ 462. Checking the "Out" or "Adverse" Conveyances of Each Owner in the Chain of Title.

The most important part of a title search is the thorough search of "out" or "adverse" claims against the persons who constitute the links in the chain of title. While an oversight by the title searcher engaged in checking the "grantee" indexes will be merely inconvenient and necessitate more work for the lawyer in picking up the thread of a back title if he omits finding a grant in the "Grantee Index," a failure to discover a grant *out* of one of the predecessors in title to particular land may result in the certification of a defective title, the client's loss of the property or his security, or the title attorney's being liable for his client's loss.

In checking each prior owner of the land from the time that he acquired the title until the time when he disposed of it, the "Grantor Index" is used exclusively. The "Grantor Index," as stated before, utilizes the family-name system whereby surnames common to the locality are positioned together. Less common names in the vicinity are arranged alphabetically. The Christian names or initials of the grantors are placed into three columns, depending on their alphabetical position. The "Grantor Index" directs the title searcher to the names of all persons making grants, the type of conveyance, the book and page number where the instrument is copied, the person to whom the grant was made, and a brief description of the land involved as shown on page 556.

GRANTOR General Index to Real Estate Conveyances — Forsyth County, N.C.

DATE OF INST	SURNAMES	GRANTORS ABCDEFGH	GRANTORS IJKLMNO	GIVEN NAMES PQRSTUVWXYZ	GRANTEES	KIND OF INSTRUMENT	Book	Page	BRIEF DESCRIPTION, LOCATION, ETC.	CAN-CELLED
1956	&	Alice D		V F	Fred H Morris Tr	D of T	699	128	Adj J Frank Idol etal	
1956	&			R L Willie M	Duke Power Co	R of W	726	291	Adj H A Michael etal U S Hwy #!?1	Can
1956	&	Helen R	J A		T W Wilcox Tr	D of T	706	108	00.75A Hedgecock Ave	Can
1956	&			Rober E Peggy P	T W Wilcox Tr	D of T	707	101	25,800 sq ft Bunker Hill R Abbotts Creek Tp	Can
1956	&	A R Carrie L	Macie K	R L	State Highway & Public Works Commission	R of W	733	59	— —	
1956	&				Hobert & Marie P Scott	Deed	733	86	Lts 39 to 50 incl Midway Park	
1955	&	A J	Isaac W Heirs		Affidavit	— —	D B 733	410	54+A Adj E M Fishel etal	
1956	& etal	Carrie L		Ray	Glen M Welborn	Deed	734	197	3+A Ray Idol Plat Abbotts Creek Tp	
1956	&	H J Evelyn R (Mrs)	J B	Sabra H (Mrs)	Southern Bell Tel & Tel Company	Permit	734	330	Tract Watkins Ford &	
1956	&	G C	Nell		&	Permit	734	330	Idlewilde Rds	
1956	&	B J			Duke Power Co	R of W	734	524	Adj Dr Fred N Pegg etal	
1956	&	Ben J	Nell P		Fred G Pegg etal	Deed of Easement	736	415	Road Pt 31 Acre Tract Abbotts Creek Tp	
1956	&	Homer B Aileen M			Wilton S & Ada Thorp	Deed	737	480	Lt 16 & Pt Lt 15 Linville Smith & Breece Prop &	
1956	&	Homer B Aileen			&	Deed	737	480	Water Right Easement	

§ 463. Compilation of the Abstract of Title.

Each conveyance located by tracing the grantees in the "Grantee Index" backward constitutes a separate link in the chain of title. The title searcher should prepare an abstract of each link in his chain of title, making notes upon the following matters, perhaps in a form similar to the following: [14]

Link #1

ABSTRACT OF TITLE to the property of Wilton S. Thorpe and wife, Ada Thorpe situated in the County of Forsyth, and State of North Carolina, Kernersville Township

Home Burch Idol and wife, Aileen M. Idol, grantors	Kind of conveyance: Warranty Deed
	Date of conveyance: 5 December 1956
	Consideration: $100 ovc
to	Did all grantors affix seals? Yes
	Date acknowledged: 7 December 1956
Wilton S. Thorpe and Wife, Ada Thorpe	Before J.P., Notary, Clerk? Notary
	Did certifying officer affix seal? Yes
	Was privy examination, if necessary, held? None
	Date recorded: 7 December 1956, 3:38 P.M.
	Book 737, Page 480
	Does the above conveyance contain full covenants? Yes
	(1) Of seizin? Yes
	(2) Of power to convey? Yes
	(3) Against encumbrances? Yes
	(4) Full warranty against the claims of all others? Yes
	Any defects of forms, executions or acknowledgements? No
	Any special limitations, reservations, or restrictions? No. But see description.
	Description

(Copy verbatim description in the first link which is the same as the present owner's deed description.)

When all of the links in the chain of title have been located and abstracted in the foregoing manner, the abstract sheets should be arranged in sequential order, beginning with the most recent conveyance and going backward chronologically to the oldest conveyance in the chain.

The title searcher can then, on separate sheets of paper, summarize his findings and list the names of the various owners, the persons who took as grantees who constitute the links in the chain of title. The abstracted

---

14. Some law firms have created variations on this form. It would seem that a check-list that must be completed as to each link in the chain of title is by far the safest practice.

links will disclose the dates that each owner took title and the dates that each owner disposed of the title. Thus the title searcher will put down under the name of each owner the years of ownership of the property in question. The title searcher is then ready to check "out" or "adverse" conveyances as against each owner to determine whether, during the period of his ownership, he made any conveyance (deed, mortgage, deed of trust, lease, option, contract of sale, express easement, or other agreement affecting his title) that will presently affect the validity or value of the title tendered for sale or as security for a loan. While theoretically it is sufficient to check "out" or "adverse" conveyances of a particular owner only from the time that he acquired the title to the time when the record shows that he disposed of it, since instruments are not always indexed in exact sequential order, the "out" or "adverse" conveyances of each owner should be checked for the entire year in which he took title and for the entire year in which he conveyed the title out. If all conveyances made during these two years and during the intervening years are checked, there is little likelihood that an adverse conveyance will be missed.

For instance, if Thorpe (in the above illustration) obtained his title on 5 December, 1956, and is offering to sell the property or is offering his title as security for a loan at the current date, the title searcher must determine whether Thorpe (and each of his predecessors for the period of the title search) has done anything during the time between the date when he acquired the property and the time when he tenders a deed or mortgage which will affect the validity or value of his title. Has he made any type of conveyance, mortgage, deed of trust, option, contract or agreement that will prevent his passing a good title to a present prospective purchaser or lender for whom the title is being searched and certified? In addition, has any owner allowed a judgment or other lien to be docketed or placed against the property during the period of ownership of each respective owner? To determine these matters "out" or "adverse" conveyances, as well as judgment and lien dockets in the clerk's office, must be thoroughly checked with respect to each owner in the chain of title.

The separate pages showing these "out" or "adverse" conveyances or claims against each person who constitutes a link in the chain of title can be set out in a check-list in the following form: [15]

---

15. Many lawyers who check titles find it convenient to prepare printed or mimeographed blank check-lists to carry with them for completion in the courthouse. This has the merit of saving a great deal of time while at the same time assuring a regularity and systematized routine which should increase accuracy.

Link #1

Wilton S. Thorpe and wife,   Date Acquired: 5 December 1956
Ada Thorpe   Date Granted: ....

Adverse Conveyances to Be Checked: From 1956 to present.

1. Adverse Conveyances:
   Book: ...., Page ....
   Book: ...., Page ....
   Book: ...., Page ....
   Book: ...., Page ....
2. Judgments:
   Book: ...., Page ....
   Book: ...., Page ....
3. Liens:
   a. Federal Tax Lien: ....
   b. County Tax Lien: ....
   c. Town-City Tax Lien: ....
   d. Local Improvement Lien: ....
   e. Welfare Lien: ....
       (Old age assistance; ambulance, some counties.)
4. Lunacy Docket: ....
5. Lis Pendens Docket: ....
6. Miscellaneous Notes:

A word of caution to the title searcher is in order with respect to "out" or "adverse" conveyances, especially to the young attorney just beginning title work. There is no segment in the examination of a land title that is more fraught with danger or which requires more careful attention than the checking of "out" or "adverse" conveyances. The title searcher cannot afford to take any chances that the subject land has been conveyed away or encumbered by an owner of the land so as to impair the validity of the title of the present holder. Not only will it be embarrassing to the title searcher and damaging to his reputation, but it may prove costly if a title which he certifies turns out to be subject to a mortgage or deed of trust or other valid conveyance which he has not discovered. The title searcher may have to make good any loss that occurs to his client. Consequently the title searcher should proceed very slowly in checking grants out of owners in the "Grantor's Index" and should recheck his work often to lessen the possibility of a fatal oversight.

Some areas of potential difficulty and possible oversight should perhaps be mentioned. The alphabetical index of initials of grantors is usually divided into three columns on the index page. Grants will be indexed in the column in which the grantor's particular initials fall, thus leading the title-searching attorney to look in a certain column where his first initial appears for the grantor's conveyances. It should be noted, however, that sometimes a grantor is not consistent in the way that he executes his instruments of conveyance. For instance, while a particular grantor may customarily sign his deeds by his initials and his surname, at other times he may use his given name. Therefore, to be safe, the title-searching attorney should check the "Grantor Index" across the page of the index book as well as down the columns in order to discover any discrepancy which might not appear by checking only initials under a particular column. All columns on the "Grantor Index" pages should be checked and double checked in order to discover every conveyance out of a particular grantor.

The title-searching attorney must be completely convinced that he locates every "out" or "adverse" conveyance of every person who has held the title during the period for which the title is searched. He must check every grantor who *may be* the person whose "out" conveyances he is checking. Hence, every grant of persons with the same initials or similar names should be checked to make absolutely sure that a particular owner has not conveyed away his title before making a grant essential to his chain of title.

Another aspect that demands extreme caution in the search of "out" or "adverse" conveyances of a particular person is the description of the *locus in quo*.[16] If the search of the "out" conveyances of a particular person in the chain of title for the period of his ownership does not reveal a description of the same land, then such conveyances may be ignored. The *recorded instruments themselves* should be looked at, however, and the title attorney should never rely solely on the brief descriptions which appear in the last column of each index page.[17]

The particular measurements of "out" conveyances must be checked with care to make sure that a particular grantor in the chain of title who has made a conveyance has retained, after such conveyance, as much land

---

16. Answers to a questionnaire sent to a number of title attorneys with respect to aspects of conveyancing that most often cause problems in title searching reveal that "faulty descriptions" rank highest on the list.

17. In Church v. Berry, 2 N.C. App. 617, 163 S.E.2d 664 (1968), it is said: "A purchaser of real property in North Carolina must examine all recorded 'out' conveyances made by prior record title holders during the periods when they respectively held title to the property to determine if any such owner has expressly imposed a restriction upon the use of the property." (Headnote.) *See* Reed v. Elmore, 246 N.C. 221, 98 S.E.2d 360 (1957).

See also Turner v. Glenn, 220 N.C. 620, 18 S.E.2d 197 (1941), in which the court said: "it is the duty of a purchaser of land to examine every recorded deed or instrument in his line of title and he is conclusively presumed to know the contents of such instruments and is put on notice of any fact or circumstance affecting his title which either of such instruments reasonably discloses."

Accord, Hensley v. Ramsey, 283 N.C. 714, 199 S.E.2d 1 (1973).

as the *locus in quo* is supposed to contain.[18] Frequently where there are several "out" conveyances from a grantor in the chain of title during a prescribed period, it is difficult to determine from the deed descriptions whether particular land has been conveyed or retained. The title searcher may have to sketch the various "out" conveyances to scale with use of square and compass to determine whether a particular grantor retained the *locus in quo* for which title is being searched. Other inquiry may be necessary to find out whether a particular instrument conveys specific property. Property is frequently conveyed with different descriptions from those used in previous conveyances of the same property. Every ambiguity must be reconciled and resolved by the title searcher in order to make sure that he does not certify a title that has been conveyed away either in whole or in part.

---

18. *E.g.*, if the owner of a tract containing X number of acres makes a conveyance that purports to convey only a portion of the tract, the title searcher must determine that the portion he retained was adequate to make his subsequent conveyances valid; that he had not already disposed of a part or all of the *locus in quo*.

CHAPTER 23

EXAMINATION OF THE SOURCES OF TITLE

Article I. Introduction

§ 464. Instruments Which the Title Searcher Must Locate and Pass On; Sources of Title.

Article II. Private Deeds

§ 465. Warranty Deeds.
§ 466. Correction Deeds.
§ 467. Quitclaim Deeds.
§ 468. Deeds Without Warranties.
§ 469. Corporation Deeds.
§ 470. Deeds of Married Persons.
§ 471. Deeds Conveying Estate by Entirety.
§ 472. Deeds by Attorneys in Fact.
§ 473. Voluntary Deeds of Partition.

Article III. Official Deeds

§ 474. In General.
§ 475. Deeds by Trustees Under Deeds of Trust.
§ 476. Deeds by Trustees Holding Title for Others.
§ 477. Deeds by Trustees in Bankruptcy.
§ 478. Deeds by Receivers.
§ 479. Commissioners' Deeds.
§ 480. Sheriffs' Deeds Under Execution Sales.
§ 481. Guardians' Deeds.
§ 482. Executors' and Administrators' Deeds.
§ 483. Tax Deeds.

Article IV. Other Sources of Title

§ 484. Title by Devise.
§ 485. Title by Descent.
§ 486. Unrecorded Deeds; Title by Adverse Possession.
§ 487. Title by Judgment of Court of Record.

Article I. Introduction

§ 464. Instruments Which the Title Searcher Must Locate and Pass On; Sources of Title.

Having considered the systematic "running of the chain of title," the instruments which the title searcher must locate and pass on should now be classified and studied. These will include (1) *private deeds,* which will include warranty deeds, correction deeds, quitclaim deeds, corporate deeds, deeds between husband and wife, deeds by attorneys in fact, voluntary partition deeds, and deeds creating or conveying tenancies by the entirety; (2) *official deeds,* which will include deeds of trustees under deeds of trust, deeds of trustees who hold title for others, deeds of trustees who hold under deeds of assignment, deeds of trustees in bankruptcy, mortgagees' deeds, receivers' deeds, sheriffs' deeds under execution, guardians' deeds, executors' deeds, administrators' deeds, and tax deeds; (3) *titles that pass by devise;* and (4) *titles that pass by judgment or decree.* In addition, the rules with respect to other sources of title such as (5) *title by adverse possession* and (6) *title by descent* must be considered, as they bear on title searches.

Article II. Private Deeds

§ 465. Warranty Deeds.

(a) *In general.* Most conveyances are by general warranty deed. The most numerous and common of the types of conveyances in an ordinary chain of title are those of general warranty. Thus the matters to be checked in warranty deeds will be set out in this subsection in some detail.

(b) *Date.* The first recital in deeds is usually the date. A date is not essential, however, to the validity of a deed. A deed is good without any date, or with an impossible date,[1] if the real date of its delivery can be proved.[2] A deed takes effect from its delivery and not from its date, since delivery is of the essence and the date is not.[3] Hence, even though a deed recites a date before the death of the grantor, if it was not in fact delivered until after the death of the grantor, the deed will be void.[4] A date is important, however, as a deed is *presumed* to have been delivered at the time of the date that it bears unless the contrary is shown by evidence *aliunde.*[5] The date on a deed creates prima facie evidence that it was delivered on that date. This evidence may be rebutted, by proof that it was not delivered on that date, and its execution must then be referred to the time when the evidence shows that the grantor actually parted with the possession for the purpose of giving effect to it.[6]

---

1. *E.g.,* in 2 BLACKSTONE, COMMENTARIES, at page 304, it is stated: "A deed is good although it mentions no date, or bears a false date, or even an impossible date, as the 30th of February; provided the real date of its being dated or delivered be proved."

2. Patterson v. Bodenhamer, 31 N.C. 96 (1848); 2 MORDECAI, LAW LECTURES 909 (1916).

3. Williams v. North Carolina State Bd. of Educ., 284 N.C. 588, 201 S.E.2d 889 (1974); Kendrick v. Dellinger, 117 N.C. 491, 23 S.E. 438 (1895); Newlin v. Osborne, 49 N.C. 157 (1856).

4. Goodson v. Whitfield, 40 N.C. 163 (1847).

5. The date recited in the beginning of a deed is prima facie evidence that it was delivered on that date. Evidence to the contrary, however, may negate or neutralize this presumption. *See* Williams v. North Carolina State Bd. of Educ., 284 N.C. 588, 201 S.E.2d 889 (1974) stating this general rule and holding that there was no evidence to rebut the presumption that a deed dated 17 April 1797 was delivered on its stated date. *See also* Turlington v. Neighbors and Turlington v. Turlington, 222 N.C. 694, 24 S.E.2d 648 (1943); Kendrick v. Dellinger, 117 N.C. 491, 23 S.E. 438 (1895); Vaughn v. Parker, 112 N.C. 96, 16 S.E. 908 (1893).

6. Newlin v. Osborne, 49 N.C. 157 (1856). *Accord,* Williams v. North Carolina State Bd. of Educ., 284 N.C. 588, 201 S.E.2d 889 (1974).

§ 465   EXAMINATION OF THE SOURCES OF TITLE   § 465

(c) *The identity of the grantor.* The title searcher must be assured that each grantor in the chain of title is the person who received the title to the *locus in quo,* either by prior grant, devise, descent or decree.[7]

A body of relatively ancient cases established the rule in North Carolina that the name of the grantor who purports to pass legal title must appear *on the face of the deed.*[8] By this rule, if the deed contains the signature of the grantor without mentioning the grantor in the body of the deed, the deed will not suffice.[9] This rule would seem to have nothing to commend it in a system of modern conveyancing where the reason for the original requirement has all but disappeared.[10] The rationale of North Carolina General Statutes, § 39-1.1 and that of Triplett v. Williams [11] and related cases ought to apply to this issue to the effect that the whole deed should be construed so as to prevent the technicalities of the common law and so as to effectuate the intention of the parties. Perhaps the better approach is that the failure to mention the grantor in the body of the deed is but one factor to be considered in determining the intention of the parties under the above mentioned statute.[12]

(d) *Grantee must be indentified.* The grantee or grantees of a deed should be so designated that there is no doubt as to the party or parties to whom the grant is made. To be valid the deed must designate an existing person or legal entity as the grantee who is capable of taking title

---

7. The title attorney must ascertain with certainty that any grantor's name corresponds with the name under which he acquired title to the *locus in quo.* If the name by which he conveyed title "out" differs in any way from that by which he took title a correction deed may be necessary in order that subsequent questions will not arise with respect to the title which may affect its marketability.

8. *See* 2 MORDECAI, LAW LECTURES 799 (1916); Kerns v. Peeler, 49 N.C. 226 (1856); Adams v. Hedgepeth, 50 N.C. 327 (1858); Gray v. Mathis, 52 N.C. 502 (1860); King v. Rhew, 108 N.C. 696, 13 S.E. 174 (1891); Estis v. Jackson, 111 N.C. 145, 16 S.E. 7 (1892). *But see* Yates v. Insurance Co., 173 N.C. 473, 92 S.E. 356 (1917), wherein a deed left a blank where the names of the grantors should have been placed and the blank was followed by the words "parties of the first part." The last clause of the deed was: "In witness whereof the said parties of the first part have hereunto set their hands and seals . . .," followed by signatures of all the purported grantors. In the *Yates* case the court held that the final clause and the signatures referring to the prior words "parties of the first part" identified the grantors sufficiently to make the deed valid notwithstanding that their names were not in the body of the deed. Thus it would appear that if a conveyance is made by a husband and wife as grantors and the husband is named by name and the wife is referred to only with designation such as "John Jones and wife, grantors," and the wife signs the deed, there would be a sufficient recital of the wife's name to make a valid conveyance.

9. *Id.*

10. *See* § 12.40 of AMERICAN LAW OF PROPERTY (Casner Ed.) at 281.

11. 149 N.C. 394, 63 S.E. 79 (1908). *See also* Whetsell v. Jernigan, 291 N.C. 128, 229 S.E.2d 183 (1976).

12. *See* Dean Mordecai's comments in 2 MORDECAI, LAW LECTURES 801 (1916), in which the author is highly critical of the rule that the grantor is not estopped by his signature where his name is not in the body of the deed.

to the land at the time the deed is delivered. A deed to a person who is dead is a nullity even though it is made to "A and his heirs"; if A is dead at the time of the grant his heirs do not take, since the word "heirs" in such case is a word of limitation and not of purchase.[13] But if the conveyance reads "To A *or* his heirs" and A is dead at the time of the delivery of the deed, the heirs of A will take.[14]

A deed to a husband and wife creates a tenancy by the entirety. A deed to two or more persons not husband and wife creates a tenancy in common. Under North Carolina General Statutes, § 59-38 (c), a deed to a partnership as grantee vests title in the partnership. A deed to a corporation as grantee vests title in the corporation. Certain unincorporated associations may be grantees, contrary to the prevailing rule at common law. Under North Carolina General Statutes, §§ 39-24 and 39-25, voluntary organizations and associations of individuals organized for charitable, fraternal, religious, social or patriotic purposes are authorized to acquire real estate and hold it in their common or corporate names.[15] Chapter 61 of the General Statutes deals with religious societies which may acquire property through trustees.[16]

While at the common law the heirs of a living person could not be grantees since it was reasoned that "the living have no heirs," under General Statutes, § 41-6 a deed to the heirs of a living person is deemed a deed to the living person's children. Likewise, a child *en ventre sa mere* can be a valid grantee under General Statutes, § 41-5. Under North Carolina General Statutes, § 41-6.1, a limitation by deed to the "next of kin" of any person is construed to be to those persons who would take under the law of intestate succession, unless a contrary intention appears by the instrument.[17] And North Carolina General Statutes, § 39-6, should be consulted with regard to revocation of deeds of future interests made to persons not *in esse*.

(e) *Consideration.* While most warranty deeds recite the payment of a consideration, usually in a recital such as "$10.00 and other valuable considerations" or "100.00 and o.v.c." (meaning other valuable con-

---

13. Neal v. Nelson, 117 N.C. 393, 23 S.E. 428 (1895).
14. Campbell v. Everhart, 139 N.C. 503, 52 S.E. 201 (1905). *Accord,* Neal v. Nelson, 117 N.C. 393, 23 S.E. 428 (1895). *But see* Morton v. Thornton, 259 N.C. 697, 131 S.E.2d 378 (1963), which states that a grant to *living* person AB *or* CD would be void as to both for uncertainty.
15. N.C. Gen. Stat. § 39-24 contains the provisos that the organization or association be organized for the purposes which are not prohibited by law; and that voluntary associations and organizations do not include, for purposes of this Article of the statutes, "associations, partnerships or copartnerships which are organized to engage in any business, trade, or profession."
16. N.C. Gen. Stat. § 61-3.
17. The statute also applies to a limitation to the "next of kin" by will or other writing.

siderations), no consideration is today necessary as between the parties to a conveyance to make it valid.[18]

It should be noted, however, that under certain circumstances it is necessary that a consideration be paid. For instance, under General Statutes, § 47-26 a deed of gift is void unless recorded within two years from the making thereof.[19] A deed of gift is good between the grantor and the grantee during the two years after its execution and delivery even though not recorded, but when two years elapse and the deed has not been recorded within that time the deed becomes void *ab initio* and vests in the grantor.[20] If a consideration is paid for the deed, the grantee need not record it except to protect himself against other purchasers for value who record or lien creditors of the grantor who docket a lien against the grantor.[21]

The question "What is a consideration?" becomes important in this regard. In *King v. McRackan*,[22] the court defines "purchaser for a valuable consideration" in the following manner: "The party assuming to be a purchaser for a valuable consideration must prove a fair consideration, not up to the full price, but a price paid which would not cause surprise or make anyone exclaim, 'He got the land for nothing! There must have been some fraud or contrivance about it.' " The same case also said that consideration is "A fair and reasonable price according to the common mode of dealing between buyers and sellers."

Another instance where the payment of a consideration for a conveyance is important is where the creditors of the grantor are interested. The want of consideration may be shown as evidence of fraud or of a fraud-

---

18. Mosely v. Mosely, 87 N.C. 69 (1882); Love's Ex'rs v. Harbin, 87 N.C. 249 (1882); Edwards v. Batts, 245 N.C. 693, 97 S.E.2d 101 (1957).

19. A deed of gift, executed without a consideration, is absolutely void when not recorded within two years after the making. Booth v. Hairston, 195 N.C. 8, 141 S.E. 480 (1928), *aff'g* 193 N.C. 278, 136 S.E. 879 (1927); Ferguson v. Ferguson, 225 N.C. 375, 35 S.E.2d 231 (1945). *Accord,* Penninger v. Barrier, 29 N.C. App. 312, 224 S.E.2d 245 (1976).

20. Winstead v. Woolard, 223 N.C. 814, 28 S.E.2d 507 (1944); Kirkpatrick v. Sanders, 261 F.2d 480, *cert. denied,* 359 U.S. 1000, 79 S. Ct. 1138, 3 L. Ed. 1029 (1959).

21. *See* N.C. GEN. STAT. §§ 47-18, 47-20.

22. 168 N.C. 621, 84 S.E. 1027 (1915).

A recital in a deed of the payment and receipt of a consideration raises a presumption that the consideration has been paid and that the deed is not a deed of gift. Pelaez v. Pelaez, 16 N.C. App. 604, 192 S.E.2d 651 (1972).

With respect to N.C. GEN. STAT. § 47-26, *see* Sprinkle v. Ponder, 233 N.C. 312, 64 S.E.2d 171 (1951), in which case the court held that an agreement by a wife to perform ordinary marital duties was not a sufficient consideration to remove the deed from the requirements of the statute. In Kirkpatrick v. Sanders, 261 F.2d 480, *cert. denied,* 359 U.S. 1000, 79 S. Ct. 1138, 3 L. Ed. 1029 (1959), the court held that payment of $100 would not constitute such a valuable consideration for the conveyance of real estate valued at $27,000 as would take the deed out of the requirements of the statute invalidating deeds of gift not recorded within two years after its execution.

ulent conveyance.[23] Furthermore, if a prior grantee has not recorded his deed and a subsequent grantee from the same grantor seeks to establish priority by recording his subsequent deed first, in order to prevail over the prior grantee, the recording grantee must be a "purchaser for value" who has paid "consideration."[24]

(f) *Operative words of conveyance.* A deed must contain apt words of conveyance. A phrase frequently used in warranty deeds in North Carolina is as follows: "Has bargained and sold, and by these presents does grant, bargain, sell and convey to said party of the second part . . . ." No particular verbiage or form is required, but it must appear that the grantor is selling or conveying the estate to the grantee by the instrument. Any form of phraseology which shows the grantor's present intent to make the conveyance is sufficient.[25] The conveyancer must be careful to see that the instrument expresses a present conveyance and not merely an intention "to convey" in the future.

(g) *Description of the land.* The descriptions of the property in the deeds in one's chain of title are of utmost importance to the title searcher. Descriptions cause perhaps more difficulties and headaches to title attorneys than any other aspect of title work. The title-searching attorney must be sure that his *locus in quo* is contained in the descriptions of each previous link of his chain of title. The title even of city lots frequently runs back to the time that the lots were described as acreage in ordinary title searches and it is imperative for the attorney to check and recheck the boundaries of the land described in the various links to make certain that the title to all of the *locus in quo* is good.

The title searcher should make it a practice in every case where a metes and bounds description in his chain of title is discovered to make sure that the description closes. He should sketch and plat out all descriptions to make sure that they describe all of the *locus in quo*.[26]

---

23. Jones v. Sanders, 254 N.C. 644, 119 S.E.2d 789 (1961); Howard v. Turner, 125 N.C. 107, 34 S.E. 229 (1899).

24. Bourne v. Lay & Co., 264 N.C. 33, 140 S.E.2d 769 (1965).

25. The Supreme Court of North Carolina has gone a long way in recognizing informal words of conveyance. In New Home Bldg. Supply Co. v. Nations, 259 N.C. 681, 131 S.E.2d 425 (1963), the purported grantor wrote these words on the back of his own deed: "I transfer this deed." He signed and sealed it. It was held that sufficient operative words of conveyance were used and the conveyance was sustained.

But see Pope v. Burgess, 230 N.C. 323, 53 S.E.2d 159 (1949), where a rather detailed instrument was held not to contain sufficient words of conveyance.

26. Many attorneys are good at reading descriptions and surveys and have no difficulty platting particular descriptions by metes and bounds and courses and distances, carefully platting and subtracting "out" conveyances in order to determine what was left in a particular grantor when he made a specific conveyance of part of his land from a larger tract. Other attorneys, particularly younger and inexperienced attorneys, may wish to procure a surveyor's services in preparing a surveyor's sketch or plat to minimize the possibility of error. It is often difficult for an attorney to plat descriptions where different sized angles are used and where a mistaken direction or length may put sketched lines on someone else's land.

§ 465 EXAMINATION OF THE SOURCES OF TITLE § 465

In locating boundaries, resort should first be made to natural landmarks referred to in the instrument. After natural landmarks, artificial monuments, adjacent boundaries, courses and distances, and finally recital of quantity of land included, are resorted to in that order.[27] In other words, there is a hierarchy of constructional rules to determine where boundaries are located where the description in a deed is unclear or ambiguous.[28] Natural and permanent objects control courses and distances. For example, if the description in a deed runs 400 feet from an oak tree, but when measured the actual distance to the oak tree is only 350 feet from the point of beginning, the deed carries and describes only to the oak tree.[29]

A statement in a conveyance of the amount of land to be conveyed is not generally controlling in establishing boundaries.[30] The specification of a number of acres in a grant, for example, being only a general description, will yield to and be controlled by more specific references to definite boundaries, monuments or courses and distances.

Courses and distances will control where the deed does not call for monuments or boundaries.[31] It should be noted that the line of an adjoining tract of land is treated as a natural boundary if at the time the deed calling for it is made the line is indicated by visible marks so that it can be identified and located.[32]

The description of lots by numbers with reference to a book of maps will control a conflicting description by metes and bounds.[33]

The title attorney must be extremely careful with respect to the descriptions of boundaries in deeds in the chain of title. There are many, many cases that have been decided by the North Carolina Supreme Court which show that defective, vague and ambiguous descriptions are prolific producers of clouds on title and litigation. The title attorney should be wary of certifying the validity of confusing, conflicting or impossible calls.

---

27. Tice v. Winchester, 225 N.C. 673, 36 S.E.2d 257 (1945).
28. Id.
29. Norwood v. Crawford, 114 N.C. 513, 19 S.E. 349 (1894); McNeely v. Laxton, 149 N.C. 327, 63 S.E. 278 (1908); Lance v. Rumbough, 150 N.C. 19, 63 S.E. 357 (1908); Wilson Lumber Co. v. Hutton, 152 N.C. 537, 68 S.E.2d (1910); Bowen v. Roper Lumber Co., 153 N.C. 366, 69 S.E. 258 (1910); Allison v. Kenion, 163 N.C. 582, 79 S.E. 1110 (1913); Wachovia Bank & Trust Co. v. Miller, 243 N.C. 1, 89 S.E.2d 765 (1955).
30. Queen v. Sink, 238 N.C. 389, 78 S.E.2d 152 (1953). However, in some cases where other descriptions are indefinite, mention of a specific number of acres may have weight and in some instances may even be controlling. *See* Wilson Lumber Co. v. Hutton, 152 N.C. 537, 68 S.E. 2 (1910).
31. Bowen v. Roper Lumber Co., 153 N.C. 366, 69 S.E. 258 (1910).
32. Batson v. Bell, 249 N.C. 718, 107 S.E.2d 562 (1959); Franklin v. Faulkner, 248 N.C. 656, 104 S.E.2d 841 (1958); Carney v. Edwards, 256 N.C. 20, 122 S.E.2d 786 (1961); Hill v. Dalton, 140 N.C. 9, 52 S.E. 273 (1905).
33. Kelly v. King, 225 N.C. 709, 36 S.E.2d 220 (1945). *But see* Lee v. McDonald, 230 N.C. 517, 53 S.E.2d 845 (1949).

§ 465   REAL ESTATE LAW IN NORTH CAROLINA   § 465

Ever present in the title attorney's mind should be the fact that he certifies "what the record shows" and not what he might think or what a court might hold if the description of a deed is challenged in litigation. Is the title that his client is taking one that is marketable? Will other attorneys certify the validity of the description? The title attorney cannot afford to take a gamble that the courts will construe a vague or ambiguous description in the same way that the arrorney does. The courts have not always been entirely consistent as to the adequacy of certain similar descriptions. The title attorney should simply report any questionable descriptions to his client in order that the client may make the decision of whether to take the title, or in order that the client can procure the attorney to clear up the faulty or questionable description if it is feasible. The ambiguity or fault may be corrected, or in some instances title insurance may be procured after disclosure of all the facts. But if the description is not certain, it is hazardous for the title-searching attorney to assume personal responsibility and potential liability if the adequacy of the description comes into litigation.

(h) *The habendum clause.* The function of the habendum clause historically has been to indicate what interest or estate is granted to the grantee by the deed. A typical example of the habendum clause is the provision: "To have and to hold the aforesaid tract or parcel of land, and all privileges and appurtenances thereto belonging, to the said party of the second part and his heirs and assigns, to their only use and behoof forever." The habendum clause has no real purpose today and for all practical purposes has degenerated into a merely useless form. The habendum clause can be omitted in a deed entirely without affecting the validity of the deed.[34]

---

34. The "granting clause" has been held to be the "heart of a deed" and indispensable to its validity. Hence, prior to 1968, the Supreme Court held in North Carolina that if the granting clause purported to convey an estate of one quality and the habendum clause (or any preceding or succeeding recital) purported to lessen, enlarge, explain or qualify the estate granted so as to be repugnant to the estate granted in the granting clause, the granting clause was held to control. Bowden v. Bowden, 264 N.C. 296, 141 S.E.2d 621 (1965). *But see* N.C. GEN. STAT. § 39-1.1, enacted in 1967, which provides that deeds executed after January 1, 1968, with inconsistent clauses will be given effect according to the intent of the parties "as appears from all of the provisions of the instrument." Thus it would appear that the content of the habendum clause will no longer be simply read out of the deed when inconsistent with the granting clause, but that it will be considered along with other clauses in the deed to determine the intent of the grantor where an inconsistency appears. It is likely, however, that the granting clause will still predominate in most cases where there is a conflict.

See Whetsell v. Jernigan, 29 N.C. App. 136, 223 S.E.2d 397, *aff'd,* 291 N.C. 128, 229 S.E.2d 183 (1976), a case which involved an 1884 deed wherein the granting, habendum and warranty clauses were regular in form as purporting to convey a fee simple title but language delimiting the fee appeared in the body of the deed following the description. The North Carolina Court of Appeals held that the limiting language appearing only at the end of the description and not referred to elsewhere in the deed should be disregarded as surplus

(i) *Warranties.* In warranty deeds, the covenant clause usually follows the habendum clause. The covenant clause is that clause of a deed wherein the grantor makes express stipulations that certain facts are true and promises and binds himself to answer for the goodness of the title he sells.

The covenants normally used in warranty deeds in North Carolina are four in number:

1. That the grantor is seised of the premises in fee;
2. That he has a right to convey the premises in fee simple;
3. That the premises are free from encumbrances; and
4. That the grantor will warrant and defend the title he conveys against the lawful claims of all persons whomsoever.

Of the foregoing four covenants, the first three are operative only between the parties; the fourth covenant is said to "run with the land" and a grantor can be sued upon his covenant of warranty to defend the title either by his immediate grantee or by a remote grantee. If an immediate grantee or remote grantee is evicted by one under a title paramount to that warranted by the grantor making the covenant of warranty, the warranting grantor will be chargeable in damages for the purchase price of the land plus interest in addition to reasonable attorney's fees expended in defending the title [35] in the event that the grantor does not defend the title after having notice of the claim against the title.

Therefore, where a grantor covenants that he is seised in fee simple and has a right to convey title in fee, only his immediate grantee can sue him if he is not in fact seised at the time he makes the conveyance and he has no right to convey title to the land. The covenants of seisin and right to convey are broken when made if ever at all, and therefore the statute of limitations begins to run immediately upon delivery of the deed in which such covenants are contained. With respect to the covenant against encumbrances the same rules apply. Only an immediate grantee may sue the covenantor for breach of the covenant against encumbrances, as this covenant also does not "run with the land." The statute of limitations as to the covenant against encumbrances also starts to run upon the execution of the instrument, as this covenant too is broken when made if ever broken at all.

The covenants of *general warranty* and quiet enjoyment, the covenants that the grantor will warrant and defend the title he conveys against the lawful claims of all persons whomsoever, are covenants that the grantor *will, in the future,* defend the title which he grants. The covenant of general warranty is not broken until the immediate grantee *or his suc-*

---

usage and should have no force and effect. *Accord,* Waters v. North Carolina Phosphate Corp., 32 N.C. App. 305, 232 S.E.2d 286 (1977). *See also* Gamble v. Williams, 39 N.C. App. 630, 251 S.E.2d 625 (1979); Johnson v. Burrow, 42 N.C. App. 273, 256 S.E.2d 811 (1979).

35. Jones v. Balsley, 154 N.C. 61, 69 S.E. 827 (1910).

cessor in title (whether remote or immediate) is evicted from the premises and the statute of limitations does not begin to run from the time of the execution of the deed, but begins to run only from the time that the one claiming under title paramount evicts the grantee or his successor in interest. The covenant of general warranty runs not only to the immediate grantee but to intermediate and remote grantees in the chain of title as well. A remote grantee of the *locus in quo* can sue any grantor in the chain of title above him who has made a covenant of warranty; no privity is necessary, nor is it necessary that there be an unbroken chain of covenants of warranty.

A distinction between "covenants of general warranty" and "covenants of special warranty" should be observed. Covenants of general warranty are assurances and guaranties that the grantor will defend the title of grantees and their successors against the lawful claims of *all persons whomsoever*. "Covenants of special warranty" are assurances and guaranties that the grantor will defend the title of grantees only against the lawful claims of persons *claiming by, through, or under the warrantor*.[36]

The title searcher will want to determine whether a deed proffered to his client contains these covenants of title and whether any have been omitted in any of the deeds in the chain of title. While a deed is sufficient to convey the title of a grantor without a covenant of warranty, there are no implied covenants that the grantor has a good title to that which he conveys. To charge the grantor with liability for failure of title it must appear that he has expressly warranted the title by an express covenant.[37] Therefore the doctrine of *caveat emptor* applies and, in the absence of express covenants for title made by the grantor, the full risk of assuring himself that he has good title falls on the purchaser or mortgagee. Hence the title attorney will be careful to ascertain the extent to which the title to the *locus in quo* has been guaranteed by the various grantors in his chain of title.

While a deed without any covenants or warranties is sufficient to convey title, such a deed is the practical equivalent of a quitclaim deed. While a deed in the chain of title without the covenants will not prevent a title from being good, the absence of the usual covenants may affect the marketability of the title to be acquired and should be carefully noted.[38]

---

36. *See* 2 Mordecai, Law Lectures 858 (1916); Spencer v. Jones, 108 N.C. 291, 84 S.E. 261 (1915).

37. Tiffany, Real Property § 681 (abr. ed. 1940); Cribbet, Principles of the Law of Property 204 (1962); 2 Mordecai, Law Lectures 888 (1916); Pridgen v. Long, 177 N.C. 189, 98 S.E. 451 (1919).

38. In the event a title insurance policy will be applied for, a break in the chain of warranties is a matter that should be reported to the company. Depending upon surrounding circumstances, a break in warranties will not necessarily stand in the way of obtaining full title insurance coverage.

(j) *Testimonial clause.* After the covenant clause in the ordinary warranty deed comes the testimonial clause which usually reads: "In testimony whereof, the said party of the first part has hereunto set his hand and seal the day and year first above written." The testimonial clause has no particular legal significance to the title searcher.

(k) *Signature.* Every grantor [39] of each deed in the chain of title must have signed the deed purporting to pass his title in order for the deed to be valid as against each respective grantor. The signature need not be subscribed at the bottom of the deed and it can be anywhere in the body of the deed.[40]

Where one is illiterate another person can sign for him and the illiterate person may adopt the signature.[41] Or the illiterate grantor may make his "mark," and it is not essential for the words "his mark" to appear or for witnesses to subscribe the deed. It is sufficient if it appears that the grantor in fact made it or adopted it.[42] Where there is a "mark" purporting to be a signature, however, the title searcher should be extremely careful and determine whether the grantor actually adopted it, because whether one has adopted a "mark" as his own signature is a question for a jury to determine; the title attorney should not gamble on what a jury will find.

(l) *Seal.* Every deed must have a seal in order to be valid in North Carolina.[43] If land is to be conveyed for a period of more than three years a conveyance is invalid unless it is under seal.[44] If the deed actually has a seal attached to it, the fact that there is no recital in the deed that it bears a seal will not impair its validity.[45] The North Carolina Supreme Court has held that the recital of the seal in the instrument raises a presumption that a seal was affixed to the original deed even though such does not appear on the face of the registered deed.[46] In the recent case of *Williams v. Board of Education,*[47] the crucial deed was not in evidence, but the record of the deed recited that "the parties have interchangeable set their hands and seals dated the day and year first above written." The

---

39. The grantor's signature may also be by an authorized agent.
40. *See* the outstanding case on signatures and seals in North Carolina, Devereaux v. McMahon, 108 N.C. 134, 12 S.E. 902 (1891).
41. Sellers v. Sellers, 98 N.C. 13, 3 S.E. 917 (1887).
42. Devereaux v. McMahon, 108 N.C. 134, 12 S.E. 902 (1891); Sellers v. Sellers, 98 N.C. 13, 3 S.E. 917 (1887); Lee v. Porter, 171 N.C. 144, 88 S.E. 217 (1916); State v. Byrd, 93 N.C. 625 (1895).
43. Williams v. North Carolina State Bd. of Educ., 284 N.C. 588, 201 S.E.2d 889 (1974); Dunn v. Dunn, 242 N.C. 234, 87 S.E.2d 308 (1955); Willis v. Anderson, 188 N.C. 479, 124 S.E. 834 (1924); Hinsdale v. Thornton, 74 N.C. 167 (1876). There was a two-year period between March 7, 1879, and March 5, 1881, in which seals were not required on deeds.
44. Patterson v. Galliher, 122 N.C. 511, 29 S.E. 773 (1898).
45. Devereaux v. McMahon, 108 N.C. 134, 12 S.E. 902 (1891).
46. Williams v. North Carolina State Bd. of Educ., 284 N.C. 588, 201 S.E.2d 889 (1974).
47. *Id.*

deed's attestation clause, signed by three witnesses, recited that the instrument was "sealed and delivered" in the presence of the witnesses. The court held that the recital of these words in the record of the deed raised a presumption that there was a seal affixed by the grantor to his signature on the original deed, and, in the absence of evidence to rebut this presumption, the contention that the deed was invalid for lack of a seal was held to be without merit.[48]

More than one person may adopt a single seal.[49] If a seal that purports to be the seal of the grantor is referred to in the body of the deed, it can be the seal of the grantor even though it is not on the line with the signature.[50] A corporate seal is also a necessary prerequisite to a valid conveyance of real estate by a corporation.[51]

Several statutes are periodically updated in North Carolina to cure certain defects with regard to seals. Under North Carolina General Statutes, § 47-108.11, where a deed, deed of trust, mortgage, lien, or other instrument entitled to be registered is recorded, and the word "seal" or "notarial seal" has been omitted, if the recorded instrument recites or shows that the grantors "have fixed or set their hand and seals," then all such documents are declared valid and binding as if the word "seal" or "notarial seal" had not been omitted. As to corporate seals, North Carolina General Statutes, § 47-71.1 validates corporate deeds executed prior to the date set out in the statute notwithstanding omission of the corporate seal.

While an instrument cannot be a "deed" and pass legal title if it does not bear a seal,[52] it may be specifically enforceable as a contract for the sale of land.[53]

(m) *Acknowledgments.* In passing on the validity of a deed and its recordation, it is especially important for the title attorney to pay close attention to the manner of its acknowledgment. While acknowledgment is not necessary to its validity, a proper acknowledgment is necessary for the deed to be recorded, and of course a proper recordation is necessary to protect a grantee against the claims of lien creditors and purchasers for value of the grantor.[54] Unless a curative statute is applicable, the regis-

---

48. *Id.* 284 N.C. 588, 595.
49. Title attorneys should be extremely careful in resolving that a particular grantor adopted a seal where the names of two grantors appear beside of one seal, since the question of whether a seal has been adopted is one of fact for the jury.
50. Harrell & Co. v. Butler, 92 N.C. 20 (1885).
51. Investors Corp. v. Field Financial Corp., 5 N.C. App. 156, 167 S.E.2d 852 (1969); Caldwell v. Morganton Mfg. Co., 121 N.C. 339, 28 S.E. 475 (1897).
52. *See* Johnston v. Case, 131 N.C. 491, 42 S.E. 957 (1902), to the effect that an unsealed instrument cannot even be *color* of title.
53. Dunn v. Dunn, 242 N.C. 234, 87 S.E.2d 308 (1955).
54. N.C. Gen. Stat. § 47-1. "Until a deed is proved in the manner prescribed by the statute, the public register has no authority to put it in his book...." Withrell v. Murphy, 154 N.C. 82, 69 S.E. 748 (1910); Duke v. Markham, 105 N.C. 131, 10 S.E. 1017 (1890); Todd v. Outlaw, 79 N.C. 235, 237 (1878).

tration of an improperly acknowledged or defectively probated deed imports no constructive notice, and the deed will be treated as if unregistered.[55] Instruments whose acknowledgment or proofs of probate are defective on their face will fail to impart constructive notice even if they are otherwise effectively recorded; i.e., if the acknowledgment or probate is *patently* defective, the recorded instrument will be treated as if unrecorded.[56] When the incapacity of the acknowledging or probating officer is *latent, i.e.,* does not appear of record, a recordation of the instrument pursuant to such defective acknowledgment or probate is valid and suffices to impart constructive notice.[57] The title attorney must, therefore, be thoroughly conversant with the provisions of Chapter 47 of the North Carolina General Statutes. The title attorney must pay careful attention to the following with respect to acknowledgments (which does not purport to be all inclusive):

1. Acknowledgments of notaries public must indicate that the notary's commission was in effect at the time of the acknowledgment and at the time the notary's seal was affixed. If a defective acknowledgment is discovered in the chain of title, the title attorney may find that a curative act has validated the defective instrument under Article 4 of Chapter 47 of the General Statutes. See also Chapter 10 of the General Statutes where certain acts of notaries are validated although irregular.

2. Prior to January 1, 1978, in order for a married woman's deed to her husband to be valid, either conveying to him a legal title [58] or creating a trust [59] for his benefit in real property, there was a statutory requirement in North Carolina that the deed be certified as not being unreasonable or injurious to the wife.[60] The purpose of this requirement was to protect the

---

55. *Id.* Hi-Fort, Inc. v. Burnette, 42 N.C. App. 428, 257 S.E.2d 85 (1979); Supply Co. v. Nations, 259 N.C. 681, 131 S.E.2d 425 (1963).

56. McClure v. Crow, 196 N.C. 657, 146 S.E. 713 (1929); County Sav. Bank v. Tolbert, 192 N.C. 126, 133 S.E. 558 (1926); Blanton v. Bostic, 126 N.C. 418, 35 S.E. 1035 (1900).

57. County Sav. Bank v. Tolbert, 192 N.C. 126, 133 S.E. 558 (1926).

But note an exception to the requirement that all deeds must be acknowledged before they are recordable. While generally it is true that all instruments should be acknowledged by the maker in order to qualify them for registration, an attested instrument may be "proved" by the oath of a subscribing witness that the maker signed the instrument in the presence of the witness or acknowledged its execution to the witness. *See* N.C. GEN. STAT. § 47-12. If the instrument required or permitted by law to be registered has no subscribing witness, or the subscribing witness is dead, the execution of the same may be proven before any official authorized to take the proof and acknowledgment of such instrument by proof of the handwriting of the maker. *See* N.C. GEN. STAT. § 47-13; Black v. Justice, 86 N.C. 504 (1882).

58. *In re* Estate of Loftin, 285 N.C. 717, 208 S.E.2d 670 (1974); Best v. Utley, 189 N.C. 356, 127 S.E. 337 (1925).

59. Garner v. Horner, 191 N.C. 539, 132 S.E. 290 (1926).

60. N.C. GEN. STAT. § 52-6, repealed by 1977 Sess. L. c. 375, s. 1, effective January 1, 1978.

Prior to 1945, every deed of a married woman to a person other than her husband had to have a special acknowledgment called a "private examination" or "privy examination"

wife who was still presumed to be under the coercive influence of her husband.[61] Without such certificate any deed of a married woman to her husband was, in theory, void *ab initio*.[62]

North Carolina General Statutes, § 52-6 was repealed in 1977 effective January 1, 1978.[63] In its place, a new sex-neutral statute, North Carolina General Statutes, § 52-10, has been enacted. Various curative statutes also limit the effect of the former statute. North Carolina General Statutes, § 52-8, for example, reads as follows:

"Any contract between husband and wife coming within the provisions of G.S. 52-6 executed between January 1, 1930, and January 1, 1978, which does not comply with the requirement of a private examination of the wife and which is in all other respects regular is hereby validated and confirmed to the same extent as if the examination of the wife had been separate and apart from the husband. This section shall not affect pending litigation." [64]

---

before a designated officer before the deed was valid. The wife was interrogated separate and apart from her husband by the Clerk of the Superior Court, by a judge or by a justice of the peace concerning the voluntariness of her deed. A married woman's deed was not valid until this examination was made. In 1945, by General Statutes, § 47-14.1, the General Assembly of North Carolina provided that all deeds, contracts and leases made by married women to persons (other than their husbands), subsequent to 1945, are valid without the necessity of a "privy examination." The 1969 General Assembly of North Carolina completely extinguished the concept of the "privy examination" with respect to married women's deeds to persons other than their husbands. By amending General Statutes, § 39-13.1, the General Assembly has provided that "privy examinations" are not required of married women who execute deeds to persons other than their husbands, whether the deeds are executed either before or after February 7, 1945.

But a special form of examination was still required on all deeds and contracts between husband and wife under N.C. GEN. STAT. § 52-6 prior to repeal of that statute effective January 1, 1978. The form of acknowledgment was set out in § 47-39 (now repealed). Until repeal of §§ 52-6 and 47-39, an attempted conveyance by a wife to her husband, directly or indirectly, without the examination and certificate as required by those statutes, was absolutely void. *See* note 64 *infra*.

61. Butler v. Butler, 169 N.C. 584, 86 S.E. 507 (1915). *Accord,* Kanoy v. Kanoy, 17 N.C. App. 344, 194 S.E.2d 201 (1973).

62. Caldwell v. Blount, 193 N.C. 560, 137 S.E. 578 (1927); Bolin v. Bolin, 246 N.C. 666, 99 S.E.2d 920 (1957). *Accord,* Kanoy v. Kanoy, 17 N.C. App. 344, 194 S.E.2d 201 (1973).

63. 1977 Sess. L., c. 375, § 1, effective January 1, 1978.

64. *See* Spencer v. Spencer, 37 N.C. App. 481, 246 S.E.2d 805 (1978), n.2, at 37 N.C. App. 488, where the Court states:

We note that G.S. 52-6 has been repealed effective 1 January 1978. The statute has been replaced by a new sex-neutral statute, G.S. 52-10. Also, over the years, the legislature has tried to limit the damage of G.S. 52-6 by passing curative statutes such as G.S. 52-8 as it stood at the time this suit was initiated. However, like Br'er Rabbit and the Tar Baby, the legislature found itself unable to turn the wretched creature loose.

See also N.C. GEN. STAT. § 39-13.1(b) which states:

(b) Any deed, contract, conveyance, lease or other instrument executed prior to February 7, 1945, which is in all other respects regular except for the failure to take the private examination of a married woman who is a party to such deed, contract, conveyance, lease or other instrument is hereby validated and confirmed to the same extent

3. If the acknowledging officer has no official seal, acknowledgments are taken "under his hand" and no private seal is required.[65] But if the acknowledging officer has an official seal he must set his official seal to his certificate of acknowledgment.

The title attorney must carefully check any acknowledgment that is unusual or novel to determine whether it is legal under Article 3 of Chapter 47 of the North Carolina General Statutes. Likewise, any attorney who drafts acknowledgments must make sure that his acknowledgments conform in every way to that statute. Defects in acknowledgment may result in defects in recordation, which may make a title vulnerable to claims of purchasers for value and lien creditors of the grantor.

(n) *Probate.* Prior to October 1, 1967, the Clerk of the Superior Court passed on all certificates of officers who took acknowledgments prior to their recordation in the office of the Register of Deeds. Since October 1, 1967, the Register of Deeds passes on the validity of certificates of proof or acknowledgments on instruments before they are recorded.[66] If the certificate of acknowledgment is in satisfactory form the deed or instrument is "probated" and admitted to registration. Until the acknowledgment is adjudicated to be in due form, which is a judicial function, the instrument is not entitled to be recorded, and if recorded it does not constitute constructive notice to purchasers for value and lien creditors of the grantor.[67] But if a probate has been omitted, the title attorney will want to determine if a curative statute has been enacted obviating the necessity for probate in a particular instance.[68] For instance, North Carolina General Statutes, § 47-50 provides that where probate has been omitted prior to December 31, 1960, and the deed has otherwise been duly recorded, the recordation is validated.

(o) *Recordation.* In North Carolina, recordation of a deed is not necessary to the validity of a deed otherwise validly executed.[69] Recordation supplies the place of the ancient ceremony of livery of seisin,[70] and is necessary only to make a conveyance valid as against other purchasers for

---

as if such private examination had been taken, provided that this section shall not apply to any instruments now involved in any pending litigation.

In addition, see Johnson v. Burrow, 42 N.C. App. 273, 256 S.E.2d 811 (1979); Faucette v. Griffin, 35 N.C. App. 7, 239 S.E.2d 712 (1978).

65. N.C. GEN. STAT. § 47-5.
66. N.C. GEN. STAT. § 47-14.
67. *See, e.g.,* Woodlief v. Woodlief, 192 N.C. 634, 135 S.E. 612 (1926). *See* cases collected in Webster, *Toward Greater Marketability of Land Titles Remedying the Defective Acknowledgment Syndrome,* 46 N.C.L. REV. 56, at 59, n.12 (1967).
68. Various curative acts, applicable to specific situations and time periods are found in N.C. GEN. STAT. §§ 47-47 through 47-108.16.
69. Ballard v. Ballard, 230 N.C. 629, 55 S.E.2d 316 (1949); Dulin v. Williams, 239 N.C. 33, 79 S.E.2d 213 (1953).
70. N.C. GEN. STAT. § 47-17.

value of the same real property from the same grantor, or as against his lien creditors.[71]

The recordation statutes, principally North Carolina General Statutes, §§ 47-18 and 47-20, called the "Connor Act," enacted in 1885, are intended to enable purchasers to rely with safety upon examination of the records and to act upon the assurance that, as against all persons claiming under the "donor, bargainor or lessor," what does not appear does not exist.[72] These statutes are designed to remedy uncertainties of title to real estate caused by persons withholding deeds, contracts, and mortgages and liens from the public records. To that end, North Carolina has developed the strict rule that "no notice, however full or formal, will supply the want of registration of a deed."[73] Therefore, an attorney checking a title can rely on the record; if a deed or mortgage is not recorded it is deemed not to exist with respect to purchasers for value and lien creditors of the same grantor.[74] In this connection, every attorney should instruct any client that he has who is to be a grantee in a deed, deed of trust or mortgage, that if the instrument is worth taking it is worth recording! If it is not recorded properly, his grantor may either reconvey the title to a grantee for value who records *his* deed first, or his grantor may have a judgment docketed against him, or a lien perfected against him, in some other way.

North Carolina General Statutes, § 47-18 relates to the recordation of conveyances of land, contracts to convey, options to convey, and leases of land for more than three years. Section 47-25 requires all marriage settlements to be registered with respect to deeds in order to be good against purchasers for value and lien creditors. Section 47-26 requires deeds of gift to be recorded within two years or else be void as against everyone, including the grantor. Section 47-28 provides for the recordation of powers of attorney. Section 47-30 provides for the recordation of plats and subdivisions. Chapter 47, Article 3 of the North Carolina General Statutes, beginning with § 47-37, sets out the various forms of

---

71. N.C. GEN. STAT. § 47-18; Bourne v. Lay & Co., 264 N.C. 33, 140 S.E.2d 76 (1965).
72. *See* Chapter 17 *supra*.
   See also Grimes v. Guion, 220 N.C. 676, 18 S.E.2d 170 (1842).
73. Bourne v. Lay & Co., 264 N.C. 33, 140 S.E.2d 769 (1965); Patterson v. Bryant, 216 N.C. 550, 5 S.E.2d 849 (1939).
74. The title attorney must be aware, however, that certain interests are not within the purview of the recordation statutes and thus will continue to exist even as against purchasers for value and lien creditors although not recorded. For instance, leases for less than three years need not be in writing to be valid. Parol leases for less than three years from the time of the making are thus valid and need not be recorded. Consequently, the title attorney should advise his client that there may be in existence an oral lease of three years or less that does not appear of record and which continues to exist.
   In addition, certain parol trusts are valid as against persons not bona fide purchasers for value without notice even though not recorded.

acknowledgment, probate and registration. Chapter 47, Article 4 of the North Carolina General Statutes, beginning with § 47-47, sets out various curative statutes with which the title searcher must be familiar.

With respect to the recordation statutes, it should be observed that a deed is not deemed to be recorded until it is indexed and cross-indexed.[75] A deed not properly indexed and cross-indexed, although it is otherwise fully recorded, does not constitute constructive notice.[76]

Some attorneys who record instruments for their clients simply rely on the bond of the Register of Deeds to protect their clients in the event the purposes of recordation are thwarted because the Register of Deeds has failed to properly index and cross-index recorded instruments.[77] Some attorneys, however, who record instruments make it a practice to check back in the office of the Register of Deeds after leaving the instrument for recordation to determine if the instrument has been properly indexed and cross-indexed so as to complete the essentials of the recordation. Whatever the case, if a deed is actually filed for recordation but is not properly indexed, it will not take priority over a subsequently filed deed that is properly indexed if that deed was filed by a purchaser for value.

§ 466. Correction Deeds.

Although the warranty deed with general warranties is the type of deed that is most commonly used in land transactions, it should be noted that there are numerous other types of private deeds in relatively common use. For instance, correction deeds are frequently given to correct some defect in a previous conveyance. A correction deed may run between the original parties to a transaction in which an error occurred or it may run from the original grantor in the erroneous instrument to the current owner of the property. The better practice would appear to be for the grantor of the instrument in which the omission or error occurred to convey directly to the current owner. Correction deeds generally have a recital therein stating the reason for the execution of the correction deed and do not include any warranties. Correction deeds are effective to correct errors in descriptions and dates, errors in references to recorded instruments, errors in names of parties, and defects in acknowledgments, probate and the like.

---

75. N.C. GEN. STAT. § 161-22; Story v. Slade, 199 N.C. 596, 155 S.E. 256 (1930); Bank of Spruce Pine v. McKinney, 209 N.C. 668, 184 S.E. 506 (1936); Johnson Cotton Co. v. Hobgood, 243 N.C. 227, 90 S.E.2d 541 (1955).

76. *But see* Johnson Cotton Co. v. Hobgood, 243 N.C. 227, 90 S.E.2d 541 (1955), to the effect that if the index and cross-index of an instrument contain sufficient matter to put a careful and prudent examiner on inquiry, the record constitutes notice as to all matters which would have been discovered by a reasonable inquiry notwithstanding some defect in the indexing or cross-indexing.

77. *See, e.g.,* Bank of Spruce Pine v. McKinney, 209 N.C. 668, 184 S.E. 506 (1936).

Correction deeds, which should themselves be recorded, are designed to remove questions from the record of title, and when in doubt it never hurts to get a correction deed where a correctable error appears. Frequently deeds are executed and filed for recordation by persons who are unfamiliar with the principles of conveyancing and many errors occur. While most of these errors are not of any major significance with respect to the validity of land titles, the title attorney is called upon to certify that a specific land title is clear for purposes of marketability. For this reason, it is frequently advisable for the title attorney to procure correction deeds or quitclaim deeds to erase any possible question about defects which may raise questions to subsequent title examiners that may curtail the marketability of the *locus in quo.*

§ 467. Quitclaim Deeds.

The quitclaim deed is employed to release and convey all of a grantor's right, title, or interest in specific property to his grantee. A quitclaim deed's practical effect is the same as that of a warranty deed with respect to the passage of title, but there are no warranties that the grantor has any title.[78] The quitclaim deed is frequently used as a form of the correction deed to clear up possible defects in title; the grantor "quitclaims" any interest that he may retain in land by reason of a defect in a prior conveyance.

§ 468. Deeds Without Warranties.

In lieu of correction deeds or quitclaim deeds, deeds without warranties are sometimes executed as "correction" deeds. These deeds simply purport to make a conveyance but do not include any warranties.

§ 469. Corporation Deeds.

Corporate deeds comprise another class of private deeds that may appear in a chain of title to specific land. A corporation, as a legal entity, is capable of owning and conveying real property in its own name.[79]

If a conveyance of a corporation is *in the ordinary course of the corporation's business,* it will be valid if signed on behalf of the corporation by its president, a vice-president or an assistant vice president and attested or countersigned by its secretary or an assistant secretary.[80] In addition, the

---

78. Hayes v. Ricard, 245 N.C. 687, 97 S.E.2d 105 (1957).

79. *See generally* Chapter 10, § 166 *supra.*

80. N.C. GEN. STAT. § 55-36(a). A 1979 amendment adds the assistant vice president to the earlier statute. A corporation deed will fail to pass title when it is not attested by its corporate secretary. *See* J. Perry Jones Realty, Inc. v. McLamb, 21 N.C. App. 482, 204 S.E.2d 880 (1974).

corporate seal should be affixed. The forms of the acknowledgment for corporate deeds are set out in North Carolina General Statutes, § 47-41.

If a conveyance of the corporation is *not in the ordinary course of the corporation's business,* the corporation may not sell, exchange, or lease *all* or substantially all of its property unless authorized by its board of directors and approved by its shareholders as provided by statute.[81] Therefore, in checking the validity of corporate deeds it is necessary to make several determinations: (1) Does a corporation exist? Is the charter properly filed in the office of the Clerk of the Superior Court, and what powers does it give to the corporation? Has the corporation been dissolved, or was it in the process of dissolution at the time of the execution of the deed? (2) Does the corporation have the authority to make the conveyance? Did it have the authority of the board of directors or the shareholders where such is necessary under the statute? (3) Has the deed been properly executed by the proper officers and attested by the proper officer; has the corporate seal been properly affixed; has the deed been properly acknowledged pursuant to the statutes relating to corporate conveyances?

It should be noted that if the corporation has been dissolved its real property may still be conveyed by a majority of its last board of directors, then living, however reduced in number, acting directly themselves or through the last officers of the corporation.[82]

See North Carolina General Statutes, § 55-36 (a) to the effect that notwithstanding anything to the contrary in the bylaws or charter of the corporation, any deed, mortgage, contract, or other instrument executed and signed by the proper officer shall with respect to third parties be held as valid as if authorized by the board of directors, unless the instrument reveals on its face a potential breach of fiduciary obligation. North Carolina General Statutes, § 55-36 (c) also provides that deeds, mortgages, contracts, and other instruments purporting to bind the corporation, which bear a seal that purports to be the seal of the corporation, are presumed to be executed by the persons who were the officers and agents of the corporation acting by the authority of the board of directors, and that such instrument is the act of the corporation.

§ 470. Deeds of Married Persons.

(a) *In General.* Subject to certain statutory provisions,[83] every married person is authorized by North Carolina General Statutes, § 52-2 "to contract and deal so as to affect his or her real and personal property in the same manner and with the same effect as if he or she were

---

81. N.C. GEN. STAT. § 55-112 (c).
82. N.C. GEN. STAT. § 55-115 (f).
83. N.C. GEN. STAT. § 52-2 is made subject to the provisions of §§ 52-10 or 52-10.1, § 39-7, and "other regulations and limitations now or hereafter prescribed by the General Assembly."

unmarried." This was not always the case with respect to married women. With respect to deeds executed prior to 1965, married women's deeds to grantees without the joinder of their husbands were absolutely void.[84] By reason of a constitutional amendment and the passage of several statutes including the above-mentioned one,[85] with respect to deeds of conveyance executed since 1965, it is not essential to their validity for a deed from one married person to a third person to be signed by his or her spouse.[86] It should be carefully noted, however, that if both spouses' signatures are not on a deed, a nonsigning spouse has a right to assert a claim of a life interest in land conveyed by his or her spouse if he or she outlives his or her spouse, under North Carolina's statutory substitute for dower and curtesy under North Carolina General Statutes, § 29-30.

Where one married person executes a deed without the joinder of his or her spouse, attention should be given to the effect of separation agreements executed between husband and wife who agree to live separate and apart. Deeds of separation provide for the release by each spouse of all of his or her spousal rights in the real property of the other. Such releases in deeds of separation are valid under North Carolina General Statutes, § 52-10, and may be pleaded in bar of any action or proceeding with respect to the recovery of rights and estates growing out of the marriage relation. Thus, if a married couple has executed a deed of separation, one of the spouses can alone convey his real property without the joinder of the other and without the other thereafter having any claim arising out of the marital relation. It should be noted, however, that while deeds of separation are valid with respect to executed portions, such deeds of separation are invalidated and rendered null and void if the spouses who have executed the separation agreement resume living together.[87] This is true even though the deed of separation is recorded. Thus, where only one spouse has signed a deed and it is discovered that such grantor and his or her spouse have signed a deed of separation which is duly recorded, the title attorney is not safe in assuming that the deed of separation is valid and binding to release all claims of the nonsigning spouse. The title attorney is well advised to see that proper affidavits are procured to assure that the husband and wife have not become reconciled and resumed living together. If the spouses have resumed living together, the

---

84. Buford v. Mochy, 224 N.C. 234, 29 S.E.2d 729 (1944).

85. *See also* N.C. GEN. STAT. § 52-1.

86. N.C. CONST. art. X, § 6.

87. Archbell v. Archbell, 158 N.C. 408, 74 S.E. 327 (1912); Jones v. Lewis, 243 N.C. 259, 90 S.E.2d 547 (1955). *See generally* Enforcement, Modification and Termination of Voluntary Separation Agreements, C. Edwin Allman, N.C. Bar Assoc. Institute on Family Law (1977), at p. III-25, III-26.

deed of separation is rendered null and void and any releases of claims arising out of the marriage relation are negated.[88]

(b) *Deeds from Wife to Husband.* With the repeal of North Carolina General Statutes, §§ 52-6 and 47-39, the conveyancing statutes became sex-neutral. Thus no special formalities are required in a deed from wife to husband.[89]

§ 471. Deeds Conveying Estate by Entirety.

The estate by the entirety, in full force in North Carolina, is an estate which is vested in both the husband and wife. A deed conveying a tenancy by the entirety must be signed by both the husband and the wife. Upon a divorce of the husband and wife who hold an estate by the entirety, or in the event the parties execute an instrument which bars the reciprocal property rights as between the parties, tenants by the entirety become tenants in common. In such case the joinder of both parties is required to convey the whole title but either alone may convey his undivided interest without the joinder of the other.[90]

§ 472. Deeds by Attorneys in Fact.

Many parcels of land are conveyed by persons who hold powers of attorney.[91] An attorney in fact may make a valid conveyance of land if all

---

88. The reconciliation of a husband and wife after they had executed a deed of separation rendered the deed of separation null and void and created serious problems prior to 1965 because every conveyance from a married woman who had a separation agreement was subject to the possibility that she had become reconciled with her husband, rendering the separation agreement a nullity. Since a married woman's deed without the joinder of her husband could not pass any title, the potential negation of the separation agreement created a real hazard for title attorneys. Since 1965, even if the deed of separation is rendered void, its only effect will be to make the deed of an individual spouse vulnerable to a claim by the nonsigning spouse for the statutory substitute for dower or curtesy under N.C. GEN. STAT. § 29-30.

89. N.C. GEN. STAT. § 52-2.

90. *See* Davis v. Bass, 188 N.C. 200, 124 S.E. 566 (1924), which is the leading case on tenancies by the entirety in North Carolina. *See also* Lee, *Tenancy by the Entirety in North Carolina*, 41 N.C.L. REV. 67 (1962). It should be noted that *survivorship* is among the chief characteristics of the tenancy by the entirety. Upon the death of one of the spouses who hold by the entirety, the surviving spouse takes the title by survivorship as if by purchase under the original instrument by which the title by entirety was acquired; the surviving spouse can therefore convey a complete title without the joinder of any other person. Where land has been conveyed to a couple by the entirety, and only one signs the deed conveying it out, it is very important to determine if and when the other spouse died.

91. Although dealing with a procedural issue, Ellis v. Ellis, 38 N.C. App. 81, 247 S.E.2d 274 (1978) is a recent example of a deed by an attorney in fact. In this case, the husband executed a power of attorney naming his wife as attorney in fact for him. The wife, acting pursuant to the power of attorney, executed a deed to herself and her husband in order to create a tenancy by the entirety in the homeplace. The husband then died and his wife claimed the homeplace.

§ 473   REAL ESTATE LAW IN NORTH CAROLINA   § 473

legal requirements have been met, but all conveyances of an attorney in fact should be carefully scrutinized upon title searches. The power of attorney should be filed of record [92] prior to the date of the conveyance and the acknowledgment should conform to North Carolina General Statutes, § 47-43.

A conveyance may be signed in the name of the grantor or grantors by the attorney in fact. Upon a title search, if the title examiner finds a deed executed by an attorney in fact, he should determine whether the power of attorney was still in existence at the time of the execution of the deed or whether it had been revoked by the death or incompetency of the grantor.[93]

§ 473. Voluntary Deeds of Partition.

Tenants in common, for instance several heirs who inherit the land of an ancestor, often desire to partition the land among themselves. To achieve this they often execute and exchange deeds conveying specific portions of the land held in common to each other. Such deeds are not strictly conveyances in the usual sense, but they operate as a severance of the possession of the various tenants in common so that each respective tenant in common thereafter owns and possesses his respective portion in severalty.

A peculiarity with respect to voluntary partition deeds should be noted where such deed is executed by one or more tenants in common to another tenant in common "and his spouse." In view of the fact that the deed creates no new title and serves only to sever the possession, it has been held that such conveyance does not create a tenancy by the entirety in the spouses.[94] By legislative enactment in 1969,[95] however, a partition deed to one of the tenants in common and his spouse may create a tenancy by the entirety provided the intent to create a tenancy by the entirety is clearly stated in the granting clause of the deed. Since the 1969 statute specifies that the instrument must express clearly the intention to create a tenancy by the entirety where a partition deed is executed to a tenant in common and his spouse, it would appear that where there is no express intention expressed, a tenancy by the entirety will still not be created.

---

92. N.C. GEN. STAT. § 47-28.
93. A power of attorney creates an agency relationship which terminates when the principal who creates the power dies. Godwin v. Trust Co., 259 N.C. 520, 131 S.E.2d 456 (1963).
94. Smith v. Smith, 249 N.C. 669, 107 S.E.2d 530 (1959); McLamb v. Weaver, 244 N.C. 432, 94 S.E.2d 331 (1956); Combs v. Combs, 273 N.C. 462, 160 S.E.2d 308 (1968); Elledge v. Welch, 238 N.C. 61, 76 S.E.2d 340 (1955).
95. N.C. GEN. STAT. § 39-13.5.

Article III. Official Deeds

§ 474. In General.

As distinguished from private deeds, there is a large class of deeds known and designated as "official deeds." These are the deeds of persons acting not for themselves, but in some official or contractual capacity.

§ 475. Deeds by Trustees Under Deeds of Trust.

The first and most important classification of official deeds is that of "trustees' deeds." The most common form of trustees' deed is that of a trustee under a deed of trust after foreclosure by power of sale authorized by the deed of trust. A deed of trust is contractual in nature and the trustee has been given the legal title to the land involved for the benefit of the holder of the indebtedness secured by the deed of trust. Deeds of trust ordinarily contain a power of sale in the trustee in the event of a default in payment of the indebtedness secured.[96]

Trustee's deeds frequently appear in the chain of title as the result of a foreclosure of a deed of trust because of default in payment of the indebtedness secured by the deed of trust. When an attorney searching a title discovers in the chain of title a trustee's deed, he must closely examine the proceedings of the sale in order to make sure that the terms of the deed of trust and the requirements of the law have been observed.

For instance, where a trustee in a deed of trust has exercised the power of sale to foreclose, in addition to the registration of the trustee's deed in the office of the Register of Deeds, the law requires a report of the trustee to be filed in the office of the Clerk of the Superior Court in the county where the land is located. The trustee's report, filed generally in the "Orders and Decrees Book" or in a book called the "Foreclosure Book," must be examined when the title search discloses the trustee's deed. The trustee's report should reveal the affidavit of the publisher showing the proper publication of the notice of sale required by law, the proper posting of notices of the sale if the same is required, orders by the Clerk if an advance or upset bid has been filed, the report of the sale, and the report of the trustee's final account. The trustee's report should include (in addition to the notices of sale posted and published as required by statute) proofs as required by the clerk, which may be by affidavit, that notices of hearing, sale and resale, if any, were served upon all parties thereto under North Carolina General Statutes, §§ 45-21.16, 45-21.17, and 45-21.29.[97]

---

96. No power of sale exists in the trustee unless expressly authorized in the deed of trust, however. Being contractual the terms and conditions under which the power of sale is authorized must be adhered to strictly. Realty Co. v. Lewis, 212 N.C. 45, 192 S.E. 902 (1937).

97. N.C. GEN. STAT. § 45-21.33(c). The purpose of this section is to have in the files of the clerk proof that the foreclosure sale was properly conducted and that the notice was published. Britt v. Britt, 26 N.C. App. 132, 215 S.E.2d 172 (1975).

If land is sold under a power of sale in a mortgage or deed of trust, all advertising requirements set forth in the instrument must be met. In addition, the requirements of North Carolina General Statutes, § 45-21.17 must be followed. The notice of sale provided for in North Carolina General Statutes, § 45-21.16A, which must be posted and published as provided in North Carolina General Statutes, § 45-21.17, shall (1) describe the instrument pursuant to which the sale is held, by identifying the original mortgagors and recording data, and if different from the original mortgagors shall list the record owner of the property, as reflected on the records of the register of deeds not more than 10 days prior to posting the notice, who may be identified as present owners, and may reflect the owner not reflected on the records if known; (2) designate the date, hour and place of sale consistent with the provisions of the instrument and Article 2A of Chapter 45 of North Carolina General Statutes; (3) describe the real property (including improvements thereon) to be sold in such a manner as is reasonably calculated to inform the public as to what is being sold, which description may be in general terms and incorporate the description as used in the instrument containing the power of sale by reference thereto; any property described in the instrument containing the power of sale which is not being offered for sale should also be described in such a manner as to enable prospective purchasers to determine what is and what is not being offered for sale; (4) state the terms of the sale provided for by the instrument pursuant to which the sale is held, including the amount of the cash deposit, if any, to be made by the highest bidder at the sale; (5) include any other provisions required by the instrument to be included therein; and (6) state that the property will be sold subject to taxes and special assessments if it is to be so sold.

After the foreclosure sale is had and the property is bid in, the trustee must make a report to the Clerk of the Superior Court within five days.[98] If no advanced bid is filed with the clerk as permitted by the statute[99] within ten days after the filing of the report of the sale, the trustee may execute a deed to the purchaser upon receipt of the purchase price. The trustee must then file his final report as required by North Carolina General Statutes, § 45-21.33 with the Clerk of the Superior Court. If an advanced bid is filed within the ten-day period, the trustee must readvertise and resell the property as provided by statute.[100] Resales may be had as often as advance or upset bids are submitted in accordance with the statute.

---

98. N.C. Gen. Stat. § 45-21.26.
99. N.C. Gen. Stat. § 45-21.27. *See also* Carlisle v. Commodore Corp., 15 N.C. App. 650, 190 S.E.2d 703 (1972).
100. N.C. Gen. Stat. §§ 45-21.27, 45-21.29 and 1-339.27 detail procedures where there is an upset or advanced bid.

§ 475 EXAMINATION OF THE SOURCES OF TITLE § 475

No title passes to a bidder at a foreclosure sale until the trustee executes a deed to the purchaser.[101] A sale under a power of sale contained in the instrument may not be consummated by deed to the last and highest bidder less than ten days after the sale, as the period for upset bid does not elapse until then.[102]

The trustee's deed which recites all the steps taken in connection with the sale is prima facie evidence of the regularity of the execution of the power of sale.[103]

With respect to trustees' deeds in the chain of title, it should be noted that if the deed of trust gives to two or more trustees the power of sale to foreclose and one trustee dies, the power of sale devolves upon the survivor.[104]

The title searcher frequently runs into deeds made pursuant to powers of sale executed by substitute trustees necessitated because of the death, resignation or incapacity of the original trustee. Where a substitute trustee has purported to foreclose a deed of trust, the examining attorney must be careful to ascertain if the substitution of the trustee was in accordance with the provisions of the deed of trust or with North Carolina General Statutes, § 45-10.

A trustee who forecloses a deed of trust under a power of sale is required by law to make a marginal entry on the recorded deed of trust showing the fact of foreclosure, the date and the name of the purchaser.[105] It would seem, however, that failure to observe this requirement will not invalidate the title given by the trustee.[106] It has also been held that the failure to make the report of the foreclosure sale to the Clerk as required by the statute does not impair the validity of a foreclosure sale.[107]

If a federal tax lien has been filed prior to the recording of a deed of trust, the tax lien of course has priority and any title passing through a foreclosure of the deed of trust is subject to the federal tax lien. In addition, under current law, even with respect to junior federal tax liens statutory notice [108] must be given to the federal government of a proposed foreclosure sale as a condition precedent to the divestiture of a junior federal tax lien which has been filed more than thirty days prior to the date of the foreclosure sale. The applicable Internal Revenue Code regu-

---

101. Spain v. Hines, 214 N.C. 432, 200 S.E. 25 (1938).
102. Shelby Bldg. & Loan Ass'n v. Black, 215 N.C. 400, 2 S.E.2d 6 (1939).
103. Little v. Harrison, 209 N.C. 360, 183 S.E. 293 (1936); Jones v. Percy, 237 N.C. 239, 74 S.E.2d 700 (1953). *Accord,* Huggins v. DeMent, 13 N.C. App. 673, 182 S.E.2d 412 (1972).
104. N.C. GEN. STAT. § 45-8; *see* Cawfield v. Owens, 129 N.C. 286, 40 S.E. 62 (1901).
105. *See* N.C. GEN. STAT. § 45-38.
106. Cheek v. Squires, 200 N.C. 661, 158 S.E. 198 (1931).
107. Peedin v. Oliver, 222 N.C. 665, 24 S.E.2d 519 (1943). It is better for the title searcher, however, to scrutinize all documents of the trustee to see that they are regular in order that a title certified will be marketable without the requirement of litigation.
108. 26 U.S.C.A. § 7425 (b), (c).

lation [109] states, in part, that if the federal tax lien is recorded more than 30 days before the date of the foreclosure sale and the appropriate district director is not given notice of the sale,[110] then "the sale shall be subject to and without disturbing the lien of the United States." [111] If the federal tax lien is filed within thirty days of the foreclosure sale and the deed of trust has otherwise been validly recorded, the government's lien is divested upon foreclosure without any notice to the government. Of course a foreclosure sale pursuant to a lien which is junior to a tax lien does not divest the tax lien even though notice of the sale is given to the appropriate district director.[112]

There have been numerous cases in North Carolina in which the title to real property has been affected by the violation of the trust relationship in foreclosure sales. Members of the bar are generally familiar with the principles which may result in the invalidation of a conveyance of the equity of redemption by the mortgagor to the mortgagee.[113] Likewise, if the mortgagee purchases the mortgaged property at his own foreclosure sale, either in person or by agent, the sale is voidable.[114] It should be noted, however, that a creditor *cestui que trust* under a deed of trust may buy at the trustee's sale unless fraud and collusion are alleged and proved.[115]

In addition to the foregoing, where the title-searching attorney discovers in connection with a foreclosure sale that the foreclosing purchaser stands in a fiduciary relationship to the seller under foreclosure, further investigation by the title examiner is indicated. For instance, if a trustee holds a foreclosure sale and the trustee's attorney bids in at the foreclosure sale, the deed is voidable by the mortgagor or his heirs.[116] Or if the trustee's or mortgagee's agent purchases at the foreclosure sale, the deed is voidable notwithstanding that the purchase price represented the fair market value of the property at the time of the sale.[117] Any person who stands in a fiduciary relationship to property and conducts a sale with respect to such fiduciary property cannot become a purchaser or sell

---

109. I.R.C. REG. § 301.7425-2.
110. In a manner prescribed in I.R.C. REG. § 301.7425-3.
111. I.R.C. REG. § 301.7425-2.
112. *Id.*
113. Where a mortgagee buys the equity of redemption of his mortgagor, the law presumes fraud, and the burden of proof to show the bona fides of the transaction is on the mortgagee. Hinton v. West, 210 N.C. 712, 188 S.E. 410 (1936); Massengill v. Oliver, 221 N.C. 132, 19 S.E.2d 253 (1942).
114. Smith v. Land Bank, 213 N.C. 343, 196 S.E. 481 (1938).
115. DeBruhl v. Harvey & Son, 250 N.C. 161, 108 S.E.2d 469 (1959). This is perhaps one reason that the deed of trust form is preferred in North Carolina over the conventional two-party mortgage.
116. Lockridge v. Smith, 206 N.C. 174, 173 S.E. 36 (1936).
117. Davis v. Doggett, 212 N.C. 589, 194 S.E. 288 (1937).

§ 475   EXAMINATION OF THE SOURCES OF TITLE   § 475

it to another to whom he bears a fiduciary relationship; such sale is voidable. For instance, if an administrator or guardian sells land to make assets and purchases the property at his own sale, either directly or indirectly, the sale can be set aside, even in the absence of any actual fraud.[118]

Particular note should be made of the situation where the trustee of a deed of trust conducts a sale. While the *cestui que trust* may take a deed from the trustee, or buy the equity of redemption from the mortgagor, where there is no fraud or collusion, in any case where the trustee sells to himself or his agent, or to anyone with whom he has a fiduciary relationship, his conveyance may be treated as a nullity. The case of *Mills v. Building & Loan Association*[119] is an important case in point. In that case the trustee was an executive officer of the defendant Building and Loan Association. He authorized the amount of the bid, sold the land as trustee, bid it in for the defendant Building and Loan Association, and then executed a deed to said defendant which resold the land to an innocent purchaser for value. In an action for wrongful foreclosure, the court held that the plaintiff was entitled to take its case to the jury. Indicating that the foreclosure sale was voidable, the court held that since the trustee was also an executive officer of the *cestui que trust* lender as well as the selling trustee he could not exercise the position of trustee in making the foreclosure sale with the disinterested impartiality required. Thus it would appear that where the trustee in a deed of trust is also an employee, agent, or attorney of the mortgage lender, he cannot convey to the mortgage lender, since to do so would put him in a position of conflicting interests.[120] While a statute, North Carolina General Statutes, § 45-21.39, was enacted in 1941 to place a one-year statute of limitations on actions attacking foreclosures like that involved in the *Mills* case, that statute has not been extended to cover transactions since 1941 and therefore a similar foreclosure to that in the *Mills* case today might be

---

118. In Graham v. Floyd, 214 N.C. 77, 197 S.E. 873 (1938), the court states: "It has long been the law that an administrator cannot purchase property at his own sale, even in good faith, fairly and for a fair price; and that he cannot in any case make the purchase without the sanction or ratification in some sufficient way manifested by those interested. This rule is well settled and founded in reason, justice and sound policy." See Tayloe v. Tayloe, 108 N.C. 69, 12 S.E. 836 (1891); Gurganus v. McLawhorn, 212 N.C. 397, 193 S.E. 844 (1937).

See also Davis v. Doggett, 212 N.C. 589, 194 S.E. 288 (1937), which held that even though the trustor was present at the sale and made no objection, and even though the price bid was the fair market value, and even though competitive bidding was not discouraged, a sale by the trustee to his own agent was voidable.

119. 216 N.C. 664, 6 S.E.2d 549 (1939).

120. As trustee one is bound to sell to every possible advantage of both the debtor and the creditor. As the purchaser or agent for the purchaser he has an obligation to make the best deal for his principal or one to whom he owes like fiduciary duties. Hence, there is a conflict of obligations. *Compare* Smith v. Land Bank, 213 N.C. 343, 196 S.E. 481 (1938); Davis v. Doggett, 212 N.C. 589, 194 S.E. 288 (1937); Furst v. Loftin, 29 N.C. App. 248, 224 S.E.2d 641 (1976).

subject to the same attack and under the same reasoning as in the *Mills* case.[121]

While considering the effects of a fiduciary buying in at his own sale, the title attorney should also be advertent to the fiduciary relationship that exists as between tenants in common with respect to mortgages and deeds of trust. Where tenants in common are jointly liable on the mortgage obligation, one tenant in common may not acquire title to the mortgaged property by purchasing at a foreclosure sale. He cannot acquire title in himself alone, either directly or indirectly. If a co-tenant purchases, either directly or indirectly, at a foreclosure sale under a mortgage or deed of trust binding on all of the co-tenants, his purchase enures to the benefit of his co-tenants and he will be regarded as a trustee for his other co-tenants and not the sole owner of the land.[122]

§ 476. Deeds by Trustees Holding Title for Others.

Where the chain of title indicates that land has been held by one "in trust" for another, the title searcher must determine whether the trustee had authority under the trust to execute a particular deed disposing of the land. Formerly, a trustee had no authority or power to convey land held by him in trust unless authority was conferred upon him under the instrument creating the trust.[123] This rule is now modified by North Carolina General Statutes, § 43-63 which provides that when an instrument affecting title to real estate describes a party as "trustee" or "agent," but does not indicate any beneficial interest, set forth his powers, or specify some other recorded instrument that sets forth his powers, then his description as "trustee" or "agent" shall not constitute notice to anyone who deals with the real property that the person so described has limited powers nor require any inquiry or investigation with respect to such trust or agency. Pursuant to this statute, the "trustee" or "agent" shall be deemed to have full power to convey or otherwise dispose of the real estate and no person interested under such trust or agency shall be entitled to make any claim on the real estate based upon notice given by such description of a person in an instrument as "trustee" or "agent."

---

121. While a title attorney should take no chances thereon, he should be aware however that such deeds executed by the trustee to himself or to his principal are not *void;* they are simply *voidable.* Therefore, *see* Council v. Land Bank, 213 N.C. 329, 196 S.E. 483 (1939), where the court states that such sale, being voidable only, may be confirmed by any of the means by which an owner of a right in equity may part with it: (1) by release under seal; (2) such conduct as would make assertion of his right fraudulent against the purchaser or against third persons, and which would therefore operate as an estoppel against its assertion; and (3) long acquiescence after full knowledge.

122. Hatcher v. Allen, 220 N.C. 407, 17 S.E.2d 454 (1941).

123. Hall v. Wardwell, 228 N.C. 562, 46 S.E.2d 556 (1948).

Authority given in the trust instrument for a trustee to sell land does not ordinarily include the power to borrow money and execute a mortgage or deed of trust on the trust realty.[124]

Of course, if the title attorney concludes that the trust is a dry, naked, passive trust, in which case it is executed by the Statute of Uses,[125] then the *cestui que trust* can transfer legal title to the land without the necessity of joining the trustee.[126]

§ 477. Deeds by Trustees in Bankruptcy.

Another form of trustee's deed is that of a trustee in bankruptcy. Title attorneys should examine carefully the bankruptcy proceedings to see that the same were in order, as the trustee usually executes his deed to the purchaser without any warranties, conveying only the bankrupt's interest in the property. Thus deeds from trustees in bankruptcy very frequently are subject to many objections, in that they are subject to existing liens against the property.

§ 478. Deeds by Receivers.

A receiver may also give a deed to real property which has come into his hands.[127] The title attorney should carefully check all proceedings had in connection with the receivership to see that all statutes have been complied with. The sale of real estate should not be made by the receiver without an order of the court, and the sale should be confirmed by the

---

124. Shannonhouse v. Wolfe, 191 N.C. 769, 133 S.E. 93 (1926).

125. N.C. GEN. STAT. § 41-7. That the Statute of Uses does not apply to resulting or constructive trusts which arise by operation of law, *see* Greer v. United States, 448 F.2d 937 (4th Cir. 1971).

126. Without knowing the specific terms of the trust, however, the title searcher has no means of determining whether the trust is active or passive. If it is active, the Statute of Uses does not execute the legal title and the trustee must join.

See generally Webster, *Doubt Reduction Through Conveyancing Reform — More Suggestions in the Quest for Clear Land Titles,* 46 N.C.L. REV. 284, 305 (1968) for the problems caused by unrecorded trusts in the search of land titles. The statutory solution proposed by the author was enacted in 1975 as N.C. GEN. STAT. § 43-63. The statute was taken from L. SIMES & C. TAYLOR, IMPROVEMENT OF CONVEYANCE BY LEGISLATION 110 (1960).

127. N.C. GEN. STAT. § 1-505 reads as follows:

> § 1-505. **Sale of property in hands of receiver.** — In a case pending in the Superior Court Division in which a receiver has been appointed, the resident superior court judge or a superior court judge regularly holding the courts of the district shall have power and authority to order a sale of any property, real or personal, in the hands of a receiver duly and regularly appointed. In a case pending in the District Court Division in which a receiver has been appointed, the chief district judge or a district judge designated by the chief district judge to hear motions and enter interlocutory orders shall have the power and authority to order a sale of any property, real or personal, in the hands of a duly appointed receiver. Sales of property authorized by this section shall be upon such terms as appear to be to the best interests of the creditors affected by the receivership. The procedure for such sales shall be as provided in Article 29A of Chapter 1 of the General Statutes.

court. The receiver, of course, takes title subject to existing liens, and the title that he conveys on a receiver's sale is no better than that which he receives.[128] But under certain circumstances the court may permit a receiver to sell encumbered property free from liens and transfer the liens to the proceeds of the sale.[129]

§ 479. Commissioners' Deeds.

Commissioners are often appointed in civil actions and special proceedings to sell real estate in accordance with the order of the court and to make distribution of the proceeds in a manner specified. Commissioners may be appointed to sell the land of minors, to sell land for purpose of reinvestment, to sell lands of a decedent to create assets, to sell land for purposes of partitioning the proceeds, and in numerous other forms of action. The title examiner must make a careful examination of any proceeding in which a commissioner is named to sell and convey real estate. The title examiner should pay particular attention to whether all necessary parties have been duly served, especially where the rights of minors or persons *non compos mentis* are involved. The title examiner should determine whether the sale has been confirmed by the court. North Carolina General Statutes, § 1-406 requires any commissioner appointed to sell land to file his final report of the sale within sixty days after receipt of the proceeds of the sale.[130]

With respect to reports of sales under partition, the title examiner should review Chapter 46 of the North Carolina General Statutes. When a report of the commissioners in a partition sale is properly confirmed by the clerk, and when exceptions to the report are not filed within ten days of the filing of the report, the report is confirmed and will not be set aside except on grounds of fraud, collusion or mistake.[131]

---

128. Pelletier v. Greenville Lumber Co., 123 N.C. 596, 31 S.E. 855 (1898); Battery Park Bank v. Western Carolina Bank, 127 N.C. 432, 37 S.E. 461 (1900); Fisher v. Western Carolina Bank, 132 N.C. 769, 44 S.E. 601 (1903); Garrison v. Vermont Mills, 154 N.C. 1, 69 S.E. 743 (1910); Witherell v. Murphy, 154 N.C. 82, 69 S.E. 748 (1910); Whitmire v. Savings & Loan Ass'n, 23 N.C. App. 39, 208 S.E.2d 248 (1974).

129. *See* N.C. GEN. STAT. § 1-507.8. *See also* National Surety Corp. v. Sharpe, 236 N.C. 35, 72 S.E.2d 109 (1952).

130. N.C. GEN. STAT. § 46-17 with respect to reports of sales under partition. When the report is confirmed, enrolled and recorded pursuant to N.C. GEN. STAT. § 46-20, it shall be binding among and between the claimants, their heirs and assigns.

See also Dunn v. Dunn, 37 N.C. App. 159, 245 S.E.2d 580 (1978) involving a lottery to determine the allotment of separate parcels by chance and holding that two of the three commissioners could validly conduct the lottery.

131. Hewett v. Hewett, 38 N.C. App. 37, 247 S.E.2d 23 (1978). The Court of Appeals noted that although there was an allegation in conclusory terms that the clerk's confirmation of the commissioners' report itself was a mistake, there were no facts alleged or proven which would constitute mistake.

§ 480. Sheriffs' Deeds Under Execution Sales.

North Carolina General Statutes, § 1-309 provides for execution sales by sheriffs and referees appointed by the court. The sheriff or referee who holds an execution sale conveys only the interest of the judgment debtor and such sales are subject to any prior liens that may exist against the judgment debtor's interest.[132]

No execution shall issue until ten days after the rendition of judgment.[133] Publication requirements and posted notice requirements as set forth in North Carolina General Statutes, § 1-339.52 should be complied with.[134] In addition to the advertisement and posted notice requirements, at least ten days before the sale the sheriff must, according to statute, serve notice on the judgment defendant if he can be found in the county.[135] The property then must be sold in the county where all or a part of the land is situated on any day of the week or month except Sunday, with hours of sale as designated in North Carolina General Statutes, § 1-339.60. Execution sales are subject to upset bids and resales as provided in §§ 1-339.64 to 1-339.66 of the North Carolina General Statutes. No execution sale may be consummated until it is confirmed by the Clerk of the Superior Court, and the Clerk cannot confirm the sale until the time for upset bids has expired.[136] Upon the Clerk's confirmation, the sheriff is obligated to tender and deliver a duly executed deed to the execution purchaser.[137]

---

132. N.C. GEN. STAT. § 1-339.68 (b).
133. N.C. GEN. STAT. § 1-310.
134. *See however* Mordecai v. Speight, 14 N.C. 428 (1832); McIntire v. Durham, 29 N.C. 151 (1846); and Burton v. Spiers, 92 N.C. 503 (1885), which construe a former statute relating to advertisement of execution sales and which cases held that such requirements were only directory; that a purchaser at an execution sale is not bound to look further than to see that the sale was made by an officer empowered to sell under an execution issued from a court of competent jurisdiction and that such purchaser is not affected by irregularities in advertising. But if the purchaser has notice of an irregularity in advertising, the sale may be set aside at the instance of the judgment defendant.
135. N.C. GEN. STAT. § 1-339.54. This section has been held to be merely directory and will not render the sale void as against a stranger who has no notice of the failure to give the judgment defendant the required notice. *See* Walston v. Applewhite & Co., 237 N.C. 419, 75 S.E.2d 138 (1953).
136. N.C. GEN. STAT. § 1-339.67. *Accord,* Questor Corp. v. DuBose, 46 N.C. App. 612, 265 S.E.2d 501 (1980).
137. N.C. GEN. STAT. § 1-339.68. *See* Questor Corp. v. DuBose, 46 N.C. App. 612, 265 S.E.2d 501 (1980) rejecting as a collateral attack an action in superior court to declare an execution sale and sheriff's deed void because the defendant-bidders did not pay their bid in cash but had, instead, cancelled judgments against the property owner. The Court of Appeals, at 46 N.C. App. 614, states:

> Plaintiffs cannot avoid the execution sale by collateral attack; they must proceed directly, either by motion in the cause or appeal. *Williams v. Dunn,* 163 N.C. 206, 79 S.E. 512 (1913); *Henderson v. Moore,* 125 N.C. 383, 34 S.E. 446 (1899). The proper remedy to set aside an execution or a sale thereunder is by motion in the cause and not by independent action. *Henderson County v. Osteen,* 292 N.C. 692, 235 S.E. 2d 166

§ 481. Guardians' Deeds.

Under certain circumstances, a guardian may sell or mortgage the property of his ward and give a deed therefor. While guardians' deeds are rare, this constitutes another form of "official deed" which the title attorney may need to pass on.

North Carolina General Statutes, § 33-31 sets out the procedures for selling or mortgaging the real property of a ward. The guardian must file a vertified petition showing that the interests of the ward will be promoted by the sale or mortgage of his property in a special proceeding. The court may grant permission to the guardian to sell or mortgage the ward's property after making appropriate findings of necessity and that it is to the best interest of the ward. No conveyance or mortgage of the ward's property will be valid without the approval of the judge of the Superior Court.[138]

§ 482. Executors' and Administrators' Deeds.

Under certain circumstances, executors and administrators may make deeds and convey title to a decedent's lands. If a will devises lands to an executor to be sold by him with directions to distribute the proceeds in a certain way, the executor may of course sell the land, subject to the outstanding debts and any liens existing against the decedent. If the power and authority to sell is given to more than one executor and any one or more refuses to administer after qualifying, shall die, resign, or for any cause be removed from the position of executor, the surviving executor or executors retain the burden of administration and may sell the land.[139] If the testator devises land and empowers his executor to convey the land but fails to name an executor or provides that his land shall be sold by his personal representative for the benefit of his estate, his administrator *cum testamento annexo* can exercise the power of sale.[140]

An administrator of a decedent's estate may sell the decedent's real property only if he obtains permission of the Superior Court of the county where the land is situated. In the administration of estates prior to October 1, 1975, a decedent's personal property had to be subjected to

---

(1977); *Finance Co. v. Trust Co.*, 213 N.C. 369, 196 S.E. 340 (1938). Where the proceeding complained of is before the clerk, the additional remedy of appeal to the superior court judge is available. N.C. Gen. Stat. 1-272.

138. Pike v. Wachovia Bank & Trust Co., 274 N.C. 1, 161 S.E.2d 453 (1968); Ipock v. Bank, 206 N.C. 791, 175 S.E. 127 (1934); Morton v. Pine Lumber Co., 178 N.C. 163, 100 S.E. 322 (1919); *In re* Dickerson, 111 N.C. 108, 15 S.E. 1025 (1892).

139. Former N.C. GEN. STAT. § 28-97, referred to in the first edition, was repealed effective October 1, 1975. Other statutes continuing the principle of survivorship of powers in surviving co-executors and joint personal representatives were enacted. *See, e.g.,* N.C. GEN. STAT. § 28A-13-9.

140. *See* N.C. GEN. STAT. §§ 28A-13-8 and 28A-17-1 *et seq.* to the same effect.

payments of his debts or claims against the estate before resort could be made to his real property. Subsequent to October 1, 1975, pursuant to North Carolina General Statutes, §§ 28A-15-1 and 28A-17-1, all types of property of a decedent, both real and personal, equitable as well as legal, are deemed assets available for the discharge of debts and other claims against the estate of the decedent, without restriction. It is no longer essential for the personal property of the decedent to be exhausted prior to resort to his real property to pay decedent's debts or other claims against his estate. Since October 1, 1975, when North Carolina General Statutes, § 28-81 was repealed and Chapter 28A of the North Carolina General Statutes became effective with respect to the administration of decedents' estates, the personal representative of a decedent may make a determination concerning what property of decedent shall be sold, leased, pledged, mortgaged or exchanged for the purpose of paying the debts of the decedent and other claims against the estate. The personal representative shall select the assets which in his judgment are calculated to promote the best interests of the estate. In the absence of a contrary provision in a will, specifying that personal property shall be first resorted to, the personal representative of a decedent may bring a special proceeding before the Clerk of the Superior Court to have a decedent's real property sold to pay the decedent's debts or claims against his estate.[141] The petition to sell real estate shall include a statement that the personal representative has determined that it is in the best interest of the administration of the estate to sell the real estate.[142]

§ 483. Tax Deeds.

A tax title differs from a title derived through ordinary sources in that it is not dependent on previous links in the chain of title. A tax title, on the contrary, is a new title independent of previous links, and a tax deed executed at the conclusion of the legal procedure for perfecting it serves to eliminate the rights of all previous parties in interest, including homestead and spousal rights, the rights of mortgagees and holders of easements.

Since a tax deed does destroy all previous interests in the land, the courts of North Carolina have been astute to require strict compliance with with all statutory procedures in order to make sure that no owner is deprived of title to his property without due process of law. Consequently the lawyer whose title rests on a tax deed must be advertent to the fact that North Carolina courts frequently strike down tax titles for defects which ordinarily would not invalidate private deeds.

The statutory procedures for the foreclosure of a tax lien and the

---

141. N.C. GEN. STAT. §§ 28A-15-1, 28A-17-1, 28A-17-2. *See generally* Aycock, *Article 17 — Sales, Leases or Mortgages of Real Property,* 11 WAKE FOREST L. REV. 35 (1975).
142. N.C. GEN. STAT. § 28A-17-2.

making of a tax deed must be followed precisely. For that reason, tax titles are looked upon by title attorneys with great distrust and suspicion. In the past, title insurance companies did not generally insure titles which were solely dependent upon the validity of a tax foreclosure. Present day competition among title companies has altered the former approach, and, depending on all of the circumstances involved, affirmative title coverage over this possible cloud on title is normally possible assuming that the tax foreclosure appears regular from the records.

Even though it may be possible to insure over any possible problem, the title attorney should remain wary of tax titles. Since there are so many potential flaws in tax forclosures that may result in the invalidation of a particular tax deed, the title attorney should perhaps presume the title to be bad until the contrary is proved. For instance, tax forclosure sales have been held invalid because the property foreclosed was not properly listed, because there was an improper publication of the notice of the tax sale,[143] because the land was listed for taxes in the name of a person other than the true owner,[144] and because the property sold under the tax deed was not sufficiently described in the listing.[145]

Before any title attorney attempts to pass on the validity of a tax title for any purpose, he should by all means make a meticulous examination of Chapter 105 of the General Statutes. He should scrutinize carefully the many cases which have held that irregularities of the slightest sort are sufficient to invalidate a title derived from a tax foreclosure. It may be imperative to obtain collateral deeds from potential outstanding claimants in order to perfect titles that may be otherwise held defective and in order to make a particular title marketable.

Article IV. Other Sources of Title

§ 484. Title by Devise.

(a) *Determination if property passed by will.* Frequently the title-searching attorney cannot locate the next preceding link in the chain of title by employing the grantee books in the office of the Register of Deeds. After discovering that he cannot locate the deed in the indexes of conveyances in the Register of Deeds' office, the title searcher will go to the office of the Clerk of the Superior Court where he will check indexes to determine if the property passed by will. The Clerk's office maintains cross-indexes to wills in both the names of devisors and devisees. In most cases where one cannot discover the next preceding link in a chain of title,

---

143. Buncombe County v. Penland, 206 N.C. 299, 173 S.E. 609 (1934); Annas v. Davis, 40 N.C. App. 51, 252 S.E.2d 28 (1979); Henderson County v. Osteen, 292 N.C. 692, 235 S.E.2d 166 (1977).

144. Wake County v. Faison, 204 N.C. 55, 167 S.E. 391 (1933).

145. Johnston County v. Stewart, 217 N.C. 334, 7 S.E.2d 708 (1940); Craven County v. Parker, 194 N.C. 561, 140 S.E. 155 (1927).

if the property has passed by will it can be discovered by looking up the name of the grantor in the deed that constitutes the last discoverable link in the chain of title in the "devisee" index. The indexes will refer the title searcher to the book and page number where a complete copy of the will and of the certificate of probate are recorded. Once it is determined that the title came to a grantor by will, the title attorney must make several further determinations.

(b) *Sufficiency of will.* For an attested will to pass title to land it must be in writing and signed by the testator, or in his presence and at his direction by another, and subscribed by at least two witnesses, who sign in the presence of the testator although not necessarily in the presence of each other;[146] or, pursuant to a statute passed in 1977,[147] an attested will may be self-proving by the acknowledgment of the testator and by affidavits of the witnesses. Both acknowledgment and affidavits must be made before an officer authorized to administer oaths under the laws of North Carolina.[148]

Land may also pass by a holographic will that meets the statutory requirements.[149] A holographic will must be written entirely in the handwriting of the testator and must be found among the valuable papers of the testator, in a safe deposit box, with a person, firm or corporation, or in some other safe place where deposited by the testator or under his authority for safekeeping. A holographic will does not require any attesting witness.[150]

(c) *Competency of testator to make will.* — The title attorney must determine whether the testator was of sufficient age to make a will, as North Carolina General Statutes, § 31-1 requires a single person to be eighteen years of age in order for his will to be valid. Whether one is the requisite age at the time he makes his will must be discovered *dehors* the records and may require an affidavit for future reference.

(d) *Witnesses to will.* North Carolina law requires two competent witnesses to sign an attested will. The testator must signify to the attesting witnesses that the instrument is his will by signing it in their presence

---

146. N.C. GEN. STAT. § 31-3.3. *In re* Will of Weston, 38 N.C. App. 564, 248 S.E.2d 359 (1978).
147. N.C. GEN. STAT. § 31-11.6.
148. *Id. See also* N.C. GEN. STAT. § 31-18.1, "Manner of probate of attested will."
149. N.C. GEN. STAT. § 31-3.4.
150. For a holographic will to be probated, however, it is essential that three competent witnesses give testimony that they believe the will is written entirely in the handwriting of the testator. The testimony of one witness as to where the will was found is sufficient. *See* N.C. GEN. STAT. § 31-18.2. Witnesses testifying with respect to holographic wills must first be shown to be familiar with the testator's handwriting and signature. Such witnesses may then testify that the will is written entirely in the handwriting of the testator and that the testator's name appearing in or on or subscribed to the will is in his handwriting. *See In re* Will of Loftin, 24 N.C. App. 435, 210 S.E.2d 897 (1975).

or by acknowledging his signature to them. The attesting witnesses must sign the will in the presence of the testator, but they need not sign in the presence of each other.[151] An executor is a competent witness,[152] and beneficiaries under a will are competent witnesses, but if beneficiaries are witnesses neither they nor their spouses shall take anything under the will that they witness unless there are two other disinterested witnesses.[153] With respect to holographic wills, however, see North Carolina General Statutes, § 31-10 (b), which provides that a beneficiary under a holographic will may testify to competent, material and relevant facts as tend to establish the holographic will as a valid will without rendering void the benefits to be received by the witness-beneficiary.

(e) *Devising clause; description of land; designation of devisee.* The devising clause of the will should be carefully scrutinized to determine that there is no doubt that the devisor intended to devise the land in question to the devisee. The property should be described with sufficient accuracy and certainty to enable the property to be identified and connected with the chain of title. A metes and bounds description is not necessary, however, and parol evidence can often be admitted to identify the property.[154] The devisee should also be named with sufficient certainty so as to leave no question with respect to the identity of the devisee.[155]

(f) *The date and manner of probate.* In order to pass title to land a will must be probated and recorded.[156] There is no time limit upon the probate of a will, and when it is properly probated it relates back to the death of the testator and passes title as of that time.[157]

It should be noted, however, that the probate and registration of any will shall not affect the rights of innocent purchasers for value from the heirs at law of the testator when such purchase is made more than two years after the death of such testator, or when the purchase is made after the filing of the final account of the duly authorized administrator of the decedent and the approval of such final account by the Clerk of the Superior Court having jurisdiction of the estate.[158]

---

151. N.C. GEN. STAT. § 31-3.3.
152. N.C. GEN. STAT. § 31-9.
153. N.C. GEN. STAT. § 31-10. *See* Vester v. Collins, 101 N.C. 114, 7 S.E. 687 (1888).
154. Of course a title searcher should be reluctant to certify any title whose description is dependent on evidence *aliunde.*
155. Again, if evidence *aliunde* is required to establish the identity of a grantee in the case of ambiguity, the title searcher will not desire to certify a title dependent on the ambiguous will prior to a lawsuit determining the question. While the title may be good, its marketability will be affected until a lawsuit is concluded.
156. N.C. GEN. STAT. § 31-29.
157. Steadman v. Steadman, 143 N.C. 345, 55 S.E. 784 (1906).
158. N.C. GEN. STAT. § 31-39. If the will has been lost, stolen or fraudulently suppressed, and an action is brought within two years from the death of the testator to obtain the will

When a will is offered for probate, the Clerk of the Superior Court must take in writing the proofs and examinations of the witnesses and must embody the substance of such proofs and examinations in his certificate of probate, which certificate must be recorded with the will.[159] The manner of probate is set out in North Carolina General Statutes, §§ 31-18.1 through 31-18.3. The recorded will should show that it has been probated in accordance with the statute. Once a will is probated in a manner that is regular on its face, it is conclusive evidence of the validity of the will until vacated on appeal or declared void by a competent court.[160] If the purported probate was improper, the defect may be cured, subject to the rights of intervening bona fide purchasers of the land for value by a new, proper probate, regardless of how long a time has elapsed.[161]

Where the land lies in another county from the one in which the will was probated, there must be recorded in the county where the land lies a certified copy of the will and the certificate of probate in order to make out a record title in the county where the land lies.[162]

North Carolina General Statutes, § 31-22 provides for the certification of a will probated in another state or country. Section 31-23 provides for probate of wills made out of state and for the appointment of a commissioner to take the examination of witnesses touching the execution of wills in order that the same may be probated in the county where the land lies. Section 31-24 provides for the examination of nonresident witnesses before notaries public in order that the will may be probated. Section 31-25 gives to the Clerk of the Superior Court of one county the power to subpoena witnesses outside the county where the land lies to prove the will and to issue commissions where necessary to take depositions of nonresident witnesses. Section 31-27 provides for the recording of certified copies of wills probated in other jurisdictions.[163]

---

or to establish the same according to law, then an innocent purchaser for value shall not get good title before the termination of such action or proceeding. *See* N.C. GEN. STAT. § 31-12. *Compare* N.C. GEN. STAT. § 28A-17-12, relating to the protection of creditors when heirs or devisees make conveyances before estates are fully administered.

159. N.C. GEN. STAT. § 31-17.
160. N.C. GEN. STAT. § 31-19. *See* Morris v. Morris, 245 N.C. 30, 95 S.E. 110 (1956), to the effect that if the decree of probate on its face shows that the will was not probated as required by mandatory applicable statutes, N.C. GEN. STAT. § 31-19 does not apply and the probate is void. *Accord,* Jones v. Warren, 274 N.C. 166, 161 S.E.2d 467 (1968).
161. Steadman v. Steadman, 143 N.C. 345, 55 S.E. 784 (1906).
162. N.C. GEN. STAT. § 31-20.
163. A will executed in another state which contains a devise of real estate in North Carolina shall be valid to pass title to real estate in North Carolina provided the will is executed according to the laws of North Carolina, notwithstanding that said will was not probated in accordance with the laws of North Carolina. The will probated outside of North Carolina, however, has no efficacy to pass property within North Carolina until probated in North Carolina on a certified exemplified copy of the will. *See In re* Mark's Will, 259 N.C. 326, 130 S.E.2d 673 (1963).

§ 484

(g) *Caveats to wills.* A title examiner, when he discovers a will in his chain of title, should determine whether a caveat has been filed with respect to any will in question, the validity of which is necessary to the validity of a particular title.

If a will has been probated in "common form," [164] it is subject to "caveat" by any person who has a pecuniary interest that will be adversely affected by the probate of the will. A "caveat" challenges the validity of the instrument that purports to be a will. North Carolina has a statute of limitations that provides that a caveat must be filed within three years of the probate of the will, except that if the person entitled to file a caveat was at the time of the probate of the will either under eighteen years of age, insane or imprisoned he may file a caveat at any time within three years after such disability is removed.[165] If the will has been probated in "solemn form," [166] wherein notice has been given to interested parties to see the probate proceedings, no caveat can thereafter be brought by any person who has been given notice of the proceedings.[167] A probate in "solemn form" can come about in two ways: (1) where the propounder petitions the Clerk to issue notices (or citations) to all interested parties to "come and see" the probate proceedings, at which time they can challenge the validity of the will; [168] or (2) where the will has been probated in common form and an interested person files a caveat to the will which raises the issue of *devisavit vel non* to determine whether or not the instrument offered is the decedent's will. When the issue of *devisavit vel non* is raised, the Clerk must transfer the issue to the civil issue docket for trial by jury.[169] When a caveat is filed, the caveator shall

---

164. A probate in "common form" is an *ex parte* proceeding based on the oath of witnesses or propounders that an instrument is the last will and testament of the decedent. No one appears before the Clerk of the Superior Court but the propounders and/or witnesses, and the Clerk simply admits the instrument to probate without question. The proceeding is deemed an *in rem* proceeding and admission of the will to probate is conclusive as to the validity of the will unless it is set aside in a direct proceeding. No notice need be given to any person when the probate is in common form.

165. N.C. GEN. STAT. § 31-32. *In re* Will of Joyner, 35 N.C. App. 666, 242 S.E.2d 213 (1978).

166. For a description of probate in "solemn form," *see* Redmond v. Collins, 15 N.C. 430 (1834). *See also* 2 MORDECAI, LAW LECTURES 1211-1213 (1916).

167. Any person not given notice or citation to appear at probate in solemn form is not estopped to assert a caveat. *In re* Will of Cox, 254 N.C. 90, 118 S.E.2d 17 (1960).

168. Where interested parties raise no issues of fact after being given notice of a probate in solemn form, the Clerk may probate the will in solemn form without the necessity of a verdict of a jury. *See* N.C. GEN. STAT. § 1-273; *In re* Will of Ellis, 235 N.C. 27, 69 S.E.2d 25 (1951).

169. *In re* Will of Roediger, 209 N.C. 470, 184 S.E. 74 (1936); *In re* Will of Morrow, 234 N.C. 365, 67 S.E.2d 279 (1951). *See In re* Will of Mucci, 287 N.C. 26, 213 S.E.2d 207 (1976), which holds that once a caveat is filed and the proceeding to probate is transferred to Superior Court for trial there can be no probate except by a jury's verdict. The trial court

cause notice of the caveat proceeding to be given to all devisees, legatees, or other persons in interest in the manner provided for service of process by North Carolina General Statutes, § 1A-1, Rule 4 (j) and (k). The notice shall advise such devisees, legatees, or other persons in interest, of the session of Superior Court to which the proceeding has been transferred and shall call upon them to appear and make themselves proper parties to the proceeding if they so choose.[170]

When a caveat is filed, the Clerk of the Superior Court must enter upon the book and page number where the probated will is recorded a notice that the caveat has been filed, the date of the caveat, and the result of the proceeding had thereon.[171] When a caveat is filed, all further proceedings with respect to the testator's property are suspended until the status of the will is decided by the court, except that such proceedings as are necessary to preserve the property, collect the debts, and to pay the taxes and debts that constitute a lien on the property may be continued.[172]

(h) *Status of titles conveyed by heirs and devisees before the estate has been fully administered.* If the first publication or posting of the general notice to creditors provided for in North Carolina General Statutes, § 28A-14 occurs within two years after the death of the decedent, all sales, leases or mortgages of real property by the heirs or devisees of any resident or nonresident decedent made after the death of the decedent and before the first publication or posting of the general notice to creditors shall be void as to creditors and personal representatives. All sales, leases or mortgages of real property by the heirs or devisees of any resident or nonresident decedent made after such first publication or posting and before approval of the final account shall be void as to creditors and personal representatives unless the personal representative joins in the sale, lease or mortgage and the transaction is approved by the Clerk of the Superior Court. Approval of the Clerk must appear in the deed, lease or mortgage, accompanied by a statement that he has made a finding that the transaction will not prejudice the payment of any valid claim against the estate. In the event the first publication or posting of the general notice to creditors as provided for in North Carolina General Statutes, § 28A-14-1 does not occur within two years after the death of the decedent, all sales, leases or mortgages of real property by heirs or devisees of any resident or nonresident decedent shall be valid as to creditors and personal representatives of the decedent.[173]

---

may not, at least where there are factual issues, resolve those issues even by consent and adjudge that the disposition in question is testamentary and entitled to probate as a matter of law.

170. N.C. GEN. STAT. § 31-33.
171. N.C. GEN. STAT. § 31-37.
172. N.C. GEN. STAT. § 31-36.
173. *See generally* Aycock, *Article 17 — Sales, Leases or Mortgages of Real Property*, 11 WAKE FOREST L. REV. 35, 38 (1975).

§ 485. Title by Descent.

Frequently the title-searching attorney cannot locate the next preceding link in the chain of title either in the index of grants in the Register of Deeds' office or in the index of wills in the office of the Clerk of the Superior Court. He may learn by a process of elimination or by independent investigation that the title passed by intestacy or inheritance. If the title examiner has no independent information it may be difficult for the thread of title to be located, even if it is properly recorded. For instance, the records relating to the administration of decedents' estates are generally indexed in the office of the Clerk of the Superior Court only in the name of the decedent and in the name of the decedent's administrator. There is no index of heirs of a decedent. Thus, if a last discoverable deed came from a grantee who was an heir of a decedent, it will not necessarily be discoverable in the index to decedents' estates unless the particular heir happened also to be the decedent's administrator. Collateral additional information is frequently necessary to discover that an estate passed to a particular person as heir by intestate succession.

Once the fact of intestacy is determined, the title examiner must examine the records of administration in the office of the Clerk of Superior Court to ascertain that a particular grantor was an heir to whom the land descended under the laws of inheritance.[174] The title attorney must satisfy himself that the recital in the records of administration that specific persons were heirs is correct. This can usually be accomplished by obtaining an affidavit from some reliable citizen in the community who knew the intestate and his family, the affidavit showing that the specified persons survived the decedent and became his heirs. That a particular person took title by descent is established by the record and is substantiated by collateral affidavit. The title attorney must be very careful to see that he has accounted for every heir's interest in such case in order that he will not end up purchasing some undisclosed heir's interest at a premium price to make his certified title good.

The title searcher must determine if the estate of the decedent has been finally settled. The record of appointment of the personal representative, the record of the personal representative's accounts, his final settlement of all debts against the decedent's estate, and all other proceedings entered with respect to the decedent's estate, should be checked where they are indexed, cross-indexed and recorded in the office of the Clerk of the Superior Court. The title examiner must make sure that all statutory requirements have been met to pass the legal title free and unencumbered to the heir in question. These facts should all be abstracted, as they

---

174. *See* N.C. Gen. Stat. ch. 29.

constitute a link in the chain of title where property has passed to a particular grantor by inheritance.

With respect to title by descent, North Carolina General Statutes, § 28A-17-12, relating to the validity of conveyances by heirs and devisees prior to the complete administration of estates, should be kept in mind.[175] Conveyances by heirs of a decedent within two years before the publication or posting of the general notice to creditors shall be void. Conveyances made by heirs of a decedent after publication or posting of the general notice to creditors, but before approval of the final account of the personal representative, shall be void unless the conveyance is joined by the personal representative and unless the transaction discloses that the conveyance was made pursuant to a finding by the Clerk of the Superior Court that the transaction will not prejudice the payment of any valid claim against the estate and the Clerk approves of the transaction.

In the event the first publication or posting of the general notice to creditors does not occur within two years after the death of the decedent, all sales, leases and mortgages of real property by the heirs of any decedent shall be valid as to creditors of the deceased.

§ 486. Unrecorded Deeds; Title by Adverse Possession.

If the title examiner cannot trace the passage of title by deed, by devise, or by intestate succession, he will run out of record sources of title and cannot proceed until additional information is procured. By investigations independent of the records he may discover that a grantor in the chain of title has taken title by deed but failed to record it. Rather frequently it is discovered that a properly executed deed, regular in every respect, has simply not been put on record. In such cases the title examiner can often procure the deed and have it recorded to make out the continuous chain of title.[176]

If no other source of title can be located, the title examiner may conclude after investigation that the property has been acquired by adverse possession by a particular grantor. While title to land can be acquired by adverse possession, either after the expiration of seven years where there is color of title [177] or after the expiration of twenty years where there is no color of title,[178] title attorneys should never certify a title purely on the basis of adverse possession. A title attorney certifies only "record title" and not matters collateral to the records. With respect

---

175. N.C. GEN. STAT. § 28A-17-12.
176. Special care must be taken in such cases to check closely for "out" conveyances and potential liens against the next preceding grantor of the unrecorded deed during the period between the time the deed was executed and the time that it was placed on the records and properly indexed.
177. N.C. GEN. STAT. § 1-38.
178. N.C. GEN. STAT. § 1-39.

to title by adverse possession, the title is not marketable since there is the ever present possibility of lawsuits, in which case the person who claims to have perfected title by adverse possession must bear the burden of proving all of the elements required for the acquisition of title by adverse possession, and he may or may not be successful, depending on the findings of the trier of facts. Thus title attorneys should never chance certifying any title dependent on adverse possession.

If a title is acquired by adverse possession, however, it can become a matter of record by the claimant bringing an action against the former owner in an action to quiet title under North Carolina General Statutes, § 41-10 in cases where the adverse claimant prevails.

§ 487. Title by Judgment of Court of Record.

Title to land may be passed by a judgment of a court of record having jurisdiction, wherein the court determines that title shall be transferred from one party to another.[179]

---

179. N.C. Gen. Stat. §§ 1A-1, Rule 70, and 1-228.

CHAPTER 24

OBJECTIONS TO TITLE

§ 488. Defects Disclosed by Records Must Be Noted.
§ 489. Prior Conveyances.
§ 490. Easements of Record.
§ 491. Mortgages and Deeds of Trust.
§ 492. Judgments.
§ 493. Mechanics' Liens.
§ 494. Security Interests in Fixtures Under the Uniform Commercial Code.
§ 495. Repeal of Liens Arising from Assistance to the Aged and Disabled.
§ 496. Liens to Recipients of Ambulance Service Provided by County or Municipality.
§ 497. Lis Pendens.
§ 498. County and Municipal Taxes.
§ 499. State Taxes.
§ 500. Federal Tax Liens.
§ 501. Assessments for Local Improvements.
§ 502. Zoning Ordinances.
§ 503. Restrictive Covenants.
§ 504. Leases, Contracts of Sale, Options, Rights of First Refusal with Respect to Land.
§ 505. Party Wall Agreements.
§ 506. Possibilities of Reverter and Rights of Entry; Reversionary Interests.
§ 507. Parol, Resulting and Constructive Trusts.

§ 488. Defects Disclosed by Records Must Be Noted.

After the chain of title has been run, the title-searching attorney, in checking the "out" or "adverse" conveyances against all parties in the chain for the respective periods during which they purportedly held the land, may find that the records disclose various defects in the title. These defects must be noted as they may constitute the basis for objections on the part of a prospective purchaser or lender who may refuse to take the proffered title. Some of the more common title defects or objections are set forth in this chapter.

§ 489. Prior Conveyances.

The title searcher must determine that no party in the chain of title has conveyed the *locus in quo* outside the chain of title during the time that he held the land in such a way as to defeat the title of the present purported owner. As discussed previously, this is determined by searching each prior owner in the "Grantor Index" for the period of time between the time that each respective owner took title and the time when he conveyed it to the next successive owner in the chain of title being searched.

The description must be carefully checked in each conveyance out of any party in the chain of title to verify that no part of the *locus in quo* has been conveyed away, or, if it has been, that it has been reconveyed to the granting party so that it is still in the chain of title. Careful note must be made that a description may be in different words and figures from those in a previous conveyance but that it may describe the same tract of land as described differently in a previous conveyance. If the property, or any part of it, has been previously conveyed away by any party in the chain of title, the title searcher's abstract of title and certificate should note the fact and its effect.

§ 490. Easements of Record.[1]

The title searcher may find an instrument that has subjected the *locus in quo* to an easement. Grantees of course take title to lands subject to duly recorded easements that have been granted by their predecessors in title.[2] Frequently easements that have been granted with respect to telephone and electric lines, pipe and water lines, or for the joint use of alleys or ways for the benefit of adjoining lands, create no problems of title as they are quite common and are necessary for the utilization of the land. Each easement granted out should be noted, however, in order that the prospective purchaser or lender may know the nature and quality of the title that he is taking. Easements for sewer lines, high voltage electrical transmission lines, gas pipelines, light and air, and easements which provide for the lateral support for adjoining land or buildings, may seriously impair the value of a title and therefore all instruments granting easements with respect to the *locus in quo* must be carefully studied, noted and reported in the title certificate.

§ 491. Mortgages and Deeds of Trust.

(a) *Generally.* The most frequent type of conveyance that a former owner may have made with respect to land while he owned it is the mortgage or deed of trust to secure loans from time to time. Mortgages and deeds of trust are indexed in the "Grantor Index" in the same manner as deeds. Any mortgage or deed of trust which describes the land for which the title search is being made executed by the owner of the land during the period of his ownership must be carefully abstracted and studied in order to determine if it creates a defect in title or outstanding encumbrance. Complete notes should be collected with respect to the mortgage or deed of trust including any marginal notations thereon. Conclusions must be drawn as to whether the mortgage or deed of trust constitutes a viable claim or lien against the land. If the attorney searching the title discovers that the land in which he is interested is in fact described in a

---

1. It should be observed that certain easements are valid against purchasers and lenders although not of record. Implied easements which do not arise from express grant, easements of necessity, and easements by prescription are some which are not discoverable from the record but which shall continue to exist notwithstanding that the land to which they are appurtenant is conveyed.
2. Hensley v. Ramsey, 283 N.C. 714, 199 S.E.2d 1 (1973).

mortgage or deed of trust, several possibilities occur with respect to the status of the title. These are discussed in the following subsections.

(b) *Cancellations.* The title searcher may find that the mortgage or deed of trust has been properly cancelled of record and that the encumbrance has been extinguished in which case it no longer constitutes a defect of title. It should be observed, however, that not every cancellation is a *proper* cancellation. Numerous cases have been litigated with respect to irregular cancellations.

A mortgage or deed of trust can be cancelled in either of the following ways:

(1) *"Personal" cancellations.* Pursuant to North Carolina General Statutes, § 45-37 (a) (1), a trustee, mortgagee, or the legal representative or attorney of either, may personally acknowledge to the Register of Deeds that the mortgage or deed of trust has been satisfied. Upon such personal acknowledgment by such trustee, mortgagee, legal representative or attorney of the trustee or mortgagee, the Register of Deeds shall make an entry of such acknowledgment of satisfaction on the margin of the mortgage or deed of trust which shall be signed by the trustee, mortgagee, legal representative or attorney and which shall be witnessed by the Register of Deeds. This is called "personal cancellation" and the terms of the statute must be followed strictly. It should be noted that by the terms of the statute neither the *cestui que trust* of a deed of trust nor his legal representative can make a valid cancellation. See, however, North Carolina General Statutes, § 45-37.1, which provides that cancellations by deed of trust beneficiaries prior to January 1, 1930 are validated.

(2) *"Exhibition" cancellations.* North Carolina General Statutes, § 45-37 (a) (2) provides for "exhibition cancellation" of mortgages and deeds of trust. This section provides that the Register of Deeds may make an entry of satisfaction of a mortgage or deed of trust upon exhibition of the mortgage or deed of trust and all notes or bonds secured thereby, if the deed of trust or mortgage and all the notes or bonds are endorsed as "paid" and "satisfied" by the obligee, mortgagee, trustee, assignee of the same, or by the officer of an active chartered banking institution in the State.[3] The Register of Deeds marks the mortgage or deed of trust "satisfied" on the margin of the recorded instrument and shall mark it cancelled. The person claiming to have satisfied the debt may retain the bond or mortgage or other instrument. If the mortgage or deed of trust recites that it is to secure a certain sum of money but does not mention any notes or bonds, then the exhibition of the mortgage or deed of trust

---

3. If the instrument secures negotiable paper transferable by delivery, the endorsement thereon of satisfaction may be by the bearer or holder, unless a prior marginal entry has been made by the Register of Deeds, showing notice to him of a claim of one who asserts such paper was lost by or stolen from him, in which event no cancellation may be entered until the ownership of the notes is determined.

alone, properly endorsed by the obligee, mortgagee, trustee, assignee, or officer of an active State chartered bank will be sufficient to obtain cancellation.

Another form of "exhibition cancellation" is provided by North Carolina General Statutes, § 45-37 (a) (3). That section directs the Register of Deeds to make a proper entry of cancellation on the margin of a mortgage or deed of trust even without an endorsement of payment or satisfaction if the mortgage or deed of trust is exhibited by the grantor or mortgagor, or his agent, attorney, or successor in title, provided the mortgage or deed of trust is exhibited along with the notes or bonds secured and the notes or bonds are more than ten years old at the time exhibited, counting from the maturity of the last note on bond. If the instruments so exhibited have an endorsement of partial payment, satisfaction, performance, or discharge, within the said ten-year period, the period of ten years shall be counted from the date of the most recent endorsement.

In any county in which deeds of trust and mortgages are recorded in the office of the Register of Deeds by a microphotographic process or by any other method or process which renders impractical or impossible the subsequent entering of marginal notations upon the records of instruments, the Register of Deeds shall record the satisfaction and cancel the record of each such instrument satisfied by recording a notice of satisfaction, which shall consist of a separate instrument, or that part of the original deed of trust or mortgage re-recorded, reciting the names of all parties to the original instrument, the amount of the obligation secured, the date of the satisfaction of the obligation, the appropriate entry of satisfaction as provided in North Carolina General Statutes, § 45-37, a reference by book and page number to the record of the instrument satisfied, and the date of recording the notice of satisfaction.[4]

(3) *Cancellation by conclusive presumption of payment; 15-year statute of limitations.* Title searchers have in North Carolina General Statutes, § 45-37 (b) a very valuable statute of limitations which solves many problems in connection with uncancelled mortgages and deeds of trust, which are sometimes uncancelled because of oversight by the parties involved. That statute provides that a mortgage or deed of trust is conclusively presumed to be paid and therefore of no subsequent validity with respect to purchasers for value and creditors of the mortgagor or grantor (trustor) from and after the expiration of fifteen years from the date of the maturity of the mortgage or deed of trust unless the holder of the indebtedness secured by such instrument has filed with the Register of Deeds an affidavit specifically stating the amount remaining unpaid on the debt secured by the instrument or some other respect in which the conditions of the mortgage or deed of trust have not been performed. The party secured by the mortgage or deed of trust may, in the presence of the

---

4. N.C. GEN. STAT. § 45-37.2.

§ 491   OBJECTIONS TO TITLE   § 491

Register of Deeds, make on the margin of the record of the mortgage or deed of trust a notation of any payment that has been made on the indebtedness and the amount still due or obligations not performed under the instrument. If such an affidavit or notation is filed, the mortgage or deed of trust will continue to subsist for a period of fifteen years as against creditors and purchasers for value but for no longer than fifteen years.

(c) *Discharge of mortgage or deed of trust by release deed.* The mortgage or deed of trust may have been discharged in whole or in part by a release deed.[5] A release deed is a deed of conveyance executed in the same form and manner as required for other deeds of conveyance. It is necessary to examine a release deed which purports to release the *locus in quo* from the lien of a mortgage or deed of trust very carefully. If the encumbrance purportedly released is a mortgage, the release deed should be signed by the original mortgagee. If the mortgage indebtedness has been assigned, the release deed should be signed by the original mortgagee and his assignee. If, however, the instrument by which the mortgage indebtedness was assigned was sufficient to pass the legal title to the land as well as title to the indebtedness to the assignee, it would seem that the release deed would be sufficient though signed by the assignee of the mortgagee alone, as he would then be the owner of the entire interest in the indebtedness and the land originally taken by the mortgagee.

If the encumbrance purportedly released is a deed of trust, the deed of release should be signed by both the trustee and the *cestui que trust* or *cestuis que trustent.* Frequently, however, provision is made in deeds of trust that the trustee may release the lien without the joinder of the *cestui que trust* upon payment to the trustee of specified sums and that a purchaser is not required to look to the application of the proceeds of the release money. In the absence of such a provision in the instrument giving to the trustee the power to release the deed of trust without the joinder of the *cestui que trust* the latter's signature should always appear. Since the notes or instruments of the indebtedness may pass from hand to hand, if the deed of trust does not specifically provide for permission to the trustee to execute a release deed without the joinder of the *cestui que trust,* the release will not be valid unless the person who is actually the holder of the indebtedness joins and signs the deed with the trustee. Title-searching attorneys are put on notice to make sure that the person signing as *cestui que trust* was the current holder of the indebtedness at the time he executed the release.[6]

---

5. Deeds of release are usually employed where the original indebtedness still remains in effect as to a portion of the property. Where the mortgage debt is paid in full, the mortgage or deed of trust should be marked satisfied of record and cancelled as provided in N.C. GEN. STAT. § 45-37.

6. For safety's sake, the title attorney should make sure that the noted indebtedness was exhibited at the time the release deed was executed. *See* Mills v. Kemp, 196 N.C. 309, 145 S.E. 557 (1928), to the effect that where a deed of trust secured "bonds" and a cancellation

(d) *Where mortgage or deed of trust has been foreclosed.* The mortgage or deed of trust discovered among the "out" conveyances of a grantor in the chain of title may have been foreclosed. If it is discovered that there has been a foreclosure against the purported present owner, he will of course have no title to the land included in the mortgage or deed of trust. While North Carolina General Statutes, § 45-38 makes it the duty of a mortgagee or trustee foreclosing any mortgage or deed of trust to make an entry upon the margin of the book and page where it is recorded showing the fact and date of such foreclosure and the person to whom the land was conveyed, the failure of the mortgagee or trustee to do so does not affect the title of the purchaser at the foreclosure sale.[7] Therefore, in order to determine that a mortgage or deed of trust discovered in a title search has not been foreclosed by the mortgagee or trustee, the title-searching attorney must add the mortgagee or trustee to his list of grantors whose "out" or "adverse" conveyances must be checked in the "Grantor Index."

(e) *Outstanding mortgage or deed of trust against property.* The mortgage or deed of trust may be an outstanding and viable encumbrance against the property. In such case, a prospective purchaser may wish to assume or take subject to the mortgage as a part of or in diminution of the purchase price. If he does not wish to assume or take subject to the mortgage or deed of trust indebtedness, then it will be necessary for the encumbrance to be cancelled of record and cancelled pursuant to North Carolina General Statutes, § 45-37 or released by a deed of release.

§ 492. Judgments.

(a) *Generally.* The title-searching attorney should check judgments in the office of the Clerk of the Superior Court in the "Judgment Index" under the names of all persons in the chain of title who have held the title during the ten years preceding the title search. Judgments for money against landowners become liens upon the land of judgment debtors when they are properly docketed in the office of the Clerk of the Superior Court in the county where the land lies.[8] The lien of a judgment attaches to real

---

was of a "bond" (singular), the title searcher was put on notice as to possible error in the cancellation, being charged with notice of all facts a reasonable inquiry would have revealed. In the case of Wynn v. Grant, 166 N.C. 39, 81 S.E. 949 (1914), where a trustee cancelled a deed of trust without making remittance of all proceeds to the noteholder, the court held that a purchaser of the land had notice of the notes and at their peril had to ascertain that the noteholder was paid. *See also* Monteith v. Welch, 244 N.C. 415, 94 S.E.2d 345 (1956), which holds that a purchaser who paid a trustee who cancelled a deed of trust without authority from the holder of the indebtedness does not get a clear title. A trustee's cancellation without the authority of the holder of the indebtedness is void.

7. Cheek v. Squires, 200 N.C. 661, 158 S.E. 198 (1931).

8. N.C. GEN. STAT. § 1-234. *See also* N.C. GEN. STAT. § 7A-193 with respect to judgments of the district courts. Transcripts of judgments rendered in another county may be docketed so as to create a lien on the land in the county where docketed. Transcripts of judgments

property acquired by the judgment debtor subsequent to the docketing of the judgment in the county where the land lies during the life of the judgment.[9] The judgment lien gives the judgment creditor the right to have the land of the judgment debtor sold under execution to satisfy the judgment debt.[10]

To be properly docketed a judgment or transcript of judgment must be entered by the Clerk of the Superior Court upon the judgment docket, the entry showing the names of the parties, the relief granted, the date of the judgment and the date, hour and minute of docketing, and it must be cross-indexed under the names of each plaintiff and each defendant.[11]

The lien of a judgment has a life of ten years from the date of rendition of the judgment.[12] The lien is lost if not enforced by a *completed* execution sale within ten years.[13] Neither part payment nor agreement will operate to extend the life of a judgment lien.[14] A judgment lien may be renewed, however, for one additional ten-year period by bringing an independent action on the previously docketed judgment within ten years from the date of the rendition of the original judgment.[15] Note should be taken,

---

of magistrate courts may be docketed to create liens on land. N.C. GEN. STAT. § 7A-225. N.C. GEN. STAT. § 1-235 provides for the docketing of judgments of the North Carolina Supreme Court. N.C. GEN. STAT. § 1-237 provides for the docketing of federal court judgments. *But see* United States v. Lumber Co., 127 F. Supp. 518 (1955), to the effect that condemnation judgments in favor of the United States Government do not have to be recorded in the county where the land lies.

9. Moore v. Jordan, 117 N.C. 86, 23 S.E. 259 (1895). The lien extends to and embraces only such estate as the judgment debtor has at the time of the docketing thereof or thereafter acquires while the judgment subsists. Thompson v. Avery County, 216 N.C. 405, 5 S.E.2d 146 (1930); Durham v. Pollard, 219 N.C. 750, 14 S.E.2d 818 (1941).

10. Bruce v. Nicholson, 109 N.C. 202, 13 S.E. 790 (1891).

11. N.C. GEN. STAT. § 1-233. The cross-indexing is an essential part of the docketing and a defect therein either as to the name of the defendant or with respect to the name of the plaintiff will defeat the lien. Dewey v. Sugg, 109 N.C. 328, 13 S.E. 923 (1891). *See* Jones v. Currie, 190 N.C. 260, 129 S.E. 605 (1925), which holds that an error in the index as to the name of the sole plaintiff prevents the judgment from being a lien upon the land of the defendant even though the defendant's name was properly shown on the index. (It should be noted, however, that in the *Currie* case not only was the index in error with respect to the plaintiff's name but the error also appeared on the docket.) In Valentine v. Britton, 127 N.C. 57, 37 S.E. 74 (1900), where two judgments were docketed on the same page of the docket book, but the cross-index showed only one, only the judgment cross-indexed was held to be a lien. *See however* Hahn v. Mosely, 119 N.C. 73, 25 S.E. 713 (1896), which held that while a judgment must be indexed under both the names of the plaintiff and the defendant in order to constitute a lien upon defendant's land, where there were multiple plaintiffs in the action it is not necessary for the name of more than one of the plaintiffs to be shown on the index of judgments.

12. N.C. GEN. STAT. § 1-234; Cheshire v. Drake, 223 N.C. 577, 27 S.E.2d 627 (1943).

13. McCullen v. Durham, 229 N.C. 418, 50 S.E.2d 511 (1948).

14. McDonald v. Dickson, 87 N.C. 404 (1882).

15. N.C. GEN. STAT. §§ 1-306, 1-47 (1); Reid v. Bristol, 241 N.C. 699, 86 S.E.2d 417 (1955).

though, that the lien of a judgment upon a previously docketed judgment does not relate back to the date of the initial judgment but will be subject to any intervening liens.[16] Therefore any judgment affecting a land title can be located by checking in the judgment index book under the names of all the owners in the chain of title for the past ten years.[17]

North Carolina General Statutes, § 1-239 provides the modes available for the cancellation of judgments. The judgment debtor may pay the amount of the judgment into the office of the Clerk of the Superior Court who shall make an entry of payment on the judgment docket of the court and who shall forward a certificate that payment has been made to each Clerk of the Superior Court of each county to whom a transcript of said judgment has been sent. The statute also permits the judgment creditor, his attorney, or agent to acknowledge personally that the judgment has been satisfied in the presence of the Clerk or his deputy. The judgment is marked "satisfied" on the judgment docket record by the judgment creditor, his attorney or agent. The Clerk shall mark the words "Paid" or "Satisfied" opposite the names of the parties on the judgment index. If anything appears upon the record that will put the title-examining attorney on notice that a judgment has not been properly cancelled or that satisfaction of the judgment has been made in a manner that does not comply with the statute, a judgment creditor will be protected as against a subsequent purchaser or encumbrancer.[18]

(b) *Priority of judgments.* North Carolina General Statutes, § 1-233 requires the Clerk of the Superior Court to cross-index judgments which affect any right to realty or the payment of money. All judgments rendered in any county by the Superior or District Court, during a session of the court, and docketed during the same session, or within ten days thereafter, are held and deemed to have been rendered and docketed on

---

16. Springs v. Pharr, 131 N.C. 191, 42 S.E. 590 (1902); McIntosh, North Carolina Practice and Procedure § 1755 (Wilson and Wilson ed. 1956).

17. There are some exceptions, however, which are not often applicable. *See* N.C. Gen. Stat. § 1-234 to the effect that the time during which the creditor is prevented from enforcing his lien by order of court, the operation of an appeal, or by reason of a statutory prohibition, the period of delay does not constitute any part of the ten years as against the defendant in such judgment, the party obtaining such orders or making the appeal or any other person who is not a purchaser, creditor, or mortgagee in good faith. In addition, the allotment and laying off of a homestead to the judgment debtor will extend the statute of limitations with respect to judgment liens as to property embraced in the homestead until the homestead terminates. *See also* N.C. Gen. Stat. § 1-369. This necessitates going further back than ten years in checking judgment indexes in certain cases.

18. A particular portion of a judgment debtor's land can be released from the lien of a judgment without marking the whole judgment paid. A marginal entry on the judgment docket can be made by the judgment creditor, his authorized attorney, or his authorized agent, to the effect that a certain portion of the lands of the judgment debtor is released. A deed of release from the judgment creditor, his attorney or agent, releasing certain land from the judgment, should likewise prove effective to estop the judgment creditor from thereafter asserting the lien of his judgment against specified land.

the first day of said session, for the purpose only of establishing equality of priority as among such judgments. This relation back provision of North Carolina General Statutes, § 1-233 does not apply with respect to purchasers for value and other encumbrancers who buy land or lend money on the security of land at any time before the date of the actual rendition of the judgment; in such case where a purchase of land is made or a mortgage or deed of trust is taken between the first day of a court session and the last day of a court session, with respect to such purchase or mortgage the time of actual rendition of the judgment determines priority. Likewise, the relation back provided by the statute does not apply to give a judgment rendered in one county priority over a judgment docketed from another county.

(c) *Property to which judgment attaches.* A judgment is a lien only on land in the county where the judgment is docketed.[19] The lien of a judgment attaches to land in remainder.[20] Once the judgment is docketed its lien attaches to property of the judgment creditor the instant that he owns it. Hence the lien of a judgment extends to and embraces only such estate as the judgment debtor has at the time the judgment is docketed or at the instant he acquires property during the life of the judgment.[21]

§ 493. Mechanics' Liens.

The title-searching attorney may find that the records disclose defects in title caused by the existence of lien claims by laborers, materialmen, architects, engineers, land surveyors, or landscape architects.[22] To the extent that the time period for filing the lien claim has not expired,[23] inchoate lien rights may be outstanding. The North Carolina General Assembly has made recent substantive changes and amendments to the lien statutes which pose new dangers and difficulties to purchasers of real property, lenders, and title attorneys. A complete discussion of this topic may be found at Chapter 20 *supra*.

---

19. King v. Portis, 77 N.C. 26 (1877).

20. Stern Bros. v. Lee, 115 N.C. 426, 20 S.E. 736 (1894). Reversionary interests are likewise subject to lien of judgment. Kirkwood v. Peden, 173 N.C. 460, 92 S.E. 264 (1917).

21. Dula v. Parsons, 243 N.C. 32, 89 S.E.2d 797 (1955); City of Durham v. Pollard, 219 N.C. 750, 14 S.E.2d 818 (1941).

22. Parts 1 and 2 of Article 2 of Chapter 44A of the NORTH CAROLINA GENERAL STATUTES.

23. N.C. GEN. STAT. § 44A-12(b). *See generally* Urban & Miles, *Mechanics' Liens for the Improvement of Real Property: Recent Developments in Perfection, Enforcement, and Priority,* 12 WAKE FOREST L. REV. 283 (1976); Humphrey, *Position, Priorities and Protection of Parties and Statutory Liens* in N.C. Bar Ass'n Foundation Institute on Troubled Real Estate Ventures and New Use and Ownership Concepts, IV-1 through IV-23 (May 1975).

§ 494. Security Interests in Fixtures Under the Uniform Commercial Code.[24]

The title searcher should be aware of the problems in title searches which may arise in real estate transactions where fixtures are involved. Article III of Chapter 2 *supra*, should be studied with respect to security interests granted by an owner of real property in fixtures which, if properly recorded under the Uniform Commercial Code, may prevent a purchaser for value of the realty, or a lender on security of the real property, from acquiring good title to the items affixed to the realty. Under North Carolina General Statutes, § 25-9-313, a title searcher for a purchaser or lender who is going to make future advances on the security of real estate apparently must check not only the real estate records but also the filings under the Uniform Commercial Code in order to assure his priority with respect to articles affixed to the real property in which security interests may have been retained.

§ 495. Repeal of Liens Arising from Assistance to the Aged and Disabled.

While a lien was formerly provided on real property to counties which furnished assistance to aged and disabled persons to the extent of the total amount of assistance paid to the recipients, this lien was terminated by repeal of the statute in 1973. While the repealing act enacted in 1973 provided that the repeal of the statute should not apply to any claims or liens created pursuant to former North Carolina General Statutes, § 108-28 prior to the effective date of the repealing act and that such previously existing claims and liens should be entitled to full and complete enforcement, the 1975 General Assembly abolished all claims and liens arising from assistance to the aged and disabled and declared them null and void except those liens which had *actually* been collected by the county attorney prior to the effective date of the 1975 amendment.[25]

§ 496. Liens to Recipients of Ambulance Service Provided by County or Municipality.

In a large number of counties a general lien upon the real property of any person who receives ambulance service at the expense of a county or municipality is subject to a lien for unpaid charges for such ambulance service from the date that such lien is properly filed in the office of the Clerk of the Superior Court in the county where the real property is located.[26] The claim of lien must be filed within ninety days of the

---

24. *See generally* Urban, *Future Advances Lending in North Carolina*, 13 WAKE FOREST L. REV. 297 (1977). *See* part G. at pp. 334 through 339 for a discussion of security interests in fixtures and revised N.C. GEN. STAT. § 25-9-13.

25. *See* 1975 N.C. Sess. L., c. 48, s. 1, which amends 1973 N.C. Sess. L., c. 204, s. 2.

26. N.C. GEN. STAT. § 44-51.1. N.C. GEN. STAT. § 44-51.8 sets out the counties to which the ambulance service lien statute is applicable.

furnishing of the ambulance service in order to be valid, and an action to enforce the lien will be barred unless brought within ten years after the date on which the service was furnished or within three years of the recipient's death. North Carolina General Statutes, § 44-51.3 sets out the methods by which the lien may otherwise be discharged of record.

§ 497. Lis Pendens.

The title searcher must check the record of *lis pendens* to determine if there is any action pending which affects the title to the real property being searched.[27] One claiming under a conveyance or encumbrance subsequently executed or subsequently recorded after the notice of *lis pendens* is properly indexed in the record is bound by all proceedings in the action as fully as if he had been a party thereto.[28]

While a pending lawsuit involving title to land will not constitute *constructive* notice to a purchaser for value or encumbrancer of the property affected thereby unless a *lis pendens* is filed and properly cross-indexed pursuant to North Carolina General Statutes, §§ 1-116 and 1-117, if the purchaser or encumbrancer of property has *actual* notice of the pendency of the litigation affecting the title to the property, he will take the property subject to any judgment that may be rendered in the pending action even though no *lis pendens* has been filed or cross-indexed.[29] The *lis pendens* statutes enable a purchaser for a valuable consideration *who has no actual notice* of the pendency of litigation affecting the title to land to proceed with assurance when the *lis pendens* docket does not disclose a cross-indexed notice disclosing the

---

27. N.C. GEN. STAT. § 1-116 provides that any person who desires the benefit of constructive notice of pending litigation affecting the title to real property, to foreclose a mortgage or deed of trust on the real property, or relating to attachment of the real property, must file a separate, independent notice of the suit with the Clerk of the Superior Court of the county where the land lies in order for notice to be effective as against bona fide purchasers for value or lien creditors. The notice of such pending litigation must be indexed and cross-indexed in a record called the "Record of Lis Pendens." The notice of such pending litigation shall contain: (1) the name of the court in which the action has been commenced and is pending; (2) the names of the parties to the action; (3) the nature and purpose of the action; and (4) a description of the property to be affected thereby.

See Bank v. Evans, 296 N.C. 374, 250 S.E.2d 231 (1978), noting that the common law rule of *lis pendens* has been replaced in North Carolina by the provision of N.C. GEN. STAT. §§ 1-116 to 1-120.1. The Court went on to hold that a claim for relief by a creditor seeking to set aside a fraudulent conveyance pursuant to N.C. GEN. STAT. § 39-15 constitutes an action "affecting title to real property" within the meaning of N.C. GEN. STAT. § 1-116, the *lis pendens* statute.

28. N.C. GEN. STAT. § 1-118; Cutter v. Cutter Realty Co., 265 N.C. 664, 144 S.E.2d 882 (1965). It should be noted that the *lis pendens* statute does not apply to situations other than those provided for in the statute. For instance, an action simply to secure a personal judgment for the payment of money has no effect as a *lis pendens*. Accord, Lord v. Jeffreys, 22 N.C. App. 13, 205 S.E.2d 563 (1974).

29. Lawing v. Jaynes, 285 N.C. 418, 206 S.E.2d 162 (1974).

pendency of such an action. If a purchaser buys real property from a defendant-vendor, *with actual notice* of knowledge that an action has been instituted against the defendant-vendor that affects the title to the specific property purchased, the purchaser will take title to the specific real property subject to any judgment or decree that may be rendered in the pending case. The burden of proof is on the purchaser to show that he is a purchaser for value without notice of such pending litigation that affects title to the specific property purchased.

The plaintiff may file his notice of the pending litigation at the time the summons is issued,[30] at any time after the complaint is filed, at any time after the real property has been attached, or at any time after an answer or other pleading has been filed setting up an affirmative defense to the action.[31]

North Carolina General Statutes, § 1-120.1 provides that actions brought within federal courts are within the requirements of the *lis pendens* statute.

Lis pendens may be cancelled by the court in which the action to which it relates was commenced at any time the action is settled, discontinued or abated on application of any aggrieved person. The Clerk may be ordered to cancel the *lis pendens* of record and shall endorse the cancellation on the margin of the record.[32] If the title-searching attorney discovers a *lis pendens* which affects the real property that he is searching, he must consult the court records with respect to the pending case to ascertain its status. It is no longer necessary for the title attorney to search the civil issue docket in the county where the land lies unless a separate *lis pendens* is filed.[33]

It has been held that one who wantonly, maliciously, without cause, commences a civil action and puts upon record a complaint and a *lis pendens* for the purpose of injuring and destroying the credit and business

---

30. *But see* N.C. GEN. STAT. § 1-117 that the *lis pendens* notice shall be of no avail unless within sixty days after it is cross-indexed the summons is personally served on the defendant or unless he is served by publication or an order is made for service by publication.

31. N.C. GEN. STAT. § 1-116(c).

32. N.C. GEN. STAT. § 1-120.

33. Under Arrington v. Arrington, 114 N.C. 151, 19 S.E. 351 (1894), and Massachusetts Bonding Co. v. Knox, 220 N.C. 725, 18 S.E.2d 436 (1942), both decided prior to 1959 when the *lis pendens* statute was rewritten, it was necessary to search the civil issue docket since the court held that where an action involving the title to land within the county where the land lay was constructive notice of the claim and lien. This is no longer the law as the statute has required a *separate independent* notice of pending litigation to be filed and cross-indexed on the *lis pendens* record since 1959. *See* Cutter v. Cutter Realty Co., 265 N.C. 664, 144 S.E.2d 882 (1965).

The *lis pendens* statutes enable a purchaser for a valuable consideration *who has no actual notice* of the pendency of litigation affecting the title to land to proceed with assurance when the *lis pendens* docket does not disclose a cross-indexed notice disclosing the pendency of such an action. Lawing v. Jaynes, 285 N.C. 418, 206 S.E.2d 162 (1974).

of another, whereby that other suffers damages, may be held liable for the tort of abuse of process.[34]

§ 498. County and Municipal Taxes.

(a) *In general.* One of the most difficult areas in the search of a land title is that in which the searcher makes sure that there are no unpaid county, city or town taxes on the land which will constitute a lien against the property being searched.

North Carolina General Statutes, § 105-361, as amended in 1973, provides that an owner of real property, an occupant, a person having a lien, estate or interest in real property, a prospective purchaser or lessee of real property, or a person or firm about to make a loan secured by real property, or the authorized agent or attorney of any such persons, may request a written certificate showing the amount of taxes due with respect to specific real property. The tax collector is required to furnish the certificate when requested and is subject to a $50 civil penalty if he fails to supply it to one entitled to request it. When the certificate has been issued to a person who requests it, or his successor in interest, and such person relies on the certificate by paying the taxes, purchasing or leasing the real property, or by lending money secured by the real property, then the tax lien on such property is released and ceases.[35]

(b) *County taxes.* Taxes which are assessed by a county which remain unpaid are a lien on the real property of the taxpayer in the county. An important aspect of the lien is that it is not simply a claim against the owner but it is rather a claim against the property, a right *in rem* against the property, as distinguished from a right *in personam* against the person. Thus if the lien attaches against a landowner it continues on the land notwithstanding a change in the ownership of the land and can be enforced against a subsequent owner. Hence the title searcher must con-

---

34. *See* Austin v. Wilder, 26 N.C. App. 229, 215 S.E.2d 794 (1975), citing and quoting Chatham Estates v. Banks, 171 N.C. 579, 88 S.E. 783 (1916).

35. The full text of subsection (b) of N.C. GEN. STAT. § 105-361 is set out below:

(b) Reliance on the Certificate. — When a certificate has been issued as provided in subsection (a), above, all taxes and special assessments that have accrued against the property for the period covered by the certificate shall cease to be a lien against the property, except to the extent of taxes and special assessments stated to be due in the certificate, as to all persons, firms, and corporations obtaining such a certificate and their successors in interest who rely on the certificate:

(1) By paying the amount of taxes and assessments stated therein to be a lien on the real property;
(2) By purchasing or leasing the real property; or
(3) By lending money secured by the real property.

The tax collector shall be liable on his bond for any loss to the taxing unit arising from an understatement of the tax and special assessment obligations in the preparation of a certificate furnished under this section.

It is important to note that subsection (d) of the statute provides that an oral statement made by the tax collector as to the amount of taxes, special assessments, and related matters, will not bind the tax collector or the taxing unit.

sult the tax records in the county where the land lies to determine if there are unpaid taxes against the land. It will be necessary for the title searcher to determine locally who is the depository of the tax records in a particular county. The governing body of each county and municipality is required by statute to appoint a tax collector to serve for a term to be determined by the appointing body and until his successor has been appointed and qualified.[36]

The lien for taxes levied on a parcel of real property shall attach to the parcel taxed on the date the property is to be listed for taxation under North Carolina General Statutes, § 105-285. The lien for taxes levied on personal property shall attach to all real property of the taxpayer in the taxing unit on the same date. All penalties, interests and costs allowed by law shall be added to the amount of the lien and shall be regarded as attaching at the same date as the lien for the principal amount of the taxes.[37]

The title searcher must check the tax records with respect to the owners of the *locus in quo* for at least ten years to see that no taxes remain unpaid since North Carolina General Statutes, § 105-378 provides that no county or municipality may maintain an action or procedure to enforce any remedy for the collection of taxes, nor can tax liens be enforced, unless the action or procedure is instituted within ten years from the date that the taxes became due.[38]

---

36. N.C. GEN. STAT. § 105-349(a). While sheriffs are no longer entitled to serve as county tax collectors as a matter of right, a board of county commissioners may appoint a sheriff to serve as tax collector if it so desires.

37. The lien dates from the date that the property is to be *listed* (January 1 of each year) regardless of the time at which liability for a tax for a given fiscal year may arise or the exact amount thereof may be determined. *See* N.C. GEN. STAT. § 105-355. Penalties, interest and costs are automatically added to the lien. It should be noted that the taxes on one parcel of real estate do not become a lien on other real estate owned by the taxpayer. *See* CAMPBELL, PROPERTY TAX COLLECTION IN NORTH CAROLINA 194 (1974).

While the law formerly provided that a lien for poll taxes attached to the real property of the taxpayer, the poll tax was abolished in 1965 by constitutional amendment. *See* N.C. CONST. art. V, § 1. In addition, since 1974 there is no lien on an owner's real property for dog license taxes, as was the case prior to 1974. *See* CAMPBELL, PROPERTY TAX COLLECTION IN NORTH CAROLINA 197 (1974). No provision of N.C. GEN. STAT. ch. 153A, nor any statute authorizing cities and towns to impose license taxes on animals, makes such license taxes liens on the owners' real property.

It has been held that an owner of the equity of redemption is considered the owner of real estate which is subject to a mortgage or deed of trust for purposes of tax listing and assessing. *See* N.C. GEN. STAT. § 105-302 (c). Since personal property taxes are a lien against an owner's real property, a mortgagor's personal property taxes constitute a lien against his real property. N.C. GEN. STAT. § 105-340 (a). Therefore, if a mortgagor defaults in payment of his personal property taxes, the taxing authority (county or municipality) has a lien against the real property even if it is purchased for value pursuant to a foreclosure of the mortgage or deed of trust. Powell v. County of Haywood, 15 N.C. App. 109, 189 S.E.2d 785 (1972); Powell v. Town of Canton, 15 N.C. App. 113, 189 S.E.2d 784 (1972).

38. Since the Machinery Act of 1971 was enacted, there is now a statewide uniform statute of limitations for property taxes.

The title searcher should note that not infrequently real property is listed on the tax books in the name of one who is not the true owner or under an assumed name, sometimes in the trade name of the owner's business. Notwithstanding that the land is listed in a name other than the name of the owner, the taxes levied on the land so listed will still become a lien on the land.[39] Therefore, the title attorney must make inquiry to determine how the property has been listed. Frequently, also, it is not easy to determine whether or not a listing for taxes covers the *locus in quo*. In such cases it is necessary to make an independent examination outside the tax records to determine if the *locus in quo* is included in a given listing. Sometimes tax listings do not appear in their proper places in the tax books; in such cases the only thing to do is for the searcher to continue his search and inquiries until the listing is found.

What if the title searcher finds that the *locus in quo* has not been listed for taxes in the county? In such cases the counties are given the authority to assess such unlisted property for the taxes due for the five preceding years.[40] Therefore the title searcher should see that the *locus in quo* is listed and that the taxes for the preceding five years have been paid before the title is cleared.[41]

Where an owner may have listed a number of tracts of land together, perhaps as one parcel, it is sometimes desirable for a part of the owner's land to be released from the taxing unit's lien when he does not make total payment of his taxes on all of his lands and personalty. North Carolina General Statutes, § 105-362 (b) provides that a taxing unit may discharge the tax lien on one or more parcels of land upon payment of all the taxes due on the parcel or parcels of land sought to be released,[42] plus all or a proportionate part of the personal property taxes [43] owed by the listing taxpayer for the particular year or years.

(c) *Municipal taxes.* Taxes levied by municipal corporations upon property within their limits constitute a lien upon the real property lying within their limits. The same general rules applicable to county taxes apply to taxes and tax liens in municipalities. The lien for municipalities' taxes attaches in the same way, has the same duration, and is allocable among the several tracts owned by the same owner within the municipal taxing unit.[44]

---

39. See CAMPBELL, PROPERTY TAX COLLECTION IN NORTH CAROLINA 198 (1974).

40. N.C. GEN. STAT. § 105-312(d) and (f).

41. N.C. GEN. STAT. § 105-312(d) and (f).

42. See CAMPBELL, PROPERTY TAX COLLECTION IN NORTH CAROLINA 87 (1974). "Taxes" include any applicable interest, penalties and costs. N.C. GEN. STAT. § 105-273 (15).

43. The proportionate part shall be a percentage of the personal property taxes equal to the percentage of the total assessed valuation of the taxpayer's real property in the taxing unit represented by the assessed valuation of the parcel or parcels to be released. N.C. GEN. STAT. § 105-362. See CAMPBELL, PROPERTY TAX COLLECTION IN NORTH CAROLINA 87 (1974).

44. N.C. GEN. STAT. § 105-362(b).

An inconvenience arises to the title searchers from municipal taxes which must be noted. The tax records of a municipal corporation are not maintained in the county courthouse. In order to determine if there is a lien for unpaid taxes due a town or city the title searcher must check the tax records of the municipality separately from the county courthouse records, usually in the town or city hall.[45]

§ 499. State Taxes.

While there is currently no state *ad valorem* tax on real property in North Carolina, all state taxes levied pursuant to the Revenue Act are made liens on the taxpayer's realty from the time the certificate of tax liability or a judgment is docketed by the Commissioner of Revenue in the office of the Clerk of the Superior Court of the county where the real estate is situated. The lien arising from the docketing of the certificate of tax liability or judgment continues to have vitality only for ten years after the docketing and loses its efficacy after that time. The taxpayer is entitled to have the certificate and lien for tax liability for state taxes cancelled after the expiration of ten years.[46]

In addition to the foregoing, pursuant to North Carolina General Statutes, § 105-20 the State has a lien for unpaid inheritance taxes due to the State from a decedent landowner's estate and where land passes to heirs and devisees this lien arises automatically without any necessity for docketing a certificate of tax liability under North Carolina General Statutes, § 105-241. The lien for State inheritance or estate taxes shall not attach or affect the land of a decedent after ten years from the date of the death of the decedent.[47] Thus when one is checking a title to land which has belonged to an owner who died within the last ten years, he must determine whether a release from state inheritance and estate taxes has been issued by the Department of Revenue; if not, the State still has a lien for any unpaid taxes.

§ 500. Federal Tax Liens.

Federal taxes, including but not limited to income taxes, may become a lien on the real estate of the delinquent taxpayer. Therefore federal taxes and liens therefor are a matter of importance to the title examiner. Federal tax liens filed in North Carolina before October 1, 1969, were filed in the office of the Register of Deeds of the county where the land is situated and are still on file in that office.[48] Federal tax liens filed in

---

45. A number of counties and cities in North Carolina have combined city-county tax offices which collect and record both municipal and county taxes and keep the tax records of both governmental units combined in one office.
46. N.C. GEN. STAT. § 105-242 (c).
47. N.C. GEN. STAT. § 105-20.
48. N.C. GEN. STAT. § 44-65.

§ 501   OBJECTIONS TO TITLE   § 501

North Carolina subsequent to October 1, 1969, are filed in the office of the Clerk of the Superior Court of the county where the land is situated.[49]

Federal tax liens have a six-year statute of limitations measured from the date that they are assessed.[50]

Since federal courts respect state concepts with respect to property, a general tax lien of the federal government does not attach to real property of a delinquent taxpayer which is held by the entirety with his spouse.[51]

§ 501. Assessments for Local Improvements.

Municipalities are empowered by statute to make local improvements by the construction and widening of streets, the construction of sidewalks, the provision of sewers, water connections and gas connections. These statutes provide a regular method for the levying of assessments against properties abutting the improvements in order to pay for the improvements. These assessments for local improvements become liens against such properties.[52]

---

49. N.C. GEN. STAT. § 44-68.1.

50. 26 U.S.C.A. § 6502. This statute raises questions, however, as to how far back the federal tax lien books must be checked in that it provides that the period for which a tax lien exists may be extended by agreement in writing between the taxpayer and the Secretary of the Treasury or his delegate. Furthermore, there are provisions for suspension of the running of the statute of limitations. 26 U.S.C.A. § 6503. Hence, it may not be safe to rely on the six-year statute of limitations to bar enforcement of the federal tax lien. While enforcement may appear to be barred by the statute, the title may still be subject to the lien of the federal government by reason of an extension given or a suspension of the statute of limitations. To be certain, it is often advisable to procure a release of the lands from a discovered federal tax lien even though it appears to have expired. 26 U.S.C.A. § 6325 (a) (1).

51. Trust Co. v. Insurance Co., 263 N.C. 32, 138 S.E.2d 812 (1964); United States v. American Nat'l Bank of Jacksonville, 255 F.2d 504 (5th Cir. 1958), *cert. denied,* 358 U.S. 835, 79 S. Ct. 58, 3 L. Ed. 2d 72 (1958).

52. N.C. GEN. STAT. §§ 160A-216 and 160A-217 set out the various purposes for which special assessments may be made. *See also* N.C. GEN. STAT. § 160A-228.

Assessments for other public improvements or purposes may be authorized. *See, e.g.,* N.C. GEN. STAT. § 160A-238 which authorizes a city to make special assessments for beach erosion control projects and for the construction of flood and hurricane protection. *See* N.C. GEN. STAT. § 160A-217 through 160A-238 generally for the *general* statutes relating to assessments for which liens may be imposed for public improvements and the procedures to be followed. In addition to the *general* statutes, *special* legislation may have been enacted in particular instances permitting special assessments of benefited real property where public improvements have been made.

See N.C. GEN. STAT. §§ 153A-185 through 153A-205 for general statutes providing authority for *counties* to make special assessments which can become liens against real property.

See also N.C. GEN. STAT. § 105-361, as amended in 1973, setting forth a method of obtaining a certificate showing the amount of "special assessments" due with respect to specific real property and entitling the person obtaining this certificate to rely upon it. *See* CAMPBELL, PROPERTY TAX COLLECTION IN NORTH CAROLINA 59-62 (1974).

An assessment made for local improvements becomes a lien from the time that the governing body of the municipality confirms the assessment roll and from the time that its clerk enters the date, hour, and minute of such confirmation of the assessment on the minutes of such governing body.[53] The title attorney should note that the minutes of the local governing body will have to be checked in addtion to any volume which is set up to collect the records of assessments. These assessments and liens must be seached in the twon or city hall where the land is located as no central recordation is required by the statutes.

The lien for assessments to real property expires after ten years from its due date.[54] If the assessment is payable in installments, the lien for any installment is destroyed after then years from its due date if the assessment is payable in that manner.[55]

Pursuant to North Carolina General Statutes, § 160A-236, where property has been or is about to be subdivided, the city council may, with the consent of the owner of the property, apportion the assessment among the lots or tracts within the subdivision. Thereafter each of the lots or tracts shall be released from the line of the total original assessment, but each lot or tract shall be subject to the lien for an improvement to the extent of the portion of the original lien assessed respectively against each lot or tract.

§ 502. Zoning Ordinances.

Zoning ordinances generally impose certain restrictions on zoned property which may prevent an owner of the property from using the property for some contemplated purpose. While most title attorneys except zoning regulations from their certificates of title, clients should be apprised that a zoning regulation may make certain land unavailable for some desired use. The title attorney should call the client's attention to the impediments to usage of land that may arise from zoning in order that independent investigation may be made. The zoning statutes of North Carolina relative to municipalities appear in North Carolina General Statutes, §§ 160A-381 through 160A-392. The zoning statutes of North Carolina relative to counties appear in North Carolina General Statutes, §§ 153A-340 through 153A-347.

Special notice should be taken that municipalities have been granted extraterritorial powers to plan and regulate the use of land beyond their borders in a number of instances.[56]

---

53. N.C. Gen. Stat. § 160A-228.

54. *See* N.C. Gen. Stat. § 160A-233, which provides that special assessment liens may not be enforced unless an action or proceeding is begun within ten years from the date that the assessment or the earliest installment thereof included in the action or proceeding became due.

55. N.C. Gen. Stat. § 160A-233.

56. N.C. Gen. Stat. § 160A-360.

§ 503. Restrictive Covenants.

In almost all high grade residential subdivisions lots have been sold subject to various building and use restrictions. The restrictions provide for the location of the house on the lot, cover such matters as setback and side lot line requirements, often prescribing the size or cost of dwellings that can be built thereon and limiting the uses that can be made of the property. Violation of these restrictions does not ordinarily result in a reversion, but their existence may impair the marketability of the land even prior to any violation since an injunction can be had to prevent the land from being used for certain purposes, perhaps prohibiting some purpose for which the property is desired by a prospective purchaser.[57] Therefore title attorneys must be careful to determine if the *locus in quo* is subject to restrictive covenants, their effects, and whether they have been violated.[58]

Whether or not restrictive covenants apply to specific real property is often difficult to determine. This is because a restrictive covenant may exist and be effective although not recorded in the direct chain of deeds to the *locus in quo.* For instance, see *Reed v. Elmore.*[59] In that case certain land, lot number 3, had been conveyed to a grantee with a restriction on lot number 3. The deed conveying lot number 3 further stated: ". . . this restriction shall likewise apply to lot number 4 retained by the grantor, said lot number 4 being adjacent to lands hereby conveyed." The court held that the recorded deed conveying lot number 3 and imposing a restrictive covenant on lot number 4 as well, constituted notice to purchasers of lot number 4 that the restriction on lot number 4 existed notwithstanding that it was not in the direct chain of conveyances with respect to lot number 4.[60]

In view of the holding of *Reed v. Elmore*[61] a purchaser of real property

---

57. Restrictions on the use of land which are validly created and recorded are enforceable against subsequent holders of the land. *See e.g.,* Sedberry v. Parsons, 232 N.C. 707, 62 S.E.2d 88 (1950); Davis v. Robinson, 189 N.C. 589, 127 S.E. 697 (1925). *See* Strickland v. Overman, 11 N.C. App. 427, 181 S.E.2d 136 (1971).

58. Sometimes restrictive covenants are buttressed by reverter or reentry clauses which provide that the land shall revert to the grantor or be subject to reentry in case of a breach of the covenant. In such cases, if the covenant has already been breached, a proffered title may have been defeated or may be subject to entry by the grantor or his heirs when offered!

59. 246 N.C. 221, 98 S.E.2d 360 (1957).

60. This was not generally thought to be the law prior to the decision of the *Reed* case. *See* Turner v. Glenn, 220 N.C. 620, 18 S.E.2d 197 (1941), and Hege v. Sellers, 241 N.C. 240, 84 S.E.2d 892 (1954), which indicate that a purchaser for value is chargeable with notice of a restrictive covenant only if such covenant was contained or referred to in a recorded deed or other instrument *in his direct line of titles. See* Church v. Berry, 2 N.C. App. 617, 163 S.E.2d 664 (1968). *Cf.,* Marrone v. Long, 7 N.C. App. 451, 173 S.E.2d 21 (1970), aff'd, 277 N.C. 246, 176 S.E.2d 762 (1970).

61. 246 N.C. 221, 98 S.E.2d 360 (1957).

in North Carolina must examine all recorded "out" conveyances made by prior record titleholders during the periods when they respectively held title to the property to determine if any such owner has expressly imposed a restriction upon the use of the property.[62] The difficulty in discovering all existent restrictive covenants that grow out of *Reed v. Elmore* is easily demonstrable. The case charges purchasers with constructive notice of all that "could be discovered by a search of the deeds and records, whether within the direct chain of conveyances or outside the direct chain of conveyances. Therefore, for safety's sake, the title examiner must look at each deed of any tract of land of both immediate and prior grantors that was executed during each one's ownership of the land in question. Furthermore, beyond requiring the title searcher to go beyond the index books into the actual deed books to look at deeds conveying lands other than the lands being searched, the title examiner must read *each* of these collateral deeds in *detail,* not merely their descriptions to find potential latent restrictions, servitudes, or easements imposed in such collateral deeds. When this requirement is considered with the rule existent that deeds are construed as a whole and meaning is given to every part without reference to formal divisions of the deed,[63] it becomes obvious that the title searcher is given an entirely impracticable and unreasonable task.[64]

All covenants restricting the use of land are considered to be interests in the land in the nature of negative easements and must be created in writing under the Statute of Frauds.[65] If duly recorded, the benefits and burdens of restrictive covenants that are appurtenant to the land pass with the land to subsequent holders of the land.[66] It should be noted that where land within a given area is developed in accordance with a general plan or uniform scheme of restriction, ordinarily *anyone purchasing in reliance on the restrictions* may sue and enforce the restrictions against any lot owner taking with record notice, regardless of whether he was an earlier or later purchaser, upon the principle that such restrictions create servitudes upon each lot in favor of each of the rest of the lots in the restricted area, which servitudes amount to mutual negative ease-

---

62. Church v. Berry, 2 N.C. App. 617, 163 S.E.2d 664 (1968).
63. *See* N.C. GEN. STAT. § 39-1.1.
64. Legislation to rectify this situation is proposed in an article by the author. *See* Webster, *supra* note 69.
65. Davis v. Robinson, 189 N.C. 589, 127 S.E. 697 (1925).
66. Davis v. Robinson, 189 N.C. 589, 127 S.E. 697 (1925); Sedberry v. Parsons, 232 N.C. 707, 62 S.E.2d 88 (1950); Higdon v. Jaffa, 231 N.C. 242, 56 S.E.2d 661 (1949). This is true even though it does not appear in the immediate deed of one's grantor. "The law contemplates that a purchaser of land will examine each recorded deed or other instrument in his chain of title, and charges him with notice of every fact affecting his title which such an examination would disclose. In consequence, a purchaser of land is chargeable with notice of a restrictive covenant by the record itself if such covenant is contained in any recorded deed or other instrument in his line of title, even though it does not appear in his immediate deed." Strickland v. Overman, 11 N.C. App. 427, 181 S.E.2d 136 (1976).

ments.[67] But if the restriction is established for the benefit of a particular grantor only, then it is only a personal covenant and only the grantor himself shall have the right to enforce it.[68] Whether a restrictive covenant is pursuant to a general plan or scheme for the benefit and protection of others who buy land with reference to it or whether it is only a personal covenant for the benefit of a particular grantor is a question of intention.[69] The determination of whether a covenant is one pursuant to a general scheme and mutually enforceable or whether it is simply a personal covenant running to the grantor, since it is a matter of intention as expressed in the instrument in which it appears, often cannot be settled with any degree of assurance except by recourse to judicial decision.

While it is the law of North Carolina that restrictive covenants will not be enforced by the courts when there has been a change of circumstances in the restricted area or a change in the character of the neighborhood to such an extent that the objectives of the covenant have been frustrated or made impractical of accomplishment or inequitable,[70] the courts will not relieve a grantee of restrictive covenants simply because they are burdensome; there must have been a radical change in the circumstances within the restricted area as will destroy the essential objects of the restriction.[71] Since this is a fact that must be judicially determined, the title-searching attorney cannot safely gamble a prediction that a "substantial" change has occurred that will relieve specific land from a restric-

---

67. Craven County v. Trust Co., 237 N.C. 502, 75 S.E.2d 620 (1953).

68. *See* Julian v. Lawton, 240 N.C. 436, 82 S.E.2d 210 (1954); Phillips v. Wearn, 226 N.C. 290, 37 S.E.2d 895 (1946); Stegall v. Housing Authority, 278 N.C. 95, 178 S.E.2d 824 (1971); Sleepy Creek Club, Inc. v. Lawrence, 29 N.C. App. 547, 225 S.E.2d 167 (1976), to the effect that for a covenant to be enforceable by a stranger it must be shown to have been impressed on land for his benefit. Thus if a restrictive covenant inserted in a deed is not made pursuant to a uniform plan of development, persons other than the grantor cannot enforce such covenant unless it is shown that the provision was made for the benefit of such persons.

69. *See* Julian v. Lawton, 240 N.C. 436, 82 S.E.2d 210 (1954). It is important to know whether a restriction is general or personal. If the former, upon clearing land from the restriction by agreement, it is necessary to get the written assent of all landowners who have purchased with reference to the restriction in order to remove certain land from the general scheme or plan protected by the restriction. If it is only a personal covenant, personal to the grantor, only his agreement will be required and the restriction will expire at the death of the grantor. Stegall v. Housing Authority, 278 N.C. 95, 178 S.E.2d 824 (1971); Sleepy Creek Club, Inc. v. Lawrence, 29 N.C. App. 547, 225 S.E.2d 167 (1976), to the effect that for a covenant to be enforceable by a stranger it must be shown to have been impressed on land for his benefit. Thus if a restrictive covenant inserted in a deed is not made pursuant to uniform plan of development, persons other than the grantor cannot enforce such covenant unless it is shown that the provision was made for the benefit of such persons.

70. *E.g., see* Muilenburg v. Blevins, 242 N.C. 271, 87 S.E.2d 493 (1955); Shuford v. Asheville Oil Co., 243 N.C. 636, 91 S.E.2d 903 (1956); Bengel v. Barnes, 231 N.C. 667, 58 S.E.2d 371 (1950); McLeakey v. Heinlein, 200 N.C. 290, 156 S.E. 489 (1930); Elrod v. Phillips, 214 N.C. 472, 199 S.E. 722 (1938); Starkey v. Gardner, 194 N.C. 74, 138 S.E. 408 (1927).

71. Tull v. Doctor's Bldg., Inc., 255 N.C. 23, 120 S.E.2d 817 (1961).

tion.[72] He must advise or effect a removal of the restriction by procuring necessary release agreements from all interested parties or by instituting court action to do so.

§ 504. Leases, Contracts of Sale, Options, Rights of First Refusal With Respect to the Land.

Outstanding leases, contracts of sale and options to purchase the *locus in quo* are objections to title, as all of these are instruments affecting the title. Purchasers for value and creditors take land subject to any outstanding leases, contracts of sale or options which have been reduced to writing and duly recorded.[68]

Recently, the North Carolina Supreme Court in the case of *Smith v. Mitchell*,[69] upheld the validity of a right of first refusal. In that case, a seller of real estate placed, inter alia, the following restrictive covenant on the property:

> If any future owner of lands herein described shall desire to sell the lands owned by him, he shall offer the parties of the first part the option to repurchase said property at a price no higher than the lowest price he is willing to accept from any other purchaser. Parties of the first part agree to exercise said option or to reject same in writing within 14 days of said offer. This covenant shall be binding on the parties of the first part and their heirs, successors, administrators, and executors or assigns for as long as W. Osmond Smith, Jr. shall live and for 20 years from the date of his death unless sooner rescinded.

The Court rejected the argument that any preemptive right on this nature constituted an invalid restraint on alienation.[75] It held that reasonable preemptive rights affecting land were valid and that since this right of first refusal was properly limited as to duration and had a provision for determining the price of exercising the right, it was not void as an unreasonable restraint.[76]

A properly limited right of first refusal, therefore, will constitute an

---

72. Brenizer v. Stephens, 220 N.C. 395, 17 S.E.2d 471 (1941). *See generally* Chapter 18 supra. Webster, *The Quest for Clear Land Titles — The Burden of Searching the Record for Instruments Outside the Vendor's Chain of Title*, 46 N.C.L. Rev. 295 (1968).

73. N.C. Gen. Stat. § 22-2; Eller v. Arnold, 230 N.C. 418, 53 S.E.2d 266 (1949). In the case of Lawing v. James, 285 N.C. 418, 206 S.E.2d 162 (1974), the Supreme Court of North Carolina held that registration of an option to purchase land was not essential to its validity as against lien creditors or purchasers for a valuable consideration of the optionor. In 1975, N.C. Gen. Stat. § 47-18 was amended to provide that options to convey land must be recorded in order to be valid as against lien creditors or purchasers for a valuable consideration of the optionor.

74. 301 N.C. 58, 269 S.E.2d 608 (1980).

75. 301 N.C. 58, 61.

76. At 301 N.C. 58, 66, the Court adopts the Rule Against Perpetuities time period as the legal limit on the duration of a preemptive right of this nature.

objection to title. The question of whether a prior transfer complied with the terms of a valid preemptive clause could certainly be a bothersome one to a title searcher.

Title attorneys should note additionally and advise prospective purchasers and lenders that there may be in existence a lease running for exactly three years or for a period of less than three years from the time of the making thereof which will be valid and binding although neither in writing nor recorded.[77] If there is such a lease for a period of less than three years, although parol, a lender or purchaser's right to possession would be postponed until the termination of the lease period.

§ 505. Party Wall Agreements.

The title attorney in examining titles to business property very often runs across party wall agreements. These are nothing more than contractual agreements for the joint use of walls between two buildings. The property line of the two owners generally runs through the center of the wall, although in some cases the wall is entirely on the land of one person with the right of the adjoining owner to fasten his building to the other's wall. In ascertaining the validity of a party wall agreement it is necessary to determine the status of the titles at the time the parties entered the agreement to make sure that they had the authority to bind the property. If they had the title to the land and buildings at the time the agreement for a party wall was entered, the party wall becomes both a benefit and burden to the lands involved and thus should be noted, with respect to the burden, as an objection to the title.[78]

§ 506. Possibilities of Reverter and Rights of Entry; Reversionary Interests.

Reversionary clauses creating possibilities of reverter and rights of entry for condition broken, if found in instruments in the chain of title, will render a land title uninsurable and unmarketable. If such clause is discovered the title attorney should list it as an objection to title.

The title attorney should be cautioned that the Rule Against Perpetuities does not apply to possibilities of reverter and rights of entry for condition broken, and once recorded, however far back in the chain of title, they may continue to exist. While the Marketable Title Act [79] will be of assistance in this regard, the title attorney is well advised to limit his certification of record title to the specific period of time for which he has checked the title.

---

77. Investment Co. v. Zindell, 198 N.C. 109, 150 S.E. 704 (1929).
78. Reid v. King, 158 N.C. 85, 73 S.E. 168 (1911).
79. *See* Chapter 25 *infra*.

§ 507. Parol, Resulting and Constructive Trusts.

While they are not matters of record, the existence of parol, resulting or constructive trusts in particular lands may constitute an objection to title, if discovered. The title attorney must be aware of the rules relating to trusts which exist although not in writing and not recorded.

North Carolina has not adopted the seventh section of the Statute of Frauds which requires that express trusts must be "manifested and proved" by a writing signed by the party declaring the trust. There is no statute in North Carolina which requires a writing to create or prove the existence of a trust in real property.[80]

In North Carolina, therefore, express parol trusts may arise in certain cases with respect to real property which is being searched. For instance: (1) Where one person, *A*, purchases land from another, *B*, and procures title to the land to be placed in still another person, *C*, who agrees orally to hold the land for *A*, *C* is a trustee for *A*.[81] Likewise, if *C* orally agrees with *A* that *C* will buy the land and take title from *B* in *C*'s name and agrees that he will hold it for the benefit of *A* and will convey the land to *A* upon *A*'s paying the purchase price, *C* will be held to be the trustee for *A*.[82] (3) Where *A*'s land is about to be sold under a mortgage foreclosure or execution sale, if *C* agrees to purchase the land and hold the title for *A* until *A* repays *C* for making the purchase, he is held to be a trustee for *A*, notwithstanding that the agreement was in parol.[83]

---

80. Thompson v. Davis, 223 N.C. 792, 28 S.E.2d 556 (1943); Taylor v. Addington, 222 N.C. 393, 23 S.E.2d 318 (1942); Atkinson v. Atkinson, 225 N.C. 120, 33 S.E.2d 666 (1945); Housing, Inc. v. Weaver, 37 N.C. App. 284, 246 S.E.2d 219 (1978).

That parol evidence may be admitted for the purpose of engrafting a parol trust on the legal title provided the declaration of trust is not one in favor of the grantor, see Tomlinson v. Brewer, 18 N.C. App. 696, 197 S.E.2d 901 (1973); Ketner v. Rouzer, 11 N.C. App. 483, 182 S.E.2d 21 (1971).

81. Shelton v. Shelton, 58 N.C. 292 (1859).

82. Electric Co. v. Construction Co., 267 N.C. 714, 148 S.E.2d 856 (1966); Martin v. Underhill, 265 N.C. 669, 144 S.E.2d 872 (1965); Paul v. Neece, 244 N.C. 565, 94 S.E.2d 596 (1956); Wells v. Crumpler, 182 N.C. 350, 109 S.E. 49 (1921); Ricks v. Wilson, 154 N.C. 282, 70 S.E. 476 (1911); Avery v. Stewart, 136 N.C. 426, 48 S.E. 775 (1904).

Where one person buys land under a parol agreement to do so and to hold it for another until he repays the purchase money, the purchaser becomes a trustee for the party for whom he purchased the land, and equity will enforce such an agreement. Bryant v. Kelly, 279 N.C. 123, 181 S.E.2d 438 (1971); Ketner v. Rouzer, 11 N.C. App. 483, 182 S.E.2d 21 (1971); Brown v. Vick, 23 N.C. App. 404, 209 S.E.2d 342 (1974).

83. Owens v. Williams, 130 N.C. 165, 41 S.E. 93 (1902); Wilson v. Jones, 176 N.C. 205, 97 S.E. 18 (1918); Rush v. McPherson, 176 N.C. 562, 97 S.E. 613 (1918); McNinch v. Trust Co., 183 N.C. 33, 110 S.E. 663 (1922); Cunningham v. Long, 186 N.C. 526, 120 S.E. 81 (1923); Hare v. Weil, 213 N.C. 484, 196 S.E. 869 (1938); Embler v. Embler, 224 N.C. 811, 32 S.E.2d 619 (1944); Bahadur v. McLean, 7 N.C. App. 488, 177 S.E.2d 898 (1970); Brown v. Vick, 23 N.C. App. 404, 209 S.E.2d 342 (1974).

Two significant points should be made with respect to the foregoing illustrations. The first point is that for one, *C,* to be held a trustee because of his agreement to be a trustee for another, *A,* the agreement to hold land in trust must have been made *prior to* or *contemporaneously with* the passage of title to the purported trustee.[84] If the person agreeing to hold the land in trust has already taken the title and makes the oral trust agreement for a purported *cestui que trust subsequent* to his acquisition of title no enforceable trust is created, a writing being required under North Carolina General Statutes, § 22-2 in such case.[85]

The second point to note is that in each of the illustrations given above the parol trust created is in favor of a person *other than the grantor.* No express trust may be created by parol agreement in *favor of a grantor* by the grantee of a deed orally agreeing to hold in trust for the grantor, in the absence of a showing of fraud, mistake or undue influence. Therefore a grantor, *A,* cannot convey legal title to *C* on an oral agreement by *C* that he shall hold in trust for *A,* whether the parol agreement is made prior to, contemporaneously with, or subsequent to the passage of the legal title to *C.*[86]

---

84. Owens v. Williams, 130 N.C. 165, 41 S.E. 93 (1902); Sykes v. Boone, 132 N.C. 199, 43 S.E. 645 (1903); Jones v. Jones, 164 N.C. 320, 80 S.E. 430 (1913); Lutz v. Hoyle, 167 N.C. 632, 83 S.E. 749 (1914); Kelly v. McNeill, 118 N.C. 349, 24 S.E. 738 (1896); Riggs v. Swann, 59 N.C. 118 (1860); Pittman v. Pittman, 107 N.C. 159, 12 S.E. 61 (1890); Blackburn v. Blackburn, 109 N.C. 488, 13 S.E. 937 (1891). *Compare,* Wall v. Sneed, 30 N.C. App. 680, 228 S.E.2d 81 (1976).

85. Smiley v. Pearce, 98 N.C. 185, 3 S.E. 631 (1887); Pittman v. Pittman, 107 N.C. 159, 12 S.E. 61 (1890); Blount v. Washington, 108 N.C. 230, 12 S.E. 1008 (1891); Loftin v. Kornegay, 225 N.C. 490, 35 S.E.2d 607 (1945); Kelly v. McNeill, 118 N.C. 349, 24 S.E. 738 (1896); Humphrey v. Faison, 247 N.C. 127, 100 S.E.2d 524 (1957); Bryant v. Kelly, 10 N.C. App. 208, 178 S.E.2d 113 (1970); Wall v. Sneed, 30 N.C. App. 680, 228 S.E.2d 81 (1976).

86. *See* Loftin v. Kornegay, 225 N.C. 490, 35 S.E.2d 607 (1945); Gaylord v. Gaylord, 150 N.C. 222, 63 S.E. 1028 (1909); Campbell v. Sigmon, 170 N.C. 348, 87 S.E. 116 (1915); Walters v. Walters, 172 N.C. 328, 90 S.E. 304 (1916); Carlisle v. Carlisle, 225 N.C. 462, 35 S.E.2d 418 (1945). However, if fraud, mistake or undue influence is shown on the part of the grantee, a parol trust may be created even in favor of the grantor. Loftin v. Kornegay, *supra. Accord,* Cornatzer v. Nicks, 14 N.C. App. 152, 187 S.E.2d 385 (1972), citing Willetts v. Willetts, 254 N.C. 136, 118 S.E.2d 548 (1961), which accords with previous cases in this note. *See also* Carwell v. Worley, 23 N.C. App. 530, 209 S.E.2d 340 (1974), which holds that a parol agreement in favor of a grantor, entered into at the time of or prior to the execution of a deed, and at variance with the written conveyance, is unenforceable in the absence of fraud, mistake or undue influence, quoting from Loftin v. Kornegay, *supra.*

But see Strange v. Sink, 27 N.C. App. 113, 218 S.E.2d 196 (1975), where a husband and wife held land as tenants by the entirety. They conveyed the land to grantees upon an oral agreement that the grantees would reconvey the land to the wife. It was contended by defendant grantee that a parol trust could not be engrafted upon a warranty deed in favor of the wife who was a grantor. The North Carolina Court of Appeals held that the husband-wife entity was "the grantor" since the land was owned by them by the entirety. Therefore, the grantees were held to have taken title on an enforceable parol trust from the entity (husband and wife) as grantor, for the benefit of a *separate* third party (the wife).

An owner of land cannot simply orally declare himself to be a trustee for another person even if for a valuable consideration.[87]

Other trusts in land that may be valid though not in writing are the *resulting trusts* and *constructive trusts.*

Resulting trusts relate to the situation where equity will raise a trust by reason of the nature of a transaction which indicates that the parties would have intended a trust to be created although none was declared. For instance, if a trust for a specific purpose is created and the trust fails or is fully performed without exhausting the trust estate, there is no inference that the trustee who has legal title to the property should have any beneficial interest in the property. The trustee is said to hold on a "resulting trust" for the person who created or attempted to create the trust or for his estate.[88] The classic example of a resulting trust is the purchase money resulting trust. As defined in *Cline v. Cline*[89] by the North Carolina Supreme Court:

> In such a situation, when one person furnishes the consideration to pay for land, title to which is taken in the name of another, a resulting trust commensurate with his interest arises in favor of the one furnishing the consideration. The general rule is that the trust is created, if at all, in the same transaction in which the legal title passes, and by virtue of the consideration advanced before or at the time the legal title passes.[90]

The North Carolina Supreme Court set out the following ways in which resulting trusts may be created in a 1925 opinion:[91]

> (1) where a purchaser pays the purchase money, but takes title in the name of another;

---

87. This has been held to violate N.C. GEN. STAT. § 22-2. *See* Frey v. Ramsour, 66 N.C. 466 (1872); Pittman v. Pittman, 107 N.C. 159, 12 S.E. 61 (1890); Wolfe v. Land Co., 219 N.C. 313, 13 S.E.2d 533 (1941); Lord & Van Hecke, *Parol Trusts in North Carolina,* 8 N.C. L. REV. 152, 154 (1929).

88. Tire Co. v. Lester, 190 N.C. 411, 130 S.E. 45 (1925); Oakhurst Land Co. v. Newell, 185 N.C. 410, 117 S.E. 341 (1923).

89. 297 N.C. 336, 255 S.E.2d 399 (1979).

90. *Id.* 297 N.C. at 344.

Illustrations: If *A* purchases land and pays the purchase price to the vendor and at his direction the vendor transfers the land to *B,* a "purchase money resulting trust" arises. Likewise, if *A* pays money to *B* and directs *B* to purchase land with the money and to take title in *B* 's name and *B* does so, *B* holds upon a "purchase money resulting trust" for *A. See* RESTATEMENT OF TRUSTS, § 440; Edwards & Van Hecke, *Purchase Money Resulting Trusts in North Carolina,* 9 N.C.L. REV. 177 (1931).

But a purchase money resulting trust does not result where *A* and *C* agree to buy a tract of land but *A* pays the purchase price and takes title in his name. In this situation, while it is possible — depending upon circumstances — that he may have other remedies, no resulting trust arises in *C* 's favor when consideration passes from him to *A* thereafter. Cline v. Cline, 297 N.C. 336, 255 S.E.2d 399 (1979) citing Bryant v. Kelly, 279 N.C. 123, 181 S.E.2d 438 (1971); Rhodes v. Baxter, 242 N.C. 206, 87 S.E.2d 265 (1955).

91. Tire Co. v. Lester, 190 N.C. 411, 130 S.E. 45 (1925).

§ 507 OBJECTIONS TO TITLE § 507

(2) where a trustee or other fiduciary buys property in his own name, but with trust funds;
(3) where the trusts of a conveyance are not declared, or are only partially declared, or fail; and
(4) where a conveyance is made without any consideration, and it appears from circumstances that the grantee was not intended to take beneficially.

The payment of the purchase money raises a resulting trust in favor of him who "furnishes" or "pays" or "owns" the purchase money, unless a contrary intention or a contrary presumption of law dictates otherwise. And it should be noted that the presumption that a resulting trust was intended in favor of the party advancing the money may be repelled, not only by showing it affirmatively, by declaration or otherwise, but also by deductions and inferences derived from the relations in which the parties stand to one another. Resulting trust decisions involving husband and wife, for example, have always been troublesome and have also been guided by a historical double standard that has recently been criticized as constitutionally suspect.[92]

---

92. *See* Tarkington v. Tarkington, 45 N.C. App. 476, 263 S.E.2d 294 (1980); Parslow v. Parslow, 47 N.C. App. 84, 266 S.E.2d 746 (1980). The traditional rules regarding husband and wife may be summarized as follows: If a husband furnishes the money and the title is placed in the wife's name, there is no presumption of a resulting trust but the presumption of a gift to the wife. Bass v. Bass, 229 N.C. 171, 48 S.E.2d 48 (1948); Carlisle v. Carlisle, 225 N.C. 462, 35 S.E.2d 418 (1945); Arrington v. Arrington, 114 N.C. 116, 19 S.E. 105 (1894); Ricks v. Wilson, 154 N.C. 283, 70 S.E. 476 (1911); Nelson v. Nelson, 176 N.C. 191, 96 S.E. 986 (1918). If the wife furnishes the money, however, and title is placed in the husband's name, there is created the presumption of a resulting trust in favor of the wife. McWhirter v. McWhirter, 155 N.C. 145, 71 S.E. 59 (1911); Deese v. Deese, 176 N.C. 527, 97 S.E. 475 (1918); Tyndall v. Tyndall, 186 N.C. 272, 119 S.E. 354 (1923); Tire Co. v. Lester, 190 N.C. 411, 130 S.E. 45 (1925); Dail v. Heath, 206 N.C. 453, 174 S.E. 313 (1934); Wise v. Raynor, 200 N.C. 567, 157 S.E. 853 (1931); Bullman v. Edney, 232 N.C. 465, 61 S.E.2d 338 (1950).

See also Skinner v. Skinner, 28 N.C. App. 412, 222 S.E.2d 258 (1976), where a wife had purchased land before she married and made all of the payments toward its purchase. After her marriage she deeded the land to herself and her husband as tenants by the entirety. Subsequently, in an action for absolute divorce, the wife asked the court to require the husband to convey to the wife his interest in the land, contending that since she had paid the purchase price for the land a resulting trust arose in the wife's favor when she conveyed the land to herself and her husband as tenants by the entirety. The North Carolina Court of Appeals held, however, that no resulting trust arose *as there was no conveyance by a third party* to the husband and wife upon consideration being furnished by the wife. The court distinguished the cases of Ingram v. Easley, 227 N.C. 442, 42 S.E.2d 624 (1947); Tire Co. v. Lester, 190 N.C. 411, 130 S.E. 45 (1925); and Deese v. Deese, 176 N.C. 527, 97 S.E. 475 (1918), wherein it was held that resulting trusts arose in favor of the wife when the wife paid the purchase price for land to a third person and the land was conveyed by the third person to both husband and wife. In the *Skinner* case, the North Carolina Court of Appeals held that the wife was attempting to engraft a trust *upon her own conveyance* in violation of the rule of Gaylord v. Gaylord, 150 N.C. 222, 63 S.E. 1028 (1909).

See Brice v. Moore, 30 N.C. App. 365, 226 S.E.2d 882 (1976), to the effect that where a husband pays for land and has the deed made to himself and his wife as tenants by the entirety, there is a presumption that the husband intends to make a gift to his wife of an

Constructive trusts arise, independently of the intention of the parties, by construction of law to prevent what would otherwise be a fraud. Where one person takes title to land by fraud, either actual or constructive, or in violation of some duty, express or implied, equity will impress a constructive trust upon the property involved in favor of one who is in good conscience entitled to it.[93]

Constructive trusts have been called "fraud rectifiers" [94] to prevent the unjust enrichment of the holder of a title who has acquired title by fraud or improper means which would make it contrary to the principles of equity and good conscience for him to hold the property for his own benefit. The forms and varieties of these trusts, which are termed *ex maleficio* or *ex delicto,* are practically without limit.[95] Constructive trusts may be declared anytime a person obtains legal title to property by the violation of a fiduciary relationship or by neglect to discharge some duty

---

interest in the property, which interest will continue when the tenancy by the entirety is later destroyed. In order to rebut the presumption of a gift to the wife and to establish a resulting trust in the husband, evidence must be introduced that is clear, strong and convincing that a gift was not intended. The husband has the burden of bringing forward facts overcoming the inference of a gift.

See also the following recent cases: Leatherman v. Leatherman, 297 N.C. 618, 256 S.E.2d 793 (1979), holding that a wife's services rendered in her husband's business are gratuitously performed absent a special agreement to the contrary, and would not be consideration for a resulting trust. Rauchfuss v. Rauchfuss, 33 N.C. App. 108, 234 S.E.2d 423 (1977), holding that when a husband makes payments on property held as a tenancy by the entirety, the law presumes that he intended it as a gift to his wife. Hood v. Hood, 46 N.C. App. 298, 264 S.E.2d 814 (1980) where the plaintiff conveyed his land to his wife to avoid any attachment of the property in the event his bootlegging activities were uncovered. Since the conveyance was for an unlawful purpose, he was precluded from asserting a resulting trust because of the doctrine of "clean hands."

If the person who supplies the money is a parent or one standing *in loco parentis* to the grantee in whose name title is placed, there is created a presumption that provision was being made for the child by way of advancement. Creech v. Creech, 222 N.C. 656, 24 S.E.2d 642 (1943); Edwards & Van Hecke, *Purchase Money Resulting Trusts in North Carolina,* 9 N.C.L. REV. 177 (1931). But where the relation between the payor and the grantee is that of brothers, sisters, uncle and nephew, or any other except that of husband and wife and parent and child, there is the normal presumption of a resulting trust because of the absence of a legal duty to support. Likewise, it would appear that if a child furnishes the money and the title is placed in the name of the parent a resulting trust would arise in favor of the child.

93. Cline v. Cline, 297 N.C. 336, 255 S.E.2d 399 (1979), where a husband and wife agreed to move onto and work a farm owned by the husband's mother in reliance on representations that the land would be conveyed to both when the mortgage was paid off. The husband acquired title in his name alone, and the Court held that the husband had breached his fiduciary obligation to his wife, and imposed a constructive trust on the land. Batchelor v. Mitchell, 238 N.C. 351, 79 S.E.2d 240 (1953); Davis v. Davis, 228 N.C. 48, 44 S.E.2d 478 (1947); Pearson v. Pearson, 227 N.C. 31, 40 S.E.2d 477 (1946); Vail v. Stone, 222 N.C. 431, 23 S.E.2d 329 (1942); Speight v. Branch Banking & Trust Co., 209 N.C. 563, 183 S.E. 734 (1936).

94. Auto Supply Co. v. Equipment Co., 2 N.C. App. 531, 163 S.E.2d 510 (1968).

95. *Id.*

§ 507 OBJECTIONS TO TITLE § 507

or obligation with respect to the property or in any other unconscientious manner.[96]

A parol trust arising as either a constructive trust or a resulting trust must be proved by clear, strong and convincing proof, a mere preponderance of evidence not being sufficient.[97] Whether the evidence is sufficiently clear, strong and convincing to establish the existence of a parol trust is for the jury to decide.[98]

Title attorneys searching land titles should be aware of the following with respect to parol trusts, whether they arise from express declaration as set out above, as a resulting trust or constructively *ex maleficio*. While they are not matters of record, the interest of *cestuis que trust* will be protected against all persons who are not bona fide purchasers for value from the trustee without notice of the trust. It should be carefully noted that to cut off the equitable interest of a *cestui que trust* of a parol trust the purchaser must be not only a purchaser for value which is sufficient under the Conner Act but he must be a *bona fide purchaser without notice* of the existence of the trust. Parol trusts do not come within the purview of the recordation statutes and protection is given to the interests of such trust beneficiaries against everyone who cannot qualify as a *bona fide purchaser for value*.[99]

---

96. *E.g.*, where property is obtained by fraud, mistake or undue influence or duress, equity will impress a trust upon the legal title. See Edwards v. Culbertson, 111 N.C. 342, 16 S.E. 233 (1892); Avery v. Stewart, 136 N.C. 426, 48 S.E. 775 (1904); Auto Supply Co. v. Equipment Co., 2 N.C. App. 531, 163 S.E.2d 510 (1968). Where one steals, embezzles or converts the property of another and exchanges the same for other property, he may be charged as a constructive trustee of the property. See Cassada v. Cassada, 230 N.C. 607, 55 S.E.2d 77 (1949). Where an agent is to buy property for his principal but buys it in his own name, a constructive trust may be declared. See Express Co. v. Pritchett, 179 N.C. 411, 102 S.E. 616 (1920); Cotton Mills v. Manufacturing Co., 221 N.C. 500, 20 S.E.2d 818 (1942). Where an administrator or executor permits foreclosure of a mortgage on lands of the estate and purchases the property at the foreclosure sale in his own name, he may be declared a constructive trustee for the benefit of the heirs of the mortgagor if there were funds of the estate available to prevent the foreclosure. Batchelor v. Mitchell, 238 N.C. 351, 78 S.E.2d 240 (1953). Where there is *any* fiduciary relationship between the parties and the fiduciary acquires title directly from the beneficiary without full disclosure and utmost fairness to the beneficiary a constructive trust may be declared. See LEE, NORTH CAROLINA LAW OF TRUSTS 79 (1st ed. 1951). In addition to the foregoing instances, a constructive trust may be declared where one takes title by reason of his committing murder. See Garner v. Phillips, 229 N.C. 160, 47 S.E.2d 845 (1948), where it is held that a son who murders his parents and acquires legal title to their property by intestate succession holds as a constructive trustee in favor of those who would have taken had the murderer predeceased his parents.

97. Colwell Electric Co. v. Realty Co., 267 N.C. 714, 148 S.E.2d 725 (1966); Martin v. Underhill, 265 N.C. 669, 144 S.E.2d 856 (1965); Vinson v. Smith, 259 N.C. 95, 130 S.E.2d 45 (1963); Hodges v. Hodges, 256 N.C. 536, 124 S.E.2d 524 (1962); McCorkle v. Beatty, 225 N.C. 178, 33 S.E.2d 753 (1945); Rauchfuss v. Rauchfuss, 33 N.C. App. 108, 234 S.E.2d 423 (1977).

98. Martin v. Underhill, 265 N.C. 669, 144 S.E.2d 856 (1965).

99. *See* Finance Corp. v. Hodges, 230 N.C. 580, 55 S.E.2d 201 (1949), where it is stated: "Where a third party is the owner of the equitable title to property by virtue of some equity

Hence, if the grantee knows of the existence of the trust or if he or his attorney has reason to suspect that the legal titleholder actually holds on a parol trust for another, there is a danger that the interest of the *cestui que trust* will not be cut off by a grant, even if a good and new consideration is given.[100]

---

resting in parol, the grantee or lienee of the apparent owner is protected against the claim of the beneficial owner only in the event he is a purchaser for value without notice, and to constitute him a purchaser for value he must have advanced some new consideration or incurred some new liability on the faith of the apparent ownership. There must be a new consideration moving between the parties, and for such purpose an existing or antecedent debt will not suffice. That is to say, claims in equity resting in parol do not come within the purview of our registration statutes."

See also Spence v. Pottery Co., 185 N.C. 218, 117 S.E. 32 (1923), to the effect that a judgment creditor of a trustee who holds on a parol trust is not equivalent to a purchaser for value for purposes of cutting off the rights of the *cestui que trust*. Likewise, a purchaser for value at an execution sale against the trustee is not such bona fide purchaser for value so as to be protected against the rights of the *cestui que trust*.

100. *See* Bunting v. Ricks, 22 N.C. 130 (1835), to the effect that one purchasing a land title from a trustee with notice of circumstances sufficient to raise a suspicion of the trust is affected with notice of the trust although the trustee declares he has perfect title. *See also* Wilson v. Jones, 176 N.C. 205, 97 S.E. 18 (1918); Corporation Comm'n v. Bank, 193 N.C. 696, 138 S.E. 22 (1927). *See generally* Lord & Van Hecke, *Parol Trusts in North Carolina,* 8 N.C.L. Rev. 152 (1929).

CHAPTER 25

MARKETABLE TITLE ACT

§ 508. Generally.

§ 508. Generally.

North Carolina adopted a Marketable Title Act in 1973.[1] The purpose of the statute, which is set out in note 8 *infra*, is to enhance the marketability of real property by making the status of land titles determinable from an examination of recent records only. After finding that nonpossessory interests in real property, obsolete restrictions and technical defects in titles which have been placed on the real property records at remote times in the past often constitute unreasonable restraints on the alienation and marketability of real property, the General Assembly has attempted to reduce the necessary period for land title searches and to clear titles from outmoded encumbrances and interests. This has been done by combining the collective features and sanctions of "curative acts," "the recording acts," and "statutes of limitations" all into one act.

The basic idea of the Marketable Title Act is to provide that by making a title search of the chain of title of particular real property backward for the specified number of years (thirty), a title lawyer and his client (prospective purchaser or lender) can know from an examination of those thirty years of records that all interests not appearing in these records (either by recordation or re-recordation) shall be deemed automatically extinguished, subject to certain enumerated exceptions. Of course, any estate, interest, easement or use restriction, or defects reflected in the muniments of title necessarily discoverable in making out a thirty-year title search of the property will not be extinguished.

The statute provides that if a person claims title to real property under a chain of record title for thirty years and no other person has filed a notice of any claim of interest in the real property during the thirty-year period, then all conflicting claims based upon any title transaction prior to the thirty-year period shall be extinguished.[2] Subject to express exceptions in the Act, a record title in a person and his predecessors in title for thirty years is deemed to be marketable as against all prior rights, estates, interests, claims or charges the existence of which depends upon any act, title transaction, event or omission that occurred prior to the thirty-year period. All such rights, estates, interests, claims or charges,

---

1. N.C. GEN. STAT. §§ 47B-1 through 47B-9. *See* Taylor v. Johnston, 289 N.C. 690, 224 S.E.2d 567 (1976) holding that the statutory presumption in favor of the State under N.C. GEN. STAT. 146-79 is not affected by the Marketable Title Act.
2. N.C. GEN. STAT. § 47B-1.

however denominated, which do not appear in the record chain of title on a thirty-year title search are declared null and void, whether owned or claimed by persons *sui juris* or under disability natural or corporate, private or governmental.[3]

While the Marketable Title Act ideally could enable a title examiner to ascertain the status of title to a particular tract of land by searching a record chain of title for only thirty years, this ideal has not been achieved by the statute as enacted and the statute does not purport to do so. A large number of different types of interests were expressly excepted from the operation of the Act [4] and will continue to be viable as against otherwise unblemished record chains of title of thirty years or more. Among the exceptions are interests in real property disclosed by and defects inherent in the muniments of title discoverable within a thirty-year search of the record title, rights of persons in actual possession, rights of any other person who also qualifies as the owner of a marketable title under the Act and who is listed as the owner of the real property on the tax books of the county, rights of the owners of mineral rights, owners of rights of way by railroads, rights of owners of easements of flowage, flooding or impounding of water in a watercourse or body of water that continues to exist, rights of owners of easements for placing and maintaining lines, pipes, cables or conduits aboveground, underground or on the surface which are useful in the operation of any water, gas, natural gas, petroleum products, or electric generation, transmission or distribution system, or sewage collection or disposal system, or any telephone, telegraph, or other communications system, or any surface water drainage or disposal system, rights of the United States, rights or interests, created subsequent to the beginning of such thirty-year period, deeds of trust, mortgages and security interests or agreements duly recorded and not otherwise enforceable, rights or interests with respect to property registered under the Torrens Law, and covenants applicable to a general or uniform scheme of development which restrict property to residential use only and are otherwise enforceable.

The numerous exceptions to the Marketable Title Act seriously reduce the Act's utility to obviate the necessity for searching land titles for more than thirty years, particularly the exceptions relating to easements, deeds of trust, mortgages and security instruments.[5] Nevertheless, the Marketable Title Act as adopted can serve to clear real property of many outmoded interests such as ancient contingent remainders, possibilities of

---

3. N.C. GEN. STAT. § 47B-2.

4. N.C. GEN. STAT. § 47B-3.

5. *See* Note, *Property Law — North Carolina's Marketable Title Act — Will the Exceptions Swallow the Rule?* 52 N.C.L. REV. 211 (1973).

reverter, rights of entry and other servitudes and defects.[6] While the title examiner must still make his title search backwards in the chain of title more than the thirty years contemplated by the concept of the statute in order to assure himself that viable excepted interests do not encumber the property being searched, the risks of both title examinations and title purchasing should be significantly reduced by reason of the Act.

The Act provides that rights and interests that would otherwise be extinguished by the Act may be preserved by registering (or re-registering) such rights and interests in the office of the Register of Deeds in a manner whereby they will always be discoverable in the record chain of title in a thirty-year title search.[7]

The Marketable Title Act became fully operative on October 1, 1976, after providing in North Carolina General Statutes, § 47B-5 for a three-year transitional extension of time from the effective date of the statute (1973) for owners of interests created prior to 1943. The purpose of this extension of time, which will not recur, was to allow a period of time within which owners of interests antedating the effective date of the statute by more than thirty years could have an opportunity to preserve such interests by recordation under North Carolina General Statutes,

---

6. Following is an example of how the Marketable Title Act will operate to clear certain land titles: Assume that in 1915 a possibility of reverter or right of entry for condition broken was created in a deed duly recorded at the time of its execution which provided that the determinable fee or fee simple on a condition subsequent would terminate or be terminable upon the happening of some event in the future. Successive transfers of the land have been made since the possibility of reverter or right of entry were created without reference to the terminating limitations or forfeiting conditions. Assume that these successive conveyances, purporting to convey a fee simple and all duly recorded, were made to *A* in 1920, to *B* in 1925, to *C* in 1935, and to *D* in 1945. In 1980, *D* wants to convey to purchaser for value. The event that would cause a reverter or give a right of reentry to the original grantor or his heirs has never occurred. If there has been no re-registration of the claim of the possibility of reverter or right to entry for condition broken under the original 1915 deed, and the existence of such interest is not discoverable on a search of the title to the land for a period of 30 years, *D* has acquired a marketable title under the Marketable Title Act and the possibility of reverter or right of entry for condition broken is extinguished.

7. It should be noted that no disability or lack of knowledge on the part of any person shall delay the commencement of or suspend the running of the 30-year period that confers a marketable title. The registration (or re-registration) of a notice of claim of an interest may be filed of record by the claimant or by any other person acting on behalf of a claimant who is under a disability, unable to assert a claim on his behalf or one of a class but whose identity cannot be established or is uncertain. *See* N.C. GEN. STAT. § 47B-4.

See also N.C. GEN. STAT. § 47B-6 which contains a "slander of title" provision to provide a remedy against persons who may abuse the privilege of filing notice under the statute for the purpose of asserting false or fictitious claims to the land.

See generally for an article advocating the enactment of marketable title legislation, Webster, *The Quest for Clear Land Titles — Making Land Title Searches Shorter and Surer in North Carolina via Marketable Title Legislation,* 44 N.C.L. REV. 89 (1965). Except for a large number of exceptions which were added to the Act by the General Assembly, the statute enacted is substantially in the same form as proposed in the article cited.

§ 47B-4. This one-time extension of time within which owners of interests more than thirty years old could record under North Carolina General Statutes, § 47B-4 to preserve such interests expired on October 1, 1976.

The full text of the Marketable Title Act is set out below:

§ 47B-1. Declaration of policy and statement of purpose. — It is hereby declared as a matter of public policy by the General Assembly of the State of North Carolina that:

(1) Land is a basic resource of the people of the State of North Carolina and should be made freely alienable and marketable so far as is practicable.

(2) Nonpossessory interests in real property, obsolete restrictions and technical defects in titles which have been placed on the real property records at remote times in the past often constitute unreasonable restraints on the alienation and marketability of real property.

(3) Such interests and defects are prolific producers of litigation to clear and quiet titles which cause delays in real property transactions and fetter the marketability of real property.

(4) Real property transfers should be possible with economy and expediency. The status and security of recorded real property titles should be determinable from an examination of recent records only.

It is the purpose of the General Assembly of the State of North Carolina to provide that if a person claims title to real property under a chain of record title for 30 years, and no other person has filed a notice of any claim of interest in the real property during the 30-year period, then all conflicting claims based upon any title transaction prior to the 30-year period shall be extinguished.

§ 47B-2. Marketable record title to estate in real property; 30-year unbroken chain of title of record; effect of marketable title. — (a) Any person having the legal capacity to own real property in this State, who, alone or together with his predecessors in title, shall have been vested with any estate in real property of record for 30 years or more, shall have a marketable record title to such estate in real property.

(b) A person has an estate in real property of record for 30 years or more when the public records disclose a title transaction affecting the title to the real property which has been of record for not less than 30 years purporting to create such estate either in:

(1) The person claiming such estate; or

(2) Some other person from whom, by one or more title transactions, such estate has passed to the person claiming such estate with nothing appearing of record, in either case, purporting to divest such claimant of the estate claimed.

(c) Subject to the matters stated in G.S. 47B-3, such marketable record title shall be free and clear of all rights, estates, interests, claims or charges whatsoever, the existence of which depends upon any act, title transaction, event or omission that occurred prior to such 30-year period. All such rights, estates, interests, claims or charges, however denominated, whether such rights, estates, interests, claims or charges are or appear to be held or asserted by a person sui juris or under a disability, whether such person is natural or corporate, or is private or governmental, are hereby declared to be null and void.

(d) In every action for the recovery of real property, to quiet title, or to recover damages for trespass, the establishment of a marketable record title in any person pursuant to this statute shall be prima facie evidence that such person owns title to the real property described in his record chain of title.

§ **47B-3. Exceptions.** — Such marketable record title shall not affect or extinguish the following rights:

(1) Rights, estates, interests, claims or charges disclosed by and defects inherent in the muniments of title of which such 30-year chain of record title is formed, provided, however, that a general reference in any of such muniments to rights, estates, interests, claims or charges created prior to such 30-year period shall not be sufficient to preserve them unless specific identification by reference to book and page or record be made therein to a recorded title transaction which imposed, transferred or continued such rights, estates, interests, claims or charges.

(2) Rights, estates, interests, claims or charges preserved by the filing of a proper notice in accordance with the provisions of G.S. 47B-4.

(3) Rights, estates, interests, claims or charges of any person who is in present, actual and open possession of the real property so long as such person is in such possession.

(4) Rights of any person who likewise has a marketable record title as defined in G.S. 47B-2 and who is listed as the owner of such real property on the tax books of the county in which the real property is located at the time that marketability is to be established.

(5) Rights of any owners of mineral rights.

(6) Rights-of-way of any railroad company (irrespective of nature of its title or interest therein whether fee, easement, or other quality) and all real estate other than right-of-way property of a railroad company in actual use for railroad purposes or being held or retained for prospective future use for railroad operational purposes. The use by any railroad company or the holding for future use of any part of a particular tract or parcel of right-of-way or non-right-of-way property shall preserve the interest of the railway company in the whole of such particular tract or parcel. Operational use is defined as railroad use requiring proximity and access to railroad tracks. Nothing in this section shall be construed as repealing G.S. 1-44.1.

(7) Rights, interests, or servitudes in the nature of easements, rights-of-way or terminal facilities of any railroad (company or corporation) obtained by the terms of its charter or

through any other congressional or legislative grant not otherwise extinguished.

(8) Rights of any person who has an easement or interest in the nature of an easement, whether recorded or unrecorded and whether possessory or nonpossessory, when such easement or interest in the nature of an easement is for the purpose of:

   a. Flowage, flooding or impounding of water, provided that the watercourse or body of water, which such easement or interest in the nature of an easement serves, continues to exist; or
   b. Placing and maintaining lines, pipes, cables, conduits or other appurtenances which are either aboveground, underground or on the surface and which are useful in the operation of any water, gas, natural gas, petroleum products, or electric generation, transmission or distribution system, or any sewage collection or disposal system, or any telephone, telegraph or other communications system, or any surface water drainage or disposal system whether or not the existence of the same is clearly observable by physical evidence of its use.

(9) Rights, titles or interests of the United States to the extent that the extinguishment of such rights, titles or interest is prohibited by the laws of the United States.
(10) Rights, estates, interests, claims or charges created subsequent to the beginning of such 30-year period.
(11) Deeds of trust, mortgages and security instruments or security agreements duly recorded and not otherwise unenforceable.
(12) Rights, estates, interests, claims or charges with respect to any real property registered under the Torrens Law as provided by Chapter 43 of the General Statutes of North Carolina.
(13) Covenants applicable to a general or uniform scheme of development which restrict the property to residential use only, provided said covenants are otherwise enforceable. The excepted covenant may restrict the property to multi-family or single-family residential use or simply to residential use. Restrictive covenants other than those mentioned herein which limit the property to residential use only are not excepted from the provisions of Chapter 47B.

§ 47B-4. Preservation by notice; contents; recording; indexing. — (a) Any person claiming a right, estate, interest or charge which would be extinguished by this Chapter may preserve the same by registering within such 30-year period a notice in writing, duly acknowledged, in the office of the register of deeds for the county in which the real property is situated, setting forth the nature of such claim, which notice shall have the effect of preserving such claim for a period of not longer than 30 years after registering the same unless again registered as required herein. No disability or lack of knowledge of any kind on the part of any person shall delay the commencement of or suspend the running of said 30-year period. Such notice may be registered by the claimant or by any other person acting on behalf of any claimant who is

(1) Under a disability;
(2) Unable to assert a claim on his behalf; or
(3) One of a class, but whose identity cannot be established or is uncertain at the time of filing such notice of claim for record.

(b) To be effective and to be entitled to registration, such notice shall contain an accurate and full description of all real property affected by such notice, which description shall be set forth in particular terms and not be by general reference; but if such claim is founded upon a recorded instrument, then the description in such notice may be the same as that contained in the recorded instrument. Such notice shall also contain the name of any record owner of the real property at the time the notice is registered and a statement of the claim showing the nature, description and extent of such claim. The register of deeds of each county shall accept all such notices presented to him which are duly acknowledged and certified for recordation and shall enter and record full copies thereof in the same way that deeds and other instruments are recorded, and each register of deeds shall be entitled to charge the same fees for the recording thereof as are charged for the recording of deeds. In indexing such notices in his office each register of deeds shall enter such notices under the grantee indexes of deeds under the names of persons on whose behalf such notices are executed and registered and under the grantor indexes of deeds under the names of the record owners of the possessory estates in the real property to be affected against whom the claim is to be preserved at the time of the registration.

§ 47B-5. Extension of time for registering notice of claims which Chapter would otherwise bar. — If the 30-year period specified in this Chapter shall have expired prior to October 1, 1973, no right, estate, interest, claim or charge shall be barred by G.S. 47B-2 until October 1, 1976, and any right, estate, interest, claim or charge that would otherwise be barred by G.S. 47B-2 may be preserved and kept effective by the registration of a notice of claim as set forth in G.S. 47B-4 of this Chapter prior to October 1, 1976.

§ 47B-6. Registering false claim. — No person shall use the privilege of registering notices hereunder for the purpose of asserting false or fictitious claims to real property; and in any action relating thereto if the court shall find that any person has intentionally registered a false or fictitious claim, the court may award to the prevailing party all costs incurred by him in such action, including a reasonable attorney's fee, and in addition thereto may award to the prevailing party treble the damages that he may have sustained as a result of the registration of such notice of claim.

§ 47B-7. Limitations of actions and recording acts. — Nothing contained in this Chapter shall be construed to extend the period for the bringing of an action or for the doing of any other required act under any statutes of limitations, nor, except as herein specifically provided, to affect the operation of any statutes governing the effect of the registering or the failure to register any instrument affecting real property.

§ 47B-8. **Definitions.** — As used in this Chapter:

(1) The term "person" denotes singular or plural, natural or corporate, private or governmental, including the State and any political subdivision or agency thereof, and a partnership, unincorporated association, or other entity capable of owning an interest in real property.

(2) The term "title transaction" means any transaction affecting title to any interest in real property, including but not limited to title by will or descent, title by tax deed, or by trustee's, referee's, commissioner's, guardian's, executor's, administrator's, or sheriff's deed, contract, lease or reservation, or judgment or order of any court, as well as warranty deed, quitclaim deed, or mortgage.

§ 47B-9. **Chapter to be liberally construed.** — This Chapter shall be liberally construed to effect the legislative purpose of simplifying and facilitating real property title transactions by allowing persons to rely on a record chain of title of 30 years as described in G.S. 47B-2, subject only to such limitations as appear in G.S. 47B-3.

CHAPTER 26
REPORT OF TITLE

§ 509. Attorney's Written Report of Title.

§ 509. Attorney's Written Report of Title.

(a) *In general.* After the title attorney completes his examination of a title, he should give to his client a written report on the status of the title searched. The report should be detailed, setting out all recorded objections and encumbrances that may affect the title or its marketability. This written report usually takes the form of a "Certificate of Title," which is furnished to the prospective purchaser or lender. The "Certificate of Title" should set forth the inclusive dates of the title search, up to the final minute to which the record has been examined. If the attorney's certificate is to go to the time of the closing of the transaction, it should recite that it covers the record of title up to the exact time that the instruments involved are themselves put on record.

If the title attorney finds that the fee simple title to property is vested in a prospective grantor or borrower who proposes to give a mortgage or deed of trust, but that the title is subject to some objection or defect, he should clearly set out such objection or defect, excepting each from his certificate. If he discovers an outstanding lease, option, easement, contract to convey, or any other instrument affecting the title, such as a deed, uncancelled mortgage or deed of trust, or if he has discovered a laborer's or materialman's lien, tax lien, record of municipal assessment, judgment, building restriction or any other impediment of title or encumbrance of any kind, the title examiner should call it to the attention of the purchaser or lender in his "Certificate of Title."

Where a title is searched for the purpose of lending money thereon, the various insurance company lenders, mortgage companies, savings and loan associations, and others who must approve loans, including title insurance companies, have developed their own forms of preliminary and final certificates of title which title attorneys must follow in making title reports.

Whatever the form of the title certificate, the title attorney should be aware that he is expected to stand behind his work with respect to all matters disclosed by the record and certified by him. The title attorney is viewed by most purchasers and lenders as an insurer of what the records disclose. If the attorney has been employed to make only a limited search of the title at the request of his client he should indicate the limits of his title search in his certificate in order that his liability will be limited to matters of record for that period. If *any* phase of a complete title examination has been omitted, an exception from the certificate's coverage should be specifically noted in writing. The title attorney should explicitly limit the area of his responsibility so as to exclude that which may arise from work not actually done.

(b) *Form of certificate of title.* Set forth below is a facsimile of a title certificate which has been used in North Carolina:

NORTH CAROLINA)

COUNTY OF ROCKINGHAM)

IN THE MATTER OF TITLE TO REAL ESTATE SITUATE)
ON THE WEST SIDE OF FAIRMOUNT STREET IN THE CITY)
OF EDEN, ROCKINGHAM COUNTY, NORTH CAROLINA, AND)   CERTIFICATE OF TITLE
KNOWN AS LOT NO. 280 OF THE HIGHLAND PARK PRO-)
PERTY, ACCORDING TO MAP RECORDED IN BOOK OF)
MAPS 1913, PAGE 66, ROCKINGHAM COUNTY REGISTRY)

        TO: MR. KERMIT R. BLACK, EDEN, NORTH CAROLINA:

        We hereby certify that we have carefully examined the record title to the following real estate:

        That certain tract of land, lying and being in the City of Eden, Rockingham County, North Carolina, and being Lot No. 280 of the Highland Park Property according to map and survey of same made by Z. V. Ward, C.E., recorded in Book of Maps 1913, at page 66, Rockingham County Registry, said lot being more particularly described as follows:

        Beginning at a point evidenced by an iron stake in the west line of Fairmount Street, which point is 160 feet distant in a southerly direction measured along the west line of Fairmount Street from the point of intersection of the west line of Fairmount Street with the south line of Thompson Avenue; runs thence in a southerly direction along the west line of Fairmount Street 80 feet to a point evidenced by an iron stake, the northeast corner of Lot No. 281 according to the aforesaid map; runs thence in a westerly direction along the line dividing Lot No. 280 from Lot No. 281, a distance of 175 feet to a point evidenced by an iron stake, the northwest corner of Lot No. 281; runs thence in a northerly direction in a line parallel with the west line of Fairmount Street 80 feet to a point evidenced by an iron stake, the southwest corner of Lot No. 279, according to the aforesaid map; runs thence in an easterly direction along the line dividing Lot No. 279 from Lot No. 280, a distance of 175 feet to the west line of Fairmount Street, the POINT AND PLACE OF BEGINNING.

        TOGETHER WITH the right to use as an alley or driveway jointly with the owner of the lot situate immediately south of the lot herein conveyed a strip of land fronting 10 feet on the west side of Fairmount Street and extending westwardly therefrom 175 feet along the dividing line between said Lots Nos. 280 and 281, which said strip of land or driveway is composed of the southernmost 5 feet of Lot No. 280 and the northernmost 5 feet of Lot No. 281, according to the aforesaid map, and is for the joint use of the owner of Lot No. 280, his heirs and assigns, and the owner of Lot No. 281, his heirs and assigns.

        We further certify that in our opinion deed from O. V. Moore and Maxine J. Moore, his wife, to Kermit R. Black, dated November 23, 1970 and filed for registration in the Rockingham County Registry at 10:00 a.m. on November 25, 1970, vested indefeasible fee simple title of record to the above described real estate in Kermit R. Black subject to the following encumbrances and conditions:

        1. Ad valorem taxes for the year 1970 on this real estate are due Rockingham County in the amount of $104.28, and the City of Eden in the amount of $141.67. (In your purchase of this property you agreed to assume and pay 1970 ad valorem taxes.)

        2. There is outstanding and uncancelled of record a deed of trust on the real estate executed by O. V. Moore and Maxine J. Moore, his wife, to Brown Trust Company, Trustee, dated July 1, 1967, recorded in Book 1476, page 994, Rock-

§ 509 REPORT OF TITLE § 509

ingham County Registry, securing a note in the original amount of $12,500.00 payable to the order of Union National Bank and bearing interest from date at the rate of 8% per annum. (You purchased this real estate subject to this deed of trust indebtedness and agreed to assume and pay the balance remaining unpaid thereon, and you obtained from Union National Bank statement certifying the balance unpaid on this deed of trust indebtedness.)

3. Subject to the right of the owner of Lot No. 281 to use with the owner of Lot No. 280 the southernmost 5 feet of Lot No. 280 and the northernmost 5 feet of Lot No. 281 as an alley or driveway; said driveway being a strip of land fronting 10 feet on the west side of Fairmount Street and extending westwardly therefrom 175 feet along the boundary line between Lot No. 280 and Lot No. 281 and being made up of the southernmost 5 feet of Lot No. 280 and the northernmost 5 feet of Lot No. 281, and being for the joint use as an alley or driveway of the owner of Lot No. 280, his heirs and assigns, and the owner of Lot No. 281, his heirs and assigns.

4. Wilton X. Nash acquired this property in 1943 by deed recorded in Book X314, at page 17, of the Rockingham County Registry. We do not find recorded in the Rockingham County Registry any conveyance of this property by Wilton X. Nash. We find in the Office of the Clerk of the Superior Court record of administration on the estate of Wilton X. Nash which states that Wilton X. Nash died without a will on May 17, 1951 leaving as his only heir at law his son Solon Z. Nash. By deed dated March 3, 1953 Solon Z. Nash and wife conveyed this property to Millicent Q. Fox, the deed reciting that Solon Z. Nash inherited this property from Wilton X. Nash who died intestate leaving Solon Z. Nash as his only heir at law. The sufficiency of the title to this property is dependent upon Wilton X. Nash having died leaving Solon Z. Nash as his only heir at law, and also upon the condition that the wife of Wilton X. Nash is dead, and this certificate is made subject to these conditions being true. (Prior to your purchase of this property we acquainted you with this situation, and you informed us that you had ascertained to your satisfaction that Wilton X. Nash left no wife surviving him, and that he never had any child except his son Solon Z. Nash.)

5. This property is subject to the restrictive covenants and building restrictions applying to the Highland Park Property, as set forth in deed from Highland Park, Inc. to J. B. Agnew recorded in Book X98, page 8, Rockingham County Registry.

6. While this certificate does not apply to any matters not appearing in the public records of Rockingham County, we called to your attention (prior to your purchase of this property) that the title to this property may be affected by the following matters, among others, which do not appear of record and which are not covered by this certificate: (a) claims, if any, for labor or services performed or materials furnished in connection with any construction or repairs to the property, and for which no notice of lien has been filed in the Office of the Clerk of the Superior Court; (b) unrecorded leases or rental agreements for three years or less relating to the property, if any; (c) rights of persons in possession of the property, if any; (d) Municipal zoning ordinances affecting the use of the property; and (e) such facts as an accurate survey of the property by a registered engineer would reveal.

Respectfully submitted,

CLAY, WEBSTER AND CALHOUN, Attorneys

By_____

This November 25, 1970
10:01 a.m.

— — — — — — — — — — —

(Note: The above example of a certificate of title merely illustrates a few of the many items which may be necessary to be included in a particular certificate, and the general treatment shown in this certificate is not represented as being adequate or appropriate for any particular title. Each certificate of title should be drafted to meet the needs of the particular situation of the title involved.)

(c) *Title searching attorney should retain copy of title report, working notes and abstract.* When the transaction for which the title attorney is employed is completed, the title attorney should arrange and keep in order his abstract sheets and place them in his files with all of his working notes, citations and authorities on which he relies in rendering his opinion of the status of the title. In that way the title attorney retains a good and complete history of the title in the event questions arise with respect to the title in the future and in case the attorney is called upon to explain some pertinent point relating to the title. It is, of course, impossible for any attorney to remember every detail about a land title. The retention of all abstracts and work sheets relating to the title, in addition to a copy of the certificate of title, is very important for future reference. Furthermore, the title attorney may be called upon to search the same land for another purchaser or lender and the abstracts and records of the title will only have to be brought up to date from the prior search's termination, saving the client considerable time and making it economically profitable for the title attorney.

CHAPTER 27

TITLE INSURANCE

§ 510. The North Carolina "Approved Attorney" System.
§ 511. Desirability of Title Insurance.
§ 512. Title Insurance Increases Marketability of Land.
§ 513. Types of Title Insurance Policies.

§ 510. The North Carolina "Approved Attorney" System.

The relationship between the real estate bar and the title insurance industry varies from state to state. In North Carolina, the approved attorney system of title insurance has evolved and received statutory support.[1] Under this system, all title insurance policies are ordered by an attorney on the approved list of the title company involved.[2] And unlike the many states where the title company performs its own search and may even have an in-house title plant containing duplicates of all necessary land records, the approved attorney performs the title search in North Carolina and then submits a title report and certificate to the title company. Upon review of the approved attorney's report on title, the title insurance company issues a binder and policy of title insurance.

As with any title insurance system, this North Carolina approved attorney framework has its benefits and detriments. The chief benefit of the system is that real estate attorneys who have developed special skills in examining local land records investigate the title. These attorneys are in the best position to become well versed in the local idiosyncracies of the register of deeds office, local customs with regard to title searching, and unique problems affecting land in their area. Perhaps the chief detriment of the system falls upon the searching attorney rather than on his or her client. In the event a claim is paid by the title company to the insured because of a defect in title erroneously missed by the searching attorney, it is possible for the title company to proceed against the attorney because the company is subrogated to the rights of the insured upon payment of a claim. While title companies do not appear to regularly exercise this right, it remains their legal option when they choose to use it.

§ 511. Desirability of Title Insurance.[3]

Frequently, if the land being searched and certified is unusually valuable, the title attorney may find it advisable to recommend the pro-

---

1. N.C. GEN. STAT. § 58-132.

2. It is now relatively easy to become "approved" for purposes of certifying title and ordering title insurance. Increased competition between title insurers has brought about this development.

3. *See generally* for an excellent recent article and bibliography relating to title insurance coverage Taub, *Rights and Remedies Under a Title Policy,* 15 REAL PROPERTY, PROBATE AND TRUST JOURNAL 422 (1980).

curement of a policy of title insurance. Many lenders require title insurance in all cases and procure a "Mortgage Title Policy." If lenders do not desire to rely solely on a simple certificate of title from the title attorney, it would certainly seem that an individual, who would ordinarily have less financial stability than corporate lenders and more to lose proportionately, should frequently be well advised to procure an "Owner's Title Policy" insuring the owner against the risk of any defect in his title.

As has been pointed out, the title attorney's certificate of title certifies only as to the status of the "record title." There are a large number of potential title pitfalls that may not appear on the records which can result in one receiving less than he purchased, or in some cases may result in a grantee not receiving any title at all! For instance, even if the title attorney has been completely thorough and accurate in his search of the records in the public offices, numerous hazards of title can exist that are not discoverable in the land title records. Some of them are set forth below:

1. *The existence of undisclosed heirs.* Where a title has passed by intestacy and has been deeded out in the chain of record title by persons who are heirs of the decedent, one or more of the heirs of the decedent may have been omitted in a deed that purports to be from all of the heirs of the decedent. Even if the records of administration show that persons executing a deed are all of the heirs of a deceased person, any heir who has been omitted will not have his rights in the land of his ancestor extinguished if he does not join in the deed. An omitted heir can still assert his interests in the property even as against innocent purchasers for value notwithstanding that the record has been thoroughly searched and does not disclose his existence.

2. *Defective delivery of deed.* Although the chain of title appears to be perfect in the records, some deed in the chain may not have been properly delivered with the knowledge and assent of the grantor. It sometimes happens that a deed is written, signed and sealed prior to the death of a prospective grantor, and before he can deliver the deed the grantor dies. If the deed is delivered subsequent to the grantor's death, notwithstanding that the record of title appears complete, continuous, and perfect, such deed is not properly delivered and all subsequent deeds in the chain of title dependent on it are nullities. That a deed has been delivered by an attorney in fact whose authority has been revoked, that the grantee was dead at the time of the delivery, that the grantee's name has been filled in after its delivery, that the deed has been stolen, or that an officer of a corporation was not properly empowered to execute an instrument, cannot be determined from the records alone and could result in the loss of title by a purchaser or mortgagee.

3. *Fraud and forgery.* Deeds appearing in the records may be the result of forgery, perhaps resulting from a fraudulent impersonation. While

every care may be taken to certify "record title," no record is any better than the instrument recorded. Hence, when a title attorney certifies a good "record title" he does not certify against possible forgeries or that a particular grantor was the owner of the land as he purported to be at the time he executed a conveyance.

4. *Mental incompetence or infancy of grantor.* The person who executed a particular deed may have been a minor or under a mental disability at the time the deed was executed. Even though a minor's deed or the deed of an insane person is recorded properly, it is voidable on behalf of the infant or incompetent even against innocent purchasers for value.

5. *Various other hidden risks which are not revealed by examination of the records.* A number of other potential risks that are not discoverable from a title searcher's examination of the records include: reverter rights which antedate the period for which the title search is made; easements which arise by operation of law, such as easements created by implication of law and easements of necessity which are not recordable; title defects that may occur by reason of the fact that a grantor who purports to be single is in fact married at the time he executes a deed, giving rise to spousal rights that do not appear of record; confusion of names, as where two persons have the same name and one of them, not the owner of property, executes a deed to the property in his own name; where a legal interpretation of an instrument is involved; where clerical errors have occurred.

6. *Known risks.* Chiefly because of increased competition between title insurers, it is now possible to obtain insurance coverage against certain risks disclosed by the certificate of title. In almost all such cases, the title defect is one which is very unlikely to ever cause a loss or even the assertion of a claim. The service of insuring over such defects is nonetheless a valuable one in certain real estate transactions.

Most of the foregoing reasons illustrate that the "record title" to real property is not necessarily "good title." While a purchaser or lender may be willing to risk an impairment of his lien or even a total loss of his title, relying solely on the records, if he is informed of the potential existence of these defects in the title which are not discoverable in the land title registration books, he may wish to protect himself by purchasing title insurance.

§ 512. Title Insurance Increases Marketability of Land.

Not only is title insurance often advisable where one desires to make expensive improvements on real property, but if a title insurance company writes a policy of title insurance on particular land its marketability is greatly improved. Should a purchaser of the land subsequently desire to sell it or use it for collateral for a loan, the existence of a title insurance policy on the land will simplify and facilitate the sale or loan. For this reason it is often wise for a purchaser or lender to procure title insurance even where there is no reason to suspect any defect in the title.

§ 513. Types of Title Insurance Policies.

The most common types of title insurance policies are the owner's policy and the loan policy. A leasehold policy is also regularly used to protect a long-term lessee. A quick summary of the nature of these types of policies is as follows:

1. *Owner's Policy.* Insures the status of the owner's title and marketability subject to enumerated exclusions and exceptions. The face amount of the policy should be the purchase price of the property. The owner remains protected by the policy even after he or she conveys the subject property to the extent that liability remains through the covenants of title given by the insured when the property was sold. The policy involves the payment of a one-time premium and is not assignable.

2. *Loan Policy.* In the most common situation, the loan policy insures that the lender has a valid first lien on the property and that the mortgagor has good title to the security. The face amount of this policy reflects the principal amount of the mortgage and the risk decreases with the debt. It not only protects the initial mortgagee, but also protects any successor of the mortgagee. If the mortgage is assigned, the successor owner of the indebtedness is insured by the original loan policy.

3. *Leasehold Policy.* This policy provides various protections to a long-term lessee including the assurance that the lessor has acceptable title to the leased premises. The estate insured by this policy is a leasehold estate.

It should be noted that where the mortgagee is requiring a loan policy, an owner's policy can be obtained at the same time at only a nominal additional cost. While the joint issuance of both loan and owner's policies by a title insurance company initially represents little additional risk assumption by the company, there are advantages to ordering both policies which should be explored by the attorney representing the buyer in the real estate transaction.

Index

A

ABSTRACT OF TITLE.
  Compilation, §463.

ACCOUNTS AND ACCOUNTING.
  Tenancies in common.
    Duty of tenant to account, §115.

ACKNOWLEDGMENTS.
  Deeds.
    Execution of deeds.
      When required, §198.

ADVERSE POSSESSION.
  Actual possession required, §288.
  Boundaries.
    Proof of possession under known and visible lines and boundaries, §295.
  Claims.
    Intent to claim title to land occupied, §293.
  Color of title.
    Constructive adverse possession, §294.
    Lappage or interlocker, §296.
    Proof of possession under known and visible lines and boundaries, §295.
  Constructive adverse possession, §294.
  Continuous possession required, §291.
  Disabilities that will delay or prevent passage of title, §302.
  Elements generally, §287.
  Examination of titles.
    Title acquired by adverse possession, §486.
  Exclusiveness required, §289.
  Generally, §286.
  Hostilities, §289.
  Intent to claim title to land occupied, §293.
  Interlocker or lappage, §296.
  Lappage or interlocker, §296.
  Means of acquiring title, §286.
  Minerals, §298.
  Mistake.
    Occupation by mistake, §293.
  Nature and extent of title acquired by adverse possession.
    Generally, §297.
    Minerals, §298.
    Property that cannot be acquired by adverse possession, §299.
  Notorious possession required, §290.
  Occupation by mistake, §293.
  Open possession required, §290.
  Periods of possession required by statute, §291.
  Persons who may acquire title.
    Disabilities that will delay or prevent passage of title, §302.
    Generally, §300.
    Tenants in common, §301.
  Property that cannot be acquired by adverse possession, §299.
  "Tacking" to make continuous possession, §292.
  Tenancies in common, §301.

ADVERSE POSSESSION—Cont'd
  Uninterrupted possession required, §291.

AGENTS.
  Real estate brokers, §§129 to 134.
    See REAL PROPERTY.

ALIENATION.
  Estates for years, §79.
  Fee simple estates, §28.
  Life estates.
    Right to alienation, §52.
  Restrictive covenants and conditions.
    Restraints upon, §390.
  Tenancies in common, §113.

ALIENS.
  Deeds.
    Grantees, §181.
    Grantors, §175.

ANNEXATION.
  Fixtures.
    See FIXTURES.

ASSESSMENTS.
  Examination of titles.
    Objections to title, §501.
  Liens, §455.
  Life estates.
    Life tenant's duty to pay local assessments, §56.

ASSOCIATIONS.
  Deeds.
    Grantors.
      Unincorporated associations' deeds, §173.

ATTORNEYS AT LAW.
  Examination of titles.
    Report of title, §509.
    Responsibilities and duties of title attorneys, §458.

B

BANKRUPTCY.
  Examination of titles.
    Deeds by trustees, §477.

BOUNDARIES.
  Adverse possession.
    Proof of possession under known and visible lines and boundaries, §295.
  Deeds.
    Description of property.
      Boundaries extend to center of monuments, §188.

BREACH OF CONTRACTS.
  Contracts for the sale of land, §§135 to 151.
    See CONTRACTS FOR THE SALE OF LAND.

BROKERS.
  Real estate brokers, §§129 to 134.
    See REAL PROPERTY.

INDEX

C

COMMERCIAL CODE.
See UNIFORM COMMERCIAL CODE.
CONDEMNATION.
  Easements.
    Acquisition of easements, §326.
  Generally.
    See EMINENT DOMAIN.
CONTRACTS FOR THE SALE OF LAND.
  Breach.
    Misrepresentation by vendor as to acreage, area or square footage, §146.
    Misrepresentation by vendor as to quality or character of property, §147.
    Parol evidence rule.
      Contract versus tort cause of action, §148.
    Remedies for breach by vendor.
      Generally, §145.
  Description of the land, §142.
  Doctrine of part performance.
    Not applicable in North Carolina, §144.
  Interim contracts, §138.
  Long-term contracts, §138.
  Memorandum.
    Sufficiency, §140.
    Writings which may constitute, §140.
  Names of parties, terms and conditions, §143.
  Options.
    Distinguished, §135.
    Necessity of consideration, §137.
    Tender of purchase price as a prerequisite to exercise, §136.
  Real estate brokers.
    Statute of frauds, §129.
  Signature requirement, §141.
  Statement of names of parties, terms and conditions, §143.
  Statute of frauds.
    Description of the land, §142.
    Doctrine of part performance.
      Not applicable in North Carolina, §144.
    Generally, §139.
    Names of parties, terms and conditions, §143.
    Signature requirement, §141.
    Sufficiency of the memorandum, §140.
    Writing which may constitute the memorandum, §140.
  Subcategories, §138.
  Sufficiency of the memorandum, §140.
  Warranties.
    Doctrine of equitable conversion, §151.
    Implied warranty where builder-vendor involved, §149.
    Remedies for breach by vendee.
      Generally, §150.
    Risk of loss.
      Doctrine of equitable conversion, §151.
      Uniform vendor and purchaser risk act, §151.
    Uniform vendor and purchaser risk act, §151.

CORPORATIONS.
   Deeds.
      Examination of title sources, §469.
      Grantors, §166.
COVENANTS.
   Covenants for title, §§210 to 225.
      See COVENANTS FOR TITLE.
   Covenants in leases, §§237 to 251.
      See COVENANTS IN LEASES.
   Deeds, §§152 to 209.
      See DEEDS.
   Estoppel by deed, §§226 to 229.
      See ESTOPPEL BY DEED.
   Restrictive covenants and conditions, §§383 to 399.
      See RESTRICTIVE COVENANTS AND CONDITIONS.
COVENANTS FOR TITLE.
   Convenants of seisin and right to convey.
      Breach.
         Damages recoverable by grantee upon breach of the covenants, §216.
         Property party plaintiff in action to recover, §215.
         Statute of limitations, §214.
         When covenants are breach, §§213, 215.
      Damages recoverable upon breach, §216.
      Generally, §212.
      Personal covenants, §215.
   Covenants against encumbrances.
      Breach.
         Damages recoverable, §218.
         Statute of limitations, §219.
         When breach occurs, §219.
      Damages recoverable upon breach, §218.
      Generally, §217.
      Proper party plaintiff in action to recover, §220.
   Covenants of warranty and quiet enjoyment.
      Actual and constructive evictions, §222.
      Breach.
         Actual and constructive evictions, §222.
         Damages recoverable upon breach, §224.
         Proper parties plaintiff to bring action, §225.
         Statute of limitations, §223.
         When breach occurs, §222.
      Damages recoverable upon breach, §224.
      Generally, §221.
      "Running with the land," §225.
   Damages.
      Covenants against encumbrances.
         Breach, §218.
      Covenants of seisin and right to convey.
         Breach, §216.
      Covenants of warranty and quiet enjoyment.
         Breach, §224.
   Estoppel by deed, §§226 to 229.
      See ESTOPPEL BY DEED.
   Feudal system, §210.
   Generally, §210.
   Statute of limitations.
      Covenants against encumbrances, §219.
      Covenants of seisin and right to convey, §214.

INDEX

COVENANTS FOR TITLE—Cont'd
  Statute of limitations—Cont'd
    Covenants of warranty and quiet enjoyment, §223.
  Types of covenants, §211.
COVENANTS IN LEASES.
  Alterations by tenant, §249.
  Assignment and subletting, §241.
  Breach.
    Anticipatory breach.
      Applicability of doctrine, §253.
    Termination of lease, §243.
  Covenant limiting use of premises by lessee, §244.
  Covenant of fitness of purpose, §242.
  Covenant of title and quiet enjoyment, §238.
  Covenant to deliver possession, §239.
  Covenant to insure premises, §246.
  Covenant to pay taxes, §245.
  Covenant to renew lease, §247.
  Covenant to repair, §240.
  Covenant with respect to assignment and subletting, §241.
  Damages.
    Doctrine of mitigation of damages applicable, §252.
  Default in payment of rent.
    Termination of lease, §243.
  Delivery of possession, §239.
  Destruction of premises, §243.
  Doctrine of anticipatory breach of contract.
    Applicability, §253.
  Doctrine of mitigation of damages.
    Applicability, §252.
  Fitness of purpose, §242.
  Forfeiture for nonpayment of rent, §243.
  Generally, §237.
  Inspections.
    Provision in lease giving landlord right of entry, §250.
  Insurance.
    Covenant to insure premises, §246.
  Limitation of use of premises by lessee, §244.
  Option to purchase leased premises, §2489
  Quiet enjoyment, §238.
  Renewal of lease, §247.
  Repairs.
    Covenant to repair, §240.
    Landlord's right of entry, §250.
  Right of entry.
    Provision in lease giving landlord right, §250.
  Rule in Dumpor's case, §254.
  "Running with the land."
    Effect of covenants that run with the land, §251.
  Subletting, §241.
  Taxation.
    Covenant to pay taxes, §245.
  Termination of lease.
    Breach of convenant, §243.
    Default in payment of rent, §243.
  Waiver.
    Rule in Dumpor's case, §254.

CREDITORS' RIGHTS.
  Tenancies by the entirety, §126.
  Tenancies in common, §114.
CURTESY.
  See DOWER AND CURTESY.

D

DAMAGES.
  Covenants for title.
    See COVENANTS FOR TITLE.
  Covenants in leases.
    Doctrine of mitigation of damages applicable, §252.
  Easements, §330.
  Leases.
    Doctrine of mitigation of damages, §252.
DEAD PERSONS.
  Deeds.
    Grantees, §178.
DEBTS.
  Encumbrances.
    Subject to life tenant's debts, §61.
  Fee simple estates.
    Owner's debts, §30.
DEEDS.
  Acknowledgments.
    Execution of deeds.
      When required, §198.
  Aliens.
    Grantees, §181.
    Grantors, §175.
  Associations.
    Grantors.
      Unincorporated associations' deeds, §173.
  Attorneys in fact.
    Examination of title sources, §471.
  Boundaries.
    Description of property.
      Boundaries extend to center of monuments, §188.
  Commissioners' deeds.
    Examination of title sources, §479.
  Conveyances of estates by entirety.
    Examination of title sources, §471.
  Corporations.
    Examination of title sources, §469.
    Grantors, §166.
  Correction deeds.
    Examination of title sources, §466.
  Covenants for title, §§210 to 225.
    See COVENANTS FOR TITLE.
  Dead persons.
    Grantees, §178.
  Defined, §152.
  Delivery and acceptance.
    Acceptance by grantee, §207.
    Conditional deliveries, §203.
      Directly to grantee, §206.

INDEX

DEEDS—Cont'd
  Delivery and acceptance—Cont'd
    Escrow deliveries, §2U3.
      Necessity for written contract to make escrow enforceable, §204.
      Wrongful delivery to grantee, §205.
    Generally, §199.
    Grantees.
      Acceptance by grantee, §207.
      Conditional delivery directly to grantee, §206.
      Delivery persumed from possession of deed by grantee, §200.
      Delivery to third person not grantee, §202.
      Escrow's wrongful delivery to grantee, §205.
    Recordation.
      Delivery presumed from recordation, §201.
    Third persons.
      Delivery to third person not grantee, §202.
    Written contracts.
      Necessity to make escrow enforceable, §204.
  Description of subject matter.
    Acres.
      Description by reference to quantity or number of acres, §192.
    Alleys.
      Rules of construction, §188.
    Boundaries.
      Extension to center of monuments, §188.
    Courses and distances, §184.
      Courses control distances, §187.
      Monuments control, §187.
    Ditches.
      Rules of construction, §188.
    "Intention of the parties," §186.
    Maps and plats.
      Description by reference, §189.
    Metes and bounds, §184.
      Rules of construction in cases of conflicts and ambiguities, §185.
    Methods of description, §184.
    Miscellaneous informal descriptions, §193.
    Monuments, §184.
      Boundaries extend to center of monuments, §188.
      Control over distances and courses, §187.
    Necessity for words of conveyance, §194.
    Prior conveyances.
      Description by reference, §191.
    Public roads.
      Rules of construction, §188.
    Rules of construction.
      Boundaries extend to center of monuments, §188.
      Cases of conflicts and ambiguities in metes and bounds, §185.
      Courses control distances, §187.
      Monuments control distances and courses, §187.
      Quantity statement least reliable guide, §187.
      Streets, public roads, alleys, ditches and streams, §188.
    Streams.
      Rules of construction, §188.
    Streets.
      Description by reference, §1909
      Rules of construction, §188.
    Sufficiency of description, §183.

657

DEEDS—Cont'd
Description of subject matter—Cont'd
  Words of conveyance.
    Necessity, §194.
Essential factors in deeds, §157.
  Nonessential factors in deeds, §158.
Estoppel by deed, §§226 to 229.
  See ESTOPPEL BY DEED.
Execution.
  Acknowledgments.
    When required, §198.
  Delivery and acceptance, §§199 to 207. See within this heading, "Delivery and acceptance."
  Grantors.
    Proper execution of deeds by grantor, §195.
  Legal and orderly execution of deeds, §159.
  Seal, §197.
  Signing, §196.
  Witnesses.
    Not required, §198.
Executors' and administrators' deeds.
  Examination of title sources, §482.
Fraud.
  Effectiveness of deeds in absence of fraud, §209.
Grantees.
  Aliens, §181.
  Dead persons, §178.
  Deed to grantee from himself, §180.
  Delivery and acceptance.
    Acceptance by grantee, §207.
    Conditional delivery directly to grantee, §206.
    Delivery persumed from possession of deed by grantee, §200.
    Delivery to third person not grantee, §202.
    Escrow's wrongful delivery to grantee, §205.
  "Heirs" of living persons, §179.
  Identification of grantee, §182.
  Nonresidents, §181.
  Persons en ventre sa mere, §177.
  Requisites to be a grantee.
    Generally, §176.
  Sufficiency of identification of grantee, §182.
Grantors.
  Aliens' deeds, §175.
  Corporations' deeds, §166.
  Execution.
    Proper execution of deeds by grantor, §195.
  Infants' deeds, §162.
    Married infants' deeds, §163.
  Married infants' deeds, §163.
  Married women's deeds to persons other than husbands, §164.
  Married women's deeds to their husbands. §165.
  Necessity that grantor read deed.
    No necessity, §209.
  Partnerships' deeds.
    Generally, §167.
    Real property held in name of one or all partners or by third person in trust for partnership, §171.
    Real property held in name of one or more partners where real property records do not disclose partnership, §170.

INDEX

DEEDS—Cont'd
  Grantors—Cont'd
    Partnerships' deeds—Cont'd
      Real property held in names of all partners, §172.
      Real property in partnership name, §168.
      Real property in partnership name conveyed in name of individual partner, §169.
    Persons non compos mentis, §161.
    Requisites to be a grantor.
      Generally, §160.
    Trustees' deeds, §174.
    Unincorporated associations' deeds, §173.
  Guardians' deeds.
    Examination of title sources, §481.
  Husband and wife.
    Examination of title sources of deeds of married persons, §470.
    Grantors.
      Married women's deeds to persons other than husbands, §164.
      Married women's deeds to their husbands, §165.
  Infants.
    Grantors.
      Generally, §162.
      Married infants' deeds, §163.
  Legal and orderly execution of deeds, §159.
  Maps and plats.
    Description of property, §189.
  Married persons.
    Examination of title sources, §470.
  Mortgages and deeds of trust.
    See MORTGAGES AND DEEDS OF TRUST.
  Nonessential factors in deeds, §158.
  Nonresidents.
    Grantors, §175.
  Partition.
    Examination of title sources, §473.
  Partnerships.
    Grantors.
      Generally, §167.
      Real property held in name of one or all partners or by third person in trust for partnership, §171.
      Real property held in name of one or more partners where real property records do not disclose partnership, §170.
      Real property held in names of all partners, §172.
      Real property in partnership name, §168.
      Real property in partnership name conveyed in name of individual partner, §169.
  Persons non compos mentis.
    Grantors, §161.
  Quitclaim deeds, §155.
    Examination of title sources, §467.
  Receivers.
    Examination of title sources, §478.
  Recordation.
    Delivery and acceptance.
      Delivery presumed from recordation, §201.
    Office where deeds, deeds of trust and mortgages are recorded, §376.
  Requisites of a valid deed, §156.
    Essential factors, §157.
    Nonessential factors, §158.
  Revenue stamps.
    Requirements generally, §208.

EASEMENTS—Cont'd
  Eminent domain.
    Acquisition by condemnation, §326.
    Termination of easements, §341.
  Examination of titles.
    Objections to title, §490.
  Extent.
    Actions to enforce rights of dominant and servient owners, §330.
    Generally, §328.
    Servient owner's right to use lands subject to easement, §329.
  Injunctions, §330.
  Licenses.
    Creation, §344.
    Generally, §343.
    Revocability, §345.
    Transferability, §345.
  Negative easements, §309.
  Profits a prendre.
    Generally, §342.
  Recordation, §382.
  Right to use land subject to easement, §329.
  Servient owner's right to use lands subject to easement, §329.
  Statutory cartway proceedings, §327.
  Termination.
    Abandonment, §336.
    Cessation of purposes of easement, §334.
    Eminent domain, §341.
    Expiration of period, §339.
    Express release, §335.
    Extinguishment by servient owner's adverse user, §338.
    Generally, §333.
    Lien creditors, §340.
    Merger of tracts into single ownership, §337.
    Transfer of servient land to purchaser for value, §340.
      Exceptions, §340.
  Transferability.
    Appurtenant easements, §331.
    Easements in gross, §332.

EJECTMENT.
  Tenancies in common.
    Actions of ejectment between co-tenants, §120.

EMBLEMENTS.
  Estates for years.
    Tenant's rights in lieu of emblements, §81.
  Life estates.
    Incidents of life estates, §53.
  Tenancies at will.
    Tenant's right, §103.
  Tenancies from period to period.
    Right to emblements, §92.

EMINENT DOMAIN.
  Appropriation of property.
    Statutory provisions authorizing, §402.
  Attempt to purchase, §404.
  Compensation.
    Rules relating to compensation in eminent domain proceedings, §406.
  Defined, §400.

INDEX

EMINENT DOMAIN—Cont'd
  Easements.
    Acquisition by condemnation, §326.
    Termination of easements, §341.
  Evidence.
    Admissibility in determining "market value," §407.
  Exercise of power.
    Persons authorized, §403.
  Fee simple estates.
    Subject to power, §34.
  Generally, §400.
  Inverse condemnation, §401.
  Market value.
    Evidence admissible in determining, §407.
  Nature of power.
    Generally, §400.
  Offsetting benefits.
    Right of condemnor, §408.
  Persons authorized to exercise power, §403.
  Purchasing attempts, §404.
  Right of condemnor to offset benefits to realty condemned, §408.
  Rules relating to compensation in eminent domain proceedings, §406.
  Special proceedings, §405.
  Statutory provisions authorizing appropriation of property under eminent domain, §402.

ENCUMBRANCES.
  Debts.
    Subject to life tenant's debts, §61.
  Improvements.
    Life tenant's duty, §58.
  Insurance.
    Land subject to life estates, §59.1.
  Interest.
    Life tenant's duties, §57.
  Life tenant's duties with respect to encumbrances on land, §57.
  Merger.
    Subject to merger, §59.
  Profits.
    Life tenant's right to profits, §60.
  Remainders and reversions.
    General standard of duty owed by life tenant, §54.1.
    Life tenant's disability to acquire outstanding title against, §62.
  Repairs.
    Life tenant's duty, §58.
  Sales.
    Unproductive land, §63.
  Title.
    Life tenant's disabilty to acquire outstanding title against reversioner or remainderman, §62.

ESCHEATS.
  Fee simple estates.
    Absence of inheritable blood, §32.

ESTATES.
  Classification of estates under common law of England, §23.
  Estates for years, §§74 to 87.
    See ESTATES FOR YEARS.
  Fee simple estates, §§24 to 41.
    See FEE SIMPLE ESTATES.

ESTATES—Cont'd
  Fee tail estates, §§42 to 45.
    See FEE TAIL ESTATES.
  Freehold estates not inheritable, §§46 to 63.
    See LIFE ESTATES.
  History, §23.
  Joint tenancies, §§108, 109.
    See JOINT TENANCIES.
  Life estates, §§46 to 63.
    See LIFE ESTATES.
  Rights of residential tenants, §§65 to 73.
    See LANDLORD AND TENANT.
  Tenancies at sufferance, §§106, 107.
  Tenancies at will, §§98 to 105.
    See TENANCIES AT WILL.
  Tenancies by the entirety, §§111, 125 to 128.
    See TENANCIES BY THE ENTIRETY.
  Tenancies from period to period, §§88 to 97.
    See TENANCIES FROM PERIOD TO PERIOD.
  Tenancies in common, §§110, 112 to 124.
    See TENANCIES IN COMMON.

ESTATES FOR YEARS.
  Alienation, §79.
  Creation, §75.
  Definitions, §74.
  Emblements.
    Tenant's rights in lieu of emblements, §81.
  Essentials, §75.
  Estovers.
    Tenant's right, §80.
  Holding over beyond stated term, §87.
  Incidents, §§78 to 87.
  Leases.
    Creation of tenancy for years, §75.
    Essentials, §75.
    Parole leases, §76.
    Requirement that lease be in writing, §76.
    Requirement that lease be recorded, §77.
    Subleases, §79.
    Termination without necessity of notice, §86.
  Liquidation.
    Requirement that lease for years be recorded, §77.
  Merger, §85.
  Notice.
    Termination without necessity of notice, §86.
  Possession.
    Tenant's exclusive right of possession, §82.
  Repairs.
    Tenant's liability to make repairs, §84.
  Statute of frauds, §76.
  Subleases, §79.
  Waste.
    Tenant's liability for waste, §83.

ESTOPPEL BY DEED.
  Covenant of warranty in deed, §226.
    No covenant of warranty, §227.
  Persons estopped by deeds, §228.
  Rebutter, §228.

INDEX

ESTOPPEL BY DEED—Cont'd
  Recordation.
    Title by estoppel as affected by recordation statutes, §229.

ESTOVERS.
  Estates for years.
    Tenant's right, §80.
  Life estates.
    Incidents of life estates, §54.
  Tenancies at will.
    Tenant's right, §102.
  Tenancies from period to period, §91.

EVIDENCE.
  Eminent domain.
    Admissibility in determining "market value," §407.

EXAMINATION OF TITLES.
  Abstract of title.
    Compilation, §463.
  Adverse conveyances of each owner in chain of title, §462.
  Adverse possession.
    Title acquired by adverse possession, §486.
  Assessments.
    Objections to title, §501.
  Attorneys at law.
    Report of title, §509.
    Responsibilities and duties of title attorneys, §458.
  Bankruptcy.
    Deeds by trustees, §477.
  Chain of title.
    Checking the "out" or "adverse" conveyances of each owner in the chain of title, §462.
    Compilation of the abstract of title, §463.
    Period of time for which chain of title is searched, §461.
    Running the chain of title, §460.
  Easements.
    Objections to title, §490.
  Execution sales.
    Sheriffs' deeds, §480.
  Executors and administrators.
    Deeds, §482.
  Guardians and wards.
    Deeds, §481.
  Importance of title examination, §456.
  Improvements.
    Assessments for local improvements.
      Objections to title, §501.
  Information to be obtained prior to title search, §459.
  Insurance.
    See TITLE INSURANCE.
  Judgments.
    Objections to title, §492.
  Leases.
    Objections to title, §504.
  Liens.
    Recipients of ambulance service.
      Objections to title, §496.
    Repeal of liens arising from assistance to the aged and disabled.
      Objections to title, §495.

EXECUTORS AND ADMINISTRATORS.
  Examination of titles.
    Deeds, §482.

F

FEDERAL TRUTH IN LENDING ACT.
  Mechanics' liens.
    Applicability, §452.
FEE CONDITIONAL ESTATES.
  Not in effect in North Carolina, §42.
  Statute de donis conditionalibus.
    Converts to fee tail, §42.
FEE SIMPLE ESTATES.
  Alienation, §28.
  Conditions subsequent.
    Distinguished from fee simple determinable estate, §37.
    Distinguished from fee simple subject to executory interest, §39.
    Illegal, impossible or repugnant limitations and conditions, §41.
    Incidents, §38.
    Termination, §38.
  Debts.
    Owner's debts, §30.
  Definitions, §24.
  Descent and distribution.
    Heirs, §29.
  Determinable fee simple.
    Alienation, §36.
    Creation, §35.
    Distinguished from fee simple absolute, §35.
    Distinguished from fee simple subject to a condition subsequent, §37.
    Illegal, impossible or repugnant limitations and conditions, §41.
    Incidents, §36.
  Eminent domain.
    Subject to power, §34.
  Escheats.
    Absence of inheritable blood, §32.
  Executory interest.
    Distinguished from fee simple subject to condition subsequent, §39.
    Example, §39.
    Illegal, impossible or repugnant limitations and conditions, §41.
    Incidents, §41.
    Rule against perpetuities, §41.
  Forfeiture for conviction of treason or felony.
    Applicability in North Carolina, §33.
  Generally, §24.
  "Heirs" as word of limitation.
    At common law, §25.
    In North Carolina, §27.
    Necessity under modern statutes, §26.
  Husband and wife.
    Spouses' rights, §31.
  Incidents of fee simple estates.
    Convictions of treason or felony.
      Forfeiture not applicable in North Carolina, §33.
    Descent to heirs, §29.
    Eminent domain.
      Subject to power of eminent domain, §34.

INDEX

FEE SIMPLE ESTATES—Cont'd
Incidents of fee simple estates—Cont'd
Escheats to state in absence of inheritable blood, §32.
Spouses' rights, §31.
Subject to owner's debts, §30.
Unlimited power of alienation, §28.
Limitations.
Illegal, impossible or repugnant limitations and conditions, §41.
Rule against perpetuities.
Applicable to fee simple estates subject to an executory interest, §41.
Spouses' rights, §31.
Words of inheritance, §§25, 26.
Words of limitation, §§25, 27.

FEE TAIL ESTATES.
Creation at common law, §43.
Forms, §43.
History, §42.
Rule in Wild's case, §44.
Statutory change in North Carolina, §45.
Converted to fee simple estates in North Carolina, §§42, 45.

FELONIES.
No forfeiture for conviction in North Carolina, §43.

FIDUCIARIES.
Tenancies in common.
Aspects between tenants in common, §116.

FIXTURES.
Annexation.
Circumstances from which permanent annexation may be deduced, §13.
Ways of deducing intention as to permanent annexation.
Character of the annexation, §15.
Circumstances from which permanent annexation may be deduced, §13.
Express agreement, §14.
Relationship of the parties.
Chattel mortgages or executed conditional sales contracts or other security interest in chattel, §20.
Disputes arising between persons claiming a decedent's personal property and persons claiming a decedent's real property, §19.
Generally, §16.
Mortgagor and mortgagee, §18.
Vendor and vendee of realty, §17.
When fixtures annexed by tenant, §21.
Defined, §12.
Generally, §11.
Uniform commercial code.
Construction mortgages, §22.4.
Effect.
Generally, §22.
Filing.
Effect, §22.1.
Generally, §22.1.
Ten-day filing period, §22.2.
Inapplicability, §22.3.
Priorities when construction mortgage involved, §22.4.
Prior real estate interests, §22.2.
Regulation of priority of security interests, §22.
Removability of fixtures, §22.5.

FIXTURES—Cont'd
  Uniform commercial code—Cont'd
    Subsequent interests, §22.3.
      Inapplicability of ten-day filing period, §22.3.

FRAUD.
  Deeds.
    Effectiveness of deeds in absence of fraud, §209.

FRUCTUS INDUSTRIALES.
  Defined, §10.

FRUCTUS NATURALES.
  Defined, §9.

G

GIFTS.
  Recordation.
    Deeds of gift must be recorded within two years, §381.

GUARDIANS AND WARDS.
  Examination of titles.
    Deeds, §481.

H

HISTORICAL PRESERVATION.
  Zoning, §396.
    Constitutionality, §396.

HUSBAND AND WIFE.
  Deeds.
    Examination of title sources of deeds of married persons, §470.
    Grantors.
      Married women's deeds to persons other than husbands, §164.
      Married women's deeds to their husbands, §165.
  Fee simple estates.
    Spouses' rights, §31.
  Life estates.
    Marital life estates, §50.
      Dower and curtesy, §49.
  Restrictive covenants and conditions.
    Conditions and restrictions in restraint of marriage, §391.
  Tenancies by the entirety.
    Disability of either spouse to convey his or her share during coverture, §125.

I

IMPROVEMENTS.
  Encumbrances.
    Life tenant's duty, §58.
  Examination of titles.
    Assessments for local improvements.
      Objections to title, §501.
  Tenancies in common, §118.

INFANTS.
  Deeds.
    Grantors.
      Generally, §162.
      Married infants' deeds, §163.

INDEX

INHERITABLE ESTATES.
  Fee simple estates, §§24 to 41.
    See FEE SIMPLE ESTATES.
  Fee tail estates, §§42 to 45.
    See FEE TAIL ESTATES.
INJUNCTIONS.
  Easements, §330.
IN REM.
  Exclusionary rights, §3.
INSPECTIONS.
  Covenants in leases.
    Provision in lease giving landlord right of entry, §250.
INSURANCE.
  Covenants in leases.
    Covenant to insure premises, §246.
  Encumbrances.
    Land subject to life estates, §59.1.
  Leases.
    Covenant to insure premises, §246.
  Mortgages and deeds of trust.
    Duty to pay insurance, §266.
  Title insurance.
    Desirability of insurance, §511.
    Increase in marketability of land, §512.
    North Carolina "approved attorney" system, §510.
    Types, §513.
INTEREST.
  Encumbrances.
    Life tenant's duties, §57.
  Tenancies in common, §117.

J

JOINT TENANCIES.
  Concurrent ownership generally, §108.
  Defined, §109.
JUDGMENT LIENS.
  Docketing of judgments of various courts, §413.
  Enforcement, §416.
  Examination of titles.
    Objections to title, §492.
  Execution, §416.
  Extent, §412.
  Generally, §410.
  Inception, §411.
  Priority where judgment debtor acquires real property after docketing of judgment, §415.
  Priority where judgment debtor owns real property at time judgment docketed, §414.
  Termination, §417.

L

LANDLORD AND TENANT.
  Covenants in leases, §§237 to 251.
    See COVENANTS IN LEASES.

LANDLORD AND TENANT—Cont'd
  Estates for years, §§74 to 87.
    See ESTATES FOR YEARS.
  Federally assisted low-rent housing projects.
    Eviction of tenants, §73.
  Joint tenancies, §§108, 109.
    See JOINT TENANCIES.
  Leases.
    Generally.
      See LEASES.
    Relationship generally, §230.
  Residential rental agreements act.
    Eviction of tenants in federal assisted low-rent housing projects, §73.
    Introduction, §65.
    Landlord's obligations, §67.
    Mutuality of obligations, §66.
    Remedies, §70.
    Retaliatory eviction, §71.
    Security deposit act, §22.
    Statutory prohibition against retaliatory eviction, §71.
    Tenant's obligations, §68.
    Unilateral withholding of rent, §69.
  Rights of residential tenants, §§65 to 73.
  Security deposit act, §72.
  Tenancies at sufferance, §§106, 107.
  Tenancies at will, §§98 to 105.
    See TENANCIES AT WILL.
  Tenancies by the entirety, §§111, 125 to 128.
    See TENANCIES BY THE ENTIRETY.
  Tenancies from period to period, §§88 to 97.
    See TENANCIES FROM PERIOD TO PERIOD.
  Tenancies in common, §§110, 112 to 124.
    See TENANCIES IN COMMON.

LEASES.
  Alterations by tenant, §249.
  Anticipatory breach, §253.
  Breach.
    Anticipatory breach.
      Applicability of doctrine, §253.
    Mitigation of damages, §252.
  Covenants in leases, §§237 to 251.
    See COVENANTS IN LEASES.
  Damages.
    Doctrine of mitigation of damages, §252.
  Defined, §231.
  Description of leased premises, §234.
  Dumpor's case, §254.
  Estates for years, §§74 to 87.
    See ESTATES FOR YEARS.
  Examination of titles.
    Objections to title, §504.
  Execution.
    Description of leased premises, §234.
    Designation of term of lease, §235.
    Generally, §232.
    Names of parties, §233.
    Statement of rent, §236.
  Generally, §232.

INDEX

LEASES—Cont'd
  Insurance.
    Covenant to insure premises, §246.
  Landlord and tenant.
    Generally.
      See LANDLORD AND TENANT.
    Relationship generally, §230.
  Mitigation of damages, §252.
  Names of parties, §233.
  Option to purchase, §248.
  Parties.
    Names, §233.
  Rent.
    Statement of rent, §236.
  Repairs.
    Covenant to repair, §240.
  Residential rental agreements act, §§65 to 71.
    See LANDLORD AND TENANT.
  Right of entry of landlord, §250.
  Rule in Dumpor's case, §254.
  Taxation.
    Covenant to pay taxes, §245.
  Tenancies at sufferance, §§106, 107.
  Tenancies at will, §§98 to 105.
    See TENANCIES AT WILL.
  Tenancies from period to period, §§88 to 97.
    See TENANCIES FROM PERIOD TO PERIOD.
  Terms.
    Designation of term of lease, §235.
  Waiver of covenant.
    Rule in Dumpor's case, §254.

LICENSES.
  Easements, §§343 to 345.
    See EASEMENTS.

LIENS.
  Assessments, §455.
  Examination of titles.
    Recipients of ambulance service.
      Objections to title, §496.
    Repeal of liens arising from assistance to the aged and disabled.
      Objections to title, §495.
  Mechanics' liens, §§418 to 453.
    See MECHANICS' LIENS.
  Real property.
    Assessment liens, §455.
    Generally, §409.
    Judgment liens, §§410 to 417.
      See JUDGMENT LIENS.
    Mechanics' liens, §§418 to 453.
      See MECHANICS' LIENS.
    Tax liens, §454.
  Taxation, §454.

LIFE ESTATES.
  Alien.
    Incidents of life estates.
      Right to alien, §52.
  Assessments.
    Life tenant's duty to pay local assessments, §56.

MECHANICS' LIENS—Cont'd
  Generally—Cont'd
    Perfection of the lien, §423.
      Amendments, §423.
      Assignment, §423.
    Priority, §425.
      Contractors' lien against federal mortgages or deeds of trust, §434.
      Contractors' lien against federal tax liens, §431.
      Contractors' lien against interests arising under the bankruptcy act, §432.
      Contractors' lien as against purchase money mortgage or deed of trust, §428.
      Contractors' lien as against security instrument security presently owned and after acquired property, §429.
      Contractors' lien as against subcontractors' lien, §427.
      Mechanics' lien against owners' homestead exemption, §433.
      Mechanics' lien as against instruments security future advances, §430.
    Waiver, §435.
  Liens of mechanics, laborers and materialmen dealing with one other than the owner of real property.
    Amount secured, §446.
    Applicability of provisions, §439.
    Definitions, §438.
    Direct lien rights of second and third tier subcontractors upon funds, §442.
    Duties and liabilities of the "obligor," §448.
    Effect of one person's waiver upon another person's rights, §447.
    Enforcement, §450.
    First tier subcontractors.
      Grant of lien, §440.
    Grant of lien upon funds.
      Direct lien rights of second and third tier subcontractors, §442.
      First tier subcontractors, §440.
      Remote tier subcontractors, §444.
      Second and third tier subcontractors, §441.
    Introduction, §437.
    Liens upon owner's interest in real property, §451.
    Lien upon funds.
      Amount secured, §446.
      Duties and liabilities of the "obligor," §448.
      Effect of one person's waiver upon another person's rights, §447.
      Enforcement, §450.
      Perfection, §445.
      Priorities, §449.
    Nature of lien, §438.
    Owner's interest in real property, §451.
    Perfection, §445.
    Priorities, §449.
    Remote tier subcontractors.
      Grant of lien, §444.
    Second and third tier subcontractors.
      Direct lien rights, §442.
      Grant of lien upon funds, §441.
      Subrogation rights, §443.
    Statutory definitions, §438.
    Subrogation rights available to second and third tier subcontractors, §443.
MERGER.
  Encumbrances.
    Subject to merger, §59.
  Estates for years, §85.

676

INDEX

MINERALS.
  Adverse possession, §298.
  Ownership, §8.
  Real property.
    Word construed, §8.

MINORS.
  Deeds.
    Grantors.
      Generally, §162.
      Married infants' deeds, §163.

MISREPRESENTATION.
  Real estate brokers, §§132, 133.

MORTGAGES AND DEEDS OF TRUST.
  Equity of redemption.
    Amount necessary for redemption, §260.
    Essential feature of every mortgage, §258.
    Foreclosure of right to redeem, §261.
    Persons who have right to redeem, §259.
    Statutory termination, §261.
    Termination of right, §261.
  Examination of titles.
    Objections to title, §491.
  Foreclosure.
    Acceleration clause, §277.
    Accrual, §277.
      Acceleration clause, §277.
    Action to foreclose, §280.
    Deficiency judgments, §282.
    Due-on-sale clause, §278.
    Nature of mortgagee's right.
      Generally, §276.
    "Power of sale" foreclosure, §281.
    Statute of limitations, §283.
    Types available in North Carolina, §279.
    When right accrues, §277.
    When right to foreclosure accrues.
      Acceleration clause, §277.
  Form of deeds of trust, §257.
  Form of mortgages, §257.
  Insurance.
    Duty to pay insurance, §266.
  Nature and effect.
    Generally, §255.
  Payment and discharge.
    Discharge of record, §284.
    Effect of payment, §§284, 285.
    Generally, §284.
    Tender of payment, §284.
  Recordation.
    Office where deeds of trust and mortgages are recorded, §376.
  Right to possession and use of mortgaged property.
    Duties of mortgagee in possession, §264.
    Duties of mortgagor in possession, §263.
    Duty to pay taxes, §265.
    Generally, §262.
    Insurance.
      Who may pay, §266.

MORTGAGES AND DEEDS OF TRUST—Cont'd
  Statute of limitations.
    Right of mortgagee to foreclose, §283.
  Taxation.
    Duty to pay, §265.
  "Title theory" in effect in North Carolina, §256.
  Transfer of mortgagee's interest.
    Generally, §272.
    Where mortgagee transfers mortgage and note or indebtedness at same time by written instruments, §275.
    Where mortgagee transfers mortgage debt only, §273.
    Where mortgagee transfers mortgage only without transferring mortgage debt, §274.
  Transfer of mortgagor's interest.
    Acquisition of mortgage security by owner of property, §271.
    Conveyance of interest in mortgaged property to the mortgagee, §270.
    Right to transfer, §267.
    When doctrine of merger applies, §271.
    Where transfer recites that mortgagor's grantee "assumes" the mortgage, §269.
    Where transfer recites that property is "subject to" the mortgage, §268.

N

NONRESIDENTS.
  Deeds.
    Grantees, §181.
    Grantors, §175.
NOTICE.
  Estates for years.
    Termination without necessity of notice, §86.
  Recordation.
    Constructive notice from recordation, §375.
  Tenancies at will.
    No prior notice required for termination, §105.
  Tenancies from period to period.
    Termination of lease, §97.
NUISANCES.
  Classification, §361.
  Generally, §360.
  Liability for nuisances, §366.
  Nuisances per accidens, §365.
  Nuisances per se, §364.
  Persons entitled to relief, §366.
  Private nuisances, §363.
  Public nuisances, §362.
  Relief.
    Persons entitled to relief because of nuisances, §366.
  Remedies, §367.
  Spite fences, §368.

O

OPTIONS.
  Distinguished, §135.
  Necessity of consideration, §137.
  Tender of purchase price as a prerequisite to exercise, §136.

INDEX

ORDINANCES.
  Zoning.
    Enforcement and remedies, §398.
    Examination of titles.
      Objection to title, §502.
    Generally, §393.
    Operation, §397.
    Validity of zoning ordinances, §395.

OWNERSHIP.
  Defined, §2.
  Exclusionary rights, §3.
  In rem rights, §3.
  Minerals, §8.
  Real property.
    Right of user, §4.
  Right of disposition, §2.
  Rights of enjoyment and duties incident to ownership of real property, §§346, 347.

P

PAROL EVIDENCE RULE.
  Contracts for the sale of land.
    Contract versus tort cause of action, §148.

PARTITION.
  Tenancies in common.
    Generally, §121.
    Practice in partition proceedings, §124.
    Restrictions on right, §123.
    Voluntary, §122.

PARTNERSHIPS.
  Deeds.
    Grantors.
      Generally, §167.
      Real property held in name of one or all partners or by third person in trust for partnership, §171.
      Real property held in name of one or more partners where real property records do not disclose partnership, §170.
      Real property in partnership name, §168.
      Real property in partnership name conveyed in name of individual partner, §169.
  Dower and curtesy.
    No dower or curtesy in real estate held by partnership, §50.

PERSONAL PROPERTY.
  Classes of property, §5.
    Significance of distinctions between real and personal property, §6.
  Disposition.
    Right of disposition, §2.
  Distinctions between real and personal property.
    Significance, §6.
  Exclusionary rights, §3.
  In rem rights, §3.
  Ownership.
    Right of disposition, §2.

PLANNING AND ZONING.
  Generally, §§392 to 399.
    See ZONING.

POLICE POWER.
  Zoning.
    Source, §395.
PRIORITIES.
  Recordation.
    Generally.
      See RECORDATION.
PROFITS.
  Encumbrances.
    Life tenant's right to profits, §60.
PROFITS A PRENDRE.
  Generally, §342.
PROPERTY.
  Classes of property, §5.
    Significance of distinctions between real and personal property, §6.
  Definitions.
    Generally, §1.
  Disposition.
    Right of disposition, §2.
  Distinctions between real and personal property.
    Significance, §6.
  Exclusionary rights, §3.
  Generally, §1.
  Personal property.
    See PERSONAL PROPERTY.
  Real property.
    See REAL PROPERTY.

R

RACIAL MINORITIES.
  Restrictive covenants and conditions.
    Restrictions upon, §390.
REAL PROPERTY.
  Classes of property, §5.
    Significance of distinctions between real and personal property, §6.
  Condemnation.
    See EMINENT DOMAIN.
  Contracts for the sale of land, §§135 to 151.
    See CONTRACTS FOR THE SALE OF LAND.
  Definitions.
    Fructus industriales, §10.
    Fructus naturales, §9.
    Land, §7.
    Minerals, §8.
  Disposition.
    Right of disposition, §2.
  Distinctions between real and personal property.
    Significance, §6.
  Eminent domain.
    See EMINENT DOMAIN.
  Exclusionary rights, §3.
  Fixtures, §§11 to 22.5.
    See FIXTURES.
  Fructus industriales.
    Defined, §10.

INDEX

REAL PROPERTY—Cont'd
Fructus naturales.
Defined, §9.
In rem rights, §3.
"Land" used as synonym for real property, §7.
Liens.
Assessment liens, §455.
Generally, §409.
Judgment liens, §§410 to 417.
See JUDGMENT LIENS.
Mechanics' liens, §§418 to 453.
See MECHANICS' LIENS.
Tax liens, §454.
Minerals.
Word construed, §8.
Ownership.
Right of disposition, §2.
Right of user, §4.
Real estate brokers.
Broker's obligations as agent of seller, §131.
Commissions.
Right to, §130.
Contracts not within statute of frauds, §129.
Liability of broker to purchaser for misrepresentation, §132.
Liability of seller to purchaser because of misrepresentation of agent, §133.
Regulation generally, §134.
Statute of frauds.
Contracts not within, §129.
Rights of enjoyment and duties incident to ownership, §§346, 347.
Users rights, §4.

RECEIVERS AND RECEIVERSHIP.
Examination of titles.
Deeds, §478.

RECORDATION.
Chain of title, §380.
Deeds.
Delivery and acceptance, §201.
Deeds of gift.
Recordation within two years, §381.
Defective or unauthorized instruments, §377.
Easements, §382.
Estoppel by deed.
Title by estoppel as affected by recordation statutes, §229.
Examination of titles.
Unrecorded deeds, §486.
Generally, §369.
Gifts.
Deeds of gift must be recorded within two years, §381.
History, §369.
Indexing, §378.
Instruments required to be recorded to effect priority under recordation statutes, §379.
Lien creditors.
Persons protected by recording acts, §374.
Priorities, §371.
Notice.
Constructive notice from recordation, §375.

RECORDATION—Cont'd
  Persons protected by recording acts, §373.
    Lien creditors, §374.
  Priorities.
    Effect of failure to record as against purchasers for value and lien creditors, §371.
    Effect of failure to record as between donees, heirs and devisees, §372.
    Effect of failure to record as between grantors and grantees inter se, §372.
    "Race" type recordation statute, §370.
  Purchasers for value, §373.
    Persons protected by recording acts, §373.
  "Race" type recordation statute, §370.
  Recordation.
    Office where deeds, deeds of trust and mortgages are recorded, §376.
  Requirements.
    Effect of recording defective or unauthorized instruments, §377.
    Indexing, §378.
    Use of indices, §378.
  Use of indices, §378.
  Use of recording system, §380.

REMAINDERS AND REVERSIONS.
  Encumbrances.
    General standard of duty owed by life tenant, §54.1.
    Life tenant's disability to acquire outstanding title against, §62.

REMEDIES.
  Contracts for the sale of land.
    Breach.
      Remedies for breach by vendee, §150.
      Remedies for breach by vendor, §145.
  Nuisances, §367.
  Zoning, §398.

REPAIRS.
  Covenants in leases.
    Covenant to repair, §240.
    Landlord's right of entry, §250.
  Encumbrances.
    Life tenant's duty, §58.
  Estates for years.
    Tenant's liability to make repairs, §84.
  Leases.
    Covenant to repair, §240.
  Tenancies from period to period.
    Tenant's duty to repair, §95.
  Tenancies in common, §118.

REPORTS.
  Examination of titles.
    Attorney's written report of title, §509.
  Title.
    Attorney's written report of title, §509.

RESTRICTIVE COVENANTS AND CONDITIONS.
  Alienation.
    Restraints upon, §390.
  Construction of language creating title subject to reverter, §384.
  Construction of language limited uses of land, §385.
  Construction of restrictive covenants, §388.
  Creation of restrictive covenants, §386.
  Enforcement of restrictive covenants, §387.

INDEX

RESTRICTIVE COVENANTS AND CONDITIONS—Cont'd
  Examination of titles.
    Objections to title, §503.
  Fee simple determinable.
    Described, §384.
  Fee simple subject to conditions subsequent.
    Described, §384.
  Generally, §§383, 385.
  Husband and wife.
    Conditions and restrictions in restraint of marriage, §391.
  Marriage.
    Conditions and restrictions in restraint of marriage, §391.
  Planning and zoning, §§392 to 399.
    See ZONING.
  Private restrictions on the use of lands.
    Alienation restraints, §390.
    Conditions and limitations on the estate granted, §384.
    Construction, §388.
    Construction of language creating title subject to reverter, §384.
    Creation of restrictive covenants, §386.
    Enforcement.
      Persons entitled to enforce, §389.
    Fee simple determinable.
      Described, §384.
    Fee simple subject to condition subsequent.
      Described, §384.
    Generally, §§383, 385.
    Marriage, §391.
    Modes of termination, §389.
    Racial restrictions, §390.
    Restraint of marriage, §391.
    Restraints on alienation, §390.
    Termination, §389.
    Validity of particular restrictions, §390.
  Public restrictions on the use of lands, §§392 to 399.
    See ZONING.
  Racial minorities.
    Restrictions upon, §390.
  Termination of restrictive covenants, §389.
  Validity of particular restrictions, §390.
  Zoning, §§392 to 399.
    See ZONING.

REVENUE STAMPS.
  Deeds.
    Requirements generally, §208.

RIGHT OF ENTRY.
  Covenants in leases.
    Provision in lease giving landlord right, §250.
  Examination of titles.
    Possibilities of reverter and rights of entry.
      Objections to title, §506.

RULE AGAINST PERPETUITIES.
  Fee simple estates.
    Applicable to fee simple estates subject to an executory interest, §41.

RULE IN DUMPOR'S CASE.
  Application to covenants in leases, §254.

RULE IN WILD'S CASE.
Forms for creating fee tail estates at common law, §44.

S

SALES.
   Contracts for the sale of land, §§135 to 131.
      See CONTRACTS FOR THE SALE OF LAND.
   Encumbrances.
      Unproductive land, §63.
   Execution sales.
      Examination of titles.
         Deeds under execution sales, §480.

SEALS.
   Deeds.
      Execution of deeds, §197.

SECURITY INTERESTS.
   See UNIFORM COMMERCIAL CODE.

SHERIFFS.
   Examination of titles.
      Deeds under execution sales, §480.

SIGNATURES.
   Deeds.
      Execution of deeds, §197.

SPITE FENCES.
   Nuisances, §368.

STATUTE OF FRAUDS.
   Contracts for the sale of land, §§135 to 151.
      See CONTRACTS FOR THE SALE OF LAND.
   Deeds.
      Necessity for written contract to make escrow enforceable, §204.
   Estates for years, §76.
   Real estate brokers.
      Contracts not within statute, §129.

STATUTE OF LIMITATIONS.
   Covenants for title.
      Covenants against encumbrances, §219.
      Covenants of seisin and right to convey, §214.
      Covenants of warranty and quiet enjoyment, §223.
   Mortgages and deeds of trust.
      Right of mortgagee to foreclose, §283.

SUBDIVISIONS.
   Regulations generally, §399.

SURVIVORSHIP.
   Tenancies in common.
      Doctrine does not apply, §112.

T

TAXATION.
   Covenants in leases.
      Covenant to pay taxes, §245.
   Deeds.
      Examination of title sources, §483.

INDEX

TAXATION—Cont'd
  Examination of titles.
    County and municipal taxes.
      Objections to title, §498.
    Deeds, §483.
    Federal tax liens.
      Objections to title, §500.
    State taxes.
      Objections to title, §499.
  Leases.
    Covenant to pay taxes, §245.
  Liens, §454.
  Life estates.
    Life tenant's duty to pay taxes, §55.
  Mortgages and deeds of trust.
    Duty to pay, §265.
  Tenancies in common, §117.

TENANCIES AT SUFFERANCE.
  Defined, §106.
  Generally, §106.
  Incidents, §107.

TENANCIES AT WILL.
  Characteristics, §98.
  Creation.
    By express agreement, §99.
    Implication or operation of law, §100.
  Definitions, §98.
  Emblements.
    Tenant's right, §103.
  Estovers.
    Tenant's right, §102.
  Generally, §98.
  Interest of tenant, §101.
  Notice.
    No prior notice required for termination, §105.
  Termination, §105.
  Waste.
    Tenant's liability, §104.

TENANCIES BY THE ENTIRETY.
  Creditors' rights, §126.
  Defined, §111.
  Husband and wife.
    Disability of either spouse to convey his or her share during coverture, §125.
  Partition, §127.
  Survivorship, §128.
  Termination, §127.

TENANCIES FOR YEARS.
  Generally, §§74 to 87.
    See ESTATES FOR YEARS.

TENANCIES FROM PERIOD TO PERIOD.
  Creation, §§88, 89.
  Definitions, §88.
  Emblements.
    Right to emblements, §92.
  Estovers, §91.
  Generally, §90.

TENANCIES FROM PERIOD TO PERIOD—Cont'd
  Interest.
    Right to transfer tenant's interest, §94.
  Notice.
    Termination of lease, §97.
  Possession.
    Right to exclusive possession, §93.
  Repairs.
    Tenant's duty to repair, §95.
  Termination of lease, §97.
  Waste.
    Tenant's liability for waste, §96.

TENANCIES IN COMMON.
  Accounts and accounting.
    Duty of tenant to account, §115.
  Adverse possession, §301.
  Alienation, §113.
  Concurrent ownership generally, §108.
  Creditors' rights, §114.
  Defined, §110.
  Ejectment.
    Actions of ejectment between co-tenants, §120.
  Fiduciaries.
    Aspects between tenants in common, §116.
  Generally, §110.
  Improvements, §118.
  Interest, §117.
  Partition.
    Generally, §121.
    Practice in partition proceedings, §124.
    Restrictions on right, §123.
    Voluntary, §122.
  Possession between tenants, §115.
  Repairs, §118.
  Survivorship.
    Doctrine does not apply, §112.
  Taxation, §117.
  Waste.
    Actions of waste between co-tenants, §119.

TITLE.
  Adverse possession, §§286 to 302.
    See ADVERSE POSSESSION.
  Covenants for title, §§210 to 225.
    See COVENANTS FOR TITLE.
  Encumbrances.
    Life tenant's disabilty to acquire outstanding title against reversioner or remainderman, §62.
  Examination of titles.
    Generally, §§456 to 507.
      See EXAMINATION OF TITLES.
  Marketable title act.
    Generally, §508.
  Reports.
    Attorney's written report of title, §509.

TITLE INSURANCE.
  Desirability, §511.
  Increase in marketability of land, §512.
  North Carolina "approved attorney" system, §510.

INDEX

TITLE INSURANCE—Cont'd
  Types, §513.

TITLE SEARCH.
  Examination of titles, §§456 to 507.
    See EXAMINATION OF TITLES.

TRUSTS AND TRUSTEES.
  Constructive trusts.
    Objections to title, §507.
  Deeds.
    Grantors, §174.
  Examination of titles.
    Parol, resulting and constructive trusts.
      Objections to title, §507.
  Parol trusts.
    Objections to title, §507.
  Resulting trusts.
    Objections to title, §507.

U

UNIFORM COMMERCIAL CODE.
  Examination of titles.
    Security interests in fixtures under the uniform commercial code.
      Objections to title, §494.

W

WAIVER.
  Covenants in leases.
    Rule in Dumpor's case, §254.

WARRANTIES.
  Contracts for the sale of land.
    Implied warranty where builder-vendor involved, §149.

WASTE.
  Estates for years.
    Tenant's liability for waste, §83.
  Tenancies at will.
    Tenant's liability, §104.
  Tenancies from period to period.
    Tenant's liability for waste, §96.
  Tenancies in common.
    Actions of waste between co-tenants, §119.

WATER RIGHTS.
  Accretion, §353.
  Avulsion, §353.
  Definitions.
    Navigable, §349.
  Drainage of surface water, §355.
  Erosion, §353.
  Federal governmental regulation, §358.
  Generally, §348.
  Governmental regulation.
    Federal, §358.
    State, §359.
  Navigable.
    Defined, §349.
  Percolating waters, §354.

WATER RIGHTS—Cont'd
  Public trust doctrine, §356.
  Public water rights, §356.
  Reliction, §353.
  Riparian owners.
    Right to take water from known and well defined channels of water above surface of earth, §352.
  Sovereign prerogative doctrine.
    Recognition in North Carolina, §357.
  State governmental regulation, §359.
  Submerged lands.
    Under navigable waters, §350.
    Under nonnavigable waters, §351.
  Subterranean and percolating waters, §354.
  Surface water drainage, §355.

WITNESSES.
  Deeds.
    Execution of deeds.
      Not required, §198.

Z

ZONING.
  Constitutionality of historical preservation zoning, §396.
  Enforcement under zoning ordinances, §398.
  Examination of titles.
    Ordinances.
      Objections to title, §502.
  Generally, §392.
    Ordinances, §393.
  Historical preservation, §396.
    Constitutionality, §396.
  Ordinances.
    Enforcement and remedies, §398.
    Generally, §393.
    Operation, §397.
    Validity of zoning ordinances, §395.
  Planning and zoning generally, §392.
    Ordinances, §393.
  Police power.
    Source, §395.
  Remedies, §398.
  Subdivisions.
    Regulations generally, §399.
  Types of zones, §394.
  Validity of zoning ordinances, §395.